EUROPE 1939

UNION OF SOVIET SOCIALIST REPUBLICS

FINLAND

LAKE LADOGA

Kronstadt
lsinki
Petrokrepost
Leningrad • Tikhvin
val
(linn)
Narva
—*Volkhov River*
LAKE ILMEN

ESTONIA

• Demyansk
Kalinin

LATVIA

• Velikiye Luki
• Rzhev ⊛ Moscow
• Nevel
Vitebsk
• Vyazma

LITHUANIA

vno
• Vilna
Orsha • Gorki • Smolensk
• Sukhinichi
• Minsk
Bryansk
• Orel
• Voronezh

stok
• Kovel
AND
• Kursk
est-Litovsk

Kiev • Belgorod
Zhitomir • Kharkov
lav Berdichev • Fastov
Lvov Cherkassy • Poltava • Izyum
• Tarnopol • Vinnitsa *Dnieper River*
Dnepropetrovsk • Kotelnikovo
• Uman Zaporozhye • Stalino Astrakhan
Dniester River Krivoi Rog Taganrog • Rostov
Prut River Nikolaev • Mariupol
Klausenburg Odessa • Kherson • Melitopol
RUMANIA *SEA OF AZOV* Krasnodar R. • Armavir
Galatz CRIMEA Kerch *Kuban* • Maykop • Grozny
• Ordzhonikidze

⊛ Stalingrad

Bucharest ⊛ • Sevastopol
• Constanta Gudauta • Sukhumi
• Nikopol **BLACK SEA** Baku •
BULGARIA
⊛ Sofia

CASPIAN SEA

Istanbul ⊛ Teheran
lonika
DARDANELLES ⊛ Ankara
REECE **TURKEY**
AEGEAN **IRAN**
SEA • Izmir
Athens

RHODES
D ⊛ Nicosia Baghdad ⊛
CYPRUS **SYRIA** **IRAQ**
CRETE
⊛ Damascus

S E A • Amman
PALESTINE
TRANS-JORDAN

Tobruk • • Bardia Marsa
Sollum Matrûh • Alexandria
• Fûka • El Alamein Suez
Cairo ⊛
EGYPT *Nile River*

| 0 | 100 | 200 | 300 | 400 | 500 miles |

Paul J. Pugliese

Dvina River

Volga River

HITLER'S WAR

HITLER'S
WAR

David Irving

The Viking Press · New York

First published in 1977 by The Viking Press
625 Madison Avenue, New York, N.Y. 10022

Published simultaneously in Canada by
The Macmillan Company of Canada Limited

LIBRARY OF CONGRESS CATALOGING IN PUBLICATION DATA

Irving, David John Cawdell, 1938—
Hitler's war.

Bibliography: p.
Includes index.
1. World War, 1939–1945—Germany.   2.   Hitler,
Adolf, 1889–1945.   I.   Title.
D757.I69   940.54'0943   76–18195
ISBN 0–670–37412–1

Printed in the United States of America

Set in Videocomp Times Roman

Contents

Acknowledgments

I like to think that I chose precisely the right ten years to work on Hitler. Any earlier, and the archives would not have begun to disgorge their captured papers; any later, and those who came closest to enjoying Hitler's confidence would have died. Hitler's secretaries and adjutants were without exception of the utmost help. Traudl Junge and Christa Schroeder provided unpublished manuscripts and letters of the period; his adjutants Admiral Karl-Jesco von Puttkamer (navy), General Gerhard Engel (army), and Colonel Nicolaus von Below (Luftwaffe) did the same, and labored through much of the resulting manuscript. Without the memories of Colonel Erik von Amsberg, Max Wünsche, Fritz Darges, and Otto Günsche, many a gap in our knowledge would have remained unfilled. But many other adjutants attending Hitler's conferences also assisted—of whom I must single out for mention Major General Ottomar Hansen, Lieutenant Colonel Ernst John von Freyend, Admiral Kurt Freiwald, and Captain Herbert Friedrichs, and particularly Johannes Göhler and Wolf Eberhard for the important diaries and letters they made available to me for the first time.

The most important documents were provided by Professor Hugh Trevor-Roper and by Lev Besymenski. Dr. Cortez F. Enloe, Washington, D.C., furnished medical records on Hitler. François Genoud, Lausanne, Switzerland, supplied key extracts from Bormann's personal files; Frau Asta Greiner, Wiesbaden, Germany, her husband's unpublished diaries and private correspondence; the stenographer Karl Thöt, Bonn, his war diary; the late Colonel Karl-Heinz Keitel, papers from his father's collection; Albert Speer, Heidelberg, Germany, his office Chronik and other papers; Reinhard Spitzy, Austria, certain letters; Günter Peis, Munich, selected items from his unique collection; and Dr. Heinrich Heim, Munich, papers originating from his period as Martin Bormann's adjutant; furthermore Hitler's doctors Professor Hanskarl von Hasselbach, Dr. Erwin Giesing, and Dr. Richard Weber provided papers or other aid.

Many of the collections deposited in the archives would have remained closed to me without the kindness of the following: Isabella Adam, Ursula Backe, Anni Brandt, Ilse Dittmar, Friedl Koller, Paula Kubizek, Baroness Jutta von Richthofen, the late Lucie Rommel, Anneliese Schmundt, Gertrud Seyss-Inquart, Ruth von Vormann, Elisabeth Wagner, Elisabeth Todt, Margarete von Waldau, Baroness Marga von Weichs, Baroness Marianne von Weizsäcker—all of whom either permitted me to see or provided me with direct access to their husbands' papers, letters, and diaries. (The Weizsäcker diaries have been expertly transcribed by my colleague Professor Leonidas E. Hill.) Frau Blanda Benteler allowed me the diaries of her husband Walther Hewel; Liselotte von Salmuth those of her husband, the Colonel General; Else Renate Nagy the manuscripts and papers of her late husband Dr. Wilhelm Scheidt—adjutant of Hitler's court historian General Walter Scherff; Frau Gerta von Radinger the private letters of her late husband, Alwin-Broder Albrecht (whom she had married in 1940). Frau Anneliese Schmundt gave me her private war diary. I am also grateful to Dr. Peter von Blomberg, Manfred Brückner, General Heinz-Günther Guderian, Joachim Hoepner, Hermann Leeb, Fritz von Lossberg, Rüdiger von Manstein, and Roland Schaub for permission to use the private papers of their fathers. The late Karl-Otto Saur, Field Marshal Erhard Milch, Major General Ivo-Thilo von Trotha, General Walter von Seydlitz-Kurzbach, Ambassador Dr. Hasso von Etzdorf, and the late Ludwig Krieger, stenographer, all made diaries and papers available to me.

Of those who gave up their time for long conversations or to write letters I must mention these: Ludwig Bahls, Werner Best, Karl Bodenschatz, Herta Berger—widow of the stenographer killed on July 20, 1944—Herbert Büchs, Eugen Dollmann, Peterpaul von Donat, Xaver Dorsch, Baron Sigismund von Falkenstein, Ambassador André François Poncet, Reinhard Gehlen, Otto-Heinz Grosskreutz, Werner Grothmann, Hedwig Haase, Ernst "Putzi" Hanfstaengl, Heider Heydrich, Ralph Hewins, Ambassador Hans von Herwarth, Professor Andreas Hillgruber, Professor Raul Hilberg, Gebhard Himmler, Walter Huppenkothen, Professor Hans-Adolf Jacobsen, Elisabeth Kaltenbrunner, Hans Kehrl, Werner Koeppen, Marlene Kunde (née Exner), Dr. O. H. Schmitz-Lammers, Helmut Laux, Heinz Linge, Field Marshal Friedrich List, Heinz Lorenz, Colonel J. L. McCowen, Johanna Morell, Josef Müller, Pastor Martin Niemöller, Max Pemsel, Leo Raubal, the late Anneliese von Ribbentrop, Walter Rohland, Jürgen Runzheimer, Professor Ernst-Günther Schenck, Henriette von Schirach, Richard Schulze-Kossens, Dietrich Schwencke, former Federal Chancellor Dr. Kurt von Schuschnigg, General Curt Siewert, Otto Skorzeny, Gertrud and Friedrich Stumpfegger, the late Helmut Sündermann, Admiral Gerhard Wagner, Winifred Wagner, Karl Wahl, Walter Warlimont, and Karin Weigl. Walter Frentz placed his photographic collection at my disposal; Peter Hoffmann his expertise; Frau Luise Jodl her husband's papers.

For most of the ten years I also plagued archives and institutes with my inquiries. I am most indebted to the exemplary Institut für Zeitgeschichte in Munich, and to its then director Professor Helmuth Krausnick and above all its head of archives Dr. Anton Hoch, who guided me as friend and mentor with great objectivity and ability from October 1966 onward; Frau Karla Götz, Hermann Weiss, and Anton Zirngibl fulfilled my often immodest demands, and Dr. Wolfgang Jacobmeyer permitted me to use his prepared edition of the Hans Frank diaries. In transferring to the Institut my entire Hitler document collection, including the interview and interrogation records, Hitler's armament decrees, the Canaris/Lahousen fragments, a correct transcription of Greiner's war diary notes, the Scheidt papers, and much else, I hope to have recompensed in part for the assistance given me. Much of the material was microfilmed by the Imperial War Museum, London S.E. 1, before I transferred it to Munich; these films are available from the museum's Foreign Documents Centre. I also transferred my collection of records on Hitler's medical history to the Bundesarchiv in Koblenz, Germany (where it is filed as item *Kl. Erw. 525*). I placed a copy of the Fritzsch Papers, 1938–39, in the Bundesarchiv-Militärarchiv in Freiburg, Germany, where Dr. Friedrich-Christian Stahl, Alfred Bottler, and Colonel Helmuth Vorwieg aided me. At the neighboring Militärgeschichtliches Forschungsamt (of the German Defense Ministry) I was guided by Colonels Karl Gundeslach, Manfred Kehrig, Rolf Elbe, and Dr. Georg Meyer through the intricacies of their own archives. At Nuremberg's State Archives Dr. Puchner and Dr. Schuhmann aided me; and at the Führungsakademie der Bundeswehr in Hamburg Colonel Helmuth Technau was kind enough to allow me to carry volumes of original records—including the important Koller diaries—to London with me to put on microfilm. In the Operational Archives Branch at Washington Navy Yard I met with the fullest cooperation of Dr. Dean C. Allard and Mrs. Mildred D. Mayeux; and Robert Wolfe, John E. Taylor, Thomas E. Hohmann, and their colleagues provided assistance at the National Archives. I must also mention Mrs. Agnes F. Peterson of the Hoover Library, Stanford, California; Detmar Finke of the Office of the Chief of Military History (OCMH), Washington D.C.; and Mr. George E. Blau, chief historian of USAEUR headquarters, Heidelberg, Germany. The U.S. Mission's Berlin Document Center provided speedy and efficient assistance while under its director Richard Bauer, as did the heads of archives of the German, French, Finnish, and British foreign offices. In London I encountered particularly useful help from Dr. Leo Kahn of the Imperial War Museum; Squadron Leader L. A. Jackets of the Air Historical Branch; Mr. Brian Melland, Mr. Clifton Child, and Mrs. Nan Taylor of the Cabinet Office Historical Section; and Mr. K. Hiscock at the Foreign Office Library. World War II researchers will find many of the special microfilms of materials prepared by me while researching this book available now from E. P. Microform Ltd., East Ardsley, Wakefield, Yorkshire, England.

This book would have been impossible without the patience and generosity of the many publishers who waited long years for the scaffolding to be removed from this *monumentum aeris* which I have erected. My editors, Alan Williams of the Viking Press and Stanley Hochman, provided me with many a stimulus and useful reproof. Without the indulgence of my wife, Pilar, in putting up with the years of turmoil and inconvenience the book might not have appeared. Nor shall I forget the nameless legions who typed, translated, or trudged the archives with me: Mrs. Jutta Thomas, the only one of my secretaries to survive the full marathon, and my colleague Elke Fröhlich, who encouraged me to persist and helped me to scale the mountains of records in Berlin, Munich, London, Freiburg, and Bonn that had daunted and dissuaded other writers and would otherwise have discouraged me.

Introduction

"To historians is granted a talent that even the gods are denied—to alter what has already happened!"

I bore this scornful adage in mind when I embarked on this study of Hitler's war years late in 1964. I saw myself as a stone-cleaner—less concerned with a wordy and subjective architectural appraisal than with scrubbing years of grime and discoloration from the facade of a silent and forbidding monument, uncertain whether the revealed monument would prove too hideous to be worthy of the effort.

In earlier books, I relied on the primary records of the period rather than published literature; I naïvely supposed that the same technique could within five years be applied to a study of Adolf Hitler, little realizing that it would be eleven years before I would lay bare the factual bedrock on which the legend of Hitler had been built. But I believe that hard rubbing has disclosed a picture of the man that nobody until now had suspected.

My conclusion on completing the research startled even me: while Adolf Hitler was a powerful and relentless military commander, the war years saw him as a lax and indecisive political leader who allowed affairs of state to rot. In fact he was probably the weakest *leader* Germany has known in this century. Though often brutal and insensitive, Hitler lacked the ability to be ruthless where it mattered most, *e.g.,* he refused to bomb London itself until the decision was forced on him in the late summer of 1940. He was reluctant to impose the test of total mobilization on the German "master race" until it was too late to matter, so that with munitions factories crying out for manpower, idle German housewives were still employing half a million domestic servants to dust their homes and polish their furniture. His military irresolution also showed through, for example, in his panicky vaccillation at times of crisis like the Battle for Narvik in 1940. He took ineffectual measures against his enemies inside Germany for too long, and seems to have been unable to take effective action against strong opposition at the very heart of his High Command. He suffered incompetent ministers and generals far longer than the Allied leaders did. He failed too to unite the feuding Party and Wehrmacht factions in fighting for the common cause, and he proved incapable of stifling the OKH' (War Department's) corrosive hatred of the OKW (the Wehrmacht High Command). I believe I show in this book that the more hermetically Hitler locked himself away behind the barbed wire and minefields of his remote military headquarters, the more his Germany became a Führer-Staat without a Führer. Domestic policy was controlled by whoever was most powerful in each sector—by Hermann Göring as head of the powerful economics office, the Four-Year Plan; by Hans Lammers as chief of the Reich Chancellery or by Martin Bormann, the Nazi party boss; or by Heinrich Himmler, minister of the interior and "Reichsführer" of the black-uniformed SS.

The problem is that Hitler was a puzzle even to his most intimate advisers. Joachim Ribbentrop, his foreign minister, wrote in his Nuremberg prison cell in 1945:

> I got to know Adolf Hitler more closely in 1933. But if I am asked today whether I knew him well—how he thought as a politician and statesman, what kind of man he was—then I'm bound to confess that I know only very little about him; in fact nothing at all. The fact is that although I went through so much together with him, in all the years of working with him I never came closer to him than on the first day we met, either personally or otherwise.

As a historian I have resorted to the widest possible spectrum of source materials. I have not only used the military records and archives; I have burrowed deep into the contemporary writings of his closest friends and personal staff, seeking clues to the real truth in their diaries or in the private letters they wrote to their wives and friends. In this way I have tried to understand the intricacies and contradictions in Hitler's last years.

The sheer complexity of that character is evident from a comparison of his extreme brutality in some respects and his almost maudlin sentimentality and stubborn adherence to long-abandoned military conventions in others. In the chapters that follow, we shall find Hitler cold-bloodedly ordering the execution of fifty or a hundred hostages for every German occupation-soldier killed; dictating the massacre of Italian soldiers who turned their weapons against the German troops in 1943; ordering the systematic liquidation of Red Army commissars, Allied Commando troops, and—in 1945—even captured Allied aircrews; in 1942 he announces to the General Staff that the entire male populations of Stalingrad and Leningrad will eventually be exterminated, and he justifies these orders to himself and to his staff by political doctrines and the expediencies of war. Yet the same Adolf Hitler indignantly exclaimed, in one of the last war conferences of his life, that Soviet tanks were flying the Nazi swastika as a ruse during street fighting in Berlin, and he flatly forbade his Wehrmacht to violate flag rules! In an age in which the governments of the democracies, both during World War II and in later years, unhesitatingly attempted, engineered, or condoned the assassination of the inconvenient—from General Sikorski, Admiral Darlan, Field Marshal Rommel, and King Boris to Fidel Castro, Patrice Lumumba, and Salvador Allende—we learn that Hitler, the unscrupulous dictator, not only never resorted to the assassination of foreign opponents, but flatly forbade the Abwehr (Intelligence Agency) to attempt it (in particular he rejected Admiral Canaris's plans to assassinate the Red Army General Staff).

The negative is traditionally always difficult to prove; but it seemed well worth attempting to discredit accepted dogmas if only to expose the "unseaworthiness" of many current legends about Hitler. The most durable of these concerns the Führer's involvement in the extermination of the Jews. My analysis of this controversial issue serves to highlight two broad conclusions: that in wartime, dictatorships are fundamentally weak—the dictator himself, however alert, is unable to oversee all the functions of his executives acting within the confines of his far-flung empire; and that in this particular case, the burden of guilt for the bloody and mindless massacre of the Jews rests on a large number of Germans, many of them alive today, and not just on one "mad dictator," whose order had to be obeyed without question.

I had approached the massacre of the Jews from the traditional viewpoint prevailing in the mid-1960s. "Supposing Hitler was a capable statesman and a gifted commander," the argument ran, "how does one explain his murder of six million Jews?" If this book were simply a history of the rise and fall of Hitler's Reich, it would be legitimate to conclude: "Hitler killed the Jews." He after all created the atmosphere of hatred with his anti-Semitic speeches in the 1930s; he and Himmler created the SS; he built the concentration camps; his speeches, though never explicit, left the clear impression that "liquidate" was what he meant. For a full-length war biography of Hitler, I felt that a more analytical approach to the key questions of initiative, complicity, and execution would be necessary. Remarkably, I found that Hitler's *own* role in the "Final Solution of the Jewish Problem" has never been examined. German historians, usually the epitome of painstaking essaying on every other subject, to whom no hypothesis is acceptable unless scrutinized from a thousand angles, suddenly developed monumental blind spots when Hitler himself cropped up: bald statements were made, legends were created, blame was laid, without a shadow of historical evidence in support. British and American historians followed suit. Other writers quoted them. For thirty years, our knowledge of Hitler's part in the atrocity has rested on inter-historian incest.

Many people, particularly in Germany and Austria, had an interest in propagating the accepted version that the order of one madman originated the entire massacre. Precisely when the order was given and in what form has, admittedly, never been established. In 1939?—but the secret extermination camps did not begin operating until December 1941. At the January 1942 "Wannsee Conference"?—but the incontrovertible evidence is that Hitler ordered on November 30, 1941, that there was to be "no liquidation" of the Jews (without much difficulty, I found in Himmler's private files his own handwritten note on this). On several subsequent dates in 1942 Hitler made—in private—statements which are totally incompatible with the notion that he knew that the liquidation program had in fact begun. In 1943, and again in early 1944, I find that documents being submitted to Hitler by the SS were tampered with so as to camouflage the truth about the pogrom: sometimes the files contain both the original texts and the "doctored" version submitted to Hitler. Small wonder that when his closest crony of all those years, SS General Josef ("Sepp") Dietrich, was asked by the American Seventh Army for an opinion on Hitler on June 1, 1945, he replied, "He knew even less than the rest. He allowed himself to be taken for a sucker by everyone."

My own hypothesis, to which I point in the various chapters in which I deal in chronological sequence with the unfolding persecution and liquidation of the European Jews, is this: the killing was partly of an *ad hoc* nature, what the Germans call a *Verlegenheitslösung*—the way out of an awkward dilemma, chosen by the middle-level authorities in the eastern territories overrun by the Nazis —and partly a cynical extrapolation by the central SS authorities of Hitler's anti-Semitic decrees. Hitler had unquestionably decreed that Europe's Jews were to be "swept back" to the east; I describe the various phase-lines established by this doctrine. But the SS authorities, Gauleiters, and regional commissars and governors in "the east" proved wholly unequal to the problems caused by this mass uprooting in midwar. The Jews were brought by the trainload to ghettos already overcrowded and underprovisioned. Partly in collusion with each other, partly independently, the Nazi agencies there simply liquidated the deportees as their trains arrived, on a scale increasingly more methodical and more regimented as the months passed.

A subsidiary motive in the atrocity was the animal desire of the murderers to loot and plunder the Jewish victims and conceal their traces. (This hypothesis does not include the methodical liquidation of Russian Jews during the "Barbarossa" invasion of 1941, which came under a different Nazi heading—preemptive guerrilla warfare; and there is no indication that Hitler expressed any compunctions about it.) We shall see how in October 1943, even as Himmler was disclosing to audiences of SS generals and Gauleiters that Europe's Jews had virtually been exterminated, Hitler was still forbidding liquidations—*e.g.,* of the Italian Jews in Rome—and ordering their internment instead. (This order his SS also disobeyed.) Wholly in keeping with his character, when Hitler was confronted with the facts—either then or, as Kaltenbrunner later claimed, in October

1944—he took no action to rebuke the guilty. His failure or inability to act in effect kept the extermination machinery going until the end of the war.

It is plausible to impute to Hitler that not uncommon characteristic of Heads of State who are overreliant on powerful advisers: a conscious desire "not to know." But the proof of this is beyond the powers of any historian. What we *can* prove is that Himmler several times explicitly accepted responsibility for the liquidation decision.

Given the brutality of Hitler's orders to "dispose of" the entire male populations of two major Soviet cities, his insistence on the execution of hostages on a one hundred to one basis, his demands for the liquidation of Italian soldiers, Polish intellectuals, clergy and nobility, and captured Allied airmen and Red Army commissars, his apparent reluctance to acquiesce in the extermination of Europe's Jews remains a mystery. His order in July 1944, despite Himmler's objections, that Jews be "sold" for foreign currency and supplies suggests to some that like contemporary terrorists he saw these captives as a potential "asset," a means by which he could blackmail the civilized world. In any case, by April 1945 whatever inhibitions he may have felt were overcome, and we find him ordering Himmler to liquidate any unevacuated prisoners from concentration camps that were in danger of being overrun by American troops.

My central conclusion, however, is that Hitler was a less than omnipotent Führer and that his grip on his immediate subordinates weakened as the war progressed. Hitler certainly realized this, but too late—in the final days, in his Berlin air raid shelter. In the last two chapters we see him struggling vainly to turn the clock back, to reassert his lost authority by securing one last tactical victory over his enemies. But there are few generals—either Wehrmacht or SS —who now heed him.

I also found it necessary to set very different historical accents on the doctrinaire foreign policies Hitler enforced—from his apparent unwillingness to humiliate Britain when she lay prostrate in 1940 (as I believe I establish on pages 152–53, for example), to his damaging and emotional hatred of the Serbs, his illogical and over-loyal admiration of Benito Mussolini, and his irrational mixtures of emotions toward Josef Stalin. For a modern English historian there is a certain morbid fascination in inquiring how far Adolf Hitler really was bent on the destruction of Britain and her Empire—a major raison d'être for her ruinous fight, which in 1940 imperceptibly supplanted the more implausible one proffered in August 1939: the rescue of Poland from outside oppression. Since in the chapters that follow evidence extracted again and again from the most intimate sources—like Hitler's private conversations with his women secretaries in June 1940—indicates that he originally had neither the intention nor the desire to harm

Britain or destroy the Empire, surely British readers at least must ask themselves: What, then, were we fighting for?

Given that the British people exhausted their assets and lost their Empire in defeating Hitler, was he after all right when he noted that Britain's essential attitude was "Après moi le déluge—if only we can get rid of the hated National Socialist Germany?"

Unburdened by ideological idealism, the Duke of Windsor suspected in July 1940 that the war continued solely in order to allow certain British statesmen to save face, even if it meant dragging their country and the Empire into financial ruin. Others pragmatically argued that there could be no compromise with Adolf Hitler and the Nazis. But did Britain's leaders in fact believe this?

Dr. Bernd Martin of Freiburg University has revealed that secret negotiations on peace continued between Britain and Germany in October 1939—negotiations on which, curiously, Sir Winston Churchill's files have officially been sealed until the twenty-first century! Similar negotiations were carried on in June 1940, when even Churchill showed himself in Cabinet meetings to be willing to make a deal with Hitler if the price was right.

Of course, in assessing the real value of such negotiations and of Hitler's publicly stated intentions it is salutary to know that in 1941 he confidentially admitted to Walther Hewel (as the latter recorded in his diary): "For myself personally I would never tell a lie; but there is no falsehood I would not perpetrate for Germany's sake!" It is also necessary to take into account a string of broken promises that kept Europe in paralyzed inactivity for the better part of a decade.

Nevertheless, one wonders how much suffering the (Western) world might have been spared if both sides had pursued this line. But modern historiography has chosen to ignore this possibility as heresy.

The facts revealed here concerning Hitler's recorded actions, motivations, and opinions should provide a basis for fresh debate. Americans will find much that is new about the months leading up to Pearl Harbor. The French will find additional evidence that Hitler's treatment of their defeated nation was more influenced by memories of France's treatment of Germany after World War I than by his respect for Mussolini's desires. Russians can try to visualize the prospect that could conceivably have unfolded if Stalin had accepted Hitler's offer in November 1940 of inclusion in the Axis Pact; or if, having been defeated in the summer of 1941, Stalin had accepted Hitler's offer to rebuild Soviet power beyond the Urals; or if Hitler had taken seriously Stalin's alleged peace offer of September 1944.

In each case, this book views the situation as far as possible through Hitler's eyes, from behind his desk. This technique was bound to yield different perspectives, while answering many questions that arose in the past as to the motives for his actions and decisions. For example, I have devoted great effort to accumulating the same Intelligence material that was presented to Hitler—like the rare intercepts of Göring's *Forschungsamt* (literally, "Research Office"), which monitored telephone lines and decoded international radio signals; these explain, for instance, Hitler's alarm in July 1940 over Stalin's intentions.

Because this tragic moment in history is told from Hitler's point of view, we inevitably *see* the sufferings of the Germans, whereas the destruction and death inflicted on other nations remains somewhat more abstract. However, it is well to keep in mind that conservative estimates are that Hitler's War resulted in 40,000,000 military and civilian deaths. Of this number approximately 2,500,000 were Germans.

In modern Germany, some of my conclusions proved unpalatable to many. A wave of weak, repetitive, and unrevealing Hitler biographies had washed through the bookstores two or three years before my manuscript (running to over three thousand pages in the first draft) was published. The most widely publicized was that written by a German television personality, Joachim Fest; but he later told a questioner that he had not even visited the magnificent National Archives in Washington, which houses by far the largest collection of records relating to recent European history. Stylistically, Fest's German was good; but the old legends were trotted out afresh, polished to an impressive gleam of authority. The same Berlin company also published my book shortly after, under the title *Hitler und seine Feldherren;* their chief editor found many of my arguments distasteful, even dangerous, and without informing me, suppressed or even reversed them: in *their* printed text Hitler had not told Himmler there was to be "no liquidation" of the Jews (on November 30, 1941); he had told him not to use the word "liquidate" publicly in connection with their extermination program. Thus history is falsified! (My suggestion that they publish Himmler's note as a facsimile had been ignored.) I prohibited further printing of the book, two days after its appearance in Germany. To explain their actions, the Berlin publishers argued that my manuscript expressed some views that were "an affront to established historical opinion" in their country.

The biggest problem in dealing analytically with Hitler is the aversion to him as a person created by years of intense wartime propaganda and emotive postwar historiography. My own impression of the war is limited to snapshot memories of its side effects: early summer picnics around the wreckage of a Heinkel bomber on the fringe of the local Bluebell Woods; the infernal organ note of the V-1 flying bombs awakening the whole countryside as they passed overhead; convoys of drab army trucks rumbling past our country gate; counting the gaps in the American bomber squadrons straggling back from Germany in formation after the day's operations; the troopships sailing in June 1944 from Southsea beach, heading for Normandy; and of course VE-Day itself, with the bonfires and beating of the family gong. Our knowledge of the Germans responsible for all this was scarcely more profound. In *Everybody's* magazine, long defunct, I recall "Ferrier's World Searchlight" with its weekly caricatures of a club-footed dwarf called Goebbels and the other comic Nazi heroes.

The caricatures of the Nazi leaders have bedeviled the writing of history ever since. Writers have found it impossible to de-demonize them. Confronted by the phenomenon of Hitler himself, they cannot grasp that he was an ordinary, walking, talking human weighing some 155 pounds, with graying hair, largely false teeth, and chronic digestive ailments. He is to them the Devil incarnate. The process flourished even more after his death: at the Nuremberg Trials, the blame was shifted from general to minister, from minister to Party official, and from all of them invariably to Hitler. Under the system of "licensed" publishers and newspapers enforced by the Allies in postwar Germany, the legends prospered. No story was too absurd to gain credence; the authority of the writers who created them passed unchallenged.

Among these creative writers the German General Staff must take pride of place. Without Hitler, few of them would have risen higher than to the rank of colonel; they owed him their jobs, their medals, their estates, their endowments. Often they owed him their military victories too—the defeat of France in 1940 (see pages 44–45, 80–81, 114, 116–18), the Battle of Kharkov in 1942 (pages 387–88), to mention just two. After the war those who survived—which was not infrequently because they had been dismissed, and thus removed from the hazards of the battlefield—contrived to divert the blame away from themselves to the erstwhile Führer and Supreme Commander. I have exposed the frauds and deceptions in their biographies. Thus in the secret files of the Nuremberg prosecutor Justice Robert H. Jackson, I found a note addressed to his investigator warning about the proposed tactics of General Franz Halder, the former German Army Chief of Staff: "I just wanted to call your attention to the CSDIC intercepts of Halder's conversations with other generals. He is extremely frank on what he thinks should be suppressed or distorted, and in particular is very sensitive to the suggestion that the German General Staff was involved in anything, especially planning for war." Usually, these tactics involved labeling Hitler a "madman" —although the medical experts who treated him are unanimous that clinically speaking he remained quite sane to the very end.

Fortunately, this embarrassed adjusting of consciences and memories was more than once, as above, recorded for posterity by the hidden microphones of the Combined Services Detailed Interrogation Centers. When General Heinz Guderian—one of Halder's successors as Chief of Staff—and the arrogant, supercilious General Leo Geyr von Schweppenburg were asked by their American captors to write their history of the war, they felt obliged to obtain the permission of Field Marshal Wilhelm von Leeb as senior officer at the Seventh Army CSDIC. Leeb replied:

> Well, I can only give you my personal opinion: . . . You will have to weigh your answers carefully when they pertain to objectives, causes, and the progress of operations in order to see where they may affect the interests of our Fatherland. On the one hand we have to admit that the Americans know the course of operations quite accurately; they even know which units were employed on our side. However, they are not quite as familiar with our motives. And there is one point where it would be advisable to proceed with caution, so that we do not become the laughingstock of the world. I do not know what your relations were with Hitler, but I do know his military capacity. . . . You will have to consider your answers a bit carefully when approached on this subject, so that you say nothing that might embarrass our Fatherland. . . .
>
> *Geyr von Schweppenburg:* The types of madness known to psychologists cannot be compared with the one the Führer suffered from. He was a madman surrounded by serfs. I do not think we should express ourselves quite as strongly as that in our statements. Mention of this fact will have to be made, however, in order to exonerate a few persons. The question is whether now is the right time to mention all this.

After an agonized debate on whether and which German generals advocated war in 1939, Leeb suggested: "The question is now, whether we should not just admit openly everything we know." The following discussion ensued:

> *Geyr von Schweppenburg:* Any objective observer will admit that National Socialism raised the social status of the worker, and in some respects even his standard of living as long as that was possible.
>
> *Leeb:* This is one of the great achievements of National Socialism. The excesses of National Socialism were in the first and final analysis due to the Führer's personality.
>
> *Guderian:* The fundamental principles were fine.
>
> *Leeb:* That is true.

I was startled and, as a historian, depressed by the number of "diaries" which close scrutiny proved to have been faked or tampered with—invariably to Hitler's disadvantage. Two different men claimed to possess the entire diaries of Admiral Wilhelm Canaris—the legendary Abwehr chief hanged by Hitler as a traitor in April 1945. The first produced "documents of the postwar German Intelligence Service (BND)" and original papers "signed by Canaris" in his support; the second, a German High Court judge, announced that his set of the diaries had recently been returned by Generalissimo Francisco Franco to the West German government. Forensic tests on the paper and ink of a "Canaris" document supplied by the first man, conducted for me by a London laboratory, proved them to be forgeries. An interview with Franco's chef de bureau—his brother-in-law Don Felipe Polo Valdes—in Madrid disposed of the German judge's equally improbable claim. Neither ever provided the actual diaries for inspection. The Eva Braun diaries published by the film actor Luis Trenker were largely forged from the "memoirs" written decades earlier by Countess Irma Larisch-Wallersee; the forgery was established by the Munich lawcourts in October 1948. (Eva Braun's genuine diaries, and her entire correspondence with Hitler, were acquired by a CIC team based on Stuttgart-Backnang in the summer of 1945; they have not been seen since. I identified the team's commander and visited him in New Mexico; he admitted the facts, but I failed to persuade him to make the papers available for historical research—perhaps he has long since sold them to a private dealer.) The oft-quoted "diaries" of Himmler's masseur Felix Kersten are equally fictitious, as for example the "twenty-six-page medical dossier on Hitler" described in them shows. Oddly enough Kersten's real diaries—containing political dynamite on Sweden's elite—do exist and have not been published. Similarly, the "diaries" published by Rudolf Semmler in *Goebbels—the Man Next to Hitler* (London, 1947) are phony too, as the entry for January 12, 1945, proves: it has Hitler as Goebbels's guest in Berlin, when the Führer was in fact still fighting the Battle of the Bulge from his HQ in West Germany. And there are no prizes for spotting the anachronisms in Count Galeazzo Ciano's extensively quoted "diaries": for example Marshal Rodolfo Graziani's "complaints about Rommel" on December 12, 1940—two full months *before* Rommel was appointed to Italy's North African theater! In fact Ciano spent the months after his dismissal in February 1943 rewriting and "improving" the diaries himself, which makes them very readable but virtually useless for the purposes of history. Ribbentrop warned about the forgery in his prison memoirs—he claimed to have seen Ciano's real diaries in September 1943—and the Nazi interpreter Eugen Dollmann described in his memoirs how the fraud was actually admitted to him by a British officer at a prison camp. Even the most superficial examination of the handwritten original volumes reveals the extent to which Ciano doctored them and interpolated material—yet historians of the highest repute have quoted them without question as they have Ciano's so-called "Lisbon Papers," although the latter too bear all the hallmarks of subsequent editing. They have all at some time been retyped on the same typewriter, although ostensibly originating over six years (1936–42).

Other diaries have been amended in more harmless ways: the Luftwaffe Chief of Staff Karl Koller's real shorthand diary often bears no resemblance to the version he published as *Der letzte Monat* (Mannheim, 1949). And Helmuth Greiner, keeper of the official OKW operations staff war diary until 1943, seized the opportunity in 1945, when asked by the Americans to retranscribe his original notes for the lost volumes from August 1942 to March 1943, to excise passages which reflected unfavorably on fellow prisoners like General Adolf Heusinger—or too favorably on Hitler; and no doubt to curry favor with the Americans, he added lengthy paragraphs charged with pungent criticism of Hitler's conduct of the war which I found to be missing from his original handwritten notes when I compared them with the published version. This tendency—to pillory Hitler after the war—was also strongly evident in the "diaries" of General Gerhard Engel, who served as Hitler's army adjutant from March 1938 to October 1943. Historiographical evidence alone—*e.g.,* comparison with the 1940 private diaries of Reichsminister Fritz Todt or the wife of General Rudolf Schmundt, or with the records of Field Marshal von Manstein's Army Group Don at the time of Stalingrad—indicates that whatever they are, they are *not* contemporaneous diaries (regrettably, the well-known Institut für Zeitgeschichte in Munich has nonetheless published them in a volume, *Heeresadjutant bei Hitler 1938–1943* [Stuttgart, 1974], rather feebly drawing attention to the diaries' inconsistencies in a short Introduction).

My exploration of sources throwing light on Hitler's inner mind was sometimes successful, sometimes not. Weeks of searching with a proton-magnetometer—a kind of supersensitive mine-detector—in a forest in East Germany failed to unearth a glass jar containing stenograms of Goebbels's very last diaries, although at times, according to the map in my possession, we must have stood right over it. But I did obtain the private diaries written by Walther Hewel, Ribbentrop's liaison officer on Hitler's staff, and by Baron Ernst von Weizsäcker, Ribbentrop's state secretary. Field Marshal Wolfram von Richthofen's widow made available to me the two thousand-page original text of his unpublished diaries too; in fact every officer or member of Hitler's staff whom I interviewed seemed to have carefully hoarded diaries or papers, which were eventually produced for my exploitation here—mostly in German, but the research papers on the fringe also came in a Babel of other languages: Italian, Russian, French, Spanish, Hungarian, Romanian, and Czech; some cryptic references to Hitler and Ribbentrop in the Hewel diaries defied all my puny codebreaking efforts, and then proved to have been written in Indonesian! For the sake of completeness, I would add that Field Marshal Fedor von Bock's diary was pruned by him, but he does not seem to have interpolated fresh material; and that General Halder's diary is completely trustworthy (having been originally transcribed from the shorthand by the British) but is best employed *without* reference to Halder's postwar footnotes.

Many sources of prime importance are still missing, although enterprising West German publishers have now obtained the full text of Goebbels's diaries. That those of Hewel and Weizsäcker remained hitherto unexplored by historians is a baffling mystery to me. They only had to ask the widows, as I did. The diaries of Hans Lammers, Wilhelm Brückner, Karl Bodenschatz, Karl Wolff, and Professor Theo Morell are missing, although known to have fallen into Allied hands in 1945. Nicolaus von Below's are probably in Moscow. Himmler's missing pocket notebooks certainly are. Alfred Rosenberg's remaining diaries are illicitly held by an American lawyer in Frankfurt. The rest of Field Marshal Erhard Milch's diaries—of which I obtained some five thousand pages in 1967—have vanished, as have General Alfred Jodl's diaries covering the years 1940 to 1943; they were looted with his private property by the British 11th Armored Division at Flensburg in May 1945. Only a brief fragment of Benito Mussolini's diary survives (see pages 541–42): the SS copied the originals and returned them to him in January 1945, but both the originals and the copy placed in Ribbentrop's files are missing now; a forgery perpetrated by two Italian nuns temporarily and expensively deceived the London *Sunday Times* some years ago, before it was exposed by the same laboratory that tested the "Canaris" document for me. The important diaries of Schmundt were unhappily burnt at his request by his fellow adjutant Admiral Karl-Jesco von Puttkamer in April 1945, along with Puttkamer's own diaries. The diary of Dr. Stephan Tiso, the last Slovak premier (from August 1944), is unaccountably held in the closed files of the Hoover Institution.

As for autobiographical works, I preferred to rely on the original manuscripts rather than the published texts, as in the early postwar years apprehensive publishers (especially the "licensed" ones in Germany) made changes in them—for example in the memoirs of Karl-Wilhelm Krause, Hitler's manservant. Thus I relied on the original handwritten memoirs of Himmler's Intelligence chief, Walter Schellenberg, rather than on the mutilated and ghostwritten version subsequently published. I would go so far as to warn against the authoritativeness of numerous works hitherto accepted as "standard" sources on Hitler—particularly those by Konrad Heiden, Dr. Hermann Rauschning, Dr. Hans Bernd Gisevius, Erich Kordt, and by Hitler's dismissed adjutant Fritz Wiedemann. (The latter unashamedly explained in a private 1940 letter to a friend: "It makes no difference if exaggerations and even falsehoods do creep in.")

With the brilliant exception of Professor Hugh Trevor-Roper, whose book *The Last Days of Hitler* was based on the records of the era and is therefore virtually unassailable even today, each successive biographer has repeated or engrossed the legends created by his predecessors, or at best consulted only the most readily available works of reference themselves. Since it proved impracticable to study in detail such a dictator's whole life within this one volume, I limited myself to his war years; I eschewed as far as possible all *published* literature, since by 1964 when I began the research it was possible to speculate that "books on Hitler" outnumbered page for page the total original documentation available. This proved a sad underestimate.

Idle predecessors had gratefully lamented that most of the documents had been destroyed. They had not—they survived in embarrassing superabundance. The official papers of the Luftwaffe Field Marshal Milch, Göring's deputy, were captured by the British and total over 60,000 pages (not that Göring's most recent biographer consulted even one page of them). The entire war diary of the German naval staff, of immense value far beyond purely naval matters, survived; it took many months to read the 69 volumes of main text, some over 900 pages long, in Washington, and to examine the most promising of the 3,900 microfilm rolls of German naval records held there too.

And what is the result? Hitler will long remain an enigma, however hard the historians burrow and toil. Even his intimates realized they hardly knew him. I have already quoted Ribbentrop's puzzlement; but General Alfred Jodl, his closest strategic adviser, also wrote in his Nuremberg cell on March 10, 1946:

> . . . But then I ask myself, did you ever really know this man at whose side you led such a thorny and ascetic existence? Did he perhaps just trifle with your idealism too, abusing it for dark purposes which he kept hidden deep within himself? Dare you claim to know a man, if he has not opened up the deepest recesses of his heart to you—in sorrow as well as in ecstasy? To this very day I do not know what he thought or knew or really wanted. I only knew my own thoughts and suspicions. And if, now that the shrouds fall away from a sculpture we fondly hoped would be a work of art, only to reveal nothing but a degenerate gargoyle—then let future historians argue among themselves whether it was like that from the start, or changed with circumstances.
>
> I keep making the same mistake: I blame his humble origins. But then I remember how many peasants' sons have been blessed by History with the name, The Great.

"Hitler the Great"? No, contemporary History is unlikely to swallow such an epithet.

From the first day that he "seized power," January 30, 1933, Hitler knew that only sudden death awaited him if he failed to restore pride and empire to post-Versailles Germany. His close friend and adjutant, Julius Schaub, recorded Hitler's jubilant boast to his staff on that evening, as the last celebrating guests left the Berlin Chancellery building: "No power on earth will get me out of this building alive!"

History saw this prophecy fulfilled, as the handful of remaining Nazi faithfuls trooped uneasily into his underground study on April 30, 1945, surveyed his still warm remains—slumped on a couch, with blood trickling from the sagging lower jaw, and a gunshot wound in the right temple—and sniffed the bitter-almonds smell hanging in the air. Wrapped in a gray army blanket, he was carried up to the shell-blasted Chancellery garden. Gasoline was slopped over him in a reeking crater and ignited while his staff hurriedly saluted and backed down into the shelter. Thus ended the six years of Hitler's War. We shall now see how they began.

— David Irving,
London, January 1976

Hitler's People

As an aid to following the narrative, brief biographical details follow of the principal German personalities referred to in the text.

ALBRECHT, Alwin-Broder: Until June 1939 Hitler's naval adjutant, his replacement was demanded by Raeder after an unfortunate marriage; Hitler demurred and made him a personal adjutant instead. He is presumed to have died in the last days in Berlin.

AMSBERG, Colonel Erik von: A former adjutant of Keitel's, he stepped in as Hitler's Wehrmacht adjutant after Below, Puttkamer, and Schmundt were injured in the July 20, 1944, bomb explosion.

ASSMANN, Admiral Heinz: Jodl's naval staff officer, who frequently attended Hitler's war conferences from 1943 to 1944.

BACKE, Dr. Herbert: The very capable state secretary in the food ministry, who virtually supplanted the minister, Richard Walter Darré, in 1942.

BECK, General Ludwig: Was Army Chief of Staff until August 1938, when he was replaced by Halder and began to intrigue against Hitler; after the July 20, 1944, bomb plot failed, he committed suicide.

BELOW, Colonel Nicolaus von: Genteel and educated, Below served as Hitler's Luftwaffe adjutant from 1937 until the Führer's suicide.

BERGER, SS General Gottlob: Chief of Himmler's SS Main Office *(Hauptamt)*.

BEST, Dr. Werner: A department head in the Gestapo, he was appointed Hitler's Plenipotentiary in Denmark in 1942.

BLASCHKE, Professor Johannes: Hitler's principal dentist—his postwar interrogation by the Americans provides the main evidence that Hitler's was the corpse found by the Red Army in Berlin.

BLOMBERG, Field Marshal Werner von: The first field marshal created by Hitler—in 1937—Blomberg was fired as war minister in early 1938 after marrying way, way below his station; but Hitler had a soft spot for him until the very end.

BOCK, Field Marshal Fedor von: One of Hitler's toughest and most successful soldiers in France (1940) and Russia (1941–42), he died in an air raid in 1945.

BODENSCHATZ, General Karl: Officially Göring's chef de bureau, Bodenschatz became his permanent representative at Hitler's HQ.

BONIN, Colonel Bogislaw von: Latterly the chief of operations in the German General Staff.

BORGMANN, Colonel Heinrich: Succeeded Engel as Hitler's army adjutant in 1943; killed by air attack on his car in April 1945.

BORMANN, Albert: Younger brother of Martin Bormann, but not on speaking terms with him; Albert was an adjutant in Hitler's Private Chancellary.

BORMANN, Martin: Rose from relative obscurity as Hess's right-hand man to position of vast personal power upon Hess's defection in May 1941. Head of the Nazi Party Chancellery, and from 1943 the "Führer's secretary" as well. He was the dynamo inside the Nazi machine, converting Hitler's half-spoken thoughts into harsh reality. Hard working, hard living—condemned to death at Nuremberg in absentia, his lawyer's appeal for clemency is still on the case file, undecided.

BOUHLER, Reichsleiter Philipp: As Chief of the Chancellery of the Führer of the Nazi party, Bouhler handled the incoming mail of German citizens; as such his office dealt with applications for clemency and thus became involved in the murderous euthanasia projects and the technicalities of the liquidation of Jews and other "undesirables." He took his own life in May 1945.

BRANDT, Dr. Karl: Hitler's accompanying surgeon from the mid-Thirties onward, he was dismissed in October 1944 by Martin Bormann; the Americans hanged him in 1947 for his part in the euthanasia planning.

BRAUCIIITSCII, Field Marshal Walther von: Appointed Commander in Chief, Army, by Hitler in 1938 for want of a better general; Hitler tolerated him only reluctantly until his ill-health provided sufficient cover for his retirement in December 1941. He died in British captivity in 1948.

BRAUN, Eva: Hitler's only known mistress from 1931 onward; she provided conversation and company, and according to Hitler's secretaries, developed from the humble laboratory assistant she had been before then into a woman of great poise and charm. He formally married her thirty-six hours before their joint suicide in April 1945.

BRÜCKNER, SA Gruppenführer Wilhelm: A chief adjutant of Hitler's, dismissed in October 1940—having, like Albrecht and Blomberg, contracted a much-criticized marriage.

BURGDORF, General Wilhelm: Succeeded Schmundt as Hitler's chief Wehrmacht adjutant and chief of the army personnel branch after Schmundt was wounded in the July 20, 1944, bomb explosion; previously Schmundt's deputy. A rough diamond and heavy drinker, he committed suicide soon after Hitler.

CANARIS, Vice Admiral Wilhelm: Chief of the Abwehr—the OKW Intelligence

Branch—until its absorption by the SS in 1944, Canaris weathered many storms. A man of few friends, with Indian manservants, Greek blood, and a liking for warm champagne for breakfast, he slipped off his tightrope between the traitors and the SS in 1944 and was hanged in the last month of the war.

CHRISTIAN, General Eckhard: He had been Jodl's chief staff officer until he married Hitler's personal secretary Gerda Daranowski in November 1942; then he rose rapidly until he was the chief of the Luftwaffe operations staff.

CHRISTIAN, Frau Gerda: One of Hitler's four private secretaries, and certainly the most attractive—as the Führer is known to have appreciated. She joined his staff before the war, retired on her marriage in November 1942, but returned a year later and stayed with Hitler until the end.

DARGES, Fritz: Martin Bormann's adjutant until 1939, he became Hitler's personal adjutant from March 1943—until Hitler sacked him in July 1944, ostensibly because of an incident with an insect during a war conference, more probably because Darges had jilted Eva's sister Gretl Braun. He was sent to the Russian front.

DIETRICH, Dr. Otto: Hitler's press spokesman.

DIETRICH, SS General Josef "Sepp": One of the Party Old Guard, he commanded the SS Leibstandarte (Life Guards) and then the SS Sixth Panzer Army.

DÖNITZ, Grand Admiral Karl: Commander in Chief of the German U-boat service until 1943, he stepped into Raeder's shoes when the latter resigned as Commander in Chief, Navy, that January. Dönitz supported Hitler's bolder strategic decisions—*i.e.,* to hold on to the Crimea and the eastern Baltic provinces—and satisfied Hitler that he was the best successor as Führer in April 1945.

DORSCH, Dr. Xaver: After Fritz Todt, one of the Reich's most outstanding civil engineers; became head of the Todt Organization building military sites in Reich-occupied countries.

EICHMANN, SS Colonel Adolf: A minor official in Kaltenbrunner's Reich Main Security Office, Eichmann was responsible for the smooth running of the Jewish deportation programs; he was one of the driving forces behind the extermination of the Jews.

EICKEN, Professor Carl von: The ear, nose, and throat specialist who operated on Hitler's throat in 1935 and again in November 1944.

ENGEL, Colonel Gerhard: Hitler's army adjutant from 1938 to 1943, he then distinguished himself as a division commander.

ETZDORF, Major Hasso von: Liaison officer between the General Staff and Ribbentrop's foreign ministry, his often cryptic penciled notes were deciphered by the Americans postwar and present vital information on Hitler's foreign strategy.

FALKENHAUSEN, General Alexander von: The aristocratic Nazi Military Governor of Belgium, he entered into a liaison with an equally aristocratic Belgian lady which resulted in his dismissal in July 1944; this probably spared him from the hangman's noose some weeks later, as his implication in the bomb plot escaped the attention of the Gestapo.

FEGELEIN, SS General Hermann: Himmler's representative at Hitler's HQ from 1944 to the end; married Gretl Braun (*see also* Darges) but left her a widow, as he was shot for attempted desertion in the last days.

FELLGIEBEL, General Erich: Chief of the Wehrmacht's and Army's Signals Branches, he was executed after the failure of the 1944 bomb plot in which he was implicated.

FRANK, Dr. Hans: One of Hitler's oldest friends and his personal legal adviser in the Thirties. Hitler appointed him Governor General of rump Poland after that country's defeat in 1939.

FRANK, Karl-Hermann: Deputy Protector of Bohemia-Moravia.

FRICK, Dr. Wilhelm: Minister of the Interior, until Himmler supplanted him in August 1943.

FROMM, General Friedrich: A deadly enemy of Keitel, Fromm commanded the Replacement Army—divisions being raised and trained in Germany; he was implicated in the July 20, 1944, conspiracy, but only vaguely—the People's Court found no evidence, for example, that he had known of the plot, but condemned him to death for cowardice in not having acted more energetically against his Chief of Staff, Stauffenberg, that afternoon.

GIESING, Dr. Erwin: Army ENT-specialist summoned from Rastenburg hospital after July 20, 1944, bomb explosion to treat Hitler's head injuries.

GLOBOCNIK, SS Brigadier Odilo: Formerly police commander in occupied Polish district of Lublin, he ranked with Eichmann as one of the Nazis behind the massacre of the Jews.

GOEBBELS, Dr. Joseph: one of the Party's Old Guard; Gauleiter of Berlin, and after 1933 Reich propaganda minister—an outstanding speaker and master of dialectics, but undoubtedly one of the evil geniuses behind the Führer. Took his own and his family's lives after Hitler's suicide.

GOERDELER, Dr. Carl: Former mayor of Leipzig, Goerdeler was political leader of the anti-Hitler conspiracy culminating in the July 20, 1944, bomb explosion.

GÖRING, Reichsmarschall Hermann: A man of many titles, but principally important as Commander in Chief of the Luftwaffe and head of the Four-Year Plan office. Alternating between bouts of laziness and spasms of intense activity, he was most closely identified by the German public with their eventual misery and defeat—but somehow his popularity remained virtually unimpaired until his October 1946 suicide.

GUDERIAN, General Heinz: Ranks as one of World War II's leading tank commanders; was dismissed by Hitler in December 1941 to satisfy Kluge and remained in a command limbo until Hitler appointed him his personal Inspector of the Panzer Service in February 1943. Even then Guderian wavered in his loyalty; he certainly had advance warning of the July 20, 1944, bomb explosion and prudently absented himself from the Führer's HQ that day—to return only hours later, to his own surprise, as the army's new Chief of General Staff until March 1945.

GÜNSCHE, SS Colonel Otto: Formerly a private in Hitler's escort squad, Günsche—a big, blond bulldog of an officer—became his personal adjutant and bodyguard, and was entrusted by the Führer with burning his corpse after his suicide in April 1945—and with giving him a coup de grâce with his pistol if necessary.

HAASE, Professor Werner: Had treated Hitler before the war, became his doctor again briefly in the last days in Berlin.

HALDER, General Franz: Succeeded Beck as the army's Chief of General Staff in 1938; generally acknowledged to have been a good tactician, Halder retained this post until Hitler could stand him no longer—in September 1942.

HASSELBACH, Dr. Hanskarl von: Dr. Karl Brandt's deputy as Hitler's accompanying surgeon until October 1944.

HESS, Rudolf: Hitler's official "deputy" until his flight to Scotland in May 1941.

HEWEL, Ambassador Walther: He had joined the Nazi party as a student in the early Twenties, shared Hitler's Landsberg imprisonment briefly in 1923, then emigrated as a planter to Java; he returned to become a member of Ribbentrop's staff—serving through the period of this book as liaison officer at Hitler's HQ.

HEYDRICH, SS General Reinhard: Kaltenbrunner's predecessor as chief of the Reich Main Security Office of the SS; as such he was more interested in the "executive" side—the building of a formidable police organization throughout Germany. Appointed "Reich Protector" of occupied Czechoslovakia in October 1941, embarked on reforms there, assassinated by British-trained agents in May 1942. As he was the brain behind the extermination camps, he merits no sympathy.

HIMMLER, Heinrich: SS Reichsführer, chief of police, and—after August 1943 —Minister of the Interior. "Himmler," said the Nazi party newspaper chief Max Amann, "considered it his duty to eliminate all enemies of the Nazi ideology and he did so calmly and impersonally, without hate and without sympathy." A rare mixture of crackpot and organizational genius.

JESCHONNEK, General Hans: A lieutenant at sixteen in World War I, he seemed marked out for a brilliant career; by 1939 he was Luftwaffe Chief of Staff —by August 1943 he was dead, a suicide.

JODL, General Alfred: A pure soldier, of unquestionable loyalty to his Führer, Jodl served as chief of the OKW operations staff *(Wehrmachtführungsstab)* from August 1939 to the very end. His strategic insight was profound. He was hanged at Nuremberg in 1946.

JUNGE, Frau Traudl: Youngest of Hitler's secretaries, she joined his staff when Gerda Daranowski married in 1942; she herself married Hitler's manservant Hans Junge, was widowed by 1944, and stayed with Hitler to the end. (Née Traudl Humps.)

JUNGE, Captain Wolf: Jodl's naval staff officer until August 28, 1943, then again from summer 1944 onward while Assmann recovered from injuries sustained on July 20, 1944.

KALTENBRUNNER, SS General Dr. Ernst: Heydrich's successor as chief of the Reich Main Security Office—but personally more interested in the Intelligence side and less in the police and executive aspects, in which "Gestapo" Müller grew in influence.

KEITEL, Field Marshal Wilhelm: Chief of OKW (German High Command) in title only; he exercised his ministerial functions well; the military and strategic side he—wisely—left to Jodl. Loyal and hardworking, Keitel shared Jodl's fate at Nuremberg.

KESSELRING, Field Marshal Albert: He held important air commands during the invasions of Poland, France, and Russia. Supreme commander of German forces in Italy (1943–1945), in March 1945 he took over from Rundstedt as Commander in Chief West. In 1947 he was condemned to death for war crimes against Italian civilians, but this sentence was later commuted to life imprisonment. He was pardoned in 1952.

KLUGE, Field Marshal Günther Hans von: A good commander of men, like Rommel—always in the battle line with his troops, but politically ambitious too. Lent an ear to various groups of plotters, but would not commit himself. Fearing implication in the failed July 20, 1944, plot, Kluge took cyanide and closed his "big blue, patrician eyes" for the last time on August 18, 1944, his personal admiration for Adolf Hitler undiminished.

KOCH, Erich: Gauleiter of East Prussia, he was appointed Reich Commissioner in the Ukraine in 1941, pursuing policies of such brutality as to achieve the impossible—a pro-Soviet Ukraine.

KOEPPEN, Dr. Werner: Rosenberg's representative at Hitler's HQ, he recorded the Führer's political Table Talk for some months in 1941.

KOLLER, General Karl: Luftwaffe Chief of Staff from November 1944 to the end; Bavarian, dour but capable, having risen from the enlisted ranks.

KORTEN, General Günther: Luftwaffe Chief of Staff following Jeschonnek's 1943 suicide, he died an agonizing death when a fragment of table pierced him after Stauffenberg's bomb exploded beneath it in July 1944. Korten was the first to campaign for a strategic bomber force in the Luftwaffe.

KRANCKE, Vice Admiral Theodor: Permanent representative of the Commander in Chief, Navy, at Hitler's HQ after September 1942.

KREBS, General Hans: Last Army Chief of Staff, he negotiated with the Russians in Berlin following Hitler's death, then committed suicide.

KREIPE, General Werner: Luftwaffe Chief of Staff from August 1 to September 21, 1944, when Hitler banished him from war conferences at his HQ.

LAMMERS, Dr. Hans Heinrich: A legacy of the Hindenburg regime, Lammers was an expert on constitutional law and, as chief of the Reich Chancellery, the most important civil servant of the Third Reich.

LEY, Dr. Robert: Party Organization chief, he took over the trade unions in 1933 and molded them into the monolithic German Labor Front (DAF).

LINGE, Heinz: Hitler's manservant until the very end in Berlin.

LOSSBERG, Colonel Bernhard von: Jodl's army staff officer.

LUTZE, Victor: Succeeded the murdered Ernst Röhm as chief of the SA brownshirt army in 1934. A heavy drinker and loose talker, he engaged Himmler's displeasure by remarks about the SS, and died in a car crash in 1943.

MAISEL, General Ernst: Burgdorf's deputy in the Army Personnel Branch—a quiet, intelligent officer manhandled by postwar writers for his unfortunate part in Rommel's death.

MANSTEIN, Field Marshal Erich von: Universally acclaimed as Germany's most outstanding General Staff product, as he displayed in offensive operations in Poland (1939), the west (1940), and the Russian campaign.

MEISSNER, Dr. Otto: Like Lammers, a leftover of the Hindenburg era; head of the Presidential Chancellery *(Präsidialkanzlei).*

MILCH, Field Marshal Erhard: Founder of Lufthansa airline, Milch was called upon by Hitler and Göring to build the secret Luftwaffe in 1933. After years of intense rivalry with Göring, Milch—who had labored to conceal a serious defect in his family tree (he was pure Aryan, but accepted popular legend to the contrary to conceal the fact that he was the product of the illicit relationship between his mother and her mother's brother)—was sacked in 1944.

MODEL, Field Marshal Walter: Monocled, highly schooled, modern in outlook, he was the antithesis of Manstein; when a front line needed holding or restoring, Hitler sent for Model.

MORELL, Professor Theo: Morell alone had been able to cure Hitler of a gastric disorder in 1936; he appointed him personal physician and turned a deaf ear on all his critics until the very end.

MÜLLER, SS General Heinrich: Chief of *Amt IV* (the Gestapo) under Kaltenbrunner, he vanished in the last days of the war and has not been positively seen since.

PAULUS, Field Marshal Friedrich: Led his Sixth Army into Soviet captivity after the Battle of Stalingrad, 1943.

PUTTKAMER, Admiral Karl-Jesco von: Hitler's naval adjutant from March 1935 to June 1938, then again from August 1939 to the end—one of the most important witnesses still surviving from Hitler's circle.

RAEDER, Grand Admiral Erich: Was already Commander in Chief, Navy, when Hitler came to power in 1933, and forcefully resigned exactly ten years later.

RATTENHUBER, SS Brigadier Hans: Chief of Hitler's police bodyguard at HQ, responsible for his security, he sought to conceal his brutal and intriguing nature beneath a veneer of Bavarian charm.

RIBBENTROP, Joachim von: Reich foreign minister after 1938, he realized that many of Hitler's foreign policies were doomed to failure but allowed the Führer to overrule him every time; hanged at Nuremberg in 1946.

RICHTHOFEN, Field Marshal Wolfram von: Perhaps the toughest Luftwaffe strike commander, Richthofen commanded first an air corps, then an air force (Luftflotte); Hitler always committed Richthofen where the battle was fiercest, and listened readily to the field marshal's extravagant complaints about his army counterparts.

ROMMEL, Field Marshal Erwin: Commandant of Hitler's HQ 1939–40, he secured command of a panzer division in time for the attack on France, fought a brilliant if reckless campaign there, and repeated his triumphs on a larger scale in North Africa, until the lack of supplies and the Allied superiority in tanks and aircraft beat him back; his loyalty to Hitler remained unchanged, but his hatred of the OKW and Jodl reached pathological proportions in 1944. Implicated by others in the July 20, 1944, conspiracy, he took the consequences —poison—in October that year.

ROSENBERG, Alfred: Verbose Party philosopher; bitter opponent of Koch, particularly after Rosenberg as Minister for the Occupied Eastern Territories had to deal with him; notorious anti-Semite.

RUNDSTEDT, Field Marshal Gerd von: Blunt, chivalrous, loyal, but elderly and easygoing in later years, Rundstedt was the senior serving German soldier; Hitler was fond of him and rightly trusted him—thrice appointing him to high commands, and thrice relieving him when expediency demanded. From 1942 to 1945 Rundstedt was—with a brief interval in the summer of 1944—Commander in Chief West.

SAUCKEL, Fritz: Gauleiter of Thuringia, Sauckel was appointed by Hitler in 1942 to take charge of the manpower procurement program of the Reich; this Sauckel achieved by contracts, inducements, or slave labor. Hanged at Nuremberg.

SAUR, Karl-Otto: Outwardly the typical Nazi—stocky, forceful, crude—Saur was first Todt's, then Speer's right-hand man in the munitions ministry; his phenomenal memory for dates and statistics made him one of Hitler's favorites.

SCHAUB, Julius: Joined the Nazi party in 1925, served as Hitler's personal

adjutant and factotum until the end; of too limited an intellect to intrigue—
hence valued highly by the Führer in his entourage.

SCHEIDT, Dr. Wilhelm: Adjutant to Hitler's court historian Scherff. After
Scherff's injury on July 20, 1944, Scheidt took his place for many months
at Hitler's war conferences. But through his friendship with Beck, Goerdeler,
and Kurt von Hammerstein, Scheidt was the source (unwittingly perhaps?) of
much secret Intelligence that reached the enemy, direct from Hitler's HQ.

SCHERFF, General Walter: Chief OKW historian, appointed by Hitler in 1942
to write the Reich war history; but he never got around to it—and on his orders
the shorthand records of most of Hitler's war conferences were burned in May
1945.

SCHMUNDT, General Rudolf: Hitler's chief Wehrmacht adjutant after 1938,
and chief of the army personnel branch after October 1942 as well; his role as
private adviser to Hitler needs intensive research. He died a lingering death,
blind and burnt, after the July 20, 1944, bomb blast.

SCHÖRNER, Field Marshal Ferdinand: Like Model, Schörner was usually assigned to sectors where other generals had failed, and he usually succeeded.

SCHROEDER, Christa: Hitler's private secretary after 1933, she stayed with him
until ordered to leave Berlin on April 20, 1945. Hitler warmed toward her,
despite her sharp tongue and feline comments on the war's progress.

SEYSS-INQUART, Dr. Arthur: A quiet-spoken Austrian lawyer, propelled by
the 1938 union between Germany and Austria into high office in Vienna as a
Nazi sympathizer, Seyss-Inquart was Hans Frank's deputy in Poland until
May 18, 1940, when he was appointed Hitler's viceroy in the Netherlands.
Hanged at Nuremberg.

SONNLEITNER, Dr. Franz von: diplomat, stood in for Hewel during his recovery from air crash injuries in 1944.

SPEER, Albert: Nominated by Hitler as architect for Berlin, despite his youth;
ambitious, vain, publicity-conscious, but possessing—like Göring—undoubted
presence and organizing ability. Hitler shrewdly appointed him Todt's successor as munitions minister in February 1942, but became disillusioned with him
in the last weeks of his life.

STUMPFEGGER, Dr. Ludwig: A well-known surgeon on Himmler's staff, who
began treating Hitler in October 1944.

TODT, Dr. Fritz: Hitler's main civil engineer, who had built the autobahn
network on his orders, and then the West Wall in 1938–39; in March 1940 Hitler
nominated him to head a new munitions ministry. When Todt was killed in
a plane crash in February 1942, Speer succeeded him.

VORMANN, General Nikolaus von: Appointed by Brauchitsch to act as army
representative at Hitler's HQ in August and September 1939.

VOSS, Vice Admiral Hans-Erich: Succeeded Krancke as naval representative at
Hitler's HQ on March 1, 1943.

WAGNER, General Eduard: Quartermaster General of the German army—until his suicide after the July 20, 1944, bomb plot failed.

WARLIMONT, General Walter: *De facto* deputy to Jodl in the OKW operations staff, Warlimont deeply felt that he should have held Jodl's position (which by rights was his).

WEIZSÄCKER, Baron Ernst von: Ribbentrop's state secretary at the foreign ministry after 1938; from early 1943 onward he was German ambassador to the Vatican.

WOLF, Johanna: Oldest of Hitler's private secretaries.

WOLFF, SS General Karl: Chief of Himmler's personal staff, SS representative at Hitler's HQ until early 1943—when he was involved in a marriage scandal —and from September 1943 chief of police in Nazi-occupied Italy.

ZEITZLER, General Kurt: Dubbed "Thunderball" *(Kugelblitz)* because of his intensive energy as Chief of Staff to a panzer corps in Russia, 1941–42; Hitler fetched him from his position as Rundstedt's Chief of Staff in France (1942) to succeed Halder as Army Chief of Staff. Zeitzler put up with Hitler's tantrums until June 30, 1944, when he simply vanished and reported sick.

PART 1

HITLER'S WAR BEGINS

"White"

Late on the evening of September 3, 1939, Hitler exchanged the elegant marbled halls of the Chancellery for the special train, *Amerika,* parked in a dusty Pomeranian railroad station surrounded by parched and scented pine trees and wooden barrack huts baked dry by the central European sun.

Never before had Germany's railroads conveyed a train like this—a cumbersome assemblage of twelve or fifteen coaches hauled by two locomotives immediately followed by armored wagons bristling with 20-millimeter antiaircraft guns; a similar flak wagon brought up the rear. Hitler's personal coach came first: a drawing room about the size of three regular compartments, a sleeping berth, and a bathroom. In the drawing room, there was an oblong table with eight chairs grouped around it. The four remaining compartments in Hitler's coach were occupied by his adjutants and manservants. Other coaches housed dining accommodations and quarters for his military escort, private detectives, medical staff, press section, and visiting guests. Joachim von Ribbentrop, Hans Lammers, and Heinrich Himmler followed in a second train code-named *Heinrich.* Göring's private—and considerably more comfortably furnished—train, *Asia,* remained with him at Luftwaffe headquarters near Potsdam.

The nerve center of Hitler's train was the "command coach" attached to his own quarters. One half was taken up by a long conference room dominated by a map table, and the other half by Hitler's communications center, which was in constant touch by teleprinter and radio-telephone with the OKW and other ministries in Berlin, as well as with military headquarters on the front. Hitler was to spend most of his waking hours in this hot, confined space for the next two weeks, while Colonel Rudolf Schmundt, Hitler's chief adjutant, valiantly kept the stream of importunate visitors to a minimum. Here General Wilhelm Keitel introduced to the Führer for the first time his chief of operations, Major General Alfred Jodl, a placid, bald-headed Bavarian mountain-warfare officer a year younger than Hitler, whose principal strategic adviser he was to be until the last days of the war. (Jodl was to be called upon by the Americans in the postwar period for his advice on the defense of western Europe, then hanged as a war criminal at Nuremberg.) Jodl took one of the chairs in the middle of the long map-table, while Keitel regularly sat at one end and Colonel Nikolaus von Vormann, the army's liaison officer, sat next to the three telephones at the other.

In the train, as at the Chancellery, the brown Nazi party uniform dominated the scene. Generally speaking, Hitler's adjutants were the only others who found room there. Even Rommel, the new commandant of the Führer's headquarters, could not live in this train. Hitler hardly intervened in the conduct of the Polish campaign anyway. He would appear in the command coach at 9 A.M. to hear Jodl's personal report on the morning situation and to inspect the maps that had been flown in from Berlin. His first inquiry of Colonel von Vormann was always about the dangerous western front situation, for of 30 German divisions left to hold the three-hundred-mile line, only 12 were up to scratch; and against them France might at any time unleash her army of 110 divisions. But contrary to every prediction voiced by Hitler's critics, the western front was curiously quiet. On September 4, an awed Colonel von Vormann wrote: "Meanwhile, a propaganda war has broken out in the west. Will the Führer prove right after all? They say that the French have hung out a banner at Saarbrücken reading *We won't fire the first shot.* As we've strictly forbidden our troops to open hostilities, I can't wait to see what happens now."

It was indeed a mystery. While Poland reeled toward defeat, her allies made ominous noises but remained inactive as their precious opportunities dwindled with each passing day.

Poland was overrun in three weeks. Neither the bravery of her soldiers nor the promises of her allies prevented this overwhelming defeat; it startled Stalin, astonished the democracies, and confirmed Hitler's belief in the invincibility of his armies. They had fallen upon Poland from Pomerania and East Prussia, from Silesia and from the protected territories of Slovakia as well; at no stage were the Poles able to establish a stable front. The gasoline engine, the tank, and the dive-bomber should not have taken the Poles by surprise, but they did. Hitler's armored and mechanized units swept through the brittle Polish defenses in the west and encircled the enemy armies while they were still massed to the west of the Vistula, where they were deployed partly in defense of their country and partly in preparation for the drive to Berlin—the thrust which would bring about an anti-Nazi revolution in Germany, as the Polish government had so naïvely been led to believe. German expectations came off somewhat better. What had been planned on the maps of the German General Staff throughout the summer now took precise shape in the marshlands and fields of Poland in September 1939.

Hitler left General Walther von Brauchitsch in unfettered control of the army's operations. He listened unobtrusively to all that went on about him in the command coach, soaking up the debates and discussions and no doubt comparing the course of the campaign with the events his self-taught knowledge had led him to expect. His being there did not distract his staff, as one member wrote, except that they were forbidden to smoke in his presence—a prohibition that fell heavily on his chain cigar-smoking naval adjutant, Captain Karl-Jesko von Puttkamer. Hitler's only strategic influence had been on the "grand pincer" plan, with its powerful southward thrust with mechanized forces from East Prussia behind the Vistula. He had attempted to veto the appointments of Generals Johannes Blaskowitz to command the Eighth Army and Günther von Kluge the Fourth Army —the latter because of Göring's personal antipathy, and the former because he recalled that in manuevers three years before, the general had not committed his tanks as he himself would have considered best; but on these appointments Hitler allowed himself to be overruled, although he did later find fault with the conduct of the Eighth Army's operations. This produced the only real crisis of the campaign; but the crisis occurred precisely where Hitler had expected, and he had ordered countermeasures in anticipation. The few days in which Kluge commanded his Fourth Army before an aircraft accident put him temporarily *hors de combat* convinced Hitler that here was a general to whom he should always entrust the most demanding operational commands; the resulting affection probably spared Kluge from the gallows, though not from death, five years later.

The Poles had committed the basic strategic error of concentrating their forces forward in the Posen (Poznan) salient, instead of establishing a main line of defense that could be more readily held, for example on the Vistula River. As it was, these forces were encircled and destroyed in the first phases of the campaign. The western border fortifications were weak and obsolete—those near Warsaw dated back to the Great War; the capital's fortifications were incorporated into its suburbs, and this inevitably resulted in heavy fighting there. But by that time the outcome was a foregone conclusion.

At eight o'clock on the morning of September 4, after his train's arrival at the front, General Fedor von Bock, the commander of Army Group North, joined Rommel in reporting to Hitler, and the three men set out on an extended tour of the battle areas. Accompanied by his adjutants and a manservant, Hitler rode in a heavy six-wheeled Mercedes, and the rest of his staff and escort followed in six identical vehicles. The little convoy, headed by two armored scout cars, with two more bringing up the rear, drove off to visit Fourth Army headquarters; seventy or more cars packed with Party and ministerial personages jostled for position behind the Führer's convoy, completely ignoring the vehicle-sequence orders the frantic Schmundt had drawn up. A choking cloud of Pomeranian dust was flung up from the unpaved country roads. At each brief halt the same undignified scenes were repeated as Hitler's generals and Party leaders elbowed their way into the foreground of the photographs being taken and then galloped back to their cars to urge their chauffeurs into even closer proximity to the Führer's Mercedes. Once when Martin Bormann angrily rebuked Rommel for these scenes of disorder the general coolly snapped back: "I'm not a kindergarten teacher. You sort them out, if you want!" Hitler affected not to notice all this—no doubt seeing it as further proof of his own popularity. During the first days of the campaign, no way could be found to shake off this horde of idle camp followers, but eventually Schmundt did manage to elude most of them by beginning each visit to the front with a short flight in the three available Junkers 52's to an airfield where a little motor convoy was waiting.

The Wehrmacht was already steamrolling northward toward Thorn, and General Heinz Guderian's armor was entering his birthplace, Chelmno (Culm). These were fields long steeped in German blood; ancient German land was coming under German rule again. Everywhere Hitler was surrounded by jubilant soldiers who sensed that this was an historic hour and that the injustices of Versailles were at last being wiped out. On the sixth he toured the battlefield of Tucheler Heide, where a powerful Polish Corps had been encircled and now desperately struggled to break out. (Apparently convinced that the German tanks were only tinplate dummies, the Polish cavalry attacked with lances couched.) Here the roads were hideous with the carnage of unequal battle. A radio message told Hitler that Cracow was now in German hands. As he had hoped, the greater part of the Polish army had been trapped west of the Vistula, while the strong force assembled at Posen for the attack on Berlin was now aimless and isolated—far from the main scene of events.

At 10 P.M. that evening, September 6, Hitler returned to his command coach. Colonel von Vormann briefed him on the western front. "The phony war continues," he wrote later that day. "So far not a shot has been fired on the western front. On both sides there are just huge loudspeakers barking at each other, with each side trying to make it clear to the other how impossible their behavior is and how stupid their governments are. Tomorrow Brauchitsch and Raeder are due here. . . . Poland's situation is worse than desperate." Vormann already talked of the dissolution of the Polish army: "All that remains now is a rabbit hunt. Militarily, the war is over." Hitler stared at him incredulously; then, beaming with pleasure, he took the colonel's hand in both of his and pumped it up and down before leaving the command coach without a further word.

The situation in the west had a comic-opera quality. From both sides of the Rhine, loudspeakers assured the enemy they would not open fire first. At some places the troops were bathing in the river. There were secret exchanges of food and drink between the French and German lines. French deserters disclosed that their frontline sentries were not permitted to load live ammunition in their rifles.

German commanders had the strictest possible instructions not to fire into French territory or permit flights over the frontier. In addition, Hitler went out of his way to avoid provoking British public opinion: when Göring begged for permission to bomb the British fleet riding peacefully at anchor at Scapa Flow, Hitler rejected the Luftwaffe commander's request as overeager. He was furious when Britain announced on September 4 that one of her transatlantic liners, the *Athenia,* had that morning been torpedoed off the Hebrides by a German submarine, with some loss of life among the eleven hundred British and American passengers. Admiral Erich Raeder checked with his submarine commander, Karl Dönitz, and assured Hitler that none of their handful of U-boats could have been near the alleged incident and that in any case they were under orders not to attack British passenger vessels. Hitler suspected that Winston Churchill, as First Lord of the Admiralty, had himself ordered the liner sunk to provoke American public opinion, and he instructed the propaganda ministry to expose this "lord of the liars" forthwith. Shortly afterward, however, Raeder advised him confidentially that a U-boat commander had now admitted the sinking. The liner, he contended, had been blacked-out and zigzagging, and he had mistaken it for a cruiser and sunk it. The damage had been done. Raeder and Hitler agreed to keep the truth to themselves, and it is doubtful that even Goebbels learned it. Submarines were henceforth forbidden to attack passenger vessels even if in convoy with naval forces.

Hitler's territorial plans for Poland were still indeterminate. He had expected to be forced to accept Italian mediation and an eventual armistice, and to improve his position at the bargaining table he had seized as much Polish territory as possible in the first days. But the armistice offer never came. As his armies surged on, his appetite grew. In a secret speech to his generals on August 22 he had set as his goal "the annihilation of the Polish forces"—an orthodox Clausewitzian objective—rather than any particular line on the map. A week later he still talked only of fighting his "first Silesian war" and wrote off eastern Poland to the Russian claim. But on September 7, when Stalin had not yet moved his armies, Hitler also mentioned to his army Commander in Chief, General von Brauchitsch, the possibility of founding an independent Ukraine.

Hitler's hazy notion was to mark the ultimate frontier between Asia and the West by gathering together the racial German remnants scattered about the Balkans, Russia, and the Baltic states to populate an eastern frontier strip along either the Bug or the Vistula river. The troops in their garrisons would be like the Teutonic knights in their castles or like the northwest frontier of India in more modern times. To the west of the 1914 Polish-German frontier, the Poles and Jews would be uprooted and displaced eastward; the land would be resettled by the skill and industry of the Germans—those whom Himmler was already extracting from the South Tyrol would populate the northern slopes of the Beskid Mountains, for example. Warsaw would become a center of German culture; or alternatively it would be razed and replaced by green fields on either side of the Vistula. Between the Reich and the "Asian" frontier, some form of Polish national state would exist, to house the ethnic Pole—a lesser species of some ten million in all. To stifle the growth of new chauvinistic centers, the Polish intelligentsia would be "extracted and accommodated elsewhere."

With this independent rump Poland, Hitler planned to negotiate a peace settlement that had some semblance of legality and thereby spike the guns of Britain and France. If, however, this rump Poland fell apart, the Vilna area could be offered to Lithuania, and the Galician and Polish Ukraine could be granted independence—in which case, as Abwehr Chief Wilhelm Canaris noted, Keitel's instructions were that his Abwehr-controlled Ukrainians "are to provoke an uprising in the Galician Ukraine with the destruction of the Polish and Jewish element as its aim." On no account was this Ukrainian nationalist ferment to spill over into the Soviet Ukraine, Keitel warned. Moscow's attitude toward Poland was still uncertain, however; the Russians were eager to amputate a slice of territory but reluctant to wield the knife in public.

Hitler's army fell upon the hated Poles with well-documented relish. Colonel Eduard Wagner, as Quartermaster General initially responsible for occupation policy, wrote privately on September 4: "Brutal guerrilla war has broken out everywhere, and we are ruthlessly stamping it out. We won't be reasoned with. We have already sent out emergency courts, and they are in continual session. The harder we strike, the quicker there will be peace again." And a week later: "We are now issuing fierce orders which I have drafted today myself. Nothing like the death sentence! There's no other way in occupied territories."[1]

Hitler's own anti-Polish feelings were comparatively new; born of his frustrated plan in the fall of 1938 for an alliance with Poland against Stalin, they were now reinforced by events in this campaign. There is no trace of his crueler plans for Poland among the documents predating the outbreak of the war. In Poland, however, Hitler and his generals were confronted by what they saw as still warm

---

[1]From unpublished letters of Wagner, in my possession. When the tide turned against Hitler, Wagner joined the opposition; he committed suicide in July 1944. By the whims of modern historiography, he was transformed into a hero of the anti-Nazi resistance.

evidence that Asia did indeed begin just beyond the old Reich frontier in the east. In the western Polish town of Bydgoszcz (Bromberg) the local Polish commander had ordered the massacre of several thousand German residents on the charge that some of them had taken part in the hostilities. Göring's paratroopers were being shot on the spot when captured by the Poles. It was also charged that the Poles had used poisonous blister-gases in manufacturing booby traps. Hitler was particularly angered by a report that a Polish prisoner who had jabbed out the eyes of a wounded German soldier had been routinely sent to the rear through regular army channels. (Hitler said he should have been tried and executed on the spot by a drumhead court-martial.)

On the evening of the eighth, moreover, Warsaw radio imprudently appealed to civilians to join in the fight to defend their invaded homeland, and this was deplored as an open incitement to franc-tireur warfare. The population was instructed, for example, to pour gasoline over disabled German tanks and set them on fire. "Against Germany the Polish people fight side by side with the Polish soldiers, building barricades and combating the German operations and positions by every means they can."

There was no acceptable explanation for Stalin's inactivity. While Hitler could easily finish off Poland alone, he was particularly eager for Russia's strategic involvement because then Britain and France would have to think twice about implementing their guarantee. As Reinhard Heydrich explained to his department heads: "Then Britain would be obliged to declare war on Russia too."[2] Above all Hitler wanted to get the Polish campaign over before the U.S. Congress reassembled on the twenty-first.

His heavy special train, *Amerika,* had left for Upper Silesia on the ninth. It finally halted in a railway siding at Illnau. The pleasing draft in the corridors ceased, and the temperature within the camouflage-gray walls and roofs rose. The air outside was thick with the hot dust-particles of mid-September. His secretary Christa Schroeder wrote plaintively:

We have been living in this train for ten days now. Its location is constantly being changed, but since we never get out the monotony is dreadful. The heat here is unbearable, quite terrible. All day long the sun beats down on the

---

[2]Britain was not in fact obliged to declare war on Russia when she invaded Poland on September 17, 1939, as by a secret clause in her August treaty with Poland she had providently specified that the only "European Power" to which the treaty referred was Germany.

compartments, and we just wilt in the tropical heat. I am soaked to the skin, absolutely awful. To top it all, there is hardly anything worthwhile to do. The Chief drives off in the morning leaving us condemned to wait for his return. We never stay long enough in one place. Recently we were parked one night near a field hospital through which a big shipment of casualties was just passing. . . . Those who tour Poland with the Chief see a lot, but it's not easy for them because the enemy are such cowards—shooting in the back and ambushing—and because it is difficult to protect the Chief, who has taken to driving around as though he were in Germany, standing up in his open car even in the most hazardous areas. I think he is being reckless, but nobody can persuade him not to do it. On the very first day he drove through a copse still swarming with Polacks—just half an hour earlier they had wiped out an unarmed German medical unit. One of the medics escaped and gave him an eyewitness account. . . . Once again, the Führer was standing in full view of everybody on a hummock, with soldiers streaming toward him from all sides. In a hollow there was this Polish artillery; obviously they saw the sudden flurry of activity and—since it's no secret that the F. is touring the front—they guessed who it was. Half an hour later the bombs came raining down. Obviously it gives the soldiers' morale a colossal boost to see the F. in the thick of the danger with them, but I still think it's too risky. We can only trust in God to protect him.

"The Führer is in the best of moods; I often get into conversation with him," wrote General Rommel. "He says that in eight or ten days it'll all be over in the east and then our entire battle-hardened Wehrmacht will move west. But I think the French are giving up the struggle. Their soldiers are bathing in the Rhine, unmolested by us. This time," he concluded, "we are definitely going to win through!"

That day, September 12, Hitler summoned Göring, Brauchitsch, and Keitel to his train at the Ilnau railway siding and flatly forbade them to provoke the French in any way. Late that afternoon he received Admiral Wilhelm Canaris, Keitel's chief of Intelligence, for a rare audience. Canaris was white-haired, weary, and elderly, a frail stooping figure with a soft lisping voice, a studied sloppiness of dress, and an apparent naïveté of manner that were designed to disarm his critics. The admiral was known widely as "that slimy Greek"—a soubriquet he sought to disprove by circulating a family tree which supported his claim to Italian ancestry.

Hitler walked into the command coach just as Canaris was outlining to Keitel the unfavorable effect a German bombardment of Warsaw would have on foreign opinion. When asked for news from the western front, Canaris craftily replied that the French were systematically marshaling troops and artillery opposite

Saarbrücken for a major offensive.[3] Hitler remained politely incredulous. "I can hardly believe that the French will attack at Saarbrücken, the very point at which our fortifications are strongest." They would also then run into second and third lines of even stronger defenses. They might, Hitler conceded, invade across the Rhine or even—though less probably—through Belgium and Holland in violation of their neutrality. Keitel agreed, and Jodl added that the artillery preparation for a major offensive would take at least three weeks, so the French offensive could not begin before October. "Yes," responded Hitler, "and in October it is already quite chilly, and our men will be sitting in their protective bunkers while the French have to wait in the open air to attack. And even if the French should manage to penetrate one of the weaker points of the West Wall, we will in the meantime have brought our divisions across from the east and given them a thrashing they'll never forget."

Before Canaris left, Keitel forbade him to brief Mussolini on the German military situation. Hitler no longer trusted the Italians, as he had found out that they were in contact with the French.

Hitler's tours of these battlefields were his first real contact with "the East." They reinforced his unhealthy fantasies about the "subhumans" and the Jews.

On September 10 he had visited the Tenth Army, busy finishing off the Polish forces encircled at Radom. The Polish countryside struck him as tangled and unkempt, as though from prehistoric times. Was this still Europe? Indiscriminately scattered about the untended acres were wretched wooden hutlike dwellings with thatched roofs; between them were miles of endless swamps with occasional farmsteads and rare, magnificent castles gleaming on the horizon. The laborers' buildings were caked with filth, the barns and sheds were dilapidated, the roads were treeless and rutted by centuries of wheels. At the roadsides, knots of submissive Polish civilians stood in the swirling dust of Hitler's motorcade. Among them he glimpsed Jews in high-crowned hats and caftans; their hair in ritual ringlets; they looked for all the world like figures out of medieval anti-Semitic drawings. Time had stood still here for centuries.

The Jews were the enemy. He had given them clear warning in a bellicose speech to the Reichstag eight months before. How often in his life had his prophecies been laughed at by them! How the Jews had mocked his earnest prediction that one day he, a humble street agitator, would lead the German

---

[3]Canaris, a confirmed anti-Nazi, had deliberately exaggerated reports of a planned minor French attack—in regimental strength—in the hope of disrupting Hitler's Polish campaign strategy, according to Colonel Lahousen, who accompanied him.

people to true greatness! Their peals of laughter had died to a croak in their Jewish throats, Hitler had jeered in January 1939. "Today I am going to be a prophet again. If the international finance-Jewry inside and outside Europe manages just once more to precipitate the world into war, the outcome will be, not the bolshevization of the earth and the consequent triumph of Jewry, but the annihilation of the Jewish race in Europe." The Berlin newspapers had headlined the Reichstag speech as one of Adolf Hitler's greatest: PROPHETIC WARNING TO THE JEWS.

Now, in September 1939, Hitler was upon the verge of world war. And Dr. Chaim Weizmann, the president of the Jewish Agency, had written to Neville Chamberlain promising explicitly that all Jews everywhere stood by him and would fight on the side of the democracies against Nazi Germany. *The Times* published Weizmann's letter on September 6, and Hitler no doubt considered it an unorthodox Jewish declaration of war. He often referred to it in later years —by which time his grim prophecy was being cruelly fulfilled. "For the first time we are now implementing genuine ancient Jewish law," he boasted on January 30, 1942. "An eye for an eye and a tooth for a tooth." And on November 8 he reminded his Party faithfuls of that unique 1939 "prophecy," adding with ominous ambiguity: "As a prophet they always laughed at me. But of those who laughed loudest then, countless laugh no longer today. Nor are those who are still laughing even now likely to laugh when the time comes . . ."

While Hitler's overall anti-Jewish policy was clearly and repeatedly enunciated, it is harder to establish a documentary link between him and the murderous activities of the SS "task forces" *(Einsatzgruppen)* and their extermination camps in the east.

For the pogroms that now began, Himmler and Heydrich provided the initiative and drive themselves, using arguments of Reich security. Hitler's only order to the Reichsführer SS, Himmler, in this context was one for the general consolidation of the German racial position; there is no evidence that Hitler gave him any more specific instruction than this, nor did Himmler ever claim so. When army generals became restless about deeds being enacted by the SS in Poland, Himmler reassured them in a secret speech at Koblenz in March 1940, of which his handwritten notes survive—though they are infuriatingly cryptic in parts. He explained that now for the first time, under Adolf Hitler, the solution of the thousand-year-old historical problem of Poland was possible: only the infusion into Poland of Germanic blood during the years of Germany's weakness had made some Poles great and dangerous; now that Germany was strong she must see to the "final annexation of the area, its purification and Germanization"; a simple merging of the peoples was impossible for racial reasons. But a "Bolshevik method"—which Himmler defined in a memorandum two months later as downright extermination of the minority races—was "equally impossible." He conceded that the "leading brains of the resistance" were being executed but this was not, stressed Himmler in this *pièce justificative,* "a wild excess by subordinate commanders—still less by me." Here Himmler's jottings show a German phrase *(Weiss sehr genau, was vorgeht)* which might be translated either as "(I) know precisely what is happening" or "(He) knows precisely what is happening."[4] Two weeks later Himmler spoke in a Ruhr city. Here his notes read: "The Führer's mission to the Reichsführer SS: the quality of the German species. Blood our most supreme value. New territories not a political, but an ethnological problem."

This ethnological mission had been assigned to Heydrich. As in Austria and Czechoslovakia, the advancing tide of German army units had been followed by his police net. In the present Polish campaign his task forces were subordinated directly to the generals. Each army had its *Einsatzgruppe,* and each corps an *Einsatzkommando* of a hundred officials in Waffen SS uniform with SD (*Sicherheitsdienst,* security service) emblems on their sleeves. Their primary role was Intelligence—seizing enemy documents—and counterinsurgency operations, or what the army orders more formally described as "combating any anti-Reich or anti-German elements in rear areas." According to Heydrich, writing ten months later, the special order directing the task forces to conduct "security operations of a political and ideological nature in these new territories" was issued by Hitler himself. But the order's practical interpretation—embodying what Heydrich calmly referred to as the liquidation of Polish leaders "running into several thousands"—evidently sprang from him. On September 7 he briefed his staff (without any mention of a Führer Order) as follows: "The Polish ruling class is to be put out of harm's way as far as possible. The lower classes that will remain will not get special schools, but be kept down in one way or another." To Heydrich, the prophylactic mission of his task forces was the essential one— hunting down the thousands of leading Poles already listed in black books and liquidating them before they could unite in opposition.

Parallel to the SS task forces attached to the armies, there was an independent "special duties" task force which rampaged through Poland under the command of the arrogant and brutal SS General Udo von Woyrsch. Most of the early savagery against the Poles and Jews was Woyrsch's work. When he was eventually kicked out of Poland on German army orders, he loudly protested that he had received direct instructions from the Führer via Himmler to spread "fear and

[4]General Ulex, who was present, recalled this after the war as "I am doing nothing of which the Führer does not know." (*Cf.* Professor Helmut Krausnick, "Hitler and the Murders in Poland," *VfZ,* 1963, 196ff.) However, nobody else recalled this. And General von Leeb, whose diary has been available to me, would certainly have mentioned such a candid statement in it, given his pronounced Christian convictions. Ulex had been humiliated by Hitler late in 1938. No other authors have bothered to transcribe Himmler's speech notes. Colonel Eduard Wagner wrote his wife on the following day: "It was highly interesting yesterday. In the evening Himmler spoke to the Commander in Chiefs at Koblenz. More about that verbally . . ."

terror" in what would seem an illogical attempt to dissuade the Poles from committing acts of violence. (Himmler's orders to Woyrsch survive, dated September 3: he was charged with the "radical suppression of the incipient Polish insurrection in the newly occupied parts of Upper Silesia"; Hitler is not mentioned.) Heydrich was nettled by Woyrsch's ouster and later ascribed the army's interference to its ignorance of the "political mission" entrusted to the task forces by Himmler, who was acting, Heydrich claimed, on the directives of the Führer and Göring; it was wrong for the army to see the task force operations as "arbitrary acts of brutality," he complained.

There is no surviving record of when—or if—Heydrich conferred with Hitler during the Polish campaign. But the German army's records of briefings by Hitler are voluminous, and they offer a curious and distasteful picture. In short, many of Hitler's generals learned from him that he planned to eliminate the Polish intelligentsia one way or another; either they welcomed it, or they joined a conspiracy of silence.

Not until October 1939 did the major "mopping up" of "potential dissidents" begin in Poland. It was evidently delayed at the request of the army, even though Heydrich was eager to get on with the job. Hitler's blood was already boiling at the ponderous court-martial procedures being implemented against Polish guerrillas—he wanted their swift and summary execution; but Heydrich had his eye on bigger game. He was quoted as saying, "We will let the small fry off; but the nobility, the papists, and the Jews must all be killed." He proposed discussing with the army ways and means of eliminating these enemies after the Germans entered Warsaw. On September 7 Hitler met with Brauchitsch in his private coach and for two hours discussed the political future of Poland. He instructed the army to abstain from interfering in the SS operations.

The next day Hitler issued a set of guidelines in which the emphasis was on the appointment of Party functionaries as civil commissars—to do the dirty work —whose task it was to parallel the army's military government in Poland. Little is known in detail of what Hitler told Brauchitsch. After talking to General Franz Halder on the ninth, Eduard Wagner noted in his diary: "It is the Führer's and Göring's intention to destroy and exterminate the Polish nation. More than that," Colonel Wagner noted in his diary, "cannot even be hinted at in writing." The same day a member of Hitler's staff—Colonel von Vormann—wrote: "The war in Poland is over. . . . The Führer keeps discussing plans for the future of Poland —interesting but scarcely suited for committing to the written word." Yet another colonel on Halder's staff joined this dumb chorus a few days later. "A lot is happening and the questions looming ahead give rise to much food for thought, above all the proposals over Poland's fate. . . . Too hush-hush to write even one

word about them." Only General Walther Heitz, the new military governor of
West Prussia, lifted a corner of this veil of secrecy in writing up a conference with
Brauchitsch on September 10: "Other business: I am to rule the area with the
mailed fist. Combat troops are overinclined toward a false sense of chivalry."

That the nature of the SS task force operations had been explained to Brauchitsch was established two days later when Admiral Canaris reminded Keitel
of the damage the planned "widespread executions" of Polish clergy and nobility
would inflict on the Wehrmacht's reputation. Keitel retorted that this had long
been decided on by the Führer, who had made it plain to Brauchitsch—who had
visited Hitler with Göring that morning—"that if the Wehrmacht wants nothing
to do with it, they will merely have to put up with the SS and Gestapo appearing
side by side with them." Hence the creation of parallel civil authorities in Poland.
On them would fall the job of "demographic extermination," as Canaris recorded
Keitel's phrase. In fact Heydrich, recognizing that time was on his side, readily
heeded the army's urgent appeal to postpone the really bloody business until it
was out of Poland. Thus, when Heydrich informed a member of Halder's staff
—Colonel Wagner—that the planned "mopping up" of Poland would embrace
"the Jewry, intelligentsia, clergy, and nobility," the army officer asked only that
the army not be compromised—in other words, that the murderous orders flow
directly from Heydrich to his task forces in the field. Preferably, even this would
not happen until full control of the occupied areas had been transferred to the
Party and its civil commissars.

But Heydrich had not in fact secured Hitler's approval for liquidating the Jews.
On September 14 he reported to his staff on his tour of the task forces. The discreet
conference record states: "The Chief [Heydrich] enlarged on the Jewish problem
in Poland and set out his views on this. The Reichsführer [Himmler] will put
certain suggestions to the Führer, on which only the Führer can decide, as they
will also have considerable repercussions abroad." Hitler, however, favored only
a deportation of the Jews, as became clear to both Brauchitsch and Himmler
when they conferred separately with Hitler at Zoppot on September 20. To
Brauchitsch he talked only of a ghetto plan for the Jews (causing Halder to warn
that nothing must happen to give foreign countries a peg for "atrocity propaganda"). Hitler's somewhat more moderate instructions to Himmler were presumably those echoed by Heydrich to his task force commanders in Berlin next
day: the formerly German provinces of Poland would be reannexed to the Reich;
an adjacent *Gau,* or district, made up of a Polish-speaking population, would
have Cracow as its capital and probably be governed by the Austrian Dr. Arthur
Seyss-Inquart. This Gau—the later *Generalgouvernement*—would be a "kind of
no-man's-land" outside the planned East Wall: it would accommodate the Polish
Jews. Hitler also authorized Heydrich to unload as many Jews as possible into
the Russian zone. To facilitate this expulsion the Jews were to be concentrated
in the big Polish cities. They would be joined by the Jews and the remaining thirty

thousand gypsies from Germany. About 3 percent of the former Polish ruling class remained, said Heydrich; they would be put in concentration camps. The educated class of teachers, clergymen, aristocrats, and demobilized officers would be rounded up and dumped in the rump Polish Gau. The working class would provide a reservoir of migratory labor for the Reich. Hitler asked Himmler to act as overlord of this resettlement operation.

For his part, General von Brauchitsch circularized his field commanders thus: "The police task-forces have been commanded and directed by the Führer to perform certain ethnographical *(volkspolitische)* tasks in the occupied territory." The commanders were not to interfere, nor would they be held responsible. The only stipulation Brauchitsch made when he met Heydrich on September 22 was that the expulsion operations must not interfere with the army's movements or Germany's economic needs. Heydrich readily agreed.

Hitler's positive enjoyment of the battle scenes was undeniable. He visited the front whenever he could, heedless of the risk to himself and his escort. It irritated him when his convoy took a wide detour around the city of Lodz en route to Eighth Army headquarters, and he ordered that on the way back the convoy was to drive right through the heart of the city (an order the unhappy army authorities fulfilled by cordoning off the entire route, clearing away the Polish population in neighboring streets and conducting Hitler's convoy at an uninterrupted fifty miles an hour, two vehicles abreast, from one end of the city to the other). He enjoyed meeting his troops and, for all we know, was exhilarated by the smell of cordite and sight of blood. At a divisional headquarters set up in a school within range of the Polish artillery, he made the acquaintance of General von Briesen, who towered head and shoulders above him. Briesen had just lost an arm leading his division into an action which warded off a desperate Polish counterattack by four divisions and cavalry on the flank of Blaskowitz's Eighth Army; he had lost eighty officers and fifteen hundred men in the fight, and now he was reporting to his Führer not far from the spot where his father, a Prussian infantry general, had been killed in the Great War. Hitler could only stare entranced as this monumental officer reported the battle situation to him. Afterward he exclaimed to his staff, "That is just what I always imagined Prussian generals looked like when I was a child!" He repeated these words a dozen times to different listeners that evening and insisted that Briesen immediately be awarded a Knight's Cross. "That is the commander I have been looking for for years for my SS"—a less than realistic appraisal of so blue-blooded an officer. On the fifteenth we find Hitler at Jaroslav, watching his soldiers bridging the river San.

———

By September 16, 1939, the greatest strategic triumph of the campaign was complete: the Polish army optimistically assembled at Posen for the attack on Berlin had been encircled, and Kutno had been captured by the Fourth and Eighth armies. In a model operation that the legendary Field Marshal von Schlieffen himself could not have improved on, a former corporal had destroyed the last vestiges of Polish military strength west of the Vistula. The bold pincer operation starting from bases nearly two hundred miles apart could have been blunted by a successful Polish stand, but now it was only a matter of days before Warsaw itself fell.

Hitler had begun to debate the fate of that city with Jodl on the fifteenth. As has been noted he was particularly eager to have the capital in his hands by the time the U.S. Congress reconvened. Since he wanted to avoid the high casualties inherent in house-to-house fighting, he hoped that the mere threat of concerted ground and air attack would bluff the city's commandant into capitulating. On the thirteenth he had repeatedly plagued General Blaskowitz for estimates on how long it would take to starve the city into submission, and a few days later he worried at his own liaison officer with the same question. The General Staff, erroneously believing that the armies parked outside Warsaw would not be immediately needed for other purposes, favored a bloodless siege of the Polish capital; but this would take weeks and Hitler could not spare the time.

Early on the sixteenth a German officer carried to the Polish lines a written ultimatum giving the commandant six hours in which to surrender unconditionally. If he failed to do so, the Germans would regard the city as a defended fortress, with all that that implied.

Hitler's bid for an easy and bloodless victory was rejected. The Polish commandant refused even to receive the ultimatum. He had spent every waking hour since September 9 preparing the capital for the German assault. The civilian population had been urged to join with the military in defending the city against the invaders; all fortifications and defenses had been strengthened; every suburban building had been reinforced by sandbags, concrete, and barbed wire, its basement linked by a honeycomb of tunnels to a network of resistance strongpoints; deep antitank trenches cut across Warsaw's main thoroughfares, and there were barricades formed of heaped-up streetcars, cobblestones, and rubble; the parks and squares bristled with heavy artillery. Surrender was unthinkable.

As Blaskowitz was later to report: "What shocked even the most hardened soldier was how at the instigation of their military leaders a misguided population, completely ignorant of the effect of modern weapons, could contribute to the destruction of their own capital."

Until then, Hitler had limited the bombardment of the capital to dive-bomber and artillery attacks on strategic targets. But whatever inhibitions he may have felt about the presence of a million civilians and nearly two hundred foreign diplomats were apparently about to break down under the demands of his timetable. At three o'clock on the afternoon of the sixteenth, Luftwaffe aircraft released over Warsaw several tons of leaflets giving the civilian population twelve hours to leave by two specified roads, and Hitler ordered a saturation bombardment for the next day.

The people of Warsaw were never able to take advantage of the leaflet offer because by some incredible oversight nobody had informed the local German army commanders of it. As a result, they of course had kept the two egress roads under heavy artillery fire. Shortly before midnight, Hitler called off the scheduled bombardment.

At midday on the seventeenth, the Germans monitored a Warsaw Radio message asking them to accept a Polish officer who would come toward their lines under a flag of truce. His mission would be to negotiate the release of the civilian population and the foreign diplomatic corps.

Hitler immediately began to suspect that the Polish commandant was playing for time—that he planned to wage a bitter house-to-house resistance and that under those circumstances civilians were likely to be encumbrances and useless mouths to feed. Better, therefore, that Warsaw's civilians should remain bottled up in the city.

At 6 P.M. the Deutschland Sender broadcast an invitation to the Polish forces to send officers to the German lines for negotiations to begin at 10 P.M. Meanwhile, Keitel telegraphed Brauchitsch that since the civilian population had failed to leave the city by the earlier deadline, that offer was now void.

Any Polish officers who turned up for negotiations were to be instructed to hand to their commandant an ultimatum calling for the unconditional surrender of the capital by 8 A.M. the next day. Arrangements for the evacuation of the diplomatic corps would be made on request, but the civilian population had to stay put. Leaflets to this effect were dropped.

When by 11:45 A.M. on the eighteenth no Polish officer had appeared at the German lines, Hitler ordered Brauchitsch and Göring to prepare at once to attack Warsaw from the eastern suburb of Praga. His attempts to obtain the city's bloodless capitulation were apparently sufficient to give him a clear conscience in ordering death to rain down on its one million inhabitants.

The Polish government and military command had already escaped to neutral Romania, thus the Russians could now claim that the Poland with whom they had concluded their nonaggression pact no longer existed. "To protect the interests of the Ukrainian and White Russian minorities," two Soviet army groups invaded eastern Poland in the small hours of September 17. The news reached Hitler's train soon after. He canceled his planned flight to Cracow and at about

4 A.M. entered the command coach of his train, where he found Schmundt waiting with Keitel and Jodl. All of them were grouped around the maps of Poland, guessing at the Soviet army's movements until the arrival of Ribbentrop, who on Hitler's instructions now revealed to the astonished generals the details of secret arrangements made with Moscow for Poland. "We decided with Stalin on a demarcation line between the two spheres of interest running along the four rivers —Pissa, Narev, Vistula, and San," the foreign minister explained as he somewhat crudely drew the line on the map. The generals frostily pointed out that Russian aircraft were evidently even now taking off without any notion of where the leading German units were, and that the Wehrmacht had suffered considerable casualties in capturing territory which was apparently a hundred miles and more beyond the demarcation line secretly agreed upon. Now joint staff talks with the Russians had to begin at once—Ribbentrop somewhat tactlessly suggested Brest-Litovsk, the scene of Russia's World War I humiliation, as a venue—and the most advanced German units had to disengage from the fighting immediately and withdraw to the proposed line.

By September 19, when Hitler and his staff drove into Danzig, the Polish campaign was all but over; it had lasted only eighteen days, a breathtaking victory that confounded all his opponents. How he now privately mocked the foreign ministry Cassandras who had predicted military disaster![5] Only the garrisons of Warsaw, Modlin, and Hela were still holding out. It was a soldier's world. He had spent two hours last evening talking with Rommel about the problems of war. "He is exceptionally friendly to me," wrote Rommel.

As the victorious Führer drove through the streets of Danzig for the first time, flowers rained down from the windows, swastika flags draped the streets, and the crowds of German Danzigers were wild with emotion. When the convoy of cars stopped outside the ancient Artus Hof, Schmundt was heard to comment to a newer staff member who was overwhelmed by this reception, "It was like this everywhere—in the Rhineland, in Vienna, in the Sudeten territories, and in Memel. Do you still doubt the mission of the Führer?" Here, in a long, columned fourteenth-century hall built in the heyday of the Germanic knightly orders, Hitler delivered a lengthy speech on which he had been working for many days. He pathetically compared the humanity with which he was fighting this war and the treatment the Poles had meted out to the German minorities after Pilsudski's

[5] *Cf.* Hewel's unpublished diary, October 10, 1941: "Triumphant conversation [with the Führer] about the foreign ministry. Who in 1939 believed in victory? The state secretary at the foreign ministry [Weizsäcker]?"

death. "Tens of thousands were deported, maltreated, killed in the most bestial fashion. These sadistic beasts let their perverse instincts run riot and—this pious democratic world looks on without batting one eyelash." In his peroration he spoke not of the blessing of Providence, but of "Almighty God, who has now given our arms his blessing."

Afterward his staff cleared a path for him through the heaving Danzig population packed into the Long Market outside. A bath was provided for the sweat-soaked Führer in one of the patrician houses, and he worked over the text of his speech for release to the press. Then he took up quarters for the next week in the roomy seafront Kasino Hotel at Zoppot, near Danzig, where Ribbentrop, Lammers, and Himmler also found rooms for themselves and their staffs. Hitler received most of his official visitors in his suite of rooms—numbers 251, 252, and 253 on the second floor—while the war conferences were conducted in Jodl's suite, rooms 202 and 203. His mood was irrepressible. At midnight two days after his arrival, followed by one of his manservants with a silver tray of champagne glasses, he burst into Jodl's room, where a number of generals were celebrating Keitel's birthday. Despite the thick fog of cigar smoke, he stayed there an hour or more drinking and talking. His Polish victory had convinced him that the Wehrmacht he had created was equal to any task he set before it.

Here at Zoppot Hitler began weighing a course of action as hideous as any that Reinhard Heydrich was tackling in Poland: "mercy killing," or euthanasia. The ostensible occasion for this formal decision was related to war needs. About a quarter of a million hospital beds were required for Germany's mental institutions; of Germany's disproportionately large insane population (a result of centuries of lax and indiscriminate marriage laws) of some seven or eight hundred thousand people all told, about 10 percent were permanently institutionalized. Others were in and out of hospitals. They occupied bed space and the attention of skilled medical personnel which Hitler now urgently needed for the treatment of the casualties of his coming campaigns. Above all they were a glaring genetic impurity marring the blood of the German race. According to Dr. Karl Brandt, his personal surgeon, Hitler wanted between 40 and 60 percent of the permanently hospitalized insane to be quietly put away.

To his suite at the Kasino Hotel the Führer now summoned his constitutional and medical advisers, and in particular Hans Lammers, chief of the Reich Chancellery, and Dr. Leonardo Conti, chief medical officer of the Reich, together with the ubiquitous Martin Bormann; Reichsleiter Philipp Bouhler, chief of the "Führer's Chancellery" (an essentially Party authority) was also present for a reason that will shortly become plain. Hitler instructed Dr. Conti that in view of the war, a program for the painless killing of the incurably insane should be initiated; this would release badly needed hospital beds and nursing facilities for patients with a greater national priority. Dr. Conti appears to have suggested restricting this program to only the most hopeless cases, and he questioned whether there was any scientific basis for assuming it would produce eugenic advantages. He believed the authorities would be justified only in aiding, for example, a terminal case of paralysis through the most painful stages to a rapid end. During the conference the word "euthanasia" was actually used, but Hitler made it plain that under no circumstances was the real cause of death to be divulged to the next of kin. There was some discussion of the actual mechanics of the program. Dr. Conti proposed the use of narcotics to induce in the patients a sleep from which they would not awaken; but in separate discussions with Dr. Brandt Hitler learned that barbiturates would be too slow to be "humane" and that most physicians considered carbon monoxide gas the fastest and most peaceful lethal dose, if somewhat unmedical in character. Hitler asked Brandt shortly to investigate which was the fastest way consequent with the least amount of pain.

After this Zoppot discussion, some time passed without any results. In fact Dr. Conti had become involved in lengthy discussions with Lammers, with the ministry of justice, and with psychiatric and legal experts, in which the legal and ethical bases of Hitler's proposals were explored. Lammers favored the enactment of a secret law which would protect the doctors and nurses involved in the program against potential criminal charges. The consequence of this delay was that Hitler bypassed both Lammers and Conti, and peremptorily dictated onto a sheet of his private stationery, which bore a gold-embossed eagle and "Adolf Hitler," an order that was both simple and unorthodox, and that considerably enlarged the scope of the euthanasia project:

> Reichsleiter Bouhler and Dr. Brandt, M.D., are herewith given full responsibility to enlarge the powers of certain specified doctors so that they can grant those who are by all human standards incurably ill a merciful death, after the most critical assessment possible of their medical condition.
>
> *(signed)* Adolf Hitler.

It was a curious confirmation of the fact that Hitler regarded the war as Germany's struggle to the end that this Führer Order was symbolically backdated to September 1, the start of what he had envisaged as his "first Silesian war." Now it was no longer a local campaign but a bloody crusade in the course of which the German people were to become ennobled by conflict and purged of the impure elements in their blood and seed.

An extensive camouflage organization was set up by Bouhler's Chancellery; census forms, ostensibly for statistical survey purposes, were circulated to doctors and hospitals as from October 9, 1939; on these forms there were separate listings of the senile debilitated, the criminally insane, and patients of non-German blood.

Panels of three assessors then decided the life or death of each patient on the basis of these forms alone. As Hitler had told Bouhler, he wanted a process untrammeled by red tape. He resisted every effort Lammers made to codify the procedure in a Reich law, for this would have led to too many ministries and officials learning what was afoot.

Hitler had been an enthusiastic advocate of the racial rejuvenation of the German people ever since the Twenties, supporting his beliefs with an inadequate grasp of the Mendelian laws of genetics. (In fact, the processes of "negative eugenics" are extraordinarily slow: if all living epileptics were sterilized, for example, it would still take three centuries for the incidence of epilepsy in a population to be reduced by one quarter!) In 1929, however, Hitler had brutally summed up his views as follows: "If Germany were to have a birthrate of a million children a year, and to put away seven or eight hundred thousand of the weakest, then the end result might even be a net increment in strength." On the pretext that—according to some authorities—20 percent of the German population had hereditary biological defects, the National Socialists had instituted a program of racial hygiene immediately after they came to power; Minister of the Interior Wilhelm Frick was a fervent advocate. In July 1933 the Cabinet had passed the first related law; it was henceforth obligatory for doctors to report on patients with hereditary diseases so that they could be sterilized. From sterilization and abortion it was an easy step to the "destruction of human beings unworthy of life," the program initiated by Hitler in 1939. An elderly Darwinian (Alfred Ploetz) whom the Reich had made a professor after 1933 was to point out in 1935 that "the contraselective effects of war must be offset by an increase in the extermination quotas." In other words, so much fine blood is lost in battle that equal quantities of impure blood must be let if the race is not to be polluted—a pseudoscientific justification which emerged openly and unmistakably in arguments adduced by Hitler in private in 1943.[6]

Frick had drafted the necessary laws concerting the operations of the local health offices in 1934, parallel to which functioned the racial-politics agencies of the Party in each Party district. In that same year, the Bavarian provincial commissioner of health affairs urged that sterilization alone was not enough. Psychopaths, imbeciles, and other subnormals must be sorted out and exterminated. "This is a policy," he added, "which has in part already begun in our concentration camps." Over the next ten years tens of thousands of senior medical officials were to pass through special courses in racial hygiene, and perhaps significantly these were attended after 1938 by senior officers and staff of all the Wehrmacht services as well. Subtle appeals were made to their latent racial

[6]See page 529 below.

psychoses, the economic burden represented by these unworthy specimens was explained, and particularly repulsive samples were fed and housed at the institutions as walking laboratory exhibits. In June 1935 a Reich law allowed abortions for genetic reasons. In the same year Hitler openly told Dr. Conti's predecessor that should war come he would "tackle the euthanasia problem," since a wartime psychology would reduce the risk of opposition from the church.

But it was not until the end of 1938 that Hitler was directly involved in any euthanasia decisions, and then it was in "mercy killing," rather than the infinitely more controversial blanket program to eliminate the insane. Bouhler's Chancellery had repeatedly submitted to him appeals from patients in intolerable pain, or from their doctors, asking Hitler to exercise the Head of State's prerogative of mercy and permit the doctor to terminate the patient's life without fear of criminal proceedings. When Hitler received such an appeal from the parents of a malformed, blind, and imbecile boy born in Leipzig, he sent Dr. Brandt early in 1939 to examine the child, and on hearing the doctor's horrifying description of the pathetic case, he authorized the doctors to put him to sleep; at the same time he orally authorized Bouhler and Brandt to act accordingly in any similar cases in the future. A ministerial decree was eventually passed in August 1939 requiring all midwives and nurses to report to the local health office the details of such deformed newborn babies; a panel of three assessors judged each case, and if all three agreed, the infant was procured from the parents either by deception or by compulsion and quietly put away with as little pain to the child and sorrowing parents as possible. From a theological expert[7] Hitler had in 1939 secured formal assurances that the church need not be expected to raise basic objections to euthanasia. Perhaps as many as five thousand children were eventually disposed of in this way.

The "mercy killing" of the few was followed by the programmed elimination of the burdensome tens of thousands of insane; and all this was but a platform for far wider campaigns of extermination on which the Reich was to embark now that it was at war.

---

[7]The rector of the theological high school at Paderborn, a Professor Maier.

Overtures

Hitler's train idled on a siding in outer Pomerania until 9:30 A.M. on September 26 and then began the eight-hour haul back to Berlin. The journey passed in heavy silence. Hitler went into the command coach, but Keitel was in Berlin and Jodl must have been in his private compartment, for only Colonel von Vormann was there, seated at his customary place next to the telephones, writing and sorting the heaps of papers that had accumulated. For the next few hours Hitler spoke no word but restlessly paced the length of the swaying carriage while the train drew closer to Berlin. There were no messages, no calls, no visitors. Just after 5 P.M. the train reached Berlin's Stettin station, unheralded by any crowds or scenes of jubilation. The motor pool had sent cars to pick them up; Hitler and his entourage drove almost stealthily to the Reich Chancellery, where dinner was served at the large round table in his residence. The atmosphere was funereal. After a while Hitler abruptly rose, bid the others good night, and retired to his rooms.

Without doubt his thoughts now revolved around the next step he must take: could the western powers be made to see reason, or must he defeat them as he had defeated Poland? In January 1944 he was secretly to address his skeptical generals with words that he might well have been thinking now. "If I am now taken to task about what concrete prospects there are of ending the war, then I should just like to ask you to look at the history of wars and tell me when in the major campaigns any concrete idea emerged as to how each would end. For the most part there was not even a concrete idea as to how the campaign should be conducted. Moltke himself wrote that it is erroneous to expect that any plan of war can be drawn up that will hold good after the first battles." In the same speech he was to explain: "In my position one can have no other master than one's own judgment, one's conscience, and one's sense of duty. Those are the only masters to whose commands I bow."

The army had already taken matters into its own hands, issuing in mid-September 1939 an order for the withdrawal of most of the combat divisions from Poland and their partial demobilization. Keitel warned General Halder that such an order was unthinkable without Hitler's consent; and when Hitler heard of it he sat sharply upright and ejaculated, "We are going to attack the west, and we are going to do it this October!"

There are small indications that Hitler had known all along that he was on the threshold of a long and bitter war with Britain—that Britain would not withdraw even now that Poland no longer existed. As early as September 5 the Führer instructed Walther Hewel—Ribbentrop's liaison officer on Hitler's staff, who as a student had spent several months with him in Landsberg prison in 1923—to use every possible diplomatic channel to rescue his disconsolate friend "Putzi" Hanfstaengl from the consequences of his own stubbornness in London and arrange his escape to Germany.[1] A few days later, the British Cabinet announced that Britain was preparing for a war that was expected to last at least three years; this blunt statement evidently jolted Hitler, for he was still referring to it three weeks later. Britain was clearly going to play for time until her rearmament was complete—and this was the one development Hitler feared most. On the evening of September 12 he confidentially disclosed to Colonel Schmundt that as soon as Poland had been defeated he would swing around and *attack* in the west; he must exploit the western weakness while he could. But he deliberately kept General von Brauchitsch uninformed of his thinking.

A few days later, on the fourteenth, he discussed with his chief engineer, Fritz Todt, architect of the West Wall fortifications, the need for a proper permanent headquarters site in the west, as his special train would be too vulnerable to air attack. One site was debated and discarded, and another near Munstereifel was eventually selected. To his adjutants, Hitler explained that his Great War experience in Flanders had taught him that until January the weather would hold good for an offensive, after which it would be imprudent to launch a large-scale campaign before May. He admitted that he did not expect the victorious campaign in Poland to influence the western powers; he proposed to make one more peace offer to Britain, but he had small hopes for it. He did not seriously expect Britain to come to terms until the Wehrmacht was arrayed on the English Channel, he said. On the twentieth, General Keitel, chief of the OKW (Wehrmacht High Command), warned a member of his staff that Hitler was planning to launch an offensive in the west as soon as it became clear there was no chance of reaching an understanding with the western powers.

---

[1] After a ham-handed joke by Hitler and Göring in February 1937 had misfired, Hanfstaengl had fled to England, believing his life to be in danger.

In a long speech, Hitler revealed this intention to his startled supreme commanders on September 27, the day after his return to the Chancellery: what disturbed the army was Hitler's insistence that since German superiority of arms and men was only temporary, the offensive against France must therefore begin before the end of 1939, and, as in 1914, it would have to be carried through Belgium and at least the southern tip of a Holland he hoped would bow before the inevitability of such action. Hitler explained that he was unconvinced of Belgium's honest neutrality, for she was clearly fortified only along her frontier with Germany, and there were indications that she would permit a rapid invasion by the French and British forces massing on her western frontier—perhaps a secret military convention already existed between Belgium and the western powers to that end. (In this belief he was mistaken.) Thus the Ruhr, seat of Germany's armaments industries, would be lost and so would the war. He ordered General von Brauchitsch to establish the earliest date by which the German buildup could be complete. Aware that Brauchitsch inwardly rebelled against this new campaign, Hitler tolerated no discussion of his decision or of the prospects. He terminated the conference by shredding his brief notes and tossing them into the fire burning in the study grate.

As he privately informed Reichsleiter Alfred Rosenberg on September 29, he intended to propose a grand peace conference to arrange an armistice, demobilization, and the general settlement of outstanding problems, but if need be he would launch an offensive in the west. He was not afraid of the Maginot line. If the British would not accept the peace he offered, then he would destroy them. And Baron Ernst von Weizsäcker recorded Hitler as saying in his presence that day that the new offensive might cost Germany a million men—but it would cost the enemy the same number, and the enemy could ill afford the loss. Hitler repeated his arguments to his army and army group commanders when he assembled them in the Chancellery the next day to receive his thanks for the Polish triumph.

Warsaw had just fallen. It had been at the mercy of German ground and air bombardment since September 10. Elsewhere in Poland the towns had largely escaped damage. In Cracow, only the railroad station and the airfield had been bombed. But this was not to be the fate of Warsaw, whose commandant Hitler suspected of stalling for time in which to fortify the city against the encircling German armies. By the twenty-first it was clear that Warsaw would have to be taken by storm. The two hundred foreign diplomats were allowed to escape through the German lines, and the artillery bombardment of the city's vital gas, power, and water installations was stepped up. On the twenty-fifth Hitler had visited the Tenth and Eighth armies; the latter had a hundred and fifty batteries of artillery drawn up for the final bombardment due to begin next day. From the roof of a sports stadium Hitler and a handful of his followers watched with binoculars as the artillery pounded Warsaw. Blaskowitz's final report states:

On September 25 the Führer and Commander in Chief of the Wehrmacht visited the Warsaw front with the Commander in Chief of the army and his Chief of Staff. He was briefed on the Eighth Army's plan of attack: according to this the main artillery assault on the fortress will commence early on September 26. Until then only identified military objectives, enemy batteries, and vital installations such as gas, water, and power stations are being bombarded by ground and air forces. Thirteenth Army Corps' attack is to begin at 0800 hrs on September 26, followed by Ninth Army Corps one day later; opportunities of improving on the opening positions before then will be exploited. . . .
  After the plan of attack has been outlined broadly to him and been given the detailed approval of the Commander in Chief of the army, the Führer, who is deeply troubled by the suffering that lies in store for the population of the fortress [Warsaw], suggests that one more last attempt should be made to persuade the military command of Warsaw to abandon its lunatic course. He guarantees that the officers of the fortress will be granted honorable captivity and may retain their daggers if they surrender forthwith, and orders that the NCOs and troops are to be assured of their early release after the necessary formalities.

Millions of new leaflets publishing these terms were dropped over Warsaw that evening. The Polish commandant made no response. Early on the twenty-sixth, therefore, the target of the artillery bombardment was changed to the city itself, and the infantry assault began. The next day it was all over; the Poles had capitulated with virtually no further military resistance. For a week there had been no water in the city; the railroads were in ruins; there was no food or electric power. Unburied in the ruins lay some twenty-six thousand civilian dead, over twice the total German military casualties of the entire Polish campaign. On October 2, General Rommel and Colonel Schmundt visited Warsaw and afterward reported to Hitler on the terrible scenes of destruction. Rommel wrote to his wife the next day: "All went according to plan yesterday. Flight to Berlin, flight to Warsaw, talks and inspection there, flight back to Berlin, report in the Reich Chancellery, and dinner at the Führer's table. Warsaw is in bad shape. There is hardly a building not in some way damaged or with its windows intact. . . . The people must have suffered terribly. For seven days there has been no water, no power, no gas, and no food. . . . The mayor estimates there are forty thousand dead and injured. . . . Apart from that everything is quiet. The people are probably relieved that we have come, and that their ordeal is over. The NSV[2] and the 'Bavaria' rescue convoy and the field kitchens are beseiged by starving,

---

[2] *National-Sozialistische Volkswohlfahrt,* the Party's civilian welfare organization.

exhausted people. It's raining here in Berlin, and there are low-lying clouds. In Warsaw the weather was fine but cloudy."

A pall of death still hung over Warsaw as Hitler flew in for his big victory parade there on October 5. The stench of rotting bodies soured the Polish air. Handpicked regiments of the finest infantry divisions stomped past in a parade-march that could not have been improved upon, but according to his closest staff the Führer was unnerved by the spectacle of the death and destruction all about. Outwardly he remained hard and callous. To the foreign journalists swarming around him as he returned to the airfield he said menacingly, "Take a good look around Warsaw. That is how I can deal with any European city. I've got enough ammunition." But when he saw the banquet that the army had prepared at the airfield, either his stomach rebelled or his instinct for bad publicity warned him not to sit at a vast, horseshoe-shaped table with spotless white linen and sumptuous food at a time when hundreds of thousands of Warsaw's inhabitants were starving. He turned on his heel and instructed Keitel and his staff to follow him immediately to the aircraft. He had wanted to eat at a field kitchen with his troops, he said.

The frontiers of eastern Europe had now been agreed upon between Germany and the Soviet Union. Hitler had insisted that his foreign minister personally fly to Moscow to settle the details. Since Ribbentrop was unenthusiastic about the mission, Hitler told him with some feeling: "Laying down the definitive frontiers between Asia and Europe for the next thousand years is after all a task worthy of the foreign minister of the *Grossdeutsches Reich!*" The partition of Poland had caused some anguish in Germany. Göring, a fanatical huntsman—a member of what Hitler called "that green freemasonry of men"—turned greedy eyes on the forests of Bialystok, rich with game, and he persuaded General Hans Jeschonnek to telephone Hitler's train to point up the importance of the Bialystok wood supply to the German economy; Hitler had bellowed with laughter. "He talks of wood and he means stags!" and he instructed that Bialystok should nevertheless be assigned to the Russian side of the demarcation line.

Ribbentrop settled the line on a small-scale map of Europe in Stalin's Kremlin office on September 28. Whereas the line provisionally agreed upon in mid-September had run along the Vistula River, it now followed the Bug River far to the east, since Stalin had also assigned to Germany the districts of Warsaw and Lublin in exchange for the Baltic state of Lithuania, which the August pact had placed within Germany's sphere of influence. So now the German troops who had advanced to the Bug, only to be ordered to withdraw to the Vistula, had to march eastward once again, spanning the difficult terrain for the third time in as many weeks. Stalin offset the only other dissatisfaction with the partition—the fact that the oil-producing region at Lvov (Lemberg) was on his side of the line—by a promise to supply Germany with three hundred thousand tons of the oil annually.

All in all, as Ribbentrop remarked to Hitler on his return to Berlin, talking with Stalin and the other Kremlin potentates he had felt he was among comrades barely distinguishable from his National Socialist acquaintances.

Rosenberg almost choked when he heard of Ribbentrop's flattery of Stalin. He saw the strategic weakness in the new eastern frontiers almost at once. The new demarcation line would give Germany no common frontier with Romania, thus Germany's sole railway link with the Romanian oil fields and the Black Sea would run through Soviet-controlled territory. As another minister commented to Rosenberg, "If the Russians now march into the Baltic states, we shall have lost the Baltic as well, strategically speaking; Moscow will be more powerful than ever and they will be able to act against us in concert with the West any time they choose." Rosenberg probably put this view to Hitler with some emphasis when he saw him on the twenty-ninth. In fact the indecent haste with which Stalin moved to take up the options extended to him gravely embarrassed Ribbentrop's ministry; it can only be explained by the Soviet leader's alarm at the speed with which Hitler's Wehrmacht had polished off Poland and by his fear that peace might break out. Under pressure from him Estonia conceded air and naval bases to Russia on September 29, and Latvia and Lithuania followed suit a few days later. Finland, however, made it clear from the outset she would offer the most determined resistance to similar Russian demands.

For the first two weeks of October 1939, Hitler unquestionably wavered between continuing the fight—which meant launching an almost immediate offensive in the west—and making peace with the remaining belligerents on the best terms he could get. The fact that he had ordered the Wehrmacht to get ready for "Operation Yellow" (*Fall Gelb,* the attack on France and the Low Countries) in no way detracts from the reality of his peace offensive. Whatever his final decision, there was no time to be lost.

Hitler saw powerful arguments against stopping the fighting while the Reich's military advantage was at its height. Nevertheless, he would probably have settled for what he had already conquered—if only to be able to return to his grandiose architectural dreams. Besides, Germany would have needed at least fifty years to digest the new territories and carry out the enforced settlement programs planned by Heinrich Himmler to fortify the German blood in the east. Thus Hitler's peace feelers toward London were sincere—not just a ploy to drive a wedge between Britain and France. Weizsäcker wrote early in October: "The attempt to wind up the war now is for real. I myself put the chances at 20 percent, [Hitler] at 50 percent; his desire is 100 percent. If he obtained peace, the thesis that Britain would sacrifice Poland would be proven quasi right. And besides, it would eliminate the awkward decision as to how to reduce Britain by military means." Early in September Göring had hinted to the British through Birger Dahlerus, the Swedish businessman whom Hitler had already accepted as an unofficial intermediary to London during August, that Germany would be willing to restore sovereignty to a Poland shorn of the old German provinces excised from the Fatherland at the end of the Great War; there would also be an end to the persecution of the Jews and a reduction in German armaments. The British response had been a cautious readiness to listen to the detailed German proposals.

But since these proposals had been made, the Russians, as per their agreement with the Nazis, had seized eastern Poland. Hitler told Göring and Dahlerus in Berlin late on September 26 that if the British still wanted to salvage anything of Poland, they would have to make haste. They would have to send a negotiator who would take him seriously, and now he could do nothing without consulting his Russian friends. As for the Jewish question, the Germans proposed that it be solved by using the new Poland as a sink into which Europe's Jews should be emptied. Hitler approved the proposal that a secret meeting take place between German and British emissaries—perhaps Göring himself and General Sir Edmund Ironside—in Holland. Dahlerus left for London at once.[3]

The German army had good reason to keep anxious track of Hitler's peace offensive. Late in September, Halder's deputy had gloomily—and wholly inaccurately—warned that the German army could not launch a frontal assault on the French before 1942. Hitler was aware of the army's reluctance to apply its mind to "Yellow"; this was one reason for his speech of September 27. But even in that speech he had referred to a western assault only as a necessary evil if the French and British failed to see reason. If that happened, then "we must resolve to batter the enemy until he gives in."

The army marshaled what arguments it could against executing "Yellow" now: the tactics which had proved so successful in Poland would not suffice against the well-organized French army; the foggy weather and short hours of autumn daylight would set the Luftwaffe at a disadvantage; the army lacked ammunition, stores, and equipment. Brauchitsch enumerated these arguments to Hitler on October 7, and Hitler—already angered by the reluctance of his soldiers to follow him—asked the Commander in Chief to leave his notes behind, an ominous sign that he was not satisfied. Over the next two days he dictated a fifty-eight-page memorandum for the eyes of Keitel and the three commanders in chief alone; in

---

[3]From the papers released to the Public Record Office in London it is clear that neither Chamberlain nor Halifax rejected Hitler's terms out of hand when Dahlerus described them. Even Churchill talked approvingly of an armistice. However, the file that evidently contains notes of Chamberlain's talk with Dahlerus on September 29, 1939, is closed until 1990, and forty-five pages of the foreign office file on Germany and future policy (F.O.371/22,985) covering the crucial period of October 3–4, 1939, are unavailable until the year 2015. A two-volume history of Anglo-German peace negotiations by Dr. Bernd Martin, of the University of Freiburg, is to appear shortly.

it he explained just why they must launch "Yellow" at the very earliest opportunity and just why time was working against Germany.

The Führer read this formidable document to his uncomfortable generals on the tenth. We shall return to it at greater length shortly. In it, he insisted that Britain's long-range goal remained unchanged: the disintegration of the powerful German bloc, and the annihilation and dissolution of this new Reich with its eighty million people. The long-range German war aim must therefore be the absolute military defeat of the West (in which the destruction of the enemy's forces was more important than the gaining of enemy territory). This was the struggle which the German people must now assume. Despite all this, he added, a rapidly achieved peace agreement would still serve German interests—provided that Germany was required to relinquish nothing of her gains.

Hitler ignored none of the various unofficial channels for negotiation with the West now that Poland had been laid low. Over the next few days, however, it became clear that while some circles in Britain—notably in the air ministry—wanted an armistice, there was in the British Cabinet a hard core of opposition to whom all talk of making a deal with Hitler was anathema. Hitler was probably right in identifying the main source of this stubborn anti-German line as Churchill, now First Lord of the Admiralty, and the clique around him. On September 29, Alfred Rosenberg secured Hitler's permission to take up feelers put out through an intermediary in Switzerland by officials of the British air ministry; but this glimmer of hope was shortly extinguished when the intermediary reported that the forces for peace in that ministry had been pushed to the wall by the more militant forces at Churchill's beck and call. Little more was heard of these diffident approaches from London.

At this stage in Hitler's thought processes there came an ostensible intervention by President Roosevelt that was as abrupt in its approach as it was enigmatic in denouement. At the beginning of October an influential American oil tycoon arrived in Berlin on a peace mission for which he had apparently received a ninety-minute personal briefing from Roosevelt. He was William Rhodes Davis, whose own personal interest lay in preventing any disruption of his oil business with Germany. He had been brought into contact with Roosevelt by John L. Lewis, leader of the CIO, the United States labor federation whose fourteen million members represented a political force no president could afford to ignore. Lewis was originally both anti-Fascist and anti-Communist, but he had, said Davis, been impressed by the significant rise in the living standards of the German worker under National Socialism. Anxious about the effects of a long war on American export markets, Lewis had obliged Roosevelt to entrust this unofficial peace mission to Davis.

In Berlin the oilman met Göring, and a seven-page summary of the discussion of the alleged Roosevelt proposals survives.[4] It was evidently given wide confidential circulation in Berlin, for sardonic references to Roosevelt's sudden emergence as an "angel of peace" bent on securing a third term figure in several diaries of the day.

> President Roosevelt is prepared to put pressure on the western powers to start peace talks if Germany will provide the stimulus. President Roosevelt asks to be advised of the various points Germany wants to settle, for example, Poland and the colonies. In this connection President Roosevelt also mentioned the question of the purely Czech areas, on which however a settlement need not come into effect until later. This point was touched on by President Roosevelt with regard to public opinion in the United States, as he must placate the Czech voters and the circles sympathizing with them if he is to exercise pressure on Britain to end the war.

Davis assured Göring that Roosevelt's main strategic concern was to exploit the present situation to destroy Britain's monopoly of the world markets. "In his conversation with Davis, Roosevelt explained that he was flatly opposed to the British declaration of war. He was not consulted by Britain in advance." Roosevelt suspected that Britain's motives were far more dangerous and that they had nothing to do with Poland; he himself recognized that the real reason for the war lay in the one-sided *Diktat* of Versailles which made it impossible for the German people to acquire a living standard comparable with that of their neighbors in Europe. Roosevelt's proposal, according to the unpublished summary, was that Hitler be allowed to keep Danzig and all the now Polish provinces taken from Germany by the treaty of Versailles, that all Germany's former African colonies be restored to her forthwith, and that the rest of the world give Germany financial assistance in establishing a high standard of living.

This was not all. If Daladier and Chamberlain refused to comply, then President Roosevelt would support Germany—Davis reported—in her search for a just, tolerable, and lasting peace: he would supply Germany with goods and war supplies "convoyed to Germany under the protection of the American armed forces" if need be. John L. Lewis had privately promised Davis that if some such agreement could be reached between Germany and the United States his unions would prevent the manufacture of war supplies for Britain and France.

Göring outlined Davis's message in detail to the Führer immediately after the meeting, and on October 3 the field marshal announced to the American that in his important speech to the Reichstag on the sixth Hitler would make a number

---

[4]Signed by Ministerialdirektor Wohlthat, this remarkable document was not published in the postwar volumes of captured German documents; nor were the German reports on the Dahlerus missions that followed.

of peace proposals closely embodying the points Davis had brought from Washington. (Hitler's more detailed proposals as described by Göring indeed went so far that their sincerity is open to question.) Göring told Davis: "If in his [Roosevelt's] opinion the suggestions afford a reasonable basis for a peace conference, he will then have the opportunity to bring about this settlement. . . . You may assure Mr. Roosevelt that if he will undertake this mediation, Germany will agree to an adjustment whereby a new Polish state and an independent Czechoslovak government would come into being. However this information is for him [Roosevelt] alone and to be used only if necessary to bring about a peace conference." Göring was willing to attend such a conference in Washington.

When Davis went back to the United States with the five detailed points Hitler proposed, he was accompanied by a German official, a "special ambassador" appointed to settle any details. Hitler hoped for an interim reply from Roosevelt by the fifth. (As Rosenberg wrote: "It would be a cruel blow for London to be urgently "advised" by Washington to sue for peace!") But something had gone wrong with the mission: when Davis reached Washington he was not readmitted to the President, and they did not meet again.

A different aspect of Roosevelt's policy was revealed by the Polish documents ransacked by the Nazis from the archives of the ruined foreign ministry building in Warsaw. The dispatches of the Polish ambassadors in Washington and Paris laid bare Roosevelt's efforts to goad France and Britain into war with Germany while he rearmed the United States and psychologically prepared the American public for war. In November 1938, William C. Bullitt, his personal friend and ambassador in Paris, had indicated to the Poles that the President's desire was that "Germany and Russia should come to blows," whereupon the democratic nations would attack Germany and force her into submission; in the spring of 1939, Bullitt quoted Roosevelt as being determined "not to participate in the war from the start, but to be in at the finish"—the United States without doubt would fight, but "only if France and Britain kick off first." Bullitt was said by the Poles to have carried with him to Paris a "suitcase full of instructions" outlining the pressure he was to put on the Quai d'Orsay not to compromise with the totalitarian powers; at the same time Washington was applying "various exceptionally significant screws" to the British. Washington, Bullitt had told the Polish diplomats, was being guided not by ideological considerations but solely by the material interests of the United States. The Warsaw documents left little doubt as to what had stiffened Polish resistance to German demands during the August 1939 crisis.

On Friday October 6, Hitler spoke to the Reichstag. His "appeal for peace" was addressed to the British in more truculent and recriminatory language than many of his more moderate followers would have wished. He singled out Churchill—who was then First Lord of the Admiralty—as a representative of the Jewish capitalist and journalistic circles whose sole interest in life lay in the furtherance of arson on an international scale.

On the ninth, he issued to his commanders in chief a formal directive to prepare for "Yellow" with all haste, in the event that "Britain and, under her command, France as well" were not disposed to end the war. His soldiers were, however, full of optimism. General Rommel wrote from Berlin on the seventh: "The reaction of the neutrals [to the Führer's speech] seems very good. The others will be able to think it over during the weekend. There is not much going on here otherwise. If the war ends soon, I hope I will soon be able to go home. . . ."

Hitler had sent Dahlerus to London for talks with Chamberlain. Late on October 9 the Swede reported to him the conditions Britain was attaching to peace negotiations: in addition to insisting on a new Polish state, Britain wanted all weapons of aggression destroyed forthwith; and there must be a plebiscite in Germany on certain aspects of her foreign policy. These were hard terms to swallow, for in public Hitler was still claiming that the future of Poland was a matter for Germany and Russia alone to decide, and Britain was blithely ignoring the growing armed strength of the Soviet Union and her expansionist policies. Nevertheless, on the tenth, Dahlerus was instructed to advise London that Hitler would *accept* these terms on principle. The Swedish negotiator saw Hitler twice that day before he departed for a promised rendezvous with a British emissary at The Hague. He took with him a formal letter from Göring and a list of Hitler's proposals—which included a new Polish state; the right for Germany to fortify her new frontier with Russia; guarantees backed by national plebiscite; nonaggression pacts between Germany, France, Britain, Italy, and the Soviet Union; disarmament; and the return of Germany's former colonies or suitable substitute territories.[5] Dahlerus noted to one German officer after meeting Hitler that "Germany for her part was able to swallow even tough conditions, provided they were put in a palatable form." He said he was taking with him to Holland more than enough to dispel Britain's smoldering mistrust of Hitler.

In Holland, however, Dahlerus waited in vain for the promised British emissary. The British foreign office asked him to describe Hitler's proposals to their local envoy and to remain at The Hague until he heard from London. Berlin optimistically viewed this request as a positive token of British interest and agreed

---

[5]The brief treatment of this episode in Sir Llewellyn Woodward's *British Foreign Policy in the Second World War*, Vol. II (H.M.S.O., 1971), page 186, includes an inadequate summary of the proposals.

that he should wait there. But Chamberlain's eagerly awaited speech to the House of Commons the next day, October 12, exploded Hitler's confident expectation that peace was about to descend on Europe after five weeks of war. Chamberlain dismissed Hitler's public offer (of the sixth) as "vague and uncertain"—he had made no suggestion for righting the wrongs done to Czechoslovakia and Poland. If Hitler wanted peace, said Chamberlain, "acts—not words alone—must be forthcoming." That same evening Hitler sent for Göring, Milch, and Udet of the Luftwaffe and instructed them to resume bomb production at the earliest possible moment. "The war will go on!" Dahlerus was asked to return from The Hague to Berlin forthwith. Édouard Daladier's reply to Hitler was no less abrupt. "Before these answers came," Weizsäcker wrote two days later, "the Führer himself had indulged in great hopes of seeing his dream of working with Britain fulfilled. He had set his heart on peace. Herr von Ribbentrop seemed less predisposed toward it. He sent the Führer his own word picture of a future Europe like the empire of Charlemagne."

To the Swedish explorer Sven Hedin a few days later Hitler voiced his puzzlement at Britain's intransigence. He felt he had repeatedly extended the hand of peace and friendship to the British, and each time they had blacked his eye in reply. "The survival of the British Empire is in Germany's interests too," Hitler noted, "because if Britain loses India, we gain nothing thereby." *Of course* he was going to restore a Polish state—he did not want to gorge himself with Poles; as for the rest of Chamberlain's outbursts, he, Hitler, might as well demand that Britain "right the wrongs" done to India, Egypt, and Palestine. Britain could have peace any time she wanted, but they—and that included that "brilliantined moron" Eden and the equally incompetent Churchill—must learn to keep their noses out of Europe.

And in a fit of anger Hitler complained to Dahlerus about "the unbelievable behavior of Mr. Chamberlain"; from now on Germany would fight Britain tooth and nail—he did not propose to bargain with her any longer. Dahlerus left the Chancellery in a huff at the failure of his peace effort, but was later soothed by Göring, who sent an important German decoration around to him that same evening.

To Hitler it was clear there was no alternative but to proceed with the war. The *urgency* of resuming the offensive was what he had most impressed on his supreme commanders in his memorandum of October 9. While German military advantage was now at its very zenith, every month that passed in idleness would see a relative weakening vis-à-vis the enemy; in Italy, moreover, Mussolini was not getting any younger; the West might succeed in blackmailing Holland or Belgium into abandoning their neutrality, or in bribing the venal Balkan countries to the same effect; Russia's attitude could easily change. And there were other reasons why Germany must strike swiftly and avoid a protracted war: as Britain patched up her military resources and injected fresh units into France, the psychological boost this gave to the French could not be ignored; conversely it would become progressively more difficult to sustain the German public's enthusiasm for war or to feed the German war effort with foodstuffs and raw materials as each month passed. Germany's air superiority was only temporary—the moment the enemy believed *he* had achieved air superiority he would exploit it regardless of any reprisals Hitler might announce. Above all the British and French knew of the vulnerability of the Ruhr industries, and the moment the enemy could base aircraft or even long-range artillery on Belgian and Dutch territory, Germany would have to write off the Ruhr from the war effort; enemy bombers would have to fly barely a sixth of the distance that German bombers would have to cover to reach important British targets from the small strip of Germany's North Sea coast. This was why Hitler was convinced that the occupation of Belgium and Holland *must* be on the western powers' agenda already, and this was how he justified ordering his army to prepare to attack France through Belgium.

If the coast of western Europe were in Hitler's hands, the advantages to Germany would be decisive if the war against Britain was to continue: for sound strategic reasons the German navy needed submarine bases west of the English Channel. (On the tenth, Raeder also proposed that Germany obtain naval bases in Norway for the same reasons.) Similarly the Luftwaffe would have a disproportionate advantage in striking power if its flying distance to British targets involved only the short shuttle route from Holland, Belgium, or even the Pas de Calais in France.

The battle performance of the arms, men, and leadership of the German Wehrmacht had been strikingly demonstrated in Poland. In the fighting in the west, Germany could field a modern army of proud and battle-hardened soldiers. Their weapons were up-to-date and plentiful, particularly in the panzer and air forces; the artillery had at least two to three times as much ammunition per gun as at the onset of the war in 1914. Hitler proclaimed himself unimpressed by France's superiority in heavy howitzers and long-range artillery. But he warned emphatically against underestimating the value of the British divisions; as each month brought more to the shores of France, it would become increasingly awkward for the French government to extricate itself from the war.

These were the reasons Hitler gave for asking the Wehrmacht to put the offensive first, attacking in the west "this very autumn," and en masse; after all this might well be the push that ended all the fighting in Europe. The German army would attack the French along a front from south of Luxemburg to north of Nijmegen, in Holland. Splitting into two assault groups on either side of the

Belgian fortress of Liège, it would destroy the French and British armies which would have come to meet it. The German armored formations would be used with such speed and dexterity that no cohesive front could be stabilized by the enemy; on no account were the tanks to become entangled in the endless maze of Belgian streets. The cities were to be bypassed, invested by lesser troops, and starved into submission. The Luftwaffe was to concentrate on shattering enemy railroad and road networks, rather than squander effort on hunting down individual aircraft. "Extreme restrictions are to be imposed on air attacks on cities themselves"; they were to be bombed only if necessary as reprisals for raids on the Reich cities. The war aim of the Wehrmacht, he drilled into his supreme commanders in this carefully-thought-out memorandum, was the destruction of the Anglo-French armies, not the destruction of public property and installations.

The German navy and air force accepted Hitler's arguments without demur, but the army leadership began a kicking and struggling that was to last until the spring of 1940. Perhaps this was because for the first time the generals clearly saw that Hitler took his position as Supreme Commander of the Wehrmacht seriously —that he now proposed to "interfere" more radically with the overall strategic direction of the war. Admiral Raeder not only shared the views expressed in the memorandum, but added an urgency of his own when he saw Hitler on the evening of the tenth of October: if Britain was to be defeated, she must be beleaguered and beseiged regardless of army objections and the risk of American involvement. "The earlier we begin, and the more brutally, the earlier we shall see results; the shorter will be the war." Hitler thought the same way and stressed the importance of maintaining the submarine construction program right through 1940. Rudolf Hess meantime furnished him with several studies urging the use of magnetic mines to blockade Britain's sea lanes. In short, everybody accepted the need to defeat the western powers except the German army: the OKH (War Department) considered the army unready for a new campaign; army group commanders Bock and Leeb echoed this skepticism with different degrees of vehemence, and army commanders like Reichenau and Kluge were equally unenthusiastic about the campaign—they would not even favor such an attack if the western powers were to invade Belgium forthwith. General von Brauchitsch found in mid-October that Hitler turned a deaf ear on his hesitations. Only a sound thrashing would make the British see reason, the Führer said. "Yellow" was provisionally to begin the third week of November; this early date would be dependent only on the weather forecast for Luftwaffe operations and not on the recalcitrant army's whims.

An indirect but readily traceable result of the British snub of his peace overture was a further hardening in Hitler's attitude to the future of Poland. After his Reichstag speech of October 6, he did not renew his offer to set up a rump Polish state. The Poland of 1939 would be subdivided, dismembered, and repopulated in such a way that it would never again rise to embarrass Germany or the Soviet Union. The eastern half, of course, had gone to Stalin; in the west, part would be absorbed by the Reich, while central Poland, *i.e.,* the districts of Warsaw, Radom, Lublin, and Cracow, would become a Polish reservation under exclusively German rule—a reservoir of cheap labor for the Reich's industries. By the end of September, Hitler had already drafted the first decrees for radical surgery of Poland's population under the overall direction of Heinrich Himmler as "Reich Commissioner for the Consolidation of the German Population." The Polish and Jewish populations in western Poland were to be displaced to a reservation in central Poland, and refugees of German descent from the Baltic states and eastern Poland would take their place.

A series of radical decrees signed by Hitler heralded this new order in Poland. On October 4 he amnestied all deeds committed by Germans "enraged by the atrocities perpetrated by the Poles." The Hitler decree appointing Himmler gave him the job of "eliminating the injurious influence of such non-German segments of the population there as are a danger to the Reich"; it was signed on the seventh. On the eighth Hitler signed a decree setting up new Reich Gaue (districts)— "West Prussia" and "Posen"—while former Polish frontier regions around Kattowitz and Zichenau were annexed to Silesia and East Prussia, respectively. As for the remaining German-occupied area, the Polish reservation, on the twelfth Hitler drafted a decree "for the restoration . . . of public order" there, subjugating these remaining regions to a German Governor General, a viceroy responsible only to himself; the new setup was to go into effect the moment the military government was withdrawn.

The Generalgouvernement was about one quarter the area of prewar Poland. As Governor General, Hitler selected Dr. Hans Frank, the Party's legal adviser; Frank, a former member of the Faculty of Law at Munich University, had specialized in industrial law. He rapidly gained a reputation for slipperiness with the army generals assigned to the eastern command, and since he shortly fell out with Himmler—who did not even attend Frank's installation ceremony at Lodz —his reign from Cracow castle was to be a lonely one.

These were the twilight days of the German army's rule in Poland. At a conference at the Chancellery on October 17, Hitler announced to Keitel, Frank, and Himmler that the army was to hand over control to the civilian administrations set up under Hans Frank and Gauleiters Albert Forster and Artur Greiser. The army ought to be glad to be rid of this unwholesome task, Hitler noted, and warming to his theme he ordered that in the Generalgouvernement it was no part of the administrators' duty to establish a model province along German lines or to put the country economically back on its feet. On the contrary, this was to become a "Polish economy"[6] par excellence! Significantly Frank's task in Poland would be to "lay the foundations for a military buildup in the future" and to prevent the Polish intelligentsia from creating a hard-core opposition leadership. The fight would be cruel, but this alone, Keitel noted in his record of Hitler's remarks, would spare Germany the need to go onto the battlefield once again because of Poland. Poland must become so poor that the people would *want* to work in Germany; the Jews and other vermin must be given speedy passage eastward. To an army colonel who arrived at the Chancellery that evening Keitel frankly admitted: "The methods to be employed will be irreconcilable with all our existing principles." According to yet another version, Hitler ended by announcing that he wanted Gauleiters Greiser[7] and Forster to be able to report to him ten years from now that Posen and West Prussia were pure and Germanic provinces in full bloom, and Hans Frank to be able to report that in the General-gouvernement—the Polish reservation—the "devil's deed" had been done.

The population surgery prescribed by the redrawn map of eastern Europe inflicted hardship on Germans too, and German refugees crowded the roads of the territories of southeastern Poland beyond the San River, an area which had been assigned to Russia. Here there were scores of villages and hamlets where the language and the culture was German, where Germans had tended land given to their ancestors by Maria Theresa and Joseph II—villages with names like Burgthal and Wiesenberg, or Neudorf and Steinfels, where the farms were laid out and worked in an orderly and scientific manner that set them apart from the farms of Polish and Ukrainian neighbors.

In the last days of October 1939, Captain Engel, Hitler's army adjutant, handed him a Fourteenth Army report on the evacuation of these thousands of ethnic Germans before the advancing Red Army troops occupied their villages. In the five days after September 22, about five thousand bewildered villagers and their livestock had been marched westward, helped by army transport of the withdrawing Wehrmacht units and looked after by NSV welfare teams. No orders had been given; none were necessary. "In the majority of cases the villagers had experienced enough during the Great War (when the Germans were transported to

---

[6] Literal translation of *polnische Wirtschaft,* a phrase of which the sense would better be given, however, by a "Polish pigsty."

[7] On March 7, 1944, Gauleiter Artur Greiser cabled the Führer that 1,000,000 Germans had been officially transplanted to his Reich Gau "Wartheland" from the old Reich, from the rest of Europe, and most recently from the Black Sea regions; the Jews had all but vanished from the area, and the number of Poles had been reduced from 4,200,000 to 3,500,000 by forced migration. This indicates the kind of population movements that Hitler set in train in October 1939. In May 1945, with the approval of the western governments, the tides were reversed, but even more dramatically. About 40,000,000 Germans, Poles, and Czechs were forcibly resettled by 1948.

Siberia) and during the years of Bolshevik rule, 1919 and 1920, for them to abandon their property without further ado and take to their heels." These were pious and deeply patriotic Germans, untainted by Polish ways, the report concluded; they would be excellent stock for the resettlement of Germany's newly won eastern provinces. As this westward movement was in progress, a more ominous eastward flow began: from their half of Poland, the Russians began deporting dangerous intellectuals and officer classes; and in the German half the Jews were being rounded up, confined, and spilled over the demarcation line into the Russian zone where possible.

Hitler's attitude toward the Kremlin at this time revealed a fascinating conflict between his short-term desire for a stable eastern front and an assured supply of raw materials, and his long-term, immutable hatred and mistrust of Stalin and communism; his imperial eastern ambitions had only temporarily been anesthetized by the rapid conquest of Poland. In private conferences with such loquacious personalities as Count Galeazzo Ciano, both the Führer and Ribbentrop spoke reverently of the treaties signed with Moscow. But secretly Hitler acted as though the Russians were infected by some contagion which must at all costs be prevented from spreading to the Reich. Contacts between the German and Soviet armies along the demarcation line were prohibited by Berlin. The repatriation of the ethnic Germans was actively encouraged, and at one time there was even a suggestion that the navy protect the interests of the German communities trapped by the Russian encroachment on the Baltic states. How long could he rely on the Kremlin to respect the demarcation line? In his long October memorandum to his supreme commanders Hitler had warned: "Through no treaty and no agreement can the lasting neutrality of Russia be guaranteed with certainty. For the present all the indications are that Russia will not abandon this neutrality. But that may change in eight months, in a year, or even in several years' time." Only the clear demonstration of Germany's superiority in arms would dissuade Stalin from tearing up his pact with Berlin the moment it suited him. This latent mistrust was voiced even more emphatically by Hitler to Keitel on the seventeenth: Poland was to be left in decay except insofar as was needed to work up the roads, the rail systems, and the signals networks to turn the area into an important military springboard; without doubt he was thinking in terms of an attack on Russia.

In a long speech behind closed doors to senior Party officials and Gauleiters on October 21, he promised that once he had forced Britain and France to their knees he would revert his attention to the east and show who was the master there. It had become clear that the Russian army was not much use, he was quoted as explaining, and that their soldiers were badly trained and poorly equipped. "Once he had [dealt with the East] as well he would set about restoring Germany to how she used to be. . . ." He wanted Belgium; and as for France,

Hitler was now thinking in terms of the ancient frontier of 1540—when the Habsburg empire of Charles V had embraced Switzerland and a multitude of duchies like Burgundy and Lorraine as far to the west as the Meuse.

In summary, Hitler proposed to exploit his alliance with Stalin as long as possible and then to attack Russia before Stalin attempted to destroy him. It was plain that Russia was prepared to pay a high price in raw materials for German industrial expertise, machine tools, modern artillery, aircraft, and ship designs. Russia even signed a trade agreement with Britain to procure the rubber and tin needed by Berlin. Nevertheless, to his closest associates Hitler betrayed his true feelings about the alliance. A week after his speech to the Gauleiters, he assembled two dozen generals and admirals for an investiture at the Chancellery, and during the banquet that followed, he suddenly asked the panzer general, Guderian, what the army reaction to his Moscow Pact had been. Guderian replied the army had breathed a sigh of relief, but this was evidently anything but the answer Hitler wanted. The Führer lapsed into a brooding silence and then changed the subject.

Incidents

By November 1939 Adolf Hitler had faced up to the fact that the war would go on. In mid-October his propaganda ministry had already instructed editors to mute reporting of peace proposals from abroad so that no false hopes would be raised in the German public. When Alfred Rosenberg came to him on November 1 with nebulous reports of fresh peace moves within the British air ministry, the Führer belittled the prospects: while he himself would still favor a German-British rapprochement, London was in the grip of a Jewish-controlled, lunatic minority against whom Chamberlain was a characterless and impotent old man. Hitler said he failed to see what the British really wanted. "Even if the British won, the real victors would be the United States, Japan, and Russia." England, even if victorious, would emerge from a war in ruins, and her fate if she were militarily defeated would be worse.

Early in November, the Belgian and Dutch monarchs appealed to the warring parties to seek ways of restoring a lasting peace, but their well-intentioned appeal was immediately rejected by Lord Halifax in a public speech using language described by Ribbentrop as of such brazenness that he actively discouraged all further unofficial feelers, and the appeal was left unanswered by Berlin. German propaganda now portrayed the British whom Hitler had unsuccessfully wooed as murderers, liars, hypocrites, and it used a veritable thesaurus of other uncomplimentary terms. Hitler gathered that the peace party in Britain had lost. British Fascist leader Oswald Mosley had put up a good fight, but he had been silenced. The only good Briton, in Hitler's view, was Lloyd George. That Britain was continuing the fight was an unpalatable truth he now had to face.

Upon his return from Poland, Hitler had equipped the big Congress Room in his official Berlin residence as a war conference room. In its center was a large map table.

Here the Führer conducted all his war conferences in Berlin until the chamber was ruined by a bomb five years later. The OKW generals Keitel and Jodl moved into neighboring rooms vacated by Hitler's adjutants. Jodl's status was still relatively weak. When he ventured an appreciation of the overall strategic situation, Hitler cut him short after the first few sentences and delivered a lecture on what *he* thought. But Hitler's regard for Jodl grew as his contempt for the army's representatives became more explicit. He told Jodl in the middle of October, when they were discussing the new "Yellow" offensive in the west: "We are going to win this war even if it contradicts a hundred General Staff doctrines—because we've got the better troops, the better equipment, the stronger nerves, and a united, resolute leadership!" Throughout that month and the next, the army's Commander in Chief and Chief of Staff showed equal determination in waging a rearguard action against "Yellow," and it is not impossible that Hitler got wind of military and political conspiracies constantly being hatched by the army generals and civilian dissidents. At any rate, that autumn he pithily commented to Luftwaffe officers waiting for one conference to begin, "Here comes my Coward Number One!" as Brauchitsch, the army Commander in Chief, came through the door, and added, ". . . and Number Two!" when Halder, the Chief of Staff, joined him.

On October 19, 1939, the reluctant war department had at Hitler's behest issued its first hasty directive on "Yellow." It envisaged a massive main attack being carried through Belgium by seventy-five divisions whose object it was to meet and destroy the British and French armies on French and Belgian soil. As a token of their distaste for the whole affair, Brauchitsch and Halder deliberately left it to General Keitel to read out the details to Hitler. While General von Bock's Army Group B and the powerful *Armeeabteilung* Niederrhein (Army Sector Lower Rhine) would deliver the main thrust through Liège and Namur, General von Rundstedt's Army Group A would follow up with a subsidiary attack on the southern wing; Army Group C, commanded by General von Leeb, would remain on the defensive with sixteen divisions behind the West Wall.

The big push into Belgium would involve crossing a fifteen-mile-wide sliver of Dutch territory at Maastricht, but at this stage Hitler hoped it might be possible to avoid hostilities with Holland over this "temporary" claim on Dutch hospitality. (If the British landed in Holland, of course, the German army must have plans ready to occupy the whole country immediately.) Meanwhile, to justify invading neutral Belgium the military and Intelligence agencies were instructed to compile detailed summaries of instances of Franco-Belgian collusion and to allow their imaginations free rein in doing so.

The military prospects of this OKH plan did not encourage Bock and Rundstedt, who expressed their pessimism in memoranda to the war department in October. Leeb added a similar study, questioning the propriety of violating Belgian and Dutch neutrality. General von Reichenau, commanding the Sixth Army, put his objections to Hitler in person more than once, and when Hitler voiced his own fear that if "Yellow" was not executed forthwith, "one fine winter's night Britain and France may arrive at the Meuse without a shot being fired," the general stubbornly retorted, "That would be preferable in my view." When Keitel returned from a brief visit to General Staff headquarters at Zossen, impressed by the arguments Brauchitsch and Halder were deploying against "Yellow," Hitler bitterly accused his OKW chief of "conspiring with the generals" against him. He insisted that in the future Keitel loyally transmit the Führer's will to the war department—an order whose implications provoked the upright, traditionalist general into offering Hitler his resignation both orally and in writing; Hitler told him not to be so touchy. Hitler's staff believed Göring was behind the Führer's growing animosity toward the army, but even Göring was uneasy about launching "Yellow" so soon; however, he failed to win Ribbentrop's support, and after Hitler turned a deaf ear on him, the field marshal privately vowed to be a good soldier and obey orders in the future.

A basic difference of opinion lay in the Intelligence estimate of the enemy, inadequate because of the Abwehr's almost total failure to establish a network in the west. The army put the strength of the French army far too high, in Hitler's view; what perturbed Hitler was the growing British force in France, for he considered each British division was worth three or four French. But the expert tactical opinions could not be ignored. Bock warned that the British would land in Antwerp and before the Wehrmacht could prevent it there would again be a long and bloody war of attrition in Belgium. Other generals pointed out that the winter nights were long and that the combination of long nights and rainy, foggy days would make a war of movement difficult. But Hitler wanted a war of movement in which his armored and mechanized formations could sweep forward, exploiting the "inflexibility" of the French and the "inertia" of the British armies, and the more he pored over the maps the less he liked the war department's proposed operational plan. In the third week of October he commented acidly to Keitel and Jodl that Halder's plan, with its strong right wing along the coast, was no different from the Schlieffen Plan drafted before World War I: "You cannot get away with an operation like that twice. I have something very different in mind. I will tell you two about it in the next few days and then discuss it with the army."

This was the alternative possibility—a vast encirclement of the enemy, spearheaded by the armored units thrusting eventually up to the coast between the Meuse River and Arras and Amiens; this was terrain he had fought on as a young man, and he knew it would be ideal for the tanks. Farther to the north, in Flanders, the tanks would get into terrain difficulties. The idea obsessed him, and at the end of a discussion with the senior "Yellow" generals at the Reich Chancellery on October 25 he tentatively put it to the Commander in Chief. Bock, who was also present, wrote in his diary that the Führer

said in reply to a question from Brauchitsch that from the very outset he has had the following wish and idea: to deliver the main offensive *only south* of the Meuse, perhaps coupled with a subsidiary attack on Liège, so that by our advancing in a roughly westerly and then northwesterly direction the enemy forces already in or pouring into Belgium will be cut off and destroyed.

   Brauchitsch and Halder are obviously taken completely by surprise, and a "lively" debate rages to and fro over this idea.

This was the germ of the campaign plan that was to bring about France's defeat. But it seemed so bold, staking everything on one card—namely whether the German armies would succeed in breaking through to the Channel coast or not—that Hitler hesitated to order such a radical change of emphasis, the more so since three days before he had provisionally ordered that "Yellow" was to begin on Sunday, November 12. But he asked the army to look into his idea, and from a side remark it was clear that he was not averse to postponing the offensive until spring if need be.

Hitler was aware that the army's opposition was not limited to objective debate of the merits of "Yellow."
   There was a clique of as yet unidentifiable officers bent on his forcible removal from power, and their contacts with the western governments made them potentially very dangerous men indeed. During October he accordingly authorized Heydrich's secret service to develop its contacts with the British Intelligence network in Holland. Heydrich's men were to pretend to represent dissident German army generals willing to risk all in a plot to overthrow the Führer. If they could secure the British agents' confidence, the names of the real German conspirators might be revealed, or gleaned from the subsequent radio traffic between the agents and their Intelligence masters in London. This was the SS plan, and it worked up to a point. After a convincing series of false starts and unkept rendezvous, the first clandestine meeting between the British agents and Heydrich's "army generals" took place on Dutch soil in the second half of October; certain questions were submitted for the British Cabinet to answer, on the assumption that the generals captured Hitler and ended the war; and an additional rendezvous was arranged for early November. Hitler was intrigued by the possibility of embarrassing the Dutch government by exploiting the evidence of Anglo-Dutch staff collaboration revealed by these SS ploys, and he discussed this with Ribbentrop and Heydrich's lieutenant, Dr. Werner

Best; a plan to kidnap the British agents was first considered, then shelved for the time being.

The Abwehr was not consulted by Heydrich. The Abwehr had its hands full with a very different kind of operation, again at Hitler's command. If he invaded Belgium on November 12, the Albert Canal and the nearby fortress of Eben Emael would present serious obstacles to the advance of Reichenau's Sixth Army. The canal linked Antwerp to the Meuse; at Eben Emael it had been designed from the outset as a moat, an integral part of the Belgian eastern defenses, and it was fortified with bunkers, blockhouses, and walls ramped to steep slopes. Only three bridges crossed the canal, and these had been built with pillboxes and demolition chambers controlled by detonating squads housed in impregnable blockhouses some distance away. The Eben Emael fortress had eighteen heavy guns emplaced in casemates and armored turrets and manned by a thousand Belgian troops living underground in the tunnels and bunkers; it commanded the Meuse and the southern reaches of the canal. Since the whole system was some twenty miles from the Reich frontier, the bridges could be demolished long before German army advance parties could reach them; the Germans would then have to cross the wide Meuse by the two available bridges on the Dutch side at Maastricht, and these had also been prepared for demolition.

This complex problem occupied Hitler as much as the rest of "Yellow's" problems put together. In the last week of October he proposed setting up a camouflaged Abwehr battalion under Reichenau's control—some four or five hundred Germans under a Captain Fleck and a Lieutenant Hokke, who were skilled in clandestine operations. This battalion would be rigged out in uniforms used by the Dutch frontier police in the Maastricht enclave. As Hitler was to say, "In wartime, a uniform is always the best camouflage. But one thing is vital— that the leaders of Hokke's shock troops be the spitting image of Dutch police officers as far as language, dress, and behavior go." Their job would be to put the detonating cables and charges out of action.

Hitler lamented his army generals' inability to come up with ideas like these. "These generals are too prim and proper," he scoffed after one such conference. "They haven't got a *ruse de guerre* among the lot of them. They ought to have read more Karl May!"[1] He had a solution for the fortress of Eben Emael as well: at the same time as the "Trojan horse" policemen were silencing the Dutch guards on the bridges, some three hundred airborne troops would *silently* cross the Maastricht enclave in squadrons of gliders and land within the fortress walls in the darkness before dawn; they were to be equipped with deadly fifty-kilo

[1]German author of popular and ingenious American Indian stories.

"hollow-charge" explosives capable of knocking out the big guns there. At the beginning of November, the Seventh Air Division commanded the immediate activation of an airborne assault unit for the glider operation; its orders were to seize the bridges, knock out the fortress, and hold these positions until the army's advance guards had fought their way up from the Reich frontier. The unit was to be ready for action by the twelfth.

There was much that could, and did, go wrong. Canaris's Abwehr bungled the preparatory work: an official of the Munster Abwehr office was detected purchasing large quantities of Dutch police uniforms in the province of Groningen; he was arrested trying to smuggle them across the frontier, and by November 5 there was a public uproar in Holland. For several days Dutch newspapers featured cartoons speculating on the manner in which the Nazi invaders would be dressed when they came. One cartoon that reached the Chancellery in Berlin showed Göring skulking in the uniform of a Dutch streetcar conductor; another had him preening himself in a mirror as a Dutch policeman.

With the attack on France and Belgium ostensibly just one week away, the German army command was in a high state of nervousness. Generals who attempted to remonstrate with Hitler had been sent away unheeded or unheard. At noon on November 5, General von Brauchitsch himself secured an audience with the Führer, and the next hour saw one of the strangest encounters in the history of their uncomfortable partnership. The General Staff was now on a different tack: with facts and figures supplied by the quartermaster general, they were trying to point up the army's unreadiness and unwillingness for a new campaign. Brauchitsch himself wrote out in longhand his answer to Hitler's memorandum of October 9.

His main concern was the state of the army in the west. In the Polish campaign the infantry had shown little verve in attack, the general contended, and at times the NCOs and officers had lost control. Brauchitsch even spoke of "mutinies" in some units, and he recounted acts of drunken indiscipline at the front and on the railways during the transfer west that invited comparison with the uglier scenes of 1917 and 1918. Reports from railway officials and of resulting courts-martial had reached Brauchitsch. On hearing this, Hitler, who had listened in silence, lost his temper and, interrupting the Commander in Chief, demanded the identities of the units involved. His hoarse, angry voice could be heard by the secretaries outside. Snatching Brauchitsch's memorandum from his hands, he tossed it into his safe and thundered at the general that it was quite incomprehensible to him how an army commander could blacken and condemn his entire army because of a handful of excesses. "Not one frontline commander mentioned any lack of attacking spirit in the infantry to me. But *now* I have to listen to this, after the army has achieved a magnificent victory in Poland!" He insisted that Brauchitsch furnish him with the reports he had mentioned, and with details of the death sentences passed in the east and west in consequence. He would fly to the units concerned immediately. Sweeping out of the room, Hitler slammed the door behind him and left Brauchitsch trembling.

Keitel afterward suggested to Hitler that it was the older recruits—the oft-mentioned "white years" of young men who because of Versailles Treaty prohibitions had not undergone early conscription and intensive training—who were to blame for these acts of indiscipline. Hitler agreed; he had fought in vain against the refusal of Brauchitsch's predecessor to train these men in good time. Later that evening he angrily discussed with his adjutants Schmundt and Engel this "army sabotage" of his plans. He dismissed General von Brauchitsch's written memorandum as a pack of lies, and Captain Gerhard Engel, Hitler's army adjutant, was ordered to visit the front and report to him on the "mutinying army units." To Fräulein Schroeder he dictated an aide-mémoire on the ugly scene with Brauchitsch; this too was locked away in the safe for future use. He also dictated a document dismissing Brauchitsch, but Keitel talked him out of this. There was no suitable successor for the courtly and pliable Commander in Chief of the German army. The Brauchitschs had served their country as officers and servants of the state for many centuries, and Nietzsche's aphorism could have been their family motto: "Rebellion is the distinguishing mark of the slave; let *your* mark be obedience." A Herr von Brauchitsch would not rebel.

Two days later Hitler provisionally postponed "Yellow" by three days, giving the weather as the reason.

That evening, November 7, his special train left for Munich—his first return to Bavaria since he had departed from the Berghof to confront an uncertain future in August. He was loath to leave Berlin, but the annual Party anniversary of the 1923 beer-hall putsch was the next day, and he must speak to the "Old Guard" at the Bürgerbräukeller. He was uneasy about the security risks involved in annual public appearances—the best safeguard against assassination was always an irregular routine. This Bürgerbräu assembly and the long march through Munich's narrow streets were annual opportunities no less inviting to an assassin than the Nuremberg rally or that approach road to the Kroll opera house in Berlin. On November 9, 1938, a Swiss waiter named Maurice Bavaud had trained a gun on him on this very march through Munich, but Bavaud's aim had been spoiled by the sudden forest of hands raised in salute. Hitler learned of the attempt only when Bavaud was stopped by railway police at Augsburg—as he was attempting to leave Germany—for not having a valid ticket. He was found to be carrying an envelope addressed to the Führer, and under interrogation he also confessed to having stalked Hitler with a gun during his daily walks on the Obersalzberg mountain in October. Bavaud was to come up for secret trial by the People's Court in December 1939.[2]

Hitler was supposed to remain in Munich until the ninth and then, after further ceremonies, fly back to Berlin; however, on the morning of the eighth his residence was telephoned from Berlin that the army was demanding a fresh decision on the next day's deadline for "Yellow," and since his chief pilot warned him that the weather forecast was against flying, he sent an adjutant to arrange for his private coaches to be attached to the regular express leaving Munich that same evening. His adjutant returned with word that this train would get him to Berlin by 10:30 the next morning, but it would be cutting things fine if he was to catch it after his speech. Hitler irritably asked if there were no later trains, but the next express to Berlin would not arrive there until too late for the army's purposes. He therefore brought forward the beginning of his speech by five minutes, to 8:10 P.M., and ordered Hess to stand in for him during ceremonies scheduled for the next day.

At seven-thirty the Munich police chief arrived to escort him to the beer hall, and an adjutant telephoned the Bürgerbräu with instructions that the speeches must begin punctually, as they now had a very tight schedule. At eight o'clock sharp, the Führer entered the cavernous beer hall, the local Party band stopped playing in mid-march, and Christian Weber (a former horse-dealer who was now one of the Party's leading figures in Bavaria) spoke a few brief words of welcome.

Normally Hitler spoke for about ninety minutes, but this time he spoke for just under an hour, standing at a lectern in front of one of the big, wood-paneled pillars. Many of the Old Guard were away at the front, so the hall was filled with other senior Party members and local dignitaries as well as the next of kin of the sixteen Nazis killed in the 1923 putsch. Hitler's speech was undistinguished, a pure tirade of abuse against Britain, whose "true motives" for this new crusade Hitler identified as jealousy and hatred of the new Germany, which had achieved in six years more than Britain had in centuries. Julius Schaub, who was responsible for seeing to it that his chief reached the railroad station on time, nervously passed him cards on which he had scrawled increasingly urgent admonitions: "Ten minutes!" then "Five!" and finally a peremptory "Stop!"—a method he had previously had to use to remind his Führer, who never used a watch, of the passage of mortal time. "Party members, comrades of our National Socialist movement, our German people, and above all our victorious Wehrmacht: *Siegheil!*" Hitler concluded, and stepped into the midst of the

[2] He was beheaded.

Party officials who thronged forward. A harrassed Julius Schaub managed to shepherd the Führer out of the hall at twelve minutes past nine. The express was due to leave from the main railway station in nineteen minutes.

At the Augsburg station, the first stop after Munich, confused word was passed to Hitler's coach that something unusual, though as yet undefined, had occurred at the Bürgerbräu. At the Nuremberg station, the local police chief, a Dr. Martin, was waiting with more detailed news: just eight minutes after Hitler had left the beer hall a powerful bomb had exploded in the paneled pillar right behind where he had been speaking. There were many dead and injured. Hitler's Luftwaffe aide, Colonel Nicolaus von Below, later wrote: "For a moment Hitler refused to believe it. He had been there himself and nothing had happened then. . . . The news made a vivid impression on Hitler. He fell very silent, and then described it as a miracle that the bomb had missed him."[3] He spoke by telephone with SS General von Eberstein, the Munich police chief (who had been flatly forbidden to encroach on this strictly Party preserve with regular police security measures), and consoled the anguished SS general: "Don't worry—it was not your fault. The casualties are regrettable, but all's well that ends well." By 7 A.M. the news was that six people had been killed (the death toll later rose to eight) and over sixty injured.

At the Anhalt station in Berlin, Hitler's chauffeur persuaded him at last to inspect the bulletproof Mercedes limousine he had ordered for the motor pool. The vehicle was driven into the Chancellery's entrance hall for Hitler's approval; its windshield was of quarter-inch laminated glass, its body of toughened steel armorplate, and its floor was extra thick in order to protect the occupants against mines. Turning to Martin Bormann, Hitler said, "In the future I will only ride in this car. You can never tell when some idiot may lob a bomb in front of you."

At first the SS security agencies ran around in circles. Himmler reported that the manager of the Bürgerbräu was known to the Heydrich office as a high-ranking freemason who "dealt only with Jews, freemasons, and other sinister elements." The Abwehr indulged in even wilder flights of fancy and suspected that the perpetrators would be found among old Party luminaries whose noses had been put out of joint. Perhaps they had even been in league with Göring! Hitler evidently hoped it would prove to be the work of agents of a foreign power. The people who feared Hitler's renewed disfavor hurried to dissociate themselves from the outrage at Munich, and for several days afterward his adjutants Brückner and Wünsche brought to the ruffled Führer telegrams of congratulation

---

[3]Below's account goes on to say that Hitler often excitedly repeated the circumstances that had led to his leaving the Bürgerbräu early (see also Rosenberg's diary, November 11). "He joked that this time the weather expert had saved his life. Otherwise, commented the Führer, the expert was pushing him into an early grave with his weather forecasts, for the weather outlook was black and likely to continue so."

from people like Admiral von Horthy, the king and queen of Italy, Benito Mussolini, the still-exiled Kaiser Wilhelm, and Field Marshal von Blomberg. Queen Wilhelmina of the Netherlands cabled Adolf Hitler:

> Herr Reich Chancellor, may I send to you my most heartfelt congratulations on your escape from the abominable attempt on your life.

Even as Hitler had been speaking at the Bürgerbräu, however, a man had been apprehended at Konstanz, attempting to cross illegally into Switzerland. On the night of November 13 this man, Georg Elser, a thirty-six-year-old Swabian watchmaker, confessed that he had single-handedly designed, built, and installed a time bomb in the pillar. In his pockets were found a pair of pliers, sketches of grenade and fuse designs, pieces of a fuse, a picture postcard of the Bürgerbräu hall's interior; a badge of the former "Red Front" Communist movement was found concealed under his lapel. Under Gestapo interrogation a week later the whole story came out—how he had joined the Red Front ten years before but had long lost interest in politics, and how he had been angered by the regimentation of labor and religion as well as by the relative pauperization of craftsmen such as himself in the early years of Nazi rule. The year before he had resolved to dispose of Adolf Hitler and had begun work on an ingenious time-bomb controlled by two clock-mechanisms for added reliability. After thirty nights of arduous chiseling at the pillar behind the paneling, he installed the preset clocks in one last session on the night of November 5, the evening after Hitler's furious altercation with Brauchitsch in Berlin. The mechanism was soundproofed in cork to prevent the ticking from being heard, and Elser's simple pride in his craftmanship was evident from the records of his interrogations. He refused to agree he had been acting on higher orders, even though the customs officials who had arrested him both described how they saw a man in a light-colored overcoat apparently waiting for him just inside the Swiss frontier. He probably was telling the truth, and there is no doubt that one watchmaker acting alone had nearly accomplished what after years of debate, planning, and self-indulgent conspiracy a platoon of officers and intellectuals were to fail to do five years later.

To Hitler it seemed an impossible coincidence that his archenemy, the Nazi renegade Otto Strasser, was at that time in Switzerland, and he later claimed that the Dutch prime minister and Anthony Eden had known of the plot. In private he assured his staff that one day he would publish the whole story but not yet, as he also wanted to round up those who had pulled the strings. Security measures were tightened. General Rommel, commandant of Hitler's headquarters, wrote on November 9: "Six feet of rubble cover the spot where the Führer spoke yesterday evening. That was how strong the explosion was. One dare not think what would have happened if the assassination had succeeded. My only hope is that now in the Führer's headquarters too the security precautions will be better organized with everything in one person's hands (mine). Because if anybody is going to take *this* responsibility, he cannot share it with anybody else." And on the fifteenth, referring to "Operation Yellow," Rommel wrote: "The Führer's mind is absolutely made up. The assassination attempt in Munich has only made his resolution stronger. It is a marvel to witness all this."

On the day after the Munich explosion Hitler again postponed "Yellow," and on November 13 he further instructed that the offensive would not begin before the twenty-second.

There is some reason to believe that Hitler himself did not intend these deadlines to be serious—that they were designed to keep the army at maximum readiness in case the western powers should themselves suddenly invade the Low Countries. Nor would the western powers have to violate Belgian and Dutch sentiment in so doing, for with the exception of Flemish minority elements, popular sympathies in the Low Countries lay with the West; the Belgian armed forces were concentrated almost wholly against the German frontier, where British and French forces could join them virtually overnight, leaving Germany's "Achilles heel," her Ruhr industrial zone, in a precarious situation indeed. Hitler did not doubt that the West had economic means enough to pressure the Low Countries into "appealing for help" at a propitious moment. "Let us not credit the enemy with a lack of logic," Hitler said later in November. "If we respect their [the Low Countries'] neutrality, the western powers will just march in during the spring."

Hitler was also under pressure from Göring and the Luftwaffe's Chief of Staff to occupy the whole of Holland rather than just temporarily violate the Maastricht enclave: possession of Holland would be vital for the future air war between Britain and Germany. After the Munich bomb attempt, Hitler came around to this view.

The time had come to compromise the Dutch. He instructed Heydrich to wind up the cat-and-mouse game being played with the British agents in Holland. Heydrich's "army officers"—who had not shown up at the agreed rendezvous on November 8—now appeared on the ninth at Venlo, just inside the Dutch frontier. The British agents drove up, there was a rapid exchange of gunfire, and they were dragged across the border into Germany together with the driver and another officer, mortally wounded; this latter turned out to be a Dutch Intelligence officer accompanying them. The Dutch government formally requested the return of the body; that was "Holland's biggest blunder," Hitler afterward ominously said. This was proof that the ostensibly neutral Dutch were working hand in glove with the British. "When the time comes I will use all this to justify my attack," he told his generals. "The violation of Belgian and Dutch neutrality is unimportant," he explained. "Nobody will ask about such things after we have won."[4] On November 12, Hitler personally presented the Iron Cross to the SS major who had directed the kidnapping.

One unexpected bonus from the Venlo incident was that the British agents turned out to be Britain's top agents in Holland; from them Heydrich's officers learned that the British secret service was evidently in touch with genuine Wehrmacht officers who were planning a revolt against Hitler. But Heydrich's ambition to establish a direct link between the Bürgerbräu explosion in Munich and the British secret service remained unfulfilled (which did not prevent Himmler from claiming later in November that proof to that effect had been obtained).

On November 13, General Jodl instructed the war department that a new Führer Directive was on its way: the army must be prepared to occupy as much of Holland as possible to improve Germany's air defense position. This was on the assumption that the British, who had already eroded Holland's neutrality by repeated overflying of RAF planes, would attempt to set foot in Holland as soon as Hitler's troops marched across the Maastricht enclave. Hitler would justify his violation of Dutch neutrality by claiming the involvement of the Dutch General Staff in the Venlo incident. Three days later he again postponed "Yellow," this time to November 26 at the earliest; on the twentieth the operation was postponed to December 3. On November 20, meanwhile, Hitler issued a further directive to the services which finally ranked the attack on Holland equal to those on Belgium and France:

> In variation of the earlier directive, all measures planned against *Holland* are authorized to commence simultaneously with the beginning of the general offensive, without special orders to that effect. The reaction of the Dutch forces cannot be estimated in advance. Where no opposition is encountered, the invasion is to be given the character of a peaceful occupation.

According to the diary of a member of Jodl's staff, during a conference in the OKW's map room Hitler expressed the opinion that "the planned attack in the west would lead to the biggest victory in the history of the world."

In the east, meanwhile, the "devil's work" was well in hand. Gruesome reports of massacre and persecution began to filter up through army channels. Not all of them reached Hitler, since Brauchitsch had in September tacitly agreed that Heydrich should have free rein for his special tasks; for Brau-

---

[4]This was an argument of some force. Who later questioned the various Allied encroachments on neutral nations: the planned invasions of Norway and Eire in 1940 (see below) and the actual occupation of Iceland that same year?

chitsch to have protested now would have been hypocritical, and besides, his row with Hitler on November 5 had made him reluctant to set foot in the Chancellery again. But consciences had to be salved, and the reports were dutifully shuttled about between the adjutants. Thus, soon after the Munich plot, Captain Engel received from Brauchitsch's adjutant a grisly set of eye-witness accounts of executions by the SS at Schwetz. An outspoken medical officer addressed to Hitler in person a report summarizing the eyewitness evidence of three of his men:

> Together with about 150 fellow soldiers they witnessed the summary execution of about 20 or 30 Poles at the Jewish cemetery at Schwetz at about 9:30 A.M. on Sunday, October 8. The execution was carried out by a detachment consisting of an SS man, two men in old blue police uniforms, and a man in plain clothes. An SS major was in command. Among those executed were also 5 or 6 *children aged from two to eight years old.*

Whether Engel showed this document and its attached eyewitness accounts to Hitler is uncertain. He returned it to Brauchitsch's adjutant almost immediately with a note: "The appropriate action to be taken at this end will be discussed orally." Apparently he asked Himmler to investigate the executions. A few days later, however, Brauchitsch's adjutant submitted a further report, this time by General Blaskowitz, the military commander in the east, protesting at the wave of illegal executions. Engel later recorded: "I showed this report, which is absolutely objective in tone, to the Führer that same afternoon. He took note of it calmly enough at first but then began another long tirade of abuse at the 'childish ideas' prevalent in the army's leadership; you cannot fight wars with the methods of the Salvation Army."

If Hitler still regretted having kindled this holocaust, it was not because of the horrors that were beginning to spread like a medieval plague across eastern Europe: they were inevitable byproducts of his program, and he was more concerned to justify them inwardly than to prevent them. What unsettled him was the unscheduled delay the war would inflict on his grand plans for the reconstruction of Germany. On nocturnal drives through the deserted, blacked-out streets of Berlin he would mentally survey and supervise the architectural reshaping of the city. One night he ordered his driver to stop outside the half-completed "House of Tourism" near Potsdam Bridge and sadly commented that it was a pity the war had to put a stop to so many of these fine building projects throughout the Reich.

In the Reich Chancellery, the large table in the old Cabinet Room, where Bismarck's Berlin Congress had assembled, was now dominated by a huge relief map of the Ardennes—the mountainous, difficult region of Belgium and Luxemburg that was twice to be the scene of Hitler's unorthodox military strategy. The Chancellery cleaning women must have dusted around the contoured models of Belgium and Luxumburg without realizing the map's significance. Many an hour Hitler stood alone in the evenings, tracing the narrow mountain roads and asking himself again and again whether his tanks and mechanized divisions would be able to get through.

By now he had been provided with the original construction plans of the bridges across the Albert Canal; previously he had only aerial photographs and picture postcards of these important targets. The blueprints showed where each demolition chamber had been built into the bridges and pinpointed each detonation fuse and bunker. From other sources he had similar details on the toughness of the concrete and armorplate of the fortress at Eben Emael. Belgian deserters proved particularly useful. A scale model of the fortress had been built, and intensive training of the glider crews had begun under top security conditions.

The bridges, and particularly those in the Dutch town of Maastricht, presented the most intractable problem, the more so since the Dutch had evidently been warned by anti-Nazi agents in Berlin and even alerted to the date originally set for the attack, for on November 12 extensive security precautions had suddenly been introduced at the Maastricht bridges.[5] Had the Abwehr's four hundred special duties agents infiltrated the border in Dutch uniforms, they would have been slaughtered. Hitler discussed the operations with Canaris and his chief of sabotage operations, Colonel Erwin Lahousen, on November 16; but he did not believe they would capture the bridges over the Albert Canal by surprise alone, and he began casting around for other means of preventing the bridges' destruction. Though he asked to meet the two Abwehr officers who would lead the clandestine operation, he also reflected that should the bridges be blown the most urgent need would be to displace the army's mechanized units from the northern to the southern wing, for it was in this thrust through the Ardennes that the main chance lay. The British and French were expecting Hitler to attack through Holland, so all their best units were in the north. He ordered a full-scale secret conference on the bridges plan, starting at 3 P.M. on November 20, and directed that Brauchitsch should come too.

General von Reichenau made it clear from the outset that since the invasion

[5]Colonel Hans Oster, Canaris's Chief of Staff in the Abwehr, had himself warned the Belgian and Dutch legations that Hitler planned to attack on November 12. The uniform scheme was not mentioned.

Oster had been cashiered from the Reichswehr over a morals scandal in 1934 and immediately conscripted into the Abwehr by Canaris. Both men were hanged in April 1945.

of Holland had already been compromised once, he had no faith in the Abwehr's "Trojan horse" plan. The "Dutch policemen" must not cross the frontier before the glider operations had begun. Since the Dutch authorities were now expecting the police uniforms to be used, as was shown by the fact that they had issued special armbands to their police, there was little prospect of the Abwehr getting away with it. Hitler replied, "Then the entire operation as at present planned is pointless!" Canaris did what he could to salvage the plan (according to Lahousen, he lied) by suggesting that the Dutch were still in the dark, as the Munster agent who had been arrested had not himself known the purpose of the uniform purchases. Hitler was unconvinced. "None of the plans is *bound* to succeed." But after they had surveyed the large relief map and all the other possibilities had been scrutinized—including attacking the bridges with light bombs to destroy the demolition cables, and rushing them with tanks and 88-millimeter guns[6]—he had to fall back on the Trojan horse. "There must be some means of getting these bridges into our hands," he complained. "We have managed to solve even bigger problems before."

When the conference ended four hours later, Hitler had provisionally adopted the sequence proposed by Göring: at X-hour proper, fifteen minutes before dawn, the gliders would land silently on the fortress at Eben Emael and the bridge at Canne; five minutes later dive-bombers would attack the other Albert Canal bridges to disrupt the demolition charges; the bombers would be followed five minutes later by the arrival of more glider-borne troops just east of the bridges themselves. At the same time the Abwehr's disguised advanced party would seize the Maastricht bridges; for this they would have to cross the frontier in Dutch uniform forty-five minutes before X-hour. Within the first hour after X, it was hoped, the tanks and artillery of the Sixth Army would be close enough to relieve them. A special liaison officer with the army would at once radio back to Hitler's staff a report on the fate of the bridges, for on this would depend the course of the rest of the campaign.

The weather was still against "Yellow." Each day the Luftwaffe's chief meteorologist was consulted on the long-term forecast. Göring, indeed, expended large sums on a charlatan who claimed to have developed an electronic machine capable of influencing the weather. (It proved on investigation to be a broken radio.) General Halder, ignoring the fact that the Führer had never consulted horoscopes, unrealistically proposed bribing Hitler's soothsayer, since he no longer heeded his generals' prophecies of doom. (When Hitler later learned the role astrology had played in persuading his own deputy, Rudolf Hess, to fly to the enemy he clamped down on astrologers in general.)

---

[6]"If it can't be accomplished by trickery," Hitler said, "then brute force must do."

Every morning, Berlin was in the grip of icy frost and fog, which lifted in the afternoon to let a weak sun filter through. On November 21 the Führer issued surprise orders for his leading generals and admirals to hear an exposure of his views two days later. Had not Frederick the Great summoned his defeatist generals to just such a talk before the battle of Leuthen? To the large audience that packed the Great Hall of the Chancellery at noon on the twenty-third Hitler depicted the coming battle as the operation that would finally ring down the curtain on the world war that Germany had been fighting ever since 1914. He repeated the compelling arguments for early action that he had first marshaled in his October memorandum. He recited the many occasions since having first decided on the arduous life of a politician in 1919, when aided only by Providence he had ignored the grim prophecies of others to exploit the brief opportunities that opened to him. How many opportunities the politicians and generals had lost in the years since Moltke's death in 1891! At that time, too, the generals had claimed that they were unready.

He, Adolf Hitler, had now provided the generals with a strategic situation unparalleled since 1871. "For the first time in history we have only to fight on one front. The other is at present open. But nobody can be certain how long it will remain so." His own indispensibility had been forcefully impressed on him by the recent assassination attempt; that there would be other attempts was probable, for what the enemy called a fight against "Hitlerism" was, he warned, nothing less than a war against the presence of any powerful, determined government in Germany. In the same degree the immediate future depended on the lifespans of Mussolini and Stalin, for if the Duce died, the basically hostile monarchy would convert Italy's imperialist strategy into a fundamentally anti-German one; and if the Russian dictator died, the treaty with Russia might become worthless. Thus there was no time to be lost. This was why the defensive strategy his cowardly army generals were calling for was shortsighted; had Moltke in his studies of 1871 and after proposed defensive strategies? On the contrary, Moltke had clearly shown that only through offensives could wars be decided. Germany's present enemies were weak and unready: here, he illustrated his point by listing in turn the number of French tanks and guns, and British ships. The United States might on the other hand prove dangerous in one or two years' time. He was convinced that Italy would join in as soon as Germany made the first move against France, just as Russia had waited before joining in against Poland.

His speech bristled with concealed barbs against the army generals.[7] While he

---

[7]Rommel wrote the next day: "The Führer spoke very bluntly. But that seems quite necessary, too, because the more I speak with my comrades the fewer I find with their heart and conviction in what they are doing. It is all very depressing."

praised the "aggressive spirit" of the navy and Luftwaffe, in an evident reference to Brauchitsch, he sneered: "If our commanders in chief are going to have nervous breakdowns as in 1914, what can we ask of our simple riflemen?" He had been "deeply wounded" by suggestions that the German army was inferior insofar as infantry was concerned, and that the officers had had to precede their men into battle, with consequently disproportionately high officer losses. He dismissed this curtly. "That is what the officers are there for." He recalled how in 1914 after months of training the infantry attack on Liège had broken up in panic and disaster; nothing like that had happened in the Polish campaign. "I will not hear of complaints that the army is not in shape. It is all a matter of military leadership. Give the German soldier proper leadership and I can do anything with him."

It was not as though Germany had a real choice between armistice and war. The West wanted war, Hitler said, therefore Germany must fight on until victory. A more tortuous argument he deployed was that since the German people had already sacrificed so much to rebuild the Wehrmacht, it would be irresponsible not to make the fullest use of it now. "People will accuse me: war and yet more war! But I regard fighting as the fate of all the species. Nobody can opt out of the struggle, unless he wants to succumb." He had spent his whole life preparing for this fight. A few minutes later he said, "Victory or defeat! And it is not a matter of the future of National Socialist Germany, but of who will dominate Europe in years to come. For this it is *worth* making a supreme effort." In a dark reference to conspirators, Hitler warned that wars could not be ended except by destroying the enemy. "Anybody who thinks differently is irresponsible." He believed the present favorable strategic situation would last perhaps six more months, but then the British troops, "a tenacious enemy," would vastly strengthen their foothold in France, and "Yellow" would be a different proposition altogether.

"My own life is of no importance," he concluded. "I have led the German people to great achievements even if we are now an object of hatred in the outside world." His was the choice between victory or annihilation. "I have chosen victory." If he had to die, he would do so honorably, because he did not propose to survive the defeat of his country. Germany would neither capitulate to the enemy nor dissolve in internal revolution.

The speech lasted two hours. Afterward, Hitler instructed his principal generals and admirals to join him in his study. According to one of them, Hitler explained that he realized it was unusual for the supreme commander to explain his decisions and orders to his subordinates. He had made this exception because he had detected the negative mood prevailing among the generals. He ended this little speech with the words: "This will be the last war Germany fights against France, because I am going to smash France to smithereens. I can clearly see that coming, with my prophetic eye." Then he shook each of them by the hand and released them from the Chancellery.

General von Brauchitsch reappeared in the evening and stiffly informed the Führer that if he had no confidence in him he ought to replace him. Hitler retorted that the general must do his duty like every other soldier; he was not oblivious to "the spirit of Zossen" prevailing in the army, and he would stamp it out. Zossen was the headquarters of the General Staff and seat of the conservative and conspiratorial elements of the German army.

Clearing the Decks

Whether or not Hitler's often expressed fears that time was working against Germany were a purely tactical device to spur his wary generals is uncertain. Until the spring of 1940, although delay after delay postponed the launching date of "Yellow"—his campaign in the west—time certainly worked in his favor: lifeblood was being pumped into his armies massing in the west far faster than the enemy could strengthen their own forces. Indeed, Hitler not only had time to remold the strategy of his campaign—he now prepared and sent an expedition to Scandinavia. This was something he had not even been contemplating in the autumn of 1939. True, the Wehrmacht had not yet reached that peak of perfection he had hoped to attain by 1944, but he was sure that this was to be only a short war; the armies that had defeated Poland would carve up France with equal facility. It was also true that there was no popular, jingoistic support for this war: on the very first day of the Polish campaign Dr. Goebbels had come to the Chancellery with a fast public-opinion poll his agencies had just conducted in Berlin; sitting on a table, dangling his legs, the propaganda minister had complacently revealed a complete lack of enthusiasm or patriotic exuberance among the Berliners—they were resigned to the coming of fresh tribulations, but it would not be a popular war, he told the Führer.

Hitler knew that his pact with Stalin was misunderstood. In his November 1939 speech to the generals he had laid bare his own suspicions about Stalin. "Russia is *at present* harmless," he assured them—and more than one of them noted the emphasis he laid on *"at present."* Pacts were respected only until they no longer served a purpose. "Russia will abide by the pact only as long as she considers it to her advantage." Stalin had far-reaching goals, and among them were the strengthening of Russia's position in the Baltic—which Germany could only oppose once she was unencumbered in the west—the expansion of Russian influence in the Balkans, and a drive toward the Persian Gulf. It was the aim of German foreign policy that Russia should be deflected toward the Persian Gulf, as this would bring her into conflict with Britain; but she must be kept out of the Balkans. Hitler hoped the present situation between Germany and Russia would prevail for two or three more years, but if Stalin were to die, there might be a rapid and ugly *volte face* in the Kremlin. There was clear evidence of a Russian military buildup that could be unleashed against Germany. Blaskowitz reported from Poland that four military airfields were being built, and two to three hundred Russian bombers had been counted, around Bialystock. In addition, wrote Blaskowitz, Russian propaganda was making plain that this was nothing less than a war against fascism: "Germany is said [in the USSR] to be planning an attack on Russia as soon as she is victorious in the west. Therefore Russia must be on guard and exploit Germany's weakness at the right moment." Blaskowitz described Russian infantry as poor, but the armored troops were considered good (if badly equipped), and the general's command had clearly identified Russian espionage and Communist subversive activity behind German lines in Poland. Moreover, he reported, the Russians were doing all they could to help the Poles establish a Polish Legion in France. In short, Hitler must conclude that war with Russia was inevitable—and that victory would go to the side which was ready first.

To strengthen her position in the Baltic, Russia now made of Finland demands similar to those she had successfully pressed against the three other Baltic states two months before. When Finland snubbed the Russians, the Red Army attacked on the last day of November 1939; Hitler was extremely embarrassed vis-à-vis his Italian ally, who was unaware that Finland had been abandoned to Soviet influence in a secret codicil to the August pact with Stalin. Russia had justified her demands on Finland as necessary to safeguard her communications to the far north and the Baltic approaches to Leningrad; but who could menace those communications if not Germany? Berlin regarded the invasion of Finland as a further token of Stalin's mistrust of Hitler. But even though German sympathy was solidly for Finland, Hitler instructed his foreign missions to adhere to an anti-Finnish line, for the integrity of his brittle pact with Stalin was to be his most powerful weapon in the attack on France. This loyalty to Stalin further tarnished Hitler's image with his allies, for Mussolini openly supplied Finland with arms and recalled his ambassador from Moscow. The Kremlin's gratitude to Hitler was expressed in a November revolutionary Comintern proclamation which lumped Germany with the other capitalist plunderers and not inaccurately predicted that once victory in the west had become clear for one side or the other, Italy would join in like a battlefield hyena.

But the Finnish war thrust the Russians further into Hitler's arms. They needed military supplies and aid. The Führer even agreed to a Russian request

for the transfer of fuel and provisions from German steamships to Soviet submarines blockading Finland. (This did not prevent the Russians from torpedoing a
German vessel steaming out of a Finnish port a few days later; the survivors were
abandoned to their fate.)

Soviet compliance was the economic key to Hitler's continued war-making
capacity. Under the economic treaty signed between the two powers on August
19, Russia was to supply Germany with such raw materials as grain, oil cake,
phosphates, platinum, and petroleum; it was also to act as a safe channel to
Germany for goods exported by Japan, Manchuria, Afghanistan, Iran, and Romania but subject to British naval blockade. The Soviet Union imported rubber
and zinc from Britain and cotton from the United States and immediately re-
exported them to Germany. Hitler also needed the oil produced in Russia and
Soviet-occupied Poland (where two-thirds of Poland's oil resources were located),
and he knew that Stalin could exert pressure to control the supply of Romanian
oil to Germany. It thus behooved him to behave like a proverbial friend in need;
and throughout the winter he was a Soviet friend indeed as he instructed his
military and economic authorities to do their utmost to meet the Russian demands. An additional trade treaty with the USSR was signed in December, and
this was supplemented by a far-reaching commercial agreement in Moscow on
February 11, 1940.

Russia's list of requirements was not easy to fulfill. The Russians wanted the
half-built cruiser *Lützow* and the aircraft carrier *Graf Zeppelin;* they also wanted
the blueprints of these and even more up-to-date German warships including the
Bismarck and the *Tirpitz.* They asked for sets of the heaviest ship's armament,
and for the 57,000 blueprints prepared for the new Krupp 406-millimeter triple-
turret guns, the fire-control sets, and the ammunition that went with them. The
Soviet navy wanted samples of accumulators and periscopes for submarines, they
wanted a supply of top-grade German armorplate for a cruiser to be built in
Russia, and they wanted hydroacoustical gear, torpedoes, and mines as well. The
German air force was to supply the Soviet Union with prototypes of its most
modern equipment—fighters and bombers, high-performance aircraft engines,
antiaircraft artillery, control gear, and bombs. The army was to hand over field
artillery, samples of modern explosives, tanks, engineer corps equipment, radio
gear, and chemicals. Hitler sided with Ribbentrop and urged on his service
commanders complete acceptance of almost all these demands. Such delays in
delivery as he did propose were clearly the result of his country's own pressing
arms requirements and shortages of raw materials, rather than of any ulterior
plotting for the future. During negotiation for the commercial agreement, he told
Keitel he wanted it signed as rapidly as possible. He told Raeder that his only
anxiety in handing over the blueprints of the battleship *Bismarck* to the Russians
was that these revealed that the vessel had been planned on a far larger scale than

was permitted by the international agreements binding on Germany at the time. Raeder assured him it would take the Russians six years to copy the *Bismarck;* however, he conceded that it would be unfortunate if the blueprints fell into British hands.

Hitler attentively followed the course of the Russian invasion of Finland. He had been alerted by the navy to the danger that the Soviet attack might bring the western powers to Finland's aid. Such a course of action would give the Allies a foothold in Scandinavia, and this would have immense consequences for Germany. For the first time, the strategic importance of Norway was forcibly brought home to Hitler.

So far, he had assigned his navy a largely passive role in the war. Raeder's small force had supported the land operations against Poland in a modest way, while the pocket battleships *Admiral Graf Spee* and *Deutschland* dispatched in August into the south and north Atlantics, respectively, had for many weeks lain low in remote waters to avoid incidents. Hitler initially forbade his submarines to attack even Anglo-French naval forces, but as the enemy's attitude hardened toward Germany he gradually stripped away these irksome restrictions until eventually all-out and unrestricted submarine warfare was the order of the day. Raeder's navy was vastly inferior to the combined Anglo-French force. Its major expansion plan had been due for completion in 1944; Raeder had canceled that and made his production capacity available for submarine and surface vessel construction. During the first year of the war, the German navy had on average only a dozen submarines with which to blockade the British Isles. Since the Luftwaffe was given priority in raw materials, the navy's steadily reduced steel allocation further limited its expansion.

In one respect, however, Raeder had an advantage over Brauchitsch and Göring: he had discouraged Hitler from interfering with naval strategy and operations, and within the broad directives which the Führer now began to issue, the navy had a free hand to dispose of its fleet as it thought best. To Hitler the sea was an unwholesome element, an area of uncertainty he did not understand, and he was relieved to trust Grand Admiral Raeder to act as he saw fit. Raeder in turn committed his crews wholeheartedly to the war effort, with none of the carping that characterized the army generals. His destroyers executed bold sorties into the very jaws of the enemy, laying magnetic minefields in the estuaries of the principal British rivers. A U-boat sank the aircraft carrier *Courageous;* another U-boat penetrated Scapa Flow and torpedoed the battleship *Royal Oak.* Toward the end of November, the German fleet attacked the British northern patrol and sank the ill-armed merchant cruiser *Rawalpindi.* Hitler had a faulty understanding of the strategy of cruiser warfare and of the long-term benefits to be drawn from such costly fleet operations, but the sinking of the *Royal Oak* by Lieutenant Guenther Prien brought scenes of wild enthusiasm to the streets of Berlin for the first time. The Führer saw the huge crowds that packed the Wilhelmstrasse when he invited Prien's crew to the Chancellery, and this was a language he understood.

In the South Atlantic the *Graf Spee* had now begun raiding enemy convoys, but the Luftwaffe—and Göring particularly—wanted to bring the war closer to Britain's shores: when on November 28, in reprisal for the German mining of the coastal waters, Britain issued an Order-in-Council blockading Germany's export shipments, Raeder advised Hitler the British order was a triple violation of the Paris Declaration of 1856. Göring and his deputy, General Erhard Milch, hurried to Hitler that same afternoon with proposals for a crushing Luftwaffe offensive against British shipyards, docks, and ports. It was suggested that the Luftwaffe attack shipping west of Britain, while the German navy dealt with the shipping off the east coast. Hitler turned down the Luftwaffe's idea, but he did issue a new directive specifying that the best way to defeat Britain would be to paralyze her trade. The German navy and the Luftwaffe were to turn to this task, in conjunction with the more tenebrous forces of German sabotage and fifth-column organizations, as soon as "Yellow" had been successfully completed. Since Hitler would then control the Channel coast, the Luftwaffe really could attack on the lines Göring had proposed.

Afraid lest Britain secure a foothold in northern Norway, in December 1939 Hitler issued the first secret instructions for a German operation against Norway to be studied. In October,[1] Raeder had left him in no doubt as to Germany's grim strategic position should the British occupy Norway: in winter all Germany's Swedish iron-ore requirements passed through the ice-free port at Narvik; German merchant ships and warships would no longer be able to traverse the neutral Norwegian waters; the British air force could dominate northern Germany from Norwegian bases; and the Royal Navy would command the Baltic. Though he had realistically advised Hitler that a Norwegian campaign might end in a massacre of the German fleet, Raeder saw no alternative to such a campaign if the strategic dangers inherent in a British occupation of Norway were to be obviated.

Raeder's view took Hitler by surprise. His own strategy had always envisaged respecting and preserving Norway's neutrality, but neither his political nor his naval advisers gave him respite once the Russo-Finnish war broke out. At noon on December 11, Alfred Rosenberg, head of the Party's foreign policy department, briefed Hitler on an idea that had originated with one of his Norwegian contacts:

[1]See page 36 above.

the Norwegian would use his organization to create disturbances in Norway, and he would then appeal to the German forces to occupy key Norwegian bases.

In the event, a different plan was adopted, but room was still found in it for Rosenberg's contact man—Major Vidkun Quisling. Quisling had been Norway's defense minister until 1933, after which he had founded his own party, the anti-Jewish Nasjonal Samling. He was a convinced anti-Communist. After World War I he had for many years been a military attaché in Moscow, and had afterward come to regard bolshevism as the greatest danger confronting Europe and, more immediately, Scandinavia. He now dreamt of a common alliance of the Germanic peoples, and he was concerned about anti-German sentiments provoked in Norway by Germany's acquiescence in the Russian assault on Finland. Rosenberg told Hitler that Quisling's idea was that Germany should invade Norway at the request of a government he would himself set up. For once Ribbentrop and his state secretary, Weizsäcker, were unanimous in warning Hitler against even agreeing to see this Norwegian. But Quisling had hard evidence that Britain had designs on Norway. Hitler thought the matter over and the next day told Rosenberg he was willing to meet Quisling and form a personal impression of him. Quisling brought the Norwegian businessman Viljam Hagelin with him. "In this conversation," Rosenberg's office recorded, "the Führer repeatedly emphasized that what he most preferred politically would be for Norway and, for that matter, all Scandinavia to remain absolutely neutral. He had no intention of enlarging the theaters of war by dragging still more countries into the conflict. But if the other side was planning such an enlargement of the war with the object of forcing a further constriction and threat upon the German Reich, then he must obviously feel compelled to take steps against the move. In an effort to offset the increasing enemy propaganda activity, the Führer then promised Quisling financial aid for his Pan-Germanic movement." Quisling had claimed that the Norwegian press was under British control and that Carl Hambro—the Jewish president of the Norwegian Storting, or parliament—had allowed the British secret service to infiltrate Norway's Intelligence service (of which he was also head) from stem to stern. Quisling said he had two hundred thousand followers, many in key positions in Norway. Since constitutionally the Hambro government—which had prolonged its tenure—would be in office illegally as of January 10, Quisling suggested that his movement overthrow it after that date and then appeal to Hitler to move troops into Oslo.

Hitler was not convinced that Quisling's following was so large, and he privately asked the OKW to draft two alternative operations, one following Quisling's suggestions, but the other projecting an occupation of Norway by force. Through foreign ministry channels, Hitler initiated inquiries into Quisling's background. The replies were not wholly satisfactory, and Hitler shortly decided *not* to rely on him for any assistance beyond the kind of subversive operations that Konrad Henlein, the Sudeten German leader, had undertaken within Czechoslovakia in 1938. Before they returned to Oslo, Quisling and Hagelin met Hewel and Schmundt, who instructed them to commence operations designed to cause economic unrest in Norway by ruining the country's shipping, foreign trade, and fisheries industries. A number of handpicked Norwegians would undergo secret guerrilla-warfare training in Germany; when Norway was invaded, they were to seize key buildings in Oslo and elsewhere, and thus present the king with a *fait accompli*. The military details of the invasion would be drawn up by a special OKW study group. No date for the operation was set.

Though Admiral Raeder had not raised the related problem of Denmark, which lay across the access route to Norway, Hitler was without compunction in ordering this little country to be occupied at the same time as Norway. He had signed a nonaggression treaty with Denmark as recently as August.

The General Staff continued their open hostility to Hitler. After his unequivocal speech to the generals in the Chancellery on November 23, General Guderian privately taxed Hitler with his astonishing attitude toward the leaders of an army that had just won such a victory for him in Poland. Hitler retorted that it was the army's Commander in Chief himself who displeased him, adding with an expression of extreme distaste that there was unfortunately no suitable replacement for the general. Brauchitsch's chief of Intelligence noted: "There is as little contact between Br. and the Führer as ever. A changeover is planned."

When Jodl toured the western front and returned to Berlin on the December 12, he confirmed that the military airfields in the west were largely waterlogged. Hitler postponed a decision on "Yellow" until after Christmas so that his troops could get some leave. He suspected the hand of the General Staff against him everywhere. When the *Deutsche Allgemeine Zeitung* published a sensational and sloppy article on the "Great Headquarters," Hitler was furious at an implicit suggestion that history was being made by the General Staff and not himself; Keitel was obliged to admonish Halder on that score. But the Führer was hard to please, for when at Christmas the *Essener National-Zeitung* ventured a seasonal comparison between Adolf Hitler and the Messiah, Goebbels confidentially informed the entire German press that the Führer would prefer them to abstain from such comparisons in the future. Through Colonel Schmundt Hitler also arranged for the suppression of General von Rabenau's biography of General Hans von Seeckt—Brauchitsch's great predecessor. It was in Seeckt's own interest, as Hitler put it. He exercised this personal censorship with increasing arbitrariness: when—evidently from telephone-tapping reports—he learned that the editor of the General Staff's *Military Weekly* had privately questioned the verac-

ity of the OKW war communiqués, he demanded the general's immediate resignation. As a military commander, however, Hitler was still only flexing his muscles.

Indeed, in moments of military crisis, Hitler was to display an indecisiveness and
lack of precision that was otherwise wholly out of character. This contributed to
the loss of the *Graf Spee.*

On December 13 the pocket battleship fell foul of three British cruisers off the
coast of neutral Uruguay. During the following night a series of disjointed radio
messages reached Berlin. The first read: "Action with *Exeter, Ajax,* and *Achilles.*
Damaged *Exeter* and light cruiser." Five hours later, the battleship signaled her
attendant supply ship *Altmark:* "On your own." Obviously, things were not going
well, but it was not until the small hours of the fourteenth that the first details
reached the Berlin admiralty. "I have taken fifteen hits, food stores and galleys
destroyed, I am making for Montevideo." To those familiar with the political
stance of Uruguay it was clear the battleship's fighting days were probably over:
the country had a pro-British president, a pro-French foreign minister, and a rich
and powerful British embassy; it was also a hotbed of British secret service
activity. *Graf Spee* could hardly have run for a more hostile haven. It would take
many days for the damage to be repaired. The government at Montevideo granted
only three days. Meanwhile British naval forces began to mass in uncertain
strength at the mouth of the Plate River, waiting for the lame warship to leave
the neutral waters.

At 1 P.M. on the sixteenth, Raeder arrived at the Chancellery with the latest
cable from the battleship. Captain Hans Langsdorff had signaled:

1. Military situation off Montevideo. apart from cruisers and destroyers [there
   are also] *Ark Royal* and *Renown.* Tightly blocked at night. No prospect of
   breakout into open sea or reaching home.
2. Propose emerging as far as neutral waters limit. Should it be possible to fight
   through to Buenos Aires using remaining ammunition, this will be attempted.
3. In event that breakout would result in certain destruction of *Spee* with no
   chance of damaging enemy, I request decision whether to scuttle despite
   inadequate depth of water? Estuary of the Plate? Or internment?
4. Please radio decision.

The German admiralty was puzzled: its Intelligence had—accurately, as we now
know—ascertained from the radio emissions of the aircraft carrier *Ark Royal* and
the battle cruiser *Renown* that both ships were still many days to the north of
Montevideo; they could not arrive before the nineteenth. But Langsdorff's signal
breathed despair.

Even before he read it, Hitler met Admiral Raeder at the door of his study with a demand that *Graf Spee* must attempt to break through to the open sea; if she must go down, at least she could take some of the enemy with her. He put a hand on the admiral's shoulder. "Herr Grossadmiral, I can well understand how you feel. Believe me, the fate of this ship and her crew is as painful to me as to you. But this is war, and when the need is there, one must know how to be harsh." But he followed this firm speech with an inexplicable act. Raeder showed him the admiralty's draft reply to Captain Langsdorff: *Graf Spee* was to stay at Montevideo as long as the authorities would allow; a "breakout" to Buenos Aires would be "approved," internment in Uruguay would not. "If scuttling, thoroughly destroy everything first." Although this reply was wholly out of keeping with Hitler's heroic demand, he nonetheless allowed Raeder to transmit it around the world to Montevideo at once. Hitler's naval adjutant was perplexed.

Hitler eagerly awaited the news of *Graf Spee*'s last battle. During the seventeenth, however, the stunning news arrived that the battleship had sailed out of Montevideo, discharged her crew onto a waiting steamer which had borne them safely to a friendly Buenos Aires, and then gently settled down onto the shallow bed of the river's estuary.[2] In a savage mood, that evening Hitler pondered the damage Langsdorff had done to Germany's fighting image. At three in the morning he ordered the official announcement of the battleship's loss altered to read: "Under these circumstances the Führer ordered Captain Langsdorff to destroy the ship by blowing her up." The neutral press appraised the episode with reserve and even respect; but Germany's enemies responded with shrieks of spiteful glee, and this exposed a further weakness in the Führer—his inability to accept misfortune with equanimity. He developed an aversion to cruiser warfare, with its doctrine of hit-and-run; out of this aversion grew a hostility toward the maturer officers of the German navy, which contrasted with his admiration of the dashing destroyer and submarine commanders. Langsdorff himself had been an officer on Jodl's staff; he had been given the *Graf Spee,* it transpired, almost as a cure for his chairbound attitudes. But the cure had apparently not worked—perhaps the injuries he had suffered when a shell hit the bridge earlier had affected the captain's judgment. He shot himself on reaching Buenos Aires.

When the *Deutschland,* sister ship of the ill-fated *Graf Spee,* returned to Germany, Hitler—fearful of the loss of prestige Germany would suffer should a "Deutschland" ever go under—ordered her renamed. *Spee*'s supply ship *Altmark,* laden with prisoners plucked from the decks of the battleship's victims, was ordered to return home to Germany.

---

[2]Her vital equipment was undestroyed, and some time later British Intelligence officers were able to examine her radar gear. Shortage of explosives was the probable reason for this.

———

Hermann Göring did what he could to use this incident to impugn the honor of the navy's big ships. His Luftwaffe's prestige was running high. With insignificant loss to the German fighter defenses, a marauding squadron of RAF bombers attacking Wilhelmshaven in broad daylight on the eighteenth was virtually wiped out. The British realized their attempts at visual daylight bombing raids were fraught with perils and decided to convert to a night-bomber force.

Hitler left Berlin for a brief respite at the Berghof. Passing through Munich, he paid his annual Christmas visit to his friends and patrons, the Bruckmanns; without Else Bruckmann's salon twenty years before, he might never have got this far. He stayed two hours, chatting about his plans to conquer Britain, to force her to her knees over the next eight months by using magnetic mines and other fabulous weaponry. In private circles such as these, Hitler had no sense of security precautions but would happily ramble on about his future strategy, revealing all. Warsaw, he said, was a desolate heap of rubble thanks to the intransigence of its defenders. Only a small area was worth rebuilding. But when peace came, he would turn to the magnificent reconstruction of the new Reich—whose Nordic dimensions he hinted at in his entry in the Bruckmanns' guest book: "In the year of the fight for the creation of the great German-Teutonic Reich!"

For three days Hitler toured the western front, joining the Christmas celebrations of Luftwaffe squadrons, antiaircraft batteries, infantry, and SS regiments. It was clear that the French were not making any move to attack. In the autumn the army's cryptographers had broken the main French codes, and the ability to decode the flood of signals transmitted by the French war ministry more than compensated for the shortcomings of Canaris's Abwehr organization. The signals revealed that the French were having problems in manufacturing antitank weapons and in activating new units in the interior; the weakness of the French Ninth Army between Sedan and Mauberge was also evident. At Spichern, near Saarbücken, the French had fallen back under local German pressure and Hitler was able to cross the French frontier for the first time since 1918. Here the famous frontier battles of 1870 had been fought.

On his return to Berlin, Hitler again postponed "Yellow," this time to mid-January. The long-range weather forecast predicted a period of cold, clear wintry weather for then; failing that, the Führer resolved, he would call off "Yellow" until the spring.

As in years past, he retreated to the Berghof to await the New Year. Here Eva Braun and her friends brought a relatively civilized touch to his surroundings, but the photographs in her albums show that even when the Führer sat faintly smiling at the delight of the offspring of Speer, Goebbels, and Martin Bormann at a Berghof children's party, he still wore the field-gray army tunic, with its solitary Iron Cross, that he had emotionally donned on the day his troops attacked Poland. In one photograph, however, Hitler is shown in somber evening dress, spooning molten lead into a bowl of water—a New Year's Eve tradition. Some believe that a man's future can be predicted from the contorted shapes the solidifying metal assumes. Hitler's face betrays a certain lack of confidence in this procedure.

At the Berghof he received a long, angry, and frightened letter from Benito Mussolini. It broke the months of silence which followed a mid-December speech in which Foreign Minister Ciano had revealed that Rome had not been consulted at the time of Hitler's pact with Stalin and that the Führer had broken promises given to the Italians about the imminence of war. Mussolini's letter marked the lowest point in Axis relations, which had been soured by Hitler's continued flirting with Moscow. As recently as December 22, Hitler had on Stalin's sixtieth birthday cabled him greetings coupled with his best wishes for the Soviet peoples; Stalin had cordially replied. In Mussolini's eyes Hitler was a traitor to the Fascist revolution; he had sacrificed the principles of that revolution to the tactical requirements of one given moment.

> You cannot abandon the anti-Semitic and anti-Bolshevist banners which you have flown for twenty years and for which so many of your comrades died; you cannot abjure your gospel, which the German people have blindly believed. . . . The solution for your *Lebensraum* is in Russia and nowhere else. Russia has twenty-one million square kilometers and nine inhabitants per square kilometer. It is outside Europe, in Asia—and this is not just some theory of Spengler's.

Not until they, the Axis leaders, had jointly demolished bolshevism would they have kept faith with their revolutions. "It will then be the turn of the great democracies. . . ." wrote Mussolini.

In this letter—which Hitler deliberately left unanswered for two months—Mussolini also voiced concern about rumors reaching him on German treatment of the Poles. He proposed that Hitler should take steps to restore some kind of Polish state.

Hitler's policy in Poland had undergone a radical change in the autumn of 1939. Initially he had regarded a future "Polish state" as a bargaining counter against the western powers. But as the prospects of an armistice receded, his attitude hardened—although he lagged perceptibly behind the SS and Party in degree. Early in October he had indicated to Governor General Frank that the Generalgouvernement was to be a kind of Polish reservation, but in November he bluntly told Frank: "We are going to keep the Generalgouvernement. We will never give it back." Although Hitler's long-standing personal friend, Frank was only a verbose and pettifogging lawyer. He did not have the Führer's confidence to the inexplicable extent that SS Reichsführer Himmler had—and it was Himmler's SS and police agencies that wielded the *executive* power in German-occupied Poland.

Himmler's rule in the east derived its authority from an official commission granted to him by Hitler in September. Though the Reichsführer made much of it in his public and private speeches, this commission did not exist in writing, and its limits became increasingly ill-defined. Basically, Himmler's job was the Germanization of the new provinces of West Prussia and Posen. On this Hitler and Himmler agreed, but thereafter their opinions differed. Hitler saw no great urgency about the matter and had himself told Himmler: "I don't want these eastern Gauleiters in a frantic race to be the first to report to me after two or three years, 'Mein Führer, my Gau is fully Germanized.' I want the population to be racially flawless, and I'll be quite satisfied if a Gauleiter can report that in ten years." (In March, Hitler even told Mussolini that he expected it would take forty or fifty years to develop these regained provinces.) Himmler, however, wanted greater urgency. Acting on a cruel directive he had issued at the end of October, the two Gauleiters concerned—Forster and Greiser—and SS Generals Krüger and Odilo Globocnik, police commanders based in Cracow and Lublin, respectively, began the ruthless midwinter expulsion from their domains of the 550,000 Jews, the post-1919 Polish settlers, and the principal anti-German and intellectual elements; they used Frank's Generalgouvernement as a dumping ground.

Himmler gave them until February 1940 to complete the job. Long forced marches took a heavy toll of these unwanted human beings. Early in January, both Göring and Lammers took protests about this impossible state of affairs to Himmler and evidently to Hitler as well—but to no avail. Yet in some respects Hitler did act as a brake. From Himmler's scrawled notes on his private confrontations with the Führer we know that he was obliged to report in person on the "shooting of 380 Jews at Ostro" on November 19; and that when at the end of November the archbishop and suffragan bishop of Lublin were condemned to death along with 13 priests for the possession of arms and subversive literature, Hitler ordered their reprieve and deportation to Germany instead.

What Himmler did not include in his notes was the fact that Heydrich—blithely disregarding Frank's authority in the Generalgouvernement—had found his own ways of simplifying the midwinter population movements. In January 1940 he converted a remote camp at Soldau, near the East Prussian border, to a liquidation center for Poles who survived the day-to-day brutalities. A ripple of protest disturbed the German armies poised in the west to unleash "Yellow."

Hitler learned that on January 22, Major General Friedrich Mieth, Chief of Staff of the First Army, had told his assembled officers about atrocities in Poland: "The SS has carried out mass executions without proper trials. There have been disturbances. There have been certain incidents between the SS and regular forces. . . . The SS has besmirched the Wehrmacht's honor." Mieth was dismissed. Soon after, the army's Commander in Chief East, General Johannes Blaskowitz, sent to Berlin a formal list of specific SS and police atrocities in Poland—including murder, looting, and general bestiality. He challenged the very basis of the occupation policies: "The view that the Polish people can be intimidated and kept down by terrorism will definitely be proven wrong. They are far too resilient a people for that." Blaskowitz added that the atrocities would provide the enemy with powerful ammunition throughout the world.

When Frank next came to the Reich Chancellery, he criticized Blaskowitz's unhelpful attitude. One of Hitler's adjutants wrote: "Reichsminister Frank . . . described the programs for the rounding-up and resettlement of the Jews. He bitterly attacked the army's Supreme Commander [Blaskowitz] and the field-administration officers. They are interfering with the work of 'pacification'; the officers 'have no instinct' and are getting in the way of his agencies. He asked the Führer to tell the army not to interfere, particularly in political matters, as it is flatly opposed to the Party line. The Führer had a fit of anger, which lasted until the war conference began."

The wording of this note, which talks of "resettlement," may mean that at this point the real fate of the Jews was being withheld from Hitler; he does, however, appear to have issued orders to Hans Frank for regular prophylactic massacres of the Polish intelligentsia, cruelly and cynically justifying this step as a security measure. The first two thousand Poles were to die as soon as "Yellow" began to cause sufficient diversion in the west. How else can Frank's confidential remarks at the end of May 1940 to his police authorities in Poland be interpreted? "The Führer has said to me, 'The problem of dealing with and safeguarding German interests in the Generalgouvernement is a matter for the men in charge of the Generalgouvernement and for them alone.' And he used these words: 'The ruling class that we have already unearthed in Poland is to be exterminated. We must keep close watch on whatever grows up in its place, and dispose of that too after a suitable time has elapsed.' " And Frank hastened to recommend to his minions: "There's no need for us to burden the Reich or its police bodies with all this. There's no need for us to cart off all these elements to concentration camps in the Reich first. That'll just result in a lot of bother and unnecessary correspondence with next-of-kin. No—we'll liquidate this business here, on the spot."

It was General von Brauchitsch who quelled the rumors along the western front. He of course had long ceased to cavil at the SS operations. Indeed, he arranged for Himmler to explain and justify them to the troubled army generals in the west, in a speech at Koblenz on March 13. When Blaskowitz submitted two further thick dossiers on SS atrocities in April, Berlin handled them as gingerly as nitroglycerine: Keitel refused to sign for their receipt; the Luftwaffe's General Milch locked his copy in a safe and threatened Blaskowitz's courier with arrest. Blaskowitz was relieved of his command in May, and when his successor wrote still more reports on the atrocities in Poland in July, Keitel abruptly instructed him to stop meddling in matters which did not concern him.

The directive issued by the Eighteenth Army on its transfer to Poland in August 1940 is an eloquent statement of the army's surrender to the Party. It forbids any criticism of the struggle being waged there against minorities, Jews, and the clergy. "For centuries an ethnological struggle has raged along our eastern frontier. To put an end to it once and for all has called for a short, sharp solution. Specific Party and government agencies have been put in charge of waging this ethnological war in the east. This is why our soldiers must keep their noses out of what these units are doing. We are not to make their job more difficult by criticizing them."

Under Party sponsorship, lawlessness flourished in the east. Hitler turned a blind eye on the excesses. An army major procured the arrest of eight Polish whores and did four of them clumsily to death in prison that evening; a fifth survived a bullet in the brain and escaped. Gauleiter Forster made representations to Hitler against executing this major for one drunken offense and—contrary to the recommendations of Brauchitsch, Keitel, and Schmundt—Hitler commuted the sentence to a prison term. In another case, one of the innumerable young SA officers appointed magistrate in Poland ordered fifty-five Polish prisoners out of their cells and shot them all in a drunken orgy. Here too the local Gauleiter, Greiser, begged the ministry of justice not to blight the young officer's promising career, and Hitler—learning that the man had a clean Party record—granted him a reprieve. In later years, it fell to Hitler's naval adjutant, Karl-Jesko von Puttkamer, to brief him on the court-martial sentences requiring confirmation by him as Supreme Commander. A level-headed and incorruptible ex-destroyer commander, Puttkamer succeeded in influencing Hitler to the necessary degree so that what were considered the most deserving cases did not escape the firing squad or, sometimes, the hangman's rope.

Within Germany itself, Himmler's police agencies were now acting as a law unto themselves. When the first German citizen was summarily shot for refusing to work on a defense project, the Gestapo quieted all criticism by informing the ministry of justice that before leaving for the Polish front on September 3 the Führer had instructed Himmler to maintain order in the interior "as he saw fit." More executions followed, although Göring warned Heydrich that no Germans were to be executed without formal sentencing. At the end of September, the minister of justice submitted to Hitler a file on summary executions of Germans; Hitler replied that he had not given Himmler any *general* instruction but that he had ordered certain executions himself, as the regular military and civil courts were not adjusting themselves to the special war conditions. "This is why he has now ordered the Teltow bank robbers to be put before a firing squad," his staff explained. But the files also show that Hitler drew much of his information on civilian crime from casual references in the newspapers. A thoughtless editor had only to headline a story MAN SWINDLED SOLDIERS' WIVES for the Führer to send Schaub scurrying to a telephone with instructions that the modest prison sentence passed on the defendant was incomprehensible and that the Führer wanted the man to be shot.

Hitler's attitude to the Party's own courts was even more ambivalent, as his reaction to the trial of Julius Streicher showed. Streicher, the stocky, balding Gauleiter of Franconia, was an insensitive and rigid member of Hitler's "Old Guard" with an obsession against the Jews and accepted morality. His enemies were legion—the armed forces as a whole, Nuremberg's mayor and police president, and above all Rudolf Hess and his bustling deputy Martin Bormann. Hitler saw in Streicher an idealist and a true revolutionary, but when the clamor against the Gauleiter reached its climax at the end of 1939 he yielded and permitted Streicher—one of the very few men allowed to address the Führer by the familiar *du*—to be put on trial by the Party's Supreme Court. The actual charges against him seem uncertain. Treason may have been among them; four days after Hitler's speech to the Gauleiters in October,[3] Streicher had revealed Hitler's military plans to local Party members in a speech, and he had repeated this imprudent step in a larger assembly a few days later. Speaking of Hitler's decision to invade neutral Belgium, Streicher had explained, "We need the coast for our attack on Britain." His recent speeches—of which the police president privately showed a dossier to the local military authorities—included blasphemous attacks on the clergy, libelous references to the generals of the Great War, and an address to a young female audience in November in which he exhorted them to find nothing improper in the desire to seduce married men. "Any woman or lady who gets worked up about this is in my eyes just a pig." According to Major Walther Buch, the Party's chief judge, Streicher was indicted for dishonest monetary dealings in the confiscation of Jewish property; for libeling Göring over the true paternity of his daughter Edda; for brutality and improper relations with a very young girl. Streicher himself said he was accused of having called war widows "silly geese," but was acquitted of this charge.

Whatever the charges, the Supreme Court—six Gauleiters and three Party

[3]See pages 40–41 above.

judges—met in February and on the sixteenth decided on a verdict against Streicher. Hitler suspended Streicher from office and forbade him to make further public speeches; but he was not ejected from the Party, as Hess had demanded, and he was allowed to continue publishing his newspapers—including the despicable *Stürmer*. To Hitler the trial smacked of a kangaroo court, and he told other Party leaders like Ley that he felt an injustice had been done to Streicher: the legalists had paid too little attention to Streicher's Party record in the past. After all, Streicher had won Nuremberg, the stronghold of the Marxists, for the Nazi party just as Goebbels had won Berlin.

On January 6, 1940 the Führer had returned from Munich to Berlin.

Over the following days he submitted to a series of medical examinations by his corpulent physician, Dr. Theodor Morell—blood-serum and sedimentation-rate tests, urinalyses, and fecal examinations. The records of these have survived, and are unremarkable except that the urine was alkaline, as was to be expected of a vegetarian, and that a routine series of tests for syphilis all proved negative. Morell's heart examination on January 9 revealed a normal pulse and blood pressure for a man of Hitler's age, and there is as yet no reference to the rapidly progressive coronary sclerosis that seems to have first been detected in mid-1941.

"We Must Destroy Them, Too!"

An icy winter descended on Germany. The canals froze, the railways were clogged with military movements, population and industry alike were starved for coal and the most elementary daily requisites. These domestic worries Hitler transferred to the willing shoulders of Field Marshal Göring. He himself was concerned only with the coming offensive against France and the Low Countries. Day and night he talked and dreamed of "Yellow"—of how the armored divisions could best be employed, of how the bridges could be seized intact, of how the Dutch government could be persuaded not to fight back, and of how each operation should be devised to shed as little German blood as possible—a consideration that weighed less on him with each successive year. By Christmas 1939 he had already decided where the big hole was to be punched through the French defenses: at Sedan; and it was indeed at Sedan that the foundations of the Nazi triumph over France were laid.

It was now January 1940, and the Führer was back at his Chancellery in Berlin. He had heeded neither the entreaties of his generals, the admonitions of his diplomats, nor the anxious counsels of his vacillating Italian ally. The frightened letter Mussolini had written early in January proved how little Hitler could rely on Italy. Why else should the Italians offer to mediate with the West unless they intended to use Hitler's inevitable refusal as an alibi? A few days later Mussolini repeated the familiar complaint that Ribbentrop had in August 1939 promised Ciano that the West would stay out of the war; what was the point of such carping observations if Italy were not planning to welsh on her obligations when the time came?

It was indeed a curious alliance, for the *Forschungsamt,* Göring's remarkable telephone-tapping and codebreaking agency, now intercepted a coded telegram in which the Belgian ambassador in Rome reported to his foreign ministry in Brussels that Count Ciano had betrayed to him Germany's firm intention of attacking Belgium and had revealed the date currently set for that adventure. Since the records show that the Forschungsamt was reading the coded dispatches from the Italian embassy in Berlin to Ciano, Hitler must have known that the military attaché General Marras had supplied this information to Rome; at any rate, when Hitler later in the month proposed spreading *false* rumors about his new plans, Marras figured significantly among those with whom the rumors were to be planted!

Hitler assured Ambassador Bernardo Attolico, "1940 will bring us victory," but at the beginning of March, though Mussolini now made loyal noises, the Italians were still sitting uncomfortably on the fence. "The Italians are strange people," wrote Weizsäcker at that time. "Loyal glances toward us, so as to share in any success we may achieve. And gifts and minor acts of treachery for the West, so as to keep in their good books too."

Hitler was satisfied in his own mind that neither Belgium nor Holland would long maintain its strict neutrality. He was (wrongly) convinced that Brussels had long since reached secret agreement with London and Paris. Not surprisingly, Belgium had shifted her main defensive effort to her frontier with Germany, and the anti-German trend of all Belgian military preparations was highlighted by a secret report submitted by German army Intelligence in January 1940: Belgium had been fortified solely against Germany; fraternization was actively encouraged between Belgians and the French and British forces in the west; since mid-October, over two-thirds of all Belgium's forces were massed in the east, apparently oblivious of the growing Anglo-French concentration in the west; the Belgian gendarmerie had received instructions to speed any French invasion of the country, and while signposts in western Belgium had been replenished and improved to that end, those in the east had been wholly removed to hamper a German invasion. In the west, throughout November the Belgians had allegedly accumulated railway stock and convoys of trucks to aid the French. Mayors of Ardennes villages were ordered to prepare billets for French troops. Mufti-dressed French soldiers "on leave" were observed on the Belgian transport systems with uniforms in their suitcases. The fortifications at Liège and on the Albert Canal were far beyond the Belgian military capacity to defend—they had clearly been designed to accommodate French and British troops as well. One glance at an Intelligence map was enough to show that the Allies were preparing the left wing of their offensive through Belgian territory. "With the exception of one division, every single mechanized infantry, armored, and cavalry division is standing on the Belgian frontier." In short, Hitler saw no reason to have compunctions about attacking this "little neutral."

Hitler still frowned on the notion that he had unleashed a second World War. Later in January he was to authorize the navy to refer to the campaign from time to time as the "English war." For more general consumption, he decided that the best overall title was the "Great German War of Liberation." Neither term caught the public imagination—perhaps the public still hoped peace was just around the corner.

On the afternoon of January 10, the Führer discussed "Operation Yellow" with his commanders in chief. The weather report was excellent—for the next ten to fourteen days they could count on clear wintry weather in the west. He decided "Yellow" would begin fifteen minutes before dawn on the seventeenth, preceded perhaps by four or five days of saturation bombing attacks on French airfields and flying schools. As January 10 ended, Germany was closer to launching "Yellow" than ever before. Two million men waited with their tanks and guns confronting the armies of France, Belgium, and Holland.

Shortly before noon the next day, however, infuriating news reached the Chancellery. A Luftwaffe major carrying a suitcase of the most secret documents had strayed in a light aircraft across the Belgian frontier and crash-landed near Mechelen-sur-Meuse. Hitler stormed into Jodl's room and demanded a complete list of all the documents the major had been carrying. "It is things like this that can lose us the war!" he exclaimed—an outburst of startling frankness when spoken by the Führer. The major had contravened a direct embargo on flying with secret papers. Even now Hitler did not waver on his decision to launch "Yellow" on the seventeenth, and at 3:15 P.M. he confirmed this.

He also issued a drastic "Basic Order No. 1" on security—a regulation that was from now on to be displayed in every military headquarters as a wallposter—stipulating that nobody was to hear of any secret matter unless absolutely necessary and that then he was to be told no more, and no earlier, than necessary. "I forbid the thoughtless dissemination, just on the basis of some distribution list or other, of orders whose secrecy is of prime importance!" As a concrete restatement of general security principles the order was sound and admirable, but in later years Hitler came to wield it as a capital weapon in his tactic of *divide et impera:* soldiers should not interfere with diplomacy, nor diplomacy with the affairs of government; one army group commander was not to learn the orders and intentions of his neighboring army group. Only Adolf Hitler, as Führer and absolute commander, had the right to know it all.

Most of the Belgian newspapers reassuringly reported that the Luftwaffe major had managed to destroy all the papers he was carrying, but one journal (correctly as we now know) stated that same evening that this was not so: the German major had hurled the documents into a stove in the room where he was being interrogated; but a Belgian officer had thrust his hand into the stove and retrieved the smoldering fragments. On January 12, Jodl set out to Hitler the maximum the Belgians could deduce from the secret documents. If they had all fallen intact into enemy hands, than the situation was indeed serious. Later that day the attaché in Brussels cabled that the major and his pilot had assured him they had burned all the papers apart from an unimportant residue, and he repeated this in person to Hitler at the Chancellery at 11 A.M. on the thirteenth.

The Mechelen incident was not enough to deter Hitler from launching "Yellow." But shortly afterward a bad weather report—of warmer air coming from the northeast and resulting in periods of fog in the west—unsettled him, and at about one o'clock that afternoon he ordered all movements stopped. "Yellow" was provisionally postponed by three days to the twentieth. But the weather picture worsened. Hitler told his staff; "If we cannot count on at least eight days of fine and clear weather, then we will call it off until the spring." And on the afternoon of the sixteenth he directed that the whole offensive was to be dismantled until then, and that its reassembling was to be made on a new basis: that of security and surprise. He left Göring in no uncertainty about his anger at the Luftwaffe's loose security regulations, for two more incidents had occurred: in one, an officer had dropped a dispatch case out of a train, in the other a Luftflotte adjutant had lost a file of secret documents. Göring reacted characteristically: he dismissed both General Helmuth Felmy, the major's superior, and Felmy's Chief of Staff, and he then calmly informed Hitler that he had consulted a clairvoyant, who had also reassured him that the most important papers had been destroyed.

The Intelligence reports from Belgium gave this Delphic utterance the lie. Extensive mobilization was carried out in both Holland and Belgium late on the thirteenth. The Belgian General Staff ordered military units stationed in southern Belgium to offer no resistance whatever to French and British troops that might march in—indeed, the frontier barriers were to be taken down to speed their entry. Since the Forschungsamt was reading the Belgian codes, it is reasonable to assume that Hitler had by now also read the telegram sent by the Belgian military attaché in Berlin, Colonel Goethals, on the evening of January 13, warning that the German invasion was due next day, according to what an *"informateur sincère, de valeur discutable"* had told him.[1] By the morning of the seventeenth, it was clear from the official *démarches* of the Belgian government that the Mechelen documents had betrayed most of "Yellow" in its original form. Belgium and Holland now knew that Germany planned to disregard their neu-

---

[1]Goethals sent further telegrams to Brussels on January 14, 15, and 17, 1940, indicating that his source was passing on to him Hitler's decisions with a time lag of about twenty-four hours; the source may have confused the beginning of "Yellow" with the preceding Luftwaffe strike, which was to take place on January 14 (later canceled). Goethals's source was his Dutch colleague, Major G. J. Sas, who saw him at about 5 P.M. on the thirteenth and told him that when Hitler had learned of the Mechelen incident he was furious. "He stormed about and ordered the immediate beginning of the offensive in the west, before the Allies could take countermeasures." Sas's source was a Colonel Hans Oster.

trality and mount an airborne landing operation at Namur; fortunately for Hitler, the documents could not have compromised the delicate plan to seize the bridges across the Meuse and the Albert Canal.

In a sense Hitler must have been relieved that this Luftwaffe *bêtise* had forced a major decision on him. Besides, the enemy would now surely concentrate his best forces in the north to meet the new German "Schlieffen-style" attack; so the prospects of an encirclement operation beginning at Sedan and ending at the Channel coast were much enhanced. Everything depended on keeping this, his real intent, concealed from the enemy, and in a series of conferences at the end of January 1940 Hitler impressed this on his army commanders. As he said on the twentieth, he was convinced Germany would win the war, "but we are bound to lose it if we cannot learn how to keep our mouths shut." He ordered the preinvasion timetable to be overhauled in such a way that he need no longer decide on the date of the attack seven days in advance. He directed that paratroop units also be employed in the north, for he now wanted the whole of Holland occupied. When "Yellow" began, a foreign ministry official would be sent secretly to The Hague to invite the Dutch monarchy to accept the Wehrmacht's "armed defense of Dutch neutrality."[2] A constant state of alert was to be maintained in the west on the assumption that "Yellow" might start at any moment. This placed an almost intolerable burden on the goodwill of the towns and villages on which the armies had been billeted since October. The army commanders reminded Hitler of the undesirable consequences for the local female residents, but he reflected that at present there was far more at stake.

At the end of January 1940, the Führer had sent his chief military adjutant on a flying tour of the western front. On his return to Berlin on February 1, Colonel Rudolf Schmundt was bursting to report what he had found at General von Rundstedt's army group headquarters at Koblenz. Rundstedt's former Chief of Staff, General Erich von Manstein, was as adamantly opposed to the current war department (OKH) offensive plan in the west as was Hitler; moreover, he was advocating a radical alternative almost identical to what Hitler had been debating with his closest staff ever since October—breaching the French lines at Sedan after crossing the awkward Ardennes region of southern Belgium and then pushing a strong armored force straight up to the Channel to cut off the British and French elite forces as they advanced into Belgium. When Hitler had toured the

[2]Major Werner Kiewitz, who had carried Hitler's first surrender ultimatum to Warsaw on September 16 (see page 17), was selected for this mission. He was to persuade Queen Wilhelmina of the futility of opposing the German invasion. In the event, the Dutch were forewarned, and they refused to issue an entry visa to him; a desperate plan to parachute him into The Hague was abandoned, as by then the queen had escaped to England.

western front over Christmas, he had talked of little else to his adjutants. But while he had contemptuously referred to the war ministry plan as "the same old Schlieffen medicine as before," Hitler had not convinced himself to the extent of issuing a concrete order redisposing the armored divisions for the attack through the Ardennes.

Hitler's respect for General von Manstein's ability bordered on fear. That Manstein had independently had the same idea as he, convinced him of its soundness; and that the OKH bureaucrats had removed Manstein from his post with Rundstedt and given him command of a corps in the rear, impressed him even more. On February 13, Hitler told Jodl of his decision to commit the mass of his armor to the breakthrough at Sedan, where the enemy would now least expect it. Jodl urged caution. It was an "underhand approach"; the Gods of War might yet catch them napping there, for the French might launch a powerful flank attack. But now Hitler was deaf to criticism. On the seventeenth he buttonholed Manstein in person when the general attended a Chancellery dinner party for the new corps commanders. Manstein assured him that the new plan was the only means by which to obtain a total victory on land; everything else was just a half-measure. The next day Hitler sent for General von Brauchitsch and his Chief of Staff and after explaining the underlying strategy dictated the new operational plan to them. On February 24, the war department issued the new directive for "Yellow."

The eventual outstanding success of the new strategy—which has gone down in history not wholly unjustly as the Manstein Plan, for it was he who elaborated it in all the staff detail of which Hitler was incapable—convinced Hitler of his own military genius. Henceforth he readily mistook his astounding intuitive grasp for the sound, logical planning ability of a real warlord. His reluctance to heed his professional advisers was ever after magnified. He told one of his elder civil servants, experts should be on tap—not on top.

To undermine the French soldier's morale Hitler ordered German propaganda to hint that the real quarrel was with the British. Millions of rust-brown "autumn leaves" were released over the French lines, imprinted with Goebbels's famous message: "*Automne. Les feuilles tombent. Nous tomberons comme elles. Les feuilles meurent parce que Dieu le veut. Mais nous, nous tombons parce que les Anglais le veulent. Au printemps prochain personne ne se souviendra plus ni des feuilles mortes ni des poilus tués. La vie passera sur nos tombes.*"[3]

---

[3] "Autumn. The leaves are dropping. We too will drop like them. The leaves die because God wills it. But we die because the British want it. Next spring nobody will remember either the dead leaves or the fallen French soldiers. Life will go on above our graves."

But Hitler's true attitude toward Britain and France was the reverse of what this melancholy warning would seem to suggest. It was for the British that he had a maudlin, unrequited affection that caused him to pull his punches throughout 1940 to the exasperation of his strategic advisers. As Halder explained Hitler's program to the chief of army Intelligence late in January: "The Führer wants to win the war *militarily:* defeating France, then a grand gesture to Britain. He recognizes the need for the empire." During lunch at the Chancellery in these weeks of early 1940, Rudolf Hess once inquired, "Mein Führer, are your views about the British still the same?" Hitler gloomily sighed, "If only the British knew how *little* I ask of them!" How he liked to leaf through the glossy pages of *The Tatler,* studying the British aristocracy in their natural habitat! Once he was overheard to say, "Those are valuable specimens—those are the ones I am going to make peace with." And how he envied the ease with which the British got away with their "trickery and double-dealing!" The Chancellery dinner attended by Manstein and the other corps commanders fell on the day after the *Altmark* incident, in which the Royal Navy had coolly violated Norwegian neutral waters under circumstances to be explained below. Hitler could talk of little else and expounded loudly on the inherent *properness* of such actions—whatever the international lawyers might subsequently proclaim. History, he explained, judged only between success and failure; that was all that really counted—nobody asked the victor whether he was in the right or wrong.

Characteristically, nobody interrupted or contradicted Hitler. A general who was present later wrote: "Among his listeners sat Manstein, his face absolutely motionless. Some time before I had heard him make comments on the Nazi creed that were of an acerbity rare in army circles. Another general sat nodding sagely at each and every remark that Hitler made, like a mandarin toy with its head on a spring. The very astute General Schmidt listened with his head cocked attentively to one side." Rommel—who had been given an armored division a few days before—left the Chancellery clutching the copy of *Mein Kampf* Hitler had just given him. It was inscribed: "To General Rommel with fond memories, Adolf Hitler, February 3, 1940." Rommel wrote that afternoon: "I am enormously pleased with it."

The *Altmark* incident had revealed the frailty of the neutrality of a small country which falls foul of the interests of two great powers. The *Altmark* was the 15,000-ton German supply ship which had ministered to the needs of *Graf Spee* in the South Atlantic; since the action off the Uruguayan coast, she had lain low, her holds packed with three hundred British seamen captured from *Graf Spee's* victims. Until mid-February 1940, the worried German admiralty had heard no sound from her, but on the fourteenth she signaled that she was about to enter northern Norwegian waters. In those waters she should be immune to enemy attack; under The Hague Rules she was entitled to passage through them, for she was not a man-of-war but a naval auxiliary flying the flag of the German merchant marine. Such defensive armament as she had boasted in the Atlantic was properly stowed away below. The Norwegian picket boats interrogated her; her captain denied the presence of any prisoners—the position in law would not have altered if he had admitted them—and the *Altmark* was allowed to proceed.

The Norwegians undertook to escort her, but in Berlin late on the sixteenth the admiralty began intercepting British naval signals which left no doubt but that an attempt was afoot to capture the *Altmark* even if it meant violating Norwegian neutral waters. By 6 A.M. next morning these fears were confirmed. A radio signal of the British commander to the admiralty in London had been decoded in Berlin: the British destroyer *Cossack* had been alongside the *Altmark,* and he and his group were returning to Rosyth. By midday a full report of this incident was in Hitler's hands, telephoned through by the legation in Oslo. Seeing the British force—a cruiser and six destroyers—closing in, the *Altmark*'s captain had sought refuge in Jøssing Fjord. Two Norwegian vessels had held the British ships at bay until dusk, when the *Cossack,* her searchlights blazing, had forced her way past them into the fjord and ordered the German ship to heave to. The *Altmark*'s report described how a boarding party had seized the ship's bridge "and began firing like blind maniacs into the German crew, who of course did not have a gun among them." Six men died, many more were injured. A handful of the crew fled across the ice which hemmed the vessel in, or they sprang into the water; the British boarders opened fire on these as well—an outrage to which the Norwegians also later testified. The three hundred prisoners were liberated, the ship and its crew were looted, and the *Cossack* withdrew. The Germans had not fired one shot.

Hitler did not have to await the official decoration of the *Cossack*'s captain with the Victoria Cross to know that this violation of Norwegian neutrality had the highest sanction in London. London had even signaled the captain the previous afternoon that the destroyers were to open fire on the Norwegian patrol boats if the latter resisted the British approach. These and other British signals were decoded by Berlin. The German naval staff war diary concluded: "From the orders of the admiralty and the steps taken by the British naval forces it is clear beyond a doubt that the operation against the supply vessel *Altmark* was premeditated and planned with the deliberate object of capturing the *Altmark* by whatever means available, or of releasing the prisoners, if necessary by violating Norway's territorial waters." Now if never before Hitler realized how real was the possibility that the Allies would use the Russo-Finnish war as a pretext for a full-scale invasion of Norway. He ordered that in the ensuing operation to recover the damaged *Altmark* Norway's neutrality was to be respected to the utmost; but his own resolve to violate it once and for all dated from this naval episode.

More than the wish to repair his prestige, injured by the *Altmark* affair—more even than the strategic need to occupy the Norwegian coast before the Allies could do so—there began to weigh with Hitler the belated consideration that since the Scandinavian peoples were also of Germanic stock they naturally belonged within the Nazi fold. There is no other explanation for his later persisting in his plan to occupy Norway, even after the initial pretext had gone.

It is important to recall that in none of his Wehrmacht directives or secret speeches to his generals had Hitler adumbrated the occupation of Scandinavia. Only after Quisling's visits in December 1939 had the Führer ordered Jodl's staff to study such a possibility, but he had sat on the resulting document for some weeks before forwarding it to the service commands on January 10. The OKW study recommended that a special working staff under a Luftwaffe general, with navy and army assistants, should devise a suitable operational plan. Assuming the code name "Oyster," this staff began work under General Erhard Milch a week later, but almost immediately Hitler ordered the unit dissolved and the OKW study withdrawn; he was not convinced that the Luftwaffe knew how to safeguard the secrecy of such planning. Instead, a top-secret unit was established within the OKW itself under Hitler's personal supervision; its senior officer was a navy captain, Theodor Krancke, and it was from the very scanty Intelligence material available that Krancke and his handful of army and Luftwaffe aides drafted the first blueprint for the campaign. He proposed simultaneous amphibious landings at seven Norwegian ports—Oslo, Kristiansand, Arendal, Stavanger, Bergen, Trondheim, and Narvik—the troops being carried northward by a fleet of fast warships; paratroops of the Seventh Air Division and waves of bombers and fighters would support the invasion. Diplomatic pressure on the Oslo government would do the rest.

Characteristically, Hitler consulted neither Brauchitsch nor Göring at this stage. The Luftwaffe's reluctance to coordinate its operations with the other services was notorious—indeed, its truculent and disastrous spirit of independence was borne out by the bombing and sinking of two German destroyers late in February with heavy loss of life. Göring refused to attach a Luftwaffe officer to Krancke's staff and remained in haughty ignorance of the Norwegian plan until early March. Hitler meanwhile accepted General Jodl's recommendation that the campaign preparations be put in the hands of an infantry general, Nikolaus von Falkenhorst, a fifty-five-year-old veteran of the

1918 German campaign in Finland; summoned to the Chancellery on February 21, Falkenhorst accepted the mission with alacrity and returned to the Chancellery on the twenty-ninth with a complete operational plan which now embraced not only Norway but Denmark as well, for the lines of communication between Germany and Norway had to be secured. Hitler had still not firmly decided whether the invasion was to be launched before, after, or even simultaneously with the attack on France and the Low Countries; but since Jodl had recommended making the two theaters entirely independent of each other, that decision could be postponed.

On March 1, Hitler signed the directive for the occupation of Norway and Denmark. Daring and surprise were the essence of the campaign. The army at once protested the introduction of a new theater. Göring stormed into the Chancellery and refused to subordinate his squadrons to Falkenhorst's command (eventually General Milch commanded Luftwaffe operations "in consultation with" Falkenhorst). Only the navy committed itself body and soul to the campaign, which was just as well, since Raeder's fleet was to suffer dearly.

Hitler wanted the campaign launched *soon*, before the British and French could beat him to it. Hewel brought him telegram after telegram from Helsinki, Trondheim, and Oslo hinting at the Allied preparations to land in Scandinavia on the pretext of helping Finland. On March 4, Hitler orally ordered the service commands to speed up their planning; it was to be completed within six days so that the simultaneous landing operations, including northern Norway, could begin on the seventeenth. "Yellow" could then follow about three days later. Göring was still discontented, and when Falkenhorst reported progress on March 5, he expressed loud contempt for all the army's joint planning work so far; but to Hitler this was a strategic crisis transcending interservice rivalries.

The risk of an Allied intervention in Scandinavia was too great. Through Rosenberg, Hitler received from Quisling's men in Oslo urgent proof that the British and French invasion plans were far advanced: communications within Scotland, just twenty-four hours from the Norwegian coast, had been blacked out. Something was clearly afoot. At lunch on the sixth, Hitler leaned over to Rosenberg and said, "I read your note. Things are looking bad."

The crisis reached its blackest point on March 12, as a torrent of dispatches from Moscow and Helsinki revealed that armistice talks had begun. If the western powers wished to act, it had to be now; if there was no war in Finland, Britain and France would have no legitimate reason to land in Scandinavia. London began desperate attempts to keep the war alive a few more days. Winston Churchill had evidently flown to Paris on the eleventh to inform the French government that on March 15 his expeditionary force was to sail for Narvik, for at 3:30 P.M. on March 12 the Forschungsamt intercepted an urgent telephone call from the

Finnish envoy in Paris to his foreign ministry in Helsinki. The envoy reported that Churchill and Daladier had promised him that if the Finns appealed for help immediately, British and French troops would be landed in Norway; the Norwegian government would merely be "notified" of this; Britain and France would then break off diplomatic relations with the Soviet Union at once. (Whether the Forschungsamt intercepted the actual date of the invasion is uncertain.) Thus the fat really was in the fire. Hitler ordered all German invasion plans accelerated, and the forces to stand by for the so-called *Immediate Op.* emergency. By next morning, however, the Russians had signed the armistice with Finland, and the immediate crisis was over.

The German admiralty's intercepts of coded British radio messages clearly indicated that the British and French had been on the very brink of a major landing in Norway. Destroyers had been attached to the British Commander in Chief Home Fleet, submarines stationed as a flank defense across the Skaggerak, and troop embarkation for an unspecified "Plan Three" completed. The fact that the troop transports had now been placed on extended sailing alert indicated that the Allies had only postponed their invasion and not canceled it altogether. German invasion preparations returned to a more leisurely pace; for the time being, Hitler withheld the executive order for the operation. "He is still searching for a sufficient reason," Jodl wrote in his diary. The true root of the Norwegian campaign was laid bare by Hitler in a remark to Rosenberg three weeks later, the day the amphibious operation began: "Just as Bismarck's Reich dates from the year 1866, so today has seen the birth of the Greater Germanic Reich."

We have seen how as Führer Hitler concerned himself not only with grand strategy—with all the chains of Intelligence combining only in his hands—but with the minutest interlocking elements of each operation: the position of the demolition charges on canal bridges, the thickness of the concrete in his fortifications, the strength of the guns commanding the Norwegian fjords. In this he was aided by a phenomenal memory and technical insight into weapons design, although his knowledge was limited to ships, tanks, and guns rather than to the weapons of air war. It was he who first demanded that 75-millimeter long-barrel guns be installed in German tanks. And it was he who pinpointed the common error in German warship design—building the forecastle so low that in heavy seas it tended to cut beneath the waves: on his birthday in 1937, the proud navy had presented him with a model of the *Scharnhorst*, and late that evening he had sent for his adjutant Puttkamer and invited him to crouch and squint along the model's decks with him; he was right, of course, and even at that late stage the forecastle had to be redesigned. On his bedside table his manservants always laid out the latest edition of Weyer's naval handbook—the German Janes'—for the

Führer to commit to memory as though he were preparing for some astounding music-hall act. His own staff had already witnessed the scene at headquarters during the Polish campaign when Admiral Raeder telephoned news of the sinking of some British warships; Hitler had beamed with pleasure, put down the telephone, and told Puttkamer the news, adding without the slightest hesitation the displacement, armament and armor thickness of each vessel. "Am I right, Puttkamer?" he had inquired, and the naval adjutant had reassured him, "Without doubt, mein Führer!" (Nonetheless he had privately checked in Weyer's immediately afterward and exclaimed to the other adjutants that Hitler's figures had been right "down to the last Pfennig!")

Did Hitler have some secret method, or was it that rarity—a photographic memory? We cannot tell. When the Red Book of arms production reached him each month, he would take a scrap of paper and, using a colored pencil selected from the tray on his desk, scribble down a few random figures as he ran his eyes over the columns. Then he would throw away the paper—but the figures remained indelibly in his memory—column by column, year after year—to confound his bureaucratic but more fallible aides with the proof of their own shortcomings. One month he pounced on a printing error in the current Red Book: an "8" instead of a "3." He had remembered the right figure from the previous month's edition. Late in 1940 Keitel took his new adjutant for an arms production conference with Hitler at the Berghof. Keitel started with figures on the total ammunition expended in the recent French campaign, and added more to allow for an extended war now; but Hitler responded that in 1916 the German armies had consumed far more 210-millimeter and 150-millimeter ammunition each *month,* and he stated the precise quantities from memory. Afterward Keitel instructed his adjutant to forward those new figures to General Georg Thomas of the OKW's munitions procurement office. "That is the new program." When the adjutant suggested they should at least check Hitler's figures Keitel wearily replied, "This is something you still have to learn. If the Führer says it, you can take it that it's right."

Hitler's seeming omniscience, and the eloquence of the arguments by which he gradually wore everybody down while apparently refreshing himself, had one disadvantage. While the less frequent visitors on technical affairs like the minister of posts, the elderly Wilhelm Ohnesorge, or the chief of naval construction, Admiral Karl Witzell, were flattered by the genuine interest the Führer displayed in their reports, Hitler's regular staff were discouraged by the feeling that since the Führer had already thought of everything himself there was little they could contribute by way of suggestion or initiative.

Although the OKW maintained its own munitions procurement office under General Thomas, Keitel readily echoed Hitler's mounting criticism of the arms production effort during the winter. He made no discernible effort to point out to Hitler that it was his own insistence on German armament in breadth for Blitzkrieg warfare—or war by bluff—rather than in depth for an extended war on many fronts, that was to blame for the present low ammunition production capacity. Again and again Hitler dinned into Keitel's head the disparity between current production programs and the achievements of the German munitions industry in World War I. In vain Keitel warned that such huge production figures could not be attained if the high quality of modern ammunition was not to be jeopardized. Hitler himself drew up a new production program in which priority was given to mine production for the naval and Luftwaffe blockade of Britain and to huge monthly outputs of artillery ammunition. He virtually doubled previous figures in a new program he issued on December 12, 1939.

Keitel issued the program to the army ordnance office—at that time headed by a sixty-year-old professor, General Karl Becker. By mid-January 1940, the latter had objected that Hitler's program could not be met "to the remotest extent": there was no point squandering scarce steel and nonferrous metal stocks manufacturing millions of shells if the chemical and explosives industry was not big enough to fill them. Keitel refused to tell this to the Führer. The Führer's munitions program must be fulfilled. If the ordnance office could not do it, the Führer would give the job to somebody else. Hitler was already toying with the idea—first put to him by Göring, who lost no opportunity to criticize the army's feeble ordnance office—of appointing a civilian munitions minister to take arms and munitions production out of the hands of the bureaucratic army staff officers. When Keitel himself asked for the power to control the arms industry, Hitler turned him down. In view of the increasing Allied strength in the West he was planning to establish ten more army divisions as well as new Luftwaffe squadrons which would concentrate on minelaying operations; he must at all costs have the increased mine and munitions production now.

When in February the army ordnance office reported the previous month's production figures, Hitler found this the last straw. Production of the most important weapons had actually declined. In the two main calibers of shell the Führer's program figures would not be reached even by April. Throughout January and February Hitler cursed General Becker's lethargic and inadequate ordnance office. Nor did he have any confidence in the ability of Keitel's staff to prod the arms industry into activity.

At the end of February, Göring appointed Dr. Fritz Todt as a special trouble-shooter to locate the bottlenecks in the munitions industry and recommend ways of stepping up production. Hitler trusted Todt implicitly, and Todt had also won the respect of the Party. He shortly convinced Hitler that if the industry was given a voice in how it was to fulfill its orders—the system of self-responsibility that had functioned so well in the construction of the autobahns and of the West Wall —Hitler's "impossible" production figures could be achieved. In March, Hitler appointed Todt his munitions minister. It was as much a rebuff to Keitel as to General Becker. But when the pained General Thomas, whose gloomy analyses of Germany's economic position had continually irritated Hitler, voiced objections, he was silenced by Keitel with the blunt comment that the less he reminded the Führer of his existence the better. Fritz Todt effectively wielded the powers Hitler had earlier denied to Keitel and Becker, for by the summer of 1940 the munitions crisis had virtually been surmounted. General Becker sensed his failure keenly, despite Hitler's endeavors to preserve his self-esteem, and he committed suicide not long after—the first of a sad band of Germans whose only common denominator was a failure to come up to Hitler's expectations.

At the end of February 1940, Hitler had secretly convened the Party leaders in the Chancellery and assured them the war would be over in six months—his new weapons would force the enemy to their knees; without doubt he was alluding to the mass minelaying operations the Luftwaffe was shortly to begin, using the deadly magnetic mine against which he believed the Allies had no defense.

Italy's uncertain stance continued to trouble him. Roosevelt had sent his undersecretary of state, Sumner Welles, to tour the engaged European capitals and sound their leaders on the prospects of peace. Hitler observed this uninvited diplomat's first port of call, at Rome, with as much disquiet as the British, though for different reasons. He was concerned that Welles's vague peace proposals might strengthen the neutralist elements in Rome, or even drive Italy into the arms of the Allies. Hitler studied the official Italian communiqués on the Rome talks and compared them closely with the Forschungsamt intercepts of the secret Italian dispatches relating to them. The Duce, however, appeared to have loyally defended Germany's claims. In his own talks with Sumner Welles, Hitler adhered rigidly to his argument that since this was Britain's war, it was up to Britain to end it. No amount of flattery by the American diplomat could cajole the Führer from this attitude. On March 4, Hitler repeated it to a General Motors vice president, James D. Mooney, to whom he granted an audience. "The current war can only be brought to an end by the other countries giving up their war aims," meaning the annihilation of Germany; Germany, he said, had no war aims.[4]

---

[4]The only American who made a good impression on Hitler at this stage was the traveling journalist Colin Ross, sent to him by Youth Leader Baldur von Schirach. Ross described to him the "fantastic slyness" and organizing talent of the American Jews, who had achieved so much that nobody in the United States now dared to support fascism openly, although there was much that was Fascist about the American government and way of life. Roosevelt's pathological envy of Hitler, said Ross, was caused by seeing how Hitler had put all his ambitious plans into practice, while he, who had come to power in the same year, had not.

Britain's heavy-handed dealings with Mussolini reinforced his Axis position. To force him to take his trade negotiations with Britain seriously, the British imposed a naval blockade on Italy's coal supplies at the beginning of March. Hitler stepped in with an immediate offer of a million tons of coal a month, to be supplied over land to his harassed Axis partner. On March 8 he sent Ribbentrop to Rome with an overlong and profuse letter replying at long last to the Duce's missive of two months before. When Ribbentrop reported back that Mussolini had at last agreed on principle to take up arms against Britain and France, Hitler asked for an immediate meeting to be arranged with the Fascist leader. He instructed Jodl's staff to provide him with a folder of charts, including one grossly faking Germany's actual military strength (crediting her with 207 divisions instead of her actual 157), and met Mussolini at the Brenner Pass on March 18.

It was their first meeting since Munich. How much of his far-reaching program Hitler had achieved since then! Mussolini, on the other hand, arrived with the air of a schoolboy who had not done his homework, as Hitler later put it. The Führer impressed upon Mussolini that the Duce could decide the best moment to declare war, but that he, Hitler, would recommend doing so only after the first big German offensive. The Duce promised to lose no time, but he would prefer "Yellow" to be delayed for three or four months until Italy was properly prepared. Hitler hugely exaggerated Germany's prospects: her armies were more powerful than in 1914, she had more ammunition than she could use, production of Junkers 88 aircraft and submarines was surging forward. As for the British, once France had been subdued, Britain would come to terms with Hitler. "The British are extraordinarily determined in defense but quite hopeless at attacking, and their leadership is poor." More than once he assured Mussolini that for Germany there could now be only one partner; however, despite all these protestations he evidently still mistrusted the Italians, for he imparted to Mussolini neither the impressive operational plan he and Manstein had evolved for victory in the west, nor the slightest mention of his intentions in Scandinavia. And in the directive he soon after issued to Keitel, a directive in which the Wehrmacht was instructed to resume staff talks with Italy, he stated explicitly that any Italian forces must be assigned a task as independent from the main German operations as possible, to minimize "the problems inevitable in a coalition war."

Italy was still angry with Germany about the pact with Russia, which had been supplemented in February by an important economic agreement. Hitler attempted in both his letter and his private talk with Mussolini to convince him that Russia was changed—though how far these words were intended for Soviet consumption is a matter of speculation. "Without doubt," Hitler had written the

Duce, "since Stalin's final triumph Russia has been undergoing a change from the Bolshevik principle to a more nationalist Russian way of life." At the Brenner meeting he reminded Mussolini that he had always wanted to march side by side with the British, provided that the British respected Germany's claims to expand eastward and returned to her the colonies lost after the Great War. "But Britain preferred war. This was why I was forced into partnership with Russia."

Yet there were surely less abstract reasons for his insistence that German industry deliver the goods to Stalin in abundance and on time—an insistence he voiced urgently throughout the spring of 1940. The British were known to be wooing the Russians even now. So long as the pact with Stalin was in force, it effectively released sixty high-grade divisions for Hitler to employ in the attack on France. Hitler's innermost intentions lay just below the surface. Perhaps the Russians should have guessed at them, for in 1940 millions of copies of the latest reprint of *Mein Kampf* went on sale, in which Chapter Fourteen, with its clear statement of his plan to invade the east, remain unexpunged. And when Hitler touched in conversation with Mussolini on the enforced evacuation of the German-speaking population from the South Tyrol—a mountainous province claimed by both Italy and Austria—he cryptically explained that he planned to resettle these people in a beautiful region "that I do not yet have but will certainly be procuring"; he must have already been looking ahead to the day when his armies would have turned eastward and be standing astride the Crimea, the region he formally assigned to the South Tyroleans in mid-1941.

On March 22, 1940, four days after his pregnant aside to Mussolini, Adolf Hitler again headed south, flying this time from Berlin to the Berghof for the Easter weekend. Captain Engel took the opportunity of this long flight to hand the Führer a lengthy report General Guderian had compiled on the wretched equipment and training standards of the Soviet troops in Finland. According to Engel, Hitler returned it with the laconic commentary: *"Auch die müssen wir vernichten!"*—"We must destroy them, too!"

Hors d'oeuvre

On Easter Monday, March 25, 1940, Hitler drove with his staff down the winding road from the Berghof and returned to the Chancellery in Berlin. The next time he was to see the Obersalzberg mountain it would be high summer, and he would be master of all northern Europe from North Cape to the Pyrenees.

The risks involved in the Norwegian operation were daunting, but he felt he must eliminate this constant source of worry implanted in his mind by Admiral Raeder—the fear that the Allies might obtain a foothold in Norway and cut Germany off from her iron-ore supplies. For the present his plans were delayed because the Baltic ports were still icebound and the transport ships he needed could not yet be assembled there. The world press slowly filled with speculation about the Allied designs on Scandinavia, but so far no word of Hitler's own daring intentions had leaked out. This was the first success of his stringent new security regulations. He had not even breathed a word of his military plan to Ribbentrop.

At noon on the day after Hitler's return to Berlin, Admiral Raeder put it to him that although a British invasion of Norway now seemed less acutely imminent than it had two weeks earlier, the Germans would do well to seize the initiative there now. It would be best to occupy Norway in a surprise operation timed to coincide with the new moon on April 7; by the fifteenth the dark nights would already be too short. Hitler agreed, but opted for a date between the eighth and tenth so that "Yellow" could begin four or five days after, if conditions were right. Raeder also asked Hitler to authorize an immediate resumption of Luftwaffe minelaying operations, as it seemed that the secret of the magnetic mine was now out; although both Keitel and Göring wanted the minelaying campaign delayed until "Yellow" began, the Führer directed that it must begin immediately. Against Göring's advice, Hitler also allowed himself to be persuaded by Raeder on another issue: the Führer had originally wanted the dozen destroyers that were to carry troops to Narvik and Trondheim to remain as a source of artillery support and to boost the morale of the troops they had landed; as he put it to Jodl one evening in his map room, he could not tolerate "the navy promptly scuttling out of the Norwegian ports." What would the landing troops make of that? But Raeder dug his heels in. The most perilous phase of the whole invasion campaign, he insisted, would be the withdrawal of the warships from northern Norway to the safety of German waters under the nose of the most powerful navy in the world. If the destroyers were detained one moment too long, they would be bottled in by the British and wiped out when they emerged. Raeder was prepared to risk his fleet for Norway, but he would not stand by and see it frittered away, and in a private clash with Hitler on March 29 he told him so. Hitler yielded to the force of argument.

Intelligence on Britain's intentions in Scandinavia hardened, although on March 22, Raeder's codebreakers found to their dismay that the British had just changed one of their most important codes; this might hamper cryptanalysis for two weeks. The Scandinavian press began to speculate on an imminent Allied operation in Norwegian waters. Raeder warned Hitler of a perceptible stiffening in Norway's attitude toward Germany. Far more important was that Hitler now learned of an Allied Supreme War Council decision in London on March 28 to develop a two-stage Scandinavian operation early in April: the cynical Allied master plan was to provoke Hitler into an overhasty occupation of *southern* Norway by laying mines in Norway's neutral waters; Hitler's move would then "justify" a full-scale Allied landing at Narvik in the north to seize the railroad to the Swedish ore fields. This first stage would later be coupled with several operations farther south. On March 30 German Intelligence intercepted a Paris diplomat's report on a conversation with Paul Reynaud, France's new premier. According to a summary in the naval staff's war diary, Reynaud had assured this unidentified diplomat that the dangers in western and southern Europe would shortly pass, as in the next few days the Allies would be launching all-important operations in northern Europe. On the same day, Churchill broadcast on the BBC a warning to Norway that Britain would no longer tolerate a pro-German interpretation of neutrality; the Allies would continue the fight "wherever it might lead them." (Churchill's designs on Norway were known to German Intelligence from a series of incautious hints he dropped in a secret press conference with neutral press attachés in London on February 2.) Small wonder that Hitler later referred more than once to the indiscretions committed by Reynaud and Churchill as providing the final urgent stimulus for his own adventure.[1]

On March 30, German cryptographers also intercepted a cable from the

[1] Ambassador Hewel recorded Hitler's dinner-table reminiscences on July 5, 1941, thus in his diary: "For instance, if we had formally declared war against Norway, we would have lost it; yet Norway is absolutely vital to the future of Germany. And vice versa, if Churchill and Reynaud had kept a still tongue in their heads, I might well not have tackled Norway. A week earlier Churchill sent his nephew [Giles Romilly] to Narvik, just typical of his American-Jewish journalistic character. Treason."

Romanian legation in Oslo conveying the impression being created by the British envoy there: conspicuous protestations that no far-reaching decisions had yet been taken in London or Paris about violating Norwegian waters were coupled with British denials that they intended to land troops in Norway. The combination finally convinced the German naval staff that "in reality a British operation against Scandinavia is imminent," and that a race between Britain and Germany was developing. An intercepted Swiss legation report from Stockholm claimed that British *and* German invasions of the Norwegian coast were imminent. Major Quisling said the situation was so urgent that the Germans should not wait for him to build up his organization first; British and French officers were being installed in key points in Norway, disguised as consular officials. Admiral Raeder nervously pressed Hitler to launch the invasion on April 7, the earliest possible date; but after spending two days investigating every detail of the operation with all the commanders involved, Hitler decided on April 2 that the first assault on Norway's coastline was to take place at 5:15 A.M. on the ninth.

The nervous strain on Hitler would have overwhelmed most men. Perhaps the very idea was too audacious to succeed? How could trainloads of South German mountain troops heading for the Baltic coast be plausibly explained? How could ponderous transport ships laden with hundreds of troops, guns, and ammunition be safely dispatched toward the Arctic without alerting the British fleet in time to wipe out the German navy? When on April 1, Hitler personally addressed the handpicked commanders, one report noted: "The Führer describes the operation . . . as one of the 'cheekiest operations' in recent military history. But in this he sees the basis for its success." He offered the familiar preventive reasons for occupying Norway but added that the time had come for Germany to win safe channels to the outside world. "It is intolerable that each generation is subjected to renewed pressure from Britain. Sooner or later the fight with Britain would have been inevitable. It has to be fought. It is a matter of life and death for the German nation."

At 2 A.M. on April 3, Hitler's operation passed the point of no return. The first three transports camouflaged as coal vessels sailed from Germany, bound with the tanker *Kattegat* for Narvik, a thousand miles to the north. Four more "coal ships"—three for Trondheim and one for Stavanger—were ready in German ports. All carried heavy equipment, artillery, ammunition, and provisions concealed beneath the coal. The initial assault troops would be carried on fast warships, some entering the Norwegian ports under cover of the British flag: ten destroyers would carry two thousand troops to Narvik, escorted by the battleships *Scharnhorst* and *Gneisenau;* another seventeen hundred troops would be landed at Trondheim by the cruiser *Hipper* and four destroyers. Thousands of assault troops would be landed at five other ports by virtually the rest of the German navy—a fleet of cruisers, torpedo boats, whalers, minesweepers, submarine chasers, tugs, and picket boats. Troop reinforcements would arrive during the day in fifteen merchant ships bound for Oslo, Kristiansand, Bergen, and Stavanger. If anything prematurely befell even one of these ships laden with troops in field-gray, the whole operation would be betrayed.

Hitler ordered the OKW to disclose the impending operation to Ribbentrop. By April 5, the admiralty in Berlin could recognize that a fresh British operation had begun. An imperfectly broken British radio message of very unusual length appeared to be an operational order to fifteen or twenty submarines; since the operation seemed to be one of particular importance, it was decided that either the British were deploying against Hitler's operation or that "the enemy has his *own* plans to invade Norway." The German naval staff correctly deduced the two-stage character of the Allied plan—first the British would lay a mine barrage, then, as soon as the Germans retaliated, the Allies would use this as justification for an invasion. Since there was no other evidence at all that the Allies might have detected Germany's strategic plan, let alone the audacious scale on which Hitler had prepared the invasion, the naval staff concluded on April 6 that "the enemy is on the threshold of conducting operations in Norwegian waters or on Norwegian soil." In Berlin, the foreign ministry learned that the Allied governments had sent to the Scandinavian governments crisply worded notes indicating that since the latter were no longer "entirely free agents" in handling their foreign affairs, the Allies reserved all rights.

In his Chancellery, Hitler feared that at any moment word would arrive that the Allied invasion had begun. On the afternoon of the sixth the war department notified him that the railroad movement of invasion troops from their assembly areas in the heart of Germany to the Baltic dockyards had begun on schedule. From Helsinki came fresh word of an imminent British operation against Narvik; Swedish and Norwegian officers tried to assure Berlin that the Allies were just trying to provoke Germany into an ill-considered preventive campaign, but Hitler remained unconvinced. He already felt that the Swedes knew more than was good for them. He had arranged for all the foreign military attachés in Berlin to tour the West Wall over the next few days—but the Swedish legation had declined the invitation, explaining that the attaché would be urgently needed at the time scheduled. Equally ominous were the telephone conversations the Forschungsamt now intercepted between the Danish military attaché and the Danish and Norwegian ministers in Berlin, in which the attaché urgently asked for immediate interviews with them as he had something of "the utmost political significance" to tell them.[2]

---

[2]The Abwehr office of the OKW had been involved in some of the dealings with Major Quisling's men and was thus apprised of the coming Norwegian invasion. Admiral Canaris's Chief of Staff, Colonel Hans Oster, warned the Dutch military attaché Major Sas of this—presumably to restore his own credibility after the many false alarms he had given in the winter. Sas passed the information on to the Danish and Norwegian legations, though neither was greatly impressed by it.

During the night of April 6-7, the German fleet operation began. The battleships, cruisers, and destroyers sailed from their North Sea ports. A further stiffening in the Norwegian attitude to Germany was detected. Norwegian coastal defenses were on the alert, troop movements were reported, lighthouses and radio beacons were extinguished. Norwegian pilots for the "coalships" waiting to pass northward through the Leads to Narvik and Trondheim were only slowly forthcoming—was this deliberate Norwegian obstructionism, or had the German admiralty simply failed to impress on these ships' captains the importance of the timetable? It was too late to speculate now, for the entire German invasion fleet was at sea. Hitler was committed to either a catastrophic defeat, with the certain annihilation of his navy, or to a spectacular victory.

Early on April 8, the German legation in Oslo telephoned Berlin with the not altogether unexpected news that British warships had just begun laying minefields in Norwegian waters. This violation of Norway's neutrality could hardly have been more flagrant, nor more opportune for Hitler's cause. Now he could present his seizure of the Norwegian coast as a dramatic, and highly effective, answer to the Allied action; and a gullible world would believe it. In Oslo, there was uproar and anger at the Allied presumption; the redoubled Norwegian determination to defend their neutrality caused Raeder to order his warships to abandon their original intention of entering the Norwegian ports under the British flag, as he could now see little profit in the deception.

The elation in Berlin at the Allied action was shattered by a second telephone call from the Oslo legation in the early evening. The *Rio de Janeiro,* a slow-moving merchant ship headed for Bergen with horses and a hundred troops, had been torpedoed a few hours earlier off the Norwegian coast. Troops in field-gray uniforms had been rescued from the sea and were presumably even now being interrogated by the Norwegians. But Hitler's luck still held. The hours passed, and although word came that the Norwegian Cabinet had been urgently called into session, it seemed to have resolved upon no clear course of action. From intercepted radio messages the British admiralty was known to have identified the fast warship groups heading for Narvik and Trondheim during the eighth. But in Berlin the naval staff was confident that the British would wrongly conclude that this was an attempted breakout into the Atlantic. Raeder had insisted on attaching battleships to the first group, and this was now vindicated, for the British were indeed deceived, and deployed their forces far to the north of the true seat of operations.

In the small hours of April 9, Berlin picked up a Norwegian radio signal reporting strange warships entering the Oslo Fjord. Now Hitler knew that the toughest part of the operation—running the gauntlet of the Norwegian coastal batteries—had begun. But shortly before 6 A.M. German signals from the forces landed at Narvik, Trondheim, and Bergen were monitored; they called for U-boats to stand guard over the port entrances. Access to Norway had now been forced. Hitler and Jodl read the signals with evident relief, though not until later did the full measure of this German victory dawn on them.

By the evening of April 9, 1940, Norway and Denmark appeared securely in German hands. General von Falkenhorst reported at five-thirty: "Norway and Denmark occupied . . . as instructed."

Hitler himself drafted the German news-agency report announcing that the Danish government had submitted, grumbling, and almost without a shot having been fired, to German *force majeure.* Grinning from ear to ear, Hitler congratulated Rosenberg: "Now Quisling can set up his government in Oslo." The unbelievably sluggish British naval command had fumbled every countermove. In southern Norway the strategically well-placed airfield at Stavanger had been captured by German paratroops, assuring Hitler of immediate air superiority— the key to the later campaign; at Oslo itself—where the seaborne forces arrived three hours late—five companies of paratroops and airborne infantry landed on Fornebü airfield. A small party of infantry marched with band playing into the Norwegian capital and Oslo fell.

At the Reich Chancellery in Berlin there was the heady scent of victory and relief. When the gold-embossed supper menu was laid before Hitler that evening, the main course of macaroni, ham, and green salad was appropriately prefaced by *smörrebröd.* Scandinavia was indeed just the hors d'oeuvre; as soon as the Luftwaffe could disengage itself from Norway, "Yellow" would begin—a feast of military conquest which Hitler was already savoring in advance.

As Admiral Raeder had predicted, the German navy had suffered grievous losses and was to suffer yet more; but Hitler confided to his adjutants that if his navy was to do naught else in this war, it had justified its existence by winning Norway for Germany. In the final approach to Oslo along the fifty-mile-long Oslo Fjord, Germany's newest heavy cruiser, the *Blücher,* had been disabled by the ancient Krupp guns of a coastal battery and finished off by torpedoes with heavy loss of life. Off Bergen the cruiser *Königsberg* was also hit by a coastal battery; it limped into port and was sunk the next day by British aircraft. South of Kristiansand, the cruiser *Karlsruhe* was sunk by a British submarine. Three more cruisers were damaged and many of the supply vessels sunk, for during their own invasion preparations the British had stationed sixteen submarines in the area; this was the operational signal the German admiralty had been unable to decipher completely.

In one incident, the cruiser *Hipper* and four destroyers bearing seventeen

hundred troops to Trondheim were challenged by the coastal batteries guarding
the fjord; the *Hipper*'s commander, Captain Heye, steered directly toward the
batteries, signaling ambiguously in English: "I come on government instructions." By the time the puzzled gunners opened fire, the ships were already past.

It was at Narvik that the real crisis began. Ten destroyers landed General
Eduard Dietl's two thousand German and Austrian mountain troops virtually
unopposed, for the local Norwegian commander was a Quisling sympathizer. But
the three camouflaged supply ships and the tanker *Kattegat* never arrived from
Germany. Only the tanker *Jan Wellem* arrived punctually from the naval base
provided by Stalin at Murmansk; as the ten destroyers could refuel only slowly
from this one tanker, they could not be ready to return before late on the tenth.
But earlier that day five British destroyers penetrated the fjord in a blinding
snowstorm; in the ensuing gunplay and the battle fought there three days later,
the aging British battleship *Warspite* and a whole flotilla of destroyers sank all
ten German destroyers—though not before they had taken a toll from the British.
Thus half of Raeder's total destroyer force had been wiped out.[3] Hitler had that
morning already radioed Dietl to hold on to Narvik at all costs. He was to prepare
frozen Lake Hartvig as an airfield ready to receive Luftwaffe supply planes. After
word came of the sinking of the destroyers, Rosenberg found the Führer slumped
deep in thought following a conference with Göring. When over the next two days
news arrived of British troops landing at Harstad, not far north of Narvik, and
at Namsos, to the north of Trondheim, the military crisis brought Hitler to the
verge of a complete nervous breakdown.

Had the diplomatic offensive in Oslo been prepared with the same thoroughness
as the military invasion, the Norwegian government could have been won over
or effectively neutralized. Thus armed Norwegian resistance would have been
avoided and the interior lines of communication secured from one end of Norway
to the other. But bad luck had dogged events in Oslo: when the *Blücher* had sunk
in Oslo Fjord, the assault party detailed to arrest the Norwegian government had
foundered with her; in addition, the airborne troops due to land at Fornebü
airport were delayed by fog. As a result, the king and government had had time
to escape the capital, and the local German envoy, Kurt Bräuer, was not equal
to the situation.

---

[3]The German destroyer commodore at Narvik was killed in the action on the tenth. His successor
notified the German admiralty that during the second raid, on April 13, the British destroyers caused
additional casualties by machine-gunning the German sailors thrown into the sea. Whatever the
substance of such wholly uninvestigated allegations, they will have contributed to the atmosphere at
the Reich Chancellery.

On April 10, both king and government—in refuge outside Oslo—had been amenable to negotiation, but Bräuer wanted them to recognize Major Quisling's new government and left the talks without awaiting the outcome of his proposals. Back in Oslo, Bräuer learned that the proposals were rejected: the king refused to violate the constitution by appointing Quisling, whom the Norwegian public regarded as a traitor. The fugitive government issued a call to arms and sabotage, and a confused but still undeclared war between Norway and Germany began. Had Bräuer not insisted on Quisling but dealt with the existing government instead, this situation would not have arisen.

Hitler's support for Quisling was short-lived. On April 14, the foreign ministry flew Theo Habicht, a Nazi revolutionary and ministry official, to Oslo to straighten matters out. His instructions were to make a last attempt to secure agreement with the king. Quisling was forced to climb down next day; but with the British operations in Narvik stiffening the Norwegian resolve, Germany's position was weaker politically than it had been four days earlier. Ribbentrop's representatives scraped together an "Administrative Council" of leading Oslo citizens including the chief justice of the Norwegian Supreme Court, Paul Berg, but progress was slow and quite the opposite of what Hitler had wanted. He was apoplectic with rage at Bräuer and Habicht for allowing these "Norwegian lawyers" to dupe them; he had wanted to see Quisling at the head of an ostensibly legal Norwegian government—not some lawyers' junta. Habicht and Bräuer were fetched back to Berlin and dismissed from the foreign service—it was all Ribbentrop could do to save them from incarceration in a concentration camp. Hitler fumed that all he desired in these northern lands was law and order; since the foreign ministry had failed, the army and Party must now try.

Next to the old Reich Cabinet Room Hitler used for his war conferences were the rooms his military advisers Jodl and Keitel occupied; additional offices were supplied for their adjutants and clerical staff. It was on this small stage that in mid-April 1940 the command crisis over Narvik was played. It shed such unfavorable light on Hitler's qualities of leadership that Colonel Schmundt, his faithful Parsifal, ordered all reference to it excised from the official records of the High Command; it showed Hitler in an all too mortal posture—when the strain upon him grew too great, his nerves cracked and he lost his powers of reason.

Neither Luftwaffe nor submarines could carry munitions, reinforcements, or artillery to General Dietl in any quantity. Eleven Junkers 52 transport planes had landed on Lake Hartvig with the components of a mountain battery, but no sooner were the aircraft unloaded than the ice thawed and all eleven aircraft sank. With his own two thousand troops now augmented by the two thousand shipless sailors of the destroyer force, Dietl could not hold Narvik—the whole point of the Norwegian campaign—once the main British assault on the port began. Together with Göring, Hitler studied one plan after another for the relief of the Narvik force. It worried him that they were mostly Austrians, for he had not yet wanted to place such a burden on the Anschluss. By April 14, he was already talking to Brauchitsch of abandoning Narvik and concentrating all effort on the defense of Trondheim, threatened by the British beachhead at Namsos and now by the onset of a fresh invasion at Aandalsnes to the south. He planned to expand Trondheim into a strategic naval base that would make Britain's Singapore seem "child's play." Over the next few days, after repeated conferences with Göring, Milch, and Jeschonnek, he ordered the total destruction of Namsos and Aandalsnes, and of any other town or village in which British troops set foot, without regard for the civilian population. He frowned at his adjutants and said, "I know the British. I came up against them in the Great War. Where they once get a toehold there is no throwing them out again."

On the fourteenth, he had somehow gained the impression that the British had already landed at Narvik. He knew of no other solution than that Dietl should fight his way southward to Trondheim. Jodl scorned the idea. "Mein Führer, I have been there. An expedition there is like a Polar expedition!" Jodl knew and trusted Dietl; he also knew Narvik, and he considered it quite possible to defend it for a long time with meager resources. But Hitler had no intention of wasting more aircraft in supplying Dietl. He announced Dietl's promotion to lieutenant general and at the same time dictated to Keitel a message ordering Dietl to evacuate Narvik forthwith. The British would now take Narvik unopposed; that Sweden would defend her iron-ore fields, as Göring believed, seemed to Hitler unlikely. Jodl wrote in his diary: "The hysteria is frightful." His deputy later recalled that when Hitler was not loudly giving vent to irrelevant suggestions, he sat glowering in one corner of Jodl's room. Hitler had acted like this once before, during a minor crisis over the capture of Warsaw. If he was plagued by nervous fits in a subsidiary campaign like this, it augured ill for "Yellow," which was to begin as soon as the Luftwaffe's paratroops and transport squadrons were released from their commitment in Norway. Jodl's staff was scandalized by the Führer's lack of comportment in these days.

In fact Hitler's radio message to Dietl was never sent. It reached the OKW offices at Bendlerstrasse, and at 10:40 A.M. on the morning of April 15 it was back in Jodl's room, in the quivering hands of his army staff officer, Colonel Bernhard von Lossberg. Lossberg angrily refused to send out such a message—it was the product of a nervous crisis "unparalleled since the darkest days of the Battle of the Marne in 1914." The whole point of the Norwegian campaign had been to safeguard Germany's iron-ore supplies. Was Narvik now to be relinquished to the British without a fight? Jodl quietly advised him that this was the personal desire of the Führer. Keitel turned his back on Lossberg and left the room. With Jodl's permission, Lossberg visited the Commander in Chief of the army and urgently begged him to talk Hitler around, but Brauchitsch curtly refused. "I have nothing whatever to do with the Norwegian campaign. Falkenhorst and Dietl are answerable to Hitler alone, and I have not the least intention of going of my own free will to that clip joint," meaning the Reich Chancellery. However, the colonel craftily persuaded Brauchitsch to sign another message to Dietl, one congratulating him on his promotion and ending: "I am sure you will defend your position, which is so vital to Germany, to the last man." Lossberg handed this text to Jodl and tore up Keitel's handwritten Führer Order before their eyes. Thus ended one day of the Narvik crisis.

It is clear Hitler feared the blow that the loss of Narvik would inflict on his prestige. Now Jodl began to assert his authority as strategic adviser. He openly rejected Hitler's muttered reproaches against the army and navy operations. When Hitler drew ugly comparisons between the scuttling of the disabled destroyers at Narvik and the ignominious end of the *Graf Spee,* Jodl pointed out that when a warship has no fuel and has expended her last ammunition she has no choice if she is to avoid capture. As each day of this Narvik crisis passed, Jodl's voice was raised with more assurance. Eventually the Allies had landed some twelve thousand British, French, and Polish troops to confront Dietl's lesser force. Jodl remained unimpressed; and when Hitler again began talking of abandoning Narvik, he lost his temper and stalked out of the Cabinet Room, slamming the door behind him with a noise that echoed around the Chancellery building.

Upon reflection, however, Jodl decided that his faith in Hitler had not been misplaced. Had not precisely the same despondency smitten Frederick the Great at the battle of Mollwitz two hundred years before? When that battle had turned against the great Prussian monarch, he had taken flight with his cavalry. And hadn't it been Schwerin and his infantry who had saved the day without him?

Jodl expressed his opposition to Hitler's policy of despair with the advice: "You should not give up anything until it is really *lost.* " Throughout the seventeenth the argument raged back and forth between them. Hitler had already drafted a radio message ordering Dietl to withdraw. "There must be some way out!" he exclaimed, leaning over the chart of Norway. "We cannot just abandon those troops." Jodl retorted in his earthy Bavarian accent, "Mein Führer, in every war there are times when the Supreme Commander must keep his nerve!" Between each word, he rapped his knuckles on the chart table so loudly that they were white afterward.

The psychological effect of this drama on Hitler was interesting. He composed himself and with deliberate controlled evenness replied, "What would you advise?" Thereupon Jodl showed him an appreciation by his staff, appended to which was a draft directive to Dietl to hold out and contain enemy forces there as long as possible. That evening Hitler signed the order; but he made it abundantly clear in a preamble that he thought the whole northern position was bound to be overwhelmed by the Allies eventually, since all the odds were against Dietl and his four thousand ill-armed men. It was not one of his more felicitously worded messages.

His fifty-first birthday passed without noticeable public enthusiasm. When Alfred Rosenberg presented him with a large porcelain bust of Frederick the Great, tears welled up in the Führer's eyes. "When you see him," he said, "you realize how puny are the decisions we have to make compared with those confronting him. He had nothing like the military strength we command today!"

But military strength, if mindlessly applied, often proves counterproductive. In Norway, Falkenhorst had begun draconian reprisals to quell the incidence of sabotage. Hostages were taken. Göring mentioned during an audience with Hitler that a mass resistance movement in Norway was growing. By late on April 18 it was clear that earlier attempts at kid-glove tactics had failed. On that day, the fugitive Norwegian government declared itself at war with Germany. All diplomatic talks ceased, and Hitler told his staff that from now on brute force was the only answer. At the war conference he announced his intention of transferring executive authority to Falkenhorst; the tough young Gauleiter of Essen, Josef Terboven, would be appointed Reich Commissioner for Norway, answerable only to the Führer himself. Keitel—rightly fearing that Norway was now to suffer as Poland was already suffering—raised immediate objections. When Hitler's only reply was to snub the OKW chief, Keitel took a leaf from Jodl's book and stormed out of the conference chamber. Afterward he privately cornered Hitler and warned that friction was bound to arise between Terboven and the military commander. Nevertheless, by that evening Terboven was already at the Chancellery; the next day saw him ensconced in private with Hitler, Himmler, and Martin Bormann; and on April 21, Terboven and his staff were en route for Oslo and ready to introduce a reign of terror to the Norwegian people.

Again Hitler was plagued by sleepless nights. What was the true situation in Norway? If the Luftwaffe generals were to be believed, Falkenhorst was in despair and already giving up Trondheim as lost. During the day, the trickle of information reaching the Chancellery along the one scrambler-telephone link between Oslo and Berlin was never enough to quench Hitler's thirst for detail. He sent one officer after another by special plane to Norway to report to him on the progress of his two divisions of infantry struggling to bridge the three hundred miles between Oslo and Trondheim.

On April 22, he sent his own adjutant, Schmundt, by plane to Oslo with Jodl's army staff officer, Colonel von Lossberg. Lossberg—a towering figure with a game leg and a fearless nature—reported back to Hitler the next evening after a hazardous flight. So struck was he by the contrast between the confident resolution he had found at Falkenhorst's Oslo headquarters and the air of dejection in the Chancellery, that he apparently forgot himself; when the downcast Führer asked in what strength the British had now landed at Namsos and Aandalsnes, he exclaimed, "Five thousand men at most, mein Führer!" This, to Hitler, was a disaster, but the colonel briskly interrupted him: "*Jawohl,* mein Führer, *only* five thousand men. Falkenhorst controls all the key points, so he could finish off the enemy even if they were far stronger. We must rejoice over every Englishman sent to Norway rather than to meet us in the west on the Meuse." When Hitler emphasized that the army must move reinforcements to Falkenhorst, Lossberg recommended that he leave matters in Falkenhorst's hands. Germany needed every division it could retain in the west for "Yellow." Hitler allowed Lossberg to lecture him no longer on elementary tactics. Perhaps the ill-concealed sarcasm the colonel had voiced over Hitler's panicky and pernickety command methods from the Chancellery had found their mark. Lossberg was curtly dismissed from the conference chamber, and for weeks afterward he was not allowed into the Führer's presence.

On the chart table, Lossberg had left behind him a small sheaf of recently captured British military documents which he had brought with him from Oslo. On the following day this little dossier was greatly augmented by additional British documents, which arrived from Oslo with one of Jodl's officers. A British infantry brigade fighting south of Aandalsnes had been put to flight by the advancing Germans, and important files captured. The immense political importance of the find sank in overnight: the brigade commander, in private life a London soap manufacturer, had previously been briefed on the plan to capture Stavanger—long before the German invasion of Norway. The British orders were dated April 2, 6, and 7! Other British landing operations had been planned at Bergen, Trondheim, and Narvik. The German operation had cut right across the British scheme, and the troop transports, which had actually been sighted by the Luftwaffe on April 9, had been recalled to port to enable the navy to engage the German fleet. These documents, in conjunction with files seized from French and British consulates in Norway, showed the whole history, dating back to January, of the Allied plan to invade Norway. It was equally clear that certain Norwegian leaders were determined the Allied operation should not be resisted.

Hitler was overjoyed. He had taken much booty since his invasion began, including a million tons of shipping in Norwegian ports, but this haul of secret Allied documents was the stroke of real luck he had been waiting for. He personally mapped out the propaganda campaign to exploit them; until the small hours of the morning, he, Schmundt, and Jodl checked over the White Book the foreign ministry was preparing. The hasty publication contained document facsimiles, translations, and statements of British officers as to the documents' authenticity. Hitler himself met and talked to the British prisoners brought to Berlin from Norway.[4] At midday on the twenty-seventh, Ribbentrop distributed the damning publication to the assembled foreign diplomats in the main Chancellery building. That afternoon, he broadcast a lengthly tirade that was heard worldwide, from North America to the Russias; in it he emphasized the cant and humbug of British assurances to the little neutrals.

The speech was due to begin at 2:30 P.M., and Hitler made it one of the rare occasions when he himself listened to the radio. Ribbentrop as usual kept his huge audience waiting several minutes before he began, and Rosenberg, the minister's archenemy, slyly observed to Hitler: "Not a very punctual start!" Hitler waved his hand in a characteristic gesture and laughed. "The foreign minister is always too late." (Once Ribbentrop had kept him waiting for several minutes before deigning to come to the telephone; Hitler had recommended that he not repeat this threadbare tactic with him again.)

There was no denying the effect Ribbentrop's White Book on the Norwegian documents had on world opinion. Well might Hitler ask, Who now dares condemn me for assailing Belgium and Holland if the Allies care so little for small states' neutrality themselves? At all events, on the very day the captured documents were released to the world, April 27, 1940, Hitler secretly announced to his staff the decision over which he had wavered these many months. He would launch "Yellow" in the first week of May.

To open the assault in the west, Hitler had marshaled 137 divisions, with over 2,400 tanks and 3,800 aircraft at their command; yet even so he was facing a numerically superior enemy. His Intelligence agencies had pinpointed the position of 100 French divisions and 11 more divisions from the British Expeditionary Force; the Belgians had raised 23 divisions, and the Dutch 13. Added to this total

---

[4]One of Halder's staff wrote at this time about the British army's problems: "And what military dilettantes they are is clear from the volumes of written material found on a British brigade commander in Norway. It is very valuable to us. . . . The first British prisoners were flown to Berlin, shown to the Führer, wined and dined, and driven around Berlin for four hours. They just could not understand how things can look so normal here and that the public is not being fed from soup kitchens. They are staggered to see the shops open and people in the streets. Above all they were in perpetual fear of being shot: that's what they had been tricked into believing." Hearing a few days later that Polish prisoners had attacked the new British arrivals, Hitler asked that next time photographers should be present to capture the scene of supposed allies at one another's throats.

of 147 divisions were 20 more holding the fortifications. The French had committed only 7 divisions, plus 3 fortification divisions—immobile units capable only of defense—to their frontier with Italy. In short, instead of launching his offensive with the traditional superiority of numbers, Hitler's army had the odds against it. Superior morale, tactics, and weaponry would have to make up for this deficiency. The weather for the Luftwaffe must be perfect from the first moment.

Hitler did not doubt the outcome of the forthcoming passage of arms. He would command this campaign himself, and by rapid initiative and superior strategy he would annihilate the enemy, whose "bureaucracy and hidebound tactics" had already proven their undoing in Norway. Jodl was years later to write: "Only the Führer could sweep aside the hackneyed military notions of the General Staff and conceive a grand plan in all its elements—a people's inner willingness to fight, the uses of propaganda, and the like. It was this that revealed not the analytic mind of the staff officer or military expert in Hitler, but the grand strategist." On the eve of the assault on France and the Low Countries, Hitler was to proclaim to his assembled staff, "Gentlemen: you are about to witness the most famous victory in history!" Few viewed the immediate future as sanguinely as he.

Now the real pressure was on. On April 29, Hitler ordered the Luftwaffe to stand by to open "Yellow" on May 5; on April 30, he ordered the entire Wehrmacht to be ready to launch "Yellow" at twenty-four hours' notice from the fifth. That day, General Jodl had confirmed to him that in Norway the German forces that had set out weeks before from Trondheim and Oslo had now linked; the Führer was delirious with joy. "That is more than a battle won, it is an entire campaign!" he exclaimed. Before his eyes he could already see the autobahn he would build to Trondheim. The Norwegian people deserved it. How utterly they differed from the Poles! Norwegian doctors and nurses had tended the injured until they dropped with exhaustion; the Polish "subhumans" had jabbed their eyes out. Moved by this comparison, on May 9, Hitler was to give his military commander in Norway an order which began as follows:

> . . . In the course of the campaign in the east German soldiers who had the misfortune to fall injured or uninjured into Polish hands were usually brutally ill-treated or massacred. By way of contrast, it must be said of the Norwegian army that not one single such incident of the debasement of warfare has occurred.
>
> The Norwegian soldier spurned all the cowardly and deceitful methods common to the Poles. He fought with open visor and honorably, and he tended our prisoners and injured properly and to the best of his ability. The civilian population acted similarly. Nowhere did they join in the fighting, and they did all they could for the welfare of our casualties.
>
> I have therefore decided in appreciation for this to authorize the liberation of the Norwegian soldiers we took prisoner. Only the professional soldiers will

have to remain in captivity until such time as the former Norwegian government withdraws its call to arms against Germany, or individual officers and men give their formal word not to take part under any circumstances in further hostilities against Germany.

The Allies had evacuated their forces from Namsos and Aandalsnes at the beginning of May, leaving only the twelve thousand troops landed at Narvik to continue the fight. The British press admitted frankly that the defeat in Norway was having a disastrous effect on public opinion. When the British submarine *Seal* showed the white flag and surrendered to a German naval aircraft on May 5, the naval staff saw it as a "sad sign of Britain's lack of resolution and readiness."

Hitler assembled his staff for a last run of secret conferences on the details of "Yellow": everybody was now standing by—the glider and parachute troops who were to seize bridges, forts, and key points in Holland and Belgium; the disguised "Dutch policemen"; the emissary who was to present to the queen of Holland a demand that the Dutch proffer no resistance; the little scout force of radio vehicles detailed by Jodl to report directly to him on the operation against the bridges and Fort Eben Emael; and two million men. The weather forecasts were of crucial importance; the Luftwaffe's chief meteorologist sweated blood over the burden of responsibility he alone now carried. On May 3, Hitler postponed "Yellow" on his advice by one day, to Monday. On the fourth he again postponed it, to Tuesday. On Sunday the fifth the forecast was still uncertain, so "Yellow" was set down for Wednesday the eighth. On this deadline Hitler was determined: he ordered a special timetable printed for his headquarters staff as part of the elaborate camouflage of his real intentions. The timetable showed his train departing from a little station near Berlin late on May 7 and arriving next day in Hamburg en route for "an official visit to Oslo."

Hitler would not brook weather delays any longer. At the end of April the SS obtained the transcript of a telephone conversation between the prime ministers of Britain and France, indicating that they were planning an operation themselves. Hitler later mentioned this as his reason for fearing that "at any moment the Allies might march into Holland and Belgium" (in fact the two prime ministers were discussing a French air attack on Russia's oil fields). But the Luftwaffe's meteorologist was adamant, in conference with Hitler on May 7, that there was still a strong risk of morning fog; so Hitler again postponed "Yellow" by one day.

Hitler was even more alarmed by what the Allies might now learn of *his* plans. On May 7, the Forschungsamt showed him two coded telegrams the Belgian ambassador to the Vatican had just sent to his government: a German citizen who had arrived in Rome on April 29 had warned that Hitler was about to attack Belgium and Holland. The Abwehr was ordered to search out the informant—

a supreme irony as the SS was to realize four years later, for the culprit was a minor member of Canaris's Abwehr network.[5] In any case, the fat was in the fire. At 5 P.M. Dutch radio announced that all leave was canceled, and by early on the eighth Holland was in a state of siege. Telephone links with foreign countries were cut, members of Anton Mussert's pro-Nazi movement in the Dutch forces were arrested, cities began evacuation measures, the government district of The Hague was cordoned off, and—most irritating of all for Hitler—the guard on important bridges was increased. Hitler wanted to wait no longer, but Göring kept his nerve and promised that although there was still fog in the morning, the weather was improving daily: May 10 would be ideal. Hitler was torn between the counsels of his experts and the whispering voice of his intuition. Against all his instincts he reluctantly agreed to postpone "Yellow" to May 10, "but not one day after that."

Early on the ninth Puttkamer, the duty adjutant, telephoned one of the westernmost corps headquarters, at Aachen; the Chief of Staff there told him there was some mist, but the sun was already breaking through and tomorrow would probably be as fine. When the naval adjutant repeated this to Hitler, he announced, "Good. Then we can begin." The service commands were informed that the final orders to attack or postpone (code words "Danzig" and "Augsburg," respectively) would be issued by 9:30 P.M. at the latest.

Extraordinary security precautions were taken, even within Hitler's own staff. Martin Bormann was left in the belief that they were to visit Oslo, and the Party authorities there made great plans to welcome the Führer. Hitler instructed his female secretaries to pack their bags for a long journey, and when these innocents asked Julius Schaub "How long?" he replied with an air of mystery, "It might be a week, it might be two. It could be a month or even years!" In fact, even Schaub, Hitler's long time intimate, did not know. During the afternoon Hitler and his staff drove out of Berlin, heading north toward Staaken airfield. But the column of cars bypassed Staaken and went to the small railroad station at Finkenkrug, a popular excursion spot. Here Hitler's special train was waiting for them. It left at 4:38 P.M., heading north toward Hamburg; but after dusk fell, it pulled into the little country station of Hagenow. When it set off again, even the uninitiated could tell it was no longer heading north. At about nine o'clock it

[5]This was Dr. Joseph Müller, a Catholic lawyer, who later became the postwar Bavarian minister of justice. Colonel Oster also repeated his earlier acts of subversion by giving the Dutch military attaché a running commentary on each postponement of "Yellow" and the final definitive warning at 9 P.M. on the very eve of the offensive. His complicated motives can be summarized thus: recognizing Hitler's immense popular support by 1940, Oster desired to inflict on him such a military defeat that a coup against him would stand a better chance; he also desired the Allies to take him seriously as a negotiating partner. The Dutch military commander considered him "a pitiful specimen."

halted outside Hanover; the telephones were linked up, and the latest weather forecast was obtained from Luftwaffe headquarters near Potsdam. It was still good. Hitler ordered the code word "Danzig" issued to the commands.

Still the secret was closely kept. Over dinner Schmundt asked the secretaries nonchalantly, "Have you got your Sick-Sick tablets?" After a while Hitler joked, "If you behave yourselves, you can all take home sealskins as souvenirs." He retired early to his sleeping quarters, but the movement of the train and his apprehensions kept him from sleeping. Hour after hour he gazed out of the carriage window, watching for the first telltale signs of fog shrouds forming. The initial success of "Yellow" depended on the Luftwaffe's striking force, and fog was Göring's worst enemy.

An hour before dawn, at 4:25 A.M., the train glided into a small station from which all the name indications had been removed—it was Euskirchen, thirty miles from the Allied lines. A column of the three-axled field limousines that had served Hitler so well in Poland was awaiting him in the semidarkness. For half an hour he and his entourage drove through the little Eiffel villages, in which the signposts had been replaced by stark yellow plates with various military symbols on them. Hitler broke the silence only once. Turning to Major von Below, the Luftwaffe adjutant sitting with Schaub on the jump seats of his car, he asked, "Has the Luftwaffe taken into account that here in the west the sun rises several minutes later than in Berlin?" Below set his mind at rest.

After a while the country lanes began to climb a hill through scattered woods. When his limousine stopped, Hitler clambered stiffly out. A former antiaircraft position on the side of a hill had been converted and strengthened to serve as his field headquarters. The nearest village had been completely evacuated, and would serve for his lesser staff. It was already daylight. The air was filled with the sound of birds heralding the arrival of another dawn. Hitler stood outside his bunker, watching the sun slowly bring color to the countryside. This was to be the first real day of spring weather. From the two main roads in the valleys on each side of this hill they could hear the heavy rumble of convoys of trucks heading westward. An adjutant pointed wordlessly to his watch: it was 5:35 A.M. Far away they could hear the growing clamor of heavy artillery begin, and from behind them swelled a thunder of aircraft engines as the Luftwaffe fighter and bomber squadrons approached.

PART 2

"WAR OF LIBERATION"

The Warlord at the Western Front

On May 10, 1940, the *Völkischer Beobachter*—chief organ of the Nazi party—rolled off the presses in Berlin, Munich, and Vienna with red banner headlines: GERMANY'S DECISIVE STRUGGLE HAS BEGUN! and THE FUHRER AT THE WESTERN FRONT. After half an hour's tough arguing, Keitel had persuaded Hitler to allow the OKW communiqué to end with the announcement that he himself had gone to the western front to take command. Hitler was loath to steal his generals' thunder, but the OKW generals, fresh from their command triumph in Norway, wanted to keep the army's General Staff firmly in its secondary place. Hitler's prestige was high. General Erwin Rommel—now commanding a panzer division in the west—had in a letter on April 21 written a private eulogy of the Führer's victory over Denmark and Norway. "*Ja,* if we didn't have the Führer! Who knows whether any other German exists with such a genius for military leadership and such a matching mastery of political leadership too!"

Hitler had patiently gone over every aspect of "Yellow" with the leading generals—with Walther Reichenau, Günther von Kluge, and the panzer general Ewald von Kleist, whose tanks would spearhead the thrust to the English Channel, and with General Ernst Busch, whose Sixteenth Army would string out a powerful flank defense south of the armored thrust. Hitler found high praise for the meticulous logistics work of Kleist's Chief of Staff, General Kurt Zeitzler.

Just as he was godfather to the strategy underlying "Yellow," so Hitler was the progenitor of the special raids which opened the campaign—the "Trojan horse" trick used to seize the Dutch bridges, the paratroop raids against Rotterdam and the Moordijk bridge in "Fortress Holland," and above all the glider landings on the key bridges in Belgium and on the daunting fortress-site at Eben Emael. "Suffice to say this," was the appraisal of one of Jodl's staff in September, "this operation against the bridges was *the* factor that would determine whether the Sixth Army could advance or not. That it came off was thanks to the Führer alone, as regards both the decision itself and the preparation."

As a military commander, Adolf Hitler remained an enigma even to his closest associates. They admired him for his past achievements for Germany but still feared for the future. In victory his generals worshipped him; but those whom he rejected turned sour, abominated him, and eventually conspired against him. The depth of hatred he stirred in the souls of these intelligent outcasts can be read in the countless essays they composed in vain endeavors to synthesize and express their memories. Alfred Jodl, perhaps his most able strategic adviser, was to write from a prison cell that he still kept asking himself whether he had really known the man at whose side he had led such a thorny and self-denying existence. "I keep making the same mistake: I blame his humble origins. But then I remember how many peasants' sons were blessed by History with the name The Great." And General Zeitzler—one of Hitler's last chiefs of the General Staff—also grappled in vain with this phenomenon, though more analytically. "I witnessed Hitler in every conceivable circumstance—in times of fortune and misfortune, of victory and defeat, in good cheer and in angry outburst, during speeches and conferences, surrounded by thousands, by a mere handful, or quite alone, speaking on the telephone, sitting in his bunker, in his car, in his plane; in brief on every conceivable occasion. Even so, I can't claim to have seen into his soul or perceived what he was after."

Zeitzler saw him as an actor, with every word, gesture, and grimace under control, his penetrating stare practiced for hours before some private mirror. He won over newcomers from the first handshake and piercing look, and paradoxically appeared the very embodiment of the strong and fearless leader, of honesty and open heart. He cultivated the impression that he cared deeply for his subordinates' well-being. He would telephone a departing general at midnight: "Please don't fly. It's such foul weather and I'm worried about your safety." Or he would look a minor official in the eye and explain, "Now I'm telling you this privately, and you must keep it strictly under your hat."

The surviving records are full of examples of the congenial impression Hitler made on others. Rommel proudly wrote on June 3: "The Führer's visit was fabulous. He greeted me with the words, 'Rommel! We were all so worried about you during the attack!' He was beaming from one ear to the other, and asked me to walk with him afterward—I was the only division commander there." Milch wrote down Hitler's words to him on April 21, 1941, after a particularly hazardous return flight from North Africa: "Thank goodness you got back!" In June 1941 Albert Speer's office chronicle noted: "The Führer sent a telephone message from the Obersalzberg begging Herr Speer to drop the proposed visit to Norway, as things are too uncertain up there and Herr Speer is indispensable to him." In February 1943 Field Marshal Wolfram von Richthofen wrote in his diary: "Finally the Führer inquired very anxiously about my health." In midwar would halt urgent conferences with hungry generals for half an hour to a.. stenographers to eat. One wrote in his diary on February 20, 1943: "The midday conference was short—57 minutes—but cold. The Führer must have noticed that we were freezing, because he mentioned it to us. I said that if you sit still a long time you do get cold. The Führer . . . then promised a heater for us. I replied, 'That would be very nice, mein Führer!' " And next day: "At the noon conference the heater promised by the Führer is indeed there—a small china stove. . . . In the afternoon, before a brief reception of seven officers handpicked for special missions for which the Führer briefs them in a short speech, he inquired in General Schmundt's presence whether the stove was warm enough for us. When we said it was, he was hugely pleased and laughed out loud."

His assessment of character was instant and deadly. A member of Jodl's staff, Captain Ivo-Thilo von Trotha, who was often present at Hitler's supper table during the French campaign, wrote in 1946: "My impression was that the Führer clearly recognized the human weaknesses of his colleagues and stood aloof from them." Hitler knew precisely how far he could go with each general. Once he snatched a document from Keitel's hands and threw it on the floor. Keitel meekly gathered it up. Hitler judged newcomers after only a glance. Of one army commander he sourly commented, "He looks like a schoolteacher!"—and since for him every teacher was a *"Steisstrommler,"* or buttock-thrasher, that general's career was clearly at an end. But his staff abounded with misfits—like his personal adjutant, the crippled nonentity Julius Schaub—whose value was in their undivided loyalty to him.

Of his gifts as a leader, even a military leader, there is no doubt. Halder was to refer to his unusual intellect and grasp, his imaginativeness, his tenacity and willpower. Jodl wrote that in the French campaign Hitler's leadership was clear, consistent, and capable; here Hitler was to prove himself a "classical commander." Jodl considered that in drafting the terms of the armistice with fallen France, Hitler ostensibly showed a generosity that gave cause to hope that of the two warring impulses within him it was the better that was gaining ground.

By decades of planned reading, Hitler had soaked up a huge amount of technical and military learning. His memory was proverbial. He had not only read the works of Frederick the Great, Moltke, Schlieffen, and Clausewitz, he could confound his generals with quotations from memory. What he lacked was the ability to assess and analyze a military situation logically, unhurriedly, and calmly —as a staff officer would have; in that respect he was still the World War I corporal who had no mastery of the time and space problems involved in the deployment of great armies. In the French campaign he was to prove as timid and cautious in the conduct of operations as he had been bold, almost brash, in designing them; in later campaigns he asserted himself to the other extreme. The classical Führer Directive, in which his commanders were given a broad mission and left to their own discretion in carrying it out, was increasingly supplemented and supplanted by Führer Orders, in which Hitler intervened in the tactical operations at every level. His victory in France confirmed him in his belief that he was a predestined military commander.

Hitler's headquarters for "Yellow" were at Münstereifel. The underground command post was very cramped. Alone in his room, with its folding bed, table, and chair, he could hear every sound made by Keitel and Jodl next door. Jodl's operations staff was billeted down in the village and worked in a wooden encampment hidden three miles away in the woods. Hitler toured it briefly one day—the only time he ever set foot inside Security Zone II. He preferred to hold his war conferences in the open air, for the spring landscape enchanted him. He privately suggested to his staff that when the war was over they should all return each year—just this little select group around him now—to Münstereifel, "my bird paradise." The site remained unchanged until 1944, with even the names of the occupants left painted on the doors; it had been intended as a permanent memorial to Hitler's "war of liberation."

As the Luftwaffe predicted, May 10, 1940, dawned fine. He rewarded the meteorologist responsible for the brilliant forecasting with a gold watch. During the night, his Luftwaffe had already begun mining the Belgian and Dutch ports. Now Göring struck simultaneously at seventy airfields, destroying between three and four hundred planes, and thus seizing for Hitler an air superiority that was to remain unchallenged for the next two weeks. Soon messengers brought him the exhilarating news that the British and French armies had begun pouring into Belgium. In October 1941, his armies now before Moscow, Hitler still remembered the thrill of that moment. "When the news came that the enemy was advancing along the whole front I could have wept for joy! They'd fallen right into my trap! It was a crafty move on our part to strike toward Liège—we had to make them believe we were remaining faithful to the old Schlieffen Plan. . . . How exciting it will be later to go over all those operations once again. Several times during the night I used to go to the operations room to pore over those relief maps."

The Belgians and Dutch were not unprepared. The Forschungsamt had intercepted a last frantic telephone warning from the Dutch military attaché to his government the previous evening, but the delicate "Trojan horse" operations went ahead—a calculated risk, in view of the enemy's foreknowledge. As one of Jodl's staff noted: "Our troops were storming an enemy who was ready and waiting for our attack to begin early on May 10." The Dutch government had cannily refused an entry visa to Major Kiewitz, Hitler's special emissary to Queen Wilhelmina. Ironically it was Canaris's Abwehr that was appointed to find out how the Dutch suspicions had been aroused; the Abwehr adroitly diverted suspicion to a senior foreign ministry official.

Extreme anxiety reigned at Hitler's headquarters as word of the vital commando-operations was awaited. One of Jodl's officers was accompanying the first wave of tanks invading Holland and Belgium with a radio truck, to report direct to Hitler on the state of the bridges over the Meuse and the Albert Canal. Between 9 and 10 A.M. the first three coded signals arrived from this officer, Captain von Trotha: the Dutch had evidently managed to blow up both bridges across the Meuse north and south of Maastricht; the railway bridge farther north had also been blown up, but was now in German hands; the Abwehr's Special Battalion 100, the "Trojan horse," had suffered fearful casualties.

But in the afternoon Trotha had better news: the Belgian bridges across the Albert Canal—where a hundred troops had silently landed in gliders as dawn broke—were intact, except for one at Canne. A Belgian infantry division close by had as yet done nothing to mop up this diminutive German holding force. By 4:30 P.M., Hitler learned that the 4th Panzer Division had actually forded the Meuse, leaving its armor temporarily behind, and was pouring into the two bridgeheads seized across the Albert Canal. At Eben Emael a band of intrepid German engineer troops armed with hollow-charge explosives had landed by glider and immobilized the entire fortress: the underground gun-crews were sealed in, their artillery was knocked out. By early next morning, May 11, a temporary bridge had been thrown across the Meuse at Maastricht, and an armored brigade had crossed. The 4th Panzer Division now spearheaded the advance of Reichenau's Sixth Army. Eben Emael capitulated at midday, and with this, Belgium's fate was effectively sealed.

In the evening, Captain von Trotha brought to Hitler the first impressions of the front line. On the approaches to Maastricht the German armor had encountered little resistance; the frontier forces had thrown their weapons away and fled by bicycle. The Dutch population had stood curiously watching the tanks and infantry pass. The people were friendly, Trotha reported; some of them gave the Hitler salute, others willingly helped the invaders on their way with directions stuttered in Dutch or broken German. As Trotha had entered Maastricht in his armored radio vehicle, two colossal detonations, shattering millions of windows, had heralded the demolition of the bridges. A stolid Dutch citizen had espied his red-striped General Staff trousers and besought advice: he had left home and crossed the bridge, hatless, just to fetch milk—how was he to get back? Trotha had replied the Germans also regretted that the bridge was down, but that all complaints were to be addressed to the Dutch military authorities. "I was opposed to it from the start," said the Dutchman. Trotha replied, "Well you must just wait until our troops have finished crossing." The Dutchman asked how long that would be. "We will try and get everybody across by the time the war ends," joked the army officer. "But what will my wife think?" "I expect the people over there will also learn in time that the war has come," responded Trotha. In fact, by afternoon the Germans were already ferrying Dutch citizens from one side of the river to the other.

In southern Holland the German troops had found the Dutch garrisons of towns and villages standing idly around without their guns or gear and passively awaiting the invaders. But in the north a four-day battle raged as the Dutch tried to wipe out the paratroops and glider-borne infantry landed at Rotterdam and The Hague; bomber squadrons had already taken off to relieve the pressure on General Kurt Student's paratroops at Rotterdam when word arrived that the Dutch were capitulating. Only half the bombers could be recalled—the rest dropped nearly a hundred tons of bombs on the town; nine hundred people died in the subsequent fires. The next day Holland formally surrendered.

It was now time for Hitler's masterstroke.

Every indication until now had persuaded the enemy that the offensive through Belgium and Holland was the somewhat unoriginal linchpin of Hitler's strategy. For month's Canaris's organization had been feeding clues to that effect to the enemy, using every conceivable method from elegant women agents to "indiscreet" telephone conversations on lines known to be tapped by the enemy.

But Hitler's main offensive was to start far to the south, at Sedan, on the other side of the Ardennes, where General von Kleist's armor had just crossed the Meuse and established a bridgehead. On May 14, Hitler directed that all available panzer and mechanized divisions were to assemble for a rapid push from this bridgehead westward and then northwestward to the English Channel; that he should have issued a Führer Directive which merely repeated what had long been ordered was an augury of the extent to which he proposed to take command himself.

> The course of the operations so far shows that the enemy has not perceived the basic idea of our own operation, the eventual breakthrough by Army Group A [Rundstedt]. They are still moving up powerful forces to a line extending from Antwerp to Namur and apparently neglecting the sector confronting Army Group A.

Bock's Army Group B was given the task of luring as much of the enemy into Belgium as possible before Rundstedt's armor cut them off in the rear by driving to the Channel. Leeb's Army Group C had meanwhile so successfully simulated preparations for a frontal assault on the Maginot line that the French had hesitated to withdraw troops from the south until it was too late, for the Luftwaffe had destroyed the railway lines. Their path now flattened before them by the bombers of Richthofen's Eighth Air Corps, Kleist's armored units rolled out of the Sedan bridgehead toward the Channel coast.

From this moment on, only a resolute commander supported by outstanding military Intelligence could have saved France. General von Rundstedt, Germany's oldest active soldier, is said to have remarked that he would have found it much more interesting to fight the rest of the campaign in the shoes of France's Army Chief of Staff, General Maurice Gamelin. It was now clear that the cream of the Allied forces had mustered north of Kleist's advance and was penetrating Belgium. German army Intelligence had located a new French Seventh Army referred to explicitly as an *"armée d'intervention dans la Belgique."* Since the end of March, Halder's Intelligence branch, "Foreign Armies West," had consistently estimated that half the Anglo-French forces were in the north, waiting to be cut off.[1]

Again, as in the Norwegian campaign, Hitler's nerve briefly left him. He was wary of his own good fortune. When Brauchitsch made his regular twice-daily telephone call, Hitler nervously bombarded him with minutiae of which the army's thorough preparations had long taken care. As Kleist's armor swept onward toward the Channel coast, on May 17 Hitler intervened to order that they halt to allow the slower infantry divisions time to catch up and consolidate the flank before the French could penetrate it. Army Intelligence argued in vain that the French were presently concerned only with stabilizing their own defensive line along the Aisne and the Somme: radio Intelligence had found a new French army headquarters west of Verdun, and aerial reconnaissance showed that the French transport movements were purely defensive. Hitler would not be convinced. He drove to Rundstedt's headquarters, nervously studied the maps, and on his return to his own headquarters spread a wholly unnecessary gloom about the danger from the south. When Halder and Brauchitsch saw him the next day, he was raging that the army was about to ruin the whole campaign and that it was needlessly running the risk of defeat. On the nineteenth Hitler had fresh occasion for alarm when army Intelligence lost all sight of the three-quarters of a million Allied soldiers believed trapped in the north; for hours on end it seemed that the bulk of the British and French forces had succeeded in escaping southward after all. Not until May 20 was this first personal crisis over. The army reported that there were at least twenty enemy divisions trapped north of the Somme; in the evening, when Brauchitsch telephoned Hitler with the news that the tanks had reached Abbeville—and hence

---

[1]The Allied superiority in tanks was vast. The French and British had 3,432 tanks, not including either the obsolete Renault F.T. or the light British tanks. The Germans had started the campaign with 2,574 tanks, of which, however, 523 were the light Mark I, and 955, the hardly better Mark II. (Among the rest were 345 Mark IIIs, 278 Mark IVs, 106 Czech Mark 35, and 228 Czech Mark 38s.)

the Channel coast—Hitler was ecstatic with praise for the army and its commanders.

He spoke with such emotion that General Keitel made a written record of his words, which is, however, lost. According to Jodl, the Führer spoke of the peace treaty he would now make with France—he would demand the return of all the territories and properties robbed from the German people these last four hundred years, and he would repay the French for the ignominious terms inflicted on Germany in 1918 by now conducting the first peace negotiations at the same spot in the forest of Compiègne. As for the British: "The British can have their peace as soon as they return our colonies to us."

According to an officer who read Keitel's missing account, Hitler jubilantly predicted that this victory would at last right the wrongs done by the Peace of Westphalia which had concluded the Thirty Years' War and established France as the dominant power in Europe. To Keitel he exclaimed, "I must not forget how much I owe to Field Marshal von Blomberg at this moment! Without his help the Wehrmacht would never have become the magnificent instrument that has reaped us this unique victory!"

But it was this victory psychosis, prematurely sprung upon his military staff, this belief that total victory had been achieved by May 20, 1940, that was to prove his undoing at Dunkirk.

Hitler now turned his attention to long-range planning.

On May 20 he had already conferred with Brauchitsch and Halder on the outline of the second phase of the campaign, code-named "Red," in which German forces would sweep southward from the Somme and Aisne toward the lower Seine and the Swiss frontier. His earlier eagerness for Italian divisions to join in a mid-June offensive ("Brown") on the Upper Rhine front had evaporated. He wrote frequently to Mussolini with word of his latest victories, but Mussolini's replies were an uninspiring amalgam of polite applause and qualified promises of later belligerency. Indeed, an awkward disparity of aims was now emerging: for Italy the main enemy was now Britain, while Hitler believed that with France laid low he could oblige Britain to come to terms with him. There were disquieting rumors that Italy was preparing to invade Yugoslavia, which might set the whole of the Balkans on fire. An urgent question of priorities would have to be faced.

When Admiral Raeder privately disclosed to Hitler on the twenty-first that the admiralty had been studying the problems of a seaborne invasion of the British Isles since November, Hitler did not noticeably welcome this diligence; and when Jodl a few days later suggested that an immediate invasion be prepared, the Führer roundly rejected the idea without explaining why. We must conclude that he believed that submarine and bomber attacks would force Britain to submit, for he indicated that after France's defeat he would concentrate on the production of submarines and Junkers 88 bombers. He left Raeder at least in no doubt that he thought the war still far from over.

In one respect Russia's posture gave immediate cause for alarm, for it could instantly shut off Germany's Romanian oil supplies. Russia's main threat to Germany was still a distant one: from the slow rate at which airfield construction was progressing in the Russian-occupied border regions, it seemed clear that Germany still had a breathing space during which the Kremlin would continue to appease Hitler. Molotov had expressed Russia's genuine relief that Germany had managed to invade Norway before the Allies had, and he had received word of "Yellow" with equal sympathy; but this honeymoon would not last any longer than served the Russian purpose. Hitler probably believed that if he could attack the Soviet Union in the spring of 1941 he would thwart Stalin's intentions. How else is one to interpret the Führer's cryptic remark to Halder on April 24, 1940: "We have an interest in seeing to it that the [Romanian] oil fields keep supplying us until next spring at the least; after that we will be freer." Romania was now exporting over 130,000 tons of oil a month to Germany—nothing must endanger these oil fields or the countries through which the Danube and the railroad links brought that oil to Germany.

At the end of May 1940 the risk did become acute as rumors multiplied of Italian plans to attack Yugoslavia; this would free Hungary to attack Romania —from Forschungsamt intercepts of the Hungarian legation's cables from Berlin, the Germans knew how hollow were Hungary's declarations of solidarity with the Axis—and Russia would use this as a pretext to invade Romania as well. On May 20 the German military attaché in Moscow quoted to Berlin reliable details of Soviet troop concentrations on the Romanian frontier. Molotov denied them, but the facts spoke for themselves. Brauchitsch (unaware that Bessarabia, or Moldávia, had already been assigned to Stalin by the secret August 1939 pact) urged Hitler on the twenty-second to do something to curb these Russian ambitions; Hitler responded that he "hoped" to limit the Russian expansion to Bessarabia. Weizsäcker wrote a curious passage in his private diary on May 23: "Assuming there *is* a crushing victory in the west, the obvious next move would be to create order in the east as well, that will give breathing space and river frontiers—an order that will endure. Whether Britain submits at once or has to be bombed into her senses, the fact is there will probably have to be one more squaring of accounts in the east. . . ." In the event, Italy undertook not to attack Yugoslavia, and after a few days this eastern crisis subsided. But all this was symptomatic of the raw nerves constantly exposed in the Balkans, where Hitler's sole interest was the economic necessity of keeping the peace at all costs. Even at the height of battle, the absolute political leader must keep more than immediate military problems on his mind.

Many intricate and interrelated factors explain how the British Expeditionary Force (BEF) escaped from Dunkirk in the last days of May 1940, while German armor was pulled back on orders first from Rundstedt and then from Hitler himself.

The first factor, often overlooked in retrospective works of history, was that the realization that the British were deserting the field of battle en masse did not dawn on the German High Command until about May 26—a full week after the decision had been taken in London. The jealousy with which the war department (OKH) guarded its own affairs from OKW interference contributed to this. Halder's Foreign Armies West branch had certainly reported as early as May 21 that the unusual number of troop transports in Dunkirk and Boulogne might indicate that British troops were about to be evacuated; and the permanent radio link between the war office in London and the BEF in France, first monitored the next day, also suggested events were being removed from French control. But to Hitler all this was unthinkable. Had he not always warned that once the British got a toehold anywhere it was almost impossible to dislodge them? He was convinced that the British would fight to the last man in France and that he must deploy his forces accordingly. Not until May 26 was this fundamental error realized. German army Intelligence intercepted a radio message from the war office in London to the British commandant in Calais just after noon. "Every hour you continue to exist is of the greatest help to the BEF." Aerial reconnaissance had sighted thirteen warships and nine troop transports in Dunkirk harbor that morning. Foreign Armies West concluded: "It is probable that the embarkation of the British Expeditionary Force has begun." Only now did Hitler permit the armored advance on—though not into—Dunkirk to begin again. His artillery would finish the job.

The sequence of events which had resulted in the halting of the armor two days before had begun with a brief local crisis on May 21, when British and French tanks launched an unexpected attack on the inner flank of the German Fourth Army at Arras. Hitler and Rundstedt both regarded this as proof that the armored spearhead of Army Group A had advanced too fast for an effective flank defense to be established, and Rundstedt ordered the Fourth Army and Kleist's armored group to delay its advance on the Channel ports until the Arras crisis had been resolved. Brauchitsch and Halder regretted Rundstedt's overcautious conduct of Army Group A operations—bearing up on the Channel ports from the southwest—and without informing Hitler they ordered control of the Fourth Army transferred to General von Bock's Army Group B, which was advancing on the ports from the east. Bock was to command the last act of the encirclement. Hitler learned of this when he visited Rundstedt's headquarters at Charleville with Jodl and Schmundt the next morning, May 24. Thus an element of contrariness, a subconscious desire to spite Brauchitsch and the General Staff, must have contributed to Hitler's peremptory cancellation of their order: the Fourth Army was not to be transferred to Bock's command—for the time being it was to stay where it was. It was tactically foolhardy, claimed Hitler, to commit their tanks, which were vital to the success of "Red," in the swampy Flanders lowlands to which the war department would have sent them.

At Charleville, Hitler found every support for his views. Indeed, the previous day the Fourth Army's General von Kluge had himself persuaded Rundstedt it would be better not to attack on the twenty-fourth but to allow Kleist's armor time to regroup for a more methodical assault on the twenty-fifth. (With gross exaggeration, Kleist was claiming that half his tanks were out of action, and this figure must have worried Hitler.) Rundstedt's proposal to Hitler on May 24 went one stage further: his armor should remain where it was, commanding the high ridge along a line of canals west of Dunkirk, and give an appropriate welcome to the enemy forces swept westward by Bock's Army Group B; this would give the tanks a valuable respite. The possibility that the British might escape to England was not discussed. Hitler was obsessed by two visions: his precious armor floundering in the swampy Flanders fields that he, Keitel, and Jodl had all seen with their own eyes in World War I; or alternatively, his tanks being pointlessly shot to pieces in the streets of Dunkirk, as they had in fact been in the suburbs of Warsaw eight months before.

There was a political factor too. Hitler desired to spare Belgium's relatively friendly Flemish population the destruction of property this closing act of "Yellow" would entail.

At all events, Hitler did not hesitate to lend his authority to Rundstedt's decision to halt the tanks. How far he was also motivated by Göring's boast that the Luftwaffe alone would annihilate the encircled enemy is open to dispute. Göring certainly telephoned Hitler to this effect. Afterward, Hitler told his army adjutant that Göring would do the job, and he contrasted the Luftwaffe's ideological reliability with that of the army leaders. At twelve-thirty the Führer's headquarters telephoned the "halt order" to the army group and army commanders: they were to stand fast west of the canal line; that same day, in a directive giving guidelines for "Red" and the campaign against Britain, Hitler merely indicated in passing that the Luftwaffe's present job in the north was to break all resistance of the "encircled enemy" and prevent any British forces from escaping across the Channel. To a protesting staff member, Jodl soothingly said, "The war is won; it just has to be ended. There is no point in sacrificing a single tank if we can do it much more cheaply with the Luftwaffe."

Thus the tanks remained "rooted to the spot," as Halder bitterly commented in his diary on May 26. Hitler had still not set the tanks in motion. One more factor had arisen. On the evening of the twenty-fifth he explained to his adjutants that he particularly wanted the SS elite brigade under Sepp Dietrich to join in this crucial action at Dunkirk. His intention was to show the world that he had troops equal to the best even such a racially advanced nation as Britain could field against him. Heinrich Himmler—who conferred with Hitler that day on his radical plans for the eastern territories[2]—may well have asked this favor of Hitler, although his own agenda makes no explicit reference to the military operations. By May 26, Sepp Dietrich's Leibstandarte Adolf Hitler—Life Guards Brigade— was in position. On that morning, too, Rundstedt's staff changed their attitude, since radio monitoring suggested that their appreciation of the enemy's intentions was wrong. Colonel Henning von Tresckow, one of Rundstedt's staff, telephoned his friend Schmundt at Hitler's headquarters about this, with the result that at 1:30 P.M. Hitler informed Brauchitsch that the tanks might resume their eastward drive at once. They were to come within artillery range of Dunkirk, and the army's heavy artillery and the Luftwaffe would do the rest. But Kleist's tank drivers were now resting, or their tanks were being overhauled, and many hours would pass before the attack began.

Meanwhile the Luftwaffe could see that the British were apparently embarking only their troops, abandoning all their weapons and equipment as they fled. The beaches were thick with waiting Englishmen, the roads were choked with truck columns fifteen miles long. Göring landed at Hitler's headquarters in a light aircraft and boasted of the carnage his bombers were wreaking in Dunkirk harbor. "Only fishing boats are getting through. Let's hope the Tommies can swim!" The reality, however, was soon different: the Luftwaffe bombers were based largely on airfields back in Germany, and either their bombs were ineffective against small ships or they exploded harmlessly in the sand dunes; more ominously, the German bombers proved no match for the short-range British fighters based just across the Channel. The Germans found that for the first time the enemy had local air superiority, and their troubles were added to by the fact that at the end of May the Luftwaffe's Eighth Air Corps was grounded by fog for three days. In Dunkirk the British rearguard fought on with undiminished tenacity as the last British and French troops were embarked.

Göring failed to see the warning signs for his Luftwaffe, which Hitler had now ordered to open direct air attacks on the British Isles as soon as possible, beginning "with an annihilating attack in reprisal for the British raids on the Ruhr." The Luftwaffe commander confidently leaned his vast bulk across the map table in Hitler's headquarters, stabbed a finger at the map, and promised that when his planes began their attacks on London no stone would be left atop another.

———

[2]See page 123 below.

While these momentous events were transpiring in the west, in Germany's new eastern domains a ruthless program of subjugation and pacification had begun. "Yellow" distracted the world's press from what was going on.

On Sunday May 25, the Reichsführer SS outlined to Hitler and the head of his Chancellery, Lammers, proposals for dealing with the various racial strains in Poland, whether Poles, Jews, Ukrainians, White Russians, Gorals, Lemkes, or Kashubs. Himmler showed the Führer his six-page plan for screening the 23 million people in these new dominions for adults and children of sufficiently pure blood to allow their assimilation into Germany. He proposed that all other children should be taught only what he saw as the necessary rudiments: "Simple counting up to five hundred, how to write their names, and lessons on the divine commandant to obey the Germans and be honest, industrious, and well-behaved." It was unnecessary for them to learn to read. Racially acceptable children could be evacuated to the Reich to receive a proper education after separation from their parents. As Himmler pointed out, in what now seems a significant explanation when the plan's recipient is considered: "Each individual case may seem cruel and tragic, but this method is the mildest and best if we are to reject as ungermanic, impossible, and incompatible with our convictions the Bolshevik method of physically exterminating a race."

After a few years of this racial sifting, a low-grade potpourri of races would remain in the east. "This population will be available to Germany as a leaderless labor force, providing us with seasonal migratory labor for special projects like roadbuilding, quarrying, and construction work. They themselves will eat and live better than under Polish rule. And, given their own lack of culture, they will be well appointed to work under the strict, forthright, and just leadership of the German nation on its eternal cultural mission." As for the Jews, Himmler's six-page plan disclosed, "I hope to effect the complete disappearance of the Jew [from Europe] by means of a mass emigration of all Jews to Africa or some other such colony."[3]

Afterward, Himmler scribbled in his notebook: "Memorandum on Poland. Führer warmly approves." Hitler commanded Lammers to provide an oral briefing for Hans Frank, the Gauleiters, top SS officials, and police officials of the eastern provinces. Himmler stipulated that the document's contents must never be quoted in any orders that these men issued (an interesting embargo).

A month later, Himmler took the opportunity of a train journey with Hitler to show him an eight-page plan for settling these eastern provinces with strong

[3]After France's defeat, Hitler decided in July 1940 that Madagascar would make a suitable destination for Europe's Jews. See page 136.

German stock. It provided for one-eighth of the indigenous population to be transplanted as racially acceptable stock to Germany; the other seven-eighths would be displaced eastward, into Hans Frank's Generalgouvernement. To provide healthy German stock, Himmler proposed that after two years of military service or four years in the SS young unmarried German soldiers be induced to settle and work the land in the eastern provinces for up to eight years before marrying and taking over a farmstead or estate. The Generalgouvernement was to serve them as a reservoir of cheap labor. The foreign laborers were to be kept in serfdom; attempts at sexual relations with their German overlords would be punishable by death or heavy prison sentences. It was the lack of racial purity, Himmler argued, that had led to the downfall of the Greek and Roman empires. He afterward noted on the document: "Shown to the Führer in the train from Freiburg i.Br. to Ottersweiser on June 30, 1940. The Führer said that every point I made was right."

By that time, as we shall see, Hitler was already considering provinces far to the east of Poland.

There is much less to be learned from an examination of the military events of the rest of the French campaign. On May 28, the king of Belgium capitulated, and by June 2 the British evacuation of Dunkirk was over. German army Intelligence estimated that half the enemy forces had been swept from the battlefield; Brauchitsch telephoned this information to Hitler that evening. The German army, with 136 divisions, was virtually intact. It would embark on "Red," the final defeat of France, with a 2 to 1 superiority.

Events were fast pushing Europe's frontiers back to those of the sixteenth century. German bomber squadrons based in the Artois region and Flanders could keep the British Isles in check. But nothing was further from Hitler's mind than an invasion of Britain now. The great strategic option, between striking north or south after Dunkirk, was not recognized at the time. His blueprint for "Red" was largely determined by short-term psychological or political factors: Verdun must be captured as rapidly as possible. Overland contact must be made with Spain—a decoded cable had just revealed that Franco had assured Britain of his neutrality and lack of aggressive intentions against Gibraltar. Paris itself would be bypassed to the east and west, for Hitler feared nothing more than that an 1871-style Communist uprising in the capital might bring his forces into armed conflict with Soviet-backed Communists. The Maginot line would be taken from the rear. "Red" would begin at 5 A.M. on June 5.

Meanwhile, surrounded by Party officials and personal bodyguards, Hitler toured the battlefields in Belgium and Flanders. At the end of May the new Italian ambassador, Dino Alfieri,[4] had brought him Mussolini's offer to attack France's Alpine frontier on June 5. Since this might well lead world opinion to believe that it was this Italian "second front" and not "Red" that brought France down, Hitler asked the Duce to wait a few days. Even so, Italy's belated belligerency and her transparent self-interest aroused the anger of the generals to whom Hitler now revealed Mussolini's intentions in conferences at Brussels and Charleville on the first two days of June. At Brussels, where Bock had assembled his senior generals, Hitler explained his Dunkirk decisions: "Gentlemen, you will have wondered why I stopped the armored divisions outside Dunkirk. The fact was I could not afford to waste military effort. I was anxious lest the enemy launch an offensive from the Somme and wipe out the Fourth Army's weak armored force, perhaps even going so far as Dunkirk. Such a military rebuff," as he put it, "might have had intolerable effects in foreign policy. . . ." Afterward he drove with Army Group Commander von Bock in an open car through Brussels— which he had last seen as a Bavarian infantryman.

At Charleville the next day, June 2, he addressed Rundstedt and his generals, by chance in the villa which had once housed Kaiser Wilhelm II during World War I. He outlined "Operation Red" to them and informed them that Italy would shortly join in. He spoke of the reparations he proposed to exact from France; then his voice softened, and he once again extolled Britain and her mission for the white race. It was not, he said, a matter of inconsequence to him which power ruled India. One general wrote in his diary: "He points out that without a navy the equal of Britain's we could not hold on to her colonies for long. Thus we can easily find a basis for peace agreement with Britain. France on the other hand must be stamped into the ground, she must pay the bill." Another general wrote: "Hitler never drew the proper consequences from his admiration of the British; his threats against France revealed his boundless greed for conquest."

As he left the villa, crowds of cheering soldiers thronged his car. Hitler, every inch the victorious warlord, acknowledged their acclaim.

To Hitler the war seemed already won. He said as much to Admiral Canaris on June 3 when the Intelligence chief came to report on the Abwehr agents who had been killed in the campaign so far. And he repeated it to Admiral Raeder the next day. Within a few weeks France would be knocked out, and German industry could resume work on equipping the navy and Luftwaffe; he would demobilize large sections of the army to provide the industrial manpower. In the far north,

---

[4]The Forschungsamt had detected the anti-German utterances of his sixty-year-old predecessor, Bernardo Attolico, and Hitler had requested his recall.

the Allies suddenly abandoned their last foothold in Narvik, losing an aircraft carrier, two destroyers, and a troop transport in skirmishes with the diminished German battle fleet that chanced upon the scene; Hitler generously credited General Jodl alone with the decision to retain Narvik in mid-April, despite his own dark hours of despair for Dietl's survival. Jodl's position on Hitler's staff was henceforth unassailable.

Hitler's occupation policy in Holland and Belgium was to establish these Germanic states as border dependencies around a mighty German core. As early as November he had drafted a decree on the administration of the countries to be occupied in "Yellow." In the version he had signed on May 9 he had deleted the words "There is to be no exploitation of the occupied regions in a selfish German interest." In Holland as in Norway he established a Reich Commissar to fill the vacuum left by the fleeing monarchy; he chose an Austrian, Arthur Seyss-Inquart, evidently on Himmler's recommendation. Seyss-Inquart had felt ill at ease with his job in the Generalgouvernement and had pleaded for an army commission so he could serve Germany as he had in the previous war; but Hitler knew the lawyer had a crippled leg and gave him Holland to administer instead, ignoring the angry outcry this civilian appointment provoked in the army. On May 22 he explained that by appointing Reich commissars in Norway and Holland he hoped to remold these countries along National Socialist lines.

In Holland, as in Belgium, there had been embryonic Nazi organizations, but Hitler had little time for them. He regarded his own rise to power as unique and inimitable. He scorned Holland's Anton Mussert and Britain's Sir Oswald Mosley as plagiarists of his own ideas, and he discarded Quisling in all but form. Only for Belgium's Léon Degrelle did he have some respect, and he betrayed real anger when at one stage of the French campaign he was told—quite falsely—that Degrelle was among a large number of foreign Nazis shot by the French in May.

Since Belgium had fought honorably and capitulated unconditionally, Hitler was inclined to leniency. He agreed to Göring's heartfelt request—the Luftwaffe chief had telephoned Hitler the moment the Belgian capitulation was announced —that King Leopold be chivalrously treated. A senior statesman, Otto Meissner, was sent to tell the king that if Belgium now acted sensibly his kingdom might yet survive—otherwise Hitler would create a new Gau: "Flanders." A telegram in German army files indicates that King Leopold was furious at the looting and wilful destruction of his country by the withdrawing French and British troops, so Hitler's political wisdom in ordering his armies to spare the cities of Flanders from unnecessary visitations undoubtedly paid dividends. But here Hitler too appointed a German military governor: General Alexander von Falkenhausen was a liberal commander and maintained liaison with the king. There was in consequence little resistance to the Nazi presence in Belgium until Falkenhausen incurred Hitler's displeasure in 1944 and was replaced by a civilian, the Gauleiter of Cologne. Hitler retrieved for Germany the former German areas of Eupen, Malmedy, and Moresnet which had been annexed by Belgium in 1918; he ordered Brauchitsch to separate the Belgian prisoners of war into Flemings and Walloons —the former, 200,000 men of trusty Germanic stock, were to be released forthwith, while the latter, 150,000 less friendly prisoners, were to be held in continued pawn.

For "Red," the second half of the French campaign, Hitler's staff had found a new headquarters site in southern Belgium—in the deserted village of Brûly-de-Pêche in a forest clearing. Fritz Todt had rapidly erected three barrack buildings to house Hitler, a dining hall, and Jodl's staff; he had converted a church to house the rest. The whole headquarters, code-named "Forest Meadow," was ready with its antiaircraft batteries and barbed-wire entanglements by the time Hitler arrived on June 6.

He never felt as secure here as at Münstereifel. Perhaps it was the swarms of mosquitoes that rose from the dense undergrowth all around to plague him. Perhaps it was a general impatience to end the war. There was less for him to do during "Red"; Brauchitsch, who had phoned him regularly during "Yellow," now came in person. Hitler had mellowed toward him, and seems to have taken him more into his confidence about his future military plans. For a while Hitler abandoned his idea of discarding Brauchitsch—he could hardly do this to the Commander in Chief of a victorious army, as he mentioned to one adjutant. Ribbentrop was also a frequent visitor. After Dunkirk he asked Hitler whether he might draft some sort of peace plan for the British, but Hitler replied, "No, I shall do that myself. It will be only a very few points. The first point is that nothing must be done which would in any way injure Great Britain's prestige; secondly Britain must give us back one or two of our old colonies; and thirdly, we must reach a stable *modus vivendi* with Britain."

A member of the headquarters staff wrote of these weeks of waiting for the French collapse: "I have the happiest memories of those weeks, partly because of the fine military victories, partly because of the magnificent landscape in the Eifel and in Belgium. Of course we had a lot to do, usually far into the night, but the work was a pleasure in contrast to the often barely tolerable weeks of tension that had gone before. Every evening the Führer ate privately with ten or twelve others, regularly joined by one or two officers of the Wehrmacht operations staff; my turn came every eight or ten days. He was on top of the world and in splendid humor, and we talked about anything but shop. I remember we all debated the reason why the cuckoo makes a point of laying its eggs in other birds' nests." And one of Hitler's secretaries wrote on June 13: "For a week now we have been out front again, in a deserted village. For the first few nights I had to sleep with the other girl in a former pigsty, which had been boarded up and was frightfully damp. Yesterday the barracks were ready for us, *Gottseidank,* so we are on dry land again. . . . Every night we get the same performance: at precisely twenty past twelve, enemy aircraft come and circle over the village. We don't know if they are looking for us or the approach road to the front. We can't get them down because they fly too high. If they don't come then, the Chief"—meaning Hitler —"inquires, 'Where's our office airman today then!' At any rate every night finds us standing until half past three or four in the morning with the Chief and other members of his staff in the open air watching the nocturnal aerial maneuvers until the reconnaissance planes vanish with the onset of dawn. The landscape at that hour of the morning reminds me of a painting by Caspar David Friedrich. . . ."

On June 10, 1940, Italy formally declared war on Britain and France. Hitler had known of the date for a week in advance and had again tried to persuade Italy to wait, as he could not spare the Luftwaffe to help Mussolini's divisions penetrate France's Alpine fortifications. He made no attempt to disguise his contempt and forbade Keitel to permit staff talks with the Italian forces. A member of Keitel's staff noted: "The Führer's view is that since Italy left us in the lurch last autumn we are under no obligation to her now." In the foreign ministry sardonic comparisons were drawn between Mussolini and the traditional circus clown who rolled up the mats after the acrobats completed their performance and demanded that the audience applaud *him;* or again, the Italians were dubbed the "harvest hands." Over dinner on the eleventh, hearing that the Italians had only now bombed Malta, Hitler commented sourly, "I would have done everything the other way around." That Mussolini had formally declared war on France instead of first launching a lightning invasion of Malta left him almost speechless with vexation. "That must be the last Declaration of War in history," he exclaimed. "I never thought the Duce was so primitive." And, waving at his adjutants Mussolini's letter announcing his intention, he added, "I always knew he was naïve, but this whole letter is a warning to me to be much more careful with my dealings with the Italians in the future."

There survives among the papers of Walther Hewel the government communiqué announcing Italy's inauspicious action, with eloquent amendments written in Hitler's own hand. Where the original text proclaimed: "German and Italian soldiers will now march shoulder to shoulder and not rest until Britain and France have been beaten," Hitler irritably crossed out "Britain" and then redrafted the latter part to read "*. . . and will fight on until those in power in Britain and France are prepared to respect the rights of our two peoples to exist.*" He commented scornfully that Mussolini evidently expected this "looting expedition" to be some kind of excursion on which he could proceed at a *passo romano* goose-step. "He is in for the surprise of his life. The French respect the Italians far less than us." He cursed, "First they were too cowardly to join in with us, and now they fall over themselves to be in on the spoils." After a while he reflected: "Declarations of war always were the mark of a hypocritical political attitude—an attempt to keep up an appearance of chivalry. They only became fashionable with the rise of civilization. In olden times they didn't Declare War —there were just sudden raids and invasions, and by and large that is the proper, healthy way. Never in my life will I sign a declaration of war. I will always strike first."

Paris was abandoned by the French government and declared an open city to prevent its destruction. At the last meeting of the Supreme War Council held in France that day, Winston Churchill, the new British prime minister, begged the French to tie the German forces down by defending Paris, or to resist until the Americans came in.[5] His appeal for yet more French blood to be spilled in Britain's cause may have rung cynically in his allies' ears; the French commanders left him in no doubt the war was lost. Hitler's Intelligence services must have worked brilliantly now, for the next day, June 13, one of Hitler's secretaries wrote: "I personally cannot believe the war will go on after June. Yesterday there was a War Council in Paris: Weygand declared the battle for Paris lost and suggested a separate peace, in which Pétain supported him; but Reynaud and some other members thundered their protests against him. . . . To know precisely what the situation is and still order your men to fight on until they die, shows complete lack of principle."

The French Cabinet resigned in the face of this defeat, and the aged Marshal Henri Philippe Pétain, veteran and hero of World War I, took over. On June 17 word reached Hitler through Spain that Pétain desired an armistice and wanted to know the German terms. One of Jodl's staff later wrote: "When he heard this news Hitler was so delighted that he made a little hop. I had never seen him unbend like that before." He decided to meet Mussolini to discuss the terms at once. Meanwhile, the Wehrmacht was ordered to keep up its pressure on the

[5]Hitler devoted some thought to keeping the United States at bay. He granted an exclusive interview to the Hearst Press correspondent Karl von Wiegand on June 13 to stress his total lack of predatory interest in either North or South America, or for that matter in the British Empire; of Britain he demanded only the return of of the former German colonies. "But as Britain lost battle after battle, her men in power besought America with tear-swollen eyes to help them. They declared that Germany was threatening the British Empire and intended to destroy it. One thing will, admittedly, be destroyed in this war—a capitalist clique which is and always has been willing to destroy millions of people for its own despicable ends."

defeated enemy—to take Cherbourg and Brest as a matter of honor, and to occupy the Alsace and particularly Strasbourg as a matter of geography.

For many days Hitler had deliberated on the armistice itself: he would invite the French to undergo the same indignities as they had visited on the defeated German generals in 1918 at Compiègne; he ordered his staff to find out precisely how the French had behaved then. It had been raining in 1918, and the Germans had been kept waiting in the downpour to humiliate them still further. Hitler at first prayed that this time as well it would rain at Compiègne. Eventually, his mood changed somewhat: it must be the purpose of *this* armistice to give France no cause to fight on from North Africa; above all, Hitler wanted to show the British how magnanimous he could be in victory.

The terms of the armistice betrayed a master hand. Weizsäcker noted approvingly: "They are so elastic that Pétain can hardly reject them. . . . On the other hand the terms leave room for an *annihilating* peace." At Munich, Hitler privately persuaded Mussolini to shelve the Italian territorial claims on France until a final peace treaty. Only northwestern France would be occupied by the Germans as far as the Spanish frontier. The rest would remain under Pétain's control. The delicate problem of the French fleet called for brilliant handling, for Hitler did not want it to escape to the British. When Admiral Raeder asked him on the twentieth if Germany could claim the fleet, Hitler replied that the German navy had no title to the ships as the French fleet was unbeaten. Besides, the French ships were beyond their reach. The armistice therefore formally renounced all claim to the French fleet: the French might retain part to preserve their colonial interests; the rest was to be taken out of commission. Otherwise the ships would be left unmolested—in fact Hitler wished for nothing better than that they might be scuttled by their crews. In short, for reasons of strategy the German armistice terms bore no comparison with the humiliating terms inflicted on Germany in 1918 or indeed with the terms of armistice recently drafted by France in anticipation of defeating Hitler.[6]

At noon on June 21, Hitler drove through the fog-shrouded roads of northern France to the forest of Compiègne. Ever since Pétain's armistice request had reached him four days before, Hitler's headquarters staff had toiled to set the scene for the world's press and cameramen. The old wooden dining car in which Marshal Foch had dictated his terms to the Germans on November 11, 1918, had been retrieved from its permanent display in Paris and set up on a short length of railway track in the same spot in the forest, near the French armistice memorial. A guard of honor awaited Hitler's arrival. Forty minutes later the French

---

[6]The captured French document, dated November 9, 1939, analyzed in particular means of ensuring that the reparations could be extracted from Germany without the errors made in 1919.

officers arrived. Hitler sat on one side of the long table set up in the dining car, while General Keitel began reading out the preamble to the three stony-faced Frenchmen.

Hitler himself had composed these words: "After a heroic resistance, France has been vanquished. Therefore Germany does not intend to give the armistice terms or negotiations the character of an abuse of such a gallant enemy. The sole object of the German demands is to prevent any resumption of the fighting, to provide Germany with the necessary safeguards for her continued struggle against Britain, and to make possible the dawn of a new peace whose primary element will be the rectification of all the brutal injustices inflicted on the German Reich. . . ." After this twelve-minute introduction Hitler rose and left with his party, while Keitel continued to dictate the terms to the Frenchmen. Schmundt had dictated the order in which the German officers were to leave at this stage, and it spoke volumes for Hitler's mentality: Hitler was to be followed by Göring, and then by Ribbentrop, Hess, and Raeder; Brauchitsch was to leave last of all. The railway coach was now shipped to Berlin as an exhibit; the French memorial at Compiègne was demolished with explosives—only the statue of Marshal Foch himself remained untouched, on Hitler's personal instructions.

The French signed the armistice document with Keitel the next afternoon and then left for Italy to bargain with the Italians. Hitler could now fulfill a lifelong dream to visit Paris and see its architecture. He sent for his three favorite intellectuals—the architects Albert Speer and Hermann Giesler and the sculptor Arno Breker—and they arrived at Brûly-de-Pêche that evening, June 22. Over dinner Hitler could talk of nothing but the next day's visit. At 4 A.M. the next morning he flew secretly to Le Bourget airport with Keitel, a handful of his staff, and the court architects clad in incongruous field-gray. Here at last, towering above him in stone and iron and stained glass, were the monuments so familiar to him from the pages of his architectural encyclopedias. He was actually *inside* the modern baroque Opéra, asking the gray-haired usher to show him long-forgotten chambers of whose existence he was aware from the architectural plans. For these three brief hours shortly after dawn he wandered around the Tour Eiffel, the Arc de Triomphe, and Les Invalides, where he stood in bareheaded awe of Napoleon's sarcophagus. When it was light enough he gazed out across the undamaged city from the forecourt of Sacré-Coeur and Montmartre. At ten that morning he flew back to Belgium. That evening he commanded Speer to draft a decree for the complete reconstruction of Berlin—it must outshine everything he had seen in Paris. He signed the document three days later, ordering the Reich capital's facelift to be completed by 1950.

The Italians and French came to terms as well. Hitler told Brauchitsch he believed the British would soon give way. An hour after midnight on June 25, 1940, a bugler of the 1st Guards Company took up station at each corner of the

Führer's village headquarters. Seated at the bare wooden table in his requisitioned cottage, Hitler waited with Speer, his adjutants, secretaries, and personal staff; he had also invited two of his fellow infantrymen from World War I to join him— one Ernst Schmidt, a master painter, and his old sergeant Max Amann, now chief of the Party's printing presses. Throughout Europe millions of radios were tuned in to this quiet forest acre. Hitler ordered the lights in the dining room switched off, and the window opened. A radio turned low whispered a commentary. At 1:35 A.M., the moment prescribed for the armistice to take effect, the buglers sounded the cease-fire.

It was the most moving moment of his life. Nobody would ever understand what this victory meant for him; for four years he had once fought as an anonymous infantryman, and now as Supreme Commander it had been granted to him to lead his people to a unique victory. After a while he broke the silence. "The burden of responsibility . . ." But he did not go on.

The Führer asked for the lights to be turned on again.

The Big Decision

While Schmundt packed up the headquarters, and a never-ending stream of telegrams and congratulations reached the Chancellery in Berlin—from the exiled kaiser in Holland, from the crown prince, from Hindenburg's daughter, and even one from Hitler's old schoolmaster in Austria—the Führer contentedly toured the Flanders battlefield of World War I with his old comrades Amann and Schmidt. He even found the house where he had been billeted as an infantryman and delightedly showed it to Schaub and the select handful who accompanied him on this nostalgic pilgrimage around those corners of his memory. At one point he darted off and clambered up an overgrown slope, looking for a concrete slab behind which he had once taken cover. His memory had not deceived him, for the same nondescript slab was still there and for all we know lies there to this day.

Schmundt had prepared for him an interim headquarters, "Tannenberg," high up in the Black Forest near Freudenstadt. Hitler did not want to return to Berlin until he had some unofficial response to the peace feelers he had extended to the British through Sweden. He would then stage a triumphal return to the capital on July 6 and make his formal offer in a Reichstag speech two days later. After that he would be free to attend to Russia in 1941.

The anti-Bolshevik urge, like some Wagnerian motif, continued to inspire his private deliberations, occasionally breaking to the surface in moments of triumph or repose—much to the consternation of his unready associates. Every time the Russians made some move, he reminded himself that this motif was his real raison d'être: he had analyzed the inexplicable Russian armistice with Finland with this in mind, and he had concluded that Stalin must have been bluffing about his military weakness; but to what end? Unlike "the alcoholic dilettante" into whose hands British power had now been thrust, Stalin was a national leader of whose strategic capability Hitler was in no doubt; he knew how to think in terms of centuries—he set himself distant goals which he then pursued with a single-mindedness and ruthlessness that the Führer could only admire.

As early as June 2, Hitler had mentioned to Rundstedt when discussing "Red" at Charleville, "Now that Britain will presumably be willing to make peace, I will begin the final settlement of scores with bolshevism." He obviously regarded the August 1939 pact with Stalin with increasing cynicism. It was a life insurance policy to which he had steadfastly contributed but which he now felt had served its purpose; his victory in France had given him a feeling of immortality.

The Russian and British problems were inseparably entangled with the British: if Russia were neutralized as a military power, Britain would be obliged to accept just the kind of *bloodless* defeat Hitler was reserving for this troublesome brother-country. Her last "Continental dagger" would be smitten from her grasp.

There is an abundance of contemporary evidence that in June 1940 Hitler was still well disposed toward the British Empire. The archives of the High Command and the navy provide examples. This was why Keitel rejected a proposal that Britain's food supplies be sabotaged, and on June 3 Hitler explicitly forbade Canaris to introduce bacterial warfare against Britain. On June 17, Jodl's principal assistant confirmed to the naval staff that

> . . . the Führer has anything but the intention of completely destroying the British Empire, as England's downfall would be to the detriment of the white race. Hence the possibility of making peace with Britain after France's defeat and at the latter's expense, on condition that our colonies are returned and Britain renounces her influence in Europe. With regard to an invasion . . . the Führer has *not* so far uttered any such intention, as he is fully aware of the extreme difficulties inherent in such an operation. That is also why the High Command has as yet undertaken *no* studies or preparations. (The Commander in Chief, Luftwaffe, has put certain things in hand, *e.g.,* the activation of a parachute division.)

Hitler also lengthily discussed his friendly attitude toward Britain with Rudolf Hess, and together with Göring he hatched a plan to offer Britain twelve divisions for "overseas purposes"—the defense of her Empire against aggression. Göring criticized the plan as meaningless, since Britain could now in increasing measure rely on the United States for military support.

Hitler persisted in believing that with the fall of France the British government would see reason. Admiral Raeder urged him to launch immediate air raids on the main British naval bases and to prepare a seaborne invasion; for the latter, of course, aerial supremacy was essential. Hitler, however, believed an invasion quite superfluous. "One way or another the British will give in." On June 25 one of his private secretaries wrote: "The Chief plans to speak to the Reichstag shortly. It will probably be his last appeal to Britain. If they don't come around even then, he will proceed without pity. I believe it still hurts him even now to have to tackle the British. It would obviously be far easier for him if they would see reason themselves. If only they knew that the Chief wants nothing more from them than the return of our own former colonies, perhaps they might be more approachable. . . ." On the same day General Jeschonnek, the Chief of Air Staff, refused to assist the OKW's invasion planning since "in his [Jeschonnek's] view the Führer has no intention of mounting an invasion." When the air member of Jodl's staff nonetheless pressed Jeschonnek to help, the general bitingly replied, "That's the OKW's affair. There won't *be* any invasion, and I have no time to waste on planning one."

Hitler felt that the British public was being deliberately misled as to his war aims. In a democracy, public opinion—and that meant *published* opinion—made it difficult to reverse one's course of action; perhaps, he reasoned, there was nobody in Britain with the courage to admit the error in declaring war on Germany. "Naturally, it matters a lot what the Britons expect the Führer's purpose to be in fighting their country," wrote Hewel to a contact in Switzerland on June 30, (the letter is important, since it appears to have been submitted to Hitler for approval.) "They were cajoled into this catastrophe by emigrés and liberal-thinking people . . . now it is up to them to find some way out of this mess. The point is, Can the British grasp the genius and greatness of the Führer, not only as a benefit to Germany but to the whole of Europe too? Can they swallow their envy and pride enough to see in him not the conqueror but the creator of the new Europe? If they can they will automatically come to the conclusion that the Führer does not want to destroy the Empire, as the emigrés duping them claim." Hitler was minded to give the British one last chance shortly, added Hewel. "If they continue to wallow in their present pigheadedness, then God help them." A few days later Weizsäcker summed up the situation in his diary: "We'd like to call it a day, put out a Germanic hand to Britain and thus win added pressure for our threat against the Russians, who are currently reaping all the advantages—which are, indirectly, against us. In addition, perhaps we automatically shy from taking over the immense task of inheriting both Europe and the British Empire. 'Conquer Britain—but what then, and what for?'—This question of the Führer's is countered by others, like Herr von Ribbentrop, with a comparison to two great trees that cannot prosper if they grow up close together." In Weizsäcker's view Britain would not give in unless clubbed to the ground—and only after Churchill had been disposed of.

Deep in the Black Forest, the Führer waited for word from Britain and planned the Reich's new frontiers. Now that victory was his, he saw no reason not to gather the spoils of war. He would throw France back to the frontiers of 1540. He personally instructed the two western Gauleiters, Josef Bürckel and Robert Wagner, to reannex Alsace and Lorraine by stealth; any formal German announcement would have prompted Mussolini to enforce Italy's territorial claims against France, or even provoked Marshal Pétain to transfer his fleet and African colonies to the enemy. Meanwhile German troops stopped the thousands of French refugees from returning to these provinces; German civilian governments were set up, and all French official protests were ignored. Many of Hitler's own staff, like Otto Meissner and Rudolf Schmundt, had been born in Alsace.

Small wonder that Hitler warned his legal experts to "put as little down on paper as possible," for the new Germany would have a western frontier not enjoyed since the late Middle Ages; it would embrace all of Holland, Belgium, and Luxemburg, and much of modern France besides. The line he envisaged ran from the Somme estuary southward; it gave Germany the Channel ports of Boulogne, Calais, and Dunkirk, much of Flanders, all of Lorraine, the Franche Comté and part of Burgundy, as far as Lake Geneva. (Hitler also asked Jodl's operations staff to draft a contingency plan for the invasion of Switzerland.) France herself was to be reduced to an impotent collection of self-governing provinces.

Under the peace settlement Hitler also intended to oblige his former enemies, as well as the pro-Axis countries, to agree on a uniform solution of the Jewish problem. France would be required to make available an overseas territory to accommodate Europe's Jews—he considered Madagascar best suited. Hitler revealed this decision to Admiral Raeder on June 20 and evidently to Ribbentrop and Himmler soon after, for experts in the foreign ministry worked eagerly on the Madagascar plan throughout the summer, and the Reichsführer SS definitely issued corresponding instructions to the police generals in the east. He told a relieved Governor General Hans Frank that the Führer had ordered an end to the dumping of Jews in the Generalgouvernement of Poland after all, as they were to be deported overseas, including those now in Poland. Gauleiter Greiser, governor of the newly annexed Warthegau, was not pleased, however, for he had herded 250,000 Jews into the Litzmannstadt (Lodz) ghetto to await their transfer to the Generalgouvernement; further delay would place a huge medical and foodstuffs burden on his administration that winter. But "of course he would bow to these instructions," he promised. At a Cracow conference, SS General Streckenbach quoted Himmler: "When and how the deportation begins, depends on the peace settlement."

It is difficult to relate the political and military developments of the summer of 1940 to the industrial—and hence longer-range—decisions Hitler took. His political posture from early June onward was one of conviction that Britain could be persuaded by diplomatic means to yield to his will. Nevertheless, in the second week of June he ordered Keitel, Göring, and the arms industry to convert to the special needs of the war against Britain: all effort must be applied to the mass production of Junkers 88 bombers and of submarines. But though the ammunition dumps were to be replenished, the peacetime consumer-goods industry was restarted. The field army was to be reduced in strength immediately by thirty-five divisions, which would provide industry with the manpower it now lacked.

The key to the uncertainty this reflected was Russia. Jodl felt that Hitler's "huntsman's instinct" told him that Stalin meant him no good, and twice during June Russian actions fed these suspicions. On the twelfth, Moscow issued an ultimatum to the Baltic state of Lithuania, followed four days later by similar ultimata to Estonia and Latvia. Soviet troops invaded these countries, and from the concentrations of troops on Romania's frontier it was clear that further moves were intended.

Now Germany's oil supplies were in real danger. Army Intelligence recorded a flood of reports that the Russians were going to invade Germany, that heavy tanks had been heard massing across the frontier, and that Germany was to receive an ultimatum to hand over Memel. The rapidity with which Hitler finally defeated France must have taken Stalin by surprise, for on the twenty-third Molotov informed Germany that despite an earlier promise to avoid war with Romania over the Bessarabian region, the Soviet Union would brook no further delay and was resolved to "use force if the Romanian government refuses a peaceful settlement." To Hitler's evident consternation, the Russians also laid claim to Bukovina, a region formerly owned by the Austrian crown and never by Imperial Russia; Bukovina was densely populated by ethnic Germans. Hitler asked Ribbentrop to refresh his memory as to the content of the 1939 pact with Stalin, but the secret protocol was alarmingly vague: "With respect to the southeast, the Soviet party stresses its interest in Bessarabia. The German party declares its total political *désintéressement* in these regions." The plurality of "regions" was an embarrassment, but the protocol bore Ribbentrop's signature, and war in the Balkans had to be avoided at all costs. Molotov agreed to limit the Russian claim to northern Bukovina, and under German pressure the Romanian government bowed to *force majeure* on the twenty-eighth.

To his adjutants Hitler expressed all the private anger about these two Russian moves—into the Baltic states and eastern Romania—that he was unable to vent in public. He termed them the first Russian attacks on western Europe and as such to be taken very seriously indeed. "This is Russia trying to safeguard her flanks." Since the autumn of 1939 Stalin had now annexed over 286,000 square miles, with a population of over twenty million people.

During the last days of June, Hitler had a number of private talks with Brauchitsch, the army's Commander in Chief, some of which General Halder also attended. Halder was concerned about Russia's growing militancy, her steadily increasing strength along the September 1939 demarcation line in Poland, and her colossal armaments program; he pointed out that the few divisions left in the east were not even sufficient for customs purposes and asked for an increase in German strength there. On June 23, Hitler discussed this at length with Brauchitsch —a long note of their decisions was taken by Colonel von Lossberg. Basically Hitler ruled that the army was to be reduced from 155 to 120 divisions (although 20 of the 35 divisions to be disbanded could be reactivated on short notice if necessary); he directed that the armored and mechanized divisions were to be doubled—itself an interesting provision; and that no fewer than 17 divisions were to be stationed in the east, together with the headquarters of General Georg von Küchler's Eighteenth Army. The Russians were to be reassured that this redeployment was merely a "transfer home."

Hitler's political appreciation of the situation was that if Britain continued to fight, it could only be because she hoped to enlist the United States and Russia on her side. Two days later, Halder is to be found briefing his staff on the new element in all this: "Germany's striking power in the east." In an order to the three army group commanders on June 25, General von Brauchitsch mentioned innocuously that the various organizational changes would be effected "partly in occupied areas, partly in Germany, and partly in the east." Discussing the reasons underlying the transfer of the Eighteenth Army to the east, in a letter to Brauchitsch on the twenty-eighth,[1] Halder wrote: "The purpose here for the time being is to demonstrate the physical presence of the German army; but it is important not to show an attitude of open hostility." Two days later he apparently told Weizsäcker that Germany must keep a weather eye on the east. "Britain will probably need a display of military force before she gives in and allows us a free hand for the east."[2] And on July 3 Halder was even more explicit in his discussion of the eastern problem. "It has to be examined from the angle of how best to deliver a military blow to Russia, to extort from her a recognition of Germany's dominant role in Europe."

Tannenberg was not one of Hitler's most attractively sited headquarters. It consisted of a number of wooden barracks and concrete block houses partly below ground level, deep in the Black Forest. The tall pine-trees sighed in the wind, and

---

[1]The letter is quoted in a restricted British monograph but is not among the files restituted to Germany; it is presumably still in British hands.

[2]In the published version of his diaries, Halder annotates the quotation to suggest that Weizsäcker was quoting Hitler *to him,* but taken in conjunction with the entry of July 3, 1940, it is difficult to defend that interpretation.

it rained heavily. There were only a few days of sunshine in the week he stayed there, beginning June 28. While Jodl's staff applied itself to the theoretical problems of defeating Britain, Hitler began to draft the speech he would deliver to the Reichstag upon his return to Berlin.

The Italian ambassador called on him here; Hitler hinted that Germany was on the threshold of "big new tasks," without being more specific. In truth, he had not yet made up his own mind which way to turn. He mentioned to Schmundt that he was turning over in his mind whether or not to fight Russia. The Wehrmacht adjutant afterward told Below about it as they walked gloomily through the dripping forest. (The scene of this exchange remained indelibly in the Luftwaffe adjutant's memory and helped to fix the time of Hitler's portentous remark in the rush of history that summer.) Hitler also seems to have discussed this possibility with his foreign minister, and one of Jodl's staff—whether on Hitler's direct command cannot now be discerned—privately began drafting an OKW plan for an attack on Russia.[3]

By late June 1940, Hitler suspected that the British had no intention of submitting; by the end of the first week in July, this suspicion had hardened to a certainty.

Not only had Germany's own unofficial soundings through Sweden met with a rebuff, but Hitler's agencies had intercepted the formal British reply to an offer of mediation by the Pope. The extent of Britain's determination was displayed vividly on July 3, when Churchill's navy opened fire on the remnants of the French fleet at Mers-el-Kebir, killing 1,150 French sailors; this was Hitler's own language and the message reached him loud and clear. Moreover, Allied documents captured in France demonstrated unmistakably the kind of war that Britain was preparing: among the records of the Supreme War Council was one of a November 1939 meeting at which Chamberlain had disclosed that the British air staff had developed a plan to use its new long-range bombers for the destruction of the Ruhr, site of an estimated 60 per-cent of German industry. Aerial photographs had been taken; plaster models had been built of the entire region. The RAF bombing offensive as planned would continue for several months and would inevitably, Chamberlain admitted, take a heavy toll of civilian life in Germany, which was a drawback from a world-opinion point of view. French War Minister Daladier had begged the British to think again, fearing that the German reprisals would fall most heavily on France.

Hitler's agents had also discovered notes written by Daladier during a visit to Paris by Churchill and British air marshals on May 16, while the archives of the

---

[3]This was Colonel Bernhard von Lossberg; for his plan ("Operation Fritz") see page 162 below.

Quai d'Orsay were being burned outside the windows. ". . . Churchill thinks the [German] salient can be cordoned off just as in 1918. I explain to him there can be no comparison between the two wars. A long technical argument with his generals, who declare to me that the German advance into France can be slowed down by bombing the Ruhr. I retort it is absurd to believe that. The Germans are interested only in pressing on into France and finishing off Britain afterward. The damage to the Ruhr won't matter two hoots to them; they won't let their spoils slip through their fingers now. . . . London must be defended *here*. Air Marshal Joubert de la Ferté and Churchill contradict, they point out the importance of defending the British arms factories. . . ." A last desperate telegram from Reynaud to Churchill appealed for the RAF to stop its futile attacks on the Ruhr and send aircraft instead in direct support of the French infantry, now standing alone in battle with the Germans. This document was also in Hitler's hands by the end of June.

So the British planned to fight on—relying on their air force for the defense of their isles and a strategic attack on Germany's rear. It was an unwelcome revelation for Hitler and the OKW operations staff. As one of Jodl's officers was later to write: "We had in truth not the slightest desire for such a passage of arms. Our worries centered solely on the gathering Bolshevik menace far in the east, against which no natural frontier protected us. This was why we had built up our costly arms industry." On June 30, Jodl drafted a first appreciation of the continued war with Britain. It was dominated by the specter of a Britain resurgent and able to strike at Germany's arms industry—in essence it was concerned with defensive and preventive strategy, with ways of breaking Britain's will, and of defeating her bomber force either in the air or in the factories themselves. Jodl regarded the invasion of Britain as an extreme to be adopted only if all else failed to bring Britain to her senses; meanwhile, the country could be blockaded or bombed into abandoning her war against Germany. Hitler ordered his service commanders to start invasion preparations since "under certain circumstances" the need might arise, but the mere thought of committing upward of thirty good divisions to an *opposed* operation "overseas" must have smitten the Führer with grave apprehension. He willingly allowed the invasion preparations to go on, but apparently only for the diversionary[4] and political effect they had on Britain and Russia.

---

[4] An unpublished OKW directive signed on June 28 by Lossberg—who certainly knew that a Russian campaign was now in the cards—ordered the Intelligence services to use all available channels to dupe the British into believing "Germany is preparing war against the British mainland and overseas possessions with all dispatch in the event that Britain desires to continue the fight." The British were to be led to believe that their blockade and bombing offensive were ineffective, that a German air offensive would start once the Luftwaffe had recovered its breath, and that there would be new secret weapons (super-artillery, tanks) by September; moreover Germany, Italy, and Russia

———

On July 6, 1940, Hitler returned to Berlin, two months after he had sallied forth to fight the French. A public holiday had been declared in the capital, the shops had shut at noon, a million swastika flags had been distributed free to the packed mass of humanity lining the streets to the Chancellery, and roses were scattered in the roads for Hitler's cars to crush. As a military band struck up the Baden-weiler march and Dr. Goebbels himself broadcast the running commentary over the radio network, at 3 P.M. Hitler's special train pulled into Anhalt station.

The strategic alternatives facing Hitler were of nightmarish magnitude. Every other decision he had taken on impulse, with an instinctive lunge after a night of deep contemplation. But the choice between attacking Britain or Russia was one that occupied him continuously until the end of July and to a lesser degree until autumn. Unexpectedly he was now confronted by two enemies, but he had only one bullet left in the breech, as he himself later graphically put it. Britain was the less urgent of the dangers; Churchill might conceal from his own people the magnitude of the defeat suffered at Dunkirk, but the debris of an army in flight, left on the beaches of northern France, was concrete evidence of Britain's inability to intervene directly on land for several years to come. That the RAF might bomb German industry concerned Hitler less than the mischief Britain might create in the Balkans—the source of Hitler's oil—where Churchill could set one jealous country at its neighbor's throat with little risk to British life and limb.

The Allied planning documents recently captured in France had been an eye-opener, betraying, as they did, the sympathetic attitude shown by Turkey, Greece, and particularly Yugoslavia toward the various moves contemplated by the Allies: the Greek war minister had secretly announced his country's readiness to allow the Allies to land troops in Salonika, and Turkey had agreed to allow French aircraft overflights from Syria to bomb the Russian oil fields in the Caucasus. In short, the Balkans could prove Hitler's undoing, and he told Italy's foreign minister as much on the day after his return to Berlin. The Italians wished to invade Yugoslavia now, but Hitler urged them not to since then Hungary could invade Romania, the Balkans would go up in flames, and Russia might cross the Danube into Bulgaria, where Communist and Pan-Slav influence was rife and the royal house dangerously insecure. "The Russians would therefore certainly advance toward their ancient Byzantine goal, the Dardanelles and Constantinople,"

---

would soon open a campaign against the British position in the Middle East—this was the "real" explanation for the five panzer divisions and the infantry divisions being withdrawn from France to the Reich. (These were the divisions being moved up against Russia.).

said Hitler. He added explicitly, "So long as the conflict with Britain has not been brought to a victorious conclusion, a Balkan conflict would present great difficulties for us. Things might go so far that Britain and Russia, under the pressure of events, could discover a community of interest."

By July 1, 1940, both General von Brauchitsch and Colonel von Lossberg, a member of Jodl's staff, had realized that Hitler proposed a Russian campaign. Brauchitsch asked the OKH to "do some operational thinking" about this, and Halder accordingly asked General Hans von Greiffenberg to start planning in the operations branch of the General Staff. In addition, "Foreign Armies East" was directed to investigate the distribution of Soviet forces confronting them. Lossberg's OKW study of a Russian campaign[5] was some thirty pages long, with a number of appendices and maps; early in July, during the subsequent sojourn of the OKW command train *Atlas* on a siding at Grunewald station in Berlin, Lossberg directed Captain von Trotha—his assistant—to obtain maps of Russia. The Lossberg study in its final form—the plan was code-named "Fritz," after his son—bore a striking resemblance to the campaign that was actually begun in the summer of 1941.

Lossberg was undoubtedly right when he later suggested that there was a psychological factor in Hitler's decision to deal with Russia first. It was not just that the Führer realized that risking a seaborne invasion of Britain despite her crushing naval supremacy might on the first day cost him a hundred thousand men—men he would one day need to achieve his distant goal, the black nugget of National Socialist ambition, the subjugation of the Soviet Union. It was the realization that victory in France had produced both in his command staffs and in the German people a smugness and a self-satisfaction and a savoring of the peace to come that threatened to undermine all hope of launching a superhuman crusade against the Bolsheviks. It was now or never: never again would Germany have a leader of such authority and following. In April 1941 he was to say:

Of course the people will never see the point of this new campaign. But the people never does grasp what must be done for its own advantage. The people must always be led by the nose to paradise. Today we are more powerfully armed than ever before. We cannot keep up this level of armament much longer. I would never be able to tackle my real peacetime ambitions otherwise.

---

[5] *I.e.,* before July 5. Sources differ as to Lossberg's inspiration. After the war, he himself privately claimed to have drafted the plan on a contingency basis on his own initiative and not, for example, on Jodl's instructions. But his cousin was to state under interrogation that "in about August" Lossberg had told him the Führer had commissioned the rough study from him.

That is why we have to use the arms we have now for the real battle—the one that counts, because one day the Russians, the countless millions of Slavs, are going to come. Perhaps not even in ten years' time, perhaps only after a hundred; but they will come.

In spite of all this, throughout the summer of 1940 Hitler allowed the invasion preparations against Britain to continue in the hope that this threat coupled with propaganda, blockade, and if need be air bombardment would bring the British people to their senses. Admiral Raeder felt that the British would not make peace without, figuratively speaking, a taste of the whip first: he urged Hitler first to order heavy air raids on some big city like Liverpool, and then to deliver his "peace offer" in the Reichstag; an invasion must be regarded only as a last resort. Hitler agreed in principle, but refused to unleash the Luftwaffe against Britain as this might stir up irreparable hatred.

The signs were in fact conflicting. It was rumored that the new British ambassador in Moscow, Sir Stafford Cripps, had predicted that an invasion was bound to succeed, forcing the government to emigrate to Canada; and the expatriate Duke of Windsor—who had served with the French military mission near Paris but had now escaped through Spain to Portugal—bitterly attacked Churchill's unnecessary prolongation of the war and categorically foresaw that "protracted heavy bombardment would make Britain ready for peace." He considered that his return to Britain would result in a powerful boost for the peace party there, and that was why Churchill was sending him away to govern the Bahamas.[6] But by July 11 it was clear that Churchill's hard line was prevailing.

Hitler was perplexed by this continued intransigence. He assumed that Churchill had deliberately misinformed his colleagues, for Cripps was heard to explain in Moscow that Britain could not make peace "because Germany would without doubt demand the entire British fleet to be handed over to her"—a charge devoid of even the smallest shred of support in the German documents. Yet, could not the British people realize, Hitler reasoned, that Churchill's opportunist war would mean the end of their empire? Halder wrote on the thirteenth: "The Führer . . . accepts that he may have to force Britain to make peace; but he is reluctant to do so, because if we do defeat the British in the field, the British Empire will fall apart. Germany will not profit therefrom. We should be paying with German

---

[6]The American ambassador in Madrid reported to Washington that on July 1 the Duke of Windsor had told him: "The most important thing now to be done [is] to end the war before thousands more [are] killed or maimed just to save the faces of a few politicians." The duke is quoted as saying that French and other societies were so diseased that they ought never to have declared war on a healthy organism like Germany. These views, stated the ambassador, reflected a possibly growing element in Britain of people "who find in Windsor and his circle a group who are realists in world politics and who hope to come into their own in event of peace." His dispatch is in U.S. government files.

blood for something from which only Japan, America, and others would draw benefit." Hitler now shared the army's suspicion that the only explanation for Churchill's stand was that through Cripps he was working out a deal with Moscow. Could Stalin be making common cause with Britain, despite all he had just learned from copies supplied to him of captured French documents about the Franco-British plans of April 1940 to bomb the Caucasus oil fields?

Hitler had postponed the Reichstag session and left Berlin on July 8. For the next ten days he drifted purposelessly about Bavaria and Austria—attending a reception for Munich artists at Bormann's house, persuading the Hungarian leaders to moderate their territorial demands on Romania, and then retiring to the Obersalzberg for a week of quiet reflection on the future. The Hungarian premier, Count Paul Teleki, had brought him a letter from his regent, Admiral Nicholas Horthy, on July 10; only Horthy's handwritten draft survives in the Budapest archives, but it shows that he strongly hinted—as in an earlier letter in November —that Germany was the only power that could prevent Stalin and the Red Army from "devouring the whole world like an artichoke, leaf by leaf." Between the lines was Horthy's undertaking to lend his forces to an anti-Soviet campaign.

With Hitler's acquiescence, Joachim von Ribbentrop had begun an extended maneuver to win the support of the Duke of Windsor, who was now staying with the duchess at the Lisbon mansion of one of Portugal's leading bankers, Ricardo de Espirito Santo Silva, prior to taking up his new post at Bermuda. Hitler's respect for the duke (whom he had met in 1937) was increased by the reports that now reached him of the latter's unconcealed loathing of Churchill and the war, as well as his conditional willingness to accept high office in a Britain humbled by armistice. The duke had assured the Spanish foreign minister he would return to Britain if the duchess were recognized as a member of the Royal Family. For the moment, German policy was limited to arranging the duke's safe arrival in an area within Germany's sphere of influence, for example southern Spain. Ribbentrop genuinely feared the British secret service had evil designs on the duke, for he sent Walter Schellenberg, chief of Heydrich's security service, to Lisbon with instructions to ensure that no harm came to him. Schellenberg was also to enable the duke and duchess, whose passports had been impounded by the British embassy in Lisbon, to cross back into Spain if they wished.

There was an air of high intrigue about the German diplomatic cables that now arrived from Lisbon and Madrid. On July 9 the news was that the duke had asked the Spanish foreign minister to send somebody he could trust to Lisbon to pick up a message. Two days later Ribbentrop confidentially cabled his ambassador in Madrid that only the Churchill clique stood in the way of peace and that if the duke so desired Germany was willing to smooth the path for "the duke and duchess to occupy the British throne." The duke told the Spanish emissary that he had been offended by the tone of Churchill's letter appointing him governor of the Bahamas and that its delivery had been accompanied by an oral threat of court martial if he disobeyed. By the last week of July it seemed Ribbentrop might succeed: the Spanish emissary quoted the duke as saying that he was not afraid of his brother the king, who was "of copious stupidity," so much as of the queen, who was shrewd and forever intriguing against the duke—and particularly the duchess. For two pins, he would break with his brother and Britain's present policies and retire to a life of peace in southern Spain—but the Lisbon embassy had impounded his passports. To Ribbentrop this cannot have seemed a serious obstacle. On the twenty-fourth, the Spanish emissary communicated to Ribbentrop that the duke and duchess had said they were willing to return to Spain. When the duke had been told the time might come when he would again play an important part in English public life, and perhaps even return to the throne, he had replied in astonishment that the British Constitution made this impossible for a king who had once abdicated. Ribbentrop's ambassador reported, "When the emissary then suggested that the course of the war might bring about changes even in the British Constitution, the duchess in particular became very thoughtful."

Hitler's suspicion of collusion between Russia and Britain was powerfully reinforced by reports of conversations of Russian diplomats in Moscow; these reports were partly intercepted by the German Intelligence service and partly furnished by the Italian government in the innocent belief that proof of the antagonism of Yugoslavia and Greece toward Germany would soften Hitler's stern opposition to any Italian adventure against Yugoslavia. Hitler was far more concerned with them as concrete proof of Soviet duplicity, however. Thus on July 5 the Turkish ambassador reported to Ankara on a conversation with Sir Stafford Cripps: Mikhail Ivanovich Kalinin, the President of the Presidium of the Supreme Soviet, had assured the Briton that Britain and Russia had many interests in common; but while it was necessary for them to arrive at an understanding he recommended that nothing be done hastily.

In Hitler's eyes, this cautious utterance exposed Stalin's hypocrisy. According to Molotov's version of Stalin's meeting with Cripps, the Soviet dictator had refused to convert his policies into anti-German ones.

Yet in mid-July the Italians supplied Ribbentrop with a decoded Greek telegram sent to Athens by the Greek legation in Moscow. It reported on a two-hour interview with Cripps on July 6, the contents of which demonstrably alarmed Hitler when he read them on his return to Berlin. Cripps had emphasized that the Russians were feverishly making war preparations (*"which is quite correct,"* noted the Greek telegram) and that if the war lasted, then within one year the Soviet Union would join in on Britain's side. Significantly the Greek envoy had retorted that "it appears questionable to me that if Germany believes the Kremlin definitely intends to attack she will give the Russians a year to get ready and not take action immediately." Cripps had claimed in reply that because Germany could not be ready to attack Russia before autumn, and even then could not endure a winter campaign, "she will be forced to postpone the war against Russia until next spring—by which time the Russians will be ready too." Until then both parties would avoid any disruption of their mutual relations. Speaking to the Turkish ambassador on July 16—it was the Hungarian foreign ministry that supplied Ribbentrop with an account of this conversation—Cripps had indicated Stalin's evident inclination to accept the collaboration proposed to him by Churchill in a personal letter; as Cripps had admitted to the Turkish ambassador, "I fully understand how delicate this matter is, but faced by imminent German attack . . . we are forced to come to some arrangement with the Russians whatever the cost."

Russia for its part seemed to be trying to set the Balkans at Germany's throat. In an "unusually cordial" interview with the new Yugoslav minister in Moscow, Kalinin had insidiously cast aspersions on sharp business practices adopted by Germany in exporting to Yugoslavia. "This is no way for the Germans to safeguard the peace," the Russian had hinted. "Indeed, they always demand more and more. No, you must struggle against it; you must be vigilant—you must stand together." The Yugoslav diplomat's dispatch on this pregnant interview was also in Hitler's hands on his return to Berlin.

On July 16, Hitler had without noticeable enthusiasm accepted Jodl's draft order to the Wehrmacht to prepare an invasion of Britain "and if need be carry it out," since Britain still failed to draw the proper consequences from her hopeless position. The army generals, exhilarated by their recent victories, were eager to go and jostling for the most favored positions on the Channel coast. But the navy was more circumspect. The withdrawal of a thousand heavy barges from the German waterways would paralyze large sections of industry; in addition, adequate local air superiority was a *sine qua non* for any invasion operation. On the fifteenth the OKW had orally asked the commanders in chief whether everything could theoretically be ready by August 15; on his arrival now in Berlin Hitler learned from Raeder that this would be quite impossible. Nonetheless the Führer ordered the stage to be set—the transport ships and crews were to be be marshaled along the Channel coast in full view of the British. His aim was transparent, for the Luftwaffe meanwhile operated with a decorum and restraint hardly compatible with the strategic objective of fighting for air supremacy.

Hitler now delivered his long-delayed speech to the Reichstag. The flower-bedecked Kroll opera house was packed to overflowing—the generals and admirals in the dress circle and the "deputies" in the orchestra. There is no need here to analyze his speech—effective as ever, now narrating, now mocking, now ranting, now appealing. Its burden was an "appeal to Britain's common sense," an appeal Hitler had long known would fall on deaf ears, but nonetheless a necessary tactic if he was to justify himself to history and the German people. What was unorthodox was that he unexpectedly announced an avalanche of promotions for all his principal commanders on the western front. He had kept them secret even from his staff, but Hermann Göring must have learned that he was to be created a *Reichsmarschall*—one rung higher even than field marshal—for he had already ordered a gaudy new uniform which he paraded before Hitler immediately after his return to the Chancellery; the Luftwaffe generals were disappointed that Göring no longer saw fit to wear Luftwaffe uniform. Among the dozen field marshals Hitler had just created, he reluctantly included Brauchitsch, although against his better judgment, as he told his adjutants. Before the day was over he privately assured the sixty-five-year-old Field Marshal von Rundstedt, who was about to return to France, that he had not the slightest real intention of launching a cross-Channel invasion; that would be quite superfluous.

Hitler evidently repeated to Brauchitsch his demand that a Russian campaign now be explored. He had established—perhaps from the Lossberg study—that the Wehrmacht could regroup for an attack on Russia within four to six weeks. Lossberg's "Fritz" draft certainly indicated that the regrouping could be very rapid, and the strategic objective Hitler outlined to Brauchitsch echoed Lossberg: "To defeat the Russian army or at least to take over as much Russian territory as is necessary to protect Berlin and the Silesian industrial region from enemy air raids. It would be desirable to advance so far into Russia that we could devastate the most important areas there with our own Luftwaffe."

The Führer was now convinced that Britain was playing for time and reposing her hopes in American and Russian intervention. By all accounts she had already lost the war, if things did not improve; the British ambassador in Washington was openly conceding that Britain had been defeated and must expect to pay. Before leaving Berlin on July 21, Hitler collected Raeder, Brauchitsch, and Göring's Chief of Staff, Jeschonnek, in the Chancellery and explained to them the need to take the necessary political and military steps to safeguard the crucial oil imports should—as was "highly unlikely"—the Romanian and Russian supplies threaten to dry up. The ideal strategy now would be to invade Britain and end the war, but this would not be just an enlarged river-crossing operation; he asked Raeder to report to him within a week on the prospects for an invasion that must be completed by September 15 at the latest. Brauchitsch was optimistic, but Raeder was not. "If the preparations cannot definitely be completed by the beginning of September, it will prove necessary to ponder other plans," Hitler concluded. By this he meant that he would postpone the decision on England until next May and attack Russia this very autumn.

While awaiting Raeder's report on the prospects for an invasion of Britain, Hitler toured Weimar and Bayreuth. What thoughts must have inspired him now, listening to *Götterdämmerung?* But now there were air raid wardens in the theater, air raid shelters everywhere, and the program in his hands included a full-page announcement on what to do if the sirens sounded. Since May the British air offensive, now conducted almost entirely under cover of darkness, had begun causing perceptible discomfiture in Germany.

On the twenty-fifth Hitler was back in the capital and Raeder again tried to dissuade him from an invasion of Britain; the admiral used economic arguments and the unreadiness of the Luftwaffe to mask his basic opposition from a naval point of view. Hitler asked him to report again on the position in a few days' time. But his final decision may have been spurred by an intercepted telegram that was shown him before he left Berlin for the Berghof late that evening. In it, the Yugoslav ambassador in Moscow, Gavrilovic, a pro-Russian member of the Serbian Agrarian party, reported to his government and quoted Sir Stafford Cripps's view that France's collapse had put the Soviet government in great fear of Germany. "The Soviet government is afraid that the Germans will launch a sudden and unexpected attack. They are trying to gain time. The Soviet government thinks Germany will not be ready for a war against them this winter."

Gavrilovic had also discussed the growing Russian military strength with his Turkish colleague. "The army's mechanization is much more advanced than people believe. The Red Army has 180 divisions according to his information, and is more powerfully organized than any other at this moment. Apparently this is all aimed at Germany, while Japan is only of subsidiary interest." The Turkish ambassador also considered war between Germany and Russia a foregone conclusion.

Hitler arrived at the Berghof in time for lunch on July 26. Over the next few days a series of meetings followed with Balkan potentates. Hitler urged the Romanians to concede the territorial claims now raised by Hungary and Bulgaria, painful though they were, coming so shortly after Russia's invasion of Bessarabia and Bukovina. The Russians were now known by the German army to have stationed in the former Romanian provinces powerful forces—

including the bulk of their cavalry and mechanized units. Small wonder that the king of Romania had begged Hitler to guarantee the rest of his country, if only because of Germany's concern over the oil wells there. But it was the proximity of the Russian air force that also nagged at Hitler. In one of these Berghof conferences, on the twenty-eighth, he explained, "The long-term political lineup in Europe must be straightened out. Only if one no longer has to fear being exposed to enemy bombing attack can one embark on far-reaching economic plans."

One morning after the regular war conference in the Berghof's Great Hall, Hitler asked General Jodl to stay behind and questioned him on the possibility of launching a lightning attack on Russia *before* winter set in.[7] He explained that he was perfectly aware that Stalin had only signed his 1939 pact with Germany to open the floodgates of war in Europe; what Stalin had not bargained for was that Hitler would finish off France so soon—this explained Russia's headlong occupation of the Baltic states and the Romanian provinces in the latter part of June. It was now clear from the increasing Soviet military strength along a frontier on which Germany still had only five divisions stationed that Russia had further acquisitions in mind. Hitler feared Stalin planned to bomb or invade the Romanian oil fields that autumn; in such an event, Germany would be open to all manner of Soviet blackmail. Hitler would then be unable to launch a winter counteroffensive, and by spring—from all that he had heard—Russia's entire military potential would be marshaled against him. Russia's aims had not changed since Peter the Great: she wanted the whole of Poland and the political absorption of Bulgaria, then Finland, and finally the Dardanelles. War with Russia was inevitable, argued Hitler; such being the case, it was better to attack now—this autumn; postponement was only to Russia's advantage. Jodl doubted whether they could be ready by autumn, but he undertook to find out at once. Hitler's decision was to start *preparations* nonetheless; meanwhile he would make one last political attempt to explore Stalin's intentions before making up his mind to attack.

A few days later Jodl returned to the Berghof with his operations staff's analysis of the prospects for an attack against the USSR. Spreading out railway maps on the large red marble table at the Berghof, he had to advise Hitler that for transport reasons alone it would be impossible to attack Russia that autumn. Hitler ordered the OKW to attach top priority to expanding the handling capacity of the railways in the east.

[7]Hitler's sudden insistence on an autumn campaign against Russia was unquestionably an echo of the mocking tone adopted by Soviet leaders in their (intercepted) conversations with Balkan diplomats. Hitler himself referred to "intercepted conversations" in this connection on July 31.

When the Führer called his OKW, army, and navy chiefs to the Berghof on July 31, 1940, his reluctance to reach a firm decision on an invasion of Britain contrasted strongly with his powerful arguments in favor of attacking Russia.

Admiral Raeder had flown down from Berlin. He sedulously gave the impression that the navy would be ready for the invasion by mid-September 1940; but he advanced formidable technical reasons why they should wait until May 1941. May and June were the ideal months, while from a moon and tide point of view in the coming autumn only two periods were attractive—from August 20 to 26, and from September 19 to 26; the first was too early for the navy, the second fell in what records showed to be a traditional foul-weather period. Hitler took the weather risk very seriously. Meanwhile, warned Raeder, the commandeering of barges and fishing ships required for the invasion was having catastrophic effects on the German economy. In passing he raised basic tactical objections to the army's plan to invade southern England on such a broad front. If Hitler waited until May, on the other hand, the navy's fleet of battleships would be brought up to four by the new *Tirpitz* and *Bismarck,* and there would also be many more smaller warships. Hitler thanked the navy for its splendid achievement so far, and the admiral returned to Berlin.

After he had gone, Hitler commented to Brauchitsch and Halder—who had flown up from General Staff headquarters at Fontainebleau—that he doubted the technical practicability of an invasion. He was impressed by Britain's naval supremacy and saw no real reason to take "such a risk for so little." The war was already all but won. With more marked enthusiasm—Halder underlined in his diary several of Hitler's following statements—the Führer turned to the other, less risky, means of dashing Britain's hopes. Submarine and air war would take up to two years to defeat Britain. Britain still had high hopes of the United States, and she was clutching at Russia like a drowning man: if Russia were to drop out of the picture, then the United States must, too, because with the USSR eliminated Japan would be released as a threatening force in the Far East. That was the beauty of attacking Russia. "If Russia is laid low, then Britain's last hope is wiped out, and Germany will be master of Europe and the Balkans."

This then was Hitler's strategy. The Wehrmacht must prepare to finish off Russia as a military power by capturing Moscow, launching a huge encirclement operation from the north and south and following this up with a subsidiary offensive against the Caucasian oil fields.

The main campaign had to be completed in one stage. There was, alas, no time to commence it that autumn, as winter would have set in before the operation could be concluded; but if it were started in the spring—May 1941—the army would have five clear months in which to defeat the Soviet Union. The army he had so recently ordered cut back to 120 divisions would now be expanded to a record 180 divisions; whereas on June 23 he and Brauchitsch had agreed to allocate 17 infantry divisions to the east, he now proposed that by spring his strength there be built up to 120 divisions, including most of his armored units. He would explain this imbalance to the Russians by stressing the need to have an area well away from the danger of British air attack in which to set up new divisions for "campaigns in Spain, North Africa, and Britain."

Neither Brauchitsch nor Halder offered any objections.

The Dilemma

Winston Churchill's resistance in the summer of 1940 overthrew the very basis of Hitler's calculations. For twenty years he had dreamed of an alliance with Britain. Until far into the war he clung to the dream with all the vain, slightly ridiculous tenacity of a lover unwilling to admit that his feelings are unrequited. When Japan joined the war in December 1941, the dream still lingered dimly on, although Britain and Germany had by then dealt each other blows of unexampled savagery. In his unpublished diary, Walther Hewel recorded Hitler's melancholy lament: "How strange that with Japan's aid we are destroying the positions of the white race in the Far East—and that Britain is fighting against Europe with those swine the Bolsheviks!" But Britain's persistent war aims were clear beyond a doubt from a secret 1939 document captured by Hitler's troops in France: Germany was to be defeated and dismembered, regardless of whether Hitler was overthrown by internal revolution or not; but these true war aims were not to be published, as they would only implacably unite the Germans behind their Führer.

As Hitler told Major Quisling on August 18, 1940: "After making one proposal after another to the British on the reorganization of Europe, I now find myself forced against my will to fight this war against Britain. I find myself in the same position as Martin Luther, who had just as little desire to fight Rome but was left with no alternative. In this fight now I will destroy the England of old, and go alone about establishing a New Order in Europe. My interests are only in northern Europe, not the south. The Mediterranean countries have always been death to the Germans."

This was the dilemma confronting Hitler that summer. He hesitated to crush the British. Accordingly, he could not put his heart into the invasion planning —Göring at least noticed this and drew the appropriate conclusions. More fatefully, Hitler initially stayed the hand of the Luftwaffe and forbade any attack on London under pain of court-martial; the all-out saturation bombing of London, which his strategic advisers Raeder, Jodl, and Jeschonnek all urged upon him, was vetoed for one implausible reason after another. Though his staffs were instructed to examine every peripheral British position—Gibraltar, Egypt, the Suez Canal—for its vulnerability to attack, the heart of the British Empire was allowed to beat on, unmolested until it was too late and its armor of fighter squadrons and antiaircraft batteries rendered it impregnable. In these months an adjutant overheard Hitler heatedly shouting into a Chancellery telephone, "We have no business to be destroying Britain. We are quite incapable of taking up her legacy," meaning the empire; and he spoke of the "devastating consequences" of the collapse of that empire.

Perhaps he felt his peace feelers had not "got through" or had been expressed in the wrong language. Rudolf Hess believed so, for early in September he told a confidant: "The Führer never wanted to batter the empire to pieces, nor does he want to now. Is there nobody in Britain willing to make peace?" If the war continued, the white race would be committing suicide, since even if Germany secured an absolute victory in Europe she was incapable of taking over the imperial legacy overseas, Hess noted. This was unquestionably Hitler's language, which makes it likely that when Hess urgently asked his friend about ways and means of communicating Hitler's serious wish for peace to leading Britons he was acting as the Führer wanted. The views of the Duke of Windsor may have influenced Hitler's assessment of the British mentality: it was reported from Lisbon that he had described the war as a crime, Halifax's speech repudiating Hitler's "peace offer" as shocking, and the British hope for a revolution in Germany as childish. The duke delayed his departure for the Bahamas as long as he could, but he explained through intermediaries he would intervene actively only if he was convinced he had the support of the majority in Britain, as his return to England might lead to civil war. He assured his Portuguese host that he could return by air from Bermuda within twenty-four hours if need be. "Undiminished though his support for the Führer's policies are," reported the Lisbon ambassador, "he thinks it would be premature for him to come right out into the open at present."

Ribbentrop—clearly with Hitler's knowledge—cabled his Madrid ambassador to send confidential word to the Portuguese banker host that Germany was determined to use as much force as was necessary to bring Britain to the peace table: "It would be good if the duke could stand by to await further developments." If the duke could not be dissuaded from leaving (a loyal friend of King George's and a handful of Scotland Yard detectives had just arrived in Lisbon to persuade him), then the banker was to arrange a private channel of communication with him. The Duke of Windsor left Lisbon for the Bahamas on August 1. In his last conversation with his host he replied to Ribbentrop's message: he praised Hitler's desire for peace and reiterated that had he still been king there would have been no war, but he explained that given an official instruction by his government he had no choice but to obey. To disobey would be to show his hand too soon—it would cause a scandal and rob him of his prestige in Britain. A code word had been prearranged with the banker for his immediate return to Lisbon.

From the reports of friendly neutrals like Spain, Hitler had a detailed picture of the situation in Britain. From an agent in the State Department in Washington he also obtained copies of the reports of the American ambassador in London, Joseph P. Kennedy, who at the beginning of August predicted that the Germans would get their way without invading Britain. They had only to continue the blockade: the east coast harbors were already paralyzed, the rest were badly damaged.

This was Hitler's view too. To Göring it was one more reason not to sacrifice his Luftwaffe in preparations for an invasion he believed would never take place —despite the fact that the primary task assigned to him in Hitler's directive of August 1 was the defeat of the British air force. Göring's proposal was to feint with a great bomber force toward London, forcing the bulk of the enemy's fighter force into the air, and then to wipe this out with the combined fighter strength of Field Marshal Albert Kesselring's and Field Marshal Hugo Sperrle's commands; he could have everything ready by August 5. The attacks would continue until the enemy air force was defeated or the weather worsened. Hitler was back in Berlin on the fourth, but Göring repeatedly postponed the attack, giving the weather as his excuse. On the sixth the army's Chief of Staff complained in his diary: "We now have a peculiar situation in which the navy is tongue-tied with inhibitions, the Luftwaffe is unwilling to tackle the task which they first have to accomplish, and the OKW—which really does have some Wehrmacht commanding to do here—lies lifeless. We are the only people pressing ahead."

On the eighth Hitler returned to the Berghof, where he awarded Frau Bormann the Mother's Cross in gold for her considerable procreative accomplishments, and he inspected the new beehives Bormann had laid out—as though there were no more pressing problems.

At the Berghof, the tapestry at one end of the Great Hall was drawn aside to reveal the projection room, and a cinema screen was set up at the other end. Every available Russian and Finnish newsreel film of their recent war was run and rerun, while Hitler and his staff studied the Russians' weapons and the tactics the film revealed. When the lights went up, little knots of officers excitedly discussed the eastern enemy. The Intelligence reports reaching Hitler were unmistakable and disconcerting: a gigantic rearmament effort had begun in Russia; in addition, according to Heydrich's organization, the Soviet trade missions were spreading

Communist propaganda and organizing cells in German factories. At the Brown House, the Nazi party headquarters in Munich, one day Hitler told Ribbentrop that he did not intend to stand by idly and allow the Soviet Union to steamroller Germany; Ribbentrop begged him not to contemplate war with Russia, and he quoted Bismarck's dictum about the unwillingness of the gods to allow mere mortals to scan the cards of Fate.

The real face of Stalinism had been unmasked in the Baltic states, where less than two months after the Red Army had taken over, the entire intelligentsia had been liquidated with a ruthless efficiency not even Himmler was achieving in Poland. When Keitel submitted a handwritten memorandum against waging war with Russia if it could possibly be avoided, Hitler summoned him to a private interview and scathingly reduced the field marshal's arguments one by one: Stalin had as little intention of adhering to their treaty as he did; moreover, Stalin was alarmed by Hitler's military successes. Keitel was hurt and suggested that the Führer find an OKW chief whose strategic judgment meant more to him. Rising to his feet, Hitler angrily denied him the right to resign—Brauchitsch too had tried that last autumn. Keitel was on his feet as well. Without a word he turned on his heel and left the room. Hitler retained the memorandum. Presumably it vanished into his safe along with his collection of other incriminating documents.

Keitel had already, on August 2, instructed his armaments staff that an upheaval in all their planning might prove necessary, as the Führer now recognized that Britain might not collapse that year. In 1941 the United States might intervene and "our relationship to Russia might undergo a change." Admiral Canaris, Keitel's Intelligence chief, was also briefed in August on Hitler's intention of attacking Russia in the spring. Ways and means must be found of camouflaging the buildup of German strength in the east. The OKW had already issued an order to that end and transparently code-named it "Eastern Buildup." According to this plan, because of the vulnerability of the western provinces to British air attack, Germany's eastern provinces were to accommodate more divisions and their transport systems were to be modernized. Eastern mapping sections were also to be enlarged for the same reason. Even Admiral Raeder was informed by Hitler during August that these growing troop movements to the eastern front were just an outsize camouflage to distract from the imminent invasion of Britain. In fact, the truth was the reverse. The OKW's war diary stated explicitly on the eighth: " 'Eastern Buildup' is our camouflage order for preparations against Russia."

Hitler's mind was on the shape of the Greater German Reich to come—and above all on how Germany was to police the more turbulent and dissident peoples that would come within the Reich's frontiers. This, he declared to Colonel Schmundt on August 6, must be the peacetime task of his Waffen SS. An elite force of "state police troopers" was to maintain the authority of the central government so that there would never be any need to call on the regular forces to take up arms against their fellow countrymen.[1] These police troopers, noted Schmundt, must be of the best German blood and unconditional champions of the Nazi ideology—a body of men of a purity and pride that would never make common cause with the seditious proletariat; to increase their authority in the eyes of the people, the Waffen SS must prove their value on the coming battlefields; they must be an elite, and Hitler laid down that the Waffen SS must therefore not exceed 5 to 10 percent of his army's peacetime size. The Wehrmacht objected bitterly to this further entrenchment of Himmler's private army, but Keitel agreed with Hitler's arguments and ordered them given the widest circulation within the army.

Among close friends at the Berghof, Hitler often thought out loud about his plans for all Europe when it was finally in his hands. He would build great autobahns far into the east, he would build new cities; on Victory Day the people of Berlin must dance in Wilhelmsplatz, and then the rebuilding of Berlin was to begin. He would be gracious and magnanimous to the vanquished enemy heads of state—even to Churchill, whom he would "give leave to paint and write his memoirs."

Göring told Hitler he needed three days of good weather to begin the air attack on the British fighter defenses. On August 12, he announced that the attack would begin the next day. At 11:20 A.M. Hitler therefore left the Berghof for Berlin. When Raeder warned on the thirteenth that the invasion of Britain was a last resort, not to be undertaken lightly, Hitler reassured him that he would first see what results the Luftwaffe obtained. Thus he postponed his decision. But those who knew him realized the invasion would never take place. "Whatever his final decision, the Führer wants the *threat* of invasion of Britain to persist," the naval staff's war diary noted on August 14. "That is why the *preparations,* whatever the final decision, must continue." In fact, Hitler's attention was already very much on Russia. It is evident that he was unsettled by signs that the USSR was preparing to swallow Finland once and for all, for he told Göring to supply the Finns secretly with war goods and particularly with antitank mines, forthwith; he asked Raeder to fortify northern Norway against any Russian designs on that area as well.

When the newly created field marshals assembled in the Chancellery on August

---

[1]At his very first Cabinet meeting on January 30, 1933, Hitler had asked that in the event of a general strike the Reichswehr not be used to put it down; Blomberg, as defense minister, expressed his gratitude for this view and emphasized that the soldier was accustomed to treating only foreigners as potential enemies.

14 to receive their magnificently bejeweled batons from Hitler's hands, he was explicit about his strategic thinking. His remarks about Britain would have bemused the British people, who even now believed that Hitler was hell-bent on destroying and devouring the British Empire. In addition to the naval staff's account of his speech, there are two surviving records by field marshals. Hitler referred to Germany's greatest strength as her national unity. Since Britain had rejected Hitler's hand of peace, a conflict was inevitable but was initially to be restricted to Luftwaffe operations. "Whether the army will have to be employed can't be predicted. In any case it would only be used if we were absolutely forced to. . . ." Hitler expressed doubts that the Luftwaffe would succeed in altering British determination before bad weather set in: should it fail, he would postpone a decision about an invasion until May 1941.

Leeb's account[2] of Hitler's revealing *political* speech toward the end of the luncheon is important enough to quote at length:

> Probably two reasons why Britain won't make peace.
>
> Firstly, she hopes for U.S. aid; but the U.S. can't start major arms deliveries until 1941.
>
> Secondly, she hopes to play Russia off against Germany. But Germany is militarily far superior to Russia. The film of Russian warfare in Finland contains quite ludicrous scenes. The loss of gasoline [from Russia] can easily be made up by Romania.
>
> There are two danger-areas which could set off a clash with Russia: number one, Russia pockets Finland; this would cost Germany her dominance of the Baltic and impede a German attack on Russia. Number two, further encroachment by Russia on Romania. We cannot permit this, because of Romania's gasoline supplies to Germany.
>
> Therefore Germany must keep fully armed. By the spring there will be 180 divisions.
>
> As for Europe: there is no justification for the existence of small nations, and they particularly have no right to big colonial possessions. In the age of air forces and armored divisions small nations are lost. What matters today is a unified Europe against America. Japan will have to seek contact with Germany, because Germany's victory will tilt the situation in the Far East against Britain, in Japan's favor. But Germany is not striving to smash Britain because the beneficiaries will not be Germany, but Japan in the east, Russia in India, Italy in the Mediterranean, and America in world trade. This is why peace is possible with Britain—but not so long as Churchill is prime minister. Thus we must see what the Luftwaffe can do, and await a possible general election.

---

[2]Field Marshal Leeb's diaries are being published by the West German government; I am indebted to Leeb's heirs and to Dr. George Meyer for access to the manuscript.

The first two days of the Luftwaffe attack were a disappointment—not that the defenses were proving insuperable, but the unpredictable English summer foiled every effort to coordinate the operations of Göring's three air forces. Hitler ruled nonetheless that the air war must go on and that invasion preparations should take September 15 as their target date. But in the latter part of August haze and even fog made the air war progressively less profitable. A "total blockade" of the British Isles was declared, but even this was a half-measure, for it was followed up a week later by an OKW compendium of practices forbidden to the German forces—the use of poison gases, unrestricted attack on certain types of shipping in specific areas, and of course Hitler's on-going embargo on air raids on London town; he forbade any kind of "terror attack" without his permission.

On August 15, Germany's Lisbon embassy learned that the Duke of Windsor had cabled his former host to let him know when he should "act"; but that time was still far off. The next evening, Hitler again left Berlin for the Obersalzberg; such hopes as he may have reposed in the Luftwaffe's campaign were temporarily disappointed.

At the Berghof Hitler busied himself less with plans for invading Britain than with other ways of crushing her people's will.

He studied an earlier Brauchitsch proposal that if the invasion were abandoned, a German expeditionary force should be sent to Libya to support an Italian attack on the British position in Egypt: Germany could spare an armored corps until the following spring. Hitler also asked Ribbentrop to explore ways of bringing Spain into the war, and Jodl's staff attracted Hitler to the idea of capturing Gibraltar with Spanish complicity. But General Francisco Franco was reluctant to declare war, for his country's economy had not yet recovered from three years of civil war; he informed Ribbentrop's Madrid embassy that Spain would need an annual supply of four hundred thousand tons of gasoline and large quantities of wheat and other imported commodities as well. Hitler instructed Keitel to examine Germany's ability to meet these requirements.

Hitler had renewed cause for anxiety about the situation in the Balkans. The Italians were pressing him to enable them to invade Yugoslavia; in addition, after a week of talks between Hungary and Romania on the disputed Transylvania region, war between those two countries became imminent on August 23. Hitler needed complete peace on Germany's southeastern border, and he urgently warned Italy against giving Britain the least excuse to station air force squadrons in Yugoslavia.[3] The Romania situation led to more far-reaching decisions: Ro-

---

[3]Marshal Pietro Badoglio assured Germany a few days later that Italy had no intention of attacking Yugoslavia or Greece.

mania appealed to Germany to arbitrate the dispute and—without consulting Moscow, as he was bound to under the pact with Stalin—Hitler agreed. Meanwhile he ordered the German army to stand by to occupy the vital Romanian oil region to prevent "third parties"—meaning Russia—from getting there first should the arbitration talks break down. Canaris already had several hundred counter-sabotage troops in the region. Hitler's decision was not determined by sheer opportunism, for there were firm reports of Russian troop movements on the new frontier with Romania. When Field Marshal von Brauchitsch visited the Berghof on the twenty-sixth, Hitler explained to him the need to safeguard Romania without "as yet" provoking the Russians too much; he now wanted ten good divisions moved eastward to the Generalgouvernement and East Prussia.

The Vienna Award of August 30, in which Germany and Italy obliged Romania to cede the disputed territories to Hungary and guaranteed these new frontiers, removed the immediate risk of conflagration in the Balkans. However, the forces Hitler had now set rolling continued in motion, and on September 2 he decided to send a German military mission to Romania at the king's request. The Russians would, of course, regard this as yet another provocative act, but Hitler had already figured out the consequences. On August 27 Colonel Schmundt flew to East Prussia with Dr. Fritz Todt to search for a suitable site for the Führer's headquarters during the coming Russian campaign.

One night late in August 1940, British aircraft appeared over Berlin for the first time and dropped a few scattered incendiary bombs. Hitler refused to believe that Churchill could have authorized such a folly, given the Luftwaffe's intimidating superiority in bombers; but in the early hours of the twenty-ninth word was telephoned to the Berghof that the bombers had again struck Berlin and that this time ten civilians had been killed. Evidently the Reich capital now faced an ordeal of fire by night. That same afternoon Hitler flew back to Berlin. He announced to Jodl that as soon as the weather was right he would permit the Luftwaffe to raid London itself in strength—as punishment for Churchill's "downright stupidity," as he told his adjutants. That night the bombers came again. On the fourth of September, Hitler authorized the Luftwaffe to attack Britain by night, too.

That afternoon he delivered one of his most forceful public orations, taunting Churchill for his recent failures and officially inaugurating the new air war. Germany was all-powerful. One year's war had brought her Norway and all Europe from the Bug River in the east to the Spanish frontier in the west; only Britain's "skill in scurrying" had saved her skin so far. He mocked the thesaurus of reassuring predictions used by British officialdom to hint at Hitler's ever-imminent downfall. "For example they say, 'We learn that,' or 'As we understand from well-informed circles,' or 'As we hear from well-placed authorities,' or 'In the view of the experts'—in fact they once went as far as announcing, 'It is believed that there may be reason to believe . . .' " It was this kind of jargon, the Führer told his delighted audience in the Sportpalast, that had made of Dunkirk a glorious feat of British arms. "I saw the vestiges of that feat of arms with my own eyes, and it looked quite a mess to me." He mocked that after Germany had thrown the Allies out of Norway they had chanted: "We only wanted to lure the Germans up there. What a unique triumph that was for us!" After France's defeat Britain had rejoiced that now she need only defend herself. "And if Britain is now consumed with curiosity and asks, Well, why doesn't he invade? I answer, Calm down, he's coming!" Britain and her pathetic collection of exiled monarchs did not frighten him. "We German National Socialists have come up through the toughest school imaginable. First we fought as soldiers in the Great War, and then we fought the fight of the German revolution." As for the night bombard-ment of Germany's Ruhr cities that Churchill had begun three months before, Hitler now announced he would reply measure for measure and more. "If they proclaim they will attack our cities on a grand scale, we will *wipe their cities out!*"

Whether Göring had formally been advised that Hitler proposed to fulfill his cherished ambition of attacking Russia is uncertain, but Jodl's staff certainly noticed on the fifth that the Reichsmarschall showed no interest in preparing for the invasion "as he does not believe it will be carried out." Perhaps Göring saw the bombing of London and the blockade of Britain as convenient and antiseptic alternatives. He established headquarters on the Channel coast and personally directed the new offensive, which opened that night with a bombardment of the docks and oil refineries east of London.

Admiral Raeder certainly saw the handwriting on the wall, for Hitler's naval adjutant had privately informed him that a Führer headquarters was already being built for the Russian campaign. On September 6 the naval chief arrived at the Chancellery with a series of powerful arguments as to why—if the invasion of England fell through—Germany ought to concentrate her attack on Britain's Mediterranean positions and on a sea and air blockade of the British Isles (which a captured Allied document showed to be most feared of all). Raeder did not as yet attempt to dissuade Hitler from an attack on the Soviet Union, a move which the admiral discreetly referred to in his notes as "the *S*-problem"; however, he warned Hitler that it would be impossible to launch both the attack on Russia and the invasion of Britain simultaneously; the navy preferred the attack to be undertaken when the ice in the Baltic was melting, as this would tilt the balance against the Russian navy. Hitler agreed to tell the OKW this and assured the admiral that if he did drop the invasion, he would eject the British from the Mediterranean that coming winter; and for the first time he mentioned that Germany and Italy must secure footholds in the Azores, the Canaries, and the Cape Verde Islands before the British—and later the Americans—could do so. As Raeder summarized it to the naval staff: "The Führer's decision to invade

Britain is by no means definite, as he is convinced Britain can be subdued even without an invasion."

Hitler's hesitation became even more marked when Raeder briskly announced on September 10 that the navy would complete its accumulation of troop transports in the Channel ports within the set time; indeed, Hitler was visibly taken aback and consequently welcomed the various doubts voiced about the seaworthiness of the barges and the probable onset of autumn gales. Hitler again postponed the fateful decision for three more days, blaming the weather and the strength of British air defenses; the weather forecast for September had indeed proven wrong—while the navy tactfully termed the current weather "wholly abnormal," Hitler went further and described it (gratefully, we suspect) as "exasperating," as the kind of conditions from which only a defender could draw profit.

When Hitler assembled his commanders in the Chancellery once more at 3 P.M. on the fourteenth—with Field Marshal Milch deputized to represent Göring, who was still on the Channel coast—he explained why he would not formally cancel the invasion even though the primary requirement, the defeat of the British air force, had not been met. He began with a political survey. "Moscow is dissatisfied with the way things have gone; they were hoping we would bleed to death." He was giving military aid to Romania because Germany needed the oil, and to Finland because of the balance of power in the Baltic. While it was difficult to see into the future, anything might happen. "New conflicts are quite possible"; but he contemplated them calmly. He did not expect America's modest rearmament, which was mostly naval, to take effect before 1944, and he certainly did not want the war to last that long. "We have attained our objectives, so we have no interest in prolonging it." He reminded them that the Reichsmarschall had asked for five or six consecutive days of perfect weather and had never gotten them, this had enabled the enemy fighter defenses to take breath between each hammering. While the exact number of British fighter planes was uncertain, the RAF had surely suffered grievously. From now on it would be a war of nerves, with the bomber attacks and the *threat* of invasion gradually wearing the British people down. "If eight million inhabitants [of London] go crazy, that can lead to catastrophe. If we get good weather and can neutralize the enemy air force, then even a small-scale invasion can work wonders." He proposed, therefore, to wait a few more days before finally canceling the operation. If it were dismantled altogether, it would come to the ears of the enemy and the nervous strain would be that much less. He would still not permit the Luftwaffe to carry out saturation bombing raids on London's residential districts, as Göring's Chief of Staff Jeschonnek had requested. "That is our ultimate reprisal!" He wanted key targets like railroad stations and water and gas works attacked first! "*Not* the population, for the time being." Three days later Hitler postponed the invasion "until further notice." His commanders knew what that meant; from now on only the *threat* of invasion was to be maintained. In reality, Hitler's mind was elsewhere.

During September and October 1940, foreign diplomats in Moscow reported mounting Soviet bitterness toward Hitler over the controversial Vienna Award and his guarantee to Romania—a guarantee which could only be directed against Russia. A secret analysis by Foreign Armies East in mid-September provided chapter and verse for Russia's hostility; anti-German propaganda in the Red Army was continuing undiminished, and there were caricatures of Hitler, Göring, the "Nazi hydra," and the omnivorous "Fascist shark" in Red Army barracks even in the newly occupied areas. In addition, as recently as August the Red Army had appealed to Finnish war veterans to fight with it "against German and Italian fascism and create a Soviet Europe in which there will be no more exploitation." German Intelligence had also learned of a meeting of the Supreme Soviet on August 2 in which while Molotov and Marshal Kliment Voroshilov, Commissar for Defense, had tried to lull their listeners with details of Russia's western frontier fortifications, others warned against trusting Germany because "certain information indicated that after her victory in the west she would start a war against Russia." "Indeed," these others had continued, "we must get in our attack before our thieving neighbor in the west can get in hers."

The heavily camouflaged German buildup in the east was due to reach its interim conclusion at the end of October. Under the now familiar rubric of "dispersing the forces tightly concentrated in the west," Brauchitsch personally signed an order for additional divisions to move east immediately on September 6. Significantly enough, Field Marshal von Bock's army group headquarters was to take over command, from Posen, and two more armies were to join the Eighteenth—the Fourth and the Second. This would bring up to thirty-five the number of divisions on the eastern frontier, among them six armored divisions. On that same day, General Jodl ordered the Abwehr to dupe Russian agents known to be taking an increasing interest in these movements by feeding to them false information indicating that the bulk of Germany's strength was at the southern end of the front; the Russians were "to draw the conclusion that we are able to protect our interests in the Balkans from Russian clutches at any time with powerful forces."

In fact for strategic reasons Jodl's staff recommended that the main military effort at the start of the attack on Russia should be in the north, even though concentrating strength in the south would have taken better account of the Russian threat to the Romanian oil. In the north, explained Colonel Lossberg in his draft campaign plan ("Fritz") submitted to Jodl later in September, there were better road and rail facilities, the Russian influence in the Baltic region could be quickly extinguished, and it would be possible to cooperate with Group XXI operating from northern Norway through Finland into Russia; above all, an attack in the north would rapidly bring Leningrad and Moscow under the German guns. Lossberg proposed occupying all of Russia up to a line easy to defend against "Asiatic Russia." Tactically, they must prevent the Russians from withdrawing in strength into their vast hinterland, as they had before Napoleon's Grand Army in 1812.

Lossberg's plan undoubtedly formed the basis of Hitler's later grand strategy against Russia.[4] The main thrust north of the Pripyet Marshes was proposed by the colonel as follows: "An attack by two army groups from the general line east of Warsaw to Königsberg, with the southern group the more powerful (the group assembling around Warsaw and southern East Prussia) and being allocated the bulk of the armored and mechanized units." The latter army group would wheel north at an appropriate moment and cut off the Russian armies to the north from the rear. Lossberg predicted that Russian military resistance south of the Pripyet Marshes would be feebler—plagued by internal unrest in the Ukraine fomented by the Abwehr's advance subversive operations. The further strategy of the campaign, and its terminal objectives, must depend on whether and when Russia caved in under the force of the initial German onslaught. Had not Hitler himself exclaimed, according to his army adjutant, "If we can just tackle this colossus the right way, it will crumple up quicker than was ever dreamed possible!"

Only one possibility remained open to Moscow—to take the offensive first in order to disrupt the half completed German invasion preparations; or even more pertinently to invade the Romanian oil fields, perhaps using airborne troops alone. It would be the job of a future German military mission in Romania to forestall such a Soviet move. In Lossberg's view, however, the Russians would be forced for political reasons to try to thwart the German attack close to the frontier; otherwise they would be abandoning the flanking positions they had so recently secured on the Baltic and Black Sea coasts.

In Romania the king had abdicated in the crisis evoked by the Vienna Award, and the ruthless but incorruptible General Ion Antonescu had been appointed the national leader. Antonescu secretly asked Hitler to modernize the Romanian army with German tanks and artillery and to lend German instructors and staff officers. In return, he would deploy his forces exclusively on the Russian frontier. When Keitel put these requests to Hitler on the afternoon of September 19, Hitler

---

[4]The only surviving copy is now in Russian archives, which explains why it escaped the attention of other postwar historians.

decided instead to send about one division of German troops into Romania as a "military mission," as Lossberg had suggested; in addition, Romania was to be supplied with captured Polish equipment rather than the superior German models, for Hitler still suspected the Romanians might use them on their neighbors. A Luftwaffe mission would also be housed in Romania. On the same day the OKW issued a document stating that while these missions' ostensible purpose was to help the Romanians reorganize and train their forces, the "real jobs"—which were not to be made apparent to either the Romanian or the German missions' members—were:

1. to protect the oil fields from the clutches of a third power, and from destruction;
2. to enable the Romanian forces to fulfill specific tasks to a rigid plan aligned with German interests; and
3. to prepare the operations of German and Romanian forces from Romanian soil in the event we are forced into war with Soviet Russia.

The reader should be reminded that even at this stage no irrevocable order for an attack on Russia had been given; Hitler was still only preparing the military machine. But as E. M. Robertson has commented: "The consequences of having set in motion the planning machinery for the eastern campaign cannot be overlooked. With forces gathering on either side of the frontier and the political situation continuing to deteriorate, only some unfortunate and prodigious event would cause a final cancellation of the most cherished venture of his career."

Molotov

The six weeks preceding the doom-charged visit of Vyacheslav Molotov to Berlin in November 1940 are a period when Hitler's foreign policy becomes almost impossible to disentangle. With the direct assault on the British Isles all but abandoned and the Luftwaffe's murderous bombardment producing no visible collapse, he took counsel with the Spanish and Italians on ways of striking the British Empire at the periphery; he brought Japan into the Axis in a Tripartite Pact ostensibly designed to warn the United States against intervention, and he even pawed over the possibility of an alliance with France. This much is clear. But what are we to make of his more determined attempts to lure the Soviet Union into joining the Tripartite Pact as well? Was it a realistic alternative to inflicting military defeat on her, or was it a cynical attempt to force Britain to give way and enable Hitler to concentrate his undivided effort in the east?

The impulse towards a *peripheral* solution was provided by Admiral Raeder —and perhaps by Göring too, although the date of his often-mentioned "three-hour argument" with Hitler, urging against a Russian campaign is still obscure Early in September Raeder had examined with Hitler the strategic options open to Germany; by the twenty-sixth, when he came for a long private talk on the same subject, he was convinced there were ways of pacifying Russia more elegant than brute force. Germany should throw the British out of the Mediterranean that winter, before the United States was roused; it should provide assistance to Italy for the capture of the Suez Canal and then advance through Palestine to Syria. Turkey would then be at Germany's mercy. "Then the Russian problem would assume a very different aspect. Russia is basically frightened of Germany" —a point on which Hitler agreed. "It is unlikely that any attack on Russia in the north would then be necessary." Hitler appeared to like this plan: they could then invite Russia to turn toward Persia and India—again on the British periphery— which were far more important to her than the Baltic. After the admiral left, the Führer mentioned to his naval adjutant, Puttkamer, that the interview had been enlightening, as it had checked with his own views and he could see how far he was right.

The key to any peripheral strategy was, however, Italy, and Italy was ruled by a vain Mussolini whose reach far exceeded his grasp. The Italians had haughtily declined Hitler's offer of an armored corps for the attack on Egypt: the attack had opened on September 13 and petered out four days later. Hitler's plan for France to join in a coalition war against Britain by fighting in the defense of North Africa—a plan inspired by Vichy's determined repulse later that month of the powerful British naval force that attempted to land General Charles de Gaulle's Free French troops at Dakar—would also depend on the extent to which Italy's distrustfulness could be overcome. North Africa was in her sphere of interest, and the Italians were reluctant to moderate their demands for the disarmament of French forces there or to allow the French fleet units stationed at Toulon to put to sea.

The most intractable barrier to Franco-German cooperation was the interest both Italy and Spain were declaring in substantial portions of France's African territories: Spain expected to be given the whole of French Morocco in return for declaring war on Britain. In other respects as well, the talks conducted in Berlin and Rome by Franco's future foreign minister, Ramón Serrano Suñer, remained unproductive. Hitler postponed reaching a final decision on problems affecting Spain and France until he could meet their leaders and Mussolini. Small wonder that the High Command's exasperated war diarist lamented: "Our command policy of late seems to be dictated only by regard for the feelings of the Reichs-marschall and the Italians."

One thing Hitler was certain of by late September 1940: it would be impossible to gratify the territorial dreams of Italy, France, and Spain simultaneously. If Spain were to join the war and seize Gibraltar, and if France were also to be encouraged to join the grand coalition, he must resort to "fraud on a grand scale," as he disarmingly put it to Ribbentrop: *each* aspirant would have to be left in the happy belief that his wishes would be largely fulfilled. The first claimant to be deceived was Hitler's senior partner, Benito Mussolini, whom he met on the Brenner frontier between Italy and Germany at midday on October 4. Hitler cunningly suggested that they lure Spain into the war by promising to deal with her colonial demands in the final peace treaty with France; in return for the loss of part of Morocco to Spain, France could have a slice of British Nigeria and the honor of defending her remaining colonies and reconquering those she had for-feited—to say nothing of the privilege of permitting Germany to establish bases in West Africa. Mussolini was promised Nice, Corsica, and Tunis. There would be something for everybody in the coalition.

———

On leaving the Brenner frontier, Hitler's train immediately headed for Berchtes-gaden. By 9 P.M. he was back at the Berghof. For three days he idled in the autumn sunshine, reflecting on the implications of his new political strategy. His timetable was clearly mapped out: he would first like to see the former French ambassador, André François-Poncet (whom he liked) in Berlin; then he would embark on a grand tour, seeing Marshal Pétain in France and next General Franco in Spain, before returning to France to settle with Pétain the terms of their future collaboration. First, however, he would write to Stalin to tempt him with a share of Britain's legacy in return for Russia's participation in the coalition. "If we manage that," Brauchitsch was told, "we can go all out for Britain." The alternative of course—war with Russia—was already being quietly prepared, and with increasing reason, for there was a steady trickle of reliable Intelligence that behind her well-disposed if occasionally frosty facade the Soviet Union was contemplating carrying the world revolution further to the west. Hitler instructed Göring to ensure that all the Russian contracts with German industry were punctiliously fulfilled so that Stalin would have no cause for complaint on that score; but he also authorized the Luftwaffe to start extensive high-altitude photo-graphic reconnaissance missions far into Russia.

On October 9, Hitler was back in the Chancellery in Berlin. Hungary, Ro-mania, and Bulgaria were all showing a willingness to join the Tripartite Pact; Spain, he decided upon reflection, seemed so torn by internal malaise as to be valueless—Germany might have to take Gibraltar without Spain's aid; Italy's value as an ally was mitigated by her generals' sloth and Count Ciano's latent hostility. This was how Hitler apparently summarized the position to Field Marshal von Brauchitsch.

In conversation with Ribbentrop, Hitler debated the best approach to Moscow. Ribbentrop suggested a summit meeting between Stalin and the Führer, but Hitler pointed out that Stalin would not leave his country. Hitler himself dictated a lengthy letter to Stalin on the thirteenth inviting Molotov to visit them very shortly in Berlin. The letter bore all Hitler's familiar trademarks—the inveighing against Britain's duplicity, the portrayal of her leaders as conscienceless political dilettantes who dragged one reluctant country after another into battle on Brit-ain's behalf and then abandoned them in their hour of need; he reminded Stalin of the captured Allied documents which revealed plans to bomb the Soviet oil fields, and he sought—though unconvincingly—to explain Germany's guarantee to Romania and her military mission there as a necessary safeguard in case of *British* sabotage or invasion. If Molotov came to Berlin, the letter concluded, Hitler would be able to put to him his concrete ideas on the joint aims they could pursue.

On October 12, Hitler had issued a secret message to the services formally canceling all invasion preparations against Britain. The army units would be needed for other purposes; the tugs and fishing boats were to be returned to the civilian economy. Göring's bombers alone would continue the war against the British people. As Hitler gloated to a visiting Italian minister on the fourteenth: "Let the British announce what they will—the situation in London must be horrific. Recently an American newspaper triumphantly claimed the Luftwaffe cannot have inflicted all that much damage, because of eighty-two American firms only eight have been completely destroyed and another seventeen damaged; but I am completely satisfied with such figures, even if the American newspaper isn't. It is far more than I expected. Let's wait and see what London looks like two or three months from now. If I cannot invade them, at least I can destroy the whole of their industry!" The aerial photographs his bomber crews brought back proved the extent of the damage done to Britain night after night. Churchill announced that over eight thousand Britons had been killed by the Luftwaffe.

What perplexed Hitler was the total lack of plan and purpose behind the British bombing offensive. Germany had feared an attempt to paralyze her transport system or, even worse, a ceaseless onslaught on her oil refineries—oil was Germany's Achilles heel—yet Churchill was making the fundamental error of attacking Germany's civilians and inflicting only negligible damage on her war effort in the process. Nevertheless, Hitler had ordered Reichsleiter von Schirach to organize the evacuation of children from the biggest cities, and he had increased the antiaircraft batteries around Berlin from nineteen to thirty. He had also sent for Fritz Todt and commanded that air raid shelters be built. The blackout was perfected, blue lights were installed in streetcars, trains, and hospitals, and the whole civil defense organization was handed over to Field Marshal Milch.

The uncomfortable realization that as yet there was no defense against the enemy night-bomber confronted Hitler with a host of new problems. If only one aircraft approached Berlin, should the entire city be sent scurrying for the air raid shelters by sirens? How long before the all clear could be sounded? On the night of October 14 a typical episode angered Hitler: first an enemy bomber arrived without any advance warning; then there was an all clear followed by a fresh alert as more enemy bombers were spotted approaching over Magdeburg. The injured and sick in Berlin's hospitals were twice forced to trek down into their shelters —this was not a burden he had planned to inflict on the *German* population at all. He sent for Milch the next day and ordered him to sort the matter out. Hitler was glad he was leaving Berlin for the tranquility of the Berghof that night.

In Berchtesgaden, his only engagement of consequence was a private visit from the Italian Crown Princess Maria-José, the elegant spouse of Crown Prince Umberto and sister of King Leopold of Belgium. Hitler entertained her at afternoon tea on the seventeenth in the mountaintop "Eagle's Nest." The tea party started well—Hitler's majordomo Artur Kannenberg had as usual prepared it exquisitely. (Hitler would never hear a word said against the obese and sycophantic Kannenberg; whether softly playing an accordion in the background while the Führer and Eva Braun warmed themselves on a sofa before a crackling log fire, or organizing the great state banquets that passed flawlessly and without incident, Kannenberg had become indispensable.) A number of Hitler's most presentable womenfolk were also invited to meet the princess—among them Henriette von Schirach and the dazzlingly attractive wife of Robert Ley. While white-jacketed servants ministered to their needs, the princess haltingly begged Hitler to allow her brother to come and meet with him secretly. She assured Hitler of Leopold's loyalty, despite the domestic troubles caused by the food shortage in Belgium and Hitler's unwillingness to release the rest of the Belgian prisoners. When Hitler refused, she steadfastly repeated her request and then pleaded for the release of at least the more ailing prisoners. Hitler was impressed by her plucky manner with what was after all now the most powerful man in Europe. After the princess left his mountain, he joked feebly with his staff: "She is the only real man in the House of Savoy!"

In the special train *Amerika,* Hitler left Bavaria toward midnight on October 20, 1940, on the first leg of a rail journey that was to cover over four thousand miles within the next week. Every hundred yards or so sentries patroled to the right and left of the railroad track; the Luftwaffe had provided exceptional air cover, too. The French leaders were still unaware that Hitler was coming to them.

Hitler had eventually abandoned his desire to meet François-Poncet, the former French ambassador, again. He had always warmed toward this Frenchman and believed he had won him over, but Ribbentrop had recently reeducated him by brandishing quantities of captured French diplomatic papers in which the former ambassador's confidential pronouncements were more pithy and colorful than either the Forschungsamt had succeeded in decoding or the French had published after war broke out. François-Poncet had no real sympathy for the spirit of National Socialism, for all his recognition of the injustices of Versailles and the wayward genius of the Führer; Hitler, warned the ambassador, was bent only on securing for Germany a hegemony in Central Europe. But "the remarks he [François-Poncet] occasionally drops about the Führer and other leading Reich figures are often so pointed and spiteful as to be incompatible with an even moderately loyal attitude." "As far as I am concerned," the ambassador had written in July 1937, "this mistrust has never left me. I am too well aware of the Third Reich leaders' powers of hypocrisy, mendacity, and cynicism to discard this mistrust one instant whatever the smiles and the amiability I outwardly adopt."

Hitler's train pulled into the little railroad station at Montoire, "somewhere in occupied France," at 6:30 P.M. on October 22. Ribbentrop's train, *Heinrich,* was already there. The station area had been freshly graveled and a thick red carpet had been rolled out. Antiaircraft batteries had been stationed on the surrounding hills. At seven, the short, stocky Pierre Laval, French deputy premier, sporting the familiar Gallic moustache and white tie, arrived by car. He had learned only a few minutes earlier that he was about to meet the Führer himself. In the dining car Hitler briefly indicated his wish to speak with Pétain in person on the lines France's future collaboration with Germany might take. The defeat of Britain was inevitable, he prophesied, and Laval earnestly assured him that he too desired this defeat, as must every red-blooded Frenchman. Britain, said Laval, had dragged France into an unwanted war, abandoned her, and then besmirched her honor at Mers el-Kebir and more recently at Dakar. That the French had not wanted the war was shown by the two million troops who had allowed themselves to be taken prisoner.[1] Hitler emphasized that he was determined to mobilize every conceivable force necessary to defeat Britain. "Perhaps the immediate future would prove this was no empty phrase"—a hint at his intention of drawing Russia into the Tripartite Pact. Laval, who had scribbled notes throughout the interview, promised to return with Pétain in two days' time.

At 4 A.M. Hitler's train left for the Spanish frontier. Upon General Franco's willingness to enter the war, and the consequent claims Hitler would have to support against France's colonial possessions, would depend the tenor of the main approach to Pétain. By 4 P.M. his train had reached the frontier town of Hendaye. A guard of honor was drawn up on the platform. Franco's train was half an hour late, but at four-thirty it drew alongside on another platform, where the Spanish-gauge railway ended. Hitler invited the Caudillo to inspect the guard of honor. Then the hard business of the day began in the drawing room of Hitler's train.

The argument that followed was to haunt Hitler to the end of his life. He later told Mussolini, "I would rather have three or four teeth extracted than go through that again." In vain he tried to persuade the plump, swarthy Spanish dictator to enter into an immediate alliance and allow German troops to capture Gibraltar. Twice during the summer Admiral Canaris had visited Spain in this connection, and mountain troops were already conducting experiments on the cliffs and caves of the Côte d'Azur in France—trying out various projectiles, explosives, and drilling techniques. Franco refused to rise to Hitler's bait. It was clear he doubted the likelihood of an Axis victory. Hours of argument brought Hitler no closer to his goal. He barely controlled his fury when Franco's foreign minister several times interrupted in a tactless way that Ribbentrop would cer-

---

[1] In fact the maximum number of French prisoners in German hands was 1,538,000.

tainly never have dared with *his* chief—usually at the precise moment when Hitler believed Franco was on the point of accepting the German terms.

Once he stood up abruptly and said there was little point in talking any longer, but talk on he did until dinner was served in his dining car. The Spanish leaders were scheduled to leave immediately afterward, but Hitler tackled Franco again, arguing with him about Spain's requirements of guns, gasoline, and foodstuffs until far into the night. When at 2:15 A.M. the Spanish leader's train left the little frontier station to the strains of the Spanish national anthem, General Franco was no nearer to joining the Axis. It was clear to all who crossed Hitler's path in these hours of his jolting journey back to Montoire that he was furious. He mouthed phrases about "Jesuit swine"—referring to Spain's Foreign Minister Serrano Suñer—and the Spaniards' "misplaced sense of pride." Over the next weeks, his anger at having been cold-shouldered turned to contempt. "With me, Franco would not even have become a minor Party official," he scoffed to Jodl's staff, and he sneered at the quirk of fortune that had made a man like Franco head of state. (Another general had started the Spanish uprising in 1936, only to meet his death in an air accident.) But history was to prove that General Franco was wise enough to outlive by twenty years the Axis that now was wooing him.

At three-thirty the next afternoon, October 24, Hitler arrived back at Montoire. Ribbentrop and his staff had stayed behind for one more round of talks with the Spanish and so returned by plane—the foreign minister seething with anger at the fresh snub he had that morning been dealt by Serrano Suñer, who had failed to appear at the meeting they had arranged, and had sent only a junior official in his place. A secret protocol drawn up between the three governments—of which only Hitler, Mussolini, and the foreign ministers were to learn—was the only tangible product of the journey to Hendaye. But Franco was rightly suspicious of the vagueness of the territorial offers it contained, and his suspicions grew stronger as Hitler's demands grew shriller in the months to come.

Hitler now set much greater store in persuading Marshal Pétain to bring France into the "continental bloc" he was organizing against Britain. Spain's territorial claims could now safely be ignored. Hitler nervously left his train after lunch to make sure that a proper guard of honor was awaiting the French leaders, and he placed Field Marshal Keitel in front of the guard of honor to greet the "victor of Verdun" as his car drew up shortly before 6 P.M. Pétain stepped out wearing a long French military greatcoat and a general's red cap, beneath which gleamed his silver hair. Laval followed. Pétain was evidently gratified at the dignity of the German welcome, but he avoided inspecting the guard of honor. Hitler conducted him to his drawing room and repeated the impressive catalog of German arms, stressing the certainty of the Axis victory.

But when he asked Pétain for his response, the latter answered evasively that he must consult his government. The marshal would go no further than to confirm in principle his country's readiness to collaborate with Germany. Nonetheless, Hitler was pleased with the outcome. Pétain's military bearing, and even his reserve, had enhanced his admiration for him. He afterward said in Schaub's hearing, "France should be proud to have such a leader, a man who wants only the best for his own country." Although he suspected Pétain would meet with opposition from his government, he believed the Montoire conferences had accomplished all he had set out to achieve, and this was echoed in the first paragraph of the next directive he issued to the forces:

> It is the aim of my policy toward France to collaborate with that country in the most effective possible way to fight Britain in the future. For the time being there will fall to France the role of a "nonbelligerent" obliged to tolerate military steps taken by the German war command in her territories, and particularly in the African colonies, and to support those steps where necessary by operations of her own defensive forces. The most urgent duty of the French is the defense—both by defensive and offensive means—of their possessions in West and Equatorial Africa against Britain and de Gaulle's movement. From this duty there can flow France's wholehearted participation in the war against Britain.

Pétain's meeting with Hitler had ended at 7:45 P.M. on October 24, a Thursday. Hitler accompanied the marshal back to his car while a guard of honor presented arms; then the marshal was driven away, never to be seen by him again.

Hitler's special train remained overnight at the Montoire station. He had planned to return to Berlin to prepare for Molotov's visit—the Russians had secretly accepted the invitation two days before—but now something unexpected occurred. Hewel brought him a long, jealous letter from Mussolini which had just arrived via the OKW's coded-teleprinter service. The letter, dated five days before, contained an impassioned appeal by the Duce to the Führer to set aside his dangerous flirtation with the French. Mussolini warned that he had information that the Vichy government was in secret touch with London via Lisbon; the French would always hate the Axis, and certainly no less now that they were in defeat. As for his own plans, Mussolini again mentioned that the British menace looming over Greece was comparable with that which Hitler had so successfully forestalled in Norway. "As far as Greece is concerned," Mussolini noted, "I am determined to act without hesitation—in fact to act very rapidly indeed."

After reading this, Hitler took fright and instructed Ribbentrop to arrange a meeting with Mussolini in a few days' time in Upper Italy. The lack of greater urgency suggests that the Duce's reference to attacking Greece was only of secondary importance to Hitler's concern to assuage Mussolini's fears about the approaches to France. Surely the Italians would not attack Greece *now,* with the autumn rains and winter snows almost upon them? That would be "downright madness"—it would be an open invitation to the British to occupy Crete and other Greek islands well within bomber range of the Romanian oil fields. Ribbentrop telephoned his Italian counterpart from the first railroad station inside the German frontier, and in the small hours of Friday morning Hewel brought the Führer a teletyped note from Ribbentrop's train, *Heinrich:* "I just spoke with Count Ciano on the phone and told him the Führer would very much like to speak with the Duce early next week. Count Ciano put this to the Duce and replied latter would be happy to welcome the Führer and Reich Chancellor on Monday in Florence.—*Ribbentrop.*"

During his Brenner meeting with Mussolini, on October 4, Hitler had probably given theoretical support for an Italian occupation of Greece if—and only if—necessary to forestall a British invasion. Admittedly the Abwehr had reported rumors of an Italian attack on Greece some days earlier; during Friday October 25 the German military attaché in Rome cabled that Marshal Badoglio himself had informed him that they now had information that the British intended to occupy Greek territory and that the Italians had for their part taken all necessary precautions to intervene the moment the first Briton sets foot on Greek soil. But he had reassured him: "I will inform you if it comes to that."

Hitler heard no more until Monday morning. His train reached Munich eventually late on Saturday, and he spent the next day killing time there. Ribbentrop's foreign ministry remained placidly unperturbed by the multiplying reports of Italian preparations in Albania, which Italy had occupied in April 1939. The two key dispatches from Rome that Sunday evening—the military attaché's discovery that Italy *was* going to attack Greece next morning, and the ambassador's report on Ciano's communication to the same effect at 9 P.M.—were not deciphered by their Berlin recipients until Monday morning and had certainly not reached Hitler, whose train left Munich punctually at 6 A.M. for Florence; so punctually indeed that Field Marshal Keitel, who had flown down from Berlin, had to leap onto the train as it was pulling away from the platform.

Mussolini's troops had invaded Greece at five-thirty that morning. The stunning news reached Hitler's train at Bologna, fifty miles north of Florence. Mussolini had obviously withheld his plan from him, to pay him in his own coin for Norway—and more pertinently for sending German troops into Romania, of which Mussolini was joint guarantor. Hitler's purpose until now had been at least to persuade the Duce not to attack Greece until after the American presidential elections, which were one week away. Hitler also wanted to be in a position to give his friend his expert advice on the best thrust direction for the offensive, and to mount a German airborne assault on Crete by divisions first moved to North African soil. Possession of Crete was after all the key to the command of the eastern Mediterranean. By the time Hitler's train steamed into Florence an hour later, II A.M., however, he had pocketed his intense disappointment at his ally's rash and thoughtless move, though he was hard put to control his anger when Mussolini strutted up to him and announced in German: "Führer—*wir marsch-ieren!*" "We are on the march!"

Seven hours of discussions followed. At one stage Mussolini hinted incoherently at his real motive for attacking Greece. "You see, I trust my soldiers; but not my generals. They can't be trusted." But Hitler's mistrust extended to *all* Italians from now on. Why had they not given expression to their military aspirations by completing their assault on Egypt? The capture of the British naval base at Alexandria would have had immense consequences for their Mediterranean position. The Italians were comparing their Greek campaign with the German campaign in Norway, but they had left Crete and the Peleponnesian Islands unmolested; had Hitler shown no interest in Trondheim or Narvik in April? There was nobody on Hitler's staff who did not see this Greek adventure as a strategic error of the first magnitude, although Mussolini was optimistic that it would soon all be over. One of Hitler's adjutants noted that Hitler "swore at all German liaison staffs and attachés who knew their way around the best restaurants but were the world's worst spies," and hinted that "this was going to spoil many a scheme he was hatching himself."

All his fears proved only too well founded. Italy had not committed enough strength to the campaign. On the day after the Florence meeting, British ground and air forces landed on Crete. On November 3 the first British army units landed on the Greek mainland near Athens. Mussolini's invading divisions were thrown back. A member of Jodl's staff noted on October 29: "At present no participation in Greece is planned; nor is anything being undertaken with regard to Crete for the time being." But within a week Hitler had been forced to order the Wehrmacht to prepare an offensive against Greece to take the pressure off his harassed and headstrong ally. Out of this plan emerged perforce the need to invade Yugoslavia as well, and the schedule for spring 1941—already crowded with possible major operations in east and west—was finally thrown out of joint. On this day in October 1940 was sown the first seed of later defeat. "There is no doubt about it," the Führer was to lament as the shadows of that defeat began to fall across him, "we have had no luck with the Latin races! While I was occupied, first in Montoire, buttoning up a futile policy of collaboration with France, and then in Hendaye, where I had to submit to receiving gaudy honors at the hands of a false friend, a third Latin—and this time one who really was a friend—took advantage of my preoccupation to set in motion his disastrous campaign against Greece."

———

Nevertheless, the signs had been there to see, had Hitler not been so afflicted with blind trust in Mussolini; nor can Ribbentrop escape his share of the blame. Hitler's naval adjutant, Puttkamer, has stated that his chief refused to take the warning signals seriously. On October 18 Jodl's staff had first heard rumors that Italy was planning to hurl up to ten divisions at Greece at the end of the month. On the seventeenth a colonel on the Italian General Staff had confidentially told a German liaison officer in Rome that the Italian attack would begin eight or nine days later. A senior official of the foreign ministry had then drafted a telegram to the German ambassador in Rome directing him to deliver a stern demarche to the Italian government, but Ribbentrop had prevented the dispatch of this telegram, saying that its tone was too strong and that the ambassador should merely direct a "friendly inquiry" to Count Ciano. Almost simultaneously Hitler was shown a telegram in which his ambassador in Rome referred to the Italian plans against Greece, and not long afterward he saw a full report by the ambassador on a conversation with Ciano. In this exchange, the Italian foreign minister pointed out: "Italy has complete freedom of action over Greece. The Führer has conceded this to the Duce"—words which caused Ribbentrop to telephone his ministry and stop even the telegram about the "friendly inquiry." The whole matter must be decided by the Führer, said Ribbentrop; and Hitler's decision was that Italy must be trusted, and that no inquiry was to be sent to Rome.

Hitler returned to Berlin. For the next two weeks—ending with Molotov's arrival from Moscow—he lost the initiative, thanks to Mussolini's untimely attack on Greece. He unenthusiastically examined one peripheral project after another: the capture of Gibraltar, support for the Italians in Egypt, the mining of the Suez Canal, and even the occupation of various Atlantic islands as bases for a possible future war with the United States. Now he began to regret that he had not invaded Britain, and the diaries of his staff show him repeating years later that the navy had smart-talked him out of it. Julius Schaub recalled, "The Führer told me afterward, 'So long as I acted on instinct I acted rightly; the moment I allowed myself to be persuaded, things went wrong—as with the invasion of Britain.'"

During this period of indecision, only the Luftwaffe bombing—which had now killed fourteen thousand people in Britain—and the U-boat blockade continued. Meanwhile, Mussolini's humiliation by the Greeks restored British morale. For a time Hitler considered the possibility of seeking an armistice with Britain at the expense of Italy or France; but his instinct was against that, and he told Göring —as chief of the Four-Year Plan—to prepare the war economy for a long fight. Some time before, on returning through France from his meeting with Franco, he had cabled Admiral Karl Dönitz, the wiry commander of the German U-boat fleet, to join his train; he had ordered him to build huge concrete shelters to protect the U-boats from enemy air attacks on new submarine bases in western France. The navy had not thought them really necessary, but on his return to Berlin now Hitler sent for Fritz Todt and showed him precisely what he wanted. By Easter 1941 the first "U-boat pens" were ready—a good example of Hitler's foresight.

The Axis alliance as such had again reached low ebb. Throughout the summer the German army had encouraged Hitler to offer Italy armored units to ensure victory in Egypt, but the Italians had proudly snubbed this offer. At the Brenner meeting early in October, however, the Duce had hinted that he could use German tanks after all, and throughout that month Hitler had prepared to send his 3rd Panzer Division to help the Italians capture Marsa Matrûh; the army had sent a panzer general to carry out an on-the-spot investigation in North Africa. By the time the general reported to Hitler at the beginning of November, the Führer had determined to let the Italians stew in their own juice all winter. He would, instead, use the spare troops to invade Greece from Bulgaria and thus secure an outlet to the Aegean Sea; and he also planned a simultaneous attack on Gibraltar together with Spain but without Italy, since he could meet Spain's territorial demands at Italy's expense. He told his army adjutant he was so angry with Italy that he was minded to send no troops to North Africa and none either to Albania—into which Italian attack divisions had retreated after a Greek counterattack.

The panzer general's report from North Africa was the last straw: the Italians were highly unready to resume their offensive; their army commanders were inadequate, the water supplies for the attacking troops were insecure, and German mechanized units would be adversely affected by engine breakdowns under desert conditions. Hitler forthwith "wrote off" all idea of sending troops to North Africa; he ordered the planning to continue on a purely caretaker basis only. Ironically, it was to General Rommel that the Führer now bluntly proclaimed, "Not one man and not one pfennig will I send to North Africa." A few days later the disgrace of the Italians was complete. They had kept their battle fleet in harbor rather than risk it in an assault on Crete; now a handful of British torpedo planes attacked the warships in Taranto harbor and crippled three battleships, including Mussolini's most modern battleship. *Schadenfreude* in Berlin was tempered by the realization that the strategic balance in the Mediterranean had been ominously tilted.

Hitler's lack of strategic purpose was most clearly expressed in his rambling discussion with his supreme commanders on November 4 and in the resulting Wehrmacht directive issued a week later. General Franco had just personally written to Hitler that he took his oral promises very seriously—which meant that he intended to declare war on Britain. Hitler now told his commanders that he wanted to speed up Spain's entry into the war and tackle Gibraltar—the key to the western Mediterranean—as soon as the political negotiations were out of the way. A wing of Junkers 88 dive-bombers would fly from French airfields, wipe out the British warships sheltering in Gibraltar, and land in Spain; at the same time powerful German ground forces would cross into Spain and invest the British fortress. Since the British would probably covet the Canaries or Portugal's Cape Verde Islands once Gibraltar had fallen, the Germans must occupy those Atlantic islands, too. The political talks were to start at once.

In the Balkans, an operation for the occupation of northern Greece (Macedonia and Thrace) was to be planned should need arise. That Hitler desired the Dardanelles to come under German control is also evident, though this would eventually mean war with Turkey. However, on November 4 he commented to General Halder: "We cannot go on down to the Dardanelles until we have defeated Russia." Russia remained the one great area where Hitler could take a bold initiative, and it came higher in his list of priorities than invading Britain. At the end of October, a member of Jodl's staff had noted that even though the Soviet Union had just occupied still more Romanian territory—three islands in the Danube estuary, on the pretext that they were part of Bessarabia—this encroachment was for the present being played down. "No orders of any kind have been issued for Case East, nor are any as yet to be expected." And in the admiralty it was optimistically believed that "Case East is no longer considered likely as things are going at present." But, on November 4, Hitler said to Halder that Russia remained the nub of Europe's problems: "Everything must be done so that we are ready for the final showdown."

What triggered Hitler's remark? From the Forschungsamt reports Hitler now knew that in Moscow Molotov had recently discussed Russia's interest in the Dardanelles with Sir Stafford Cripps and had even demanded a naval base there. The ultimate clash between Germany and the USSR seemed inevitable if Hitler could not deflect Moscow's interests toward the Persian Gulf and India. But the Nazi party also seems to have reminded Hitler where his real mission lay. On the last day of October, the ruthless Gauleiter of Posen, Arthur Greiser, lunched with Hitler and Bormann at the Chancellery and complained at the way the eyes of the German people were currently turned west instead of east. The conquests in the west had brought Germany a bigger population to feed, and this was the very opposite of the Lebensraum policies Hitler had preached to the Party: Lebensraum could only be assured by conquests in the east. "The Führer agreed that this opinion was a correct one," noted Bormann, "and emphasized that when peace is concluded absolutely every young and capable civil servant aspiring to promotion will have to serve a number of years in the eastern territories."

On the eve of Molotov's arrival in Berlin, Hitler visited Field Marshal von Bock, his formidable new Commander in Chief in the east. Bock wrote:

The Führer called, sat half an hour at my bedside, and was very friendly and concerned. The overall situation was covered in detail. He is furious at Italy's escapade in Greece; not only did Italy keep it secret from us, she actually denied it when we taxed her with it. The Führer described how he tried to prevent the mischief by going down to Florence, or at least to keep things on ice long enough for us to lend a helping hand; but in vain—Mussolini had announced he could no longer call off the operation that had begun. The ultimate—and highly undesirable—outcome is that the Romanian oil fields will be threatened by the British air force units from Salonika. This danger is so great that it may oblige us to take countermeasures. . . . What will transpire in the east is still an open question; circumstances may force us to step in to forestall any more dangerous developments.

The outcome of Molotov's visit would determine whether or not Hitler would attack the Soviet Union. In the secret directive he circulated to his service commanders on November 12 after a week of drafting and redrafting, Hitler approved this wording: "*Russia.* Political discussions have been initiated with the aim of establishing what Russia's posture will be over the coming period. Irrespective of the outcome of these discussions, all the preparations orally ordered for the east are to continue. Directives thereon will follow as soon as the army's basic operational plan has been submitted to and approved by me."

Molotov had his first encounter with Hitler at three o'clock that day.

The Soviet foreign minister arrived at Anhalt station with a big bodyguard. Ribbentrop's state secretary, Weizsäcker, described them as "good gangster types for a film"—he found it depressing that 130 million Russians were being represented by such a shabby bunch. The station building was brilliant with fresh greenery and flowers, Russian flags waved, and a military band greeted the delegation. Every member seemed to be under his neighbor's surveillance. Molotov had even had to radio Moscow for permission to eat in the German dining car. He was accompanied by a young official, ostensibly an interpreter, though he spoke not one word to the Germans. Weizsäcker wrote in his diary: "Molotov seems to be a thorough worker. His men are timid. All are obviously afraid of us. Many of them quote Bismarck and his concept of a German-Russian collaboration. . . . From our viewpoint too a cooling off in the east is worthwhile. This summer it has become *à la mode* to wish for war with Russia or regard it as necessary." And in an entry he added some days later: "Why not let them stew in their own stupid bolshevism? So long as the country is ruled by officials like those we have seen here, it's less to be feared than when the czars were in power!"

Not since his talks with the British before Munich, in 1938, had Adolf Hitler heard such tough language as Molotov used on November 12 and 13. Hitler had always contended that the Soviet Union and the Reich were two different worlds, but might try to live together. As Ribbentrop had done before him, he harangued the Russian minister as though he were at a Party rally. He put it to Molotov candidly that it was in their interests to stand back to back, rather than try to outstare one another. If Russia wanted to share in the booty as the British Empire fell apart, then now was the time to declare Soviet solidarity with the Tripartite Pact powers. He was not asking for an outright military alliance from Russia; he sympathized, he said, with Russia's desire for an outlet to the high seas and suggested she should expand southward from Batum and Baku toward the Persian Gulf and India; Germany would expand into Africa. As for Russia's interest in the Dardanelles, Hitler restated his willingness to call for the renegotiation of the 1936 Montreux Convention, which governed the straits, to bring it into line with Moscow's defensive interests.

Molotov—one year younger than Hitler, a stocky, nondescript figure who reminded Weizsäcker of "a schoolmaster type"—itemized with an occasional frosty smile the price demanded by the Soviet Union for any explicit alignment with the Axis. Stalin himself had dictated these points to him before he left, he said. Russia wanted another stab at Finland—she intended to occupy and annex the whole country, which had, after all, been assigned her by the 1939 pact Molotov had signed with Ribbentrop in Moscow. But Hitler was adamant that there must be no fresh war in the Baltic; he was at war, and he needed Finland's nickel and timber supplies. When Molotov complained—"crudely," as he himself apologetically noted—that Hitler's recent guarantee to Romania and the troops he had just sent there could only be directed against Russia, Hitler acidly reminded him that Romania had herself asked for them. And when Molotov announced Russia's intention of inviting Bulgaria to sign a nonaggression pact which would permit the establishment of a Soviet base near the Dardanelles and would guarantee the safety of King Boris, Hitler ironically inquired whether Bulgaria too had *asked* for such assistance; pressed later by Molotov for a reply to Soviet terms, Hitler evasively answered that he must consult Mussolini!

Molotov was unconvinced: he was unconvinced that Hitler was serious in his offer of partnership; since Italy's crippling reverses in Greece and at Taranto, he was unconvinced of Axis supremacy; above all he was unconvinced that Britain's days were numbered. Each of his conferences with Hitler was terminated by the warning of approaching British aircraft, and his dinner at the Soviet embassy on the thirteenth ended abruptly for the same reason. Ribbentrop invited him to the concrete shelter at his home and here—who will ever know what prompted Molotov's untimely candor?—the Soviet foreign minister revealed that Moscow's long-range interests extended far beyond the Balkans—as though that was not ominous enough! Molotov asked Ribbentrop whether Germany really was interested in preserving Sweden's neutrality, and he declared that Russia could never entirely forego an interest in the western approaches to the *Baltic* either—the Kattegat and Skagerrak.

When Ribbentrop told the Führer of Molotov's revelations in the shelter, Hitler was stunned. Like Italy, the Soviet Union had suffered only military disgraces—most recently in Finland—while Hitler's Wehrmacht had crushed the resistance of one country after another. Yet Molotov had made immense demands. "He demanded that we give him military bases on Danish soil on the outlets to the North Sea," Hitler was to recall in the last week of his life. "He had already staked a claim to them. He demanded Constantinople, Romania, Bulgaria, and Finland—and *we* were supposed to be the victors!" While the public was deliberately fed the impression that the formal discussions had been harmonious and successful, within the OKW and Hitler's Chancellery there was no doubt that the parting of the ways had come. Keitel's adjutant recalled that when he entered the Führer's daily war conference the next day it was like entering the house of a dying man: a funereal aura clouded the proceedings. One of Hitler's own adjutants wrote: "[The Führer] says he never had expected much from it all. The discussions have shown, he says, which way the Russians' plans are lying: M[olotov] has let the cat out of the bag. He (the Führer) is vastly relieved, this won't even have to remain a *mariage de convenance.*"

Irrevocable and terrible in its finality, the decision Adolf Hitler now took was one he never regretted, even in the jaws of ultimate defeat.

The "Barbarossa" Directive

After Molotov's trainload of advisers and secret police officials had crossed the demarcation line back into Russia's share of Europe, an air of uncertainty and gloom shrouded Hitler's Chancellery. One of his adjutants recorded his conviction that the Führer himself was at a loss which way to turn next: his confidence in his own military commanders—and particularly in Göring's Luftwaffe—was waning. Perturbed at Britain's unexpected tenacity, uncertain about Russia's true military strength, again and again he repeated that he alone would decide the next move. The talks with Molotov had betrayed Russia's designs on Europe. He could not afford to surrender the Balkans; it would be awkward enough to have Finland in Russia's sway. As for Ribbentrop's deal with Stalin in August 1939, Hitler now admitted: "That pact never was an honest one, because the gulf between the ideologies was just too wide."

Opinion among Hitler's principal advisers was divided about the Russian campaign. Ribbentrop had been convinced there was no alternative. Brauchitsch certainly did not oppose it. Halder gave no clear lead one way or the other: his papers show him to have regarded now Britain, now Russia, as Germany's most important opponent; his mind was in confusion. Keitel's opposition had been stilled. Jodl unquestionably regarded the Russian campaign as inevitable and was optimistic about the outcome. The Party leaders gloated in anticipation of the new empire awaiting them. Only Göring and Raeder voiced pertinent objections.

The Reichsmarschall confronted Hitler with them on November 13: it would be foolish to court a war with Russia. His Luftwaffe had only just got its teeth into Britain's industrial flesh; in addition, Germany could never police such a huge area in the east. Far better to let Russia attack Finland and advance toward the Dardanelles, since this must surely bring Britain into open conflict with Russia (such was also Papen's advice). Hitler replied that the danger from Russia was so singular that it must be met squarely before the Soviet industrial buildup was complete. He evidently also explained to Göring that in a long war Germany could beat Britain's food blockade only by expanding to the east; similarly, the oil requirements of large-scale air war against Britain—and no doubt the United States—could only be covered by capturing the Caucasian oil fields. Göring was told to assume that the attack on Russia would start on May 1, 1941, and last only a few months; he thereupon ceased objecting, and instructed Keitel's chief economic officer to supply him with a dossier on Russia's arms economy. On the fourteenth, it was Raeder's turn to voice the admiralty's emphatic opposition to attacking Russia before Britain had been defeated, and the admiral maintained this vigorous criticism of the plan until the end of the year.

Heinrich Himmler probably echoed Hitler's views most closely in a November speech to Party officials in which he pinpointed the frontier between Europe and Asia. People suggested it was the Ural Mountains, but the Mongol strains permeated the people both sides of that barrier too strongly to escape Himmler's racialistic scrutiny:

> That is why this Russian people will never make a purely European or even a pure Asiatic race. It must be treated as a potpourri of races and kept within its frontiers. By brute force if by no other means. At present there is no need for that; we have our friendship pact with Russia. But this friendship pact is not a love affair; it's a pact designed to meet the most elementary requirements of our two nations. Up to now, by means of this pact Russia has subjugated entire countries and nations, apart from Finland, without drawing her sword from its scabbard; she has annexed large territories on her western and southern frontiers. Her appetite threatened to grow gigantically, so it became necessary for us to map out our mutual interests to each other afresh. In his long overdue visit to Berlin, Molotov has been given the necessary instructions. If what I have heard is true, then Stalin is not permitted to start any wars for the moment, or any fighting, as otherwise he will be dealt a sharp rebuke by our own guns. This order holds good both for her [Russia's] evil designs on Finland and for any she may have in the south or southeast. She is permitted to launch military operations only with the Führer's express permission. To put muscle into our orders, we have based enough troops along our eastern frontier for the Red czar in Moscow to take them seriously. Anyway, as I said in my last speech, Russia is militarily quite harmless. Her officer corps is so poor that they do not even bear comparison with our NCOs; her army is as badly equipped as trained. They cannot possibly be any danger to us.

Before ten days had passed, it was clear the Russians' aims were irreconcilable with Hitler's. Ribbentrop had submitted to Moscow a draft treaty embodying in secret protocols the substance of Hitler's oral offer to Molotov: Germany's territorial expansion would take place in Central Africa; Italy's in north and northeast Africa; Japan's in the Far East; and the Soviet Union's toward the Indian Ocean. On November 25, Molotov submitted the four conditions on which Russia would sign. The first two—a demand that Hitler evacuate from Finland the troops sent in August 1940, and that Bulgaria conclude a pact with Russia granting her military bases within range of the Bosphorus—were wholly unacceptable to Hitler. He instructed Ribbentrop to make no reply at all.

The Führer had retreated from these traumatic events in Berlin on November 16 and spent the next few days at the Berghof. He had, of course, privately notified King Boris of Bulgaria of the proposals Molotov had outlined for Soviet "protection" of his country, and on the seventeenth Hitler conferred with the king at the Berghof. He had a certain mistrust of all kings, but the short, swarthy Bulgarian monarch spoke fluent German and had an easygoing manner which tended to win over the Führer. (During this private visit to Germany he stayed at the Hotel Vier Jahreszeiten in Munich, where he caused consternation to his personal detectives by slipping out of the hotel's back door and strolling through Munich's bohemian quarter and the English Gardens.) Boris was a shrewd businessman, and provided that Hitler did not compromise him too early—after all, Bulgaria was exposed to attack from Turkey and the Soviet Union—he was willing to let German divisions cross Bulgarian territory when the time came to attack northern Greece. Hitler offered him western Thrace as an outlet to the Aegean if Bulgarian troops would participate, but in the king's view this was going too far. Boris also warned Hitler that road conditions were so poor in winter that it would be advisable to postpone the assault on Greece until early March. Bulgaria was also reluctant to join the Tripartite Pact at present.[1]

By the end of the following week, Hungary, Romania, and Slovakia had all joined the Tripartite Pact. The Greeks had now started a counteroffensive into Albania. Italy begged Hitler to supply German trucks to replace the inferior Italian transport, but Hitler refused. He saw no realistic way of helping Italy until the spring. In Vienna, the Hungarian prime minister agreed to allow German troops to cross into Romania. Yugoslavia would have to be cajoled into refraining from molesting the German movements toward the Greek frontier: to the chagrin of the Italians—who had designs of their own on Yugoslavia—Hitler insisted on luring Yugoslavia toward the Axis by offering her part of northern Greece (Salonika) and guaranteeing her possessions. The greatest impression on Hitler was made by the new Romanian leader, General Antonescu, who paid a first visit to Berlin on the twentieth. His contempt for the Slavs, his admiration for the National Socialist movement, and his soldierly bearing won the Führer immedi-

---

[1] She joined on March 1, 1941, simultaneously with the entry of the first German divisions. See page 208 below.

ately; Antonescu announced that in signing the Tripartite Pact, Romania was not just acting out a formality but was ready "to fight sword in hand beside the Axis powers for the victory of civilization." Hitler adroitly hinted that the anti-Romanian Vienna Award might yet be rescinded in Romania's favor when peace came.

Italy's disgrace made it easier to reshuffle Spanish and Italian claims on African territory—all the more necessary now that the Gibraltar operation's importance had been enhanced by the British foothold in Greece. When General Franco's foreign minister, Serrano Suñet, had visited the Berghof on the eighteenth, Hitler had given him "the friendly advice" to declare war on Britain as soon as possible: "Any hesitation by politicians can easily cost thousands of brave soldiers their lives!" He bluffed the Spaniard with fictitious figures of Germany's armed might and glibly promised to supply all the wheat and oil Spain would need; but he had no real answer to the minister's argument that the Spanish people were not psychologically ready for a new war, and he could make no concrete moves to replace the vague assurances he had offered both at Hendaye and in a secret agreement Spain had since signed with Italy and Germany concerning the African territories it was to receive. Hitler knew that if he made public the inroads that were to be made in Morocco, the French there would immediately declare for de Gaulle.

There were already signs that Pétain was treating with the enemy. The Spanish foreign minister advised Hitler that Pierre Laval was one of the most hated men in France for collaborating with Germany, and that this fact indicated the true sentiments of the French people. Hitler instinctively agreed—he feared that every weapon he provided to Vichy would one day be turned against him. When Washington announced the appointment of an admiral as ambassador to Vichy in place of its present lowly chargé d'affaires, Hitler's suspicions of the "old fogy" —Pétain—intensified. The Forschungsamt had reported on November 11 that secret talks were going on in New York between emissaries of Pétain and Churchill.

Hitler for his part did nothing to strengthen the French people's affection for Laval. He authorized Gauleiter Josef Bürckel, the civil administrator of Lorraine, to expel a hundred thousand hostile French citizens from the province, and later in November nearly seven thousand German Jews from Baden and the Palatinate were on Hitler's orders transported into Vichy France. Both actions aroused Pétain's indignation. Meanwhile the Franco-German talks on military collaboration were conducted desultorily at the German embassy in Paris. The fact that Hitler appointed only Major General Walter Warlimont, Jodl's deputy, as Germany's representative showed how little importance he attached to them.

Hitler's timetable began to take shape, dominated by the need to program the commitment of his scarcest resources most efficiently—in this case the Junkers 88 dive-bomber squadrons, which were only gradually coming off the production lines. Their commitment in Spain must be over by February if they were to be available for the attack on Greece (an operation now code-named "Marita," after the daughter of one of Jodl's junior staff). On May 1 the attack on Russia would begin. (This had not prevented Hitler from "confidentially" informing the talkative Ciano that he would be invading Britain in May).

A number of untidy residual problems remained. King Leopold of Belgium, now a prisoner, had been brought to the Berghof on November 19, where he had hinted that if Hitler would broadcast an explicit guarantee of Belgium's future independence—as the British were doing—the Belgians might be open to military and political agreements. Hitler did not rise to the bait: he saw no need. Nor would he release the Belgian prisoners, as they supplied him with a useful labor force, whereas Belgium already had widespread unemployment.

The second area that briefly attracted Hitler's attention was southern Ireland, which had remained neutral though with pronounced pro-German sympathies. In mid-November, the OKW had examined the possibility of an appeal from Dublin for German aid; but it was not until the twenty-second that Hitler directly considered the matter.

Early that morning German army Intelligence picked up a British radio message reading: "Fifty wireless operators (no Jews) are to be provided for transferring GHQ. Depart Carlisle November 22 1940 1300 hrs for operation Ireland. Starting point for operation Ireland is Rosslea in Ulster." Taking the political situation into account, the German High Command deduced that a British invasion of southern Ireland was imminent. This would provide Britain with airfields and submarine and escort bases which would gravely set back the German U-boat operations west of Ireland. To deprive London of her apparent motive, the German foreign ministry denied any German intention of occupying Ireland, and this was welcomed by Eire's President Eamon De Valera; Berlin believed that Dublin's determination to beat back any British invasion had given London second thoughts. Hitler's attention, once attracted to the Emerald Isle, characteristically lingered on, however. On the twenty-seventh he asked his High Command to analyze the pros and cons of invading Ireland, whose fall into German hands would spell the end of Britain. Perhaps no episode illustrates so vividly the whims which inspired Hitler's *ad hoc* military strategy as the winter of 1940 approached. It was not difficult for Admiral Raeder to demonstrate that a prolonged German occupation of Ireland in the face of Britain's huge naval superiority was quite out of the question.

Despite the remarkable resilience of the British people under heavy air attacks, all Hitler's advisers—and particularly Admiral Raeder—saw the continued

bombing of British industry and dockyards—coupled with the submarine campaign—as the most likely way to bring Britain to her knees. Nothing was to be
allowed to distract effort from this remorseless campaign. Coventry, and now
Birmingham, had been devastated by night attacks before once again worsening
weather forced a halt to German raids. (Indeed, bombers were one reason why
Hitler wanted the Azores, which provided his only chance of striking at the
United States with long-range Messerschmitts—still on the drawing board, but
he had seen a mock-up at Augusburg in 1937—and forcing the Americans to set
up their own system of air defense at the expense of helping the British.) But
Hitler still lacked the determination needed to use the strategic bomber force to
maximum effect. On the morning after Birmingham's first raid he told a Hungarian visitor that he was sorry about the fine cities and the people being destroyed in Britain; it was all the fault of incompetent British politicians. Perhaps
he admired the ability of the "Germanic" British to stand up to the bombers.
Himmler explained to Party officials: "The Führer had no desire to destroy the
British people or their empire. The British are a race related to our own and in
their bones they are as uncowed as ever. This is displayed by the unheard-of
toughness with which the British people has taken its beating from the Luftwaffe,
month after month. The bombardment of London and the wiping out of entire
cities has not sufficed . . ."

Bored by the failure of his squadrons in the Battle of Britain, Reichsmarschall
Göring had gone on an extended hunting leave on his estate at Rominten. On
November 25, Hitler explored with Field Marshal Milch and Chief of Air Staff
Jeschonnek ways of attacking the British position in the eastern Mediterranean
from Italian-controlled airfields. The most important target would be the British
fleet at Alexandria, but this could not be tackled until the Italians had taken
Marsa Matrûh; the Luftwaffe was to prepare to mine the Suez Canal, though the
Italians were still unwilling to agree. Meanwhile, until the German attack on
Greece started in the spring, the Luftwaffe was to help the Italians out of their
predicament by attacking military targets in Greece. The Italian squadrons which
had briefly assisted in the attack on Britain were to be transferred to Albania.
Hitler complained to the air force generals that the Italians failed to realize how
grave the situation was: they were "frittering" their forces away, and had brought
the British bomber squadrons so close that Germany must now supply sorely
needed antiaircraft batteries to Romania (to protect her oil interests) and to
southern Germany.

On December 4, Milch brought Hitler details of Göring's proposals: by basing
the Tenth Air Corps, with two squadrons of Junkers 87 dive-bombers, on Sicily,
and two more squadrons of Junkers 88 dive-bombers (the heavier, longer-range
aircraft) in southern Italy, Germany could effectively block the narrows between
Sicily and North Africa. Jeschonnek's deputy wrote after this conference: "Dis-

cussion between Führer and Milch on possibilities of battering British position in Mediterranean. This is necessary as the Italian disaster in Greece is having psychological effects quite apart from any military disadvantages: Africa and Spain are beginning to waver in their attitude toward us." Hitler handed Milch a letter to carry immediately to Mussolini. In it he warned the Duce that he must have these squadrons back by early February for use elsewhere. By the seventh, Milch and the Deputy Chief of Air Staff were back from Rome, reporting to Hitler on Mussolini's optimism about the situation in Albania. "Midday, back in Berlin," wrote Jeschonnek's deputy. "Conference with Führer, who is considerably upset by the unpleasant consequences of the situation in the Mediterranean. He fears this may have an effect on Spain's attitude."

That this was no idle fear was shown a few days later. On November 28, Ribbentrop's ambassador in Madrid had reported that General Franco was willing for the proposed preparations for Spain's entry into the war to proceed; Hitler assumed that this meant "proceed immediately," and on December 4 he sent Admiral Canaris to Franco with a personal letter proposing that German troops formally cross the Spanish frontier on January 10, which would mean starting the assault on Gibraltar, six hundred miles from the frontier, in the first week of February.

Field Marshal von Reichenau would command the assault; it would start on February 4 or 5 and last four weeks. By mid-May 1941, Hitler could have the troops back for other purposes. The Führer demanded that the assault open with a saturation bombing attack on Gibraltar—particularly on the fleet units and dockyard there. Then the gun batteries were to be silenced, and the Rock itself battered with thousands of rounds of artillery fire; the level ground between the Rock and the Spanish frontier was to be plowed through and through to neutralize enemy minefields. The heaviest available tanks would tackle the British troops sheltering in the galleries, and the remnants would be driven out by colossal demolition charges. "The principle must be to use as much equipment as possible to avoid [German] bloodshed."

Like so many other projects, the capture of Gibraltar was an operation Hitler had vividly pictured in his imagination night after night.

The directive for the Gibraltar operation, code-named "Felix," had already been prepared, and General Jodl was already packing his bags for Madrid, where he was to explain the plan to Franco, when a telegram arrived from the Spanish capital bringing everything to an abrupt halt. In a long audience on the evening of the seventh, Franco had stated that for economic reasons Spain could not be ready by January 10: what good would Germany's deliveries do Spain if her transport network could not distribute the foodstuffs to the starving populace? Besides, Britain would seize the Canary Islands and Spain's other overseas possessions. It was in both their countries' interests, Franco suggested, that he decline Hitler's proposal; he did not want Spain to become a burden on the Axis.

Hitler ordered Keitel to ask by what date Spain *could* be ready; Canaris replied from Madrid that Spain could only join in the war if Britain was on the brink of collapse. The alacrity with which Hitler now abandoned "Felix"—though in later years he again toyed more than once with this idea—suggests that his instinct was screaming warnings against accepting obligations toward a second Latin nation. In the immediate aftermath of Franco's rebuff he lamented this further proof that Mussolini's misadventures in the Balkans had undermined the awe in which the world held the Axis. He also greatly regretted forfeiting the psychological bonus the capture of Gibraltar would have bestowed.

Molotov's negative reply to Hitler's proposals at the end of November 1940 dispelled whatever hesitations Hitler still had about attacking Russia. Visiting the sick General von Bock again briefly on December 3, the field marshal's sixtieth birthday, Hitler warned that the "eastern problem" was now coming to a head; there seemed to be links running between Russia and the United States, and this in turn made a joint Anglo-Russian enterprise more likely. "It would be dangerous to sit back and wait for the end of a development like that. But if the Russians are eliminated, Britain will have no hope whatever of defeating us on the Continent, particularly now that America is prevented from interceding effectively by Japan, whose rear is free of danger now." To Brauchitsch, two days later, Hitler announced, "The hegemony of Europe will be decided in the fight with Russia."

Hitler's strategic timetable took shape. He would execute "Marita" early in March. Of course, if the Greeks saw the light and showed their British "guests" the door, he would call off "Marita" altogether—he had no interest whatever in occupying Greece. Then he would attack Russia during May. "In three weeks we will be in Leningrad!" Schmundt heard him say.

This confident prediction was symptomatic of the German army's crass underestimate of their Russian opponent's strength. Virtually nothing was known about the Red Army: a complete search of archives in France—Russia's own ally!—had yielded nothing. Hitler was confident that the German Mark III tank with its 50-millimeter gun provided clear superiority over the obsolete Red Army equipment; they would have one thousand five hundred by spring. "The Russian himself is inferior. His army has no leaders," he assured his generals. "Once the Russian army has been beaten, the disaster will take its inevitable course."

At 3 P.M. on December 5, Hitler's military advisers—Brauchitsch and Halder of the army, and Keitel and Jodl of the OKW—came to the Chancellery to argue out each phase of the coming operations and their tactical details. Now for the first time the two varying concepts of the Russian campaign—the meticulous studies drawn up and exercised by Halder's staff and the draft operational plan submitted by Jodl's Colonel Lossberg—were brought into informal synthesis. Halder's proposal was distinguished by a particularly powerful main drive toward Moscow, the hub of the Soviet political and transport system; Lossberg's "Fritz" attached more weight to the northernmost army group and the occupation of the Baltic coast.[2] Lossberg's plan was evidently not actually discussed at this conference, but its influence on Hitler is clear, for in his reply to Halder the Führer now drew heavily on Lossberg's arguments. Both Halder's plan (which had been originated by General Erich Marcks and completed by General Friedrich Paulus) and Lossberg's assumed that the Russians must of necessity defend the western areas of the Soviet Union and the Ukraine; and both stated that the Russians must be prevented from staging an ordered retreat as in 1812—the Russian front must be pierced by armored spearheads, encircled from the rear, and liquidated. The army and OKW were also agreed that they must occupy as much Soviet territory as necessary. This would prevent the Russian air force from reaching Reich territory; it would also enable Göring's bomber squadrons to attack Russian industries and thus prevent a resurgence of armed Soviet might. Halder proposed that the offensive end along a line from the Volga River to Archangel.

Where Hitler took exception, though at first with noticeable mildness, was to Halder's insistence that nothing detract from the main assault on Moscow. Hitler wanted the Russian forces in the Baltic countries to be encircled first; a similar huge encirclement action by Army Group South, south of the Pripyet Marshes, would liquidate the Russian armies in the Ukraine. Only after that should it be decided whether to advance on Moscow or to bypass the Soviet capital in the rear. "Moscow is not all that important," he explained. This was the first hint of a strategic controversy that was eventually to rage between Hitler and the General Staff in the summer of 1941, though neither Halder nor Brauchitsch took it seriously as yet. Indeed, when the first draft directive for the Russian campaign was brought to Hitler by Jodl, it still conformed with Halder's recommendation of a main thrust toward Moscow ("in conformity with the plans submitted to me"). But Hitler ordered the document redrafted in the form *he* had emphasized: the principal task of the two army groups operating north of the Pripyet Marshes was to drive the Russians out of the Baltic countries. "Only after this, the most urgent task, has been accomplished, followed by the capture of Leningrad and Kronstadt, are the offensive operations to be continued with the object of seizing the vital transport and armaments center, Moscow."

Hitler's motives for seizing the Baltic coast first were clear. The admiralty

[2]Details of the Lossberg plan, dated September 15, 1940, are summarized on page 162 above.

attached particular importance to restoring peace in the Baltic as soon as possible. The Baltic was the navy's training ground and the route Germany's ore supplies from Scandinavia must take; besides, when the Russians had been destroyed in the Baltic countries, great forces would be released for other operations. The Russian campaign would be a short one; indeed, it must be settled together with all other continental problems before 1941 was over—for from 1942 onward the United States would be capable of intervening.

Toward the United States, where Roosevelt had just been elected for a third term, Hitler was to display unwonted patience despite what he regarded as extreme provocations for one long year. Technically neutral, the United States under the Roosevelt administration had violated neutrality time and again; both Roosevelt and Churchill yearned for the incident that would swing American public opinion around toward open intervention. Until then American aid was limited to the trade of over-age destroyers for British bases in the Western hemisphere, the exporting of aircraft and munitions, and a fringe of illegal military activities: American citizens fought in the Royal Air Force; a blind eye was turned on British violations of the Pan-American security zone; and United States warships chased, harried, and shadowed Axis merchant ships plying their trade in transatlantic waters. These warships were ostensibly escorting the German steamships for their own safety, but the admiralty in Berlin knew from its radio reconnaissance and decoding sections that in reality the Americans were passing on to the British all the information they could about these blockade-runners.

In vain Admiral Raeder protested to Hitler about this "glaring proof of the United States' nonneutrality." He asked whether this active hostility was to be allowed to go unchallenged, and whether this was "compatible with the honor of the German Reich." But to Hitler the United States was still a *quantité négligible* and he wanted it to stay that way in 1941. Nothing must happen to increase the tension between Germany and the United States. Throughout the year that followed, the dossier of American violations thickened; and now that the foreign ministry and Forschungsamt were also reading the American diplomatic ciphers, the evidence against Roosevelt hardened. But nothing would alter Hitler's determined refusal to take up the gauntlet flung down to Germany.

His eyes were now fixed on Russia. On December 18, Jodl brought him the final version of the campaign directive, retyped on the large "Führer typewriter." "Fritz," Lossberg's code name for the coming campaign, was replaced by the more majestic-sounding "Barbarossa," the name by which the first Emperor Friedrich had gone into history eight hundred years before as the founder of a mighty empire. Partly the handiwork of Jodl, a master stylist whose spoken German was very clear and simple, and partly the product of Hitler's pen, the eleven-page document instructed the Wehrmacht to be prepared to "overthrow Soviet Russia in a rapid campaign even before the war with Britain is over." The Luftwaffe would have a purely support role, rather than one of strategic bombardment. All preparations were to be complete by mid-May 1941; he, Hitler, would give the word for the necessary troop concentrations to begin eight weeks before the chosen date "if Russia should fail to change in her attitude toward us." Nine copies of the directive were signed for the commanders in chief and the OKW; those let into the dreadful secret were to be kept to an absolute minimum, and every single phase was to be camouflaged against Russian scrutiny.

From now on his intention of disposing of the Soviet menace was the one constant in Hitler's grand strategy. His goals in Africa and his policies toward Spain and France had been reduced to a shambles by Italy's military ignominy. He expected General Maxime Weygand, the French Resident in North Africa, to declare for de Gaulle at any moment. Franco's rebuff robbed Hitler of direct access to Morocco. At short notice the army and OKW drafted a campaign plan, "Attila," in case Germany had to occupy Vichy France as well and stop the French home fleet from crossing to North Africa.

Mussolini blamed his political and military advisers for the Greek calamity: they had promised him it would take little more than a "military two-step" to invade Greece, but now the Greek army was deep inside Albania, outnumbering the Italian divisions more than 2 to 1. Badoglio, chief of the Italian armed forces, resigned; Mussolini replaced him with General Ugo Cavallero and sent the Italian ambassador with a pathetic appeal to Hitler to speed Yugoslavia's entry into the Tripartite Pact as a warning to Greece. Hitler responded that the only methods that would halt the Italian army's headlong flight were barbaric ones "like putting the guilty generals and colonels before the firing squad and decimating the other ranks." Yugoslavia had little love for Italy and refused even to allow German trucks to pass through to the Italian forces in Albania. Hitler supplied a squadron of transport planes to help Mussolini fly divisions from Italy, and he suggested that the Duce come and see him personally on December 10. But on the ninth a further disaster began for Italy as the British army in Egypt opened a counteroffensive which was to throw back the Italian forces into Libya and result within a matter of days in the capture of thirty-eight thousand Italian troops and four of Mussolini's generals. British casualties were a little over a hundred men.

Not that Italy's disgrace was wholly a disadvantage, for now, as Hitler explained on the ninth to General Halder, "There is no need to pay any significant attention to the Italians." In addition, Franco's rebuff had absolved Hitler from keeping the pledges he had given since Hendaye. In short, he could promise France everything—and in particular that it would keep its territories intact if it would collaborate with the Axis. This honeymoon was to last less than a week, however.

In the early hours of December 14 the text of a personal letter from Marshal Pétain reached Hitler. He thanked the Führer for his honorable intentions in transferring to Les Invalides in Paris the mortal remains of Napoleon's beloved son, the Duke of Reichstadt, which had since 1832 reposed in Vienna; but he also advised Hitler that he had dismissed Pierre Laval, the deputy premier with whom the German leaders had so recently conferred at Montoire, and replaced him by Admiral Jean François Darlan who would continue the policy of cooperation and in whom Vichy had greater confidence. In vain Ribbentrop tried to secure Laval's restoration; the luckless minister was held incommunicado on Pétain's orders. Even greater was the further affront to Hitler of Pétain's refusal to attend the ceremony at Les Invalides. The marshal initiated the rumor that this was just a German trick to lure him to Paris and kidnap him—a canard which enraged Hitler. He again withdrew the hand he had extended toward France. Who needed France anyway? A vision still haunted him—the possibility of signing a peace with Britain, but this time at France's expense.

Something distantly resembling the spirit of Christmas overcame Hitler. He instructed the Luftwaffe to suspend bombing missions against Britain until Christmas was over.[3] A fortnight of aimless meandering ensued. He spoke at noon on December 18 to the new batch of officer cadets—2,375 from the Luftwaffe alone —and submitted to various medical tests in a checkup by Dr. Morell. With the "Barbarossa" decision made, a forced levity entered his conversation. On the nineteenth, when Ribbentrop's lanky SS adjutant Richard Schulze came to announce the birth of the foreign minister's son, Hitler was sitting on a bench in the Chancellery entrance hall, his hands characteristically clasped around one knee. He asked Schulze to stand beside his brother, Hansgeorg, who was one of the Führer's own SS aides, and quizzically inquired, "How big do you have to be to get into the Leibstandarte regiment?" "Six feet tall, mein Führer." Hitler sighed. "Then that rules me out. It will be back to the infantry for me!"

Keitel, Halder, and much of Jodl's staff had gone on leave. Protected by extra antiaircraft trains, Hitler set out with his personal staff on a Christmas tour of the western front. He wanted to inspect the big gun batteries which Todt's organization had installed to command the Channel coast—the sites had names like "Great Elector," "Siegfried," and "Gneisenau"—and he wanted to celebrate

---

[3]Much to the annoyance of the British foreign office, who had prepared to reap propaganda capital. See Sir Alexander Cadogan's *Diary*.

the holiday with the aircrews of Göring's fighter and bomber squadrons. (Göring himself was spending a comfortable Christmas and New Year at his Rominten estate, some twenty miles from the Russian frontier in East Prussia.) Only one frosty interview with Admiral Darlan, Pétain's "crown prince," chilled the atmosphere of Hitler's special train; Darlan recounted how his family had always hated the British and had been fighting them now for three hundred years—a perhaps inappropriate confidence, given Hitler's present mood. One of Hitler's secretaries wrote to a friend: "We have not stopped moving since December 21. Christmas on the French coast—Calais and Dunkirk. As we were eating dinner in the dining car of our special train on the twenty-third at Boulogne, the British came and started bombing, and our antiaircraft roared back at them. Even though we were shunted into a safe tunnel"—guarded by antiaircraft trains at each end—"I couldn't help feeling 'a bit queer'. . . . On New Year's Eve the mood was more than painful. . . ."

Hitler had returned to the Berghof to spend New Year with Eva Braun and his "family" of adjutants and staff. Goebbels would be making the traditional speech to the Reich. Hitler had already seen and approved the script, and marked it with spidery ink amendments of a trivial, grammatical nature, except for one: where Goebbels had wanted to proclaim "Never will we capitulate, never will we tire, and never will we be despondent," Hitler had expunged the first four words.[4]

[4]In June 1943 he again censored a Goebbels speech in the same sense; see below, page 523.

Let Europe Hold Its Breath

Hitler entered the new year, 1941, with two distantly related ambitions: to knock out Soviet Russia and thus force Britain to submit with no injury to her empire, and to rescue fascism in Italy from threatened oblivion. All else was subsidiary to these aims. He had no designs on Greece and fervently hoped that now the Greeks had thrown the Italian invaders out they would rid themselves of their British guests as well; then he could cancel the "Marita" operation against Greece. Through Admiral Canaris he had offered, using obscure Spanish and Hungarian diplomatic channels, to mediate between Greece and Italy, but in vain. As for the Italian defeats in Africa, he would not have been alarmed by them were it not for the danger that Mussolini's regime might collapse in consequence. "The fact is, for better or for worse Germany is tied to the Duce," explained Hitler on January 4. "In the long run you can only make history by loyalty," he mused virtuously. Hitler's loyalty to Mussolini is indeed worthy of an odd niche in history.

In North Africa, Hitler saw no problems that a small force of German tanks and aircraft could not put right. In the Balkans, however, a dangerous situation had developed since Italy's ill-timed attack on Greece in October. Over Hitler's broad desks at the Chancellery, and now at the Berghof, flowed the dispatches from Ribbentrop's experts. Familiar and unfamiliar Balkan potentates and diplomats were ushered past—the queen mother of Romania, prattling endlessly about the problems of Europe's other monarchs, about cousin Christian of Denmark, and about her brother King George II and Crown Prince Paul of Greece; then in January the prime minister of Bulgaria, followed a week later by King Boris again, still promising to join the Tripartite Pact but genuinely fearing that the Russians, and possibly Turkey too, would invade the moment the Germans set foot in Bulgaria, which the Russians were loudly proclaiming was in *their* sphere of interest. Here too was Antonescu, reaffirming the Romanian willingness to fight for Hitler but asking now for mines and for big guns to defend his Black

Sea port of Constanta (where seven hundred thousand tons of German oil was stockpiled) against Russian attack. Walther Hewel brought Hitler file after file of top-secret Forschungsamt intercepts and surveys. From these sources Hitler gained confidence that Turkey would not as yet intervene. Nonetheless he had ordered that the divisions assigned to "Marita" be split into three groups—one to protect Romania against Russian invasion, one in southeastern Bulgaria to dissuade Turkey from interfering, and one for the actual operation against Greece.

No terrain could be less promising for a modern army than the Balkans. Before his armies could even get into Bulgaria, they would have to throw pontoon bridges across the swirling Danube River, nearly a mile wide; the one existing railway bridge could handle only six trains a day. The roads were virtually impassable in winter and became morasses when the snow thawed. The crumbling bridges crossing the countless Balkan streams and dikes would never support the loads an army would impose on them.

Nevertheless, the Wehrmacht overcame all these obstacles: in the remaining weeks before "Marita" German staff officers in plain clothes and Volkswagens were sent throughout Bulgaria to supervise the strengthening of the bridges and the resurfacing of the roads. And when the campaign was over, Hitler was to relate to the Reichstag: "In barely three weeks this triumphant campaign has extinguished the fighting in two countries, following rutted tracks, demolished roads, across jagged slopes and boulders, along the narrowest rocky paths, through raging torrents, over towering mountain passes, across demolished bridges and bare mountainsides!"

To Hitler, early in 1941, the Balkans meant two things: the Ploesti oil field in Romania, now well within the reach of the RAF bombers even if the Athens government still refused them the necessary overflight permission; and Salonika, in northern Greece, from which the Allies had launched their deadly assault on Austria-Hungary in World War I. That must not happen this time. In 1918 there was no great power waiting on the sidelines to benefit. This time there was the Soviet Union, her eyes firmly fixed on the Dardanelles.

Hitler called together his leading military advisers and Ribbentrop for a council of war at the Berghof. It began on January 7 and ended on the ninth with a major secret speech in which he outlined the reasoning underlying his grand strategy at a length and level of frankness unfamiliar since his harangues of 1939. Keitel and Jodl were already at the Berghof; they were joined on the eighth by Raeder's chief of operations, the studious and intellectual Rear Admiral Kurt Fricke, and Halder's deputy, Paulus; and by the ninth, the afternoon of the speech itself, Brauchitsch and the army's chief of operations, Adolf Heusinger, had also been driven up the snow-covered lanes to the Berghof with General Jeschonnek, the Luftwaffe's Chief of Staff.[1] Jeschonnek was a slim, cool-headed, ruthless staff officer of an ability outstanding for his youth: at sixteen he had been an infantry lieutenant in World War I, then a fighter pilot; still only forty-one, he had a typically Silesian mentality—an abrupt, single-minded attitude with neither the ability nor the inclination to argue with those who disagreed with him. It was Jeschonnek who had confidently predicted that Britain would cave in under the pressure of the Luftwaffe bombing offensive. Now, not even Hitler accepted that: the British people's "toughness" was a wholly unexpected factor, he admitted.

As for Britain, Hitler had long since decided that an invasion would be a "crime" unless the country was so paralyzed that his army would have the kind of walkover the French had had in the Ruhr in 1923 when Germany failed to keep up reparations payments. "Terror raids by the Luftwaffe have little point or prospect of success," he explained. The Luftwaffe must concentrate on reinforcing the naval blockade of Britain's imports and on attacking bottlenecks in the arms industry. This combined offensive could produce results by July or August 1941; Britain was already admitting a 10 percent loss in arms output, and as her aluminum imports were being stifled, Hitler was skeptical about the British air force's prospects of expansion without direct American aid. Rumors of Britain's growing military strength could easily be discounted by the simplest analysis of the raw materials position: Germany had produced as much pig iron as Britain and France put together; at present she was producing twenty-four million tons a year compared with less than eight million in Britain. Germany produced far more aluminum, and as a dictatorship she could marshal far greater reserves of manpower; in Britain the number of jobless was actually increasing—a sure measure of the enemy's industrial problems. The German naval blockade was only just beginning: fifty submarines were in training, three would be in service by January, five in February, eight in March; from June onward, there would be fifteen new submarines a month. "The destruction of the English mother country is inevitable in time," Hitler concluded.

Britain, of course, realized this and the fact that Germany could be defeated only here, on the continent. "Britain," asserted Hitler, as he had consistently since the fall of France, "is propped up by her faith in the United States and Russia." Her wooing of Stalin was betrayed by many clues: Churchill had two weeks before appointed Anthony Eden, whom Hitler suspected of having pronounced pro-Bolshevik sympathies, to the foreign office;

---

[1] Jeschonnek is presumably the author of the hitherto unpublished note on Hitler's speech of January 9, 1941, which I found among the papers of his deputy, Hoffmann Waldau.

from intercepts and other sources, Hitler was aware of the diplomatic overtures Britain was preparing in Moscow; Britain had announced her lack of
interest in the Dardanelles; and Russia's chorus of increased demands since
the summer of 1940 was unlikely to be coincidence. Stalin was infinitely the
cleverest and most cautious of Hitler's opponents—he must be seen as an ice-
cold blackmailer who would not hesitate to tear up every written treaty if it
served his purposes. Russia's *Drang nach dem Westen* would lead Stalin to
exploit every temporary indisposition of Germany or her allies, and the British would do everything to egg him on.

Apart from Russia, Germany's position was now impregnable, at least for the
coming year, Hitler noted. Norway was safe from invasion—at most the British
might launch minor prestige raids for their nuisance value. Occupied France
wanted an end to the war; the unoccupied half still dreamed of a reverse in its
fortunes, but he had prepared "Operation Attila" to occupy this sector and seize
or immobilize the French fleet at Toulon should General Weygand, that "German hater," declare North Africa for the Allies. He was still undecided about
Spain: Franco had more than once broken his promise concerning Gibraltar, and
he would still go no further than agree to enter the war once Britain was down
and almost out—a promise that had come to Britain's ears. In the Balkans, only
Romania was deliberately and unreservedly friendly; Antonescu had made "the
best impression imaginable" on Hitler. Bulgaria was loyal, had feared Russian
intervention until recently, but would join the Tripartite Pact in good time.
Turkey would take no action at this time. Hungary was "usable" at present.
Yugoslavia was cool. Poland was no longer any problem.

Therefore Russia must be Britain's last hope. "They will only give up when we
have smashed this last hope on the continent to smithereens." The British were
no fools, said Hitler; they must realize that if they lost this war they would no
longer have the moral authority to hold their empire together. "On the other
hand, if they can pull through and raise forty or fifty divisions, and if the United
States and Russia help them, then Germany will be in a precarious situation. That
must not be allowed to happen." He had always believed in destroying the
enemy's most powerful positions first. "That is why Russia must now be defeated." If Britain did not give in even then, Germany need leave only some fifty
divisions in the east; her army could be cut back to provide manpower for the
Luftwaffe and naval construction programs, for the antiaircraft defenses, and for
the dispersal of industry out of reach of the British bombers. Meanwhile Russia's
defeat would enable Japan to put pressure on the United States, and Roosevelt
would have second thoughts about attacking Germany.

Since Russia must be defeated, it must be defeated now. "True, the Russian
forces are a clay colossus with no head, but who knows how they will develop
in the future?" He believed the Russian arms industry was still hamstrung by

development problems.[2] The defeat of the Soviet Union must be swift and final; under no circumstances must the Russians be allowed to regroup after the first, brutal breakthrough. Again he called for the rapid occupation of the Baltic coast first of all. The generals' strategic targets were the annihilation of the Russian army, the capture of the most important industrial regions and the destruction of the rest, and the occupation of the oil fields at Baku—on the Caspian Sea. Though immense and new, this latter demand should not, however, daunt them; their armies had also covered immense distances in the few weeks of the French campaign, Hitler reminded them. He concluded, "Germany will then be unassailable. The vast spaces of Russia will yield hoards of incalculable wealth. Germany must dominate them economically and politically, without annexing them bodily. Thus we will have all we need to be able to fight whole continents in the future, if need be; we will be invincible. When we fight this campaign, let Europe hold its breath!" From now until June 1941, Hitler made no mention whatsoever of Russia in his public speeches.

Mussolini was still loath to meet with Hitler. Small wonder, for on January 5 a small British force had captured the Italian fortress of Bardia in Libya, taking forty-five thousand Italians prisoner. There were now only five Italian divisions left in Cyrenaica and five more in Tripolitania. Meanwhile the Luftwaffe corps Hitler had transferred to the Mediterranean had opened its attack on January 6, sinking a British cruiser and damaging an aircraft carrier. Mussolini finally agreed to come to a meeting later in January but stipulated that there must be no fuss and no photographers—he even suggested their two trains should meet somewhere in the open countryside.

Hitler sought for ways of helping the Italians out of their self-created mess without hurting Mussolini's prestige at home. He considered sending a mountain division to Albania and a small "blocking force" of German tanks and engineers to help the Italians hold on to Tripoli; his ambassador in Rome accompanied Ribbentrop to the Berghof on the ninth and urged that Germany exert a greater influence on Italian strategy in the Mediterranean, but Hitler characteristically refused to do anything that would damage the Duce and thus impair the "most valuable link in the Axis," the mutual trust between Mussolini and himself. Two days later he signed the directive ordering the army and Luftwaffe to prepare to support the Italian defense of Albania and Tripolitania.

Hitler collected Mussolini from a small railroad station near Salzburg at 10 A.M.

---

[2]In April 1941, Hitler learned for the first time how advanced the huge Soviet arms industry was. See page 237.

on January 19. Two days of conferences and strolls about the snow-clad Obersalz-berg followed. Hitler had one 90-minute talk privately with the Duce, but from the record of the other conferences it is clear he revealed nothing he had not already stated to his own generals on the ninth, except that he made no mention of his plan to attack Russia soon. Indeed, he again averred that so long as the wise and prudent Stalin was alive Russia would adhere to her treaties. (On January 9, according to a note taken by Admiral Fricke, Hitler had explained he had no intention of revealing his own plans to the Italians because of the very real danger that the Italian monarchy would forward this Intelligence to Britain.) He did, however, reveal that "in the British Cabinet's secret meetings Churchill referred to the helping hand Russia would perhaps one day lend, in addition to America." Britain, however, would lose the war before then. "The British may get used to living a troglodyte existence, or to having no windows in their houses and the like," states the record of Hitler's comments, "but when their food imports are no longer safe they will have no option but surrender. This is why Germany is trying to sink as much shipping as possible—particularly refrigerated vessels, as they take a long time to build. In the three such ships sunk in recent weeks Britain has lost two whole weeks' meat supplies."

This meeting brought to an end Mussolini's dream of fighting an independent war, parallel to Hitler's, in the Mediterranean. He accepted the offer of a "block-ing force" for Tripoli but could not accept the mountain division for Albania, as he needed the Albanian port space for his own reinforcements. On January 22, Tobruk with twenty-five thousand Italians fell into British hands. The whole of Tripolitania was now in peril. The panzer specialist General Hans von Funck, sent to North Africa in mid-January, reported to Hitler on February 1 in the most pessimistic terms at the Chancellery in Berlin: the Italians had no will to resist the British onslaught in North Africa. What was needed was not a defensive "blocking force," but a force capable of launching a determined counterattack on the extended British mechanized units. "The crazy feature is," said Hitler after-ward to his staff, "that on the one hand the Italians are shrieking for help and cannot find drastic enough language to describe their poor guns and equipment, but on the other hand they are so jealous and childish that they won't stand for being helped by German soldiers. Mussolini would probably like it best if our troops could fight in Italian uniforms there, and our aircraft flew with the Italian fasces on their wings!"

In conference with his army and Luftwaffe chiefs two days later, Hitler again declared that militarily the loss of Italian North Africa would mean little; how-ever, its political and psychological effects could be devastating, for Britain could then deal with Mussolini at pistol point and force him to make peace. Conversely, if Hitler could win quick successes for the Axis in Libya, this might speed a peaceful settlement in the Balkans. He decided to send more than just a "blocking force" to North Africa; he would send a light infantry and a panzer division to Libya, with a German corps staff. Who should command this Afrika Korps? Erich von Manstein and Erwin Rommel were suggested to him. He chose Rommel. (In August 1942 he explained to Italy's Ambassador Alfieri: "I chose Rommel because he's like Dietl—he knows how to carry his troops forward with him; and this is absolutely vital for the commander of an army fighting under extremes of climate, be it in North Africa or in the Far North.") Son of a Württemberg schoolmaster, Rommel had won the *Pour le Mérite* medal fighting the Italians in World War I. Between the wars he had written a brilliant manual, *Infantry Attack*. In the French campaign of 1940 he had fought his 7th Panzer Division through to the Channel coast heedless of personal risk and exhaustion; as recently as December, Schmundt had shown Hitler an illustrated divisional history Rommel had devised of the French campaign—for the future "desert fox" was nothing if not a capable public relations man, too.

On February 6, 1941, Rommel and General Enno von Rintelen, the military attaché in Rome, were briefed by Hitler in Berlin. Rintelen was instructed to ask Mussolini to put all the Italian mechanized units in Libya under Rommel's new command. That evening Hitler leafed through the British and American illustrated weeklies to show Rommel what his enemies in Cyrenaica looked like. These magazines and boys' adventure books were Hitler's main source of information. ("Your experts should read more Karl May and attend fewer courses," he said in rebuke to the Luftwaffe's Field Marshal Milch in October 1942. "Then they'd be of more use in this war!") Rommel was instructed to hold Tripolitania for the Axis powers, tying down the British and preventing them from breaking through to the French in Tunisia. "Saw army's Commander in Chief [Brauchitsch] first," wrote Rommel in his hotel afterward. "Then the Führer. There's no time to be lost. My luggage is being sent on afterward. . . . My head reels to think of all that can still go wrong. It will be months before things take effect!" On February 9, Mussolini's agreement to hand over tactical command to Rommel arrived, and after some delay Rommel's first troops and equipment began disembarking at Tripoli on the twelfth. It was a beginning, but it would be April or May before the last of his corps was finally assembled there.

Spurred on by Admiral Raeder, by the ambiguous attitude of Vichy, and by the deteriorating situation in the Mediterranean, during January 1941 Hitler put renewed pressure on General Franco to revise his views on Gibraltar. He could not understand why the Spanish dictator had rejected his offers of material aid, for the British were certain—he argued—to let Spain down in the end. When Mussolini came to the Berghof, Hitler also persuaded him to pressure Franco at a forthcoming personal meeting: Gibraltar in the hands of the Axis would put a new complexion on the whole North African dilemma. Air bases and two German divisions in Spanish Morocco would soon keep General Weygand in his place.

At Salzburg on January 18, Ribbentrop briefed his ambassador to Madrid on the tough line to adopt with the Caudillo, but this new approach did not bring possession of Gibraltar any nearer. Franco, of course, had no inkling of the strict timetable Hitler had already drawn up for the attacks on Greece and Russia, a timetable into which "Felix," the attack on Gibraltar, must be slotted, if it was to take place at all; this explains the increasing irritability of Ribbentrop's telegrams to Madrid over the next two weeks. On the twentieth the ambassador cabled from Madrid that Franco had cleverly skirted around the central issue— "As to *whether* Spain would enter the war there is no question, that was settled at Hendaye; it is only a question of *when.*" If Germany would not send food supplies until Spain entered the war, they would arrive too late. The ambassador had replied that if Germany was expected to send food shipments in advance— for example, the one hundred thousand tons of grain tantalizingly held up in ships in Lisbon—then Germany must be permitted to stipulate the date of Spain's entry into the war, and Franco must agree to it in advance.

Ribbentrop's ploy was not likely to flatter Franco's self-esteem. The ambassador was instructed to read out to Franco six points, of which the first was: "Without the help of the Führer and the Duce there would not be any Nationalist Spain today. Nor any Caudillo." If Franco did not abandon his "vacillating attitude," then the end of Nationalist Spain was only a matter of time. Franco angrily denounced this as unjust: he had never vacillated, and he still intended to enter the war; but the ambassador cabled Ribbentrop that the Caudillo seemed more hesitant than before. Ribbentrop cabled him to see Franco yet again and read out a message beginning: "Only the immediate entry by Spain into the war is of any strategic value to the Axis." (This was the harsh truth.) Given the necessary promise Germany would at once release one hundred thousand tons of grain from Lisbon. In a lengthy reply to Ribbentrop's earlier demarche the Spanish government amiably reminded Berlin of the German foot-dragging the previous summer—Germany had still not sent the economic experts Spain had asked for in September; the Spaniards also suggested the German High Command had taken little account of the extremes of weather encountered in southern Spain in the winter. Ribbentrop now concentrated his venom on his ambassador, for having allowed Franco to slither away from a clear Yes or No answer to the question of whether or not he was willing to enter the war at once.

On January 28, Jodl pointed out to Hitler that even if they could resume preparations for "Felix" on February 1, it would be impossible to launch the actual assault on Gibraltar before mid-April, which meant that the hundreds of artillery pieces and troops involved could not be released for "Barbarossa" in mid-May. Hitler told Jodl they must dispense with "Felix," but evidently he still pinned some hopes on Mussolini's talks with the Caudillo on February 12. A few days beforehand he wrote the Caudillo a personal letter suggesting that in times of crisis nations could be saved "less by prudent foresight than by a bold heart." This poetic appeal made no impression on Spain's realistic leader. On the fourteenth Ribbentrop telephoned to the Berghof a message from the Duce, which the Italian chargé in Berlin had just delivered to the foreign ministry. Hitler's senior secretary, Fräulein Wolf, took the telephone message down in shorthand. By raising demands which it was clear Hitler would not accept, Franco had made it abundantly clear that Spain would not join the war. Spain was to be given military and economic aid; the Hendaye secret protocol was to be reworded more precisely, so as to grant Spain the whole of French Morocco; and the assault on Gibraltar was to be executed by *Spanish* forces, perhaps with German support. Mussolini's general impression was that Spain was in no position to declare war. To Hitler, however, Franco was failing to honor a promise. Walther Hewel, Ribbentrop's liaison with Hitler, wrote in his diary that day: "Telegram from Rome on Mussolini's meeting with Franco. Negative, as we expected. The Führer is going to drop Spain. They will just go under."

"In the evening, we sat for a long time with the Führer around the fireside," continued Hewel's diary. "The Führer talked about his pension—that of a middle-grade civil servant! He is going to write books—a third volume of *Mein Kampf* . . . entitled *Collected Broken Promises,* and books on Frederick the Great, Luther, and Napoleon." Earlier that afternoon he had spent two-and-a-half hours nervously trying to persuade the Yugoslav prime minister to join the Tripartite Pact. By now Field Marshal Sigmund Wilhelm List's Twelfth Army preparations in Romania were so far advanced that bridge-building across the Danube—the frontier with Bulgaria—could begin the next day if need be. But so many uncertainties were involved in occupying Bulgaria, let alone attacking Greece, that Hitler was still looking for alternatives; not until the end of the month would he finally allow the bridge-building to begin.

The Yugoslav prime minister indicated that his country was no keener to join the Axis than it had been in November. The most he would offer was to mediate between Italy and Greece. Hitler suggested that it was illusory to expect the British to evacuate their foothold in Greece now. "Only when our dive-bombers and armored corps appear will they get out of Greece as hastily as they have on every other occasion we employed these means. Germany has no demands whatever against Greece. Here as elsewhere Britain is the root cause of all the difficulties.''[3] Of course, added Hitler, he was aware from the Allied documents captured in France (which were duly published) of the extent to which the Greeks had offered their country as a front for Britain. What he did not say was that a recently intercepted French diplomat's report from Belgrade recounted a conversation with the state secretary in the Yugoslav foreign ministry: "Yugoslavia is trying to gain time until May. Britain has assured her that from May onward Britain's military strength and the entry of the United States into the war will change the whole situation."

"England will be annihilated," Hitler warned his Yugoslav visitors. "If the British now announce they are a country of long wars and adduce the course of the Napoleonic wars as evidence for this theory, then let me point out that the only reason the British could hold out so long then was because they had the Prussians fighting for them"—a reference to Blücher's opportune arrival at the battle of Waterloo. The Yugoslavs offered one suggestion—that they form a Balkan bloc with Bulgaria and Turkey—but this would have made impossible any attack designed to oust the British from Greece; Hitler dismissed it privately as "a British insinuation." When the Yugoslavs left the Berghof they said they would report to the prince regent in Belgrade and let Hitler know. On the outcome would depend "Marita," and Hitler had reason to be nervous.

The first wave of divisions was now moving toward the frontier with Russia— only a slow procession as yet; not until mid-March would the second wave begin. As Lossberg had pointed out, the German railway network was so superior to the Russian system that when the real race began, Germany could muster seven divisions a day and the Russians only five; the farther west the "Barbarossa" divisions waited the better—"the bigger will be the Russian surprise when the German troop concentration begins." The whole military jigsaw puzzle would be fitted together, each piece numbered and timetabled by the General Staff, in the last weeks before the attack. Only when the puzzle was unveiled would Stalin find Hitler ready to attack Russia.

When Field Marshal von Bock reported to Hitler on February 1, their conversation drifted through the problems of basing great decisions on the rackety foundations provided by Italy's disasters. The attack on Russia would divert world attention from the African calamity. Britain was proving a tough nut to crack; there was no talk of invasion now. But "the people in Britain aren't fools," said

[3]Had Italy not attacked Greece, the difficulties would not have arisen. But Hewel was echoing his master's views when he wrote to a friend on January 23, 1941: "It is actually regrettable that we are forced to smash and destroy so much that we do not want to smash and destroy and that should not have been destroyed for European culture and the mastery of the Germanic races."

Hitler. "They just *act* like fools! They will realize there is no point in fighting on once Russia too is beaten and eliminated." Bock agreed that *if* the Russians stood their ground and fought, they would be defeated; and he wondered whether they could be forced into an armistice? This might be one consequence of the German capture of the Ukraine, Moscow, and Leningrad, replied Hitler; otherwise the Wehrmacht must advance toward Yekatarinburg. "Anyway," he concluded, "I am glad that we carried on with arms manufacture so that we are now strong enough to be a match for anybody. We have more than enough material and we already have to begin thinking about converting parts of our industry. Our Wehrmacht manpower position is better than when war broke out. Our economy is absolutely firm." The Führer rejected out of hand any idea of yielding—not that Bock had hinted at it. "I am going to fight," he said; and "I am convinced that our attack will flatten them like a hailstorm."

Two days later Field Marshal von Brauchitsch brought Chief of the General Staff Halder to the Chancellery to outline the army's operational directive on "Barbarossa." Halder put the Russian strength confronting them at about 155 divisions —in short, numerically a little more than the German strength but vastly inferior in quality. Although army Intelligence believed the Russians might have as many as 10,000 tanks, compared with their own 3,500, the Russian armored vehicles were a motley collection of obsolete design. "Even so, surprises cannot be ruled out altogether," warned Halder—with some perspicacity, for by June 1941 the Red Army had 967 ultramodern T-34 tanks on the front, and the Germans did not have an antitank gun powerful enough to use against that model. As for the Russian soldier, Halder believed the Germans were superior in experience, training, equipment, organization, command, national character, and ideology. Hitler naturally agreed, but he challenged the army's estimate of Russia's huge manpower reserves and arms potential. He was convinced, however, that the Soviet dictatorship was so hated, particularly by the young Russians, that it would crumble under the first victorious German onslaught. As for Soviet armament, he was something of an expert on arms production, he said; and from his "memory" he unlocked a ten-minute statistical lecture on Russian tank production since 1928, proving in the process just how thinly armored each type was.

Hitler approved the army's directive but once again emphasized the capture of the Baltic coast and of Leningrad. The latter was particularly important if the Russians were falling back elsewhere, as this northern stronghold would provide the best possible supply base for the second phase of the campaign. Finland would assist in the northern theater, dividing her forces for operations against the Murmansk railway in the far north and against Leningrad on the Baltic. Hitler knew that Halder had just had a first round of talks with his Finnish counterpart, General E. Heinrichs, in Berlin. Hitler was convinced the Finns would make ideal allies, although Finland's political strategy would be problematical as she wished to avoid a complete rupture with the United States and Britain. Hitler had said to his staff. "They are a plucky people, and at least I will have a good flank defense there. Quite apart from which, it is always good to have comrades-in-arms who are thirsting for revenge. . . ."

The army's timetable produced some interesting side-effects which had obviously not occurred to Hitler up to now. Once the second wave of divisions started eastward from western Europe in mid-March, "Attila" (the emergency occupation of Vichy France) would become virtually impossible. With the third wave in mid-April the maximum-capacity transport plan began, and the troop concentrations could no longer be concealed except as a vast decoy operation "to distract from an invasion of Britain"; but when the fourth and final wave of panzer divisions that had been reequipping and resting in central Germany started rolling eastward from April 25 onward, an invasion of Britain would become an obviously impossible cover story. Hitler admiringly agreed with all that Halder had said. "When 'Barbarossa' gets going, the whole world will hold its breath— it won't move a muscle!"

The army directive was forthwith issued. The next day, Admiral Raeder set out the navy's somewhat smaller role (the navy's main enemy was still Britain). Afterward, Raeder told the admiralty that the navy's principal task in "Barbarossa" would be to establish a supply line to Leningrad.

Probably no major campaign has ever been launched upon less Intelligence. The services had furnished Hitler—to say nothing of their lower commands— with only the most inadequate information on the Russians. They were certain of only one thing: the German fighting man's inborn superiority. All else was the product of rumor, speculation, and fragile calculations. Admiral Canaris told Keitel the Abwehr had drawn a blank in Russia. Conditions for espionage were impossible. Maps were nonexistent. The range of the army's radio-monitoring stations was strictly limited. Foreign Armies East appealed to the Luftwaffe to intensify photographic reconnaissance missions, as it would take eight weeks to print the maps and issue them to the troops. The Russian aircraft industry was an unknown quantity on which the veil was only gradually being lifted. Recent indications were that it was being expanded at a disconcerting speed. Göring, apprehensive that the Russian air force might prove more formidable than the army Intelligence figures indicated, arranged for a team of his air ministry engineers to inspect the Soviet air industry, but not until early March did permission for their trip arrive.

This lack of proper Intelligence was the root cause of the ultimate disaster. For while Halder had confidently advised the Führer on February 3 that they would oppose only a small Red Army superiority in numbers, 155 divisions, by early

April that figure had been raised (as the Finns and Japanese had always recommended) to 247 divisions; and four months later, when it was too late to retreat, the army admitted it had now identified *360* Soviet divisions in combat with them.

The whole of Hitler's strategy was based on the assumption that Russia would be laid low in a Blitzkrieg of only a few months. Germany's oil and rubber stocks would not hold out much longer. Repeatedly during the latter months Keitel had warned the services to economize on oil consumption so that a stockpile could be built up for "Barbarossa." Now, on February 8, Keitel learned from his staff that while the Luftwaffe and navy would have enough fuel to last until the coming autumn, gasoline and diesel fuel for the army's tanks and motor transport would not hold out beyond mid-August if supplies from Romania dried up—unless of course the oil fields of the Caucasus could be reached in time. Keitel ordered further economies. The rubber situation allowed for even less leeway. Much of Germany's rubber supplies had reached her from the Far East along the Trans-Siberian railroad. War with Russia would cut that link, leaving only an uncertain trickle supplied by blockade-running ships. Later in February the OKW submitted to Hitler and Göring a full survey of the economic side-effects of "Barbarossa." Göring was forced to agree with the OKW's view that possession of the Ukraine would not be enough: Germany would need the oil fields of the Caucasus as well, whatever the cost. Keitel's economics expert General Thomas noted after meeting Göring on February 26: "He shares the Führer's opinion that when German troops march into Russia the entire Bolshevik state will collapse, and that for this reason we need not fear the destruction of the stores and railway system on a large scale, as I do. The main thing is to get rid of the Bolshevik leaders rapidly first of all." Göring's anxiety was the weakness of the German supply lines. "He recalled that supply failures had proved Napoleon's undoing. For this reason he has kept urging the Führer to concentrate more on the supply organization and less on activating fresh divisions, some of which would not come under fire." But far from pulling in his horns, Hitler was already thinking beyond the end of "Barbarossa." On the seventeenth, Jodl instructed his staff that the Führer wished them to study the problems of assembling troops in Afghanistan for an assault on India.

On Sunday February 16, Hitler's chief Wehrmacht adjutant, Rudolf Schmundt, who had flown to North Africa with Rommel the week before, reported back to the Berghof with photographs of Rommel's arrival and a first analysis of the position.

Hitler saw a possible crisis zone in Libya, for if the Italians were driven out altogether, the British could transfer forces to Syria with complex side-effects on

"Marita" and "Barbarossa." Not surprisingly, he awaited Rommel's operations "feverishly," as Schmundt wrote a few days later. Colonel Schmundt described the enthusiasm with which Rommel had thrown himself into his task. Hitler sanctioned all his requests—for antitank guns, mines, and Luftwaffe reconnaissance and close-support aircraft. Rommel's first troops had disembarked at Tripoli in one night and then covered the 350 miles to the Italian front west of El Agheila in twenty-six hours—an accomplishment not without effect on the demoralized Italian troops. Rommel organized a military parade of his troops, whose new tropical helmets and gear gleamed in the African sun. Before he left Tripoli he set up the rapid manufacture of scores of dummy tanks mounted on Volkswagen chassis to dupe the British into thinking he had a powerful armored force. By the twenty-first, the first 35 dummy tanks had arrived at his headquarters—another 170 were being built. His troops had already withstood their first howling *ghibli* (sandstorm) and were advancing on El Agheila. The British were withdrawing from their position there, and the Italians were already acquiring new heart—though their fighter pilots still lacked verve. The letters Rommel sent to Schmundt (which the colonel undoubtedly showed to Hitler) exuded optimism from every line. Hitler decided to send out the 15th Panzer Division as soon as he could.

How eerily different was this new battlefield for Rommel's soldiers—city dwellers or farmers for the most part. The Cyrenaican desert was an almost treeless, shadowless lunar landscape baked by a fierce sun; however, as soon as darkness fell, the temperature plummeted toward zero. There were few valleys, and the monotonous expanse of white or reddish-yellow sand was broken only by occasional herds of sheep and camels tended by migrant Arab tribes. At the end of February Rommel had lost only one man—killed in the dark by his own troops. In mid-March he reported to Hitler in person and then returned to Africa. He detected the weakness of the British forces opposing him—a weakness resulting from the dispatch of over sixty thousand British troops to Greece; without waiting for the new armored division to arrive, and against the explicit instructions of both the German war department and the Italian Supreme Commander, Italo Gariboldi, he launched a bold assault in early April; he did not halt until he had reached the Egyptian frontier and taken three thousand British prisoners, including five generals.

By March the last major crisis before "Barbarossa" had been overcome—or so Hitler believed. At 7 A.M. on February 28, since Greece still proudly refused to offer peace terms to Italy, the German Wehrmacht began throwing three mighty army bridges across the mile-wide, fast-flowing Danube from Romania into Bulgaria.

After several false starts, Hitler dictated to Fräulein Wolf an important letter assuring Turkey's President Ismet Inönü that he saw "no reason, either now or in the future, why Germany and Turkey should ever be enemies." He assured Inönü that the Wehrmacht would stand many miles off the Turkish frontier—unless of course Turkish measures forced him to revise this attitude. (The General Staff and OKW had both worked out contingency plans for a tank campaign against European Turkey in alliance with Bulgaria.) Inönü replied calmly that Turkey's sole desire was to safeguard her integrity, and he warmly recalled her comradeship with Germany in World War I. Hitler was well pleased.

On March 1 we find him in Vienna, where the German-speaking King Boris signed Bulgaria's formal entry into the Tripartite Pact. Who could then have foreseen that this document would prove the death warrant of the king, poisoned by an unknown hand in 1943; or that Fräulein Wolf's shorthand pad with the letter to Inönü would be found by American soldiers raking through the ruins of the Berghof in 1945? So far, however, all Hitler's calculations were again proving correct; within one week, by March 7, 1941, the first German soldiers would be standing on the Greek frontier, facing British and Greek troops as they had in 1918. This time would surely be different: neither Turkey nor Russia would move a muscle. Nothing could save Greece.

Behind the Door

One incident of the climactic summer of 1941 must be examined here lest it become submerged in the noisier events of Hitler's attack on Russia. It serves to illustrate the atmosphere in which that year's more controversial decisions were taken.

A few days after Hitler's combined armies invaded Russia, Sweden as the protecting power gave Germany discreet permission for the Soviet embassy buildings in Paris to be searched. The embassy staff refused to let the police unit in, so the building was forcibly entered by a major general of the German police and a squad of forensic experts of Heydrich's security service. If the reports shown to Hitler—admittedly of Nazi origin and hence possibly tainted—are to be believed, horrifying evidence of the activities of the GPU, the Soviet secret police, was found. Heydrich's summary report to Ribbentrop related: "There were twenty-six Soviet Russians in the building. Five of them (four men and a woman) had locked themselves into strong rooms specially shielded by heavy armorplate steel doors; they were busy destroying documents and other materials in four furnaces specially constructed and installed in there. They could not be prevented from doing this, as even using special technical gear it would still have taken hours to force the rooms open. After the materials had been incinerated, the rooms were then opened from within by their occupants." Heydrich's officers were less impressed by the undiplomatic haul of radio gear, time fuses, detonators, and explosives than by the outside laboratory-type furnaces found in the special wing of the building used by the GPU. Investigation indicated that they had been used for cremating bodies.

Ribbentrop brought this report to Hitler, but Hitler had already heard the details firsthand from Admiral Canaris, one of whose department heads had himself inspected the Paris building. He had recorded: "The inspection yielded an exceedingly interesting insight into the GPU's activities. The completely isolated wing of the embassy in which the GPU's offices and execution chambers were located can only be described as a criminals' and murderers' workshop of the most outstanding technical perfection: soundproof walls, heavy, electrically operated steel doors, hidden spyholes and slots for guns to be fired from one room into another, an electrical furnace, and a bathtub in which the corpses were cut up, completed the macabre inventory of these rooms, in addition to housebreaking implements, poison capsules, and the like. Thus there is every probability that General Miller, and perhaps General Kutiepoff as well, together with many an awkward White Russian emigré or opponent of the Soviets in France, vanished in this way—they literally 'went up in smoke.' "

Hitler ordered the Soviet embassy buildings in Berlin unsealed and searched at once. At first the Swedes refused to allow the safes to be blown open, but eventually they agreed to look the other way. In the Soviet trade mission headquarters at 11 Lietsenburgerstrasse the same armored strongrooms with the same furnaces were found, and again there were stocks of guns and ammunition.

Hitler was a realist. There was no reason why these finds should have shocked him, and there is no evidence that he regarded them as of anything more than propaganda value (not that he could exploit them, for diplomatic reasons). He expected the war in the Soviet Union to be merciless and to obey no conventional rules. For twenty years he had been fighting bolshevism, and its face had changed but little in those two decades. Bolshevik methods were familiar to him, and they had also impressed themselves on those European nations which had however briefly tasted the fruits of bolshevism.[1] The horrors of the Cheka were part of history, but the brutality of the Bolsheviks in the Spanish civil war, in Stalin's half of Poland, and most recently in the hapless Baltic states—occupied by the Soviets in the spring of 1940 under the Ribbentrop-Molotov pact—indicated that this was a permanent trait. In the French campaign, German troops had found ten of their infantry comrades bound hand and foot with their eyes torn out, and an antiaircraft gunner with his feet sawn off; the culprits turned out to be Spanish Red Guards (all were executed). In the Baltic countries Stalin had appointed commissars who had supervised the deportation and liquidation of the entire intelligentsia within a matter of weeks (as had been done in Poland already); these commissars—said to have been Jewish—had then been replaced by Russians who had disposed of their predecessors.

---

[1] In a cynical entry in his unpublished diary of August 1941, Goebbels wrote: "A search of the Soviet embassies in Paris and Berlin has brought surprising terror weapons to light. These Soviet embassies are in fact the refuges of criminals. This is inevitable. If a criminal gang comes to power, then they will use criminal means to conduct their policies. It is a good thing that bolshevism is being got rid of once and for all in our eastern campaign. There was after all no room for the two of us in Europe, in the long run."

In the western campaigns Hitler had instructed the Wehrmacht to fight with discipline. In the armistice that followed he had explicitly ordered all troops and civilian personnel in the occupied territories to perform their duties "flawlessly" and with proper reserve toward the former enemy populations; any drunkenness or violence was to be severely punished—if necessary by "death and dishonor." In the interests of the armistice, he had not insisted on the extradition of enemy "war criminals" for trial by German courts. In March 1941, Hitler took no action when his ambassador in Paris recommended executing former Prime Minister Reynaud and Minister of the Interior Georges Mandel on the charge of having organized bands of ununiformed franc tireurs to gun down German parachutists during "Yellow."

In the eastern campaign, however, no holds would be barred on either side. A member of Jodl's staff later wrote: "For Hitler the Russian enemy has two faces, and one of them is bolshevism, his ideological deadly enemy, which Hitler as Europe's champion intends to put to the sword and 'eradicate with ruthless, remorseless lack of mercy'—you have to hear it from his own mouth, rasping and rolling every 'r.' For Hitler, bolshevism is not an enemy with whom one chivalrously crosses swords. In his view we must expect all manner of knavery and cruelty. So Hitler proposes to meet him with the same fighting methods from the start. He states that 'Them or Us' is to be the pitiless motto of this clash." To some extent the Bolshevik leaders had themselves paved the way for this development by formally renouncing czarist treaties, including the various conventions governing warfare, and by having refused to sign the Geneva Convention of 1929 on the treatment of prisoners of war.[2] They could do what they liked with German prisoners in their hands, but they could expect no quarter from Hitler either.

Göring's previous hint to General Thomas concerning the advisability of rapidly getting rid of the Bolshevik leaders was now—on Hitler's direct orders to Jodl—to be entrenched as a principle in the special guidelines issued to the Wehrmacht for "Barbarossa":

> The coming campaign is more than just a clash of arms. It will result in a conflict of two ideologies. Given the vastness of the country, it will not be enough to defeat the enemy armed forces if the war is to be ended. The entire area must be split up into states with their own governments, with each of whom we can sign peace agreements. . . . Every revolution of any size creates facts which cannot just be wiped away. Wishful thinking alone will not rid

[2]On August 8, the Soviet government offered through Sweden to observe The Hague Convention of 1907 on land warfare, and the Geneva Conventions of 1925 and 1929 on poison-gas warfare and prisoners of war, respectively. By that time the Russians had lost a million soldiers as prisoners to the German army.

modern Russia of the socialist idea; so this alone can act as the domestic political basis for the creation of these new states and governments. The Jewish-Bolshevik intelligentsia as the present "subjugators" of the people must be got rid of. The former bourgeois aristocracy, in so far as it survives abroad, is also useless—they are rejected by the Russian people and are anti-German in any case. . . . In addition we must do everything to avoid allowing a nationalist Russia to supplant the Bolshevik one, as history shows it will always be anti-German. Our job is to set up as soon as possible, with a minimum of military effort, socialist mini-states dependent on us. These tasks will be so difficult that they cannot be entrusted to the army.

The war aims Hitler thus revealed to Jodl were very different from the colonization of the east which was alone his driving inspiration. In July 1943 he was to make this clear. "I consider it a cardinal and catastrophic error, something with the gravest consequences, to take the slightest step that might cause a man to say to himself: 'We are getting out of here anyway; we are not going to remain; there are going to be national states founded here, so we will have to get out.' " A soldier needs "positive war aims" to fight body and soul for his country. What war aim can equal a crusade of imperialist conquest? Hitler's outspoken philosophy in July 1943 was this: "In the end man lives from the soil, and the soil is a goblet passing from lip to lip, which Providence allows to linger longest with the nation that fights for it."

Jodl's staff redrafted the special guidelines for "Barbarossa" during March 1941, as Hitler had asked. The army's actual zone of operations was to be a belt as shallow as practicable, while in the rear Himmler's SS and various "Reich commissioners" would see to the founding of the new state governments. The OKW records speak obscurely of the need to put "all Bolshevik headmen and commissars" out of the way, and they quote Hitler as having stipulated that the political administrations were to start functioning as soon as possible "so that the struggle between the ideologies can be waged simultaneously with the clash of arms." Himmler had been ordered by Hitler to carry out on his own responsibility "certain special duties" of a kind to be expected in a fight between two diametrically opposed political systems. The army's records portray Hitler's purpose more bluntly. Halder recorded the Führer as telling him: "We have to set up de-Stalinized republics. The intelligentsia appointed by Stalin must be destroyed. The Russian empire's command machinery must be smashed. In the whole of Russia it will be necessary to employ the most naked brute force. The ideological ties are not yet strong enough to hold the Russian people together. Once the officials are disposed of, the nation will burst apart." Again there is no evidence that the General Staff contested this broad view.

Halder's quartermaster general (traditionally responsible for army occupation policy) attended that conference; after discussing police matters with Heydrich, a few days later he drafted an army order giving the SS "task forces" a free hand to execute certain grim assignments within the army's zone of operations. In a lengthy speech to his army and Luftwaffe generals at the end of the month—to which we shall return in another context[3]—Hitler also prepared them for the different character of the coming fight in Russia. Communist ideology was compared to legalized criminality. "We must put the arguments of soldierly comradeship right out of our minds," he told his generals. "The Communist is no comrade and never will be." He again explicitly referred to the "annihilation of the Bolshevik commissars and the Communist intelligentsia," and he emphasized that "commissars and GPU officials are criminals and must be treated as such." In conclusion, Hitler noted: "I do not expect my generals to understand my orders to this effect. But I demand that they obey them."

Early in March 1941 the British navy executed a lightning raid on the Lofoten Isles in Norway, shelling the town of Svolvaer, sinking several ships in the harbor, and taking about two hundred German merchant seamen prisoners. Militarily the raid was insignificant, but Hitler treated it as a monstrous blow to German prestige, and it roused in him wholly disproportionate fears for Norway's security. Norway was to be the key to German naval supremacy in future decades—he had commissioned Albert Speer to construct at Trondheim a major new city and naval dockyard, and Todt's labor battalions were already engineering superhighways to the far north, the like of which Norway had never seen before.

While snow settled suddenly around the Berghof, blotting out premature signs of spring, Hitler issued orders for the immediate investigation of the Lofoten raid and the execution of all Norwegians who had aided the enemy. The army was to install 160 gun batteries along the Norwegian coast forthwith, and Admiral Hermann Boehm, the admiral commanding Norway, was summoned to the Berghof. At this conference Hitler decided it would no longer be possible to release 40 percent of the (very considerable) military strength in Norway for "Barbarossa"; indeed, he actually ordered the Narvik and Kirkenes regions reinforced. For the next three years the fear that the British would mount an invasion of Norway never left him.

As the ice thawed in Central Europe, the Wehrmacht's timetable began to unfold. One of Hitler's secretaries, Christa Schroeder, wrote at the Berghof on March 7:

[3]See page 221.

"I feel so cut off from everybody here, so shut in, that it is as though I were deaf. It will soon be time to return to Berlin; we have been down here long enough. We will probably be back in Berlin in the middle of the month. . . . We have to be injected again against cholera and typhus—and that happened before all our big journeys!"

Göring had now returned from his extended leave, and on March 6 he secured a long interview with Hitler in which he repaired the fences that had been broken —particularly by his hated rival Admiral Raeder—in his absence. Raeder had especially regretted the continuing reduction of naval air power that had begun early in 1940, and he had lost no opportunity of criticizing the Luftwaffe commander and exposing the hollowness of his claims to Hitler. From the moment Göring had gone on leave in November, the admiral had argued with the Führer that the surest means of defeating Britain was the blockade of her imports by air and submarine forces operating under a unified—meaning his own—command; his submarine officers at least had a right to adequate aerial reconnaissance over the Atlantic. Hitler had initially regarded the continual in-fighting between Raeder and Göring as proof of the need for a much more powerful OKW. (Another bone of contention between the two commanders was whether torpedo-bomber attacks on enemy shipping were better controlled by the air force or the navy. Hitler irritably declared this was "completely unimportant," all that mattered was that the weapon be effectively employed.) At this time Göring's prestige was low following his defeat in the Battle of Britain. He was also embarrassed by the exaggerated claims of his pilots when "destroyed" enemy aircraft, battleships, and aircraft carriers turned up intact. It is significant that although Göring referred to himself in February 1941 as "the second man in the state," Hitler was privately explaining to Keitel and Jodl that one reason why a powerful OKW would become necessary in the future was that "a man might later step into his shoes who might well be the best statesman but might not have as much military knowledge and ability at his fingertips as he did." This could hardly refer to Göring.

Raeder had become bolder in his attacks on the absent Reichsmarschall, producing air photographs of Portsmouth, Plymouth, and Cardiff to show the ineffectiveness of the Luftwaffe attacks and pointing out that the crescendo of RAF attacks on Germany was proof that the enemy air force was anything but defeated. Only in bombing the sea lanes could the Luftwaffe be used to best advantage. These arguments were accepted by Hitler in his directive for economic warfare against Britain on February 6. He identified the loss of British merchant shipping as the most potent factor in the destruction of the war economy; the effect of Luftwaffe attacks on the British arms industry was noted as "more problematic." In a direct reference to Göring's present tactical directives, Hitler emphasized: "No decisive effect is to be expected from systematic terror raids on residential areas or attacks on coastal fortifications." Hitler ordered the Luftwaffe to transfer control of No. 40 Bomber Wing, equipped with the long-range Focke-Wulf 200, to Admiral Dönitz, the submarine fleet commander, for reconnaissance purposes. Furious, Göring summoned Dönitz on February 7 and bitingly informed him that the navy was laboring under a delusion if it imagined that in this way it was going to scrape together a naval air force; only over his dead body would any of his precious Focke-Wulf 200s be supplied to Dönitz for such unspectacular purposes as aerial reconnaissance. Now that Göring had returned from leave, Hitler wearily yielded to his tantrums.

Hitler nevertheless remained unimpressed by the Luftwaffe attacks on Britain. A French diplomat who had left Britain in December reported to the German authorities that although the night bombing of London and Coventry had affected public morale to some extent, Newcastle, where he had been stationed, had hardly suffered. Hitler personally underlined with blue pencil the man's remarks that "massive attacks on Newcastle had not taken place up to his departure. He was puzzled by this as at present the Vickers Armstrong shipyards at Newcastle were building an aircraft carrier (due to be finished in about six months), two battle cruisers (finished in five or six months), a light cruiser, six or seven destroyers, and three or four submarines." Hitler ordered this oversight brought to the Luftwaffe's attention, but still he refused to injure Göring's pride—as he himself put it—by giving the navy direct control of the air force units that it needed. Indeed, now that Göring's leave was over, Hitler laid down a final reorganization of Luftwaffe reconnaissance duties, splitting them up into naval (North Sea) and Luftwaffe (Atlantic) zones, a compromise that positively invited disaster.

In Albania, the minor offensive Mussolini had so pompously launched on March 9 folded up within five days. Hitler was secretly pleased that the Duce had again burned his fingers. Now the Greek general commanding the northern army secretly let the Germans know that they would agree to an immediate armistice in Albania if the Italian troops there were replaced by Germans; they would also talk about territorial claims, provided that there were no Italians at the conference table; unless these provisos were met, the Greeks would fight to the finish. Hitler wanted the British thrown out of Greece and the Peloponnesus, but he told both Brauchitsch and Raeder that even if Greece would now agree to do so, Germany would still have to occupy the whole country so that the Luftwaffe could command the eastern Mediterranean. He nonetheless viewed the coming war with Greece with undiluted distaste. He admired the Greeks as a nation and had still not broken off diplomatic relations with Athens; as a result, there was a continuous flow of information on the mood there—and the mood of the people was that the "holy war with Italy" must be fought to final victory.

By March 24, when Hitler departed for Vienna, the British were believed to have disembarked up to forty thousand troops in Greece. The OKW instructed the German military attaché in Washington to see to it that the size of the British force in Greece was given maximum publicity. "The bigger the British talk, the better will be the propaganda effect of their defeat." In Vienna, the documents attaching Yugoslavia to the Tripartite Pact were at last to be signed, and Hitler was in high spirits as his train pulled into the station. He caught sight of Ribbentrop's corpulent young liaison officer, Ambassador Hewel—easily the most eligible bachelor on his staff—and teasingly suggested that this was his thirty-seventh birthday and high time to be married. "I hope in my old age you will allow me to say, Send all the little Hewels to come and see me. . . ."

Hitler and his entourage stayed at the Imperial Hotel, redolent with memories of March 1938. When the day was over, Hewel entered in his diary: "Ceremonial signing of Yugoslavia's entry to the Tripartite Pact at the Belvedere. Afterward conferences with [Dragisha] Cvetković"—the Yugoslav prime minister—"and Ciano. Afterward dinner with Schirach, very pleasant. Maria Holst, Fräulein Caspar, etc., were there. Führer spoke the whole time about my getting married." Indeed, among Hewel's possessions is the menu of that dinner—simple enough, but signed by everybody present: Hitler's personal photographer Heinrich Hoffmann, Dr. Karl Brandt, his adjutants, Bormann, and the young Viennese beauties Schirach had selected to grace the table. Hitler scribbled at the top, "To the peacock, from a well-wisher.—Adolf Hitler."

Before Hitler returned to Berlin, his adjutants allowed a "Frau Wolf" in to see him—his younger sister, Paula, working incognito as a secretary for doctors in a military hospital. For a while they chatted about family affairs. Paula said, "Sometimes when I am in the mountains and I see a little chapel I go in and pray for you." Hitler was deeply stirred, and after a time replied, "Do you know it is my absolute conviction that the Lord is holding his protecting hand above me?" Paula had been eleven when their mother died, and Adolf eighteen. He had not seen her for thirteen years after that, but he had let her have his share of their orphans' pension, while he had worked as a laborer in Vienna. In the years of his rise to power, he had annually sent her a ticket to the impressive Nuremberg rally, but she remained of the opinion that it was a pity he had not become an architect as he had always wanted. This was the last time he saw Paula.

It had taken all of March to persuade the ambiguous Yugoslavs to sign the pact, but the psychological blow to Britain was well worth the time invested; in addition, Hitler's armies fighting in Greece would depend on a line of communications extending for some 250 miles along, and only 12 miles away from, the Yugoslav border, so even hostility short of war would be most undesirable. The regent, Prince Paul, had visited him unofficially at the Berghof and explained how touchy public opinion in his country was. It was not until Germany agreed to Paul's terms—Yugoslavian territory would not be crossed by Axis troops, and though Yugoslavia was to make no military contribution herself, she was to receive Salonika as a reward—that the Yugoslav privy council agreed to the signature; however, anti-Italian feeling was running so high in Belgrade that several ministers resigned over the issue. Once the pact was signed, Hitler sent for Keitel and expressed his pleasure that there would be no further unpleasant surprises for them in the Balkans, but when he made the same remark to Ciano he qualified it thus: "Yugoslavia's domestic affairs could still take a complicated turn despite everything." This was not an example of his famous intuition; the Abwehr report on Yugoslavia had that day noted: "The mood of large circles is black toward Germany. Incidents and provocations are multiplying, particularly in the provinces and villages. The state of affairs is enough to give rise to fears that the government will lose control of the situation. . . ." At 10:20 P.M., Hitler's train left Vienna for Berlin, where he was to meet the Japanese foreign minister on the afternoon of the twenty-seventh.

Seldom was a pact shorter-lived than this one with Yugoslavia. Early on March 27, Hewel brought Hitler the stunning news from Belgrade that there had been a coup d'etat; the prince regent had been overthrown, and with him the Cvetković government. Hitler's first reaction was that this was a bad joke, but the putsch was real enough: crowds were demonstrating outside the German legation, the German tourist office had been destroyed, the Swedish envoy had been mistaken for a German and beaten unconscious, and British flags—distributed by the British legation—were appearing everywhere. There were some American flags as well. Crowds were singing "The Red Flag" in the streets. Serbia was in an uproar; Croatia was still calm. The coup had been engineered by Yugoslavia's air force commander, General Dušan Simović; a Serb known to be hostile to Germany, he was an exponent of Pan-Slavism and perhaps even a Russian agent. His revolutionary Cabinet did not ratify the entry into the Tripartite Pact, but made continuing protestations of loyalty toward Germany. Hitler set little store by them—he had mouthed enough of his own in the past. He stormed that this revolution was as though somebody had smacked his fist into a basinful of water.

The traumatic effect of the Belgrade putsch on Hitler became apparent only later. He saw it as a timely warning never to trust the Slavs. A month later he privately noted:

> To go through something like that teaches caution. Nations today are governed less by logic and reason than by hatred and perhaps by money interests as well, and this is how it has happened that one nation after another has been precipitated into misfortune by British promises and lies—Poland, to whom I offered

the most favorable terms,[4] France, who did not want a war at all, Holland and Belgium, Norway, and now Greece and Yugoslavia. You may say, the people themselves cannot help it, but I have to deal not with the people but their governments.

On first receiving the news, he had sent for Keitel and Jodl, met them in their conference room, and showed them the Belgrade telegram. His initial anger had yielded almost immediately to delight at the new strategic openings. As a result of his Austrian upbringing, he had always been uneasy about the chauvinistic Serbs in Belgrade. This uneasiness had been reinforced by Intelligence reports that Churchill's agents were plotting the overthrow of Prince Paul. Now he had been forced to abdicate and an officer camarilla had dumped seventeen-year-old King Peter on the throne. Hitler could hardly credit his good fortune that all this had happened now. In mid-May, "Barbarossa" was scheduled to begin; had the overthrow of Prince Paul occurred only then, it would have enormously complicated Hitler's plans. "Luckily the enemy unmasked themselves now, while our hands are still free!" he crowed. Now he would wipe Yugoslavia off the map. Hewel wrote in his diary: "—Göring, Brauchitsch, and Ribbentrop are sent for immediately. Decisions are rapidly taken. The mood is exhilarating. The Hungarian and Bulgarian envoys are summoned forthwith." At 1 P.M. Generals Halder and Brauchitsch arrived. Hitler, sparkling with excitement, took them and Ribbentrop to the map table, where he announced, "I have decided to destroy Yugoslavia. How much military force do you need? How much time?"

Almost at once, Hitler was informed that the Hungarian envoy, Döme Sztójay, had arrived. The war conference was adjourned. The generals had their orders anyway. Ribbentrop had not spoken. Hitler told the Hungarian envoy that now that the Italians had been made a laughingstock by Greece, the whole world thought the Axis powers were finished. His message to the regent of Hungary, Horthy, was this: the hour had struck for Hungary's revenge; the Führer would support her territorial claims to the hilt. "March back into the Banat!" he advised her, and he offered Hungary an Adriatic outlet which Admiral Horthy—the last commander of the Austro-Hungarian navy in 1918—must surely desire: the port of Fiume. After hearing these words, Sztójay was flown to Budapest. Shortly afterward Hitler received the Bulgarian envoy, Draganoff, and offered him what would have been Yugoslavia's share of Greece—Macedonia. "The eternal uncertainty down there is over," he rejoiced. "The tornado is going to burst upon Yugoslavia with breathtaking suddenness."

The next evening the Hungarian, Sztójay, arrived back with a secret letter from

---

[4]He was referring to the sixteen-point proposals "offered" to the Poles in August 1939. At the time he had described them privately as terms on which the Poles should "choke."

Horthy: the regent would be pleased to help, but turned down the offer of territory. Hitler was delighted that Germany and Hungary would now confront the Slav menace shoulder to shoulder, and mused to the envoy, "Now that I reflect on all this, I cannot help believing in a Higher Justice. I am awestruck at the powers of Providence."

In the brief war conference with Halder, Brauchitsch, and Ribbentrop, Hitler had settled the broad plan of attack in the Balkans. "Politically it is vital for the blow to fall on Yugoslavia without mercy; militarily, she must be defeated in one lightning swoop." Göring undertook to withdraw the necessary bomber and fighter squadrons from the west immediately. The Luftwaffe would open the campaign with wave after wave of bombers to destroy Belgrade. By the small hours of the morning following the war conference, the OKW's formal directive was in Hitler's hands: "Yugoslavia is to be regarded as an enemy and is therefore to be destroyed as rapidly as possible, whatever protestations of loyalty she may utter for the time being." General von Rintelen was sent to Mussolini with details for the Italian armed forces.

The attack on Russia must now be postponed for up to four weeks, as the directive made clear. It was a decision Hitler had not taken lightly, for he was well aware of the implications of allowing "Barbarossa" to drag on into the Russian winter. In the event, however, even here fate was on his side: the spring of 1941 had brought unusually heavy rains to Central Europe, and the ground would have been too marshy for the panzer divisions which were the backbone of "Barbarossa" to operate earlier than they did; the rivers and dikes were flooded throughout western Russia. The divisions Hitler now committed to the Balkans would have remained idle until June anyway.

Punctually at 4 P.M. on March 27, outwardly unruffled by the breathtaking events of the past few hours, Hitler received the Japanese foreign minister, Yosuke Matsuoka, at the Chancellery. Some 150,000 Berlin citizens marshaled outside in the Wilhelmplatz thundered a welcome for an ally Germany had always held in higher esteem than Italy.

Hitler saw in Japan's territorial aspirations in the Far East a further powerful means of bringing about Britain's submission. The purpose of his present foreign policy was to urge the Japanese to join the fray now, while the British were still at a disadvantage. In September 1940, Japan had occupied bases in northern Indochina with Vichy approval, but she feared to embark on fresh military exploits while Russia menaced her in the rear. Interestingly enough, given his foreign policy goal, during the first five months of 1941 Hitler refrained from telling the Japanese outright of "Barbarossa" and went no further than oblique hints. We are entitled to ask why, for he himself had emphasized that the Japanese could always be trusted to keep a secret. (The Forschungsamt had long given up as a fruitless exercise the tapping of Japanese embassy telephones, and to German code-experts the Japanese cyphers seemed impregnable.)

It was Admiral Raeder who had first brought Hitler's attention to Singapore, the key to British supremacy in the Far East. Late in December, Raeder had shown him a letter from his naval attaché in Tokyo, reporting that certain Japanese naval circles were seriously in favor of capturing Singapore as soon as possible; Raeder suggested to Hitler that this need not necessarily drag the United States into the war and that it would be very much in Germany's interest if Japan became embroiled with Britain, however lengthy and profitless her campaign. Hitler approved the Japanese proposal, but disappointingly little more was heard from Tokyo. He hinted obscurely to the departing Japanese ambassador, Saburo Kurusu, in early February that "mutual friends could one day become our mutual enemies"—meaning Germany and Russia—but this message left no visible impression on Tokyo. In the middle of the month Foreign Minister Matsuoka had however announced his intention of visiting Berlin. Japanese policy had two broad aims—to keep the United States out of the current war, and to prepare a preventive attack on Singapore *if* this attempt should fail. Japan also wanted to improve her relations with the Soviet Union. To Hitler, these policy aims were inadequate, and he instructed the OKW to draft a plan for wide-ranging joint consultation between Germany and Japan. He rebuked Raeder for expecting everything of Tokyo and offering nothing in return. The Wehrmacht and German industry must give their ally generous insight into all their most up-to-date secret weapons and designs, in the tacit hope that Japan would "take active steps in the Far East as soon as possible," thus simultaneously bringing about the defeat of Britain and keeping America out of the war. In an OKW directive issued early in March, it was pointed out that the attack on Russia would provide Japan with an ideal opportunity to launch her own campaigns, but that "no hint whatsoever is to be given to the Japanese about "Operation Barbarossa."

Matsuoka's personal visit to the Chancellery at the end of March 1941 had been preceded by conversations a month before in which Hitler and Ribbentrop had urged the new Japanese ambassador, General Hiroshi Oshima, to recommend an attack on Singapore. (Ribbentrop had merely indicated to the ambassador that Germany was keeping calm where Russia was concerned, but that if the Reich should be forced to fight in the east, the outcome would be a total eclipse of the Soviet Union.) The German foreign minister wanted "a lightning strike, if possible without a declaration of war," but Oshima said that Japan now felt it must prepare for war not only with Britain but with the United States and that this would take time; the preparations for attacking Singapore would be concluded by the end of May. On February 27, Ribbentrop therefore cabled his ambassador in Tokyo: "Please use every means at your disposal to get Japan to take Singapore as soon as possible." But the naval attaché in Tokyo reported that the Japanese navy had decided against attacking Singapore alone. Hitler still refused to play his trump card—revealing to the Japanese his firm plan to attack Russia; in response to General Halder's urging on March 17 he merely agreed to drop a hint as to the possibility when Matsuoka saw him; Raeder made the same proposal next day privately, but Hitler again refused.

Hitler and Ribbentrop both chose their words with extreme care throughout Matsuoka's visit. The Reich foreign minister only hinted that a Russo-German war was entirely within the realm of possibility. Hitler observed how cagey Matsuoka was about Singapore—the visitor stressed in painful detail how little weight his voice carried on this issue in Tokyo—and made his own most direct reference to "Barbarossa" in an aside to General Oshima at the luncheon given for Matsuoka on the twenty-eighth. After indicating that the Soviet Union had been behind the Belgrade putsch the day before, he noted: "If the Soviet Union were to attack Japan, then Germany would not hesitate to launch an armed attack on the Soviet Union." This, echoed Ribbentrop, was an "absolute guarantee." When a few days later Matsuoka passed through Berlin again on his way back to Tokyo from Rome, Hitler offered him a similar guarantee in the event that Japan should—through attacking Singapore—find herself at war with the United States. On April 10, Ribbentrop was to be even more explicit, stating that even if the Soviet Union did *not* attack Japan, "Germany might still start a war against the Soviet Union before the year is out; it depends on how she behaves." From intercepted documents, both the German foreign minister and Hitler were by now well aware of Churchill's attempts to panic the Russians into drawing closer to the British camp.[5] But the Japanese response was disappointing—indeed, while passing through Moscow on his return to Tokyo, Matsuoka signed an agreement of neutrality between Japan and Moscow.

Once more, on March 30, 1941, Hitler's generals and admirals were summoned from all over Nazi-occupied Europe to hear a secret speech in Berlin. The Führer chose the New Chancellery's Cabinet Room for his setting as its wood paneling provided the best acoustics. Scores of gilded chairs were fetched from the nearby

---

[5] This being so, there seems no logical explanation for Göring's revealing to his Swedish intermediary, Dahlerus—who would no doubt rapidly transmit it to London—between March 24 and 27, 1941, that Hitler was preparing to attack Russia; moreover, in the second week of June 1941 Göring again summoned Dahlerus to Berlin and informed him of the precise date of the attack. There is no indication that Hitler was aware of this.

propaganda ministry—the speech was to last three hours. Despite the imminence of "Marita," and now the attack on Yugoslavia too, Hitler's speech covered the whole European war theater, with most emphasis on the eastern front, and he only touched briefly on the tactical problems in the Balkans during the discussion that followed the simple luncheon.

He explained at some historical length his decision to attack Russia, starting significantly with Britain's refusal to make peace in June 1940. He spoke scathingly of Italy's misfortunes, charitably distinguishing between the plucky but poorly led Italian soldiers and their bumbling, devious political and military commanders. "Why has Britain fought on?" he asked. He identified two primary reasons—the influence of the Jews and of Britain's international financial involvements, and the dominant influence of the Churchill clique. Britain had floated off the sandbanks of despondency by means of purely psychological bubbles: although she had demonstrably lost four hundred thousand tons of shipping at Dunkirk, she had camouflaged the rout as a victorious retreat; the RAF's night bombing of Germany boosted home morale far more than it damaged German industry; British cockiness had been restored by the failure of the dreaded Wehrmacht invasion to materialize, and by Mussolini's defeats in the Mediterranean.

Now Britain was hitching her fortunes to the United States and Russia, declared Hitler. Of the United States he was not afraid—it could never match Germany's soaring aircraft, tank, and submarine production; not for four years would American arms output be going at full blast, and then there was the problem of transporting the arms and troops to the European theater. But Russia must be defeated now. "Now we have the chance to smash Russia while our own back is free. That chance will not return so soon. I would be betraying the future of the German people if I did not seize it now!" Once this land-forces problem had been settled, in about two years, Germany could set about mastering her other duties in the skies and oceans of the world. He urged his generals to have no moral compunctions about violating their treaty with Russia. It was quite clear why Stalin had cynically signed it; but he also urged them not to underestimate the Russian tanks or air force, or to rely too heavily on Germany's allies in this fight. "The fate of major German formations must not be trusted to the steadfastness of Romanian divisions"—a warning he was himself to ignore at Stalingrad.

Hitler also drilled into his generals that this would be a war between great ideologies, and as such very different from the war in the west. "In the east cruelty now will be kindness for the future." The Russian commissars and GPU officials were criminals and were to be treated as such. "It is not our job to see that these criminals survive."

In a masterpiece of rapid General Staff work, the entire Balkan campaign plan was dismantled and remounted within nine days to include the improvised invasion of Yugoslavia by German forces, with Hungarian and Italian troops in walk-on roles. It was a feat of planning Hitler recognized, but only tacitly.

Hitler meanwhile decided how the carcass of Yugoslavia was to be carved up —the rich and fertile Banat region would be returned to Hungary, the Dalmatian coast and Montenegro assigned to Italy, and Serbia placed under German military rule. Of the former Austrian territory Germany would require only the return of Carinthia and Styria to the Reich. Croatia was to become an autonomous state and choose its own ruler; Greek Macedonia was to be annexed by Bulgaria. It all seemed a very satisfactory end to the Balkan nightmare. Russia's Balkan stance remained uncertain, and in the last few days before launching the invasion of Greece and Yugoslavia, Hitler was in the same agony of apprehension that had gripped him before "Yellow" and the invasion of Norway. Rumors multiplied. Was Stalin offering Yugoslavia's new regime a nonaggression pact? Had he secretly offered the Yugoslavs arms and supplies, as an intercepted message between Belgrade and Moscow had implied? The Russians hotly denied the suggestion—Hungary would never allow Russian arms to cross her territory; but Hitler knew there were other routes to Belgrade, through the Aegean ports of Greece, for example. He warned Antonescu to increase the guard on Romania's frontiers as tension between the Axis and Belgrade rose. On April 5 the Romanian General Staff—regarded by Foreign Armies East as the best source of Intelligence after Finland—reported that the Russians were stepping up photographic reconnaissance sorties over Romania, that sixty or more Russian aircraft had suddenly arrived at Leofa, and that a new paratroop school had just opened at Kiev.

All these warnings sinisterly shaded the Belgrade regime's obvious attempts to gain time. Hitler instructed Ribbentrop to ignore any fresh protestations of loyalty from Belgrade. When Count Ciano telephoned after dinner on March 31 with the news that the deputy premier of Yugoslavia was asking to see Mussolini, Hitler advised, "Yes, but keep him away for the next few days." On April 5 the political clouds suddenly began to clear: Hewel brought him a disturbing Forschungsamt intercept proving that Stalin was on the point of signing a pact with the new anti-German regime in Belgrade (it was signed within the next twenty-four hours). It was, therefore, now or never. All through the fifth, Hitler was on tenterhooks, and he sat up with Hewel and his personal staff talking until five in the morning. Twenty minutes later, his armored and infantry divisions began storming the frontiers of Greece and Yugoslavia; his heavily escorted bomber squadrons were already in the air heading for Belgrade.

A Bitter Victory

To the rest of the world Hitler's lightning campaign against Greece and Yugoslavia proved once more the invincibility of the German Wehrmacht. Within the inner sanctum of his own headquarters, however, it demonstrated the grating lack of harmony within the Axis: the Axis always had been more myth than reality, but never more so than now. Hitler had fully taken into account the susceptibilities of his new allies; in a directive issued at the beginning of April 1941, he stated that while he would himself assign the necessary campaign objectives for the Italian and Hungarian forces he would endeavor to do so in such a way that Mussolini and Horthy might yet appear to their people and armed forces as "sovereign military commanders." Horthy was no problem, but the Duce—his *amour-propre* injured by a succession of defeats—obliged Hitler to adopt public postures and contortions on Italy's behalf that for once united the OKW, the foreign ministry, the army, and the navy in a seething, uncomprehending anger at their Führer's indulgence of his inept ally. But Hitler had a higher aim; he wanted to strengthen the slackened Axis bonds in time for the supreme ordeal yet to come: "Barbarossa," the assault on Russia.

Within twelve days Yugoslavia, her thirty-four divisions rent by the national rift between Serb and Croat, was defeated. The Greek armies capitulated following a heroic struggle shortly after, leaving the British Expeditionary Force fighting a hopeless rearguard action against the German armored and mountain corps which had comfortably sidestepped the formidable Metaxas line to pour into Yugoslavia and Greece. The British had committed their first blunder in purchasing the coup d'etat in Belgrade; the second error was in overestimating the resisting power of the Yugoslav army. When Hitler's Second Army, operating out of Austria, offered the Yugoslav general negotiating the armistice the use of a German plane to consult his government, the worthy officer had to struggle visibly with his qualms about entering such a newfangled device. "I am an old man and have never flown before—but I will do it for my Fatherland!" Besides,

Yugoslavia's forces were equipped with German weapons firing German ammunition; how could she possibly have fought a long war?

Hitler had ordered the attack to begin with the saturation bombing of Belgrade—with an eye to the deterrent effect on other powers, notably Turkey and the Soviet Union. Nearly five hundred bomber and dive-bomber sorties had devastated the Yugoslav capital within hours after the campaign opened. Water, gas, and power supplies failed, as many as 17,000 civilians were killed, and the government was forced to flee to the suburbs without having made any provision for this eventuality; robbed of their nerve center, the Yugoslav armies caved in. Over 340,000 Yugoslav soldiers were taken prisoner; the Germans lost only 151 dead. Throughout the campaign, the Italians and the Hungarians—who since Hungary had signed a treaty of friendship with Yugoslavia tactfully waited until Croatia had declared her independence before marching in—displayed a marked reluctance to attack until the enemy had first been soundly beaten and demoralized by the German troops. Hitler fully sympathized with Admiral Horthy's predicament: the latter's prime minister had shown his disapproval of the attack on Yugoslavia by committing suicide on April 3. Horthy expressed to the German liaison officer in Budapest the pious hope that in the coming fighting the Hungarian armies would not lose too much blood or be "led too far astray from Hungary"; at that time he had no knowledge of Hitler's plans for a coalition war against Russia within three months.

On the afternoon of April 9, German radio broadcast the first string of six special bulletins on the victories in the southeast. The Greek army defending Salonika had capitulated. Hewel noted the "magnificent mood" at Hitler's Chancellery. The mood was dimmed briefly that night when fifty British bombers arrived over Berlin, cascading high-explosive and fire bombs over the acres between the Victory Monument and Alexanderplatz. Hitler took refuge in his air raid shelter and, after the raid was over, sent Hewel to tour the blitzed area with a police general. Bellevue Castle, the crown prince's palace, the State library, and the university had been badly damaged; in the State Opera House Unter den Linden the fires were out of control, and when dawn came, this fine building in which the Führer had delivered some of his most significant speeches was a smoldering shell. The raid had killed eleven people. In revenge, a week later Hitler sent the Luftwaffe to raid London continuously for ten hours with a thousand tons of bombs.

Late on April 10 his train left Berlin for Munich; and late on the eleventh he continued through Vienna toward Graz. Here a tunnel took the single-track railway through the Alps. The OKW command train, *Atlas,* halted on the far side of the ice-cold, three thousand-yard-long tunnel; Hitler's *Amerika* stopped before entering it, near the little station of Mönichkirchen. Each train could be shunted into the tunnel in case of air attack. This heavily guarded area was to be his headquarters for the next two weeks. His only contacts with the outside world were the OKW's communications system, the twice weekly showing of rough-cut newsreels at the nearby Mönichkirchener Hof Hotel—projected without sound-track, while an adjutant read aloud the accompanying script—and the visits of his generals and ministers. It was here that a young Luftwaffe lieutenant, Franz von Werra, reported to him. Shot down over Britain, he had escaped from a prison train in Canada. He was a mine of information gleaned in captivity—for example, from German submarine crews, who told him their boats had been detected by some British device called "Asdic."

On April 12, the Nazi banner was already flying over the ruins of Belgrade. On the fourteenth the Greeks began evacuating Albania. On the fifteenth the OKW learned that the British Expeditionary Force was in full flight toward its ports of embarkation. Broadcasting to the Yugoslav nation, Churchill offered deceptive comfort: the British knew what it was like and were still standing right behind them, an awkwardly ambiguous statement which Goebbels instructed his press media to exploit to the full.

Hitler ordered his army and Luftwaffe to use all available means to prevent the escape of the British troops in Greece. Late on the seventeenth, Radio Athens was monitored announcing the inevitability of defeat and appealing to the people to remain calm. Hitler's instructions to the OKW were that if Greece surrendered, all Greek prisoners were to be released—as a mark of his admiration for the valor with which they had defended their frontiers. Prime Minister Alexander Koryzis committed suicide, and on April 20, as Hitler's birthday was being ceremonially observed in his command train at Mönichkirchen, he learned that what was left of the Greek army had surrendered to the SS Leibstandarte, or Life Guards.

In an OKW order of April 19, Hitler had laid down the principle that surrender offers were always to be accepted by German commanders, however small the enemy unit involved. Field Marshal List had therefore formally accepted the army's surrender on April 21 even though the Greek commander, General Tsolakoglu, made it plain that he was *not* surrendering to the Italians, whom his forces had soundly defeated (and indeed not seen for some days). Hitler endorsed List's action, hoping no doubt to present the Duce with a *fait accompli*. Victory over Greece was a bittersweet accomplishment, and in a gush of sentiment, on April 19 he told a Hungarian diplomat that he had not had his heart in fighting the Greeks. "I am fighting a war against Britain, not against these little coun-tries." He claimed that had Greece not allowed the British forces in, he would never have attacked her; now he was bound to disarm her, but he did so without relish and he would take no Greek prisoners.

After this high point Hitler's moral stance toward Greece rapidly deteriorated. Mussolini was speechless with rage that the Greeks had not offered their surrender to the Italians, and bluntly refused to stop the fighting unless the Greeks appealed to *him* for an armistice. Italy, blustered the Duce, had been fighting with 500,000 men and lost 63,000 dead in her six months of war with Greece. Then suddenly the SS Life Guards had advanced so far that they held a bridge which actively blocked the Italian pursuit of the Greeks! Hitler reluctantly backtracked and told Jodl that List was wrong to have accepted the surrender and that the fight must go on until the Greeks surrendered to the Italians too.

The army was furious at this public rebuff. So was Ribbentrop, who visited Hitler that very afternoon, April 21. Hewel noted: "The Chief with the Führer. Reports that the Italians are making the most brazen demands. Surrender talks are in progress with the Greek army. Obstacle: the Italians. Everybody is furious, even the Führer. He is always torn between soldier and politician. Keitel against Ribbentrop." Mussolini's haughty demands brought a comic problem to the Greek tragedy: not only had the Greek army surrendered to the Germans and laid down its arms, but the greater part of it was already in captivity; how were the Greeks now to continue fighting for Italy's benefit? Hitler sent word to the Duce's headquarters that perhaps the Italians would like to send a representative to assist Jodl in settling the surrender terms with the Greeks the next morning, April 22. But Mussolini's forces had opened a bedraggled offensive on the Epirus front as soon as word of the Greek surrender to List reached him; the Greeks were not only still fighting there, they were inflicting heavy casualties on the Italians.

The OKW rushed a draft of the surrender terms to Rome, but Mussolini still churlishly refused to play any part unless the Greeks first offered to capitulate to the Italian commander. He sulkingly announced that he could have finished off the Greeks without Hitler's help—if the five hundred thousand Italian troops had not sufficed, then he would have sent a million. When he read in the draft that the Führer wanted to allow the Greek officers to retain their swords and daggers, he protested in exasperation that these were an enemy who had inflicted nameless indignities on the Italians; but here the Germans were adamant—the whole world had marveled at the Greek army's prolonged resistance, and Hitler considered it proper to recognize their bravery. Apart from this Hitler blindly accepted the Italian demands. To the fury of Admiral Raeder he announced that the Yugoslav and Greek navies were to be handed over to the Italians when they arrived to replace the German troops; to the fury of both the OKW and army, Hitler also bowed to Mussolini's demand that the Axis troops stage a ceremonial entry into Athens, with Italians and Germans side by side. (He himself considered this an unnecessary and objectionable humiliation of a brave enemy.) The nearest Italians were still a week's march away from Athens, which did not make things easier.

When the surrender conference began at Salonika late on April 22, the Italian general present announced that he was not empowered to sign. Inquiries in Rome revealed that Mussolini had personally ordered this; the general would be authorized to sign only if the Greeks offered to surrender on the Epirus front first. For a time Hitler toyed with the idea of leaving the Greeks and Italians to fight it out, west of a certain line to be blocked by German troops. But during the night the Greeks bowed to the inevitable and offered surrender to Mussolini's generals too. At Salonika the surrender document was signed by all three parties on the afternoon of April 23, after Mussolini had played his final trick on Hitler. The Führer had forbidden premature release of the surrender news, but at 10 A.M. the Italians had already suddenly broadcast it to the world. "The enemy armies of Epirus and Macedonia have laid down their arms. The surrender was tendered by a Greek military delegation yesterday at 9:04 P.M. to the commander of the Italian Eleventh Army on the Epirus front. The details of the surrender will now be worked out in complete agreement with our German allies." Discreet inquiries in Rome revealed that Mussolini had personally ordered the early announcement. Hewel summed it up in his diary: "The Italians are acting like crazy idiots."

In Croatia—the northern region of Yugoslavia bordering on Italy and Austria— a breakaway movement had been fomented by Canaris's underground forces. General Sladko Kvaternik, an officer of the old Austro-Hungarian army, had seized power in Zagreb, aided by the Abwehr's "Jupiter" organization, and with Hitler's blessing he had set up an independent state with Dr. Ante Pavelić, the leader of the Ustashi movement who had spent long years exiled in Italy, as its *Poglavnik,* or chief. Major General Edmund von Glaise-Horstenau was appointed German liaison officer responsible directly to Keitel and the OKW. His task would eventually be to build up a Croatian police army of about six divisions. A diplomat of SA general's rank—an increasingly familiar animal in Ribbentrop's ministry—would be Germany's envoy to Croatia.

Hitler's decision to transfer the Dalmatian coastal region of Croatia to Italy caused intense resentment in Zagreb, and Glaise-Horstenau protested vehemently to Hitler at this amputation. However, the Führer closed his eyes to the hatred Germany would reap from the Croats by this action. Meanwhile the Serbs, despised as conspirators and traitors who had sold Yugoslavia to the British and the Bolsheviks, need expect short shrift from Germany. The Luftwaffe's General Helmut Förster was appointed military governor in Serbia, with orders to rule with an iron hand.[1]

---

[1]Ribbentrop's specialists had searched the Yugoslav foreign ministry and war department buildings in Belgrade for, *inter alia,* files relating to Serbian secret organizations. Among the documents found was a proposal for the Yugoslav General Staff to poison awkward personalities.

In Dalmatia, the Italians needed no prompting to act likewise. On April 24, Canaris's lieutenant, Colonel Lahousen, interviewed General Kvaternik, the new Croat war minister in Zagreb (referred to as "Marshal Kvaternik" by his overenthusiastic followers). Lahousen found that this ancient, upright nationalist's admiration for Germany and her Führer was boundless, but so was his hatred of the Italians, who were now wreaking their revenge on Dalmatia. (The Italians had already posted warnings that they were introducing corporal punishment there.) "The Croats are a people of honor, with a long military tradition," complained Kvaternik, "and it is bitter beyond words to be trodden down and humiliated now by an army that has not been able to pin one victory to its colors." He told Lahousen that when Pavelić had initially returned from his Italian exile, his first private question to him was, "Ante, have you made any kind of deal with the Italians on Croatia?" Only when his old comrade had categorically denied this did the general offer him his hand. Nonetheless, Lahousen reported to the OKW that the new Croatian leaders would swallow Italy's annexation of Dalmatia—if only because they were sure Mussolini could not hang on to this, the eastern coast of the Adriatic, for long. A few days later Canaris himself met Kvaternik in Zagreb. The general had fresh reports of Italian outrages—soldiers urinating on the Croatian national flag, tearing down the Reich insignia, actively inciting Serbian elements against the Croats, and looting foodstuffs and goods; Kvaternik feared—prophetically, as events turned out—that this "completely irrational political attitude of the Italians" would sow the seeds of serious future danger.

On April 24, 1941, the Hungarian regent, Admiral Horthy, visited Hitler's train —their first meeting since 1938. In the interval, Hitler had received from the admiral many letters, written in a quaint, archaic German style. The most recent had come in mid-April; only Horthy's handwritten draft survives, in Budapest archives. In it, Horthy once more suggested a German attack on Russia and hinted that Hungary would participate if the whole of Transylvania—at present partly under Romanian rule—were promised to him. "Nobody else knows I have written this letter, and I will *never* mention it, even in any memoirs I may write." Horthy warned that an invasion of Britain was fraught with a thousand dangers. "But if Russia's inexhaustible riches are once in German hands, you can hold out for all eternity." On April 19, Hitler acknowledged to the Hungarian envoy Sztójay that Horthy obviously felt deeply—as this letter showed—about the Russian menace; he nevertheless inwardly rejected making any commitment to Hungary at Romania's expense. So now, on the twenty-fourth, he charmed and flattered Horthy, and the regent fawned on him—according to Hewel's diary the Hungarian "talked and talked" during the luncheon, and even argued, using one of Hitler's favorite phrases, that Greece had been defeated because she was a democracy, where "the votes of two idiots count for more than that of one wise man."

Keitel lunched silently with them, listening to Horthy's endless tales from his civilian life as horse breeder, farmer, and racehorse owner. Then Keitel lured him into hunting anecdotes, knowing that Hitler abominated huntsmen as a "green freemasonry" bent only on the cowardly murder of nature's most beautiful creatures—usually, as the Duke of Windsor had once pointed out at the Berghof—from a safe distance and with telescopic sights. Those who knew Hitler well were familiar with his loathing of horses too. (When three years later, SS General Hermann Fegelein, Himmler's new liaison officer, clanked in wearing riding spurs, Hitler sardonically invited him to "gallop next door" to fetch a certain document; purpling with rage, Fegelein vowed never to wear spurs again.)

But nothing could now darken Hitler's mood. The British were in full flight to their ships, albeit destroying every bridge to impede the Wehrmacht's pursuit. When the British evacuation ended five days later, Hitler had killed or captured another twenty-two thousand elite troops. Of the fifty thousand others who escaped, some sailed to Egypt. The rest were on the isle of Crete, and on Jeschonnek's suggestion Hitler ordered an airborne assault on Crete prepared as well. Inexplicably for Hitler, Churchill also survived this second Dunkirk-type fiasco. Through Lisbon, Hitler received word that Churchill was very popular in Britain, and Anthony Eden was being publicly identified with the humiliation in the Balkans.

Hitler's own mind was made up on the Russian campaign, but he still wanted to convince Ribbentrop. He knew he would not win over the foreign ministry as such. He considered its ways conservative, its procedures ponderous, and its attitude to the Party reactionary. Since its failure to give him advance warning of the Belgrade putsch, the ministry's stock had sunk even lower in his estimation. Hitler's tendency to direct foreign policy himself, using Ribbentrop only as a secretary, was strongly exposed again in "Barbarossa." He had decided to appoint not the foreign ministry, but the Party's chief thinker, the Baltic-born Alfred Rosenberg, to manage the new eastern domain—impressed, apparently, by Rosenberg's early writings on the Bolshevik menace. Small wonder that Hewel's diary shows Ribbentrop "off sick" for most of April 1941—malingering, furious at this fresh erosion of his powers.

On about April 25, Hitler telephoned Ribbentrop in Vienna, summoned him to his special-train headquarters, and told him he had decided finally to attack Russia. Ribbentrop later recalled:

He said that all the military Intelligence reaching him confirmed that the Soviet Union was preparing in a big way along the entire front from the Baltic to the Black Sea. He was not willing to be taken by surprise once he had recognized a danger. Moscow's pact with the Serbian putschist government was a downright provocation to Germany and a clear departure from the German-Russian treaty of friendship. In this conversation I recommended that he listen first to our [Moscow] ambassador, Count [Werner von der] Schulenburg, . . . I wanted to try a diplomatic settlement with Moscow first. But Hitler refused any such attempt and forbade me to discuss the matter with anybody; no amount of diplomacy could change the Russian attitude, as he now recognized it, but it might cheat him of the important tactical element of surprise when he attacked. He requested me to put on a show of complete support for his view, and explained that one day the West would understand why he had rejected the Soviet demands and attacked the East.

Thus, Hitler regarded "Barbarossa" as that most controversial of campaigns—a preventive war.

"What can a war historian tell us about the problems of fighting preventive wars?" he asked Wilhelm Scheidt at this time. Scheidt, a young, well-groomed cavalry captain, had just been introduced as adjutant to Colonel Walter Scherff, Hitler's personal historian. Scheidt knew about "Barbarossa," and replied, "Only somebody with the deepest sense of responsibility can take such a decision, and then only after looking at it from every possible angle. Because he will be risking immense dangers in starting such a war." He would have to accept the odium of being the aggressor, in return for the tactical advantages of surprise. But Hitler mused out loud, "Britain will just have to climb down, once we have defeated her last ally on the continent. If she does not, we shall destroy her, with all the means that we shall have when all Europe as far as the Urals is at our feet."

On April 26, Hitler's train left Mönichkirchen for the former Yugoslav frontier. He motored to Maribor—newly renamed Marburg—and toured the German-speaking provinces his Second Army had regained for the Reich. Everywhere there was a huge and fervent welcome, especially at Marburg's town hall. "Then by train back to Graz," recorded Hewel. "An enormous reception there. . . . The Führer is very happy—a fanatical welcome. Wonderful singing. The museum. Lunch at Hotel Wiesler, then left for Klagenfürt in the evening. On the way Rintelen and Ambassador Benzler joined the train. A conference on setting up a Greek opposition government.[2] Coffee at the castle, with infintely ugly

---

[2]On April 22, 1941, General Tsolakoglu, now a captive, had offered to establish a new government in Athens. Keitel instructed the army to release him so that the new government could be set up as soon as Mussolini formally assented.

Benzler was the former German envoy in Belgrade, who now became Ribbentrop's plenipotentiary to the German military governor of Serbia.

maidens provided from the Gau's leadership school. But they could sing very nicely." Here in Klagenfürt, Hitler the next day met his old history teacher, Professor Leopold Poetsch. Of this man he had written in *Mein Kampf* that it had perhaps altered the whole course of his life that fate gave him such a history teacher—able to bring the subject alive.

By April 28, with the swastika over the Acropolis, German paratroops astride the Isthmus of Corinth, and the SS Life Guards Brigade in the Peloponnesus, Adolf Hitler was back in his Chancellery in Berlin.

At five-fifteen that evening, Ribbentrop's ambassador in Moscow was ushered in to him. Count Schulenburg had not been officially informed of "Barbarossa"; (Hans Krebs, his military attaché, had been forbidden to tell him.) But Schulenburg was no simpleton. The rumors sweeping Central Europe, the evasive responses from Berlin, Hitler's failure to reply to the Soviet proposals of November 25, 1940—these told him all he needed. At Ribbentrop's behest the ambassador had prepared a memorandum begging Hitler to accept the Russian proposals; but in Berlin this document had been toned down by Ribbentrop's own advisers, who pointed out that otherwise Hitler would toss it aside unread. Hitler granted Schulenburg just thirty minutes of his time. To the ambassador it seemed that the Führer had drawn all his preconceived ideas from Vidkun Quisling, who had for many years been Norway's military attaché in Moscow and had first whispered to Hitler that Stalin's empire was already falling apart—that after the very first military defeats the unpopular Bolshevik regime would collapse, and that the Ukraine and other states were struggling to secede from the USSR.

"The Führer receives Schulenburg," noted Hewel. "A superficial conversation about Russia." Hitler asked him, according to Schulenburg's own record, what devil had possessed the Russians that they had signed that pact with the anti-German putschist regime in Belgrade—was it an attempt to frighten Germany? The ambassador's opinion was that the Russians were just openly staking their claim on the Balkans; they were very uneasy about the rumors of a coming German attack as well. Hitler retorted that it was the Russians who had begun the mobilization race, but the ambassador suggested it was characteristic Russian over-reaction to German moves. If Stalin had not allied himself with France and Britain when both were still strong and intact, he would hardly opt for them now. (To Hitler this was a facile argument: in 1939 Stalin had *wanted* to encourage war between Germany and the West; how could he have foreseen that Hitler would emerge victorious so soon?) When Schulenburg referred to all the indications that Stalin was desperate to reinforce the friendly ties between Germany and Russia, and was even hinting that he could supply five million tons of grain in 1942, Hitler turned away and ended the interview. His secretary, writing a private letter in the secretaries' room beneath the Chancellery stairs, ended it abruptly with the words: "Oh dear, I must stop now as the table is just being laid. The Chief comes every afternoon to have coffee with us in our 'stair cupboard.' "

The next day Hitler spoke to nine thousand officer candidates in the Berlin Sportpalast. "If you ask me, 'Führer, how long will the war last?' I can only say as long as it takes to emerge victorious! Whatever may come! As a National Socialist during the struggle for power I never knew the word 'capitulation.' And there is one word I will never know as leader of the German people and your Supreme Commander, and again it is 'capitulation'—that is, to submit to the will of another. Never, never! And you too have to think like that." He also hinted that he might yet have to make decisions that some of them might not comprehend, but he justified himself thus: "Where would we be now if we had waited just one week more in the south?"—meaning the Balkans.

His divisions were already pulling out of the Balkans and regrouping for "Barbarossa." He decided now that "Barbarossa" would begin on June 22, a Sunday, with the onset of the final top-capacity transport program one month earlier. On the Russian front the Wehrmacht would have the upper hand only in the central section, while in consequence of the Balkan campaign—which had left the Twelfth Army in southeastern Europe—and the considerable Russian reinforcements pouring into Bessarabia and Bukovina, the German armies in the south would be numerically inferior to the enemy. This was the real strategic cost of "Marita": Army Group South could not mount the pincer movement originally planned to destroy the Russian forces south of the Pripyet Marshes but had to attempt an almost impossible encirclement action with its northern wing while the southern wing was restricted to a tactical defense role. Nonetheless, Brauchitsch was still confident that after four weeks of stiff fighting on the frontier the initial Russian resistance would melt away.

During May the OKW was to begin staff talks with Finland and—less hopefully—with Hungary. The final month in which the real assembly for "Barbarossa" could no longer be concealed was to be camouflaged as a colossal diversion from Hitler's supposedly real intention—to invade Britain.

By this time the most persistent rumors of "Barbarossa" were sweeping Moscow once again. The first wave of reports that Germany was planning to attack Russia had reached Moscow in August 1940—perhaps significantly—but it had ebbed during the autumn only to come thundering back in March. Most of these reports could be traced back to the British embassy, but travelers in Germany were bringing back enough hair-raising and evidently significant tidbits of Intelligence to alarm even the most complacent Kremlin dweller. The most substantial evidence had reached Moscow from Romania and indirectly from Belgrade. Hitler had been most frank in his overtures to General Antonescu—indeed, the Romanian leader had positively canvassed "Barbarossa"; and when Göring had seen him in Vienna on March 5 about increasing Romania's oil output he had explained unambiguously that "one day the other oil supplier might drop out." Göring had asked how many Romanians now lived on Russian territory, and he had made a scooping gesture with his hand by way of explanation. Almost at once Moscow came into possession of photocopies of a document establishing that Hitler had promised that Romania should recover Bessarabia after Russia had been defeated; Hitler learned of this leak by mid-April. At the same time he learned of another, more intriguing leak from Belgrade.

Evidently Hitler had told Yugoslavia's prince regent privately about "Barbarossa" at the Berghof on March 4. In any case, British Foreign Secretary Eden had just told Sir Stafford Cripps as much; Eden had identified his source as King George of Greece, the prince regent's brother. The excellent Hungarian Intelligence service learned of this in Moscow and passed the information back to Admiral Canaris on April 11. In short the rumor was all over Europe. A few days later the unsuspecting German naval attaché in Moscow was cabling that Cripps was now predicting that Hitler would attack Russia on June 22, a canard so "obviously absurd" that he would do all he could to kill it.[3] The OKW evenly dismissed all these rumors as a British attempt "to poison the wells" and instructed its attachés abroad to spread counter-rumors that in the first half of May there would be major shifts of Wehrmacht strength to the west.

Stalin's reaction to the warnings was illuminating. At Cripps's suggestion the Yugoslav envoy in Moscow had at the beginning of April warned Stalin about "Barbarossa." Stalin had hedged a guess at the probable date and cockily replied, "Let them come. We will be ready for them!" Hitler's rapid victory in the Balkans literally wiped the smile off Stalin's face. An extraordinary period ensued in which the Soviet government tried desperately to appease Hitler: whereas the Soviet-German trade pact of January 1941 had been followed by a noticeable slowing down of Russian deliveries to Germany, now grain, petroleum, manganese, and other materials began flooding westward, and the Soviet government even laid on a special goods train to rush rubber to Germany along the Trans-Siberian railway. But no words spoke more eloquently than the sensational scene at Moscow's railroad station on the day the Japanese foreign minister departed for Tokyo. Stalin did what he had not even done for Ribbentrop—he made a stunning personal appearance on the platform, embraced the Japanese officials, and then searched out Ambassador Schulenburg and loudly pronounced in front of the

[3]At this time, April 24, Hitler himself had not fixed the date of June 22 for certain. But in the first week in April he seems to have discussed June 22 or 23 with Brauchitsch as possible dates. Lossberg meanwhile advised Jodl that since the troop movements would not be completed until the twenty-third, the operation should begin two days after that. Cripps's rumor seems therefore to have been based on a lucky guess.

assembled diplomatic corps, "We must remain friends, you must do all you can for that!" He put his arms around the German envoy's shoulders—perhaps he was drunk, for his left eye was half closed, he groped for the right words, and he looked much older.

As if that were not enough, Stalin swung around toward Colonel Krebs, the acting military attaché, satisfied himself that Krebs was German, and promised loudly, "We will always remain friends with you—whatever may happen!" Hitler had studied all the reports, including one submitted by the Forschungsamt, on this puzzling Moscow scene, and he wondered what to make of it. Equally remarkable was the studied politeness of the Soviet remonstrance over eighty German violations of Soviet air space in the first half of April (one aircraft had landed and been found to contain cameras, exposed films, and a topographical map of Soviet territory); the Soviet protest was mild compared with Jodl's cynical list of "deliberate provocations" by Russian aircraft—eight on April 17 alone— and his warning about the "momentous frontier incidents" that might soon occur if the Russians did not mend their ways. In fact the OKW was worried about this very Soviet reasonableness. After a secret conference with Keitel on Abwehr subversive and sabotage operations planned inside Russia, Admiral Canaris noted: "After my discussion with the chief of the OKW, General Jodl disclosed to me in a conference that they are greatly worried about the Russians' soft and indulgent attitude toward us, and he added half in jest, in a reference to our No. 800 'Special Duties' Training Regiment Brandenburg,⁴ 'If these chaps'—meaning the Soviet Russians—'keep on being so accommodating and take offense at nothing, then *you* will have to stage an incident to start the war.' "

Finding a suitable incident was traditionally the difficulty of launching a premeditated preventive war, which is what Hitler's eastern crusade had now become. Neither Hitler nor his military advisers were any longer in doubt as to Stalin's long-term intentions. Halder was to state that if the Russian deployments were shown to an impartial military expert he would have to concede that they were offensive in design. Throughout March, Russian troop movements close to the frontier had been so intense, with a heavy flow of reinforcements from Moscow toward Smolensk and Minsk, that eventually Halder felt anxiety about the threat of a Russian preventive action. The danger would be acute at least until April 20, for until then the Russians would have great superiority in strength. "The disposition of Russian forces gives food for thought," Halder wrote on April 7. "If we discount the catchword that the Russians want peace and won't attack

⁴The German commando regiment.

anybody themselves, then it has to be admitted that the Russian dispositions could allow them to convert very rapidly from defense into attack—and this could prove highly embarrassing for us." He had Jodl ask Hitler whether the top-capacity "Barbarossa" transport plan should be thrown into action now, six weeks early, but Hitler was against it.

The Führer himself was in no doubt. Stalin's pact with Belgrade, coupled with a communiqué of March 24,[5] provided further justification for "Barbarossa." At the end of it all he was to say, "I didn't take the decision to attack Moscow lightly, but because I knew from certain information that an alliance was being prepared between Britain and Russia. The big question was, Should we strike out first or wait until we were overwhelmed some time in the future?" According to his army adjutant, Hitler's decision was reinforced by Intelligence reports on feverish airfield and arms dump construction by the Russians throughout the spring; there were also reports from Polish agents of Russian troop movements from as far away as the Far East, and of the creation and deployment of new armies for what could only be offensive purposes. The Russians were also instructing their com-missars, for example in Leningrad, to get ready for a long and grueling war with Germany.

German Intelligence collected concrete evidence of long-range Soviet planning. The naval attaché reported from Moscow that the Soviet naval construction program was in the process of building three battleships, eleven cruisers, *sixty-one* destroyers, and nearly *three hundred* submarines; most of this fleet would be concentrated in the Baltic. On April 4 the German naval code-breakers noticed that the Russians had suddenly adopted completely new radio- and code-systems for two days—evidently a test of war procedures. After April 7, the German embassy in Moscow observed a steady call-up of reservists and raw recruits. On the eighth, the families of the Russian trade mission began leaving Berlin. Train-loads of the paraphernalia of war were observed moving westward from Kiev to the Polish border. On the ninth, the military attaché in Bucharest reported that Marshal Semën Timoshenko, believed to be the only capable Soviet commander, had just held a council of war at Kiev and ordered an alert for all units on the

---

[5]Russia had reaffirmed her nonaggression pact with Turkey to encourage her to adopt a more aggressive role against Germany in the Balkans. The Soviet Union had steadily overcome her tradi-tional distrust of Turkey. On February 18, the Forschungsamt had intercepted a description by the Turkish ambassador in Berlin of his conversation with the Russian ambassador, Vladimir Dekanozov, who had hinted that Turkey and the Soviet Union should exchange ideas on the Balkans. The Germans had then also intercepted the Turkish secret cables from Moscow, in which the ambassador there reported that on March 9 Molotov's deputy Andrei Vyshinsky had first proposed such a communiqué, and explicitly stated that the Soviet Union would "understand" any operation Turkey was forced to launch against "the threat of an attack"; Turkey's acceptance and reciprocation of this assurance on March 14 was also intercepted.

western front. Rumors swept the Generalgouvernment that Russia would exploit her present brief superiority of arms to strike into Germany, destroying the "Barbarossa" assembly and capturing the huge arms dumps Hitler was moving into the front line. On April 13, Hitler was shown a Forschungsamt summary on the multiplying rumors of war with Russia. On the twenty-third there were fresh reports from Bucharest of immense Soviet reinforcements in Bukovina and Bessarabia, some of the reinforcements arriving from as far away as the Caucasus and Finland; the next day the German military attaché in Bucharest reported that the Russians were evacuating the civilian population along their side of the Prut River front and that shiploads of Red Army troops were arriving at Odessa and being transported by rail to the Bug and Dniestr. On the twenty-fifth the naval decoders intercepted the British military attaché's report to London from Moscow. A thousand people a day were now being called up in Moscow alone, he said, many of them being sent to the Baltic states. "Our military attaché in Budapest, who was traveling to Moscow a few days ago, saw at Lemberg [Lvov] at least one tank brigade . . . on the railway line between Lemberg and Kiev heading westward; he passed seven troop trains of which four were conveying tanks and mechanized equipment and three troops." The German attachés undertaking similar journeys also saw many military transports heading west between Minsk and Baranovichi. By May 5, Antonescu was able to tip off the Germans that Soviet troops were massing between Kiev and Odessa and that reinforcements were still pouring westward from Siberia. "The thing worth noting is that factories around Moscow have been ordered to transfer their equipment into the country's interior."

According to Hitler's Luftwaffe adjutant, the Intelligence brought back by a team of Göring's engineers from a tour of Soviet aircraft factories late in April convinced the Führer there was no time to be lost. These air ministry experts had been allowed to tour eight or nine of the biggest Russian factories producing ball bearings, alloys, aircraft, and aeroengines, and to see the advances made by Soviet research. It was clear that the Soviet air force was a far greater menace than Hitler had bargained for—both in size and aircraft performance. The aircraft factories themselves were the biggest and most modern in Europe—and more were under construction. When the German experts attended a dinner party, the leading Soviet aircraft designer, Mikoyan (who later designed the MIG fighters), stated explicitly, "Now you have seen the mighty technology of the Soviet fatherland. We shall valiantly ward off any attack, whatever quarter it comes from!" Years later Hitler was to describe this commission's report on the Soviet air force as having finally convinced him of the need to attack Russia now.

The voice of Ambassador Schulenburg was a lone voice in the wilderness. In vain he interpreted Stalin's sudden appointment to a government post—Chairman of the Council of People's Commissars—on May 6 as a public rebuke to

Molotov for having allowed German-Soviet relations to cool. Undoubtedly it was a historic event in Soviet history, but it could also be interpreted in a more sinister light, as could Stalin's urgent recall of his Berlin ambassador, who a few days earlier had returned to Moscow for consultations. In his May Day speech Stalin had proclaimed: "The Red Army is ready, in the interests of the socialist state, to ward off every blow struck by the imperialists. The international situation is full of unexpected events. In such a situation the Red Army must step up its defensive readiness." Since early May the German military attaché had noted the call-up of the youngest age-group some six months early; and now on Red Army orders foreign diplomats were prevented from traveling freely. On May 13 a German consul in the heart of China, with access to Soviet secret diplomatic circulars, reported that six days before, Moscow had instructed all missions to ascertain the probable attitude of other countries in the event of a German-Soviet conflict. On the sixteenth the Russian envoy in Stockholm was reported to have stated that at no time in Russian history had more powerful troop contingents been massed in the west (which confirmed the estimate of the Swedish air attaché in Moscow that by mid-March alone 60 percent of the Red Army had been massed in western Russia, particularly confronting Romania). And Antonescu's Intelligence service learned that Stalin was saying that "the Soviet government must accept grave sacrifices in order to win time," because the coming war could be postponed, but not prevented; to postpone it, the supply of raw materials to Germany must continue.

The trainloads of rubber, ores, oil, and grain kept rolling westward to Hitler's Germany even as June 22, the date for "Barbarossa," approached; but the date on which Stalin proposed to resume the Soviet program of expansion, now temporarily halted by Hitler's obduracy, also came closer. A year later, the proof of this was in German hands; it will be dealt with in its proper sequence, except for one episode which can for the purpose of this narrative best be related here. On May 5, two secret speeches were delivered at a Kremlin banquet by Stalin to a thousand officers graduating from Moscow's staff colleges. Among the officials who passed through the Kremlin's Trinity Gate that evening were Molotov, Mikoyan, Voroshilov, Kalinin, and Lavrenti Beria; there were also two generals and one major who later fell into German hands and independently described the speeches to German interrogators with a high degree of unanimity.[6] Had Schulen-

---

[6]Ribbentrop claimed in 1943 that agents supplied details of the speeches to Hitler almost at once. There is no trace of this in surviving German files. Göring made a similar claim after the war.

burg—who heard merely that Stalin had delivered a forty-minute speech—been there, perhaps even his optimism about the Soviet Union's designs would have been dispelled.

Marshal Timoshenko had opened the proceedings with a speech and a toast to "our great and wise Stalin." After a formal report by the director of staff studies, Stalin launched into a sober account of the need to modernize the Red Army's weaponry and prepare for the coming war with Germany. He set out these preparations in detail and pointed to certain shortcomings in infantry equipment and tactics. He promised that in two months Russia would have some of the best and fastest aircraft in the world.

> New tank models, the Mark 1 and 3, are on their way; these are excellent tanks, whose armor can withstand 76-millimeter shells. In the near future there will also be a new tank graced with my own name. This tank will be a veritable fortress. Today we have up to a hundred armored and mechanized divisions which still need to be organized into an entity. Our war plan is ready, we have built the airfields and landing grounds, and the frontline aircraft are already there. Everything has been done by way of clearing out the rear areas: all the foreign elements have been removed. It follows that over the next two months we can begin the fight with Germany. Perhaps it surprises you that I tell you of our war plans. But we have to take our revenge for Bulgaria and Finland.

As for the pact with Germany, that was just camouflage, said Stalin. He explained to his perhaps uneasy listeners that France had only collapsed because her army was without the solid grass-roots support of the French people—it was an army without authority. "Girls even hesitated to marry a French soldier." Hitler on the other hand had enjoyed the unalloyed support of his people so long as he was fighting the obvious injustice of Versailles. But the moment Hitler crossed into Russia he would forfeit the German people's support. The partisan movement painstakingly built up throughout Europe by the Comintern since the war began would assume a vast scale and paralyze the German army's supplies. By the end of the first year Germany would have exhausted her limited stockpiles of scarce raw materials, but Russia was a land of plenty. Above all Germany did not have Russia's limitless reserves of manpower. "Germany may be able to build aircraft and tanks, but she will lack the warriors themselves." Stalin emphasized: "There is no such thing as an invincible army, whatever the country of its allegiance."

A lavish banquet followed in the George Hall of the Kremlin, with drinking far into the night. Perhaps Stalin was drunk by the time he made his second speech—the sources are in conflict on this point. One of the generals, the director of the famous Frunze military academy, was toasting Stalin's genius for "preserving the peace" of Europe when Stalin irritably waved for him to stop, tottered to his feet, and delivered a speech of his own.

The slogan of peaceful policies is now obsolete—it has been overtaken by events. During the years of the capitalist encirclement of the Soviet Union we were able to make good use of the slogan while we expanded the Soviet Union's frontiers to the north and west. But now we must discard this slogan for the reactionary and narrow-minded slogan that it is, as it will not serve to win us one more square inch of territory. It is time to stop chewing that particular cud, Comrade Chosin: stop being a simpleton! The era of forcible expansion has begun for the Soviet Union. The people must be schooled to accept that a war of aggression is inevitable; they must be in permanent mobilization.

In *this* connection Germany was not explicitly mentioned as the target, but all three of the men interrogated by the Germans said they had no doubt that that was what Stalin meant. (One of them also noted that at the Soviet General Staff college problems of strategic attack alone were analyzed throughout the winter of 1940–1941.) When the director of the chemical warfare academy proposed a toast to their continued friendship with Germany, Stalin angrily interrupted that the German army's victories had only been obtained against small nations up to now. "Many of our officers wrongly overestimate the German army's success. Let's see how good the German army is when it meets an enemy of equal stature!" Raising his glass, Stalin announced a new toast: "Drink to the new era of development and territorial expansion that has begun! Long live the active policy of aggression of the Soviet nation!"

As the storm of applause subsided, Stalin's friend and companion Nikita Khrushchev sprang up and emotionally declaimed: "Never did I dream that in my old age I would live to be given a command in the army of the proletarian world revolution. And now the day is not far off when we who sit here will take the helm and steer our 'ship of history,' not on the slow and stately course we followed hitherto, but . . ." Khrushchev was interrupted by an even more inebriated Marshal Timoshenko. Great—if not always sober or coherent—was the rejoicing within the Kremlin walls that night.

Hess and Bormann

"As a German and as a soldier I consider it beneath me ever to belittle a brave enemy," exclaimed Hitler to his assembled Reichstag deputies on May 4, 1941. "But it seems necessary to me to do something to protect the Truth from the boastful lies of a man who is as miserable a politician as soldier, and is as wretched a soldier as politician." Hitler was declaiming on the Wehrmacht's fresh Balkan triumph.

> Just as he did after Norway and Dunkirk, Mr. Churchill—he also began this campaign—is trying to say something that he might yet be able to twist and distort into a British victory. I don't think that very honest, but in the case of this man it is at least comprehensible. If ever any other politician had met such defeats, or a soldier had encountered such catastrophes, he would not have kept his job six months—unless he was possessed of the same talent that alone distinguishes Mr. Churchill, the ability to lie with devout mien and distort the truth so that in the end the most frightful defeats turn into the most glorious victories. Mr. Churchill may be able to put down a smokescreen before his fellow-countrymen, but he cannot eliminate the results of his disasters.

Hitler went on to say that the British prime minister's appeal three days before to the German people to desert their Führer was explicable only as the fevered outburst of a paralytic or the delirious shout of a chronic drunkard; the same brain had spawned the ill-conceived Balkan expedition as a vain attempt to set southeastern Europe ablaze. Now the brave Greek people had paid for their pro-British monarch's folly. "I regretted it from the start. For me as a German born and bred to revere and respect the art and culture of this country whence the first rays of mortal beauty and dignity emerged, it was a hard and bitter experience to see this happening and be able to do nothing to prevent it." From the French and British documents found in France he had realized how far the Greek government had drifted into Britain's arms. He heaped praise on Ribbentrop's "unique patience and genius for perseverance" in finally bringing Yugo-slavia into the Tripartite Pact; he lavished more praise on the General Staff for their brilliant campaign planning. "One sentence will suffice to distinguish this campaign: to the German soldier nothing is impossible!"

Rudolf Hess, constitutionally "Deputy Führer" of the Party since April 1933 and second in line of succession after Göring, had sat between Hitler and Ribbentrop during the lengthy speech. Ribbentrop was to say a week later that Hess's eyes had looked completely abnormal all evening and that he had seemed mentally disturbed. Hitler did not notice. Hess was an eccentric, a beloved member of the Party's Old Guard, a believer in the supernatural and in herbal remedies; but he also had a brain of surprising shrewdness and a personal courage to match. He had been born in Egypt and was unabashedly pro-British. An enthusiastic pilot whose wings had been officially clipped by Hitler since 1933, he nevertheless found opportunities to fly the latest planes through his personal friendship with the director of air armament, Ernst Udet, and the aircraft designer Willy Messer-schmitt. Since the outbreak of war he had taken a keen interest in strategy. Hitler's Luftwaffe and naval adjutants have both stressed Hess's active support for blockading the British Isles as a relatively antiseptic way of imposing Ger-many's will on Britain, and it was Hess who had persuaded Hitler to force Göring to take the aerial torpedo seriously. Long before the war he had submitted lengthy studies to Hitler on the mass employment of mines in British waters; Hitler had ordered the admiralty to take the matter up, and heard no more until it reemerged as an admiralty proposal.

At the end of Hitler's Reichstag speech, Hess spoke with Hitler privately for about half an hour; no record survives. Hitler disclosed a few days later that on this occasion Hess persistently inquired whether he, the Führer, still stood by the program he had set forth in *Mein Kampf*—of marching side by side with Britain; and that he had confirmed he did. We also have Hess's statement, ten days later, when he was already in enemy hands, that "as recently as May 4, after his Reichstag speech, Hitler declared to me that he had no oppressive demands to make on England."

At eight-fifteen that evening Hitler left by special train with his private staff for the naval dockyard at Gotenhafen, on the Baltic, to inspect Raeder's mighty new capital ships, the *Bismarck* and the *Tirpitz*. The last time he had seen the latter was at her launching at Wilhelmshaven two years before; he still recalled the keen, honest features of the shipyard workers—"A real aristocracy of the working class." But now the battleship was fitting out here in the dismal port of Gotenhafen, beyond the reach of the British bombers, and the *Bismarck* was already straining to sail on her first Atlantic sortie. Gotenhafen itself—the former Polish port of Gdynia—was an economic white elephant built by the Poles in an attempt to ruin Danzig's trade between the wars. It was one of the ugliest cities in western Europe, a sprawling collection of endless suburbs and soulless slums, a sorry contrast to the neat Hanseatic appearance of Danzig. The two huge new battleships dominated the dockyard.

Hitler arrived on May 5 without Admiral Raeder, who wished his fleet commander to see the Führer alone. The navy's plan was to transfer the *Bismarck* and the new heavy crusier *Prinz Eugen* from the Baltic to the Atlantic coast. Hitler was ferried across to the battleship—a breathtaking spectacle of armor and machinery—in a naval tender. The crew lined up for Hitler's inspection, and he was shown around. There was a moment of levity when Hitler's physician, the portly Professor Morell, became briefly wedged in the slim entrance to one of the 380-millimeter main gun turrets. The *Bismarck,* with her twenty-eight thousand miles of electrical circuits and her radar-controlled guns, was the most advanced warship afloat. Indeed, she was considered unsinkable, and Admiral Günther Lütjens, the gaunt-faced fleet commander, emphasized this to Hitler in his cabin.

He reported on the brilliant marauding operation he had commanded with the pocket battleships *Scharnhorst* and *Gneisenau* during the first three months of the year, raiding Atlantic convoys bringing war supplies to Britain from the United States; and he explained the purpose of the new operation he would command with the *Bismarck* and the *Prinz Eugen.* Hitler was inclined to leave the navy to operate as it saw fit; though it retained its imperial traditions and its antipathy toward all political doctrines, it was fired by a common purpose and fighting spirit of which the National Socialists could approve. (Unlike the services garrisoned in the Reich, the navy was unaffected by prevailing trends of anti-Hitler rebellion, and only three of its officers were to be implicated in the 1944 plot.)

When Hitler did voice his qualms at Lütjens's proposal to risk the capital ships alone against the Atlantic convoys, the admiral put his mind at rest. "Mein Führer, there is virtually nothing that can go wrong for me, with a ship like this. The only danger that I can see is torpedo-aircraft coming at us from aircraft carriers."

Hitler returned to Berlin and then continued south to Berchtesgaden, where he was to meet Admiral Darlan on May 11.

The Führer had belatedly decided to back the Arab "liberation movement" that had broken out in Iraq, and this could best be done with Vichy support from Syria. It is characteristic of Hitler's *ad hoc* strategy that he had hitherto paid no attention to Iraq, a desert country with oil fields in the north and occupied by only small British forces under a ten-year-old treaty. But on April 2 a coup d'etat had brought the anti-British general Rashid Ali el Gailani to power, and when the British thereupon landed in strength at the port of Basra on the Persian Gulf, Rashid Ali's small army encircled the big British air base at Habbaniya some twenty-five miles west of Baghdad and fighting broke out. The Iraqis appealed to Germany for aid. Hitler ordered Vichy arms cached in Syria to be released to them, and German military experts were flown out, followed by a diminutive force of Messerschmitt and Heinkel aircraft, which Darlan allowed to land on the airfields in Syria. The prospects of a Franco-German entente thus seemed auspicious—were it not that a stunning blow now befell Adolf Hitler.

That evening a bulky packet from Rudolf Hess was delivered to the Berghof. Assuming it to contain more of the minister's interminable memoranda, Hitler pushed the packet aside. Toward noon next day, Sunday May 11, he was standing with General Karl Bodenschatz—Göring's representative—in the Berghof's Great Hall when there was a commotion and one of Hess's adjutants burst in, ignoring the protests of the guards. He handed Hitler a slim envelope. Hitler turned it over to Bodenschatz to slit open. There were two pages inside, which the general handed back to him unread. Hitler put on his eyeglasses and began to glance over it indifferently. Suddenly he slumped into a chair and bellowed in a voice that could be heard all over the house: "Oh my God, my God! He has flown to Britain!" A crowd of the curious appeared at the doors, but they were ushered out. Hess's adjutant stated unashamedly that his chief had taken off at Augsburg airfield at 5:40 P.M. the previous evening; when Hitler furiously asked why he had not told anybody until now, the adjutant gave his loyalty to Hess as the reason. Hitler swung around on Bodenschatz. "How is it, Herr General, that the Luftwaffe let Hess fly although I forbade it? Get Göring here!" But the Reichsmarschall was relaxing at his family castle north of Nuremberg.

It was found that the bulky packet from Hess contained about fourteen pages —a long-winded account of his motives for flying and his proposed peace plan. Apparently written in October 1940, it dealt with technical aspects of a peace settlement—for example, reparations to be paid to Germany. In the shorter letter —which Bodenschatz had just opened—Hess explained that he was flying to Glasgow to meet the Duke of Hamilton, a true friend of Germany whom he had met in 1936; he wanted to try for peace between Germany and Britain before the Russian campaign began. He promised not to betray "Barbarossa" to the British. According to this letter, since November Hess had made three other attempts to reach Scotland; each time an aircraft malfunction had forced him back.

How Hitler's head must have reeled to read all this! Bodenschatz was now on the telephone to Göring. The Reichsmarschall was petulantly asking *why* he was required at the Berghof. Hitler snatched the telephone, shouted, "Göring—you are to come at once!" and slammed the instrument down. Ambassador Hewel telephoned for Ribbentrop: the foreign minister was in conference with Admiral Darlan. That too was abruptly curtailed. Hess's adjutant, the unfortunate bearer of the ill-tidings, was arrested and led away.

A wave of hysterical speculation gripped the Berghof. Could Hess have been a British agent? Might he in fact have gone to Russia? *"Every possible* construction," wrote Schmundt's wife in her diary.

Hitler refused to believe Hess would be disloyal, but pacing nervously up and down his study he confided to Julius Schaub what he feared. "Never mind what he says. If Hess really gets there just imagine: Churchill has Hess in his grasp! What lunacy on Hess's part. . . . They will give Hess some drug or other to make him stand before a microphone and broadcast whatever Churchill wants. I cannot challenge it, because it's Hess's voice and everybody knows it."

Bodenschatz began immediate technical inquiries. He found out that Willy Messerschmitt had himself supplied the advanced Messerschmitt fighter Hess had used, and that Hess had availed himself of the Y-beams navigation system used by the bomber squadrons. Ernst Udet was ordered to come to the Berghof at once: perhaps Hess might have crashed en route, or run into foul weather? But further investigation revealed that ever since August Hess had been supplied with regular weather reports on Britain; giving some innocent excuse, he had also arranged with two radio stations to make a certain broadcast at a specific time so that he could fix his position.

Admiral Darlan—Pétain's deputy premier, foreign minister, navy minister, and minister of the interior—arrived after lunch with Ribbentrop. German-French relations had remained in a limbo of indecision since Montoire; now that Hitler had decided on "Barbarossa," his interest in the Mediterranean had waned, and his inborn mistrust of the French and his anxieties about de Gaulle were not easily overcome. In the Yugoslav files captured in Belgrade, a document had been found strongly indicating that General Weygand was preparing to transfer his allegiance to de Gaulle and that the American ambassador to Vichy had stated that the United States would supply him with equipment and ammunition in that event. The Italians certainly shared Hitler's mistrust. Count Ciano wisecracked to Ribbentrop's interpreter: "The people of Paris say that the British are winning the war. The people of Vichy say that *those pigs* the British will win. *Voilà la différence!"*

Canaris was to note after a meeting with Keitel at this time:

. . . When I turned to our Abwehr subversive operations in Syria and Iraq, the field marshal explained that the Führer is inclined to be skeptical about the

French attitude over this issue, as he is indeed about their whole attitude toward collaborating with Germany. He, the chief of the OKW, would in fact term himself a super-skeptic, while Herr von Ribbentrop's views on this were somewhere about the middle. The chief of the OKW mentioned in passing a discussion between the Führer and Herr Ribbentrop on the subject of de Gaulle in the course of which the Führer interrupted Ribbentrop—who had uttered a derogatory remark about de Gaulle—with the words: "Now, now, my dear Ribbentrop, if you found yourself in the same situation you would be the first to become a Gaullist!"

Ribbentrop had seriously flirted with the notion of collaboration with France since February, perhaps in the hope of presenting Hitler with a credible alternative to "Barbarossa" for the defeat of Britain. Late that month he had shown Hitler his ambassador's reply to a secret questionnaire in which he had asked whether a future French government might be cajoled into "declaring war on Britain, placing the French fleet at the disposal of the fight against Britain, and conceding bases to us in French Africa"; Ambassador Otto Abetz had replied that an outright declaration of war would be unlikely, but that a state of war might practically be brought about under certain conditions in which Weygand might even unconditionally follow Pétain. Hitler, however, remained skeptical and cool toward Darlan. A break for tea was taken at five-thirty, but Hewel noticed that the Führer's mind was elsewhere, and the conversation among the dozen people present was stilted and uncomfortable. (Only Ribbentrop continued, in a talk with Darlan next day, to press France to declare war on Britain.) Hitler's mind was on Hess.

The Reichsmarschall arrived at 9 P.M. and threw a quizzical look at Bodenschatz, but the latter had been sworn to secrecy. Now Hitler's resentment was turned on his Luftwaffe commander. (Hewel recorded that night: "According to Bodenschatz's version [Göring] was just as agitated. A long discussion with the Führer downstairs in the Hall: the Führer, foreign minister, Göring, Bormann. Very irritable. Much speculation.") The British had not yet announced anything; throughout this day and the next the argument raged back and forth at the Berghof as to whether Hess had arrived in Britain or was long dead. "A very upset day," wrote Hewel on the twelfth. "Investigations into Hess's flight. . . . Göring and Udet believe Hess could not have managed the difficult flight to Glasgow, as this would call for the utmost flying ability using the most modern equipment. But the Führer thinks Hess *could* have done it."

It was Ribbentrop who sagely pointed out that if they waited any longer, the British might announce the news at any moment to the world—indeed, they could claim that Hess had brought an official offer for a separate peace between Germany and Britain. It might just split the whole Axis wide open.[1] Hitler was aghast. He ordered Ribbentrop to telephone Ciano, and he at once began to dictate the text of a communiqué to the German people. Investigations had meanwhile established that Hess had suffered from a bile complaint for some time and had fallen under the sway of nature healers and astrologers. This facilitated the announcement that while Hess had evidently acted from idealistic motives he was in fact quite mad. "The Führer decides to go ahead with the announcement," wrote Hewel. "He insists on including the passage about it being the action of a madman." By late afternoon the tenth redraft of the communiqué was complete and passed by Hitler. In an agony of fear that the British might still launch their propaganda campaign first, assuming Hess *had* safely arrived, Hitler switched on the radio. At 8 P.M. the German communiqué was broadcast: the Party officially announced that "in a hallucinated state" Hess had taken off from Augsburg in an aircraft and not been seen since. "It is to be feared that Party-member Hess has crashed or met with an accident somewhere." Hitler, noted Hewel, was now "somewhat less tense and more lively." Hours passed and then the BBC finally stirred: Rudolf Hess had landed by parachute in Scotland two nights before. The tension at the Berghof relaxed; indeed a mood of laughter took its place. "Führer wants to wait until the morrow," Hewel ended that day's momentous entries. "The chief is staying at the Berghof."

The Party's anguished investigation into the Deputy Führer's defection continued. For advice on the English mentality, Hess had relied on Albrecht Haushofer, a Berlin professor of geopolitics and son of Munich's eminent Professor Karl Haushofer. The younger Haushofer had been befriended by Hess much earlier and shielded from outrages he might have been subjected to on account of his part-Jewish wife; he had attracted Party hostility by outspoken commentaries on Anglo-German relations in his father's monthly *Zeitschrift für Geopolitik*, with prognoses diametrically opposed to those of the National Socialists. (He had since mid-1938 warned of the growing Anglo-American military alliance and of the futility of Germany's efforts to achieve economic self-sufficiency.) Albrecht Haushofer was summoned to the Obersalzberg on May 12 and ordered to explain his behavior. He admitted that he had made many attempts to correspond with the Duke of Hamilton through Lisbon and Switzerland but said he had received no reply.[2] Haushofer was allowed to return home, but his tele-

[1] In September 1943 Hitler was to tell Goebbels: "The British muffed their biggest political opportunity of the war on this occasion."

[2] There is a curious echo of this in British government files on Hess. The Duke of Hamilton first learned of Haushofer's letters from Hess and complained to the government that these peace feelers had never reached him. The secret service requested him to take the matter no further in the national interest.

phone was tapped by the Forschungsamt and his house was watched.

On May 13 the Party recovered its composure and circulated a second communiqué: papers left behind by Hess—who was more familiar with the Führer's genuine peace proposals than any other person—suggested that he suffered from the hallucination that if he took a personal step with Englishmen known to him from earlier times, he might yet manage to bring about an entente between Germany and Britain. Hitler debated with his advisers about what to do should the British send Hess back. Ribbentrop gained the impression that Hess would be shot. Hans Frank—whom Bormann summoned posthaste to the Berghof along with all the other Party leaders and Gauleiters—later quoted Hitler as telling him: "This man is dead as far as I am concerned: whenever and wherever we find him we will hang him." Frank, who had been through many crises with Hitler as his personal lawyer, found him more upset than he had ever seen him "since the death of his niece Geli Raubal." (Geli had infatuated him and then committed suicide under mysterious circumstances in 1931.)

In time, Hitler's anger softened, though the feud was carried forward by Martin Bormann. Schaub later wrote: "In the years that followed, Hitler seldom mentioned Hess, but when he did it was always to emphasize how highly he had esteemed him—he had always been an upright and honest man until he was led astray." Bormann, of course, was like a dog with two tails to wag—especially since this affair had happened while the Führer was at the Berghof and thus within Bormann's domain. There were many who believed Bormann was morally to blame for Hess's flight, that he had undermined Hess's position so much that the minister had felt compelled to undertake this drastic act to restore his faded status with Hitler. Hitler was certainly not blind to Bormann's pathological ambition, yet in this hour of crisis he wavered. When Göring now asked him whether he proposed to appoint Bormann as Hess's successor, the Führer shook his head and said that he had earmarked Bormann to succeed the Party treasurer Franz Xaver Schwarz; the Reichsmarschall replied succinctly that Hitler was wrong "by a long shot" if he thought that would slake Bormann's ambition. "I care nothing about his ambition," retorted Hitler. Bormann would continue as head of the Party Chancellery; Göring was to look for a suitably youthful candidate to be "Party minister." When Robert Ley also bluntly warned Hitler against appointing Bormann as Hess's successor, he got a similar answer. Small wonder that Bormann's subsequent meteoric rise was to astound them all.

Propaganda Minister Goebbels had by this time also arrived from Berlin. As Goebbels saw it, Hess's act was a momentary aberration, the act of a man who had lost his nerve. After consulting with Hitler, he instructed the propaganda media to pass over the affair as briefly as possible. "We will ignore it for the time being. In any case there is shortly to be a military event which will enable us to distract attention from the subject of Hess to other things." (This must have been a reference to the imminent parachute assault on Crete.) At 3 P.M. Ribbentrop left for Rome to put Mussolini's mind at rest.

By this time the Berghof was packed with the Party leaders and Gauleiters Bormann had summoned. From four until six-thirty, Bormann and Hitler spoke to them about the Hess affair: it was now known that Hess had been "manipulated" by various astrologers, mindreaders, and nature healers who had influenced him to fly to Britain; in doing so he had put the Reich in an impossible predicament with her allies, particularly Italy and Japan. Hewel later described the scene in his diary. As Göring stands behind him with earnest mien "Bormann reads out the letters left by Hess. A dramatic assembly, heavy with emotion. The Führer comes, speaks very humanly, analyzes Hess's act for what it is, and proves he was deranged from his lack of logic: the idea of landing near a castle he has never seen and whose owner, Hamilton, is not even there, etc.; and Hoare is in Madrid.[3] Then from foreign affairs standpoint, and finally the domestic repercussions. A deeply moving demonstration. Sympathy [from the Gauleiters]: 'Nothing is spared our Führer.' Afterward, lengthy discussions." Hewel concluded that Hitler was pleased he no longer had a formal deputy.

After he had finished speaking, Hitler leaned back on the big marble table in front of the Great Hall's picture window, while the sixty or seventy Gauleiters and others pressed around him in a silent semicircle. He caught sight of Gauleiter Ernst Bohle, the Bradford-born Gauleiter of all Germans abroad, and asked him pointedly, "Tell me what you knew of the affair." Bohle guiltily replied that in October Rudolf Hess had asked him to call one evening at his home in Wilhelmstrasse, sworn him to secrecy, and asked him to translate into English a letter he was writing to the Duke of Hamilton; on no account was he to tell Ribbentrop about it. Over the next three months Bohle had several times been called to Hess's

---

[3] Sir Samuel Hoare was the British ambassador in Madrid.—Hitler could not have known that Hess had in fact succeeded in navigating in pitch darkness to within twelve miles of his target, had then parachuted safely (no mean feat for a man of forty-seven on his first attempt), and was actually in conversation with the Duke of Hamilton within a matter of hours. Under interrogation, Hess, speaking good English, explained that this was his fourth attempt to fly to Britain. He had got the idea when he was with the Führer during "Yellow," in June 1940. He had deliberately refrained from attempting the flight while Britain was scoring successes in Libya in case his proposals were interpreted as a sign of German weakness. With the Nazi victories in North Africa and the Balkans the situation had, however, changed. His knowledge of the Luftwaffe's expansion plans and the submarine construction program made him confident in Germany's ultimate victory. But Hitler had no desire to inflict slaughter and defeat on Britain: From a long and intimate knowledge of the Führer which had begun eighteen years before in the fortress of Landsberg he could give his word of honor that (unlike the Americans) the Führer had never entertained any designs against the British Empire. Nor had he ever aspired to world domination. Mr. Churchill would not, however, be an acceptable negotiating partner. Hess stated that he had come unarmed and of his own free will, and he asked for his release on parole. Churchill ordered his incarceration for the rest of the war.

office to continue work on the letter, and it was finished by January 7. At this point Hitler took Bohle aside, showed him the letters Hess had left, and asked him to point out paragraph by paragraph which passages had been in the letter Hess carried to the Duke of Hamilton. Hitler was furious that the Gauleiter had aided and abetted Hess, but Bohle cleverly cited the *Führerprinzip* in his defense: he had assumed that Hess was acting on the Führer's authority. He escaped unscathed.

Not so the rest. Haushofer joined Hess's two adjutants in a concentration camp. Hitler intervened on behalf of Frau Ilse Hess, but Bormann even had his children, Rudolf and Ilse, rechristened, and ordered his former superior's name to be expunged from the history books. Himmler, his new-found intimate, toadied to Bormann—sending him the letters Hess was writing from British captivity. Even Göring curried favor with Bormann now. Himmler took to greeting Bormann with an exaggerated affection, while the other took both Himmler's hands in his own. They were frequently on the telephone to each other. Woe betide those who fell afoul of Hess's dynamic successor, or strayed from the Party line. Precisely one year later, on May 13, 1942, Party headquarters in Munich telephoned Bormann that the obstreperous Gauleiter Carl Röver of Oldenburg was going the way Hess had gone. Following bouts of paralysis, visits by faith healers, and hallucinations, Röver had that day announced his intention of flying to see Churchill—after first calling at the Führer's headquarters—"as the whole world is mad." By that afternoon Bormann's agents were already on their way to him, armed with *"top level"* instructions. Two days later Röver had died a timely death, Hitler could order a state funeral, and Goebbels could sigh in his diary: "There goes one more member of the Old Guard." Euthanasia had its uses.

On May 12, Hitler had formally replaced Hess's old "Office of the Deputy Führer" with a Party chancellery headed by Bormann; two weeks later he conferred on him the rights of a Reich minister. Bormann now gathered powers the like of which Hess had never had, but Hitler grudged this hard-working, unobtrusive, ruthless manager none of them. A secretary overheard him command Bormann: "Just keep the Gauleiters off my back!" And the forty-year-old Bormann —who in 1930 founded the Party's financial fortunes by an insurance scheme under which millions of SA members paid thirty pfennigs monthly and stuck stamps onto a yellow card which in case of injury in the street fighting proved that they were paid up—did just that. He took the load off Hitler's mind. In alliance with the crafty constitutional expert Lammers, Bormann established a civilian bottleneck through which all state affairs had to pass on their way to Hitler; Bormann had the knack of presenting them to Hitler in a rapid, deliberate way that required only a Yes or No as answer. Hitler's whim, no sooner spoken, became a Führer Command, noted down by Bormann, elaborated by the expert lawyers he had drafted to his staff, duplicated and circulated by Party channels and teleprinters almost instantly. From eight each morning until far into the night Bormann was at Hitler's disposal; he ran the Reich while Hitler directed his war.

Bormann achieved that most dangerous of attributes—indispensability. Hitler ignored the man's sinister side and boorishness: Bormann's one and only public speech, at a Gauleiter conference, was a fiasco. Behind a steering wheel he was reckless in the extreme. Privately Hitler could never forgive Bormann for what he and the Party had done to his Obersalzberg; a future pilgrim's mecca of the worst possible taste, the Berghof was ringed by more and more buildings. The Führer even mentioned to Schaub that he was thinking of moving his permanent residence to Linz or Mohn or Bayreuth because of this. Hitler also disagreed with Bormann's approach to problems dealing with the Church and Jews. Yet Bormann survived until the end, dreaming of the day when he might step into the Führer's shoes. "Bormann clung to him like ivy around the oak," Robert Ley was to say, "using him to get to the light, and to the very summit."

Late on May 14, Ribbentrop returned from his emergency visit to Mussolini. Hewel fetched him from the airport and noted that night: "He reported this evening to the Führer up the mountain: positive." On the sixteenth and seventeenth Hitler was shown the Forschungsamt intercepts on the Italian ambassador's comments on the Hess case. Heydrich meanwhile personally interrogated Gauleiter Bohle.

For Hitler the case was already closed; his eyes again reverted east. The Second Air Force had already begun uprooting its ground organization in the west; by the end of May only a large radio-spoofing organization would remain to deceive the enemy into thinking that Kesselring was still there. On May 10 and 13 the Luftwaffe made its last mass attacks on London, causing immense damage. After that only a skeleton force of aircraft would remain to harass the British defenses and simulate invasion preparations. "Barbarossa" was to be disguised as a master deception plan: "The closer the date of the attack approaches," directed the OKW, "the cruder will be the means of deception we can employ (in the Intelligence channels as well)." The very airborne invasion of Crete was to be referred to openly as "a dress rehearsal for the invasion of Britain," and several ministries were instructed to start planning for the occupation of Britain immediately.

It was also time to start putting out cautious feelers to Russia's other bruised western neighbors. Hungary could not be approached until the last days of May, and Romania even later; but there were military reasons why Finland must be approached now. A grotesque formula had to be adopted by the OKW: despite the friendly contractual relations between Germany and Russia, there was a completely unmotivated Russian buildup on the frontier. The OKW formula explained: "This obliges Germany to concentrate forces there too. In the immediate future a political settlement is intended. If this proves impossible, it will almost certainly be necessary to apply a military settlement, if the choice of date is not to be left to Russia." The staff talks proposed with Finland would establish the basis of their cooperation should war thus break out this summer. In view of Finland's casualties in her recent war with the Soviet Union no heavy burden would be foisted onto her; it would be left to her to decide how to meet the German requests. "The course of this putative war will definitely be as follows: after Russia has lost a certain area on account of the participation of many small nations (a crusade against bolshevism) and in particular on account of the German Wehrmacht's superiority, she will be unable to fight on. The collapse in the north will come fastest and the Baltic will rapidly come into our hands. After the onset of the Russian catastrophe Germany will be the leading and impregnable power in Europe; she can cut back her army to step up Luftwaffe and naval construction programs and defeat Britain, which still rests her hopes on Russia."

Jodl proposed to the foreign ministry that Dr. Julius Schnurre, Ribbentrop's trade expert, who was on friendly terms with the Finnish prime minister and foreign minister, should go to Finland and invite her to send staff officers to Germany at once. Hewel's diary[4] of May 15 notes:

> After lunch the Chief [Ribbentrop] comes with Schnurre up the mountain. Schnurre is given instructions on discussing Russian problem in Finland, and negotiating with [Rysto] Ryti [the Finnish president]. He wants to return via Stockholm, but the Führer is very hostile toward Sweden. Says their ruling class is basically pro-British. If they did show any interest [in "Barbarossa"] then it would only be so they could immediately report what they heard to Britain. He does not want Schnurre to drop any hints at all there except that he had had talks in Finland on the Russian problem. (But even this the Reich foreign minister afterward prohibits.) Schnurre is more optimistic. The Führer reads out a memo by Paul (press department) Schmidt, says it is much too optimistic: it also notes that it would be extremely useful if the whole of Scandinavia joined the Tripartite Pact. The Führer considers this impossible, says even the Reichsmarschall [Göring] has been cured of his infatuation for Sweden. Sweden would willingly sacrifice Finland if Germany lost the war. She is afraid of losing her dominant position in Scandinavia, of encirclement by Finland, Germany, and Norway. Russian ambitions.

Hitler instructed Schnurre to tell Ryti that he had rejected the Soviet demands on Finland during Molotov's November visit to Berlin.

On the eighteenth, French haggling for alleviation of the armistice terms in

---

[4]These extracts are quoted at length, as the diary of the diplomat Walther Hewel has not previously been available to historians.

return for Vichy support in the Middle East again clouded the Berghof atmosphere. "The Führer is still nervous," an entry in Hewel's diary noted. "The French problem is acute. The Führer bitterly reproaches the foreign ministry and especially Ambassador Abetz for tossing concessions to the French; this refers particularly to the release of prisoners. A furious scene. At 7 P.M. Ribbentrop and Abetz in conference with the Führer. Führer somewhat more affable, but is still reluctant to go wholeheartedly into the French affair. Does not want to commit himself too much to France.[5] He always asks himself whether Darlan can hang on at all."

The next day Hitler was more lively and relaxed, and even found words of approval for Italy. "It is quite clear that the Duce is one of the greatest men in modern history. He has extracted from the Italian people every ounce of what there was to be extracted—and what he has extracted from the Italian people is quite marvelous. If he did not get any further, it was simply because he had reached the extreme limit of their capabilities. After him there will not be another with his energy and talents for a long time, so events in Italy will definitely run downhill later." On the following morning, May 20, as Göring's paratroops began their costly assault on the isle of Crete, Hitler drove down to Munich for two days in the quiet seclusion of his apartment there.

Anxieties gnawed within him as he pored over the great charts of Europe, trying to divine what nasty surprises the British might yet spring on him. Earlier in May he had feared the British might invade Portugal or Spain: he briefly received the Spanish ambassador and warned him of the British activities in Morocco and told him of Abwehr reports on British plans to invade the Iberian peninsula. He took the risk seriously enough—why else should enemy propaganda be harping on alleged German designs down there?—to issue an OKW directive for a contingency plan to expel any British expeditionary force. Spain would present no problem to the Wehrmacht. But Hitler privately admitted to an adjutant, "We must remember that Franco is not a leader like Mussolini or myself—he has a much more omnipotent dictator over him than the Duce or I do, namely the Pope and the Church." Later in May, his anxieties concerned "Barbarossa": was the eastern front not suspiciously quiet now? The OKW circulated to the operations staffs a succinct warning: "The Führer again reminds you that over the coming

---

[5]The fly in the ointment was always Italy, as an entry by Hewel on April 25, 1941, indicates. "Great exasperation at the Italians. Rommel in serious difficulties in Libya"—because of the Italians' failure to transport supplies to him. "Führer uses violent language. In the evening I sat in on a long discussion with the Führer. The invitation to Darlan. Führer: 'France on the one hand, Italy and Spain on the other.' "

weeks Russian preventive measures are possible and that steps must be taken in defense against these."

Grand Admiral Raeder came to see him on May 22, and the feeling of coming disaster seems to have grown even more strong within Hitler; when Raeder almost casually mentioned in a discussion of the Battle of the Atlantic that the *Bismarck* and the *Prinz Eugen* had just sailed from Gotenhafen for their first sweep in the North Atlantic, Hitler remembered all the premonitions only half-voiced in his private talk with Admiral Lütjens aboard the battleship at Goten-hafen. He complained uneasily that it seemed a great risk to run for so small a potential profit, and he mentioned Lütjens's own reservations about enemy tor-pedo-aircraft. He now asked Raeder outright, "Herr Grossadmiral, can't we fetch the ships back?" Raeder however advised him that the warships had already passed into the open North Sea, that enormous preparations had been made— five tankers and two auxiliary ships had been sent out in advance with submarines to rendezvous positions in the North Sea and the Atlantic. To recall the warships now would have a catastrophic effect on naval morale.[6] Hitler bowed to the admiral's experience and raised no further objections.

According to Hitler's naval adjutant, another factor in his anxiety was the wish to avoid provoking the United States by sending the most powerful battleship in the world to cruise on the threshold of its announced sphere of interest. All German policy was geared to depriving Roosevelt of any justification for war— at any rate, as yet. "War with the United States will come sooner or later," he had told his adjutants late in March. "Roosevelt, and behind him the big Jewish financiers, want war—they have no choice, because a German victory in Europe would cause the American Jews enormous capital losses in Europe. I only regret we still have no aircraft able to bomb American towns. I would dearly like to teach the Jews of America what it's like." Exasperating though Lend-Lease was, he said, it had one advantage: the Americans had given him the justification he needed for war. Hitler's policy of nonaggravation meantime did bear fruit: late in April his chargé d'affaires in Washington reported that in contrast to 1917 the American people were not demanding war, as they did not feel the Germans were provoking them. The German admiralty grudgingly conceded that the Führer's policy thus seemed justified, but the restrictions he continued to impose on the hard-pressed U-boat crews in the North and South Atlantic irked nonetheless. They were not to attack American warships or merchant ships, not to board those suspected of carrying war goods to the enemy, not to use their armament even

---

[6]Raeder, who knew Hitler could not sleep when his capital ships were at sea, evidently refrained from telling him that at 6:20 A.M. the previous day a British aircraft control station was monitored reporting that RAF aircraft had just been dispatched with orders to search for "two battleships and three destroyers."

if the Americans were flagrantly violating their neutrality—reporting German movements to the enemy, for example—unless the Americans fired the first shot. Roosevelt, whom Hitler seriously believed to be ill and perhaps even mentally unsound in consequence of his polio,[7] hinted that the American navy would start *convoying* its shipments of war supplies to Britain, which was certain to lead to open hostilities. Hitler approved Raeder's idea that the German press immediately publish an "interview" in which the admiral warned the American people of what Roosevelt's convoy idea must entail.

Hewel's diary of May 22 illustrates Hitler's dilemma over the United States.

> . . . Drove up the mountain. Conference with the Chief [Ribbentrop], Raeder, and Keitel on naval strategy, convoy issue, the Raeder "interview," and on Dakar, the Canaries and *the Azores!*[8] Very interesting. The Führer still vacillates in his attitude toward America, as "you cannot peer into Roosevelt's mind." If he wants a war, he will always find the means, even if legally we are in the right. *Japan* holds the key.

This was because Japan was bound by the Tripartite Pact to declare war only if the United States was clearly the aggressor.[9]

> Even though he has still not made his mind up it is better to keep the U.S.A. out of the war than perhaps to sink a few hundred thousand more tons of shipping. Without the U.S.A. the war will be over this year; with the U.S.A. it will go on for long years to come. A "warning" is agreed on.
>
> Negative comments on Italy's warfare at sea. Mosley is on the Isle of Man!
>
> Six P.M. the Italians come, under [Ambassador Dino] Alfieri. Speech on the occasion of second anniversary of the Axis pact. Tea. Got a date for Cudahy.

John Cudahy, Roosevelt's former ambassador in Brussels and now a *Life* magazine correspondent, was brought up to the Berghof next afternoon to interview Hitler for the American press. Cudahy was a rather naïve, open-faced outsider to the world of power politics, and Hitler's responses were short-tempered and impatient. Right at the start he rasped, "Convoys will mean war!" and tried to put out of his visitor's mind the "ludicrous" notion that the Nazis might ever invade the Americas. This was just a wicked lie invented to convert Ameri-

[7]According to Julius Schaub, Hitler often discussed this possibility with his physician, Dr. Theo Morell.

[8]Hitler had more than once raised the possibility of occupying the Azores as a staging point for long-range bombers to operate against the United States, perhaps this very autumn of 1941. The navy admitted that the Azores could probably be captured, but they could not be held in the face of British and possibly even American attack.

[9]In a cable of May 23 the German military attaché in Tokyo reported that the Japanese confirmed they would declare war if the United States attacked Germany, but that they could not commence hostilities immediately as they must conclude the conflict with China first.

can public opinion, said Hitler; indeed, he laughed out loud, dismissed it as a childish suggestion, and exclaimed, "That is on a level with claiming that America plans to conquer the moon!" Mindful of the propaganda meant to distract from "Barbarossa," Hitler added that his OKW was not planning expeditions to the moon but was busy with projects of rather shorter range—like Crete, at a range of sixty miles, or Britain at a range of only twenty. Hewel wrote afterward: "Three P.M., Cudahy, the U.S. envoy in Belgium, a friend of Lindbergh's. Questions from another world, childish, as in the years of struggle twenty years ago. But positive. Cudahy deeply impressed."

Hitler's message seems to have been understood by Roosevelt, for overnight a change was observed in the president's belligerent stand. Whereas on May 27 in a speech broadcast to the world Roosevelt appeared to utter a solemn commitment to enter the war, at a press conference the very next day he airily dismissed any suggestion of using his navy to convoy shipments to Britain or of asking Congress for a change in the Neutrality Law. Nevertheless, in his speech he had said outright, "From the point of view of strict naval and military necessity, we shall give every possible assistance to Britain and to all who, with Britain, are resisting Hitlerism or its equivalent with force of arms. Our patrols are helping now to insure delivery of the needed supplies to Britain. All additional measures necessary to deliver the goods will be taken." He had ended the speech with a proclamation of Unlimited National Emergency.

It was a provocative speech but, as Hewel's diary shows, Ribbentrop begged Hitler not to rise to the bait. "Roosevelt speech—weak but a propaganda danger. The man must be stopped from continually getting away with it. The Chief [Ribbentrop] comes to see Führer: a long discussion on this topic. The Führer would dearly like to make a speech, if only because he gets a kick out of it. The Reich foreign minister fears it will degenerate into a mutual abuse match and that the Führer's speech won't get a hearing in the U.S.A: Backward and forward.— In the afternoon we strolled in brilliant weather to the teahouse."

Since Raeder's visit Hitler had been distracted by a domestic incident from closely following the *Bismarck*'s steady progress toward the Americas. A drunken remark made by one of the Reich's senior press officials, Professor Karl Bömer, at a Bulgarian legation reception in mid-May threatened to betray the "Barbarossa" operation. "In four weeks the Russians'll be finished. Rosenberg's going to be Governor General of Russia. I'm going to be my old boss's undersecretary." From the intercepts that resulted, Hitler found out about the incident, summoned Heydrich to the Berghof, and ordered an investigation. Bömer was arrested, but Goebbels sprang to his defense and Heydrich found no evidence of deliberate or accidental treason. Hitler was not satisfied: he wanted Bömer's blood and ordered him tried by the People's Court. "From now on I will take ruthless action against everybody who can't hold his tongue!" Bömer ended up in a punishment battalion on the eastern front.

In Crete the bloody struggle for the island, launched on May 22, was approaching its climax. At Iráklion (Candia) some Greek companies had even joined the German paratroops in fighting the British: war was full of surprises. Late on May 24, Raeder telephoned from Berlin. On leaving the Denmark Straits south of Iceland, the *Bismarck* had stumbled on two British battleships sent to intercept her. She had dispatched the *Hood*—Churchill's most powerful battleship—in less than five minutes. The other British battleship, the *Prince of Wales,* had suffered heavy damage and turned away. But the elation at the Berghof was diminished as further signals came from the admiralty. The *Bismarck* herself had been hit twice, though without casualties, and she was bleeding oil; her speed was reduced, and the British warships seemed to be operating some kind of radar, a possibility not previously admitted. Admiral Lütjens proposed to put into the French port of Saint-Nazaire, leaving the *Prinz Eugen* to continue by herself into the Atlantic, but he could not shake off the pursuing enemy warships. He suggested that Dönitz marshal all available submarines in one area through which he would try to lure the enemy, but next day he announced that his oil was so low that he must steer directly for Saint-Nazaire.

By now the German admiralty knew that every enemy warship from Scapa Flow had sailed against the crippled *Bismarck.* Late on the twenty-fourth Lütjens had reported the first air strikes, so the British aircraft carrier *Victorious* was clearly within range. At the Berghof, Hewel noted: "Frightening hours on the *Bismarck*'s account." Further torpedo attacks were delivered by the aircraft during the midnight hours, but Lütjens dismissed them as "unimportant." By noon of the twenty-fifth, he had at last managed to shake off his pursuers. But for how long? From radio monitoring it was clear the British were throwing all they had into pinning the *Bismarck* down. Göring ordered his commanders to push out air cover as far as possible toward the limping battleship, but the range of his aircraft was insufficient. Hitler grimly radioed Lütjens greetings on his birthday. The mood at the Berghof was further soured by the presence of Heydrich and Goebbels, who were wrangling over the Bömer affair.

When Hitler rose on the twenty-sixth the news awaiting him was that the *Bismarck* had been found by the enemy; shadowed by an enemy aircraft, she still had six hundred miles to go to Brest. Soon after 9 P.M. Lütjens radioed that the aircraft had scored torpedo hits amidships and astern, and at 9:50 came the dread news that the battleship's steering was out of action: the unsinkable *Bismarck* was afloat and her guns were primed, but at best she could only steer a slow and stately circle while the British battle fleet closed in. From radio monitoring, the German admiralty identified at least four battleships and two aircraft carriers closing for the kill; the stormy seas prevented Raeder's destroyers from putting to sea, and Dönitz's submarines were too far off to engage the enemy in time. Shortly before midnight, Lütjens radioed: "Ship unmaneuverable. We are fighting to the last shell. Long live the Führer!" And to Hitler himself, he signaled: "We shall fight to the end trusting in you, mein Führer, and with our faith in Germany's victory undestroyed." Hitler instructed the admiralty to reply, "All Germany is with you. What can be done will be done. The way you do your duty will strengthen our nation in its fight for survival. Adolf Hitler."

During the early hours of May 27 the Luftwaffe scoured the area and ventured ineffectual attacks on British cruisers and destroyers. Ocean-going tugs put to sea. The Spanish government was asked to send out rescue ships. Lütjens's last radio message had come at 6:25 A.M.: "Position unchanged. Windstrength 8 to 9." From then onward there was silence. A funereal gloom descended over the Berghof. An adjutant's wife whispered that mourning clothes might seem in order. At noon Hitler learned that the British government had announced the sinking of the *Bismarck* an hour before.

Disabled and her last ammunition spent, the *Bismarck* had proved unsinkable to the end. She had scuttled herself under the guns of the British navy and sank with her colors honorably flying and the loss of some twenty-three hundred lives. Hitler's sorrow turned to anger. The OKW received instructions that no battleship or cruiser was to put to sea without his previous consent. The gallant Admiral Lütjens had himself warned in one of his last signals that the enemy use of naval radar would force a revision of the German navy's Atlantic cruiser warfare strategy. Hewel wrote on May 27:

> *Bismarck* sunk. Mood very dejected. Führer melancholy beyond words. Uncontrollable fury at the naval staff:
> 1. The ship should never have been sent out raiding;
> 2. After finishing off the *Hood* she should have dealt with the *Prince of Wales* too, and not run away;
> 3. She should have returned straight to Norway and not run straight into the lions' den.
> Red tape and wooden-headedness in the navy. Won't tolerate any man with a mind of his own.
> Reich foreign minister comes in the afternoon. Führer speaks his mind to him, swears and curses and then calms down. A walk to the teahouse. The Führer picks up again, talks about new types of ships and the airborne torpedo as a weapon.

Raeder answered Hitler's criticisms soberly when he next came to the Berghof; he particularly emphasized that for the *Bismarck* to have returned through the northern passages to Norway would have been more risky than continuing into the Atlantic. Hitler asked the admiralty to adopt a policy of conservation of strength until the effect of "Barbarossa" on Britain was known. "Should Britain's collapse threaten to become imminent, some very important duties might present themselves to our surface warships." Though Hitler did not admit it, the *Bismarck*'s loss had certainly not been in vain. She had drawn off no fewer than eight battleships, two aircraft carriers, eleven cruisers, and twenty-one destroyers, creating a diversion which more than ensured the successful conclusion of the invasion of Crete; and the capture of Crete in turn reduced Britain's naval influence in the Mediterranean and paved the way for Rommel's future triumphs in North Africa.

Hitler meanwhile had issued a belated OKW directive ordering support for the Arab "liberation movement" against Britain. Jodl's chief assistant, General Warlimont, had been sent to Paris for a week to resume the military talks broken off in December, and a protocol had been signed granting the French concessions in return for assistance in Syria and Iraq, as well as the future use of the Tunisian port of Bizerte to supply Rommel's troops in North Africa; more reluctantly, the French agreed on principle to let Hitler operate their port at Dakar as a submarine and Luftwaffe base on the west coast of Africa. They also secretly agreed to remove General Weygand from his command, though this was not specifically mentioned in the protocol. It was signed in Paris on the twenty-eighth, and the next day Warlimont flew to the Berghof to report.

Events in Iraq were overtaking Hitler, however. The British were already advancing on Baghdad, and the end could not be far off. In private Hitler cursed the "banqueting diplomats" who had misinformed him. "Unfortunately the Arabs are unreliable and venal. The British and French have grasped that fact. But we cannot give a helping hand everywhere. The Middle East by itself would have been no problem if our other plans"—meaning "Barbarossa"—"were not irrevocable. When they succeed, we can open a door into the Middle East from there." Mussolini was opposed to abandoning the Iraqi rebels and sent word to Hitler thus: "I, Mussolini, am in favor of active support, as this is an opportunity to raise the entire population of the Middle East against Britain. But if Iraq collapses, they will all lose heart again. If the German High Command also decides on active support, then it seems to me necessary to occupy Cyprus as well —after the reduction of Crete and Rhodes—since it lies off the Syrian coastline and holds the key to the entire Middle East." With Crete and Cyprus in Axis hands, the British fleet could scarcely stay safely in Alexandria; the Duce felt the capture of Cyprus would be easier than that of Crete as it was less mountainous and not so heavily fortified. Hitler's first reaction was an outburst: "Mussolini thinks Cyprus should be taken now as well!" And Hewel recorded: "The Führer proposes to agree, and to tell him to do it himself." Nonetheless, Hitler did ask Göring and Jeschonnek whether Cyprus would be possible. The Reichsmarschall winced, reported on the blood the Luftwaffe had lost over Crete—150 Junkers 52 transports alone—and advised against invading Cyprus. "Since war broke out the Luftwaffe has known no rest. From Crete we shall now be fighting a pitched battle against the British fleet and Tobruk."

Hewel made a lengthy record of Hitler's worried conference with Ribbentrop and the OKW generals on May 29:

> The point under debate is how far to bring in France or to get her involved in a war with Britain. The Führer's view is that the French will only fight, and Weygand will only stay loyal, if they know that they can thereby retain the French empire and are persuaded that the soil on which they fight will by that fight remain French. If Syria could be isolated from the rest, this could be done; but it cannot be isolated, it has to be regarded in its larger context: Syria, Tunisia, Algeria, Morocco, and Dakar. The French are making Bizerte available to us in Tunisia. But now the Italians also want a port there "on principle." Obviously they want to get their foot in the door there, and this is why the French will never give way. . . .
>
> The Führer curses the Italians. He hates the Spanish. Of Italy he says that you can't keep making concessions to somebody who is always running around with his bottom black and blue from beatings, nor will the German people stand for it. And on top of that they are an arrogant bunch. . . . The Führer's view is that when "Barbarossa" is over, he won't need to pay any more attention to Italy! We will then automatically be able to come together with the French. They are counting on kicking the Italians out of Tunisia after the war. He wants to have a talk with Mussolini shortly.

Later that day the foreign ministry's Dr. Julius Schnurre expounded at length but with precision on Finland and Sweden. The Finns had sent generals to negotiate with the OKW and the General Staff in Germany; they had been asked to prepare two divisions to support the operations of Hitler's army in Norway against northern Russia. " 'Barbarossa' is a gamble like everything else," said Hitler after Schnurre left. "If it fails, then it will all be over anyway. If it succeeds, it will have created a situation that will probably force Britain to make peace. What will the United States have to say when all at once Finland is on our side! When the first shot is fired, the world will hold its breath."

Pricking the Bubble

The dazzling heat of high summer had come to the Berghof. It was now early June 1941: with a suddenness that caused an almost perceptible lurch the last echelon of assault troops had set out from Germany for the eastern front—the twelve panzer divisions and twelve mechanized divisions whose location by an enemy must surely unmask Hitler's true intentions beyond all doubt. In less than three weeks "Barbarossa" would begin. It was time to start dropping hints to his prospective allies.

Hitler's last major anxieties had been overcome. Crete was in German and Italian hands. Only Iraq remained a "blemish," though through no fault of Germany's. Rashid Ali had fled to Iran, and the victorious British were evidently regrouping for an invasion of Syria. Yet Hitler was not downhearted. "If we tote up the results of two years of war," he told Göring, "it has to be said: 'There's got to be a limit somewhere.' Iraq was a blemish—so what? I cannot help it. After all, I am not an Arab and the Arabs are no Germans. All in all the Arabs did right"—meaning in their rebellion against the British, now shown to have been premature. "If they had waited any longer, more and more British would have poured in and a coup d'etat would have been quite impossible."

His nagging suspicions about Japan had also been removed. A few weeks before, he had been unsettled by rumors that Washington was offering Japan a nonaggression pact; he had examined this risk from every angle with Ribbentrop here at the Berghof, for both realized that such a pact would be an open invitation to Roosevelt to intervene in the European war. Admiral Kichisaburo Nomura had privately warned Hitler through Raeder that Japan's naval construction program would not allow her to tackle her Far Eastern problem until 1946, as only then would she be strong enough to take on Britain and the United States. To Hitler Japan's Foreign Minister Matsuoka was dangerously inscrutable. "He combines the hypocrisy of an American Bible missionary with all the wiles of a

Japanese oriental," he told Mussolini. But at the end of May he breathed again when Matsuoka loudly proclaimed his unswerving allegiance to the Tripartite Pact.

The first hint was dropped to Mussolini, but the dictator seems not to have grasped its meaning and Hitler did not repeat it. He had asked the Duce to join him at the Brenner Pass on June 2. Hewel accompanied Hitler's party. "Journeyed in wonderful weather to the Brenner. Arrival at 10:15 A.M., followed by talks and lunch at 2:30." Hitler talked alone with Mussolini for two hours before the two dictators were joined by their foreign ministers. When at four o'clock the train set out again for Berchtesgaden, Hewel sat with the Führer. "He is contented; says Mussolini is very confident and sure of victory. Has dropped a hint on Russia 'if the shipping losses alone do not suffice,' " meaning suffice to knock Britain out of the war. No whisper of his latent inclinations to do a deal postwar with France at Italy's expense came through, but he did talk to Mussolini of the possibility that David Lloyd George might succeed a defeated Churchill. "Then we must see what possibility there is of settling our differences."

To the Japanese ambassador, General Oshima, whom he urgently summoned to the Berghof the next day, Hitler put on the appropriate "anti-British" act. Oshima correctly interpreted Hitler's hint at "Barbarossa" and after being lectured by Ribbentrop as well, he personally cabled Matsuoka in strictest confidence. "Both gentlemen gave me to understand that a German-Soviet war probably cannot be avoided." Hitler had bluntly stated on the third that he would always be the first to draw his sword if he detected any hostility in an opponent, and although he did not expressly say so, his remarks to Oshima implied that while the Tripartite Pact was *expressis verbis* not intended as an instrument against the Soviet Union, such was the obligation on Japan—and he would expect the Japanese to honor it. Ribbentrop assured Oshima that the campaign would be over in two or three months—he could not say when it would begin, but "if Japan should find it necessary to prepare for this eventuality, then he would advise her to do so in as short a time as possible." On June 4, Hitler received King Boris of Bulgaria for two hours. Hewel took notes on the encounter, but they appear to have been lost, and since the Bulgarian records fell into Soviet hands in the course of the events Hitler was about to unleash, we are unlikely ever to learn what they discussed.

Now the Soviet Union began to reap the harvest of the hatred she had sown. The Finns confirmed to German officers sent to Helsinki that they were aware of the "historic hour" that was dawning and they would provide Finnish troops, territory, and airfields to assist in "Barbarossa." Antonescu came to Munich and again offered to support the attack with all the military and other resources at Romania's disposal. Even the Turks, Britain's last formal ally, were softening under Papen's pressure, and a treaty with Germany, the victor of the Balkans, was in the cards. Perhaps the activities of the British sabotage agencies influenced them. Not many weeks before, the Turks had intercepted a British launch laden with sabotage materials and explosives heading for their coast; in addition, Turkish police had uncovered a British sabotage ring in Istanbul. In Crete the Germans had uncovered a veritable arsenal of explosives in the house of the British vice-consul at Iráklion, a Major Pendlebury. Pendlebury—real name Kustos— was head of the British secret service in central Crete. His private diary revealed that British secret service headquarters in London had instructed its agents to ignore the prevailing laws and conventions of war.

As for himself, operating on the principle that no questions are asked of the victor, Hitler authorized orders to his Wehrmacht—even in advance of "Barbarossa"—which were so shocking that Keitel later had all copies of them destroyed. Hitler's staff, however, accepted the idea that such orders were necessary. His naval adjutant had himself seen how mercilessly the Reds fought in the Baltic states in 1919. Jodl—convinced that Hitler was of impeccable morality and pursuing only one lofty ideal, a German victory—also decided that his orders were to be obeyed whatever their character.

The decision to liquidate the political commissars attached to Red Army units was to Hitler a logical extension of the fight against the tentacles of Soviet authority—the eradication of the ruling classes. The commissars could be identified as such by the red star embroidered with a golden hammer and sickle on their sleeves. Evidently at Hitler's dictation, Jodl drafted an explanation of the decision to liquidate the commissars (though not all of them). The Bolsheviks could not be counted on to fight "humanely." The commissars in particular would subject German prisoners to spiteful, cruel, and inhuman treatment, for they were the "originators of these barbaric Asiatic fighting methods." Hitler ordered: "If they are caught fighting or offering resistance, they are to be shot out of hand without exception and immediately." They were francs-tireurs and as such not entitled to be recognized as soldiers. The less active commissars, defined as "political commissars guilty or suspected of committing no hostile acts," were to be spared: Rosenberg had pointed out that initially he would be needing many of the top Russian officials to help him administer the eastern territories. General Warlimont sent out this document, although it was evidently never signed by Hitler, directing the army and Luftwaffe that the orders it contained were to be passed on only by word of mouth below a certain command level.

The role played by Halder and the army General Staff, not to mention the German military lawyers, in drafting these orders was less than glorious. After

Hitler had undoubtedly given the initial impetus in his blunt secret speech of March 30,[1] Brauchitsch's staff had drafted two separate orders in weeks of tedious bureaucratic paperwork and discussed them with the OKW. The first was this commissar order, and the second an order restricting the jurisdiction of courts-martial on Russian soil (basically to enable the SS task forces to operate at will). The army wanted Russian civilians to be subject to military law, while the OKW lawyers and General Jeschonnek recalled that Hitler had always been irked by the ponderous procedures of the army courts, believing that only speedy conviction and execution was a true deterrent. It was Halder, however, who proposed the clause reading: "Immediate collective punishments will be enforced against towns and villages from which ambushes or treacherous attacks on the Wehrmacht are made, on the orders of an officer of not less than battalion commander's rank, if circumstances do not permit the rapid arrest of the individual perpetrators." Apart from this, the army's arguments were ignored. In the formal order issued by Keitel on Hitler's behalf in May, the Wehrmacht was instructed that offenses against Russian civilians would *not* be punishable by courts-martial; that francs-tireurs were to be wiped out in battle or "trying to escape." This aroused intense feeling among the army commands. In May, Brauchitsch partially qualified the order by issuing a supplementary order on the maintenance of army discipline, but many of his frontline generals were sick at heart when these two "Barbarossa" orders reached them.

To Hitler, however, the Red Army was not an enemy to be handled with kid gloves. In a Berghof conference on June 5 he again warned his staff of the extensive use the Russians would make of tactics not sanctioned by international convention, and he ordered printed instructions to be prepared for the troops—though not distributed as yet, so as not to put ideas into the enemy's head. Hitler anticipated that the Russians might, for example, contaminate long stretches of their roads of retreat with poison gases, or use poisonous additives to spike the food stocks and fresh-water supplies or kill livestock in the areas overrun by the Wehrmacht.

Hitler prepared to leave the Berghof, resolved perhaps not to return until Russia had been defeated. He had recently taken to gathering his friends, his adjutants, and their wives about him in the evenings and rambling on endlessly about Christianity and the Roman Empire. On June 8, Hewel entered in his Berghof diary:

[1]See page 212–13 above.

Raining. The British are marching into Syria. A long conversation alone with the Führer about Russia. Says it will be a "tough proposition" but he trusts in the Wehrmacht. [Russian] air force: numerical superiority in fighters and bombers. He is a bit frightened of air raids on Berlin and Vienna. "The area we are to occupy will not be much bigger than from Denmark to Bordeaux in size. Russians have massed their entire strength on their western frontier, the biggest concentration in history. If "Barbarossa" goes wrong now, we are all lost anyway. As soon as that is all over, Iraq and Syria will take care of themselves. Then I will have a free hand, and I will be able to thrust on down through Turkey as well.

If the French lose Syria—and I am convinced that Syria *is* lost—then there is only the one danger left, that they will lose Algeria as well. If that happens, I will thrust straight down through Spain at once and barricade the Mediterranean against the British. It is just this wretched waiting that makes one so nervous!

A few days later the OKW asked the supreme commanders for their views on a draft directive for the period after "Barbarossa": basically, after sixty divisions and one Luftflotte had been left astride the territories won in the east, the remaining military units would be used to feed manpower back into the naval and Luftwaffe construction industries and to coerce France, Spain, Turkey, and Iran into joining the fight against Britain. A contested invasion of Britain itself was not contemplated in this document. On the eleventh, Hitler sent Schmundt to check if the headquarters being built for him near Rastenburg in East Prussia was ready.

Luftwaffe reconnaissance photographs showed some four thousand Russian aircraft packing the airfields just across the frontier; radio reconnaissance suggested over a thousand more were waiting farther back. On the diplomatic front something akin to hysteria was overtaking Moscow as the realization of Hitler's mobilization dawned: the Russian shipments to Germany were stepped up; false rumors of German political demands on the Soviet Union multiplied; troop movements and the widespread call-up of Russian reservists were noticed. On June 9 the German embassy in Moscow smuggled a naval officer into a Communist party indoctrination session at which a functionary delivered a violently anti-German talk warning his audience to be on guard over the next few weeks. The speaker said that nobody in Moscow had expected Hitler to conquer the Balkans so rapidly, but once the war became a war of raw materials like petroleum and ore, Germany would be at a disadvantage; for bolshevism, the advantage was that any war of attrition must lead to the annihilation of the middle classes. The Soviet Union's interests would best be served by a period of national peace—while the rest of Europe bled white in war.

Hitler arrived back in Berlin early on June 13 obsessed with the coming campaign. Again he told Hewel his belief that "Barbarossa" must mean the end of Britain's resistance. In his diary Hewel judged the prospects more soberly: "I cannot share this belief, as the British will regard it as a weakening of Germany for a long time to come." In Berlin Dr. Goebbels reported to Hitler on the pre-"Barbarossa" propaganda campaign. Goebbels himself had told his staff that the planned eastern campaign was canceled, and that since the invasion of Britain was imminent, they must now prepare for that eventuality. Through Party channels a wave of rumors had been sent swirling around Germany—that Stalin was to visit Germany, or that he had agreed to lease the Ukraine to Germany for ninety-nine years. On the morning of Hitler's arrival in Berlin the police raided every newspaper outlet in the capital and seized the latest *Völkischer Beobachter;* but enough copies escaped seizure for the impression to be conveyed that in Goebbels's leading article, "Crete as an Example," he had unwittingly betrayed that within two months Britain would be invaded and "Mr. Churchill would be laughing on the other side of his face." But Goebbels was not in disgrace for this lapse—he was seen next day in Hitler's residence, cackling out loud over the success of his rumor-mongering, and the Führer was laughing uproariously and slapping his thigh at each fresh detail of his canny propaganda minister's devices.

It was Saturday the fourteenth. The Reich Chancellery was packed with the Wehrmacht commanders summoned for an all-day series of briefing conferences on the coming campaign. Secrecy was essential, so (paradoxically) uniforms were to be worn. Everybody was assigned different street-entrances by which to arrive at the sprawling Reich Chancellery complex, so that passersby might not sense the urgency of the conferences proceeding behind the tall granite walls that Albert Speer had built three years before. Brauchitsch would arrive through the garden gate in Hermann-Göringstrasse, Göring would enter through Wilhelmstrasse, and the army group commanders through the New Chancellery in Vossstrasse; the first would arrive shortly before 11 A.M., the last just before lunch.

At two o'clock Hitler broke for lunch, which he took sitting at a long oval-shaped table with twenty-eight of his top generals. An hour later he called for silence and spoke of his military reasons for attacking Russia. An unpublished note taken by a Luftwaffe general survives:

> *Hitler's after-luncheon speech.* The main enemy is still Britain. Britain will fight on as long as the fight has any purpose; this is typical of the British, as we have seen from their individual soldier's conduct in Flanders, and it was demonstrated again by Dunkirk, by Greece, and by Crete. But Britain's fight only makes sense as long as they can hope that American aid will take effect and that they may find support on the continent. This explains why they have high hopes that the Russians will intervene and tie down the Germans, wearing down our war economy while the balance of power is tilted by American aid. At present this is very meager; it will not become effective until the summer

of 1942, assuming they have enough shipping tonnage to bring it over here; and the shipping losses are increasing.

The proof of [Britain's] advances to Russia is the complete uniformity in their press treatment of Cripps's journey.[2] Russia's attitude is perpetually obscure; she exploited every moment of political or military preoccupation elsewhere to raise immediate political demands. We can see this happening in Russia's intervention in the Polish campaign, and again against the Baltic states and Finland, and now in the Balkans (Bessarabia, and the treaty of friendship with Yugoslavia).

Our attempt to "clarify the position" met with the following objections from Molotov. First question, What does our guarantee to Romania mean and would we object to a Russian military mission? Second question concerning the Dardanelles, and the third about Finland. In other words continual efforts to push in somewhere. Since these efforts coincided chronologically with various temporary weaknesses in the German position, we would have to expect them to use every chance they can in the future to act against Germany's interests. The Russian armed forces are strong enough to prevent us from demobilizing soldiers and feeding them into the arms and consumer-goods industries so long as this latent Russian threat persists. Even if we made peace with Britain this would still be so. We want this conflict to come early, however; indeed it is absolutely vital if we are not to forfeit the favorable conditions that prevail. The bulk of the Russian forces are standing on the frontier, so we have a good chance of defeating them right there.

Hitler rounded off his speech with a warning that the Russian forces outnumbered the German, but that German command leadership, equipment, and experience were superior. Even so, he warned them against underestimating the Red Army.

It was probably on this occasion that when Göring loudly proclaimed to a cluster of other generals that this would be a victory on the same scale as those that Hitler had already won, the Führer took him by the arm and soberly corrected him. "Göring, it will be our toughest struggle yet—by far the toughest!" Göring asked him why, and Hitler replied, "Because for the first time we shall be fighting an *ideological* enemy, and an ideological enemy of fanatical persistence at that." Three years later Hitler ruefully reminded his generals of these words.

The old familiar bouts of insomnia began to attack him as the last days before "Barbarossa" dragged by. By night he lay awake and asked himself what loop-

---

[2]The British ambassador, Sir Stafford Cripps, had left Moscow a week before to consult with the foreign office in London.

holes in his grand design the British might yet exploit. He believed he had plugged them all: he had sent Göring's deputy, Milch, on an extended tour of Germany's air raid defenses; he had ordered an urgent reinforcement of Holland's coastal defenses; and suspecting that his successful paratroop operation against Crete might stimulate the British to similar ventures against the Norwegian coast or the two Channel Isles as soon as his hands were tied in Russia, he had ordered the island garrisons increased and extensively reinforced with tanks and artillery —the more so as he intended to keep Guernsey and Jersey in German hands after the final peace treaty with Britain. Yet Hitler could still only get to sleep with sedatives, even after staying up until three or four each morning discussing Turkey, Russia, war, and warfare with dutiful but weary henchmen like Himmler, Ley, Hewel, Ribbentrop, and Seyss-Inquart.

On June 18, with the newspapers of every country but Germany openly asking when Hitler's attack on the Soviet Union would begin, the Russians unwittingly caused him his most anxious hours ever when the Soviet ambassador in Berlin, Dekanozov, asked for an interview with Ribbentrop's state secretary, Baron von Weizsäcker. Hewel, at Hitler's Chancellery, wrote an agitated note in his diary: "Big problem: Dekanozov has announced he is to see the state secretary. What is he bringing? Is Stalin going to bring off a major coup even now? A big offer to us, etc. etc.? [Führer has] a long discussion with foreign minister; Engel [Hitler's army adjutant] and myself going over every possible angle. The Führer and foreign minister will have to vanish—so they can't be reached. Much plotting: Sonnenburg, Karinhall, or Berghof; the train; Wildpark.³ Then one day lying low in the Reich Chancellery." Hewel concluded the entry as follows: "These last days before an action are the most nerve-racking: something unexpected can still occur." The next evening, however, as Hitler was in the middle of dictating his "Barbarossa" proclamation—"To the Troops of the Eastern Front!"—Ribbentrop telephoned that Dekanozov had called on his state secretary at 6 P.M., had discussed purely routine affairs, and had left after cracking a few jokes.

The proclamation was printed and issued secretly to the services on the twentieth. This time its language must have been far above the average soldier's head —it was a *tour d'horizon* of Germany's foreign policy since the war began in 1939; but in its four closely printed pages there were some lines worthy of attention. Here Hitler even claimed that the German people had never wished ill to the inhabitants of Russia. "But for two decades the Jewish-Bolshevik rulers of Moscow have endeavored to set not only Germany but all Europe alight." Hitler said he had never tried to export the Nazi ideology to Russia the way the Kremlin

---

³Sonnenburg was Ribbentrop's country home; Karinhall was Göring's; Wildpark was the site of Luftwaffe headquarters, outside Potsdam.

had tried to convert the rest of Europe to communism by means of subversion. In a cynical oversimplification, Hitler reminded his troops: "You, my soldiers, know for yourselves that until a very few weeks ago there was not one German panzer or mechanized division on our eastern frontier." The historic proclamation ended:

> At this moment, soldiers of the eastern front, an assembly of strength the like of which in size and scale the world has never seen is now complete. In league with Finnish divisions, our comrades are standing with the Victor of Narvik [Dietl] on the shores of the Arctic in the north. German soldiers under the command of the Conquerer of Norway [Falkenhorst], and the Finnish heroes of freedom under their own Marshal [Mannerheim] are protecting Finland. On the eastern front stand you. In Romania, on the banks of the Prut, and along the Danube right down to the beaches of the Black Sea are German and Romanian troops united under Antonescu, the head of state. When this, the biggest front line in history, now begins its advance it does so not just to provide the means of ending for all time this great war, or to defend those countries currently concerned, but for the salvation of our entire European civilization and culture.
>
> German soldiers! You are thus entering upon a harsh and demanding fight —because the fate of Europe, the future of the German Reich, the existence of our nation now rest on your hands alone.
>
> May the Lord God help us all in this struggle.

At the same time he ordered Jodl to advise the Wehrmacht by the prearranged code word that the attack would begin, as planned, early on June 22. Hewel wrote: "A long conversation with the Führer. Expects a lot of the Russian campaign. Wishes he was ten weeks on from hence. After all there must always be a big element of risk. We are standing outside a locked door. [Will we run into] secret weapons? The tenacity of the fanatic? He now has to take sleeping pills to fall asleep. He is still dictating. He told me that this morning [June 20] he again pored over every minute detail, but found no possibility for the enemy to get the better of Germany. He thinks Britain will have to give in—and he hopes it will be before the year is over."

The coming occupation of fresh territories in the east suggested to Hitler an alternative solution of the "Jewish problem." Since the summer of 1940 experts in the foreign ministry had studied the possibility of settling Europe's uprooted Jews on the island of Madagascar. On June 2, 1941, Hitler told Mussolini that after the war every Jew must get out of Europe. "Perhaps we can settle them in Madagascar. Considering our own population density, the island could find room for fifteen million people." (Madagascar is over twice as big as Britain or West

Germany; its prewar population was four million.) Hitler did not want the Jews to remain in their present settlement region around Lublin, as the standards of hygiene resulting from the living conditions now imposed on them raised the danger of epidemics. But for the duration of the war the Madagascar plan was out. Hans Frank's Generalgouvernement of Poland would have to accommodate Europe's displaced Jews for the time being. On October 2, 1940, Hitler had discussed this with Frank and Baldur von Schirach, Gauleiter of Vienna. Schirach pointed out that his fifty thousand Viennese Jews were the first due for deportation. Frank reported that Warsaw and other Polish cities had concentrated their Jews in restricted areas—"ghettos"—and complained that he had no accommodation available for a fresh influx of Jews. But Hitler had dreamed of ridding Europe of the "Jewish plague" since 1921, if not earlier, and he had strong popular support for this program in the Reich. The German army commander of Vienna wrote to the war department in February 1941 welcoming the deportations, as he considered the Jews the principal rumor-mongers; he asked only that an exception should be made for former Jewish officers wounded in World War I. Hitler agreed.

Thus Hitler overrode Hans Frank's practical objections to using the Generalgouvernement as a dumping ground. The problem with the Madagascar plan in wartime was, he told Martin Bormann, how to transport the Jews that far. "I would dearly like to devote my entire fleet of *Kraft durch Freude* (strength through joy) ocean liners[4] to it, but in wartime that's not so easy. I don't want my German crews being sunk by enemy torpedoes." In private—to Keitel, Bormann, and Speer—Hitler described it as his eventual ambition to eliminate all Jewish influence throughout the Axis domains. It would solve many of the infuriating legalistic problems still bogged down in the ministries of Justice and the Interior, about the rights of Jews in the law courts, the status of half-Jews, etc. On June 7, 1941, Dr. Hans Lammers wrote to Martin Bormann: "The main reason why the Führer has not approved the ruling proposed by the Ministry of the Interior is that in his opinion there won't be any Jews left in Germany after the war anyway."

As "Operation Barbarossa" approached, it occurred to Hitler that the new eastern empire would enable him to humor Hans Frank's loud objections to the dumping of Jews on his Generalgouvernement territory and Himmler's growing influence there. Three days before the Wehrmacht attacked Russia, Hitler announced this explicitly to Frank; and the latter accordingly briefed his staff that no fresh ghettos were to be established, "since the Führer expressly stated to me on June 19 that in due course the Jews will be removed from the Generalgouverne-

---

[4]Pleasure liners built by and for the mass German labor union, DAF.

ment—and that the Generalgouvernement is to be, so to speak, only a transit camp." Seven months later, the Madagascar plan died a natural death. A foreign ministry official would then write: "The war against the Soviet Union has meanwhile made it possible to provide other territories for the final solution. Accordingly, the Führer has decided that the Jews are not to be deported to Madagascar but to the east."

What exactly did Hitler mean by "east" of the Generalgouvernement? On the twentieth, Rosenberg had revealed to Canaris, Heydrich, and a host of other Party and Wehrmacht leaders that White Ruthenia—the area around Minsk—was to be set aside for "undesirables" and antisocial elements from Germany's dominions. Was this to be the new Israel, or did Hitler now use "east" just as a vague generic term, whose more precise definition would be: perdition, oblivion, extermination? The documents at our disposal do not help us.

Two days remained, and Russia was still an enigma behind a sealed door. During a coffee break snatched with his female secretaries in their "stair cupboard" in the Chancellery, Hitler noted that there was something sinister about Russia— something that reminded him of the ghost ship in *The Flying Dutchman*. And when Fräulein Schroeder, a clever, critical, and often dangerously outspoken thirty-three-year-old stenographer who had loyally served Martin Bormann before attracting Hitler's attention in 1933, asked why the Führer kept emphasizing how the "Barbarossa" decision had been the toughest he had ever taken, Hitler frankly replied, "Because we know absolutely nothing about Russia. It might be one big soap-bubble, but it might just as well turn out to be very different."

At 9 P.M. on June 20, Colonel Schmundt, his Wehrmacht adjutant, brought news from the admiralty that showed how fragile was the thread restraining the whole world from war. A German submarine had proudly reported attempting to attack the U.S. battleship *Texas*, since it was encountered ten miles within the North Atlantic blockade zone proclaimed by Germany. Hitler cannot have been pleased, for as recently as June 6 he had patiently explained to Admiral Raeder why he wanted to do everything possible to avoid incidents with the United States. On top of this, a U-boat sank the American freighter *Robin Moore* outside the Atlantic blockade zone, claiming it was carrying contraband goods for the enemy. The U.S. government protested less loudly than the U.S. press—Raeder attributed this to his forthright warnings in May—but again Hitler directed that "for political reasons incidents with the United States are to be avoided completely for the time being."

On the *Texas* incident, Raeder stated the U-boat had acted quite correctly, though he now proposed forbidding attacks on American warships up to twenty miles inside the blockade zone, to rule out navigational errors. Hitler at first agreed, but during the night he had second thoughts and telephoned the admiralty that no attacks whatever were to be made on American warships anywhere in the blockade zone. The following afternoon Raeder came in person to argue against this. The two incidents were a warning to Roosevelt that Germany meant business. Hitler would not budge; there must be no incidents with the United States until the outcome of "Barbarossa" was clear. The same order was issued to the Luftwaffe.

Less than twelve hours remained of the last, tense day before the attack. The foreign ministry telephoned with the unsettling news that the Soviet ambassador was again urgently demanding to see Ribbentrop. The foreign minister became unavailable: Dekanozov was fobbed off with word that he was away from Berlin until evening and that an appointment would be made on his return. In fact Ribbentrop was in the Chancellery and paid several visits to Hitler. Hitler was dictating a proclamation for home consumption and letters to Mussolini, Horthy, and Finland's President Rysto Ryti.

During the afternoon the German naval attaché, who had left Moscow late on the nineteenth (his recall was in response to the fact that the Russians had suddenly recalled their naval attaché from Berlin) arrived by train in the Reich capital and rendered a vivid description of the panic that had broken out in Moscow diplomatic circles; nevertheless, on returning by rail through Poland he had seen less military activity than at any time over the last four months, and certainly far less than he had observed in the Baltic countries recently. Both he and his assistant, who arrived back in Berlin the next day, encountered closed prison trains escorted by blue-uniformed GPU troops—evacuating Polish "undesirables" from eastern Poland. Ambassador Schulenburg meanwhile remained in Moscow. Ribbentrop cabled him to destroy the embassy's code books and radio equipment and to arrange an immediate interview with Molotov at which he was to read out a long rigamarole ending with the words ". . . the Führer has therefore ordered the German Wehrmacht to stand up to this menace with all the means of force at its disposal."

At nine-thirty, Dekanozov was allowed to see Ribbentrop's state secretary. To everybody's relief he was only delivering a formal Soviet complaint about repeated violations of its air space. The parallel complaint delivered simultaneously by Molotov to Schulenburg sounded so wistful that it brought the house down in Hitler's Chancellery when the telegram was read out upon its arrival there in the small hours of the morning. "A series of symptoms gives us the impression that the German government is dissatisfied with the Soviet government . . ." grumbled Molotov. One hour later, along a frontier extending from the Arctic Ocean to the Black Sea, over three million German troops, supported by three thousand tanks and nearly two thousand aircraft, attacked the USSR. Surprise was complete.

His thoughts far from the Chancellery, Hitler sat up with his private staff far into the night. Then he briefly retired to bed, remarking to his adjutants, "Before three months have passed, we shall witness a collapse in Russia the like of which world history has never seen!"

What Hewel described as a "tranquil, self-possessed mood" descended on the Chancellery during the morning of these tumultuous events. It was almost like any other Sunday, except that Hitler and Ribbentrop fell fast asleep after lunch. The foreign minister had summoned the Soviet ambassador at three-thirty that morning to break the grim news to him, and then in rapid succession he summoned the representatives of Germany's allies—Italy, Japan, Hungary, Finland, and Romania. At five-thirty Dr. Goebbels had spoken, and at six Ribbentrop had addressed the press, surrounded by his assembled staff. Many of Hitler's adjutants, wilting under the Central European sun, went swimming.

By the time Hitler awoke late that afternoon, his armies were already many miles inside the Russian frontier, and the first reactions of the world were being monitored. Italy had honored her obligations with notable speed: at 3 P.M. Rome had cabled that Italy regarded herself as at war with Russia since five-thirty that morning. Romanian troops had crossed the Prut and were fighting in the provinces invaded by Russia twelve months before. Madrid telephoned that a Spanish volunteer legion was being recruited to join the crusade. An ecstatic Admiral Horthy exulted at the "magnificent" news and told the German ambassador that this was a day of which he had dreamed for twenty-two years—mankind would thank Hitler for this deed for centuries to come. Hungary dutifully broke off diplomatic relations with Moscow before Hitler retired to bed, but this was as far as it would as yet go. At 6 P.M. a disappointed General Jodl telephoned his liaison officer in Budapest to remind the Hungarians of the historic importance of the hour; but Horthy had gone off to play polo, his Chief of Army Staff was "unavailable," and the defense minister had gone fishing. Just as Hitler expected, the Hungarians, canny as ever, wanted to see the first results of "Barbarossa" before committing themselves.

Again he sat up late with his staff listening to the military reports. The Luftwaffe had bombed Kiev, Kovno (Kaunas), Sevastopol, Murmansk, Odessa, and Zhitomir. The bulk of the Russians' forward air force had been smashed on the ground—over twelve hundred Soviet aircraft had been destroyed. Thousands of prisoners had already been taken. From North Africa came heartening news from Rommel. Of this day Hewel wrote: "11:30 A.M., [Alessandro] Pavolini [the Italian education minister] to see the Führer. I accompany the Führer; he is in a brilliant mood on account of the huge successes in Russia (Luftwaffe) and Sollum (tanks)."

As so often before, Hitler and his staff drove through the sun-drenched streets of Berlin to his special train at the Anhalt station. At half-past noon he left for East Prussia—the twin locomotives hauling him throughout the afternoon and evening across Pomerania, those fields and cities so recently "liberated" from the Poles. Over tea he reminisced with Hewel and the others. "Russia," he said at one point, "is still a big question mark." Long after midnight he was being driven in a column of cars past cordons of sentries guarding a wood about ten miles outside the dreary East Prussian township of Rastenburg. Deep inside this wood was his new headquarters—during the train journey he had decided to call it the Wolf's Lair *(Wolfsschanze)*. When a secretary inquired, "Why Wolf again—just like the other headquarters?" Hitler replied, "That was my code name in the Years of Struggle." It was 1:30 A.M. when he first set foot inside the forbidding compound. From here he planned to command the defeat of the Soviet Union.

PART 3

CRUSADE INTO RUSSIA

The Country Poacher

Thus Adolf Hitler at fifty-two set out to conquer Russia.

In a terrible, unceasing onslaught his gray legions of Wehrmacht and Waffen SS troops fought forward across the drab and windswept plains, the glowing yellow fields of Ukrainian sunflower crops, the swamps around Lake Ilmen, the barren steppe, and the rocky deserts and inhospitable tundra of the north, humming with myriads of unseen mosquitoes, until the spent Nazi tide finally lapped the Caucasus Mountains.

Within a few days Field Marshal Leeb's armored spearheads had reached Dvinsk (Daugavpils); Field Marshal Bock's tanks were encircling a long oval-shaped pocket from Bialystok to Minsk in which eventually 350,000 Russian prisoners would be taken. Within a month Smolensk itself would be in German hands and Rundstedt would be at the gates of Kiev. As the Germans advanced, they found Russian trains still laden with grain and raw materials destined for Germany. Ironically, Hitler's tanks were running on the oil he had procured from Russia.

Yet there were disturbing auguries. Stalin had proclaimed a "patriotic war," and this was a slogan of dangerous magnetism. Moreover, his tanks and aircraft were significantly more modern and plentiful than Hitler had been told; the German General Staff's red-bound manual on the Soviet forces soon became known as the "Red Donkey." Most ominous of all was the frightening tenacity of the Soviet soldier. He was willing to die; he was brave and dogged. Frederick the Great once said, "You've got to shoot every Russian dead twice, and still turn him over to make sure." More than one German officer inspecting a bloody battlefield paid with his life for ignoring this warning. Chief of Staff Halder wrote privately on July 16, 1941: "The Russians drive their men forward into counterattacks without the least artillery support, as many as twelve waves one after another; often they are raw recruits, who just link arms and—their muskets on their backs—charge our machine guns, driven by their terror of the commissars and their superiors. Sheer weight of numbers has always been Russia's *forte,* and now the Russian command is forcing us to slay them, because stand aside they won't." But the Russian soldier was poorly led, his armored units were wrongly employed, and analogous errors were made with the Soviet artillery.

A more fundamental obstacle to the invasion was the nature of the Russian terrain, of which the "Red Donkey" had made no mention at all. Hitler had been undaunted by the sheer distances involved, since unlike Napoleon in 1812 he had the internal combustion engine and the airplane—indeed, he had tempted providence by launching "Barbarossa" on the very anniversary of Napoleon's invasion. But in the months to come Hitler was to learn that horses did have certain advantages over mechanical transport. The Russian roads dissolved into bottomless morasses when the rains came; railroads were few and far between, and only tracked vehicles remained mobile when it rained, so the gasoline for the tanks had to be hauled the immense distances from the railheads by relays of farm carts and tractors.

We shall not analyze the Russian campaign in great detail, except to point out where it bore the stamp of Hitler's own personality or of his ability to inspire faith in his subordinates. It was a gamble: he had held forty-eight divisions in reserve during "Yellow," but he was attacking Russia with only ten or fifteen in reserve. However, the extent of the gamble was concealed from all but his closest intimates. When Ribbentrop came on June 27,, Hitler laughingly exclaimed that he felt like the legendary horseman who having unwittingly ridden across the frozen Lake Constance died of horror when he learned what he had done: "If I had had the slightest inkling of this gigantic Red Army assemblage I would never have taken the decision to attack."

Perhaps it was an unconscious foreboding that caused him two days later, even as the German radio was blaring out the first seven special communiqués on "Barbarossa" victories, to think again of his own death and sign a secret constitutional instrument appointing Hermann Göring his successor.

Today Rastenburg is part of Poland, and all that remains of the Wolf's Lair are the ruins of bunkers built to defend Hitler from enemy bombing or parachute attacks that never came. Massive concrete slabs tilt at awkward angles among the trees.

"Security Zone One" was in 1941 a cluster of wooden barracks and single-story concrete blockhouses which were divided into smaller compartments. "Cold and clammy bunkers," wrote one civil servant, "in which we freeze to death at night, can't sleep for the constant rattle of the electric ventilation system and its frightful draft, and wake up every morning with a headache." The whole compound was invisible from the air, concealed by camouflage netting suspended from the treetops. A few hundred yards away, on the other side of the road leading from Rastenburg to Angerburg (General Staff HQ), Jodl's operations staff occupied a similar encampment, "Security Zone Two." When Hitler had predicted that "this whole headquarters will one day become a historic monument, because here is where we founded a New World Order," Jodl had drily replied that it would be better suited as a garrison detention center for Rastenburg. It had in fact been built in one of the marshiest places in Masuria. "No doubt some government department found the land was cheapest here," sighed Hitler. Jodl's staff diarist complained in a private letter dated June 27: "We are being plagued by the most awful mosquitoes. It would be hard to pick on a more senseless site than this— deciduous forest with marshy pools, sandy ground, and stagnant lakes, ideal for these loathsome creatures."

One of Hitler's two private secretaries wrote a closely observed account of her impressions of the Wolf's Lair on June 28. This worm's-eye view of one of the most powerful men on earth deserves quoting at length if only for the scene it sets:

This time we girls . . . are accommodated as well as the men are. The blockhouses are scattered in the woods, grouped according to the work we do. Each department is kept to itself. Our sleeping bunker, as big as a railway compartment, is very comfortable-looking, paneled with a beautiful light-colored wood; it has a concealed wash basin and a mirror, a small Siemens radio on which we can pick up clear broadcasts of very many stations, and we even have electric heaters (which are admittedly not on) and a good bright light in attractive wall lamps; there is a narrow, hard mattress filled with hay. It is a tight fit but not so tight as to be uncomfortable, and now that I have put a few pictures on the bunker wall it all makes an agreeable impression. There are communal shower rooms, but we have yet to use them as at first there was no warm water and now we like to sleep, as usual, until the very last moment. As the air-conditioning noise bothered us and the draft went right past our heads . . . we have it switched off at night with the result that . . . we walk around with leaden limbs all next day.

Despite all this it is wonderful except for an appalling plague of mosquitoes. My legs have been stung to bits and are covered with lumps. The antimosquito stuff they give us only works for a short time, unfortunately. The men are better protected by their long leather boots and thick uniforms; their only vulnerable point is the neck. Some of them go around all day with mosquito nets on. I tried it all one afternoon, but found it too much of a nuisance. Indoors it is not so bad with these little monsters. Wherever a mosquito turns up, it is hunted down. In the first few days this led to immediate problems of jurisdiction, as the Chief [Hitler] says it should be the Luftwaffe's job only. Meantime flyswatters of wire mesh have arrived and anybody not doing anything else is sent mosquito-hunting. They say the small mosquitoes are replaced by a far more unpleasant sort at the end of June, and their bites will be far more powerful. God help us!

The temperature here is a pleasant surprise. It is almost too cool indoors. . . . The forest keeps out the heat: you don't notice how much until you go out onto the street, where the heat clamps down on you.

Shortly after 10 A.M. we two go to the mess bunker, No. 1 Dining Room— a long whitewashed room sunk half-underground so that the small gauze-covered windows are very high up. On its walls are wood engravings, one of baskets, another of Henry I, etc. A table for twenty people takes up the entire length of the room; here the Chief takes his lunch and supper with his generals, his General Staff officers, adjutants, and doctors. At breakfast and afternoon coffee we two girls are also there. The Chief sits facing the maps of Russia hanging on the opposite wall, and this naturally prompts him to make repeated remarks about Soviet Russia and the dangers of bolshevism. . . . He must have suffered heavily of late, since the so-called friendship treaty was signed with Russia. Now he makes a clean breast of his apprehensions, again and again emphasizing the enormous danger bolshevism is for Europe and saying that if he had waited just one more year it would probably have been too late. . . .

We wait in this No. 1 Dining Room each morning until the Chief arrives for breakfast from the map room, where meantime he has been briefed on the war situation. Breakfast for him, I might add, is just a glass of milk and a mashed apple: somewhat modest and unpretentious. We girls for our part can't get enough to eat, and after we have eaten our own share (with its small butter portion) we switch place settings while nobody's looking so that we get two or three shares each. Meanwhile we get the Chief to tell us first what the latest war situation is.

Afterward we go at 1 P.M. to the general situation conference in the map room, where either Colonel Schmundt or Major Engel [Hitler's army adjutant] does the briefing. These briefing sessions are extremely interesting. The statistics on enemy aircraft and tanks destroyed are announced—the Russians seem to have enormous numbers, as we have already annihilated over 3,500 aircraft and over 1,000 tanks including some heavy ones, forty-tonners—and our troops' advance is shown on the maps, etc. Now we can see how strenuously the Russians are fighting, and that it would have been fought on even terms if the Russians had any logical leadership, which thank God they have not.

After all we have seen so far, you can say it is a war against wild animals. If we are amazed to have taken so few prisoners, the answer is that the Russians have been whipped up by their commissars into believing the atrocity stories they tell them about our "inhumanity," about what would happen to them if they fell into German captivity. They have been told to fight to the end and to shoot themselves if need be. And they do; for example, at Kovno this happened: our troops sent a Russian prisoner into a Russian bunker to tell the Russians there to surrender, but he seems to have been shot himself by the commissar in there for having agreed to act as intermediary at all. Then the entire bunker was blown up by its own occupants. In other words, perish rather than surrender. There is a GPU commissar attached to each unit, and the commanding officer has to bow to him. Away from their leadership, the troops are just a rabble; they are absolutely primitive, but they fight doggedly on—which is of course a danger of its own and will lead to many a hard struggle yet. The French, Belgians, and so on were intelligent and gave up the fight when they saw it was pointless, but the Russians fight on like lunatics, shivering with fear that something will happen to their families if they surrender—that's what Moscow threatens them with anyway. What is the use of having so many aircraft if they don't have any brains? In the Russian squadrons it has happened, for example, that the squadron commander flew ahead and the others followed him without knowing what the target was, they just flew behind him. If he was shot down, they couldn't even find their own way home as most of them did not even know how to read a compass. . . .

Well, back to the daily routine: after the situation conference it is time for lunch, which is in No. 2 Dining Room for us. As this is very often just a hot pot we mostly pass it up. Anyway, that's what we do when it's peas and beans. If there is nothing important to be done, we sleep a few hours after lunch so we are bright and breezy for the rest of the day, which usually drags on till the cows come home. Then, around 5 P.M., we are summoned to the Chief and plied with cakes by him. The one who grabs the most cakes gets his commendation! This coffee break most often goes on to 7 P.M., frequently even longer. Then we walk back to No. 2 Dining Room for supper. Finally we lie low in the vicinity until the Chief summons us to his study where there is a small get-together with coffee and cakes again in his more intimate circle. . . . I often feel so feckless and superfluous here. If I consider what I actually do all day, the shattering answer is: absolutely nothing. We sleep, eat, drink, and let people talk to us, if we are too lazy to talk ourselves. . . .

This morning the Chief said that if ever the German soldier deserved a laurel wreath it was for this campaign. Everything is going far far better than he hoped. There have been many strokes of good fortune, for example, that the Russians met us on the frontier and did not first lure us far into their hinterland with all the enormous transport and supply problems that would certainly have involved. And again, that they did not manage to destroy their two bridges at Dvinsk. It would have been a big waste of time if we had first had to rebuild those bridges. I believe that once we have occupied Minsk our advance will surge forward. If there are any isolated Communists left among our own ranks, they will definitely be converted when they see the "blessings" of life on the other side. . . .

By June 30 the encirclement of Minsk was completed. Army Group Center destroyed 20 Soviet divisions here, capturing 290,000 prisoners, 25,000 tanks, and 1,400 guns. A captured Russian corps commander confirmed that there were no Red Army forces of any importance east of the Dvina and Dnieper rivers. Halder reflected the optimism at General Staff headquarters when he boasted in his diary on July 3:."It's probably not overstating the case if I maintain that the campaign in Russia has been won in two weeks. Of course that doesn't mean it's *over.*" In a letter on June 29, Jodl's war diarist Helmuth Greiner showed that the OKW agreed the campaign was going far better than expected. "With the capture of Dvinsk and Minsk we have covered in one week one third of the way to Leningrad and Moscow; at this rate we would be in both cities in another fourteen days— but we can assume it'll be even sooner."

Hitler shared this view. Staring at the wall map in his dining room, he proclaimed within his secretaries' earshot, "In a few weeks we'll be in Moscow. Then I'll raze it to the ground and build a reservoir there. The name Moscow must be expunged." Ribbentrop addressed his senior diplomats in similar terms a few days later. "In six or eight weeks the Russian campaign will be over. The war against Britain may go on for another six months or for ten years." At about the same time Hitler assured Ambassador von der Schulenburg, who had been repatriated from Moscow: "By August 15 we shall be in Moscow. By October 1 the Russian war will be over."

Hitler had every reason to scent victory throughout July 1941. On July 2 he was shown a decoded Turkish report quoting both Stalin and Marshal Timoshenko as privately conceding to foreign diplomats that they had already written off Leningrad, Minsk, Kiev, and even Moscow, but that they had taken this into account in their calculations. A decoded morale report from the American embassy in Moscow described air raid precautions there and anxiously noted the food situation and rumors that the Russians were already evacuating their gold reserves to safety. Over lunch with Ribbentrop on July 4, Hitler was already enlarging on his plans for colonizing Russia, as Hewel's diary shows, and contrasting the pure nihilism of the Bolshevik revolution with the basic orderliness of the Fascist revolution. "Where there is no compulsion man will always revert to a rabbitlike existence," he explained. "The Russian peasant doesn't work willingly. This is why the Communist slogans failed, and they had to resort to the collective system—with commissars instead of landowners. It's all the same thing. Slavs can't organize, they can only *be* organized. They need to be in bondage."

The next day, July 5, 1941, with the Russian campaign seemingly drawing to an end, Hitler explained to the same select lunchtime audience why he had attacked Russia without a formal declaration of war or even the pretext of an "incident." "Nobody is ever asked about his motives at the bar of history. Why did Alexander invade India? Why did the Romans fight their Punic wars, or Frederick II his second Silesian campaign? In history it is success alone that counts." He, Hitler, was answerable only to his people. "To sacrifice hundreds of thousands [of troops] just because of the theoretical responsibility-issue [for starting the war] would be criminal. I will go down in history as the destroyer of bolshevism, regardless of whether there was a frontier incident or not. Only the result is judged. If I lose, I will not be able to talk my way out with questions of form. Look at Norway—we would never have succeeded if I had announced my intention first, yet it was vital for the fate of Germany. And vice versa: if Churchill and Reynaud had kept a still tongue in their heads I would probably not have tackled Norway."

Hitler calculated that he would capture Smolensk in mid-July but that it would take until August to assemble his infantry for an attack on Moscow, so meanwhile his tank formations could "mop up" in the north. He was noticeably uncertain about how high to rank Moscow itself on his list of objectives; to him it was just a place-name, he said, while Leningrad was the very citadel of bolshevism, the city from which that evil creed had first sprung in 1917. Strategically he was right to emphasize that victory would hinge not on the capture of Moscow but on the destruction of Soviet military strength; but the General Staff disagreed with him noisily, and this problem, of how best to employ his tanks after the Dnieper and Dvina rivers had been crossed, continued to beset him throughout July. "I constantly try to put myself in the enemy's shoes," he told his generals on July 4. "They have virtually lost the war already. It is good that we wiped out the Russian tank and air forces right at the start. The Russians cannot replace them now." But should he retain his own tank forces for the assault on Moscow or divert them to help Field Marshal Leeb's drive toward Leningrad? "It will be the toughest decision of the whole campaign," Hitler admitted to his staff.

By this time the coalition was complete: Slovakia had declared war on June 23; Hungary and Finland had decorously waited a few more days, until Russian aircraft attacked them, then they too declared war. The Vichy government broke off diplomatic relations with the USSR, and thousands of Frenchmen responded to the call for volunteers to fight bolshevism: 150 airmen volunteered, among them 20 of France's foremost bomber pilots. From Denmark, Norway, Spain, France, Belgium, and Croatia came word of legions being formed to fight in Russia. Hitler directed that those from "Germanic" countries were to be organized by the SS, while the Wehrmacht would attend to the rest. All must swear allegiance to him. Sweden and Switzerland remained the exceptions— "Nations on Furlough," as Hitler contemptuously called them. As he had predicted, the battle against bolshevism was proving a rallying point for all Europe. On July 10, Hewel observed of Hitler: "He predicted it. 'I was forced into this fight step by step, but Germany will emerge from it as the greatest national Power on earth.' He believes that Churchill will topple all at once, quite suddenly. Then in Britain an immense anti-Americanism will arise, and Britain will be the first country to join the ranks of Europe in the fight against America." And Hewel added jubilantly: "He is infinitely confident of victory. The tasks confronting him today are as nothing, he says, compared with those in the years of struggle; particularly since ours is the biggest and finest army in the world."

The Vatican also let it be known that it "welcomed the war" with Russia. That Churchill had broadcast his immediate offer of aid to Russia on the first day of "Barbarossa" did not surprise Hitler. (In private he mocked the strange spectacle of "Churchill, Stalin, and Roosevelt as fighters for freedom!") But that the exiled Dutch queen should broadcast over the BBC her deepest sympathy for the Russian people conveniently revolted him, and he instructed that the Dutch royal family's remaining wealth in Holland was to be confiscated forthwith. Meanwhile, a Dutch East Company was founded in Holland to organize the provision of food for the Netherlands from the Ukraine and to negotiate contracts for Dutch specialists and workers to emigrate to the east. Japan alone shunned what Hitler regarded as her obligations to the Axis: Hitler believed that with "Barbarossa" proving such a crushing success, Axis interests would now best be served by Japan attacking the Soviet Union. He preferred land contact between the Japanese and German armies along the Trans-Siberian railway to an attack on Singapore. The Japanese were forcefully reminded that their foreign minister had himself declaimed in Berlin that no Japanese statesman could uphold Japanese neutrality if Germany became involved in war with Russia. But Japan viewed Hitler's immediate prospects soberly. On July 2, Weizsäcker commented, in his diary: "The Japanese are still playing us along. All we know is that they don't want to attack Singapore as yet. If and when they will help against Russia remains to be seen."

When early victory had seemed certain, Hitler's mind turned to future campaigns. On July 8, 1941, he instructed Brauchitsch not to send any new tanks to the eastern front; the panzer divisions there were to be reduced in number, and idle tank crews were to be sent back to Germany to train fresh tank divisions. On the thirteenth, he confirmed this in an OKW order: in addition to the twenty existing panzer divisions, the army was to establish sixteen more by May 1, 1942—twelve for the east and twenty-four—a whole panzer army—for other tasks. The next day Hitler ruled that after the Soviet Union's defeat, the army would be cut back (apart from these panzer divisions) and naval construction would be limited to requirements for the war with Britain and the United States. The Luftwaffe, however, was to be expanded on a colossal scale, and its factories were to be working at full blast by the spring of 1942. Of his real future aims at this time we are only meagerly informed. Hitler seems to have envisaged a future war—perhaps not in his lifetime—between the New World and the Old. Later in July, gossiping one night about the Englishman's innate sense of authority, he remarked, "I'm sure the end of this war's going to mark the start of a lasting friendship with Britain. But if we're to live in peace with her, we shall have to give her a knockout blow first—the British expect that from anybody, if they are to respect him properly."

Yet there were disturbing facets to that summer of 1941. Stalin had obviously laid immense plans for an offensive into Europe. The Red Army was far stronger than Hitler's experts had believed. Its air force had some eight thousand aircraft, and Soviet industry was turning out tanks at a rate which Hitler would have dismissed as impossible—had his Intelligence agencies so advised him. On July 15, Jeschonnek's deputy, touring the conquered territories, wrote in his diary: "The Red Army's equipment staggers us again and again. . . . They had laid out enormous fortifications, mostly still incomplete, to guard their Lemberg [Lvov] salient. In this region, sixty-three huge airfields alone, each with two runways and all still incomplete, bear witness to the Russian attack preparations." The next day Stalin's son Jacob, a lieutenant in a Soviet tank division, was captured near Vitebsk. Among "other proof that the Russians were just waiting to get at the Germans" was, according to the Luftwaffe's General von Richthofen, the huge booty of artillery and tanks taken at Dobromysl. "In part they come from the young Stalin's tank division. He has admitted that they were standing by for the big offensive and were smashed to pieces by my squadrons' surprise attack." Hitler learned that on Jacob Stalin there had been found a letter from a friend mentioning that before their "outing to Berlin" he was going to see his Anushka one more time. Interrogation of Stalin junior and the dictator's captured former secretary revealed that Stalin planned to exploit the German intelligentsia to improve the Russian population's caliber; Europe and Asia would then become the invincible bastions of bolshevism, and the victory of the Communist world revolution would be assured.

As a self-professed weapons expert, Hitler was particularly awed by the new Soviet armored fighting vehicles that crawled out of the forests like primeval monsters of whose existence his experts had breathed no word to him: here was a tank of fifty-two tons, its armorplate so thick that only the Luftwaffe's 88-millimeter antiaircraft guns made any impression on it; and here, south of Dubno, were tanks weighing a hundred tons. On July 4, OKW war diarist Greiner—who again stated that in fourteen days they would be in Leningrad and Moscow—confidently asserted: "The Russians have lost so many aircraft and four thousand six hundred tanks that there can't be many left." But by mid-July Hitler's weary gunners had knocked out eight thousand Russian tanks and still they came. At the end of July *twelve thousand* tanks had been captured or destroyed.[1] Visiting Army Group Center on August 4, Hitler wanly admitted to his panzer commander General Guderian: "Had I known they had as many tanks as that, I'd have thought twice before invading."

The complete failure of his Intelligence agencies rattled Hitler. An Abwehr colonel apprehensively recorded on July 20: "C[anaris] has just returned from the Führer's headquarters and describes the mood there as very jittery, as it is increasingly evident that the Russian campaign is not 'going by the book.' The signs are multiplying that this war will not bring about the expected internal collapse, so much as the invigoration of bolshevism.—C. warns in particular that attempts are being made to brand the Abwehr as the culprits, for not properly informing people about the true strength and fighting power of the Russian army. For example the Führer is said to have remarked that had he known of the existence of the super-heavy Russian tanks he would not have waged this war." Greiner speculated the next day: "What matters is how much material and manpower they can salvage from these debacles. . . . Nobody discussed this at lunch with the Führer yesterday. At first he was very taciturn, and just brooded away, so I took the opportunity to stuff my belly with the best of everything. Then he came to life and delivered a monologue of an hour or more on our brave and gallant Italian allies and the worries they are causing him. . . . You can't help being astonished at his brilliant judgment and clear insights. He looks in the best of health and seems well although he seldom gets to bed before 5 or 6 A.M."

For the ordinary German soldier, the eastern front already had something of a nightmare quality. To this nightmare, Stalin also added the specter of long-prepared partisan warfare.

On July 3, Hitler had been brought the radio monitoring service's transcript of Stalin's first public broadcast since "Barbarossa" began. Effective and cunning —though Stalin had never been much of a rhetorician—it echoed the May 5 secret speech to the generals of which Hitler was to learn shortly. Stalin asked his radio audience: "Are the German Fascist troops really invincible, as their loud-mouthed Fascist propaganda chiefs trumpet to the world? Of course they are not!" He referred to Hitler and Ribbentrop as monsters and cannibals, and

---

[1]General von Waldau, Jeschonnek's deputy, noted that by July 30 the Germans had taken:
   Army Group South: 162,680 prisoners 4,574 tanks 2,894 guns
   Army Group Center: 580,910 prisoners 5,571 tanks 4,300 guns
   Army Group North: 56,320 prisoners 1,880 tanks 1,200 guns

claimed that Hitler's ambition was to restore the landowners to power, to bring back the czars, and to destroy the national cultures of the independent constituent republics of the Soviet Union. "He will Germanize them and turn them into the slaves of German princes and barons." He appealed to patriotic Russians everywhere to destroy everything of value in the path of the advancing Wehrmacht—railway rolling stock, crops, fuel, and raw materials. They were to form partisan units behind German lines, to blow up roads and bridges, burn down forests, destroy arms dumps and convoys, and remorselessly hunt down and wipe out the enemy and his accomplices. "This war with Fascist Germany must not be regarded as an ordinary war."

Hitler piously noted: "Thanks to Stalin's slogan that everything is to be destroyed, millions must now starve." The partisan war provided the SS task forces with a fresh rationale for their mass-extermination drives, in which Russian Jews increasingly came to be regarded as "partisan material" and hence ripe for prophylactic massacre. The identification of Jews with partisans was so fixed in Hitler's pathological mind that on July 10 we find him telephoning Brauchitsch about the pointlessness of committing panzer divisions to the assault on Kiev: 35 percent of the city's population were Jews, so the bridges across the Dnieper would not be found intact. Another factor now also weighed with Hitler: should the Red workers rise in response to Stalin's appeal, the vast, sprawling conurbations of Leningrad and Moscow would become deathtraps if Hitler's precious tanks entered them.

Thus he eventually decided that Moscow and Leningrad were to be destroyed, but not necessarily occupied. This destruction he would achieve with the bomber aircraft and by mass starvation. Two days after Stalin's radio speech Hitler told his private staff that Moscow would "disappear from the earth's surface" as soon as its riches were safely in German hands. Unlike his General Staff, who regarded the capital as a strategic target, Hitler saw it only as the seat of bolshevism; on July 8 he told Brauchitsch and Halder that its devastation was necessary to drive out its population, whom they would otherwise have to feed in the coming winter. He ordered the Luftwaffe to disrupt Moscow with a terror raid—ostensibly in reprisal for the attacks on Finnish and Romanian cities—hoping for the kind of national catastrophe that the overcentralization of government in Moscow seemed to invite. "If an earthquake destroyed Moscow today," he explained to the Japanese ambassador, "the whole of Russia would perish." On July 21 and 22 the Luftwaffe raided Moscow, against Jeschonnek's better instincts; but the intercepted dispatches from the city showed that the results were far short of Hitler's expectations.

Emotionally Hitler was far more attracted to the destruction of Leningrad. On July 16, Bormann noted: "The Leningrad area is being claimed by the Finns. The Führer wants to raze Leningrad to the ground—then he'll give it to the Finns."

Its capture had been confidently expected by mid-July, but even as the evacuation of the last awkward terrain of marsh and forest west of the city was in progress, a new Russian general took command and ordered the troops not to retreat one more step. Henceforth the Russians clung grimly on with a success that was not without effect on Hitler. It was now that Hitler began seriously to consider detaching General Hermann Hoth's tanks from the army group advancing on Moscow to help Leeb's Army Group North encircle Leningrad; he would then also divert Guderian's panzer group from the Moscow front to Army Group South. This would leave only infantry armies for the final assault on Moscow. On July 21, he visited Leeb's headquarters. The army group's war diary records: "The Führer emphasized that he expects a bitter enemy defense south of Leningrad, as Russia's leaders fully realize that Leningrad has been held up to the nation as a showpiece of the revolution these last twenty-four years, and that given the Slav mentality, which has already suffered from the fighting so far, the loss of Leningrad might result in a complete collapse." As to the fact that this concentration on Leningrad would leave only infantry armies for the assault on Moscow. "The Führer is not concerned by this, since to him Moscow is only a geographical objective."

It was a difficult decision, and flatly condemned by the General Staff. Halder —plagued like Hitler by the mosquitoes and torrid climate—had already noted in his diary on July 14: "The Führer's constant interference is becoming a regular nuisance." Now the general wrote an irritable private letter on July 28. "He's playing warlord again and bothering us with such absurd ideas that he's risking everything our wonderful operations so far have won. Unlike the French, the Russians won't just run away when they've been tactically defeated; they have to be slain one at a time in a terrain that's half forest and marsh; all this takes time and his nerves won't stand it. Every other day now I have to go over to him. Hours of gibberish and the outcome is there's only one man who understands how to wage wars. . . . If I didn't have my faith in God and my own inner buoyancy, I'd go under like Brauchitsch, who's at the end of his tether and hides behind an iron mask of manliness so as not to betray his complete helplessness."

Out of the "preventive war" an old-style war of colonial conquest had emerged. Raw materials such as oil, chrome, and manganese would soon be his in the measure that the Russians were deprived of them. He would construct an oil pipeline from the Caucasus oil fields to Germany. On July 14, Hitler told one visitor to the Wolf's Lair: "We shall not lose our heads as we press onward; we will not advance beyond what we can really hold on to." But there seemed no limit to his territorial ambitions. Germany's domains would extend to the Urals and two hundred miles beyond. The Crimea would become the Riviera of the Reich, settled exclusively by Germans and linked to the fatherland by a broad autobahn. He was overheard to remark: "I entered this war a nationalist, but I shall come out of it an imperialist." It was a role he thoroughly enjoyed. In the relaxed company of his private secretary, walking in the pitch darkness one night among the blockhouses he made a bantering remark that again illustrated this. She had left her flashlight on his desk and kept stumbling in the darkness. An orderly sent to fetch the flashlight reported it missing. In mock-righteous tones that mimicked a Swabian businessman's thick accent Hitler assured her: "Look, I poach other people's countries—I don't pinch their flashlights!" And he added with the loud belly-laugh of which he was still capable in spite of the death and destruction he had loosed: "And that's just as well, because it is the small fry that get strung up. The big fish get away with it."

At a five-hour conference with his chief minions—Rosenberg, Lammers, Keitel, Göring, and Bormann—on July 16, Hitler hammered home the point that Germany alone was entitled to benefit from defeating the Soviet Union. As for their secret aims, while they must be concealed from the world at large the German leaders must themselves be in no doubt: just as she had in Norway, Denmark, Holland, and Belgium—where Germany had already staked her territorial claims in secret, whatever she might publicly profess for tactical reasons—so too in Russia must Germany adopt the pose of a protector. "But let there be no doubt in *our* minds that we shall never depart from these territories." The Crimea and Galicia in particular must be annexed. As for the rest, this "giant cake" must be so cut that Germany could dominate it, rule it, and exploit it properly. "Never again must there be any military power west of the Urals, even if we have to fight a hundred years' war to prevent it." Germans alone must be permitted to bear arms—this was why Hitler would not allow the Slavs, or Czechs, or Cossacks, or Ukrainians to join in his crusade. Since the Ukraine would be most vital as Germany's granary for the next three years, Hitler wanted Gauleiter Erich Koch appointed Reich Commissar—a tough, cruel viceroy who had shown his mettle in the economic management of East Prussia. Gauleiter Hinrich Lohse would rule the Baltic countries, with Siegfried Kasche in Moscow, Alfred Frauenfeld in the Crimea, Josef Terboven in the Kola peninsula, and Schickedanz in the Caucasus.

In Russia—the "future German empire" as he was to describe it some days later—he would encourage neither schools nor religion, a position on which he met the opposition of Alfred Rosenberg and the strongly Catholic Franz von Papen. Papen had sent him a long study urging that now was the right moment to reintroduce Christianity into Russia; Hitler would not hear of it. Wisecracking in his usual way in private, he noted that he might eventually consider letting *all* the Christian sects in "so they can beat each other's brains out with their crucifixes." In this new German empire, soldiers with twelve years of service would automatically inherit a farmstead fully equipped with cattle and machinery. During the last two years of their military service these peasant-soldiers would be trained on similar farmsteads. He asked only that some of this new peasant breed should marry girls from the countryside. They were to retain their weapons, including machine guns, so that they could answer any fresh call to arms against the Asiatic hordes. The NCOs—particularly those of the Luftwaffe and mechanized divisions—were to manage the gasoline stations along the big autobahns. Given a future standing army of 1,500,000 men, about 30,000 would be discharged each year. This soldier-peasant would above all make a far better teacher than the university-trained elementary school teacher, who would always be dissatisfied: not that Hitler planned to educate the Russian masses. "It is in our interest that the people know just enough to recognize the signs on the road," he said.

On July 17, Hitler signed the formal decrees putting these plans into effect. Parallel to Ribbentrop's jealous foreign ministry he set up an East Ministry under Alfred Rosenberg to handle the occupied territories; to complete the parallel he allowed Rosenberg to appoint a liaison officer, Dr. Werner Koeppen, to the Führer's headquarters as a counterpart to Walther Hewel. Heinrich Himmler and Hermann Göring were given sweeping powers to police and exploit these new domains. On July 31, Göring—as head of the Four-Year Plan set up in 1936 to make Germany self-sufficient—signed a document empowering Reinhard Heydrich as chief of the security police to "make all necessary preparations as regards organization and actual concrete preparations for an overall unraveling of the Jewish problem within Germany's sphere of influence in Europe." This amplified his January 1939 order to Heydrich to enforce Jewish emigration from Germany itself.

In some regions, particularly the Baltic countries, the "Jewish problem" had already solved itself since 1939. According to German reports, two days after the Soviet invasion of Lithuania in 1940 all the local businessmen had been ordered into the streets at 7 A.M. "to clean them"; the Russians had then mown them down with machine guns while commissars reported to be Jewish had taken over their businesses for the state. It was this story which at the onset of "Barbarossa" touched off such primitive and bloody pogroms in Latvia and Lithuania that Himmler's task forces complained that only a few hundred Jews remained for them to deal with when they arrived. Leeb's army group brought these massacres by Lithuanian "irregulars" to the attention of Hitler's headquarters on July 5; Colonel Schmundt replied that German soldiers were not to interfere with "these political questions"; it was part of "a necessary mopping-up operation" *(Flurbereinigung).*

The spirit inspiring Hitler in his war against the European Jews is clear from the entry in Hewel's diary on July 10:

> . . . Stayed up until 3 A.M. with the Führer in his bunker. Very hot and very exhausting, interesting though the conversation was.
> He says, "I feel like the Robert Koch of politics. It was he who discovered the bacillus, thereby opening up new paths for medical science to explore. And it is I who have discovered the Jews as the bacillus and ferment that causes all decay in society. And what I have proved is this—that nations can survive without Jews; that the economy, culture, art, and so on can exist without Jews and in fact better. That is the cruelest blow I have dealt the Jews."

He reverted to this imagery of the Jewish bacillus a few days later when explaining to the Croatian defense minister why every single Jew must be evicted from European soil. "Because if just one country, whatever the reason, tolerates one Jewish family in its midst, then this will become the seat of a fresh bacillus infection. Once there are no more Jews in Europe the unity of the European nations can no longer be disrupted. It is unimportant where the Jews are sent—whether to Siberia or to Madagascar." He planned, he said, to approach each country with this demand. The last country in which the Jews would hold out would inevitably be Hungary; the remaining European nations must then send her a joint inter-European summons, calling on her to bend to the "iron will" of Europe. At this stage Hitler spoke of habitual criminals who were to be liquidated since "if upright, valuable human beings are risking their lives at the front, it is a crime to preserve these villains," but he did not yet specifically mention Jews in this category. When he next employed this argument, early in 1943, Jews and incorrigible criminal elements were lumped into a single category.

Hitler's part in the unfolding Jewish tragedy cannot be usefully analyzed *in vacuo*. Jews and Bolshevik leadership were pathologically identified in his mind. Given this obsession it was an easy progression to draw the same conclusion about leadership in the United States. In 1939 Hitler had once confided to a bemused General Friedrich von Boetticher, the German military attaché in Washington, that he possessed documents proving Roosevelt's Jewish ancestry and that one day he would release them to an astounded world. In August 1941 in conversation with a Spanish diplomat he reverted to this theme. "The arch culprit for this war is Roosevelt, with his freemasons, Jews, and general Jewish-bolshevism." Three months later he told the Finnish foreign minister, "Be clear about one point: the whole of World Jewry is on the side of the Bolsheviks."

It was to these unidentified Jewish-Bolshevik influences that Hitler ascribed Roosevelt's attempts to provoke a shooting war with Germany in a way that would justify his declaration of war before a reluctant Congress. American troops relieved British forces that had preemptively occupied Iceland in May 1940, thus bringing the United States into the German war zone for the first time. Hans Thomsen, the German chargé d'affaires, telegraphed from Washington that Roosevelt, in conversation with Wendell Willkie, had four times reiterated his firm determination to get into the war as soon as possible. But Hitler was equally determined to avoid war with the United States at this time. On July 13 the diplomat Etzdorf quoted Hitler as saying, "So long as our eastern operations are still running, we won't let ourselves be provoked. Later the Americans can have their war, if they absolutely must." Admiral Raeder begged him to regard the Iceland occupation as sufficient cause, as a *de facto* declaration of war on Germany. Again the diplomat quoted Hitler as refusing; he would do his utmost to prevent Roosevelt from entering the war for one or two more months because the Luftwaffe was still committed to the Russian campaign. Besides, as Raeder informed the naval staff: "The Führer still presumes that a victorious Russian campaign will affect the posture of the United States." Keitel, Raeder, the admirals, and even the army generals writhed under the rigid prohibitions Hitler now imposed. He forbade even the mining of Icelandic harbors. Field Marshal von Bock snorted in his diary on July 25: "Keitel says it isn't easy to take the American occupation of Iceland lying down, and that we've had to restrict our U-boats to attacking only ships definitely identified as enemy so as not to hand the Americans the *casus belli* they are seeking. . . . We did the same thing in World War I, and I fear that—just as happened then—the Americans will find another cause."

Evidence supporting Raeder's point of view kept coming in. It was reported that the American navy had been ordered to fire without warning or provocation on *any* German warship; if the Germans survived long enough to relate this illegal act, the American commander concerned was instructed to deny responsibility and to suggest that a British unit was involved. Thus Roosevelt hoped to provoke countermeasures. The "neutral" United States had meanwhile furnished the British admiralty with sets of her secret codes. All these facts Hitler learned from intercepted U.S. naval code signals. In a speech to his staff on July 17, Ribbentrop said, "If the United States continue to provoke us after Russia's defeat, later they can have their war. We are not fearful of a common front between Britain and the United States."

Three days later Canaris reported: "A certain disenchantment is to be discerned in the Reich foreign minister von R[ibbentrop]. Thus he himself now accepts America's entry into the war as imminent, and for the first time he spoke disparagingly of the 'journalistic' reporting of Thomsen and Boetticher." Ribbentrop's stock with Hitler was currently at its lowest. "The Führer again curses the foreign ministry: 'sluts,' etc.," wrote Hewel. And a few weeks later

Hewel quoted Hitler as telling him, "I could not stick working three weeks under your boss!" Hitler, whose lanky SS adjutant Hansgeorg Schulze had just been killed on the Russian front, had recruited his brother, Richard, to replace him; Richard Schulze had formerly been adjutant to Ribbentrop and he and Hewel had often been encouraged by Hitler to make fun of their boss, the foreign minister. "In the evening Schulze and I told funny stories about *kepala orang,*"[2] Hewel wrote circumspectly in his diary. "The Führer laughed a lot, then was lost in thought."

It was no joke to Ribbentrop, however. Ever jealous of his rights, on June 9 Ribbentrop had asked Hitler to transfer the Party's foreign organization (AO, Auslands-Organisation) to his ministry, but Hitler had refused. In July, the question as to whether Rosenberg or Ribbentrop should conduct propaganda in Russia—for example, over the capture of Stalin's son Jacob and on Russian atrocities—caused a further row; Hitler characteristically decided to allow *both* ministers a free hand. Rosenberg's new ministry, set up in mid-July to handle all of Russia and the Baltic countries, was to the foreign minister like a red rag to a bull.

On the twenty-eighth Ribbentrop picked a violent quarrel with Hitler, challenging his very decision to attack Russia. It was a stiflingly hot summer day. Hitler was so enraged that he feigned a stroke, collapsed into a chair, and gasped at the petrified Ribbentrop that he must never challenge his decisions again. Ribbentrop gave his word. He appears to have suffered the more permanent damage himself, for from that date developed the splitting hemicranial headaches and occasional functional paralysis of the right arm and leg that plagued him until his execution five years later. At this point, Ribbentrop came as near as he ever did to being replaced as minister. By whom? Perhaps by Goebbels, who had schemed patiently for the day when he could supplant him. But Hitler charged Lammers to inform the foreign minister that in time of war the diplomatic service must stand aside, until the guns had finished speaking. Perhaps it was a wider dissatisfaction with the trend of events—he even suspected that the Japanese had made a secret deal with Roosevelt giving him a free hand in Europe—that motivated Hitler's aversion to the foreign ministry.

Adolf Hitler's own health was poor, for the first time in five years. The influence of this on military events in the summer of 1941 cannot be ignored.

---

[2]Malayan: "head man." Hewel had spent twelve years of his youth in the Dutch East Indies and entered his more private thoughts in his diary in this tongue.

After the conclusion of the French campaign a year earlier, he had complained of breathing difficulties and he had been X-rayed in Munich; Dr. Morell had feared pleurisy. The stress of the Russian campaign, coupled with the hot, malarial climate in which the Wolf's Lair had been sited, told severely on the dictator. Worse, the brackish waters of Masuria had infected him with dysentery, and for fourteen days until mid-August he was afflicted by diarrhea, stomach pains, nausea, aching limbs, shivery feelings, and high temperatures. As the crucial strategic controversy developed in these weeks between Hitler and his generals, his ability to overrule them was impaired by his own physical weakness; his own grand strategy, which was to set up a vast encircling movement by Army Groups North and South, enveloping Moscow from the rear, was opposed and circumvented by Brauchitsch and his staff, who favored a direct assault on Moscow by Field Marshal von Bock's Army Group Center. Brauchitsch stayed in Berlin and ignored Hitler's orders; Hitler was confined by circumstances to his field headquarters. When the army Commander in Chief did pay a rare visit to the Wolf's Lair, Hitler vainly warned that the way things were going the fronts would inevitably become static, as they had in World War I. Halder certainly recognized that Hitler was too ill to oppose the army. "Despite his medical indisposition," the general wrote on August 8, "the Führer has given the Commander in Chief the closest instructions on how he wants the air force squadrons used. . . ."

Hitler was still very weak when Goebbels visited him on August 18. "Unhappily, he looks somewhat strained and sickly," the propaganda minister wrote. "This is probably a result of his dysentery, and perhaps also of the drain on his strength of these last few weeks." Only later was Hitler's military plan recognized to have offered the better prospects, for Bock's armies were still outside Moscow when winter set in. "Today I still believe," Göring was to tell his captors, "that had Hitler's original plan of genius not been diluted like that, the eastern campaign would have been decided by early 1942 at the latest."

The illness in mid-1941 cost Hitler more than Moscow, however. On August 14, Dr. Morell performed an electrocardiogram study of Hitler's heart. The graphs were sent to a leading authority on heart conditions, Professor Karl Weber, director of the heart institute at Bad Nauheim; Weber was instructed only that the traces were of a "very busy diplomat." From them Weber diagnosed beyond a doubt that "Patient A." was suffering from a virtually incurable heart disease: rapidly progressive coronary sclerosis. In a man of Hitler's age it was not abnormal, but from now on there would always be the danger of angina pectoris —a violent paroxysm of pain behind the chest bone—or of an embolism—the sudden plugging of a blood vessel, with possibly fatal consequences. There is no evidence that Hitler was told of this heart diagnosis, but his subsequent references to having only two or three more years to live may have been an allusion to this.

More likely Morell kept the truth from him, for in the Führer's presence he later insisted that Hitler's heart and other organs were working well. In private, however, Morell began to study textbooks on the heart, and additional medicines were added to Hitler's overflowing cabinet. For repeated periods of two to three weeks Morell took to injecting 0.02 milligrams of a heart tonic, Strophantin, into Hitler's veins; and this he alternated with Prostrophanta, which contained the same ingredients but also glucose and vitamin B complex (nicotinic acid). To overcome the insufficiency of Hitler's circulatory system, Morell was also occasionally administering Cardiazol and Coramin internally to Hitler during the rest of 1941. In the following spring, Morell added to this growing list yet another medicine: Sympathol. A solution about one-hundredth as effective as adrenalin, it was meant to regulate Hitler's heart activity and overcome his heart-vessel insufficiency.

Throughout the coming winter Morell was a daily visitor to the Wolf's Lair. Hitler passively accepted his portly physician's explanations for the growing volume of medication being injected into his veins. "Morell told me my energy consumption is as high as in the tropics, because of my uninterrupted intensive work," Hitler repeated to another doctor. And, "Morell is still researching and his works are still expanding." Yet Morell's "Patient A." was not a medical ignoramus; he was better informed than most laymen. "He knew the connection between blood coagulation and thrombosis, the effect of nicotine on the heart muscles, and the possible relationship between the teeth and an inflammation of the maxillary sinus," commented a doctor who had long conversations with Hitler.

"Long conversations" is perhaps a misnomer. Hitler's conversations were monologues, delivered in a rich Austrian dialect to a handful of cronies assembled in his bunker, or over lunch or dinner at the long oblong table with Jodl at his left, an outside guest like Speer or Goebbels at his right, and his headquarters staff —the liaison officers, the younger adjutants, and secretaries—at their alloted places. Hitler would talk about the Party and Christianity. "We must not try to combat religion, but let it wither away!"

One of Hitler's devoted secretaries wrote in mid-July 1941:

In our evening discussions with the Chief the Church plays a big part. . . . It is all so convincing, what the Chief says, when for example he explains how Christianity by its mendacity and hypocrisy has set back mankind in its development, culturally speaking, by two thousand years. I really must start writing down what the Chief says. It's just that these sessions go on for ages and afterward you are just too limp and lifeless to write anything.

The night before last, when we left the Chief's bunker, it was already light. We did not turn in even then, as ordinary people would have, but made for the kitchen, ate a few cakes, and then strolled for two hours toward the rising sun, past farmyards and paddocks, past hillocks glowing with red and white clover in the morning sun, a fairyland on which you just could not feast your eyes enough; and then back to bed. We are incapable of getting up before 2 or 3 P.M. A crazy life . . . A strange calling like ours will probably never be seen again: we eat, we drink, we sleep, now and then we type a bit, and meantime keep him company for hours on end. Recently we did make ourselves a bit useful—we picked some flowers, so that his bunker does not look too bare.

Kiev

In his New Year proclamation Hitler had promised the German people the war would be over by the end of 1941. By mid-August he knew this promise would not be fulfilled. Indeed, by the end of the year none of even his interim objectives —Leningrad, Moscow, or Rostov—had been captured because the invading armies—caught between the doctrines of the General Staff and the intuition of the Führer—were halted by the onset of winter.

The General Staff argued that the enemy's military strength must always be destroyed first; in August 1941 this was the Red Army mass assembled by Marshal Timoshenko in front of Moscow. Field Marshal von Bock's Army Group Center must therefore advance on Moscow; the other two army group operations in the north and the south were seen as strictly subsidiary. Bock, a tall, bony, upright Prussian professional, agreed. But when Hitler visited him on the fourth, as the battle for Smolensk was drawing to its end and another three hundred thousand Russian captives were already being marched westward, it was clear that the Führer had not yet made up his mind on how to fight the next phase of the campaign. For one thing, Hitler was still intoxicated by Bock's "historic triumphs," and his mind was on the New Order he planned for the east. "Now we will put things in order here for a thousand years," he had exclaimed on leaving his headquarters early that morning. For another, what precisely *was* Russia's "military strength"? Halder himself would wanly admit that everybody had underestimated the Soviet colossus. "When we attacked, we assumed there were 200 enemy divisions. To date we have already counted 360. . . . And if we destroy a dozen of these, the Russians throw another dozen in."

Clearly the enemy's military strength was not the finite quantity it had been in "White" and "Yellow." Russia's manpower reserves were virtually limitless. Halder felt that the answer was to attack Soviet industrial conurbations like Moscow. To Hitler the more immediate and final solution lay farther afield—in Russia's raw material centers, the sources of her food, her iron ore, coal, and oil, and particularly the Donets region beyond Kharkov: "That is the entire base of the Soviet economy." To a visiting diplomat he explained, "Soon we will occupy the richest Russian economic regions, bearing 61 percent of their iron and 35 percent of their molybdenum; and when we cut off their oil supplies from the south the fate of bolshevism will be sealed."

By August 6, visiting Rundstedt and General Antonescu at Army Group South headquarters in the dreary Ukrainian town of Berdichev,[1] Hitler's mind was all but made up. He would make his main push southeastward toward the oil fields, while the northern advance on Leningrad from the Luga bridgeheads began. Moscow would be left for last. Meteorologists had assured him the dry weather would remain longer in the center than the south anyway. Yet even so no firm directive was issued.

At the Wolf's Lair Hitler began holding war conferences each morning and evening. These were to become nightmares for their regular participants—theatrical performances dominated by the insistent monologues of the Führer, rambling discourses on generalities intermingled with sudden snap decisions intervening in even the lowest echelons of the army's command. The conferences lasted for hours on end, sapping the energy of his generals, who were grimly aware that they had more urgent business elsewhere. It was not a pleasant atmosphere. Individual generals hesitated to speak their minds in front of such a large and compliant audience. Of Hitler's regular staff only his army adjutant, Major Engel, had a ready wit and biting tongue; the other adjutants were more diplomatic in their approach. As for his commanders, they found out that in private Hitler could be frankly spoken to; but there were few—among them Rundstedt, Reichenau, Guderian, Manstein, and later Milch, Zeitzler, and Ferdinand Schörner—who had the requisite courage.

Life within Security Zone One revolved around Hitler; when he was away visiting the frontline headquarters, it was as though the dynamo had been wrenched bodily out of the powerhouse. Favored indeed were those with special passes to the compound. To these officers and Party officials it seemed an almost unforgivable act on Hitler's part to have brought his female staff with him to this sacred half-acre; Hitler, however, guarded his ladies with an almost comic jealousy, snapping at the young Walther Hewel for getting Gerda Daranowski, Hitler's attractive secretary, to do some typing for him instead of employing a clerk of his own. One of the secretaries wrote:

> It's a thorn in some people's side that even in wartime the Chief has his personal staff around him, and particularly of course that we two females are included.

---

[1] Rundstedt's headquarters was in a former Soviet military school. Hewel noted that day: "We strolled through Berdichev. Ruined monastery church. Opened coffins, execution, ghastly town. Many Jews, ancient cottages, fertile soil. Very hot. Three hours' flight back."

An orderly told me of late-night comments in No. 1 Dining Room; I am furious about them, because we aren't here on an outing but because the Chief wants us and maintains he can't work without us. More than once he has stressed in these gentlemen's presence that without us . . . he would be in a hopeless mess. . . . It cannot have been a very pleasant situation when a few days after these utterances the Chief asked his Wehrmacht adjutant [Schmundt] whether a tent has been laid on for his ladies at the next headquarters. The reply was in the negative, so the Führer angrily ordered that accommodation was to be provided for us. "Oh, they had imagined they were only going to stay there in a tent encampment a few days, so we would not be needed!" All these excuses show how much they want to get rid of us. But the Chief has no intention whatever of being talked into it. An omnibus had to be laid on at once for us to sleep and work in. This episode quickly rid me of the illusion that the officers concerned could ever have friendly feelings for us women, whatever the late-night hours spent together in the dining room might suggest: that was just an alcoholic mirage. . . . The men have only one thought—to show themselves in the best light possible. The most ludicrous picture I think is when the Chief is standing with a cluster of his men, and the photographer begins to focus his Leica. At that moment, moving like lightning, they all crowd as close to the Chief as possible—like moths around a flame—so they too can get into the picture. I find this conduct quite absurd.

Three weeks later the same secretary was again complaining of the monotony. "We have now been here nine weeks, and the rumor is we shall stay here until the end of October. . . . I am so sick of inactivity that I recently tried to convince the Chief he needs only *one* secretary . . . but he changed the subject straight away so that I could not even touch on my request to be of some use somewhere else for the duration of the war, either in a hospital or an arms factory." Yet indirectly this secretary was serving a purpose for history, for her writings unmistakably reflect Hitler's inner thoughts. Thus on August 20 we find her recording:

A few days ago we saw here a British newsreel that reached us from America, showing the horrifying devastation of entire streets in London: all the big department stores, Parliament, and so on are in ruins. The camera showed the huge fires raging, as it panned across whole sections of the city, with warehouse after warehouse forming one sea of fire. The commentary says says that the British are sticking it out in the knowledge that Berlin looks just the same. Oh, if the poor British could only guess that the damage they are causing to Berlin is a mere shadow of this in London I am sure they would never go on fighting. Captured British officers themselves say their government is acting wholly irresponsibly. And that is really saying something, if the British admit this, and officers at that. . . .

I long for nothing more fervently than that the British should come forward with peace proposals once we have dealt with Russia. This war with Britain can only result in us smashing each other's cities to smithereens. And Mr.

Roosevelt chuckles in gleeful anticipation of the day he will inherit Britain's legacy. I really cannot understand why the British won't listen to the voice of reason. Now that we are expanding to the east, we have no need for their colonies. I find it all so much more practical that everything will be right on our doorstep: the Ukraine and Crimea are so fertile we can plant everything we need there, and the rest (coffee, tea, cocoa, etc.) we can obtain by barter from South America. It is all so simple and obvious. God grant that the British soon come to their senses.

Hitler's was not an isolated view. From Lisbon came word that the Duke of Windsor had privately written to his former host there confirming that he believed Britain had virtually lost the war already and that the United States would do better to promote peace rather than war. Those in authority were, however, bent on Hitler's extinction. In the second week of August, Churchill and Roosevelt had met aboard their warships off Newfoundland, and proclaimed the eight-point Atlantic Charter, affirming that they sought no territorial aggrandizement, that they frowned on all territorial changes that did not accord with the freely expressed wishes of the people concerned, and that all nations should enjoy equal access to the raw materials of the earth and to its oceans. (Russia, which had lost the European territories it had annexed in 1940, subscribed to the Charter in 1942 along with some twenty nations that were then at war with Germany.) On August 25, Britain and Russia invaded Iran, on the pretext of warding off a similar Axis plan. (In fact Hitler had been aware since early July, through an indirect tip from King Farouk, that the British chiefs of staff had decided to occupy the Iranian oil fields.)

More serious than the propaganda dimensions of the Charter were the secret covenants that accompanied it. The United States now took over the naval watch of the Denmark Straits (south of Iceland) and undertook escort duties on North Atlantic convoys. Clearly the distinction between neutrality and belligerency was being increasingly blurred. Goebbels favored publishing the eight points in full, but Hitler was against it. He did, however, approve Goebbels's mischievous idea of immediately following Clement Attlee's broadcast on the Atlantic talks (as Churchill's deputy) with two OKW special communiqués, announcing that the Black Sea ports of Odessa and Nikolaev were now under siege and that the Soviet iron-ore fields were in German hands. In private,[2] Goebbels—not without reason—scoffed at the Charter's meager content. "There is to be no territorial aggrandizement. *Very* impressive, coming from two powers who own half the earth's surface. They wish to see self-government restored to those who have been forcibly deprived of it. This is also thoroughly understandable, as this self-govern-

---

[2] An unpublished segment of his diary.

ment is to perpetuate the atomization of Europe which is so much in British and American interests. They'll give all countries equal access to the world's raw materials—note that: 'to the raw materials,' and not 'to the *sources* of the raw materials' . . . And disarmament is essential—only of the aggressor-nations, of course, while the peace-loving countries are to remain in possession of their weapons."

Hitler had asked Propaganda Minister Goebbels to come and see him on August 18, 1941. Apparently he was prompted by the growing Catholic clamor against the Nazi euthanasia program.

Early in July the Bishop of Munster, Count von Galen, had blown the lid off the scandal in a pastoral letter, and on the twenty-seventh he had instituted private criminal proceedings against persons unknown, explaining from his pulpit on August 3 that under German law he was obliged to report any knowledge of a crime being committed. For the Nazi party and government alike it was acutely embarrassing: Hitler's arbitrary 1939 law authorizing euthanasia had never been published. Bormann was eager to bring the Party's fight against the Church right out into the open and submitted to Hitler a memorandum on the desirability of executing the bishop. But short of treason by the bishop there was no way. Goebbels supported Bormann, arguing that Galen had spiced his sermon with wholly unfounded charges—that permanently disabled Wehrmacht battle casualties were being murdered, for example. But Hitler sagely disregarded Goebbels's advice, and instead on August 24 he ordered the entire secret euthanasia operation shut down immediately.

It was characteristic of his slackening grip on domestic affairs in Germany that the euthanasia operation continued nonetheless.[3] Immersed in "Barbarossa," Hitler was even unaware that Martin Bormann was already waging open war on the Church. Hitler's movie cameraman Walter Frentz heard Hitler say *in jest* to Bormann over lunch in 1941, "If you had your way, Herr Bormann, all the monasteries would be shut down!"—which was precisely what Bormann was doing. On another occasion Hitler said, "If my mother were still alive, she'd definitely be a churchgoer and I wouldn't want to hinder her. On the contrary, you've got to respect the simple faith of the people." Goebbels uncomfortably noted this in his diary. But according to Hitler's doctor, Hasselbach, the spectacle of the worthies of the Church of England now praying for the victory of bolshevism satisfied the Führer that all clergy *were* hypocrites. (He seemed to have forgotten that he himself had temporarily allied himself with bolshevism.) He

---

[3] It continued until February 1945, evidently on the local initiative of Gauleiters and doctors.

assured Goebbels and Rosenberg that he would not easily forgive the German church leaders their behavior during this emergency period. But first the war must be won, and until then the Party must proceed slowly against the Church. On July 30, 1941, Bormann personally circularized all the Gauleiters on Hitler's orders, instructing them to refrain from any persecution of the religious communities, since this would only divide the nation Hitler had so arduously united.

Goebbels brought with him to Hitler's headquarters on August 18 radical proposals for intensifying the surveillance and persecution of the remaining Jews in Germany. "In the eastern campaign," his memorandum read, "the German soldier has seen the Jew in all his cruelty and repulsiveness." Jews had allegedly mutilated German soldiers or shot them down from the rear. "Clearly when the soldier comes home from the wars, he must not find any Jews here waiting for him." Ever since the summer of 1940 Goebbels had impatiently prepared for the rapid deportation of Berlin's seventy thousand Jews to the east—to Poland; but the war needs for transport overrode his ambitions, and he told the Berlin police that they could not begin the big roundup until the war was over. Now, in August 1941, Goebbels and Heydrich jointly proposed harsh measures to hound and intimidate the Jews—banning them from certain districts, from all public entertainment and eating places, and from non-Jewish shops. On August 17, Heydrich recommended to Bormann that all Jews should be forced to wear a distinctive emblem, to make their surveillance as potential enemies of the state easier. Goebbels supported him. "One only needs to imagine what the Jews would do if they had us in their power, to know what we must do now that we are on top."

Afterward Goebbels wrote: "I manage to get my way completely with the Führer on the Jewish matter. He agrees we can introduce a large, visible badge for all the Jews in the Reich, to be worn by all Jews in public, so as to obviate the danger that the Jews will act as grumblers and defeatists without being detected. And in future we will allocate to Jews who don't work smaller food rations than to Germans; this is only right and proper—those who don't work won't eat. After all, of Berlin's 76,000 Jews, for example, only 26,000 work; the rest are sustained not only by the toils but also by the food rations of the Berlin public! Incidentally, the Führer agrees that as soon as the first transport possibilities arise, the Berlin Jews will be deported from Berlin to the east. There they will be taken in hand under a somewhat harsher climate."

Goebbels noted that Hitler also reminded him of his January 1939 Reichstag speech.

The Führer is convinced that the prophecy he uttered then in the Reichstag —that if the Jews once more succeeded in provoking a world war, it would end with the destruction of the Jews—is coming true. It is coming true these weeks and months with a dread certainty that is almost uncanny. In the east the Jews will have to square accounts; they have already footed part of the bill in Germany and they will have to pay still more in the future. Their last refuge will be North America, and there too they will one day, sooner or later, end up footing the bill. Judaism is a foreign body among the cultured nations, and its works these last three decades have been so devastating that the popular reaction to it is absolutely comprehensible, necessary, indeed one might almost say self-evident. At any rate in the coming world the Jews will have little cause for mirth. . . .

Heydrich ordered that in the future Jews would have to wear yellow-and-white armbands to distinguish them; early in September, when the law was published, it was amended to a yellow star. As soon as "Barbarossa" was over, Hitler had agreed, the deportation of Berlin Jews could commence.

August 18 was a beautiful summer day at the Führer's headquarters, and Hitler's dysentery had passed, so he spent the four hours of his talk with Goebbels strolling in the woods—the first time he had done so in five weeks. Goebbels detected the strain in Hitler's features, but for a man of fifty-two the Führer's vitality and application were remarkable. He asked Goebbels about the mood in Berlin, which had recently undergone small-scale British and Russian air attacks. He had no worries about the morale of his people as a whole, though he strongly distrusted the intellectuals, and he promised Goebbels he would speak to the nation in the autumn.

The Wehrmacht's big push southward would shortly begin. "The Führer is not concerned with occupying particular regions or cities," wrote Goebbels. "He wants to avoid casualties if at all possible. Therefore, he does not intend to take Leningrad [Goebbels wrote "Petersburg"] or Kiev by force of arms, but to starve them into submission; once Leningrad has been cut off, his plan is to destroy the city's lifelines with his Luftwaffe and artillery. Probably not much will be left of this city. This is presumably justified by expediency. No doubt," gloated Goebbels, "there will be a degree of chaos among its millions of inhabitants. But the Bolsheviks would not have it otherwise. Our first Luftwaffe attacks will hit the water, power, and gas stations." Even as they were talking, a message was handed to Hitler that, true to the letter of Stalin's orders, a Russian town had burned its entire food stocks shortly before its capture. Hitler ordered the town left to starve so that other towns might have second thoughts about relying on the Wehrmacht's benevolence.

The exhausted German panzer divisions would shortly recuperate, continued Hitler to Goebbels. He hoped to be beyond Moscow by the time winter set in— presumably in mid-October. He put Stalin's losses at three million dead already. Perhaps, he mused wistfully, Stalin might even now sue for peace. "He has of course little in common with the plutocrats in London; nor will he let Britain dupe him as it did the potentates of those minor countries who allowed London to lead them to the slaughter. He is a hard-bitten realist, and the moment he sees that the Bolshevik system itself is on the verge of collapse and can only be salvaged by surrender, then he will certainly be willing to do so." When Goebbels asked what then, Hitler disclosed that he would agree to a peace request provided he was given considerable territorial safeguards and the Red Army was dismantled to the last rifle. "Bolshevism without the Red Army is no danger to us." Peace, thought Hitler, might come upon them quite unexpectedly—after all, nobody had expected at the beginning of January 1933 that thirty days later Hitler would be in power.

"The Führer is convinced that Moscow and London were in the same line of business long before June," wrote Goebbels. Their aim had been identical, the destruction of the Reich. He was overwhelmed at the very thought of what it would have meant if the Bolshevik hordes had swarmed into highly civilized central and western Europe. "Perhaps we still do not fully know the precarious position we were in this June. Autumn would definitely have brought the showdown." He admitted that German Intelligence had been grossly misled on Russian tank and aircraft strengths, and this had led to errors of judgment. "For example the Führer had estimated there were five thousand Soviet tanks, whereas in reality they had something like twenty thousand. We thought they had around ten thousand aircraft; in fact they possessed over twenty thousand, albeit largely unsuitable for battle." Hitler consoled himself with the idea that had he known the truth he might never have ordered "Barbarossa," but he could not conceal from his shrewd propaganda minister his inner annoyance at having been fooled by the earlier reports from the Soviet Union. "He has worried a lot over this," observed Goebbels. And—indignantly—"The Bolsheviks deliberately set out to deceive us."

The advancing German armies had certainly found concrete indications of Stalin's true disposition toward western Europe. Captured Russian generals admitted they had been hampered in their enforced retreats by a total lack of maps of their own country; on the other hand, they had been furnished with entire truckloads of maps of Germany. While some German division commanders began "Barbarossa" with nothing more detailed than maps torn from automobile club handbooks, they found the enemy had better large-scale maps of Germany, Austria, and Silesia than they did themselves. Air reconnaissance now revealed that Stalin had established a huge complex of arms factories beyond the Urals. The Russians had also built several completely unpublicized highways along which they advanced, while the Wehrmacht adhered to the only roads they were aware of—the lanes that turned to swamps as soon as the rains fell. It also appeared that the German war department had been furnished by Communist agents with maps depicting completely fictitious roads and obstacles. In Red Army barracks were found dummy German soldiers that had been manufactured for target practice long before June 1941. From the absence of any Soviet written orders for actual operations in western Europe, it seems unlikely that anything *was* planned as early as the autumn, but most of Hitler's commanders—including Bock, Kluge, Richard Ruoff—agreed that the Führer had selected the proper time to strike.

Hitler properly realized that fast-flowing transport of supplies to his armies was the key to victory. Aided by thousands of prisoners, army engineers labored around the clock to repair the demolished Russian railway lines and re-lay them on the different German gauge. By mid-August a twin track extended as far as Smolensk. As Hitler repeatedly remarked, he was not going to make the mistakes "a certain other famous man"—meaning Napoleon—had made.

On the seventeenth, he had educated his staff on the dangers of overoptimism. "Always credit the enemy with doing just what you least want," he told Hewel. For example, he tried to envisage what Stalin would do if the Pripyet Marshes did not exist. On August 19, Martin Bormann quoted Hitler as remarking, "It'd be a good thing if the German people had a war every fifteen or twenty years. An army whose only job is keeping the peace ends up playing soldiers—look at Sweden and Switzerland!" And, "If it is held against me that my warmaking has cost one hundred thousand or two hundred thousand lives my answer is this: through my activities so far the German nation has already gained over two-and-a-half *million* people. Even if I ask ten percent of this as a sacrifice, I have still given ninety percent."

On August 18, the day of Goebbels's visit, Brauchitsch submitted to Hitler a written argument for the immediate resumption of the attack on Moscow, as the city's capture would take at least two months and Guderian's and Hoth's tanks first needed overhauling. The OKW operations staff agreed—though Colonel von Lossberg, Jodl's army aide, seemed pessimistic. Hewel noted: "A wager with Lossberg. I say the war will be shorter than World War I; he says it'll be longer."

Hitler rejected Brauchitsch's memorandum outright. It was most urgent, in his view, to deprive Stalin of his raw materials and arms industry. Besides, a rapid advance southward would encourage Iran to resist the Anglo-Russian invasion which he already knew was in the cards; in any case, he wanted the Crimea in German hands: it was from Crimean airfields that Russian bombers had recently attacked Romania. Hitler was plagued at night by a recurring nightmare—the petroleum fields of Ploesti, ablaze from end to end. His panzer generals Hoth and Guderian lamented that their tanks were largely in need of overhaul. Hitler did not believe them, as he had heard the same story before Dunkirk. After meeting with them at Borisov on August 4—where Guderian had claimed that he alone needed three hundred new tank-engines—Hitler told Keitel in exasperation that the two generals were obviously just claiming that their tanks needed overhauling to conceal their own arrogant disapproval of his grand strategy.

Well, he was Führer, and now he was in better health too. On August 21 he dictated a brusque letter to Brauchitsch beginning with the words "The army's proposal for continuing the operations in the east, dated August 18, does not accord with my intentions. I order the following"—and he restated the objectives he had been demanding since December 1940. In the north, the isolation of Leningrad; and in the south, the capture of the Crimea, the Donets industrial and coal regions, and the Caucasus oil fields. Field Marshal von Bock's Army Group Center, facing Moscow, was to remain on the defensive.

This rude rebuff caused uproar in the army. Halder literally wept over Hitler's "pamphleteering," as he believed that Hitler was throwing away the year's main chance. Brauchitsch suffered his first mild heart attack. For many nights his adjutant heard him arguing with Hitler in his sleep. He lacked the courage to resign as yet. Halder, made of sterner stuff, wrote to his wife on August 23: "Tortured days lie behind me. Again I offered my resignation to stave off an act of folly. The outcome was completely unsatisfactory. . . . The objective I set myself—namely to finish off the Russians once for all before the year is out—will not be achieved. . . . History will level at us the gravest accusation that can be made of a High Command, namely that for fear of undue risk we did not exploit the attacking impetus of our troops. It was the same in the western campaign. But there the enemy's internal collapse cast a merciful veil over our errors."

Bock's diary bespoke an equally anguished heart. "I don't want to 'capture Moscow'! I want to destroy the enemy's army, and the bulk of that army is *in front* of me!" He telephoned Colonel Schmundt asking that the Führer at least give a hearing to Guderian, who was warning that his tanks urgently needed rest and rehabilitation. Guderian's controversial midnight conference with Hitler on August 23, without Halder, can be reconstructed from his private letters and the diary of his Chief of Staff. After hearing Hitler's case for the main thrust to continue now toward the south, Guderian recognized that the Führer was right and pocketed his own doubts; but he made one condition—that his Panzer-Gruppe should be committed in its entirety to this thrust and not to two divergent campaigns. Hitler agreed. "I returned," wrote Guderian afterward, "on the twenty-fourth, well satisfied and with high hopes." Hitler had been "as always very nice and clear-thinking, and unambiguously insistent on the direction I am now taking."

Bock's wrath and Halder's indignation, when they learned of Guderian's "defection," were immense and deviously expressed: Guderian commenced his southward thrust on August 25—but Halder confiscated his most powerful corps, the Forty-Sixth Panzer, and assigned it to the Fourth Army on the Moscow front. With only two corps, Guderian's offensive limped and stumbled, although his troops fought well. "Since the twenty-seventh I've been fighting for reinforcements, but they are granted me only in driblets and too late," he wrote in one letter. His Chief of Staff observed in his diary that Guderian "has the impression that [Bock and Halder] are still hanging on to their old plan—the advance on Moscow." By early September it was clear, as bad weather arrived, that the Red Army north of the Desna River had eluded him. Not until September 19 did Kiev fall to Reichenau's Sixth Army. A week later the huge encirclement action to the east of Kiev was over, with four Soviet armies wiped out and 665,000 prisoners taken; it was a famous victory, but the war was far from won.

At the end of August 1941, Hitler again found time for his allies. Italy had dispatched an expeditionary corps to the Ukraine, presenting the German army transport officials with the unenviable choice of transporting either the unloved Italians or the supplies essential to the Wehrmacht offensive. Goebbels had recently told Hitler that the Italians planned a North Africa propaganda film in which the part played by Rommel's forces would be ignored. Mussolini might need such a film for domestic consumption, but it would have fateful consequences in Germany. Hitler instructed Goebbels to refuse the Italian request for assistance. At the German première of another Italian film, there were hoots of laughter when the Italian troops were praised as "speedy"; Hitler ordered the offending sound-track obliterated before the film's release. "Otherwise, particularly in Austria, the entire Axis relationship would be damaged." His cynicism was manifest when in August Mussolini's son Bruno was for a time reported missing in action. "It's a pity that Mussolini's son was not killed in action after all. Fascism could have done with that at present."

The Duce arrived at the Wolf's Lair on August 25. Hewel noted: "War conference, then a communal meal in the dining bunker and a talk with my Chief [Ribbentrop]. In the evening a cold buffet in the garden. Vittorio Mussolini is particularly unattractive and dumb. . . ." The next day Hitler showed Mussolini over the battlefield at Brest-Litovsk, where the two-ton projectiles of his 620-millimeter mortars had reduced the citadel to ruins. He admitted that his military Intelligence had grossly misinformed him about the Soviet powers of resistance, but he predicted that final victory would be his by the spring of 1942. He was already manufacturing the extra naval and Luftwaffe equipment needed to invade Britain—or so he told Mussolini.

That evening both dictators left for the Führer's southern headquarters site in

Galicia. Their two trains were shunted into specially modified tunnels for the night, and Mussolini joined Hitler for a confidential talk—pouring his heart out for the first time about the very real difficulties his Fascist revolution was in.[4] In 1943 Hitler reminisced: "We were speaking that night about the Russian commissar system, how you could not have two masters, and so on. He began to brood, and I went and dined in his train. Then he suddenly said to me, 'What you were saying, Führer, about not having two masters in one army, is quite right; but tell me, what can you do if you have got officers with reservations about the regime and about its ideologies . . . who say—the moment you talk of your ideology or of *raison d'état*—'We are monarchists: we owe our allegiance to the King!' " This admission of impotence in face of the Italian monarchy was a shock to Hitler, and he never forgot Mussolini's words.

The next day, August 28, both dictators flew across the fertile Ukrainian countryside for hours until they reached Rundstedt's command post at Uman. Keitel was to write: "The impression left by the sheer expanse of black soil and the—by German standards—immense harvest-lands of the Ukraine was overwhelming. For miles on end one often saw in the gently undulating open and treeless landscape nothing but the shocks of one enormous, endless wheatfield. One could sense the virginity of the soil." Three months later, in talking to a foreign diplomat Hitler described his own vivid impressions—how he had found himself surveying areas where the milk and honey flowed, where the soil was more fertile than anywhere else in Europe, "and yet the people were pitiful and impoverished beyond comprehension. I must have seen thousands of women there, but not one of them was wearing even the cheapest ornaments. In their wretched hovels there was neither cutlery nor other household goods. And this misery prevailed in a region whose soil was capable of the biggest harvest imaginable. Today there still lives there this terrified, scared mass of people, trembling with constant fear of their commissars. Only when these pitiable creatures saw with their own eyes the commissars being shot did they gradually turn back into human beings again."

And Joachim Ribbentrop on his return from the Ukraine to Hitler's headquarters wrote his own private—and premature—panegyric on the Wehrmacht's achievement in conquering the east. "The Führer is exceptionally pleased with

[4]On August 30, 1941, Canaris returned to Berlin from talks with his Italian counterpart, Colonel Cesare Amé. He told his Abwehr staff: "A. describes the situation in Italy as very grave and hinted particularly at serious ill-feeling in army circles toward the Duce and the Fascist regime. A. believes that when the three hundred thousand Italian prisoners of war return they will want the System to give a very clear explanation of why this war was fought. The surprise caused by the eastern campaign has had an extremely unpleasant effect on the Italian people, and A. has great apprehensions about the coming winter of war."

the way things are going. I firmly believe we will reach our target by winter—we shall have finally annihilated the fighting remnants of the Red Army and captured the main centers of population, raw materials, and industry so that even if the Soviet Union does not collapse completely it will be virtually incapable of regeneration in the coming winter, *i.e.,* they will in effect cease to be of value as an ally to Britain. And perhaps then after all the moment will come when the west adopts a different tone of voice, and we can achieve (albeit after a considerable detour) what we had in mind these last few years"—meaning concord with Britain. But he added: "Admittedly the interests of our allies now have to be taken fully into account." Hitler had evidently told Ribbentrop nothing of his secret talks with Mussolini; the foreign minister had to glean what information he could from the Forschungsamt's intercepts of the Italian ambassador's subsequent reports to Rome on *his* conversations with the Duce.

The summer would soon be over. At the end of August, Christa Schroeder wrote:

Our stay here at the headquarters gets longer and longer. First we thought we would be back in Berlin by the end of July, then they talked of mid-October; and now they are already saying we will not get away before the end of October, if even then. It is already quite cool here, like autumn, and if it occurs to the Chief to spend the winter here we shall all be frozen. This protracted bunker existence can't be doing us any good. The Chief does not look too well either, he gets too little fresh air and now he is oversensitive to sun and wind the moment he goes out in his car for a few hours. I would have loved to stay in Galicia—we were all in favor of it—but security there is not good enough. They say there are incidents there every day, and as they can't cordon off the area there as at our present headquarters the danger would be too great. But the countryside down there has a surprising charm, with woodland on one side and gentle slopes on the other and the cattle silhouetted against the blue sky while the farmers plod behind their plows. How romantic the peasant cottages look, all battered and windblown, with thatched roofs and scarcely a window in them, a wishing-well in front of them with a bucket on a rusty chain and a few sunflowers; the women are suntanned and barefoot with large dark cloths wrapped around their heads and reaching down to their waists—they stand there beside their cow, a little mournful, a little mysterious, but absolutely part of the landscape. It reminds me somehow of home.

The whole countryside there is freer. Here in the forest it all crowds in on you after a while. Besides, there you didn't have the feeling that you were locked in: you saw the peasants working in the fields and it made you feel free, while here we keep stumbling on sentries and are forever showing our identity cards. Well, I suppose that wherever we are we're always cut off from the world —in Berlin, at the Berghof, or on our travels. It is always the same sharply defined circle, always the same circuit inside the fence.

Just what Hitler's New Order would be in Europe was a secret he closely kept. That Slavs and Bolsheviks—particularly if they were Jewish—would not prosper under it was obvious; but the positions of countries like Italy, France, Hungary, and even Russia were still undefined. Hungary's astute military experts were not optimistic about "Barbarossa," and public opinion in Hungary frowned on Horthy's associations with the Nazis. The pro-German army Chief of Staff, General Henrik Werth, had been replaced by the isolationist General Ferenc Szombathelyi, and when Horthy visited Hitler on September 8 it was to ask for his divisions to be withdrawn from the battlefield. They visited Marienburg (now Malbork) in East Prussia together, and Horthy was deeply impressed at the genuine popular acclaim for the Führer. "We don't have your Jewish problem," Hitler pointedly explained. To his private staff he observed as the regent left, "Hungarians will always be Hungarians."

Oddly enough, it was Mussolini who had raised the New Order issue, although Italy by the extravagance of her claims on France was doing most to hinder it. Hitler's naval adjutant, Puttkamer, wrote revealingly on August 11, 1941:

> At lunch yesterday the Führer spoke about our relationship with France. This elicited for the first time the reason why he doesn't take up any of the proposals made about it. He said he thought that a man like Darlan is being perfectly honest and that it was quite possible to achieve a bearable relationship with France by progressing from armistice to a preliminary peace. This was absolutely possible, in his view, even if we made stiff demands: France expected them, would uphold them, and would join the war at our side. So—*if* we were alone—everything could be attained. The decisive obstacle was however Italy's claims—Tunis and Corsica. No French government could uphold these. But he couldn't persuade the Italians to drop them; he had to associate himself with these claims too. He couldn't barter our ally Italy against France, he said. So that's the real reason, which was news to both me and Jodl, whom I discussed it with.

On September 8—the day of Horthy's arrival—Hitler told Hewel: "These are all just alliances of expediency. For example, the German people know that our alliance with Italy is only an alliance between Mussolini and myself. We Germans have sympathies only with Finland; we could find some sympathy for Sweden, and of course with Britain." Here he must have sighed, for he added: "A German-British alliance would be an alliance from people to people! The British would only have to keep their hands off the Continent. They could keep their empire —and the world if they wanted!"

However, Churchill was still in power, and any New Order must take account of that. Hitler's conquest of the Ukraine would mean that he no longer needed the raw-material regions of France. As he explained to his ambassador in France, Otto Abetz, on September 16, the Soviet iron-ore fields at Krivoi Rog alone would yield a million tons of ore a month. Hitler would insist only on Alsace and Lorraine, and the Channel coast facing England—he had thought a lot about the latter, but felt he could not relinquish it now, as he might have to reconquer it in years to come. Nor could he overlook the need for France to participate in the defeat of Britain. Given what he saw as modest claims, Hitler assured Abetz that France would certainly have a share of the pickings from the New Order. Turkey's position was more ambivalent. Britain had tried to restore her own standing after Ankara signed its ten-year treaty with Germany on the eve of "Barbarossa"; but the Turkish foreign minister secretly assured Hitler's shrewd ambassador, Franz von Papen, that every true Turk longed in his heart for a German victory.

In his diary of September 15, 1941, Weizsäcker described Hitler's foreign policy in these words: "The quasi-depression of four weeks ago has been cured, probably the physical malaise too. An autobahn is being planned to the Crimean peninsula. There is speculation as to the probable manner of Stalin's departure. If he withdraws into Asia, he might even be granted a peace treaty. . . . He's unlikely to be replaced, let alone eliminated by a general." The next day, Papen also raised Stalin's future with Hitler, and the Führer repeated what he had told Goebbels a month before—that once the Wehrmacht had occupied a certain forward line in Russia, it might be possible to find common ground with the Red dictator, who was after all a man of enormous achievements. As another diplomat—Hasso von Etzdorf—noted on September 22: "[Hitler] sees two possibilities as to Stalin's fate: either he gets bumped off by his own people, or he tries to make peace with us. Because, he says, Stalin as the greatest living statesman must realize that at sixty-six you can't begin your life's work all over again if it will take a lifetime to complete it; so he'll try to salvage what he can, with our acquiescence. And in this we should meet him halfway. If Stalin could only decide to seek expansion for Russia toward the south, the Persian Gulf, as he [Hitler] recommended to him once [November 1940], then peaceful coexistence between Russia and Germany would be imaginable."

Papen for his part impressed on Hitler the need to promote a "constructive peace plan" after Russia's overthrow, a plan capable of inspiring all Europeans. From what Ribbentrop learned, Hitler agreed with Papen and planned a series of bilateral agreements with each European country, rather than one overall conference—except perhaps for the final grand act of ratification.

"The Führer then turned to his plans for the east," relates the only existing record of Hitler's conversation with Abetz on September 16:

Petersburg [Leningrad], the "poisonous nest" from which for so long Asiatic venom has "spewed forth" into the Baltic, must vanish from the earth's surface.

The city is already cut off. It only remains for our artillery and Luftwaffe to bombard it to pieces, destroying the water mains, the power stations, and everything the population needs to survive. The Asiatics and the Bolsheviks must be hounded out of Europe, this "episode of two hundred fifty years of Asiatic pestilence" is at an end. The Urals will be the frontier beyond which Stalin and his like can do as they please. But he [Hitler], by launching occasional expeditions across the Urals, will also ensure that Stalin gets no respite there either.

After the expulsion of the Asiatics, Europe will never again be dependent on an outside power, nor need we "care two hoots" about America. Europe will meet its own raw material needs, and it will have its own export market in the Russian territories so we will no longer need the rest of the world's trade. The new Russia this side of the Urals will be "our India," but far more handily located than that of Britain. The new Greater German Empire will embrace 135 million people, and it will rule 150 million more.

The backbone of the new empire would be the Wehrmacht and above all the SS—the capable new elite, alone in Hitler's view entitled to rule the Slavs and the inferior races of the east.

Himmler and Heydrich were frequent guests at the Wolf's Lair. On one occasion in September Hitler found himself lunching with Himmler and six SS generals (albeit some of only honorary rank: Bormann, Dietrich, Schaub, and Karl-Hermann Frank). In public Hitler talked with Himmler only of innocuous matters—architecture, the salon of Frau Bruckmann, or the relative nutritive values of the potato and the soya bean. In private they elaborated ways of fighting the growing Hydra-headed partisan movements throughout the Nazi-occupied territories. Hitler linked these movements with Stalin's July broadcast, and he condemned as far too mild the treatment so far meted out to captured offenders. On September 7—as Himmler was at the Wolf's Lair—he ordered that if the murderer of a German NCO in Paris was not found immediately, fifty hostages were to be shot; and in future the ratio was to be a hundred "Communists" for each German life taken. (The German military commander admittedly protested, and Hitler left the final scale of reprisals to his discretion.) The partisan threat was particularly severe in the Balkans, and on the sixteenth Hitler signed an order giving his local army commanders special powers; but the enemy purpose was being achieved, for more and more divisions would have to be diverted to this counterinsurgency campaign, and the differences between an initially passive population and their German occupiers hardened into an implacable hatred.

The siege of Leningrad symbolized the brutalization of this war. Four million people now packed the city's streets. By mid-September Leeb had taken the last high ground to the south. Already his tank crews could see the glittering gold spires of the admiralty building. The Russians had evacuated the main munitions factories in July, and a chaotic attempt at getting the women and children to safety had begun. But with the German capture of Petrokrepost' the city was now cut off; in a formal directive, Number 35, issued on September 6, Hitler ordered Leningrad to be so thoroughly isolated by his ground forces that by mid-September at the latest he could recover his tanks and Richthofen's air squadrons for the main assault on Moscow after all. On September 9 the Luftwaffe began around-the-clock bombing operations. Jeschonnek's deputy wrote in his diary: "We hope to have achieved a tight encirclement of Leningrad within a week. Food already appears to be short there." On the tenth, Rosenberg's liaison officer reported to him from Hitler's headquarters:

> For three days now our 240-millimeter guns have been firing into the city. Richthofen's bombing has destroyed the big waterworks. The Russians have only evacuated the Stakhanovite and other top-grade workers needed to expand their industry beyond the Urals; apart from that the entire population has remained and actually been swollen by the evacuation of the surrounding suburbs. Already it's almost impossible to get bread, sugar, and meat in Leningrad. The Führer wants to avoid house-to-house fighting, which would cost our troops heavy casualties. The city is to be just shut in, shot to pieces by artillery and starved out. A few days or weeks here or there make no difference, as the besieging army won't have to be very big. The Finns have suggested diverting Lake Ladoga into the Gulf of Finland—which lies several meters lower—to wash away the city of Leningrad.

On September 12, General Halder emphasized to Leeb's army group that his tanks would shortly be needed for the attack on Moscow. This provoked angry protests from the tank commanders. General Hans Reinhardt protested at the shattering effect this order to halt was having on his men. "The city is spread out before them, and nobody is stopping them going right on in!" But Hitler agreed that the tanks should not be committed; Leningrad should be destroyed by bombardment instead. Admiral Raeder asked him to spare at least the dockyards for the German navy; this too Hitler refused, but as regards the tanks Keitel telephoned Leeb to postpone their withdrawal by forty-eight hours. On the twelfth the Luftwaffe commander, Richthofen, entered in his diary: "Colonel Schmundt came this afternoon to lecture the higher echelons of the army on how the Führer sees things. Very necessary, unfortunately, as Halder and Brauchitsch either told them nothing at all or got it all wrong. [Schmundt] talked about the problem of Finland and Leningrad. Over L. the 'plow shall pass!' " On September 16 the tanks were finally halted, and their withdrawal to the Moscow front began. As for Leningrad, on September 27 the naval staff learned that "any surrender offer is to be rejected."

Kiev at least was in German hands. The news broke at Hitler's headquarters late on September 19. For days afterward he spoke at lunch and dinner of his plans for Europe. Dr. Fritz Todt came, and so did Gauleiter Koch, whose mission would be to tame the Ukraine for western Europe's needs. Dr. Werner Koeppen, Rosenberg's liaison officer, recorded these historic conversations:

Lunchtime, September 19

Dr. Todt related his impressions of his latest journey to Oslo and Trondheim, and of the first ground broken for the major traffic link between Germany and Denmark. The Führer talked about his plan to rebuild Trondheim afresh in terrace-form, so that every house will be in the sun all day long; this presents no traffic problems, as Trondheim's main traffic will always rely on its waterways. The Führer then spoke of the need to build one autobahn to Trondheim, and another down to the Crimea. After the war the German citizen shall have the chance of taking his Volkswagen and looking over the captured territories in person, so that if need should arise he will also be willing to fight for them. We must never repeat the prewar error of having the colonial idea the property of only a few capitalists or corporations. In the future the road or autobahn will play an incomparably larger part in public transport than the railway, which will take care of goods transportation. Only road travel enables you to get to know a country. The railway traverses distances, but the road opens them up.

He planned the New Order as a deliberately European *Raumpolitik*. Earlier, as he told Seyss-Inquart on the twenty-sixth, it was downright absurd that though a vast only sparsely populated empire lay in the east with almost inexhaustible resources and raw materials, western Europe struggled to meet its needs by imports from colonies far overseas. In time of war those sea lanes could always be endangered. "This is why it is unimportant how long we have to go on fighting in the east. Once we have securely occupied the vitally important European regions of the Soviet Union, the war east of the Urals can go on a hundred years, for all we care." Meanwhile the 130 million people living in Europe's new eastern empire would be a captive market for virtually every industrial product Europe manufactured, from a simple water-glass to the largest artifact. The east would supply raw materials. Hitler had just learned, for example, that rubber was being grown near Kharkov—he had himself already seen excellent samples of it. "The giant farms Stalin has introduced will probably be the best way to use the land in the future too, as they are probably the only way of cultivating the land intensively . . ." He felt that most Russians had become quite accustomed to being treated like animals.

The Ukrainians, he had said at lunch a few days earlier, were lazy, amorphous, nihilistic, and Asiatic in their ways; they would never understand such concepts as duty or the ethos of work; they responded only to the whip. "This is why Stalin is one of the greatest living men, because he succeeded in forging this Slav rabbit family into a nation, albeit only by the cruelest coercion." Both Hitler and Koch rejected any notion of a "Free Ukraine" for this reason. Chaos came naturally to the Ukrainians, it was their natural ambience. Half an education would make them dissatisfied and anarchistic; hence Rosenberg's ambition to found a university at Kiev must be rejected. If the occupying authorities controlled the alcohol and tobacco supplies, they would have the population eating out of their hands. In private conference with Hitler and Keitel, Koch emphasized the need to be brutal right from the start if the errors of 1917–18, stemming from vacillating occupation policies, were to be avoided. Hitler agreed. He suggested that the British rule over India must be the model for their own administration of the east. Koch departed from the Wolf's Lair amid the congratulations of Hitler's staff: Koch was undoubtedly the "second Stalin" the Ukraine needed.

"The frontier between Europe and Asia," reflected Hitler over dinner on the twenty-third, "is not the Ural Mountains but there where the settlements of Germanically inclined people end and unadulterated Slav settlements begin. It is our task to push this frontier as far east as possible, and if need be far beyond the Urals. It is the eternal law of nature that gives Germany as the stronger power the right before history to subjugate these peoples of inferior race, to dominate them and to coerce them into performing useful labors. I admit this has nothing to do with Christian ethics, but the very fact that it is according to the more ancient and well-tried laws of nature makes it the more likely to last a long while."

In the "Protectorate" of Bohemia-Moravia, draconian measures succeeded. By 1941 Hitler had incarcerated twenty-five hundred Czech "opponents," but in October 1940 he had stipulated that "the trials are to be postponed until the war's over, when they will be drowned by the noise of victory celebrations." For insurgents and rebels Hitler preferred to use the firing squad—formal trials just produced folk heroes like Andreas Hofer and Leo Schlageter (Germans executed by the French occupation forces in the Twenties). But since "Barbarossa" a wave of opposition had appeared in the Protectorate. Crops had been sabotaged, there were slowdowns and stoppages and terror incidents. Rumor reached Hitler that a full-scale uprising was being plotted. "Only now do they realize that there is no escape. As long as the great Russia, mother of all Slavs, was there they could still hope." Obviously the ailing and respectable Baron Konstantin von Neurath was too inefficient as Reich Protector to crush the mutiny at birth. Koeppen quoted Hitler's remarks at lunch a few days later: "He keeps repeating that he knows the Czechs of old. To them Neurath was just a friendly old duffer whose blandness and good humor they rapidly mistook for weakness and stupidity. . . . The Czechs are a nation of 'cyclists'—they bow from the waist upward, but the legs still kick!"

On Bormann's advice Hitler sent Neurath on extended sick-leave and appointed the feared SS General Reinhard Heydrich—head of the SS main security office—Acting Protector. ("It was at my suggestion that Heydrich was appointed!" Bormann later crowed in his diary.) When Bormann, SS Reichsführer Himmler, Heydrich, and Karl Frank (Neurath's state secretary) came to the Wolf's Lair on September 24, Hitler told Heydrich his job would be "a fighting mission," of only limited duration. He gave Heydrich carte blanche, signed in his own hand, to do as he saw fit, and he pointed out: "You observe that wherever I believe the unity of the Reich to be at risk I appoint an SS commander to safeguard it." Heydrich proudly flew to Prague on September 27 and arrested the rebellious ringleaders—among them General Alois Eliaš, the prime minister. The next day Heydrich phoned Himmler that Eliaš had confessed to being in contact with the exiled Beneš government in London. Eliaš was tried in public and condemned to death. But Hitler decided he was of more value as a hostage for the Czechs' good behavior, and he survived until May 1942.

Hitler briefed Heydrich fully on the position of his Protectorate in the New Order. Heydrich reported this secretly to his local German governors in Prague on October 2: Germany was to remain permanently in occupation of certain European countries. Norway, Holland, Flanders, Denmark, Sweden, and—because of the fifth- and sixth-century Germanic invasions—Britain too were nations of Germanic origin; they would be led humanely and justly into a closer alliance with the Reich. Heydrich also closely followed Hitler's "thoughts on the final solution" of the vexing Slav problem. One day the Protectorate would be permanently settled by Germans. "This does not mean," said Heydrich, "that we now have to try to Germanize all Czech rabble. . . . For those of good race and good intentions the matter is simple; they will be Germanized. For the rest, those of inferior racial origin or with hostile intentions, I shall get rid of them—there is plenty of room in the east for them." Inferior but well-meaning Czechs would probably be sent to work in the Reich. The more difficult category—those of good racial characteristics but hostile intentions—would have to be liquidated, if all attempts at Germanizing them failed; it would be potentially too dangerous to turn them loose in the east.[5]

[5]Hitler had used the same language to Neurath, State Secretary Karl-Hermann Frank, and the minister of justice in September 1940: "Czechs turned down on racial grounds or anti-Reich in attitude were not to be assimilated. This category was to be eliminated *(sei auszumerzen).*" In conversation over lunch on October 6, 1941, Hitler announced that the Jews in the Protectorate were all to be deported eastward. "If the Czechs still don't behave themselves then, the Führer will amend their protectorate status: Moravia will be completely detached from Bohemia and large parts handed over to the Lower Danube Gau. Gauleiter Dr. [Hugo] Jury has been waiting long enough for his missing capital city Brünn [Brno]. After this war the Führer proposes to transplant all the racially valueless elements from Bohemia to the east."

Hitler advised Heydrich to introduce the Czech workers to both the carrot and the stick. In any factory where sabotage occurred, ten hostages were to be shot; but in factories with a good output and a sabotage-free record the workers were to get extra rations. Heydrich went much further, introducing the Czechs for the first time to the full Bismarckian social security program. This social experiment lasted until May 1942, when Heydrich was assassinated in Prague by Free Czechs agents parachuted into the country.

"The Czech workers have accepted the liquidation of the conspirators quite calmly," Koeppen had written when Heydrich first reported back from Prague, over dinner on October 2. "The most important thing to them is to have enough food and work. . . . One worker has even written to Heydrich, stating his full name, saying that Czech history has always been like this: each generation has to learn its lesson and then there is peace for a time. He added that nobody would object if another two thousand of them were shot, either." The Nazis rose to the occasion.

For Hitler the last act of "Barbarossa," as he thought, had now begun. At five-thirty on the morning of October 2, 1941, Field Marshal von Bock's army group—nearly two thousand tanks commanded by Guderian, Erich Hoepner, and Hoth, and the armies of Maximilian von Weichs, Günther-Hans von Kluge, and Adolf Strauss—opened the first phase of "Operation Typhoon," the attack on Moscow. Hitler calculated that four weeks of fighting weather still remained.

At 11:30 P.M., after his supper with Heydrich, he took his special train to Berlin, where he was to speak to the German people.

Cold Harvest

Only the weather could now thwart him. On October 2, 1941, as "Typhoon" began, lunch started fifty minutes late at his headquarters as he listened to the first reports on this last battle, designed to destroy Marshal Timoshenko's armies. When the meal began, he was at first unusually silent, brooding on the great events unfolding five hundred miles to the east. He broke the silence only to ask about the weather prospects for the next few days, and then again, in a forced attempt to put his mind elsewhere, to reminisce about the Berghof—where even now Martin Bormann's construction crews were carrying out still further architectural "improvements" to the mountainside.

Yet Russia's weather was in no way unpredictable: the first daytime frost always comes on the eighteenth of October (while frost at night might come as early as the end of September). Peter the Great knew this, for he had forbidden ships to leave the Baltic ports after October 18 for fear of the winter storms. The Russian winter reaches its peak every eighteenth of January—with the notorious "Jordan's frost"—with Fahrenheit temperatures of zero in Leningrad and minus five in Moscow itself. No snow would actually stick until late November, however; and once, in 1913, there had been no snow until February.

As soon as Hitler had believed Leningrad encircled and Rundstedt's operations at Kiev far enough advanced, he had ordered the army to prepare this attack on Timoshenko's forces west of Moscow, using the armored divisions and Luftwaffe units no longer needed by Leeb or Rundstedt; he would have liked "Typhoon" to begin in mid-September, but the army had explained why the attack could not be launched before the end of the month. The Luftwaffe command showed the earliest apprehensions about "Typhoon's" prospects. Indeed, as early as August 14, Jeschonnek's deputy, Hoffmann von Waldau, had privately written at Luftwaffe headquarters: "It is all getting very late: at the end of October the war will die out in the snow." And on September 9, three days after Hitler issued the directive for "Typhoon," Waldau gloomily predicted: "We are heading for a winter campaign. The real trial of this war has begun. My belief in final victory remains." West of the Russian capital, meanwhile, Timoshenko had prepared line after line of defensive positions, while an apparently inexhaustible flow of new divisions poured into the front, making a mockery of the German army theoreticians' dreams of eliminating the enemy's military strength.

In an exultant proclamation to his three million soldiers on the eve of "Typhoon," Hitler appealed to them to to give "the last mighty heave necessary to smash the enemy before winter breaks upon us." He opened their eyes to the scale of the effort already made since June—two thousand road bridges built for the troops, over four hundred railway bridges constructed, eighteen thousand miles of railway track restored to working order, including ten thousand miles already relaid to the standard European gauge. Now he was to speak to the ordinary Berliners. "Quite apart from the transport problem," mocked Hitler over lunch on October 1, "Russia won't be helped much with one week's British tank output allocated to her, as she is losing more tanks in a day than Britain can turn out in a week. The only palpable relief for Russia would be if Britain could force us to withdraw tanks and aircraft from the eastern front, and this she can only do by invading the Continent. Churchill has warded off this Stalin demand by arguing that the invasion danger increases with the approach of dull and foggy weather again, and that he needs his forty-five divisions to defend the British Isles." Hitler made fun of the British suggestion that he had not spoken in recent months as he had nothing cheerful to tell the German people. "Over this period Churchill has admittedly made almost a dozen speeches, but if you compare actions and achievements, then I am quite content to stand before history as I am." His table companions laughed heartily; two days later they recognized that Hitler had just tried out his next big speech on them.

At 1:30 P.M. on October 3, 1941, his train arrived in Berlin. He lunched with his staff, then drove through streets of cheering crowds to the Sportpalast, where he now delivered one of the most stirring speeches of his life—wholly *ex tempore* and hence "enormously devout," as Hewel afterward reported. Hitler was exhilarated by the welcome the capital gave him. "It was the same atmosphere as at the most wonderful of our meetings during the years of struggle. The reason was that no special tickets had been distributed—the audience really was a cross section of the people. The enthusiasm and acclaim of the Berliners lining the streets to the stadium were also bigger and more genuine than for a long time. The ordinary people really do make the most appreciative audience, they are the people who deep down inside know they support me. They are marked by that kind of stability that can stand the heaviest burdens—while our intellectuals just flutter here and there."

In his tumultuous speech he outlined his unifying role in Europe—how Italy, Hungary, the Nordic countries, and then Japan had come closer to Germany. "Unhappily, however, not the nation I have courted all my life: the British. Not that the British people as a whole alone bear the responsibility for this, no, but there are some people who in their pigheaded hatred and lunacy have sabotaged every such attempt at an understanding between us, with the support of that international enemy known to us all, international Jewry. . . . As in all the years I strove to achieve understanding whatever the cost, there was Mr. Churchill who kept on shouting, 'I want a war!' Now he has it." Hitler scorned the Churchill clique who were claiming that in these last three months he had met defeat after defeat in Russia; the truth was that the Wehrmacht's divisions had advanced from one victory to the next, tirelessly and courageously, the infantry marching two thousand miles and more since the spring. "If people now talk of lightning [*Blitz*] wars, then it is these soldiers who are responsible for it; their achievements are like lightning, because never in history have there been advances like these. . . . Of course there were also a few historic lightning retreats too," he scoffed, talking about the British regiments, "and these certainly beat our operations for speed; but then there were not such great distances involved, as they always kept that much closer to the coast!"

Within an hour Hitler's train was bearing him back to headquarters. Victory in Russia seemed certain. Guderian was approaching Orel. Like two fishermen's nets flung out over the sea, Bock's armies were hauling in their catches at Vyazma and Bryansk. Another 673,000 prisoners would be found inside. On the Sea of Azov, Rundstedt destroyed the Soviet Eighteenth Army and took another 100,000 prisoners. In front of Moscow Timoshenko seemed unaware of what was happening to his own armies—some were attacking, others retreating, while all the time Bock's nets pulled tighter.

A grim jocularity overcame Hitler—he began talking freely at mealtimes again, gossipping about the different kinds of caviar and oysters and the mysterious bacteria that had massacred the crabs some decades before. Russia? "We are planning big things for our share of the territory, 'our India'—canals and railroads, the latter with a new gauge of ten feet. The population . . . must vegetate. For Stalin's rump-empire [beyond the Urals] bolshevism will be a good thing—our guarantee of their permanent ignorance." Thus wrote Weizsäcker of Hitler's ambitions. They were an open secret. In his mind's eye, Hitler transported himself fifty years onward, to when there would be five million German farmers settled there to tend the crops. "He does not attach the slightest importance to overseas colonies," wrote Koeppen. "On this score he would most rapidly reach agreement with Britain. Germany only needs a little colonial soil to cultivate tea and coffee —everything else he would produce on the Continent itself. Germany's colonial needs would be satisfied by the Belgian Congo. Our Mississippi must be the Volga —not the Niger."

Outside the dining bunker at midday on October 5, Hitler espied a large table, groaning under a display of agricultural products from East Prussia, for this was Harvest Thanksgiving day. He jested that this vegetarian display with its many hues and colors was far more attractive than if, for example, a pile of "butchered animal carcasses" had been put there—a comment that enjoyed only a mixed reception since there were the most luscious pork chops for lunch that day. At dinner the next day, Hitler was again in an expansive mood. Major Engel, his ebullient army adjutant, had been bitten by a dog, so Hitler uncorked a stream of witticisms about the fearful consequences if rabies should take hold at his headquarters. Dinner was short, so that the latest uncensored newsreel films could be shown. Hitler saw for himself his troops battling forward under General von Manstein, now commanding the Eleventh Army in the assault on the Crimea; he also saw the northern armies frustrating the frantic Russian attempts to relieve Leningrad.

By October 7, the Bryansk pocket was completely sealed, and the armored divisions were about to close the other huge ring around Vyazma. Jodl stated that the Red Army was about to lose seventy-two divisions in the two pockets, and that so far radio reconnaissance had only located one solitary division outside them. Gripped by this military drama, Hitler did not eat that day—although Himmler was guest of honor, it being his forty-first birthday. Hewel marveled in his diary: "Vyazma has been captured. The net tightens around Timoshenko's army. Jodl says, 'The most crucial day of the whole Russian war,' and compares it with Königgrätz."

Intercepted code-messages from diplomats in Moscow suggested that the end there was not far off. The Turkish ambassador told of tens of thousands of casualties and an indescribable turmoil and confusion; parts of the city's population were already fleeing for the Ural Mountains. Immense German plans were hatched in this flush of victory—the General Staff looking beyond Moscow, Hitler looking to the south. For a time, elated by his SS Life Guards' capture of Mariupol (Zhdanov) on the Sea of Azov, Hitler considered throwing them a hundred miles forward to Rostov on the Don—the very gateway to the Caucasus and the oil fields there. ("The fact that in the not too distant future we'll have used up every last drop of gasoline makes this a matter of the utmost urgency," Keitel told Canaris later in October.) General Eduard Wagner, the army's quartermaster general, wrote privately late on October 5: "Now the operation is rolling toward Moscow. Our impression is that the final great collapse is immediately ahead, and that tonight the Kremlin is packing its bags. What matters now is that the panzer armies reach their objectives. Strategic objectives are being defined that would have stood our hair on end at one time. East of Moscow!! Then I think the war'll be over and perhaps we'll see the collapse of their system too, which would see us a fair bit further on in the fight against Britain. I keep having to marvel at the Führer's military judgment. This time he is intervening—and one can say, decisively—in the operations, and so far he has been right every time. The major victory in the south is *his* work alone."

On October 8, Jodl repeated his triumphant verdict: "We have finally and without any exaggeration won this war!" At dinner Hitler exultantly scoffed at the distortions being put about by London's "Press Jews"—claims so foolish that a schoolboy with an atlas could refute them. In France Admiral Darlan had now spoken out in favor of a German-French entente. "Success," commented Hitler, "is always the best basis for bargaining."

On the eastern front it had now begun to rain.

In Kiev—and later in Odessa—there was an urban variation on the scorched earth theme: the Russians had booby-trapped entire buildings, to blow them up by remote control after the Germans moved in. According to the Soviet radio, Leningrad had been similarly prepared. Moscow would be no different. On October 7, Hitler signed an OKW order forbidding Bock to accept Moscow's surrender, if offered; no German troops were to set foot there or in Leningrad—these cities were to be encircled and wiped out by fire and bombardment. Small gaps might be left on the far side of the Moscow ring, to allow the citizenry to flee eastward into the Soviet lines and increase the chaos there. A few days later, Heydrich asked Himmler to make it clear to the Führer that responsibility for the effective destruction of Leningrad and Moscow rested solely with the Wehrmacht commanders. He said the SS agents who had penetrated into Leningrad reported that the damage so far was quite negligible, and that if they had learned anything from Warsaw it was that artillery alone was not enough—massive use had to be made of fire bombs and high explosives.

The coming victory over Russia promised to relieve Hitler of immense strategic burdens. Japan would then be free to wade into the United States, which would then hardly be in a position to come to Britain's aid in her final fight with Germany. Roosevelt for his part increased his efforts to swing American public opinion around to supporting war with Hitler now, and he sent Averell Harriman to assist Britain's Lord Beaverbrook at a Moscow conference on ways of rushing military support to Stalin. On October 6, Hitler was handed the decoded text of Roosevelt's letter introducing Harriman to Stalin:

Harry Hopkins has told me in great detail of his encouraging and satisfactory visits with you. I can't tell you how thrilled all of us are because of the gallant defense of the Soviet armies. I am confident that ways will be found to provide the material and supplies necessary to fight Hitler on all fronts, including your own. I want particularly to take this occasion to express my great confidence that your armies will ultimately prevail over Hitler and to assure you of our great determination to be of every possible material assistance.

Hitler had the text of this letter released throughout the Americas, without revealing how he had obtained it; he also, to the intense irritation of Roosevelt, amended the president's salutation ("My Dear Mr. Stalin") to "My Dear Friend Stalin"; and where Roosevelt had prudently concluded with "Yours very sincerely," the German propaganda text ended with an oily "In cordial friendship."

Roosevelt had long gone beyond strict neutrality. Early in September a U-boat had given him the welcome chance by attempting to torpedo the American destroyer *Greer* (which had reportedly been cooperating with a British plane chasing the submarine); as a result of this attack, on the eleventh Roosevelt ordered the navy to "shoot on sight" any warships of the Axis powers encountered in seas, "the protection of which is necessary for American defense." Hitler no longer believed the isolationists could keep the United States out of the war, in spite of efforts such as those by Charles Lindbergh, who used the American radio networks to denounce "warmongers," among whom he included not only Roosevelt and the British but the Jews as well. Admiral Raeder implored the Führer to permit German warships to meet force with force, since Roosevelt's announcement was tantamount to a localized declaration of war under international law; but after discussing this from every angle with Raeder and U-boat commander Admiral Dönitz—as well as with Ribbentrop—Hitler remained unconvinced that the military advantages would outweigh the political risks involved in firing back on any U.S. naval attackers, and his restrictions on the warships remained in force. He was not frightened of Roosevelt or the United States. Handed an American magazine which quoted annual statistics on tank and aircraft production in the United States, Hitler scoffed that the figures were ludicrously low—less than one month's output of the German munitions industry. As for quality, he rocked with laughter when he saw the first newsreels of the United States' two mechanized divisions on maneuvers (the film reached him through South America).

Hitler could not conceal his disappointment at the current aimlessness of Japanese foreign policy, which he had closely followed through the telegrams intercepted by the Forschungsamt and foreign ministry decoders. The Japanese had refused to show the Germans the texts of their secret exchanges with the Roosevelt administration, but in September Hitler explained to his staff that he was loath to put pressure on Tokyo to enter the war in case this was construed as proof of German weakness. By October 1941 Hitler no longer feared this construction; he even somewhat prematurely directed his press chief, Dr. Otto Dietrich, to announce to the world—and Tokyo in particular—that the Russian campaign had been won. But Tokyo's secret talks with Washington still continued; her economy was suffering from the overlong interruption of the Trans-Siberian railway by "Barbarossa"—far longer than the "two months" Hitler had promised—and on October 16 the Japanese Cabinet resigned. To Hitler's annoyance the new prime minister was General Hideki Tojo, and his foreign minister was Shigenori Togo, the former Japanese ambassador to Berlin; Hitler intensely mistrusted the latter, despite his German wife. He saw in all this just Japanese playacting designed to assuage domestic public opinion, while the Japanese continued to wriggle out of their commitments for a few more months. The truth was, as he revealed by an aside to Ciano on October 25, that Hitler was completely in the dark as to Japanese war plans. "We cannot expect Japan to pursue anything but a purely Japanese foreign policy," he had also said in September. "We must just contrive to wait until they themselves consider the time ripe for intervention." As for North America, Hitler learned that Pope Pius XII had instructed Roosevelt's special emissary Myron C. Taylor that any extension of the war by the United States would be frowned on. Indeed, the Vatican had flatly refused to pronounce the war of the democracies against National Socialism a "just war"; Hitler learned this on October 7.

That same day Field Marshal von Bock was ordered to proceed with his drive on Moscow and the first snow drifted out of the sky onto Hitler's headquarters. On the sixteenth a fighter pilot arriving at the Führer's headquarters to receive the Knight's Cross announced that six inches of snow was covering the whole countryside. On the seventeenth the temperature at Leningrad fell to 32°F.; in the far north it was 5°. The next day for the first time the weather was so bad as to prevent any noticeable change in the front lines. Bock's army group was paralyzed by the snow, slush, and slime. Nothing could move except on foot or in the lightest of handcarts, for the roads were few and far between and it was on these that the Russians now concentrated their defense. The only good highway —from Smolensk to Vyazma—had been booby-trapped with high-explosive shells, whose remote-controlled detonation caused sudden craters thirty feet wide and eight feet deep. Each night the temperatures fell and froze the snow and mud; each morning the thaw set in, and the roads were again impassable.

"The Russian roads beggar description," wrote one of Canaris's aides touring the eastern front. "They are frequently up to one hundred yards wide and people use them as they choose. Their surface is a thick, cloying layer of slime of varying depth: if you drive slowly, it bogs your truck down, and if you drive faster, you start sliding and skidding; despite the width of the roads it is enormously difficult to take evasive action, for all the traffic in both directions tries to keep to the same beaten tracks; as these ruts are very difficult to get out of, collisions occur." As the German troops struggled to advance through this filth and slush they encountered mournful columns of Russians trudging westward into captivity. There were hundreds of thousands of them, and they presented the German military authorities with problems of feeding, transportation, and accommodation they had never clearly envisaged. "The columns of Russian prisoners moving on the roads look like half-witted herds of animals," Canaris's aide noted. Barely guarded and kept in order by the fist and whip, these wretched prisoners marched until they were exhausted by hunger or disease; they were then carried by their comrades or left at the roadside. "The Sixth Army [Reichenau's] has ordered that all prisoners that break down are to be shot. Regrettably this is done at the roadside, even in the villages, so that the local population are eyewitnesses of these incidents." In the prison camps the food was so meager that cannibalism broke out. "The population," the report continued, "greet the German soldiers as liberators from the yoke of bolshevism. But there is a danger that this extremely useful mood, which is displayed by their great hospitality and many gifts, will turn into the opposite if dealt with wrongly."

The first big anti-Jewish SS action occurred at Kiev at the end of September. The report to Canaris by the previously mentioned aide noted: "Orders are that the Jews are to be 'resettled.' This takes place as follows: the Jews are ordered at short notice to report to specific collecting points with their best clothes and their jewelry on the following night. No distinctions are made as to class, sex, or age. They are then taken to a preselected and prepared site outside the town concerned, where they have to deposit their jewelry and clothes under the pretext of having to complete certain formalities. They are led away from the road and liquidated. The situations that arise in the process are so horrifying that they can not be described. The effects on the German squads are inevitable—the executions can usually only be carried out under the influence of alcohol. An SD officer ordered to act as an observer related how he had nightmares of the most terrible kind for days afterward. The native population react to this liquidation program, of which they are fully aware, calmly and sometimes with satisfaction, and the Ukrainian militia actually take part." There were even protests that some Jews were escaping the net cast by the SS task forces.[1]

The actual origins of the Kiev pogrom are obscure. The report of the security police suggests that the massacre was a reprisal impatiently demanded by the Ukrainians themselves, since it was the Russian Jews who were reported to have acted as NKVD agents and set fire to the city after the Germans moved in. Whatever the origin, on the last two days of September 33,771 Russian Jews were executed at Kiev. One month later the figure had risen to 75,000.

There are compelling indications that all this was planned long before "Barbarossa" began: at a course for SS task force commanders at Düben in June, Heydrich had instructed them—according to Walter Blume, one such comman-

---

[1]Thus a renegade Russian major named Chumak wrote in a report in December 1942 (forwarded by Colonel Gehlen, the new head of Foreign Armies East, to his superiors): "Take the Ukraine: for twenty-three years this nation had to bear the Jewish yoke without protest and in far greater degree than any other nation in Russia. . . . Yet even though all the Jews were shot between September 28 and October 1 [1941], Kiev is now swarming with them again, and all of them have been issued Russian papers."

der—that these *Ostjuden* were the intellectual reservoir of bolshevism and "in the Führer's view" were to be liquidated. Himmler, the SS Reichsführer, had orally briefed them in the same sense in May, and late in September he toured the task force headquarters and announced to them—for example to Otto Ohlendorf, commanding Task Force D, in a speech at Nikolaev—that he alone "in association with Hitler" was responsible.

Himmler's formulation was perhaps purposefully vague. There are documents which strongly suggest that Hitler's responsibility—as distinct from Himmler's —was limited to the decision to deport all European Jews to the east, and that responsibility for what happened to Russian Jews and to European Jews after their arrival in "the east" rested with Himmler, Heydrich, and the local authorities there—who took full advantage of the atmosphere of hatred and contempt for human life created by their Führer. On September 18, 1941, Himmler wrote to Arthur Greiser, the brutal Gauleiter of the Wartheland—that is, the Polish territories annexed in the German invasion two years earlier:

> The Führer wishes the old Reich territory and the Protectorate [of Bohemia-Moravia] to be cleansed and rid of Jews, from west to east, as soon as possible. As a first step I am therefore endeavoring to transport—this year as far as possible—all the Jews of the old Reich and Protectorate into the eastern territories annexed by the Reich in 1939 first of all; next spring they will then be deported still further eastward [into Russia].

The first sixty thousand, Himmler advised, would be sent to the Lodz ghetto soon to spend the winter there. Heydrich would be in charge of this "migration of the Jews." Evidently the second phase, dumping them into Russia itself, could not be begun until the Russian campaign was finished and the military pressure on the railroads was relaxed.

Hitler's own attitude is illuminated by an incident at this time. On September 20, he learned that the Bolsheviks were maltreating the large colony of ethnic Germans on the Volga: thousands were being liquidated, and the rest deported to Siberia, according to his sources. The foreign ministry recommended "reprisals against Jews in the occupied eastern territories," or even against those in the Reich. But Baron Adolf von Steengracht, Ribbentrop's representative, noted that "the Führer has not yet decided," and the next day Koeppen recorded that Hitler had decided to reserve reprisals against the Jews "for the eventuality of an American declaration of war." When Goebbels saw him two days later, he wrote in an unpublished section of his diary, only: "The Führer's opinion is that bit by bit the Jews must be got out of Germany altogether"—so even to Goebbels, his most trusted and anti-Semitic minister, Hitler made no specific mention of any extermination of either the German or the Russian Jews.

The Russian Jews had few champions. There was almost no German army opposition to their liquidation—it was regarded even by Manstein as a salutary preventive measure, wiping out the reservoirs of partisan activity before they became active. Reichenau, commanding the Sixth Army, justified it as part of the German mission to rid Europe permanently of the "Asiatic Jewish danger." In a message to his troops he proclaimed:

> In the east each soldier is not only a warrior abiding by the usual rules of war, but also the uncompromising bearer of a pure German ideal and the avenger of the bestialities committed against Germans and related races.
>
> This is why the soldier must understand why we have to exact a harsh but just retribution from the Jewish subhumans. This serves the added purpose of stifling at birth uprisings in the rear of the Wehrmacht, since experience shows that these are always conceived by Jews. . . .

Hitler considered the proclamation "excellent," and Quartermaster General Eduard Wagner circulated it to other commands as an example.

Yet no direct report by Himmler or Heydrich to Hitler on the barbarous massacres of Russian Jews they themselves had witnessed has ever come to light. At supper on October 5, for example, Himmler, who had just returned from his extended tour of the Ukraine on which he had visited Kiev, Nikolaev, and Kherson, related to Hitler his impressions of Kiev. Werner Koeppen, who was a guest at Hitler's table that evening, recorded Himmler's comments: "In Kiev . . . the number of inhabitants is still very great. The people look poor and proletarian, so that we could 'easily dispense with 80 or 90 percent of them!' The Reichsführer proposes (and the Führer immediately agrees) that the oldest Russian monastery at Kiev should be confiscated to prevent its becoming the focus of orthodoxy and nationalism. The monastery is at present being guarded by German troops because of its priceless religious treasures."

Hitler's surviving adjutants, secretaries, and staff stenographers have *all* uniformly testified that never once was the extermination of either the Russian or European Jews mentioned—even confidentially—at Hitler's headquarters. Even SS General Karl Wolff, Himmler's Chief of Staff and liaison officer to Hitler, was at this time ignorant of the program that now got under way.[2] Colonel Rudolf Schmundt, a regular visitor to the Russian front, appears to have suspected what was going on there; for when Hitler's movie cameraman Walter Frentz willingly accompanied Himmler to Minsk on an outing with stage designer Benno von Arent, he found himself the horrified witness of a mass open-air execution; Schmundt advised him to destroy the one color photograph he took, and "not to poke his nose into matters that did not concern him."

---

[2] He began to suspect in August 1942. See page 393.

By mid-October 1941, despite the foul weather, the Russian front was cracking in every joint. Hitler was still fired with optimism. On the thirteenth he and Ribbentrop first began laying the foundations for a Nazi version of a united Europe. Hewel wrote: "Reich foreign minister visits the Führer: first thoughts on a European manifesto. Probably in the economic sphere first of all, and probably at the beginning of the winter. Führer is in very best and relaxed mood." Over dinner he revealed that he had been thinking of calling together the economic experts of Denmark, Norway, Holland, Belgium, Sweden, and Finland to bring it home to them that Russia was an outlet for all their surplus population and a source of all the raw materials they might require. "I think it not impossible they would then come over into our own camp with flags flying." He unfolded his economic ideas—based on European self-sufficiency—to his own minister of economics, Walther Funk, the same day; Funk was enthusiastic. Hitler had a vision in which the Danube, which is linked by the Black Sea to the Dnieper and Don, would now be joined by canals to the Main and Oder. "All those who have a feeling for Europe can join in this work," meaning the colonization of the east. And: "Everybody will be able to participate, in one form or another, in this European economy." (A month later he was to say, "With our new economic organization, the political center of Europe is shifting. England will be nothing but a vast Holland. The Continent is coming back to life.")

His feelings toward the British people remained unchanged. One evening, an English magazine was passed around the little group chatting in his bunker. One photograph showed seven or eight RAF airmen clustered in front of their bomber aircraft; all were young and keen-looking. Hitler tapped the picture and sighed, "I wonder how many crews like these Göring could show me!" But there was an underlying bitterness against the "uncomprehending" British government which had followed its invasion of Iran with a demand that the Iranians surrender to them the German colony there of 220, and hand over 21 to the Russians. Hitler, who had agreed in secret negotiations to repatriate 1,140 sick British prisoners, partly from the hospitals of Dunkirk, in exchange for 44 German prisoners in a similar condition, stopped the exchange when the British interned and flatly refused to release the German colony in Iran.

When Todt and Fritz Sauckel—Hitler's manpower commissioner—dined with Hitler on October 17, they were brimming with everything they had just seen in the east. Again Hitler dreamed aloud of the vast construction projects whereby he would open up the east in a manner similar to the way the Americans had colonized the west. "Above all we must lay roads," Koeppen wrote that night.

He told Dr. Todt he must expand his original projects considerably. For this purpose he will be able to make use of the three million prisoners for the next

twenty years. The major roads—the Führer spoke today not only of the highway to the Crimea but also of one to the Caucasus and of two or three through
the more northern territories—must be laid across the areas of greatest scenic
beauty. Where the big rivers are crossed, German cities must arise, as centers
of the Wehrmacht, police, administration, and Party authorities. Along these
roads will lie the German farmsteads, and soon the monotonous steppe, with
its Asiatic appearance, will look very different indeed. In ten years four million
Germans will have settled there, and in twenty years at least ten million. They
will come not only from the Reich but above all from America, and from
Scandinavia, Holland, and Flanders too. And the rest of Europe shall play its
part in this opening up of the Russian wastes as well. No Germans will set foot
in the Russian towns, insofar as they survive this war (which Leningrad and
Moscow certainly will not); let them continue to rot away in their filthy
vegetable existence far from the great highways! The Führer then reverted to
the theme that "contrary to what some people think" no education or welfare
is to be laid on for the native population. Knowledge of the road signs will
suffice, there will be no call for German schoolmasters there. By "freedom" the
Ukrainians understood that instead of twice they now had to wash only once
a month—the Germans with their scrubbing brushes would soon make themselves unpopular there. He as Führer would set up his new administration there
after ice-cool calculations: what the Slavs might think about it would not put
him out one bit. Nobody who ate German bread today got worked up about
the fact that in the twelfth century the granaries east of the Elbe were regained
by the sword. Here in the east we were repeating a process for a second time
not unlike the conquest of·America. For climatic reasons alone we could not
venture further south than the Crimea—he did not mention the Caucasus at
this point—even now hundreds of our mountain troops on Crete had malaria!
The Führer kept repeating that he wished he was ten or fifteen years younger
so he could live through the rest of this process.

The remorseless advance of the German armies to the east and southeast
continued. The Ninth Army took Rzhev, the Romanians took Odessa, German
tanks rolled into Taganrog, mountain troops captured Stalino, Reichenau captured Kharkov and Belgorod, and Manstein's Eleventh Army at last broke
through into the Crimean peninsula.

At the same time, the next phase of the deportation of Europe's Jews began.
The evidence is that Hitler's intention was twofold—to establish a Jewish labor
force for his grandiose plans in the east, and to hold them hostage. (The "Jewish
hostage" motif appears again late in 1943.[3]) There was no word of massacring
them. On October 6, 1941, Hitler again pronounced at lunch, as Koeppen noted:
"All the Jews must be removed from the Protectorate—and not just to the

[3]When Hitler forbade the liquidation of Rome's Jews: see page 575.

Generalgouvernement but right on to the east. It is only our heavy need for war transport that stops us doing this right now. At the same time as the Jews from the Protectorate, all the Jews are to disappear from Berlin and Vienna too. The Jews are everywhere the grapevine along which enemy news reports filter into every nook and cranny of our nation with the speed of the winds." Hitherto Adolf Eichmann, one of Himmler's leading experts on Jewish affairs, had continued holding regular conferences with his regional officials on the various problems associated with the "Madagascar plan"—for example, the reeducation of professional Jews into the laborers, farmers, and artisans that would be needed in the new island-state. But on October 18, Himmler scribbled on his telephone pad the message he had just dictated to Heydrich: "No emigration by Jews to overseas."[4] Instead, on October 15, 1941, the big exodus from Europe to the east began—the Jews being herded initially into camps in Poland and the Lodz ghetto. "In daily transports of a thousand people, 20,000 Jews and 5,000 gypsies are being sent to the Lodz ghetto between October 15 and November 8," Heydrich informed Himmler on October 19. For the time being Himmler reluctantly kept the able-bodied Jews alive for the work they could perform; but farther east the Gauleiters had no intention of preserving the unemployable Jews: a letter dated October 25 in SS files states that Adolf Eichmann had now approved Gauleiter Lohse's proposal that those arriving at Riga should be killed by mobile gas-trucks. This initially *ad hoc* operation gathered momentum. Soon the Jews from the Lodz ghetto and Greiser's territories were being deported farther east—to the extermination camp at Chelmno. There were 152,000 Jews involved in all, and Chelmno began liquidating them on December 8.

At this stage of the Jewish massacre it is possible to be more specific about the instigators, because on May 1, 1942, Greiser himself mentioned in a letter to Himmler that the current "special treatment" program of the hundred thousand Jews in his own Gau had been authorized by Himmler "with the agreement of" Heydrich. Hitler was not mentioned. Meanwhile, from mid-November 1941 onward, the Reichsbahn trainloads of Jews—rounded up in Vienna, Brünn (Brno), Bremen, and Berlin—headed direct to Minsk, while others went to Warsaw, Kovno, and Riga. At Kovno and Riga the Jews were invariably shot soon after. At Minsk the Jews did not survive much longer: Richard Kube, Rosenberg's general commissioner of White Ruthenia, recorded on July 31, 1942, that 10,000 had been liquidated since the twenty-eighth, "of which 6,500 were Russian Jews, old folk, women and children, with the rest unemployable Jews largely sent to

---

[4]On February 10, 1942, a foreign ministry official noted that since "Barbarossa" had acquired other territories suitable for a solution of the Jewish problem, "the Führer has accordingly decided that the Jews are to be deported not to Madagascar but to the east."

Minsk from Vienna, Brünn, Bremen, and Berlin in November last year on the Führer's orders." It is not without evidentiary value that Himmler's handwritten telephone notes include one on a call to Heydrich on November 17, 1941, on the "situation in the Generalgouvernement" and "getting rid of the Jews"; two days later Heydrich circulated invitations to an interministerial conference on the Final Solution of the Jewish Problem—delayed until January 1942, it became notorious as the Wannsee Conference.

No documentary evidence exists that Hitler was aware that the Jews were being massacred upon their arrival. His remarks, noted by Bormann's adjutant Heinrich Heim late on October 25, 1941, indicate that he did not favor it: "From the rostrum of the Reichstag I prophesied to Jewry that if war could not be avoided, the Jews would disappear from Europe. That race of criminals already had on its conscience the two million dead of the Great War, and now it has hundreds of thousands more. Let nobody tell me that despite that we cannot park them in the marshy parts of Russia! Our troops are there as well, and who worries about them! By the way—it's not a bad thing that public rumor attributes to us a plan to exterminate the Jews. Terror is a salutary thing." Hitler added that, just as he was sidestepping an open clash with the Vatican by postponing the final reckoning with Bishop von Galen until later, "with the Jews too I have found myself remaining inactive. There's no point adding to one's difficulties at a time like this."[5] Hans Lammers testified later that this was undoubtedly Hitler's policy, for when he tackled Hitler on a statement by Himmler that the Führer had charged him with deporting the Jews from Germany, Hitler confirmed this but added, "I don't want to be bothered with the Jewish problem again until the war is over."

This does not gainsay the fact that Hitler felt a deep revulsion for Jews. On November 5, for example, Koeppen noted after dinner: "The Führer denies that Jews have any talent for anything. They surpass the other races in only one respect—the art of the lie and its unscrupulous application. . . . Shut them up together with only their own kind, in other words where their lying loses its effectiveness, and their 'talents' desert them and the Jew descends into squalor and poverty. While the Aryan races are improved the more they are allowed to coexist with their racial equals, the Jews suffer by it and degenerate into animals. With their lie that they are a *religious* community, and by calling their money

---

[5] In March 1942 a memo was inserted in a Reich justice ministry file of correspondence with Lammers's Reich Chancellery to the effect that Hitler intended to postpone solution of the "Jewish problem" until after the war. The memo was catalogued as Item No. 4 on a "Staff Evidence Analysis Sheet" (Nuremberg document 4025-PS) when the file was first examined by Allied investigators at the Ministerial Collection Center in West Berlin in June 1946. It is now missing. Dr. Robert Kempner, the Nuremberg prosecutor who certified copies of those items produced as trial exhibits (US-923) in August 1946, evidently did not find this document.

markets temples, they pulled the wool over the eyes of tolerant bygone generations right up to the present day. In reality no Jew has ever delved into the metaphysical—their whole religion is based on the laws of race."

In most circumstances Hitler was a pragmatist. It would have been unlike him to sanction the use of scarce transport space to move millions of Jews east for no other purpose than liquidating them there; nor would he willingly destroy manpower, for which his industry was crying out. Heinrich Heim recalls one exasperated comment by Hitler when Allied radio broadcast an announcement that the Jews were being exterminated: "Really, the Jews should be *grateful* to me for wanting nothing more than a bit of hard work from them." It was Heydrich and the fanatical Gauleiters in the east who were interpreting with brutal thoroughness Hitler's decree that the Jews must "finally disappear" from Europe; Himmler's personal role is ambivalent. On November 30, 1941, he was summoned to the Wolf's Lair for a secret conference with Hitler, at which the fate of Berlin's Jews was clearly raised. At 1:30 P.M. Himmler was obliged to telephone from Hitler's bunker to Heydrich the explicit order that Jews were *not to be liquidated;* and the next day Himmler telephoned SS General Oswald Pohl, overall chief of the concentration camp system, with the order: "Jews are to stay where they are."[6]

Yet the blood purge continued. The extermination program had gained a momentum of its own. Hans Frank, announcing to his Lublin cabinet on December 16, 1941, that Heydrich was calling a big conference in January on the expulsion of Europe's Jews to the east, irritably exclaimed, "Do you imagine they're going to be housed in neat estates in the Baltic provinces! In Berlin"—and with Hitler in East Prussia this can only be taken as a reference to Heydrich's agencies —"they tell us: why the caviling? We've got no use for them either. . . . Liquidate them yourselves!"

During October 1941 the Russians stubbornly prevented Hitler from encircling Leningrad completely when the Finnish and German armies advancing on either shore of Lake Ladoga were unable to meet. Partly for political reasons, Mannerheim—the Finnish commander—ignored Hitler's appeals to penetrate more steadfastly onto Russian territory; Field Marshal von Leeb was unable to advance the whole way to meet him. To encourage Mannerheim to resume the offensive, Hitler ordered Leeb to strike with his Sixteenth Army toward the city of Tikhvin —which would cut the sole railway line between Leningrad and Moscow.

By this time, mid-October, Moscow's fate seemed sealed. The Communist

[6]Himmler's original note on his telephone conversations of November 30, 1941, appears as a facsimile illustration, page 505.

party headquarters, the government, and the diplomatic corps had been evacuated. On the night of October 16 the files of the Frunse military academy—to which Stalin had delivered his anti-German speeches in May—were burned. Nobody knew who had started the panic or ordered the evacuations. Then the rains came and "Operation Typhoon" slithered to a halt. Bock's army group foundered in an unprecedented autumn morass of mud, rain, and slush. His generals had never seen anything like it. Trucks sank up to their axles and had to be winched out. Many were literally torn apart in the attempt. Of half a million vehicles, suddenly the German army lost 150,000. The enemy was fighting only a few miles from his arms factories and arsenals, and could use an intact network of railways around Moscow. But as they had withdrawn, they had methodically ripped up every railway track and tie to deny this weatherproof form of transport to the Germans. The Luftwaffe's deputy chief of staff General Hoffmann von Waldau, who had confidently predicted on October 10: "As long as the weather does not continue to deteriorate (and at present it is fine, 28° to 22°) the enemy will not be able to prevent us from encircling Moscow," followed this with a frustrated diary entry six days later: "Our wildest dreams have been washed out by rain and snow. . . . Everything is bogged down in a bottomless quagmire. The temperature drops to 11°, a foot of snow falls, and then it rains on top of the snow." Leeb's tanks attacking Tikhvin had to be left behind; on October 24, Hitler decided to abandon the operation, but two days later Leeb came in person to Rastenburg and persuaded him—against Hitler's better instincts as the army group's war diary records—to allow it to proceed. In the Ukraine low clouds, icing, and snow were grounding the Luftwaffe. In the attack on Rostov, General von Kleist's tanks were running out of gasoline.

Thus Hitler's bold hopes for the *rapid* overthrow of Stalin's regime were thwarted by the weather. Now all the other strategic issues which he had optimistically adjourned—the Battle of the Atlantic, North Africa, the partisan war, the British second front, and the enemy's bombing offensive, not to mention the possibility of open war with the United States in 1942—had to be squarely met. In the northern theater, an unusually early winter had begun. Over lunch on October 26, Hitler asked the army's quartermaster general, the ebullient Eduard Wagner, to what extent he had provisioned the eastern armies with winter gear. Both the Luftwaffe and the SS had prepared for their winter campaign in Russia in February or March 1941, and during the summer Hitler had continually reminded Wagner to see to army winter needs. However, Wagner's private letters indicate that he had only addressed himself to the problem on October 19; but now he assured Hitler that by October 30 both Leeb and Rundstedt would have received half their winter equipment, while the numerically far bigger Army Group Center would have received only one-third. (He mentioned that the Russians' destruction of the one railway along the Sea of Azov would delay supplies to the south.) "The Führer was extremely nice and friendly to me," wrote Wagner.

In fact, Wagner and the General Staff were more optimistic than Hitler. On October 29, Wagner noted that an enemy pipeline had been captured, still spewing forth gasoline, and this would enable the tanks to press on into Rostov. "Everything else is also moving again, and we're convinced we'll shortly finish off Moscow." The Crimea was captured, and Manstein's advance troops were already outside Sevastopol—the ancient fortress at its southern point. But winter was unmistakably closing in: on October 30, Admiral Canaris flew in to Rastenburg, his plane almost colliding with another in the fog. Hitler ran into him on the way to the map room, and asked what weather Canaris had seen at the front. Canaris told him "Bad!" and Hitler gestured with annoyance. (A member of the admiral's staff wrote: "They're all getting on each other's nerves—a bad case of the camp jitters.") The next day snow settled on the Wolf's Lair too. On November 1, Hitler spent an hour at General Staff headquarters, inspecting for himself the winter equipment Wagner had organized. He made no comment, but Wagner noted: "He looked at and listened closely to everything; he appeared fresh and lively and was in a good mood."

But a mood of restlessness, of uneasiness and annoyance, beset him. The war might now go on for two more years, he realized; and what would be left of Germany and the flower of her manhood when it was over? Already a hundred and fifty thousand men had died since "Barbarossa" began; a war like this was bound to disrupt the national metabolism, if the good blood was being constantly drained away while the evil and pernicious elements were leading their "charmed" existence in the concentration camps, and all because the Russians had proved tougher than he had bargained for, and because that "drunken poltroon" Churchill refused to admit the mess he was getting his empire into. Thus Adolf Hitler argued with himself in the months to come. From reliable sources he knew Stalin had warned Roosevelt that his munitions would be exhausted by early December, but he also knew—from radio intercepts—that Churchill was moving heaven and earth to start shipments of arms to Archangel. Hitler ardently hoped that one day the opposition to Churchill's war policies would cause his undoing. "It's significant that Britain has already had to lock up over nine thousand people in concentration camps for this reason," he remarked on October 22. "Unfortunately the leading pro-Germans like Rothermere and Lord Londonderry are too deeply in the Jewish thrall to be able to put up any real opposition."

Even at this late date he still longed for the great Anglo-German concord which would restore immediate peace. However, from a remark made by Lord Halifax in Lisbon it was clear that Churchill was just waiting for some such hint of an offer—presumably after Russia's seemingly inevitable defeat—to give him a chance of publicly rebuking the Führer and restoring Roosevelt's faith in Britain. Hitler did not expect Roosevelt to start massive arms deliveries to Russia at this point, and even if Stalin did manage to discharge his present military bankruptcy, what was there the United States could offer? At best an obsolete tank model, for American artillery was useless, and the much vaunted Flying Fortress bombers were—Göring had assured him—of such poor quality, thanks to mass-production methods, that they would be easy prey for any German fighter. In short, neither Britain nor the United States could save Russia. Thus he deceived himself.

Hitler's continued wooing of Britain was both illogical and detrimental to his own war effort. It was the reason he gave Colonel Wilhelm Speidel for rejecting the French offers of collaboration—that it would stand in the way of the later concord with Britain. And when Raeder's Chief of Staff, Admiral Fricke, argued with compelling logic that Britain's military defeat was necessary for any New Order in Europe, and that this defeat could only be achieved by concentrating on the submarine war in the Atlantic, Hitler explained that he was even now ready to make peace with Britain, as the territory Germany had already won in Europe was adequate for the German people's future needs. The admiral gathered that to Hitler a colonial empire in central Africa was of only secondary interest. "Evidently," the admiral reported, "the Führer would be glad for Britain, once the eastern campaign is over, to show signs of sense (*not* that the Führer expects it of Churchill) even if it meant that Germany could not win further ground than she already occupies." Hitler was not bothered about any "formalized, legalized" termination of the war, the admiral concluded.

Hitler's attitude toward Britain was a disappointment to his naval staff. In a nutshell, Hitler's strategy was governed by the need to avoid defeat by Britain, rather than by the necessity of defeating her outright now. Britain's bombing offensive against the northwest coast (and, of course, Italy) was becoming a serious nuisance to morale; Hitler ordered Göring to increase aircraft and antiaircraft production. Britain would not risk invading the French mainland yet, but she might attempt to seize back one of her Channel Isles. Hitler therefore sent Colonel Schmundt to inspect those islands' defenses; afterward, he ordered the army to appoint particularly active garrison commanders to each island and to multiply their infantry and artillery defenses. Britain might invade northern Norway and cut off Germany's iron-ore and nickel supplies; here too Hitler ordered the reluctant navy to take precautions, although Raeder thought it unlikely Britain would risk such an invasion in winter. Most promising for the enemy would seem to be an invasion somewhere in the Mediterranean, perhaps on Sardinia or Pantelleria.

The Mediterranean had quietly become one of the most vulnerable areas of Axis operations, particularly now that Mussolini's very position was threatened by domestic unrest. The British, with sea and air superiority in the Mediterranean, were slowly but surely throttling the seaborne supplies to North Africa, of which Rommel and the Italian troops needed some five thousand tons a day. Hitler sadly reflected that if he could capture Gibraltar it would solve the whole problem with one blow, but without Spain's consent this was impossible. As Rommel's supply predicament worsened, Hitler angrily complained that the Wehrmacht commanders had not kept him informed of the situation; but this was not true, for Raeder had predicted this since early July and had demanded that Göring divert Luftwaffe units to safeguard the supply line to Tripoli. In September, Hitler had ordered the Tenth Air Corps to do so, but Jeschonnek had got him to change his mind by arguing that the Luftwaffe was barely capable of fulfilling its "Barbarossa" tasks as it was. In vain Raeder cabled Hitler that victory in Russia would hardly depend on whether or not thirty or forty aircraft were switched to the Mediterranean. Not until mid-October did Hitler tell Mussolini in a letter that Göring would furnish Luftwaffe support, but by then the rot had set in.

At the end of the month he ordered the navy virtually to abandon the Battle of the Atlantic and switch its submarine force to the Mediterranean too. Italy's tottering regime must be militarily buttressed at all costs. The food shortage and British bombing raids had badly impaired Italian morale. Hitler told Admiral Fricke on the twenty-seventh that the Italian royal family, the anti-Fascist elements, the freemasons, and the Vatican were all deeply opposed to the war. "Let there be no mistake—the Fascist regime is not as secure as the German government. Any change of government in Italy would spell the end of the Fascist regime, and Italy would unquestionably cross into the enemy camp." Large sections of the Italian public were pro-British. The defection of Italy would moreover lead to the loss of France to the enemy as well, and hence the defection of Spain. The "safeguarding of our Continental territory is now our first strategic commandment for the time being," Hitler ordered. Because of this, the active war against Britain must be abandoned: the *Schwerpunkt* (focus) of U-boat operations must be moved from the Atlantic to the Mediterranean; he wanted twenty-four submarines stationed there as soon as possible. In vain Fricke argued that now —with Russia on the verge of collapse—was no time to remove the noose from Britain's neck, and that Italy must do more to escort the supply convoys to Tripoli herself—either by sealing off the Straits of Sicily with minefields or by eliminating Malta.

In Hitler's view the risk to Italy, to the soft underbelly of Europe, was too real to let the rot in the Mediterranean go on.

A Test of Endurance

In Stalin, Hitler unquestionably now knew, he had met his match. As the Soviet resistance hardened despite each fresh catastrophe inflicted on its armies, Hitler's admiration for his Bolshevik adversary grew. "This Stalin is obviously also a great man," he kept telling his baffled generals. "To claim anything else would not make sense. Historians of the future will have to set out from the fact that today's events are governed by the collision or collusion of great, towering personalities whose paths cross like this only once in many centuries."

The Wehrmacht had captured over three million Russian prisoners. No estimate could be put on the Red Army's casualties. The Soviet Union had lost most of its aluminum, manganese, pig iron, and coal resources. As soon as Hitler's armies could penetrate beyond Rostov into the Caucasus, Stalin would lose 90 percent of his oil as well. This was why Hitler could only smile confidently when he read in Intelligence reports that Stalin was rebuilding his armies beyond the Urals. Hitler learned that Averell Harriman said in confidence early in November 1941 that the Russian leader took three days to agree to the western condition that the Soviet Union must not make a separate peace with Hitler, and even then he made his agreement conditional on receiving adequate war supplies from the West. In Moscow, meanwhile, tens of thousands of people were being evacuated. Some of those who had to stay in the capital tried to obtain swastika flags and German dictionaries in anticipation of the city's capture.

For the first two weeks of November the German armies were held immobile by the mud and mire. The Russians were able to build line after line of defensive positions. There were those generals—Erich Hoepner among them—who bitterly criticized their army superiors for not giving the panzer *Gruppen* their head in the October offensive but rather tying them rigidly to the infantry armies; this overcautiousness, bordering on defeatism, had deprived Hoepner of the chance of destroying all the Russian reserve forces as well. Now these reserves, augmented by workers from the Moscow factories and freshly arrived Siberian divisions—magnificently equipped with winter gear—were pouring into the capital's defenses and bracing for the frost, which would give the Germans firm ground on which to resume the attack.

Germany had still suffered no military reverses, and this was a position of strength from which Hitler was willing to envisage offering peace terms to the enemy. There are several indications of this. The most curious is the manner in which he and Ribbentrop allowed the unsuspecting former ambassador to Rome, Ulrich von Hassell, to pursue his clandestine peace feelers with American officials from September on; Heydrich submitted a full report on Hassell's activities to Ribbentrop early in November and inquired whether the ambassador was "acting with the consent or instructions" of the government. Since the secretary of the principal American involved was one of Heydrich's agents, and she and Hassell conversed freely on the telephone, it is not surprising that this conspiracy was known to the authorities. The American had asked Hassell to meet him in Lisbon; Hassell proposed Switzerland instead and sent the American a memorandum— which also fell into the hands of the German authorities—to the effect that many intelligent Germans, even if they did not fear losing the war, dreaded the devastation that even victory would entail. Since "that man down south"—meaning Mussolini—was also said to think the same way, perhaps the memorandum to the United States ambassador to Rome, William Philipps, should suggest puting out feelers to the Duce too. "At present not clear as to the How of peace—but great haste called for as otherwise danger that the various parties will go too far out onto their respective limbs to be able to go back." Hassell urged the Americans not to insist at this stage on "top authority"—meaning Hitler's written sanction for the dialogue.

By early November, Ribbentrop's diplomatic seismographs detected other signs that the Führer wanted peace. Etzdorf, Ribbentrop's liaison officer to the General Staff, listed them thus: "Ambassador von Bergen is to be replaced at the Vatican by a more active personality, one better able to monitor the peace possibilities coming through there. Everything relating to peace in the [foreign] press is to be carefully collected and immediately submitted. The same procedure is to be followed with regard to Russia's domestic situation." As for Japan: "The Führer is not particularly interested in Japan entering the war; it would only make peace more difficult." Weizsäcker, Ribbentrop's state secretary, held out no hope of peace to the army, however. He told Halder that there was no evidence that Britain was inclined toward a cessation of hostilities; he felt that any moves initiated by Germany would be rebuffed.

By the end of the month Hitler knew Weizsäcker was right. British foreign office instructions to ridicule any "peace offensive" by Hitler reached German hands. Churchill had emphasized in a Mansion House speech that to talk of Europe's future was not the sole prerogative of "those who are causing the cold blood of execution yard and scaffold to flow between the German race and other European countries." An economically self-contained Europe was, he warned, equally impracticable. "The present peace offensive," the foreign office instruction continued, "comes not, as it was intended to do, at a moment of victory over Russia, but when Germany is further away from victory than at any previous time. Hitler doubtless intended to proclaim the New Europe from the Kremlin. He is now an ersatz victor making an ersatz peace offer from an ersatz Kremlin." Hitler reminded one minister arriving in Berlin for the fifth anniversary of the Anti-Comintern Pact that Lord Halifax had bragged of being "a strong enough man" to ignore the countless letters from all over England demanding peace in 1940; this was proof, said Hitler, that the "Jewish-Bolshevik" suicidal forces still had the upper hand in London. Wistfully he added that what irritated him most was that "that cretin Churchill" was interrupting him in his mighty task of cultural reconstruction.

For Hitler, the thrills of warmaking had long palled; but not for the generals. Halder's private letters home proudly reveled in the advances "his" army had achieved. Although his own Intelligence staff warned that the Russians were moving reinforcements west of Moscow, Halder turned a blind eye on these unpalatable signs and commanded Bock's army group to delay its Moscow offensive until the logistics buildup would support a far more ambitious offensive. The Ninth Army would lunge far beyond Moscow toward Kalinin, the Volga reservoir, and Selizharovo; the Third and Fourth Panzer Gruppen would make for Vologda, and Guderian's Second Panzer Army was even assigned Gorki as its final objective for the winter. Hitler pocketed his doubts and approved the plans. On November 11 Jodl signed a directive to the army groups setting out these far-flung ambitions to be achieved before the heavy snowfalls began: "The goals would justify an extreme exertion to sever the two supply lines used by Anglo-American war materials, and to improve and safeguard our restricted petroleum supplies, by advancing on Stalingrad and a rapid capture of Maykop in the south, and the capture of Vologda in the north." Halder stoutly defended these aims at a staff conference in Orsha on November 13—optimistically counting on six weeks' campaigning before winter really closed in—but neither Bock nor Rundstedt would hear of them; thus a limited advance on Moscow only was finally approved. Had Halder's grand strategy been adopted, Hitler would undoubtedly have lost his entire eastern army in the catastrophe that shortly unfolded.

In fact Hitler was on the horns of a dilemma. Even if the nearest Russian oil fields at Maykop *could* now be seized, he lacked the tankers to bring the oil to the Mediterranean theater, where it was most needed by Italy. He had postponed his assault on the main Caucasus oil fields until 1942, but since these were likely to be so thoroughly destroyed that it would hardly be possible to produce any oil until 1943, Keitel's petroleum experts questioned whether there was any real point in invading the Caucasus at all. To Hitler, there was; he wanted to rob Stalin of his oil resources, and he had heard of British plans to establish a front in the Caucasus as well.

In another sense, Hitler showed a curious optimism. Halder wrote: "All in all he gave an impression of anticipating that when both warring parties realize that they are incapable of destroying each other there will result a negotiated peace." It was the vision of a second Verdun that kept recurring to Hitler; and the condescendingly chivalrous notion that since Stalin had fought well and fearlessly, he should be spared the fate he no doubt otherwise deserved.

With the return of the long nights, the British bombing had resumed. On November 7 no fewer than four hundred RAF bombers attacked Berlin, Mannheim, and half a dozen other targets. When Hitler arrived in Munich the next afternoon to speak at the annual beer-cellar gathering of his Old Guard, the city's population had all but fled in fear of the almost inevitable nightly air raid.

That same night a most severe blow befell the supply lines to Rommel's force in North Africa. Although Italian warships had provided strong cover, an entire Italian supply convoy of seven ships was sunk by a small British force comprised of two light cruisers and two destroyers. Admittedly there was compensation in the fact that one of Raeder's U-boats sank the aircraft carrier *Ark Royal* a few days later and another sank the battleship *Barham* before November was over, but when the British counteroffensive opened in North Africa on the eighteenth the German and Italian divisions besieging Tobruk were weak, low in fuel, and short of men and materials. Supply shipping losses were now running at sixty thousand tons a month. Rommel managed to inflict heavy losses on the enemy, but he then took the hard decision to abandon Cyrenaica. In December, however, the tide turned again in his favor: Field Marshal Kesselring arrived in Rome as Hitler's newly appointed "Commander in Chief South," and with him he brought the air power needed to regain air supremacy in the Mediterranean. On the nineteenth, bold Italian midget submariners disabled Admiral Sir Andrew Cunningham's last two battleships at Alexandria, the *Queen Elizabeth* and the *Valiant,* and he lost more big warships the next day in a minefield off Malta. Soon the British possessed only three cruisers and a handful of destroyers and submarines in the area between Gibraltar and Alexandria. New blood began to flow into Rommel's Afrika Korps.

The unexpected prolongation of the war faced Hitler with fundamental decisions on armaments policy—for soon he expected to be confronting three world empires. The wasteful use of scarce resources might have been tolerable in the

Blitzkrieg economy of 1940, but it would be no longer. His munitions minister, Fritz Todt, returned from a tour of the Russian front and in a private talk with Hitler on November 29, 1941, summed up his prognosis thus: "Given the arms and industrial supremacy of the Anglo-Saxon powers, we can no longer militarily win this war!" Hitler calmly inquired, "How am I supposed to end it, then? I can't see much possibility of ending it *politically.*"

Even before "Barbarossa," Hitler had realized that German arms production was inefficient. The aircraft industry was beset by prima-donna personalities and producing a plethora of outdated aircraft. The Luftwaffe had no long-range aircraft for reconnaissance or bombing far into the Atlantic or beyond the Urals. The new generation of fighters which Göring had promised was still unfit for squadron service. General Ernst Udet, the director of air armament, recognized his share of the blame and shot himself in November. To succeed Udet, Hitler appointed Field Marshal Erhard Milch, Göring's bustling deputy who had founded Lufthansa and built the secret prewar Luftwaffe. But it would be 1943 before Milch's appointment could have any real effect. In the last week of his life Hitler ruefully admitted that he had erred in so blindly accepting Göring's advice about Luftwaffe matters all along.

Tank design was different. Here Hitler considered himself an expert, and he was indeed far ahead of the professionals. By November 1941 he feared that the tank's useful offensive life would soon be over as the Allies had clearly got wind that summer of the German army's secret antitank shells with tungsten cores. Hitler's still-embargoed other secret weapon, the Redhead "hollow-charge" shell, would soon have to be given its debut as well. All this meant that the German panzer divisions would have to complete Hitler's program of territorial conquests quickly, and this meant building tanks stronger and in greater quantity than the British or Russians could. The huge Russian tank output, and the appearance of the Soviet T-34, had shaken him badly; when Todt now told him of two more new Russian types he had examined at Orel, Hitler exclaimed in exasperation, "How can such a primitive people manage such technical achievements in such a short time!"

Nine months had passed since Hitler had called his own first tank-design symposium at the Berghof on February 18, 1941. Then he had demanded the modification of the Mark III and Mark IV tanks to mount much heavier caliber long-barreled guns—50 and 75 millimeters, respectively—despite the design objections raised by the experts. When Keitel demurred at releasing twenty thousand skilled workers from the army for tank production, Hitler snapped that it was better than losing perhaps ten times as many soldiers because of the lack of a powerful tank force. The modified tanks were demonstrated to him at the Chancellery six weeks later. Hitler climbed all over them and asked for the turret to be rotated. The gunner explained that he first had to duck his head inside—

at which Hitler angrily stopped the demonstration. "Obviously the gunner must be able to keep his eye to the eyepiece at all times!" A further symposium followed on May 26 at the Berghof: Hitler demanded an even heavier gun in future tanks and instructed both the Henschel tank works and Professor Ferdinand Porsche to produce prototypes mounting the 88-millimeter heavy gun. The designers were aghast, but Hitler announced that in future campaigns his tanks would travel to the battlefields "in the outer reaches of Europe" by train, so the load-bearing ability of roadbridges would no longer impose a limit on his tanks. He pictured to them the "morale and physical effect" of a direct hit by such a shell on a cast-steel tank turret—it would burst asunder. In Greece his SS Life Guards had destroyed enemy tanks at ranges of up to seven thousand yards with this fearful weapon.

Much had happened since that February symposium. The enemy's T-34 was vastly superior to the newest German Mark IV. At an arms conference on November 29, Hitler again warned Todt and Brauchitsch that the age of the tank would soon be over; he asked them to concentrate on three basic tank designs— a light tank for reconnaissance, like the present Mark III; a medium tank, the Mark IV; and a heavy tank (the later Panther) to outclass the Russian T-34. A superheavy tank was also to be blueprinted by Porsche for the future.

In mid-November 1941 Field Marshal von Bock's drive toward Moscow was resumed. He was confident of success, and General Halder swallowed his own misgivings and gave Bock free rein. Bock's northern wing began to move on the fifteenth, followed by the southern wing two days later. All Hitler's commanders had assured him that the Red Army lacked depth; but the enemy's resistance before Moscow was ominously vehement, and he began to suspect that he had again been wrongly advised. He saw victory at Moscow slipping through his fingers; he bluntly told the ailing Field Marshal von Brauchitsch—who had suffered a fresh heart attack a week before—that it was a question of the army's *will* to victory.

Meanwhile, General von Kleist's First Panzer Army had managed to seize Rostov on the Don, only to be thrown back again on November 28. Temperatures of 14°F. gripped the front. Fuel and equipment shortages dogged every move. The troops lacked ice axes, glycol antifreeze had to be flown in, the tank engines refused to start. (The army's quartermaster general had not informed lower levels of a simple "cold-start" procedure first demonstrated by the Luftwaffe in 1939.) Hitler's generals were gripped by apathy. Reichenau's Sixth Army had found comfortable winter quarters which they were very loath to leave; this enabled the enemy before them to regroup against the desperately harassed Kleist.

The temperature was still falling all along the front. Ribbentrop came on the twenty-second, no doubt to discuss the big demonstration of European solidarity he was about to stage in Berlin. But on the twenty-fourth Hewel noted: "Führer is dissatisfied with Ribbentrop's draft speech, lots of corrections, etc. His mind is on Africa." And one of Hitler's adjutants, Major Engel, wrote the next day: "In the evening a further lengthy debate on future operations. The Führer explains his great anxiety about the Russian winter and weather conditions, says we started one month too late. The ideal solution would have been the surrender of Leningrad, the capture of the south, and then if need be a pincer around Moscow from south and north, following through in the center . . . but time is his greatest nightmare now."

Hitler listened to Ribbentrop's Berlin speech on the radio. It was an important address to the ambassadors and foreign ministers of Germany's allies and friendly neutrals; "Europe's struggle for freedom" was its theme. Had the Soviet Union been on the brink of defeat it would have been timely and well-chosen; but Ribbentrop made the British government the butt of his leaden witticisms, goaded by the constant and effective British propaganda charge that he as Hitler's foreign minister was to blame for this war. Ribbentrop lauded Hitler's unexampled and benign patience toward Britain in these words: "If any sane person examines the advantages offered by the Führer's foreign policy to Britain, then he must clutch his head at the thought of the blindness with which the British statesmen were stricken, because the Führer not only offered a comprehensive territorial and maritime guarantee to the British Isles but even offered to supply German forces to help safeguard the British Empire." Ribbentrop referred to his own endeavors to bring the two countries together: "I will be happy to leave it to History to judge whether the sapient British propagandists are right in claiming that I advised the Führer that Britain would never fight, and that I was ignorant of the British and their national character."

Soon after Ribbentrop's radio broadcast was over, he himself was on the phone asking if Hitler had liked his speech. The Führer had not, and he was still fulminating against Ribbentrop, the foreign ministry, and the speech when his train left headquarters to take him to Berlin at 7 P.M. that evening.

In Berlin a round of receptions for the new signatories of the Anti-Comintern Pact began. They made a curious bunch. The Hungarians had to be kept apart from the Romanians. Serrano Suñer had to be received jointly with Ciano. Ciano was accorded the same frozen politeness as had been his lot on his recent visit to the Wolf's Lair. The Turks, who had also been invited to join the pact, had refused point-blank; from decoded British admiralty telegrams Hitler knew that Turkey was again playing a double role and negotiating with the British for destroyers and submarines; and her Chief of Staff had even taken to referring to the Germans as *les boches* in conversation with British officers. Vichy France, despite Pétain's jostling for German favors, was not invited to join the pact, as Hitler still evidently hoped to treat with Britain some day at France's expense. A French volunteer legion was now fighting under Bock's command, and from decoded American cables the Germans knew that Pétain had commended Germany for adhering to the armistice conditions. Hitler had kept his promises, and Pétain accordingly supported his plans for a New Order, from which he felt that France could only profit. But Hitler's latent resentment had its psychological roots too deep in recent history to be easily overcome, as his surly reply to a letter from the French marshal showed: Hitler reminded Pétain that France had declared war on Germany, not vice versa, and he said that Germany's recent execution of French "Communists" in reprisal for the assassination of German officers doing their "lawful duty" was fully justified. The Führer drew a passionate comparison between what he presented as Germany's restrained presence now in France and the French troops' unruly behavior in the Rhineland between the wars, when they had driven German citizens from the sidewalks with their riding crops, and the rape of more than sixteen thousand German women had gone unpunished.

A major source of discontent in France was that Germany—like France after World War I—was still detaining over a million French prisoners of war. Hitler could not dispense with this labor force, for the German agricultural and armament economy relied heavily on prisoners. Hitler had recently put Göring in charge of employing three million Russian prisoners, remarking that such stubborn fighters must make good workers too. But the army had paid scant attention to their welfare and accommodations; hunger, exhaustion, lack of medical care, and fierce typhus epidemics took their toll. Albert Speer, Hitler's chief architect, had asked him on November 21 to provide forced labor for his work in rebuilding Berlin. (Now that Hitler was in the capital again, Speer lunched with him and then showed him the latest scale-models of Berlin's new buildings, set up in the Model Room at the Chancellery—finely detailed miniatures of the vast Great Hall, the Office of the Reichsmarschall, and the new stadium.) Hitler granted Speer's request for thirty thousand Russian prisoners to help in the construction work. The Führer assured Speer that he proposed to start work on this huge reconstruction of Berlin before the war was over—no war was going to keep him from putting these plans into effect.

While he was in Berlin, on November 27, Hitler learned that the protracted talks between Japan and the United States had broken down. He had a private meeting with the Japanese ambassador, General Oshima, who tried unsuccessfully to warn him of what was coming; two weeks later Hitler admitted to his military staff that he should have paid closer attention to the cautious hints that Oshima dropped. Unlike Ribbentrop, who wanted the Japanese to strike northward into Russia, Hitler preferred that they should thrust southward to embarrass the British. He felt that attacking Vladivostok would not help now, as he considered "Barbarossa" all but over. Indeed, at the end of October Hitler had been against any Japanese involvement, as this would have made the peace settlement more complicated. Militarily, Japan was an unknown quantity. Her population was bigger than Germany's, so she could raise perhaps 120 divisions; but the world knew nothing of any Japanese tank, aircraft, or warship capabilities.

The United States was also evidently having second thoughts about fighting a war in Europe. Several American destroyers and merchant vessels had recently been sunk by U-boats, but Roosevelt had shown little firm reaction. The German foreign ministry answered General Halder's inquiry about whether Roosevelt was likely to declare war with a decisive negative. As late as December 6, Hitler would be shown dispatches from Hans Thomsen, his chargé d'affaires in Washington, listing the reasons why the United States would not declare war yet. This firm suggestion that Roosevelt—alarmed at the Soviet Union's imminent collapse—now wanted to avoid armed conflict until his rearmament was ready, persuaded Hitler that war between the United States and Japan might serve his purposes after all: it would tie this powerful enemy down in the Pacific at least throughout 1942, which would give him time to realize his own ambitions in Russia. Admiral Raeder and the hard-pressed U-boat commanders in the Atlantic would certainly welcome such a showdown.

As Hitler's policy toward the United States swung around during November 1941, so did that of Japan as hopes dwindled in Tokyo that Roosevelt would relax the oil and economic sanctions imposed on Japan. The German attachés in Tokyo both warned Berlin that Japan would enter the war before the year was out. Indeed, the naval attaché cabled on November 5 that a senior Japanese naval officer had advised him that "the government has as good as made up its mind to fight America. The southern campaign will most probably begin this year." In due course Tokyo would approach Germany for a pact binding each country not to make a separate peace with the United States so long as the other was still fighting. Sure enough, such a request was received by Ribbentrop on the eighteenth; he agreed "in principle," fearing that otherwise Japan might reach a compromise with the United States. For the next week the reports reaching Hitler were conflicting.

Then on November 28 he received one from Hans Thomsen in Washington reporting that Cordell Hull had handed to the Japanese what amounted to an ultimatum which "is bound to result in the immediate breakdown of the talks." The Americans demanded a nonaggression treaty, the evacuation of Indochina, and Japan's withdrawal from the Axis. Hitler discussed the implications of this with his political and military advisers at the Chancellery late that day, then sent Ribbentrop to inform the startled General Oshima—startled, for the ambassador himself was unaware the Japanese-American talks had collapsed—that if Japan did reach a decision to fight "Britain and the United States," they must not hesitate, as it would be in the Axis interests. Oshima inquired in puzzlement whether he was to infer that Germany and the United States would soon be at war, and Ribbentrop replied, "Roosevelt's a fanatic. There's no telling what he'll do." Ribbentrop then gave the Japanese the assurance they had wanted:

> If Japan becomes engaged in a war against the United States, Germany will of course join the war immediately. There is no possibility whatever of Germany entering into a separate peace with the United States under such circumstances. The Führer is adamant on that point.

Even so, Ribbentrop does seem to have had doubts. On the train carrying them both back to East Prussia the next day, November 29, he asked Hitler what Germany's posture would be if Japan actually *attacked* the United States; the Tripartite Pact only obliged Germany to assist if Japan was the victim of an attack. Hitler cast these diplomatic niceties aside; if Germany welshed on Japan in the event of Japan's attacking the United States, it would be the end of the Tripartite Pact. "The Americans are already shooting at us—so we are already at war with them."

Some days passed before Hitler's attention was again called to Japan, for he was virtually incommunicado—touring his army headquarters on the tottering eastern front. Only then was he shown the latest telegram from Tokyo, reporting Roosevelt's ultimatum to Japan; the Japanese had assured the German ambassador they would honor Germany's interests, and they again asked for Germany and Italy to stand at her side under the Tripartite Pact. In fact the secret instructions to Ambassador Oshima in Berlin were couched in even plainer terms: he was to inform Hitler and Ribbentrop confidentially that war between Japan and the Anglo-Saxon powers might be ignited "quicker than anybody dreams"; and he was to propose an agreement binding Germany and Italy to join in too.

Oshima saw Ribbentrop forthwith, on December 2, and again the next day; but the Nazi foreign minister had to prevaricate because he still could not reach the Führer. By scrambler-telephone he evidently managed this late on December 4. That night Rome was asked to approve the German counterproposal for an agreement, and at 4 A.M. Ribbentrop handed Oshima the agreed text of a German-Italian-Japanese treaty. This more than met Japan's requirements. It did not even ask for Japanese intervention against Russia as the price. "Our view," Ribbentrop cabled his man in Tokyo, "is that the Axis powers and Japan regard themselves as locked in one historic struggle."

Neither he nor Hitler realized that Japanese aircraft carriers had already sailed with war orders ten days before.

Hitler's eyes were of course elsewhere. As winter closed in, barbarous fighting erupted everywhere on the Russian front, where the army's all-out assault on Moscow was beginning. The fighting was of unexampled savagery. On both sides, prisoners were frequently shot out of hand—the Spanish "Blue Division" took the fewest prisoners. Villages were starved to feed the Germans and razed to the ground to deprive the Russians of cover; and warm clothing was stripped off captives. A captured Russian battalion commander related what happened to three Waffen SS soldiers in his area: "When the regiment's commissar, Zhukenin, of the 508th Infantry Regiment, asked an officer what he was fighting for, he replied, 'For Hitler!' So the commissar kicked him in the groin and shot him." The other two shared his fate. A captured Russian order stated that only three prisoners were to be taken in an infantry division's coming attack; the rest were to be slain. Meanwhile autopsy reports revealed that Russian troops defending the beleaguered Leningrad had resorted to nature's most primitive crime—cannibalism. German corpses found behind the Russian lines lacked parts of their bodies, although the uniforms nearby were undamaged.

The cruel Russian winter fell equally on the opposing armies, but it was unequally felt. Stalin's troops were well-clad, skilled in winter warfare, with skis and equipment adapted to sub-zero temperatures; they were also fighting close to their industrial base. Not so Hitler's armies. While the Luftwaffe and SS were more adequately provided, the German army's meager winter supplies were still bottled up by the chaotic railroad system at Minsk and Smolensk far to the rear. Different and feuding railroad authorities operated the networks in Germany, Poland, and occupied Russia. German locomotives were not only the wrong gauge, but their external "gossamer" of plumbing and pipework made them easy prey for the sub-zero winters. The retreating Russians had methodically wrecked the water towers, bridges, and railroad installations as well as the rolling stock. In consequence, the supply of food, equipment, and ammunition to the entire eastern front suddenly choked to a halt. Instead of seventeen supply trains a day, each army on the Leningrad front was lucky to get one; instead of eighteen, Guderian's Second Panzer Army was getting only three. It became apparent that the German railroads had unloaded their most infuriatingly feckless and inept staff members onto the Polish and Russian networks.

When at last winter clothing did reach the fighting troops, it was useless against the Russian winter. Many weeks earlier Brauchitsch had paraded before Hitler a dozen soldiers outfitted with the army's special new winter gear. Only now did Hitler learn that those dozen outfits were all the army had. The blame for this fraud lay squarely on the General Staff. Meanwhile Hitler's armies were trapped in blizzards and snowdrifts outside Moscow—and were slowly freezing to death.

The reverse suffered by the First Panzer Army on the Don at Rostov was a bitter pill for Hitler to swallow, because now an Intelligence report confirmed that his own original strategy—of conquering Russia's southern petroleum oil fields first —was what the Soviets had feared most. Marshal Timoshenko had just delivered a secret speech to the supreme defense council in Moscow:

> If Germany succeeds in taking Moscow, that is obviously a grave disappointment for us, but it by no means disrupts our grand strategy. . . . Germany would gain accommodation, but that alone will not win the war. The only thing that matters is oil. As we remember, Germany kept harping on her own urgent oil problems in her economic bargaining with us from 1939 to 1941.
>
> So we have to do all we can (a) to make Germany increase her oil consumption, and (b) to keep the German armies out of the Caucasus until the oil shortage in Germany begins to hurt.

So far, Timoshenko continued, Marshal Semën Budënny had had to wage a scorched-earth campaign and ignore his own colossal military casualties. "This first phase of the war has been decisively won by *us,* however much a glance at the map may give the public a different impression." The Red Army's task now was to throw the Germans back just far enough to destroy the caches of tanks and ammunition it had built up for the Caucasus offensive. This would win a few precious months for new Soviet armies to be raised, for Britain's General Archibald Wavell to establish his Caucasus front in Iraq and Iran, for the evacuated Soviet factories to resume production, and for the American supplies to start to flow.

How Hitler must have cursed the General Staff for having foisted its Moscow campaign on to him. With winter upon him, he had no option but to see it through, although the armies' reserves were at an end and the physical conditions were brutal in the extreme. How far the army faithfully called his attention to these adverse conditions is controversial even now. The two army group commanders, Bock and Rundstedt, believed that Hitler was not being told the blunt facts; so did Kleist's Chief of Staff Zeitzler. Guderian—commanding the Second Panzer Army south of Moscow—blamed his immediate superiors too. "We must face the melancholy fact," he wrote privately, "that our superior command has overreached itself; it didn't want to believe our reports on the dwindling combat strength of our troops, it made one fresh demand after another, it made no provision for the harsh winter, and now it's been taken by surprise by the Russian temperatures of − 30°F. . . . While the Luftwaffe is methodically commanded, we in the army have to put up with horrifying bungling and aimlessness."

This lack of *Zivilcourage* was first brought home to Hitler by the immediate sequel to the loss of Rostov. First, the city proved far larger than shown on the General Staff's maps. Second, Kleist's frantic warnings about his panzer army's long exposed left flank and the severe icing conditions were withheld from Hitler. When Kleist was forced to withdraw his spearhead—intending to fall back on the Mius, which had been adequately prepared for a long defense—Hitler had on November 30 vetoed this: Rundstedt, the army group commander, was to order Kleist to defend a line five miles forward of the Mius. In the course of the evening, Brauchitsch received Rundstedt's uncompromising reply refusing to carry out what he evidently believed to be only Brauchitsch's order. "If my superiors have no faith in my leadership, I must ask to be replaced as Commander in Chief." Hitler sacked Rundstedt that same night, replacing him with Reichenau; the newcomer was ordered categorically to halt the panzer army's retreat.

Hitler backed this order with a personal visit to Kleist's battle headquarters at Mariupol (Zhdanov), on the Sea of Azov. He took no General Staff officers with him—just his adjutants. He had intended sacking both Kleist and Zeitzler, but SS General Sepp Dietrich, whose SS Life Guards Division had been in the thick of the fighting, pluckily defended his superiors; and Schmundt told Hitler that Zeitzler had now shown him copies of the panzer army's frantic signals before the Rostov operation. These messages had accurately predicted this very outcome. Hitler was astonished that they had been withheld from him. He exclaimed, "So the panzer army saw it all coming and reported to that effect. It bears none of the blame, then." He telephoned Jodl's staff in this vein on December 3: Kleist's panzer army bore none of the blame for the Rostov crisis. "It reported to the army group as early as November 21 and 22 about its great anxiety over the threat to its eastern flank and the complete lack of any reserves. Army Group South has moreover claimed that it forwarded details of this menacing situation to the war ministry." Clearly the messages had been suppressed by the General Staff. Thus Hitler's confidence in Rundstedt was restored—though characteristically of Hitler the dismissal remained in force.

The Rostov setback paled into insignificance against what now occurred at Moscow. General Kluge's powerful Fourth Army had begun its big push on December 1 through the forests and swamps west of the capital; Hoepner's Fourth Panzer Army and Guderian's Second Panzer Army began an enveloping action to the north and the south, respectively. On December 2, through snowstorms and blizzards, a reconnaissance battalion of the 258th Infantry Division reached Khimki, on the very outskirts of Moscow; but it was driven back by armed Russian workers. Thus German troops came within twelve miles of the city center before exhaustion overcame them.

This was the German army's trauma. Moscow was being evacuated; its streets and public buildings were being mined for demolition. Yet by December 4, with temperatures of −6°F., both Hoepner's tanks and Kluge's infantry were at a standstill. Guderian, visiting the battlefield, found his tank crews still optimistic, while their corps and division commanders were not. But Field Marshal von Bock warned the OKW by telephone that his troops would soon be able to proceed no farther. "If the attack is not called off until then," he warned Jodl, "it will be almost impossible to go over to the defensive." On the fifth, Guderian—up at the forefront of his army with the 296th Infantry Division—realized that his own attack was hopeless too. His Chief of Staff recorded in his diary: "Twenty-five degrees below zero this morning. Tank turrets frozen solid, frostbite taking heavy toll, artillery fire has become irregular as gunpowder evidently burns differently." As the hours passed, the temperature sagged to *thirty-five degrees* below zero. "Our troops no longer had the strength to carry the attack victoriously through to Moscow," Guderian described privately on the eighth. "And so with a heavy heart I had to decide late on December 5 to call off the now pointless attack and fall back on a relatively short line I had already chosen earlier, which I can just about hope to hold with my remaining forces. . . . Fortunately we have been able to hang on to our fine tanks—at least insofar as they they are still running."

On December 5, as Hitler's offensive slued to a halt, four Soviet armies opened their counterattack north of Moscow. Next day ten more armies—one hundred divisions—fell upon Bock's exhausted and frozen troops on a two hundred-mile front on either side of Moscow. Thus the real emergency began. The Luftwaffe was grounded. Gasoline fires had to be lit in pits under their tanks for four hours to thaw out the engines. The telescopic gunsights were useless, and every caliber of gun and cannon jammed. The oil congealed in the tank tracks. The Russians used special winter oils and lubrication techniques, and now their formidable T-34 tank appeared en masse, with its armor impregnable to the standard German 37-millimeter antitank shell. "From the depths of Russia, undreamed-of masses of humanity were hurled against us," recalled an OKW staff officer. "I can still see the situation maps of the next days and weeks: where until now the blue of our own forces had dominated the picture, with the enemy's red only sparsely sketched in, now from Leningrad right down to the Sea of Azov thick red arrows had sprung up on every sector of the front, pointing at the heart of Germany. Only thin blue lines wound their tortuous way around this broad-arrowed on-slaught."

Meanwhile the paraphernalia of modern war accumulated by the Wehrmacht in its seven years of preparation for this moment congealed into frozen impotence, paralyzed by the icy grip of a sub-Napoleonic winter. If battle casualties were not dragged under cover, they were dead within half an hour from exposure. Guderian lost twelve hundred men to frostbite in one division in one day. On the ninth, one corps reported fifteen hundred cases; three hundred fifty men had to have limbs amputated. Eleven hundred army horses perished every day.

"In wave after wave of densely packed soldiers, the enemy offensive rolled across the snowscape toward us. Our machine guns hammered away at them without letup, you could not hear yourself speak. Like a dark and somber carpet a layer of dead and dying stretched across the snow in front of us, but still the masses of humanity came on at us, closer and closer, seemingly inexhaustible. Only when they came within hand-grenade range of us did the last of these attacking Russians fall to our machine guns. And then, as our gunners began to breathe again, there was a fresh stir in the distance, a broad dark line on the horizon, and it all began again." Thus a German officer described the rearguard actions north of Moscow.

Even a healthy commander would have quailed inwardly before such an onslaught. But Field Marshal von Brauchitsch was already a sick man: he had suffered heart attacks in November, and the tongue lashing to which Hitler had recently subjected him had not aided his convalescence. On December 6, as the great Russian offensive began, he tendered his resignation to Hitler. He must have known that he would otherwise be made the scapegoat. Hitler stalked up and down the room for ten minutes without answering; then he replied that he could not agree to any change at this moment. Brauchitsch left the room without a word.

From the Russian front came the ominous sounds of an impending avalanche. But even Hitler now saw that Brauchitsch was a sick and exhausted man. Who could replace him? The names of Manstein and Kesselring were whispered to him. Colonel Rudolf Schmundt persuasively urged Hitler to become his *own* army Commander in Chief, issuing orders directly through Halder to the army. Hitler said he would think it over. In fact he had already begun to act the role—or rehearse it: by early December 7 it was obvious that the corps holding the embattled salient at Tikhvin despite blizzards and catastrophic losses was in danger of being encircled. Hitler decided to abandon the city, which was largely gutted and ruined anyway, and confirmed this in a direct telephone conversation with Leeb, commander of Army Group North, at 7:04 P.M. He did not consult Brauchitsch at all. Halder sorrowfully wrote in his diary: "Today's events are again stunning and shameful. The Commander in Chief [Brauchitsch] is barely even used as postman now. The Führer deals over his head with the army group commanders direct. The terrible thing is, however, that the High Command does not grasp the condition our troops are in, and is relying on patchwork operations where only bold decisions can be of use."

Yet the High Command—and that meant Hitler—was all too aware of Germany's precarious position now that her offensives had been halted. The uneasiness of the German people was as nothing compared with Hitler's own private nightmare, for only in him were all the threads of foreign Intelligence and strategic decisions combined. As the usual faces gathered in his bunker after dinner that Sunday evening, December 7—the women secretaries, Bormann's adjutant Heim, a doctor, and Walther Hewel—Hitler reflected that the emergency collection of warm winter clothing now beginning throughout Germany on behalf of the troops on the eastern front was an admission of bad planning intelligible to even his most loyal followers.

Toward midnight the buzz of conversation was stilled as Heinz Lorenz, a press officer, burst in. An American radio station had just announced a surprise Japanese air attack on the U.S. fleet in Pearl Harbor, Hawaii. Japan was at war with Britain and the United States.

It was so unexpected—Hitler's immediate reaction was to slap his thighs in delight and joyously proclaim, "The turning point!" Then he bounced out of the bunker and ran through the icy darkness to show the news bulletin to Keitel and Jodl. To Hewel, Hitler rejoiced: "Now it is impossible for us to lose the war: we now have an ally who has never been vanquished in three thousand years, and another ally"—he added, paraphrasing a remark Napoleon had also made about the Italians, a remark which he had read in Talleyrand and which had been drifting around his magpie memory ever since—"who has constantly been vanquished but has always ended up on the right side."[1]

In Berlin, the Japanese ambassador was calling on Ribbentrop. Ribbentrop assured him that Germany and Italy would immediately declare war on the United States too. In fact, Hitler took two days over this decision (the records give no indication of a reason). Meantime the news of Japan's triumph hardened. In a carbon copy of the Japanese attack on the Russians at Port Arthur in 1904,[2] torpedo planes had sunk five battleships and badly damaged three more at Pearl

[1]Napoleon had said, "The Italians have never yet ended a war on the same side as they started it—except when they changed sides twice."

[2]Liddell Hart effectively quoted the 1904 *Times* on the Port Arthur attack: "The Russian squadron was open to, and invited attack. The invitation has been accepted with a promptness and punctuality that do high honor to the navy of our gallant allies," *i.e.*, the Japanese. (*History of the Second World War*, London, 1970.)

Harbor; air bases in the Philippines had been bombed, and the northeastern corner of Malaya had been invaded at Kota Bharu. The British battleships *Prince of Wales* and *Repulse* were sent to combat the invasion and sunk two days later by Japanese aircraft.

Hitler issued to the admiralty orders that German submarines and warships might forthwith open fire on American ships as and where they met them; and before he left for Berlin on the evening of the eighth, he discussed at length with his staff how best to declare war on the United States so as to make a good impression on his own people. That he would declare war was a foregone conclusion; not even Göring, Hitler's second man, was consulted on that point. In Washington the mood was reported to be grave; public opinion was consoled with the bromide that the United States had not yet lost a war, but late on the eighth, the west coast of the United States was panicked by a false air raid warning, followed the next noon by an alert on the Atlantic seabord, with warnings broadcast on the radio that German bomber squadrons were approaching! Hitler scoffed some weeks later, "Roosevelt declares war"—presumably meaning the covert shoot-on-sight phase existing since September—"and thereupon not only allows himself to be thrown out of East Asia wholly unprepared, but lets his merchant shipping ply peacefully back and forth along the American coast for us to pick off like sitting ducks. He drives pell-mell out of Washington because of air raid dangers, onto his estate, then back to Washington. . . . He makes his whole country hysterical, the way he goes on."

Hitler arrived in Berlin with Keitel, Jodl, Schmundt, and other members of his staff at 11 A.M. on December 9. The German chargé in Washington had now confirmed that Roosevelt was unlikely to demand war with Germany and Italy under the circumstances, unless he felt it necessary to beat Hitler and Mussolini to such a declaration for reasons of personal prestige; Roosevelt would do all he could to avoid open war in the Atlantic, a war on two fronts. To Hitler, however, this was the delicious moment when he could deliver to that "lout" Roosevelt the public smack in the eye he deserved. Late on the ninth the Washington embassy was instructed to burn its secret files and code books. Hitler began to prepare a speech for the Reichstag; the foreign ministry furnished him with a list of all Roosevelt's violations of neutrality.

Shortly after 2 P.M. on the eleventh Ribbentrop read out Germany's declaration of war to the American chargé in Berlin: now President Roosevelt had the war he had been asking for, Ribbentrop concluded.

There was little to distinguish Hitler's Reichstag speech that afternoon: he referred to the *Chicago Tribune,* which had recently published "war plans" revealing Roosevelt's intention of invading Europe in 1943, and he read out the text of the agreement just signed with Japan. Yet deep within, instinct was warning the Führer that he ought *not* to be welcoming the events that must now unfold. Major von Below, his Luftwaffe adjutant, who had met him at the railroad station in Berlin, found him uneasy about the long-term effects of Pearl Harbor. Ribbentrop also professed (later) to have been distraught at the manner in which the Tripartite Pact, made to keep the United States *out* of the war, had now brought her into direct confrontation with the Reich. But neither he nor Hitler raised any obstacles to the military convenant drafted by the Japanese and dividing the world into operational zones: west of the meridian of 70 degrees east, Germany and Italy would operate; all the world east of that line, including British India, would fall to Japan. Only this, the German leaders reasoned, would bring Japan into a sharp and prolonged conflict with Britain and exclude any possibility of a separate peace.

Despite the strategic benefits—Japan's advance on Singapore and Australia would force Britain to withdraw Indian and Anzac forces, particularly from the Mediterranean, and the United States would have to cut back her arms supplies to Britain and the Soviet Union—Hitler was heard to mutter, "I never wanted things to turn out like this. Now they"—meaning the British—"will lose Singapore!"[3] It was after he had returned to the Wolf's Lair, with the "Barbarossa" campaign on the brink of its first winter crisis, that he made to Walther Hewel the remark that has already been reported: "How strange that with Japan's aid we are destroying the positions of the white race in the Far East—and that Britain is fighting against Europe with those swine the Bolsheviks!" His foreign minister soberly warned him: "We have just one year to cut off Russia from her American supplies arriving via Murmansk and the Persian Gulf; Japan must take care of Vladivostok. If we don't succeed and the munitions potential of the United States joins up with the manpower potential of the Russians, the war will enter a phase in which we shall only be able to win it with difficulty." To this Hitler made no reply.

---

[3] And see Hitler's revealing remark on the fall of Singapore, page 373 below.

Hitler Takes Command

In the dark months of that winter Hitler showed his iron determination and hypnotic powers of leadership. We shall see how these qualities and the German soldier's legendary capacity for enduring hardship spared the eastern army from cruel defeat that winter. Where his generals saw an ignominious withdrawal as their only salvation, Hitler told them to stand firm until the spring thaw arrived to halt the enemy offensive. When they demurred, argued, and disobeyed, Hitler dismissed and disgraced them, and himself took command of the German army, until a new spirit gradually prevailed along the eastern front.

Hitler's powers to influence were remarkable. A division was reported to be retreating. Hitler telephoned its commander. The general's dejected voice reached him—barely a whisper, from a frozen, inhospitable wilderness hundreds of miles away. Hitler rebuked him: "You know perfectly well that it's just as cold thirty miles further back! The eyes of the German people are on *you.*" His few words implanted a new sense of purpose in the general, and the division stood its ground. Soon hardened commanders were swearing they had seen Hitler in the thick of battle—"We thought it was all over, but then the Führer toured our sector calling for one last ounce of effort from us, and we pulled through!" But many more months would pass before he risked leaving his headquarters.

I had to act ruthlessly. I had to send even my closest generals packing, two army generals, for example, whose strength was gone and who were at the end of their tether. . . . In winter one of them came and announced, "Mein Führer, we can't hold on any longer, we've got to retreat." I asked him, "Sirrrr, where in God's name are you thinking of retreating to? How far?" "Well," he answered, "I don't really know!"—"Do you plan to drop back thirty miles? Do you think it isn't all that cold there, then? And do you imagine your transport and supply problems will be any better there? And if you retreat, do you intend to take your heavy weapons with you, can you take them?" This man answered, "No, it can't be done."—"So you're planning to leave them to the Russians.

And how do you think you're going to fight further back if you haven't got any heavy weapons?" He responded, "Mein Führer, save at least the army, whatever happens to its guns." So I inquired, "Are you planning just a retreat to the Reich frontier, or what? Where do you plan to call a halt?" "Well, mein Führer," he rejoined, "we probably won't get any choice." I could only tell these gentlemen, "Get yourself back to Germany as rapidly as you can—but leave the army in my charge. And the army is staying at the front."

After declaring war on the United States, Hitler remained briefly in Berlin. The public mood was grim. The churches were full—a disturbing sign, but Hitler admitted to his secretaries that there was nothing he could do against the churches until the war was over. As in the case of the "Jewish problem," Hitler felt he already had enough on his plate.[1]

In the east military disaster was looming. The Soviet counteroffensive had torn open a thirty-mile-wide gap between Kluge's and Guderian's armies. Bock's Army Group Center had no more reserves. On December 9 Guderian had warned him: "Something like a crisis of confidence has broken out among the troops." More and more Russian troops and tanks poured through the breach. The most effective antitank weapon, the Redhead shell with a hollow-charge warhead— which Hitler had first seen demonstrated on November 25—had immediately been embargoed by him to keep it secret from the enemy. Whenever Russian tanks appeared, the German infantry were taking to their heels. The fear of Russian captivity, and the lack of weapons, fuel, fodder for the horses, and reserves, produced a crushing sense of inferiority.

Hitler sent the army's ailing Commander in Chief von Brauchitsch to the Moscow front to see the situation for himself. Guderian met him on December 14 at Roslavl; he wrote afterward: "It took a twenty-two hours' drive through the blizzard to reach him. I think he got the most urgent points I made." Brauchitsch ordered Guderian to hold the line forward of Kursk and Orel, but like Bock and Kluge the tank commander knew only one solution: retreat while the going was still good! Hitler turned a deaf ear on them all. "I can't send everybody home just because Army Group Center is beginning to leak," he argued; and he was encouraged by anguished appeals from the other sector commanders not to let a general rout begin.

Army Group Center's most urgent need was for reserves. Late on December 14 Hitler ordered Jodl to find out how much could be scraped together in the Reich; General Friedrich Fromm explained that his Replacement Army had a

---

[1] After discussing a proposed Sportpalast speech with Hitler on December 14, 1941, Rosenberg noted: "I said I took the view that I shouldn't mention the stamping out of Judaism. The Führer took my point and commented that as they had thrust this war onto us and brought about all this destruction, it was no wonder if they were the first to feel the consequences."

number of divisions under training, convalescing, or temporarily released to industry. Half an hour after midnight Hitler ordered Fromm to come to the Chancellery. The general undertook to raise four and a half divisions at once from all over Germany, equipped with winter clothing and skis. At 1 P.M. the next day Hitler telephoned Field Marshal Leeb, who was now asking permission to pull back his army group (North) to the Volkhov River; Hitler pointed out that this would open up the railroad link to Tikhvin for the Russians and enable them to pour more troops and supplies into Leningrad. Again he could not trust Brauchitsch or Halder to make this plain enough. He ordered Leeb to bring General Ernst Busch—commander of the Sixteenth Army besieging Leningrad—to the Wolf's Lair in person the next day.

As his special train left Berlin that evening, Hitler drafted his first Halt Order to the eastern front. "Any large-scale retreat by major sections of the army in midwinter, given only limited mobility, insufficient winter equipment, and no prepared positions in the rear, must inevitably have the gravest consequences." The Fourth Army was ordered not to fall back one foot. This controversial order was hotly debated during the night. Its critics argued that what mattered now was not clinging to frozen territory but preserving the army's fighting power for 1942; others, among them Jodl, replied that only such a holding order made sense. A colonel argued that it was time for strategic command of the war to be delegated to an acknowledged expert like General von Manstein; Jodl—emerging from Hitler's conference car—pointed out that the Führer could not stand that general too near him. "Besides, the Führer has already decided on a different way of resolving the command problem."

It was 11 A.M., December 16, when Hitler arrived back at the Wolf's Lair. His Halt Order was dictated to Bock over the telephone by Halder at 12:10 P.M. Hitler made it obvious that he was going to ignore Brauchitsch and deal directly with the army groups in the future. But the damage had already been done. When Leeb now came, Hitler had to agree to Army Group North's proposed withdrawal. "If you had been given the Third Panzer Group as I wanted, at the time the enemy south of Lake Ladoga was still weak, you would have encircled Leningrad immediately and made land contact with the Finns." This plan the General Staff had prevented.

Indeed, Hitler no longer trusted Brauchitsch's judgment. On December 16 he had his chief adjutant, Rudolf Schmundt, flown to the Moscow front; and that afternoon Schmundt returned with an accurate account of Guderian's litany of worries, told him in an hour-long conference on Orel airfield. At last the truth was reaching Hitler. Waiting for the Führer to telephone him about reinforcements that evening, Guderian—racked by sciatica—wrote to his wife: "I only hope it's not too late. The consequences don't bear thinking about. We've been put in a hideous position by our total underestimation of the enemy and the haphazard preparation for a winter campaign in Russia. Heaven knows how we're going to extricate ourselves. . . . I'm just glad that the Führer at least knows what's happening, and I hope he'll come to grips with his customary verve with the bureaucratic wheels of the war department, railroad, and other machinery. . . . I lie awake at night racking my brains about how I can help my poor men, who have no protection against this fierce winter weather."

Toward midnight Bock telephoned Schmundt with the text of his three-day-old report to Brauchitsch, openly warning that a momentous decision would shortly confront them. It read: "The Führer must decide for himself whether my army group must stand and fight, thereby risking its total destruction, or retreat, entailing precisely the same risk. If he decides on retreat, then he must realize that it is unlikely that enough troops will ever get back to the new line to hold it, and that it will be unprepared for them and not all that much shorter." Brauchitsch had suppressed this report rather than show it to Hitler. Over the phone Bock now added that his 267th Infantry Division had that very day been forced to abandon its entire artillery in the retreat. Hitler telephoned him in person. "In this situation there is only one answer, and that is not to yield one inch—to plug the gaps and hold on!" Bock grimly replied that his front might cave in any moment. Hitler responded clearly, "That is a risk I must just take."

"There is only one thing that ails our front," he explained to Brauchitsch and Halder a few moments later. "The enemy just has more soldiers than us." This was why they must rush the simplest reinforcements—riflemen, each provisioned with eight or ten days' canned food, alcohol, and chocolate—by train to the Russian front. A thousand trucks must be supplied to Bock as well, and two thousand SS troops must be flown east from Cracow. At 3 A.M. he telephoned Guderian with details of the reinforcements that he was airlifting to the front.

Later that day, December 17, General von Richthofen came to the Wolf's Lair with Göring. The Luftwaffe corps commander wrote in his diary:

Jeschonnek and I went in to see the Führer. He's a bundle of nerves, but clearheaded and confident. . . . I kept emphasizing that what matters now is keeping our troops alive and fighting where they are. What the front lacks is riflemen, winter gear, and food, but above all the will to stand fast. . . . I emphasized the need for him to appeal to each soldier in person, then it will be all right. . . . The Führer listened with enormous interest and concentration. He's planning a major proclamation. Reichsmarschall [Göring] and I were very persuasive. Führer swears loudly about the army commanders responsible for much of the foul-up. Is grappling with big reshuffle. Brauchitsch already out, Halder, Keitel, etc. are to follow him. He asks my opinion on various army commanders: not a pleasant job, but I spoke my mind bluntly while stressing my own bias.

Hitler himself signed the famous order that now went out to the eastern front. After minor frontline corrections, Army Group North was to stand fast to the last man. Army Group South was also to stand fast. The same went for Bock's Army Group Center.

> Major withdrawal movements cannot be made. They will result in the complete loss of heavy weapons and equipment. Under the personal leadership of commanders and officers alike, the troops are to be forced to put up a fanatical resistance in their lines, regardless of any enemy breakthrough in their flanks and rear. Only this kind of fighting will win the time we need to move up the reinforcements I have ordered from the home country and the west.

Richthofen was to receive one long-range fighter and four bomber squadrons from the west. The chief of air training was to release five transport squadrons to the front, and the aircraft pools of every ministry and headquarters unit were to be ruthlessly stripped of all but the most essential transport planes as well. "The most important thing is to *furnish riflemen* (in simple replacement battalions) to the weakest of the divisions. There is less urgency for the transport of tanks."

This was no time to respect personal feelings, either. If Bock was unwell, then a tougher commander must replace him: Hitler ordered Field Marshal von Kluge to take over Army Group Center. Hitler attached no blame to Bock and asked Schmundt to make this plain to the field marshal.

Less cordial was his parting now with Field Marshal von Brauchitsch, the army's Commander in Chief. Hitler clearly held him responsible for withholding from him, whatever the motives, urgent and serious messages from frontline commanders. The impression he had gained on his visit to Rundstedt's army group two weeks earlier was confirmed by the inexplicable suppression of Bock's alarming message of the thirteenth. Later in December, Hitler issued a Basic Order to all Wehrmacht commands, reminding them of the need to respect such reports as an indispensable instrument of leadership—"It is the duty of every soldier to report unfulfilled orders and his own errors truthfully"—and to report without exaggeration or dangerous embellishment.

More serious were the recent indications of Brauchitsch's inability or reluctance to execute Hitler's orders. According to Major von Below, Hitler's Luftwaffe adjutant, the incident that was the last straw had occurred in Berlin, in that midnight conference between Hitler and General Fromm. "Here Hitler found out that the orders that had reached the Replacement Army were different from those he had issued. After this nocturnal conference Hitler decided that Brauchitsch would have to resign his command of the army." Several days had followed in which Hitler thought of appointing another general in his place. By December

19, however, his mind was made up: he would follow Schmundt's advice and take command of the army himself. He knew of no general capable of instilling the National Socialist spirit into the army, he explained to Brauchitsch in a loud voice that day, and he added almost inaudibly, "We will remain friends."

He repeated to Halder his motives for taking command himself. He explained that Halder would have to carry on as before, while Keitel assumed the ministerial functions of the war ministry. It surprised many that Halder had not shared the fate of Brauchitsch; but Hitler needed the Chief of General Staff for his ability and experience, and the ambitious general learned to swallow his aversion as a professional to the "upstart" dictator. Meanwhile, Hitler and Schmundt composed an Order of the Day to the soldiers of the army and the Waffen SS: "Our country's struggle for freedom is approaching its climax. We are faced by world-shaking decisions. The prime bearer of the struggle is the army. As of today I have therefore taken command of the army myself. As a soldier in many battles of World War I, I share deeply with you the determination to win through." A second document he signed that day was a letter to the commanders of the Luftwaffe and the navy in which he formalized his action:

> As of today I have decided to take command of the army myself.
>   The Chief of the Army General Staff will be subordinated directly to myself.
>   The Chief of the Wehrmacht High Command, Field Marshal Keitel, will exercise on my behalf the remaining powers of the army Commander in Chief as the supreme commanding and administrative authority of the army . . .
>   *Adolf Hitler.*

General Guderian was the next to go. It had slowly dawned on his superiors that he was ignoring Hitler's Halt Order and preparing his Second Panzer Army's retreat; this was clear to Halder from the way the tanks were being regrouped around Orel and the army being echelonned in depth. Kluge, who had succeeded Bock, was no friend of Guderian, and when the panzer general arrived at Hitler's headquarters on December 20 Kluge angrily telephoned Halder and Schmundt to warn them that Guderian had obviously lost his nerve.

Guderian dramatically set out to the Führer the condition of the Second Panzer Army: his troops were exhausted and outnumbered; it was impossible to dig in, as the ground was frozen solid. Hitler retorted, "Then use your heavy artillery or mortars to blast out craters and install trench heaters in them." At one stage he caustically inquired of Guderian: "Do you believe that Frederick the Great's grenadiers enjoyed dying for their country either?" Guderian for his part hinted that it was high time for Hitler to rid himself of chairbound experts like Keitel, Jodl, and Halder, who had never seen the front line. (He had just written in a private letter: "They simply signal impossible orders to us and turn down all our requests and demands. What gets on my nerves is the feeling that I'm not getting through to them—that I'm powerless to prevent my being sacrificed to these conditions.") He flew back to Orel the next day and briefed his commanders on Hitler's renewed Halt Order. But his tanks' stealthy withdrawal still continued. Finally, on December 25, Kluge refused to work with Guderian any longer: one or the other of them must go. Shortly before midnight Hitler telephoned Kluge back: Guderian was being relieved of his command forthwith.

Something of the loneliness of absolute power must have gripped him in these weeks. Could he be certain that his single-handed decisions were right—or would the ultimate blame for military disaster now attach to him? There was nobody to whom he could unburden himself. With Eva Braun he could not discuss the war, and anyway she was far away in Bavaria. The women on his staff occasionally glimpsed the inner man. A few days earlier a record player had been installed in the Führer's Bunker—the concrete blockhouse in which he lived, in case of an enemy bombing raid or paratroop assault—and every evening he listened to Richard Strauss and Hugo Wolf *Lieder*—and of course to Wagner. How the girls loved to listen to Strauss's "Heimliche Aufforderung" as Heinrich Schlusnuss sang it, or to the gentle tenor voice of Peter Anders. "How beautiful these *Lieder* are," wrote one of the secretaries. "They envelope you in warmth and love, and even the Chief seems touched by them, because yesterday evening he told us two girls, 'Children, you must use every hour that's given you!' "

But with the command of the German army, an avalanche of work descended on him. He had ordered Halder to attend his war conferences each day in person with his staff, but Halder was no glutton for responsibility, and it was this that weighed so heavily. For weeks on end Hitler knew no regular routine. His midday meal used to start at 2 P.M.; now it was taken hours later—once as late as 6 P.M. This in turn dislocated the supper times, and the tea-party routine which previously had begun regularly in his bunker at 10 P.M. now never started before midnight. Once that winter it started after 2 A.M., which meant that his weary partners were unable to retire to bed before four or five. There was no exercise for anybody: the bunkers were warm, but outside it was cold and the roads were blocked by snow or treacherous with ice. While his secretaries preferred the warm, cozily furnished offices, Hitler slept in his bunker, with the ventilation system humming all night and the draft blowing on his head.

At the conference Guderian had attended on December 20, Hitler had issued a string of further draconian orders to steady the ragged eastern front. He told

Halder: "The will to hold out must be brought home to every unit!" He recognized the troops' natural tendency to cling to the sheltering villages, but he demanded that heated dugouts be improvised between them too: the men must learn to dig in and "put up with" enemy breakthroughs. Any Russians who did penetrate must be mopped up by hunting parties in the rear. Indeed, the rear area must become one vast defense zone in which the enemy would be forced again and again to stand and fight—every field bakery must learn to defend itself, as must the Luftwaffe's ground organization. The attacking Russians must find no shelter, no stone standing atop another. This was the ruthless policy Stalin had employed in his retreat that summer; how much more effective it would be in winter. Every village the Germans had to abandon must be burned down regardless of its inhabitants. Their warm clothes were to be taken from them. Any villages or woodlands falling into Russian hands were to be methodically destroyed by the Luftwaffe. The enemy must live from hand to mouth. Above all the morale of the troops had to be restored, and their fear of the Russian enemy and winter dispelled.

He embodied these principles in a new order to the three army groups in the east. Every officer and man must realize one thing: a retreating army must expect a far crueler winter than the army that held out where it was—however ramshackle its positions. "The Russians will follow hard on the heels of any withdrawing army, allowing it no respite, attacking and assailing it again and again; nor will such an army come to any halt, as it lacks any kind of prepared positions in the rear. The phrase 'Napoleonic Retreat' is threatening to come true." Hitler held out one hope to his commanders: the Russians would slowly bleed to death in their own offensive. They were already throwing their very last reserves into the fight, and these were no match for the German soldier.

Hitler's message was distributed to every officer on the eastern front. If his armies could only hold out long enough, he would transport to them fresh riflemen and ammunition, and they would win time to salvage precious equipment disabled near the Russian lines.

Christmas at Hitler's headquarters was always a cheerless affair, very different from that celebrated at the Berlin ministries, for example. Hitler received his staff in turn, handed them an envelope containing a small sum in Reichsmarks, and sometimes sent them a packet of coffee with a typed note of good wishes. Hewel wrote in his diary on the twenty-fourth: "A dejected Christmas. Führer's thoughts are elsewhere. No candles lit." Two days before, Hitler had learned from Kluge that the General Staff were sending hundreds of half-frozen troops by air to Smolensk without weapons or winter gear. He had shouted into the telephone: "Another *Schweinerei!* I was told that everbody going to the eastern front was being equipped with machine guns and rifles." Kluge warned him: "I have a feeling we shall be facing a major decision tomorrow." Hitler confidentially gave him the authority to withdraw sectors of his army group if need be—a measure of his trust in this field marshal. More important, Hitler also lifted the embargo on the Redhead hollow-charge antitank shells.

A fragment of another famous diary, that of Canaris, graphically portrays the atmosphere:

December 24, 1941.

A grave crisis is looming up on the eastern front, particularly for Army Group Center. If the Russians keep up their pressure it may end in catastrophe. Fateful consequences are now arising from the fundamental errors made in planning the operations of October 15 (no single main point of effort) and in allocating our forces (no tactical reserves anywhere, let alone strategic), and above all from our downright criminal underestimation of the enemy. General Schmundt is drawing comparisons with 1812 and talks of the "moment of truth" for National Socialism. The equipment losses are horrifying: trucks, guns, and aircraft have to be destroyed or abandoned because we lack the fuel to bring them back.

All this has a grim effect on our soldiers' fighting morale, as they suddenly realize that they are being badly led. The Führer's actions (retiring von B[rauchitsch] and a number of commanders) are quite right and have befallen those who are by no means blameless, whatever people may say about them. . . .

Our own treatment of Russian prisoners is having awful consequences. In the retreat from Moscow we had to abandon German field hospitals as well. The Russians dragged out the sick and injured, hanged them upside down, poured gasoline over them, and set them on fire.[2] Some uninjured German soldiers had to watch this torture; they were then kicked in the groin and sent back to the German lines with instructions to describe how the Bolsheviks were reacting to news of the mass executions and barbaric treatment meted out to their comrades in German captivity. On another occasion German prisoners were beheaded and their heads laid out to form the SS symbol.

The Russian army communiqué never reports numbers of prisoners taken, but just registers laconically that "fifty officers and two thousand enlisted men were liquidated"—meaning the modes of execution described above.

Hitler also received ample evidence from the Forschungsamt intercepts that the Red Army was shooting German prisoners of war. When the International Red Cross now proposed that both sides return to the accepted conventions, Hitler

[2]Jodl's naval staff officer, Commander Wolf Junge, described similar reports, adding: "When a major German field hospital had to be abandoned to the enemy at Kaluga in December 1941, our troops laid a pistol on each invalid's bed; we left them the choice of whether or not to fall alive into Russian hands" (unpublished memoirs of Junge).

refused, telling Keitel and Jodl that he did not want his troops to get the idea that the Russians would treat them decently in captivity; besides, if he had to furnish lists to the enemy, the Russians would soon observe that many of their prisoners in German hands were no longer alive (a consequence of the heartless neglect and epidemics to which they had been exposed).

The year's end had come. They had attained none of their strategic objectives. Almost hourly Hitler was to be seen clinging to the long-distance telephone linking him with Kluge and the eastern front. The dam might break at any moment. Kluge was again asking for minor withdrawals, and Hitler was grimly observing that they might just as well fall back on the Dnieper or even the Polish frontier. The Russians were not even first softening up the Germans with artillery bombardment. Hitler related to the field marshal how as a simple infantryman in Flanders he and his comrades had withstood ten days of ceaseless bombardment and nevertheless had held the line. Kluge rejoined that Hitler had not been fighting at twenty-five degrees below zero. "My corps commander has told me that if the 15th Infantry Division is ordered to stand fast, the troops are so exhausted they will not obey." Hitler angrily said, "If that is so, then it is the end of the German army," and he ended the conversation.

None of Hitler's staff would forget the New Year's Eve that followed. In the far south, Manstein's first assault on the fortress Sevastopol had failed—indeed, General Hans von Sponeck had surrendered Kerch to the enemy. Throughout the day Kluge had been on the phone to General Halder, begging for permission to withdraw the Fourth Army, the right wing of Hoepner's Fourth Panzergruppe, and the Ninth Army into a new line. Hitler flatly refused. Any strategic retreat was bound to touch off a general collapse; he demanded a fight to the finish in order to win time until the reinforcements arrived. Kluge phoned Halder soon afterward: if General Strauss's Ninth Army stood fast, it would be wiped out in the next two or three days. Then they would have no alternative but to witness the honorable collapse of the entire army group within a week.

Supper was again served late. Hitler dozed off afterward, exhausted, while the last minutes of the old year ticked away. His staff gathered expectantly in the mess and waited for him. But at eleven-thirty Kluge phoned urgently from the front, and for the next *three hours*—the time is graven in the diaries of Bormann, Hewel, and the army group itself—Hitler wrangled with the field marshal, arguing and cajoling—stopping only for a half-hour debate with Halder—on the need to stand fast. Kluge argued for a compromise—something between the extremes represented by Guderian's stealthy retreat and the Führer's adamant orders, as he put it. He asked Hitler to trust him. Halder, however, supported Hitler completely.

Hitler refused outright to grant Kluge freedom to withdraw what amounted to a ninety-mile section of the front over twenty miles. Again Kluge was ordered to hold the front. Not until 2:30 A.M. did Hitler arrive for tea with his intimate staff. "I am glad I know how to overcome even the greatest difficulties," he said. "Let's hope 1942 brings me as much good fortune as 1941. The worries can stay. So far the pattern has always been this: the hardest times come first, as a kind of preparation for the really great events." Turning to Hewel, who had shared his captivity in Landsberg prison, he added, "You have been through times like this yourself!" In the corner the phonograph was playing Bruckner's Seventh, but nobody was in a mood to appreciate it.[3]

It was on this occasion that Ribbentrop first broached with Hitler the possibility of an armistice with Russia. But Hitler merely replied that only a clear victory or defeat was now possible in the east. Over the next weeks and months there were to be many attempts at mediation, but Hitler ignored them all. On January 1, 1942, he was shown an intercepted Italian dispatch from Tokyo indicating that Japan wanted to mediate. The problem remained Britain: she had sworn never to negotiate a peace with Hitler, and only the severest military setbacks would make her reverse this decision; Ribbentrop's officials also argued that Germany must show she was a fit partner to negotiate with, and this meant an end to the "barbarism" in Europe. If Britain would now concede, Germany would leave the British Empire—minus the conquests by Japan—intact; however, in the future Britain must keep her nose out of Europe. As for France, Hitler quoted Bismarck's sentiments after the French capitulation at Sédan: the individual Frenchman might nurture some friendly feelings for the Germans; the French as a nation would always hate them. He proposed therefore to leave France outside the New Europe, outside the three great walls he was now thinking of—an East Wall from Leningrad to Rostov, a North Wall along the Norwegian coast, and a West Wall along the new frontier with France.

————

[3]One of Hitler's secretaries wrote two weeks later: "On New Year's Eve we were all in a cheerful enough mood at supper in the No.2 mess. After that we were ordered over to the regular tea session, where we found a very weary Chief, who nodded off after a while. So we accordingly kept very quiet, which completely stifled what high spirits we had been able to summon up. After that the Chief was away for three hours in conference, while the menfolk who had been mustered to offer New Year greetings hung around with doom-laden faces not daring to allow a smile to pass their lips. I just can't describe it—at any rate it was so ghastly that I broke down in tears in my bunker, and when I went back over to the mess I ran into a couple of the lads of the Escort Command, who of course saw at once that I had been crying—which set me off all over again, whereupon they tried to comfort me with words and alcohol, successfully. And then we all sang a sea chantey at the tops of our voices —'At Anchor off Madagascar, and We've Got the Plague Aboard!' "

Hitler's ruthless leadership stabilized the front for just long enough. In mid-January 1942 he could authorize Kluge to withdraw the more exposed sections of his army group. But by now a new defensive line had been prepared, reserves were arriving, warm clothing had been contributed by the German public, and most of the heavy equipment could be salvaged in time.

The winter crisis had been mastered. But the cost in officers was high—ousted by Hitler *pour encourager les autres*. General Otto Förster, the engineer-general who had already incurred Hitler's displeasure once in a 1938 dispute over fortifications, was dismissed for withdrawing his corps; General von Sponeck, who had abandoned Kerch, was sentenced to be shot (though Hitler later commuted this sentence). General Hoepner, who prematurely withdrew his panzergruppe to the winter line on January 8, was dismissed from the army in disgrace. (He and Sponeck were both executed three years later in another context.) Field Marshal von Leeb was retired from Army Group North. General Strauss was sacked from the Ninth Army. Many lesser commanders shared their fate. The Luftwaffe, and particularly Richthofen, kept Hitler zealously briefed on the army generals' shortcomings. Field Marshal von Reichenau was killed by a stroke; Bock, his health miraculously recovered, was appointed to replace him at Army Group South.

One new face drew Hitler's attention. In January the First Panzer Army's Chief of Staff lunched with him one day and reported on the imaginative emergency measures he had taken to protect the army's southern flank, suddenly exposed when the Sea of Azov froze hard enough for the enemy to cross: he had improvised squads of soldiers convalescing along the coast, fitted them out with guns and ammunition and even ice yachts for patrolling the sea. "The panzer army has really done everything it could!" said Hitler in congratulation. Eight months later it was this general—Kurt Zeitzler—whom he selected to replace Halder as the Chief of General Staff.

Over the next weeks, Hitler rejected every effort made to lighten his burden by relaxing his direct control. On January 16 he refused to sign two decrees drafted by Lammers to that effect. Indeed, he shouldered still more authority. General Hoepner, outraged at the loss of his "well-earned pension rights," instituted a lawsuit against the Reich in the Leipzig courts and won. Hitler, enraged by the blindness of the legal profession to the disciplines of war, declared himself above the law and summoned the Reichstag on April 26 to endorse a decree to that effect.[4] The decree gave him powers over every person in the Reich "regardless of their so-called well-earned rights." It puzzled many Germans that an absolute dictator should need to arrogate seemingly superfluous powers to him-

---

[4]See page 381 below.

self, but as Goebbels learned, Hitler's aim was to legalize in advance the radical steps he planned against "reactionaries, civil servants, lawyers, and certain sections of the officer corps."

The tactical withdrawal he had ordered in mid-January in Russia was followed a month later by an immensely more dramatic withdrawal in the west, as the navy's battleships at Brest were forced to abandon the Atlantic theater on Hitler's orders.

Here his motive was primarily one of preventive strategy. Throughout December and January, Intelligence reports had trickled into his headquarters indicating an Anglo-American plan to invade northern Norway in the spring. The sources were ominously similar to those proven accurate in the anxious spring of 1940: on December 25, Berlin learned from a decoded dispatch that the Finnish envoy in Washington had quoted his colleagues there about Allied preparations to invade northern Norway. A British raid on the Lofoten Isles soon after was regarded by Hitler not only as a personal insult but as a forerunner of a later invasion. It also reminded him of his reliance on Swedish iron and Finnish nickel supplies from Petsamo (Penchenga). He suspected that the enemy had secretly promised Narvik to Sweden; while Sweden's king and army were said to be pro-Hitler, her financial institutions and Social Democrats were not and might well cut off all the iron ore if Britain ever did occupy Narvik.

With this in mind Hitler ordered the reinforcement of Norway, particularly by his navy. The time for sweeping forays into the Atlantic was over anyway. The battleships *Scharnhorst* and *Gneisenau,* still denied access to French North African and Spanish ports, had been bottled up at Brest on France's Atlantic coast since the spring and had been regularly crippled by bomb damage ever since. Hitler was impatient at their enforced idleness. On December 26 his naval adjutant put to him the admiralty's request for extra air support for their next exercises. This was the last straw. "I was always a champion of big ships before," Hitler announced. "My heart was in them. But they've had their day. The danger of air attack is too great." He sent for Raeder to discuss withdrawing the battleships—to Norway, where, out of RAF bomber range, they would have a new lease on life. On December 29 he told Raeder to bring them back from Brest. Since routing them around the British Isles would invite certain disaster, Hitler suggested taking the British channel defenses by surprise—sailing the warships back through the English Channel. The navy was aghast; but Hitler bluntly gave them the alternative of that or decommissioning the warships where they lay and employing their armament and crews elsewhere.

Hitler explained to his naval adjutant on January 4 that surprise was of the essence. "Therefore any steps which might somehow alert the British must be avoided," the adjutant noted. "If the withdrawal comes off, he would like to see every ship possible transferred to Norway. This is the only step likely to have a deterrent effect on the British. Since Churchill has stated that the British still have the bloodiest sacrifices to bear, he considers an invasion of Norway quite likely. Naturally Churchill may have meant something else, but he, the Führer, will not rest in this respect until our fleet is there." The navy outlined its plan to him a week later, while Colonel Adolf Galland, the famous fighter ace and commander, explained how he proposed to give the warships air cover during their Channel dash. Hitler was taken aback by Vice Admiral Otto Ciliax's insistence on reaching the seventeen-mile-wide Dover Straits at high noon, but this was inevitable if the warships were to slip out of Brest under cover of dusk. Raeder was unhappy about the whole venture, but the alternative did not bear thinking about. The attempt would be made in one month's time.

It was probably not until early February 1942 that Hitler could form any realistic picture of the Moloch of defeat from which he had snatched his army. By January 10 the army had registered 30,000 frost casualties, with 2,200 soldiers suffering amputation, but this proved only an interim figure; by February 20 the army had counted 112,627 frost victims, of which no fewer than 14,357 were amputees. "Barbarossa" had now cost the German forces close on 1,000,000 casualties, including 200,000 dead. The bitterness within the army's ranks was directed not at Hitler but at his generals.

One vivid narrative by an ordinary soldier filtered up through SS channels to Martin Bormann and probably reached Hitler too. It recounted how his battalion had marched about aimlessly for some three hundred miles before being hurled into action on the Donets, where the Russians had already overwhelmed the defenses.

> Too late and without any heavy guns, without even a single antitank gun our battalion was thrown into the breach as a so-called stopgap force. The Russians came at us, of course, with heavy tanks and enormous masses of infantry and pushed us back. Our machine guns wouldn't fire because of the bitter cold, and our ammunition ran out. For one whole day our battalion was encircled in a village where we had dug in. We tried a breakout by night as a last hope, an act of madness, but it came off. Meantime the entire front was beginning to cave in, about sixty miles across. Everywhere troops were flooding back in disorder, losing their heads. In vain officers confronted them at pistol point trying to restore order in this chaos; panic had broken out everywhere. . . . You saw scenes we had never witnessed even with the Russians, and only rarely with the French in France: columns of troops streaming back, often several side by side on one road; steel helmets, guns, gas masks, and equipment littered the

whole area. Hundreds of trucks set on fire by our own troops because they could not move them for lack of gasoline or because of the frost and snowdrifts; blazing ammunition dumps, clothing stores, food depots. The roads of retreat strewn with dead horses and broken-down vehicles. Upon this scene of chaos there pounced *German* dive-bombers, adding the final touches of perfection to the destruction. . . . The injured lay where they fell. Shapeless huddles of misery, swathed in blankets, their legs wrapped in rags and bandages, hobbled along the roads looking like something from scenes of Napoleon's retreat. For four days our battalion fought on, screening this hideous retreat. By the fifth day the Russian tanks had overtaken us, shot us to pieces, and wiped out the rest of our battalion. I myself escaped the tanks—which took a fiendish pleasure in hounding down each of our men until he was flattened beneath the tank tracks—by running into a deep pit where the snowdrifts barred the tanks' pursuit. . . .

With his own eyes this man had seen the three divisions in his sector wiped out. "We, the survivors of this catastrophe, have only one wish: that the Führer wreak a terrible judgment on the guilty ones."

Long before the passing of the old year, Hitler's thoughts had been with the coming spring offensive. He hoped to begin advancing Army Group South into the Caucasus as soon as the weather cleared—perhaps late in April 1942. As he explained to the Japanese, from whom he concealed none of his true ambitions, a southern thrust rather than the capture of Moscow offered many advantages: it would cure the oil problem, it would keep Turkey neutral, and if all went well the autumn of 1942 might see the Wehrmacht advancing on Baghdad. He disclosed his strategic plan to Field Marshal von Bock on January 18, before Bock flew to take command of his Army Group South at Poltava, seven hundred miles away. But Hitler already realized that the war would continue into 1943: on February 9, Göring conferred with him on "responsibility for the prompt provision of locomotives for the winter of 1942–43"; the equipment was to be of a kind capable of surviving the Russian winter.

Hitler's allies were initially unenthusiastic about a spring offensive. Finland feared war with the western powers. Mannerheim virtually declined to advance on the vital Murmansk railroad; he demobilized 180,000 of his troops that spring and went over to the defensive. But Field Marshal Keitel in an undoubted feat of diplomacy persuaded both Romania and Hungary to increase their contingents on the eastern front. Romania agreed to restore her expeditionary force to its previous strength, and Hungary, not to be outdone—and fearing that Hitler would favor the Romanians in the inevitable postwar struggle for the Transylvania region—followed suit, offering a complete Hungarian army of two hundred thousand men. Italy also agreed to send more divisions east. Hitler for his part tactfully respected everybody's feelings: the allied armies would not come under

German command; and the Hungarians and Romanians would nowhere find themselves adjacent, so they could not get at each other's throats. Bulgaria, with its strong pro-Russian currents of sympathy, remained nonaligned. Her king, although an admiring follower of Hitler's, was pleased that the Führer expected nothing more of Bulgaria's army than that it dissuade Turkey from foolish undertakings. Turkey's feelings were evidently warming toward Hitler anyway, even as the spring thaws melted northward across Russia; the Turkish president privately assured Franz von Papen that he was as convinced as ever of Germany's ultimate victory and was resolved to withstand British pressure on Turkey to abandon her neutrality. Learning from Forschungsamt intercepts that a disgruntled Britain was discontinuing her arms supplies to Turkey, in April Hitler agreed that Germany would supply the Turks with tanks, guns, submarines, and aircraft.

Neutral nations and Germany's allies were not the only ones demanding the products of the German arms industry. The catastrophic material losses of the German army that winter had to be made good. Anticipating a swift defeat of Russia, in mid-1941 Hitler had ordered production effort switched to the navy and Luftwaffe, and now the army's needs, particularly in ammunition, could barely be covered. In November 1941 the economics ministry had declared its virtual bankruptcy: General Hermann von Hanneken saw no way of increasing arms production on the present raw materials basis. Hitler himself had to devise the ways and means of rationalizing arms production and surmounting red tape. Seated in his private plane on December 3, while flying to the eastern front, he had dictated to Munitions Minister Fritz Todt a three-page decree ordering the simplification and expansion of arms production. Basically, future arms manufacture was to be concentrated in the most efficient factories, turning out standardized and unsophisticated weapons by mass-production means. Todt initiated a radical reform of the arms industry's structure. On January 10 Hitler ordered the industry to revert to its earlier preferential treatment of the army's needs at the expense of the Luftwaffe and navy (although "the long-term objectives remain unaltered," *i.e.,* the focus of the fighting effort of the latter two services was to be directed against the western Allies). At the end of January, Todt outlined to Hitler his detailed proposals—basically the arms combines would supervise their own projects and a "fixed contract price" system would be introduced to dispose of the current iniquitous "cost-plus-profit" system, with its inherent deterrent to any factory to cut weapons production costs. As a result of Todt's reforms, between February and July 1942 German arms production was to increase by 55 percent. On February 7, Todt reported to Hitler and dined with him at the Wolf's Lair; by 9:45 A.M. the next morning he was dead, his charred remains lying in the wreckage of his Heinkel which had crashed on takeoff at Rastenburg airfield.

Hitler was desolate at the loss of this old friend. He ordered the air ministry to design a cockpit-recorder, to install in future planes, to register the cause of any accidents. His Luftwaffe adjutant witnessed Hitler's receipt of the news from the airfield. "He showed the barest flicker of emotion. The only thing he said was, after a few minutes, that only Albert Speer could be considered a suitable successor. As that day wore on, and more frequently with the passing years, he talked of Dr. Todt and how grievous a blow his death was for him." Speer had just arrived the previous evening from a hazardous tour of the construction gangs he had late in December supplied to the eastern front to speed up the relaying of railroad track and reconstruction of transport installations. Hitler called him into his office and informed him of his selection as Todt's successor.

For the second time in two weeks Hitler returned to Berlin, this time to bury his loyal friend, Munitions Minister Fritz Todt.

These were momentous hours. As his train pulled into the Reich capital, his battleships were in the English Channel. At noon they would be passing through the Straits of Dover, and still the British seemed totally unaware of them. In the Far East, the final Japanese assault on Singapore, bastion of the British Empire there, had just begun. It looked like the end of India, too. In North Africa, General Rommel's corps, nourished with fresh tanks and men, had gone over to the counteroffensive and thrown the British back three hundred miles and out of Cyrenaica. From decoded British foreign office instructions to missions abroad Hitler could savor the harsh mood of realism now again pervading London in view of the German army's unbroken powers of resistance and his imminent spring offensive. Yet his feelings on the coming British disgrace were mixed. To the Japanese he seemed to relish every moment. "If Britain loses India, their world will cave in on them. India is the heart of the British Empire. It is from India that Britain has won her entire wealth." But to his staff he showed a different face. To Goebbels on January 29 he had lamented the sad losses being inflicted on the White Man in the Far East. In speaking to Antonescu on February 11 he referred to the latest dispatch from Singapore as "perhaps a somewhat melancholy piece of news." It was rumored that he privately went so far as to admit he would dearly like to send the British twenty divisions to help them throw the Yellow invaders out.

Yet the clock could not be turned back. Hitler mentioned to Goebbels that every Englishman he had met before the war had agreed that Churchill was a nincompoop—"even" Chamberlain took that view. The propaganda minister did not share Hitler's and Ribbentrop's evident belief that these February disgraces would lead to Churchill's final downfall, though both would have liked to see Sir Stafford Cripps take his place.[5] Hitler believed Cripps even more inept than Churchill ("It's not enough to be called Cripps, you've got to have *Grips* [brains] as well," he wisecracked). Goebbels agreed that in any normal country a Churchill would long ago have got his just deserts; but the British were an odd folk, and probably too inert to take action.

By the early hours of February 13, the German fleet's strategic withdrawal from the Atlantic to northern waters had been successfully completed. The *Scharnhorst* had reached Wilhelmshaven, despite minor damage from two mines. The *Gneisenau* had reached Kiel, also dented by a mine. The *Prinz Eugen* had got through completely unscathed. In the belated air battles the British had lost twenty bombers, sixteen fighters, and six torpedo planes; Galland had lost only seven fighters. The London *Times* commented hotly: "Vice Admiral Ciliax has succeeded where the Duke of Medina Sidonia failed. . . . Nothing more mortifying to the pride of sea power has happened in home waters since the seventeenth century." Hitler, who had remained in hourly contact with the admiralty, and who had "trembled for the safety of our ships," as Goebbels witnessed, now breathed again.

Next day he spoke to ten thousand newly commissioned lieutenants assembled in Berlin's Sportpalast. The photographs show him—looking stern and flanked by Keitel, Milch, and Himmler—gripping the speaker's lectern. He made every officer present believe that in this hour of crisis he alone could turn the tide. Normally such speeches ended in silence, but as he left the platform a thunderous cheering broke out, and out of the clamor swelled ten thousand voices united in the national anthem. Despite the reverses in Russia, his prestige was at its height. The next evening, February 15, his train bore him back toward his headquarters in East Prussia. Toward midnight, Joachim Ribbentrop came along the swaying corridor with news that Churchill had just broadcast the fall of Singapore: Lieutenant General A. E. Percival had capitulated that evening with his seventy thousand men to General Tomoyuki Yamashita, commander of the Japanese Twenty-fifth Army. To Fräulein Schroeder, Hitler's secretary, the foreign minis-

---

[5]The German admiralty also believed Churchill impregnable. Etzdorf recorded: "In Ambassador [Karl] Ritter's view, the political leadership has certain hopes that the loss of Singapore might have far-reaching effects on the British public as far as the dropping of Churchill and a willingness for peace are concerned. The naval staff thinks otherwise. There is no hope *whatever* of the British suddenly giving way to make peace." The admiralty felt that even if Australia and India were lost, Churchill, in view of his ties to the United States, would probably reform the Empire as a British Commonwealth of Nations with Canada as its centerpiece.

ter dictated a gloating draft communiqué for the Axis press to publish next morning. Hitler read it with an expression of distaste. Then shaking his head he advised Ribbentrop: "We have to think in terms of centuries. Who knows, in the future the Yellow Peril may well be the biggest one for us."[6] He tore the document in half.

[6]Yet a few weeks later the same Hitler privately scoffed at the foreign journalists who accused him of betraying his own race and conjuring up a "Yellow Peril" through his alliance with Japan. "It was the British who appealed to the Japanese in World War I to give us the *coup de grâce* . . . the essential thing is to win, and to that end we are quite ready to make an alliance with the Devil himself."

Hitler's Word Is Law

The first half of 1942 was again to bring the Soviet Union to the brink of defeat. From the intercepted messages passing between east and west, Hitler could follow Stalin's exasperated demands for an Allied Second Front and his veiled threats to conclude a separate peace with the Nazis. But now that he had survived the winter, Hitler no longer wanted to settle his differences by negotiation. As soon as the ground dried out and he had restocked his depleted divisions in the far south, he would go over to the offensive. The German soldier's self-confidence had been restored: with the Führer's prodding they had mastered the terrors of the Russian winter, where even a Napoleon had failed. At the end of February the foreign diplomats in Berlin were informed that the Führer had now decided to fight to the bitter end. All further attempts at mediation, of which the latest were quietly proposed by Turkey, were discouraged.

Initially, as Hitler's secretary vividly described, the mood at his headquarters upon his return from Berlin was bleak. "After two days of warmer weather the temperature suddenly dropped again," she wrote on February 27, 1942. "Although by day it is only about zero, the biting east wind makes the cold far far worse. . . . The Chief is always dog-tired, but he won't go to bed, and this is often a torment for the rest of us. We used to play records most evenings, and then you could fall back on your own thoughts; but since Todt's unfortunate end the music evenings have been few and far between, and as his tea circle always consists of the same faces, there is no stimulus from outside and nobody has any personal experiences to relate, so the conversation is often tedious and indifferent to say the least. In fact, the conversations run around and around in the same circles. Thank goodness we have a cat that often sits up with us. Its playful antics . . . are a welcome relief and help to bridge the awkward silences. I like him most of all, because if he jumps on to my lap I can warm my freezing hands under his soft fur—it's bliss! There is also a Scotch terrier, but he is not all that popular as he is obstinate and capricious (besides which the Chief says he looks like a

374

scrub brush and he'd never let himself be photographed with it). . . ." Goebbels found the terrier still being given the run of Hitler's bunker at the end of March. "At present there is no creature closer to him," observed the propaganda minister.

Hitler's health had suffered from the winter, but he allowed himself no respite. In December he had jibed to Halder: "You fine generals only play ball so long as everything's going well. The moment things get sticky you report sick or tender your resignation!" If Germany was to survive, *he* could not resign; the worry, the extremes of temperature, and the general strain on his sclerotic arteries began to tell on him. Dr. Morell added an ever-increasing variety of medicines to the Führer's medicine chest: the heart tonics "Strophantin" and "Prostrophanta" first, then the stimulants "Cardiazol" and "Coramin" to overcome the insufficiency in Hitler's circulatory system. In 1942 Morell began administering "Sympathol." Hitler passively accepted Morell's increasing doses. "Morell tells me that my intense rate of work uses up so much energy that he has to give me so many injections—just as if I were in the tropics," he would explain. Or again: "Morell is still researching. He is still pushing out the frontiers of our knowledge." His faith in Morell's "Vitamultin" vitamin tablets was so great that he ordered billions of them dispensed regularly to the armed forces despite expert opinion that they were valueless. And when the winter of 1941 brought a plague of lice to the eastern front, it was Morell's invention, "Russla" powder (a foul-smelling concoction), that was prescribed to the reluctant troops. Morell's royalty profit was commensurate.

For all Morell's endeavors, visitors to Rastenburg that spring found Hitler gray, drawn, and ailing. He confided to Goebbels that he suffered attacks of giddiness; and as he described the winter crisis he seemed to age visibly. "The Führer describes to me," wrote Goebbels of a conversation on March 19, "how close we were these past few months to a Napoleonic winter. Had we weakened for just one instant, the front would have caved in and a catastrophe ensued that would have put Napoleon's far into the shade. Millions of fine soldiers would have been exposed to death by starvation and cold, and our workers—not to mention the intelligentsia—probably forced into bondage. Most of the blame for this is Brauchitsch's. The Führer has only words of contempt for him: a vain, cowardly wretch, unable even to grasp what was happening, much less master it. By his constant interference and disobedience he completely wrecked the entire plan of campaign in the east, which had been devised in crystal clarity by the Führer. The Führer had a plan which was bound to lead to victory. Had Brauchitsch done what was asked of him and what he should in fact have done, then things in the east would look very different than they do today. The Führer had no intention whatever of aiming for Moscow; he wanted to cut off the Caucasus [from the rest of Russia], thus hitting the Soviet system at its most vulnerable point. But

Brauchitsch and his General Staff knew better: Brauchitsch kept hammering on about Moscow. He wanted prestige victories instead of real ones."

In retrospect, the issues all seemed much clearer to Hitler than at the time.

For the coming German offensive in the east, Hitler had again established a clear list of priorities. This time General Halder accepted them. As Hitler set them out in a conference on March 28, 1942, a carefully phased series of campaigns would begin in the far south as soon as the ground dried out: in the Crimea, Manstein would destroy the Russian forces in the Kerch peninsula; he would then storm Sevastopol, using the techniques of World War I—sheer weight of artillery bombardment. Then Bock's army group would attack the Izyum salient east of Kharkov. The main summer offensive, "Blue," would open with the capture of Voronezh on the Don; then the armies would roll southeastward down the Don toward Stalingrad, digging in along the river for winter quarters. Hitler assured Goebbels that by October his armies would be able to go into these winter quarters. By early September he hoped they would have reached the Caucasus Mountains. Depending on the summer victories, he would decide later what operations to undertake in the center and against Leningrad. The directive for "Blue" was issued on April 5. After the defeat of Stalin's main armies, Hitler planned to construct an immense East Wall beyond which there might well rage a Hundred Years' War against the scattered remnants of the Bolshevik forces. "Russia will then be to us what India is to the British," he told Goebbels.

More than one voice doubted the prospects of this great offensive. Keitel mentioned—but only to his subordinates—as early as December 1941 the possibility that it might fail; his staff experts correctly suspected that damage to the Caucasus oil fields might be so extensive as to render their capture pointless. General Fromm, commander of the Replacement Army, doubted there would be enough manpower or munitions to execute "Blue" over such vast distances. Göring also doubted whether the Russians would be defeated that summer. However, Hitler had no real option but to strike out toward the Caucasus oil fields. He needed the oil; and so did Stalin—so the Red Army would surely stand and fight rather than withdraw beyond the Don. Already the Soviet Union had lost the iron ore of Krivoi Rog and the manganese of Nikopol; the armorplate of their latest tanks was consequently of poor quality. But if "Blue" succeeded, Stalin would have no coking coal, or oil either. Now even General Halder saw the point, and when the admiralty persisted in arguing for the capture by Rommel of the Suez Canal the general impatiently replied that Rommel's army would be too weak to withstand the enemy's counterattack from the Middle East and Red Sea *unless* the German armies were also astride the Caucasus. Besides, Halder pointed out: "The Caucasus operation is still absolutely vital for our oil supply position." He held that only victory in the Caucasus would ensure the Reich's ultimate survival in the war.[1]

The oil shortage was certainly a compelling argument to use with the admiralty. The German and Italian navies were virtually immobilized; production of aviation fuel was just enough to cover monthly requirements, but so low as to make expansion of aircraft production pointless; and in May 1942 Keitel also had to find 60,000 tons of fuel for agricultural purposes in the Ukraine and for Atlantic defensive projects. The 1942 output of gasoline for motor transport would be 77,000 tons a month less than the average monthly consumption (219,000) in 1941. Hitler signed a government decree restricting the use of motor cars to official use only—and even then a bona fide justification was needed.

Unaware that Rommel's army stood astride undreamed-of oil fields in Libya, Hitler still relied on Romania's resources. Hungary showed little inclination to part with her supplies, and Hitler had evidence that both she and Romania were secretly stockpiling oil for the private war they were planning to wage on each other in the future. But he was unwilling to put pressure on Marshal Antonescu to increase oil deliveries. Antonescu claimed that 80 percent of Romania's output was already earmarked for the Axis, and Hitler, fearful that something might happen to this loyal friend, instructed Keitel that the Romanians were to be given "kid glove treatment" and there was to be no question of imposing a military "petroleum dictator" on Antonescu. With blithe lack of vision, Antonescu's government insisted that Germany pay for all her oil with gold, and in advance; had Romania foreseen into which neighbor's coffers that gold would eventually vanish, she might have acted otherwise.

Hitler had always been a champion of the radical act. In every SS barracks hung one of his favorite Nietzsche texts: *Praised be that which toughens.* Much of his admiration of Stalin was inspired by the dictator's successful brutality. He, Hitler, would try to emulate him, but often did not succeed: he had not determined to bomb London until too late. To the Japanese ambassador, General Oshima, he mentioned that he intended to kill all survivors of torpedoed Allied merchant ships out of cruel "necessity"; but when he put this idea to the admiralty as a means of intensifying the tonnage war, Raeder would not hear of it.

The fear of reprisal did not dissuade the British from opening up in March 1942 a massive area-bombing offensive against German and German-occupied cities.

---

[1]Halder's words are quoted as above by his naval liaison officer in German admiralty archives. After the war, he and departmental heads like General Adolf Heusinger claimed to have been unanimous in opposing the Caucasus campaign.

On the night of March 3, RAF planes dropped over 450 tons of bombs on a Paris arms factory, killing 800 French civilians. Hitler ordered the Luftwaffe to execute an immediate reprisal on a British target. "The main thing is to achieve the maximum shock and terror effect." But a few days later he canceled the order, explaining to Jeschonnek that he wanted to avoid provoking air raids on German cities; besides, the British were not coming to Germany in any strength, he argued, and the Luftwaffe was incapable of meting out appropriate annihilation raids on English cities. A week later, a force of 200 RAF bombers laden primarily with incendiaries all but destroyed the medieval Baltic town of Lübeck, leaving 320 dead and hundreds of injured in the ruins. It was a Saturday night, and Hitler's temper was not improved when it was found impossible to reach anybody at Berlin's civilian ministries or military headquarters: all of them were closed— apparently from lunchtime on Saturday until 9 A.M. on Monday! Nobody knew where the ministers themselves could be reached.[2] The raid was a clear attempt to provoke Hitler into withdrawing Luftwaffe strength from the Russian front for reprisals; in this it was unsuccessful, for Jeschonnek firmly believed the Russian threat must be liquidated before all else. But Hitler did order reprisal attacks on English towns, to be chosen for their defenselessness and cultural value—the same criteria as Churchill had applied. Exeter was the first town to suffer; London was explicitly embargoed from attack. After a series of Allied fire-raids on the Baltic port of Rostock, Hitler told Goebbels that terror could only be answered with terror. "The British belong to that class of human beings whom you can only talk with after you have smashed their teeth in."

It was an unedifying sight—the two opposing leaders, well-bunkered in their respective capitals, trading blows at each other's innocent citizenry. How Stalin, who had long learned to "think in terms of centuries," must have relished it![3] During the spring, it became obvious that the British regarded their new area-bombing offensive as the second front that Moscow was clamoring for.

The British had no alternative as yet. To invade Norway or North Africa would require a shipping fleet they would soon no longer possess, thanks to the U-boats.

---

[2] This was typical of the comfortable life led by most of the Nazi ministers. Only a week earlier, on March 21, Hitler had issued a secret decree insisting that these ministers and generals set an example to the public and warning that he would act ruthlessly and without regard for rank against any of them dealing, for example, in the black market. Somehow Göring escaped censure, though he was the worst offender.

[3] The Soviet ambassador in London allegedly remarked to Sir Alexander Cadogan at the end of 1940 that his country was content to see the two sides exhaust themselves. He was in the daily habit, he said, of totting up the aircraft losses in the Battle of Britain together, in one column; whereas Churchill and Hitler were more myopically setting them down against each other.

From Stockholm, Hitler learned that Churchill had promised the exiled Norwegian government not to invade Norway—not in 1942, anyway; and the king of Sweden privately assured Hitler that he would oppose any Allied designs in northern Scandinavia. As for the Continent, the British would be foolish to count on an internal uprising in Europe, Hitler told Mussolini. (There was no more opposition in Germany—in Berlin he had fewer than two thousand critics, or so he believed. The cheering Berlin crowds after his Reichstag speech on April 26 were seen as proof of that.) However, his intuitive sense of strategy warned him late in March that the Cherbourg and Brest peninsulas might be the target of an Allied invasion. On March 27 he ordered all available reserves "immediately" moved into the region west of Caen and Saint-Nazaire, and he gave instructions that the U-boat base at Saint-Nazaire itself was to be closely reinforced. The very next morning the British launched a commando raid on the base.

The aging destroyer *Campbelltown,* accompanied by a swarm of torpedo boats and motor launches laden with commandos, had entered the base before dawn on March 28, rammed the lock gates of the huge dry-dock, and been abandoned. The warships had flown the German ensign and employed secret German signal codes, but this should not have surprised the defenses to the extent it did. The commandos were wiped out by the port's defenders, and only four of the eighteen torpedo boats and launches employed escaped destruction. French dockyard workers and sightseers were still clustered curiously around the abandoned *Campbelltown* at 11:45 A.M., when its hidden cargo of time-fused explosives blew up, killing sixty of them—though not before the ship's secret papers had been salvaged by the Germans, including what was apparently the latest chart of Allied minefields. The naval staff was well pleased, but Hitler was not. He sent for Raeder and expressed his displeasure at the fact that the raiding force had sailed so far up the Loire; and more importantly he ordered the Atlantic defenses still further strengthened to make such raids impossible in the future.

Over 140 British prisoners had been taken at Saint-Nazaire. Hitler sent his interpreter Paul Schmidt to interrogate them. The interrogation reports submitted to Hitler showed them to be the cream of Churchill's forces—well-informed, proud, and patriotic. Schmidt found most of them bitter that they should be fighting Germany, a brother country. They no longer believed Britain could win, he reported, but felt that the war would "just fizzle out." Goebbels's English-language propaganda was said by these prisoners to have a big listening public but to be using the wrong approach. Most riveting were the remarks of a territorial army major, a London industrialist and friend of Anthony Eden, who said that his war-weary countrymen would make peace the next day if they could be convinced their country's very existence was not threatened. According to this major, the British hated the Japanese but nevertheless felt that Britain ought to be in the same camp as the Germans, not fighting them. "We all like the Germans. . . . It's just that we are certain that Hitler is planning to conquer the world." Told that Hitler had no designs on Britain at all, the major is said to have exclaimed, "Then why not tell our government and people that! I would be willing to go to the British government and tell them what your peace terms are, and I give my word of honor to return to captivity here. But for God's sake do it now, before the hundreds of thousands who will die on both sides in this summer's fighting are sacrificed!"

This offer was not taken up, but many of Hitler's coming decisions—for example his rejection of the joint "India Declaration" approved by Italy and Japan and designed to encourage mutiny in that endangered dominion—were guided by a desire to preserve the prevailing undercurrents of peace perceptible to him in Britain. The British authorities continued, however, to represent Hitler's war aims to the British people very differently, for example there was a pronouncement soon afterward by Lord Vansittart, diplomatic adviser to the Cabinet, that Germany intended to exterminate twenty million Britons or transport them as slaves to Africa. So the British fought gamely on.

Hitler was now fifty-three. On his birthday there were letters from Eva Braun and her mother, and from his sisters Angela and Paula. He wrote back thanking them and sending them ham he had just received from a Spanish admirer—with a warning to them to cook it thoroughly before eating. Raeder, Göring, Milch, Ribbentrop, and a host of lesser dignitaries attended the birthday luncheon held in a dining room decked out with tablecloths and flowers. The headquarters officers and staff were given a glass of Piesporter Goldtröpfchen and cups of real coffee. All the children of the neighborhood were marshaled outside by SS adjutant Schulze and photographed plucking at the Führer's uniform and thrusting flowers into his hands. After lunch the first two Tiger tanks were demonstrated to him. From Berlin Goebbels had sent a newfangled device, a tape recorder with tapes of many symphonies and orchestras. Hitler could hear for himself how much better the Berlin Philharmonic was than its Vienna counterpart, which had an aged string section; and now he discovered Hans Hotter as the up-and-coming baritone who would be ideal for Bayreuth.

In the east the roads and fields were drying out; the snow had vanished almost everywhere. In the Crimea spring was already in full bloom. Never in his life had Hitler yearned so painfully for the onset of that season. He never wanted to see snow again. It had cost him six months of his precious last years—the vital years. After a certain age, he reflected, man's creative genius gradually abandons him. The strenuous bunker life in East Prussia had sapped his strength. The first white hairs were appearing on his head.

Hitler's doctors prescribed the solitude of the Berghof, and he himself was only too eager to put the horrors of the Russian front out of his mind. (Only a few days earlier a Russian deserter had brought over nauseating details of the one million dead in Leningrad and of the cannibalism widespread among the beleaguered Russian army units and population there.) He therefore asked Ribbentrop to arrange an early meeting with Mussolini, and to make plain that he would prefer Salzburg to some Italian venue. Mussolini meekly agreed, and Hitler's train left the Wolf's Lair late on April 24 on the first leg of the long journey to Bavaria; it was followed by Ribbentrop's equally impressive train. "A wonder that the foreign minister allows anybody to take precedence over him!" joked Hitler, long aware of Ribbentrop's tiresome vanity.

In Berlin he was to address the Reichstag, asking for powers that would neutralize the meddling lawyers of the ministry of justice for all time. He himself drafted the necessary decree and showed it to Hans Lammers four hours before the speech began on April 26. Lammers he could trust—he knew how to manufacture the quasi-legal tools needed to buttress the affairs of an authoritarian state. "He doesn't get legalistic theorizing confused with the realities of life," Hitler said some days later. Lammers suggested that it would suffice for the Reichstag to pass the law by acclamation; Göring would follow Hitler's speech with a formal approval of the law as President of the Reichstag. The little charade was performed at the end of the afternoon's speeches. The Reichstag records show Hitler thundering:

> . . . I do however expect one thing: that the nation give me the right to take immediate action in any way I see fit, wherever I do not find the obedience unconditionally called for by service of the greater cause. This is a matter of life and death to us. *(Loud applause.)* At the front and at home, in transport, civil service, and the judiciary there must be obedience to only one idea, namely the fight for victory. *(Stormy applause.)* Let nobody now preach about his well-earned rights.[4] Let each man clearly understand, from now on there are only duties.

Göring appealed to the deputies to empower the Führer to do "everything in the cause of, or contributing to, the fight for victory." Regardless of rank or position, Hitler could punish any German as he saw fit, dismissing him from any office or command without the need for regular procedures. As one man the Reichstag deputies rose from their seats and signified their assent with shouts of Heil and a singing of the national anthem. At 4:24 P.M., when the session ended —the last time the Reichstag would ever meet—Adolf Hitler was himself the Law.

---

[4]A reference to General Hoepner's lawsuit. See page 366.

That evening Hitler continued his journey to Bavaria. The days in Munich and at the Berghof passed all too rapidly. Unfortunately, the Obersalzberg was carpeted with fresh fallen snow as he arrived—snow seemed to dog him everywhere. But the snapshots Eva Braun pasted into her album show a misty-eyed Führer affectionately playing with Herta Schneider's children and fondling Bella, the new Alsatian bitch he had just bought from a minor postal official in Ingolstadt to keep Blondi, his other Alsatian, company. The advantage of taking Bella for walks was that she would not start talking politics or war with him.

The two days of talks with Mussolini yielded nothing new. The atmosphere was more cordial than on their previous meeting in August 1941. In the first meeting at Klessheim, near Salzburg, Hitler painted the German position in Russia in optimistic terms. Mussolini responded by quoting the *New York Herald Tribune*'s assessment that Russia had "a dying army." When the Duce mentioned the growing grain shortage in Italy, Hitler promised that in 1943 the Ukrainian harvest would yield at least seven million tons. Both agreed that a watchful eye was needed on France; but at the other end of the Mediterranean, Turkey was slowly but surely edging around to the Axis camp, if only in consequence of her hatred of the Russians. There was ample proof of this. Turkey had recently imposed a crippling fine on the British envoy to Bulgaria, whose luggage had mysteriously blown up in a Constantinople hotel! She had vigorously prosecuted the Soviet agents behind a recent bungled attempt at assassinating Franz von Papen in Ankara. And she was currently negotiating with Germany for the purchase of German submarines, tanks, and guns.[5]

The second meeting between the dictators was at the Berghof. Generals and field marshals took the place of the foreign ministers who had attended the first meeting (but no admirals, as the German naval staff later lamented). The Italians pressed their case for an early capture of Malta, "Operation Hercules." Hitler conceded that if successful, "Hercules" and the subsequent destruction of the British stranglehold on the Middle East would be a turning point for the Axis, but he viewed the operation with scarcely concealed distaste—not only because it was to be a primarily Italian operation (and hence in his eyes predestined to

[5]Hitler wanted to make the sale of U-boats conditional on Turkey's allowing a similar number of German submarines to slip clandestinely through the Dardanelles into the Black Sea. This the Turks rejected. Hitler withdrew a similar proposal about torpedo boats, to be disguised as merchant ships, when he was reminded that plans were far advanced to transport these down the autobahn to Linz and from there along the Danube directly into the Black Sea.

ignominious failure), but because despite all the arguments of Raeder, Kesselring, and the Italians to the contrary, he still argued that the war could only be won in the east. The Mediterranean theater was a sideshow of value only for tying down enemy forces. In deference to the alliance, Hitler paid lip service to the needs of "Hercules": since April 2, German and Italian bomber forces had been mercilessly softening-up Malta for invasion, attacking airfields, dockyards, and warships with savage side-effects testified to by the appeals reaching Hitler via neutral channels to allow British hospital ships through to the island. In mid-April, he had also agreed to supply German parachute troops for the eventual invasion, provided the British did not in the meanwhile spring surprises on him in Norway or France. This was the basic offer he repeated to Mussolini at the Berghof, but his heart was not in it. He knew from the aerial photographs spread out before them that the island was heavily fortified and unsuitable for glider landings. Rommel's offensive in North Africa must begin before the British could start theirs, and given the limited Axis air strength in the Mediterranean, "Hercules" would have to be postponed at least until after that. Early in May, therefore, the OKW laid down that Rommel should launch "Theseus," as his offensive was called, at the end of the month, with "Hercules" postponed until mid-July or mid-August. The actual objectives of Rommel's offensive were themselves a matter of disagreement: the Italians wanted him to halt on a line between Sollum and the Halfaya Pass, but Hitler wanted Egypt. A Finnish report had claimed that 90 percent of the Egyptian population was anti-British, so it must be "ripe for revolution" in Hitler's view.

At the beginning of May, Hitler returned to the Wolf's Lair in East Prussia. Bella went with him, sleeping in his train compartment and lying at the foot of the camp bed in his bunker. Perhaps Hitler saw in the massive Alsatian something of a watchdog, for over the last few days reports had trickled in of a plot to assassinate him; there were indications that Russian assassins were being sent to do the job.

Bella did have her disadvantages, though. She woke regularly as clockwork at 9 A.M. in the pitch-dark bunker bedroom, bounded onto Hitler's bed, and began to paw him affectionately. Since he seldom went to bed before three or four, this was a nuisance; besides, he liked to lie in bed for an hour or two each morning, catching up on his reading. His intake of information was staggering, a necessity if the Führer principle was to be maintained. The breakfast trolley outside his bedroom door groaned with fresh files each morning. Ambassador Hewel logged over eleven hundred different diplomatic papers passing through his hands to Hitler in 1941; by early April 1942 he had already submitted over eight hundred more. Now as Commander in Chief of the army he assumed a workload that would have crushed many men. He boasted: "Although the Russian front is three times as big as the front was in France, there is not one regiment or battalion there whose situation is not followed three times a day here at Führer Headquarters."

We shall never know all the Intelligence data on which Hitler based his decisions. The Forschungsamt archives were later destroyed, and the remarkable output of the post office went from his hands straight to the document-shredder machine. (A few weeks earlier the Post Office had begun unscrambling the enemy's sole radio-telephone link between London and Washington, and a regular flow of transcripts had reached Hitler through Himmler ever since March 1942; the transcripts included even the top-secret conversations between Roosevelt and Churchill.) Missing too are the secret cables decoded by Ribbentrop's cryptanalysts—Swiss, Turkish, British, Italian, American, French, and a host of other codes. Decoded confidential Turkish and Yugoslav dispatches from the Soviet capital enabled Hitler to follow Stalin's guesswork over Germany's coming offensive—Hitler's aim was to feign transport and other preparations for a renewed offensive against Moscow, to distract attention from his real objectives: Voronezh and the south. He also learned of the crippling Russian famine, of the arrival of American tanks and aircraft, and details of Russian aircraft production. The decoded American telegrams from Cairo to Washington were even better: in February, the Italians deciphered one in which Washington inquired about the possibility of invading northwest Africa. At the end of April, Cairo was heard advising Washington of the crucial position in Malta: antiaircraft ammunition was running out, and there was no gasoline for the motor transport. Other American messages betrayed the strength and dispositions of the forces opposing Rommel. The Abwehr units in the east were also functioning; late in April they were able to quote a member of the Soviet party leadership, Nossenko, on a resolution of the latest session of the Central Committee's presidium—"to snatch the operational initiative out of German hands before their offensive begins." The Red Army would go over to the offensive on the symbolically significant first of May (in fact, the offensive began soon after).

Hitler also learned much from orthodox diplomatic sources. Early in April he heard from Buenos Aires that Britain was mass-producing one-kilo bombs with long time-fuses. He at once ordered the Luftwaffe to begin its own mass production of such weapons. From diplomatic sources too he heard the first rumors that Vice-Admiral Sir Louis Mountbatten was preparing an amphibious invasion of France. Probably one of the more damaging items was the confirmation blurted out by Churchill—who evidently forgot the wartime slogan "walls have ears"— that the mounting shipping losses were bringing Britain to "the brink of her most critical moment since war broke out." This quotation reached Hitler through Spain and encouraged him to step up his U-boat and Luftwaffe offensive on the Atlantic and Arctic convoys. In the last week of May, convoy PQ. 16 to North Russia was attacked; 7 ships were sunk, with 32,400 tons of war supplies including

147 tanks, 77 aircraft, and 770 motor vehicles. Every Allied vessel sunk reduced the threat of a Second Front. From the intercepted enemy cables Hitler also knew precisely the terms of the Anglo-Soviet pact being hammered out in London: Stalin was demanding the restitution of his pre-1941 frontiers (which included the Baltic states and parts of Finland and Romania) and much of southeast Europe; Anthony Eden, Churchill's foreign minister, was inclined to agree, but the Americans as yet were not.

During May 1942 Hitler's armies regained the military initiative in the east. Only the growing partisan menace in the rear of Kluge's Army Group Center gave cause for concern. Persuaded that Moscow was the objective of Hitler's summer offensive, the Russians had infiltrated and parachuted tens of thousands of partisans into this area (though Hitler forbade his staff to refer to them as "partisans," just as in an internal edict he denied the bombers of Rostock and Lübeck the right to the title "Royal Air Force").

The partisans were blowing up railways and bridges, burning down factories and food stores, and intimidating the relatives of Russians working for the Axis. In the eyes of many Germans a great opportunity had been lost—that of winning at least the traditionally anti-Soviet Ukrainians to their cause. This had been Reichenau's last message to Hitler before he died in January 1942. It was the advice of Goebbels, and particularly of Rosenberg as well. The latter, officially Hitler's minister for the eastern territories, watched in despair as one plenipotentiary after another muscled in on his regional governments—each with Hitler's special warrant, like Albert Speer's for the construction of roads and railways, or Fritz Sauckel's for the procurement of workers for the Reich. Rosenberg bitterly told Hitler on May 8 that with greater tact those workers could have been procured voluntarily; by rounding them up like slaves, Sauckel—as Hitler's manpower dictator—was merely driving hordes of Russians before him into the forests, thus supplying new recruits for the partisan armies. Gauleiter Erich Koch, his own Reich Commissar of the Ukraine, was even worse than Sauckel and quite out of Rosenberg's control. "I know that we always used to say the Slav liked a good whipping," said Rosenberg, who went on to complain that some Germans in the Ukraine were taking this literally and strutting around with whip in hand; this was a bitter blow to the Ukrainians' self-esteem. Hitler approved an order Rosenberg had drafted curbing Koch's excesses, but in private he believed Koch's doctrine was the proper one. Göring also supported the tough line, telling his generals in April after a conference with Hitler: "The Russians are an enemy with barbaric methods. We are not going to introduce such methods ourselves, but it will be necessary for us to express ourselves more harshly."

Large-scale antipartisan sweeps with code names like "Hanover" and "Brunswick" began in May. The Hungarian contingent counted 117 prisoners and 4,300 dead in one such operation alone. Hitler welcomed the idea of using Russian prisoners themselves to help fight the partisans, but nobody, certainly not Rosenberg, could persuade him to appoint at least "puppet" Russian governments in the conquered regions. And so the increasingly barbaric struggle behind the German lines went on, with more and more of the local population being won around to harbor and encourage the partisan fight against the Germans.

The General Staff suggested that Hitler allow the use of poison gas to combat the partisans—thereby countering illegal warfare with illegal weapons. Hitler would not hear of it—even though he was to say when the analogous problem of fighting Tito's guerrillas in Serbia was discussed that the situation there was just like that in Russia: it would be impossible to be too tough with them. "We can only get our way by acting brutally and casting off all our European inhibitions." Similarly, he flatly forbade the General Staff to study the problems of bacterial attack, except in a purely defensive light. What may have been a hangover from his own gasing experience in World War I kept him adamant to the end. Although the British employed phosphorus in their bombs, Hitler forbade its use in the Luftwaffe's, as it caused skin injuries and its fumes were poisonous. Since German scientists had developed nerve-gases (Sarin and Tabun) and bacterial weapons to a degree of sophistication unknown to the enemy, Hitler's otherwise inexplicable inhibitions were not without effect on the war effort.

For the coming summer offensive, Hitler's armies would rely heavily on their own "partisan" operations, though they were not on the massive scale employed by Stalin. In mid-April he summoned Colonel Lahousen, Canaris's chief of Abwehr subversive and sabotage operations, to discuss these with Jodl and himself at his headquarters. The final plans, as described by Lahousen to army representatives in May, relied heavily on "what we may term reeducated prisoners of war" in addition to the regular commando regiment, the "Brandenburg" Regiment, which in earlier campaigns had performed classic holding operations at the bridges of Gennep, the Dvina River, and the Vardar bridge at Aziupolis. The Russian prisoners who had volunteered proved surprisingly effective, filtering in their own uniforms or plain clothes through Russian lines to execute clandestine missions against their former comrades; furnished with the necessary passwords, they were able to return through the German lines unscathed. Army Group South, and particularly the Seventeenth Army, had high praise for them.

During April, single pairs of Abwehr agents had already parachuted into Voronezh, Stalingrad, Krasnodar, and other areas to sabotage key railway lines, power stations, and pipeline installations. Special task forces had also been trained—one to defend the Maykop oil fields, another to cut the railway

line from Moscow through Rostov to Baku, and a third to organize an uprising in Georgia. In each force one-third were German specialists, the rest, native emigrants or prisoners of that region. The biggest force had been organized for the Caucasus offensive that coming summer—the "Bergmann"
Battalion, 200 German language experts and 550 "reeducated" Russian prisoners from the North Caucasus and Caucasia (Georgia, Azerbaijan, and Ar-
menia). When the hour struck, their task would be to infiltrate into the
Caucasus Mountains to clear and hold key passes and to arm the anti-Soviet
sections of the population. These were operations in which neither Germans
nor Russians could expect any mercy if captured.

Casualties were high. On May 22 the first major operation began—"Grau-
kopf," devised by Army Group Center: 350 Russians wearing their original
uniforms infiltrated the Soviet lines, disarmed 500 troops, destroyed communications, liquidated political commissars, and spread panic and suspicion; only 100
survivors returned to the German lines. And more than one Abwehr raiding party
left the German lines in a painstakingly rebuilt Russian aircraft, only to be shot
down in flames within minutes by alert German antiaircraft gunners.

With overwhelming air superiority, the German spring offensives were opened by
General von Manstein's Eleventh Army in the Crimea on May 8, 1942. Within
four days he had all but won the battle for the Kerch peninsula. By May 15, some
170,000 Russians were his prisoners. The remaining Soviet forces in the area were
dead or hiding out for a fanatical last stand in caves and quarries, or had
committed themselves on rafts to the Black Sea.

The second offensive, "Fridericus," was scheduled to begin on the eighteenth,
with Kleist's *Armeegruppe* and the Sixth Army pinching off the Izyum salient east
of Kharkov. But the Russians launched a spoiling attack first, throwing an
unprecedented weight of tanks into the salient on the twelfth, in a drive for
Kharkov. This sent tremors around the entire southern front and threatened to
unhinge the whole summer campaign. By evening the Soviet tanks were less than
fifteen miles from Kharkov. Field Marshal von Bock, the army group commander, telephoned Halder that evening that "Fridericus" would have to be abandoned in favor of a frontal defense of Kharkov. But the Chief of General Staff
replied that Hitler thought differently. No troops were to be redeployed for the
repair of "minor blemishes." Bock retorted, "This is no 'blemish'—it's a matter
of life and death!" He saw their only salvation in withdrawing three or four of
the infantry and armored divisions allocated to Kleist for "Fridericus" and giving
them to General Paulus's Sixth Army to stall the Russian onslaught on its right
wing, south of Kharkov. He telephoned this suggestion to General Halder urgently on May 14—the most crucial day of the battle. Hitler would not hear of

it.[6] With the main Crimea fighting over, he could release the Luftwaffe squadrons at once to aid Bock. He ordered that "Fridericus" was to commence as planned in the south—indeed, one day early, on the seventeenth. He telephoned Bock himself, explaining to the harassed field marshal that at a time like this a counterattack was the very best solution possible, as it would inevitably take the weight off the Sixth Army. To ensure that there was no "misunderstanding," Hitler ordered Halder to confirm the instructions to Bock's army group in writing.

For two days there was crisis after Kleist's offensive began. Hitler insisted that his generals keep their nerve. Sooner or later the Russians would realize they were about to be encircled. The resulting battle, heavy with carnage, was later seen as one of the boldest and most interesting operations of the war. By the twenty-second, Kleist had linked up with the Sixth Army and encircled the enemy. Within the next week 239,000 prisoners and over 1,240 captured or destroyed tanks were counted on the bloody battlefield, and Hitler had regained the Donets River.

Hitler's ebullient mood emerges from the diary of Richthofen, who lunched with him on May 21. "Führer very nice to me, calls me his specialist, etc. At lunch he held forth to our immense amusement with an endless flood of easy arguments as to the 'Special Privileges of Smokers'—for example, the right to drive off mosquitoes from all nonsmokers; and on the idiocy of winter sports, on the protests of mountaineers at the building of mountain roads and railways, on hunting and the raising of deer in order to shoot them, on deer themselves as foodstuffs (after they've eaten five times their own weight in foodstuffs first), and on trophy-hunting: 'Why don't soldiers mount the jawbones of dead Russians in their rooms, then?' And so on."

Victor of the battle of Kharkov, Hitler returned briefly to Berlin. He told Goebbels on the twenty-ninth that the grand objective of "Blue's" first operations would be the Caucasus. "Then we'll strangle the Soviet system at its Adam's apple, so to speak." The Russians were starving and lacked tanks. Halder persistently assured him that Stalin's reserves were drying up. Rumors that Stalin was mobilizing a reserve of over one hundred divisions beyond the Urals for the coming winter—not to be tapped even if Moscow itself was endangered—were discounted.

A record of Hitler's secret speech to the new officer generation on May 30 survives. It was a summary of Social Darwinism, the survival of the fittest—a eulogy of toughness and brutality. Just as Charlemagne had used harsh measures to build his empire, the little nation of Prussia unifying all the Germans in Europe

---

[6]Afterward everybody claimed paternity of this bold decision. Halder even added a footnote to his published diaries, where he had originally entered only that Bock's "proposal is turned down," to the effect that this was on his, Halder's, advice to Hitler. But the war diaries of the OKW historical section and of Bock himself show beyond the shadow of a doubt that the decision, and hence the credit for the victory, was Hitler's, and that Halder had argued *against* it.

by using force to impose its will on the reluctant, so the new Wehrmacht must employ brute force in the east if it was to win the new *Lebensraum* that the Reich needed to survive. Perhaps Hitler's experiences in World War I had made him callous of human life. Wilhelm Scheidt, the assistant of Hitler's court historian, once heard him say, "I want to raise a younger generation that will put fear into the hearts of the world—in its eyes I want to see the fires of a savage beast!" More than once in private he commended Stalin's harsh leadership, for this alone had saved the Red Army from extinction. "If we cannot emulate their toughness and ruthlessness," he began saying, "we might as well give up the fight." Yet he was also fiercely proud of the ordinary German soldier: he drew comparisons between a beleaguered garrison which had just withstood a Russian siege of four months, and the American troops who surrendered the fortress of Corregidor in the Philippines with hardly a casualty, even though they still had food for another two months. Thought-provoking though the captured Russian newsreels of the nightmare battle for Moscow were, with the abandoned German tanks, guns, and trucks heaped black against the snow and the thousands of ill-clad, hungry German prisoners being herded away to an uncertain fate, it was the faces of these unknown, unsung soldiers that gave Hitler hope, for he was convinced that they betrayed no trace of fear or *personal* surrender.

The cloak-and-dagger war of agents and assassins was by no means confined to the east. As early as January 1942, Canaris had warned of the arrival of the first Allied agents in Denmark; two had parachuted from an aircraft south of Copenhagen on December 28, and since one parachute had failed to open, the *corpus delicti* was there for the Danish police to find the next morning—complete with ten pistols, a wireless transmitter, and a device whereby a pistol strapped to the man's ribs could be fired by raising his hands, ostensibly in surrender. By May, Allied secret service activity in Norway was also evident: aircraft were being blown up by altitude-activated sabotage devices; German officials were being assassinated. Josef Terboven, Reich Commissar for Norway, was summoned to confer with Hitler, and Himmler reported the results to Heydrich soon after. On the twenty-seventh, Heydrich's own turn came—he was mortally wounded as he drove into Prague in his open Mercedes.

In this ugly underground war the Allied aim—later admitted—was to "set Europe on fire" by provoking savage Nazi countermeasures against the indigenous population. Such cold-blooded tactics had Hitler's approval. In revenge for Heydrich's death the Germans liquidated Lidice, the village found to have harbored the Czech-born assassins, and Heydrich's short-lived attempt to woo the Czechs with socialist experiments ended. But Hitler's own aim was clearly to present a minimal profile to the Czechs. In an urgent circular to the Gauleiters, which was prompted by the growing public demand for the deportation of the

Czechs from Bohemia and Moravia to follow that of the Jews, Bormann admonished: "On the Führer's instructions I am to make it clear that there is to be no open discussion of the Czech problem in Party meetings, let alone in public."[7]

The second British provocation was an air raid, and clearly designed to impress the Russian allies. At this very moment, as Hitler knew from his Forschungsamt decoders, Molotov was conferring secretly with Churchill in London. As Hitler's train bore him back to East Prussia, after speaking to the officer candidates in Berlin, alarming reports reached him of a colossal British air raid on Cologne. The local Gauleiter reported that the damage was vast. Göring, however, comfortably holidaying at his castle outside Nuremberg, claimed that since his air defenses had destroyed nearly forty of the bombers and "only seventy or eighty" had actually attacked, the occasion had been an overwhelming Luftwaffe victory. Hitler believed the Gauleiter in preference to Göring—the more so when Churchill announced that a thousand bombers had taken part in the bombing; even Churchill could hardly get away with exaggerating by a multiple of ten, reasoned Hitler. He was prepared to accept that the RAF had sent over perhaps three hundred, no doubt as a gesture to the Kremlin. When General Jeschonnek insisted on the Luftwaffe's less credible version, Hitler abruptly replied, "I have never yet capitulated before an unpalatable truth. But I must see straight, if I am to draw the right conclusions." The obvious conclusion after Cologne was that the enemy had decided to make their interim Second Front a determined attempt to attack the civilian population, killing as many as possible until the Nazi regime surrendered. Some five hundred died in Cologne, and another forty-five thousand were made homeless. Frustratingly, Göring made no secret to Hitler of the Luftwaffe's inability to exact revenge.[8] Hitler now regretted his own "reticence" with the Luftwaffe's bomber force in earlier campaigns. Warsaw had first been given a "fair" chance to surrender; he had not bombed Brussels or Paris at all, let alone Copenhagen or Oslo. "It would have been a scandal if these cities' priceless treasures had suffered from air bombardment," he told a neutral diplomat. But now the boot was on the other foot: quite without their wanting it, the peoples of Europe were breathing a new climate of brutality.

Germany's contribution to this new climate, the elimination of the Jews from central Europe, was now gathering momentum. Hitler's radical followers saw the eleven million Jews as "Europe's misfortune"—as an eastern plague threatening

---

[7]Bormann's circular was dated June 8, 1942. Four days later Himmler approved an outline *"Generalplan* East" providing for the eventual resettlement of eastern Europe's inhabitants (the Poles, Czechs, Ukrainians, and Ruthenians) in Siberia.

[8]In mid-August 1942, Hitler was advised that from now on no real effect could be expected from the Luftwaffe's attacks on Britain.

friend and foe alike. Hitler felt that in time all Europe would understand his hatred. "Somehow we must get rid of them, if they are not to get rid of us," reasoned Josef Goebbels. It seemed no coincidence that the Jews were at the bottom of the spreading partisan movement everywhere.

The precise mode of "elimination" met with varying interpretations. Hitler's was unquestionably the authority behind the *expulsion* operations; on whose initiative the grim procedures at the terminal stations of this miserable exodus were adopted, is arguable. In January 1942, Reinhard Heydrich, chief of the Gestapo, had briefed the leading government officials in Berlin thus: the Führer had sanctioned the evacuation of all Jews to the eastern territories, substituting this for the overseas deportation originally planned. In the east they would build roads, until they dropped. At a further Heydrich conference early in March the awkward problem posed by half- and quarter-Jews was examined. One solution would be to sterilize them, but it would take ten days' hospital treatment to sterilize each of the seventy thousand people involved, so this procedure would have to wait until the war was over; a "top level" opinion—*i.e.,* Hitler's—was quoted to the effect that a sharp distinction must be made between Jews and non-Jews, as it would not be acceptable for a mini-race of semi-Jews to be perpetuated in law. In a paper circulated early in March 1942, Heydrich's office advised the ministries that Europe's eleven million Jews were to be concentrated "in the east" for the time being; after the war they might be allocated a remote territory like Madagascar as a national home. Thus the official version.

The actual operation proceeded differently. Starting in March and April the European Jews were rounded up in occupied France, Holland and Belgium, and in the eager Nazi satellite Slovakia; for political reasons Hungary—which had nearly a million Jews—and Romania were not approached yet but were told that their Jewish "problems" would be left unresolved until the war was over. From Hans Frank's Generalgouvernement of Poland too—beginning with the ghettos of Lublin—the Jews set out eastward under the direction of one of the cruelest SS leaders, Brigadier Odilo Globocnik, the Trieste-born former Gauleiter of Vienna. Upon arrival at Auschwitz and Treblinka, four in every ten were pronounced fit for work; the rest were exterminated with a maximum of concealment. Two documents shed some oblique rays of light on the level of responsibility for this. At a cabinet meeting in Cracow on April 9, Hans Frank disclaimed responsibility for the disruption in the work process caused by the order to turn over all Jews for liquidation. "The directive for the liquidation of the Jews comes from higher up."[9] In a letter of June 26 it became clear that Himmler was anxious

---

[9]The semantics are significant. Frank said ". . . from higher up" *(von höherer Stelle).* Were the allusion to Hitler, Nazi usage invariably preferred *"von höchster Stelle,"* i.e., the *"top level,"* which actually occurs in the previous paragraph, or even *"von allerhöchster Stelle."*

to conceal the massacre, for Globocnik was quoted as being eager to get it over with as quickly as possible in case one day *force majeure* should prevent them completing it: "You yourself, Reichsführer, once mentioned that you felt the job should be done as quickly as possible if only for reasons of concealment." The concealment was almost perfect, and Himmler's own papers reveal how he pulled the wool over Hitler's eyes. On September 17, while the murder machinery was operating at peak capacity, the Reichsführer still calmly jotted down in his notes for that day's Führer conference: "Jewish emigration—how should we proceed?" And in March 1943 he was to order a too-explicit statistical report rewritten to remove a stray reference to the massacre of Europe's Jews before it was submitted to the Führer![10]

The ghastly secrets of Auschwitz and Treblinka were well kept. Goebbels wrote a frank summary of them in his diary on March 27, 1942, but evidently held his tongue when he met Hitler two days later, for he quotes only Hitler's remark: "The Jews must get out of Europe. If need be, we must resort to the most brutal methods." Hitler repeated the gist of this to Goebbels on April 26, adding that he had put Himmler in charge of resettling Germany's Jews in the eastern ghettos. Goebbels did not enlighten him. Over lunch on May 15, Hitler again merely spoke of transporting the Jews eastward and indignantly referred to the misplaced sympathies of the bourgeoisie. How well the Jews were faring, compared with the German emigrants of the nineteenth century—many of whom had even *died* en route! Over lunch on the twenty-ninth (as Goebbels's unpublished diary records) Hitler again dwelt on the best postwar homeland for the Jews. Siberia was out —that would merely produce an even tougher baccilus strain of Jews; Palestine was out too—the Arabs did not want them; perhaps central Africa? At all events, he summed up, western Europe must be liberated of its Jews—there could be no homeland for them here. As late as July 24, Hitler was still referring at table to his plan to transport the Jews to Madagascar—by now already in British hands —or some other Jewish national home after the war was over.

In reality, Himmler was simultaneously throwing the murder machinery into top gear, while he was careful not to place responsibility for the massacre itself on Hitler in writing. (Thus on July 28 he wrote to SS General Gottlob Berger: "The occupied eastern territories"—meaning Poland—"are to be liberated of Jews. The Führer has entrusted me with the execution of this arduous order. Nobody can deprive me of this responsibility.") On July 19, three days after seeing Hitler, Himmler ordered the "resettlement" of the entire Jewish population of the Generalgouvernement to be completed by the last day of 1942. Each day after July 22 a trainload of five thousand Jews left Warsaw for the extermination center at

[10]See page 504 below.

Treblinka; each week two trains left Przemysl for the center at Belsec. Moreover, in August the first informal approach was made to the Hungarians to begin deporting their one million Jews to the east immediately. Count Döme Sztójay, the Hungarian envoy in Berlin, warned Budapest on August 15 that this was a "radical departure" from Hitler's previous ruling that Hungary's "problem" could be left until after the war. "The Germans are determined to rid Europe of the Jewish elements without further delay, and intend—regardless of the nationality of these Jews and provided that transport facilities exist—to deport them to the occupied territories in the east, where they will be settled in ghettos or labor camps and put to work. . . . According to absolutely reliable information, Reichsführer Himmler has informed a meeting of SS leaders that the German government desires to complete these deportations within a year."

What had inspired Himmler with this urgency? Undoubtedly—according to the retrospective view of his Chief of Staff, General Karl Wolff—it was the assassination of Reinhard Heydrich in Prague. Initially the Nazis blamed it on Jewish agents and believed it. Eyewitnesses have described the traumatic effect on Himmler: he appeared for dinner that day with Hitler ashen-faced and barely able to speak. Since a Jewish congress meeting in Moscow had according to Goebbels's diary just broadcast directives to world Jewry to launch a war of assassination, the Nazis assumed Heydrich was the first victim. Goebbels ordered the arrest of five hundred Jews in Berlin as hostages and persuaded Hitler on May 29 that every remaining Jew should be evicted from the city forthwith. Hitler instructed Speer to replace the Jews in the arms industry by foreign workers. As a worried Goebbels put it, there were still forty thousand Jews with "nothing more to lose" at large in Berlin, and the prospect of some *Ostjude* pumping bullets into him was not an appealing one.

By August 1942 the massacre machinery was gathering momentum—of such refinement and devilish ingenuity that from Himmler down to the ex-lawyers who ran the extermination camps perhaps only seventy men were aware of the truth. It is conceivable that Hitler was unaware that his November 1941 order forbidding the liquidation of the Jews[11] was being violated on such a scale. Early in August, Himmler made to Wolff the melancholy confession that for the sake of the German nation and its Führer he had shouldered a burden of which nobody could ever learn, in order that the "Messiah of the coming two millennia" might remain personally uncontaminated. At the time, Wolff was unable to elicit from Himmler precisely what that burden was.

[11]See page 332.

"Blue"

In mid-1942 Hitler launched his rebuilt armies into "Operation Blue"—the summer campaign that he hoped would leave him master of all Europe as far as Astrakhan, Stalingrad, and Baku. This was the big push that would indeed bring him to the Volga by September—and to the Caucasus Mountains, beyond which lay the Caspian Sea and the Middle East. Yet great though the advances the Wehrmacht now made were, strategically the Soviet command remained the victor as autumn approached, for after Kharkov, which Hitler considered one of Stalin's most costly errors, the Red Army was never again to allow the Germans to encircle them. Each successive phase of "Blue" netted a smaller haul of prisoners and booty than the last. The Russian commander Marshal Timoshenko no longer committed his forces to fixed pitched battles but instead withdrew and regrouped to the far side of the lengthening German left flank as the Sixth Army advanced on Stalingrad.

We shall see how through the stubbornness of his army generals like Bock and Hoth, and the persisting inadequacy of the army's supply arrangements, Hitler was cheated of the ultimate autumn victory; his armies were never quite fast enough to catch up with, and scythe down, the withdrawing enemy. And when the Red Army did stand and fight, it was on its own terms: with winter drawing on and at the extreme limit of the German lines of supply.

Yet the summer operations started promisingly enough. Emboldened by the victory at Kharkov, Hitler's attention was attracted to the two Russian armies orphaned by the disaster—the one east of Izyum and the other, far larger, northeast of Kharkov. He decided on a short postponement of "Blue," the main summer campaign, while two preliminary battles ("Fridericus II" and "Wilhelm," respectively) were fought to wipe out these tempting enemy concentrations. He flew to Field Marshal von Bock's headquarters at Poltava on June 1 and won his generals' support, explaining that this was an opportunity they would be foolish not to seize while they could. "What we defeat now can't interfere with our later "Blue" offensive," he said. "Wilhelm" began nine days afterward, followed by "Fridericus II" on the twenty-second. Meanwhile General von Manstein had begun the long-drawn-out final bombardment and assault on the Crimean fortress of Sevastopol.

"Blue" itself—originally scheduled for mid-June— was provisionally set down for the twenty-second. In the interval Hitler ministered to his coalition.

On June 4, 1942, he made one of his very rare flights outside the Reich frontiers, to honor Finland's Marshal Mannerheim on his seventy-fifth birthday. In the dining car of Mannerheim's special train, its broad windows overlooking the unique Finnish landscape and sunlit Lake Saimaa, Hitler was tempted by the polished and fertile speech of President Ryti to rise in reply himself. While the local German envoy looked on disapprovingly, he delivered *ex tempore* a tactful speech on his difficult position during Finland's 1940 winter war with Russia. One witness, General Waldemar Erfurth, was so taken with the Führer's charm that he said that "there can be no doubt that on June 4, 1942, Hitler was in complete possession of his mental faculties." After Hitler's four-engined Focke-Wulf took off again, a flattered Mannerheim commented, "He is phenomenal!" and his Chief of Staff agreed.

Two days later Hitler received Miklos von Kállay, the new Hungarian prime minister. Kállay had brought a secret written undertaking from Horthy to bury the hatchet with Romania—but only until the war was over. Thereafter the Hungarians desired "both the Lord God and the Führer"—as Hitler laughingly put it the next day—to turn a blind eye on their fight with Romania. It would be, Kállay ingeniously suggested, a struggle between Europe and Asia, since the Hungarian frontier was where the Orthodox ceased to hold sway.

Flying back from Finland, Hitler heard that Heydrich had died of his wounds.

In private he bitterly regretted the foolhardy bravado—riding in an open car —which had cost the life of such an irreplaceable man. He ordered Heydrich's name graven on the Party roll of honor; an SS regiment on the eastern front was named after him. The state funeral was held in Berlin on June 9 in the Chancellery. Czech president Emil Hácha and his government attended. Six hundred of Germany's leading men gathered behind Hitler to pay homage to the Gestapo chief most of them had inwardly feared. Hitler used to call him "the man with iron nerves"; according to his historical officer, Scheidt, Hitler was even grooming Heydrich to become his successor and had appointed him Acting Protector of Bohemia and Moravia in Baron von Neurath's place in September 1941 as a first step in this direction. In Prague, Heydrich had modeled himself on Hitler, eliminating the noisy intellectual opposition and winning the workers over. He had introduced the first social security system they had ever known, and by the time of his assassination the first twenty workers' convalescent homes had already been built. On the day he died, fifty thousand Czech workers demonstrated against the British-inspired act in Prague. As Siegfried's "Funeral March" died away, Himmler spoke, recalling the day Heydrich had taken up the reins in Bohemia and Moravia: "There were many in Germany, and many more among the Czechs, who thought the dreaded Heydrich was going to rule by blood and terror." But he had not, Himmler explained. He had merely acted radically against the "unruly dissidents," restoring respect for German rule and beginning his internal social reforms soon after. Himmler—who had had cause enough to fear him in the past—spoke with evident emotion now that Heydrich was safely dead. Hitler laid his wreath, and then Heydrich's remains were borne in stately procession to east Berlin, to be buried at the Invalidenfriedhof cemetery along with those of Ernst Udet, Fritz Todt, and many of Hitler's other friends. All their tombs and monuments have vanished now.

Before President Hácha left Berlin, Hitler advised him to keep the Czechs in rein. If there was any repetition of the anti-German outbreaks that had caused him to appoint Heydrich in September, he would seriously consider deporting all the Czechs from Bohemia and Moravia. Hácha asked permission to warn his people of this grim prospect. Hitler recommended that he do so. At 11:10 P.M. the Führer left for Bavaria.

The records show him fulfilling few engagements. At the Osteria restaurant in Munich the next day he lunched with the architect Frau Gerdi Troost and Winifred Wagner's family. In Eva Braun's album a couple of photographs dated June 14 show the Führer and her walking their respective dogs on the Berghof terraces. But the war conferences continued.

On the fifteenth, Admiral Raeder came up to the Berghof for one of his rare meetings with the Führer; he was anxious to press the case for the attack on Malta and to obtain permission for the battle fleet in Norway to launch its most ambitious operation against the Arctic convoys yet—code-named "The Knight's Move." Hitler's enthusiasm for capturing Malta had long since waned, even though the parachute general Kurt Student spoke highly of the German and Italian paratroops he was training in southern Italy, and the Chief of Air Staff, General Jeschonnek, also strongly supported it. German air raids on Malta had long dwindled, and the island's air defenses were being reinforced with fresh aircraft, crews, and fuel. In May, Student had briefed Hitler on British fortifications and defenses in Malta; to Hitler it seemed that more was known of the probable British tactics than the Italian. Jodl's naval staff officer had told the admiralty: "The Führer has little confidence in the operation's success, as the

Italians' assault strength is wholly inadequate and the Italians don't have the least idea of secrecy. It seems to be a particularly difficult task, far tougher than Crete, which was difficult enough as it was." Hitler offered a string of specious arguments against invading Malta: even if they succeeded, the Italians could not keep the island garrison supplied (to which the admiralty acidly pointed out that at present the far more difficult supply line to Rommel's army in North Africa was still open). Even more farfetched was Hitler's claim that Malta served their strategy better in British hands, as its supply convoys then offered sitting targets in the antishipping war. Admiral Raeder was at loggerheads with Hitler over other matters and unable to put his case—that the capture of Malta was the *prerequisite* for any advance on the Suez Canal—more strongly. Hitler had allowed the "theoretical planning" for Malta to continue during May, but now, on June 15, he offered the admiral little hope. On no account could the Axis run the risk of failure through Italian shortcomings again. One suspects, however, that a different factor operated too—that Malta was *British,* and Hitler's "soft" line toward Britain still prevailed; nothing must prejudice the chance of an Anglo-German settlement in the autumn, after "Blue" had brought Russia to her knees.

Over 200 submarines were now in or entering German service—a fruit of the prudent policy of conservation Hitler had enforced in 1940. On May 1 there were 85 prowling the Atlantic alone, with 19 in the Mediterranean, 20 in northern waters, and over 100 fitting out in the Baltic. The submarine admiral, Dönitz, had made a fine impression on Hitler at their last meeting in East Prussia in mid-May. Hitler regretted not having devoted more shipyard capacity to submarine construction rather than to big warships—costly white elephants, rendered obsolete by the aircraft carrier and the airborne torpedo. Capital ships, in Hitler's eyes, served only a deterrent purpose, tying down enemy warships far from where the enemy would like to commit them. For this reason he had at first been averse to the admiralty's plan for "The Knight's Move," in which the entire German battle fleet in Norway—the *Tirpitz,* the *Hipper,* the *Lützow,* the *Scheer,* and a dozen destroyers—were to seek to wipe out the next Allied convoy, PQ. 17, bearing supplies to North Russia. On no account must the *Tirpitz* go the way of the *Bismarck.* But Raeder's liaison officer assured him early in June that no risk would be involved at all, provided that the Reichsmarschall was ordered to give them Luftwaffe support and—above all—adequate aerial reconnaissance. Given the right circumstances, the operation might annihilate the convoy down to its very last ship. When Admiral Raeder left the Berghof on June 15, he had Hitler's cautious permission to proceed—provided that Allied aircraft carriers in the vicinity had first been precisely located and bombed to a standstill.

On the Russian front, operation "Wilhelm" was over. The enemy was tensely awaiting Hitler's next move. Intelligence agents reported that Stalin had held a two-day council of war in Moscow beginning on June 10 and that he had opted for a purely defensive strategy, regrouping along the Don and Volga and keeping the Germans out of the Caucasus. It seemed clear that the Russians were no longer deceived by Kluge's noisy preparations west of Moscow—indeed, on June 16 an Allied press agency in Moscow quoted German strategic designs for the summer at such length that it was obvious there was a leak in German security somewhere. Hitler was perplexed and furious; Halder's General Staff must be the culprit, he suspected. Either somebody had been talking too much on the telephone, or—just as had happened before the invasion of Poland, Norway, and the Low Countries—it was deliberate treason.[1] History seemed to be repeating itself with a vengeance: Hitler was infuriated to learn that the senior General Staff officer of a panzer division had crash-landed in no-man's-land with the complete secret plans for the first stage of "Blue"—the tank thrust to the Don at Voronezh —just as had happened in the notorious Mechelen affair in 1940. His generals had apparently learned nothing from that incident. He decided to make an example of them: the staff officer involved this time was beyond punishment, having been killed by the Russians; but Hitler sacked all the officer's superiors, including the corps commander. Nor was Field Marshal von Bock spared a tongue-lashing when Hitler saw him the day after his return to the Wolf's Lair.

Hitler himself signed a new order expanding the security rules he had laid down after the Mechelen incident. "Security during the preparation of major operations is of particular importance because of the prime risk that operational orders falling into enemy hands might be exploited in time; this would jeopardize the entire success of the operation, or at the very least the negligence or disobedience of individual officers would be paid for in the blood of German soldiers." Not even the scrambler telephone was safe for discussing strategic plans, he warned. Couriers were to be armed and provided with means for igniting secret documents. No secret documents were to be carried by plane to headquarters forward of army level. As it was, he hoped the Russians could not react fast enough, since "Blue" was due to begin before June was over; he coolly ordered the strategic plan to be left unchanged.

Toward midnight on June 21, Hitler's train left Munich for Berlin. Bock's operation "Fridericus II" (east of Izyum) was to begin at 2:15 A.M. Hitler's thoughts must have gone back to that night twelve months earlier, when he had spent agonizing hours waiting for the onset of "Barbarossa." If it had not been for his stubborn army generals last summer, Russia would have long been defeated!

[1]Some months later an extensive espionage network centering on a Luftwaffe staff officer was uncovered. See page 426.

During the night, his train pulled into a station for twenty minutes. The telephones were linked up—and there was joyous and totally unexpected news from North Africa: the fortified port of Tobruk, which had withstood Rommel's siege for eight months in 1941, had fallen in as many hours. Thirty-three thousand British prisoners surrendered to the German and Italian troops, together with five generals and a vast quantity of tanks, guns, gasoline, and supplies.

Now Rommel must strike while the iron was still hot. In Berlin there was a letter from Mussolini clearly stating the Italian view that Rommel must pause while "Hercules," the assault on Malta, was launched. But already Rommel was preparing to sweep eastward into Egypt. He still had fifty tanks, and two hundred more were being repaired after the month's battles. Hitler cabled Rommel immediately, promoting him to field marshal. He trusted him implicitly. When Goebbels now referred at lunch to Rommel's irrepressible popularity—along with Dietl, Rommel was the very personification of the ideal German soldier-type— Hitler enthusiastically agreed: Rommel's ability was above question. For example, back in May Rommel had predicted every detail of this last offensive—even that the British would fall right into his trap by withdrawing into what might seem to them an ideal triangle of territory but which was actually one in which German 88s could shoot them to pieces. Hitler told his staff that he would, if need be, telephone Mussolini to give Rommel a free hand by postponing "Hercules" until the end of August. The message he then telegraphed to Rome was high-flown and urgently persuasive; without even mentioning Malta, he described the victory wrought by the German and Italian divisions in Libya as a turning point in history. Churchill's Eighth Army was practically in shreds. Since the British themselves had obligingly built a railroad from Tobruk almost as far as Egypt, a relentless pursuit must now follow. He closed thus: "The battle's Goddess of Fortune draws nigh upon the commanders only once; he who does not grasp her at that moment will seldom come to grips with her again." Mussolini allowed himself to be persuaded. "Hercules" was postponed until early September. Late on June 23, Rommel's *Panzerarmee Afrika* crossed into Egypt on a broad front. Within a week he hoped to be in Cairo.

The Italian command and Field Marshal Kesselring, Hitler's Commander in Chief South, watched Rommel's eastward progress into Egypt with mounting apprehension. Each mile lengthened his supply lines and shortened the enemy's; each mile brought the enemy airfields in the Nile Delta closer. Hitler remained optimistic. Although Rommel had received barely three thousand tons of supplies for the entire army during June, Hitler saw Egypt already in his hands. "Rommel must be given all the supplies he needs," he announced at supper on June 28, when the news arrived that four enemy divisions were now encircled in the fortress of Marsa Matrûh. He agreed with Keitel's prediction that "when the Germans captured Alexandria the *entire* British public would be thrown into a far greater rage than at the surrender of Singapore." It would stir them up against Churchill.

"Let's hope that the American legation in Cairo continues to keep us so excellently informed of British military plans with its badly enciphered cables." To Hitler and his ministers it must have seemed that the British public's morale was cracking; otherwise thirty-three thousand men could not have surrendered Tobruk with barely a fight. After "Blue" was over in the autumn, an Anglo-German settlement seemed certain.

The British fleet evacuated the harbor at Alexandria and escaped to the Red Sea. But the British army was preparing to hold out some sixty miles west of Alexandria, at El Alamein, and Field Marshal Rommel now had only seventy tanks and armored cars at his disposal.

"Operation Blue," Hitler's great summer offensive in Russia, had begun early on June 28, 1942. German and Hungarian divisions commanded by General von Weichs punched through the Russian front and swept eastward toward the Don city of Voronezh. Two days later General Paulus's Sixth Army began an advance that was eventually to take it southward along the Don. Hitler—encouraged by the evidence presented to him by Halder—believed the Russian reserves were all but exhausted; so sure was he of a swift collapse that he began thinking of taking two armored divisions from "Blue" for a later assault on Moscow. Yet the auguries of impending disaster were there: the army's quartermaster general warned that their fuel would last them only until mid-September. And the outcome of both "Wilhelm" and "Fridericus II" in terms of prisoners and booty was disappointing—a sign that the Russians had learned their lesson at Kharkov and a similar disaster on the Volkhov River far to the north; they were no longer rash enough to let themselves be encircled. Hitler had anticipated an elastic strategy from Marshal Timoshenko, his Russian adversary in the south, but he hoped to thwart this by moving his tanks down the Don fast enough to prevent the enemy's withdrawal beyond it.

Once again his generals thwarted this bold plan, though this time his own tongue-tied inability to speak forcefully to his top commanders—and especially those of the aristocracy—was to blame. The General Staff had proposed gaining time by launching Phase II of "Blue" with infantry divisions alone, but Hitler and Bock maintained that only tanks could move south fast enough to prevent the enemy's escape. This did not prevent Bock from acquiescing in General Hoth's armored drive toward Voronezh. Remembering Dunkirk in 1940 and Leningrad in 1941, Hitler feared that Voronezh would swallow up his precious armor for days on end, and he expressed growing impatience as the days passed. Keitel recognized all the familiar omens of trouble and begged him to fly out to Poltava in person and order Bock to leave the city alone. At this stage the capture of the city was unimportant, provided the railways and aircraft factories could be destroyed.

Tactically this was right. Hitler made the three-hour flight to Poltava, arriving at 7 A.M. on July 3; but confronted by the granite-faced field marshal, he lost his tongue. He became affable and friendly, joked about the way Churchill sacked every general who had a run of bad luck, explained why he did not fear an Allied Second Front, hedged about the risk that the Russians—who knew the German overall plan—might yet elude his armies, and assured Bock that the Red Army had sapped its last reserves. Far from flatly forbidding Bock to take the city of Voronezh, he wrapped up his directives in a double negative so vague that as the Führer was leaving Bock queried, "Am I right in understanding you as follows: I am to capture Voronezh if it can be done easily or without bloodshed. But I am not to get involved in heavy fighting for the city?" Hitler confirmed this with a silent nod.

Back at the Wolf's Lair his courage returned to him. As the days passed, it became more evident that neither Weichs nor Bock appreciated the urgency of making ground to the south. He watched impatiently; the city was captured easily enough on July 6, but the two armored divisions there were immediately subjected to a fierce Russian counterattack. As the unwanted battle for the city developed, precious time was being wasted. He ordered the two divisions out and to the south, but now they had to await the arrival of supporting infantry; not until the eighth could they disengage themselves from Voronezh, and after one day's southward progress their fuel ran out. The army's quartermaster general, Eduard Wagner, should have provided for this unexpectedly rapid offensive in his logistics, but he had not; at the Wolf's Lair he unjustly laid the blame on Bock. Two full days had been wasted by Voronezh. Boiling with anger, Hitler could see the Russian forces slipping away. Was this not the same Bock who had thwarted his grand designs in 1941? And had not Bock—against his own staff's advice, as they had just told Schmundt at Poltava—argued for the purely defensive treatment of Kharkov in May? Bock was having a run of bad luck; Hitler discussed him with Keitel and Halder on July 13—and then sacked him. He told Schmundt he still admired the man, but in the present crisis he could work only with generals who followed his directives to the letter.

The damage was already done, however. Keitel later told Bock: "For months afterward the Führer kept harping on 'those forty-eight hours lost at Voronezh' as time wasted to catastrophic effect." When the first phase ended on July 8, Weichs had rounded up only 28,000 prisoners and 1,000 tanks; and the Sixth Army had accounted for only 45,000 prisoners and 200 tanks. A week later, the second phase, an attempted encirclement of the enemy north of the Donets River, ended with the capture of Millerovo; this time there were only 14,000 prisoners. In retrospect, it should have been clear at once that the majority of the Red Army had escaped. But Hitler, ill-advised by his General Staff, evidently considered these low hauls further proof that the Red Army was on its last legs: how else can we interpret his decisions during July 1942 to transport five divisions of the Eleventh Army from the Crimea to the far north, and to withdraw some of his finest units to the western front as well?

Since the second half of June 1942 Hitler had felt insecure in the west. On the twenty-first, the Third Air Force had brought back photographic reconnaissance Intelligence from southern England revealing nearly three thousand small craft assembled between Portsmouth and Portland, and numbers of unfamiliar craft drawn ashore at Southampton and Poole. In occupied France the sabotage of railroads and cables was increasing. Hitler had visions of massive paratroop and glider landings—cutting the vital rail and road links to prevent him moving up reserves when the main seaborne invasion started. Halder suggested sending an armored division to the west; Hitler agreed, and ordered that three others already in reserve there should remain, together with the SS division "Das Reich" and the Seventh Air Division of paratroops. On June 26 he decided that "if the Russian resistance during the coming operations should be less than expected," the two SS divisions "Adolf Hitler Life Guards" and "Death's Head" would also be transferred to the west. Three days later he conferred with Rundstedt's new Chief of Staff in the west, the bustling General Zeitzler, with Speer, and with the general in charge of engineering and fortifications, Alfred Jacob, on their western defenses. He explained that in view of the enemy's political obligations, a major Anglo-American invasion attempt was quite possible. Having thrown the British out of the Continent once, he did not fear them; he told foreign diplomats he was relishing the chance of teaching the Americans a lesson too—his Waffen SS elite were just itching to get their hands on American troops.

With remarkable prescience, Hitler predicted in a directive of July 9 that the Allies would most probably invade either somewhere between Dieppe and Le Havre or in Normandy, as these coastal areas were within Allied fighter range and suitable for small-craft crossings. "In the event of an Allied invasion I will proceed to the west and take command myself." Whether Hitler expected a full-scale Second Front *soon* is uncertain. He believed that Churchill's recent visit to Washington had been to advise against such an invasion until 1943 and that Stalin was consequently being advised to stave off defeat until then.[2] There might still be a diversionary maneuver in the west, but it was unlikely. On the other

---

[2] This may have been deduced from the intercepted radiotelephone traffic between London and Washington (see page 407). Hitler mentioned "Churchill himself as proof." His belief was confirmed by General Franco, who had it from a reliable agent that Churchill's main purpose in Washington that June had been to convert Roosevelt to a position opposing Stalin's demand for a Second Front in 1942. Churchill had, reported Franco, warned that on no account must such an invasion fail—it might be the beginning of the end.

hand, desperate leaders might be driven to desperate remedies. True, Rommel's Egyptian offensive had been halted at El Alamein, but elsewhere the outlook was black for Britain. On July 1, Manstein took Sevastopol and was promoted to field marshal. In the Arctic German submarines and bombers sank twenty-four of the thirty-six Allied merchant ships bound for North Russia in convoy PQ.17; the *Tirpitz* and the battle fleet had not even had to go into action. In the west, therefore, Churchill might find his hand forced over a Second Front—anything was possible.

At the daily war conferences, Hitler's advisers were confident of victory in the east. General Halder studiously curried Hitler's favor. An adjutant noted one day that July: "The Chief of Staff is visibly at pains to sweeten the atmosphere. Luckily for him the situation is obviously well under control. Von Gyldenfeldt [a staff officer] and I are furious at the way he misses no opportunity of denigrating the former Commander in Chief [Brauchitsch] in his absence—and sometimes quite cleverly too—and tries to put the blame for all the previous decisions and ideas that were contrary to Hitler's. Today [Halder] said, 'Mein Führer, had the field marshal listened to you and me a bit more often, we would have been standing there or there by now.' "

In Hitler's eyes the east was already a German empire. On July 9 he discussed with Himmler the final plans for settling the South Tyroleans from Italy in the Crimea once the war was over. On the sixteenth he told Himmler he had no intention of overtly annexing Transcaucasia to the German empire; it would suffice to put a guard on the oil fields and frontiers and leave a Resident-General to protect German interests in the "Free Caucasian Protectorates," as they would be known. On the twenty-third he instructed Bormann to issue to Reichsleiter Rosenberg broad guidelines for population control in the east: the native population was to be kept down by encouraging abortion and contraceptive techniques; German standards of sanitation and public health would not be enforced (*i.e.,* the natives were not to be immunized or vaccinated). When Hitler learned that his troops had fathered over a million offspring with Russian women, he instructed Himmler to identify all the children concerned, select those that were racially promising, and "recover" them for Germany; if the mothers were also sound and racially acceptable, they could come too, otherwise they would not see their children again. Still uneasy at the prospect that in later generations even the rejected offspring might "improve" the Russian bloodstock, Hitler ordered the widest distribution of contraceptives to his troops in the east forthwith. As for education, Himmler told his police officials: "I can only repeat what the Führer has asked. It is enough if, firstly, the children are taught the traffic signs at school so that they won't run under our cars; secondly, they learn to count to twenty-five;

and thirdly, they can write their names as well. No more is necessary."

With mounting public unrest over food rationing in Germany, Hitler also ordered a more ruthless exploitation of the occupied countries. Göring told the Gauleiters assembled in Berlin: "Why should we hunger! Let the people in the countries we occupy eat Cossack saddles!" To Gauleiter Koch, his viceroy in the Ukraine, Hitler confirmed all Himmler had said. People everywhere in Europe ate better than those in Germany, he felt. It was setting back arms production; and if the bread ration was not increased, he foresaw political problems too. Koch was made responsible for extracting at least three million tons of grain from the Ukraine forthwith; the Ukrainian people were racially "inferior"—they would find some other way to survive soon enough.

For the final heave on the eastern front Hitler transferred to a forward headquarters in the Ukraine, code-named "Werewolf," at Vinnitsa. At 8:15 A.M. on July 16 his entire staff flew in sixteen planes to the new site. A secretary wrote soon after: "The airfield was an imposing sight—with the great aircraft lined up ready to take off, their engines turning over, and the air filled with the deep roar of vibrating wings and wires until one after another they rolled down the runway and lifted into the air." Three hours later they touched down at Vinnitsa. Krupp and Mercedes automobiles carried them along rustic lanes to the three-cornered copse concealing Werewolf—a summer camp of log cabins and wooden huts. Here Hitler's commandant feared only a Soviet paratroop attack, perhaps disguised in German uniforms, so the Führer found none of the concrete bunkers characterizing the Wolf's Lair at Rastenburg. But the cabins were damp, the climate was humid, and the site swarmed with deadly anopheles mosquitoes.

Each evening everybody had to swallow Atabrine, a bitter anti-malaria concoction against which the tongue rebelled. The windows were screened with gauze, but still the mosquitoes got in. At night it was icy cold. By day Vinnitsa sweltered in the Ukrainian high summer. Hitler detested the camp. He suffered splitting headaches and could not think straight. The newly creosoted wood gave off an acrid stench in the baking sun. He easily found fault with everybody. OKW diarist Greiner noted privately: "The climate and heat here get the Führer down. He longs for his old bunker [at Rastenburg], which is a sure sign of where we'll be quartered this winter. . . . By then our operations in the Caucasus will be virtually completed anyway."

Throughout July 1942 Hitler based his command decisions on the assumption that the Red Army was on its last legs. It was a fatally incorrect assumption, but there is no evidence whatever that General Halder advised him differently until August, and by then it was too late to undo the damage already done. Soon, he felt, Rommel would be astride the Suez Canal; the old strategic vision of crossing the Caucasus Mountains and advancing southward through Georgia recurred to Hitler. These would be the two arms of a pincer whereby he would conquer the Middle East. He informed Albert Speer that in future the army's supporting industry—manufacturing tanks and guns—would have equal priority with the Luftwaffe's. With Transcaucasia a German dominion, his oil nightmare would be banished. Once he said, "If I cannot capture at least Maykop, I cannot fight on." If he could get the oil fields at both Maykop and Grozny, producing five million tons a year, and even more if his armies captured the Baku oil fields south of the Caucasus, then Stalin would have to concede defeat. This was the reward at stake in August and September 1942.

There seemed sound evidence that the Russians were collapsing. In front of Paulus's Sixth Army the enemy was in full flight toward Stalingrad. Mass Soviet desertions were reported by Kleist's First Panzer Army. The Russian command seemed to be losing control. In a string of directives issued late in July, Hitler confidently asserted that the three-week campaign had thus far attained virtually all the targets he had set for the southern front. The operations against Marshal Timoshenko had gone "far better and faster" than expected. Hitler claimed: "Only puny elements of Timoshenko's armies have managed to escape encirclement and get south of the Don." Already he had divided Army Group South into two new army groups, A and B; to the former he had reluctantly appointed Field Marshal List, and to the latter, General Baron von Weichs. These two groups would now *diverge* across the Don—List's group, by far the weightier, to encircle the escaping Russians south of Rostov and then conquer the Caucasus and the Black Sea coast; and Weichs striking southeastward toward Stalingrad and the Volga. If Stalingrad itself could not be overrun at once, it was important to reach the Volga south of that city, as Hitler was convinced that the river was Stalin's main waterway from the oil fields to central Russia. After Stalingrad, the armored divisions would roll down the Volga to Astrakhan on the Caspian Sea.

These directives—inspired by the belief that Timoshenko was finished—were already a momentous departure from his April 1942 directive for a *phased* campaign in the south, and Hitler went even further, ordering Field Marshal von Küchler's Army Group North to prepare a fresh assault on Leningrad in September, followed by an attempt at cutting the Murmansk railroad at Kandalaksha in the autumn. Then Stalin would be deprived of both the Caucasian and the northern routes of Allied supplies.

Over the last week of July 1942, however, Hitler's attention was drawn back to Stalingrad, to the capture of which he had assigned only one of the four German armies in the south, Paulus's Sixth Army. All the signs were that the enemy was preparing a last stand there, rather than on the Don. The General Staff learned on July 15—and presumably told Hitler—of a high-level Moscow council of war two days before called by Molotov, Voroshilov, and General Boris Shaposhnikov, the Soviet Chief of Staff, with Allied representatives. Shaposhnikov announced a strategic retreat to the Volga, to force the Germans to winter there. "Counterattacks are to be attempted at two places, the first north of Orel and the second north of Voronezh. Air force and armored troops will take part. A diversionary thrust will be made at Kalinin. Stalingrad, Novorossiisk [a Black Sea port], and the Caucasus are to be held."

Nobody had foreseen that Stalin would voluntarily yield so much ground for a dubious strategic advantage, but the Intelligence certainly seemed confirmed by reconnaissance and other sources. Rostov, far to the west, was captured after fierce fighting on July 23, but the enemy escaped, blowing up the bridges behind him. Two days later the entire west bank of the Don was in German hands as far as Voronezh. Hitler's spearheads were about one hundred miles from Stalingrad. In a directive on July 23, Hitler predicted that Timoshenko would reinforce his armies at Stalingrad from the Caucasus region and defend the city with great tenacity. But again the German army's supply organization broke down. For days on end the Sixth Army's tanks were stranded without gasoline; violent rainstorms were blamed for delaying the German supply columns (without, mysteriously, delaying the simultaneous Russian retreat). Worse still, on July 25, Quartermaster General Wagner switched all logistics effort away from the Sixth Army to the Caucasus operation. For the first (and only) time Hitler heard the voice of General von Weichs on the telephone, pleading for the decision to be reversed; Hitler overruled Wagner, but for ten days the Sixth Army was emasculated by this lack of fuel and ammunition, while the gloating Russian commanders had time to build a line of defense far to the west of Stalingrad.

In the stifling atmosphere of Hitler's Ukrainian headquarters violent arguments broke out in the thin-walled wooden conference hut—Halder raging in private at this layman's "grotesque" ignorance of strategy, and the Führer retorting that Halder had repeatedly ignored his orders to transfer a panzer corps from the Rostov group to support the Sixth Army. Uglier still was the enmity smoldering between Jodl's staff—Hitler's military "think-tank"—and Halder's General Staff. "The General Staff is the last of the Masonic Lodges," Hitler lamented. "Unfortunately I forgot to dissolve it."

His troops fought on. On July 26, List's army group swept across the Don for the attack on the Caucasus; it was supported by Richthofen's Fourth Air Force. Three days later the last railroad linking the Caucasus with central Russia was blown up by German tanks.

Now Hitler considered the Caucasus his for the taking, and he refocused his attention on the fighting west of Stalingrad. Halder wrote the next day, July 30: "At the Führer's conference General Jodl took the floor and bombastically pronounced that the fate of the Caucasus will be decided at Stalingrad." This was what Halder had been arguing for a week himself. It was decided to transfer the

Fourth Panzer Army from List to Weichs at once. In vain List protested when Halder phoned him that evening that the transfer would leave his left flank exposed; he pointed out that now his group too was suffering fuel delays, and he underlined the gamble they were taking by driving southward into the Caucasus with such a weak force, unprotected on its flank. When he asked that at least the "Gross Deutschland" Division should not be transferred to France, Halder was equally adamant. (Hitler had rhetorically asked him only a few days before: "What is the use of victories in Russia if I lose western Europe?") In a directive signed by Halder the next day, the Fourth Panzer Army was ordered to the Stalingrad front. Halder said that while the enemy could no longer move significant reinforcements up against List from the Russian interior, they must assume that "the enemy will concentrate all available strength on Stalingrad to keep the vital Volga artery open."

Thus two German armies, each with less dependable allied forces in train, were assigned to each of Hitler's southern strategic targets—Stalingrad and the Caucasus. If the enemy's reserves *were* finished, this was an adequate disposition; if they were not, it was not.

From the documents available it is clear that Hitler did not fear any serious risk of "losing western Europe" until 1943, but there were persistent rumors that something more immediate was in the air. An Abwehr agent in British embassy circles in Madrid reported that Britain was assembling twenty-four hundred launches—calling them in from as far afield as Gibraltar, the Mediterranean, and West Africa—for a determined "invasion attempt" on the Channel or French Atlantic coast toward the end of August. On July 18 a week of talks between Churchill and Roosevelt's confidant, Harry Hopkins, began in London. Two days later a batch of intercepted transatlantic telephone conversations was sent to Himmler—and no doubt Hitler—with an SS general's comments: "Although only code words are employed in these intercepted telephone conversations, I deduce the following: today and tomorrow there must be a highly important meeting between the British and Americans. This conference will probably determine where the Second Front is to be established and when. The main people speaking are General Staff officers, ambassadors, and ministers."[3] On August 13

---

[3]On July 24, 1942, the London conference approved Britain's proposal for an invasion of Northwest Africa, "Gymnast"—shortly rechristened "Torch"—rather than the American plan to invade Cherbourg or Brest—"Sledgehammer."

The archives are silent on just what the intercepted conversations revealed. Others, less revealing, between Churchill and a Mr. Butcher in Washington on July 22, and between General Mark Clark, General Snyder, etc., were returned by Hitler to Himmler and are in his files.

a highly trusted Abwehr agent in southern England reported that the invasion target would be the Channel port of Dieppe.

Hitler was confident he could thwart any immediate British adventures; of those that might be launched in 1943 he was less certain. By mid-August he had 29 divisions in the west under Rundstedt's command, including the "Hermann Göring," 2 parachute, 2 SS, and 4 panzer divisions; the crack infantry division "Gross Deutschland" was also transferring from the eastern front. He had no fears for Norway so long as the nights were short; what might happen outside Europe did not concern him either. But the more he studied the bulky military atlases his experts had compiled on the Channel and Atlantic coasts of France, Belgium, and Holland, the more apprehensive he became: the maps and overlays spoke glibly of "field-type defenses" and used vague military jargon that he suspected concealed a multitude of weaknesses. He sent out Walter Frentz, his staff movie cameraman, to tour the coastline and photograph what he could find. The color photographs revealed that the whole coastline would be wide open to a determined Allied assault; what had already been built was useless—the very first wave of enemy bombers would pulverize the structures. Mile after mile of coastline was bare of any fortification whatever. He resolved to build an impregnable fortress line along the entire Atlantic coastline facing Britain.

Albert Speer and the military experts were summoned to the Werewolf headquarters on August 13 and informed of this decision. Hitler lectured them in detail on his requirements for this "Atlantic Wall": it must be such that with an armed force of half a million troops the entire coastline could be defended; assuming 150,000 troops in reserve, the rest would man 15,000 bunkers. A girdle of bunkers spaced at fifty-yard intervals would protect each of the ten most vital war bases; the rest would be spaced at hundred-yard intervals along the entire coast. Cost was no obstacle. "Our most costly substance is the German man. The blood these fortifications will spare is worth the billions!" Decoy sites, minefields, barbed-wire entanglements, and tank traps would complete the defense of western Europe. The Wall was to be completed by the end of April 1943. The submarine bases and naval gunsites were to get special treatment—walls and ceilings of twelve-foot-thick concrete capable of withstanding the heaviest bombs or naval gunfire. Hitler wanted his troops able to sleep or perform their bodily functions undisturbed by the heaviest bombardment. Heavy machine-guns, tanks, and antitank guns must all come under cover, for Hitler predicted that any invasion would begin with the saturation bombardment of the entire area. "It is wisest to consider our own Luftwaffe so weak in the west as to be nonexistent," Hitler warned. The individual bunker design must take everything into account. The Russians were not expected to initiate poison-gas war, but Hitler felt that the Americans probably would, and he suspected that they had developed a brand of gas capable of penetrating existing German gasmasks. He therefore ordered that all bunkers must be gas-tight and have oxygen supplies on hand. The Allies might use napalm bombs, so the bunkers must have steps and ledges to check the flow of blazing oil. Each bigger bunker must have flame-throwing gear. The whole Atlantic Wall must be so formidable that the enemy would think twice about even testing it; and when an invasion did begin, it would have to be in such strength that it would be no problem for Hitler to distinguish the real *Schwerpunkt* from any diversionary feints.

The Atlantic Wall's purpose must be to prevent the enemy from even securing a foothold in western Europe. It would take Hitler two or three days to rush reserves to the main landing zone, by which time the enemy could have landed up to three hundred thousand troops—once that foothold was granted them. He predicted to his generals now, in August 1942, that the invasion proper would be preceded during the night by waves of parachute and glider sabotage troops with orders to disrupt the transport and signals systems and to disable headquarters units; next would come wave after wave of heavy bombers, saturation-bombing the invasion defenses. The invasion would follow at dawn, with three or four thousand landing craft and total enemy air superiority. But by 1943 the Atlantic Wall he had envisaged would be a match for all that. Of course, as he told a Balkan diplomat on August 14, those mad British might venture something *before* then. "If only soldiers had the say in Britain, this operation they are peddling around as their 'Second Front' would not take place. But as lunatics like that drunkard Churchill, and Maccabeans and numskulls like that brilliantined dandy Eden, are at the tiller, we have to be prepared for just about anything!"

What occurred just five days later was indeed a baffling *coup de théâtre* by the British: two brigades of Canadian troops were landed with thirty tanks and British commando detachments on either side of Dieppe. Within less than nine hours the raid had ended in a complete debacle. The Germans, alerted by the chance meeting of a coastal convoy with the raiding force, wiped out the entire force. The British lost a destroyer, 33 landing craft, over 100 planes, and 4,000 troops, of whom 1,179 lay dead on the beaches or the few yards they had penetrated along the promenade. As the minute-by-minute reports from the Luftwaffe and army flooded into Hitler's headquarters in the Ukraine he was unperturbed; Rundstedt's radio message at 6:15 P.M. that no armed Englishman was left ashore provoked the barest flicker of a smile. Hitler sent his chief interpreter, Paul Schmidt, to question the prisoners. Schmidt wrote a few days later: "Militarily speaking, Dieppe was a total fiasco for the British. They ran slap into an ambush on the beaches and nothing worked out for them. The troops probably fought as well as ever, but their top commanders must be frightful. One prisoner bluntly told me: "The men who ordered this raid and those who organized it are criminals and deserve to be shot for mass murder!" Yet all the prisoners thought highly of Churchill, despite his blunders; he was the only leader capable of pulling Britain through the war, they felt.

Politically, Churchill's Dieppe decision was inept. Apparently—as the captured maps and 121-page British operation orders revealed—all this bloodshed and military effort had been squandered only in order to destroy Dieppe harbor and some guns and radar sites; Stalin's chagrin at the failure was obvious. Hitler was nonplussed that Churchill had even dispensed with paratroops: had these landed in the rear and fought off the reserves, Dieppe might have ended very differently. He was encouraged by the appalling quality of the new British "Sten" gun and of the Churchill tanks and equipment the enemy had obligingly ferried across and left on permanent display on the beaches and promenade of Dieppe. But he knew the real invasion would be different. For political reasons he ordered the OKW to proclaim that Dieppe *was* the Second Front; but in September, secretly addressing his western commanders, he predicted that in the real invasion the enemy would rely far more on air power. "We must realize that we are not alone in learning a lesson from Dieppe. The British have also learned. We must reckon with a totally different mode of attack—and at quite a different place." The Atlantic Wall would now play a vital role. "If nothing happens in the west next year, we have won the war."[4]

He considered his personal impressions of the western enemy as largely confirmed. British morale was evidently as brittle as the low-grade steel of the tanks stranded on the beaches. The sophistication of the Canadian assault troops was minimal. One had never heard of Roosevelt; another, asked if he knew of any Germans, replied, "Yes, General Rommel and Lili Marlene." Few even of the officers believed in a British victory now, Schmidt reported.

True, the Allies had no cause for complacency. In mid-August a Mediterranean relief convoy bound for Malta had met with a disaster even more crippling than PQ.17. Only five of the heavily escorted tankers and merchantmen reached harbor: in three days the Germans had sunk the aircraft carrier *Eagle,* badly damaged the carrier *Indomitable,* and sunk the cruiser *Manchester;* and the Italians had sunk the cruiser *Cairo* and torpedoed the cruisers *Nigeria* and *Kenya* as well.

In the Far East, British and American possessions were falling into Japanese hands. Singapore, Hong Kong, the Philippines, Java, and Sumatra; after the monsoon season, late in September, the Japanese might attack Ceylon and India too. Yet the basic weakness of the Axis was becoming clear: not only could Hitler and Ribbentrop not agree on their policy toward Japan, but the Japanese showed no inclination to pursue a joint military strategy. Ribbentrop wanted Japan to strike northward into Russia and counseled Ambassador Oshima to that effect. But Hitler rebuked his foreign minister and pointed out that this was just what

[4]This unpublished speech of September 29, 1942, is referred to at greater length below, page 428. Captain S. W. Roskill, the British official historian, suggests in *The War at Sea,* Vol. II, page 251, that the Germans drew the wrong conclusions from Dieppe. This was certainly not true of Hitler.

Churchill wanted, as it would take Japanese pressure off Australia and India. Halder and the naval staff both shared this view: Japan must shift her naval effort to the western Indian Ocean, at the expense of her ambitions in the Pacific.

The Japanese kept their own counsel, while Hitler, on the other hand, apprised Tokyo of even those most secret plans he dared not impart to the talkative Italians, and he also entrusted all Germany's military inventions and techniques to Japan; he received nothing in return. Late in July 1942 the General Staff noted with resignation that nothing was known even to the Führer of Japan's actual intentions; and when joint staff talks between General Jodl and a Japanese mission were held on August 5, the latter flatly rejected all the German advice. "You must not demand too much of Japan," the Japanese said.

The Black Spot for Halder

Once before, in July 1918, German troops had invaded the Caucasus. The Turks had caved in the Russian front and marched into Transcaucasia, and the Germans had followed from across the Black Sea; then too the Ukraine had been in German hands. The analogy between then and now, the late summer of 1942, was close indeed! But if in 1918 the Germans had needed the oil only for their military machine, in 1942 they needed it for the Ukraine too. Hundreds of thousands of useless tractors littered the collective farms, unable to sow or harvest until once more the oil of Baku began to reach them. The projected eight million tons of Ukranian grain for Europe would remain a dream unless Hitler could get to Baku.

Between his armies and Baku stood the Caucasus—seven hundred miles of untamed, jagged mountains capped by an eighteen-thousand-foot extinct volcano, Elborus. Flanked at one end by the Black Sea and at the other by the Caspian Sea, these mountains had throughout history proved a sure barrier to military ambitions. The Alps had repeatedly been crossed, from the time of Hannibal down through that of the medieval German emperors. Not so the Caucasus: the Mongol invaders, Timur, the Seldshuks and Osmans, had all skirted around its eastern end; Islam had to take to the Caspian in its northward crusade; so did Peter the Great when he invaded northern Persia. The Caucasus itself was impregnable. The German occupation forces had held its passes with a solitary company of riflemen in 1918.

Hitler had long ago decided to set a historic precedent. Field Marshal von List's army group had been directed to cross the mountains to the Black Sea coast so that the Russian navy there would be finally eliminated. The Führer was unimpressed by the obstacles. At one war conference Göring leaned over the maps, tapped the mountain range with his sausage fingers laden with glittering rings, and coolly announced, "There is not all that much difference between the Caucasus and Berlin's Grunewald!"

From now on, however, the campaign in Russia suffered from the faulty planning and Intelligence of the summer. Hitler's armored divisions outpaced their supply lines and came to a halt; they relied on one solitary low-capacity railroad running eastward from the Donets Basin, but this ended far short of the battlefields and there was not enough truck transport to bridge the gaps. Oil and gasoline were available, but they were at the wrong places. In the center and northern front, guerrilla warfare behind the German lines increased, and Hitler had to sign a special directive on uniform countermeasures. Ill-advised by Halder and army Intelligence throughout the summer on Stalin's remaining reserves, Hitler had committed his armies to too many campaigns on too many fronts, leaving the uncertain divisions of his allies to guard the flanks. But these allies—Romanian, Hungarian, and Italian—were low in morale and inadequately equipped, and out of thin air the enemy was producing fresh divisions all along the front. Hitler had no reserves to meet this unexpected situation. A tug-of-war developed over every German division temporarily withdrawn from the battlefields. Meanwhile the Russian generals captured in the fighting just smiled faintly when interrogated about the forces still at Stalin's disposal: "You are in for the surprise of your lives!"

Hitler was determined not to be surprised. The Russians would unquestionably first strike at the Hungarian and Italian armies on the Don; several times during August he asked Halder to back up the Hungarians with German artillery and antitank defenses, and on the sixteenth he shrewdly prophesied that Stalin might repeat the 1920 ploy used against the White Russian army—attacking across the Don at Serafimovich and striking toward Rostov. The Italian Eighth Army would probably collapse, and the entire southern front would then be threatened. Repeatedly throughout August Hitler ordered Halder to shift the 22nd Panzer Division from the Stalingrad fighting to an area behind the Italian army. Halder paid no heed; there is no reference to Hitler's order in Halder's diary or in the records of the army group concerned. History was to show that Hitler's fears were well founded.

Russia's strength was anything but exhausted. On August 2, Halder's chief of eastern Intelligence, Colonel Gehlen, had indicated that in July alone Stalin had produced 54 new infantry divisions and 56 new armored divisions. Halder sent all Gehlen's figures to Hitler the next day, frankly admitting that earlier Intelligence figures had been underestimations; but he added that the enemy had achieved this feat only by employing far more female labor than had Germany, and he suggested that since Stalin could now fall back only on eighteen-year-olds for recruits they need expect only 30 more divisions to be raised at most. In addition, once Stalin had raised these divisions he would still have to solve the problem of equipping and arming them. In July the Red Army had lost 3,900 tanks, and since they were importing only 400 and manufacturing less than 1,000 a month, sooner or later their tank supply would be exhausted. But even Halder's forced optimism evaporated two weeks later. Gehlen's new figures now gave Stalin the equivalent of 593 divisions, of which an awe-inspiring number was being held in reserve. Hitler pathetically clung to his earlier information—his entire strategy in Russia had been based on it. As the truth finally dawned on him, his anger at Halder and the army's generals increased. He nevertheless insisted that Gehlen must have been duped by the Russians. According to Halder, Hitler foamed: "I, the head of the greatest industrial nation—I, assisted by the greatest genius of all time," referring to Albert Speer, "I, whose drive makes the whole world tremble, I sweat and toil to produce just six hundred tanks a month. And you are telling me that Stalin makes a thousand!" But it was too late to turn back now. Hitler's only hope lay in depriving the Russians of the economic basis for continued defense.

That basis lay in the Caucasus.

On August 9, General Ruoff's command had captured Krasnodar, and Kleist's tanks rolled through Maykop; but the oil fields were in ruins. Hitler called on Field Marshal List to strike through the mountains to the ports of Tuapse and Sukhumi as rapidly as possible, thus depriving the Russian fleet of its last sanctuaries and enabling the German army to ferry supplies to the Caucasus by sea. But only one road crossed the mountains, that from Armavir through Maykop to Tuapse. The Fourth Air Force were optimistic still. But on August 11 the OKW Intelligence chief, Canaris, visiting Hitler's headquarters, wrote in his diary: "Keitel more candid than usual this time, does not share Richthofen's optimism. He does not doubt that the Russians will try to hold the western Caucasus and in particular block the road from Armavir to Tuapse." Six days later Kleist's armor reached the eastern end of the mountain ridge, where it was stalled by stiffening enemy resistance and air attacks. The Russians had marshaled over three thousand planes in this theater, including trainers and Lend-Lease aircraft. Time was running out for Hitler. Seized by uncertainty, he sent one after another of Jodl's officers to investigate on the spot and spur the army generals on. He suspected them of frittering away their strength in the Caucasian Highlands instead of building up their main thrusts to Tuapse and Sukhumi. Speer has testified to Hitler's cold fury on August 21 when List's mountaineers proudly announced that they had scaled the Elborus and raised the swastika from its peak. Army cameramen had filmed the dramatic scene. Hitler raged that his army's ambition should be to defeat the Russians, rather than conquer mountains. Jodl —a Bavarian and mountaineer like List himself—defended the field marshal and for the first time Hitler rounded on Jodl too. He fumed at List in particular and at the army's leaders in general, storming at their "arrogance, incorrigibility, and sheer inability to grasp fundamentals." By the end of August, List's offensive had petered out—defeated by impassable roads, wrecked suspension bridges, dense fog, and driving rain and snow.

To the northeast, Weichs's Stalingrad offensive was faring better, despite the oppressive heat of high summer in the arid steppes. General Hoth's Fourth Panzer Army, plagued by fuel and ammunition shortages and nonexistent roads, halted just south of the city. But on August 23, Paulus's Sixth Army covered forty miles, and at 4 P.M. one of his corps commanders reached the Volga at a point just north of the city. With 88-millimeter guns the first Soviet ships were sent to the bottom of the Volga before night fell, but here too the Red Army's resistance was stiffening.

Hitler had no reserves left. Since early August fierce Russian attacks had gnawed at the marrow of Field Marshal von Kluge's Army Group Center. Hitler had ordered him to erase a Russian salient at Sukhinichi—one hundred fifty miles southwest of Moscow—left over from the winter crisis; this attack, "Whirlwind," would create the platform for a possible later attack on Moscow itself. Russian spoiling attacks on General Walther Model's Ninth Army at Rzhev and Subtsoff left Hitler unconcerned. Perhaps he hoped to repeat his Kharkov victory.[1] When Kluge appealed for permission to cancel "Whirlwind" and use the five hundred tanks to save the Ninth Army instead, Hitler would not hear of it. Provided the armored divisions held their thrust tightly together, like a rapier lunging toward Sukhinichi, "Whirlwind" was bound to succeed. Kluge stomped out of Werewolf saying, "Then you, mein Führer, must take the responsibility!"

The attack began on August 11, in difficult terrain—heavily fortified, marshy forests alternating with treacherous minefields. Kluge allowed the divisions to splay out; their casualties were horrifying. Halder remained optimistic of success; General Adolf Heusinger—chief of his operations staff—roundly disagreed. The attack failed.

Again summoned to Werewolf on August 22, Kluge was rebuked by a disappointed Hitler and instructed to recast "Whirlwind" as a purely holding operation. This first major setback of 1942 vexed Hitler deeply. Four months later he complained, "Our worst mistake this year was that attack on Sukhinichi. It was a copybook example of how *not* to stage an attack. They attacked in just about every direction that they could, instead of holding it tightly and narrowly together and thrusting rapidly through with the five armored divisions. We had some five

[1]There was an essential difference. "Fridericus" at Kharkov (page 387) was a pincer attack; for lack of reserves Hitler could mount "Whirlwind" only with the southern arm of the pincer, the Second Panzer Army.

hundred tanks committed to the attack on Sukhinichi. And what did they do? —Splattered them all over the place: that was a 'famous victory'!"

Model's Ninth Army at Rzhev began bleeding to death. Hitler injected the "Gross Deutschland" Division into its rump, but at a stormy war conference at noon on August 24, Halder demanded permission for Model to retreat, as his army's casualties could not be sustained. One regiment had lost eight commanders in a week. The army was in danger of burning itself out.

Hitler's hatred of the General Staff boiled over. Perhaps it was the insufferable heat; perhaps it was Halder's dry, monotonous voice, or his perpetual sneer, or the Mafia-like cluster of staff officers around him. More likely it was the parallel with the winter Moscow crisis that suddenly reminded Hitler that Halder was a reactionary relic of the Brauchitsch era. "You always seem to make the same suggestion—retreat!" he rebuked the general. This idea had to be stamped out in the army, once and for all, he stormed. If Model complained that the reinforcements being sent him were useless, then he must be made to realize that the Russian reinforcements were even more so. Hitler ended his furious tirade by saying, "I must demand the same toughness from my commanders as from my troops." For the first time, Halder lost his temper. "I *am* still tough, mein Führer. But out there our fine riflemen and lieutenants are dying by the thousand just because their commanders are denied the only possible decision—their hands are tied." To everybody's embarrassment Hitler interrupted him with a calculated injury: "What, Herr Halder—you who were as chairbound in the Great War as in this—what do you think you can teach me about the troops! You, who haven't even got a wound stripe on your uniform!"—and he pounded the black stripe on his own chest.

Halder visited Hitler in private afterward and tried to reason with him: it was a crime against German blood to set tasks to sons of German mothers that were downright impossible. Hitler accused him of turning soft and of losing his nerve now that the troops were beginning to suffer casualties again.

Field Marshal von Manstein, the conqueror of Sevastopol, had been among the hushed and embarrassed witnesses of Hitler's outburst against Halder. Manstein had arrived from the Crimea, en route to the north where his Eleventh Army was slated to launch the final assault on Leningrad in September.

Beleaguered since September 1941, Leningrad was the key to the fighting both in the Baltic and in Finland. Until it was destroyed, Hitler could not release his divisions there to strengthen General Dietl's army in Lapland, where the enemy might at any time seize the only nickel mines under German control; neither Jodl nor Dietl thought either side could secure strategic victories in such formidable terrain, but Hitler disagreed. Were he Stalin or Churchill, he would risk anything to knock out those nickel mines: within a few months no more German tanks or shells could be produced. In late July he had directed the army to storm Leningrad early in September. For this operation, "Northern Lights," he promised Field Marshal Georg von Küchler, the commander of Army Group North, a veritable orchestra of artillery unparalleled since Verdun—nearly a thousand guns marshaled around the city's flat outskirts to pave the way for the infantry assault by "sheer brute force." Among the siege artillery was the 800-millimeter "Dora," a colossal weapon with only forty-six rounds of ammunition left over from Sevastopol; there were two 600-millimeter, two 420-millimeter, and six 400-millimeter howitzers as well. On August 8, Küchler had told Hitler that he hoped to finish off Leningrad by the end of October, but Jodl interjected that this was too long; "Northern Lights," he noted, was not an end in itself so much as a preparation for the campaign in Lapland. At Jodl's suggestion, Hitler brought in Manstein to direct the assault on Leningrad, since Küchler appeared to lack the necessary impetus.

The trainloads of artillery arriving from the Crimea had not passed undetected by the enemy. By late August the outlying population was flocking into Leningrad, until perhaps a million refugees were there. Stern measures of defense had been prepared, including the preparation of demolition charges around the biggest buildings. The German navy eagerly awaited the day when it could take over the huge shipyards, and it begged Hitler to avoid damaging them.

Hitler feared that the Russians would spoil the attack by striking first at the narrow German salient west of Lake Ladoga—a vulnerable bottleneck of German troops which sealed off Leningrad by land; the Russians only kept the city alive by hazardous shipments across the lake itself. Throughout August, Hitler had anxiously ordered Halder to ensure that the Eighteenth Army had enough tanks and artillery to defend the bottleneck without draining away the strength Manstein's Eleventh Army would need for "Northern Lights." Halder, apparently bent on documenting his disapproval of Hitler's leadership by petty obstructionism, at first refused the demands then bluntly disobeyed them.

On August 23, Hitler told Küchler he was putting Manstein in charge. Together they pored over the air photographs of the city. Hitler was apprehensive about house-to-house fighting breaking out in this endless maze of streets and buildings. As Küchler pointed out, when the assault began, hundreds of thousands of workers would down tools, reach for their rifles, and stream into the trench fortifications. Only days of terror-bombardment, directed against the factories, munitions works, Party buildings, and control posts would prevent this. (Manstein later told Küchler he did not believe, from his experiences with Sevastopol, that the Russians could be terrorized by bombardment.) Hitler feared a more fundamental danger—that Stalin would attack the bottleneck first. He knew that the first nine Tiger tanks were on their way from Germany. "I would set up the first Tigers behind the front line there," he told Küchler. "Then nothing can go wrong. They are unassailable. They can smash any enemy tank onslaught." Hitler decided that Manstein should launch "Northern Lights" on September 14, after Richthofen had spent three days softening up the city with his bomber squadrons. With Richthofen at Stalingrad, Hitler told Jeschonnek, that battle was already 100 percent won; with Richthofen at Leningrad, the odds on victory would rise to 150 percent.

Manstein was less hopeful, and on August 24 he told Hitler as much—particularly if the Finns would not attack Leningrad simultaneously from the north. On August 27 the Russians struck just where Hitler had feared, at the vulnerable bottleneck. Deep wounds were riven in General Georg Lindemann's Eighteenth Army here, and the Eleventh Army had to divert its strength to his support. The attack on Leningrad receded ever further into the future. The much vaunted Tiger tanks were a disappointment.

And all the time the thermometer at Hitler's headquarters camp continued to rise as the Ukrainian sun beat down. The ground was rock-hard, the grass had turned brown and dry, the trees and shrubs were grimy with dust, and clouds of dust hung in choking layers over every road. "Much though we long for rain and cool weather," wrote the OKW diarist Greiner from Werewolf on August 31, "we dread them too because then it rains in torrents and every lane will become a quagmire within minutes and the humid heat here is said to be particularly grim. In the forest camp we can just about bear the heat, but we mustn't try to leave the forest shade." As he ended the letter the first rain began to beat down on the wooden roof, and steam rose from the undergrowth.

In Egypt weeks of enforced inactivity had blunted the edge of Rommel's offensive. Ahead of his German and Italian divisions lay Montgomery's Alamein line—a forty-mile-long swath of minefields powerfully defended by tanks and aircraft.

With the revival of Malta, after a British convoy had reached the island in June, the supplies getting to Rommel had dwindled to a trickle. Hitler's instinctive dropping of the "Hercules" plan to invade the island now cost the Germans dear. As the water drought had tormented the British defenders at Hacheim in June, now in July and August the lack of gasoline tortured Rommel. In June and July his aircraft had flown twelve thousand sorties. But by early August he was down to his last few hundred tons of gasoline. Under cover of increasing air supremacy, the British attacks began. The first signs of panic were seen in the Italian divisions. The Germans had to regroup to plug the gaps, and every mile of desert cost Rommel more precious gasoline. The enemy's fighter bombers roamed the desert almost unimpeded. Jodl's deputy, Warlimont, flew out to North Africa at the end of July to see for himself; he reported vividly to Hitler on the plight of Rommel, who was confronting an enemy growing stronger each day on the ground and in the air. Hitler impatiently swung around on Göring: "D'you hear that, Göring! Saturation bombing raids in mid-desert!"

It was not even as though Hitler intended to *stay* in the Mediterranean. This was Italy's *Lebensraum* in his view; Germany had no title to it—indeed, not only was its climate wrong for the Germanic races, but the south had always been a source of mischief in German history. He was already thinking of turning Crete over to Mussolini. The Italians were not slow to stake a formal claim to the island on the pretext that Rommel's coming offensive in Egypt would make a strong Italian contingent unavoidable. Admiral Raeder demurred, since the naval staff wanted Crete retained to strengthen Germany's postwar hand in the south. Jodl's staff proposed to filibuster against the Italian claim; but Hitler adhered to his doctrinaire attitude, favoring Mussolini. Anti-Italian feeling ran high among the Germans, particularly since the Italian *comando supremo* favored its own contingent in North Africa with three times the volume of supplies that was provided to the Germans, although there were nearly a hundred thousand German troops there compared with only forty-eight thousand Italians! When Rommel launched his long-prepared assault at El Alamein on August 30, the enemy outnumbered him so heavily, and his oil reserves were so low, that by September 3 his Panzer Army Africa was back where it had started.

Raeder and the naval staff warned insistently that this was a turning point in the war. The army refused to agree. Halder believed that Rommel would demonstrate his superior leadership and seize the initiative as soon as the British launched their own offensive, "presumably next spring"; Jodl also persuaded Hitler that the Egyptian offensive had not failed, as the enemy would scarcely succeed in penetrating Rommel's Alamein position. Therefore no steps were taken to restore Germany's lost air supremacy in Africa. Hitler was convinced that no harm could come to the Axis there—and certainly not in 1942.

It was autumn. In the fine oak forests around Hitler's headquarters the scent was unmistakable. The fields had been harvested, the sunflowers had been laid out to dry on the roofs, and bulging watermelons—used here only as cattle fodder—lay everywhere; the poppies were blackening, the ears of corn yellowing, and summer was truly over. Hitler did not know it, but ahead of him lay only an unbroken succession of defeats, withdrawals, and disappointments.

He was already preparing for a long war. He had postponed the capture of Baku until 1943. He harried his subordinates into speeding up construction of the Atlantic Wall. He turned a baleful eye on partisan activity in Holland and Denmark. He ordered Kluge to speed the construction of a rear line of defense along the central eastern front. When General von Weichs arrived at Werewolf in mid-September, Hitler also ordered him to build a defensive line north of Stalingrad as soon as it had been captured and the armies were pressing on to Astrakhan.

Tantalizing and provocative, Stalingrad seemed to Hitler and his field commanders as good as theirs—there lay the rub. Hitler told Halder he wanted the virulently Communist city's entire male population "disposed of" and the women transported away. Paulus's troops were already fighting in the outskirts, from house to house and street to street. Each day, Richthofen's bombers were pouring a thousand tons of bombs into the Russian positions; Richthofen himself—tough and dynamic—was personally supervising the operations from a fighter airfield ten miles west of Stalingrad. But ground conditions were truly appalling. A two-mile-high pall of choking dust lay over the battlefields. Progress was slow. Richthofen voiced biting criticism of the field commanders Paulus and Hoth, claiming that with more spirit they could have taken Stalingrad in two days. He himself had found difficulty in spotting any enemy at all, while from his plane he had seen German troops bathing in the river instead of fighting.

In the Caucasus, Field Marshal Wilhelm List fared little better. His mountain divisions were at a virtual standstill in the narrow passes—still twenty miles and more from the Black Sea coast. Hitler's army adjutant, Major Gerhard Engel, returned with a vivid description of the mountain terrain. There were only four mule paths across the mountains, and the modern and highly mechanized German divisions could scarcely make use of them in their attempt to reach the sea. Hitler was impatient at List's slow progress. Jodl courageously defended the army group's achievements and pointed out that it was a consequence of the Führer's own orders for "Barbarossa" that the mountain divisions had neglected their specialized equipment and were thus now little more than glorified infantry divisions; Hitler claimed he had ordered their proper fitting out as mountain divisions before "Blue" began, in July, but Jodl replied that Hitler's memory was at fault. It was symptomatic of the deteriorating situation that even these two men were falling out with each other. Previously, the OKW's outstanding chief of operations had schooled himself to accept Hitler's orders implicitly; once Jodl had explained to Halder that he always remembered what his grandmother had told his mother on her wedding day: "In matrimony the husband is always right! And if he says, 'The water's running uphill today' my answer is, 'Yuh, Yuh, it's up there already!' "

At the end of August, Hitler had summoned List to headquarters. Faced with the conservative, powerfully religious field marshal, Hitler's tongue again clove to the roof of his mouth. He swallowed all his private dislikes—his complaint that List had prevented the SS tanks from breaking into Rostov, his anger at the Elborus flag-planting incident, his impatience over the lengthy delay in ferrying the Romanians across from the Crimea, and List's general insubordination. He engaged List in affable conversation, lunched privately with him, then sent him back to the Caucasus. Once the field marshal had left, Hitler critized the way he had arrived armed only with a 1:1,000,000 map of southern Russia without any of his forces shown on it—although standing orders prohibited taking strategic maps on plane journeys. To Hitler, List seemed hopelessly "at sea." List for his part did not elaborate on the formidable mountain terrain barring his advance to the coast. Meanwhile, two of Jodl's officers sent to investigate the delays in the crossing of the Strait of Kerch had scored some success in getting things moving; two days later the crossing was successfully accomplished, and a slow advance along the coast road itself began. Hitler failed to see why the crossing could not have been made a month before, as he had directed in July; did none of his commanders appreciate the urgency of their campaigns? From Hitler's mood his adjutants guessed that a storm was about to break.

His antipathy toward General Halder, the Chief of General Staff, still smoldered. He complained in private of Halder's animosity and negative attitude. "With Jodl I know where I am. He says what he thinks. But Halder just stands there like somebody with a guilty conscience." He could not abide specialists; his verdict on the Halder type was summed up in a *bon mot* coined in happier times—"A specialist is a man who explains to me precisely why something can *not* be done!" Halder had done nothing to wed the army to National Socialism. To Hitler's staff it was plain that the general had been passed the Black Spot; thus Halder was now treated as though he had an infectious disease. In his absence, there were debates at the war conferences on who ought to succeed him. Hitler observed that he really needed an old-fashioned "quartermaster," a man of drive and imagination, and he recalled that Kleist's panzer army had had such a Chief of Staff in Kurt Zeitzler. Göring's imminent arrival was announced, and his liaison officer General Karl Bodenschatz slipped out to meet him. When the Reichsmarschall entered the hut he announced portentously, "Mein Führer, I have been racking my brains all night on a successor for Halder. What about General Zeitzler?" This was characteristic of the way the Göring-Bodenschatz team worked. Jodl spoke out on Halder's behalf in the days that followed. Together with General Scherff, Hitler's court historian, he drafted a memorandum proving that Halder's staff had only been following Hitler's own orders in the weeks before the impasse in the Caucasus. But Hitler—tormented by the heat, the rows, and the realization that victory in Russia was finally slipping from his grasp—was already beyond reason.

The storm broke on September 7. Jodl himself had flown out to Stalino to confer with List and his mountain corps commander General Konrad, a close friend of Jodl's since they had been cadets together in Bavaria. He returned to Vinnitsa that evening and reported to Hitler in private, giving a horrendous picture of the conditions in the Caucasus. The Fourth Mountain Division was being asked to advance on the Georgian coastal towns of Gudauta and Sukhumi along a mountain path over sixty miles long. All its supplies would have to be carried by mule, of which nearly two thousand were still needed. The Russians would only have to demolish all the bridges. The simultaneous advance on Tuapse, the port farther west, would be incomplete before winter set in. The generals felt there was no alternative to withdrawing from these Caucasus passes and concentrating on the "road" to Tuapse.

Jodl courageously quoted these views to Hitler. It provoked a furious scene. Hitler ranted that Jodl had been sent down there to get the offensive moving again; instead, he had allowed his insubordinate Bavarian comrades to hoodwink him. ("All generals lie," was Hitler's favorite watchword.) The Führer said that not since the notorious Hentsch affair in World War I had an army been so betrayed.[2] He ended the conference and stalked out, refusing for the first time to shake hands with Keitel and Jodl as he went—a snub he persisted in until the end of January 1943. And whereas at midday he had entertained his staff and guests—Milch, Speer, and Koch—at luncheon, as he had done regularly since May 1940, he announced that he proposed to dine alone in his own quarters from now on. He left them in no doubt of his mistrust of them.

The real cause of Hitler's anger remains a matter for conjecture. His subsequent actions give some clues. After supper he sent for Julius Schaub, his personal majordomo; the crippled minion hobbled in, and Hitler asked him to arrange for a "Wehrmacht hut" to be erected nearby. Then he sent for Bormann and asked him to provide teams of stenographers to record every word spoken at the war conferences; the stenographers were to be housed in the Wehrmacht hut. Never again would Jodl or anybody else be able to put words into his mouth. Evidently Jodl had tactlessly suggested that it was Hitler's own directives, faithfully complied with, that had caused the Caucasus stalemate, for Hitler now also demanded to see every scrap of paper referring to the command of List's army group. Jodl could have kicked himself for such an elementary *faux pas.* His own rule had always been that the dictator's reputation for infallibility must remain immaculate; the blame must always be laid upon insubordinates, for they were many—never placed on Hitler, for he was only one.

---

[2]The German army's High Command had sent Lieutenant Colonel Hentsch, a General Staff officer, out to inspect the armies on the Marne. He was then blamed for the resulting retreat of those armies.

The clean sweep began at once. Over the next days Hitler contemplated replacing Keitel with Kesselring; he told Jodl he could not work with him any longer either and proposed replacing him with Paulus as soon as the general had taken Stalingrad. On September 9, the day the first Reichstag stenographers flew in from Berlin, he repeated his intention of ridding himself of Halder, as the general's nerves were evidently not equal to the strain. That afternoon he sent Keitel to drop the necessary hint to Halder. Keitel was also to tell Halder that Field Marshal List's resignation was required. For the time being he, Hitler, would command Army Group A in the Caucasus—the ultimate in anomalies, for he was after all Commander in Chief of the Army and Supreme Commander of the Wehrmacht as well. Keitel took the news to List in person.

List resigned that same evening, but Halder seems to have believed the ax would not fall on him as well. After all, Jodl continued in office and so did Keitel. But with Jodl the situation was different: Hitler still warmed toward him; his balding pate was a familiar sight across the map table, and above all he was loyal —apart, of course, from the one lapse about the blame for the Caucasus stalemate. Jodl commented to his own deputy, "The Führer will have to cast around a long time to find a better army general than me, and a more convinced National Socialist!" So he stayed on, while Hitler treated him with silent contempt for many weeks. Meanwhile the war conferences no longer took place in Jodl's map room but in his own quarters. They were conducted in monosyllabic brevity by an angry Führer while relays of stenographers recorded every word and interjection.

Under Martin Bormann's supervision the first three stenographers were sworn in on September 12 and a second batch two days later. The verbatim record of proceedings in the Wehrmacht hut came to some five hundred pages a day, every page checked and doublechecked by Hitler's adjutants and then locked away. "When we win a battle, my field marshals take the credit," Hitler explained. "When there's a failure, they point at *me.*" He could trust nobody—but the SS. After the stenographers had been sworn in, he turned to SS aide Richard Schulze, promoted him to Personal Adjutant, and ordered him to sit in on every military meeting, no matter how confidential. The towering SS captain became a familiar sight.

Two years later Hitler, in conversation with a medical specialist, revealed a further motive for introducing the stenographers. The doctor mentioned that Kaiser Wilhelm II had suffered an ear complaint similar to Hitler's and inquired whether the Führer had ever read J. D. Chamier's biography of the Kaiser; Hitler had, and admitted that English though the author was the Kaiser had emerged well—perhaps better than he deserved. The doctor's note of this conversation continues:

Hitler then said that a foreigner probably finds it easier to pass judgment on a statesman, provided that he is familiar with the country, its people, language, and archives. "Presumably Chamier didn't know the Kaiser personally, as he was still relatively young," I said. "However, his book not only shows a precise knowledge of the archives and papers, but relies on what are after all many personal items like the Kaiser's letters and written memoranda of conversations with friends and enemies. Of course in the Kaiser's time ideas were communicated far more frequently in writing than nowadays when we have the telephone, telegraph, aircraft, and car." Hitler then said that for some time now he has gone over to having all important discussions and military conferences recorded for posterity by shorthand writers. And perhaps one day after he is dead and buried an objective Englishman will come and give him the same kind of objective treatment. The present generation neither can nor will.

By mid-September 1942 the General Staff had reverted to the comforting theme that the Russians were finished—their lack of strategic reserves demonstrated by their urgent transfer of divisions from along the front to the Leningrad and Stalingrad crisis areas. Hitler optimistically spoke to Weichs and Paulus of future campaigns and of the capture of Astrakhan on the Caspian Sea. On September 13 the systematic assault on Stalingrad began. The next day even Richthofen believed the Russians were flagging. In his private diary Weizsäcker quoted his friend General Halder thus: "He says that above all he's leaving his post without worries for the army. The Russians are too far weakened to be the danger to us they were last winter. The weak spot is Africa." (Halder hated Rommel.)

But now the Russians began a heroic struggle for Stalingrad, contesting every street, every ruined building, and every yard of the battered city. Throughout late September Hitler's anxiety about the Don front, defended only by his poorly armed and unenthusiastic allies, mounted. Halder still had not executed Hitler's order for the 22nd Panzer Division to be placed in reserve behind the vulnerable Italian Eighth Army on the Don. On September 16, Hitler again ordered the transfer. Was it inertia or pigheadedness on Halder's part? Hitler, seething over the gradual stagnation of the summer offensive, suspected the former. It was time for Halder—who had identified himself so closely with Hitler's military ambitions and cast of thought in the first months after Brauchitsch's dismissal—to be ejected from the war machine like a spent cartridge case. On September 17, Hitler finally resolved to appoint the bustling General Zeitzler in his place; he turned down Keitel's suggestion that either Manstein or Paulus would be better, and he sent Schmundt, his chief adjutant, to Paris the next day accompanied by General Günther Blumentritt, who was to replace Zeitzler as Rundstedt's Chief of Staff.

It was late on September 23 before Schmundt arrived back at Hitler's

Ukrainian headquarters, bringing a puzzled—and still unenlightened—Zeitzler with him. An hour after midnight Hitler had him fetched from the guest house, and launched into an impassioned monologue on List and Halder—the latter was "more of a professor than a soldier." When the red-faced Zeitzler tried uncomfortably to defend his chief, Hitler cut him short, rose to his feet, and announced that Zeitzler was to replace Halder forthwith. "I hereby promote you to full general." Thus at forty-seven Zeitzler was one of the army's youngest three-star generals and suddenly catapulted into the highest post of the army's General Staff. A rotund, florid, jovial soldier—known throughout the army as "Thunderball" because of his dynamic years as Chief of Staff to General von Kleist—he provided a change from Halder that could hardly have been more dramatic.

Halder attended his last frosty war conference the next midday. Afterward Hitler took leave of him, while Keitel and the stenographers stood by; he rebuked the general for losing his nerve and for lacking the kind of fanatical idealism that Moltke had displayed on behalf of the monarchy. When Major Engel, the army adjutant, collected Halder outside the door the general was still weeping—as another general put it, Halder had been kicked out like a dog caught piddling on the carpet. A victory mood reigned among the OKW officials, who rejoiced at the disgrace Hitler had inflicted on the General Staff. Schmundt proclaimed that the last barrier had fallen; the "spirit of Zossen" would now be stamped out, and the German army steeped through and through in the true spirit of National Socialism.

The new Chief of Staff was certainly more closely aligned with the Party than Halder, but he was by no means complaisant. Keitel accordingly warned him: "Never contradict the Führer. Never remind him that once he may have thought differently about something. Never tell him that subsequent events have proved you right and him wrong. Never report on casualties to him—you have to spare the nerves of this man." But Zeitzler retorted, "If a man starts a war he must have the nerve to hear the consequences." Court historian Scherff shared Keitel's view. Once he told an army general that there had been errors, but it would be harmful to draw the Führer's attention to them as he might then lose faith in his "instinctive touch"; it was the overall picture that mattered.

Hitler tolerated Zeitzler's robustness willingly at first. He hoped Zeitzler would succeed in remolding the General Staff, and he even drafted two orders for Zeitzler to deal with first: the one dispensing with the older army commanders —some of them were over sixty—and the other scrapping the traditional redstriped trousers and insignia of the General Staff. Zeitzler refused to inaugurate his office with such radical decrees. The traditions of the General Staff could not be disposed of at a stroke, even by an absolute dictator. Yet there was sound reasoning behind the desire for younger commanders—as the successes of Rommel, Model, Paulus, and Dietl, all in their early fifties, showed. In a third decree, Hitler subjected the personnel decisions of the General Staff to the Army Personnel Branch instead of to the Chief of Staff, and he also made his own chief adjutant, General Schmundt, head of that branch—thus for the first time acquiring absolute control over all senior army appointments. The brazen "freemasonry" of General Staff officers must lose its monopoly within the army. Hitler ordered:

a) There is only one officer corps. The best officers are to be given additional training to equip them for early entry to high front-line commands;
b) There is to be no limit on the number selected for training. . . .

In this way a tidal wave of youthful, active frontline commanders, equipped with the skills of the General Staff, promoted in leaps and bounds while still at the peak of their mental and physical abilities, would flood new life into the weary outer reaches of the German army. Halder's replacement by a general eleven years his junior was therefore just the forerunner of a much more fundamental revolution.

Hitler's aversion to the professional staff officer found further justification late in September: the Gestapo pounced on a Communist espionage ring extending across western Europe, one of whose principals was a staff officer attached to the air ministry. They had transmitted to their Russian paymasters details of Hitler's headquarters, his planned offensive in the Caucasus, and exaggerated statistics on German aircraft production and much else. The short-wave radios were distributed by the Soviet embassy in Berlin just before "Barbarossa" began, and they were serviced by a young Communist, Hans Coppi, aided by the Countess Brockdorff-Rantzau. The leading figure was Dr. Arvid Harnack, a civil servant in the economics ministry. The spy ring was a polyglot mixture of nobility and plebs, although Hitler scornfully observed that not one German worker had chosen to identify himself with them—the 117 members finally rounded up were either "warped intellectuals" like Lieutenant Harro Schulze-Boysen of the air Intelligence staff, who fancied himself as the defense minister in a Red Germany, or small fry trapped into betraying their country for sexual or monetary favors.

The first trials began some months later. The American-born Frau Mildred Harnack, was sentenced to six years' jail, the countess to ten years'; the rest were to be hanged—a mode of execution stipulated by Hitler as befitting this offense; he also demanded a retrial of the two women, and they were eventually hanged.

The summer of 1942 was over; as Hitler flew back to Berlin on September 27, the first autumn thunderstorms were drenching the capital. A mood of melancholy gripped the people—tired of waiting for the word that Stalingrad had fallen. The Reich press chief had already ordered the printing of special editions, but the event itself was thereby brought no closer. In bloody house-to-house fighting Paulus's troops stormed factory after factory, captured the waterworks, the South Station, and almost all the Volga River bank; the swastika had been hoisted above Communist party headquarters. Hitler was optimistic but failed to inspire even his most dedicated followers with the same hope.

Domestic morale was sagging: the British night-bombing raids on city centers were proving more than the fighter and antiaircraft defenses could handle. He ordered the Luftwaffe to build flak towers in Munich, Vienna, Linz, and Nurem-berg—the fear that these cities might be laid waste was a "constant nightmare," he told his staff. During September heavy raids were made on Bremen, Duisburg, Düsseldorf, and Munich. On other nights isolated aircraft sent millions of city dwellers and factory workers to shelters and basements for hours on end. The Luftwaffe, itself in a period of technical innovation, had neither long-range strate-gic bombers nor high-speed fighter-bombers comparable with those of the enemy; the four-engined Heinkel 177 was a failure, plagued by engine failures and still totally unfit for squadron service, and the much-vaunted Messerschmitt 210 fighter-bomber had had to be scrapped outright earlier in 1942. Its outstanding successor, the Messerschmitt 410, had only just made its first flight. Hitler under-stood nothing about aircraft and had confidently left the Luftwaffe's future in Göring's hands. He began to suspect that his confidence had been misplaced. Increasingly he turned to the Chief of Air Staff, the youthful General Jeschonnek, for advice, excluding the pained and pompous Reichsmarschall Göring; or he discussed Luftwaffe policies with the eminently more capable Number Two, Field Marshal Milch, and the Reich's economic affairs with the munitions minister, Albert Speer, or with Goebbels.

To Goebbels he admitted that he was glad Munich had been bombed—he even found perverse relief in the damage to his own apartment there. The bombing would do the dour Bavarians good. The citizens had turned their backs on the war to such degree that he was pleased the British had drawn their attention to it again. Standing with Goebbels in the Chancellery galleries, where prewar Berlin had seen such spectacular gatherings, Hitler spoke of his longing for peace, which would enable him to return to these elegant surroundings with an easy conscience. Goebbels found him lively and good-tempered; the Führer had just addressed twelve thousand young officers and been fortified in spirit and resolution by the experience. Hitler confided that despite the winter, once Stalingrad had fallen he expected to fight on southward through the Caucasus, as the climate there would permit the campaign to continue. By early 1943 he hoped the huge power station at Zaporozh'ye would be working again, and then the mines and quarries of the Donets would begin producing for Germany.

In one respect Hitler still seemed too indulgent to Goebbels; the propaganda minister pointed out that in every offensive they lacked that final 10 percent of effort that decided between failure and outright success. The German public was awaiting a command for the total mobilization of its resources. Germany was confronted by a totalitarian state wholly committed to the war, while she herself was permitting useless expenditure of effort on, for example, gilding the trappings of Hans Frank's palaces in Poland. Hitler, inexplicably, still hesitated to proclaim a Total War, and thus the precious months were squandered.

Anxiety about the western defenses never left him. For example, Germany's possession of the Finnish nickel mines at Petsamo (Pechenga) was vital to her war effort. Thus he ordered every available warship to remain in northern waters now that the nights were lengthening again. In Holland, Hitler knew that the British secret service was parachuting tons of sabotage material to its agents. Himmler's Gestapo had long penetrated the spy net and ambushed each successive shipment of agents and equipment—a self-perpetuating "England Game" on which the Führer was kept constantly informed.

Even placid little Denmark, the crucial link with Scandinavia, was growing restive. On King Christian's birthday, September 25, Hitler had sent the customary greetings; he received a reply that could only be regarded as deliberately brusque. As Goebbels put it, Europe's monarchs needed socking on the jaw now and then to stuff some sense into them. So Hitler recalled his envoy and military commander from Copenhagen, sent the Danish diplomats in Berlin packing, rejected the apologies belatedly offered by the crown prince, and—after keeping the luckless Danes in agitated suspense for four weeks— delegated the former Gestapo official Dr. Werner Best to act as his strongman in Copenhagen. He instructed Best to ignore the Danish monarchy completely and ensure that Danish Nazis were introduced into a new government —which was to be "legal and complaisant," though "with no support among the Danish people." If the aged king should die, the Wehrmacht was forbidden to join the official mourning.

What Hitler most feared, however, was an enemy invasion of France. The Dieppe raid had shown that this was not impossible. "As you all know," he reminded Göring, Speer, Rundstedt, and a handful of selected generals in the Chancellery's Cabinet Room on September 29, "I have never capitulated. But let us be quite plain about one point: a major enemy landing in the west could precipitate a real crisis." The enemy would have absolute air supremacy. The invasion defenses would be pummelled by bombers and ships' artillery. Only the strongest concrete bunkers and antitank defenses along the entire coastline could ward off an invasion.

The army's transcript of his three-hour secret speech noted:

Finally the Führer repeated that he saw only one remaining danger for the outcome of the war and that was the emergence of a Second Front in the west, as the fighting in the east and the home base would be directly endangered by this. The enemy could launch their Second Front anywhere else they liked, as long as it was as far as possible from Europe. At present he saw his main job as being to spare his country from being turned into a battlefield, which would be the immediate result of an invasion in the west. If we can prevent that until the spring [by which time the Atlantic Wall's fifteen thousand bunkers would be built] nothing can happen to us any longer.

We have got over the worst foodstuffs shortage. By increased production of antiaircraft guns and ammunition the home base will be protected against air raids. In the spring we shall march with our finest divisions down into Mesopotamia, and then one day we shall force our enemies to make peace where and as we want it. Once before the German Reich suffered from its own excessive modesty. The new German Reich will not make the same mistake in its war aims.

The next day he spoke to the German people—for the first time for many months, he apologized, as he had less time for speechmaking than a prime minister who could cruise for weeks around the world in a white silk blouse and floppy sombrero or some other ludicrous garb.

It is of course impossible to talk with these people about Beliefs. If somebody believes that Namsos was a victory, or Andalsnes—if somebody describes even Dunkirk as the biggest victory in history or sees in some nine-hour expedition [Dieppe] a flabbergasting sign of national triumph—obviously we cannot even begin to compare our own modest successes with them! . . . If in these last few months, and in this country there are only a few months available for campaigning, we advance to the Don, finally reach the Volga, overrun Stalingrad and capture it—and of that they can be certain—in their eyes this is nothing! If we advance to the Caucasus, that is as unimportant as that we occupy the Ukraine, have the Donets coal in our domain, have 65 or 70 percent of Russia's iron ore, open up the biggest grain region in the world for the German people and thus for Europe, and also take over the Caucasian oil wells. All that is nothing! But if Canadian troops, wagged by a tiny English tail, come over to Dieppe and just manage to hang on there for nine hours before they are wiped out, then that is an "encouraging, astounding proof of the inexhaustible, triumphant energy typical of the British Empire!" What are our Luftwaffe, our infantry, our tanks against these? What is the effort of our engineers, our railway construction teams—what are our gigantic transport systems, built by us to open up and rebuild half a continent in a matter of months, compared with these? . . . If Mr. Churchill now says, "We want to leave the Germans to fret and ponder on where and when we will open the Second

Front," then I can only say, "Mr. Churchill, you never gave me cause to worry yet! But that we must *ponder*—you've got a point there, because if my enemy was a man of stature I could deduce fairly accurately where he would strike; but if one is confronted by military nincompoops, obviously one hasn't the faintest idea, for it might be the most lunatic undertaking imaginable. And that is the only unattractive feature—that with paralytics and drunkards you can never tell what they'll be up to next."

Africa and Stalingrad

Hitler believed he had good reason to face the coming winter with optimism. The railway transport crisis had been overcome. The harvest throughout occupied Europe was better than expected. Albert Speer was harnessing Germany's latent industrial might to mass-produce tanks and guns. Under Field Marshal Milch the Luftwaffe's production lines were being reorganized. The Atlantic coast was being fortified. The navy was in Norway; the submarines were blocking the Allied convoy routes in the Arctic. The Reich's domains extended farther than ever before in history.

On October 1, 1942, Field Marshal Rommel—amiable and reserved—visited Hitler at the Berlin Chancellery. He explained why he had had to abandon his offensive against the British El Alamein position, attributing it solely to the shortcomings of the Italian officers and British air supremacy. But when Rommel reported that British planes were knocking out his tanks with 40-millimeter shells Göring scoffed, "Out of the question—the Americans only know how to make razor blades!" Rommel retorted, "Herr Reichsmarschall, I wish we had blades like that." Hitler showed him the prototypes of new self-propelled assault guns Albert Speer had collected at the Chancellery that morning—formidable low-chassis armored vehicles mounting the well-proven 105-millimeter guns and presenting a remarkably small target profile to the enemy. He told Rommel of the new Tiger tanks and promised to send forty of them and all the gasoline Rommel needed across to Africa by means of countless Siebel ferries—small flat-bottomed ferries with powerful antiaircraft defenses. The promises remained unfulfilled. Rommel later wrote that Hitler had been misled by his armaments production experts, but even Speer had only promised Hitler a dozen of the assault guns by the end of October. Hitler was an optimist, however; he told Rommel of a weapon of such appalling power it would blast a man off his horse two miles away. Evidently his imagination had run riot on Speer's sober account of Germany's modest atomic research effort some months before.

He liked Rommel, too—he was planning to make him Commander in Chief of the army when the time came.

Hitler returned to the Ukraine on October 4. Halder was finally gone. Zeitzler's verve infected every war conference, evoking from Hitler Napoleon's maxim *"activité, activité, vitesse!"* Zeitzler took control of the eastern front, while Jodl and the OKW controlled the other theaters—a division of responsibility reflected in the war conferences at headquarters, where Zeitzler first briefed Hitler on the Russian front, not infrequently in strict privacy, followed by Jodl on the "OKW theaters." Hitler encouraged the innovation, seeing in Zeitzler the tactical experience needed for Russia and in Jodl the broad strategic vision Zeitzler lacked for the other theaters. Zeitzler toured the southern front at once, returned to Vinnitsa, and issued over Hitler's name a string of realistic orders designed to increase the army's fighting strength—from the proper use of modern weapons, ammunition, and minefields down to the introduction of special rations for combat troops.

Nor were either of these military advisers sycophants. On one occasion the stenographers caught their breath as General Jodl, propped on an elbow on the map table, glanced briefly at Hitler and replied, "Mein Führer, that is an order I will *not* comply with." On another occasion Zeitzler warned that unless a certain salient was withdrawn, the troops would lose confidence in their leadership. Hitler, his awe of the newcomer now diminished, thundered at him, "You're just a staff officer. What do you know about the troops!" Zeitzler sharply reminded the Führer that in August 1914 he had gone to war as an infantry ensign —his knapsack on his back and his rifle on his shoulder—to fight in Belgium. "For bravery in the face of the enemy I was promoted to lieutenant. For three years I commanded a company and for one year I was regimental adjutant. I was wounded twice. I think my combat experience is as good as yours." Hitler paled, instructed the general to proceed with the conference, and avoided attacking him personally after that.

Thus Zeitzler's position became entrenched. Keitel, by way of contrast, had long forfeited Hitler's esteem. Hitler took to making "good-humored" fun of his absent commanders. "My field marshals are great tacticians," he guffawed once. "By tactics, of course, they mean retreating!" Enjoying the dutiful laughter he added, "My field marshals' horizon is the size of a lavatory lid!" Field Marshal Keitel did not move a muscle as the others laughed. The next day an adjutant informed Hitler that Zeitzler wanted a brief private word with him; the meeting took place at midnight. He cordially shook the general's hand. "What can I do for you?" "Mein Führer," replied Zeitzler, "I must speak my mind. As an army general I take exception to the language you used about our field marshals. May I ask you not to use expressions like that in my presence again?" Hitler was dumbfounded, then gave him his hand. "I thank you." As Zeitzler later put it, the Führer was unpredictable. When Antonescu visited him three months later,

Hitler introduced Zeitzler to him with the words "This is my new Chief of General Staff. A man of iron nerves and great war experience."

The war had taken on many new dimensions since 1939. In the east and southeast armies of partisans and bandits were fighting a new kind of campaign. In the west too the Allies were emulating—and far surpassing—the tactics of the Abwehr in commando warfare. These peripheral successes struck a raw nerve in Hitler, whether the target was a secret radar site in France or a German oil dump in North Africa. He showed little inclination to mercy when the commandos were caught: in August, six Britons captured in North Africa behind the lines had caused great damage and many German casualties; two of them were wearing items of German uniforms. Hitler ordered their execution. As he warned his western commanders in October, unless they closed their hearts and acted ruthlessly against the Allied commandos, they would find themselves enmeshed in a partisan struggle no less gruesome than that in the east. Never before had "illegals" played such a part in war—disrupting transport, intimidating the pro-Germans, and sabotaging vital installations. One saboteur could paralyze a power plant and thus deprive the Luftwaffe of thousands of tons of aluminum. The British commandos concealed their uniforms under civilian clothing, so they could escape or surrender as they chose—"The worst possible abuse of the Geneva Convention," said Hitler, conveniently forgetting the tactics he had devised for the invasion of Holland.

A commando-training manual fell into his hands, with diagrams on how to slit human throats and how to truss prisoners so that a noose around their neck would strangle them if they moved. Some corpses trussed like this had been found. Similar instructions captured in North Africa had been commendably disowned by the British government. In September he was told that the British had machine-gunned the survivors of a sinking German minelayer. "It is essential that we give the British as good as we get—an eye for an eye and a tooth for a tooth," fulminated Hitler. "We must declare at once that henceforth parachuting airmen will be fired on, that our submarines will shell the survivors from torpedoed ships, regardless of whether they are soldiers or civilians, women or children! . . . The British are realists, devoid of any scruple and as cold as ice; but as soon as we show our teeth, they become propitiary and almost friendly!" He ordered the navy to commence reprisals, but Raeder demurred. German career officers were too steeped in the traditions of "old-fashioned" wars—the kind fought before the strategic bomber and the atomic weapon—to accept Hitler's radical ideas.

On his return to Vinnitsa on October 4 news reached him of a British commando raid on the tiny Channel island of Sark the night before. The island was guarded only by a rifle company. The commandos had seized five army engineers sleeping in a hotel, manacled them, and then shot and stabbed them to death before withdrawing. Hitler immediately ordered all the prisoners taken at Dieppe manacled as a reprisal until the British government undertook not to repeat such methods; the British proclaimed they would retaliate against the same number of Axis prisoners in their own camps. Hitler had meanwhile drafted a text for the daily OKW communiqué broadcast on the seventh: "The terror and sabotage squads of the British and their accomplices act more like bandits than soldiers. In the future they will be treated as such by the German troops and ruthlessly put down in battle, wheresoever they may appear."

General Jodl urged Hitler to leave it at that—the warning words would alone deter, no need actually to put them into practice. Hitler disagreed. He grumbled about his generals' timidity and their unwillingness to carry out even his order for the liquidation of the Soviet army commissars. "The war ministry is to blame; they always wanted the soldier's profession to be on a par with the parson's!" Keitel and Jodl refused to draft the new order, so Hitler dictated it to one of his own secretaries. He justified it by referring to the commandos' methods as being outside the Geneva Conventions. "Captured papers show that they are ordered not only to manacle their prisoners, but to kill their defenseless prisoners out of hand the moment they feel such prisoners might become a burden or hindrance to them in the prosecution of their purposes." Jodl, unhappily distributing Hitler's order to the commanders on October 19, urgently warned them not to let it fall into enemy hands.

Thus the reported tactics of the British commandos had tragic consequences for many others who fell into German hands. A thirst for revenge also played its part. For example, the record of Hitler's war conference on October 23 began: "In reprisal for the fresh British air raid on a casualty clearing station in Africa the Führer has ordered the immediate execution of the Briton captured during the sabotage attack on the power station at Glomfjord." A week later an attempt by six British sailors to destroy the battleship *Tirpitz*—wintering in a Norwegian fjord—came to grief when their two-man torpedoes were lost in foul weather. Himmler reported to Hitler that all were in plain clothes and that their ship had flown the Norwegian flag. Norwegian frontier guards had captured them, but the six had opened fire with concealed weapons, and five had escaped into Sweden; technically, they were clearly illegals. Hitler ordered the sixth, a twenty-year-old seaman who had been shot through the legs by his Norwegian captors, to be executed. Three weeks later the same fate met the fourteen British survivors of a commando-style attack launched on a hydroelectric power station in Norway: the first glider had crashed into the sea, killing all aboard; the second had crashed with its towing aircraft into a hillside. The Norwegian police rounded up the survivors. The Germans found extensive sabotage equipment in the wreckage. In accordance with the new Commando Order, all fourteen were shot before darkness fell.[1] Some of them *had* been in uniform, and this may have given Hitler misgivings, for when Britain formally protested months later, Hitler dictated to Jodl a note of reply: Insofar as they were in uniform and executing an obvious military mission, enemy soldiers would be treated according to the Convention; but soldiers "dropped behind our lines for clandestine sabotage operations" in unorthodox or civilian clothing, or equipped with "treacherously concealed firearms," would be put to death.

In the Balkans a partisan war of unexampled ferocity was raging, thanks to the devious policies of the Italians and the ineptness of the puppet governments Hitler had established. In April 1941, Yugoslavia had been dismembered into Croatia, governed by a "Poglavnik," Ante Pavelic, and Serbia, which came under German military rule. The Italians had occupied Montenegro and part of Croatia, and they were annexing large stretches of the Croatian coastline. By May 1941 partisan warfare had broken out throughout what was formerly Yugoslavia. In Serbia it was ruthlessly quelled by the Germans; but in Croatia rival armies of guerrillas and bandits roamed the land, terrorizing the pro-Germans, robbing and plundering and murdering, paralyzing the new Croatian state's machinery from the outset. The Četniks, led by Draža Mihajlovič, were fighting for the restoration of the monarchy in Yugoslavia; the partisans, led by Tito, were fighting for Communist ideals; the Ustasha, the Croatian government troops, were fighting an ineffective campaign against them all, hampered by a lack of even the simplest weapons, since the Italians were failing to supply them. Mussolini complained that the Croats were persecuting the Serbian minority and had killed two hundred thousand men, women, and children. His own Second Army, commanded by the controversial General Mario Roatta, sided not with the Ustasha but the Četniks —even to the extent of arming them against Tito's partisans. The Italians were weaving a tangled web indeed.

It was not only that all this laid bare the growing divergence of German and Italian aims. Croatia was of great strategic importance: across the country passed the German supply lines to Saloniki and North Africa; and it exported oil and two hundred thousand tons of bauxite to Germany annually. Order and control were imperative to the Nazis. But the Italians were suppressing the Croat population and actively shielding the Jews—the very subversive elements against whom

---

[1]The target, the Vemork power plant at Rjukan, had been selected because of its importance for the German atomic research program.

the Poglavnik was struggling to apply repressive laws similar to those enforced in Germany. Hitler thrashed out this explosive situation with the Poglavnik and the German military commanders late in September. He had two divisions in Croatia, and a Croat battalion was already fighting before Stalingrad; more were being trained—an entire foreign legion—by the Waffen SS, but now the Poglavnik would need them to restore order in Croatia. All this was the result of Roatta's strange dealings, but Hitler was loath to embarrass Mussolini, and the papers sent down to Rome were stripped of any references that might offend Italian suscep- tibilities. As Ribbentrop wrote in mid-October: "The German-Italian alliance is and always has been the basis of our foreign policy."

In private Hitler regretted the Italians' kid-glove treatment of the Serbs. Only brute force bereft of inhibitions would work—just as only brute force would work in the war against the partisans in Russia. "On principle, when combatting illegals, anything that works is right—and I want that hammered into every- body," he laid down. "This gives everybody the freedom of action they need. . . . If the illegals use women and children as shields, then our officer or NCO must be able to open fire on them without hesitation. What matters is that he gets through and wipes out the illegals." Hitler wanted no "pedantic" disciplinary action against the officer afterward. Himmler took the hint. In August, Septem- ber, October, and November his security forces counted 1,337 dead Russian partisans and executed a further 8,564 taken prisoner. His report to Hitler for the same period listed 16,553 "partisan accomplices and suspects" captured, of which 14,257 were executed; an additional 363,211 Russian Jews were claimed to have been executed under the same heading.

Hitler could look east without qualms. General Ruoff's Seventeenth Army was still struggling through the mountains toward Tuapse and the Black Sea. Yard by yard Stalingrad was being overrun. Soon his armies could have their well- earned winter respite. On October 14 he issued orders for winter positions to be built along the current front line—making rigorous use of prisoners, civilians, and women to aid in their construction. The next day Field Marshal von Richthofen, one of Hitler's favorite Luftwaffe commanders, called. Richthofen's diary reports: "The Führer was in good humor because of Stalingrad and of having got rid of Halder. Particularly affectionate to me . . . The Führer curses with vehemence (and justification) the name of List. My operational plans [in the Caucasus] are approved. I tell him something of our infantry weakness, our tactics, and above all our difficult terrain. Zeitler is stout and cheerful. . . ."

A few days later, Ruoff's campaign finally ground to a halt. In the last week of October the spirit of Paulus's troops in Stalingrad also flagged. Richthofen wrote: "The main reasons lie in the weariness of the combat troops and command- ers, and in the army's pedantic tolerance of a ration strength of twelve thousand men per division, of whom only a thousand are actually in the front line. . . . I tell Paulus of this, but he naturally doesn't agree." Zeitzler still spoke highly of Paulus to Hitler. But on October 26 he admitted at Hitler's war conference: "In the Sixth Army's view the enemy's resistance at Stalingrad is so stiff that the fighting will not result in the city's capture until November 10."

The capture of the Caucasian oil fields was impossible before winter, so on October 7, Hitler had ordered the Luftwaffe to destroy the Soviet oil fields around Saratov and Grozny. Two weeks later he added Astrakhan and Baku to the target lists. Maykop had been in German hands since August, but it was a shambles—the oil wells either blown up or cemented over. The army's petroleum brigade reported that a year's reconstruction effort would be needed. Now Hitler was told that much more convenient oil fields were available in the Taman peninsula. For three months the petroleum brigade had done virtually nothing at Maykop on the blithe assumption that Baku and Grozny would shortly be in German hands. After Hitler's orders for the bombing and sabotage of those oil fields, the severity of the oil crisis became apparent to everybody. The Italian navy shrieked for more oil without satisfactorily explaining what it had done with the thousands of tons Germany had already supplied. The German admiralty pointed out that the transfer of the *Scharnhorst, Nürnberg, Prinz Eugen,* and *Lützow* to Norway would alone cost nine thousand tons of fuel oil, leaving only one thousand tons for actual operations in November and two thousand tons in December.

German manpower was an equally scarce war commodity. Industry relied on the 6,000,000 foreign workers procured by Hitler's labor dictator, Fritz Sauckel —but while Sauckel insisted they must be properly fed, the local Gauleiters often thought differently. Speer promised to raise three divisions from German munitions workers, but he shortly reduced his offer to only a quarter of the 50,000 men he originally spoke of; the divisions never actually materialized. The army itself was 1,000,000 men under strength. Not so the Luftwaffe: Hitler had always believed its strength was only 1,600,000 men—now he learned that it was bloated to 1,980,000 men in anticipation of the doubling of its squadron strength, something long since abandoned by Hitler as impracticable. Hitler ordered both the navy and the Luftwaffe to transfer manpower to the anemic army, but Göring decided instead to create twenty Luftwaffe "field divisions" rather than see his airmen forced into the army's reactionary field-gray ranks. Thus to satisfy Göring's stubborn vanity 220,000 of his troops were to find themselves fighting —often at the most crucial sectors—inadequately trained and with no combat experience.

Coupled with these manpower and materials shortages was the complete bankruptcy of Hitler's Intelligence services by the autumn of 1942. Colonel Reinhard

Gehlen's army Intelligence consistently predicted until early November that the Russian offensive would open not in the south but against Smolensk or even Velikiye Luki, on the northern front. Admiral Wilhelm Canaris's Abwehr produced equally convincing evidence that the Allies were planning a Second Front not, for example, in North Africa, but against the Cherbourg peninsula. As General Fromm—responsible for raising the new divisions—commented, "If the attacks on Cherbourg and Velikiye Luki coincide, they may cost us the war." Moreover, Hitler was still misled as to Stalin's coming strength. (On October 21, Keitel said, "The Führer is convinced the Russians are collapsing. He says that twenty million will have to starve.") The first three Luftwaffe field divisions were sent to Velikiye Luki, as were sections of the Eleventh Army—which meant finally abandoning the assault on Leningrad. But a Russian attack on Smolensk would be even more likely, in Hitler's view, so he transferred the Seventh Air Division paratroops and the 20th Panzer Division there as well. These were fatal errors.

Yet Hitler did not accept Gehlen's judgment willingly. By October 26 he was clearly rattled by concrete evidence of Russian plans to cross the Don just where the Axis front was weakest—held only by the reluctant Italians and Romanians. The army group interpreted the dense night traffic toward Serafimovich as unimportant replenishments, but when the enemy started constructing heavy bridges across the Don, Hitler knew differently; he had built bridges across rivers himself and knew what it presaged. He ordered more Luftwaffe field divisions moved into the endangered Italian and Romanian sectors. He was convinced Stalin planned to strike westward toward Rostov—and strike before 1942 was over! The General Staff disagreed. On November 6, Gehlen insisted there were no signs of any Soviet offensive in the south in the near future; far more likely was a drive against Smolensk, followed by a thrust to the Baltic to cut off the whole of Army Group North. Thus the Russians would wipe out the threat to Moscow and win a prestige victory relatively easily, while in the south the logistical and transport difficulties would surely dissuade them. Nor, stated Gehlen, would the Russian offensive begin before the ground froze over. He was to prove wrong on all counts.

Hitler also saw no cause to suspect that the Mediterranean theater would soon be in an uproar. In mid-October indications had multiplied that the Allies might invade West Africa; however, the OKW considered this unlikely before spring. But the Führer's agents in Spain could see the Allied shipping build up at Gibraltar, and this indicated some operation *within* the Mediterranean. Respect for Mussolini's feelings figured among his reasons for not reinforcing the Vichy French forces in French North Africa. The Italians were less sanguine and actively prepared to invade Tunisia (a French domain) the moment the enemy should arrive.

Rommel was in Germany on sick leave. He had told Hitler that the El Alamein position was virtually impregnable. But late on October 23, General Montgomery launched a massive and unheralded attack with 150,000 men supported by over 1,000 tanks and 800 planes. The Axis was outnumbered nearly 2 to 1. Rommel's stand-in was killed by a heart attack and by the next day one panzer division had only 31 of its 119 tanks left. The enemy's American Sherman tank seemed invincible. Rommel, who hurried back to Africa, found his army's fuel and ammunition almost at an end. Despite the Luftwaffe's around-the-clock bombing of Malta, the Axis supply convoys to North Africa had been cut to pieces. The Italian sectors of Rommel's front dissolved overnight; tens of thousands surrendered to the British. His supplies dried up. The Luftwaffe commander in the Mediterranean wrote in his diary: "The blackest day was October 26: a big tanker and a smaller merchantman were sunk just short of Tobruk after we had escorted them successfully for two days. Thus a crisis of undreamed-of proportions has emerged for the panzer army. The failure of the Italian fighter escort is to blame—it just did not show up. . . . Kesselring came, worried out of his mind. Lunch was like in a mortuary. . . . Everybody's hopes were pinned on the second tanker, which sailed on October 28. In the night it was reported sunk." On the thirty-first he wrote: "The situation at the front is slightly better. The British have taken some heavy blows and have to regroup. They will begin again in one or two days. A weak relief is the docking of the *Brioni* on the thirtieth, bringing some ammunition and fuel." Indeed, both Rommel and Kesselring—and the Italian High Command— were confident that the crisis had been overcome. Hitler willingly believed them.

In what now followed, the human element weighs as heavily as the military. Hitler was preoccupied by the eastern front; besides, his headquarters was in the midst of returning from the Ukraine to East Prussia—forty-nine trainloads of officers and men, machinery and paraphernalia. On November 2 all hell broke loose in North Africa again, as General Montgomery hurled his tanks and artillery against Rommel's well-fortified minefields at El Alamein. The line was breached, and enemy armor began to pour through. In his interim report, received by the OKW that evening, Rommel suddenly sounded despondent and anxious:

> Despite today's defensive success, the army's strength is exhausted after ten days' tough fighting against British ground and air forces many times its superior. Therefore the army will no longer be capable of impeding the strong enemy tank formations expected to repeat their breakthrough attempt tonight or tomorrow. For want of motor transport it will not be possible for the six Italian and two German nonmotorized divisions to withdraw in good order. A large part of these units will probably fall into the hands of the enemy's mechanized formations. But even our mobile troops are embroiled in such heavy fighting that only part will be able to disengage themselves from the enemy. Such ammunition stocks as there are lie close to the front lines, while

in the rear there are no stocks worth talking of. Our meager fuel supplies will not permit any withdrawals over long distances. It is certain that the army will be attacked day and night by the British air force on the one road available to it.

In this situation the gradual destruction of the army must therefore be assumed as inevitable, despite the heroic resistance and exemplary spirit of the troops.

sgd. ROMMEL, *Field Marshal*

At II P.M. Hitler telephoned Jodl's staff officer, Colonel Christian, to ask if there was any more news from Rommel, and to check with Rome to find out. There was no news. In North Africa, however, Rommel had succumbed to a black despair. Still a sick man and cowed by the ceaseless British bombardment, he had already ordered his army to abandon El Alamein—without notifying anybody to that effect. The retreat began at 10 P.M. To cover himself, Rommel later dispatched to his superiors a lengthy but seemingly routine daily report, near the end of which he surreptitiously buried the announcement that he had bowed before the enemy's strength and would withdraw from El Alamein the next day, November 3: "The infantry divisions will already be withdrawn during the coming night, November 2–3." To announce a strategic decision in such a furtive way was, as Jodl's deputy, Warlimont, later pointed out, against all accepted military usage. The result was that Rommel's illicit retreat was already twelve hours old when Hitler first learned of it.

At midnight, Rome advised Colonel Christian that the routine report from Rommel was just being decoded, and it arrived by teletype at the Führer's headquarters at 3 A.M. But Jodl's night duty officer, an elderly major of the reserve, overlooked the vital sentence announcing the retreat and left the report unforwarded until morning. It was belatedly rushed over to Hitler at 9 A.M.: thus he was awakened with the news that Rommel was retreating. In the angry scene that followed, he blamed Keitel in particular for the OKW's lackadaisical attitude. For a time he suspected that the OKW had deliberately sat on Rommel's report in order to confront him with a *fait accompli* in Africa. "At this critical moment Rommel turned to me and the Fatherland!" he exclaimed. "We should have been stiffening his resolve. If I'd been awakened I would have taken full responsibility and ordered him to stand fast. But our Mr. Warlimont is snug asleep while Rommel is appealing to me!"

Hitler believed he could still give Rommel—a sensitive, almost childlike personality—the inspiration he seemed to be begging for. While the chief of the Italian *comando supremo* signaled Rommel to hold the El Alamein position "whatever the cost," at 1 P.M. on November 3 Hitler radioed to Rommel the following message, finely attuned to the susceptibilities of the field marshal:

With me the entire German people is watching your heroic defensive battle in Egypt, with rightful confidence in your leadership qualities and the courage of your German and Italian troops. In your situation there can be no thought but of persevering, of yielding not one yard, and of hurling every gun and every fighting man available into the battle. Considerable air force reinforcements are being transferred over the coming days to Commander in Chief South [Kesselring]. The Duce and the *comando supremo* will also do their utmost to furnish you with the means to keep up the fight.

Despite his superiority the enemy must also be at the end of his strength. It would not be the first time in history that the stronger will has triumphed over the stronger battalions of an enemy. To your troops therefore you can offer no other path than that leading to Victory or Death.

sgd. ADOLF HITLER

The night duty officer was fetched. Hitler questioned him in person, warning, "If you don't tell me the absolute truth, I'll have you dead inside ten minutes!" Rommel also was interrogated by radio, asked to state the precise time that the infantry retreat had begun. He radioed back: "In the latter part of the night"— so it seemed that, but for the report's inexcusable delay, Hitler could still have stepped in to forbid the retreat. Punishment was swift: the major was reduced to the ranks and sent to the front; his superior, Warlimont, was evicted from the OKW and the Führer's headquarters that same day. But Rommel's reply was, of course, a lie: his retreat had begun at 10 P.M., before his report had been dispatched. On Schmundt's insistence, Warlimont was reinstated, and even the major's lapse was not held against him long.

Another field marshal would have paid dearly for this deceit. Guderian had been sacked, Hoepner discharged from the army, and Sponeck condemned to death for just such actions as this. But by adroit public relations Rommel had developed a charisma which made even a popular dictator hesitate to take disciplinary action.

Rommel wavered throughout the day. He rescinded his order to retreat, but already it was too late. Half his troops and 40 percent of his artillery were lost. As November 3 ended, he had only twenty-four tanks left. The next day he and Kesselring reported separately that the battlefront no longer existed, and formally asked permission to revert to "mobile warfare," defending every foot of ground until the new line at Fûka was reached. Hitler sourly replied that evening, "In view of the way things have gone, I approve your decision." He had no choice, though privately he doubted Rommel could hold the Fûka or any other line. He felt Rommel's nerve had failed him.[2] Two years later he brooded: "He should have stood his ground up front [at El Alamein], that was his only chance of saving

[2]See Hitler's remark in December 1942, page 460. Throughout November, Rommel's private letters betrayed an increasing despondency. On December 11 he actually wrote his wife: ". . . I would be grateful if you would send me by secret courier a small English-German dictionary. I think I'm going to need it."

anything. He didn't compensate for the enemy's superiority of numbers by heading for the wide-open spaces—that was where their superiority really began to take effect. At that bottleneck, just forty miles across, you could just about survive an attack. But the moment you were forced out and lost the cover of the [Qattara] depression to your left, all the lessons of desert warfare showed you were liable to be leapfrogged again and again by the enemy. . . ." Too late, Hitler ordered reinforcements rushed to North Africa—the deadly Tiger tanks, guns, ammunition, fuel, two fighter squadrons from Russia, and a bomber squadron from Norway. These steps "would have brought far more realistic relief if only one-quarter fulfilled two weeks ago, than at this present juncture of the battle," a local Luftwaffe commander observed. In Africa a rout that was to end dismally in Tunis six months later had begun.

Hitler's attention was still captured by events in the east, where he feared his armies were about to lose the initiative. As the rumored Russian offensive against Velikiye Luki in the far north failed to materialize, he began to plan his own attack, now that he had been duped into moving his reserves up there.

While at the southern end of the front the First Panzer Army's advance on Ordzhonikidze was going well, in Stalingrad the infantry was losing heart. Perhaps Paulus himself was to blame. Field Marshal von Richthofen was to note in his diary in mid-November:

> . . . Telephoned Zeitzler about the need for really energetic leadership in the battle for Stalingrad, or for the attack to be called off otherwise. If the mopping-up is not done now, with the Volga icing over and the Russians in Stalingrad in dire distress, we will never pull it off. Besides, the days are getting shorter and the weather worse. Zeitzler promised to tell the Führer; he shares my view. During the night a Führer Order came to the Sixth Army in line with my telephone suggestion. But I still don't think it will work. I stressed to Zeitzler that the commanders and combat troops in Stalingrad are so apathetic that only the injection of a new spirit will get us anywhere. I suggested the commanders—who are otherwise trustworthy enough—should be sent on leave for a while to let very different types take their place. But "up top" there isn't the toughness for that.

As with Rostov the year before, the sheer size of Stalingrad had taken Hitler by surprise; it sprawled over an area about the distance from Berlin to Brandenburg. But he accepted Paulus's assurances that the battle was all but won.

Hitler was still hypnotized by the obvious Russian preparations north of Stalingrad. The OKW historian recorded: "War conference with Führer on November 2: . . . The Russian attack feared across the Don toward Rostov is again discussed. More and more Russian bridges are being built there. The Luftwaffe is to submit reconnaissance mosaics. The Führer orders very heavy air attacks on the bridge sites and troop assembly areas suspected in the forests on the other river bank." On the fifth the historian noted: "According to Chief of General Staff [Zeitzler], a council of war was attended by all supreme commanders in Moscow on November 4: the Big Push is apparently planned for the Don or central fronts before this year is out." Soon after, two thousand enemy vehicles were glimpsed massing north of Kletskaya, and the headquarters of a new Russian army group, the "Southwest Front," was detected at nearby Serafimovich. But even now Gehlen's estimate was that the Russians just planned to cut the one railroad supplying Paulus's army in Stalingrad from the west.

Hitler feared that Stalin was capable of more.

Before this fear materialized, momentous events occurred in the Mediterranean, shaking the Axis partnership to its very foundations.

Throughout October the Abwehr and SS Intelligence agencies had been swamped with "enemy invasion plans." Some spoke of Norway, others of the Channel coast or the Mediterranean. Hitler intuitively believed only the latter: as the Italian divisions marched into enemy captivity in Egypt, Mussolini's prestige was already crumbling. Air raids on Italian towns had sapped morale. A further military setback in the Mediterranean might force Italy out of the war—indeed, diplomatic sources in Rome detected the first neutralist undercurrents in government circles there. The whiff of treason was already in the air. Hitler's military liaison reported on November 6 that Mussolini thought the time now ripe to make amends to Stalin. Small wonder that Hitler believed he could postpone his next meeting with the tired and ailing Fascist dictator no longer, urgently though he himself was needed at his East Prussian headquarters.

Besides, he had gradually become aware that an immense fleet of ships was assembling at Gibraltar, a fleet far bigger than the harbor at Malta could accommodate; so this was no mere supply convoy. Hitler had recently suspected that the enemy would invade Sardinia or Corsica prior to striking at the Italian mainland itself. Much of the Luftwaffe's strength had been withdrawn eastward from Sicily, but Hitler had ordered all available German submarines to the western Mediterranean. As late as November 4 the navy would have none of this, insisting that the enemy was just preparing to fight a big supply convoy through to Malta. If this was an invasion fleet, where were the troop transports? On the sixth they changed their tune. The armada had sailed, and Italian Intelligence now reported what the German Abwehr had not—that the vessels had trucks and invasion tackle on their decks and they were joining convoys of ships streaming eastward through the Strait of Gibraltar. The navy judged that the enemy planned to invade Libya, in Rommel's rear; less likely targets would be Sicily, Sardinia, or the Italian mainland; French North Africa was considered least likely of all, as the enemy would hardly drive France into Hitler's arms. Though both Mussolini and the Luftwaffe believed an enemy invasion of Algeria far more likely—beyond the range of Axis air power—Hitler had by November 7 bowed to the navy's judgment that the likely targets were Tripoli or Benghazi, and he ordered emergency measures there, including street barricades.

He personally radioed to the handful of submarines and torpedo boats in the Mediterranean: "Army's survival in Africa depends on destruction of British naval forces. I expect determined, victorious attack." But the navy had stationed these ships in the central Mediterranean, far to the east of where the enemy's invasion designs lay. The failure of Hitler's Intelligence service was thus to cost many German lives over the months to come.

Early on the afternoon of November 7, 1942, Hitler's train left Rastenburg for Berlin and Munich—where he was to meet the Italians.

At a 7 P.M. war conference, Jodl briefed him on the latest position of the enemy armada in the Mediterranean: it was still heading due east and would probably pass through the Strait of Sicily. But one of the last Intelligence reports had mentioned Oran as an invasion target, and Hitler's ears had pricked up at this, for Oran would lie outside Axis aircraft range. Toward the end of the conference, the naval staff telephoned Hitler's train with confirmation: from the armada's 6 P.M. position and the ships' speeds, the Italians deduced that it *must* be an invasion of Algeria—they would hardly risk forcing the Strait of Sicily in broad daylight. Hitler accepted this calculation. It was a bitter pill to swallow, and his disappointment at his Intelligence agencies must have been profound. But he remained outwardly calm and detached.

His train was halted by a signal at a little railroad station deep in the Thuringian forest. Walther Hewel was called to the stationmaster's telephone—the foreign ministry was on the line. British radio stations were announcing that an American invasion force was disembarking at Algiers, Oran, and Casablanca.[3]

---

[3]The various enemy invasion convoys had suddenly headed sharply south, soon after the Italian sighting at 6 P.M. As Hitler sourly pointed out in April 1944: "The few invasions they have carried out so far completely escaped our notice. . . . Take the North African invasion!" And Keitel agreed: "We were saying right up to the last moment that they'd sail on through. Their vanguard was off Sicily, and we said they were going right on through. Then all at once they made a right-about turn and did a beeline for the shore."

Before the train moved off, Hitler ordered all the necessary countermeasures put into effect. In a speech some hours later, President Roosevelt was heard justifying the invasion action as being necessary to thwart a threatened invasion by the Axis. Roosevelt appealed to the Vichy French forces not to resist, but the aged Marshal Pétain, deeply shaken by Roosevelt's "perfidy," ordered his troops to defend France's African possessions to the bitter end.

Ribbentrop could not be reached, so at 2:30 P.M. Hitler ordered the train stopped again, and Walther Hewel telephoned to the foreign ministry the text of urgent new instructions that Hitler wanted transmitted immediately to Ambassador Otto Abetz in France:

> Ambassador Abetz is to approach the French government immediately and is to inquire whether they are seriously willing to fight with us against the British and Americans. This would entail that France not only break off diplomatic relations with those two countries, but also declare war on them as if she had been attacked by an enemy. If the French government makes an unambiguous declaration like this, then we would be ready to go through thick and thin with the French government.

At Bamberg railroad station, shortly before Munich, Ribbentrop stepped aboard Hitler's train. He had hastily flown down from Berlin after arranging for Count Ciano to come at once to Munich—Mussolini being indisposed. Hitler wanted to discuss this new opportunity of reversing Germany's policies toward France, but Ribbentrop brimmed with gloomier topics. From the latest Allied figures on the size of their invasion fleet, it was obvious the Germans had overestimated their U-boats' abilities to strangle the western powers. The entire Axis position in the Mediterranean was endangered—unless Hitler could let up on commitments elsewhere. "Give me permission to put out peace feelers to Stalin, via his ambassadress in Stockholm, Madame Kollontay," appealed Ribbentrop, "even if we have to sacrifice virtually everything we have conquered in the east!" Hitler rose angrily to his feet, reddened, and refused to discuss anything but North Africa. A momentary military weakness was no time in which to put out peace feelers to an enemy poised to strike.

At 3:40 P.M. on the eighth, the train pulled into Munich. As always the actual occurrence of the feared event had lifted the torturing burden of uncertainty and indecision. At last he knew where the Second Front was—and it was not the European mainland. Now he must airlift troops to Tunisia to bar the American advance. Now the Italians must occupy Corsica. Now Germany must make Crete the mightiest bastion of Axis power in the Mediterranean. Now France must join the Axis cause.

At six o'clock, in a buoyant mood, he delivered his anniversary speech to the

Party's Old Guard at the Löwenbräukeller. Two passages of the rambling, defiant rhetoric need quoting here. In the first he reminded them of his 1939 Reichstag prophecy concerning the fate of the Jews. "Of those who laughed then, countless already laugh no longer today; and those who still laugh today will probably not laugh much longer either." The second passage he must later have regretted; too willingly believing a message from General Georg von Sodenstern, Chief of Staff of Army Group B, that Stalingrad was virtually theirs, Hitler boasted: "I wanted to reach the Volga—at a particular spot, at a particular city. By coincidence it is blessed with Stalin's name . . . it is a vitally important city, because there you can cut off thirty million tons of river transport, including nine million tons of oil, it is there that the grain of the mighty Ukrainian and Kuban regions flows in for transportation to the north, there the manganese ore is processed—it was a huge shipment complex. That was what I wanted to capture, and, do you know, modest as we are—we've got it too! There are only a few more tiny pockets! Now some may say, 'Then why don't you fight faster?'—Because I don't want a second Verdun, that's why." Unable to eat his words just two weeks later, Hitler found himself politically committed to a strategy in Stalingrad which increasingly proved to be untenable.

Hitler's newfound fondness toward the French, inspired by glowing accounts of the fierce fight put up by French warships defending Casablanca and Oran against the American invaders, lasted less than one day. As the hours of November 9 ticked away he began to suspect that the French commanders were trying to make a deal with the enemy, if indeed they had not clandestinely done so long before. On the eighth he had still believed General Henri-Honoré Giraud to be in France; the next day he found out that Giraud had slipped across to Africa aboard an enemy submarine to act for Eisenhower in Algiers. Admiral Darlan, the French Supreme Commander, had "by chance" been in Algiers for some days and appeared to be directing the French resistance, which in the port itself collapsed on the first evening. But Hitler believed that Darlan and General Alphonse Juin were still loyal—perhaps they were in enemy hands and being forced to issue the cease-fire orders to their troops.

Giraud's switch to the Allies was too blatant to ignore, however. Captured in May 1940, he had broken parole two years later and escaped to unoccupied France, where he had resisted Hitler's blandishments to "do the decent thing" and report back to the prison camp. The reprisals that his behavior had inflicted on his fellow officers in German hands failed to make Giraud reconsider. He gave his word to Hitler's emissary that he would never go to North Africa but would remain in unoccupied France. He gave his written undertaking to Marshal Pétain to do nothing against Germany. All these promises Giraud had now broken.

Hitler's fury at Giraud's escape to Africa was matched by his contempt for Himmler's secret agents who had constantly shadowed him but failed to prevent it.[4]

By the time Count Ciano was ushered into his study at the Führer Building in Munich late on the ninth, profusely apologizing for Mussolini's inability to leave Rome, Hitler's old hostility toward France had rekindled in full. He barked at the Italian foreign minister that he had decided to occupy the rest of France —the French were incorrigible, they would never learn to love either the Germans or the Italians. An Axis bridgehead must be established in Tunisia forthwith. Whatever France's Premier Laval—due at 10 P.M.—might say, Hitler's mind was already made up. His troops were already massing along the demarcation line in France. "Strike, strike, strike!"—It was the old Prussian remedy when all else failed.

Laval was delayed by fog; his car arrived in the small hours of the night. Hitler postponed seeing him throughout the tenth, as the mists in North Africa were clearing. He was seen deep in conference with Ribbentrop, Himmler, and the generals. Himmler's files bulge with the Intelligence reports the SS put to Hitler that day: his agents at Vichy had intercepted Darlan's message to Pétain during the night demanding the execution of renegade officers. But Darlan seemed to be playing a double game, for the SS agents also learned that French reserve officers were being called up, that Darlan's staff was preparing to leave Vichy, and that all his war ministry files were being burned. General Auguste Noguès, the French resident-general in Morocco, was believed to be making a deal with the Americans. At midday, Darlan's name appeared on an order for all resistance to cease. For twenty-four hours, Hitler continued to hope that Darlan's name was being abused by the enemy. But Pétain broadcast Darlan's dismissal early that afternoon, November 10, which strongly suggested that Darlan *was* a traitor to the Axis cause. The luckless Pierre Laval was received now with barely concealed brusqueness. Hitler told him of his demands for immediate access to Tunis. Laval temporized and was coldly ushered out.[5] At twenty past eight that evening Hitler issued the order for his troops to occupy a Tunis bridgehead and the rest of France the next morning. It stated that as far as the French authorities were concerned "the occupation is being carried out in accord with the wishes of the French

[4]One of the many legends created by the postwar trial at Nuremberg is that Hitler ordered Keitel to arrange for the assassination of Giraud. No documentary evidence whatever has come to light for this. Hitler's contempt for governments that worked by assassination *is* well-documented, curiously enough—though in his own mind he evidently considered it proper to liquidate those he considered guilty of criminal treason, for example, Ernst Röhm or Otto Strasser. It is a fine distinction.

[5]According to Jodl's naval staff officer—though not according to the official record of the meeting —"Laval was willing at Munich to request us to march in, *à la Hácha;* but only if the Italians would not march in too, and that was the end of that idea."

government." "Just like 'Otto' in 1938?" the Luftwaffe generals in Paris asked General Jeschonnek in Munich. "Jawohl, just like Austria."

This time there were no cheering crowds. In southern France the occupation was greeted with a mixture of apathy and official correctness. The real French hatred was reserved for the Italians occupying Corsica and the Riviera—with a sluggishness that infuriated Hitler—and arriving in Tunisia in the wake of the Germans. The Italians in southern France had far overstepped the lines agreed on with the French. Hitler learned that Laval had been overheard on the twelfth shouting into a telephone that if Italy did not withdraw her troops in twenty-four hours he would declare war on her! This was a feud Hitler wanted to keep out of, and when Göring asked if German antiaircraft guns could be stationed in the new Italian zone, he would not hear of it: the German and Italian zones must be clearly separated by the Rhone. The Italian antics drove Hitler's last few supporters in France into open hostility and defection. But a member of Jodl's staff reported late on November 14: "The Führer's actions are governed by his consideration for Italy. He believes it absolutely vital to bolster the Duce in every way we can, and this is why he categorically refuses to oppose Italy's claim to leadership in the Mediterranean, including the coast of southern France, or to present the Italians with *faits accomplis.*"

"Operation Brown," the hasty creation of an Axis bridgehead in Tunisia, was going well, but on November 12 the French forces in North Africa capitulated to the enemy. Upon Darlan's recognition by the Allies the next day as French head of state there, his defection could be doubted no longer. Hitler realistically assumed that no Frenchman could be trusted to collaborate with him. For two weeks, however, he simulated trust in the French navy. He had no option, as he had no *military* means of detaining the French fleet of three battleships, an aircraft carrier, and over thirty destroyers at Toulon; he therefore accepted perforce the loyal promises of the navy's senior admirals not to open hostile action against the Axis and to defend Toulon themselves to the best of their ability; in return, Hitler excluded Toulon from occupation by the Italians. For a brief period a regular French infantry division defending the coast between Toulon and Marseilles actually came under German command. But Hitler silently prepared for the worst. A Luftwaffe general noted on November 16: "The Führer fears the French will create an enclave paving the way for an Anglo-American invasion; that must be prevented." Intercepted telephone conversations of French naval officers revealed that the renegade Admiral Darlan was secretly being toasted in Paris as a national hero. The Germans also learned to their chagrin that the apparently senile Pétain could have been communicating secretly with Darlan all the time by underwater cable; so much for his protestations of loyalty broadcast by radio! Hitler ordered the Luftwaffe's bomber and minelaying squadrons to stand by on two hours' notice in case the French fleet suddenly set sail, and on November 18 he decided to make a clean sweep—all Pétain's armed forces were to be disarmed, and the Toulon enclave overrun. A date eight days hence was set for "Operation Lilac." Mussolini was not informed (Hitler wanted absolute secrecy); but in spite of Raeder's frantic objections, Hitler stipulated that the Italians should nonetheless be given the Toulon dockyard and the French fleet —or whatever remained of it.[6] "Lilac" began before dawn on the twenty-seventh; by noon the French fleet no longer existed, its battleships blazing, stranded hulks, all but a handful of the rest scuttled or blown up by their crews. Hitler gave the Italians the wreckage to pick over. The French people seemed undistressed. They had lost their army, their navy, and their empire; "America will see us through all right," was the average Frenchman's philosophical belief. Throughout occupied France new painted slogans appeared overnight on a thousand walls: *Vive l'Amérique!* and patriotically, *1918!*. Germany's defeat was regarded as a certainty now.

All this was reported to Hitler. By now he had resigned himself to a long stay in south Germany and was living at the Berghof. Snow gripped the mountains as far as the eye could see. He badly needed respite. North Africa was causing ominous rumblings everywhere. Even neutral Sweden was becoming rambunctious, and the partisans in the Balkans were encouraged to redouble their insurgency. In Germany the public stoically steeled itself for eventual defeat. East Prussia would fall to Poland or even Russia; Germany would be maimed and dismembered. The diplomats again hinted that this was their last chance to extend feelers toward Stalin—while the Red Army was still being held at bay. Hitler hesitated. That a huge Russian offensive was coming he knew—but surely it was not coming yet. How else could he interpret the army's Intelligence reports? There was still time!

But there was not. On November 19, 1942, the phone rang at the Berghof and General Zeitzler, the army's Chief of Staff fighting an almost forgotten war from his headquarters in East Prussia, came on the line. A heavy artillery bombardment had begun on the Don front north of Stalingrad; it had become a saturation barrage, and now masses of tanks, black with Russian troops, were swarming forward. The Romanians were in full flight. It was all happening just where Hitler had predicted. The next day another offensive started, this time south of the city. Two days later Stalingrad was encircled, and the fiercest drama of the war began.

---

[6]Hitler also ordered all stores and ships at Marseilles turned over to Italy, except for oil dumps. Italy's oil demands were a sore point, especially since Raeder had learned that the last five thousand tons he had sacrificed to Italy had been deliberately contaminated with gasoline to render it unfit for the Italian navy's use—though suitable for civilian purposes. After Italy's defection in 1943, the Germans discovered tens of thousands of tons of oil secretly hoarded by the Italians.

PART 4

TOTAL WAR

Trauma and Tragedy

Few events in World War II were to rouse greater controversy than Stalingrad; around even fewer was to be woven a more intricate, yet durable, fabric of lies and legends in the postwar years. This is, however, understandable, for Stalingrad marked the end of German military initiative in the east; it cost perhaps two hundred thousand German lives, and it exploded the dream of empire which had fired Hitler when he came to power ten years before.

German army Intelligence had consistently reported that the Red Army was on its last legs, yet Stalin continued producing unsuspected masses of tanks and infantry out of thin air. Jodl was seen, white-faced, exclaiming, "The Russians are stronger than in 1941!" Hitherto the Russian command had been wooden, hesitant, and bureaucratic. Now suddenly it was flexible, deliberate, and far-sighted, operating its tank forces as the Germans had in 1939, but with the entire might of the Soviet war potential behind them.

The blame for the disaster was diverted onto Hitler. In later years memoirs were fudged by field marshals, fake diaries were concocted, guilty sentences were expunged from the OKW's war diary, and "contemporary" judgments on Hitler's leadership were slotted in.[1]

Nobody had expected the Soviet offensive to begin so soon.

The Russians achieved tactical surprise as well through an uncharacteristic display of cunning. The very first word to reach Hitler was of two infantry assaults on the Romanian Third Army's sector—seemingly the usual enemy

---

[1]Thus in the published war diary of the OKW an account of a crucial argument between Hitler, Jeschonnek, and Zeitzler on December 21, 1942, at the height of the Stalingrad crisis, includes the following sentences: "As usual, however, again no bold decisions are taken. It is as though the Führer is no longer capable of doing so." These sentences are a 1945 fabrication not included in the 1942 text.

"spattering" without either tanks or artillery preparation; the Romanians were confident, even when a gradual artillery barrage did begin. No use was made of the panzer corps stationed in reserve behind them and commanded by General Ferdinand Heim. At 5 A.M. on November 19, however, a colossal Russian artillery barrage suddenly began, and at 7 A.M. wave upon wave of tanks laden with infantry assailed the Romanians. They fought heroically—three of the four Romanian generals were killed in enemy bayonet charges, and every Romanian company commander fell in the ensuing battle—but their military equipment was not good enough. A rout began. At 10:10 A.M. General von Weichs's Army Group B ordered Heim (Forty-eighth Panzer Corps) to counterattack to seal the worst breach, but by midnight it was clear that he could not. He had begun the day with the 22nd Panzer Division, the 1st Romanian Panzer Division, and a battlegroup of the 14th Panzer Division under his command: but the 22nd was still exhausted from the battle for Stalingrad itself; the battlegroup of the 14th was removed from his control during the day; and the Romanian 1st Panzer Division had evidently abandoned the field of battle—Heim had no idea where it was, because all attempts to raise it by radio remained unanswered.

Barely trained, and totally inexperienced of battle, the Romanians in the front line itself had no hope. Half their tanks were immobilized because field mice had made a meal of their wiring. The enlisted ranks lacked discipline, tending to stop work most afternoons at four. Weichs had hoped that they would hold the front long enough for Heim's corps to arrive, but they did not, and their headlong flight barred the advance of Heim's tanks. Still searching for his own missing 1st Romanian Panzer Division, Heim was further beset by appalling weather—by freezing fog and rain, by sleet and snow. Weichs ordered him to go over to the defensive that evening.

Zeitzler, calling from East Prussia, had scarcely been off the telephone to Hitler at the Berghof since the crisis began. Hitler clearly realized it as such, although the General Staff situation reports painted it in a misleadingly pastel hue. By 9:30 P.M. he had authorized Weichs to abandon all further assault operations in the city of Stalingrad so as to release forces to patch up the main front line. He also ordered Field Marshal von Manstein to abandon the planned attack at Velikiye Luki and to establish a new army group on the Don, between Army Groups A and B, thus relieving Weichs of direct responsibility for the two Romanian armies, and for the Fourth Panzer Army and the Sixth Army at Stalingrad. He was furious at Heim's "delay" in launching the counterattack, and during the night he ordered him to attack again regardless of any risk to his flanks and rear. On Hitler's charts the panzer corps was a thick blue circle boasting of over a hundred tanks. Again Heim failed. This time his corps was engulfed in the Russian flood and extricated its few remnants only with difficulty.

The Romanian Third Army evaporated. From Bucharest came the most indignant sounds. Hitler needed an immediate scapegoat; he ordered Keitel: "Send for General Heim at once. Strip him of his insignia and arrest him. He is to blame!" To appease Antonescu, Heim was sentenced to death some months later, but when Schmundt, Hitler's chief Wehrmacht adjutant, reasoned with him, the Führer relented and commuted the sentence to a term of imprisonment.[2]

Such were the shocking events northwest of Stalingrad. To the south of the city, a Russian bridgehead of equal menace had spewed forth hundreds of tanks on November 20. The enemy's preparations here had totally escaped detection until two days before. The eastern flank of the Fourth Panzer Army had withstood the blow, but three adjacent Romanian divisions crumpled with scarcely a sigh. By the twenty-first it was clear that the two great pincer arms of the Red Army offensive would join around Stalingrad the next day unless the weather cleared long enough for the Luftwaffe to strike.

It was natural that the endangered Sixth Army should see its survival as depending on an airlift. When he arrived at Berchtesgaden on November 20 from his headquarters in East Prussia, the Luftwaffe's Chief of Staff, Jeschonnek, certainly did not reject the idea—if he had, Hitler would subsequently have acted very differently in the view of his Luftwaffe adjutant Major von Below. A hundred thousand men had been successfully sustained in the Demyansk pocket for many months the previous winter by such an airlift; in addition, Richthofen's squadrons had regularly airlifted fuel to the southern front during the summer—as well as engineer battalions and antiaircraft batteries to the Sixth Army—to compensate for the inadequate railroad supplies. On the afternoon of the twenty-first, Hitler therefore decided the Sixth Army must stand fast "despite the danger of its temporary encirclement"; the railroad line was to be held open as long as possible. "As to airlift, orders will follow." With Jodl he meanwhile discussed ways and means of rushing reinforcements to Weichs's army group.

Loud and weighty objections were raised against the airlift idea. Richthofen telephoned Göring, Zeitzler, and Weichs that there were not nearly enough transport aircraft for an airlift. (Transport squadrons were heavily committed in the Mediterranean.) His subordinates seconded his objections. The Sixth Army would need many hundreds of tons of food, oil, and ammunition airlifted to it every day. Ever since July it had been living from hand to mouth; it needed nine or ten supply trains daily, but in the twenty-four hours before the only railroad

---

[2]In 1944 Hitler authorized Heim's "rehabilitation" as commandant of a beleaguered Channel port; to his chagrin the general surrendered the port to the Allies without much ado, and Hitler decided not to allow other army "delinquents" a second chance in the future.

line was cut not one train had got through. Hitler, however, neither saw nor sought any alternative: in his speeches of September 30 and November 8 he had committed himself before the entire German nation—he could not relax his grip on Stalingrad and the Volga now. Late on the twenty-first he again ordered Paulus to hold on.

At what stage Hitler consulted Göring on an airlift is uncertain. Jeschonnek, prompted by Richthofen's remonstrances and the gloomy calculations of his own staff, very shortly reversed his opinion. But Hitler telephoned Göring, and the Reichsmarschall assured him the Luftwaffe would do all in its power to meet the army's needs. (Göring later explained to Richthofen: "The Führer was optimistic. What right had I to be the pessimist?") It is improbable that Göring gave his assurance unconditionally; but then Hitler himself expected the encirclement to last only temporarily—until the damaged army group front had been repaired and the infiltrating enemy annihilated. Late on the twenty-second, Paulus radioed that the Sixth Army was encircled: his ammunition and food stocks would soon be exhausted, and his fuel would last only six more days. (Since his trapped army was to survive for two more months, Paulus seems to have painted a deliberately dark picture; Hitler may have taken this into account.)

At midday on November 22 Hitler had realized he could postpone his return to East Prussian headquarters no longer. At five to ten that evening his train left Berchtesgaden station. Keitel, Jodl, Jeschonnek, and the adjutants accompanied him. Foul weather evidently prevented him from taking his plane at Leipzig, and for a whole day he was confined to the train as it headed for the Wolf's Lair. Every four hours or so the train was halted for brief telephone contact to be established with General Staff headquarters. While Hitler strolled about or looked gloomily out of the windows, Keitel and Jodl inked the latest grim details onto the Stalingrad chart; as soon as the train jolted into motion again, Hitler came to see and hear the worst for himself. Hitler and Jodl began elaborating a daring plan for General Hoth's Fourth Panzer Army to attack the encircling ring and thus relieve Stalingrad. It would take about ten days to prepare, but might inflict on the Russians just the defeat Hitler now gravely needed. When Zeitzler telephoned him during their next halt, imploring him to instruct the Sixth Army to abandon the Volga and break out westward before it was too late, Hitler rebuffed him. "We have thought of a new way out. Jodl will tell you. We will discuss it in person tomorrow."

Hitler arrived at his East Prussia headquarters late on November 23. Zeitzler was waiting outside his concrete bunker. The Führer stepped forward, his hand outstretched in welcome and a forced smile on his lips. "You have done all you could. I could not have done more myself had I been here." With calculated pathos he added, "One finds one's own true greatness in the hour of deepest misfortune—like Frederick the Great." Zeitzler was unimpressed and reported that the army group commander, Weichs, now shared his view that the Sixth Army was doomed if it held fast.[3] Hitler thumped his desk. "We are not budging from the Volga!" During the night Paulus radioed to Hitler a frantic appeal in the same sense: unless every division was withdrawn from Stalingrad, the army was doomed to "abrupt destruction." They would certainly lose most of their equipment, but at least they would save their troops. Hitler's reply was transmitted to Paulus in the early hours of the twenty-fourth: the Sixth Army was to stay where it was because an "airlift by a hundred more Junkers is getting under way."

The week that followed was ruled by Hitler's unshakable conviction that he was right; it would not be the first time that he alone had kept his head in a crisis. But optimism also prevailed around him—an optimism that has been effectively masked by postwar alteration of the few headquarters records that survive. Firstly, the military situation was not all but hopeless: reserves were moving up, ready for the relief offensive Manstein was to direct. Secondly, according to army Intelligence, Russian prisoners said that their officers were disconcerted by their own success so far and were wavering about how to proceed. Thirdly, the Sixth Army's supply position, on which the crisis hinged, was not as bad as feared (though the statistics on its needs, and even on its fighting strength, varied). On November 24 the army's quartermaster asked for 200 tons of fuel and 200 tons of ammunition a day, with an unspecified quantity of flour after the twenty-seventh. But on the twenty-fifth the OKW historian wrote that Paulus's "demand for 700 tons" was evidently exaggerated;[4] gradually the figure of 300 tons a day was accepted. Richthofen's objections that there were not enough Junkers available were disbelieved. His telephoned advice that the Sixth Army must break out to the southwest was discounted. "Führer gives me a good hearing," he wrote in his diary, "but decides against, as he believes army can hold on and does not think we would reach Stalingrad again." Richthofen's attempts to reach Göring failed: the Reichsmarschall was in Paris.[5] The air staff was evidently optimistic, for twice the OKW historian noted that 298 Junkers transport aircraft were available, with a daily capacity of 600 tons.[6] Admittedly few were reaching Stalingrad yet—only some 20 or 30 a day—but once the weather improved and the airlift got under

---

[3]According to Weichs's Chief of Staff, General von Sodenstern, in 1950, Zeitzler telephoned him at about 2 A.M. that he had at last managed to persuade Hitler to let the Sixth Army break out. But the promised order never came; Zeitzler had probably misinterpreted a remark by Hitler.

[4]Greiner, author of the OKW war diary, removed this sentence in 1945, and it does not appear in the text subsequently published.

[5]In his "diary" entry of November 25, 1942, Major Engel nonetheless transplanted Göring to the Wolf's Lair for a dramatic conference with Hitler!

[6]Greiner "improved" his record—with hindsight—in 1945 to read: "Only 298 transport planes are with the Fourth Air Force; about 500 are needed."

way things would be different; so Hitler was assured. On November 27 the OKW's note on Hitler's afternoon conference read: "Enemy's dispositions around Stalingrad could hardly be more favorable for Sixth Army's intentions. The Stalingrad food situation is better than we thought." Paulus's planned withdrawal of his northwestern front was going well. On the twenty-ninth, the conference record referred to Field Marshal von Manstein's appreciation of the situation: "Arrives at same conclusion as Führer."[7]

Manstein's opinion was highly valued by Hitler and unquestionably strengthened his determination here. On November 24, arriving at Weichs's operations room, Manstein had emphatically rejected the general's judgment that Paulus had no alternative but to abandon Stalingrad and break out; obviously a breakout was still possible and "the surest way"—Manstein's report said—and staying put was highly risky in view of the ammunition and fuel situations, but

> Nonetheless I am unable to share Army Group B's enthusiasm for a breakout as long as there are still adequate supplies—at least of armor-piercing ammunition, infantry ammunition, and fuel. This is vital.[8]

Manstein added that a relief operation would be possible with the reinforcements being moved up by the beginning of December; only if these latter movements were blocked by the enemy might a breakout by the Sixth Army become necessary; but he would ask for this only if "worse comes to worst." At the same time he radioed Paulus: "We shall do everything to hew you out of there." In a further report four days later Manstein added that the Sixth Army would need at least four hundred tons of supplies a day. But by this time Hitler's mind had long been made up.

Manstein himself was engrossed in planning a relief offensive by General Hoth from Kotelnikovo toward Stalingrad, but the forces placed at his disposal were steadily whittled away to buttress the vulnerable Italian and Hungarian sectors of the Don front north of Stalingrad. From November 28 onward the storm signs there multiplied—it was here that ever since mid-August Hitler had expected Stalin's strategic push toward Rostov to develop. Richthofen uncomfortably observed: "It seems the Russians are going to attack the Italian sector too—a bad thing, as they will probably run faster than the Romanians." He blamed Weichs's army group—and its Chief of Staff Sodenstern in particular—for treating these allies like the Cinderellas of the eastern front. Hitler, anxiously investigating the fighting fitness of the Italians and Hungarians, now observed that their provision

---

[7] This compromising sentence was omitted altogether by Greiner from his improved 1945 text.

[8] The original document has survived. In his published memoirs Manstein "improves" the damning wording I have quoted: Sixth Army should wait to be relieved, since its best chance of breaking out had passed, but *"only if"* it could be adequately supplied by air.

with antitank guns had been badly neglected; he ordered this omission repaired immediately from captured French stocks. Manstein, meanwhile, was optimistic. On December 9 he announced that the relief offensive would begin two or three days later; by the seventeenth it should have restored contact with Paulus's Sixth Army. Jodl's deputy dictated into the OKW war diary that day: "The Führer is very confident and plans to regain our former position on the Don. The first phase of the Russian winter offensive can be regarded as finished, without having shown any decisive successes." Jodl himself depicted Hitler's grand strategy in the east as to stabilize the front line for the winter so that he could resume the offensive in at least one sector in the spring of 1943.

Hitler contemplated minor losses of ground in the east philosophically. It would matter little in the end if his armies there were pressed back forty or eighty miles; but for the Axis to lose comparable ground in Europe would be catastrophic. This was why North Africa—as Europe's "outfield"—was significant. This was why he was pouring troops and armor, including the very latest Tiger tanks, into Tunis. No longer did he envisage an offensive by Rommel across the Suez Canal; Rommel was a write-off, a nervous wreck in need of rest and recuperation. To General Hans-Jürgen von Arnim, commanding the new Fifth Panzer Army in Tunisia, Hitler confided that eventually he planned to throw the enemy right out of Algeria and French Morocco. Early in December the Germans inflicted a convincing defeat on the British armor attempting to seize Tunisia. Here at least Hitler had the initiative. Seven months later he was to brag: "By occupying Tunisia we succeeded in postponing the invasion of Europe by half a year; and even more important, Italy has stayed in the Axis."

These were political considerations of which his generals had little understanding. On November 28, Rommel had arrived unannounced at the Wolf's Lair— with neither the knowledge nor consent of his Italian supreme commanders—and hinted bluntly that Hitler had best brace himself for the loss of Africa altogether. Hitler's reaction to this fresh insubordination was to humiliate the field marshal: when Rommel described the desperate retreat his men had fought across eight hundred miles of North Africa since El Alamein, and how his fifteen thousand combat troops had only five thousand rifles among them, Hitler shouted at him that the troops had thrown the other rifles away. When Rommel bitterly criticized the Italian supply shortcomings, particularly of gasoline, Hitler ordered Göring to escort him personally to Rome to speed up the shipments. He flatly refused Rommel's suggestion that his present stronghold at El Agheila be abandoned. He disbelieved Rommel's claim that he lacked the gasoline to fight on. "A giant army drove back on gasoline from El Alamein to here [El Agheila]," commented Hitler sarcastically later. "They didn't drive on water!"

Göring's visit to Rome was not an unqualified success. Mussolini accepted Rommel's opinion that in view of the two hundred miles of waterless desert behind it El Agheila could not be held for long. Kesselring, the German Commander in Chief South, was as optimistic as Rommel was pessimistic—indeed the latter openly wept on the shoulder of Milch, whom Göring had brought to Rome as well. The Reichsmarschall evidently spared no detail in his report to Hitler, but Hitler understood the strain that a long series of retreats—however brilliantly executed—had placed on Rommel's nerves. "Perhaps we should have recalled him right away and put a proper bulldog in his place with the strict order, 'You are to hold this position!' " As it happened, it was fortunate that Rommel did not stand and fight when the British assault on El Agheila began, for the enemy plan was to ambush him from the rear; but Rommel's army escaped in time and lived to fight another day.

Göring reported back to Hitler on December 11, but he had evidently telephoned the Führer the burden of his Rome impressions several days before. Mussolini was wallowing in despair—he had advised the Germans to wind up their pointless Russian campaign as best they could, to husband their depleted armies for what really mattered: the war in the Mediterranean. Hitler knew how precarious his ally's personal position now was. A series of enemy air raids had inflicted heavy casualties in Naples and Turin; but the population in West Germany had put up with far worse for far longer. But he was clearly worried that Italy might make a deal with the enemy even now is indicated by the fact that he ordered Kesselring to start stockpiling maps of Italy in case Germany had to take over her defense. And on December 6, SS channels had warned him of the latest secret peace deal offered by Myron Taylor, the American ambassador to the Vatican. Hitler decided to bluff. Kesselring was instructed to draw the Italian *comando supremo*'s attention to the grave disparity between the enemy's shipping effort to North Africa, and the Italians' effort, on which both Arnim and Rommel depended. On the "binding answer" the Italians gave would depend "far-reaching decisions" the Führer proposed to take—a clear hint that he might abandon North Africa entirely.

Hitler began planning on the ninth a lengthy sojourn at the Berghof "to clear his head for fresh decisions"; as soon as Manstein's relief-offensive had begun, he would leave for Berlin, where he would see Laval on the fifteenth, and then go to the Obersalzberg, where he would see Mussolini and Antonescu. Events in Russia were to disrupt this plan.

Consideration for Mussolini's feelings—the staple of all German diplomacy—was to cost Hitler dearly. A hundred sorely needed heavy antiaircraft batteries had been sent to northern Italy. The six hundred thousand tons of French shipping captured at Marseilles was transferred to the Italian merchant marine. Tunisia was declared an Italian sphere of interest—although in private Hitler scoffed, "If we ever go over to the offensive there, you can bet your boots the Italians won't join in with us." On December 5 five hundred expert saboteurs of Admiral Canaris's "Brandenburg" commando regiment had disembarked in Tunis, for operations behind enemy lines; these too were placed under the Italian supreme command. But when the Grand Mufti of Jerusalem offered to stir up a pro-Axis insurrection of his Mohammedan subjects throughout Tunisia, Algeria, and French Morocco, Hitler turned him down. The Mufti's condition was that North Africa must be promised its eventual freedom, and even a secret letter to the Bey of Tunis couched in these terms would have been totally incompatible with Hitler's loyalty toward Mussolini.

Before returning to the doleful events of December 1942 on the eastern front, we can review the possible sources of fresh danger to the Axis in the Mediterranean now that the enemy had secured a firm base at its western end. Hitler himself undertook such *tours d'horizon* more than once that December.

Initially he deduced that if the Axis did lose North Africa, the enemy's next thrust would be into the Balkans. They would probably bypass Crete, as it was such a bulwark of German military strength as to make its capture a most formidable proposition. But the islands of Rhodes or the Peloponnesus might seem more attractive, particularly if Churchill planned to rehash the old Salonika campaign. Since Germany's eastern campaign was again halted, Turkey's friendship had cooled perceptibly; Hitler therefore deemed it expedient to furnish fresh arms to the neutral Bulgarians to dissuade Turkey from any hostile adventures. He set out a list of priorities among the recipients of Germany's scarce arms exports: first and foremost Italy's forces in the Dodecanese, Crete, and Greece; then Bulgaria; then Romania's shattered armies and Italy's other forces; and finally Spain and Hungary.

His anxiety about Spain had grown in December. At first he had turned a deaf ear on Franco's plea for modern weapons in case the enemy swept from North Africa into Spain or her African possessions. Hitler believed that the Spanish were too tenacious an opponent, and their country possessed too few advantages, for that; but the admiralty pointed out that if the enemy occupied northern Spain, this would spell the end of Germany's submarine campaign in the Atlantic. In addition, evidence that the Americans had trained Spanish Communists in Mexico and shipped them to North Africa roused Hitler's fears anew. Instructing the Abwehr to step up its Intelligence activity throughout Spain and Portugal, Keitel explained to Canaris, "The Führer is particularly alert as to Spain, because Britain has already begun a 'Stop Thief!' propaganda campaign such as usually precedes her own military operations." Hitler was in a quandary; he could ill-afford the antitank, antiaircraft, and other guns and armament Franco was appealing for. Despite the advice of Raeder and some of his own staff, his instinct told him that Spain would be better neutral. But arms deliveries would be useless if they came too late for the Spanish to install and train with them. "If Spain's only aim is to remain neutral, let her procure the arms from America," he told General Muñoz Grandes. Nonetheless he agreed to entertain the Spanish needs, provided that Franco solemnly undertook to use the weapons to ward off any British or American aggression.

Neither Hitler nor his advisers could understand why the British had so willingly allowed Roosevelt to lay hands on the eastern hemisphere. "Any sensible Englishman must say to himself that Britain is going to have to pay the bill," he told the Dutch Fascist leader Anton Mussert in mid-December. "We have not the slightest reason to fight Britain. Even if we win we gain nothing from Britain. . . . Britain ought to be glad to have in Germany a bulwark against Russia." The day when Germany and Britain would join to rise up against American imperialism seemed farther away than ever.

The uncertainty about France's loyalties was, however, banished now forever. New Forschungsamt intercepts revealed the full extent of Darlan's long-planned treachery and even hinted that Pétain had been a willing party to it. Henceforth Hitler would exploit France ruthlessly for the Axis cause. De Gaulle's supporters would be transported to the eastern front, compelled to perform the most menial tasks. British, American, and Spanish "Communists" in France would be arrested and brought to Germany. General Weygand—hero of the Battle for France —was already in German custody, bitterly protesting at being treated like a criminal.[9] General Maurice Gamelin, Léon Blum, and Édouard Daladier would have to follow. When Heinrich Himmler came to headquarters on December 10, Hitler authorized him to remove the six or seven hundred thousand Jews from France as well; at Himmler's suggestion those with influential relatives in America were to be held in a special camp "under conditions that will keep them alive and well." (Himmler's notes do not indicate that he mentioned to Hitler the alternative fate of the others.) Hitler ordered the occupation costs paid by the French increased to the maximum that the French economy would bear. The

---

[9]Weygand informed his SS captors that he had been *adoré* by the Arabs as French high commissioner in Syria; the British never got on with them, while the Americans in Africa were committing one *bêtise* after another. He particularly condemned the Americans for repealing the French government's anti-Jewish laws there. "I myself am an anti-Semite. I had a lot to do with the Jews in Syria too. But I must stress I never had problems with the local Jews. The other kind of Jews, the political ones, the Zionists, were even fought by the local Jews: they often came to me for help and protection against the monied Jews spreading across the country buying everything up and ruining the Arabs in the process." Himmler sent Weygand's remarks to Hitler in January 1943.

spirit that had restrained his demands at Compiègne was dead. Apart from a possible later *phalange africaine* to recapture France's lost colonies, her armed forces would be limited to an enlarged police force and *garde mobile.* "The French police are good," cackled Hitler. "We'll harness them, we'll work only with the police. Himmler knows his policemen! He employs the most reprehensible methods himself, so this will make them all partners in crime. It will be a police alliance!"

Hitler relished his private conferences with Himmler. The SS chief was always bringing something new. It was Himmler who was most assiduously propagating the new "European" spirit: in the SS panzer division "Viking," now fighting in the Caucasus, the young men of Scandinavia and the Netherlands were united with the finest German troops. He was purging occupied Europe of its undesirables. He was keeping potential dissidents like Halder and Brauchitsch under discreet surveillance. But at the same time he offered an ear to malcontents within such rival departments as the army or the foreign office. It was Himmler who first secured access to Hitler for the rocket scientists of Peenemünde. Through high officials in the Wilhelmstrasse, Himmler was also working toward the overthrow of Ribbentrop. "For your information," Himmler cabled his Intelligence chief on December 5, "the Führer is very satisfied with our reports." Ribbentrop could not make the same claim after the fiascos in the Mediterranean.

Among Himmler's reports to Hitler three deserve mention here. On December 4, 1942, the Gestapo secretly announced the "taking out" of a major arsenal of the Polish underground in Warsaw: the four-room house harbored not only the usual quantities of explosives and detonators, but also "three flasks of typhus bacilli, seventeen sealed rubber tubes presumably containing bacteria, and one fountain pen with instructions for use for spreading bacteria"; captured documents revealed that twenty pounds of arsenic had also passed through the house. A few days later Himmler produced a year-old NKVD order covering instructions to the indigenous Russian population on the poisoning—again with arsenic —of German occupation troops. A more enigmatic Himmler document is a letter to the Gestapo chief Heinrich Müller, in which he stated that "the Führer has authorized the transmission of such Intelligence data as the OKW and foreign minister agree to, in order to keep up the 'radio game' with Moscow, even though this would be *prima facie* tantamount to treason normally."[10]

---

[10]This may have been the origin of the suspicious radio messages to Moscow which led Gehlen and Canaris to suspect there was a traitor operating from Hitler's headquarters. See Gehlen's memoirs, U.S. edition, pages 70–71.

It was the night of December 11–12, 1942; for the first time in many months Hitler's insomnia had returned. He lay in his sparsely furnished bunker bedroom, sleepless with worry about the coming week. He knew that rumors were sweeping Germany that an entire army, the Sixth, had been encircled by the enemy at Stalingrad. Manstein's relief offensive was slated to begin in a few hours' time. But the Sixth Army's supplies were running out—the eighteenth was the last possible day for the offensive to succeed. Göring had kept his promise by marshaling a huge armada of transport aircraft for the airlift; and yet the airlift was clearly failing. On December 1, Richthofen had controlled 221 Junkers transports and 95 Heinkel 111s; but only 15 Junkers and 25 Heinkels had actually reached the besieged city, while two days later none flew in at all because of the icing and fog.[11] Were it not for the Italians Hitler might still have snatched some sleep, but during the eleventh a Russian infantry attack had developed on the Italian Eighth Army sector northwest of Stalingrad; though it was still moderate in strength, and although the terrain and their superiority in artillery favored the Italians, Hitler had steeled himself against the inevitable catastrophe the moment the Russians began the main assault. He guessed they were only waiting for the Luftwaffe to be grounded by foul weather. There were virtually no reserves behind the Italian front. Fearing the worst, he had ordered the 17th Panzer Division unloaded there, although it might make the difference between success and failure for Manstein's relief operation that it must now begin with only the 6th and 23rd panzer divisions in its spearhead.

Was it the right decision? Manstein felt it was not—he feared that his two divisions would not get through the iron Russian ring; nevertheless, between them they had 233 good tanks, more than the Russian divisions opposing them. "We've got enough tanks," Hitler told Zeitzler the next day. "But what might of course happen is this: the rogues might rapidly dismantle in front"——the general completed the Führer's thought——"and pinch us off with one group here, this side, and one group there, on that side." "The armored divisions *ought* to manage it," Hitler reemphasized. Jodl reasured them both. "He'll manage everything," meaning Manstein. "It is just that the area is so vast and our divisions so few. The enemy just flows around behind them again." Zeitzler said, "The attack mustn't get bogged down. Time is of the essence."

It was the sense of uncertainty that kept Hitler awake. Should they have

---

[11]Engine freeze-ups caused the greatest problems, until Milch's technical experts reminded the local air commanders late in January 1943 of the simple basic "cold-start" procedures—thinning lubricating oil with gasoline. By then it was too late.

abandoned Stalingrad three weeks ago? But they would never have recaptured it if they had. They would have had to leave huge quantities of army artillery in the city. In addition, the whole point of the Russian campaign would have been lost. "We have shed too much blood for that." "Barbarossa" had now cost the German army 371,000 dead—and Hitler did not expect many of the 86,000 missing to survive Russian captivity. But might not a wrong decision now cost the 300,000 men in Stalingrad their lives? Two days earlier Bormann had recorded Hitler as saying he would never capitulate; he would keep fighting even if he had to draft fourteen- and sixteen-year-olds into the battle. "It would still be better for them to die fighting the East than for us to lose the war and see them tortured and sold into slavery." In his mind's eye Hitler could already see the glorious moment six days hence when the siege of Stalingrad would be lifted. First a narrow corridor—and the taut-faced columns of Manstein's troops, disheveled from battle, would come pouring through with food- and gasoline-laden trucks bringing up the rear. In the city itself the word would pass from starving mouth to mouth that salvation was there. This was the vision that sustained him. The uglier possibility was banished from his mind. He could not believe that Manstein would fail—unless, of course, the Italian front caved in first. He bitterly reproached himself for not having swept straight through Stalingrad that summer. "Things would have gone faster if we hadn't got bogged down in Voronezh." Lastly, he tormented himself with the question of whether or not he could now risk going to the Berghof to see Mussolini; during the train journey they would be in touch with the outside world only every two or three hours, and there was no way he could receive *pictures* of a sudden crisis developing. "We will just have to see how things go today and tomorrow," he told Zeitzler.

The attack began well the next morning. An atmosphere of euphoria pervaded the OKW. "Little worry about carrying attack through as the enemy's tank strength is strongly reduced," noted their official historian. Nonetheless, Hitler decided to let Manstein have the 17th Panzer Division after all. The field marshal even suggested the Russians were only feinting toward the Italian front to tie down Hitler's reserves. Hitler, however, refused to be led astray by the OKW's impatient optimism.[12] Stalin was after a far bigger prize: he also wanted to cut off the retreat of the entire army group in the Caucasus, half a million men.

Russian resistance stiffened as Manstein's relief attack pushed closer to Stalin-

---

[12]In the OKW war diary, Greiner's *original* note for December 15, 1942, read: "The major attack anticipated against the Italian Eighth Army has not yet begun. It seems the enemy just intends to tie down our reserves by repeated feeler-operations. The Führer, however, has not yet drawn any conclusion from this." (In the published text the word "however" has been excised.)

grad. On the fourteenth, the 6th Panzer Division destroyed forty-one tanks, but Richthofen warned that the main Russian force still lay ahead; soon the 17th Panzer Division would be joined to the attack. Already it was halfway to Stalingrad. Then, on the sixteenth, came the event Hitler had feared, as the Russians hurled three armies at the narrow sector of the Don front he had entrusted to his Italian allies northwest of Stalingrad. Two bomber wings were diverted from Richthofen's support operations for the relief attack, to help the Italians—a diversion Richthofen angrily labeled "abandoning the Sixth Army—it's murder." Manstein agreed, but both Jeschonnek and Zeitzler bowed to Hitler's decision that the Italians must be saved.

How well would even German troops have fought against such odds? The Italian Eighth Army had been ill-trained, it deployed its heavy weapons wrongly, and it lacked tough officers. After two days of plucky fighting it took to its heels, tearing an immense breach between Manstein's and Weichs's army groups and leaving nothing between the Russians and Rostov but open countryside.

Foreign Minister Count Galeazzo Ciano encountered a forbidding atmosphere at the Wolf's Lair when he arrived with Marshal Cavallero at noon on December 18. Hitler had abandoned all thought of going to the Berghof. He determined to speak bluntly with the Italians. No reference was made to the Italian Eighth Army's inglorious dissolution, but he used plain language in demanding that Italy make sacrifices to keep supplies flowing into North Africa. Germany was preparing to send her four finest divisions over to Tunis. He asked that Italy's civil transport and indeed her navy make a comparable effort. Neither Ciano nor Cavallero commented on this. Ciano's main purpose in coming was to deliver Mussolini's "hypothetical" question: given that 1943 would probably see major enemy operations in North Africa, southeastern Europe, and the west, would it not even now be possible to reach a *political* settlement with Russia à la Brest-Litovsk? Hitler patiently replied that this would be irreconcilable with his objective of Lebensraum. Besides, after six months of truce Germany would have to fight Russia all over again—a Russia immensely refreshed and reinforced. It was a false illusion for Mussolini to believe that Germany could ever abstract divisions from the east to ward off possible defeat in the Mediterranean.

Hitler sugared the pill with caustic references to the French. He revealed that he was maintaining the fiction of a "French government" under Pétain only because the unbelligerent French colonials in North Africa willingly accepted Pétain's order not to fight for the Allies.[13] He no longer had any trust

---

[13] According to an (unpublished) note by Greiner on January 7, 1943, Hitler ordered all French prisoners taken in Tunis to be released in France and paid a French government pension.

in the French. Not that he trusted the Italians now either. As the Italians left, Keitel instructed Admiral Canaris to keep an eye on Italy ("even though it is not to be anticipated that she will defect"). A member of Ciano's entourage inquired of the OKW whether the Italian Eighth Army had suffered heavy casualties; he was told: "None at all. They never stopped running."

With the collapse of the Italian army, a terrible new situation confronted Germany's Sixth Army in Stalingrad. Only two alternatives were left to it: to push a battle group southwest to meet the relieving panzer divisions, while still retaining the strategic stranglehold on Stalingrad and the Volga; or to implement "Thunderclap," a breakout by the entire Sixth Army—abandoning its heavy equipment and tens of thousands of wounded troops to the mercies of the enemy. Zeitzler put Manstein's case for "Thunderclap" to Hitler during the war conference late on December 18. As their expert scrutiny switched from one sector of the front to the next, an adjutant spread maps across the table, while Hitler, clutching a bunch of colored pencils in one hand, watched the ominous red arrows of the Red Army's offensive plunge ever closer to the airfields from which the Luftwaffe was mounting its airlift into Stalingrad. The logistic difficulties of launching "Thunderclap" seemed insuperable: Paulus demanded no less than 1,800 tons of food and 4,000 tons of fuel first; although the Luftflotte managed to fly in all of 270 tons that day, this was twice the average so far. Richthofen telephoned Zeitzler that evening saying he would need enormous reinforcement of his improvised air transport fleet.

By December 19 the three divisions of Manstein's relief force had reached the Myshovka River, some forty miles from Paulus's perimeter. The next day, one last push was made, only to be firmly blocked by the Russians. Hitler had ordered three more divisions rushed east from France, but it would take three weeks even to get them moving. (On December 19 he ordered Himmler to raise two new crack SS panzer-grenadier divisions—the 9th and 10th—in France by mid-February to replace them.)[14]

At 6 P.M. on December 19, Manstein radioed to the Sixth Army an order to begin "Operation Winter Storm"—an attempt to extend the southwestern perimeter by a limited tank attack under General Hube, thus linking up with the relief force outside. Paulus was also directed to stand by for "Thunderclap" in case Hitler gave permission. During the afternoon Manstein asked Zeitzler to secure Hitler's permission. But time was already running out. Paulus could not disen-

---

[14]Hitler kept a close eye on the raising of these divisions, telephoning his liaison officer SS General Karl Wolff twice on January 13, 1943, to stress that they "must work night and day on completing them as fast as humanly possible." The divisions fought historic battles in 1944 on the eastern front and in Normandy.

gage enough forces for "Winter Storm" without losing his grip on Stalingrad altogether; and he would need five days at least to prepare for "Thunderclap," as he had eight thousand casualties to fly out and the fuel would first have to be flown in. At present his tanks had fuel for less than fifteen miles. Paulus himself referred to "Thunderclap" as a "catastrophic solution."

It was a heartrending situation and one that the lesser commanders were glad to pass to Hitler for decision. He knew that Paulus's army was already tying down over seventy Russian divisions and brigades. On December 21 Manstein made it clear that the relief offensive could bring help no nearer to Stalingrad. If the Sixth Army pulled out now, the enemy might move to cut off the entire southern front. On the twenty-third Manstein had to take the 23rd Panzer Division out of the relief force to plug gaps west of the Don. Two days later Russian tanks overran one of the two vital airfields, and a powerful counterattack pushed the rest of the German relief force back to the Akssai River. All prospects of relieving Stalingrad that winter faded.

Hitler steeled himself against the noisy counsels of his commanders. Göring and Jeschonnek supported him; Manstein impertinently remarked to Zeitzler that if the Reichsmarschall was so sure the Stalingrad situation was not grave, then he should himself take command of the army group and its associated Luftflotte! Hitler refused to speak on the telephone with Manstein or to see him personally. Zeitzler and Manstein nonetheless argued loudly that only the immediate withdrawal of Kleist's Army Group A from the Caucasus would release enough reserves to prevent a catastrophe. When Zeitzler returned to his demand that the whole Sixth Army be ordered to break out, Hitler irritably replied, "The Sixth Army must stand fast. Even if I cannot lift the siege until spring." Göring assured him the airlift was working well. Keitel and Jodl supported Hitler with varying degrees of enthusiasm. Zeitzler accused the Reichsmarschall of lying about the Luftwaffe's capabilities and afterward reported the true airlift tonnage daily to Hitler each morning. On December 21 over 360 tons had been flown in, but now that the two closest airfields had been overrun, and the figure was soon barely a tenth of that amount. General Martin Fiebig, whose Eighth Air Corps was now wholly engaged in the airlift, wrote: "One wonders whether the Führer has got the picture—whether he really knows the state of our men and their capacity for effort, and whether the Russian strength isn't being underestimated once more."

In this atmosphere of despondency Hitler kept his nerve; but this time nerve alone was not enough. A year later he explained his grim philosophy thus in a secret speech to his downhearted generals: "Let this much be understood— nothing shocks me, whatever may happen. Some may think me heartless to insist on fighting to the last man just because the enemy will also let more blood that way, rather than to undertake this maneuver or that. It has nothing to do with heartlessness, only with my realization and conviction that *this* is the action to be taken. . . . It is a matter of supreme indifference to me what posterity may think of me."

At the time of Stalingrad, Hitler radiated outward confidence that the Sixth Army would shortly be liberated, though his private feelings may have been somewhat different. His generals trusted him—had he not proved them all wrong as recently as the Battle of Kharkov in May? Richthofen consoled the mutinous Luftwaffe generals with this argument: the Führer had been right before, even though his experts had advised otherwise, and nobody had understood him then either. "Perhaps we will all be chuckling over this crisis when May comes!" But Fiebig for one was unconvinced. "Richthofen mentioned yesterday that entire armies are often lost without any effect on the outcome of the war. But what can the Führer himself be thinking? It is a matter of two hundred fifty thousand human beings—we can't just sacrifice them, as there are no replacements. What will the Russians do with this quarter-million? They can but kill them, they haven't the food for them. Death will take a huge toll. Each man one last bullet for himself!—What does the Führer want to document with the fate of this army? There must be some purpose, otherwise one might lose faith."

Throughout December General Zeitzler pressed for the evacuation of Kleist's army group from the Caucasus in good time. Hitler at first refused. "First wait and see the outcome of our relief operation against Stalingrad. That will change the whole picture at one stroke." The prophecy had been fulfilled, but the outcome was not what Hitler had expected. On December 27 when issuing instructions to the army for the coming months, Hitler decreed that Kleist was to defend his existing line. The eventual liberation of the Sixth Army must guide all other considerations; thus the town of Kotelnikovo must be held too, as a starting point for that offensive. Meanwhile the SS panzer division "Viking" would be moved up from the Caucasus and the 7th Panzer Division brought from France early in January. A new battalion of Tiger tanks would also be provided. But these instructions were overtaken by events: the Romanian divisions guarding the flanks of the relieving force which had attacked on December 12 collapsed, and its depleted armored spearhead barely managed to extricate itself.

That evening, December 27, Zeitzler ambushed Hitler by arriving unannounced at the Wolf's Lair and bearding the Führer in his private bunker despite his adjutants' protests. He was moodily listening to records of Beethoven. The general spoke earnestly, and ended with the words: "If you do not order the withdrawal of the Caucasus front now, you will have a second Stalingrad on your hands." Hitler brooded, then curtly told him: "Very well, do as you wish!" But he regretted this almost immediately and telephoned the General Staff's nearby headquarters several times to try to intercept Zeitzler on his return. Eventually Zeitzler himself came to the phone. Hitler said, "About the withdrawal from the Caucasus—wait a bit. We'll have another talk about it." Zeitzler's voice came back: "Too late—the order has already gone out." Hitler paused, said, "Very well, then," and irritably replaced the receiver.

Given the collapse of the Romanian and Italian armies it was undoubtedly the right decision, but he may have sensed that now a retreat from Russia was beginning that would not be halted at the frontiers of Germany.

Retreat

Hitler saw in the New Year, 1943, sitting alone in his bunker with Martin Bormann, his Party secretary, until after 4:00 A.M. This itself presaged the coming times: in the year that followed a significant part of Hitler's domestic authority was delegated to a three-man cabal—Bormann, Keitel, and Lammers—convening significantly in what had been the Cabinet Room of the Berlin Chancellery, while Goebbels hovered like a predator calling impatiently for the mantle of "Führer of the home front" to descend on him.

Hitler was rarely in Berlin. He dedicated himself to his war, sustained by the prospect of coming offensives, of the growing U-boat campaign, of increased panzer and aircraft production, and by "evidence" that Stalin's manpower reserves were at last declining. Victory would surely go to the combatant with the strongest nerves, with the greatest resilience. His troubled conscience over Stalingrad he kept to himself—betraying his true feelings only by chance remarks to his secretaries or doctors. At night he could not sleep, for before his eyes there danced the arrow-covered maps of the evening's war conference, crowding in on him like childhood nightmares until at last the sedatives he had taken dragged him down into unconsciousness. For the next six months he proved more accessible to the advice of the General Staff. His tactical decisions were sound, and the retreats that marked these months were considerable military achievements. But he had lost forever the venturesome spirit that was his forte. Only at Stalingrad and in the first disordered retreat to the Donets did the army lose equipment of any consequence. Thereafter the withdrawals were planned and fought so as to inflict the maximum hardship and casualties on the enemy. Still sure of their superiority, the German soldiers felt that they were being overwhelmed by circumstance, not the Russian army: by lack of oil, by inclement weather, by unreliable allies. Their trust in Hitler remained unshaken,[1] but the security service

---

[1] As the generals showed on March 13, 1943. See pages 498–99, based on an unpublished note by Greiner.

reports indicated that at home the first mutterings of popular discontent were becoming audible.

General Eberhard von Mackensen's First Panzer Army began its withdrawal from the Caucasus on January 1, 1943, and completed it thirty days later, having covered over four hundred miles under appalling conditions for infantry and artillery alike—eighteen-horse teams struggled to haul the heavy guns through the mountains. Some 25,000 casualties were evacuated in time from the field hospitals; all the equipment except for about a hundred guns was saved. Simultaneously General Ruoff's Seventeenth Army withdrew from the western Caucasus. Thus at a cost of 226 lives an entire army group, some 700,000 men, was saved from the fate currently befalling those in Stalingrad. Against Zeitzler's advice, however, Hitler directed only four of Mackensen's divisions to Rostov; the rest were added to Ruoff's army, which was ordered during January to hold a bridgehead on the Taman peninsula—just over the narrow straits from the Crimea. This would have psychological value, argued Hitler; it would show friend and foe alike that in 1943 he again intended to go over to the offensive. With Albert Speer he even adumbrated plans to build across the Strait of Kerch a giant bridge linking the Crimea to the "Goth's Head," as the Taman bridgehead was termed.

Meanwhile, in the dying days of the old year Hitler had conceived a grand operational design to relieve the starving Sixth Army and turn the Russian onslaught into a rout. He would speedily transfer the three most powerful SS divisions—Sepp Dietrich's "Adolf Hitler Life Guards," "Das Reich," and "Death's Head"—from France and the crack "Gross Deutschland" infantry division from Army Group Center, assemble them southeast of Kharkov, and strike north of the Don toward Stalingrad as soon as the weather improved. That would be mid-February. Paulus's spirits were raised by Hitler's convincing assurances. When the one-armed panzer general Hube arrived at the Wolf's Lair from Stalingrad with word that the army's meat supplies would not last beyond January, Hitler ordered Quartermaster General Wagner to furnish concentrated food-stuffs such as were provided to Polar expeditions. When Paulus reported that bad weather sometimes prevented any airlift operations at all, Hitler promised that the Luftwaffe would carry 750 tons of supplies in on days when the weather was good. Göring did his best: already 480 Junkers and Heinkels were committed solely to the airlift; but the frontline squadrons, particularly of the Junkers, found their spirit cruelly assailed by the cold and by their inadequate leadership, and only a fraction of the available planes were actually flying each day. This was not realized at Hitler's headquarters, and still more planes were sent to the airlift—100 more Junkers, 10 Focke-Wulf Condors, and several of the troublesome Heinkel 177 heavy bombers too. A visit by a responsible Luftwaffe commander would have been more fruitful, but Jeschonnek could not spare the time and Göring averted his gaze from the seemingly inevitable disaster. The local air commander,

Fiebig, wrote that somehow the supply rate had to be maintained for six more weeks until the new relief operation got through. "If all goes well then, we have won the battle for Stalingrad and perhaps the war. We just don't know the potential strength of the other side."

Within Hitler the sense of public relations still stirred. Despite his Stalingrad worries, he telephoned Frau Troost in person from East Prussia to congratulate her on the solid gold cassette she had designed for Göring's warrant as Reichsmarschall—correctly speculating that this female *arbiter legendarium* would noise his evident well-being abroad. But his misgivings in fact were multiplying. Below, his Luftwaffe adjutant, had shown him a private letter from a relative trapped in Stalingrad, and its references to the Sixth Army's commanders were not encouraging. A question mark was placed against Paulus's name; General Arthur Schmidt and General Walter von Seydlitz were marked "sack 'em," but Hube was praised: "He's the man!" On January 8 the General Staff reported that General Konstantin Rokossovski had publicly called on Paulus to surrender. "Paulus asks what he should do now!"

The year had opened with an exasperating series of errors over an Allied convoy to North Russia. According to naval Intelligence it was escorted only by destroyers when it was sighted by a U-boat south of Bear Island early on December 30. Raeder's naval liaison officer, Admiral Theodor Krancke, asked Hitler for his blessing for a sortie by the *Hipper,* the *Lützow,* and six destroyers to attack the convoy; the pocket battleship *Lützow* would afterward break out into the Atlantic —"Operation Aurora." Throughout New Year's Eve the Führer was left in virtual ignorance of the progress of the battle. Under his impatient pressure Krancke somewhat tactlessly showed him the only two radio messages bearing on the battle's outcome. Admiral Kummetz had merely radioed: "Break off attack, no enemy cruiser with convoy, not possible to detach *Lützow* for 'Aurora.' " But the shadowing U-boat had radioed as the Arctic dusk engulfed the scene: "I see just red!"

Hitler badly needed a morale booster and interpreted the above messages optimistically. Evidently the enemy warships were ablaze. When Ribbentrop telephoned at midnight with New Year felicitations, Hitler bragged that the navy had just won a "magnificent victory." Not until next afternoon did he learn the woeful truth: British cruisers had been lurking nearby, his own task force had fumbled and run for cover, the cruiser *Hipper* was so badly damaged that at times she could make little more than fifteen knots. A German destroyer had mistakenly joined the enemy and paid dearly for her error. The convoy itself had escaped unscathed. Hitler raged at the incompetent navy radiomen and the inadequate naval spirit. The least his big ships could do was fight with as much determination as the U-boat crews or common soldiers in the east. He announced that he was going to lay up all the big ships, and he ordered Krancke to inform Raeder of this by telephone. The navy Commander in Chief was to come to the Wolf's Lair at once, but Raeder asked for time to conduct a postmortem on the fiasco first.

His stock with Hitler was already low. He had been a less frequent visitor to the Führer than his critics, of whom Speer and Göring were the most vociferous. Out of jealousy, Göring had furnished Hitler with a string of complaints about the admiralty. Speer had done the same, to further his own causes; he had picked holes in Raeder's tradition-based claim to the flotsam left on the beaches of Dieppe after the British raid—in error, as it turned out. As recently as January 4, Speer had reported the navy to Hitler for hoarding sixty oil-paper-wrapped 105-millimeter antiaircraft guns in a depot. (He had been unaware that they were there for ranging and calibration tests.) Speer also insidiously declared to Hitler that Raeder was hated throughout the U-boat arm for his attempts to suppress Dönitz's popularity. Raeder's true shortcoming, in Speer's eyes, was his refusal to abrogate control over naval armament to the Speer munitions ministry. Now Speer's campaign paid dividends.

The admiral arrived late on January 6. Hitler berated him for ninety minutes on the big ships' failure ever since 1864 to fight a single naval action right through. Neither its mutiny in 1918 nor its scuttling in 1919 were exactly glorious episodes. He wanted the ships laid up, their crews transferred to the smaller, more active vessels, and the armament built into the coastal defenses. At Raeder's request, Keitel and the two stenographers withdrew; the admiral then tendered his resignation—offering to postpone it until the Party's tenth anniversary in power at the end of January to stifle any further scandal. Hitler asked him to submit the names of two possible successors. Raeder suggested Admiral Rolf Carls or alternatively —though with marked distaste—Dönitz. But Carls was himself a champion of the big ships and was turned down. On January 14, Raeder also submitted the written reply Hitler had requested, predicting "shrieks of triumph" from the enemy when they learned that the Germans had mothballed their own biggest ships. Hitler heaped sarcasm on the document, but Krancke could see that he was impressed nonetheless.

The next months in the east would be crucial, but the idea of seeking even a conditional armistice did not enter his head. As he told Marshal Antonescu on January 10, the day the Russians opened their all-out offensive at Stalingrad, neither in the Punic wars nor in the Thirty Years' War nor in the Seven Years' War had any of the statesmen been able to predict how it would all end; yet their fanatical resolve and single-minded purpose had brought them victory.

Two days later the Russians weighed into the Hungarian Second Army, toward

Svoboda, just as Hitler had also predicted. Army Intelligence was also reporting rumors of enemy plans to invade the Crimea. In the north a major Soviet relief attack designed to lift the siege of Leningrad began. The Hungarians south of Voronezh suffered a defeat no less complete than that of the Romanians and Italians: 30,000 dead and 50,000 captured within days; as a result the German Second Army was threatened with encirclement and a similar catastrophe.

Hitler's tactical measures—rushing antitank guns to the Hungarians and calling in three more divisions from France—came too late. But strategically he was already thinking of 1944 and attending to the interlocking problems of raising fresh divisions and providing them with weapons and ammunition to replace those lost in this new winter of disaster. On the entire eastern front, he learned later in January, he had less than five hundred tanks; the Russians had five thousand.[2] With the help of Goebbels and Bormann he himself planned to wring a million troops out of the German population by mid-1943: in December he ordered German industry to release two hundred thousand men for call-up by the end of March; a month later the demand was stepped up to eight hundred thousand men. But who could replace the skilled aircraft workers or electronics engineers thus thrust into uniform, and even worse how would the German madam survive without her servants? Germany, which Hitler had made a world power by cunning and lightning wars, had too much domestic inertia to combat the manpower potential of the United States or the massive forces of Stalin's Soviet Union.

Providing the extra tanks and artillery was no less urgent, particularly now that he could no longer ignore American armament capacity. Twice in January Speer was called to the Wolf's Lair. Hitler wanted bigger, better, and more tanks. On the seventeenth he telephoned Walter Rohland, the tank production expert, secured his agreement to increase assault-gun, Panzer IV, Panther, and Tiger tank production from May, and decided to launch a new production program, the "Adolf Hitler Tank Program." He buttonholed Admiral Krancke after the conference and unemotionally told him that all warship construction larger than destroyers was to cease forthwith so that Speer could have the manpower he would now need for tanks. "Even if it is only five thousand men it will help," Hitler noted. The military crisis in the east was so grave that all else must bow to the tank program's needs. When Krancke protested, Hitler again harked back to the inconsequential naval action off Bear Island—the navy should have finished the job and annihilated that convoy whatever the toll in sailors' lives. "The tanks

---

[2]On January 23, 1943, Army Group A had 34 serviceable tanks, Army Groups Don and B had 291 between them, Center had 167, and Army Group North only 3. In early December the Germans had had about 1,300 and the Russians about 4,800.

it brought through have now probably cost many more soldiers their lives south of Lake Ladoga." (The next day the Russians announced the recapture of Petrokrepost on Lake Ladoga, thus restoring land contact with Leningrad.) Krancke reminded Hitler of his standing orders against risking the big ships against any superior enemy; but Hitler referred to the *Graf Spee* and *Bismarck* episodes as proof that it was the spirit of their crews that was wanting. Speer arrived on the night train from Berlin, drafted a decree for the tank program, and issued it over Hitler's signature together with the Führer's dramatic appeal to the workers not to let the army down. Not long afterward, Dönitz stood before Hitler, eagerly conniving at the consignment of the big ships to the wreckers'; but soon he too recognized the folly of such a decision and effortlessly persuaded Hitler to leave the ships in service. Before Raeder retired into obscurity, he begged Hitler to protect the navy from Göring, and he warned his successor not to put his trust in Speer.

The high point in Hitler's affection for Göring was reached on January 12, the Reichsmarschall's fiftieth birthday. Thereafter a series of Allied night air raids on the German and French population affected Göring's prestige. In mid-January Hitler sent for Göring's deputy, Milch, and put him in personal charge of the airlift to Stalingrad—a step which the jealous Göring had urgently counseled against, and with good cause, for Milch embarrassed the Reichsmarschall by achieving the near impossible in the two weeks that remained.

Along the southern front as far north as Voronezh a Soviet avalanche of troops and tanks was pouring through the breach created by the Romanian, Italian, and Hungarian collapse. Hitler's object was to keep Paulus's army fighting for six more weeks at least—until it could be relieved by Paul Hausser's SS panzer corps —or at least long enough to preoccupy the enemy. But what then? General von Weichs cabled him that his army group was left with barely seven divisions— mostly exhausted, dispirited, and improvised—along a two-hundred-mile front; he saw no possible way of holding up the enemy's relentless march westward. At any moment the Russians might encircle the Second Army. From within Stalingrad strong protests were now emanating from the Sixth Army, too. "Mein Führer!" Paulus radioed on the seventeenth. "Your orders on the supply of my army are not being obeyed." The planes were no longer landing at Gumrak airfield; they were just throwing out their loads in midair. The loads were thus largely wasted, and the thousands of injured waiting to be flown out were left to suffer. The Luftwaffe generals denied Paulus's allegations. Göring later bitterly accused Paulus—at the time no doubt to Hitler himself—of being too soft a commander; he was feeding thousands of Russian civilians and useless injured German soldiers. "One can't burden oneself with wounded men beyond hope of recovery; they must be left to lapse into the hereafter." The army generals did not share this attitude. General Hube, again flown out of Stalingrad, feelingly reproached Hitler. "The Luftwaffe airlift has failed. Somebody must be to blame for that. Why don't you kill off some of your Luftwaffe generals—it's always the army generals who go to the wall!" Hitler replied in level terms, "I know the grim position you are in at Stalingrad. But soon things will get better. I have got it all in hand." But Hube's reproach nettled the Führer, and he quoted it to Göring with equal feeling later. Hube was assigned to Milch's emergency staff.

Hitler turned a deaf ear on Hube's advice to appoint a Commander in Chief East, suspecting as he did that the advice had come from Manstein. Richthofen has painted a vivid portrait of Manstein in this month of crisis. "In my view Manstein is a write-off, trembling in every limb and looking years older. . . . He has been deprived of all possibility of command, as every single battalion is still being directed from On High.[3] Again and again the mistrust from above is blazoned forth against army- and army-group commanders alike. An excruciating war." Disaster seemed inevitable; already Richthofen was blaming Manstein and Göring, Göring was blaming Manstein and Paulus—for allowing the airlift's airfields to be overrun—and Paulus and his Chief of Staff were blaming the Luftwaffe. Within the Luftwaffe, Milch was not talking to Jeschonnek, and Jeschonnek was not on speaking terms with the quartermaster general; all three were responsible for the airlift.

At Hitler's headquarters, Zeitzler pointedly introduced "Stalingrad" rations for his staff, and he visibly lost weight. Milch had now discovered that the ignorance and negligence of the local air transport commanders—particularly of the Junkers 52 squadrons—accounted for most of the disappointing serviceability of their planes. On January 22 the enemy again called on Paulus to surrender. Manstein and Zeitzler both now argued that he should comply, but Hitler replied that the Russians would abide by no conventions—no prisoners would survive long; on the other hand, every day the Sixth Army fought on, no matter how hopelessly, would help stabilize the other fronts. Paulus radioed a dignified response to Hitler's instructions: "Your orders are being executed. Long live Germany."

Hitler deemed that the word of his soldiers' heroism at Stalingrad would itself be worth many divisions in the months to come. Whenever in the future Hitler's soldiers were encircled, they would fight with like tenacity. The legend of Stalingrad would enhance each later fortress's invincibility in enemy eyes. Thus, when Goebbels came to map out their propaganda on the coming total war campaign, Hitler instructed that absolute frankness be observed by the press in describing

[3] *"Von allerhöchster Stelle."* See page 391 above.

the situation of German soldiers in Stalingrad. In this way, Hitler hoped to mobilize in Germany the same latent strength that Churchill had called on in England after Dunkirk. Above all, the coming Bolshevik victory communiqués were to pass unchallenged—the better to bring a bracing shiver of apprehension to the peoples of the West. On January 24, German newspapers for the first time revealed the death throes of the Sixth Army. Speer, arriving in Berlin that day from the Wolf's Lair, telephoned Milch that Hitler sorely regretted not having called in Milch to run the airlift from the start. Twenty-nine thousand injured troops had been evacuated by the time Paulus's last airfield was overrun. His soldiers had been allowed to write one last letter home. When the last Heinkel took off, it brought out nineteen injured soldiers and seven bags of mail.

In Stalingrad, Paulus's ragged army had been severed into two pockets. In the smaller, southern pocket, Paulus despondently predicted defeat on the twenty-fifth, but his men fought on, the swastika banner still flying symbolically from the ruins of the highest building. Twenty thousand untended injured were lying in the streets. Paulus ordered the dwindling food supplies issued only to those still fit enough to fight. The Luftwaffe crews matched the courage being demanded of the soldiers, flying two and sometimes even three sorties a night to discharge food and ammunition over Stalingrad. "On the anniversary of your assumption of power," Paulus radioed Hitler, "the Sixth Army sends greetings to the Führer. The swastika still flutters over Stalingrad. May our struggle stand as an example to generations as yet unborn, never to surrender no matter how desperate the odds. Then Germany will be victorious. Heil, mein Führer!" Hitler's reply was a proclamation broadcast to the German nation as long-range Luftwaffe fighters arrived over Stalingrad for the first time. It ended: "In this fight we will have the Almighty on our side. We will not shy from shedding our own blood, because one day a new land will blossom from the sacrifices of the fallen. And our teutonic state, our German nation, shall emerge victorious!"

This was his rejoinder to the call for unconditional surrender just raised by Roosevelt at Casablanca.[4]

At Zeitzler's instance—though not without misgivings—Hitler telegraphically promoted Paulus to field marshal. Since no German field marshal had yet sur-

---

[4]On January 24, 1943. Not until later did Goebbels seize on it as a propaganda weapon. It certainly stiffened the German people's resolve to fight on under Hitler. In an April 1944 memorandum Churchill wisely—though mendaciously—disowned unconditional surrender. "This matter is on the President. He announced it at Casablanca without any consultation and I backed him up in general terms. Subsequent correspondence with the President has shown him very much disinclined to remodel his statements now." (A doctored version of the memorandum is in his memoirs.)

rendered he thus pressed the pistol into Paulus's hand. At 7:35 A.M. on the thirty-first Sixth Army headquarters radioed: "In our bunker we listened to the Führer's Proclamation and saluted the national anthem for perhaps the last time." Almost at once they added, "The Russians are outside the door," and then, "We are destroying . . ." The radio went dead.

Hitler probably spared little attention for Stalingrad that day, for alarm bells were ringing throughout his domain. In Italy, Keitel's counterpart, Marshal Ugo Cavallero, had been replaced by General Vittorio Ambrosio without explanation; English newspapers hinted that he had been at the center of an anti-Fascist clique. Ciano was retired as foreign minister. In North Africa Rommel was retreating toward Tunisia, outnumbered eight to one by the enemy; Tripoli—and thus Libya itself—had been abandoned by the Axis. In northwest Germany, American heavy bombers had just attacked Wilhelmshaven in broad daylight; and on January 30 fast British bombers had penetrated to Berlin at noon.

Long before the war Hitler had called for Luftwaffe bombers just like these— and now the enemy had them but not he. "An impertinence! It's called the Mosquito! And it's made of wood!" The Luftwaffe's own heavy bomber, the Heinkel 177, which should have been available in time to bomb Moscow when "Barbarossa" began in June 1941, was still not perfected. Nineteen sorties had been flown to Stalingrad: no Heinkel 177 had been lost to enemy action, but six had been destroyed by engine fires in midair: the bomber's engines were coupled in pairs onto one propeller shaft—a technical monstrosity conceived by General Udet, who had put a bullet in his brain in connection with Luftwaffe production failures. How Hitler would have liked to send thirty Heinkel 177s—each with a ton of bombs—to smash Stalin's war plants at Sverdlovsk and even farther afield!

It was infuriating. Here was Germany, with her magnificent corps of commanders, her outstanding soldiers, and her vaunted weapons technology—yet compelled to retreat along the entire eastern front. Kharkov itself was in danger; Hausser's SS panzer corps must move in. In the Demyansk pocket south of Leningrad, so jealously defended by Hitler these many months, supplies were running low; it would have to be given up at last. There seemed to be concrete evidence that the Allies would soon invade Portugal; thus divisions were tied down in the west. Equally disturbing for Hitler was the persistent incompetence of his Intelligence agencies. Unconditional surrender perturbed him far less than the failure of both Canaris and the SS to advise him that Churchill and Roosevelt were meeting at Casablanca (the SS placed them both in Washington).

Hitler had turned in at 2:30 A.M., earlier than usual, that first day of February. He was shortly awakened with word from Moscow: Paulus had meekly surrendered, and was thus still alive—as were eleven German and five Romanian generals. Hitler's chagrin was huge. That his field marshal should have chosen the Tartarus of Soviet captivity to the Valhalla that Hitler had opened unto him, that he had lacked the routine courage of every captain who had gone down with his ship, that he had not mustered the same bravery as had a score of Soviet commissars and commanders in identically hopeless situations—this he could never forgive Paulus. He instructed his naval adjutant, Puttkamer, to find out if it was too late to cancel Paulus's promotion, but it was already in the newspapers. "The others stick together, form a phalanx, and keep the last bullet for themselves. Imagine, even a woman with an ounce of pride in her will lock herself in and put a bullet in her brain just because she has heard a few insulting words! . . . Here is a man who can look on while fifty or sixty thousand of his troops are dying and defending themselves with courage to the end—how can he give himself up to the Bolsheviks?" When Speer's deputy, Karl Saur, telephoned the Führer at 3 A.M. with the January production figures, for the first time Hitler did not want to hear them.

Throughout February appalling crises gripped the eastern front. Weichs was removed—his army group had virtually dissolved. Through the yawning gap thundered the Soviet avalanche. "I won't be able to sleep again without sedatives until the breach is plugged," declared Hitler. Only his staff stenographers shared his awful, all-embracing knowledge of the true picture. The diary of one of them reveals that a stenographer who had arrived as recently as December had suffered a nervous breakdown by mid-February. He was apprehended just as he was about to burst into the Führer's bedroom, screaming, "The Führer wants to speak to me. I must see him!" Martin Bormann rushed him off to a Berlin hospital. Meanwhile, frightened of fresh bloody nightmares, Hitler postponed retiring to his camp bed longer every night—wearying his obedient secretaries and physicians with endless somber monologues in an atmosphere that reminded the youngest secretary, newcomer Traudl Humps, of a cemetery on a wet November day. Hitler explained to an army doctor two years later: "I have to relax and speak about something else, otherwise I keep seeing the staff maps in the dark, and my brain goes grinding on and it takes me hours on end to drop off. If I then switch on the light, I can sketch exactly where every division was at Stalingrad. Hour after hour it goes on, until I finally drop off around five or six."

In two months the Red Army had demolished five armies—German, Romanian, Italian, and Hungarian. By the end of February the Russians had recaptured Kursk, Belgorod, Kraznodar, Demyansk, and even Rostov and Kharkov. Hitler might yet even have to abandon the Donets Basin, on whose coal and iron resources he and Speer had planned to hinge the expansion of the arms industry for the final overthrow of Russia. "I will have to think it over," he declared on February 1—referring to abandoning the Donets Basin. "But one thing I can say now: if I do, there will be no further possibility of bringing the war in the east to an *offensive* conclusion. Let's make no mistake about that!" Four days later he was quoted in Greiner's private diary to this effect: "I can't abandon the Donets Basin. If I do, I can't continue the war any longer."

Nor would Hitler as yet contemplate a political solution with Stalin. Japan's Ambassador Oshima had called on January 20 and left disappointed in this respect; indeed, Hitler now reversed his earlier stand and urgently demanded a Japanese attack on Stalin in the Far East. As for the public clamor, Goebbels successfully steered it into more productive channels—toward the totalization of the national war effort. Ribbentrop favored an appeal to the rest of Europe—a Hitler proclamation which would promise the western Europeans a degree of independence, and the eastern Europeans the same, though rather less: Poland would become a Protectorate, the Baltic states would be kept in tow like Slovakia, and Italy would make parallel concessions to Croatia, Greece, Albania, and Serbia. But Hitler still wanted Germany to go it alone. When Hewel brought him Ribbentrop's renewed proposal for peace feelers toward Moscow, Hitler refused even to read it. "First we must win a major military victory," he told Ribbentrop afterward. "Then we can see."

In presenting his plans to mobilize the native populations against Stalin, Rosenberg fared no better than Ribbentrop. By early 1943 the Germans had over 130,000 "Eastern troops" organized in battalions ready to fight for them, and there were Russian generals willing to lead them against Stalin; but Hitler could still not bring himself to accept this aid; in addition, he suspected it would be playing with dynamite, for it would merely be a rekindling of Russian nationalism under a different management. Now that the great retreat had begun, he temporized—ordering his armies to evacuate the anti-Stalin population of the Caucasus to spare them Soviet reprisals for collaborating with the Axis, but still unwilling to accept Rosenberg's appeal for a major propaganda offensive to win over Stalin's other subjects.[5] Rosenberg's blunders in the Ukraine and elsewhere had lowered him in Hitler's eyes. When in February 1943 Rosenberg read him a lengthy proposal for replacing the Soviet collective system with private enterprise and property again, raising legions from all the Soviet Union's ethnic groups (not just the Russians), restoring their freedom of religion, and issuing a suitable political proclamation to them, Hitler remarked that all this seemed inopportune at present. He would perhaps return to some of the proposals "after the coming spring

[5]On February 13, 1943, "for humanitarian reasons" Himmler ordered his police commanders in Russia to evacuate all able-bodied men and women—together with their children—from the regions being abandoned by the army; if they did not afford to the public that had collaborated this protection from Soviet wrath and reprisal, they would forfeit the public's trust in the future. A similar Hitler Order was issued the next day. Thus in one February day 1,500 German troops and 780 Russian civilians were evacuated from the Caucasus to the Crimea.

offensive began." When Zeitzler mentioned to him that the captured Russian general Andrei Andreyevich Vlasov was willing to lead a "National Army of Liberation" against Stalin, Hitler saw in the general only a useful propaganda tool. "What a swine Vlasov must be," he commented to his own staff. "He owes everything to Stalin. It was Stalin who made a general out of him. Now he bites the hand that fed him." Not that he expected Paulus to act any differently. A few weeks in the Lubyanka prison and he would say anything. "Just wait and see. . . . It won't be long before he's speaking on Moscow radio."

The cost of Stalingrad had been high. Göring's Luftwaffe had lost 488 aircraft and about a 1,000 airmen in the airlift, the equivalent of an entire air corps. Only 108,000 of Paulus's troops had survived to enter Soviet captivity, of which only 6,000 were ever to see Germany again. But on February 4, Gehlen's Intelligence division estimated that 107 Soviet divisions and brigades had been tied down by the battle for the city, together with 13 tank regiments.[6] This and the blocking of the rail and road links through the city had hampered all enemy operations on the southern front. In consequence a noticeable indecision marked the enemy's next moves; Gehlen could do little more than guess at where Stalin's next offensive would begin. Admittedly he had detected an increase in the enemy reserves early in January, but these were not new troops—merely divisions taken out of the front line for rehabilitation. Hitler was still optimistic that shortages of food and raw materials would defeat Stalin. His agencies had captured a Russian document listing their casualties by now as 11,200,000 dead, missing, and injured. It seemed well worth fighting on.

Hitler spent February 1943 mending the fences torn by the winter's storms. On Sunday February 7 he invited the Gauleiters to his headquarters and briefed them on the disaster. Herbert Backe dictated this summary to his wife the next day:

> Sunday with the Führer. The Führer spoke. First words were: "What you are witnessing is a catastrophe of unheard-of magnitude. The Russians broke through, the Romanians gave up, the Hungarians didn't even put up a fight, for five days German troops from the rear held the front in a thin line thrown across the breakthrough locations. We've lost four armies in and around Stalingrad." Compares our situation with Kolin and Kunersdorf, says that if Frederick had had weapons like ours, they'd never have called him The Great because

---

[6]Greiner's war diary note for the OKW was, despite its obvious significance, not included in the text published in 1963.

then his Seven Years' War would have been over in two months. The Führer again praised Speer. . . .

The Führer also said: "If the German people fails, then it does not deserve that we fight for its future; then we can write it off with equanimity." Not the right attitude of mind.

The Gauleiters were satisfied by Hitler's speech. But the damage to the generals' confidence in him was not so easily repaired. It took all his cunning and eloquence to play them off against each other during February, until Manstein's successful spring campaign quieted them again. General Schmundt, whom he had sent on a fact-finding tour of Army Group Don just before Stalingrad fell, must have faithfully reported the ugly mood brewing there—that Manstein, Milch, and Richthofen were unanimous that so long as Hitler directed each battalion in person the army would always lack the rapid, incisive direction from above that it needed for victory; in short, that Hitler should at least appoint a Commander in Chief East. They clearly favored Manstein, but though Hitler accepted him as their greatest military commander when on the offensive, in their present dilemma he felt they needed a tough, tenacious bulldog of a man—though with a flair for improvisation—such as Admiral von Schroeder, the legendary "Lion of Flanders" who had dominated the bloody battlefield in World War I; and Hitler knew of no such general now. In this outlook he was strengthened by Göring—jealous of Manstein's warlord aura—and by Keitel and Jodl too, who had sour memories of Manstein's hostility toward the OKW principle of a unified Wehrmacht command.

Milch, who flew straight in from the Stalingrad front with Hube on February 3, deserved a close hearing, for he had performed consistently well both in expanding aircraft production and in boosting the flagging airlift to Stalingrad. But Hitler fobbed him off until March: admittedly Göring had just bragged that two thousand new aircraft had been manufactured in January, an all-time record. Hitler snubbed Milch: "Let's see if you can keep it up!" Changing the theme of their talk, he stressed the need for the Luftwaffe to mass-produce a cheap, primitive transport plane capable of making the return flight of Africa without refueling. Milch was so severely rebuked for the calamitous record of the Heinkel 177 bomber project that a few days later the field marshal gasped, "I stood in front of the Führer like a very small boy who has not done his sums properly." Manstein and Kluge, summoned to the Wolf's Lair on the sixth, fared no better. No doubt through Göring, Hitler had prior knowledge of Manstein's intention of demanding his resignation as Supreme Commander of the army. Göring evidently advised Manstein against even broaching such heresy. Hitler himself charmed the field marshal with a frank admission that he alone was responsible for Stalingrad—not Göring. "He is the man I have chosen as my successor, and that is why I cannot burden him with the blame for Stalingrad." And after a four-hour display of obstinacy, he flattered Manstein by agreeing to his demand that the eastern Donets region should be abandoned to release the Fourth Panzer Army for the coming German offensive on his army group's western flank. His batteries visibly recharged, the field marshal flew back to the eastern front. Kluge fared no better. Hitler would make no adjustments in his leadership—only in the front line. At long last he bowed to Zeitzler's recommendation that the un-economical three-hundred-mile-long salient around Rzhev and Vyazma should be abandoned in favor of the far shorter chord-line in the rear; but Kluge had to promise to make the twenty-one divisions thus released available for a great spring offensive. The fighting retreat from Vyazma and Rzhev—code-named "Buffalo"—began in March, the first German tactical triumph of 1943.

The field marshals were putty in Hitler's hands. Once when an English newspaper mentioned one of them as the kingpin of the anti-Hitler movement, he guffawed to his staff: "The British are living in the past if they imagine a field marshal really is something nowadays. The moment he lifts his arm in salute he is just another wretched sausage to me!"

General von Richthofen, the choleric, restless Fourth Air Force commander, was an admirer of Hitler's, but educated and critical. He arrived at the Wolf's Lair with Göring on February 11. A tougher nut to crack, Richthofen refused to allow Hitler to sidetrack him with tactical issues but said bluntly that now that this *Schweinerei* had occurred they must get a grip on the ground organization of the army. Of course they would be short of men as long as divisions twelve thousand-strong still put only six hundred actual combat troops into the line. "The Führer asked me point-blank what I think of Manstein," Richthofen wrote in his diary. "I said he is the best tactician and combat commander we have . . . but that Manstein, like all army commanders, is only really interested in operations and tactics." An iron hand was needed in the rear zones. "I stressed to the Führer that the army commanders were all right . . . but must be given tactical freedom to act as their own local experience dictated. Leading them by the scruff of the neck as though they were children just did harm. The Führer said if he hadn't led them like that they would have been fighting in Germany by now. I flatly contradicted him and said that if he didn't trust his top men, he should replace them. . . . Above all I suggested that it was absolutely essential for him to have personal contact with them. If—and this particularly concerned him as Führer—he couldn't visit the armies for some reason or other I was not aware of, then they must be summoned at least once a month to talk over plans and possibilities with him. . . . The Führer cursed his immediate advisers; he tells them everything but they brief him falsely and do nothing. He took it calmly when I retorted that this wasn't of the slightest importance either to us at the front or to future historians. He alone is answerable. There is no point in cursing anybody."[7] Hitler decided it was time Richthofen was made a field marshal too.

Much of the advice given Hitler did sink in, however. He accepted that 1943 would be a "year of clenched teeth," of strategic defense everywhere until production of Speer's tanks, Milch's aircraft, and Dönitz's U-boats increased. When the Gauleiters mustered at the Wolf's Lair for lunch on February 7, Hitler congratulated Goebbels on the post-Stalingrad propaganda but warned that on no account was the failure of "certain allies" to be revealed as the cause of the three-hundred-mile-wide breach torn in the eastern front. He now unconditionally approved the propaganda minister's oft-stated demand for total war. It was what "the people" wanted. To Hitler the opposition was an infinitesimal, misguided minority that had to be dealt with ruthlessly. When a handful of Munich students scattered mimeographed leaflets calling for Hitler's overthrow, the ringleaders were arrested and—young though they were—condemned to death by the People's Court. "Perhaps there are those who say it is incomprehensible that the People's Court acts so ruthlessly," Hitler thundered in a secret speech to his generals later. "A man who just distributed leaflets—and a senior civil servant at that—is condemned to death; or another, a university professor, and two students, who also distributed leaflets are also executed. But if the professor and students responsible had been at the front, they might be just as dead now, who knows? It's a risk every soldier takes all the time. I took it myself, and if need be today I would do so again. . . . But at a time when I expect young girls at home to buckle on their steel helmets and do their duty under heavy air raids, I will have any person making even the slightest attempt to stab my soldiers in the back stood before the People's Court and liquidated. Let that be known." The generals applauded.

Manstein's newly created Army Group South had its headquarters at Zaporozh-'ye on the Dnieper. The huge hydroelectric power station there had just been rebuilt by AEG, a major German electric corporation, and electricity was again flowing to the coal mines and munitions plants of the surrounding Ukraine. Speer had recently shown Hitler the completion dates of his Project Ivan—the rapid expansion of the heavy chemical, nitrogen, and explosives industries of the Donets region. Hitler had anxiously ordered extra antiaircraft batteries and ground

---

[7]Hitler believed that the failure of the army's organization branch to implement a number of his orders was partly to blame for Stalingrad. (See page 413 in this respect.)

Over lunch, Richthofen observed Hitler's method of dealing with Göring: when the Reichsmarschall raised an unwelcome topic, he began reminiscing about the old Vienna Burg Theater—to which "only Munich's Residenz Theater" was now comparable. (Göring was responsible for actor-director Gustav Gründgens's State Theater and sulked in silence.)

defenses to protect the power station, but unless Manstein's sluggish counter-offensive in the Ukraine gathered momentum, it was clear that the whole region would soon be overrun. To the consternation of Hitler's staff, Zeitzler suggested Hitler should fly out to Zaporozh'ye in person. Göring indignantly objected, as did Keitel, to the risk; but Zeitzler sardonically pointed out: "The Reichsmar-schall will be able to darken the skies with fighter squadrons. There's no risk!" Hitler did not agree with this estimate of the situation, but that night his staff stenographer wrote in his diary: "At this evening's conference the Führer an-nounced his decision to go to the front and take over command of Army Group South; this means breaking camp here."

The next day, February 16, Bormann explained in a letter: "Our southern sector is by no means a 'front' even now. Over vast areas we have just a void. To master this extremely tricky and dangerous situation the Führer . . . is going to fly out there with a small escort of intimates." Hitler in fact decided to take just Zeitzler and Jodl—to whom he had once again extended his hand on January 30—with him, together with Schmundt, Hewel, and Dr. Morell. Keitel, Bormann, and the other adjutants stayed behind at the Wolf's Lair. Puttkamer was sent ahead to open up Werewolf, the old summer HQ in the Ukraine. The long flight south began as soon as it was light on February 17, 1943.

"By afternoon the Führer's bunker was deserted," wrote a newly arrived private secretary. "It was strange, the hush that suddenly descended on the whole compound. It was as if the main dynamo of the concern had stopped. This was the first time I sensed how much Hitler's personality acted as a mainspring for all these men—the puppet-master, who held all the marionettes' strings in his hands, had suddenly let them fall."

No secret was made of Hitler's arrival at Manstein's Zaporozh'ye headquarters. Field Marshal von Richthofen arrived shortly, driving a Volkswagen. "There were cordons everywhere," he wrote in his diary. "Everybody that I asked in the streets where army group HQ was smiled scornfully, 'You won't get near it—the Führer's there!' . . . Found the Führer in thick of big war conference. I reported to him. Much beating about the bush, no real opinions, mutual tension, an atmosphere you could cut with a knife. Führer then withdrew to his quarters without reaching any decisions. . . . I saw Field Marshal von Manstein, who shares my view on situation and intentions.—Manstein against all innovations: systems of government, personalities, Luftwaffe devices, and anything else he didn't learn in his youth. . . . Führer very pleasant to me, placid, clear-thinking: question is, has he the necessary implements and ability to convert his clear thoughts into orders?" Hitler directed the Luftwaffe to concentrate on a few hot-spots in the coming offensives. Richthofen and General Otto Dessloch, a local Luftwaffe commander, arranged for two hundred antiaircraft guns to be arrayed as a last-ditch defense against the unceasing Russian tank onslaught, with orders to fight to the last shell.

The next evening, February 18, German radio broadcast throughout occupied Europe Goebbels's defiant Sportpalast speech, whipping his vast audience of Berliners—everybody from the government to the munitions workers—into a frenzy with his proclamation of total war. Now every able-bodied person in the Reich would be harnessed to the war machine; no pleas for exemption would be heeded. Hitler, too busy to listen in person, thoroughly endorsed the extracts he had read. Next morning he himself addressed an effective proclamation to Manstein's and Richthofen's troops on the eve of their counteroffensive between the Dnieper and Donets rivers, on which so much depended:

> Soldiers of Army Group South, airmen of the Fourth Air Force! The outcome of a crucial battle depends on you! A thousand kilometers away from the Reich's frontiers the fate of Germany's present and future is in the balance. . . . The entire German homeland has been mobilized. Everybody down to the last man and woman is being called to serve your battle's needs. Our youth are manning the antiaircraft defenses around Germany's cities and workplaces. More and more divisions are on their way. Weapons unique and hitherto unknown are on the way to your front. . . . This is why I have flown to you, to exhaust every means of alleviating your defensive battle and to convert it into ultimate victory. If every one of you will help, we shall once again succeed, with the Almighty's aid.

At noon Hitler called a further war conference. It was obvious that Manstein and Kleist could not stand each other. Richthofen wrote: "Each is always trying to score over the other in the Führer's eyes. After a final summing up and after due deliberation, the Führer announced in favor of Kleist. Everybody grinning except Manstein, who was furious." By this time Russian tanks were approaching Zaporozh'ye; there was nothing between them and the Luftwaffe airfields. Hitler was loath to leave, but valued his person too highly to stay too long. Richthofen privately suggested that it would make a bad impression if the Führer had to make a hasty exit under the Russian guns, and when Hitler mentioned that he had ordered General Guderian to meet him soon at Vinnitsa—he had given in to Schmundt's badgering and decided to make the truculent general his inspector of panzer troops—Richthofen recommended that Hitler immediately fly there for a couple of days and return to Zaporozh'ye if the Russian threat was thwarted. It was a diplomatic solution.

The gunfire of the Russian tanks was audible from the airfield. Hitler took off for Werewolf immediately. However, in Warlimont's opinion the Führer's presence at the front was certainly to contribute to the great success of the German offensive that now followed.[8] The First and Fourth panzer armies struck northward on February 22, destroying, encircling, and capturing the enemy units in

---

[8]Warlimont confidentially made this observation in a 1945 study for the Americans. In his published work *Im Hauptquartier der Wehrmacht,* page 328, he adopted the more fashionable opposite view.

their path. A bridgehead was soon thrown across the Donets at Balakleya, and by early March a fourth battle for Kharkov was about to begin. The Führer's confidence in Manstein was restored—he was heard to comment privately in admiring language on both the field marshal and General Zeitzler. At last the huge breach wrought that winter in the Axis lines had been plugged; the eastern front had been stabilized—now Hitler could turn his attention to his other affairs of state.

Strychnine

Until mid-March 1943 Hitler remained in the Ukraine, seven hundred miles from Berlin. Werewolf in winter was a bleak and dreary site. Battle-scarred aircraft stood around the local airfield; the countryside was neglected; impoverished Ukrainian peasants with starving horses trudged the fields and forests collecting wood to warm their wretched hovels. The thaw was coming—blessed by the soldiers for the respite it afforded, but turning field and road alike into the now familiar bottomless muddy swamps.

In the bare wooden hutments Hitler contracted first influenza and then a more serious complaint which Morell diagnosed as a brain inflammation; according to medical authorities, this could have resulted from the severe mental strain of Stalingrad, and normally several weeks of rest would have been imperative. Hitler could not afford the time. Soon he was experiencing splitting headaches on one side, and one arm developed a tremor to which he drew Morell's attention; Morell suspected it was of hysterical origin, and he noticed Hitler was dragging one leg slightly too. Hitler sat in his badly ventilated quarters, brooding and worrying; his staff were anxious about his lack of exercise. He was seized by moods of black depression, which Morell tried to combat with injections of Prostakrinum hormones (an extract of young bulls' seminal vesicles and prostate) every other day. As the daily appointment book maintained by his SS orderlies clearly establishes, from now on Morell was nearly always the first visitor to Hitler after his private staff had awakened him each morning. He could not sleep without sedatives; for a time he tried to induce sleep by secretly drinking a glass or two of beer, but fearing fatness even more than insomnia, he soon stopped.

Stalingrad had left deep scars within him. Outwardly he was callous, ordering a new Sixth Army created forthwith and obliterating all trace of the old. But he also ordered Schmundt to arrange for the most generous provision for the next-of-kin. The most delicate problem was raised by the letters the survivors were now writing from Soviet captivity—and indeed by the "last letters" that the Luftwaffe had flown out of the "fortress" itself. The latter were duly delivered, but not those from the Soviet prison camps. Of 1,900 letters that had arrived by mid-February only 45 slipped through to contaminate the German public's already frail belief in ultimate victory. Hitler's rationalization for ordering the letters to be intercepted was that few of the letter-writers were still alive. Why rouse false hopes among their families? and why afford Stalin gratuitous support for his propaganda tactics? Thus the letters were destroyed, adding to the guilty pressure on Hitler's mind. Guderian, who had not seen him since December 1941, found a changed man at Vinnitsa on February 21, 1943. "His left hand trembled, his back was bent, his gaze was fixed, his eyes protruded but lacked their former luster, his cheeks were flecked with red. He was more excitable, easily lost his composure, and was prone to angry outbursts and ill-considered decisions in consequence." For this, however, his self-medication bore much blame.

Even deeper were the scars that had been left in the Axis alliances and within the Axis itself—symbolized at their ugliest by the hand grenade tossed with fatal consequences at a German panzer general as he drove past a surly column of Italian troops marching back from the southern sector of the eastern front. These rifts tested Hitler's diplomacy to the utmost. His immediate reaction had been to "hand back the Eighth Army" to Italy and "write off" the Romanians altogether. But he learned to stifle his anger at these fitful allies. "I never want to see another soldier of our allies on the eastern front," he growled in private to Goebbels. "We can only finish off the Bolsheviks with our own soldiers—and particularly the SS." When Mussolini offered another seven hundred thousand men, Hitler disdainfully commented that there was no point in equipping them with scarce German arms which they would surrender at the first opportunity. "They can't even be assigned 'defensive' combat duties." The Italian Eighth Army, which had gone to battle with a truly splendid artillery, had proved to be incapable from the head down.

Yet when he learned in February that the bedraggled remnants of the Hungarian, Romanian, and Italian armies were being insulted and reviled, and that the Italian ambassador had complained that German units had refused any succour to the unarmed, dispirited, and hungry retreating troops, Hitler piously reminded his generals of the need for common decency and cameraderie—besides which the Reich had a powerful interest in preventing their total disintegration. In an internal policy conference with Keitel and court historian Scherff on May 31, Hitler ruled against any overall communiqué on the winter campaign. "He particularly stressed," wrote Scherff, "that the Stalingrad operation cannot be depicted without passing judgment on our allies. However, for political reasons this historical fact would have to be stood on its head, and then our allies would be able to use this in their favor later on."

Hitler's respect for the Romanian contingent was less affected by their defeat; some of their generals had fought with great distinction, and he was pleased that Antonescu permitted eight divisions to remain in the Crimea and the bridgehead across the Kerch strait. But Hungary's attitude was more ambivalent. On January 22 Germany had invited both her and Italy to withdraw their armies from the eastern front. Hungary had, it must be said, suffered the bloodiest casualties, for her army was less than four years old; 80,000 Hungarian soldiers were dead or missing since the January 12 offensive, and another 63,000 had been injured. Hitler had at once ordered the Reich air ministry to increase its industrial and antiaircraft support for Hungary. Though the murmurs of Magyar discontent grew menacing and insistent, Horthy's military remained largely loyal to the Axis cause. The Second Army's commander, General von Jány, rebuked his men with a famous document (of which Himmler's agents later obtained a photocopy for Hitler), beginning: "The Hungarian Second Army has lost its honor, for only a few men did the duty that was expected of them under their oath. . . ." And General Szombathelyi, the Chief of Staff, accepted Hitler's suggestion that the Hungarian army's new purpose should be to defend the Balkans from Anglo-American invasion.

But though Horthy's generals seemed loyal, his diplomats were more devious. The Forschungsamt and Ribbentrop's cryptographers decoded foreign radio messages that established beyond doubt that the Hungarian prime minister, Miklas von Kállay, was attempting through intermediaries in Turkey, Switzerland, and the Vatican to open secret negotiations with Britain and the United States, and that Kállay had eagerly grasped at Churchill's bumbling proposal to the Turkish government for a new Balkan League (consisting of Turkey, Hungary, and Romania) aligned against both the Soviet Union and the Axis powers. Himmler's agents had obtained word of Kállay's recent secret speech to the foreign policy committee of his Parliament, a speech which proved that he was not to be trusted. Impregnable though Crete now was, Hitler feared that the enemy might land somewhere in the Balkans that spring. He decided personal pressure must be brought to bear on Horthy to rid himself of Kállay and his dangerous doctrines.

So effective was the smokescreen of spurious Intelligence being laid down before both Canaris's Abwehr and Himmler's agencies that Hitler had only his vaunted strategic intuition to rely on in guessing where the war in the Mediterranean would turn next. Spain and Portugal were particularly vulnerable targets; their occupation would prevent Hitler from seizing Gibraltar, impede his U-boat offensive in the Atlantic, and deprive him of their iron, tungsten, lithium, and tin. Canaris was twice sent to Madrid but reported unenthusiastically. Spain neither could nor would voluntarily enter the war unless her neutrality were directly threatened. Hitler decided to furnish Franco with the weapons he would need. He may also have been the source of Franco's information that in August 1942 Churchill had "promised Russia predominant influence in Europe east of the Rhine."[1] On January 16 Himmler's report on an agent's long confidential talk with Franco was in Hitler's hands, and it showed how worried Franco was about both the bolshevik peril looming over Europe and the hardly less disconcerting shadow of American imperialism over North Africa. Conversely, there was also evidence that Churchill had secretly promised Franco a slice of French Morocco.

By February it seemed clear that the British and Americans were in fact massing strength near the border of Spanish Morocco, even at the expense of their front in Tunisia. Through Stockholm came fresh agents' warnings of an early invasion of the Iberian peninsula. Canaris went to Hitler's headquarters on the ninth and tried to kill these rumors, but Hitler ordered divisions moved up to the Spanish frontier ready for an immediate occupation of northern Spain should an enemy invasion occur. At a war conference on the tenth he predicted that it would be coupled with simultaneous invasions of the Channel and Atlantic coastlines, where his Atlantic Wall was still some months short of completion. He warned the defenses to stand by for possible mass parachute landings in the rear. A naval participant wrote after the conference: "As to Spain's attitude, the Führer's mind was suddenly completely at ease. He had certain information, I don't know where from. At any rate he said everything had been cleared up to our satisfaction." Hitler and Göring positively exuded optimism that Spain would now fight to defend herself, but Richthofen, meeting them the next day, was less sure. "I said we shouldn't expect any gratitude for the help we rendered from 1936 to 1939. The Spanish always only think of Spain; they are utterly selfish—which is natural enough—and they regard us as God-damned heretics." What Hitler and Göring knew was that one of the war's most secret treaties had just been signed in Madrid: in return for modern German weapons in sufficient quantities, Franco now committed his country in writing to fighting the British and Americans the moment they set foot in Spain, Portugal, or any Spanish possessions in the Mediterranean, Atlantic, and Africa.

The enemy might equally well exploit the partisan chaos in the Balkans; an Allied invasion there would bring the Romanian oil fields within bomber reach. Despite

[1]On January 19, 1943, Franco warned Churchill in a secret message that "the longer the war goes on, the more Britain will be obliterated by her Allies—Russia and the United States." He advised Britain to negotiate with non-Nazi elements in Germany while there was still time. Churchill did not welcome Franco's message, though the Caudillo's claim to have seen detailed accounts of his talks in Moscow may have roused his curiosity.

the mounting bomber offensive against Germany, Hitler therefore ordered fresh antiaircraft defenses supplied to Romania. He arranged for Bulgarians in German uniforms to police the more restless areas of Greece. He eloquently directed his military commander in the southeast, General Löhr, to restore peace there—"the peace of the graveyard, if need be."

In Croatia as elsewhere Italy was at the root of Hitler's troubles. General Roatta's Second Army had persistently pursued policies dramatically athwart both Hitler's and Mussolini's. When Tito's partisan forces had become too powerful, the Italians had merely ignored Germany's protests and abandoned territory wholesale. Roatta had continued to arm the Četnik (Serbian) irregulars against the partisans even though many a Četnik bullet now winged toward a German or Croatian soldier. Though in December Ciano had unenthusiastically agreed to Hitler's demand that the Četniks be disarmed, the army ignored Mussolini's directive to that effect. Soon the vital bauxite mines of Mostar were abandoned to the partisans. Every joint Italian-German sweep against them failed, the Germans felt, because of Italian sloth and ineptitude. Tito escaped time after time, until gradually Hitler came to extend to him an admiration he had previously reserved for Stalin. Late in February, he sent Ribbentrop to Rome with a strongly worded letter demanding more active Italian support, particularly against the Četniks; he furnished dozens of radio messages intercepted and decoded by his agencies, proving beyond doubt that the Četnik irregulars were fighting for General Draža Mihajlović and thus for London. But while the Duce was willing to accept German demands, his soldiers were not. The new Chief of Staff, General Ambrosio, furnished various excuses for not proceeding against Mihajlović: for example, the Italian troops were needed for the defense of Italy. Löhr came to Vinnitsa and asked for a saturation air raid on Mihajlović's headquarters at Collasin in Montenegro, and he proposed pacifying Croatia by installing at every level a German civil administration backed by local gendarmes to be supplied by Himmler. Hitler's patience with the Italians was exhausted; he ordered Mostar and the bauxite mines recaptured, and he began planning a short, sharp war of annihilation against Mihajlović and the Četniks. "On account of the intimate relations between the Mihajlović commanders and the Italian authorities, the Führer attaches particular importance to camouflaging our object and all the preparations." But not until mid-May would this operation, code-named "Black," begin.

If it were not for the political effect the loss of Tunisia would have had on Italy, Hitler would have long since withdrawn his divisions there and made more profitable use of them—just as Mussolini had urgently requested the repatriation of 290,000 Italian workers in Germany. His own interest in this distant desert war was negligible. He considered that Rommel had missed his chance, a view shared by Kesselring and Göring. "Without optimism, military command is impossible," Hitler meditated afterward. "I see Rommel—though he has limitations—as an extraordinarily bold and clever commander, but he lacks staying power; everybody thinks so." Given the Italian inability to protect supply ships—during January alone 22 out of 51 had been sunk—it was obvious the holding action in Tunisia would not last much longer.

In Tunisia Rommel was a sick man, and his future was uncertain. But General von Arnim's Fifth Panzer Army, facing westward, was in better shape. Warlimont returned from Tunis in mid-February quoting Rommel's description of the bridgehead as a "house of cards" which would collapse the moment Montgomery attacked—presumably one month hence, when the moon was full. Ominously, the Allies had a new 57-millimeter shell capable of piercing the Tiger tank, the pride of Hitler's armor.[2] But Arnim detected a weak spot facing him, the American Second Corps; on February 14 General Heinz Ziegler struck at these inexperienced soldiers and drove a big salient toward the vital Kasserine Pass, taking hundreds of American prisoners. German interrogators claimed that a surprising number of Americans were ex-convicts, adventurers, and mercenaries. "Politically speaking they are naïve," remarked Hewel to Hitler. "They are rowdies who take to their heels rather than stand fast at a crisis. . . . You really ought to see their war posters, quite incredible."—"I don't doubt," replied Hitler, "that of the Anglo-Saxons the British are the best." But the German offensive failed, and Canaris quoted Arnim as saying, "With the supply position as it is" —twenty-five thousand tons instead of the requisite eighty thousand tons had arrived in February—"you can work out with pencil and paper when the end will come." Canaris reported that nobody knew whether Kesselring or Rommel was in overall command of the newly created Army Group Africa.

Exactly why Rommel was given the army group, and not Arnim as had been planned, is not evident from the records. A specialist had checked Rommel's health and reported to Hitler that he would have to go on leave by February 20 at the latest; but the moment he was given the army group, with one German and one Italian army to defend Tunis, his illness mysteriously cleared up. Rommel was also cheered by word from Schmundt that the Führer was deeply concerned about him; Hitler evidently hoped that if properly pepped up, this petulant commander would put his heart into the final decisive strike at Montgomery's Eighth Army before departing for his convalescent leave. But Rommel did not gain heart. He took counsel of his two army commanders, Arnim and Messe, and on March 4 Hitler was handed his discouraging opinion: the present Tunis

---

[2]The Tiger was still having teething troubles. Hitler jealously called for details of the training of every Tiger tank crew whose tank was knocked out in Africa. The results were embarrassing for the army. Himmler hastily ordered that only the best crews were to man the Tigers allocated to the SS panzer corps.

battlefront was over 400 miles long, the enemy had 1,600 tanks, 1,100 antitank guns, and about 210,000 combat troops; unless Hitler would authorize Rommel to withdraw to a far shorter front, of about 100 miles, the two armies under his command would be overwhelmed. Not without justification Hitler noted: "That is a complete contradiction of his earlier contention"—namely that a retreat to Tunisia would solve their strategic shortcomings. Jodl pointed out that Rommel's plan would make a gift of vital airfields to the enemy and allow Montgomery and Alexander to join forces against the bridgehead. With 140,000 German troops alone, Rommel was not numerically all that inferior to the enemy. Hitler refused to allow the withdrawal. "This is the end," he predicted nonetheless. "They might just as well be brought back."

Hitler particularly wanted the final enemy offensive fought off long enough for the rest of the German divisions to arrive and the mass production of small transport ships to take effect. "On superior orders," as Rommel querulously wrote, he launched his last attack on March 6, on Montgomery. But that same day he returned to the line fortified at Mareth, outfought and outgunned by the British army. As Hitler had predicted, it was the end. From all appearances—arranged by the British secret service, which had read Rommel's cipher telegrams—captured Italian officers had betrayed Rommel's plans to Montgomery, so Hitler did not reproach him. He decided on the eighth to recall "the Desert Fox" before he could be tarnished by the eventual defeat in Tunis; for the time being, however, Rommel's recall remained a closely guarded secret—the *reputation* of Rommel would soldier on, *in absentia.*

He flew into Vinnitsa late on March 9 and spent the evening alone with Hitler. Again Hitler turned a deaf ear on the idea of shortening the bridgehead's battlefront; he betrayed his obvious conviction that Rommel had become a defeatist. Hitler intended to retain Tunis at all costs: he would increase the supply rate to 150,000 tons a month, he said, and when Rommel's health was better he was to return to Africa and direct the offensive westward to Casablanca. The next day Reichsmarschall Göring, summoned by Hitler, arrived in his special train from Rome and eagerly lent his not inconsiderable weight to Hitler's optimism—as did Kesselring on the fourteenth. Kesselring and Dönitz were flown immediately to Rome to put pressure on the Italians to increase the rate of supply across the Strait of Sicily. Dönitz was instructed not to mince words with the Duce; and Kesselring was to hand Mussolini a stinging written reproach by Hitler on the supply problem. It read in part:

> . . . for whatever posterity may think of Field Marshal Rommel, he has been well loved by his troops and of course by all the German troops in every one of his commands. To his enemies he was a feared opponent, and still is. It is

a tragedy that this man, one of my most courageous officers and distinguished by exceptional capability, should have come to grief on the problem of logistics —a problem which can only be solved by stepping up the sea transports to a maximum.

To Rommel, the "has-been," Hitler secretly awarded the diamonds for his Knight's Cross; the Italians refused to emulate this distinction.

Göring's prestige was plummeting with every fresh ruinous air attack on Germany's proud and ancient cities. That was why Hitler had rudely ordered his return from Rome. On March 1 hundreds of night bombers had rained high explosives and incendiaries on Berlin, leaving thirty-five thousand people homeless and over seven hundred dead. Hitler's doctors and staff reported that far into the nights that followed, he was troubled by anguished images of humble Berlin families who had lost not only their homes but two or three children before their eyes as well. The finest fighter aircraft or antiaircraft defenses were of no avail against bomber hordes like these! Only counterterror would deter the British! But Field Marshal Sperrle's emasculated Third Air Force could stage only the weakest retaliatory raids, and London barely noticed them. "The British write that our latest raid was a mere phantom," fumed Göring to his staff, "and that the lot fell in open countryside. It drives you mad! Bombing through dense cloud, *they* can hit an egg in a railroad station—yet our fellows can't even find London." A low-level Luftwaffe fighter-bomber attack on London on March 5 had been scrubbed, as Hitler was apologetically told, because of fog and the "dead calm sea"—evoking Hitler's natural astonished query: "Do our planes *swim* over, then?" (In fact without visible waves to guide them the low-flying pilots *were* in danger of crashing.) Hitler blamed the indolent and sybaritic Sperrle and called for a younger man to direct the attack on Britain. "When does the Reichsmarschall get back?" he had demanded. "Things can't go on like this; we will never wear down the British like this."

That night, March 5, a crippling attack was made on Essen, heart of the Ruhr's steel industry, destroying three thousand houses and buildings and killing hundreds of workers. When Goebbels arrived on March 8 with Speer, Hitler was still furiously inveighing against the complete failure of the Luftwaffe in comparison to the army now that Zeitzler was in charge. Göring was less to blame than the mendacious and incompetent generals around him, said Hitler, but the next six months might see many of their cities in ruins and thousands of civilians dead. Toward midnight, sitting in his bunker with Speer and Goebbels, Hitler was just saying sourly that he only had to picture his generals in mufti to lose every shred of respect for them when he heard that a colossal air raid had just been launched against Nuremberg—the medieval gem of Bavaria and seat of the Party's affairs.

Hitler had General Bodenschatz, Göring's cynical lieutenant, roused from his sleep, and rasped that the Reichsmarschall must return from Rome forthwith.

Hoping to preserve him as the vehicle of their political ambitions, Speer and Goebbels both defended Göring that night; this alone had warded off Hitler's wrath, for he had hinted to Bodenschatz that he might even assume overall command of the Luftwaffe himself. How many orders he had given the Luftwaffe both before 1939 and after—and how few had been carried out! "The generals always knew better than I; now the German public is paying the price." Göring —when he arrived on the eleventh—gratefully adopted the same line. "I told the Führer I am not an aircraft designer or technician, so I can't build the planes myself, nor can I develop new engines or equipment," he said a week later. His generals and experts had always bluffed him; his radar specialists had even excused their inability to test blind-bombing devices by pleading bad weather. Over the next nights Munich and Stuttgart were the bombers' targets. Now Hitler overrode Göring; he ordered the air war against Britain stepped up, and he appointed the youthful Colonel Dietrich Peltz "Attack Commander, England" —responsible not to the sluggish Sperrle but to Jeschonnek (and hence to Hitler) alone.

A naïve plan by Goebbels, Speer, and a handful of their disgruntled contemporaries to use Göring and his Reich Defense Committee as a front whereby they could divert absolute power from Lammers, Keitel, and Bormann to themselves was temporarily placed in limbo.

Hitler flew for the morning of March 10 to Manstein's headquarters at Zaporozh-'ye, for he was well satisfied with events on the southern front. His high hopes in the SS panzer divisions had proven justified. Here he awarded Manstein the Oak Leaf Cluster for his Knight's Cross in recognition of his achievements. Manstein's two panzer armies had left 23,000 Russian dead on the first battlefield between the Donets and Dnieper rivers; 615 tanks, 354 guns, and enormous quantities of other equipment had fallen into his hands. Thereupon, an offensive against Stalin's Voronezh army group had resulted in the destruction of the enemy's Third Tank Army southwest of Kharkov. In this operation, some 12,000 of the enemy were killed. Now Manstein's Fourth Panzer Army, with its powerful SS panzer corps, was embarking upon the fifth battle fought over Kharkov since "Barbarossa" began. Meanwhile Hitler had issued detailed orders for defensive lines to be excavated and built everywhere to the rear of the eastern front. To do this, he made ruthless use of forced labor, just as the Russians had in similar circumstances.

Thus the mood at Zaporozh'ye was one of elation, for the generals' morale was again high. Richthofen noted:

The Führer lands at 10:40 A.M. Manstein and I drive in Führer's car to army group HQ, with Führer in pretty good mettle. Fiebig at last gets the Oak Leaves.—Every army commander from both army groups and my own [Luftwaffe] corps commanders present. Army commanders deliver briefings on their situation, which tell me nothing new. Then the Führer on the coming operations and Manstein on his own intentions; nothing new either. . . . Manstein keeps up a hate campaign against Kleist [commander of Army Group A] the whole time, and Führer prompts Manstein to make hostile comments about Kleist and Kluge, his two neighbors. Führer enjoying every minute. Ribs me mercilessly but kindly; for some reason addresses everybody as "Herr Feldmarschall" today as a joke. . . . Says he never wants to hear of the Romanians or our other gallant allies again: if he relies on them he only gets worked up because they don't stand firm; and if he arms them but *doesn't* use them, he gets just as worked up to see them standing around doing nothing.

The snows were melting, turning the eastern front into its seasonal morass. The three-hundred-mile nightmare breach had almost been stitched together, proof in Hitler's eyes that the Red Army had no reserves up its sleeve after all. Already the Russians were drafting their seventeen-year-olds; perhaps the great collapse was in sight at last. Admittedly the eight-hundred-thousand-man call-up he had himself projected was proceeding less smoothly than he had hoped, and a new Russian thrust between the Second Panzer and Second Armies at Kursk and Orel was still causing concern. But in the south the recapture of Kharkov was now certain. And west of Moscow "Operation Buffalo"—the careful withdrawal of two armies to a well-fortified new line between Spass Demensk and Byelyi—was drawing to its brilliant conclusion. The Red Army, puzzled at this uncharacteristic retreat, had followed only hesitantly, stumbled upon well-laid minefields and booby-traps, and suffered heavy casualties at no cost to the Germans. The retiring Germans had destroyed or dismantled everything of value to the enemy. "A battle won," concluded Kluge's army group.

On March 13, Hitler flew back from Vinnitsa to the Wolf's Lair, calling first that afternoon at Smolensk, headquarters for Kluge's Army Group Center. Three days before, on March 10, Himmler had telephoned to Hitler's police bodyguard a warning to be on the lookout for parcel bombs.[3] Hitler showed no concern. He

---

[3]In fact Kluge's Intelligence officer, Colonel Rudolf von Gersdorff, and others claimed after the war that they planted a parcel bomb in Hitler's aircraft before it left Smolensk on March 13, 1943. (If they did, it failed to go off.) Admiral Canaris, one of the plotters, wrote in his own notes of the flight he made to Smolensk on March 8: "I conveyed time fuses and explosives in my plane to the Army Group's Abwehr II sabotage unit." Since Canaris dined for two hours with Himmler on March 10, shortly *before* Himmler put through his telephone warning to Hitler's police bodyguard, it is tempting to assume that Canaris made an incautious remark to him about the bomb plot; but Himmler's files show that since March 3 parcel bombs posted by the Polish underground were causing some concern, and his phone call to SS Brigadeführer Hans Rattenhuber, chief of Hitler's bodyguard, was probably

was inspired by the buoyant mood of Kluge's officers at Smolensk. They were delighted at the tactical victory of the Fourth and Ninth armies, which had succeeded beyond all their expectations in disengaging from the enemy and withdrawing without any loss of men or equipment, while at the same time carrying out extensive demolitions in their wake. Initially the Russians had whipped their armies into hot pursuit—with consequent heavy casualties in the intricate and well-planned minefields the Germans had laid. The Russians captured only their own wrecked equipment. The new "Buffalo" line was already built—a formidable line of barbed wire entanglements, bunkers, and antitank ditches. When Kluge asked if the objective of their coming summer campaign could be disclosed to them, Hitler astonished both Kluge and his staff with its modesty: "To hold the eastern front just as it is." That evening he was back in East Prussia.

Yet the prospect of a year on the defensive galled him. "I can't just let a whole year go to waste," he said. All the indications were that the Soviet Union might yet be about to collapse. Zeitzler agreed; the new East Wall was all very well, but "they will flatten us first, before we can finish it." Hitler responded, "They are in such a state now that we would be lunatic not to exploit it." The fragmentary records of his war conferences reveal him already plotting with Zeitzler a partial resumption of the offensive in order to regain the initiative in the central front. Zeitzler hinted at April 15 as a suitable date, though Manstein thought that too early. "One thing we must *not* say," insisted the Führer, "is—this year just a few prods at the enemy, next year the Big Push. Perhaps *this* year we can win the war!" Before March 13 was over Hitler had signed Zeitzler's order laying the foundations of "Citadel," a combined attack by Kluge's and Manstein's army groups on a tempting enemy salient at Kursk.

The next day Sepp Dietrich's SS troops retook Kharkov. Hitler exuberantly telephoned Goebbels, but the canny propaganda minister was against any special radio fanfare—it would undermine the very "Dunkirk spirit" he had labored to contrive in Germany. Hitler, however, wanted the gallantry of his SS Life Guards properly recognized, and insisted; half an hour later he heard the announcement on the radio, though preceded by the less pompous Horst Wessel fanfare this time rather than the one from Liszt's *Préludes*.

That evening Goebbels appealed to be allowed to revive the anti-Jewish propaganda motif and pestered him to complete displacing Jews from the entire Reich

---

just a reprimand for not having issued warnings to the Reich ministries yet. A remarkable coincidence nonetheless.

as soon as possible. Hitler indulgently agreed that Goebbels could go ahead, but when Himmler himself arrived at the Wolf's Lair on the seventeenth, with the creation of fresh SS corps and divisions on his agenda, the Führer apparently felt it necessary to speak a word of restraint, for the next day Himmler telephoned Gestapo Chief Müller in Berlin that there was to be "no deportation of the privileged Jews[4]" from France. Again it does not behoove the historian to speculate or embroider on the precise significance of the words employed.

For the first time in six years, Hitler's stomach spasms had begun to recur. The doctors advised him to retire for a week or two to the Obersalzberg. With the eastern front now paralyzed by the thaw, Hitler bowed to their advice. Besides, he wanted to speak in Berlin on March 21, Memorial Sunday, to kill the persistent rumors that he was gravely ill; and at the Berghof he would be closer to the Mediterranean theater. While the invasion of Spain and Portugal predicted by Jodl for February 22 had failed to materialize, Admiral Canaris had twice warned that the enemy would occupy Sicily, Sardinia, and Corsica during March, and Zeitzler's Intelligence officers agreed. (Thus convincingly had they been hoaxed by the Allies.) In Tunis, General Montgomery had just begun the offensive against the Mareth line. It seemed high time for Hitler to meet the Duce—and his other coalition partners too.

He had himself lighted on a cure for his stomach pangs. In 1936 his SS doctor, SS General Dr. Ernst-Robert Grawitz, had prescribed "Dr. Koester's Antigas Tablets," a German patent medicine, for his tender gastrointestinal tract, and at his request Dr. Morell supplied several gross of these. Hitler was relieved to experience the same well-being these apparently harmless black pills had given him six years earlier and began to consume them regularly—from eight to sixteen every day—until an appalled visiting doctor examined them in October 1944 and read the legend on the small flat aluminum tin: "Extr.nux.vomic. 0.04; Extr. bellad. 0.04." The doctor then announced that they were principally based on the poisons strychnine and atropine, and that Hitler had from time to time been imbibing nearly lethal doses. Only then were relevant entries in the poisons manual read out to a chastened Führer. "Atropine acts on the central nervous system first as a stimulant, then as a paralyzer. In humans it primarily affects the forebrain, manifesting itself in a state of psychic exaltation. A state of cheerfulness develops, coupled with vivid flights of ideas, talkativeness, and restlessness, visual and aural hallucinations, and fits of delirium which may be peaceful and serene but may equally degenerate into acts of violence and frenzy." Strychnine, on the

[4]Those with influence in the United States. See page 462.

other hand, accumulated in the body, acting on the nervous system to increase all the senses' acuteness. "After heavy doses the accentuated sensitiveness to light may turn into downright aversion to light; and the other senses show similar changes. The senses of hearing and touch are accentuated, and for a time the senses of smell and taste may become more acute." So dramatically could strychnine amplify the reactions of the nervous system that lockjaw could result from a normally harmless stimulus. The significance of Hitler's self-medication beginning in the spring of 1943 should not be scanted.

Thus Hitler left the Wolf's Lair, though for many weeks longer than he originally planned. His car brought him to the local railroad station, where his special train was waiting, and as soon as he, his servants, and his Alsatian bitch Blondi were aboard it began to move. His compartments were of a luxury strange to him after the strenuous bunker life of Rastenburg—there were silken sheets for all his staff, highly polished woodwork and brass lamps, and a soft carpet on the floor. Surrounded by his private staff, he took dinner in the dining car with its red-leather-covered chairs. At his command the three secretaries joined him— Johanna Wolf, the most senior and self-effacing; the forthright Christa Schroeder, who had served her apprenticeship with Bormann; and Traudl Humps, the newcomer. Schaub, Hewel, Bormann, and Morell sat in as well—the portly doctor wading into the meal with an appetite that was as audible as it was evident. Hitler contented himself with mashed potato, an egg, and a dry biscuit.

Traudl Humps later wrote: "I was taken aback by the informal nature of the conversation. Bormann above all was gentle and friendly. . . . The Führer spoke softly and with restraint. After the meal he asked for the ceiling lights to be switched off. He preferred subdued light as his eyes were rather sensitive." A pot of caraway tea was served. "Delicious," exclaimed Hitler, but nobody accepted his offer of a cup. At intervals the train halted, and telephone messages were received. Hitler summoned a manservant: "Take Blondi for a walk outside." Then the train began again, the dining car gently swaying, Morell snoring lightly, and the one small table lamp casting a dim glow.

At Rügenwalde in Pomerania the next morning he stayed for a few hours to inspect Krupp's new giant gun, "Long Gustav," and various new tank prototypes undergoing trials on the ranges. Here at last was the new Ferdinand tank, a seventy-ton monster powered by two diesel-electric sets, all but impregnable with its eight-inch-thick armorplate and formidable 88-millimeter gun. These and the Tigers would surely overwhelm the Russians when "Citadel" began. Speer and his dynamic Nazi deputy Karl-Otto Saur boarded the train for an informal conference on the new weapons programs, as it continued toward Berlin. Hitler was undaunted by the prevailing fear of Russian "armies" that were a mere shadow of their name. "I am convinced the rogues are so weak . . ." the stenographers heard him say; and "All they have against us are 'formations,' but . . ." (The fragments alone exist, but they seem clear enough.) He invited Speer and Goebbels to dinner in the Chancellery, showed them the damage survey of Munich after the last British air raid, and mentioned the high hopes he vested in Dönitz's U-boat war. Goebbels recommended that the Luftwaffe bomb London's plutocratic districts rather than the slums. When he channeled the conversation around to the Jews, Hitler congratulated him on having evacuated most of them from Berlin. "The war is enabling us to deal with a whole series of problems we could never have dealt with in normal times," Goebbels quoted him as saying. Yet Hitler obviously found the propaganda minister's company distasteful, for he refused to make time available for a further private meeting with him until May. Thus far had Martin Bormann's influence over Hitler progressed.

Half an hour after midnight on March 22 his train left Berlin for Munich. He spent the day with Frau Troost, lunched in the Osteria, and looked at the latest paintings. That evening Eva Braun joined the train for the short journey to Berchtesgaden; a long column of Mercedes cars brought them up the mountain to where the Berghof lay, its Great Hall window palely reflecting the moonlight and the snow; Frau Mittelstrasser, the housekeeper, welcomed the couple; Hitler's coat and cap were hung up in the vestibule, and he withdrew to his quarters.

Few records survive of his conferences and decisions of the following weeks. A minute-by-minute logbook of his movements, kept by his manservants, shows him rising regularly around noon, lunching at two or three, and going to bed far into the night; supper was a very movable feast indeed. Apart from "Citadel," we know that Hitler was looking ahead to a further offensive against Leningrad in the summer. But he was also casting around for some way of regaining the initiative in the west too: "Gisela," a Nazi occupation of northern Spain, was one; but he had begun to reconsider a lightning invasion of Iceland too—"Operation Ikarus," which Raeder had barely talked him out of in 1940. Mussolini was not due to come until April 7; before then Hitler had only a little-publicized meeting with King Boris, one of his trustier allies; the monarch confirmed that Bulgaria would fight on Hitler's side if Britain and Turkey should invade the Balkans. No record was made of the meeting; it was so informal that at one stage one of Hitler's secretaries made an unheralded appearance munching an apple and clutching a pair of tennis rackets. "Don't worry yourself," Hitler consoled her afterward; "even kings are only human."

In these weeks at the Berghof, Hitler looked briefly into some Third Reich problems he had too long ignored. Others he studiously avoided, but many more were kept deliberately from him. Thus when Reichsführer Himmler came on

March 30 the discussion revolved solely around the military affairs of the SS, according to Himmler's note—and no mention was made of the Black Chapel scandal which was about to disclose the dubious loyalties of Admiral Canaris's Abwehr.[5] An Intelligence chief who had produced as little hard information as Canaris had, should long since have been dispensed with. His predictions had invariably proven wrong. For example, initially he had prophesied that Britain and France would march at the time of Munich and that France was about to attack Germany in mid-September 1939. In addition, he had known nothing of Stalin's huge tank production in 1941, of the North African invasion plan in 1942, or of the Roosevelt-Churchill Casablanca meeting more recently. But so long as Keitel shielded Canaris, his subordinate, Himmler was loath to burn his fingers by impeaching him for treason. Canaris knew of this—perhaps he had some hold over Himmler. We can imagine with what concealed contempt Canaris recorded, after a heart-to-heart talk with the visibly dejected field marshal in 1941, that Keitel had ("verbatim") confided to him: "If I did not have such loyal friends in my department as you, my dear Canaris, I would have chucked it all up long ago. Only the knowledge that I have such reliable colleagues consoles me and keeps me going."

Nor did Himmler evidently raise with Hitler the progress made on the "Jewish problem" during their two-hour mountain stroll on March 30—Hitler wearing a soft peaked cap to shade his eyes against the Alpine glare. Earlier in 1943 Himmler had submitted to him a statistical report on a similar topic—the population migrations he had sponsored since Hitler's written order of October 1939; the report[6] was typed on the special large-face typewriter and clearly went to the Führer. But did Hitler ever see the statistical report the Reichsführer had commissioned at the same time on the "Final Solution of the Jewish Problem in Europe"? In dry tones, Himmler's chief statistician, Dr. Richard Korherr, had analyzed the fate of the world's estimated 17,000,000 Jews: Europe's 10,000,000 had dwindled by 45 percent since 1937, owing to emigration, the high natural mortality rate, and the enforced "evacuation" that had begun with the prohibition of emigration late in 1941. To Himmler's annoyance, on reading the sixteen-page document on March 23 he found that it stated *expressis verbis* on page 9 that of

[5]Following the routine arrest of a Munich Abwehr agent involved in a sordid currency racket, the Gestapo had uncovered evidence linking Canaris's principal officials with treasonable communications to the Vatican. On March 24, 1943, Himmler had a telephone conversation with the Gestapo chief, Müller, in Berlin on the "Black Chapel complex." On April 5 the Abwehr headquarters was raided, and key Canaris aides including Dr. Hans von Dohnanyi and General Hans Oster were arrested.

[6]In three years Himmler had resettled 629,000 ethnic Germans from outside the Reich; 400,000 more were still to come. In the same period 365,000 Poles were dumped in the Generalgouvernement of Poland, and 295,000 French citizens were evicted from Alsace, Lorraine, and Luxemburg.

the 1,449,692 Jews deported from the eastern provinces 1,274,166 had been subjected to "special treatment" at camps in the Generalgouvernement and a further
145,301 similarly dealt with in the Warthegau. Himmler knew too well that the
Führer had in November 1941[7] ordered that the Jews were *not* to be liquidated.
On April 1 he had the report edited "for submission to the Führer"; and a few
days later—lest he had not made himself plain—instructed that in the version for
the Führer he "did not want there to be any mention of 'special treatment of Jews'
whatever." According to the new text, the Jews would have been "channeled
through" the camps to Russia—not "subjected to special treatment" at the
camps. As he wrote on April 9, the report would serve magnificently for "camouflage purposes" in later years.

Mussolini arrived at Salzburg station on April 7. The sun glinted on the snow-clad
mountains, the sky was postcard blue, but the Duce himself was a sick man—
his eyes lusterless, his cheeks hollow, he had to be helped out of his carriage by
two companions. There were rumors that he had cancer, but Hitler privately
believed it was just a psychological depression. While it was understood that the
fall of Tunis was probably inevitable, at least he could inspire Mussolini with the
coming campaigns in the east. Mussolini and his *de facto* foreign minister, Gi-
useppe Bastianini, were housed at Klessheim—an enchanting baroque chateau
near Salzburg which had been lavishly restored by Hitler—and here a short series
of what Zeitzler contemptuously dubbed "gala war conferences" were held for
Mussolini's benefit. Here Göring, Zeitzler, and Jodl rehearsed the daily situation
in optimistic tones (though Zeitzler refused Hitler's suggestion that a fake map
of the eastern front should be employed, as had been customary in Halder's day
on such occasions). They banqueted together, Hitler consuming his vegetarian
concoctions, Mussolini's meals first sampled by an unenthusiastic "taster" as in
Roman times.

The conferences were short, out of regard for the Duce's health, but even so
he had difficulty following them. The two dictators were moved by different
purposes. Mussolini still wanted an armistice with Stalin, to enable the Axis to
throw all its might against Britain and the United States; and he handed Hitler
a memorandum on the possible negotiations. Given the Allies' poor showing over
the Russian convoys and a Second Front, Stalin had good cause to be upset. The
Duce believed Spain would voluntarily join the Axis. To Hitler all this was
disappointingly naïve: from the Forschungsamt intercepts he knew just how
closely the "Jewish Bolsheviks" of London, Washington, and Moscow were

[7]Page 332.

Himmler's telephone notes of November 30, 1941. At 1:30 P.M. the SS chief telephoned Heydrich in Prague from Hitler's bunker at the Wolf's Lair, ordering that there was to be "no liquidation" of Jews.

collaborating in Germany's defeat; and there were alarming signs that even Spain had come under their sway. If fascism in Italy was not to be overthrown, so he advised Mussolini, Tunis must be held if at all possible. This meant that the Italian navy must abandon its pride and throw every fast cruiser and destroyer it had into the supply operations for Tunisia. It would be impossible to salvage Arnim's army group in defeat. The Duce asked for more oil for the ships, and Hitler agreed to supply it. An hour-long Hitler monologue on Frederick the Great and Prussian steadfastness did the rest; Mussolini returned to Rome visibly improved in body and mind.

The distinction between Hitler's private and his public views was as marked as the contrast between Klessheim and the Berghof. In private he was cynical about the New Order. How would the Duce have reacted to hearing the Führer mutter to his staff: "Our neighbors are all our potential enemies. We must squeeze what we can out of them. But we neither can nor should make them any promises."

Each evening Hitler was driven back up to the Berghof, where he was greeted by the barking of Eva Braun's two untidy black scotties and by Eva herself, elegantly clad in the latest fashions. Her favorite dress was of close-fitting Nile-green wool, with long sleeves and a broad strip of leopard skin around its hem. Hitler kissed her hand and chatted with the others of her house party—her pretty sister Gretl, Frau Herta Schneider, and Frau Marion Schönmann were frequent guests, as were the wives of Below and Dr. Karl Brandt. Eva organized regular film shows in the basement bowling-alley, but Hitler piously stayed away. "In wartime, with the people called upon to make such sacrifices, I cannot watch movies.—Besides, I must save my eyesight for reading maps and dispatches." The same priggish considerations militated against his wearing more comfortable clothes. A Churchill, he noted, might gambol about the world dressed in silk blouses and cowboy hats—but not the Führer of the Reich. "As long as we are at war I will not take off this uniform. My knees are white as chalk anyway, and that looks awful in short trousers. —But the moment the war is over, I am going to hang my uniform on a nail, retire here, and let somebody else take over the government. As an old man I will write my memoirs, surrounded by clever, intellectual people—I never want to see another officer. My two elder secretaries will stay with me and do the typing . . ."

They were long evenings that spring, for Hitler refused to go to bed until the last enemy bomber had left Germany's airspace. British and American bombers had already carved black swaths far into central Europe. In March alone eight thousand tons of bombs had rained down on Germany, sometimes a thousand tons a night on single cities like Duisburg, Essen, and Berlin. On April 4, 228 civilians were killed in Paris and 221 in Naples in American air raids; on the fifth an American raid on the Belgian port of Antwerp accounted for 2,130 civilians. Göring's Luftwaffe was powerless to defend or deliver adequate reprisals. Hitler's interest in the army's long-range missile project increased, and on March 29 he approved Speer's blueprints for a huge concrete missile site on the Channel coast, from which Britain would be bombarded once missiles were available. It was the first of several "secret weapon" projects that were—however improbably—to sustain his own hope of final victory.

As Göring's prestige declined, the rivalry of the other satraps increased. Speer was an almost permanent visitor to the Berghof throughout April, but Bormann was lord of the manor here. He had secured Hitler's signature to a document appointing him his official "Secretary"—giving him express control over Hitler's security and affairs: he had the right to attend all conferences and "communicate the Führer's decisions and opinions to the Reich ministers and other departments and agencies"—a formidable prerogative. He alone would decide which nonmilitary supplicants might see Hitler and which documents would be shown to him. Bormann's powers became vast. His eyes were everywhere; his energy was prodigious; his loyalty was beyond question. When Baldur von Schirach, the thirty-five-year-old Gauleiter of Vienna whom Hitler had regarded as his possible successor, challenged Bormann's domestic policies, the Reichsleiter outmaneuvered him—summoning him to Hitler on March 26 for a tirade about his "decadent" cultural speeches and art exhibitions. Speer and Goebbels followed through. Schirach gamely accused Ribbentrop of failing to build bridges to the enemy. Hitler rejoined that since Casablanca and "unconditional surrender" there was no alternative. Afterward he angrily remarked to Bormann that the Gauleiter had become infected by Vienna: he too had contracted defeatism.

Clutching at Straws

By the spring of 1943 the Axis alliance was a myth, and Hitler knew it. In Tunisia, Montgomery's offensive had succeeded and the Axis bridgehead was being inexorably crushed. Late in February the Italians had already hinted that the loss of Tunis might bring about a new situation, and one month later Churchill had only evasively answered Parliamentary questions about possible Axis armistice feelers. Finland was already searching for a way out of the war. From the decoded messages shown to Hitler, it was clear that both the Hungarian and Romanian governments had in neutral capitals official emissaries who were sounding out the western enemy on the prospects of peace. Now Vidkun Quisling and Gauleiter Terboven—Reich Commissar for Norway—separately warned Hitler that in the event of an enemy invasion of Norway, Sweden would support the Allies. Hitler, who had just personally instructed his new envoy to Stockholm that his sole purpose must be to keep Sweden neutral—to safeguard Germany's iron-ore supplies—now resorted to more drastic measures: after one routine Berghof conference he detained Jodl and a handful of trusted advisers and instructed them to draft outline plans for a lightning invasion of Sweden should need arise. Only the success of "Citadel," regaining the initiative on the eastern front, would bring all these peripheral nations back into line.

Romania's Marshal Antonescu, invited to the Berghof on April 12, accepted Hitler's reproaches with a fatalistic air; for him as for Hitler himself there could now be no compromise between a clear victory or complete annihilation. When Hitler read him the Forschungsamt records of incriminating telephone conversations and other documents proving the disloyalty of Romanian ministers—and their clandestine negotiations with the enemy in Ankara, Bucharest, Budapest, Berne, and above all Madrid—the marshal made a convincing display of indignation (though he himself had authorized the feelers). Hitler gave the Hungarian regent, Horthy, a far rougher ride a few days later when the admiral flatly denied that the Forschungsamt records could be true; he supported Prime Minister

Kállay to the hilt and thrice denied that Hungary was in contact with the enemy. Hitler with good reason trusted neither Horthy nor Kállay. "We are all in the same boat," he said. "If anybody goes overboard now, he drowns."

Nor was the language Hitler and Ribbentrop used to prod the Hungarian regent into taking a sterner line over his Jewish citizens very delicate. The Nazis found it intolerable that eight hundred thousand Jews should still be moving freely around a country in the heart of Europe—particularly just north of the sensitive Balkans. For many months Germany had applied pressure for the Hungarian Jews to be turned over to the appropriate German agencies for deportation to "reservations in the east." It was argued that so long as they remained, they were potential rumormongers, purveyors of defeatism, saboteurs, agents of the enemy secret service, and contact men for an "international Jewry" now embattled against Germany.

Events in Poland were pointed to as providing an ugly precedent: there were reports of Jews roaming the country, committing acts of murder and sabotage. The eviction of the Jews ordered by Hitler had recently been intensified by Himmler's order that even those Jews left working for armaments concerns in the Generalgouvernement were to be housed collectively in camps and eventually to be got rid of as well. In Warsaw, the fifty thousand Jews surviving in the ghetto were on the point of staging an armed uprising—with weapons and ammunition evidently sold to them by Hitler's fleeing allies as they passed westward through the city. Himmler ordered the ghetto destroyed and its ruins combed out for Jews. "This is just the kind of incident that shows how dangerous these Jews are."

Poland should have been an object lesson to Horthy, Hitler argued. He related how Jews who refused to work there were shot; those who could not work just wasted away. Jews must be treated like tuberculosis bacilli, he said, using his favorite analogy. Was that so cruel when one considered that even innocent creatures like hares and deer had to be put down to prevent their doing damage? Why preserve a bestial species whose ambition was to inflict bolshevism on us all? Horthy apologetically noted that he had done all he decently could against the Jews: "But they can hardly be murdered or otherwise eliminated," he protested. Hitler reassured him: "There is no need for that." But just as in Slovakia, they ought to be isolated in remote camps where they could no longer infect the healthy body of the public; or they could be put to work in the mines, for example. He himself did not mind being temporarily excoriated for his Jewish policies, if they brought him tranquillity. Horthy left unconvinced.

What had prompted the earthier language Hitler now employed? It is possible to recognize the association in his mind of certain illogical ideas; half were unconscious or the result of his own muddled beliefs, but half had deliberately been implanted by trusted advisers like Himmler and Goebbels: the Jews had started the war; the enemy was the international Jew; the most deadly of the Bolsheviks, like Stalin's propagandist Ilya Ehrenburg, were Jews; Ehrenburg and the Jews behind Roosevelt were preaching the total extermination of the German race. The saturation bombing of German cities, their blasting and burning, was just the beginning.

In his warning to Horthy that the "Jewish Bolsheviks" would liquidate all Europe's intelligentsia, we can identify the influence of the Katyn episode—an unexpected propaganda windfall about which Goebbels had just telephoned him. Strange frozen mounds had been pointed out to German soldiers in a forest near Smolensk in February; now they had thawed and been opened to reveal the mummified remains of twelve thousand Polish army officers. The diaries and letters on the corpses were last dated April 1940—when the region was in Russian hands. They had all been shot expertly in the nape of the neck. Hitler warmly approved Goebbels's suggestion that Katyn should be linked in the public's mind with the Jewish question.

But the most poisonous and persuasive argument used to reconcile Hitler to a harsher treatment of the Jews was the bombing war. From documents and target maps recently found in crashed bombers he knew that the British aircrews were instructed to aim only at the residential areas now and to disregard the industrial targets proper. Only one race murdered, he told the quailing Horthy, and that was the Jews, who had provoked this war and given it its present character against civilians, women, and children. He returned repeatedly to this theme as 1943 progressed; in 1944 it became more insistent; and in 1945 he embodied it in his Political Testament, as though to appease his own conscience and justify his country's actions.

Nor was Hitler minded to treat even the non-Jewish Russian peoples with kid gloves. Throughout the spring of 1943 a noisy squabble raged between Alfred Rosenberg, the endlessly verbose minister for the eastern territories, and Gauleiter Erich Koch, Rosenberg's primitive and unruly minion in the Ukraine. Hitler had wanted Rosenberg's ministry to confine itself to political guidance in the east; instead he had established an unwieldy and bureaucratic executive apparatus. Rosenberg—supported by Ribbentrop, Zeitzler, and Goebbels—wanted to win the Russian peoples' support in the fight against Stalin, and he complained that Koch's brutal methods were incompatible with this. For example: to create a private hunting preserve, Koch had liquidated all the peasants in a certain forest. His pasha lifestyle was incompatible with the spirit of total war. At Christmas he had sent a special plane to Rostov to collect two hundred pounds of caviar at a time when General Paulus's soldiers were starving in Stalingrad.

Party dignitaries rose up in arms to demand Koch's expulsion from office and Party alike; yet Hitler, Bormann, and—more circumspectly—Himmler defended him. Rosenberg and his circle of Baltic emigrés might theorize about the future cultural life of the Ukraine, but Koch's harsh duty was to squeeze every ton of grain and every slave laborer he could out of the region. That was what war was about—and apparently the ability to fulfill this task excused all else.

The idea of harnessing Russians voluntarily to the war against Stalin was a chimera, said Hitler. "I have always felt there are only a handful of men who can really keep their heads in a major crisis, without being waylaid by some phantom hope or other. The saying that drowning men clutch at straws is only too true." When Ribbentrop identified himself with General Vlasov's previously mentioned idea for a Russian army of liberation, Hitler rapped his knuckles. "There are to be no such political operations. They are useless and unnecessary. They will only result in our people fraternizing with the Russians. Besides, it will be seen as a token of weakness on our part." Field Marshals Kluge and Küchler were also rebuffed when they supported the Vlasov project. Vlasov and Zeitzler's Colonel Gehlen had put their names to millions of leaflets dropped over the enemy lines; they announced that the Wehrmacht was fighting only Stalin and not the Russian people, and they spoke of a "National Committee" in Smolensk as though it were the Russian government being groomed for the post-Stalin era. To Hitler this idea was madness; as he angrily told Zeitzler, to let the Ukrainians set up their own government would be tantamount to throwing away the Nazis' entire war aim. The Russians would start off as a satellite state such as Poland had been in World War I, and Germany would end up confronting an entirely independent state all over again.

On May 19, Hitler brought Rosenberg and Koch face to face and refereed the match himself. Rosenberg firmly repeated that Koch's policies were damaging the Reich and supplying the enemy with thousands of partisans; Koch was accused of being disobedient, rebellious, and libelous about Rosenberg's "conspiring with emigrés." Koch defended himself and justified his methods. With a sense of justice worthy of a comic-opera character, Hitler adjudged that both were right, though Koch was righter. In the future only the Führer would authorize any proclamations to the peoples of Russia—"not some idiot or other in the war ministry or at the front." As for the partisan argument, if Rosenberg were right, there would be fewest partisans where the "particularly crafty generals" spoke in the most honeyed tones; this was not the case. Nor could slave labor be procured except by Koch's methods. "Only feeble-minded generals imagine we can win any manpower by sweet-talking." And as for Koch's executions in the Ukraine: "How many of our compatriots are losing their lives in air raids here at home?" Hitler laid down that in the future neither Koch nor Rosenberg was to employ foreigners as advisers. "If they work *against* their own country, they are devoid of character. If they work *for* it, they are useless as advisers to us."

The military aspects of the Vlasov "Russian army" project were analyzed in a heated session between Hitler, Keitel, and Zeitzler some weeks later. Hitler knew that the German army's Georgian and Armenian battalions had deserted en masse to the enemy, and he had little patience for this new project. He did not object to employing hundreds of thousands of Russian volunteers in noncombatant duties (General Lindemann's Eighteenth Army alone had forty-seven thousand). But he would not approve of the Vlasov project beyond its sheer propaganda value in enticing Soviet soldiers to desert: the deserters were to be transported into Germany, "decently treated," and employed in the coal mines. Vlasov himself would be needed only for his photograph and signature on the leaflets; otherwise, his activities were to be curbed. History, said Hitler, had proven that in times of crisis such nationalistic movements only rounded on the occupying power. Keitel accordingly ruled that no "National Committee" was actually to be set up in occupied Russia; the Führer would permit Vlasov's propaganda leaflets only on condition that German agencies realized that nobody must take them seriously.

General Zeitzler's prestige with Hitler had risen in the same measure as the OKW's had declined, with the crumbling of its North African theater. Hitler had given the army's General Staff a free hand in devising a plan for "Citadel" to the success of which he attached considerable importance: a modest offensive victory in Russia would inspire the neutrals and halfhearted allies too; it would stabilize the front for the rest of 1943, long enough for him to release armored divisions to thwart any enemy molestation of Italy or the Balkans; in addition, the home economy badly needed the slave labor that "Citadel" would harvest in its wake.

Even though they were half a continent apart, the interreaction of the Mediterranean and eastern theaters naturally made for a variety of difficulties. During March and early April various operational concepts for "Citadel" had been examined and cast aside. Zeitzler's final proposal was that the objective—an inviting rectangular salient 130 miles wide and thrusting 80 miles out toward the German Second Army—should be excised in a classic pincer attack by the Ninth Army from the north and the Fourth Panzer Army from the south, their spearheads meeting just east of Kursk. Zeitzler drafted a pompously worded operational order ("The victory at Kursk must shine as a beacon to the whole world") and Hitler signed it on April 15. It made grim provision for the rounding up and smooth westward dispatch of the hundreds of thousands of able-bodied Russians expected to fall into the German net. "Citadel" was set to begin on the third of May.

Once this much had been settled, Zeitzler flew back to his headquarters in East

Prussia, but a few days later he received a telephone call from Hitler: the Führer had thought "Citadel" over and now felt it would be better to abandon the idea of a pincer attack—which was so obvious that the enemy would be certain to be ready and waiting for it—and instead combine the assault forces of Army Groups South and Center in one frontal thrust, piercing the very center of the bulge and thus splitting the enemy's massed strength in two.[1] Zeitzler would not hear of it; redeploying the two armies would inflict a crippling delay on "Citadel," and he made a special flight to Berchtesgaden on April 21 with the maps and statistics to prove it. Hitler yielded. Zeitzler had proved right at Stalingrad; his own sureness of touch, his strategic instinct, had failed him then. Worse still, now that "Citadel" had become Zeitzler's baby, Hitler's heart was no longer in it.

General Model, commander of the Ninth Army, had originally asked for two days to punch through the Russian defenses, but late in April he raised this estimate to three days. His superior, Kluge, impatiently pointed out that with 227 tanks and 120 assault guns the Ninth Army was stronger than ever before, but Model claimed he still needed 100 more tanks. Zeitzler agreed to rush 50 from the west, with 20 more Tigers and 40 assault guns. But the "three-day" estimate worried Hitler: three days of uninterrupted battle against an experienced enemy would result in the massacre of the assault troops. "When Model told me before 'Citadel,'" Hitler said a year later, "that he'd need three days—that's when I got cold feet." He asked Model to fly to the Berghof. On April 27 the wiry, dark-haired general was standing before him in the Great Hall; his aerial photographs appeared to confirm the claim that twelve-mile-deep Russian fortifications with immensely powerful antitank artillery had to be overcome before the Ninth Army could advance on Kursk. Moreover, Model warned that even the Mark IV tank was vulnerable to the new Russian antitank rifle. Hitler postponed "Citadel" to May 5. On April 29 he ordered a further postponement to the ninth, to give the armies a few more days to stockpile tanks and guns.

Out of "a few days" grew weeks, then months. General Guderian, who began attending the war conferences on May 2 in his capacity as inspector of panzer troops, gave Hitler his own impression of tank production prospects if "Citadel" could be delayed long enough. At present the Tiger was plagued by gear and steering faults, and the advanced Panther tank production had repeatedly broken down. But Guderian told Hitler that during May two battalions of each of the different tank types—Panthers, Ferdinands, Tigers, and Hornets—would be activated; the existing tanks on the Russian front would be reinforced with armored

---

[1] In postwar captivity, General Johannes Friessner met one of Hitler's adjutants and asked why the Führer had not mounted just such an offensive. Given the comparative weakness of the Russian defenses in the center of the bulge, Friessner—who had commanded a corps under Model's Ninth Army—believed it would have succeeded.

"aprons" against antitank shells; in addition, tank output itself was increasing. The Speer ministry had promised 939 tanks in April, 1,140 in May, 1,005 in June, and 1,071 in July. In short, suggested Guderian, it was well worth holding up "Citadel" for a bit. In reality he was opposed to the offensive altogether, for he wanted to conserve German tank strength throughout 1943 in order to meet the enemy's operations in the west thereafter.

Hitler—his own mind already made up for an even longer postponement—summoned his leading generals to Munich for a three-hour conference on May 4. No stenogram survives, and recollections differ as to the standpoints adopted by each general (a common phenomenon after a defeat). However, the Chief of Air Staff, Jeschonnek, rendered a contemporary description to one diarist (Richthofen), and it throws a piquant sidelight on the personalities around the Führer.

[On April 27] General Model declared he was not strong enough and would probably get bogged down or take too long. The Führer took the view that the attack must be punched through without fail in shortest time possible. [Early in May] General Guderian offered to furnish enough tank units within six weeks to guarantee this. The Führer thus decided on a postponement of six weeks. To get the blessing of all sides on this decision, he called a conference [on May 4] with Field Marshals von Kluge and von Manstein. At first they agreed on a postponement; but when they heard that the Führer had already made his mind up to that effect, they spoke out for an immediate opening of the attack—apparently in order to avoid the odium of being blamed for the postponement themselves.

There is nothing to be gained from referring here to the postwar versions of Manstein or Guderian. Jeschonnek, Richthofen, and Zeitzler all opposed any further delay, arguing that time would operate solely in favor of the Russians; their fortifications, minefields, and artillery emplacements would become more formidable with each passing day. Nonetheless, Hitler now postponed "Citadel" to mid-June.

Another factor now bore on his decisions: the imminent Axis defeat in Tunisia.

Starved of ammunition, food, and fuel, General von Arnim's quarter of a million troops had fought a stubborn rearguard action in its ever shrinking bridgehead. Bereft of Italian naval support, supply ships were not getting through; and enemy fighters were inflicting cruel losses on the Junkers transport planes. By the end of April, Arnim had only seventy-six tanks left and was distilling what fuel he could from low-grade wines and liquors. Dispatching General Warlimont to Rome to renew pressure on the quivering Italian navy, Hitler told him to say that tanks and divisions were just as "nice to look at" as warships. "There are no moral reasons not to fight. The only moral act is to fight and win this war. What is immoral is to lose, and then scuttle your ships without having fought." The appeal availed him naught—the Italian navy stayed in harbor; indeed, some days later Hitler heard that the battleship *Vittorio Veneto* had secretly radioed British headquarters at Malta details of German supply convoys putting to sea. On May 6, overcoming Arnim's defense of the mountain passes, the British First Army broke through to Tunis. Two days later the Luftwaffe—faced now by forty-five hundred fighter and bomber aircraft—abandoned its North African airfields. Keitel wrote that day: "The Führer and Duce are determined to continue the fight in Tunisia as long as possible," but one by one Arnim's divisions were enveloped as their last ammunition was spent.

Warlimont returned from Rome on May 7 with comforting news about Mussolini's health and his personal assessment that provided Il Duce kept a tight rein on events, the coming loss of Tunis need not spell disaster within Italy. Hitler was not so sure. "The Duce and the Fascist party are resolved to stand by Germany through thick and thin," he told his staff at noon. However "a section of the officer corps—more at the top, fewer lower down—is inclined to make peace already. Certain influential circles are capable of treachery." He announced that he planned to furnish armed support to the Fascists in Italy to bolster her powers of resisting the enemy. Meanwhile, every week Arnim could fight on was vital to the Axis cause. He asked Field Marshal Rommel to come to see him.

Hitler had slept the last three nights at Martin Bormann's villa outside Munich. On May 6 he turned his back on the Mediterranean and returned by train to Berlin. Viktor Lutze, SA Chief of Staff, had just died in an autobahn accident, and Hitler intended to use the next day's state funeral to underline his lingering nostalgia for political militias like the SA. He had had a bellyful of army generals —liars and cheats, they were reactionary and hostile to the dogmas of National Socialism.

It was a good funeral. The routine selection from *Götterdämmerung* stirred him deeply. At four o'clock, after banqueting the Party leaders, he gave them a stern if banal warning against the autobahn madness that seemed to go with high office. Then he addressed the Gauleiters on the meaning of the present war. It had begun as a fight between bourgeois and revolutionary states, in which the former had been easily overthrown. But now they were facing in the east a *Weltanschauung*-state like their own, its Jewish-Bolshevist ideology permeating its army with a zeal and spirit which only his own SS divisions could match. This was why he, Hitler, had decided that "the Jews must be thrown out of Europe." He had come to believe that in the great prewar purge Stalin had not ruined the Red Army after all; quite the contrary. And the introduction of political commissars had vastly increased the army's effectiveness. The Russian solidarity behind Stalin was complete: for twenty-five years he had ruthlessly eliminated his opposition; he had no Church elements to restrain him as Hitler had in Germany. The Führer often feared that the Herrenvolk could not forever maintain their superiority over the enormous manpower reservoirs of the east. Ghengis Khan's hordes had penetrated far into the heart of Europe—the glittering jewel—without Germandom having possessed the strength to hold them back. Now too Germany alone must bear the brunt of the struggle against Asia. Speer's gigantic tank program would ensure victory in the east, while Dönitz's U-boats kept the Jewish-fostered warmongers of the West at bay. Hitler told the Gauleiters that Stalin had lost over thirteen million troops since "Barbarossa" had started. The summer offensive would be modest in scale but carried forward by dependable German troops alone. Postwar Europe would dispense with the present "hodgepodge of small states." The time would come, announced Hitler, when Germany would dominate all Europe.

He wrote off the Tunis bridgehead in North Africa, even though small bands of Axis troops were continuing to hold out. But he had not turned his back on Mussolini. (He had never forgotten the Duce's benevolence over Austria in 1938. "I told him then 'I will never forget you for this!' And I never will," Hitler admonished his less forgiving staff.) He was worried about the Duce's health, but he worried far more that treacherous, royalist generals would betray Italy into the enemy's hands. This was why he had recalled Rommel from his convalescence to Berlin—Rommel, rather than the gullible and popular Field Marshal Kesselring, who refused to believe that the Italian generals were as dark-hearted as the Führer sensed them to be, was the one to command Hitler's troops in Italy.

Rommel flew into Berlin on May 9 and reported to Hitler at 1 P.M., looking fit and well. That he was not still in Tunis was a secret Hitler had not yet revealed to his people; now was the time to dissociate this valuable commander from the debacle in Africa. Hitler kept the ambitious field marshal on tenterhooks. Rommel wrote in his diary: "Afterward I attended the war conference. No special job as yet. Field Marshal Keitel hinted at my utilization in Italy with the Duce if things should turn sticky there." Rommel spent the rest of the day being lectured by Goebbels. The next day he recorded: "I stressed to both the Führer and Goebbels the meager fighting quality of the Italians and their reluctance to fight." On the twelfth Hitler published the news that Rommel had been in Germany since March, when he had awarded him the highest medal; but, aware that the field marshal was spurned by the Italians (as Göring and Kesselring reminded him) as "the man who lost Libya," he refrained from releasing the text of his extravagant letter of praise to Rommel. At 6 P.M. that evening, Hitler and his staff flew back to his East Prussian headquarters.

Why he did so is a mystery. Perhaps it was a blind, an attempt to deceive the enemy into believing that "Citadel" was imminent. He had no fear of an enemy invasion in the west as yet—the Atlantic Wall allayed that peril. No, he knew that the Mediterranean was still the most dangerous theater. As early as May 1 he had believed both the western Mediterranean and the Peloponnesus of Greece most vulnerable to invasion. A week later an adjutant had announced at the war conference a startling Abwehr scoop which seemed to substantiate Hitler's fears: a corpse found floating off the Spanish coast had yielded sealed envelopes bearing ostensibly genuine letters from the British war office and Lord Mountbatten to Admiral Cunningham and General Dwight D. Eisenhower, betraying the enemy's most secret plans after the capture of Tunis. Two invasion operations were to be mounted, one in the western Mediterranean and one in the Peloponnesus (code-named, apparently, "Brimstone" and "Husky"); these would be covered by dummy invasions of Sicily and the Dodecanese, respectively. The envelopes had been expertly resealed and turned over to the British by the Spanish foreign ministry. Admiral Canaris fell hook, line, and sinker for their contents. Hitler was less gullible, for at the end of the war conference he turned on his heel and spoke his thoughts to Jodl's staff officer: "Christian, couldn't this be a corpse they have deliberately played into our hands?"[2] There was no way of knowing. Both Zeitzler's Intelligence staff and Canaris ruled out the possibility, and for the next month the Peloponnesus and Sardinia—presumed to be the target of the real assault in the western Mediterranean—attracted most of Hitler's attention.

Albert Speer and his principal arms barons came to see him at the Wolf's Lair on May 13. Hitler bestowed a rare award, the "Doctor Todt Ring," on the munitions minister, for his reorganization of the armaments industry had yielded amazing results. Germany was turning out six times as much heavy ammunition as in 1941 and three times as many guns. Between February and May heavy tank production had doubled, testifying to the indomitable spirit of the workers despite the paralyzing air raids. "In the autumn," Speer reminded Hitler, "you instructed us to deliver specific quantities of arms by May 12. Today we can report that we have met every one of those figures and in some cases far exceeded them."

To Goebbels, Speer afterward commented that the Führer looked worn out with worry: it was the anxiety over Italy. What use indeed were the new weapons

---

[2] The stenographer—himself a close aide of the famous Intelligence chief Colonel Nicolai in World War I—recalls the scene vividly. The corpse was indeed a brilliant if gruesome ploy of the British secret service.

Speer had demonstrated within the headquarters compound the next day—the mighty hundred-ton Mouse tank, the new assault guns, and the deadly Blowpipe bazooka (Pusterohr)—if Italy changed sides, the enemy landed in the Balkans, and the Romanian oil fields were reduced to ruins?

The fighting in Tunis was now over. The Afrika Korps' last radio emission had arrived: "Ammunition spent. Arms and equipment destroyed. The Afrika Korps has fought till it can fight no more, as ordered." A hundred thousand of Hitler's finest troops were being marched into British and American captivity; some 150,000 Italians had been taken prisoner. The blow was softened in Hitler's eyes by its gradualness, its inevitability given Italian shortcomings, and the realization that these captives would at least be spared the torments that faced prisoners in Soviet hands. Yet the Italian posture now raised fresh alarm. Hitler offered Mussolini five divisions to restore the blood to Italy's anemic arteries. The Duce's reply, obviously drafted by the devious General Ambrosio—Keitel's counterpart as chief of the *comando supremo*—stated that the three German divisions left on Italian soil as a backlog of the transport movements to Tunisia were quite enough: but he wanted three hundred tanks, fifty antiaircraft batteries, and hundreds of fighter aircraft. When Admiral Dönitz reported back to Hitler on May 14 after personally grilling the Italian commanders in Rome, he could only reinforce Hitler's suspicions. Hitler responded, "A man like Ambrosio would be happy to see Italy an English dominion."

Dönitz stated that the Italians expected the British to invade Sicily next. Obviously forgetting his earlier suspicions, Hitler replied that the letters on the British corpse indicated that the target would be Sardinia; Sicily was too heavily defended, and it would take up to four weeks to sweep the Strait clear of the Axis minefields. One thing was clear—colossal enemy bombardments of the ports and railway networks of Sardinia, Sicily, and Corsica had begun. Dönitz had tried to impress on the Italians that if they did not employ every available ship—big and small—to pump troops and stores into these islands now, the dismal story of North Africa would be repeated all over again. Mussolini had weakly accepted this; Ambrosio had not—submarines and cruisers were there to fight, not act as transport vessels. When Dönitz quoted Mussolini as saying that the British press was bragging that the capture of Sicily would release two million tons of shipping presently obliged to detour around the Cape, Hitler irritably interrupted ". . . and then our fine submarines must sink them." "And on top of that," continued Dönitz, "we are coming up to our worst U-boat crisis, since the enemy has new detecting gear which makes submarine warfare impossible for the first time." Suddenly they were losing over fifteen U-boats a month. "The losses are too high," exclaimed Hitler. "We can't go on like this."

His insomnia returned. If he lost the Balkans, he would lose his last allies, forfeit Romania's oil, and lose the bauxite, chrome, and copper mines on which

Speer's factories depended. Zeitzler, jealously husbanding his divisions massed for "Citadel," refused to release a panzer division for possible use in the Balkans; but the road and rail network in the Balkans was so primitive that Hitler knew he could not leave it until the last moment. With Italy the problem was less acute: the railways were better, and if worse came to worst he could always barricade Italy off from the Reich; but not the Balkans. He ordered the Luftwaffe field division on the Isthmus of Corinth strengthened, and a panzer division transferred to the Balkans from the west.

The next fortnight in Italy would be crucial. Rommel might have to storm the Italian frontier and go to the Duce's rescue if his generals betrayed him. After the noon conference on May 15, Hitler made a two-hour secret speech to his generals, including Rommel, on the dangerous situation left by the defeat in North Africa. It is so important that the note taken by one officer present, Captain Wolf Junge, is quoted here at length:

The enemy's victory in Africa has not only opened up the east-west passage through the Mediterranean for him, but released eighteen to twenty divisions and considerable air and naval forces. They will also exploit the new situation for a political offensive designed to use bluster and blandishments to persuade Germany's weak allies to defect. Quite apart from the military position, this is particularly dangerous in Italy and Hungary. Bulgaria and Romania can be regarded as secure. . . .

In Italy we can rely only on the Duce. There are strong fears that he may be got rid of or neutralized in some way. The royal family, all leading members of the officers' corps, the clergy, the Jews, and broad sectors of the civil service are hostile or negative toward us. Their motives are partly deliberate enmity, partly shortsighted incompetence and blind egoism. The broad masses are apathetic and lacking in leadership.

The Duce is now marshaling his Fascist guard about him. But the real power is in the hands of the others. Moreover he is uncertain of himself in military affairs and has to rely on his hostile or incompetent generals (Ambrosio!!!) as is evident from the incomprehensible reply—at least as coming from the Duce —turning down or evading the Führer's offer of troops.

In the present situation a neutral Italy would not be bad at all; but it could not be neutral now—it would defect voluntarily or under pressure to the enemy camp. Italy in enemy hands is the Second Front in Europe we must avoid at all costs; it would lay open the western flank of the Balkans too. Our main purpose now must be to prevent a Second Front in Europe. "Europe must be defended in its outfield—we cannot allow a Second Front to emerge on the Reich's frontiers." It is for this objective that we may have to make sacrifices elsewhere.

It is good that we have not yet attacked in the east ["Citadel"] and still have forces available there; because the decision has been taken to act as soon as a crisis breaks out in Italy. To this end, of the eighteen mobile divisions available in the east, eight armored and four infantry divisions will have to be rushed to Italy to get a firm grip on her and defend her against the Anglo-Americans (or throw them out again). No resistance of note is expected from the Italians (according to Rommel). Collaboration of the Fascist political forces is hoped for.

At the same time Hungary will be occupied.

The consequences on eastern front will be: defensive evacuation of the Orel Bend; acceptance of risk to the Donets region; if worse comes to worst even withdrawal in the north to the Luga line. Zeitzler demanded that the bridgehead on the Kuban should also be given up; but the Führer did not express an opinion on that.

Zeitzler was instructed to work out a timetable for the troop movements [from Russia to Italy]. The next one or two weeks are crucial. . . . Every week is vital to us, because after about eight weeks the newly activated "Stalingrad" divisions in the west will become operational, which would obviate the need to raid the eastern front for divisions.

Thus the main points of the Führer's remarks.

It was certainly a remarkable speech. Quite apart from the first hint at enforced German occupations of Italy and Hungary, it destroys the myth that Hitler always refused to abandon territory voluntarily in Russia, when it was strategically necessary. It also puts "Citadel," the Battle of Kursk, into its proper perspective in history: it was subordinated to the need to prop up a crumbling dictatorship in a country whose military value was nil.

All eyes turned to Italy. Hitler began planning an urgent personal meeting with Mussolini again.

Out of regard for Mussolini's feelings he scrapped the official communiqué on the Tunis fighting, which put the blame on the Italians. When British newspapers, week after week, mocked the German soldiers for surrendering, Ribbentrop begged the Führer to publish the war diaries and documents proving how heroically they had fought against impossible odds in Tunisia. Hitler's stubborn refusal was telephoned by Hewel back to Ribbentrop: "We have to be clear that we have suffered a painful defeat in Africa. If you have taken a knock, you mustn't try and talk your way out of it or pretty things up. You will soon end up like the Italians—who make a veritable saga of every defeat they suffer until the whole world laughs at them. There is only one thing to do at times like this: *Hold your tongue and prepare to counterattack.* Once the counterattack is delivered, all talk of any insufficiency in German soldiers vanishes. Stalingrad is an example: the stories that the German divisions' morale was collapsing stopped the moment we struck back hard at the Russians again, at Kharkov."

Before leaving for the Berghof again, Hitler conferred in detail with Keitel, Kesselring, and Löhr on the defense of the Mediterranean position; his aim was to prevent a "boundless bankruptcy" from loosening their stranglehold on the Balkans the moment the *Schweinerei* in Italy began. Rommel—given his deep personal hatred of them now—would be the ideal commander to confront the Italian generals with.

On May 18, Hitler ordered him to set up the skeleton staff of a new army group for what was, after all, the occupation of Italy. Rommel would report directly to him. His interim headquarters would be in Munich. The operation—code-named "Alarich"—was so secret that Hitler declined even to sign the OKW's draft directive. "This time we've got to be fanatically careful with bits of paper," he said. A similar directive, "Konstantin," provided for filling the vacuum in Greece and Croatia should the Italian army suddenly pull out. Initially, Rommel's worry was that the Alpine fortifications being hastily completed by the Italians against the Reich frontier might be manned, especially on the Brenner Pass, to keep German divisions out—thus deliberately letting Italy fall into the enemy's hands. Rarely can two ostensibly allied armies have contemplated each other with such veiled mistrust.

Zeitzler had calculated for Hitler that the first reinforcements could be flooding from the Russian front into Italy within ten days of any trouble there. Every two days would then bring a fresh infantry division, spearheaded by three SS armored divisions—the troops with the closest ideological ties to the Fascist leaders. A speech by Mussolini's Foreign Minister Bastianini early on May 20 convinced the Führer that dirty work was afoot. "We must be on our guard, like a spider in its web. Thank God I've a good nose for things like this, so I usually get wind of anything long before it breaks out."

How far Admiral Canaris reliably warned of the treason blossoming in Italy is uncertain from the records. But Himmler's officials left Hitler in no doubt. SS Specialist [*Sonderführer*] von Neurath brought hair-raising details back from Sicily: the local people hated the German troops and were making unabashed preparations for "postwar"; government officials were turning a blind eye on anti-German outrages; the Italian Sixth Army based on Sicily was now commanded by General Roatta of Balkan ill-repute, and Roatta obviously regarded defeat as certain. Perhaps he even relished the prospect. His staff were anglophiles; some had even married Englishwomen. "Crafty?" exclaimed Hitler, on hearing Roatta's name. "He is the Fouché of the Fascist revolution, a spy totally devoid of character. A spy is what he is!" Hitler's field marshals shared this view. Curiously enough, the attaché reports from Rome spoke only in the highest terms of both Roatta and Ambrosio; this may have been because one of Canaris's assistants, Colonel Emil Helfferich, was attached to the attaché's staff.

At 1 P.M. on May 21, 1943, Hitler flew from East Prussia to Berchtesgaden, after a brief treatment session with his personal surgeon, Dr. Karl Brandt. His health was still impaired: ten days earlier, a fresh electrocardiogram had revealed no improvement in the rapid progressive coronary sclerosis affecting his heart vessels. He had discussed his stomach problems with Romania's Marshal Antonescu, and the latter recommended to him a Viennese dietician, Frau Marlene von Exner. Much against her will, Dr. Morell induced her to cook exclusively for the Führer by paying her a two thousand-Reichsmark bribe and a tax-free salary of eight hundred marks a month as a reward. Young, attractive, and good-natured, she soon shared the Führer's table with the other female headquarters staff. She brought back memories of old Vienna to her new employer, and he humored her cheerful protests at the way National Socialism favored Linz above Vienna. But whereas she had been able to display her culinary talents to Antonescu in a welter of oysters, mayonnaise, and caviar delicacies, with Hitler's austere meals she was at her wit's end. A typical Berghof menu was that on June 7, 1943: orange juice with linseed gruel; rice pudding with herb sauce; crispbread with butter and nut paste. Hitler adored her.

Mussolini could not come and see him; the records do not explain why. Probably he feared to leave Italy even for a few hours.

According to Jodl's deputy, Warlimont, Himmler submitted to Hitler a detailed plan for launching an operation against Italy if need arose. Hitler's own plan was to infiltrate four divisions into Italy more or less by stealth; at least sixteen more were to follow under Rommel the moment an enemy invasion occurred. But Rommel greatly feared that enemy bombers—or for that matter Italian officer renegades—would block the Alpine frontier passes. Hitler ordered the Luftwaffe to furnish antiaircraft batteries for the Brenner Pass; if the Italians demurred, then "British air raids" were to be faked, using refurbished unexploded RAF bombs hauled out of the ruins of German cities. On June 5, Warlimont briefed Canaris on this at Berchtesgaden. Canaris offered "Brandenburg" Division commandos who would become members of the gun crews and so be in a position to combat any attempted sabotage on the Alpine passes. But Jodl's deputy warned that no measure casting doubt on Italy's will to fight must ever become public; not even the general commanding the "Brandenburgers" must know. Canaris mouthed agreement; he was willing to risk "acting disloyally" toward the Italians, but he doubted whether the "true objectives" of the military preparations could be totally concealed from them. To Keitel he suggested that OKW fears of Italian defection were exaggerated, and he persuaded the guileless field marshal to cancel the antisabotage provisions. He also asked for Hitler to attach an Abwehr representative to Rommel's top-secret working party. Then he flew to Rome.[3]

Hitler's June 1943 sojourn at the Berghof was dismal and depressing. What price victory now? Bormann brought him a seventy-six-page speech Goebbels was planning to deliver to Berlin munitions workers on the fifth. Hitler crossed out whole pages or inked in spidery alterations. Where Goebbels proclaimed that their long-suffering fellow citizens would all receive generous compensation for their sacrifices "when victory is ours," Hitler thoughtfully altered this to read "after this struggle is over."[4]

The black outlook in both the submarine campaign and the air war contributed to this subtle distinction. At the end of May, Dönitz had frankly outlined the catastrophic U-boat situation in the North Atlantic to Hitler: enemy air patrols had been stepped up, and they were evidently using some secret device to detect the U-boats; in May, 38 submarines had been lost compared with 14 in April. As recently as March submarines had been able to destroy 875,000 tons of enemy shipping, and Hitler had spoken highly of their future prospects to the Gauleiters in Berlin on May 7: but the very next day 5 U-boats had been destroyed in one convoy battle, and on the twenty-fourth Dönitz had had to call off his attack in the North Atlantic if he was not to lose his entire front line. It was a tragedy for the German navy. Their Intelligence departments were successfully cracking the enemy codes that told Dönitz precisely where the convoys would be routed; there was talk of a "Hedgehog" in some messages, but this appeared to be just a patterned release of depth charges. The Germans had learned of the enemy's advances in centimetric radar after examining the remains of a bomber shot down near Rotterdam in February. Dönitz—correctly—believed the same equipment lay behind his submarine losses, but there was no evidence. Keitel instructed Canaris to find out as a matter of urgency.

Hitler had long expected just this setback to the U-boats—he was surprised they had done so well so long. Thus he did not reproach the navy. Dönitz had immediately fitted his submarines with multiple-barreled 20-millimeter antiaircraft guns and ordered that in the future they were to stand and fight back when aircraft approached. Ten U-boats were equipped to carry only antiaircraft guns. But these were improvisations. Until the acoustic homing torpedoes entered service in October as "destroyer busters," the U-boats would be restricted in their

---

[3]At this point the surviving fragments of Canaris's diary end.
[4]See facsimile on page 524.

hat das mehr bedauert als wir. Aber die braven Volks-

genossen, die ~~dabei~~ Beruf, Geschäft und den Genuß

dadurch zunächst

eines manchmal jahrzehntelangen Fleißes einbüßten,

können schon heute das Bewußtsein haben, daß ihr

Opfer nicht umsonst war. Sie werden dafür nach Mög-

lichkeit jetzt schon und besonders nach dem ~~Siege~~

Ende dieses Ringens

in ~~großzügigster~~ Weise entschädigt werden. Heute aber

gerechter

gilt es, alle Kraft auf den Sieg zu konzentrieren.

Im Rahmen dieses gigantischen Umschichtungs-

prozesses sind im Vorlaufe der vergangenen fünf

Monate fast 3½ Millionen Meldungen von Arbeits-

kräften eingelaufen. Von diesen Meldungen sind

bisher 2½ Millionen bearbeitet. Hunderttausende

von Männern konnten aus dem Produktionsprozess für

Hitler censors Goebbels' speech of June 5, 1943. Where Goebbels wanted to say "when victory is ours," Hitler altered it to read, "after this struggle is over." (The handwriting above Hitler's is Martin Bormann's.)

usefulness. Hitler knew that unless Dönitz could sink enemy shipping faster than it could be built, the war could not be won. He ordered Dönitz's submarine program increased from thirty to forty new boats a month, and he approved Dönitz's suggestion that all naval construction work be transferred to Speer's ministry. On June 15, however, the admiral arrived at the Berghof with a staggering demand for nearly 150,000 men to implement this naval expansion. Hitler told him: "I just don't have the men. The antiaircraft and night-fighter defenses have got to be increased to protect our cities. The eastern front has got to be strengthened. The army needs divisions for its job defending Europe."

Dönitz's energy was in stark contrast to Göring's indolence and lethargy that summer. From Gestapo morale reports, Hitler knew that his people were prey to a growing conviction that nothing could halt the enemy bombing campaign. Every night the British bombers visited a different town or city of the Ruhr, methodically heralded their arrival by chilling showers of colored pyrotechnic flares, and unloaded one or two thousand tons of bombs over the streets and houses. Their losses, sometimes thirty or forty bombers in one night, seemed not to deter them. A handful of bombers breached the Ruhr dams, unleashing the reservoirs on the sleeping populaces below. (Goebbels informed Hitler that the enemy press gave credit for this diabolical plan to a former Berlin Jew.) By day the American bomber formations completed the destruction in the ports or bombed targets in France and Italy. Sometimes the British sent small fast bombers by daylight deep into Germany, causing more insult to public morale than injury to industry. Or lone Mosquitoes, each with a one-ton sting, would circle for hours on end above Berlin, forcing its millions of inhabitants to take refuge until the all clear sounded. Though Milch warned that when Berlin's time really came, the people would no longer heed the sirens, Hitler still commanded that the sirens must sound each time, even if they saved only one or two lives thereby. Göring's solution was to propose that Germany's bombed-out citizens be evacuated to Burgundy—but this was hardly likely to commend itself to the Ruhr workers. Besides, in one night over a hundred thousand people lost their homes in Dortmund alone. Not until November could the Luftwaffe expect to strike back in force. Milch hoped to be manufacturing over three thousand fighters and bombers every month by then.

Unquestionably air superiority was the key to this war. This was why Hitler now ordered bomber squadrons transferred from the west to the Mediterranean and why he placed Field Marshal von Richthofen—his most trusted air commander—in command of the Second Air Force there. This incidentally was further proof that "Citadel" ranked lower in his order of priorities than keeping the enemy at bay in the Mediterranean. But even Richthofen could not prevent the huge enemy air onslaught that preceded each ground operation there. Six thousand tons of bombs were discharged over the tiny fortified island of Pantelleria, commanding the shipping routes in the Strait of Sicily. The Italian defenders suffered few casualties but were so demoralized that without firing a shot they offered to capitulate. On June 11 the Germans heard the island's commandant, Admiral Parvesi, radioing to the enemy in Malta: "We offer surrender; out of water." By that evening the island was firmly in Allied hands. That the Italian soldiers had been unable to withstand the kind of bombardment German civilians —men, women, and children alike—were enduring night after night certainly did not augur well for the coming Mediterranean campaigns, Hitler noted.

Correcting the Front Line

No month brought such concentrated high drama as July 1943. "Citadel" began, the enemy invaded Italian soil, the Russians sprang their own great summer offensive, and Mussolini was ousted by his monarch just as Hitler had always predicted. (Had he not written in October 1939 of the Italian monarchy: "For a pittance they would be willing to sell Italy's own birthright in the Mediterranean, in their own stupid shortsightedness, and then to join Germany's enemies as well"?) Finally, the war in the air reached a climax in prenuclear barbarism as over forty thousand civilians were burned, blasted, or poisoned to death in Hamburg.

Until the end of June Hitler had waited at the Berghof, watching events in Italy, fearing to trigger off "Citadel"—the battle for Kursk—in case Mussolini's generals staged a mass defection while his back was turned, or the enemy launched their invasion of Sardinia (which he believed must be their next target). Thrice he had ordered fresh postponements of "Citadel." On the sixteenth General Guderian had come, and explained why his earlier tank-output estimates had proved overoptimistic. With the Panther tank it was the old story: mass production had begun before its trials were completed. Guderian suggested this promising battle tank should not be put into action until at least five hundred were available. Jodl's staff also argued against executing "Citadel" in its original form, and Zeitzler probably took the same line now: he proposed staying their own hand until the Russians had pushed out westward themselves, and *then* launching a counterattack; tactically it was an attractive idea, but Hitler's objection was that Stalin had no reason to oblige him by attacking before events on the Mediterranean front compelled Germany to send divisions there, and this objection could not be faulted. On June 18, after a fresh conference with Zeitzler and Guderian, Hitler had committed himself to the offensive solution and three days later set July 3 as the date—finally postponed by two more days upon reasoned objections stated by General Model on June 25. Kluge and Manstein approved the decision.

Yet Hitler clearly anticipated failure, for he forbade the OKW to proclaim "Citadel" publicly, so that he could deny its existence if success was denied to him.

When Goebbels had come to the Obersalzberg on June 24, Hitler had lengthily justified his strategic thinking to him. He had abandoned forever his old dream of capturing the Caucasus and waging a campaign in the Middle East; the winter had swallowed up too many divisions for that. Nor could his armies contemplate advancing on the Urals. Despite the superior quality of the new Tiger and Panther battle tanks, he had decided to sit tight and conserve strength until 1944, to render the eastern front impregnable to winter crises like those of the past two years. He regarded the imminent operation only as a "minor correction" of the line, which might well rob Stalin of a few armies or even an army group but which would hardly swing neutral world opinion to a view of Germany as victor again. In the Mediterranean he expected the Allies to assail Sardinia first and then lunge toward the Peloponnesus. "The Führer believes he can hold this line," wrote Goebbels the next day. "Under no circumstances will he fall back from the Italian mainland. He has no intention of falling back on the Po River, even if the Italians do defect; in that case the war in Italy will just have to be fought by us alone." The Duce himself was old and worn out, said Hitler, and his people were limp and listless; this was why he was determined not to become too powerfully engaged in Russia—it would tie him hand and foot if Italy collapsed.

In the Generalgouvernement of Poland, in Russia, and in other regions where there was heavy partisan activity, Himmler's SS brigades fought to restore order, if not law, for the vital links between German industry and the front line were themselves under constant attack. In vain Hans Frank and his provincial governors complained that it was Himmler's own doctrinaire and muddled policies that contributed most to the unrest and fed the partisan cause. Several times since August 1942 Frank had even tendered his resignation, only to have it rejected by the Führer. Meanwhile the SS rampaged regardless of Frank's political authority, ruthlessly arresting "suspects," rounding up able-bodied Poles for labor service, or simply terrorizing and intimidating. Himmler's forced resettlement programs in the Lublin district—with whole villages being expelled overnight and repopulated with bemused German peasants as a "Germanic bulwark" against the East —caused uproar and resulted in the indignant resignation of Frank's governor at Lublin. Outwardly a strongman, Frank was weak and vacillating. He took his complaints personally to Hitler early in May 1943, but Hitler told him his problems were nothing to those of the occupied eastern territories and sent him back to Cracow. Hitler's chagrin at the lengthy April ghetto uprising in Warsaw was so great that he would dearly have liked to replace Frank by a tougher viceroy, but by whom? Only his Gauleiters were tough enough. For two hours he debated with Bormann, Ley, and Goebbels the Party's debilitating lack of first-class leadership material. He might even have to appoint a Gauleiter as the new SA Chief of Staff.

Eventually he decided that Hans Frank must stay. Frank could not help his failure, Hitler admitted; the job was beyond anybody's ability. "He has to extract food supplies, prevent the unification of his people, ship out the Jews and yet at the same time accommodate the Jews from the Reich, he has to step up arms production, refrain from rebuilding the ruined cities, and so on." Frank bitterly opposed Himmler's methods, but after a four-hour walk with the Reichsführer on the Obersalzberg on June 19, Hitler endorsed the SS position: in the future, fighting partisans and guerrillas was to be Himmler's responsibility alone; no blame was to be attached to the SS for the current increase in partisan activity in Poland or elsewhere. Himmler noted that day: "When we discussed the Jewish problem the Führer spoke in favor of the radical completion of the evacuation of the Jews, despite the unrest this will still cause over the next three or four months—that will just have to be put up with." The vicious SS General Erich von dem Bach-Zelewski took overall command of antiguerrilla warfare.

The "Jewish problem" was taboo at the Berghof. Only once was it mentioned, during an uncomfortable scene in June a few days after Himmler's visit. Baldur von Schirach and his pretty wife—court photographer Heinrich Hoffmann's daughter Henriette—were in Hitler's house party. They joined the fireside circle, slumped in the deep armchairs in the semi-darkness; the drawing room was lit only by the single floor lamp in one corner and the candles on the mantelpiece. While Hitler drank his special tea and the others their wine or cognac, Henriette exclaimed that she had just witnessed at Amsterdam the loading of Jews into trucks for deportation. "It is horrifying to see these poor people being packed into open trucks. Do you know about it? Do you permit it?" Her outburst was greeted by an icy silence. Hitler retorted, "They are being driven off to work, so you needn't pity them. Meantime our soldiers are fighting and dying on the battlefields!" Later he added, "Let me tell you something. This is a set of scales"—and he put up a hand on each side like the pans—"Germany has lost half a million of her finest manhood on the battlefield. Am I to preserve and minister to these others? I want something of our race to survive a thousand years from now." He reproached her: "You must learn how to hate!" Henriette countered with a line from Goethe's *Iphigenie:* "Man is made to love, not hate." This was probably the occasion on which Hitler irritably asked Schirach to tell his wife not to come with her "warpaint" on again: her eyelids were silvered, and her lashes heavy with mascara. It irked Hitler that Schirach had used his wife to plead his case for him.

The next evening, June 24, Goebbels wickedly brought the fireside conversation around to Vienna. Until after 4 A.M. Hitler drew savage comparisons between Schirach's Viennese and Goebbels's Berliners until tears welled up in Henriette's eyes: the Berliners were hard-working, intelligent, and politically shrewd; Vienna's musicians were either not themselves Viennese or had to die first before they were recognized. Hitler's abruptness with Henriette unsettled even Goebbels. "The behavior of Schirach and his wife charged the evening with a certain tension," Goebbels wrote. "Frau von Schirach in particular acted like a silly cow . . . and later summed up her unhappiness by saying that she wanted to go back to Munich with her husband and would the Führer send [Gauleiter] Giesler to Vienna instead." "Tell me," Hitler challenged her, "is your husband our Reich representative in Vienna—or is he Vienna's man in the Reich?" By the time the last air raid reports came in, it was long after dawn. Hitler kissed Eva Braun's hand and withdrew to his quarters—his shoulders hunched, his head sunk, his gait firm. The Schirachs departed for Vienna in a huff the same night, without seeing him again.

In the Ruhr town of Wuppertal, three thousand civilians had been killed by British bombers in half an hour that night. Over two thousand had died in the same town in a raid one month before. Hitler decided to deliver a fresh homily to Göring the next day. As Goebbels—who had just toured the blitzed Ruhr towns himself—said, the Reichsmarschall's stock had hit rock-bottom. The ravaging of these ugly Ruhr conurbations did not perturb Hitler overmuch; one day, he predicted, Germany would have ten million Volkswagens and five million other cars to contend with, and these towns would have had to be rebuilt with broad boulevards and streets anyway. But Speer was having to divert a hundred thousand men to repair the Ruhr, and the people's morale was brittle. Hitler promised to make an early surprise visit to the Ruhr. But at present grand strategy required that he turn the other cheek: the bombers were needed for "Citadel" and Italy. He had ordered the antiaircraft and night fighter defenses increased, he told Goebbels; and now at last they were getting the heavier armament that Udet and Mölders in their wisdom had thought unnecessary. One fighter armed with the new 30-millimeter cannon had recently shot down five bombers in a single night. By autumn the army's rocket missiles should be raining down on London from launching sites on the Channel coast, he assured the propaganda minister. "For the time being we've just got to be patient."

His forebearance with Göring was truly monumental. The Reichsmarschall gently let things slide and lost his grip. Hitler had arrogated direct control of the air war against Britain to himself. But the technical stagnation of the Luftwaffe was a mystery to him. Without Göring's knowledge he invited the leading aircraft manufacturers to see him. He wanted to find out the truth, but the absence of both Göring and Milch had the reverse effect. Professor Ernst Heinkel excused his failure to produce a satisfactory heavy bomber by citing Göring's persistent demand that the Heinkel 177 be a dive-bomber—although Göring had forbidden precisely that use ten months earlier. And when Hitler questioned Professor Willy Messerschmitt about the new Me-262 jet aircraft, the brilliant designer—whose vanity had been injured by Milch's closing down an obsolete piston-engined fighter project, the Me-209, in favor of the Me-262 one month earlier—pointed out that the jet aircraft's fuel consumption would be far higher than the Me-209 and thus secured a Führer Order reversing Milch's decision. (Hitler was not told that the jet used low-grade fuels which were more plentifully available than high-octane aviation fuel.) This half-truth by Messerschmitt set back jet-aircraft production in Germany by many months.

The immediate prospect for Speer's arms factories seemed grim. The Abwehr had just received a long report on a top-secret conference held by the British ministry of aircraft production at the beginning of the week. The Abwehr's agent, "Hektor," claimed to have been one of the few people present, and quoted Sir Stafford Cripps as insisting on an increase of heavy-bomber production to five hundred a month. "Cripps said almost verbatim that after talks with Portal and Harris he has the impression that Germany might be softened-up to such an extent by the present around-the-clock bombing that a costly invasion in the west could be dispensed with altogether. The main thing now, he said, is to flatten one town after another in Germany and especially the Rhine–Ruhr area. Deliberate attacks on the civilian population are also intended, as there are reports that morale in Germany is beginning to crumble."[1] All the mysterious "Hektor's" messages so far, and those of his controller in the legation in Stockholm, were unanimous in stating that the air offensive against Germany was only just beginning. Hitler at once signed orders for Speer to begin the immediate evacuation of arms production to the occupied areas of eastern Europe.

At midday on June 29, 1943, Hitler decided to transfer his headquarters back to the Wolf's Lair. He believed "Citadel" could safely begin in six days, on schedule. The Italians had handed Kesselring the text of an urgent telegram from the British naval liaison office in Washington to the admiralty in London. It was dated June 23, and taken in conjunction with remarks of a British naval officer overheard in Alexandria it appeared to show that the Allied invasion operations

---

[1] Sir Stafford Cripps was minister of aircraft production, Sir Charles Portal was Chief of Air Staff, and Sir Arthur Harris was Commander in Chief of RAF Bomber Command.

in the Mediterranean had been postponed and even changed: there was now explicit reference to *three* islands, and a distinction was drawn between commando assaults and the main invasion operations, which Hitler's Intelligence experts found significant. Moreover, there seemed clear proof that Stalin was as apprehensive about "Citadel" as the German General Staff was confident: on June 21, Hans Thomsen, the German envoy in Stockholm, cabled that the Soviet diplomatist A. M. Alexandrov had arrived there and "wants to meet with a gentleman from the German foreign service with whom he is acquainted." The next day Moscow again expressed dissatisfaction with the absence of an Allied Second Front—without one, "victory over Germany is impossible." On July 1 an authoritative Soviet magazine article derided the "collective guilt" theory propagated by the West against Germany and hinted that the Reich might even keep Poland and the Sudeten territories.

Hitler arrived back at the Wolf's Lair on July 1. Fresh wooden barracks had sprouted everywhere, invisible under the camouflage netting. It was unseasonably cold here. That evening he addressed a major policy speech to his "Citadel" commanders, assembled at Zeitzler's nearby HQ. He explained why he had kept postponing "Citadel"—he now had two thousand tanks ready for the battle, although admittedly half were only the older Mark III. "In a grave, clear, and confident voice he made the following points," recorded an infantry corps commander, General Friessner:

Our situation. The blame for our misfortunes must be laid squarely on our allies. The Italians let us down completely. If, as the Führer repeatedly demanded, they had made timely use of their fleet to escort and transport their troops to Africa, Africa would not have been lost. Now their ships are being smashed in their harbors. Comparison with World War I, where we too conserved our fleet too long until it was too late.—Italians failed on the eastern front, in Greece, etc. Hungary likewise: . . . Romania unreliable: the marshal's brother, Prime Minister [Mihai] Antonescu, is a devious character. Finland at the end of her tether; internal troubles with Social-Democrats, fostered and fed by Sweden.

What's at stake? Germany needs the conquered territory, or she will not exist for long. She must win hegemony over Europe. Where we are—we stay. Soldiers must see this, otherwise they'll regard their sacrifices as in vain. Balkans must not be lost whatever happens; our most vital raw materials for war are there. The Italians have pulled out of Greece and been replaced by Germans. Feel safer since then. Crete is firmly in our hands; thus we prevent enemy from getting air bases. Greater Germany and Europe must be defended far beyond our frontiers; so far we have managed this perfectly. German troops are now occupying the isles of Rhodes, Sicily, Sardinia, and Corsica—the Italians would have long surrendered them, just as they did without fighting in Pantelleria.

Eastern front. We will yield nothing without a scrap. . . . The Russians are biding their time. They are using their time replenishing for the winter. We must not allow that, or there'll be fresh crises this winter. So we've got to *disrupt* them.

(The last sentence indicates how limited "Citadel's" objective was.) Hitler concluded: "The die has been cast. The attack is on. Everything must now be done to ensure its success."

The operation itself was barely discussed. General Model repeated his misgivings, and the Ninth Army's situation was examined on the map. The only moment of anger occurred when Manstein tactlessly asked for Richthofen to be recalled from Italy to restore the vigor of the Luftwaffe on the eastern front. This upset Richthofen's stand-in, General Otto Dessloch, and brought a bellow of rage from Göring, who was jealous enough of Richthofen's prestige. Göring and Manstein otherwise shared the general optimism about "Citadel." Only Jodl did not, fearing that a long-drawn-out battle lay before them. But Hitler reassured his generals that Stalin had lost up to fourteen million troops so far and was facing a crippling famine. Of course the attack was a risk, he admitted, but he felt it had to be taken.

In Hitler's words, "Citadel" had to procure a victory "to dispel the gloom of our allies and crush any silent hopes still stirring within our subjugated peoples' breasts." His field commanders had high hopes that it would. They saw Luftwaffe squadrons amassed in a strength never before witnessed on the Russian front. The armored and infantry divisions were eager and well equipped, the troops were confident and refreshed by the months of resting. Elaborate steps had been taken to deceive the Russians.

"Citadel" began early on July 5—the Russians had evidently been forewarned, for their artillery heavily bombarded the German lines shortly before. An immense and bloody battle ensued. Longing for word of great victories once more, Hitler telephoned Zeitzler and Jeschonnek repeatedly for the latest news. Zeitzler could tell him little at first, but by evening it was clear that the battle was going well. General Dessloch's and General Robert Ritter von Greim's combined Air Forces (the Fourth and Sixth) had flown 4,570 sorties, destroying 432 Russian planes. Manstein had plunged eleven miles northward into the enemy fortifications; Kluge had come seven miles south toward him. Between their spearheads lay the city of Kursk—and 3,000 tanks which Stalin—willing to stake everything on the outcome of the battle even where Hitler was not—had thrown into the defense. The familiar euphoria gripped the Wolf's Lair, though all knew it would be a hard fight: line after line of fortifications extended before the Germans, reaching up to two hundred miles eastward into enemy territory. The Soviet tanks were well dug-in and flanked by treacherous minefields. Mass rocket-launcher regiments were waiting for the invaders too. In the first three days there were 30,000 German casualties, but Zeitzler could report that tank losses were at an acceptable level. By the eighth, 460 enemy tanks had been destroyed; Hoth's Fourth Panzer Army knocked out 195 that day alone.

But in the south the technical inadequacy of the much vaunted Panther battle tank drained Manstein's offensive badly. It was to await the arrival of 200 Panthers that "Citadel" had after all been delayed until July 5; but on that first day alone, all but 40 broke down, and a week later barely more than 16 were still in action. Nonetheless, while in the north Model's Ninth Army found it could penetrate no farther, little now lay ahead of Manstein in the south. Rommel noted in his diary at the Wolf's Lair on July 9: "Noon, at war conference with Führer: attack in the east is going well."

That afternoon, however, Hitler received the first reports that a large enemy invasion operation was again under way in the Mediterranean. Luftwaffe aircraft sighted the ships after they sailed from Malta and Pantelleria. By late evening it was clear they were heading for Sicily and not Sardinia. Hitler ordered a paratroop division thrown into action as soon as it could be ferried down to Sicily. There were reports of enemy paratroop landings and a heavy naval bombardment of the island's main harbors at Syracuse, Catania, and Augusta. The next morning the invasion began. Hitler was told at his noon conference that three hundred ships were involved.

The invasion's timing was totally unexpected. As recently as July 6, Kesselring, Commander in Chief South, had considered that the reinforcement of the Italian islands with German troops would give the enemy second thoughts about attempting an early invasion. Schmundt, Hitler's chief adjutant, had gone on leave. The invasion could hardly have come at a less propitious moment for Hitler's strategy, unless the German and Italian divisions in Sicily could throw the enemy into the sea without fresh reinforcement. The enemy paratroops were mopped up during the first day, and the "Hermann Göring" Division fought well against the Americans. On July 10 the naval staff considered that "the fight now beginning offers us every chance." Much would hinge on the Italian navy's willingness to do battle with the enemy's seaborne lines of supply: it was like the Tunis position, but reversed in favor of the Axis. Admiral Dönitz ordered every German torpedo boat into the fray, and he asked his Italian counterpart, Admiral Arturo Riccardi, to do likewise; he obliquely hinted that the Italian battleships should also be "brought up in closer proximity to the battle zone." It was clear from aerial reconnaissance that the enemy had committed his entire invasion fleet to Sicily, but even now the Italians opted for a policy of conservation of their warships.

Moreover, the most disturbing accounts reached Hitler about the actions of Italian officers in Sicily. Admiral Priam Leonardi, the commandant of Augusta, had falsely reported that on July 11 enemy assault craft had landed there. According to the local German brigade commander, Colonel Wilhelm Schmalz, the Italian defenders at once blew up their guns and ammunition and set fire to their fuel dumps; the fires were still raging. The antiaircraft batteries at Augusta and Priolo had fired their entire ammunition into the sea and blown up their guns as well. "On the afternoon of July 11 there was not one Italian soldier left in Schmalz's brigade area under any kind of command. Every single officer had abandoned his troops during the morning and was heading for Catania on bicycles and motor transport. Italian troops are drifting around the countryside and roads singly or in clusters of up to five men. Many have thrown away their weapons; some have discarded their uniforms too and donned blue denims."

By July 12 the enemy had landed 160,000 men and 600 tanks on Sicily. With a few exceptions, the Italian fleet lay idle under the hands of its older-generation officers. A strategic decision, which he could no longer ignore, now confronted Hitler.

On July 12, Stalin launched his own counteroffensives.

Before, however, we proceed to analyze Hitler's strategic decisions, it will be appropriate to examine the origins of his continued buoyancy. With hindsight, we can recognize July 1943 as the month the tide finally turned against him. Why did he not see this too? Hitler felt that even if "Citadel" were called off, it would still have drawn the Soviet dragon's teeth: Manstein alone counted 24,000 prisoners by July 13; and he had also captured or destroyed 1,800 enemy tanks, 267 artillery pieces, and 1,080 antitank guns. In consequence, no Soviet counterattack of strategic significance need be feared before the autumn. The Berlin view was that if nonetheless Stalin had had to counterattack now, it was because famine and unrest were sweeping his country. This was well supported by Zeitzler's Intelligence experts, who had sorted through hundreds of bags of captured Russian mail. There were comparisons between 1943 and the disastrous Soviet killer-famine of 1921. One letter described a girl's forty-mile trek through wolf-infested country just to get fifteen eggs. "The letters often afford heartrending glimpses into human destinies," the army digest read by Hitler said. "A mother describes to her husband at the front how their children are growing up and sketches the outline of their tiny hands. A twelve-year-old girl writes to tell her father that her mother has died, and imparts to her lines all the sympathy that her suddenly grown-up heart can bestow. A young wife dispels all her husband's fears that her love won't outlast their separation, which has already gone on three years, in words of deep and powerful sensitiveness. These are no subhumans who wrote these letters." Hitler was probably more impressed by the recurring theme in them: the Soviet Union was at its last gasp.

Above all, Hitler now had the prospect of German "secret weapons" to sustain him until 1944. On July 8, Dönitz came with blueprints of the new Type XXI submarine, all-electric, with an underwater speed so high that it would frustrate all the enemy's defensive tactics. His experts hoped the first boats would be ready by November 1944, but he had discussed with Speer ways and means of producing them much faster. As for the enemy's deadly radar detection equipment, Dönitz hoped to fit out all his U-boats soon with a simple device that would give them ample warning that a radar set was homing onto them. A new antishipping mine had been developed—so potent and so difficult to combat that for the present Hitler would not even allow his navy to employ it for fear the enemy would capture one and use the device in far greater numbers against Germany. As Speer came in, Hitler turned to him. "The most vital thing is to build this new U-boat." Speer replied, "We all agree on that. We have already ordered that it is to take priority over everything else."

That same day Speer brought to him the top scientists of the army's rocket research laboratory at Peenemünde on the Baltic. Hitler knew that Göring and Milch had a team at Peenemünde developing a pilotless flying bomb, but he had been cool toward the army's A-4 rocket project. Todt had expressed dismay at the lavishness of the Peenemünde site's installations and doubted that anything practical would emerge from the complex of engine-test rigs, launching pads, and wind tunnels. But Brauchitsch had backed the A-4 project, and General Friedrich Fromm, commander of the Replacement Army, had been a dedicated benefactor; he had shown Speer over Peenemünde in June 1942 and the new minister had been captivated by the grandeur of the project and lent it his authority. Hitler frankly and realistically told Speer some months later that the A-4 would be pointless unless five thousand were available for the first salvo and production ran at the rate of three thousand a month—a cool appraisal from which he was, however, to depart in the intoxication of the hour of revenge. After all, the rocket had only a one-ton warhead, yet cost as much as one hundred of Milch's flying bombs. In June 1943 Himmler saw an A-4 being launched and learned of its impacting accurately over one hundred miles away. He also commended it to Hitler— oblivious to its disadvantages: it was fueled by such exotic substances as liquid oxygen and pure alcohol, and its fourteen-ton weight was largely aluminum and electronics equipment, both of which were needed far more urgently for the Luftwaffe's industry. But Speer turned a blind eye on this, for he was not, after all, accountable for the aircraft industry as yet. On July 8, Speer introduced to Hitler the men behind the A-4 project: Gerhard Degenkolb, the man who had revolutionized the locomotive industry in 1942 and was now to mass-produce the rockets; General Walter Dornberger, commandant of Peenemünde; and a young, flaxen-haired chief scientist, Wernher von Braun. Hitler gripped his hand. *"Professor* von Braun!" he greeted him. Both the army and the Luftwaffe assured Hitler that their missiles would be operational against England before the year was out.

Two days later, July 10, Heinrich Himmler came to the Wolf's Lair. The A-4 rocket was at the top of his agenda: the wide diversification of Himmler's interests is testified to by the fact that within a year the SS was to have complete control of rocket plants and launching batteries.

Himmler never disappointed Hitler, let alone bored him. One minute he was discussing the use of "Russian poisons in Africa," or the case of the exiled Russian Archduke Vladimir; the next it was the procurement of foreign currency, the bombing war, or the SS panzer corps. Today Himmler wanted to advocate turning the Polish underground army against Stalin. Hans Frank was also demanding a new line over Poland, and the SS was clandestinely fostering a Polish underground group, "The Sword and Plow," to ferret out the rival pro-Allied underground army. The latter was bitterly disillusioned now that Churchill had openly torn up Chamberlain's costly guarantee to Poland, and when the Gestapo captured the Polish underground's chief, General Stefan Rowecki, Himmler felt the whole army could be swung around to fight Stalin instead of the German occupation forces. Hitler read Rowecki's *vita* and admitted that he had had the same idea. But he decided against it: Rowecki was obviously a leader, and such men were dangerous. Himmler noted: "The Führer then reiterated the basis of our Polish policies. These I was aware of and fully understand."

Hitler willingly used non-Slav soldiers in the fight against Stalin. Himmler regularly reported on his SS volunteer divisions raised in the occupied countries. Hitler particularly wanted to attract British captives into joining the fight. Hewel had noted after a conversation with Hitler on November 29, 1942: "He believes that countless patriotic Englishmen must be suffering under their present regime, as they see the future danger of the Jews, and particularly the Bolsheviks, taking over the Empire. He considers it quite possible that given suitable treatment a British legion could be raised to fight in British uniforms against bolshevism. Such a legion would be more welcome to him than one of any other nationality." The problem was that while the Russian captives would, the British would not fight for Hitler; and the one legion Hitler would not even contemplate was a Russian "liberation army."

As he had told his generals on July 1, his soldiers must have the animal satisfaction of knowing that the ground they were fighting for would become theirs for all time. "When our fine peasant lads march into action now they are not thinking, 'Thank God we can liberate this soil for the wonderful Ukrainians.'

They are saying, 'What land this is! Here I come—and here I stay!' " As for the "partisan-infested" regions of the northern Ukraine and the central front, Hitler accepted Himmler's radical proposal that the entire population should be evacuated forthwith; the adults would labor for the Reich, their children would be taken away from them and housed in camps on the periphery, to work in the *Kok-sagys* rubber plantations Himmler planned to cultivate in those regions. *Kok-sagys*—a species suited to temperate climates—was another child of the Reichsführer's fertile brain.[2]

After the Russian counteroffensive began north of operation "Citadel," with Orel as its target, Hitler placed General Model in tactical command of both the Ninth and the Second panzer armies there. The northern pincer of "Citadel" could advance no farther, and on July 13, the Führer summoned both army group commanders, Manstein and Kluge, to discuss the operation's future. Kluge wanted "Citadel" called off. Manstein, still brimming with optimism, took the opposite view. His armies were on the brink of victory—if he could add the Twenty-Fourth Panzer Corps to them, it would tilt the balance finally against the defenders of Kursk; the Russians had thrown their last reserves into the battle —now Hitler must commit his. He could still encircle and destroy half the troops defending Kursk. If the battle was tamely abandoned, the enemy would be free to cause trouble later elsewhere along the front. When Kluge declared that the Ninth Army could not resume the attack either now or later, Hitler irritably exclaimed, "The Russians manage everything, and we manage nothing at all!" Thus the battle was stopped—neither defeat nor victory. Hitler had not excised the Kursk pocket and herded off its inhabitants to slave labor as he wanted; he had lost some 20,720 men, including 3,330 dead. "That's the last time I will heed the advice of my General Staff!" he proclaimed to his adjutants; but he generously shielded Zeitzler himself from the criticism that now sprang up against him. Hitler had himself agreed to the operation and issued the orders for the attack; the responsibility was, he admitted, his and his alone.

But the Russians had suffered the heavier losses in "Citadel"—17,000 dead and 34,000 prisoners. Their tactical reserves had been decimated. Accordingly, the next weeks were to see the Russian summer offensive faltering: when they launched an attack on Manstein's southern front on July 17, Mackensen's First Panzer Army and General Karl Hollidt's new Sixth Army were able to beat them back, taking 18,000 prisoners and destroying 700 tanks in two weeks. When Stalin issued his order of the day on the twenty-fourth announcing his victory at Kursk—

---

[2]Hitler had just appointed him Special Commissioner for all Rubber Plant Affairs.

he claimed that 70,000 Germans had died, and 2,900 German tanks been destroyed—Hitler remarked, "My feeling is: this proves he has called off his own show . . . Stalin has abandoned all hope of pushing on here in one big *furioso.*" It seemed that stability had returned to the Russian front.

In Sicily, meanwhile, there was crisis. Unless Hitler could move reliable divisions into Italy and the western Balkans, the Allies would soon land there too. The Italians were barely putting up the pretense of a fight. All the indications were that Mussolini's renegade generals and the king were plotting his overthrow. Why otherwise had Ambrosio played the familiar Italian card of raising impossible demands for modern tanks and aircraft to be supplied forthwith by Germany? He demanded two thousand planes late in June: it was like August 1939 all over again, only this time both countries were fighting a determined invader, immensely superior in arms and men, with his command unified, resolute, and nearby; as for the Axis, Mussolini was in Rome, where he was surrounded by men the Führer saw as knaves, weaklings, and intriguers, while Hitler was in East Prussia over a thousand miles away.

The American army mopped up the Italians in western Sicily, but the British Eighth Army was soon held up by a tough, predominantly German-manned line of defense forward of Mount Etna. However, unless the Italians showed more fight, Hitler was loath to risk committing more German divisions to the island. He had ordered Colonel Schmalz's report on Admiral Leonardi's behavior at Augusta to be shown to Mussolini, and Mussolini had promised an immediate investigation; but the Duce also made a perceptible effort to push the blame for what now seemed the inevitable loss of Sicily onto the Germans for having failed to meet Ambrosio's supply demands. On July 13 thirty Italian torpedo boats did sally forth to attack enemy ships off Syracuse, but they returned unscathed, lamely pleading that they had not found any Allied shipping. Richthofen, commanding the Second Air Force, sneered in his diary: "As expected, the Italian fleet has not even put to sea 'to save its honor.'" Dönitz telephoned Hitler's headquarters that if Hitler so commanded he was willing to take over the Italian navy at once, so as to bring at least the loyal destroyers and submarines into action.

While Hitler would not go as far as that yet, he did ride roughshod over Italian sovereignty elsewhere. He decided that the defense of Sicily could only be entrusted to the Germans, and he directed an army corps staff to be flown in to reconnoiter the best line forward of Mount Etna. He personally sent a major to Sicily with the top-secret oral instruction that the German corps commander was to take over the battle himself, "unobtrusively excluding" Italians from control. A German commandant was also nominated for the Strait of Messina; the Italian batteries there were if need be to be manned with German crews. Dönitz eagerly supplied 1,723 naval gunners from the 10 batteries he had lined up in France for a possible occupation of northern Spain. On the fourteenth, the OKW brought its contingency plans for a lightning German action against Italy and the Italian-occupied Balkans up to date. If the Italians did an about-face, Rundstedt would force the mountain passes between France and Italy, and General Student's paratroops would take over the Brenner Pass.

On July 14, Hitler showed Mussolini's letter—drafted by Ambrosio—demanding 2,000 aircraft to Milch. He had already ordered one fighter and four bomber squadrons added to Richthofen's air force in Italy. But the Italian ground organization would have to be overhauled. In the last three weeks 320 aircraft had been destroyed in attacks on Italian airfields; 36 fighters out of a squadron of 40 had just suffered tire damage, for the Italians had not bothered to sweep the runways clear of bomb fragments after a raid; Richthofen had had to turn down the Luftwaffe's finest antishipping squadron because the Italian runways were too short and primitive to handle it. "Otherwise," Milch assured the Italian ambassador, "the Führer could hardly have provided better air support for Germany than he is providing for Italy. Hundreds of aircraft are already on their way to Italy and hundreds more are on their way at the expense of the night-fighter defenses of our own western air space." The navy and Luftwaffe were both contributing their heaviest gun batteries—literally hundreds of guns—to the defense of the Strait of Messina. But Hitler rightly hesitated to commit his armored divisions to Sicily. As Jodl warned, it seemed likely that Ambrosio was plotting to lure as many elite German divisions as possible to the south, where they could be cut off and turned over to the enemy on a platter when the time came. Hitler agreed with this stark appraisal of their allies' ulterior intentions. Somehow he had to prevail on Mussolini to rid himself of General Ambrosio, his own appointed gravedigger; German generals had to take over the most endangered areas. Dönitz supported Jodl's view and asked that the Italian admiralty also be frozen out, to reduce its present unholy influence on the campaign.

Hitler decided to meet Mussolini again. Meanwhile he picked General Hube, the veteran of Stalingrad, to command all ground troops in Sicily. Göring tried hard to get his own Luftwaffe's General Rainer Stahel appointed, but Rommel outargued him. Hitler had intended giving Rommel overall command in Italy, but now Göring got his revenge. On July 18, Rommel wrote in his diary: "At midday with the Führer. Field Marshal Kluge also there . . . I learn that the Führer has been advised not to make me Commander in Chief in Italy, as I am supposed to be hostile toward the Italians. I assume the Luftwaffe is behind this. Thus my employment in Italy recedes into the dim and distant future again.— Apparently the Führer's going to meet the Duce."

Two new army groups were now created: B, to be commanded by Rommel from Salonika, covering Greece, Crete, and the Aegean; and E, commanded by General Löhr from Belgrade to control the rest of the Balkans. In the event, Rommel's new appointment lasted just one week.

On July 18, Hitler flew down to the Berghof. He sat just behind the cockpit, his papers spread out on the folding table, meditating that it was all turning out just as he had feared. "This was precisely why I was so apprehensive about launching our offensive in the east too early," he said a few days later. "I kept thinking that at the same time we'd find our hands full down south."

His strategy now was this: somehow they must tempt the enemy to pour huge reinforcements into the island of Sicily—then the Luftwaffe would bomb the supply ships to pieces and starve the invader into submission; what he wanted was Tunis in reverse. He had therefore resolved to confront Mussolini with a personal ultimatum: either Sicily must be effectively defended—with a view to reverting to the offensive later on—or it should be abandoned, and the decisive battle fought on the Italian mainland. But first the Duce would have to tighten his grip over the Italians and his armed forces.

The one-day meeting between the Axis leaders had been planned for later but advanced to July 19 by events in Sicily. Mussolini—who had originally wanted several days with Hitler as he had had in April—probably wanted to impart to the Führer that his country could no longer fight on. But Hitler did not give him a real opportunity to speak his mind—not even during the time they spent together in the Duce's shabby, old-fashioned train with its jostling staff in comic-opera costumes. The account rendered in Mussolini's later diary describes how things went from the moment Hitler arrived at the Treviso airfield:

Punctually at nine the Führer landed. He inspected the guard of honor and we proceeded to the railroad station. After about an hour the train left us at a station outside Feltre. An automobile bore us onward to the villa selected for our meeting, the house of Senator Gaggia, a veritable labyrinth of rooms and salons which are still a nightmare in my memory. We arrived there after an hour's drive in an open car under a scorching sun, during which I merely exchanged polite small talk with the Führer.

The actual meeting began at noon. . . . The Führer began the talking, and continued for two hours. His words were taken down in shorthand and the complete text of his speech is in foreign ministry files. Scarcely had he begun when my secretary came in with a telephone message from Rome: "Since 11 A.M. Rome has been under intense air bombardment." I informed the Führer and the others. The news charged the atmosphere with tragedy—the atmosphere crowded in on us with each fresh telephone message reporting the exceptional length of the raid, the number of bombers employed, and the severe damage (including the university and the church of San Lorenzo).

When the Führer had concluded his speech, a first confidential exchange of opinions took place between the two of us. He imparted two important facts to me: firstly, the U-boat war was about to be resumed with other means; and secondly that at the end of August the German Luftwaffe would begin reprisal attacks on London, razing it to the ground within a week. I replied that in anticipation of the reprisals this would provoke, Italy's air defenses would have to be [strengthened].[3]

I was then called away to receive fresh reports, whereupon it was time to return. Only during the hour-long train journey could I make one thing plainly understood to him: that Italy is now withstanding the entire weight of two empires—Britain and the United States—and there is a very real and growing danger of her being crushed beneath them. The bombing of our cities damages not only our public's morale and powers of resistance, but also our main war production. I told him again that the campaign in Africa would have ended very differently had we been at least equal, if not superior, to the enemy air force. I also warned that the nervous tension within my country is now at an extreme and dangerous pitch.

He told me the Italian crisis was a leadership crisis, and hence a human one. He would send reinforcements for the air force and new divisions to defend the peninsula. He declared that the defense of Italy is also in Germany's highest interests. His choice of words was friendly at all times, and we parted on the best of terms. The Führer's aircraft took off soon afterward.

Hitler was curiously satisfied with the outcome of this—as it happened, his last —visit to Italy. He believed he had revitalized the Italian war effort. His generals were unimpressed. Field Marshal Richthofen wrote that day: "Landed at Treviso at five to nine. As is right and proper, the Duce and Kesselring met me there. . . . At the villa the Führer delivered a two-hour speech without a break to the Duce, his military staff, and other companions on how to fight wars and battles. Nobody apart from the Duce understood a word. Afterward, Ambrosio observed with a smirk that it was not so much a *coloquio* as a *disloquio*. . . . The Führer was tired from so much energetic speaking, but looked well, much better than the Duce. Then the same trek back to Treviso. The whole show has probably produced less than one could conceal under a little fingernail."

"On parting," Richthofen wrote, "the Führer was again most cordial. The routine query as to my well-being. Particularly pressed me not to risk my health

---

[3]Mussolini omitted the word *assicurare.*—The German record indicates that Hitler told him of the radar warning-devices being fitted to the submarines and of the decoy buoys and new U-boat types arriving early in 1944. "Finally the Führer also mentioned a weapon on which he did not want to impart precise details, but which would enter service against the British when the winter began and against which there was no defense"—evidently meaning the A-4.

or myself—saying I would make a fine trophy for the British if they could get their hands on me. I could only respond that I would look even more unsightly stuffed than I do now."

As he flew back from the Berghof to East Prussia on July 20, Hitler was despondent about Mussolini's future. The previous evening Martin Bormann had shown him an Intelligence report cabled by Himmler to the Berghof; it contained clear evidence that "a coup d'etat is being planned to get rid of the Duce and install Marshal Badoglio to form a war cabinet." Himmler's report said: "B[adoglio] is known to be a leading Freemason in Italy. His aim is said to be to commence immediate peace talks the moment the Anglo-American troops have completed their occupation of Sicily." The cable was long and circumstantial. There was no point in warning Mussolini—he was of an almost childlike naïvete. On the railroad station he had blurted out to the Führer: "I just don't know what my generals can be thinking of, stationing such strong forces up here in the north. They are supposed to be defending Italy!"

Shortly afterward, German railroad officials on the border tipped off the OKW to the fact that the Italians were steadily stockpiling ammunition in the fortifications facing the Reich, for example at Tarvisio.

Rommel was summoned to see Hitler on July 20 and entered in his diary: "At Führer's evening conference: major breach in the eastern front at Army Group Center, aimed at Orel. All quiet in Sicily. His talk with Duce yielded no real clear decisions. Duce unable to act as he would wish. I am to take command over Greece, including the islands, for the time being, so that I can pounce on Italy later." The next day he wrote: "Morning conference: eastern front somewhat firmer, but big breach at Orel. Russians still have 8,700 tanks operational." That afternoon he saw Jodl: "The Duce is aware of his colleagues' political intentions." On July 22, Rommel wrote: "At the Führer's midday conference: eastern front now stable apart from Orel." He flew off the next day to begin his thankless task in Greece, where apart from the questionable Italian Eleventh Army he would command only one German panzer division and three German infantry divisions. Admiral Canaris's Abwehr still maintained that the main Allied invasion was not that in Sicily, but still to come in the Balkans.

Meanwhile, an ominous calm had overtaken the murderous bombing war. The Luftwaffe had abandoned its costly and ineffective raids on London and provincial cities, as the bomber squadrons were needed in Italy. Since mid-June long-range German night fighters had begun harassing Allied bombers over their own English airfields, but Hitler disapproved of such intruder-operations: the German public wanted revenge for their own dead and maimed—what did it care for minelaying operations or pinpricks against enemy airfields? When Göring and

Milch came to see him on July 23, he emphasized: "You can only break terrorism by counterterrorism. We have got to counterattack—anything else is useless!" When Colonel Peltz defended the intruder-operations, Hitler variously replied, "At present we can be pleased with ourselves if our crews even find London!" "Can't find London—a disgrace!" "If this goes on, the German public will go raving mad!" "The British will only stop bombing if their own cities are being flattened, and not otherwise!"

The next day, July 24, the first storm signals were hoisted over southern Europe. Unsettling and indeterminate news reached Hitler that the Fascist Grand Council was being convened that evening in Rome for the first time in many years. Roberto Farinacci, a radical and independent Fascist agitator, evidently intended thereby to force Mussolini to adopt more extreme measures against his opponents; but this was in fact playing straight into his critics' hands. As midnight passed without fresh word from Rome, Hitler grumbled that if a Farinacci had pulled a trick like that on him, he would have had Himmler haul him off straight away. "What good can possibly come of such a meeting? Just empty chatter!" At 3 A.M., the *consiglio* was still in session. Before Hitler retired for the night, word reached him that the British had attacked Hamburg with up to a thousand heavy bombers, that the port city was a blazing inferno, and that for some as yet undetermined reason the radar defenses had failed to function.

The first photographs of the hideous scenes there were shown to him the next morning. Corpses of men, women, and children littered the streets—the women with their hair in curlers, the men clutching suitcases, the children seeking shelter in the arms of fire-fighters. In one parish alone eight hundred civilians had died. At his noon conference Hitler learned that the enemy had begun jamming the ground and airborne radar sets by the very means the experts had feared all along: "They have released cascades of hundreds of thousands of strips of metal foil into the sky." The antiaircraft gunners and fighter pilots were fighting blind from now on; the bombers could maraud everywhere with virtual immunity. During the week that followed, Hamburg was to suffer three more night attacks. In one, an immense firestorm began, the huge fires creating hurricane-strength winds that sucked trees, rooftops, debris, and people into their flames; the tens of thousands sheltering in the massive concrete bunkers were incinerated alive, poisoned by monoxide fumes, or drowned by the flood of bursting water mains. Part of Hamburg's antiaircraft batteries had been sacrificed for the defense of Italy.

Even the terror of the first night failed to presage the fact that over forty thousand more people would be killed there in the week to come. But Hitler steeled his heart. For the present, Rome was more important. He swung around on Ribbentrop's liaison official. "See that you find out what you can, Hewell!"

Hewel replied, "They adjourned their *consiglio* at three this morning. I will find out the moment anything else comes through." But by the time the conference ended at 2 P.M. he could still report only that wild rumors were sweeping Rome.

Later that day word came that Marshal Badoglio had asked the German ambassador to see him. Mackensen declined, but the aged marshal insisted on a meeting. Badoglio then dropped his bombshell: Benito Mussolini had resigned. The king had asked the marshal to set up a military government. "Badoglio has taken over," exclaimed Hitler to Keitel that evening. "The blackest of our enemies!"

"Axis"

In the week immediately following Mussolini's overthrow, Hitler vacillated between two extremes: his initial instinct was to send paratroops to Rome, flush out the monarchy, the traitors, and the Vatican, and restore the "wronged" dictator to power. He refused to believe that the Duce had willingly abdicated; he assumed that his restoration alone would bring back the Fascist organization that had seemingly melted into nothingness overnight. As July 26, 1943, dawned, he even sent out orders for his troops to abandon Sicily forthwith, leaving their tanks and equipment where they were; for between Sicily and the Brenner Pass there were virtually no German troops at all, apart from Field Marshal Kesselring's headquarters staffs outside Rome and the naval detachments based in certain Italian ports. It was indeed a chilling situation: a thousand miles of Italian coastline along which the enemy might at any moment land and be positively welcomed by the new regime in Rome. Were he, Hitler, in Churchill's shoes he would have struck at once to reap such a rich reward. Yet as the days passed and more moderate advisers came to the Wolf's Lair, reason prevailed; the enemy was as perplexed by the new situation as he was, and now time worked in Hitler's favor. Throughout August the Wehrmacht foothold in Italy was steadily strengthened, in spite of Badoglio's protests. A brilliant rearguard action was fought in Sicily after all. And when in September Badoglio and his generals finally fulfilled the Führer's gloomiest predictions and hoisted the long-prepared white flag of surrender, Hitler was ready to step in.

These weeks of drama were not devoid of comedy or bereft of bitterness. The stenographic records of Hitler's first conferences after word came from Rome show how effectively he could grapple with major crises. Sepp Dietrich's SS Life Guard Division must be rushed from the eastern front to Italy at once; the seventy thousand German troops in Sicily must be brought back to the mainland—abandoning their heavy equipment if need be. "Their pistols are all they'll need. . . . they can make short work of the Italians with pistols too"; there must be an evacuation of Sicily "like Dunkirk" in 1940. The 3rd Panzer-Grenadier Division must seize Rome, arrest the government, and kidnap the king and above all the crown prince, who would be retained as hostages to guarantee that Italy abide by her pact with Germany; Badoglio must be captured dead or alive; Mussolini must be found and rescued, if he had not already been put to death, in which case his body must be recovered to prevent the enemy from putting it on public display. And Rommel! "Find out where Rommel is!" The field marshal was run to earth in Salonika: at 11:15 P.M. on July 25 the OKW telephoned him to return to the Führer's headquarters at once.

From all over Germany they flew in to the Wolf's Lair—Himmler, Guderian, Goebbels, Göring; Speer was already there; Ribbentrop, convalescing from a lung ailment, arrived looking pale and drawn; Dönitz decided to come with several of his staff; Schmundt was ordered back from leave; Roberto Farinacci was flown up from Munich, whither he had escaped from Rome. (Hitler contemplated using him—pending Mussolini's rescue—to set up a puppet Italian government to rival Badoglio's, but he abandoned the notion the moment he talked with the weedy Italian—indeed, he began to suspect that Farinacci had been bribed by Badoglio to convene the *consiglio* which had brought about the Duce's downfall.) What disturbed all the Party leaders most was this vivid proof that dictatorships could be toppled with such ease. As Jodl bluntly put it, ruminating out loud to Hitler: "The fact is, the whole Fascist movement went pop, like a soap bubble!" Hitler directed Himmler to ensure that nothing went pop in Germany.

Yet while Hitler mastered the initial details of the crisis, his statesmanship abandoned him, swamped by the signals transmitted by his enraged emotions. For several days he was tempted to adopt rash expedients that would have put him wholly in the wrong and brought the entire Italian people solidly behind Badoglio and the king. The very existence of General Hube's soldiers in Sicily depended on the Italian railwaymen and dockers; and the longer these continued to work, the better were Hitler's chances of infiltrating additional German divisions into northern Italy.

But Hitler felt outraged; that Mussolini, a leader bound to him by destiny, should have been so ignobly deposed by traitors and vassals of the monarchy, made his blood boil. He did not doubt that Badoglio was already working hand-in-glove with the enemy. "We can be clear on one score: traitors that they are, they will of course proclaim their intention of continuing the fight. Of course! But it will be a betrayal." He smiled contemptuously. "We shall be playing the same game, leading them on until we suddenly drop like lightning on the whole bag of them and round up the entire gang." On July 26 he sent Captain Wolf Junge, Jodl's staff officer, to Kesselring with oral orders to stand by to seize Rome and prevent the Italian fleet's escape. Hitler instructed the Second Paratroop Division to fly to an airport outside Rome the next day without advance warning to either Kesselring or the Italians. The 3rd Panzer-Grenadier Division was also to move to the outskirts of the capital. Hitler would give the code word the moment Badoglio moved a muscle against Germany's interests; if that fateful twitch occurred too soon for full-scale intervention, then Kesselring and General Student would have to occupy Rome with what forces they could muster from the headquarters staffs there—the proverbial German cooks and clerk-typists who had on occasion also wrought havoc on Americans troops in Tunisia.

In the teahouse of the Wolf's Lair Himmler had lined up half a dozen Luftwaffe and army special agents as candidates for the job of rescuing the mislaid Fascist dictator, now known to have been arrested on the king's orders on leaving the palace. Otto Günsche, Hitler's bodyguard, took them into the Führer's study. Hitler asked each in turn: "What do you think of the Italians?" The last of them, a burly scar-faced Waffen SS captain, growled: "What a question, mein Führer! And me an Austrian!" Hitler picked this man, Otto Skorzeny, and assigned him a secretary to note down everything he would need. Skorzeny would leave with Student for Rome next morning. The latter parted from Hitler with the words: "A tough but particularly rewarding mission, mein Führer!"

Worn out, that evening Hitler ate alone. No less than thirty-five people packed the following war conference. Two factions were clearly crystalizing: the one, led by Dönitz and Jodl, decried precipitate action against Italy; the other, led by Hitler, wanted Student to strike as soon as he was ready. Rommel wanted the whole operation adequately thought out and prepared, but Goebbels felt that the British would hardly wait a week while Rommel was doing his thinking and preparing. Göring had already stated his opinion at midday: "Our opponents will obviously scream to the Allies for help and beg for protection." Hitler pointed out: "But it will still take them some time to get ready to invade." At first the British would be nonplussed—they always were. Everybody, particularly Goebbels and Ribbentrop, opposed Hitler's plan to sweep through the Vatican as well; "apologies afterward" would never repair the harm this would do to Germany's image abroad. Meanwhile Kesselring and Richthofen insisted from their Italian headquarters that Badoglio would stay loyal to the Axis cause; Badoglio—cunningly adjudging Kesselring's marked sense of military chivalry—had received him that evening with a copy of Napoleon's *Italian Campaigns* open on his desk. "You see, Field Marshal," he explained disarmingly, "this is the problem that gives me sleepless nights. How to lead a defeated army on to victory?" Kesselring reported innocently that Badoglio had only replaced Mussolini to provide the strong war leadership needed to restore honor to Italian arms. Hitler could only chuckle at Kesselring's gullibility.

———

Militarily, Hitler knew he could not defend the entire Italian mainland when Badoglio defected. "In the course of events we shall obviously have to fall back along here somewhere," he had said on July 25, tapping the map of Italy. "That is quite plain." In addition to the divisions he was already moving into northern Italy from southern France, he wanted three SS armored divisions taken out of Manstein's Army Group South: the SS divisions were most politically akin to fascism. Their transfer would in turn necessitate withdrawing the German salient at Orel to release divisions for Manstein. Kluge, brought before Hitler on the twenty-sixth, was aghast. "Mein Führer! I am bound to point out that there is nothing we can release at this moment. That is quite out of the question at present!" Only when his army group had fallen back on the new "Hagen" line, along the Dnieper, could he offer any help; but this sector of the East Wall had only just been begun and would not be ready for occupation before September. Hitler feared that Badoglio would have defected long before then. "September is quite impossible, Field Marshal!" he retorted. And he angrily commented, "The swine on the other side shovel out a line in two days, and *we* can't throw *them* out!" For the time being, however, he had to make do with Sepp Dietrich's Life Guards alone.

The next evening Field Marshal von Richthofen arrived from Rome. The crowded war conference with Hitler lasted until nearly midnight. "Everybody very rude about Kesselring," wrote Richthofen in his diary. "I counterattack. Some of his dispatches are admittedly psychologically tactless, but by and large objective and accurate. I identify myself with them. . . . Rommel knows nothing, thank God says nothing, and is just reveling in feelings of revenge against the Italians, whom he hates. Dönitz is moderate and sensible. Everybody else, especially Ribbentrop, just repeating whatever the Führer says."

Richthofen stubbornly stuck to his guns: premature action by Student would be a catastrophe. Jodl backed him up, and so did Dönitz. Richthofen did predict that Marshal Badoglio might raise impossible military demands and use their nonfulfillment as a pretext to deal with the enemy; almost on cue Ambassador Mackensen's telegram arrived from Rome, announcing just such Italian demands. Richthofen urged Hitler to appear to accept everything in order to win time to infiltrate Rommel's divisions into Italy. But Hitler's big worry was that he was missing the bus—that in silent agreement with Badoglio the British would suddenly arrive by air and sea in Italy. On this score Richthofen had to agree. Hitler ordered: "Student is to fulfill his mission as soon as possible." When Rommel left for Munich to join his new Army Group B headquarters the next morning, he had Hitler's secret instructions for the invasion of Italy in his pocket; but on no account were he or any of his more famous officers to show themselves south of the Reich frontier for the time being. Canaris's Abwehr was ordered to give Rommel every support, using its agents in Italy to find out what Badoglio and his frontier troops were up to.

———

It was at this moment that a blustering speech by Churchill rescued Hitler from his dilemma.[1] Speaking in the House of Commons, he said that nothing short of "wholesale unconditional surrender" would prevent Italy from being "seared and scarred and blackened from one end to the other"; he expected the new Italian government to take some time reaching a decision. "We should let the Italians, to use a homely phrase, stew in their own juice for a bit." Secretary of State Cordell Hull issued an equally intransigent statement in Washington. Badoglio and the king were evidently between the devil and the deep blue sea. They can scarcely have expected an armistice to prove so unattainable after the Allied wooing and blandishments of the past month. Now Hitler knew he would have *time* after all. A message was sent to Kesselring reminding him not to let General Student unleash "Operation Black," his plan to occupy Rome, "through any misunderstanding."

An immensely self-satisfied Führer joined his field marshals for lunch that day, July 28. By evening his mind was made up against precipitate action. Richthofen wrote: "From 9 P.M., Führer's war conference. Militarily speaking, all quiet. The sensible solution has at last won through for Italy. Obviously southern Italy will (now!) be pumped full of forces to meet the real enemy and all other eventualities. Our only purpose now is to play for time. With this in view all Italy's demands will be accepted." To the chagrin of the Italians, Hitler's divisions now began rolling singly over the Brenner into Italy.

Despite the curiously reassuring appreciations of Admiral Canaris's Abwehr and its associated Foreign Armies West branch of the General Staff, Hitler had more than enough direct evidence of Badoglio's stealthy and treacherous maneuvers. The reliability of Himmler's SS Intelligence channels cannot have failed to impress him in these weeks. It was through the SS-fostered "Post Office Research Institute" that Hitler obtained on July 29 the transcript of a radio-telephone conversation held soon after midnight between Churchill and Roosevelt. Ignoring the possibility that the enemy could unscramble this link, they had gossiped about the "imminent armistice with Italy" in language that told Hitler that Roosevelt at least was in secret contact with King Victor Emmanuel but that many days would pass before Italy would defect, because first the terms of the armistice would have to be thrashed out. Churchill wanted to prevent the sixty thousand British prisoners in Italy from being shipped to "Hunland." But by his very

---

[1]Since he made no reference to the speech in his memoirs, Winston Churchill evidently belatedly realized this. As the German naval staff crowed in its war diary the next day: "Churchill's speech has thrown a cold douche on patriotic circles in Italy and been a boon to us."

garrulousness he was ensuring that Hitler would propel enough divisions into Italy to do just that.

On July 30, Rommel's army group reported that the Italian defenses along the Brenner were being stealthily reinforced, and demolition charges laid. Hitler learned reliably from the Croatian Poglavnik that General Roatta, the Italian army Chief of Staff, had recently told a fellow general that Badoglio's protestations of loyalty were just a ploy to win time; indeed, on the thirty-first the Italian minister at Zagreb told the Poglavnik that Italy was not merely going to desert the Axis—she was going to join the enemy.

Nevertheless, Canaris's Intelligence agencies played all this down. When it was learned that the *comando supremo* had burnt its secret files two days before the Duce's overthrow, Colonel Alexis von Roenne (chief of Zeitzler's Foreign Armies West) swore that this did not indicate that treason was in the air. At the beginning of August, Canaris came to Hitler's headquarters and reported on a meeting he had just had with General Amé, his Italian opposite number: the Abwehr chief blandly assured Keitel that Badoglio was resolved to fight on. "There is no question of any peace negotiations."[2] During August, the discrepancy between these assessments by Canaris and Roenne and those by the SS, the foreign ministry, the Forschungsamt, and the frontier Gauleiters in Austria grew so wide that the German admiralty raised a scandalized comment in its war diary. By this time Italian obstructionism was at its height. The railways were purposefully jammed with civilian traffic to impede the entry of fresh German divisions; Hitler according-ly ordered them to enter on foot, despite the scorching Mediterranean sun. There were gunfights between Italian and German officers. At staff talks with Keitel and Ribbentrop in Tarvisio on August 6, General Ambrosio again assured the Germans that Italy "wanted to fight on at Germany's side," but his lack of interest in se-curing more German arms and material told Ribbentrop all he needed to know. He telephoned Hitler immediately—this was "treason, one hundred per-cent."

When Ribbentrop's belief was subsequently confirmed by events, this should have led to Canaris's final downfall. But he was too slippery for that. In Septem-ber he trumped his SS challengers with a file of miraculously accurate Abwehr dispatches and accused Keitel of having withheld them from the Führer. Thus Canaris survived.

----

[2]General Amé has stated that Canaris met him in Venice on July 30 with the whispered congratula-tion: "We hope *our* July 25 will also soon come!" Canaris begged Amé to do everything to prevent the entry of more German troops. The SS learned of this, but Himmler declined to unmask Canaris to Hitler at this stage. Both Canaris and Roenne were later hanged for treason.

Under the new code word "Axis," Hitler's planning for the occupation and disarming of Italy and the seizure of her idle fleet at La Spezia continued throughout August 1943. Mussolini had still not been found by the Führer's agents. All that was known was that he was still alive, because Hitler's sixtieth birthday gift to him—a twenty-four-volume set of Nietzsche—was duly acknowledged by the deposed dictator. Meanwhile the hunt went on.

The Anglo-American air offensive had not lessened, but Hitler paid scant attention to it. After the first big Hamburg raid he had greedily signed Albert Speer's draft decree for the mass production of the army's A-4 rocket missile— the later V-2—to bombard London that autumn; heedless of the effect on the Luftwaffe's aircraft industry, Hitler had on July 25 ordered all available skilled labor, raw materials, machine tools, and electric power devoted on high priority to the rocket missile. "You can only smash terror with counterterror," he had reiterated that day. "Otherwise the time will come when the people here just lose faith completely in the Luftwaffe." Speer was as yet doing nothing to support the Luftwaffe's plea for proper emphasis on the fighter defenses. Milch had already stepped up fighter output to one thousand a month and was planning to treble this over the next year; and highly effective new night-fighter tactics had been improvised in the wake of the Hamburg catastrophe, abandoning the rigid but thin line of radar-guided fighters in favor of packs of two to three hundred at a time, fighting the enemy freelance over the actual burning target area. On August 1, Albert Speer dismally predicted to Hitler that if six more cities were given the Hamburg treatment, the war would be over. But in commending the A-4 rocket to Hitler he was mistaken, for what Germany needed were fighters for the defense of the home base.

Göring's influence over Hitler was now weak; and General Jeschonnek, the Luftwaffe Chief of Staff, had reached the end of his tether—torn between Hitler's demands and Göring's reproaches. Hitler ordered the women and children moved out of the Reich capital at once. Berlin was evacuated of one million civilians in grim anticipation of the raids to come. On August 13 the American bombing of Wiener Neustadt resulted in a four-hour row between Hitler and Jeschonnek. Four days later the Americans bombed the ball-bearing works at Schweinfurt and Messerschmitt's plant at Regensburg, killing four hundred workers. That night the British saturated Peenemünde with bombs, killing seven hundred scientists and slave laborers. Jeschonnek committed suicide, and Milch at last persuaded his successor, General Günther Korten—whom the Reichsmarschall presented to Hitler on the twentieth—to transfer fighter squadrons back to the defense of the Reich. From the British bomber-loss figures supplied to Berlin by the imaginary agent in the British air ministry, Hitler decided that the night air-war at least was tilting slowly back in Germany's favor.

On August 20 Hitler discussed with Dr. Ley and leading architects how to take care of the survivors and the bombed-out families. When Ley offered to build

350,000 homes a year, Speer interrupted: "I will not provide the materials, because I cannot." His counterproposal was for the nationalization of all homes, but Hitler would not hear of that. "I need a million new homes, and fast. Each about ten feet by twelve; it is immaterial whether they are of wood, concrete, or prefabricated slabs. I am even thinking in terms of mud huts or at worst just holes in the ground simply covered over with planks. The houses should be built singly in individual plots, around towns and villages, where possible scattered about among the trees." He did not expect each house to have a lavatory, or gas, water, or electricity—just the barest essentials in a form that even old women or children could easily erect, for their menfolk were at the front: two benches, a table, a cupboard, and nails to hang their clothes on. "We are forced to build as spartanly as possible, so there must be no distinction between them. The main thing is for these people to have a roof over their heads when winter comes; otherwise they will perish."

Speer's inability to provide materials for Ley's program to house the homeless was not unconnected with his own massive support for Hitler's secret weapons projects. On this same visit he persuaded Hitler to authorize the manufacture of an immense gunsite on the Channel coast; the guns were to have four-hundred-foot barrels and be theoretically capable of maintaining a permanent attack on London: several propelling charges were to be detonated in sequence to give each shell the necessary velocity—a principle which worked on a small scale but not when it eventually came to the test. The huge underground gun battery swallowed up hundreds of thousands of tons of urgently needed concrete, and it never fired a single shell at England. Himmler was afflicted with the same strategic blindness, having himself been intoxicated by visits to Peenemünde. He offered Speer concentration camp labor to build missile factories and man the assembly lines; he also offered him the use of the SS proving ground at Blizna, Poland, for the rocket-launching trials. Hitler ordered Speer and the SS chief to make the maximum use of caves, tunnels, and bunkers for what all three evidently considered a significant element of Germany's coming strategy.

In Berlin, Dr. Goebbels marshaled the ministers and Party officials for a pep talk to restore their battered morale; the Führer remained in East Prussia, directing the war in Russia and the Mediterranean. The German people must at all costs stand fast during the trying months to come: until the fighter and antiaircraft defenses mastered the bombing terror, until the missile attack on London could begin—and until the monolithic Anglo-American and Soviet facade began to crack.

Hitler believed that the evidence justified his hopes that one day the western Allies would turn against Moscow and decide they had committed a blunder in continuing to assail Germany. The first straw in the wind had been Stalin's rejection of General Wladyslaw Sikorski's London-based Polish exile government in April, and the creation of a puppet Polish committee in Moscow. In July, Stalin had followed this with a "Free Germany" committee consisting of exiled Communists and renegade generals captured at Stalingrad. Now British newspapers at last scented where Moscow proposed to lay the postwar boundaries of the bolshevik empire. Conversely Stalin's recall of his ambassadors from London and Washington, and his absence from Churchill's conference with Roosevelt at Quebec, indicated Soviet dissatisfaction with the Allies. There were rumors that Stalin wanted peace talks with Germany. "I fully recognize that at present a ruthless desire to destroy us has the upper hand in Britain and America," reflected Hitler. "But the British have got it all quite wrong! They declared war to preserve the 'balance of power' in Europe. But now Russia has awakened and turned into a state of the highest technical and material caliber. . . . This means that the onslaught from the east can in the future only be met by a united Europe under German leadership. That is in Britain's interest too." The time must come, in Hitler's view, when the Allies would realize their political mistake and reason would replace their present campaign of hatred and destruction against the most potent power in Europe.

Until Italy's future was more certain, however, Hitler could not speak his mind to the German people. For the same reason, he hesitated to order General Hube to evacuate his sixty thousand troops from Sicily to the mainland: on the one hand Admiral Dönitz protested that giving Sicily to the enemy would provide them with easy access to southern Italy and the Balkans; but on the other, General Jodl warned that the moment military operations were launched for the rescue of Mussolini or the capture of Rome and the Italian fleet at La Spezia, the Italians would cut off all the supply routes to Sicily and the sixty thousand men would be lost. Everything thus hinged on the loyalty of Badoglio to the Axis. Kesselring, Mackensen, and Rintelen all reported that he could be trusted. But the contrary evidence was overwhelming. From his Gauleiter in the Tyrol Hitler learned that the Italians had stealthily moved three divisions—two of them known for their anti-German inclinations—into Bolzano and Merano. "These steps were obviously taken to satisfy the Anglo-American requirement that Italy must take positive action against Germany if she is to get better peace terms."

Kesselring wanted southern Italy packed with German troops, but Hitler felt this was risky and unnecessary, as the British would be unlikely to invade a malarial zone. He told General Heinrich von Vietinghoff, whose new Tenth Army would take over the two corps stationed there, that he proposed eventually to evacuate Lower Italy and "would not be happy until all those divisions from southern Italy and Sicily were standing south of Rome." For the time being, Hitler instinctively rejected Rommel's insistent demands for Kesselring to be recalled so that he, Rommel, could exercise the supreme command in Italy— south as well as north; he anticipated that the time might well come when

Kesselring's infuriating optimism would stand Germany in good stead, and he adhered to the split command. Rommel's political plus was his blind faith in Hitler. "M[ussolini] probably won't be coming back," he wrote from his Munich headquarters. "The Fascist party was evidently very corrupt and was swept away in a matter of hours. . . . On the other hand it suits us well, as now there is only one great man to lead in Europe." Admiral Dönitz shared Rommel's sentiments about Hitler, writing with trembling hand after forty-eight hours at the Wolf's Lair: "The enormous energy the Führer radiates, his unerring conviction, his prophetic analysis of the situation in Italy—all these have very much brought home to us these last few days what poor worms we all are in comparison to the Führer!"

Rommel came up from Munich on August 11, arriving in time for the noon war conference:

Göring, Dönitz, Student, and Himmler are at the conference. Eastern front: heavy fighting at Kharkov, big Russian breach west of the city. At Leningrad a battle of attrition, with day-long artillery barrages; offensive expected on August 12.

Discussing Italy, the Führer agrees with my own views. Führer appears to intend sending me in quite soon. Like me he doesn't believe in the honesty of the Italians. . . . The Führer says the Italians are playing for time; then they will defect. The probable object of the Churchill-Roosevelt meeting is just to lure the Italians into treason, particularly since the Italians are obviously taking part in the talks. . . . The Führer evidently wants to adhere to his old plan of restoring fascism to power, as this is the only way to guarantee that Italy will unconditionally stand by us. He has sharp words of condemnation for the work of Mackensen, Rintelen, and Kesselring, as they—and particularly Kesselring —still totally misinterpret the Italian situation and blindly trust the new regime. . . .

Zeitzler is very aloof toward me, and reserved. Worried about the eastern front?

Lunch with the Führer. I sit on his left. A very spirited discussion, with the Führer evidently delighted I am there. Again and again I find that he has complete confidence in me. . . .

Before supper I confer with Jodl. His plan, based on our proposal, was for me to take command in Upper Italy. My new draft has me in command of all Italy, with two armies (north and south), while being myself under the Italians; the army group HQ near Rome so as to exert influence over the *comando supremo* and the regime. After I refute his objections, Jodl agrees.

Then supper with the Führer, and evening conference. . . . He approves my proposal to fight a delaying action in Sicily and to fall back on Italy only when forced to do so, and meanwhile to establish four lines of resistance [across the peninsula]—the first from Cosenza to Taranto, the second at Salerno, the third at Cassino, and the fourth and ultimate line along the Apennines. . . .

One last attempt was made to force the Italians to show their true intentions. Hitler ordered Rommel and Jodl to confront the Italians with a putative plan for a joint defense of Italy and to study their reactions. The meeting took place at Bologna on August 15. General Roatta took the news that Rommel would command all German forces north of the Apennines very badly. He icily submitted a map which would in effect deploy the Italian divisions in a barrier across the peninsula, where they could trap the Germans in the south; the motive was clear.[3] (On the same day the Italians declared Rome an "open city"—evidently for no other reason than to prevent the Germans from using its railway lines to the south.) Rommel wrote a twenty-page memorandum on the Bologna meeting. Jodl more succinctly cabled the OKW that evening: "Grounds for suspicion remain undiminished." Hitler ordered the evacuation of Sicily to begin.

While even the overt relations between Germany and Italy were thus deteriorating, Hitler had continued patching up his defenses in the Balkans. King Boris of Bulgaria was invited for a two-day informal visit to the Wolf's Lair. According to records kept by Hitler's manservant, they lunched together for three hours on August 14 and again the next day before Hitler himself accompanied Boris to Rastenburg airfield. He had asked the king to provide two more Bulgarian divisions for security purposes in Greece, but Boris was reluctant in view of the potential risk to his country from Turkey; besides, he wisely pointed out, the Greeks hated the Bulgars, so such a move might only increase the disturbances. Bulgaria's military position was precarious: in return for rich territorial concessions from Hitler, she had declared war on the Allies but not on Russia; but the Soviet Union was known to be grooming divisions in the Caucasus for an invasion of Bulgaria, and a powerful Communist movement was emerging in the land.

Two weeks later King Boris was struck down by a disease of mysterious suddenness. The German air attaché in Sofia provided immediate air transport for the king's German physician, Dr. Seitz, on August 24; Seitz reported that the king was dying. Ribbentrop's staff warned of the grave consequences to Bulgaria's policies. "Without the king, the Bulgarian people would be leaderless and uncertain of themselves, and they might come under the influence of the Communist and pro-British opposition." Seitz provisionally diagnosed a bladder disease, and Professor Hans Eppinger was summoned for consultation from Vienna. Complications set in, and the famous neurologist Professor Maximilian de Crinis was

---

[3]At that very moment an Italian general, emissary of Marshal Badoglio, was in Madrid informing the British ambassador there that if the Allies were now to land in Italy the regime was willing to make common cause with them against Germany. Not surprisingly, the main records of the Italian ministries involved in this affair remain classified in Rome to this very day.

flown in from Berlin on the twenty-eighth; but at 4:20 P.M., the king died. The government communiqué spoke of angina pectoris. Upon the doctors' return, Hitler instructed his minister of justice to discharge them from their oath of secrecy and to question them; they were unanimous that the cause of death was not angina pectoris but an exotic snake-poison. It was the characteristic "Balkan death," as Eppinger put it.

Hitler was disconsolate at the loss of this stabilizing influence in Bulgaria. Enemy radio broadcasts rejoiced at Boris's death. He ordered a powerful delegation to attend the state funeral, including Admiral Raeder, Keitel, and an impressive assembly of army generals. His instinct told him that the House of Savoy lay behind the murder: rumor had it that Boris's queen—Giovanna, third daughter of the king of Italy—was a leading figure in the Bulgarian underground; and was it not suspicious that Princess Mafalda, her sister, the wife of Prince Philipp of Hesse and "blackest carrion in the Italian royal house" (as Hitler luridly described her), had spent some weeks in Sofia quite recently? Curiously, while the Bulgarian government had agreed to allow the German doctors to perform a postmortem, the king's own family had refused. Gradually the pieces of Hitler's crossword puzzle were clicking into place. From the Forschungsamt he learned that Prince Philipp had recently dictated groups of ciphers over the telephone to Mafalda, evidently employing some private code. But to arrest him would be to alarm the Italian monarchy too soon. So Hitler invited the prince to be his guest at headquarters, treated him with continued hospitality—and told his guards not to let him out again.

Hitler's Intelligence agencies stubbornly contrived to distract his attention to his western front and Scandinavia—rumoring enemy invasion plans throughout August. Hitler took these threats very seriously and attributed their nonmaterialization only to the worsening weather. His edginess increased, and where a shrewder statesman would have wooed the subjected peoples with diplomacy, he resorted to brute force. This only increased the unrest and guerrilla activity.

Denmark—straddling his lines of communication to Norway—was a classic example. On the evening of August 21, Hitler had invited his staff movie cameraman, Lieutenant Walter Frentz, whose birthday it was, to take supper with him. Frentz had just returned from another tour of the Atlantic Wall project, and he mentioned that several guerrilla bomb incidents, including one at his own hotel, had marred his visit to Denmark. Hitler ordered Jodl to obtain daily reports on this "guerrilla war" in the future, and he berated Ribbentrop for being taken in by the bland dispatches of his diplomats. A few days later—alarmed by the reports the OKW commander, General von Hanneken, was now submitting— Hitler ordered Ribbentrop to issue an ultimatum to the Danish government; it was to declare a state of emergency, ban public meetings, outlaw strikes like those currently paralyzing half the country's ports, and introduce draconian measures against guerrilla activities. As Hitler evidently anticipated, the ultimatum was rejected, and the Danish forces were disarmed early on August 29 almost without a shot being fired; the generals were rounded up, the king and crown prince were placed under house arrest, and the Danish navy was surrendered to Admiral Dönitz.

Over the weeks that followed, Heinrich Himmler assumed police control of the luckless peninsula. Hitler ordered him to deport all Jews, discounting warnings that this might increase the political unrest in Denmark; several thousand Jews escaped to Sweden, but 477 were rounded up by the Germans and taken to the Theresienstadt concentration camp in October. Quixotically he ordered the release of the fifteen thousand Danish officers and men who had been interned in August, and thus the bitter pill was sugared.

Hitler's trust in Himmler and the SS was now absolute. While at the beginning of 1943 the SS chief had complained of his maltreatment by the Führer—who seemingly remembered him only when he needed fresh divisions raised—now Himmler's star was firmly in the ascendant. Hitler was sure that Germany would never forget the heroism of the Waffen SS divisions that had recaptured Kharkov in March and dispelled the gloom of Stalingrad. In his eyes the regular army was corrupt and slothful, incapable even of retreating without cramming its trucks and baggage with tons of looted property, while the SS troops could be relied on to fight well and strike terror into the enemy's heart. Himmler's pocket diary shows him attending Hitler's conferences with increasing regularity; sometimes Hitler phoned him in person; they lunched together two or three times a week or dined far into the night.

Now more than ever Hitler needed Himmler. He did not doubt the growing precariousness of his position. Events in Italy had sparked off a mood of defeatism in Germany. Himmler—in a secret January 1944 speech—epitomized the mood thus: "The Duce arrested, the Fascist party dissolved! How smoothly it went! Oh how glorious!—And then the murmurs begin: So, a Duce can be arrested. Very interesting. And many a rash mind poses the question, Why not here in Germany too! Then we'll be rid of the Nazis, we can make peace with the British, the British will guarantee Germany against Russia—and everything will be all right!"

Throughout August 1943 the Reichsführer and Gestapo rounded up German dissidents. The aged and infirm were let off with a warning. The more able-bodied, "not more than 150 in all" Himmler boasted, were put to the guillotine. The most dangerous group was, however, left at large: in March, Himmler had warned Hitler that certain nuclei of ex-ministers and dismissed army generals were beginning to plot a coup d'etat. There was General Franz Halder, whom he code-named "Reservist" ("As he's holding himself in reserve to take over the German army," Himmler sneered in August 1944); and he was also keeping watch on the former finance minister, Johannes Popitz, and his circle under the code name "Baroque" ("Because that's just what they were: baroque!"). For months Popitz had been trying to establish contact with Himmler through an intermediary, a lawyer called Carl Langbehn. The lawyer explained to the crafty Reichsführer that the war must be stopped, peace made with Britain, and the Führer pensioned off. Himmler at once told Hitler: "I'll bump him off right now—what cheek!"—meaning Popitz. But Hitler laughed. "No, not that. Hear him out first. Send for him, and if in that conversation he puts his cards straight on the table, *then* you can arrest him!" Himmler—appointed minister of the interior on August 20 in place of Dr. Wilhelm Frick, whom Hitler found infuriatingly timid and legalistic —sent for Popitz three days later and secretly recorded the entire conversation on magnetic wire. Gestapo officials stood by to arrest the man, but—Himmler ruefully admitted later—Popitz would not be lured out of his reserve and he left the building a free man.[4]

Thus Himmler was in the ascendant, and the "moderates" were on their way out. Once Frick had proposed to Hitler setting up a Reich Senate of academics and clergy as a supreme constitutional body—the very image, Hitler now re-marked, of the Fascist grand council that had just proven Mussolini's undoing. Hitler appointed Frick Protector of Bohemia and Moravia in Neurath's place. At the same time he up-rated Karl-Hermann Frank's powers as deputy protector in Prague, so as to vest absolute authority in him. As Göring later disarmingly put it: "It became increasingly clear that the Führer was turning more and more to the representatives of brute force."

Jodl's account of the Bologna meeting of August 15 convinced Hitler that Italy was about to defect.

Rommel was instructed that if necessary he was to "make ruthless use of his weaponry to get his way." On August 17 an Italian general forced a German unit at gunpoint to hand over American parachutists they had taken prisoner in northern Italy. Late the next day Hitler issued a further directive to the southern front, beginning thus: "In some form or other it is expected that Italy will surrender to enemy pressure, sooner or later." He ordered Vietinghoff's Tenth

---

[4]Popitz was executed after the failure of the attempted assassination of Hitler on July 20, 1944; Langbehn was also executed. Halder was arrested. There is no proof for the postwar legend that Himmler ever plotted against Hitler with them—quite the reverse.

Army to move three mechanized divisions to the coastal area most in danger of invasion, the stretch between Naples and Salerno. The Italians had now assembled nearly seven divisions around Rome, leaving only one division to defend all Apulia.

Two formidable Allied convoys were sighted by agents, passing eastward through the Strait of Gibraltar. One was reported laden with seventy thousand troops and their equipment. Kesselring now assessed the enemy's total strength in the Mediterranean at twenty-five divisions, apart from those in Sicily. Hitler deduced that this was too significant a concentration for just an operation against Sardinia or Corsica: responding to Soviet pressure, the enemy must be about to invade the continental mainland. The admiralty agreed. Southern Italy was most likely, though even southern France could not be ruled out. "There is no precise evidence as to the enemy's intentions." The sentence exposed the bankruptcy of Canaris's Intelligence networks. Himmler's were working well. Early on August 26 he alerted Hitler to an agent's urgent message from Rome: "Badoglio has asked Britain for an armistice regardless of conditions. The British have promised to reply by Saturday, August 28, 1943, and want to send in a strong convoy meantime with the most up-to-date weapons to enable temporary resistance to be offered to German troops." Jodl asked the Luftwaffe to mount a rigorous air surveillance off the coasts of Italy. The tension still mounted. There were fresh clashes between the Italians and Rommel's troops in the north, now entering Slovenia with Tiger tank regiments. The Italians were detected making plans for resistance in Toulon; Hitler ordered the port's immediate occupation by his Wehrmacht.

Late on August 30, the OKW issued a revised directive for "Axis," under which Italy was to be occupied by German forces. When that code word was issued, the Germans were to disarm the Italians, seize their weapons—particularly the tanks of the "Centauro" armored division—and prepare a gradual fighting retreat northward to Rome. Northern Italy was to be pacified and a Fascist government restored. Kesselring's forces were to link up with Rommel's. The retreating troops were to burn and destroy "as though on enemy soil." Corsica was to be held (eventually General Frido von Senger und Etterlin was given command). Field Marshal Weichs would assume command of the entire southeastern front, the Balkans. Meantime, Canaris was instructed to raise a secret army of South Tyroleans to watch over the German supply routes; and he was given responsibility for ensuring that no harm came to the generating stations supplying the vital Brenner railroad. All this while, the Italian generals and government were expressing pained surprise that Hitler showed so little faith in their loyalty to the Axis cause. Hitler had replaced his two credulous diplomats in Rome—Mackensen and Rintelen—with two from a more skeptical school: Ambassador Rudolf Rahn and Colonel Rudolf Toussaint. Their dispatches spoke a more realistic language about the future.

From late September 2 on, it was plain that an invasion of southern Italy was imminent. At 6 A.M. the next day one hundred landing craft disgorged two divisions of the British Eighth Army on the southernmost point of the peninsula, at Reggio di Calabria. Hitler could do little to interfere. The Italians imposed a virtual news blackout and offered little resistance themselves. In the afternoon a British message was decoded: "Six hundred prisoners taken, including two colonels; no minefields, no Germans, civilians are friendly." The Germans had only the 29th Panzer-Grenadier Division down there; it began a fighting retreat, inflicting heavy casualties on the British all the way. Ironically, in view of what is now known,[5] the German naval commander in Italy, Admiral Wilhelm Meendsen-Bohlken, reported that day that Badoglio's government could be trusted. The report blandly assured Hitler: "They are stifling anything redolent of peace demonstrations." The Italian navy in particular had promised him that there could be no question of "a repetition of Scapa Flow or Toulon" with their fleet. Hitler marveled at the admiral's gullibility.

When Romania's Marshal Antonescu visited that day, Hitler told him to expect no gratitude from the Italian monarchy. He was convinced the king of Italy was dealing with the enemy. The Führer begged Antonescu to be on guard against poisoning attempts, and he repeated this warning to Rommel on September 4. Rommel—like Hitler—knew that the latest British operation was only the thin end of the wedge. "The thick end in the western Mediterranean has still to come. I am to have an audience of the king shortly. The Führer has forbidden me to eat anything there, out of concern for my health." In his diary that day he entered:

Immediately after arriving at the Wolf's Lair I joined the [1 P.M.] war conference. General Glaise-Horstenau was also at the Führer's conference.

Afterward lunched with Führer until 5 P.M. The Führer makes a tranquil, confident impression. He wants to send me to see the king of Italy soon. He agrees to my Italian campaign plan, which envisages a defense along the coastline, despite Jodl's objections (which don't hold water in a modern war). —The Führer considers it still too early for the countries of Europe to unite. —Himmler wants to send us Hausser in exchange for Sepp Dietrich. At my request this plan is dropped.

On eastern front the situation has reached the crisis point; the Russians have managed to break through.—In Calabria the British are not going to be attacked; Calabria is to be abandoned.

8.30 P.M. Dinner with the Führer. Previously with Jodl. Führer advises me to take care when I see the king.

[5]That same day, September 3, 1943, the Italians signed their armistice with the Allies at a conference in Sicily. It was kept secret for five days, to give the enemy the maximum tactical benefit.

It was at about this time that after one war conference, Hitler was observed sketching with his colored pencils a new flag for a Republican Italy.

He had given Antonescu a reasonably forthright account of Germany's military position—although he had tended to minimize the resurgence of the Soviet threat. Instead, he referred to the disastrous Russian harvest and to Stalin's fifteen million casualties. "The first one to lose his nerves will lose the war as well," said Hitler.

During August, while Hitler was reinforcing his strength in the Mediterranean, Stalin had cleverly exploited the strategic impasse to mount a series of attacks all along the eastern front. Manstein repeatedly warned that Stalin's objective was to cut off his own Army Group South and Kleist's Army Group A in the Crimea and Kuban bridgehead, and he demanded that either at least twelve new divisions be provided him to reinforce his northern flank, or that Hitler permit him to withdraw from the coal-bearing Donets region. This would shorten his front by one-third and thus provide him with the reserves he needed. At 7 A.M. on August 27, Hitler flew down to his old headquarters in the Ukraine; Manstein told him that without reinforcements he could not prevent the Russians from sooner or later breaking through to the Dnieper River. Hitler stayed five hours, listened calmly, promised to transfer divisions to Manstein from Kluge's Army Group Center and from Army Group North; then he flew back to East Prussia. His promise to Manstein was broken within one day, for Kluge had his own enemy breakthrough to contend with; he arrived at Hitler's headquarters the next day and talked the Führer out of further weakening Army Group Center.

For several days Hitler was in the grip of indecision as he waited to see which way the cat jumped in the Mediterranean. But while Hitler hesitated, Stalin did not. On the Sea of Azov, General Hollidt's new Sixth Army was breached and a corps briefly encircled. On his own responsibility, Manstein told Hollidt to fall back—the first irrevocable step toward abandoning the rich Donets Basin. Hitler had repeatedly warned Zeitzler: "If we lose the Donets Basin, we lose the coal we need for our arms factories. And then the war will be over in eleven months." But Speer and his coal experts had assured Zeitzler that this was not so, and Hitler had no choice but to allow Manstein to withdraw. However, he ordered him to destroy anything of value to the enemy first. This decision was announced to Manstein at the Wolf's Lair on September 3.

The next day Hitler also authorized the withdrawal of General Ruoff's Seventeenth Army from the Kuban bridgehead across the Strait of Kerch. As recently as June, Speer's engineers had put into service an overhead cable railway across the four-mile-wide strait; it was capable of transporting a thousand tons of supplies a day from the Crimea to the bridgehead. For many months Stalin had confronted the bridgehead with over fifty divisions, but now he was no longer impressed by Hitler's ability to mount a new offensive and was deploying them elsewhere; Marshal Antonescu agreed with Hitler that the bridgehead had become a liability. Liquidating it would release nearly four divisions for the rest of the front. Kleist was ordered to speed up the fortification of the Crimea. How Hitler longed for the autumn rains to return!

Thus the eighth of September 1943 arrived—a hot and airless day. Hitler had slept only four hours but was awakened at 5:45 A.M. because he had to fly down to Zaporozh'ye to see Manstein again. The field marshal had cabled a frantic picture of his army group's plight the day before: over fifty-five Russian divisions were now confronting his forces, and still Hitler could offer no solution. The Russians had again pierced the Sixth Army, and at the frail weld between Manstein's and Kluge's army groups the dam had finally burst and the enemy was pouring westward toward Kiev and the middle reaches of the Dnieper.

An inexplicable restlessness gnawed at Hitler here in the Ukraine. Was it Italy? Two days before, Jodl had shown him a breakdown of the Wehrmacht's commitments and hinted that only from southern Italy could divisions possibly be spared for the eastern front. But suppose Badoglio's eighty divisions then defected to the enemy? It was a tangled web. On the seventh Hitler had suggested "unraveling it by brute force." Here at least he could take the initiative by putting a blunt political and military ultimatum to Badoglio: either provide a satisfactory explanation for his machinations, manipulations, and troop movements—or take the immediate consequences. The ultimatum was being drafted at this moment. Now, after barely ninety minutes at Manstein's headquarters, Hitler could stand the uncertainty no longer. He bolted back to his Condor aircraft, was airborne at 12:45 P.M.—leaving Russian soil for what was to prove the last time—and was back at the Wolf's Lair in conference by five.

Again his sixth sense had served him well. He found that two hours earlier an ominous SS teletype indeed had arrived—a four-day-old report by an agent on the Italian air staff. He had just overheard Ambrosio's *comando supremo* secretly telephoning this message to the air force: "Italian peace proposals by and large accepted by the British. We are trying to iron out difficulties raised by Americans." Other reports were conflicting. The Allies' morning newspapers were noisy with rumors of armistice. But the king of Italy had just assured Rahn that his country would fight on, and Badoglio had told the envoy the same: "Germany has still to learn what an Italian general's word of honor means!" Worn out by events, Hitler dozed in his room for half an hour.

Almost at once he was awakened by an adjutant. The BBC had just announced Italy's "unconditional surrender." No details were given, but shortly afterward General Eisenhower broadcast a proclamation from Algiers radio: "The armistice was signed by my representative and representatives of Marshal Badoglio and takes force immediately." At 6:30 P.M. Hitler summoned a full war conference, with Ribbentrop as well. He telephoned Goebbels to come at once on the night train. Jodl put in a direct telephone call to his generals in Rome. Both were at that very moment seeing General Roatta—and the army's Chief of Staff was hotly refuting the Allied broadcasts as wicked libels on the honor of Italy. Consternation gripped Hitler's staff, as Roatta's denial still robbed him of the freedom to issue the code word "Axis." Jodl drafted a monition alerting all commands, but before it could be teletyped, Ribbentrop learned from Rome that at 7:15 P.M. Badoglio had confessed that Italy had indeed surrendered.

The OKW acted like lightning. At 7:50 P.M. Jodl's adjutant telephoned the code word to the south. Within half an hour it was confirmed in writing. There was precious little advance warning, but as Jodl later pointed out, even the two hours' advance notice given by the BBC had given Germany some opportunity to issue orders before the Italians could react. It was unlikely that the Italian fleet could be kept from escaping; at 8:45 P.M. Admiral Cunningham was heard radioing the Italian ships to run for the nearest Allied haven.

The German admiralty commented: "The consequences of this vile act of treachery—unique in military history—will be very different from what Italy had hoped. The countryside will become a battlefield between the betrayed allies of yesterday and the ruthless conquerors of today." Alas, no record of Hitler's conversations that evening remains. Long after dawn the group disbanded. As Prince Philipp of Hesse—nephew of the Kaiser, son-in-law of the king of Italy —went out, the chief of Hitler's police bodyguard stepped forward and arrested him; he was consigned that same night by car to the Gestapo at Königsberg, and he remained in a concentration camp until the war was over.

Relieved that the clouds of uncertainty had been dispelled, Hitler fell into bed at 5 A.M. to snatch five hours' rest after a working day of twenty-three. He alone had steadfastly predicted this treachery.

Feelers to Stalin

While in the north Hitler's troops stood their ground, the Russian offensive during September and October 1943 swept over Novorossisk, Bryansk, Poltava, Smolensk, Dnepropetrovsk; and on November 6, Kiev itself fell. Army Groups South and Center had fallen back on the new "Panther" line—primarily along the Dnieper River—but Stalin rapidly built up fresh bridgeheads here as well. Hitler stormed at General Zeitzler, his Chief of Staff: "You see! I gave you permission to build the Dnieper line you were always asking for, and where is it? The troops found nothing ready for them!"

That much was true. But it is difficult to pinpoint the blame for the failure of the East Wall project. The causes are buried too deep in papers and memories to emerge with any clarity. The earliest blame attaches to Hitler and his stubborn determination to keep the fighting as far from the Reich as possible. After the winter crisis of 1941 1942 he had argued that a strongly fortified rear position would actively tempt his frontline generals to fall back on it. During 1942 he reversed this view, and he encouraged the army to fortify the stabler sectors of the front using impressed labor drawn from the local Russian population. Kluge had done little, causing Hitler to exclaim—after Mussolini's overthrow and the failure of "Citadel"—"If only he had done some construction here, instead of talking so much hot air and making explanations!" On the southern front the position was different. With his armies advancing on Stalingrad and the Transcaucasus there was no cause to construct walls far in the rear; but now that they were falling back, it was too late. While the West and Atlantic walls were built under virtually peacetime conditions, now every train in the east was needed for men, munitions, and the paraphernalia of war.

Speer's papers show Hitler repeatedly discussing with him in February and April 1943, the erection of improvised fortifications in the east. But neither Speer nor Zeitzler had set wheels in motion. Speer recorded on July 8: "Changing his earlier position, the Führer now fully agrees that the construction of the East Wall must be speeded up," but this is clearly an attempt to establish an alibi for himself before the judgment of history. The files of both Speer and the army are strongly flavored with the kind of jealous squabbling over rights and privileges that seems to have inflicted more damage on the German war effort than all the enemy's armies and bomber squadrons combined. In early September the rivalry was still raging. Zeitzler was loath to allow Speer's Todt Organization engineers to direct the East Wall project. Hitler ruled that only these engineers had the know-how to provide big, permanent fortifications, but Zeitzler favored earthworks and more primitive sites. Speer thereupon secured Hitler's signature to a decree consolidating his own absolute control of the Todt Organization throughout the Reich and occupied territories. A long feud, however, smoldered between Speer and the organization's director, Xaver Dorsch. Besides, the architect Speer had displayed in the Atlantic Wall project little of the inspiration and energy that distinguished the engineer Fritz Todt's work on the 1938 West Wall. Speer was primarily a munitions *minister,* and he had his eyes on higher targets still: his redesignation by Hitler early in September as minister of armaments and war production led to authoritative rumors that Speer was a future minister of war. He was collecting his own court around him—Goebbels, Milch, and Himmler, to whose SS General Hans Kammler he had just relinquished control of the army's A-4 missile production program.

Parallel to the high-level bickering over construction of the East Wall ran a debilitating argument over the precise route it should follow. Zeitzler had always favored following the Dnieper, as its western bank was a steep cliff towering often 150 feet above the eastern plains. In summer the river was a raging flood sometimes two miles wide and virtually unbridgeable. But it was over a hundred miles behind the lines, and initially Hitler would not agree to such a fatalistic view of the future. Now the stalling of "Citadel" and Mussolini's overthrow left him no choice. On August 12, Zeitzler ordered the army groups to start building the East Wall immediately, provisionally following the Dnieper in the central front; it was to go from the Kerch peninsula in the south to Lake Peipus and Narva in the north. The OKW, the Luftwaffe, and the navy raised immediate protests about this route. One of "Barbarossa's" original objects had been to push the closest Russian bomber airfields out of striking range of the Reich, while at the same time providing airfields from which Heinkel 177 bombers could devastate the Urals industries; the proposed East Wall route would defeat both objectives. In addition, abandoning the Black Sea naval base of Novorossisk to the enemy would not only sour Germany's political relations with Turkey, Romania, and Bulgaria but jeopardize the German sea transport to Sevastopol and the Crimea. In the south the Germans would be forfeiting the coal and grain of the Donets Basin and the Central Ukraine. If at least a bridgehead around Zaporozh'ye could not be defended, then the loss of the hydroelectric power station there would make it impossible to mine the manganese of Nikopol and the iron ore of Krivoi Rog, or operate the blast furnaces at Dniepropetrovsk. Thus Speer's plan to establish a munitions industry in the Ukraine would collapse.

Equally, both Army Group North and the naval staff objected to the proposed route of the northern section. An East Wall built from Velikiye Luki to Lake Peipus and Narva—as Zeitzler proposed—meant the final loss of Leningrad; and the Russian fleet could again maraud in the Gulf of Finland and jeopardize both the German navy's training programs in the Baltic and the iron-ore shipments from Sweden; the important oil-shales in Estonia would also have to be written off. But Zeitzler wanted a defensible East Wall built by the end of October, and on September 4 he issued orders to the army groups to that effect: east of the line, the population and property along a twenty-five-mile-wide belt was to be ruthlessly exploited for the project; a swath of total destruction in this zone must make it impossible for any enemy to survive the elements there. "The outlying area must become a desert."

Field Marshal Georg von Küchler, commander of Army Group North, came a week later to protest in person to Hitler. He agreed with Zeitzler that only his army group's withdrawal to the East Wall could release any significant reserves to the High Command—nine divisions in all. But it would be like losing a battle. His men had gained and valiantly defended their present lines at Leningrad in two years of bloody fighting; they would not like seeing the graves of thousands of their comrades abandoned to the enemy without good cause. Zeitzler would not accept his arguments, but Hitler was clearly loath to act prematurely. He could not ignore the political consequences on Finland of a withdrawal from Leningrad, but equally, he feared that Stalin was hatching a winter offensive from Velikiye Luki toward the coast at Pleskau or Riga, cutting off the whole army group's retreat. He postponed a decision.

For several days after Badoglio's capitulation there was utter confusion in Italy; not so at the Wolf's Lair. When Goebbels and his state secretary, Werner Naumann, arrived there early the next morning, September 9, 1943, the headquarters compound was bathed in an almost deathly hush. Hitler himself was calm and collected. As Martin Bormann wrote that day: "Marvelous to see the Führer's poise in face of fantastic complications in the east, the south, and elsewhere! The coming months are going to be very difficult. But now is the time to stand fast with iron determination."

Yet Hitler had not closed his mind to the possibility of an armistice with either Stalin or Churchill. A split between West and East seemed inevitable sooner or later. Ribbentrop—whose stock had fallen so sharply that Hitler could now contemptuously address him in front of his generals as "Herr Foreign Manager"—

had extended feelers to the Russians again during August. First he had sent Rudolf Likus to Stockholm to seek clues as to Stalin's peace terms. Then, in mid-August, he had ordered his subaltern, Dr. Peter Kleist, to pick up his earlier threads with a certain non-Aryan Baltic businessman in Stockholm, Edgar Klauss, known to have contacts with the Soviet embassy there. Klauss claimed that the former Russian ambassador in Berlin, Vladimir Dekanozov, was coming on September 12 and hoped to meet a German negotiator then; Kleist reported this to Ribbentrop at the Wolf's Lair on the tenth. According to Ribbentrop, Hitler proved more receptive this time; they went over to a map, and he sketched in a possible demarcation line to be agreed on with Stalin. But during the night he changed his mind and told Ribbentrop he would have to think it over more carefully. In conversation with Goebbels on the ninth he had shown a greater affinity for the British than for Stalin; but again Churchill was the obstacle. Hitler decided to wait until Dönitz could resume his submarine offensive, until the army's missile attack on London began—again provisionally postponed until the end of January 1944—and until the Allies had been dealt the kind of military reverse that, in Hitler's calculus, must always precede a secret offer of armistice.

Operation "Axis" had been smoothly completed as planned. Rome had been seized and a tough commandant, General Stahel, appointed for the city. The disarming of Italy's armed forces was proceeding rapidly. In Milan and Turin Communist rebellions had begun; in Florence the Germans were up against Italian tanks. In the Aegean, Rhodes and Corfu were still battlefields between the Germans and Italians; when the Corfu garrison was finally overwhelmed, Hitler ordered the Italian commandant's execution. Late on the tenth an ultimatum was issued to all Italian troops still resisting instructing them to lay down their arms; otherwise their commanders would be shot as francs-tireurs. Often the Italians gave their arms to the partisans—particularly to Tito's guerrillas in Dalmatia; wherever this was found to have occurred, Hitler ordered their officers to be stood before firing squads and the men to be deported to the eastern front to swell his army's labor force. The Italian fleet sailed on the ninth on a pretext: Luftwaffe bombers equipped with guided missiles sank the battleship *Roma* and injured her sister ship *Italia;* the rest defected to the enemy. In Nice, when a German officer was killed by an Italian hand-grenade, the railroad garrison was put before a firing squad in revenge. Such was the German troops' hatred of their former Italian allies.

Badoglio and his turncoat comrades had done their utmost to wound Germany. When the American Fifth Army's seaborne invasion at Salerno, south of Naples, began on September 9, the Germans realized from decoded American radio messages that their minefields had been betrayed to the enemy. There was evidence that Rome had radioed the British a warning that the ports of Trieste, Monfalcone, Bari, Metković, and Ragusa (Dubrovnik) were now in German hands. An Italian naval lieutenant put the fuel dumps in Naples to the torch—"thus possibly sealing the fate of every German soldier in southern Italy," observed Richthofen. Meanwhile Badoglio, Ambrosio, and Roatta had fled to the enemy, accompanied by the king and Crown Prince Umberto. With grim satisfaction Hitler read the latest intercept of an Anthony Eden telephone call to Winston Churchill in Washington, where he was reported by *The Times* to be waiting for a military triumph to illuminate his return to London. Eden was discussing the problems Umberto was causing by refusing to accept an English officer as aide-de-camp. Only now did the Germans learn that Badoglio had secretly concluded the armistice as early as September 3; yet the American bombing of Naples, Viterbo, and other targets had continued—no doubt as a blind. Badoglio had invited American paratroops to land on the airfields around Rome, but Hitler's troops had seized them first. Courier planes had shuttled between Badoglio and Eisenhower, while the Italian antiaircraft guns were ordered not to fire. On occasion, American officers had been driven in full uniform through Rome. As for the Duce, Badoglio had promised to relinquish him to the enemy. He would be tried forthwith. According to the Führer's secretaries, Hitler's heart went out to him, wherever he now was.

"Understandably"—Hitler was broadcasting to his people late on September 10, surrounded by Himmler, Göring, and his staff—"I am grieved by the sight of the unique injustice inflicted on this man [Mussolini] and the degrading treatment meted out to him, whose only care these last twenty years and more has been for his people, as though he were a common criminal. I was and am glad to call this great and loyal man my friend. Nor am I one to tailor my convictions to the demands of expediency, let alone disown them; some may think differently, but my belief is that in the affairs of nations as in those of men loyalty is a virtue beyond price. Without it, society must totter, and its organizations will sooner or later wither away." It sounded very much like an obituary for Mussolini.

The vultures crowded in. Hitler had appointed a National Government under Alessandro Pavolini to save what was left of fascism in Italy; SS General Karl Wolff was attached as police "adviser" to Pavolini. North of the Apennines, Italy was now officially "German occupied territory," with a military governor; to the south was the "operations zone." Kesselring was ordered on the twelfth to defeat the American divisions at Salerno if he could; if he could not, he was to fall back on Rome, blocking the enemy's advance by destroying roads, bridges, tunnels, and railway installations as he retreated. The southern Italians and Sicilians had openly abetted the enemy; now their countryside would pay the price. On the eleventh the OKW ordered that everything of value in the south—goods and raw materials—was to be stripped and shipped north "on behalf of the new Fascist government." On the twelfth, Speer persuaded Hitler to vest this power in him alone. While Hitler's order of the eleventh provided for industry in northern Italy to continue operating, Speer's superseding order of the twelfth empowered him to dismantle precious machine-tools from anywhere in Italy "in danger of air attack" and ship them back to the Reich. For Speer's purposes everywhere south of the line from La Spezia to Ancona was deemed "in danger of air attack"— the whole of the Italian "boot."

To Hitler's ministers, Mussolini's exit was something of a relief. As Goebbels wrote: "Politically speaking I do not regret it much. We must judge it all from the standpoint of expediency." On the twelfth, two of Hitler's frontier Gauleiters came for lunch—Franz Hofer from the Tyrol and Friedrich Rainer from Carinthia. Hitler signed decrees subjecting large provinces of northern Italy to their Gau administration; this was the very overture to annexation he had adopted in Alsace and Lorraine. The future Germany was intended to reach the frontiers of Venetia. By 4:40 P.M., when the conference ended, Hitler had signed all three decrees—those for the two Gauleiters and the one enabling Albert Speer to dismantle Italian industry.

At what stage Hitler learned the startling news of Mussolini's rescue is uncertain. Himmler had certainly known since 10:30 A.M. that the operation was under way, and at 2 P.M. the fallen Duce was already free. Speer suggested that under the circumstances the three decrees should be canceled, but Hitler would not hear of it and changed their date from September 12 to 13, so that there could be no doubt that the Duce's liberation had not in the least affected his decisions on Italy's future. At 9:45 P.M., as he was having supper with Himmler, an SS general telephoned from Vienna that Mussolini had just arrived there with Otto Skorzeny. Hitler spoke himself with Skorzeny, congratulated him, and awarded him the Knight's Cross for this spectacular success. According to a manservant, he exclaimed afterward, "When news of the rescue gets out, it will hit the world like a bombshell—particularly the British. That'll show them I never turn my back on a friend—that I'm a man of my word. The British will say, 'He's a friend indeed!' "

Two days later, at 2 P.M., Hitler drove from the Wolf's Lair to the local airfield to meet the plane bringing the tired Italian dictator up from Munich. Mussolini was dressed in a simple dark blue suit; gone was the bombast and the bonhomie. He was a broken man. Before they all lunched together, Hitler summoned SS General Ernst Kaltenbrunner—whose SS agents had contributed to the rescue— and Skorzeny to relate Mussolini's hair-raising escape to him. Kaltenbrunner explained that until July 28 the Duce had been imprisoned in the Carabinieri barracks in Rome; during August he had been transferred to Ponza, and then to the island of St. Maddalena. Two weeks ago he had been whisked up to the Campo Imperatore hotel high up in the Apennines. A glider-borne force of paratroops and SS agents had crash-landed around the hotel and robbed the Carabinieri of their precious charge without loss of life to either side.

It was a very different Mussolini who conferred with Hitler over the next few days. Shorn of his authoritarian powers, Mussolini was an ordinary man whose future was at best that of a glove puppet, to act as his envied friend the Führer now directed. He protested that he was still ill, and for a while Hitler believed that Mussolini had been poisoned too; but Morell took him under his scrutiny, sent for the Italian medical records, X-rayed the dictator, and found nothing wrong with him. Mussolini's moral decay and softness toward his enemies repelled Hitler, who had expected him to exact a terrible revenge on Count Ciano, Dino Grandi, and all who had betrayed the cause of fascism. A few days later Edda, Ciano's wife, who had been brought to Germany, appealed to Hitler for enough Spanish currency to enable her to emigrate with the count through Spain to South America; but Hitler gathered that Ciano planned to write his "memoirs" (which would certainly not flatter Germany), and ruled that he was to remain in German hands. Besides, his agents had intercepted a threatening letter from Edda to her father: if the Duce did not take her out of Germany, she would cause the name of her father to be cursed and hated throughout the world. For hours on end—until three in the morning—Hitler paced up and down the map room with Goebbels, speculating what Edda's stranglehold over her father could possibly be. He himself suspected that Mussolini had for months been searching for ways and means of ditching Germany: could it be that? Despite his disillusionment, Hitler advised the former dictator to put his family's affairs in order before applying himself to the new order of Italy and the Fascist party.

To Ribbentrop's astonishment, Hitler remarked to Mussolini that he planned a compromise with Stalin. But the very next day he changed his mind again and admitted to the minister in private: "You know, Ribbentrop, if I come to terms with Russia today, I would be at her throat again tomorrow—it's in my nature." Ribbentrop replied that that was hardly the way to earn respect for one's foreign policy. Hitler was torn between Stalin and the West. When Goebbels asked whether he refused to deal with Churchill on principle, he retorted: "In politics you can't let personalities and principles stand in your way. It's just that Churchill is inspired by hatred, not common sense." In one way, he would far prefer to deal with Stalin—but then Stalin could hardly grant the Reich what it was demanding in the east. On September 18 he accompanied Mussolini back to Rastenburg airfield and watched him take off for Munich, where he was to begin piecing together his new regime.

Hitler had now regretfully abandoned hope of throwing the American Fifth Army back into the sea at Salerno. Hube's four divisions had all but succeeded during the previous nine days: initially the Americans had encountered only the 16th Panzer Division, but Richthofen's rocket-firing fighters and the 88-millimeter guns of an antiaircraft regiment had wrought havoc on the invasion ships; on the thirteenth a German counterattack by two panzer and one panzer-grenadier division began, and routed two American divisions defending Salerno. But the counterattack came under heavy bombardment from Allied warships offshore—a new dimension in beachhead operations. Thus the beachhead remained; the Americans were joined by Montgomery's troops, who had landed at Taranto, and Kesselring prepared to fall back toward Rome.

Hitler's staff rejoiced at the "thrashing" meted out to the Americans. Jodl set their value far below that of Montgomery's seasoned troops. Though British and Americans had been committed in equal numbers, over nine-tenths of the prisoners who had surrendered were Americans: American paratroops were "usable," but the rest "surrender the moment the position is hopeless" and "never attack so long as a single gun is left firing from the German lines." Hitler wrote off the threat of an enemy invasion elsewhere for many months to come. "No more invasions for them! They are much too cowardly for that. They only managed the one at Salerno because the Italians gave their blessing." The bungling Allied planning comforted him greatly over the next weeks. Why did they not immediately invade the Balkans, where the natives were waiting for the Allies with open arms? Why had they not ventured a bold invasion north of Rome when Badoglio defected? Why had they not at once occupied the islands of Rhodes, Cephalonia, and Corfu? Why were they making such slow progress up Italy?

Italy's defection had profited the Reich in terms of material. Hitler rudely stripped southern Italy of every antiaircraft battery—whether German or Italian—in favor of the north and Germany. No longer did Germany have to feed Italy with coal, oil, and foodstuffs. Nearly 50,000 Allied prisoners had been removed from Italian into German custody; here they were joined by their former jailers, for by the end of September the first 268,000 Italian prisoners had already been transported to the Reich. "Operation Axis" had also yielded a big haul of Italian weaponry: 449 tanks, 2,000 guns, and 500,000 rifles. Eight hundred thousand Italians had been disarmed. But the strategic cost of "Axis" had been high, because—apart from the SS Life Guards temporarily withdrawn from Russia—the divisions pumped into Italy had drained the central reserve, which thus also indirectly weakened the eastern front. Moreover, Hitler had been duped for many weeks into expecting an early invasion of France, where the enemy had bombed ports, alerted the underground, and ostentatiously swept offshore minefields. Late in September Hitler still believed that only bad weather had stopped the invasion.

The Abwehr's remarkable agent "Josephine" now claimed that at Quebec the

Allies had agreed to postpone the invasion "of northern France" until 1944, as they lacked shipping space and the bombing offensive would not reach its climax until April. This agent seemed most reliable.[1] On August 21 he had predicted that the night-bombing offensive would resume two nights later (as it did, against Berlin). He had also reported controversy in the RAF about the value of such sporadic raids; but the British air minister, Sir Archibald Sinclair, and the war Cabinet had overruled them and demanded that the attack on Berlin begin. The British were manufacturing seven hundred four-engined bombers a month, according to "Josephine." These reports evidently reached Hitler and influenced him.

Three heavy night raids had been launched against Berlin but failed to repeat the catastrophe of Hamburg. The new freelance night-fighting tactics were proving effective. Goebbels's evacuation order had spared the lives of many thousands; in the raid on September 1 only 13 Berliners died, and in the final raid two nights later, of 346 dead only one was a child. But worse was expected: in the big cities painted arrows were to be seen everywhere—telling the people which way to flee if firestorms broke out again.

To the German people the war in the air *was* the Second Front. By September 1943, as Milch stated in a secret speech on October 6, Germany was defended by 8,876 antiaircraft guns of 88-millimeter caliber, and a further 24,500 of lighter calibers; her fighters had destroyed 48,268 enemy aircraft, and the guns a further 12,774, for the expenditure of over 26 million shells. Hitler's bombers had scattered over 35 million bombs in Europe, Africa, and Asia. But now the boot was on the other foot. By day and night the bombers ranged over Germany, sometimes as far as Danzig or East Prussia. From the newly captured airfields around Foggia in southern Italy they could reach any target in Austria and the Balkans. The American bombers now also had radar and were escorted as far as the German frontiers; soon long-range fighter escorts would appear. The bombers were heavily armored: eighteen of them, in tight formation, could concentrate 200 heavy machine-guns on any attacking fighter planes. Hitler learned that the German fighters had still not been equipped with 30-millimeter cannon, although he had seen the prototype MK 101 demonstrated in a twin-engined fighter at Rechlin in July 1939. He now ordered the fighters fitted experimentally with the

---

[1]Hitler and the Wehrmacht attached great importance to this Abwehr source. Not until late 1944 did Luftwaffe Intelligence deduce that "Josephine," like "Hektor" and "Ostro"—two other star agents —were the fruity product of various Abwehr attachés' imaginations, coupled with their zealous reading of the popular press. Trick questions about nonexistent British aircraft factories finally tripped them up.

50-millimeter KWK antitank gun, to enable them to open fire from well outside the bombers' defensive radius. General Adolf Galland, commander of the day fighters, opposed this, but the weapon became one of the most feared items of the day fighters' hardware.

The inadequacy of the current fighter armament sorely affected pilot morale, and this in turn was felt by the people. On October 4 the Americans bombed Frankfurt on a brilliant autumn day—their glittering squadrons droning high over the city "as ours used to, in peacetime," Hitler complained that day that the Germans had known Frankfurt would be the target, from an agent, but no fighter had challenged these bombers over the city. Hitler bitterly reproached Göring, saying that his Luftwaffe had lost the confidence of both the people and the troops. "I must insist, as spokesman of the German people, that whatever the cost, these mass daylight attacks have got to be stopped." The Reichsmarschall passed this rebuke on to General Galland: "The German public doesn't care two hoots about your fighter casualties. Try going to Frankfurt and asking what impression your fighter losses that day made on them. They'll tell you, 'You must be joking! Look at our *thousands* of dead!' "

Between them, Göring and Galland brought discipline to the fighter squadrons and inflicted savage wounds on the American bombers in October. In three days' raids up to the tenth the enemy lost 88 bombers and nearly 900 men. When they attacked the ball-bearing factories at Schweinfurt on October 14, the day fighters —each flying several sorties—brought down 60 and severely damaged 17 more.[2] Meanwhile, at night the battle ebbed and flowed: on the lakes around Berlin bobbed myriads of metal radar-reflectors intended to deceive the bombers; new radar jammers had been designed; airborne receivers enabled the night fighters to home in on the bombers' own powerful radar emissions, and their tactics were adapted to the Schwerpunkt tactics of the enemy. Germany's enemies fought back cunningly—with decoy raids, split raiding forces, and German-speaking broadcasters countermanding the orders transmitted by the German ground controllers. It was a growing nightmare. But the Nazi defenders resorted to trickery as well: unloading fake target flares over the open countryside or patrolling the enemy airfields, waiting for the exhausted bombers to return. Hitler was impatient at this unspectacular activity and demanded fresh raids on Britain's cities. Their scale was immaterial. "Aerial terrorism is only effective as a threat," he now pontificated, "not in its actual fulfillment. . . . How often these last three hundred years have entire cities or great buildings been consumed by flames? The devastation actually works in our favor, because it is creating a body of people with

---

[2]Galland in fact flew 882 fighters against the bombing force that day and lost 14: each side's newspapers claimed their aircraft shot down 121 of the other.

nothing more to lose—people who will therefore fight on with utter fanaticism."
He ordered Speer to begin planning the reconstruction of the ruined cities—more
elegant and modern than before. On October 22, a second firestorm occurred; it
ravaged Kassel, and six thousand citizens died between dusk and dawn. It made
no impression on Hitler; those Germans who learned of it, accepted it with a
numb sense of inevitability.

Yet the brutalization of the war—the cloying smell of death clinging to the ruins
of these cities—was in a way to result in new suffering for Hitler's enemies too.
He intensified his pressure for the secret weapons to terrorize London—the A-4
rocket, the flying bomb, and the multiple-gun battery near Calais sinisterly known
as the "High Pressure Pump." The same ruthlessness permeated his feelings
toward the Badoglio Italians. When their garrison on Cephalonia was finally
subdued late in September—it had held out in hope of a British invasion—Hitler
ordered the four thousand Italians taken prisoner to be executed as francs-tireurs;
only the deserters were to be spared their lives. A few days later he dropped a
broad hint to Göring that one of the big Allied-occupied cities in southern Italy,
like Brindisi or Taranto, should be stricken by a heavy Luftwaffe night attack
before the enemy had time to establish a fighter defense; this would remind the
Italians and Germany's other reluctant allies that allowing the enemy in was no
passport to paradise.

Early in October the remaining Jews were deported from Denmark. Himmler
also considered the eight thousand Jews in Rome a potential threat to public
order; Ribbentrop brought to Hitler an urgent telegram from his consul in Rome
reporting that the SS had ordered from Berlin that "the eight thousand Jews
resident in Rome are to be rounded up and brought to Upper Italy, where they
are to be liquidated." Again Hitler took a marginally more "moderate" line. On
the ninth Ribbentrop informed Rome that the Führer had directed that the eight
thousand Jews were to be transported to Mauthausen concentration camp in
Austria instead, where they were to be held "as hostages." It was, Ribbentrop
defined, purely a matter for the SS. (The SS liquidated them anyway, regardless
of Hitler's order.)

Coincidentally, it was at this time that Himmler first revealed to two audiences
—of SS Gruppenführer (generals) on October 4, and Gauleiters on October 6—
an awful secret which he forbade them to discuss in public: by the end of 1943
the last Jews in occupied Europe would have been physically *exterminated*. That
Himmler's intention was to make all his SS generals and the Gauleiters, regardless
of their guilt, accessories after the fact to the massacre is strongly suggested by
one curious document in his files: a name-by-name list of those who had *not*
attended his speech! Against the fifty-one names were checks marking whether

or not they had since read his speech or otherwise "taken cognizance of it." The shorthand record and magnetic recordings show that he did *not* yet claim to be acting on Hitler's orders.[3] Himmler clearly considered his standing with the Führer impregnable, to admit so openly that he had disregarded Hitler's veto on liquidating the Jews all along. The same Gauleiters were Hitler's guests at the Wolf's Lair on October 7; from this point on, he could no longer logically plead ignorance of what his "faithful Heinrich" had done.[4]

The SS stood high in Hitler's esteem that autumn. Between them, Himmler and his Gestapo chief, Müller, had strangled the incipient murmurings of unrest in Germany that echoed the events in Italy. Kaltenbrunner, as Heydrich's successor, had rapidly organized an Intelligence network that clearly surpassed the Abwehr's uninspiring achievements; without Kaltenbrunner's agents, Mussolini's rescue would have been impossible. Princess Mafalda had also been found and lured into German custody; even now she was languishing in a concentration camp—a useful hostage to assure the king of Italy's good behavior.[5] Himmler had inspired his Waffen SS troops, moreover, with a fanatic's loyalty to Nazi Germany. Late in October he showed Hitler a passage in a recent letter from a young SS brigadier on the eastern front: "If the others had not been there, I would so much have liked to tell the Führer how much his soldiers revere him and are devoted to him. Even if his orders sometimes seem merciless or cruel—when the order is, 'Hold on to the last man'—one feeling is supreme among the men fighting for their fatherland with rifles in their hand, that they have as their leader a man second to the Lord God alone." This was Hermann Fegelein: a few days later Hitler selected him as his liaison officer to Himmler; in June he married Eva Braun's sister; a year later he was facing Hitler's firing squad as a deserter in the ruins of Berlin.

"The Führer is confident," said Bormann in a secret speech at this time, "but he is not just an optimist; in fact, he is on principle pessimistic as far as all reports

---

[3]To the SS generals on October 4, 1943, Himmler praised the toughness of those who had had to carry out the massacre: "This is a page of glory in our history which has never been written and is never to be written." To the Gauleiters two days later he referred to "the Jewish problem" as the most difficult he had handled. "The Jews must be exterminated," was easier said than done. Even where women and children were concerned he, Himmler, had opted for a clear solution. "I did not consider myself justified in exterminating the menfolk—that is to kill them or have them killed—while leaving their children to grow up and take vengeance on our sons and grandsons. The hard decision had to be taken to make this race disappear from earth." He could not have been more explicit as to his own responsibility.

He first hinted at having had superior orders on May 6, 1944 (page 630).

[4]Milch, Dönitz, and several of their aides had addressed the Gauleiters on the morning of October 6; whether they stayed to hear Himmler's speech that afternoon is not clear from their diaries. Speer certainly did. Kaltenbrunner—who at Nuremberg pleaded that he had known nothing until 1944—was certainly in Berlin, and SS General Wolff was in Italy until the seventh, when he visited Hitler.

[5]Princess Mafalda died in the American bombing raid on Buchenwald concentration camp.

to him are concerned. He no longer believes what is not proven to him. He is skeptical about every cable and dispatch he receives." Even so, he was confident of the future. The very lack of communiqués from the Moscow foreign ministers' conference suggested a widening split between Russia and the West. Stalin was most probably demanding a Second Front and sidestepping all his allies' suggestions that the world's postwar frontiers should be agreed on first. Stalin was in a position of consummate strength; and thus—as Hitler had himself argued in 1933—he was in a position to dictate to the world. To this Hitler knew only one reply: "The most important thing is to keep up the fight and never falter, but spy out the enemy's weaknesses and exploit them without the least thought of capitulation or 'understanding' . . . Who can guarantee that one day a bombshell won't burst among the Allies, who will suddenly discover differences they can't plaster over anymore? . . . Just one internal collapse among our enemies and their whole enemy front might just cave in!" When fresh feelers reached Hitler now from Britain, he thrust them aside.

On October 15, Himmler's chief of foreign Intelligence, Walter Schellenberg, learned that the British trade chief in Stockholm, David MacEvan, who was known to report directly to Churchill, had offered to come secretly to Germany for a conference ostensibly on economic affairs. Schellenberg deduced there was more to it than that—that the British, fearing Russia's encroachment on western Europe and the Middle East, now wanted to start armistice negotiations. Himmler provisionally forbade MacEvan's journey and asked Ribbentrop to secure a decision from Hitler. Simultaneously, Hitler learned that the Swiss legation in London had reported to Berne in a note which—"according to Eden's private secretary"—the Americans had termed an intolerable interference in Allied strategy that Stalin had vetoed any Allied invasion of the Balkans.[6]

One reason for Hitler's rebuff to these vague Allied feelers was that under Kesselring's command the campaign in Italy was proceeding far better than he had dared to hope. Rommel, commanding Army Group B in northern Italy, had prophesied the total loss of southern and central Italy within days of Badoglio's defection; overawed by Rommel's warning, Hitler had refused Kesselring's appeal for two more divisions to be sent from Rommel's forces to the south. With these Kesselring might have routed the Allies, but even so his strategic defensive was a setback for Churchill and Roosevelt. At the end of September, Hitler had even asked Kesselring to study a German counterattack in Apulia—around the Foggia air base—to deprive the enemy of any springboard into the Balkans; but

[6]There is no record of such a note in published volumes.

Kesselring found it would be impossible to raise enough divisions. Hitler therefore ordered the line from Gaeta on one coast to Ortona on the other to be fortified and held, south of Rome. On October 9 he received at the Wolf's Lair the venerable Italian Marshal Rodolfo Graziani, who was to be Mussolini's new Commander in Chief, and he approved the activation of a small new Italian army on training grounds outside Italy.

Once again Rommel had misjudged. A year later Hitler recalled: "In Italy too he predicted our collapse as being just around the corner. It still has not occurred. Events have proved him completely wrong and thoroughly justified my decision to leave Field Marshal Kesselring there—whom I saw as incredibly naïve politically but an optimist militarily; and my view is that without optimism you cannot be a military commander." To both Hitler and General Rudolf Schmundt, chief of army personnel, it was plain that Rommel and Kesselring would always be at each other's throats; and that since Rommel was still tormented by his defeat in Africa, it would be better to give him another command far from Italy.

On October 15, Hitler sent for Rommel. At their meeting two days later, Rommel again cut a gloomy figure. A few days later Hitler gave Kesselring a fresh hearing, and on the twenty-eighth he decided in his favor. Rommel would be withdrawn from Italy and given a different assignment—as yet undecided.

On October 23, 1943, the main attack on the Sixth Army's sector of the East Wall, the southernmost portion, began: the next day Melitopol was overrun. Kleist and his commanders lost their nerve. A headlong retreat began. Farther north a gap was torn in the German lines between Dniepropetrovsk and Kremenchug that was to yawn a hundred miles wide within two weeks. Hitler appealed to Marshal Antonescu to rush Romanian divisions to help stem the Soviet flood swirling toward Bessarabia and Transnistria—the Black Sea province annexed in 1941 by Antonescu. But Antonescu feared for the seven divisions he had already committed to the Crimea, where along with two German divisions over 210,000 troops might any day be cut off from their overland supplies. In a reply received on October 27, the marshal advised Hitler to get out of the Crimea while the going was good.

Hitler demurred. Abandoning the Crimea without a fight would not impress Turkey or Bulgaria, and it would bring Stalin 250 miles closer to the Romanian oil wells and refineries on which Hitler and the Wehrmacht relied. He hoped to parry the Soviet thrust before it reached the coast at Nikolaev; but even if he could not, the Red Navy was not powerful enough to prevent him from evacuating the Crimean troops by sea after a protracted holding action. With this in mind, on the day he received Antonescu's reply Hitler summoned Göring, Dönitz, Zeitzler, and Jodl to a special war conference at 4:30 P.M. Zeitzler was optimistic that the eight divisions being supplied from other theaters would suffice to overcome the crisis. The Crimea had enough munitions to survive any immediate isolation. Admiral Dönitz agreed that a seaborne evacuation of the Seventeenth Army from the Crimea would be possible, although the job would be a long one and risky because of the powerful Russian air force. Hitler, Dönitz, and the Reichsmarschall were unanimous in believing that the Crimea must be held, and in the meantime provisioned by sea. Zeitzler "indicated his agreement." The records are plain on this score.

Only Field Marshal Kleist, commanding Army Group A, thought differently. The day before, he had—without consulting Hitler—ordered the evacuation of the Crimea to begin on the twenty-eighth. Zeitzler canceled the order that same evening. On November 1 the Russians reached the Dnieper's broad estuary into the Black Sea, thus cutting off the Crimean peninsula in the rear. How long could the 210,000 men there hold out?

The war conferences of October 27, 1943, vividly illustrated the complexities of fighting wars on many fronts—and in many mediums—with dwindling resources. Rundstedt had just submitted a horrendous account of Germany's military weakness in France. Pitched battles were being fought with Communist insurgents and guerrillas in the Balkans. At night the skies of Europe were loud with bomber engines and alight with the burning cities left behind. Speer needed workers to clear the rubble, build the new factories, and operate the machinery; Milch needed manpower for his new aircraft industry; Dönitz needed crews to man the hundreds of new submarines launched against the Allies. Above all Hitler needed fresh divisions to repair the breaches in the eastern front. With heavy heart he signed an order late in October for industry to release 210,000 German males— coincidentally the same number trapped in the Crimea—to the army over the next three months; he had already had to waive the draft deferment allowed to the sole surviving sons of families. Speer warned that declines in coal, iron, petroleum, and arms production would immediately result; but Hitler saw no alternative. On October 27, while strolling in the woods around the Wolf's Lair, Göring put in a special plea for his aircraft factories to be spared the ax, but failed to win his point.

Hitler evidently blamed bureaucracy for swallowing up industrial manpower. He told the Reichsmarschall of a British cartoon he had seen—a man told to save paper, but shown sitting at a desk throwing away sheet after sheet of it. "What on earth are you doing?" "I used too much paper, so now I've got to write a thousand times *I must save paper!*" Göring gave Hitler a concrete example of the shortage of manpower: Willy Messerschmitt, the aircraft designer, had bluntly told him a few days earlier that for want of four thousand workers his jet aircraft, the Me-262, would be held up by three or even six months. According to Göring, Hitler "almost had a heart attack" on hearing this news. Professor Messerschmitt had spoken to him of the Me-262 as a possible high-speed bomber for attacking Britain, and in his own lively imagination Hitler had already assigned this jet bomber a key role in stopping any Allied invasion attempt in France. In his mind's eye—forewarned by the newsreel film of similar events in Italy—Hitler could see the hours of utter chaos as Allied landing craft disgorged tanks, guns, and troops onto the beaches in the spring of 1944. His own troops would be pinned down in their bunkers by heavy naval and air bombardment; the air would be full of enemy fighters. At this moment his new jet bombers should appear—thundering along the beaches with cannon blazing, hurling bombs at random into the jammed invasion troops, spreading panic and confusion for vital hours until Hitler could bring up his mobile reserves. Göring promised the Führer he would get his jet bombers by May.

Hitler's strategic thinking had undergone a startling change since Italy's defection. Göring portrayed it thus to his generals on October 28: "In Russia we have won an immense outlying area in which we can resort to flexible tactics; but in doing so we must remain firmly resolved to amass sufficient troops by a certain time—this spring at the latest—to throw the Russians back out of the areas they have now regained. Seen like that, this breach [of the East Wall] is of no import: it does not affect our vital interests. Whether the Russians are at Krivoi Rog or get a hundred miles closer to us or not is not vital; what is, is that by spring at the latest we can muster enough maneuverability to stand fast in the west and stop the Second Front before it starts. Only air power can do that. The Führer made this abundantly clear yesterday in Dönitz's presence. The Führer says the [Me-262] jet fighter with bombs will be vital—because it will hurtle at top speed along the beach at just the right moment and hurl its bombs into the throngs forming there." (Göring added, "I thought to myself, 'Who knows if we'll really have the Me-262 by then?' ") If an enemy army ever set foot on French soil, concluded Göring, it would spell the end for Germany; whereas even if every German city was in ruins, the German people would still survive to fight on.

In a bulky report to Hitler, Field Marshal Rundstedt reached broadly the same conclusion: the defense of France would stand or fall at the Atlantic Wall; and, the Wall itself, he warned, was largely bluff and propaganda. But any German retreat here would provide the enemy with the harbors that he needed, and deprive Germany of her U-boat bases and coastal convoys. Besides, Rundstedt's divisions were too weak in both men and equipment to fight a war of movement against a superior enemy. At Hitler's conference on October 30, Jodl supported Rundstedt's main contention that—whatever *else* the Allies might undertake in Scandinavia or the Balkans—a spring 1944 invasion of France was a certainty, because only the loss of the Ruhr would finally defeat Germany; besides, Churchill would want to neutralize the A-4 missile sites in northern France. Given the likelihood that the Atlantic Wall would be breached eventually, Jodl demanded an immediate stop to the drain on Rundstedt's divisions for the benefit of the eastern front and a massive effort to reinforce the Channel defenses using impressed French labor for the purpose. Hitler agreed; indeed, he went further, for he now secretly ordered Rundstedt to send a team to reconnoiter a possible line to be defended along the Somme and Marne rivers down to the Swiss frontier—which implicitly assumed that all of France would be overrun by the enemy.[7]

He also found a neat solution to the Rommel-Kesselring dilemma. On November 5 he told Rommel that Kesselring alone would now command all of Italy, as Commander in Chief Southwest; Rommel's army-group staff was to inspect the western coastal defenses and suggest how they could be improved, and at the same time study ways and means of mounting counteroffensives against an enemy lodged in western Europe. He was to begin with Denmark and work his way south. Rommel was piqued by what seemed such an uninspiring mission—far from the limelight in which he had fought his famous battles. He wrote a few days later: "Nobody knows if the new job is a way of shelving me or not. Various people have taken it as that. I am loath to believe it, and the Führer spoke quite differently. The envious are legion—but these times are so grave that there is really no room for envy and strife." Only his love for Hitler spurred Rommel on. On November 8 the Führer delivered his annual address to the Old Guard in Munich's Löwenbräu beer cellar. "What power he radiates!" wrote Rommel in intoxication. "What faith and confidence he inspires in his people!"

---

[7]This order again dispels the legend that Hitler was loath to allow his army commanders to make timely provision for retreats. The proposed line, incidentally, still left Germany with the French provinces Hitler had decided in 1940 to annex.

"And So It Will Be, Mein Führer!"

In four years, the wheel had turned full circle, and Hitler had once again to attend to the western front. Throughout the winter it remained his constant preoccupation as he devoured Intelligence reports or enemy dispatches that had fallen into German hands, and pored over aerial photographs, trying to deduce where the Allies would set foot in Europe—and when. With his predilection for weapons technology and for designing gadgets, he began to sketch the infernal mantraps and instruments of death with which he hoped to thwart the enemy—batteries of automatic flamethrowers, impenetrable minefields, and barrels of oil that could be exploded in the sea so that the invasion troops would have to wade in through a wall of fire. More than once he was heard to exclaim that if the Allied invasion established a beachhead, the war was lost for Germany.

On November 3, 1943, he underlined this in his Directive Number 51:

> These last two-and-a-half years of tough and bloody struggle against bolshevism have strained our military strength and energy to the utmost. It was appropriate to the magnitude of the danger and the overall strategic situation. Now the danger in the east remains, but an even greater one is emerging in the west: the Anglo-American invasion! The sheer vastness of the eastern spaces allows us to countenance even a major loss of territory if the worse comes to the worst, without it striking fatally at Germany's vital arteries.
>
> Not so the west! . . . I can therefore no longer tolerate the weakening of the west in favor of other theaters of war.

Hitler expected the enemy to invade in the spring and perhaps even earlier; they would probably land near the A-4 rocket sites and the V-1 flying-bomb catapults currently being erected along the Channel coast by armies of French laborers. The political and strategic profit to the Allies of an invasion of Denmark meant that its shoreline would also have to be defended.

———

The Balkans cried out for reinforcements too. The Italian collapse had created pandemonium there: believing an Allied invasion was imminent, the guerrillas came out into the open; the few German divisions had to concentrate along the coastline, leaving the interior largely in guerrilla hands. Hitler's attempts to bolster the Poglavnik's tottering government in Croatia failed, even though the country now regained the Dalmatian coastline it had lost in 1941 to Italy. Several times during September and October Hitler conferred with his generals and ministers on the Balkan problem. Field Marshal von Weichs, his Commander in Chief there, toured the Balkan capitals and reported that while an Allied invasion was unlikely before the spring, "the most dangerous enemy is Tito." The partisan commander had built up within Croatia a regular Soviet state based on a solid civil administration; moreover, he had a hundred thousand men under arms, with Russian officers to organize them and British officers to tender expert advice. In his diary Weichs wrote:

> The grim partisan situation puts a completely different complexion on things. Not that you can speak of "partisans" anymore—under Tito, a powerful bolshevik army has arisen, rigidly led, acting on directives from Moscow, moving from strength to strength, and growing deadlier every day. It has strong British support. Tito's present objective is to break into Serbia and then defeat the nationalist guerrillas led by D[raža] M[ihajlović].
>
> Seen in this light the impotence of the Croatian government is an increasing menace. Should the enemy invade Dalmatia and Albania, we can expect general Communist uprisings to break out there.

The Italian withdrawal had left a vacuum in Albania, where there was only one German battalion to defend the coastline. If the Allies had landed even one regiment here, they could have controlled the country in two weeks.

Hitler's response to this situation was a significant political realignment, since he lacked the military strength to solve the problem by force. On Himmler's advice, he had become markedly skeptical about the Croatian government's future, and supported by Weichs and Kaltenbrunner he decided to enlist the aid of the Serbs. On October 29 he vested in Ribbentrop's very able special envoy to the Balkans, Hermann Neubacher, sweeping powers to fight communism there; in particular he could make contact with the nationalist partisan leaders like Mihajlović if need be. The Serbs were tempted with the restoration of Montenegro, the removal of Göring's notoriously corrupt economic envoy Neuhausen (who landed in Moabit prison), and special favors for Prime Minister Milan Nedić —a man whom Hitler found he could trust and like.

One thing was plain: Hitler could not abandon the strategically important Balkan peninsula with its oil, copper, and bauxite. Thus he ordered its perimeter defense to be tightened, along the cordon of islands from the Peloponnesus and Crete to Rhodes. Kos was taken in October; and on November 11 a modest

German force landed on the island of Leros, held by ten thousand British and Italian troops, and recaptured it in five days' bloody fighting. Samos was taken on the twenty-second, and thus the whole Dodecanese returned to German control, one of the last German victories under Hitler's dictatorship.

Meanwhile Romania was hypnotized by Stalin's ten-mile-a-day advance on her frontier, and Hungary was already known to be longing for an armistice; but Hitler had sent Admiral Raeder to Budapest with a yacht as Horthy's birthday present, and the regent wrote back assuring Hitler of his undying loyalty. The truth was that Badoglio's humiliation by the Allies was a chastening deterrent to imitation. Besides, Hungary and Romania were busy sharpening their knives for each other's throat. In Bulgaria, meanwhile, three regents had established a pro-German government after Boris's death, but it was weak in the face of the Turkish military buildup and a pro-Russian undercurrent in the country.

Hitler hated the Balkans! "If the British said Germany's job will be to keep the Balkans in order," he said at one war conference now, "we'd be busy for the next thirty years—marching in and out and back again, banging their heads together and getting out again."

From Himmler's Intelligence sources Hitler knew that the British were applying powerful pressure on Turkey to abandon her neutrality; at present, Turkey was resisting. Himmler's principal source was the astounding "Cicero"—an Albanian manservant employed by Sir Hughe Knatchbull-Hugessen, the British ambassador in Ankara—who had contacted Franz von Papen's embassy there early in October and been equipped by the police attaché L. G. Moyzisch with a Leica camera, skeleton keys, and large sums of Turkish currency. In return, he was secretly photographing all the British ambassador's papers during the hour or so that the diplomat bathed and breakfasted. Moyzisch had already secured from the Turkish secret service a telegram in which the Turkish ambassador in Moscow reported on the foreign ministers' conference there. (The ambassador accurately stated that Stalin had reluctantly agreed that the Second Front could be postponed until 1944 provided the Allies delivered war materials and food on the largest scale.) Once he began supplying photocopies of documents from the British embassy, he was recalled to Berlin and closely questioned about Cicero —who had by now already supplied eighty films of top secret British documents. Moyzisch described how the SD Gestapo had developed this agent, who was motivated solely by greed and therefore indubitably authentic.

Moyzisch hurried back to Ankara on November 9, as the British ambassador was due back from a meeting in Cairo, where Eden had just spent three days talking with the Turkish foreign minister. By the tenth, Ribbentrop already had Cicero's dispatch. "In Cairo Eden has demanded Turkish airfields for fighter operations in view of precarious British military situation in the Aegean." Eden had added that Germany's military strength was not to be feared, and he cited her inability to do more than utter a weak formal protest to Portugal when Britain had recently established bases in the Azores. The Turkish foreign minister refused to discuss Eden's demand without consulting his government, however; and it was clear to British and Germans alike that this meant the demand would be turned down. Papen himself lunched with Hitler at the Wolf's Lair on the seventeenth. Next day German Intelligence sources in Ankara—not Cicero this time—reported:

1. The Turkish ambassador in Moscow reports, "British ambassador here told Stalin of Turkish refusal, to which Stalin replied the Turkish mistrust annoyed him and the Three Powers would shortly have to put pressure on Turkey."
2. Eden informed Hugessen in Cairo that he had formed a bad impression of the Russian army: it seems to be in confusion and at the end of its strength.

Hitler hoped that Stalin's army would not last much longer. "We must not think of it as some kind of medieval giant that gets stronger every time it topples to the ground," he rebuked his generals. "One day its strength must also fail."

On November 1, Russian troops again set foot in the north and east Crimea but were held at bay. On the third General Hoth's Fourth Panzer Army was convincingly breached; Kiev fell, and the Russians reached Fastoff, forty miles to the southwest, before slogging to a halt on the seventh—in Hitler's view, worn out by their exertions. Hitler sacked the weary Hoth. With this "Jeremiah" gone he was given details on the cancer of "defeatism" spreading among Hoth's soldiers. "His men have only just found the courage to report all this to me," complained Hitler weeks later. Zeitzler commented, "Any army is the image of its commander." Hitler agreed. "If a commander says it's pointless to try influencing his men, I can only say, 'For *you* to try influencing them is pointless because you haven't got it in you to influence men.' " This was why he admired such Party faithfuls as Koch, Sauckel, and Ley—Gauleiters who had in their time converted Communist Gaue into Nazi party strongholds. "The good Gaue were always under the good Gauleiters." He was convinced it was the same in the army.

The security service, which censored soldiers' letters home, reported that the men no longer believed in victory. Goebbels wrote with mixed feelings that morale at the front was now lower than at home. Himmler felt that Manstein was at the bottom of the eastern front's defeatism, and when Hitler sent for him on November 7 it was widely believed the field marshal would be retired. Instead, Hitler insisted that Manstein prepare a thrust from the bridgehead at Nikopol toward the Crimea—an operation he trusted would restore land contact to the vital peninsula. First the situation southwest of Kiev had to be restored, but suddenly the long-expected rains began just when they were least needed. Sepp Dietrich's Life Guards began the attack on the fifteenth, recaptured the city of Zhitomir, then slid to a halt in the mire, after killing 20,000 enemy troops and destroying or capturing 603 tanks, 300 guns, and 1,200 antitank weapons. These figures alone revealed the colossal reserves at Stalin's disposal. "Where will it ever end!" wrote Goebbels. "The Soviets have reserves of which we never dreamed in even our most pessimistic estimates."

On the northern front, squabbles between Küchler and Kluge prevented their adjacent army groups from coordinating their counterattack on the Russians at Nevel—the key city on their common boundary—whose recapture would block the enemy's further advance on Latvia. On November 8, Kluge executed a costly attack and reached his objectives, but Küchler refused to attack the next morning as arranged, and Kluge had to retire to his opening position; his casualties had been in vain. With more than a little truth Hitler complained: "The whole catastrophe of Nevel can be blamed on the petty selfishness of the two army group commanders."[1]

This was not entirely true. Fundamental to the permanent crisis of arms was the lack of reserves. In mid-November Hitler discussed with his political advisers the possibility of recruiting more Estonians and Latvians for the defense of their native soil, but Rosenberg pointed out that unless the Baltic states' autonomy was assured, they would be unwilling to spill their own blood for the German cause. Hitler "was inwardly opposed to making such far-reaching concessions in difficult times," Rosenberg wrote afterward.

He preferred to drain his own industrial labor force before making any kind of territorial concessions. His armaments chiefs were aghast. Göring insisted that the army already had a vast surplus of manpower in the rear; Milch had himself sworn that he could, given the chance, "round up 2,000,000 men from the army's rear for the battlefront within three weeks;" he complained that of the 8,000,000 German soldiers barely 260,000 were actually on the eastern front. Hitler agreed there was an imbalance and asked Göring and Dönitz to discuss with him ways

[1]On November 14, 1943, Küchler's Chief of Staff, General Eberhard Kinzel, was bluntly instructed at the Wolf's Lair that Küchler must withdraw enough strength from the army group's northernmost (Eighteenth) army to deal with Nevel. But Nevel was never recaptured.—Kinzel was, it can be remarked, the former chief of Foreign Armies East Intelligence, whose faulty appreciations had irreparably harmed the "Barbarossa" campaign until his removal in April 1942. He took his own life in April 1945.

of increasing the combat strength. But Göring felt himself so vulnerable because of his sinking prestige that when the conference began on November 24 he actually declared that he was convinced the Luftwaffe had a large number of men to spare. The army was not mentioned. Three days later Hitler signed a strongly worded command for at least 1,000,000 men to be extracted from the Wehrmacht's "fat" and sent to the front line. Theoretically it should have been possible, but the practical result, sadly recorded by Schmundt some months later, was a disappointment. "Unhappily it has not been a big success. By bureaucratic procedures the command's execution was first postponed, then not applied with the absolute harshness that was necessary. No use was made of the penal provisions laid down by the Führer. Instead of 1,000,000 men only 400,000 were extracted." During December only 20,000 troops were supplied to the eastern front, barely 10 percent of its casualties.

Göring's prestige was low because Berlin had now begun to suffer, though not on the Hamburg scale. Night after night up to a thousand heavy bombers cascaded fire bombs and demolition bombs crudely known as "blockbusters" over the capital. Often there was ten-tenths cloud, and the German night fighters could neither take off nor land; the enemy had superb radar gear, while Göring's bombers and fighters were still groping in the dark. After the big raid on November 22, the government quarter was in ruins: Speer's ministry was gutted, the admiralty was blazing, the air ministry was in ruins, and the Chancellery was badly damaged. For days on end the city had no telephones, gas, water, or electric power. The Alkett factory, where most of Hitler's self-propelled assault guns were made, was devastated. In some raids over three thousand people died, but despite the choking layers of smoke polluting the streets for days on end, the Berliners proved as tough as the people of Hamburg in July—for which Hitler repeatedly congratulated Goebbels, the city's Gauleiter. In London, some newspapers claimed that a million had died in Berlin and that the whole city was in ruins; Goebbels was careful not to deny these claims.

Hitler could only console himself with the thought of the coming reprisal attacks on Britain. Under Himmler's control, slave laborers were toiling to complete an impregnable underground factory in the Harz Mountains for the partial manufacture and assembly of the A-4 rocket—at the rate of nine hundred a month. The first big launching silo at Watten, in northwest France, had been destroyed by enemy bombers before it was complete; now Hitler accepted the recommendation of Speer's engineers that a new site be chosen at nearby Wizernes. A million-ton dome of concrete would be emplaced on the edge of a chalk quarry first, then the missile-launching complex excavated beneath it. Hitler was "unconvinced it would ever be completed," but his skepticism about the missile system was dispelled by high-pressure salesmanship from the Peenemünde team, who adroitly covered up the backwardness and costly ineffectiveness of the A-4 missile. Late in October, as Hitler was being assured that the A-4 would be operational by the end of 1943, the Luftwaffe's new Chief of Staff, General Günther Korten, had interrupted: "We are aiming at that date too"—meaning the flying bomb. But Jodl retorted that his information was more reliable than Korten's, and according to his sources the flying bomb was a long way behind the rocket. In reality, as Speer's manufacturing experts knew, the A-4 rocket had only just begun launching trials with live warheads—and these were all prematurely exploding from the heat of reentry. Speer learned on November 8 that "the research is not as complete as the development team would have people believe." Nobody told Hitler; that same day in Munich he was proclaiming: "Our hour of revenge is nigh!"

The Luftwaffe's flying bomb had meanwhile gone into mass production at Volkswagen's Fallersleben factory in September; but it was plagued by production and navigational faults, and the production line halted in November. On November 3 the Luftwaffe learned that firing trials might be complete by early February 1944. The launching organization—96 special catapult sites erected by tens of thousands of French workers and Todt engineers along the Channel coast facing England—would be ready by mid-December 1943, and the two giant launching bunkers would be operational in March. On November 26, Hitler and Göring inspected the Luftwaffe's latest secret equipment at Insterburg airfield, an hour's train journey from the Wolf's Lair. He was shown the flying bomb and asked an engineer when it would be ready. The man replied, "By the end of March!" Hitler fell abruptly silent, as the date was the latest he had yet been told (in fact the engineer was referring only to the trials, which was even worse). But at least Hitler had been told about delays on the flying bomb, while he was kept in the dark over the A-4. On December 15 he instructed Jodl that the reprisal attack on London was to begin on February 15, preferably on a foggy forenoon at 11, with a barrage of as many missiles as possible. The OKW, which had established a special corps to direct the three secret weapons' operations—the third was the long-barreled underground gun for shelling London from Calais—followed this a week later with an order to open fire in mid-*January*. The corps commander, an elderly artillery general, replied that this was out of the question: there could be no certainty about the flying bomb until January, and in his view the whole A-4 project was a costly extravaganza which should be scrapped. His lone voice of sanity was not heeded. Jodl wrote in his diary after seeing Hitler on December 25: "A-4 and [flying bomb] are dawdling." By that time the American bomber force—trounced at Schweinfurt—had diverted its attentions to the 96 catapult-launching sites for the V-1 in France; soon 73 had been destroyed, but now this mattered little, for a new system of prefabricated launchers had superseded them and the 96 were little more than decoys. Hitler drew much comfort from the fact. "Obviously the things are getting on their nerves. If they were to start erecting such things and we knew they were for wiping out Berlin, then we'd get nervous too and set *our* Luftwaffe on *them.*"

Meanwhile, on the day after the Insterburg inspection, the Reichsmarschall had sworn to Hitler that within two weeks the Luftwaffe would bomb London and take revenge for Berlin's suffering. He planned to muster 300 bombers, to fly 500 sorties during the first night, followed by 150 more sorties the next morning. Hitler and Jodl pored over the population-distribution maps of London and Birmingham, and Göring left for France to command the operation in person. However, Chief of Air Staff Korten had his heart in a different project—the creation of a long-range bomber force for strategic attacks on Soviet industrial centers such as power stations and aeroengine factories. But "two weeks" grew into two months; not until January 22 was a fleet of 462 aircraft assembled for the London attack.

After the first raid the British gloatingly announced that only thirty bombers had found their way to London. The wretched Heinkel 177 had suffered heavy losses. "That rattletrap is quite the worst junk ever manufactured," lamented Hitler. "It's a flying Panther"—referring to the equally paralytic tank—"and the Panther is the crawling Heinkel!" Hitler refused to believe that less than three hundred or four hundred had reached London. "You've got agents," he challenged Korten. "We find out the most precious secrets of their war councils, their most confidential plans and ideas! But as to whether three buildings have been burned down in London, or a hundred or five hundred—we haven't a clue!" Korten mumbled, "We've put all our star agents on to it." These agents were in fact fictitious, the product of an Abwehr attaché's imagination.

One relief to Hitler in this darkening month of December 1943 was the steadfast refusal of Turkey to declare war on Germany. The top-secret British documents being photographed by Cicero on his master's desk in Ankara revealed this and much more. Hitler, Ribbentrop, Himmler, and Papen were satisfied that the photocopies now arriving almost daily from Ankara by air courier were authentic —angry telegrams stamped "Of Particular Secrecy" from Eden and Churchill, records of the meetings with Stalin at Teheran and with Turkey's President Inönü at Cairo, and a letter from Allied headquarters in Cairo confirming that because of the German victory in the islands of Kos and Leros operations in the Aegean had come to an abrupt end. The Abwehr played no part in this Intelligence coup; it was the SS who took the credit, and Hitler trusted them.

The picture that emerged was of mounting and abrasive pressure by Britain on Turkey to live up to its alliance and enter the war on February 15. This date was to be preceded by weeks of stealthy infiltration of the country by RAF ground staffs to prepare key airfields to accommodate twenty squadrons at one swoop, airfields from which the British could command the air in the southeast. Meanwhile British submarines would enter the Black Sea to operate against the Crimea and the Romanian coastline; moreover, with Turkey in the war Bulgaria would have to withdraw her nine divisions presently policing Serbia and Greece. But the Cicero papers showed that Turkey was fearful and suspicious of Russia's still unannounced postwar plans for the Balkans; Turkey knew from Hitler that Molotov had demanded Soviet bases in the Dardanelles in November 1940, and she saw no cause to help the hangman weave the noose. In Cairo, the Turks realized that Churchill and Eden had written off the Balkans and eastern Europe to Stalin. "The President [Inönü] returned from Cairo horrified," the Turkish foreign minister told Papen, "and said that if he had seen this coming, he would never have gone there." Turkey had no desire to share Iran's fate—occupied, divided into spheres of interest, and anesthetized with a nice declaration of her independence. Soon Hitler was reading the British ambassador's enraged telegram to Churchill on the thirteenth, reporting that the Turks were demanding impossible amounts of armaments before they would agree to terms—a ploy familiar to the Führer from his dealings with the Italians. The ambassador suggested that either the talks be broken off, or a last attempt made in staff talks to secure "agreement on the deadline of February 15," or allow them to jog hopefully on *sine die.* "We have already shown the Turks the big stick," replied the British foreign office on the eighteenth; but there was no denying that if the Allies finally broke with Turkey there would be repercussions both in Germany and the Balkans. The three commanders in chief, Middle East—Air, Army, and Navy—were therefore sent to visit Ankara in person; but the Turks refused to meet them. Eden accepted temporary defeat and cabled the following to his ambassador:

> To sum up. Our object is to get Turkey into the war as early as possible, and in any case to maintain a threat to the Germans from the eastern end of the Mediterranean, until Overlord is launched. . . . We still have not given up the idea that our squadrons should fly in on 15th February.

"Overlord" was evidently the code name for the 1944 invasion in the west.[2] Hitler's conclusion from studying the Cicero papers was that it would not come until mid-February. "There's not the slightest doubt that the attack in the west will come in the spring; none whatever." As the Turkish foreign minister said to

---

[2] According to Hitler's Luftwaffe adjutant Colonel von Below, a further Cicero document actually identified the location of "Overlord" as the Normandy peninsula. Below can still hear Hitler's puzzled exclamation: "But why on earth should the British have found it necessary to tell their ambassador in Turkey *that?*" Late in February 1944 Hitler certainly began insisting that Normandy must be reinforced, while refusing to explain why.

Papen imploringly, "We are at the most critical pass in our recent history. But since the Balkans are to be sacrificed to the Russians . . . we have no alternative but to keep playing our hand the way we are doing, in the hope that the German eastern front holds firm."

This was the political significance of the Crimea in Hitler's eyes, a significance which Manstein either could not or would not accept. Bitter though a decision to withdraw Army Group North from the Leningrad front would be, its political effect would be mild compared with the loss of the Crimea. "The Finns can't just jump overboard; when all's said and done they will still have to defend themselves." Not so Turkey, Bulgaria, and Romania. Stalin recognized this too, for his main winter offensive when it opened on December 24 was against the Fourth Panzer Army's sector west of Kiev—the left shoulder of Manstein's army group. Manstein's new headquarters at Vinnitsa was at the very focus of the Russian offensive, and he cabled an alarmed report to the Wolf's Lair the next day, beseeching Hitler to gain twelve divisions by giving up the uneconomic "bulge" along the Black Sea and the bridgehead at Nikopol while there was still time. Politically, this would be disastrous; but even militarily Hitler doubted whether Manstein was right. He was enraged by the "white lies" in Manstein's telegram: it spoke of German "counteroperations" where it meant "decamping"; and it vaguely observed, "We might hope that the enemy . . . will attempt to strike west through Cherkassy and Kirovograd, through Krivoi Rog or across the lower Dnieper, thereby finally exhausting his strength in the frontal attack on us." Hitler angrily lectured Zeitzler: "The enemy's not going to do what we *hope,* but what will damage us the most!"

Manstein was acting as if his army group was the orphan of the eastern front. In fact, since October Hitler had sent him five first-class panzer divisions and three infantry divisions. "The ratio of his forces to the enemy's is better than anywhere else on the entire eastern front and always was. If his troops are badly demoralized, then it's because of the spirit permeating them from above." Through Party channels, and particularly from Gauleiter Koch, Hitler had learned of the defeatism infecting Manstein's headquarters. Characteristically, the field marshal warned that there were 47 Soviet infantry divisions and 9 tank corps confronting him. Hitler refused to acknowledge that these could be anything but worn-out divisions which had been "reconditioned" and fed back to the battlefields; he "knew" the enemy troops' morale was low. "How can he maintain that those are 47 brand-new divisions that nothing can stop?" Hitler asked Zeitzler. With heavy sarcasm he commented, "Our German divisions are 'all rotten formations,' the Russians are all 'fresh as a daisy.' " If the retreat shortened the German front, it would shorten the enemy front by an equal amount. "But if we retire here, then this"—presumably jabbing at the Crimea on the map—"is lost." Zeitzler blurted out: "The Crimea is as good as lost anyway sooner or later." Hitler disagreed. "I'll think it over during the night again. . . . You know, Zeitzler, we can all put on airs and say, It's as good as lost. But when the time comes and it *is* lost, it won't be Manstein who accepts the blame: the responsibility is *ours.*" It was the political effect on Turkey that alarmed him. "They [the British] are trying to blackmail Turkey into joining the war on February 15," he reminded Zeitzler. ". . . Herr Manstein won't take any responsibility for that. He'll just say, 'That's a matter for the politicians.'" In addition, if Antonescu lost his army in the Crimea, he might be overthrown. "That is why we are duty-bound to defend this second Stalingrad if at all possible."

For many nights Hitler worried over the strategic decision. If he allowed Manstein to retreat, he would lose the Crimea, the iron-ore fields of Krivoi Rog, the manganese of Nikopol, and the foodstuffs of the Ukraine. He asked Zeitzler early on December 29 to work out how many divisions Küchler could release to Manstein if Army Group North was withdrawn to the East Wall line from Narva to Lake Peipus, and soon afterward he authorized Küchler to fall back on an intermediate line. When the field marshal came to the Wolf's Lair on December 30, Hitler flatteringly noted that Küchler's was the elite army of the entire eastern front, indeed an outright provocation to Kluge and Manstein. "You are lucky the other army groups don't know your strength-ratio, otherwise we couldn't save you from them!"

Admiral Dönitz, however, voiced emphatic protests against falling back on the East Wall in the north without good cause, and on January 5, 1944, Hitler forbade any voluntary withdrawal. The consequence was that when the Russian offensive began there nine days later, Küchler's weakened army group was no longer strong enough to withstand it, and it was thrown back onto the East Wall line anyway. Küchler was replaced by General Model, Hitler's stoutest defensive expert, and he halted the Soviet onslaught. Hitler felt that Küchler had been lured into retreating by the fatal East Wall mentality. "If we are going to withdraw to it anyway, why bother to hold on!"

As for the Allies, despite Cicero, the end of 1943 saw Hitler completely ignorant of their intentions. An early cross-Channel invasion was expected, but even here an Allied bluff was not impossible. A regular participant in the war conferences, Captain Heinz Assmann, wrote on December 29:

> The questions occupying the Führer and Wehrmacht operations staff now are primarily these:
>
> 1. Is all the Anglo-American huffing and puffing about an invasion in the west —speeches, articles, new appointments, and newspaper reports—really serious or just an immense bluff to dupe Germany and perhaps Russia too? Are

they trying to lure units away from the eastern front or prevent us from reinforcing that front at the crucial moment of the Soviet winter offensive?

2. Is the invasion hubbub a diversion for a major operation in the *Balkans,* either via Crete, Rhodes, and the Aegean, or via Turkey, or both?

3. Is the invasion planned *not* for the west but perhaps in Denmark–Norway after all?

4. Is Turkey as reliable as she seems, or has she perhaps already resigned herself to the passage of British troops and the use of her airfields?

5. Can we hold on to the Ukraine, which is vital for feeding the German people? Where can we still cut back on strength to help the worst pressure points on the eastern front? Where is the first infallible clue as to their real invasion intentions?

6. Will the U-boat campaign with the new submarine types result in the desired successes?

Much would depend on the new secret submarine types. The need to train them in the Baltic was one powerful argument Admiral Dönitz had voiced against allowing Küchler's Army Group North to fall back any farther, and recent naval events had greatly enhanced Dönitz's standing at the Wolf's Lair.

Once again the navy had shown an aggressive spirit which Hitler sadly missed in his field marshals. On Sunday December 26 the battle cruiser *Scharnhorst* had attacked an Allied convoy in the Arctic. Previous experience had indicated that the enemy was prudently reluctant to fight Dönitz's big ships in the dark, and in December there would be no light at all in those northern latitudes. But at 7:35 P.M. Dönitz telephoned Hitler with the alarming news that British warships had picked up the *Scharnhorst* while they were still thirty miles off, and had evidently destroyed her. An hour earlier, the bewildered Rear Admiral Bey had signaled Berlin: "Enemy firing at us by radar at a range of over eighteen thousand meters," followed barely six minutes later by a grim farewell: "To the Führer! We fight to our last shell." Then there had only been silence, interrupted by English signals like "Finish her off with torpedoes!"—"Fire a star shell!"—"Clear the the target area except for those ships with torpedoes and one destroyer with searchlight." Hitler accepted the warship's loss philosophically. If the enemy's radar was so good—according to Dönitz the British had pinpointed in their radar every waterspout thrown up by the shells—then the *Scharnhorst* had been like a blind man boxing with a prizefighter.

Hitherto radar research had been controlled by Göring. It was a conspicuous failure. The British night bombers could bomb Berlin accurately through ten-tenths cloud, and a new 3-centimeter radar had just been found in a downed bomber, but the Luftwaffe could still not operate even a 10-centimeter radar system. Under pressure from Speer and Dönitz at the Wolf's Lair on January 2, Hitler transferred all radar and electronics research to Speer's unified control.

In a lightning war like those with Poland and France in 1939 and 1940, fought by largely professional armies, the political indoctrination of the troops was of little moment. In the bitter, protracted contest the war had now become, however, with four-fifths of the fighting men recruited from German civilian life, Hitler recognized—too late—that such indoctrination was as important as material armament. By early 1943 troop morale was already suffering, particularly from the frontline soldier's uncertainty about the fate of his wife and family after the heavy British night attacks. Hitler expected his generals to explain the purpose of the struggle to their men, and when all but a few—like Walter Model, Ferdinand Schörner, and Lothar Rendulic—proved unequal to the task he called upon the Party to instill the necessary spirit. He had addressed the generals assembled by Bormann for this purpose at the Wolf's Lair on October 16 and reassured them that he would not emulate the hated political commissar system of the Bolsheviks: he would not be putting Party lecturers into army uniform, but elevating loyal and politically conscious officers to positions in which they could influence their comrades.

There is no doubt that Hitler was finally impelled to issue his order of December 22, 1943, establishing an OKW National Socialist Leadership Staff under General Hermann Reinecke, by the uncomfortably effective subversion campaign being directed against the eastern front by the renegade German generals taken prisoner at Stalingrad. Late in August his former orderly, Hans Junge—now a Waffen SS officer in Russia—had visited him briefly. "The most dangerous developments at the front at this juncture," Hitler asserted later, "are definitely the [anti-Nazi] proclamations printed by General Seydlitz. Various people told me so, most vividly Junge, who's got his head screwed on. The proclamations arrive in black-white-and-red"—the colors of the Reich—"and the ordinary soldier can't tell what's true and what isn't. Besides our soldiers have always taken officers to be men of honor." The troops were completely taken in by trick photomontages published by these Moscow renegades. How were they to know that Stalin's League of German Officers—of which Seydlitz was chairman—was as Hitler said just "a herd of unprincipled swine who have sold their souls to the Devil"?

The December 22 order gave the Party its first bridgehead into the Wehrmacht. Early in January General Reinecke announced to Hitler that he and Martin Bormann's Party chancellery were recruiting a small fanatical leadership staff from old, experienced Party warriors and young battle-hardened army officers; in this undertaking they had Himmler's active support. Schmundt assured Hitler that the army had been clamoring for it for a long time. But while the new Party-indoctrinated "leadership officers" would undoubtedly influence the lower command levels to which they were temporarily attached, Hitler himself had to speak to the senior generals, who would otherwise remain immune. Hitler strongly wanted to crack the whip over them again, for unsettling reports had recently reached him—including one broadcast by the BBC—that certain disaffected generals were plotting his overthrow or even assassination. But he hesitated. "It would be hard to bring them all together at the same time." Bormann, however, was eager. "If it could be done, it would be the biggest success."

Keitel reminded Hitler that they needed to appoint a specially capable "leadership officer" for the army. Hitler replied without hesitation, "Schörner. He is a fanatic!" Until recently commander of the bridgehead at Nikopol, Schörner was a tough general not given to defeatism. Only recently he had ended a letter to Schmundt with the words: "You know the position here. But we will pull through." How different from the melancholy Manstein, who saw his fame as a commander withering before his eyes!

Manstein arrived in agitation on January 4, 1944, and again demanded permission to withdraw his entire southern sector—thereby abandoning Nikopol and the Crimea forever—to find the means to buttress his damaged northern sector, where the Fourth Panzer Army had now been thrown back on to the former Polish frontier. Again Hitler refused. Manstein asked for the others present to leave the room and in Zeitzler's presence alone launched a sober and forceful critique of Hitler's overall military command in the east. Hitler tried to stare him down—like "an Indian snake charmer," in Manstein's words; but the field marshal could not be charmed. He recommended that Hitler appoint a Commander in Chief East like Rundstedt in the west and Kesselring in Italy. Hitler had heard all this before. He pointed out that nobody had as much authority as he had, "and even I am not obeyed by my field marshals. Do you think they would obey *you* any better?" He could offer Manstein no fresh divisions: Dönitz had persuaded him not to shorten the front of Army Group North any further; in the west they must first wait until the invasion had been defeated, or the British had got bogged down in Portugal—his latest *idée fixe*. Hitler explained to Manstein that he was fighting to gain time—time to raise new armies, time for the U-boat campaign beginning in May 1944 to bite, time for the smoldering East-West dispute to blaze up into the open. Russia's frontier changes in Poland were already provoking near hysteria in London and Washington. In the event, Manstein's soldiers were able to withstand the winter onslaught, yielding almost no ground to the Russians; where there was a will, Hitler concluded, there was evidently a way.

During these first days of 1944, Hitler laid down the material foundations of the coming year's campaign. He personally besought Dönitz, Speer, and their submarine experts to keep to production targets. He had ordered Göring to concentrate production effort on the jet fighters and jet bombers, and—just in case the jet ran into snags—on the unique Dornier 335 fighter-bomber, which had a propellor at each end and was attaining speeds almost as high as the jet fighter. He ordered jet-engine production to be housed underground at the Central Works tunnel-factory already producing A-4 rockets near Nordhausen, and on January 4 he again told Speer and Milch how much he was relying on the new secret U-boat types and the jet aircraft. "If I get the jets in time, I can fight off the invasion with them"—and again, a few days later—"If I get a few hundred of them to the front line, it will exorcise the specter of invasion for all time."

Finally, on January 4 he applied himself to the overriding manpower problem. During 1944 Germany somehow had to raise more than four million new workers. The whole afternoon was devoted to a conference between Keitel, Speer, Milch, and Herbert Backe, agriculture minister, as the "employers" and Sauckel and Himmler as the "manpower procurers." Speer's belief was that French workers were more productive in "protected" factories in France, but Sauckel raised powerful arguments for continuing the conscription of French labor for war plants in Germany. He emphatically contended that even by taking Italian forced labor into account he could not guarantee the 4,050,000 new workers needed for 1944. Hitler was still loath to employ female workers on a scale comparable to Russia, Britain, and the United States, explaining that there was no comparison between "our long-legged, slender women" and the "stocky, primitive, and robust Russian women."

Sauckel counted heavily on Italian forced labor. But once again the "Italian problem" thwarted Hitler. To please Mussolini, he had agreed to the raising of a modest new Italian army—four divisions; the Italian internees had only to volunteer for these to escape labor service, but few of the "volunteers" ever reached the divisions. The only ray of sunshine in this darkness had been Mussolini's unexpected arrest of Count Ciano: together with his "fellow conspirators" he was tried and condemned to death by a Fascist court in Verona in January. His wife, the former Edda Mussolini, managed that very day to escape to Switzerland, having addressed this letter to Hitler:

> Führer! Twice I believed your word, and twice I have been cheated. Only the soldiers lying on the battlefields prevent me from deserting to the enemy. If my husband is not released . . . nothing but that will stop me: for some time now the documents have been held by people authorized to make use of them if anything were to happen to my husband, me, my children, or my family.

A similar letter had gone to Mussolini himself: if Ciano was not in Switzerland within three days, Edda would make use of every document she possessed. Hitler took no action to intervene, and Ciano met the Fascist firing squad at 9 A.M. the next day, January 11.

The spectacular failure of the Allies to make any headway in Italy was a huge comfort to Hitler. Since early September the enemy had managed to advance only forty kilometers—little more than six miles per month—despite immense naval and air superiority. A year later Jodl was to comment on the Allies' bad strategy. "I still cannot understand why they began right down at the bottom and fought a laborious land campaign northward instead of using their colossal naval and other strength to leapfrog northward on a huge scale." This, coupled with Hitler's stubborn defense of the Crimea, undoubtedly impressed Turkey to remain neutral. While General Jodl maintained his instinctive fear for the Balkans for some months yet, Hitler concluded correctly from the Cicero reports that he could safely draw on his Balkan contingents to strengthen the Russian front. On January 12—Cicero's microfilmed documents revealed—the British foreign office had secretly cabled in exasperation to the British ambassador in Ankara that Turkey was unlikely now to enter the war soon. "We must now concentrate our main effort on maintaining the threat to the Germans from the eastern Mediterranean. At the same time the situation on the Russian front is moving rapidly and may be followed by developments which will cause a change in the Turkish attitude." Ribbentrop advised his ambassador to disclose to the Turks that the evidence was that *provided* Turkey remained intransigent Britain could not afford to break completely with her. According to the Cicero documents, Britain's ambassador was informed that Turkey was required to enter the war at the same time as "Overlord"—the invasion from British soil—began; this finally convinced Hitler that enemy strategy in the Balkans would be limited to diversionary operations only, rather than be the main invasion assault. (Furthermore an air raid was being planned against the Romanian oil refineries at Ploesti after March 15; it was code-named "Operation Saturn.") The Turkish foreign minister, Menemencioglu Numan, meanwhile informed a furious British ambassador: "We are not so stupid as to get dragged into a war against our own interests for the second time in twenty-five years." Ribbentrop instructed that a quarter of a million gold marks was to be paid to Cicero; it was money well spent.

Despite Manstein's misgivings, his Army Group South had staged a brilliant defense of the Dnieper bend and the bridgehead at Nikopol, but as the position of the Fourth Panzer Army on his left flank grew increasingly precarious he wrote urgently first to Zeitzler and then to Hitler himself appealing for reinforcements before his entire army group was encircled. Hitler dismissed the letters as a typical attempt by Manstein to justify his inevitable failure to future historians.

Hitler next saw Manstein on January 27. At Schmundt's suggestion, he had summoned the principal generals from the Russian front to hear a two-hour secret speech designed to put fresh fire into their veins. Row upon row, the generals sat before him in the dining room of a converted inn in the OKW's Security Zone II, near the Wolf's Lair. For two days they had listened to speeches by Goebbels, Rosenberg, and other Party leaders at Posen (Poznan). Now—after a communal lunch—they heard Hitler lecture articulately and, if the shorthand record be taken as a guide, powerfully on war and nations, and on the influence of leadership and racial character on a nation's morale. He hinted at new torpedoes, new submarines, new radar equipment, and secret weapons which would turn the tide in their favor after May 1944; until then they must grimly hold out. For this, National Socialist indoctrination—that same "holy conviction" that distinguished the Reich from the merely skeletal administrative structure that had been fascism in Italy—was indispensable.

Toward the end of his speech, something incredible occurred. For the first time, he was loudly interrupted. He had just addressed this challenge to the generals: ". . . If the worse comes to the worst and I am ever abandoned as Supreme Commander by my people, I must still expect my entire office corps to muster around me with daggers drawn—just as every field marshal, or the commander of an army, corps, division, or regiment expects his subordinates to stand by him in the hour of crisis." As he paused in his rhetoric, Manstein's voice came from the front row, loud and—possibly—reproachful: "*And so it will be,* mein Führer!" The interruption created a sensation at the Wolf's Lair, where it was talked about for days. Hitler hoped at first the field marshal had meant to reassure him of their loyalty, but Bormann and the adjutants told him the generals had interpreted the outburst otherwise: that the worse would indeed come to the worst. It was an interruption of exquisite ambiguity.[3]

Shortly afterward Hitler sent for the field marshal. "Field marshal, I must forbid you ever to interrupt a speech by me to my generals again." Then he referred sarcastically to Manstein's recent letter asking for reinforcements. "No doubt you wanted it in your war diary to clear your name before the historians!" Manstein angrily retorted that his letters to the Führer never went into the diary. "Forgive me for resorting to an English expression, but *I* am a *gentleman.*" At that evening's war conference Hitler melted toward Manstein again. Perhaps it was innate respect for this outstanding commander; perhaps it was just because General Erwin Jaenecke spoke confidently of his Seventeenth Army's ability to hold the Crimea, during the conference. The other army- and army-group commanders were equally optimistic now, though none of them viewed the future exactly rosily. This was the effect of Hitler's rhetoric.

Twice that day—both in his speech and in the private evening circle—Hitler again formulated his goal as winning for Germany the "world domination" for

---

[3]It resulted, according to Schmundt's diary, in Manstein's eventual dismissal. See page 616.

which she was "predestined." That night he told Bormann of his unorthodox ideas for making good Germany's disastrous casualties, for otherwise in population terms she would lose the war even though victorious militarily. Hitler remarked that Germany's most important asset, the fertility of entire generations of German women—perhaps three or four million of them—would be wasted unless men could be found for them. A great campaign must begin for every sound German woman, married or not, to bear as many children as possible to safeguard Germany's future. Writers, poets, and artists must henceforth extol the unmarried mother. As in animal breeding, the finest specimens of manhood must do their bit, and German womanhood must be educated to abandon their fanatical insistence on marital fidelity—"a fetish they often ignore themselves until they are married," Hitler slyly observed. Otherwise one day Germany, and with her all Europe, would be overwhelmed by the Asiatic hordes of which the current Russian plague was but a part. "We must look at the population charts of Europe and Asia in 1850, 1870, and 1900," said Hitler, "and try to visualize what the map of 1945 will be."

Trouble from Providence

The Hitler of early 1944 was unlike the confident Führer who had set out for the Polish front in his train in September 1939. His animal energy and abnormal willpower remained unsapped, but his appearance had undergone a shocking change. Werner Best found him a tired, broken, and elderly man, dragging his feet and stooping so low that he seemed to bow. His features were sunken and lined with worry and anger. His eyes stared with an almost reproachful gaze. Hitler's secretaries noticed that sometimes his knees would begin to shake, or he had to grasp his trembling left hand with his right; the tremor when he had to lift a cup to his lips was too marked to be concealed. Yet he refused to take these symptoms seriously, and Dr. Morell loudly proclaimed his patient to be in the best of health. We know from his papers that for five months after September 1943 he continually urged Hitler to submit to a further electrocardiogram, without success. Not until September 1944 did Hitler agree: again the diagnosis of the electrocardiogram was "coronary sclerosis." It was the same with X-rays; several times Morell noted in his papers that his patient should be X-rayed, but there is no trace of any X-ray after 1940, with the exception of those of Hitler's head in September 1944. When Hitler's adjutants reproved Morell for his lackadaisical treatment of the Führer, his exasperated reply was invariably the same: "*You* try treating a patient like the Führer!"

For all his obesity—his weight hovered around 230 pounds—and hirsute repulsiveness, Morell retained Hitler's affections. Each evening at Hitler's midnight tea party, Morell would be snoring loudly within minutes of slumping into an armchair. Hitler's eyes were alive with sympathy and indulgence at this spectacle. "Without Morell I would probably have died long ago, or at least be incapable of working on. He was and is the only one who can help me." A secretary described the doctor thus: "With his podgy, hairy hands clasped across his potbelly, he fought back his sleepiness. In some strange way, his eyes closed from the bottom upward—it looked hideous behind his thick-lensed spectacles. Nor was he a good conversationalist. Sometimes Colonel von Below [Hitler's spry, elegant Luftwaffe adjutant] gently nudged him. Then he would wake up and chuckle, assuming that the Führer had told a joke."

Hitler's private milieu had also changed. He rarely came in contact with people from the world outside his headquarters. His horizon was the perimeter fence, with its guards and minefields. Schmundt and Schaub introduced what new faces they could to the evening conversation parties—the architect Hermann Giesler, the wives of the adjutants and headquarters commandant, and former members of Hitler's staff like Hans Pfeiffer and Hans Junge, both of whom would die shortly in France. Morell lamented in one letter that Julius Schaub had been injured in a Munich air raid, and the old familiar faces were gone. "Reichsleiter Bormann is mostly away on business in Berlin and Munich. Heini Hoffmann [Hitler's bibulous personal photographer and court jester] only puts in a guest appearance every four weeks or so. Scarcely anybody of the old clique is still here. The headquarters has outgrown itself, and most people are preoccupied with themselves. I for my own part have become a recluse, doing scientific research and working on my business undertakings in what time I can." Albert Speer had also vanished from Hitler's sight—at first recovering from a grave illness, then afflicted by a pathological fear that his colleagues were trying to usurp his powers; not until spring did Hitler see the armaments minister again.

Bormann's influence over Hitler was now immense. Rosenberg, Lammers, and the other Cabinet ministers rarely penetrated the Party secretary's protective shield around the Führer. In vain the finance minister, Count Schwerin von Krosigk, demanded to report to Hitler on the threatening inflation and the loss of public confidence in the Reichsmark. Hitler was told only what Bormann (and Himmler) wanted him to know about internal Reich affairs.

The long-delayed visit by Dr. Hans Frank, Governor General of occupied Poland—on February 6, 1944—provides a further significant example. The Russian army was now fighting on Polish soil, but Hitler—"exceptionally forthright and looking the picture of a healthy, dynamic, and active man" as Frank wrote that day—assured the Governor General that he would not allow the General-gouvernement to become a battlefield. "Yes, my dear Frank, it *is* odd: previously we regarded the Generalgouvernement as something of a backwater; today it is our bulwark against the east." He applauded Frank's new policy, aimed at securing Polish assistance in the fight. Frank told him of the fortifications built along the frontier and showed him maps of Polish petroleum production, population distribution, forestation, and agricultural output. But even Hans Frank seems to have been pulling the wool over his Führer's eyes; in his eighteen-page diary record of the discussion—which Bormann also attended—Frank touched on the Jewish problem only once: "I said that getting rid of the Jews by getting them out of the Generalgouvernement[1] had taken a great load off the country's general situation."

Afterward Frank ran into Morell. "I asked him," wrote Frank, "about the Führer's health. He claimed it is better than ever before. His stomach pains are gone and his appetite has returned—a particularly good sign. He said he was proud of this achievement." Shortly after, Hitler's appetite failed again, however, though for a different reason. When Frau von Exner, the Viennese dietician recommended by Antonescu, became engaged to an SS adjutant at headquarters, it was learned that she had a Jewish great grandmother. Hitler had to dismiss her, after refusing to eat for many days. "You will understand that I must pay you off," he told her. "I cannot make one rule for myself and another for the rest." But he did order Martin Bormann to put her family papers in order—giving them full Aryan "clearance"—and his annoyance was intense when he learned many months later that Bormann, who had himself been rebuffed by the girl, had in fact resorted to petty persecution. Her relatives were ejected from the Party, a step which had severe financial effects on them.

In Italy, the Allies were being held at bay. Hitler's real fear was of the invasion threat looming in the west. "*If* only they would land half a million men," he reflected on December 30, "and then foul weather and storms cut them off in the rear—then everything would be all right!" Rommel's tour of inspection in Denmark was complete, and that day Hitler had instructed his representatives in Copenhagen to resort to criminal terrorist tactics to stamp out acts of sabotage and assassination by underground agents in Denmark. Since it was considered counterproductive to try and then execute these agents—and thus make martyrs of them—Hitler ordered Himmler's agents to strike back under cover against leading Danish opponents and their property. The next day an SS marksman gunned down a journalist, and a few days later the spiritual leader of the Danish resistance, Pastor Kaj Munk, was assassinated. "You can't smash terrorism by philosophizing," Hitler told his generals secretly on January 27, 1944; "you have to smash it by using even greater terror."

By early 1944, Rommel was confidently asserting his authority in preparing the defense of France. Hitler was cautiously optimistic; the Allies, he felt, had secured footholds in Africa and Italy only because of the Italian traitors. "But they won't find any here—they'll get the thrashing of their lives!" He also said,

---

[1]Literally, *"Die Beseitigung der Juden aus dem Generalgouvernement."* In fact they had been got rid of *in* that domain; but the wording was in deference to Hitler's insistence on their deportation for forced labor in the east.

"I am convinced that when the time comes it will be a huge relief—just like Dieppe." Meanwhile Hitler applied his own mind to the Atlantic defenses. He insisted on digging in the scores of useless Panther tanks as gun batteries in France, since they had proved a liability on the battlefields of Russia. He ordered extra concrete pumped into the forward defenses. He commanded that pillboxes for three thousand new antitank and other guns were to be built by the end of April at the very latest. Most important of all, he gave Rommel's army group tactical command of the armies along the Channel coast. Rommel toured these areas from January until May and struck the fear of God into officers and men alike, rudely awakening them. Hitler knew that Rommel had many critics among the generals but he counted on the Desert Fox to light a bonfire under them—before the Allies could in the spring. On January 15, General Jodl reported to Hitler on his own tour of the Atlantic defenses. He was unimpressed by the pace of fortification activity; large sections of the defensive works were incomplete, and the Germans were fraternizing with the French coastal population. The Luftwaffe had not planned ahead at all.[2] He supported Rommel's contentions wholeheartedly.

For six weeks from January 12, Rommel stood in for Rundstedt as Commander in Chief West and began implementing tactical concepts strongly opposed to those of Rundstedt, who remembering the lessons of the Russian front had planned a flexible defense on French soil, with a powerful mobile reserve of panzer divisions in the rear. Rommel convincingly argued that the Allied invasion attempt must be defeated on the very landing beaches; the enemy, once ashore, could marshal such colossal and overwhelming material strength that he could never again be dislodged. Thus the panzer divisions must be brought right up to the coast; otherwise they would arrive on the battlefield too late— or not at all, if the enemy destroyed the road and railway links before them. This tallied well with Hitler's vision. "With every month the invasion is delayed the probability grows that we will get at least one squadron of jet aircraft. . . . The main thing is that the moment the invasion begins the enemy must be smothered in bombs—that'll force them to take cover, and even if there's only one jet airborne, they'll still be forced to take cover and this will waste them hour upon hour. But in half a day our reserves will be well on their way!" This delay would also enable Hitler to take stock: "Which is the decoy—and which is the real invasion!"

---

[2]"Yesterday," wrote Rommel on December 29, 1943, "I was in P[aris] again and spoke with Field Marshal Sp[errle, Commander in Chief Third Air Force]. The prospects here are not all that good. From what I had heard I expected a lot more from this Service." And Jodl wrote in his diary several days later: "How on earth is the air war against the invasion going to be conducted?" Not until August 1944 was Sperrle dismissed by Hitler.

Rommel's activity changed the whole face of the Atlantic defenses. With his Party backing and influence on Hitler, he was able to start fresh divisions moving to the west. He demanded millions of mines per month, to lay along the coast. He prepared to flood or swamp low-lying areas. He conferred with the Todt Organization's chief, Xaver Dorsch, on an ingenious arsenal of deadly gadgets to meet the invaders: submerged barriers of massive spikes designed to gash open the hulls of landing boats, and nutcracker mines supported on iron girders, staggered and echeloned along the beaches, some visible, some below the water's surface. Tempted by the cash rewards, the male French population willingly assisted, while their womenfolk made rush-matting for sand traps or helped to erect antiparatroop defenses. According to Rommel, they worked with a will and finished each day "singing lustily." All France knew, he said, what would happen to their towns and villages if Germany's enemies landed and made a battlefield of them.

From the Cicero documents Hitler knew that the Allies had scheduled the capture of Rome for the end of January 1944. All the indications were that this was the objective of the powerful offensive begun by a British corps in Italy on January 17. But wholly unexpectedly—and without even a hint from the German Intelligence services—on January 22 an American corps staged a sudden seaborne landing south of Rome at Anzio—to the rear of the German lines.

Misled by Canaris's assurances, Kesselring had denuded the Anzio coastline shortly before, and only two German battalions met the American troops debouched by three hundred ships along a twenty-mile stretch of shore. But both sides fumbled. Kesselring delayed his counterattack for a week, to allow further panzer divisions and heavy units to arrive in Italy. The Luftwaffe's Richthofen scornfully noted in his diary: "Thus we violate the cardinal rule of war accepted for many millennia—to lay into enemy beachheads with everything you've got immediately, so as to exploit the disorder always reigning in the first few days. In theory this decision has already cost us the battle for Rome." But the Americans were even more hesitant in consolidating their beachhead. "Politics play a big part," Hewel reminded Hitler. "No general over there can afford big defeats. Questions get asked, and if an over-risky gamble he's begun doesn't pay off, he gets hauled over the coals." Hitler realized that an American bloody nose at Anzio would be a big prestige boost after the dark months of 1943. He even said, "If we can wipe them out down there, then there won't *be* an invasion anywhere else"—Roosevelt could not take such a risk in a presidential election year. But Hitler's sixth sense urged caution on him too, telling him that Anzio was less a Battle for Rome—whatever the dramatic, purple prose he used in his messages to Kesselring[3]—than a sly enemy attempt to lure the high-grade German reserves like the brand-new 9th SS Panzer Division away from France into a peripheral war of attrition in Italy; and after the long-delayed counterattack by Mackensen's Fourteenth Army failed to throw the Americans back into the sea, he was content to see the beachhead merely contained.

"We were completely surprised by those few invasion operations they have launched so far," Hitler was to say in April. He asked Jodl to determine precisely why Intelligence had failed to predict Anzio. Kesselring claimed that the few clues that reached him in mid-January were dismissed by Admiral Canaris as erroneous. Early in February, the defection to the British of an important Abwehr agent in Turkey put the last nail in the admiral's long-prepared coffin. Erich Vermehren, a young junior-grade official in the Abwehr's main Middle East headquarters at Istanbul, had vanished with his countess wife, who was eight years his senior and a fervent Catholic. This blew the Abwehr in the eastern Mediterranean wide open and brought even Cicero's operations to an abrupt end. The Abwehr frantically tried to divert the blame to the SS or even to Ribbentrop's ministry, but Hitler had had enough of Admiral Canaris and told Himmler so at two meetings on February 9 and 11. Hitherto he had respected the OKW's sovereignty, but now he accepted the SS accusations. Canaris was disgraced and suspended from office. On February 12, Hitler signed the order for Himmler to set up a "unified German secret Intelligence service." But even now Canaris escaped arrest—shielded from criticism by his gullible superior, Keitel, and even put in charge of the OKW's economic-warfare unit outside Berlin.

On the Russian front, Hitler clung fanatically to his belief that Stalin's military strength was waning. Later in February, Zeitzler's staff produced estimates that over 18,000,000 of the 46,000,000 able-bodied men available to Stalin in 1941 had now been eliminated by battle casualties or loss of territory. Russian casualties were outnumbering German by seven to one. Stalin's manpower reserves had now shrunk to barely 2,100,000 men, according to Zeitzler. This was why Hitler still fought on, defending every centimeter of ground even though the Russians were still moving men and equipment into their battlefront faster than he himself could. And as that front moved ever closer to German soil, Hitler's willingness

---

[3]On January 28, 1944, Hitler radioed: "In the next few days the 'Battle for Rome' will break out. . . . It must be fought in holy wrath against an enemy who is waging a pitiless war of extermination against the German people, who shuns no means to that end, who is devoid of all higher ethical purpose, and who is intent only on the destruction of Germany and thereby of our European culture." The enemy must realize that his main 1944 invasion would be an undertaking that would choke on the blood of the British and American soldiers, the document concluded.

to permit operational retreats like the "Buffalo" movement of 1943 disappeared. From now on the German soldier would fight where he stood, holding out until the inevitable breach between East and West came to his salvation: such was Hitler's strategy.

In the north, Model's army group was preparing its final withdrawal to the East Wall (Panther) line. In the center, Busch had fought a series of successful defensive actions, and his line was still intact. But a gap of over 150 miles yawned north of Manstein's Army Group South, exposing it and Kleist's Army Group A to extreme danger. Since January 28, 54,000 German troops had been encircled at Cherkassy on the Dnieper River, and the same fate threatened the garrison of the Nikopol bridgehead. Hitler ordered a counterattack to cut off the Russians encircling Cherkassy; but snow and rain thwarted the operation, and after weeks of harrowing fighting Hitler reluctantly authorized the garrison there to break out as best they could, leaving most of their injured to the mercies of the enemy. The dramatic breakout began on the night of February 15—led by a silent phalanx of troops with fixed bayonets, followed by the artillery and heavier equipment; but instead of the Second Panzer Corps waiting to receive them in a designated position, they were greeted by heavily armed Russian units instead. The heavy gear was abandoned, but the men fought on to the westward. They were confronted by a river, sprang into the icy waters and forded it or were drowned. Only 30,000 of the 54,000 who set out reached the German lines. Transport aircraft had flown out 2,400 of the luckier injured men.

The Cherkassy pocket had irritated the Russians out of all proportion to its size. It was here that Stalin again employed his deadly psychological weapon, the League of German Officers—the organization of turncoat German prisoners in Russian hands. Seydlitz and his fellow generals broadcast appeals over Moscow radio to their encircled former comrades to lay down their arms. Officers in German uniform infiltrated into the pocket to commit acts of sabotage, issue conflicting orders, and deliver secret letters from Seydlitz to the generals still faithful to their Führer: each of the corps commanders in Cherkassy, Stemmermann, and Lieb received such letters; so did General Kruse. Their authenticity was beyond doubt. Elsewhere Seydlitz-letters were slipped into the hands of Field Marshals Rundstedt and Küchler, Generals Model and Lindemann. Some of Seydlitz's emissaries were captured, and revealed—before their execution—that they had been brainwashed and trained by the Russians at a special camp near Krasnogorsk. On hearing this Hitler cited Scripture: "Lord, forgive them—they know not what they do!" His revulsion toward the German officer corps as a whole was further increased by the revelations of corruption and debauchery at the highest level in the military government of Belgium, brought to light when members of military governor General von Falkenhausen's staff were put on trial in Berlin.

The Seydlitz and Falkenhausen affairs had a strange sequel. To restore Hitler's faith in his officers, General Schmundt took it on himself to secure every field marshal's signature to a declaration of personal loyalty to the Führer. Flying first to Rundstedt in France—most senior of Germany's serving soldiers—and satisfying him of the authenticity of Seydlitz's treachery, Schmundt then went on to Model, Rommel, Kleist, Busch, Manstein, and Weichs in turn (Kluge appears not to have signed the document). Weichs wrote in his diary: "Such a reaffirmation of our oath of allegiance seems unmilitary to me. An officer's loyalty ought to be taken for granted." But Weichs admitted that in the Party's history similar declarations of loyalty by the Gauleiters after various disgraceful affairs—like the alleged plot by Ernst Röhm in 1934—had succeeded in restoring Hitler's confidence in them. Perhaps it would work for the army too.

For a variety of reasons, Hitler decided it was time to leave the Wolf's Lair for a while. He planned to meet Antonescu (to ask him to his face about Romania's loyalty). He also wanted to be closer to the Italian front. "We have built headquarters in just about every other corner of the Reich," he wanly joked, "but never dreamed that we should one day need one near Italy!" Another reason for leaving was so that he could address the Nazi faithfuls at the Party Foundation Ceremony in Munich. But above all, the truth was that he could no longer take the risk of an enemy air raid on the Wolf's Lair, whose bunkers had been built only to withstand the pre-blockbuster type of bombs. The British bomber force had a month earlier dropped twenty-four hundred tons of bombs on Berlin in one night; both British and American daylight formations—currently blasting Göring's fighter-aircraft factories—had East Prussia well within their range. Sooner or later Churchill or Roosevelt might consider the Führer a worthwhile target. Thus he entrained for Munich on February 23, 1944, while the Todt Organization moved in to erect even stronger bunkers at the Wolf's Lair.

It is unlikely that he glimpsed the bomb-torn ruins of Posen, Cottbus, Leipzig, and Nuremberg as he passed through. He consistently and consciously avoided seeing the misery his enemies had wrought—a harsh but in retrospect a proper attitude, for an enraged mind cannot make sober and logical decisions. Besides, the blinds were drawn to shield his painful retinas. For two weeks now he had been troubled by a stabbing pain and increasingly opaque veil in his right eye, of such turbidity as to rend him virtually blind when he closed his left eye. As he was driven along the snow-swept autobahn toward Berchtesgaden that evening, the sirens were already sounding, searchlights were fingering the sky, and pathfinder flares were bathing the countryside in a hostile glare: a heavy British attack was beginning on Schweinfurt, and six hundred bombers were over Bavaria. The crack of the antiaircraft batteries was still echoing around the sleepy

Berchtesgaden valleys when Hitler arrived at the Berghof at 10:15 P.M., his driver having missed a turning in the deep snow and headed some distance in the general direction of Vienna by mistake. A staff stenographer wrote: "The war conference was slated to begin at 11:30 P.M. As we stood by in the anteroom the Führer came in with Reichsleiter [Martin] Bormann, Gruppenführer [Albert] Bormann, and the rest of his staff, having toured the air raid shelter tunnels built here in recent months. He welcomed us with a friendly grin. The conference began at 11:45 P.M. and ended at five past midnight."

Camouflage netting covered the Berghof, and at midday only a melancholy twilight filtered through the famous window of the Great Hall. On March 2 a leading Berlin eye specialist examined Hitler's blue-gray eyes, gently palpated the eyeballs, and peered into their recesses with an opthalmoscope and magnifying mirror. He diagnosed "minute hemorrhages in the vitreous humor," and Hitler heard him recommend to Morell that the Führer submit to two quarter-hour periods of complete relaxation every day with heat treatment by sunlamp if possible. He was to avoid all "unnecessary excitement, particularly during the period immediately before the night's rest." Hitler's nine-year-old spectacles were quite inadequate, and a new pair of bifocals were prescribed.

Everybody who saw Hitler was shocked by his physical transformation. Defeat —Manstein's army group was now in near flight from the Ukraine—was carving deep hollows in his features. Hungary was secretly negotiating with the Allies. The two German counterattacks at Anzio had failed to eradicate the American beachhead. The new German divisions would not be ready until May. The aircraft industry was in smoking ruins. Small wonder that when Eva Braun gently reproached him for walking with a stoop, he would reply, "That's because of the burden of worries I'm carrying all the time," or again, "It's the heavy keys I'm carrying in my trouser pockets," or, "It's so I suit you better: you wear high heels, and I stoop a bit—then we are just right for each other."

On March 5 the two armaments "dictators" Milch and Saur came to the Berghof —their respective bosses being indisposed: Göring on leave and Speer convalescing. Their report on future aircraft, tank, and gun production was optimistic despite the crushing blows dealt by the enemy bombers. A Fighter Staff had been created to mobilize industry for the defense of the Reich's airspace. Hitler agreed to make fighter aircraft production a top priority and demanded that the two planned bunker-factories—with seventeen-foot-thick concrete roofs—should each have at least seven million square feet of floor space, capable of housing everything needed for aircraft manufacture from the forging of the crankshafts and smelting of the steel down to the finished product. He released sixty-four miners to Saur from the gangs tunneling air raid shelters under the Berghof and advised him to train at least *ten thousand* more; he must not rest until Germany's entire war industry was underground.

At the Central Works underground factory near Nordhausen, Himmler's slave laborers were already tooling up the production lines for jet aircraft, A-4 rockets, and the Luftwaffe's V-1 flying bombs. At the Volkswagen's works, mass production of the flying bomb had at last begun in January, and the missile was now functioning flawlessly—covering 175 miles or more with barely any deviation in its Peenemünde trials. On March 5, Milch gleefully urged Hitler to begin the flying-bomb attack on England on April 20—Hitler's birthday—sending off fifteen hundred in the next ten days and the rest in May. "It will be the most evil torture you can imagine, just picture for yourselves a large high-explosive bomb falling on Berlin every half-hour and nobody knowing where the next will fall! Twenty days of that will have them all folding at the knees!"

Hitler, however, delayed the flying-bomb attack. Not until mid-May did he make up his mind on a date. Perhaps he had wanted all the "revenge" weapons to open fire simultaneously—A-4 rocket, flying bomb, "high-pressure pump," and Krupp's "Gustav" long-range guns, coupled with a saturation attack on London by the Third Air Force. He also wanted the attack to coincide with the Allied invasion. But the A-4 rocket was still far from ready. In January only 50, in February only 86 A-4s had left the underground Central Works—far short of the target figures. (In May, General Dornberger, chief of the rocket project, wryly reported: "Our main problem is getting the missiles to the target in one piece"; most of them were blowing up in midair. Of the 57 test-launched from the SS proving ground in Poland by mid-March, only 26 lifted off, and only 4 reached the target area intact.) In Speer's absence, loud criticism was voiced against this costly if spectacular weapon. The OKW pointed out that liquid-oxygen output alone would limit the rate of fire to about 25 A-4s a day. Even Saur, Speer's closest adviser, recommended on March 5 that Hitler consider converting the Central Works factory from A-4 assembly to fighter-aircraft manufacture: the tunnels were big enough to house a plant turning out a thousand planes a month. Hitler appeared to agree, but someone changed his mind again—perhaps it was Speer himself, whom Hitler visited two weeks later bearing a bouquet of flowers on the minister's thirty-ninth birthday. Or perhaps Himmler—by now a daily visitor to Hitler—may have tendered this advice.

Göring and Ribbentrop now counted for little in Hitler's esteem. He took to summoning low-ranking officers to the Berghof, knowing he could trust them to speak out openly. For several days he interviewed soldiers from platoon right up to divisional rank about the fighting at Anzio. They told him of the crushing enemy artillery superiority, of the slime and filth, of the inferior German radio gear and faulty hand-grenades. (As a consequence, Hitler ordered Kesselring to apply the lessons of 1918 trench warfare to Anzio; remorseless pressure must be put on the enemy by the long-forgotten techniques of storm-regiments and artillery bombardment.) A panzer general, Gerd von Schwerin, later described one such reception at the Berghof that March. Schmundt—who first privately expressed doubts as to whether Hitler's constant interference on the battlefield was really salutary—ushered him in. "I couldn't help feeling that while Hitler was trying to be sincere, his mind was elsewhere." Outside, Schwerin met Göring and Himmler, and he related how the Russians had kept their notorious wet-weather offensives rolling by rounding up thousands of women and making each one wade ten miles through the slime to the front lines with a shell on her back.

Schmundt, the general reported, told him laughingly that "nobody takes Göring seriously any more." Beside Bormann, the new force in Hitler's life was undeniably Grand Admiral Karl Dönitz. It was the admiral who had cajoled Hitler into preventing the earlier withdrawal of Army Group North to the Panther line (with grim consequences for Küchler's troops). It was Dönitz too who had demanded the retention of the Crimea. And now that Hitler's health was poor, it was Dönitz whom he sent to preside over the Memorial Day parade in Berlin and to address the ten thousand new officer-candidates in Breslau.

Ribbentrop was deeply wounded by Hitler's loss of faith in him and privately made an offer to Hitler which showed that he certainly made up in personal courage whatever he might lack in diplomacy. As Walter Schellenberg, chief of Himmler's foreign Intelligence service, later wrote:

Ribbentrop told me he was very familiar with my special reports on Russia, and he had given the whole situation much thought. He had then gone to the Führer and told him frankly that their biggest and most dangerous enemy was the Soviet Union and that Stalin had as much military ability and statesmanship as Churchill and Roosevelt put together, if not more. The Führer shared this view and even mused out loud that Stalin was the only one he could find the necessary respect for, if one day he was going to reach a compromise peace with somebody after all. But he—Ribbentrop—had then put to the Führer the idea that everything possible should be done to liquidate Stalin, as the Soviet regime would then no longer be able to withstand the burdens of the war. Therefore he [Ribbentrop] had announced to the Führer his willingness to sacrifice his own life, if he could save Germany thereby. His plan was to do all he could to lure Stalin once more to the conference table; then he would gun him down. For a long time the Führer had turned this over in his mind, and then finally replied, "No. I don't like anything like that. It would be asking for trouble from Providence."[4]

---

[4] I have relied on Schellenberg's own handwritten text, rather than on the heavily "edited" published *Memoirs*.

At the end of February the Turkish foreign minister had confidentially warned Germany that unless the eastern front could be stabilized before the Russians crossed the Dniester River, the Balkans would disintegrate and Germany would eventually lose the war; Turkey would have to declare war too, if only to save her own skin.

The upshot was Hitler's dramatic meeting with Admiral Horthy, the Hungarian regent, on March 18. Hitler had reacted to Italy's defection in September by ordering contingency plans for the armed occupation of Romania and Hungary (code-named "Margarethe I" and "II") should either Antonescu or Horthy follow Badoglio's example. Antonescu had sworn continued loyalty, and Hitler believed him. Horthy, however, was something else. Hungary had not only refused formal recognition to the new Mussolini government, but had accepted legations from *both* the Badoglio and the Fascist regimes; and she had noisily demanded the return of her nine light divisions policing the rear areas on the Russian front—most recently in a letter from Horthy dated February 12—maintaining that she needed them for the defense of her own mountain frontier, the Carpathians, against the Red Army. In February, Ribbentrop received a long secret service report proving that Hungary was clandestinely dealing with the enemy. In mid-March Himmler learned from agents in Budapest that Prime Minister Kállay was advocating the sabotage of German military trains running through Hungary to Manstein's and Kleist's army groups. In short, the circumstances were almost identical to the situation in Italy the previous summer.

Originally, "Margarethe I" projected using Slovak, Croat, and Romanian troops as well as Germans for the invasion of Hungary. On March 8 Hitler selected Sunday the nineteenth as the invasion date but decided—probably on Kaltenbrunner's advice—to use only German troops; use of the hated satellites would provoke Hungarian resistance and destroy economic stability. Moreover, an attempt to secure Horthy's agreement to German demands would be made first; in particular Kállay's government must be replaced by an unambiguously pro-German one, under Béla von Imrédy for example. Göring believed Horthy would comply, but Hitler evidently did not. The OKW order for "Margarethe I" was issued on the eleventh; if the Hungarians did resist the German invasion, their army was to be disarmed and the ringleaders shot.

On March 15, after a fresh meeting with Himmler and Ribbentrop, Horthy was sent a loaded invitation to present himself at Klessheim castle near Salzburg in two or three days' time. Since Hitler offered in the invitation to deal with the military points raised in Horthy's letter of February 12—which he explained he had been unable to answer earlier because of illness—Horthy would probably bring his military chiefs with him; thus Hungary would be leaderless if "Margarethe" did result in a pitched battle. Horthy agreed to come with his generals on the eighteenth. On the day before, Hitler plotted with Ribbentrop, Jodl, and

Himmler the precise scenario for the confrontation: the regent's train would arrive at ten-thirty, and the talks would begin half an hour later. Every word spoken would be monitored by hidden microphones and recorded on disks in the castle's control room.[5] At twelve-thirty there would probably be a break for lunch; this would enable Hitler to decide whether or not the Hungarians would have to be disarmed. "If Horthy permits the invasion and there is no resistance, then we defer decision on disarming and demobilizing them," Jodl wrote in his diary. This time Hitler would accept no "lame excuses" from the slippery regent of Hungary.

Sure enough, Horthy objected next morning to the presence of Hitler's regular interpreter and insisted on talking with him in German and in complete privacy —or so he thought. Even so, the actual sequence of events is clouded by uncertainty; the disks must be presumed destroyed. Eyewitnesses saw Horthy suddenly burst out of Hitler's room, red-faced and protesting loudly, before vanishing into his own quarters, with Hitler hard on his heels in an attempt to preserve at least a semblance of protocol. Hitler had told him bluntly that he "was taking steps" to ensure he was not caught unawares by Hungarian treachery: he had insisted that Kállay be replaced by Imrédy as prime minister, and he had decided to send twelve divisions into Hungary to "assist" the new government; he demanded that Hungary's entire economy be geared to the war effort and that her numerous divisions mobilized against the Romanian frontier be sent to the Russian front instead. When Horthy lamely replied that then Hungary would be bombed just as Germany was being bombed, Hitler retorted, "This harsh certainty is better than any amount of uncertainty." Hitler hinted that the Romanians, Slovaks, and Croats would join the invasion—a particularly hateful prospect for the proud Hungarians. Believing perhaps that Hitler was still bluffing, Horthy had then charged out of the meeting room, exclaiming, "If it's all been decided already, there's no point in my staying!" At a given signal from Hitler, the air raid sirens sounded and a smoke screen was laid across the castle; Horthy was told that his train could not leave in the middle of an air raid. After lunch with Himmler and the generals, Hitler inquired loudly of Keitel whether the invasion could be postponed; Keitel replied that the troops were already on the move and could not be recalled.

Thus Horthy was left with an ultimatum calling for his consent to the invasion. The alternative was not spelled out, but it was clear to him that he had been ambushed. Toward 8 P.M. he accepted—a climb-down for which Hitler was

---

[5]"He's a cunning rogue," Hitler had told Zeitzler after the April 1943 meeting with Horthy. "Yesterday, I got him to agree to everything I wanted, in private. And today he comes back and says, 'You know, I'm very hard of hearing. It seems I only understood half of what you were saying yesterday.' "

totally unprepared. Evidently Ribbentrop's plain speaking to the Hungarian envoy Döme Sztójay in another room resulted in this volte-face. Horthy cabled coded instructions to his Cabinet in Budapest to permit the invasion. Hitler's only concession had been to agree not to occupy Budapest itself, apart from a "guard of honor" for Horthy. Now wreathed in smiles, the Führer conducted the aged regent to his train at nine o'clock; it was the last time he was to see him. The all clear had sounded. On Austrian soil, the train was unaccountably halted for several hours—since Hitler maintained telephone contact with SS General Kaltenbrunner, who was on the train, it appears that Horthy's safe return was dependent on his Cabinet's honoring the agreement. Four battle groups invaded Hungary concentrically at 4 A.M. No blood was shed, and now all Hungary— with its oil and vital raw materials—was in Hitler's hands. At the Citadel, Horthy's official residence, a German guard of honor, immaculate and ominous, was awaiting him when he arrived at eleven.

This, Hitler's last conquest, was truly an outstanding coup. Strategically, the cost of "Margarethe" had been high: the divisions had been subtracted from the Anzio battlefield and virtually every other front. But Hungary's industrial potential was well worth the cost. That very night of March 18, Hitler sent for Saur and instructed him to harness Hungarian industry to the war effort at once. The lower echelons of the Hungarian forces actually welcomed the invasion. Eventually the Hungarian contingent on the Russian front was doubled. Marshal Antonescu could also increase the Romanian contingent, now that he need no longer fear war with Hungary. Even so, it took a long time to dispel Hitler's doubts about Hungary. Field Marshal von Weichs, Commander in Chief Southeast, whose headquarters now transferred to Budapest, wrote after seeing Hitler on March 28: "The Führer mistrusts the Hungarians and particularly hates the regent, who no doubt equally loathes Germany. The links with the enemy powers still exist. Her defection is still to be reckoned with, a colossal danger for the eastern front. Thus as few Hungarians as possible are to be under arms, though it will be impossible to disarm the army completely."

Two other totally unrelated but interesting scenes took place that same Sunday, March 19, 1944, as German troops rolled into Hungary. The Führer sent his favorite secretary, Gerda Christian, to take flowers and champagne to his other secretary, Christa Schroeder, lying gravely ill in the hospital on her birthday; and he wrote her a rare handwritten letter of encouragement. The invalid was the most querulous member of his staff, but she was so touched that she wrote him an emotional reply and even promised to *give up smoking*—a minor triumph for the Führer, but a pleasing one. Hitler read her letter aloud to his fireside circle.

That same day Hitler had conferred at the Berghof with his leading field marshals—Rundstedt, Rommel, Kleist, Busch, and Manstein. Rundstedt stepped forward and read to an impassive Führer the declaration of personal loyalty all the field marshals had now signed; the field marshal then handed the document to him. Thus Seydlitz and his ilk were cast from the ranks (they were tried *in absentia* some weeks later, and condemned to death). The next day Hitler delivered to all the leading generals of the western front an unusually uninspiring and pallid speech. Salmuth, commanding the Fifteenth Army, was shocked at Hitler's personal appearance. "To my horror, it was an old, stooping man with an unhealthy, puffy face who came into the room. He looked downright worn-out, weary—I would even say ill." He spoke distantly of the new jet aircraft and submarines, without stating precisely *when* they would arrive. He warned the generals to be on guard against enemy parachute drops in the rear. The rest was a combination of rambling remarks and solecisms. "At tea afterward I sat at the Führer's round table," wrote Salmuth, "next to Rundstedt who was in a foul temper." Hitler conferred alone with Rommel—although the latter was technically Rundstedt's subordinate—and announced afterward that he was also giving Rommel control of the First and Nineteenth armies, as well as greater influence over the motorized divisions which were Rundstedt's only tactical reserve. Rundstedt saw little point in being Commander in Chief West, but stayed nonetheless. Now it was Rommel who was the optimist. "We have the utmost confidence that we'll get by, in the west," he wrote privately. Hitler had warned the generals, as the shorthand record of his speech shows, that he believed the enemy would establish their main beachhead in either Normandy or Brittany.

The Allied bombing of German cities continued, and now Budapest as well was the target of American bomber raids. When the Russians tried and executed as war criminals certain German officers—primarily from the SS—Hitler decided it was time to follow suit. On March 23 he told Hewel: "British and American war criminals must also be condemned to death and their confessions must also be publicized after their execution." Allied airmen accused of machine-gunning civilians, for example, were to be put on trial; he also wanted to punish captured American airmen who labeled their bombers "Murder Incorporated." Jodl suggested that since the enemy automatically executed all German agents, they should do the same with the plainclothes British and American agents and saboteurs who had fallen into their net in Hungary—some five hundred already, according to Kaltenbrunner. "The Führer mentioned that some had special assignments to murder and spread bacilli epidemics," Hewel noted.

On the night of March 24 the British again poured nearly twenty-five hundred tons of high explosives and incendiary bombs onto Berlin—though this time they lost over seventy bombers. No Geneva Convention protected the war's civilians;

the urge to punish the bomber crews was powerful, yet there was no legal way around the convention protecting prisoners of war. When the next morning Himmler announced at the Berghof that eighty Allied airmen had just escaped from a Wehrmacht prison camp at Sagan, and spoke of the millions of manhours the manhunt would cost, Hitler impulsively ordered all the escapees recaptured to be turned over to the secret police. "Himmler, you are not to let the escaped airmen out of your control!" (Jodl later claimed there was no word of "executions," just of "turning them over" to the SS; but Bodenschatz remembered Hitler asking those concerned to stay behind to see him after the war conference.) Fifty of the escapees were shot on Himmler's orders.

Many of Hitler's ministers wanted all captured bomber crews executed for attacking civilian centers—especially Ribbentrop. During May 1944, the enemy began machine-gunning civilian targets; Bormann initiated a campaign for Party officials and school teachers to advise the public, and school children in particular, on how to take cover when Allied fighters approached. Hitler asked Göring to select isolated cases of such machine-gunning and—where an accused airman fell into German hands—execute him. Jodl's staff suggested oral instructions be given to the commandant of the prisoner-collecting camp at Oberursel to turn such airmen over to the SD for "special treatment," but the technical problems —particularly of identification—proved insuperable. Kaltenbrunner had no such airmen in his cells. Keitel was opposed both to a regularized "lynch law" and to normal court-martial procedure. Göring, mindful of the hundreds of Luftwaffe airmen in enemy hands, suggested that clear cases of murder could be dealt with by the proper courts. The foreign ministry pointed out that the Geneva Convention required a three-month stay of execution of death sentences on prisoners of war. By this time it was late June 1944, and Hitler had more pressing problems on his mind.

By late March 1944 a seemingly irreconcilable difference emerged between Hitler and Manstein. At his noon conference on March 25, the field marshal was fighting for permission to withdraw General Hube's encircled First Panzer Army to the northwest before a second Stalingrad resulted.

Hitler insisted that Hube retain his existing battlefront between the Dniester and Tarnopol—a town he now declared a "fortified area." (He had just introduced this new fortress-like concept for key coastal towns in the west. They were to be commanded by tough, handpicked army generals who would not lose their nerve or honor when the enemy tide swept past their strongholds.) But Manstein said this would be impossible and demanded reinforcements for General Erich Raus's Fourth Panzer Army, whose task would be to mount a relief attack toward Hube's force; these reinforcements, suggested Manstein, could easily be spared from the armies which had occupied Hungary and from the western front. Hitler was adamant. "I can't release any strength to you so long as I have to reckon with an invasion in the west." He blamed Manstein for the present dilemma of the First Panzer Army: Manstein had tolerated one withdrawal after another, although Göring had reported that his troops were being put to flight by only a handful of Soviet tanks. Insulted by these remarks, Manstein told Schmundt afterward that he was quite ready to lay down his command. At that evening's conference, Hitler agreed to give him the reinforcements he wanted from Hungary, and the Second SS Panzer Korps from the west. With these units Raus's Fourth Panzer Army began its relief offensive on April 5, and the First Panzer Army fought its way out of the ring. It was the high point on the eastern front that spring; but Manstein was no longer in command.

Field Marshal von Kleist had followed him to the Berghof on March 27 to plead for the withdrawal of his Army Group A. Shortly after he had left, Hitler told General Zeitzler: "I have decided to release Manstein and Kleist." Zeitzler recognized from his tone of voice that arguing was no use; he asked to be relieved of office too, and when Hitler refused, he sent around an adjutant with a formal letter of resignation. Hitler sent for the Chief of Staff and rebuked him: "A general cannot resign."

The Führer sent his plane to fetch the two field marshals back to the Berghof on March 30. Probably Göring and Himmler lay behind Manstein's dismissal. Some weeks earlier General Scherff, Hitler's court historian, had warned a war correspondent not to mention Manstein by name in future dispatches; and a recent study of the field marshal in the Nazi weekly *Das Reich* had probably upset Hitler too. The famous Manstein interruption during Hitler's January speech to the generals was a further provocation. But when he told Manstein that evening, before the main conference, that what the southern front needed was a new name, a new slogan, and a commander expert in defensive strategy—he meant Model, who had just halted the rout in the north—he was probably speaking the truth. There was no bitterness between them. Hitler told an adjutant long afterward that should he ever come to mount great offensives again, Manstein would be their first commander; and in the autumn he donated a great estate to him. Manstein had after all been the only general to speak out for the Sedan breakthrough strategy in 1940—and that, Hitler reminisced now that he had steeled himself to sever their partnership, was something he would not easily forget.

Model and Kleist's successor, General Ferdinand Schörner—a Party faithful and personal nominee of Heinrich Himmler—were already waiting outside. Hitler offered Manstein his hand. The field marshal took it and said, "I hope for your sake your decision today turns out right for you."

The Most Reviled

Thus the Ukraine was lost—the fertile countryside for which Hitler had invaded Russia. The German invaders had been driven out by the Soviet armies and—not least—by the disappointed, deceived, and angry Ukrainians themselves. "If the rest of this war and its victorious conclusion should ever see these territories vouchsafed to us again," a Gauleiter wrote, "then there must be a radical change in our attitude to and treatment of the native population." Erich Koch had achieved the seemingly impossible in one year: converting the forty million Ukrainians who had greeted the German invaders with garlands and lauded them as their liberators from the hated Bolshevik yoke into a sullen, seething people, driven as partisans into the forests and swamplands of the north Ukraine.

In the early weeks of the Russian campaign, when Hitler's fifth Blitzkrieg victory seemed likely, Koch's brutal sledgehammer policies were arguably best suited to produce the maximum effect in the shortest time. But as one ugly surprise after another confronted Hitler that year, the same critical Gauleiter quoted above—Alfred Frauenfeld, governor of the Crimea—now pointed out that Hitler should have found the moral courage to replace Koch by someone with more elastic policies. It was not enough to draw on Britain's "brutal colonial policies" as an excuse. Koch had proclaimed the serfdom and inferiority of the Slavs with such raucous insistence that "even a disaster policy deliberately planned and paid for by the enemy could hardly have done more harm." Koch had frequently stormed, for example: "If I find a Ukrainian fit to sit at my table, I must shoot him!" Koch had closed down the schools laboriously reopened by the Wehrmacht, robbed the farmers of their last cows, dispensed with Ukrainian doctors and vets alike—without reflecting that diseases and epidemics were no respecters of the German occupation forces—and deported the able-bodied to Germany in a manner reminiscent of "Arab slave traders." When Hitler had instituted medals for bravery and hard work, Koch had waited nearly a year before unwillingly issuing any to the Ukrainians. In mid-April Koch was described to Himmler as looking like "an alcoholic on his last legs"—his face a pasty bluish-white, lined and pock-marked from one ear to the other. "He is incapable of orderly debate. Even the soberest instruction throws him into a rage, and he rejects it with a volley of oaths."

How far Hitler still sympathized with his raucous Gauleiter is uncertain. But his determination to *reconquer* these lost Russian territories—a prize glittering at the end of the coming bloody year—remained undimmed. He told the trusted Marshal Antonescu in March and Karl-Otto Saur in April that once the invasion threat had passed—either gloriously defeated by Rundstedt and Rommel or exposed as a shameless fraud—he would bring back his victorious armies from France to the eastern front and deliver the knockout blow. Instinct and intuition, those twin insidious sources of comfort to the Führer, assured him the Red Army was almost exhausted; he said as much to Kleist on March 30, when the dismissed army group commander advised him to make peace with Stalin. On April 8, a grim battle began to rage in the Crimea. Hitler would not relinquish his goal. In spite of Zeitzler's appeal that "thousands of German soldiers in the Crimea will be lost if you don't act now," Hitler refused to order their evacuation. "One thousand more or less are of no consequence." Manstein, inspired by Hitler's speech of March 19, shared this view; he admitted to Admiral Dönitz: "Perhaps the Führer is *right* in not yielding one foot of ground voluntarily." Antonescu, moved by Hitler's arguments, agreed that the Crimea must be held.

Hitler told his adjutants he would never let history reproach him for losing faith in final victory just when it was almost within his grasp—as had happened to Germany in November 1918. New secret weapons, new armies, were on the way. For the reconquest of Russia in 1945 he would need tanks and self-propelled assault guns above all. "The air force can't win wars," Saur told the Fighter Staff after a long talk with Hitler on April 7. "Its job is to protect the tank production lines and keep them working. The Russian campaign can only be ended with tanks. That's why the Führer said yesterday, 'If this tank production program is realized, then it will win the war for us.' But the prerequisite for this is that our Luftwaffe production targets are met one hundred percent, so that we can keep the enemy at bay and the tank factories rolling." Saur promised to increase aircraft production fivefold during 1944. A big new factory would be built in Hungary, turning out five hundred new fighters a month.

When Admiral Dönitz attempted on April 13 to obtain production priority for certain naval items, Hitler flatly refused. "Tanks and assault guns are my lifeblood too, but nonetheless we've got to put up a fighter umbrella over the Reich first of all. That is the alpha and omega of it."

He asked Göring what had become of the underground factories Speer's ministry had been ordered to build the previous autumn, and when Göring gave no satisfactory answer Hitler instructed Xaver Dorsch, chief of the Todt Organization, to present himself at the Berghof the next day. Dorsch pointed out that his organization did not operate within the Reich frontiers—the factories were the responsibility of Speer's own construction chief, Carl Stobbe-Dethleffsen. Hitler angrily retorted, "I've had enough of these petty squabbles! I want the Todt Organization to build the factories—at once!" The six-month-old blueprints were fetched from Berlin; Hitler passed them at once and ordained that in the future, Dorsch's organization was to construct all the major building projects in the Reich. Dorsch was embarrassed at this rebuff to his absent chief, Speer, and—after Bormann and the two obligatory stenographers had been asked to withdraw—he pointed out that it was Reichsminister Speer's will that the Todt Organization should not function within the Reich frontiers but only in the occupied countries. Hitler was unrepentant. On April 16 he ordered Dorsch to build ten mushroom-type bombproof hangars for the fighter squadrons, and a bombproof aircraft factory, the first of its kind, near Landsberg in Bavaria. Göring undertook to place the Luftwaffe's construction organization at Dorsch's disposal too. On Hitler's instructions, Göring summoned all the construction experts—except Speer and Stobbe-Dethleffsen—on the nineteenth. "I will brook no further delays," Hitler had told him.

Speer's reaction to this organized dismantling of his empire was immediate. On April 19 a voluminous and pained letter arrived at the Berghof, and its bearer—one of the minister's staff—orally added that Speer was minded to resign all his offices, a threat he had not however included in his letter. Speer's hypnotic command tended to dissipate in his absence. While it was unquestionably Speer who had achieved the production miracles—typified most sensationally by the launching on April 17 and 19 of Dönitz's first two Mark XXI U-boats six months ahead of schedule—it was Saur and Dorsch who were the frequent Berghof visitors, while Speer took a leisurely five-month convalescence in the Tyrol mountains. And it was Saur who stood beside the Führer as the brand-new armor rumbled past him at Klessheim castle on his birthday, April 20—the outstanding new 38-ton pursuit tank, and Vomag's heavy, fast, low-profiled hunter-killer tank, with its ultralong 75-millimeter gun. Once these birthday presents were in mass production, Hitler planned to turn the tide of battle on the eastern front decisively in Germany's favor. But that afternoon Field Marshal Milch begged him not to let Speer go, and he asked for some message of comfort with which to repair the minister's injured vanity. Hitler drummed his fingers absently on the windows, then curtly answered, *"Jawohl, gut!* Tell Speer from me that I am very fond of him. Is that enough?"

———

Milch returned from the Tyrol the next day, but Hitler was too grieved to notice him. That afternoon, he had received General Hube at the Berghof, decorated him for his First Panzer Army's magnificent fighting escape from the Soviet encirclement, and promoted him to four-star general. Hitler had mentioned to Schmundt and the other adjutants the previous evening the possibility that he would soon appoint the one-armed general Commander in Chief of the army. Hube had asked permission to fly back to Berlin that night for personal reasons; Hitler had agreed, although the general's pilot lacked night-flying experience. Now he regretted it, for the Junkers had flown into a mountain outside Salzburg. Hube was dead and the jovial Walther Hewel had received terrible burns and injuries.

A melancholy Führer welcomed Speer on the Berghof steps on April 24. Speer charmed him away from his previous designs; having realized that Xaver Dorsch now had Hitler's fullest confidence, Speer himself proposed making him overall director of Reich construction work—*inside* his ministry. Hitler told him to do as he thought best. It was the same with the A-4 projectile. On the twenty-fifth General Korten, the Luftwaffe's Chief of Staff, added his authority to the long-standing appeal by Saur, Milch, and Göring's technical adjutant, Colonel Ulrich Diesing, for A-4 production to shut down in favor of fighter—and now tank—production. ("We won't see the A-4 this year," Milch predicted.) Hitler refused. In the pilotless bombardment of England he saw an important means of striking at the morale of the enemy invasion troops—weren't his own soldiers in Russia sick with worry when the British bombed their home towns? Rommel—the only surviving candidate for army Commander in Chief now that Hube was dead—emphasized this psychological element of the battle that might now begin with any dawn. "The big air raids here probably mean the invasion preparations have already begun," wrote Rommel privately on the twenty-sixth. "Here at the front the damage is slight so far, and it's good that our troops get accustomed to this saturation bombardment. Morale in Britain is rock-bottom, one strike after another, the screams of 'down with Churchill and the Jews' and cries for peace are growing louder. Bad omens for such a risky offensive. . . ."

Before considering Rommel's preparations to meet the Allied invasion, we must first investigate what was for Hitler the most disturbing event of that spring —the premature and seemingly unnecessary loss of the Crimea. On April 10 the Sixth Army had been forced to abandon Odessa, the port through which the navy had been keeping General Jaenecke's beleaguered Seventeenth Army in the Crimea supplied; but the roots of the catastrophe went back much further—some would say to the "Crimea psychosis" induced by Jaenecke's furtive attempt to abandon the peninsula as early as October. Thereafter, both army and navy commanders in the Black Sea had contrived to keep Hitler, and even their own superiors, in the dark about developments. Thus, Zeitzler had sincerely assured Hitler that Nikolaev, the Russian naval dockyard, was in no danger—it was, in fact, overrun two days later. And Kleist had informed Hitler on March 27 that Admiral Helmuth Brinkmann had ordered the evacuation of the naval base at Odessa two weeks earlier—an arbitrary act of which even Dönitz was unaware when Hitler furiously telephoned him. Hitler had to resign himself to the loss of Odessa itself, consoled by the thought that at least there would be time for the demolition of its dockyards and the mining of its approaches. He dismissed Kleist three days later.

With General Schörner's appointment to Kleist's command, renamed Army Group South-Ukraine—a provocative hint at Hitler's undiminished plans of conquest—a fresh spirit swept through the troops. Schörner's Crimean orders were harsh and his methods unorthodox. He lured one Romanian division after another into the German lines and "intermarried" them irrevocably with German units so that Antonescu could not withdraw them if he wished. Now that the Seventeenth Army had fallen back on Sevastopol, the fortress harbor at the southern end of the Crimean peninsula, he ordered any troops abandoning their positions shot for cowardice; if Russian tanks—and over five hundred had poured through the breaches into the peninsula—broke through these last positions, they were to be knocked out in the rear and the lines themselves repaired. Any soldier destroying an enemy tank with a bazooka was to get an immediate three-week mainland leave.

Dönitz predicted that the loss of Odessa by Kleist's army group would make the eventual loss of the Crimea inevitable. Though the Seventeenth Army had enough food and ammunition to hold out for many months, the navy would then be able to ferry only about thirty thousand tons a month from Constanta, in Romania, to Sevastopol. Operating from Odessa, the Russians—ignoring the German minefields—would be in a position to interrupt the lighter coastal traffic; in addition, the route from Constanta to Sevastopol was far longer.

On April 3, Zeitzler confidentially informed the OKW that Odessa could not be held, but that lower echelons were not yet to be told; this time Dönitz and Hitler did learn in advance. Indeed, Zeitzler subsequently used Dönitz's own memorandum on the importance of Odessa for the Crimea to support his own argument for the peninsula's immediate evacuation. Dönitz responded pathetically that only the Führer could take in the whole strategic situation and that as soon as the invasion of France had been thwarted, the lost territories in Russia would be reconquered. Zeitzler rejoined that 180,000 troops were at risk in the Crimea—troops urgently needed for the defense of the South Ukraine and of Romania herself.

In spite of the points made in his earlier memorandum, Dönitz advised Hitler to hang on to the Crimea even if Odessa was lost. He telephoned the Berghof on April 8, emphasizing that the Seventeenth Army had supplies for a siege of five of six months. Recalling his own World War I experiences, he now argued that the Russians were unlikely to disrupt the German supply operations from Odessa and Nikolaev. Two days later, however, General Jaenecke ordered the evacuation of the Crimea to begin. He was acting on his own responsibility again, though with Schörner's subsequent approval, since a hundred Russian tanks were pouring southward following the collapse of the Romanian 10th Infantry Division on the northern front. But again Hitler had not been informed, and again he canceled Jaenecke's order—calling instead for an evacuation of the Kerch peninsula while the northern front was repaired.

But events were now moving faster than Hitler's orders, and the breach was too wide to repair. Even as Hitler was telephoning Dönitz that evening that not until the next day would he reach a decision on whether or not to abandon the Crimea, Jaenecke was informing the navy that his army was already in full flight toward Sevastopol. When the navy in turn put this startling news to General Jodl, he replied it was not an OKW concern—the Russian front was Zeitzler's affair. Hitler issued the only order possible on the twelfth—all nonessential personnel were to be evacuated from the Crimea. He added, however: "I have decided to hold on to the Sevastopol battlefield itself as long as humanly possible, to tie as many enemy forces as possible to that front." He feared that the loss of Odessa—which would bring Russian naval strength back to the western Black Sea again—and of the Crimea had already caused irreparable damage to Germany's political position. To stave off these effects, he ordered the army and navy to rush antitank guns, ammunition, bazookas, and above all food to Sevastopol. Dönitz promised that his navy would make every sacrifice necessary to keep the fortress provisioned, and he at least kept his word.

However, the effect of the Crimean debacle on Turkey was immediate. On April 20 she bowed to mounting Allied pressure, announced that she was no longer neutral but a pro-Allied country, and would cease the vital chrome deliveries to Germany within ten days. Privately the Turkish foreign minister apologized to Germany that his country had been threatened with war by Russia and with blockade by the Allies. It was a language Hitler fully understood, having employed it himself in more propitious circumstances.

Several days passed before the Russians began their all-out assault on Sevastopol—days during which they rebuilt the airfields and brought 27 divisions and some 200 tanks into position along the fortress's twenty-two-mile perimeter. Dönitz had evacuated 100,000 pioneers and nonessential troops to Constanta, leaving perhaps 35,000 manning the front line and 90,000 more in the rear—an imbalance which was the object of Hitler's later criticism. Their material position seemed hopeless: in the precipitous retreat into the fortress, Jaenecke had lost most of his army's guns and ammunition. He had 81 pieces of artillery, 36 antitank guns, and 9 tanks; their ammunition was low. Neither he nor his naval counterpart, Admiral Brinkmann, believed the siege could be withstood for long. Hitler disagreed: he ordered the war ministry to rush guns and ammunition to Sevastopol. Zeitzler even asked for Field Marshal Milch to be put in charge—for there were many similarities with Stalingrad. Hitler, however, left Zeitzler and his logistics generals in command, and this was a fatal error, for again they proved unequal to the task—whether it was premeditated treachery or incompetence we cannot tell.[1] At all events, Zeitzler shortly complained to Hitler that the navy's ships docking at Sevastopol to evacuate the prisoners, injured and "useless eaters," were arriving *empty* instead of bringing the army supplies Hitler had ordered; Hitler's inquiries revealed that those supplies had still not reached Constanta, so it was not the navy's fault. Dönitz now changed his tune, since he feared that a "sudden crisis" in the fortress might result in an equally sudden demand for the navy to evacuate its entire garrison in an impossibly short time. On April 24 he telegraphed to the Berghof—to put himself on record thus: "The Commander in Chief, navy, has never adjudged [whether Sevastopol could be held or not]; this is the army's concern alone." *Privately* he now accepted Zeitzler's view that the garrison was doomed; but the Führer must decide—the Führer must have his reasons for hanging on to Sevastopol.

Hitler in fact feared that the loss of Sevastopol would actually bring Turkey into the war and set off a similar chain-reaction in the other neutral lands. On April 25, Dönitz's two local commanders personally assured him at the Berghof that sufficient supplies for a hundred thousand troops could be convoyed to Sevastopol—provided they arrived at Constanta. Only Jaenecke spoke out against Hitler's decision to keep fighting; and even then his tongue failed him at the Berghof on April 29, and he had to speak his real mind in a carping five-page letter to Hitler the next day. He blamed Kleist's tactical errors for the loss of the Crimea; the imminent Soviet assault on the Seventeenth Army was bound to succeed. "Would it not be better to snatch this prey, over which the Bolsheviks are already crowing, from under their very noses and transfer the forces to Army Group South-Ukraine?" It was a tempting argument, but Hitler was a realist. The Sevastopol troops would arrive dispirited, exhausted, and virtually unarmed— useless as reinforcements for the main front; on the other hand, the twenty-seven Russian divisions presently besieging the fortress could immediately be thrown

---

[1] Both Eduard Wagner, the quartermaster general, and Zeitzler's general of artillery, Fritz Lindemann, were conspiring against Hitler; Hitler's adjutants particularly suspected Lindemann of active treason over the Crimea.

against the main front. The Führer had no use for an army general who could not see that, and he dismissed Jaenecke from his command. General Kurt All-mendinger replaced him. Some days later, Hitler ordered Jaenecke court-mar-tialed in order to establish just why the fertile Crimea peninsula had been lost with such staggering speed.

The throttling of Germany's only chrome supplies put a time bomb under Hitler's strategy, though the fuse was longer than he at first feared: the OKW calculated that the Reich's chrome stocks—vital for the high-grade steels needed for Hitler's tank production—would last another eighteen months.

Parallel to this uncertainty about the war, or perhaps because of it, his health was worsening. His tremor was so pronounced by early May 1944 that his left leg shook uncontrollably even when he was in bed. While the Föhn mountain wind did not affect him, the incessant snow, sleet, and rain did. He needed Morell, but the portly doctor was unsettled by the rarefied air and lived down in Berchtes-gaden itself, ascending the fifteen hundred feet to the Berghof only for two hours each midday. For weeks on end the whole mountainside was swathed several times a day in acrid smoke screens as enemy bombers approached, until Morell imagined he was suffocating and had to summon doctors to attend to himself. His Berlin assistant, Dr. Richard Weber, had to tend to Hitler; the jealous Morell would not trust his patient or consultation notes to either Dr. Brandt or his deputy, Dr. Hanskarl von Hasselbach.

Morell's consultation notes on two typical sessions with Hitler, on May 4 and 5, 1944, show that the Führer was no easy patient. Hitler's stomach spasms had returned. Morell had prescribed massage; Hitler had previously refused, and now refused again. The doctor advised an early retirement each night, but Hitler was already resting ten hours a day, and he refused to go to bed earlier. "That is impossible because of the British air raids!" He would not retire until the last bomber left German territory. Again Morell advised him to imbibe less liquid, less than two pints a day. "Fortunately drinking and smoking are not involved," he noted; in view of Hitler's heart condition he advised him to gulp down some coffee or take Cardiazol if he felt unwell suddenly, and meanwhile he ought to try breathing pure oxygen two or three times a day. He administered intravenous injections of glucose and of Testoviron—a sex hormone produced by a reputable Berlin firm.[2] In the following weeks he also injected Septo-Iodine, a recognized treatment for respiratory infections and heart condition, varying doses of Glyco-

[2]Hitler startled his secretaries by making sudden sexual allusions—completely out of character. When they told Morell, he smirked, and explained he had just given the Chief these injections.

norm and liver-extract, his own proprietary Vitamultin-Calcium preparation, and Tonophosphan, a tonic for Hitler's nerves and muscles. Hitler also continued to consume quantities of Dr. Koester's antigas pills. It was an incredible volume of medication for an intelligent man to submit to, but Hitler preferred it to the alternatives—spasms, fatigue, time-wasting exercise, and massage.

Since early April 1944 he had expected to be awakened in his ice-cold Berghof bedroom one morning with word that the Anglo-American invasion had begun. From December to April he had half hoped that the invasion clamor in the enemy newspapers was just bluff. "The whole show the British are putting on looks suspiciously like a charade to me," he had opined hopefully on April 6. "These latest reports of censorship and security measures over there—you don't go doing that if you are *really* up to something." Keitel had agreed: "No, you keep your mouth shut!" "I can't help feeling the whole thing will turn out to be a shameless charade," repeated Hitler.

This conformed with his estimate of the Allies' fighting ability—Kesselring was keeping them at bay in Italy with "his little finger," as Hitler put it. Enemy bomber superiority made no impact on German troops; in Italy, they had only slit-trenches for cover from the bombardment—but the Atlantic Wall fortifications were covered with concrete up to twenty feet thick. To thwart attempted airborne landings, Hitler had ordered virtually the entire light antiaircraft defenses of the Reich concentrated in France. He and Rommel were confident that the invasion—assuming it ever came—would end in disaster for the Allies. "From day to day we are growing stronger," Rommel wrote on May 6. "My inventions are coming into action. Thus I am looking forward to the battle with the profoundest confidence—it might be on May 15, or perhaps not until the end of the month."

Only the date was uncertain. While Rommel and Rundstedt believed the enemy would land on either side of the Somme estuary and thrust by the shortest route toward Paris, Hitler had long been convinced that the enemy's main invasion would occur far to the west—either in Normandy or Brittany—so that the Cherbourg peninsula could be made into a strategic bridgehead. He had said as much on March 4 and again to the western generals in his speech on March 20; he confidently repeated it to Antonescu on the twenty-third; he adhered to his opinion staunchly, despite the avalanche of contrary Intelligence reports from Foreign Armies West. "I am for bringing all our strength in here," he said on April 6, tapping the Normandy coastline on the charts; "particularly the forces we don't absolutely have to have anywhere else." As soon as Hube's army had fought itself free of the encirclement in Russia, Hitler ordered the crack "Das Reich" Division moved into Normandy. Rundstedt's and Rommel's papers reveal with what obstinacy they clung to their different appreciation of Eisen-hower's intent. But on May 1 both of them were sharply reminded by Jodl's staff that Hitler expected the invasion in the Seventh Army's area, not the Fifteenth's; and on May 6, Hitler was again to have Jodl telephone Rundstedt's Chief of Staff that he "attached particular importance to Normandy."

In western Europe, a violent air assault on communications had begun—bridges, railway lines, locomotives, passenger trains, and canals were the targets. The French people suffered sorely: American aircraft killed 400 Frenchmen in Rouen on April 24 alone. Laval besought Hitler to try once more to win the French around to a combined defense of France, but Hitler—confident that another "Dieppe" fiasco was awaiting the Allies—refused to pay the price Laval de-manded. The night bombing of Germany had temporarily ended in a clear victory for Göring's night fighters and the antiaircraft defenses.

Late on April 30, Saur telephoned Hitler with the latest tank and aircraft production figures; despite the almost total destruction of the factories in Febru-ary and March, in April they had manufactured 1,859 new fighters and over 1,500 armored fighting vehicles. Hitler used the word "magnificent" in his reply. That his armaments workers were willing to work seventy-two hours a week indicated that morale was still high. Germany just had to hold out until the great East-West clash occurred—history books assured him that most great coalitions fell apart before five years were over. The bones of contention were already there: the oil of the Middle East, Russian aims in the North Sea, Soviet expansion toward India, the latent feud between Britain and the United States. "America is quietly and without much ado skinning Britain alive, pawning her into penury," he chuckled to Mussolini. "If we just sit tight and hold on without flinching, the big break between Britain and America is bound to come one day." When the British realize that the Americans are after their world position "then some Englishman *must* stand up against it." Politically, time was on Germany's side. What Hitler feared most was that he personally might not live to see the final victory—or that some military landslide might occur to snatch the political victory from his people's grasp.

With totally unexpected swiftness, the Russian armies now stormed and pene-trated the Sevastopol fortress on the Crimea and wrote the end to the chapter Manstein had begun there so brilliantly two years before. The assault began on May 5. By late on the seventh, Schörner telegraphed to Zeitzler that the Seven-teenth Army had lost 2,795 men; he was flying in all available reserves, 220-millimeter howitzer assault-guns, and heavy antitank guns, but few had yet reached the Black Sea from Germany; 120 heavy antitank guns had been promised to the army, but 40 were still en route by air to Constanta and the rest held up in railway transports on the Hungarian-Romanian frontier. Late on the eighth, Hitler conceded defeat and ordered the Seventeenth Army brought out by sea and air from Sevastopol—officers were to enforce order during the evacuation by the use of firearms if necessary. Only 37,500 German and Romanian troops were brought to the Romanian mainland before the enemy overran the last pocket of resistance five days later.

Hitler was furious at this fiasco. To shame the army, he ordered Zeitzler to transport these salvaged remnants of an army back to Germany, as they were fit only to work in the arms industry; as soldiers they were failures. Schörner—reporting to Hitler through the Reichsführer SS as well as through Zeitzler—bitterly blamed Kleist, his predecessor: the field marshal had allowed discipline to rot, his noncombat troops had worked a pleasant six- or seven-hour day, and the wines of the Crimea had done the rest. He praised Antonescu, but not the Romanian General Staff. Himmler told Hitler that in Schörner's view "radical solutions" were called for in Romania, *i.e.,* rooting out everybody—and particularly General Erich Hansen, the feckless German military attaché in Bucharest —except Antonescu himself. But Antonescu valued Hansen, so Hitler knew he could not recall him. Schörner's subordinates meanwhile demanded that the navy's Black Sea admirals—whom Dönitz now caused to be decorated with high medals—be court-martialed. Angry Seventeenth Army officers complained of navy cowardice; bloody and filthy from the carnage of Sevastopol, they had disembarked at Constanta and found naval officers in spotless uniforms sunning themselves, indifferent to whether their ships ran the gauntlet of the Russian defenses or whether they offered lame excuses for returning empty. But the real culprits were in the German General Staff, who had failed to supply the guns and ammunition fast enough. In the five-week battle for the Crimea, over seventy-five thousand Germans and Romanians paid for this failure with their lives.

An unnatural calm fell upon the whole eastern front until late June.

Parallel to the expanded tank output, Hitler still wanted a sizeable bomber production. The impact of the American raids on German industry and transport was an example of what the Luftwaffe should be capable of in the east. The Luftwaffe had executed its first hesitant strategic bombing raids in June 1943, when T34 tank factories, oil refineries, and ball-bearing plants in Gorki and Saratov were attacked on several nights running with great success. When General Karl Koller, a Bavarian, became chief of the Luftwaffe operations staff in September, he reassigned the Fourth Air Corps under General Rudolf Meister; its mission was to destroy Stalin's seven key electric-power stations. But in

February 1944 Hitler intervened and called on Meister to retrain his crews for a methodical attack on the Red Army's rear communications—bridges, railway junctions, and marshaling yards; as it happened, by April few worthwhile Russian industrial targets could be reached from airfields still in Luftwaffe hands.

Saur's fighter production program also made great inroads into the bomber factories. In February, March, and April the reeling aircraft industry had produced 567, 605, and 680 bombers, respectively. But the Fighter Staff's new program would cut the target to 550 bombers a month, which would support only 40 squadrons; this meant that eleven others would have to be disbanded. And if an even more radical plan was adopted, only 284 bombers would be assembled every month; this would mean that after October there would be sufficient support for only 26 squadrons. General Korten, Chief of the Air Staff, described this plan as the death of the bomber arm. Koller highlighted this danger in a report to Hitler on May 5 and on the nineteenth followed it with a persuasive study of the bomber strength needed to maintain German hegemony in Europe. At a conference with Göring on May 22, Hitler dismissed the planned targets as quite unacceptable, and the next day the Reichsmarschall announced to the Fighter Staff that he wanted an armada of at least twenty-six hundred bombers—which would require the manufacture of over eight hundred a month, including the four-engined Heinkel 177—in addition to nearly seven thousand fighter aircraft. Göring also gave Hitler a progress report on the Me-262 jet (unaware that three prototypes had crashed over the last few days for no apparent reason). Hitler—who was partly relying on these jet bombers to defeat the invasion—congratulated him. "Now they'll get there on time!" But a rude shock awaited him almost immediately.

It was May 23. Field Marshal von Richthofen had come up from Italy, where a troublesome enemy offensive had begun at Cassino on the twelfth—a patent attempt to lure German reserves and Luftwaffe units away from France; and that very morning a more serious thrust had begun from the Anzio beachhead. Richthofen wrote in his diary: "3 P.M. with the Führer. He's grown older, good-looking, very calm, very definite views on the military and political situation, no worries about anything. Again and again one can't help feeling this is a man blindly following his summons, walking unhesitatingly along the path prescribed to him without the slightest doubt as to its rightness and the final outcome. . . . The unpleasant military occurrences at Cassino and—since this morning—at the [Anzio] beachhead are contemplated by him quite calmly: as he puts it, we can be thankful that we are still fighting so far down. After all, last September we all thought, and he did too, that this summer would see us fighting in the Apennines or even in the Alps." Time was on their side, Hitler reminded the Luttwaffe commander; politically, Germany had won the war long ago.

At this moment Göring, Milch, Saur, and the aircraft specialists were ushered into the Great Hall. Hitler wanted to examine their aircraft production targets in person. He gazed out of the great picture window, listening absently, as the Fighter Staff's program figures were read out. When the Me-262 jet-fighter production was mentioned, he interrupted, "Jet *fighter?* I thought the 262 was coming as a high-speed bomber?" This, after all, was the order he had given last autumn. Milch replied, "For the time being it is being manufactured as a fighter!" Hitler persisted: "How many of the 262s already manufactured *can* carry bombs?" "None, mein Führer. The Me-262 is being manufactured exclusively as a fighter aircraft." An awkward silence followed, and then Milch explained that to carry a thousand-kilo bomb the jet would require an extensively strengthened airframe and undercarriage; the first one hundred being built were designed exclusively as fighters. Hitler lost his composure. The wonder aircraft on which —perhaps unrealistically—he had reposed his hopes of disrupting the invasion was not even being built. "Never mind!" he interrupted. "I only want one two-hundred-fifty-kilo bomb!" The aircraft was so fast that it needed neither cannon nor armorplate, noted Hitler. How much did they weigh? ("Who pays the slightest attention to the orders I give?" he complained. "I gave an unqualified order and left nobody in any doubt that the aircraft was to be fitted as a fighter-*bomber.*") Saur said the cannon, armor, and ammunition weighed over five hundred kilos. "Then it can all be taken out!" said Hitler triumphantly. Colonel Edgar Petersen, the chief of the Luftwaffe experimental station at Rechlin, nodded. "That can be done without any difficulty." In desperation Milch appealed to Hitler to think again, but he was subjected to a torrent of abuse. "Mein Führer," exclaimed the field marshal, "the smallest infant can see this is a fighter, not a bomber aircraft!" Hitler turned his back on him for the rest of the discussion. *"Aufschlagbrand!"* —crashed in flames!—whispered somebody: the reference was to Milch's career.

Hitler ordered the Me-262 to be manufactured solely as a high-speed bomber now. But there was a snag. Göring came the next day and confessed that his engineers had reminded him that the armor and cannon were all *forward* of the plane's center of gravity; to alter this would mean a major redesigning job, perhaps even changing the position of the wings. Because of the production pipeline, it would take five months to effect any change. "You gentlemen appear to be stone-deaf," Göring had raged at the Luftwaffe engineers on his return from the Berghof. "The lot of you! I referred again and again to the Führer's order. He doesn't care two hoots about getting the Me-262 as a fighter, but wants it only as a bomber. . . . And now suddenly it is impossible! The Führer says, 'For all I care you can put the fighters on a bonfire.' He wants an aircraft which can force its way through by virtue of its sheer speed, despite the enormous mass of fighters that will be guarding the invasion forces. What no civilian dares to do—simply ignore orders—you gentlemen dare time after time after time." In a further meeting, Hitler permitted the testing of the Me-262 fighter version to continue, but only the bomber version was to enter service as yet—attacking the enemy's embarkation movements on the far side of the English Channel, from a few thousand feet up, or bombing the disembarking mass of tanks and troops swarming around the invasion beaches. The Reichsmarschall personally promised that none of his staff would "go behind his back" again.

At Klessheim castle in March 1944, Horthy had assented to Hitler's demand that Hungary turn over her Jews to Germany. Working from Budapest, a task force under SS Colonel Adolf Eichmann deported four hundred thousand Jews over the next four months.

The motives of Hitler and Himmler still diverged, though the Führer's attitude had noticeably hardened. Hitler was primarily concerned that this potential Fifth Column be removed from the Balkans and was callous about their subsequent fate; but Himmler—however much he protested that he was not just "bloodthirsty"—was eager to see what he called an "uncompromising," an irrevocable, and above all a Final Solution. When Hitler instructed him in April to provide two 100,000-strong contingents of Hungarian Jews to work on Saur's bombproof tank and fighter factories in the Protectorate and elsewhere, the Reichsführer SS expressed unconcealed displeasure at this "singular" arrangement. But on May 24, Himmler assured an audience of generals: "Not one of them will in any way cross the German public's field of vision."

As part of the Nazi indoctrination project, during the spring he and Hitler separately made several secret speeches to groups of generals. Hitler's speech of April 26 has not survived. But Himmler's talk on May 5 to an audience including General Hans-Jürgen Stumpff and Hermann Reinecke (and a member of Hitler's own staff, Admiral Hans-Erich Voss) has: it was taken down by stenographers, stylistically improved, and like most of his main speeches retyped on a large-face "Führer" typewriter. Since only carbon copies are left in Himmler's files, Hitler *may* have been sent the top copies of each of Himmler's speeches. In theory he might therefore have found the passage in Himmler's seventy-page speech of October 6, 1943, where he bluntly disclosed to Albert Speer and the Gauleiters that he, Himmler, had decided to murder Jewish women and children as well as adult males. ("I took the decision that a clear-cut solution had to be found here too.") On May 5, 1944, however, Himmler tried a new version—or adapted it to his audience of generals. After revealing in now stereotyped sentences that he had "uncompromisingly" solved the "Jewish problem" in Germany and the German-occupied countries, he added: "I am telling this to you as my comrades. We are all soldiers regardless of which uniform we wear. You can imagine how I felt executing this soldierly order issued to me, but I obediently complied and carried it out to the best of my convictions." Never before, and never after, did Himmler hint at a *Führer* Order; but there is reason to doubt he dared show this passage to his Führer.[3]

Consider too Himmler's speech of May 24, in which again speaking before generals he explained his stance somewhat differently. He recalled how in 1933 and 1934 he had thrown habitual criminals into concentration camps without trial, and boasted, "I must admit I have committed many such illegal acts in my time. But rest assured of this: I have resorted to these only when I felt that sound common-sense and the inner justice of a Germanic—and right-thinking—people were on my side." With this in mind Himmler had confronted the "Jewish problem" too: "It was solved uncompromisingly—on orders and at the dictate of sound common-sense." One page later, Himmler's speech again hinted that Jewish women and children were also being liquidated.[4] The fact remains that in his personal meetings with Hitler, the Reichsführer continued to talk only of the "expulsion" [*Aussiedlung*] of the Jews, even as late as July 1944.

When the same generals came to the Obersalzberg on May 26, Hitler spoke to them in terms that were both more philosophical and less ambiguous. He spoke of the intolerance of nature, he compared Man to the smallest bacillus on the planet Earth, he reminded them how by expelling the Jews from their privileged positions he had opened up those same positions to the children of hundreds of thousands of ordinary working-class Germans and deprived the revolutionary masses of their traditional Jewish ferment:

> Of course, people can say, "Yes, but couldn't you have got out of it . . . more humanely?" My dear generals, we are fighting a battle of life and death. If our enemies are victorious in this struggle, the German people will be extirpated. The Bolsheviks will butcher millions upon millions of our intellectuals. Those who escape the bullet in the nape of the neck will be deported. The children of the upper classes will be taken away and got rid of. This entire bestiality has been organized by Jews. Today incendiary and other bombs are dropped on our cities although the enemy knows he is hitting just women and children. They are machine-gunning ordinary railroad trains, or farmers working in their fields. In one night in a city like Hamburg we lost over forty thousand women and children, burned to death. Expect nothing else from me, but that I do just what I think best suits the national interest and in the manner best serving the German nation.
>
> *(Prolonged loud applause.)*

Kindness here as indeed anywhere else would be just about the greatest

---

[3]Page 28 of the large-face typescript, containing this pregnant sentence—for only Hitler was empowered to issue a "soldierly order" to Himmler—was manifestly retyped and inserted in the transcript at a later date, as the different indenting shows.

[4]This page alone was also retyped and possibly inserted at a later date in the typescript.

cruelty to our own people. If the Jews are going to hate me, then at least I want to take advantage of that hatred.

(Murmurs of approval.)

The advantage is this: now we have a cleanly organized nation, in which no outsider can interfere.

Look at the other countries . . . Hungary! The entire country subverted and rotten, Jews everywhere, Jews and still more Jews right up to the highest level, and the whole country covered by a continuous network of agents and spies waiting for the moment to strike, but fearing to do so in case a premature move on their part drew us in. Here too I intervened, and this problem is now going to be solved too. If I may say this: the Jews had as their program the extirpation [*Ausrottung*] of the German people. On September 1, 1939, I announced in the Reichstag, if any man believes he can extirpate the German nation in a world war, he is wrong; if Jewry really tries that, then the one that will be extirpated is Jewry itself.

(Spirited applause.)

In Auschwitz, the defunct paraphernalia of death—idle since late 1943—began to clank again as the first trainloads from Hungary arrived.

An oppressive uncertainty lay across the Obersalzberg. The invasion had still not come. On May 24, General Korten, the Luftwaffe's Chief of Staff, told Göring: "The invasion appears to have been postponed, otherwise we wouldn't be having these big [American] air raids on the Reich again." And Speer, who had now finally returned from sick leave, echoed this optimism. "If nothing has happened by July or August we can assume we will be left in peace all winter." The German command was even uncertain as to whether the invasion, when and if it came, would begin when dawn coincided with a high tide in France, or two hours after *low* tide as a recent Allied invasion exercise suggested. Rommel's fiendish underwater fangs along the possible invasion beaches relied on the former assumption. The field marshal was still confident, however. "Everything is going very well indeed and just as planned," he wrote on May 19. "Two days ago I telephoned the Führer for the first time. He was in the best of spirits and did not stint his praise for the job we have done in the west. I hope now to get on faster than ever. The weather meanwhile is still cold and at last it's raining. The British will just have to be patient a while." To his son Rommel wrote a shade more realistically. "These last months and weeks we have achieved the impossible, but we are still not as ready as I would have liked: more mines, even deeper submerged obstacles, better antiparatroop defenses, even more artillery, antiaircraft guns, mortars, and rockets!! So far their heavy bombing of the Atlantic Wall has not had much effect; damage and casualties have been slight."

It was time to begin wheeling the secret weapons out from under their elaborate camouflage. But what remained of them? Hitler had been deceived over the Me-262—Göring now told him that three and perhaps even six months would be needed before the bomber version reached the squadrons. The A-4 rocket had overcome its worst problems but would not be operational until September. The aircraft industry had delayed far too long over Hitler's recent demand for the 50-millimeter cannon—originally designed for tanks—to be installed in twin-engined fighters. The huge underground gun battery built near Calais for shelling London was ready, but the gun barrels themselves were still far from trouble-free —and the specially designed projectiles were still not capable of the necessary range. Only the Luftwaffe's pilotless flying bomb was standing by—its original ninety-six launching sites in France were admittedly in ruins, but these were only decoys now; still undetected by Allied aerial reconnaissance, the real catapults were well-concealed and awaiting last-minute assembly in a belt of countryside farther back. With these, Hitler assured Mussolini, he would "turn London into a garden of ruins" the moment the invasion began. (He also hinted that German chemists had developed a poison gas—in fact the first nerve gases—against which even German gas masks afforded no protection.)

In mid-May the Führer ordered the flying-bomb offensive to start with an all-out attack on London one night in mid-June, coupled with a fire-raising attack by Sperrle's bomber squadrons; thereafter, intermittent salvos were to be fired night after night—and by day too if bad weather hampered the British defenses. "Panic will break out in England," Hitler gloatingly told his private staff. "These flying bombs have such an unnerving effect that nobody can stand them very long. I am going to pay those barbarians back for machine-gunning our women and children and sacking our culture!" On about June 4 he decided that it was time to begin, and the flying-bomb regiment was instructed that by the tenth its prefabricated catapult equipment was to be moved from the hidden dumps up to the launching sites. In this way he would force the enemy's hand, he hoped: public outcry would leave Churchill no alternative but to launch a premature and hence disastrous invasion of France. "If the British came to us now with any kind of peace feelers," Hitler told Slovakia's Prime Minister Josef Tiso: "I would prefer to tell them to keep their feelers—until after the invasion." With the invasion defeated, he would revert to the conquest of Russia.

Hitler doubted that the invasion was imminent, but the waiting irritated him. He allowed Admiral Dönitz to go on leave on June 1 for the first time since war began. Rommel wrote with a trace of nervousness on May 29: "The nonstop Anglo-American bombardment is admittedly continuing. The French are suffering particularly cruelly—three thousand civilian dead these last forty-eight hours alone, while our own casualties are mostly low. Many decoy sites are being bombed."

In Italy, now that the Anzio forces had linked up with the main battlefront Rome itself could well become a battlefield, just as Stalingrad had. This produced another instance of Hitler's strange conception of morality. The same Führer who was indifferent to the fate of defenseless Jewish children was piously proud to have defeated Belgium without defiling Brussels, and France without attacking Paris—his enemies, it was noted, had just bombed the Rouen cathedral and attacked, quite pointlessly, the famous monastery at Monte Cassino. As early as February Hitler had turned down Kesselring's suggestion that in an emergency the Tiber bridges in Rome should be destroyed, as the river's steep embankments would check the most determined enemy's advance. In fact Hitler had reiterated that Rome's status as an "open city" must be strictly preserved. While he could jest to Mussolini: "You and I are the most reviled men in the world," he did not want to go into history as the man who caused Rome to be destroyed. Therefore, Wehrmacht troops had been forbidden to set foot there without special passes, and even during the fiercest fighting at Anzio all military transports had been tediously diverted around the outskirts of Rome.

This forbearance brought no Allied response. When Kesselring formally suggested to the enemy, through the Vatican, on June 3, that both sides continue to respect the "open city," they made no reply but instead appealed to the city's populace to join the battle. Sir Henry Wilson, the Supreme Allied Commander in the Mediterranean, broadcast the falsehood that the Germans were defending Rome, and the British and American tanks speedily penetrated to its very heart the next day. To impede further pursuit of his withdrawing army, Hitler should now have blown up the bridges, but he did not. Late the next evening, June 5, Roosevelt broadcast news of the victory. He attributed to the skill of his generals the fact that Rome had escaped damage.

It was after midnight when Hitler went to bed. The last Luftwaffe reconnaissance of southeastern England, a week before, had shown hardly any landing craft assembled at Dover—facing the Dunkirk-Dieppe coastline, where the latest saturation air raids led both Rommel and Rundstedt to believe that the invasion might eventually occur. The rest of Britain's south coast had eluded the Luftwaffe reconnaissance. Luftwaffe meteorologists forecast several days of poor weather. Thus Hitler did not suspect that five thousand vessels laden with the enemy were at that very moment bearing down upon the coast of France.

PART 5

THE WORMS TURN

Man with a Yellow Leather Briefcase

During the night the news of the parachute and glider landings in Normandy hardened, and ships' engines were heard offshore. But the Führer was not awakened; his adjutants consulted with Jodl, who pointed out that the situation would not clear up until daybreak anyway. It followed from this that until the full situation was put to him at the midday war conference, Hitler took no decision on the—increasingly frantic—appeals by Rundstedt to release the OKW panzer reserves to counterattack. By that time wave after wave of landing craft had disgorged tanks and men onto the landing beaches after annihilating naval and air bombardments, and the Seventh Army admitted that the Allies had already established west of the Orne River a beachhead some fifteen miles wide and two miles deep inland.

Thus by the time Hitler's war conference began, the Battle of France was already lost—if Rommel's dictum about the necessity for defeating the enemy on the very beaches had meant anything. The events of the next days disclosed that the movements of any German reserves by day were impossible, so overwhelming was the enemy's air superiority. That the enemy had not been defeated on the beaches was due in part to the weakness of the Atlantic Wall in Normandy—despite all Hitler's warnings since February 1944, the Wall was only 18 percent complete in the Seventh Army's sector, compared with 68 percent in the Channel sector commanded by Salmuth's Fifteenth Army—and in part to the sluggishness of German Intelligence, which had accurate evidence that the invasion would occur on June 6 or 7 but failed to alert all the echelons concerned—in particular General Friedrich Dollmann's Seventh Army.

Hitler subsequently ordered an investigation of this renewed Intelligence failure, which had resulted in Rommel leaving his French headquarters for Germany on the fourth, Dollmann being absent on a map exercise at Rennes, and Sepp Dietrich being in Brussels. Working in conjunction with the SS, the Abwehr in France had since early 1944 penetrated numerous Resistance "cells" in France;

637

thus they had learned that two lines of a Paul Verlaine poem broadcast by the BBC's French service would be the invasion-alert. On June 1 the first line was heard for the first time: *les sanglots longs des violons de l'automne.* This, Intelligence knew, indicated that the invasion was due in the first half of the month. At 9:15 P.M. on the fifth the BBC broadcast the second line: *blessent mon coeur d'une langueur monotone.* This was the prearranged signal for the Resistance to start sabotage operations for an invasion beginning within forty-eight hours of midnight. Salmuth's radio operators picked this up and alerted every lower echelon as well as the HQ of Army Group B—where Speidel was acting in Rommel's absence. Rundstedt's headquarters also subsequently claimed to have intercepted the signal and warned "all echelons concerned." But for some reason neither the OKW, nor the Berghof, nor the Seventh Army was warned—and it was Dollmann's army, in Normandy, that took the blow. This is all the more inexplicable as German Intelligence in Paris had analyzed the BBC secret messages—125 invasion-alerts were transmitted on the afternoon of June 1 alone—and found that nearly all 28 that were transmitted to cells penetrated by the Germans were in the Normandy–Brittany area. The results of Hitler's investigation are not known; the noisy tread of history approaching soon took his thoughts elsewhere, and if the culprits were either Colonel Georg Hansen, Canaris's successor as chief of military Intelligence, or Colonel Alexis von Roenne, chief of Foreign Armies West, both were shortly executed in another context.

Far more serious was the incorrect estimate of initial Allied strength in England. Hitler's last information was that 90 divisions and 22 brigades were under arms in the British Isles; the real number of divisions available for invasion operations was only 37. There is strong evidence that since early 1944 Zeitzler's faltering Intelligence branches had begun deliberately inventing "ghost" enemy divisions to frighten some common sense into Hitler; more recently a well-laid British deception campaign had fed substance into these phantoms—with success beyond the wildest dreams of the British, because throughout June Hitler dared not throw everything he had in France into the Normandy battle in case the enemy's "other" invasion army then appeared elsewhere. Thus while on D-Day morning Rundstedt cautiously adjudged the Normandy operation to be "quite serious after all," as the enemy's employment of three airborne divisions and paratroops at the root of the Cherbourg peninsula showed, his morning telegrams to Hitler stressed that he could not yet say with certainty whether this was the real invasion or only a decoy. Hitler released the meager OKW panzer reserves—two divisions—at about 2:30 P.M.; Rundstedt was instructed to destroy the beachhead by nightfall, as more Allied airborne and amphibious troops were probably on their way.

It is easy to smirk now, but this was the prevailing mood. Hitler and his generals were overconfident. In his unpublished memoirs, the Fifteenth Army's commander, General Hans von Salmuth, wrote of that invasion morning: "At 6 A.M., since it had been daylight for an hour and a half, I had my Chief of Staff telephone Seventh Army again to ask if the enemy had landed anywhere yet. The reply was, 'Fleets of troop transports and warships big and small are lying at various points offshore, with masses of landing craft. But so far no landing has yet taken place.' Thereupon I went back to sleep with a calm mind, after telling my Chief of Staff '—So their invasion has miscarried already!' " According to a manservant, Hitler's mood was equally cocky. "The news couldn't be better," was how he welcomed Keitel that morning. "As long as they were in Britain we couldn't get at them. Now we have them where we can destroy them." And to Göring: "They are landing here—and here: just where we expected them!"

The Luftwaffe High Command remained optimistic throughout the day. Although they too had been caught napping in France—in spite of the fact that a master plan drawn up in February and constantly updated since, had provided for nineteen squadrons of fighters to be rushed to the west the moment the invasion started—Göring and Korten, his Chief of Staff, retained their composure. On that sixth of June the Luftwaffe could raise only 319 sorties over France, compared with the enemy's 10,585, and only *12* fighter-bomber sorties were flown into the beachhead area itself (in which 10 of the pilots released their bombs prematurely); but the Luftwaffe assured Hitler that within three days they would reach maximum strength. On June 7, Richthofen wrote: "The Channel fighting is still assessed very optimistically by the Luftwaffe High Command."

Not until June 8 was Göring's optimism damped. By that evening he had only five ground-attack aircraft and ninety-five fighters operational against the invasion. He had eight hundred crews available for fighter squadrons, but not enough aircraft. The Allies' total air supremacy over the Normandy beachhead was a fact. Since even far inside the German-controlled area all daytime movement of men and materials was impossible, the immediate counterattack by the OKW reserves and the 21st Panzer Division failed. The artillery bombardment by offshore enemy warships guided by spotter planes was so deadly that when Göring announced the formation of a squadron of suicide-pilots willing to fly Focke-Wulf 190s laden with two-ton bombs (since no fuel load would be needed for a return flight) for several days Hitler considered dispatching them against these ships. Dönitz's U-boats could not get near them. General Guderian summed up the situation to Hitler a few days later: "Even the greatest bravery of the tank soldiers can't make up for the defection of two other Services." Gathering his forces, Rundstedt planned to mount an armored counterattack from under an impenetrable "wall of fire" put up by the Third Antiaircraft Corps west of Caen early on the eleventh; but on the evening of the tenth, he had to cancel the attack when an enemy tank assault disrupted the assembling forces, driving them to the defensive.

Thus by June 10 German optimism had evaporated. Dönitz conceded: "The invasion has succeeded. The Second Front has come." Loud recriminations began at the Berghof. When Göring blamed the navy for having assured everybody that the enemy would not risk his capital ships in a Channel invasion and for objecting to the earlier laying of the secret "pressure mines" off the French coast. Dönitz bridled: "Discussion of such matters does not seem opportune at this moment." It was obvious that the enemy planned to capture the deep port of Cherbourg next. If this could not be prevented, warned Rundstedt on June 11, the Führer might be confronted with a situation requiring "fundamental decisions." Rommel echoed this in a letter to Keitel the next day. Hitler now realized that his optimism had been misplaced, and belatedly ordered two high-grade SS panzer divisions (the 9th and 10th)—which had been standing by to attack a minor Russian salient near Kolomea—to entrain immediately for the Normandy front instead. "If I had had the 9th and 10th SS panzer divisions in the west," he grumbled at the end of August, "all this would probably never have happened." With these reinforcements Rundstedt was ordered to destroy the Normandy bridgehead piecemeal.

On the afternoon of June 6, 1944, the OKW had ordered the flying-bomb attack against London to begin. But first six days had to be spent in bringing up the heavy steel catapult rigs from their camouflaged dumps and transporting them to the sixty-four prepared launching sites along the Channel coast. The launching crews exchanged their Todt Organization camouflage for blue-gray Luftwaffe uniforms, and the regiment's command staff moved into its new bunker at Saleux; but on the eleventh it was clear that all was not well, as disastrous Allied bombing of the French road and rail networks had resulted in trains being split, catapult sections being delivered to the wrong sites, and vital components vanishing completely. Despite this—with none of the sites operational—the OKW insisted that day that the attack begin the next night.

How Hitler thirsted for the moment! Here at the Berghof he had joined the rest of Germany in the "front line" of the bombing war. By day he watched the American bomber squadrons glittering high overhead on their way from Italy to targets in southern Germany. By night the British flew the other way into Austria and Hungary, the Obersalzberg sirens driving the entire Berghof staff out the back door to the large steel portals masking the entrance to the tunnels now honeycombing the mountain. Hitler himself was loath to go down the sixty-five steps until the antiaircraft batteries began firing; he stood close to the tunnel exit, taking care that nobody tried to leave before the all clear sounded. Often the red glow of fires burning in Munich could be seen reflected in the skies. His housekeeper had begged him to move his town apartment's contents to somewhere safer, but he had refused. "Frau Winter, we must set an example."

His impatience with Göring's fighter defenses rose with each successful raid. In the raid on Munich on June 9, Eva Braun's close friend, Heini Handschuhmacher, the well-known actor, was killed with his wife. Eva and her women friends returned in tears from the funeral and pathetically described the misery caused by the raids. "Hitler listened with a mournful face," wrote a secretary later, "swore vengeance, and promised that he would repay everything onehundredfold with the Luftwaffe's new inventions."

The flying bomb—shortly christened V-1 by Goebbels—was one of the war's most terrifying weapons: a cheaply built pilotless plane with a one-ton warhead of high explosive, it was propelled so fast by its simple jet device that few modern fighter aircraft could engage it; its engine resonated with a deep organlike growl, awakening the whole countryside over which it passed—its sudden silence being the signal that it was about to impact. Göring proudly took the credit.

On the night of June 12 the flying-bomb attack on London began. The launching sites were still not ready, and the result was a fiasco: of ten V-1s catapulted, four crashed at once, two vanished without trace, one demolished a railway bridge in London, and the other three impacted elsewhere. Now Göring anxiously informed Hitler that Milch—the same field marshal who had deceived them over the Me-262 jet aircraft—was the author of the V-1. Two more days passed while the catapult rigs were properly adjusted. Late on June 15 the offensive was resumed; no fewer than 244 V-1s were launched against London by noon the next day; spotter aircraft reported fires sweeping the British capital.

The new campaign took the British completely by surprise. Though Hitler did not know it, Churchill had to order a complete redistribution of the British antiaircraft and fighter defenses: bombing of the V-1 sites now assumed a priority above the destruction of German cities, aircraft factories, and oil refineries. Göring retracted his earlier statement about the authorship of the weapon; but at 5:35 P.M. on the seventeenth Hitler telephoned Milch to congratulate him in person, and a few days later he jubilantly ordered Speer to throttle back A-4 rocket production to release manpower and materials to increase V-1 and jet-bomber production.

Surely the enemy would now have to launch their "second invasion" force against the Pas de Calais to neutralize this V-1 threat? Both Hitler and Jodl had recognized as early as the twelfth that defeating such a second invasion was now probably the only hope. Besides, the Russians were clearly winding up for a main offensive on the eastern front; war on two fronts, the nightmare Hitler had avoided in 1939, was about to become a reality.

Late on June 16 four Focke-Wulf Condors flew Hitler and his staff to Metz, while the entire fighter force along the route was grounded, and antiaircraft batteries forbidden to fire in order to avoid accidents. After dawn the next morning, while Luftwaffe fighters patroled the highway from Rheims onward, he drove to W2, the Führer's Headquarters built near Soissons, to confer with Rundstedt and Rommel and to congratulate the flying-bomb commander, General Erich Heinemann. The immediate purpose of Hitler's flight was to restore the two field marshals' confidence, shaken by the enemy's success in consolidating his bridgehead at Normandy. By the skillful use of airborne troops, the Americans had torn open the front and were bound to isolate the whole Cherbourg peninsula sooner or later. Hitler appears to have reproached Rommel, and Rommel evidently blamed the poor quality and equipment of the Normandy divisions —with some justice, for throughout the spring, Zeitzler had steadily drained away the best divisions to the eastern front. Hitler was also told of the crushing enemy air superiority.

Two aspects of the coming battle were discussed that day: the coming battle for Cherbourg and a future counterattack by four SS panzer divisions from west of Caen and Falaise—which was Hitler's own proposal. By 10 A.M., Hitler's first order for the defense of Cherbourg had been telephoned by Rommel's Chief of Staff Hans Speidel to the army group HQ. "The fortress Cherbourg is to be held at all costs. . . . A retreat in one stage only will not take place." The German troops were to make a fighting retreat into the fortress, delaying the enemy's advance by obstacles, minefields, and deception, while the time was used to stock up Cherbourg for a long siege and demolish the port facilities—starting immediately—so that the enemy could not use it. Before the SS counterattack, Hitler called for a clear Schwerpunkt in Normandy east of the Orne; this Schwerpunkt was to be established at the expense of the First and Nineteenth armies but not of Salmuth's Fifteenth Army in the Pas de Calais, where Rommel and Rundstedt both expected the "second invasion" to come. The navy and Luftwaffe would be ordered to concentrate on the enemy's warships and shipping tonnage; the new "pressure mines" would be used for the first time. Both field marshals were visibly impressed by Heinemann's report on the V-1 attack: all morning hundreds of enemy bombers had been bombarding the launching sites, though with scant effect. Hitler left Soissons—near the battlefield where as a corporal he had won his Iron Cross a quarter of a century before—late that afternoon.

Back at the Berghof the next evening, the news was that the Americans had, as feared, reached the west coast of the Cherbourg peninsula. At 11 P.M. he said accusingly to Jodl, "They are stating quite bluntly that they've got through. Now, have they or haven't they!" "Jawohl," conceded the general; "they got through."

The convincing details of the coming secret weapons probably account for Rommel's renewed exuberance. His next report exuded optimism again: the enemy had landed twenty-five divisions, but with heavy casualties; the local French population were still overwhelmingly on the German side. Admiral Friedrich Ruge, his naval aide, marveled at Rommel's new faith and surmised in his diary that Hitler must possess "sheer magnetism." Hitler seriously counted on the new secret mines to foil the second invasion; on June 18 he insisted that a barrage also be laid outside Le Havre—"so they can't stage a repeat performance there."

He had also spoken of the Messerschmitt jet bomber. Göring's propellor-driven fighter-bombers were being massacred in France, just as Hitler had feared. During June he closely followed the jet bomber's production progress and studied the photographs of the underground factories being built. General Korten appealed for the immediate appearance of twelve to fifteen Me-262 bombers at the battle front—whether piloted by civilians or officers was immaterial—and for three more to be used, despite Göring's misgivings, as high-speed photographic reconnaissance planes. Production of the Heinkel 177 heavy bomber was to be stepped up as well, with a corresponding cutback in medium-bomber (Junkers 188) production. On June 20, Hitler accepted Speer's proposal that all aircraft production be transferred to his armaments ministry. At last Hitler was taking a more personal interest in the Luftwaffe's equipment.

Since the Russians had overrun Sevastopol, little had occurred in the east. On June 10 they had attacked the Finns, and for several days Hitler had drawn political comfort from the significant failure of the Russians to assist the Normandy invasion by attacking German-held sectors of the eastern front instead. But Stalin would not postpone his summer offensive forever, and the question was, Where would the blow fall?

In May, Hitler had detected an enemy Schwerpunkt only at Kovel, which Model's Army Group North-Ukraine had relieved in April. Model had wanted throughout May to promote an attack here, and the Fifty-sixth Panzer Corps— with virtually all Army Group Center's tanks—had been transferred to him "temporarily" for this purpose. On June 11, however, Hitler canceled the Kovel attack when divisions had to be switched to the Normandy front. The upshot was that of his forty-five original divisions, Field Marshal Busch (Army Group Center) had only thirty-seven left in June to defend an eight hundred-mile perimeter should the Russians now attack it.

Almost complete radio silence had descended on the Russian front. Intuitively, Hitler suspected that Stalin would now go all-out for Army Group Center; the gathering storm-signs that reached him confirmed his view. But throughout May, General Zeitzler's eastern Intelligence expert, Colonel Gehlen, had scented the main Soviet Schwerpunkt opposite Model's Army Group North-Ukraine, consistent with what he called "the Balkans solution"; and even when Russian reinforcements were reported moving northward from there to the center—to Gomel and Smolensk—Gehlen would go no further on June 13 than to suggest that the Red Army might launch an initial attack on Army Group Center as a holding operation, albeit one with far-ranging objectives (even Minsk). The next day, both Zeitzler and his chief of operations, General Heusinger, reemphasized this view: the Soviet Schwerpunkt would for the first time come up against a German Schwerpunkt—Model's army group.

Zeitzler rejected all the conflicting evidence. On June 17, the OKL telephoned him directly to warn of evidence of an imminent Red Army offensive near Smolensk. A captured Russian cipher officer revealed that three corps of fighter planes, including one from the Crimea, had just arrived at Smolensk; over four thousand five hundred aircraft were suddenly confronting Army Group Center. Soviet reinforcements had been moved from Kovel, after the German attack had failed to materialize there, to Gomel and Smolensk, and they were confronting the Ninth and Fourth armies, respectively. On June 18 and 19, Hitler called for the Fourth Air Corps, the last great air reserve in the east, to bomb the Gomel armies, and he refused to transfer the corps to Normandy for minelaying operations for just this reason. As late as June 20, General Zeitzler was still obstinately maintaining that the real Soviet offensive would shortly come against Model's front. Hitler ignored his advice. From the Berghof, the Luftwaffe was informed the next day: "The general appreciation is that the expected attack on Army Group Center begins tomorrow." Once more, toward 2 A.M. on June 22, Hitler personally ordered the Sixth Air Force to stand by on full alert for that attack within the next few hours.

Before we record the catastrophe that now indeed befell Army Group Center, we must look briefly at two of Hitler's concurrent preoccupations—the bombing war and Finland.

On June 21, 2,500 American aircraft had attacked Berlin in broad daylight, releasing over 2,000 tons of bombs on the capital. Forty-four bombers were shot down, and in one of them was found a map revealing that 114 had flown on to Russian airfields in the Ukraine. Hitler ordered General Meister's Fourth Air Corps to raid them there that very night. Two-thirds of the bombers were destroyed and the rest crippled beyond repair. It was a satisfying and sudden end to the American "shuttle-bombing" raids.

Hitler's guest at the Berghof war conferences on June 21 and 22 was his favorite Bavarian general, Dietl, commander of the German Twentieth Army in Lapland. Since February Hitler had been aware of secret Soviet-Finnish armistice talks, but these had collapsed in March as the Russian terms were too harsh. Suspicious that this all-too democratic government might abandon the war at any moment,

Hitler stopped arms deliveries to Finland in April, and when Marshal Mannerheim promised him in May that the weapons would never end up in Russian hands Hitler privately dismissed this "platonic assurance" as quite valueless. Mannerheim's determined resistance to the Russian offensive of June 10 impressed him, however, and two days later Hitler decided: "As long as the Finns keep warring we'll support them; the moment they start jawing, the deliveries will be stopped." He ordered Göring to rush a fighter squadron to Helsinki and Guderian to supply a battalion of assault guns. At the evening conference on June 21 he nonetheless expressed disappointment that Mannerheim had withdrawn his troops so far. Dietl went red in the face, slammed his fist on the red marble map table, and dismissed Hitler's criticisms as typical of a "chairbound general" unencumbered by any expert knowledge of the terrain; he would fly back to Finland and support Mannerheim to the hilt. After the general left the Great Hall, Hitler turned to his gaping staff and exclaimed, "Gentlemen—that's the kind of general I like!"

Dietl and his corps commanders had spent two days listening to speeches by Keitel, Rosenberg, and Himmler at the SS training college at Sonthofen.[1] Himmler's speech—which again may have later been shown to the Führer—covered the familiar ground, though he no longer claimed to be murdering the Jews on *Hitler*'s orders. He conceded that ("at most") fifty thousand Germans were now in concentration camps, including some fifteen thousand political prisoners. He asked for the generals' sympathy in having had to eliminate the Jews: Germany could not have withstood the bombing terror if the Jewish germ had remained, he argued, nor could the front line have been held east of Lemberg (Lvov) if the big Jewish settlements had still existed in that city—or in Cracow, Lublin, and Warsaw. And using the familiar arguments he answered their unspoken question as to why the Jewish children had to be murdered too.

Next afternoon, on June 22, the same generals listened to a secret speech by Hitler on the Obersalzberg, on the nature of war and revolution. The shorthand record has survived in Bormann's files. To frequent storms of applause, the Führer expounded his philosophy that in war as in nature the weakest must go to the wall, and that a nation which failed to recognize this would as surely vanish from the face of the earth as had countless prehistoric species. "Nor can there occur a revolution in the Germany of today. The Jews have gone; and the born

---

[1] Of Keitel's speech on June 20, 1944, we know only that he had optimistically proclaimed that the Red Army would not attack until the Allies had scored major victories in the west and that its Schwerpunkt would lie in the south and not the center. This was not, of course, Hitler's view.

leaders I have already singled out long ago, regardless of their origins, for positions of authority." If any man now turned to the outside world against Germany, then a death sentence would be meted out to him. The generals fiercely applauded Hitler's image of the "little worm" of an infantryman in a slit trench, confronting ten or more Russian tanks with only a grenade in his hands, while democrats at home plotted his country's surrender. "How can one expect the brave little rifleman to die for his country on the battlefield, while at the same moment others at home are doing no less than plotting the betrayal of these men's sacrifices!" When people asked him, "How easy is your conscience now?" he could only respond that he could often not sleep, but that he never for one instant doubted that Germany would survive every danger. "I still have not made my ultimate appeal to the German nation," he reminded the generals, and they responded with frenetic applause and shouts of "Heil!"

The plane carrying Dietl and his generals back to Lapland crashed into the Semmering Mountain a few hours later, killing everybody aboard. Agonized by the fear that this loss might finally prompt Finland's defection, Hitler ordered absolute secrecy about the tragedy until Ribbentrop's mission in Helsinki— securing the Finnish government's unconditional agreement to reject any further Soviet peace proposals—was accomplished. Dietl's generals were quietly buried by the Party in Carinthia; Hitler himself attended the state funeral for Dietl at Salzburg on July 1.

The simultaneous loss of Cherbourg was not only bitter but also a mystery to Hitler. Jodl had spoken well of General Karl Wilhelm von Schlieben, the port's commandant, and Hitler had radioed him on June 21: "I expect you to fight this battle as Gneisenau once fought in the defense of Colberg." But that night the general called for urgent supplies to be airlifted to him, and Hitler caustically commented at the next day's noon conference: "Two years they've had to stock up Cherbourg, yet within two days of being cut off they are already clamoring for air supplies." Only now did he learn that far fewer German troops were in the port than he had supposed—and indeed ordered. Of the 77th Infantry Division only sixty men had arrived; the rest had either been wiped out or—against his orders—broken through the American line to the *south.* The low combat strength of the other divisions derived in part from Hitler's earlier order for every yard of the peninsula to be defended in a fighting retreat. He nonetheless asked some very angry questions of the Seventh Army that afternoon, and the answers supplied to him at the evening conference did not satisfy him. Although Cherbourg had in theory enough food and ammunition for an eight-week siege, its stock of antitank weapons was nonexistent. Rundstedt and Rommel claimed to have warned of this deficiency throughout their area for months.

Hitler considered desperate measures—a counterthrust into the rear of the American corps attacking the port, which Rundstedt rejected out of hand, or an airlift of three thousand paratroops. General Student was willing, but the OKL was not, unless a full moon could be provided. Hitler fumed: "It must be possible to put down three thousand troops in our own territory!" But given the Allied air supremacy, it was not; on June 25, 118 German fighter aircraft set off to support Schlieben, but all were beaten back. That afternoon an Anglo-American battle fleet appeared offshore and began blasting the port. At 7:32 P.M. Schlieben's radio operators faintly broadcast: "The final battle for Cherbourg has begun. General is fighting with his troops. Long live Führer and Germany." Then the sign-off prefix, and "Heil the Führer, Heil Germany!"

Far into the night Hitler debated with General Guderian and General Walter Buhle ways of providing Rundstedt with long-range artillery capable of engaging such enemy battle fleets from the shore. The next afternoon, June 26, Keitel ordered court-martial investigation of the negligence and omissions that had so weakened the Cherbourg garrison; everybody involved from Seventh Army downward was to be examined. Early on June 28, the Seventh Army's commander, Friedrich Dollmann, took poison. Hitler was told the general had died of a heart attack, believed it, and authorized a generous obituary.

"If people now say, 'Look, the British are in Cherbourg,' I reply, 'To you that is the beginning of their reconquest of France, but I look at it differently.' " Thus Hitler pacified his generals. "After all, we already hounded them out of France once; so Cherbourg is just the last ground they still hold. When war broke out, it was not we who were in France, but they . . . and the enemy was barely a hundred miles from Berlin, standing on our eastern frontiers." And in a way it was fortunate that the Germans were now hypnotized by the western front, for the events in the east were far grimmer.

The Russian offensive on June 22 had begun with deceptive mildness: company-strength infantry attacks on Army Group Center left two minor breaches torn temporarily on either side of Vitebsk. Zeitzler had continued to direct Hitler's attention to the apparent threat to Army Groups South- and North-Ukraine. But then great Russian tank formations had appeared, and poured through the breaches, while overwhelming operations by ground-attack squadrons had neutralized the German artillery, the backbone of the defensive system; the Sixth Air Force had only forty fighter aircraft operational that day. A month before, at the Berghof, Hitler had personally briefed Field Marshal Busch, summoned from Army Group Center headquarters at Minsk. He was to hold the present line and in particular defend the "fortified places" of Vitebsk, Orsha, Mogilev, and Bobruisk to the last man. By June 25, however, the Red Army was about to engulf the entire Fourth Army and most of the Ninth; moreover, the sheer scale of the Russian offensive only dawned slowly on the Germans. Believing that disaster could still be staved off, Hitler bluntly refused frantic appeals by Busch and Zeitzler to abandon the "fortified places" while there was still time; thus Busch lost six divisions tied down in their defense. When he came to the Berghof he appealed for Army Group North to be pulled back too, so that strength could be released to his own front. But now that Mannerheim had just pledged Finland's loyalty, Hitler refused to let him down like that. Himmler blamed this "incomprehensible collapse" on Busch. "In my view the army group's command was too soft and war-weary," he wrote on June 26. Hitler evidently agreed, for two days later, as a penalty for failure, he sacked the field marshal.

This was the only remedy he knew in such a desperate situation, and he applied it liberally. Others would follow Busch into the wilderness that same week, and at its end, Hitler—his determination to win through unimpaired—was even his own Chief of General Staff, for General Zeitzler had also disappeared, either sick or sickened by events.

Hostility toward Zeitzler had mounted at the Berghof. Early in May he had formally complained about General Guderian's disparaging comments on the attitude of the General Staff and tendered his resignation—an offer Hitler left temporarily unanswered. Some weeks later Göring slandered Zeitzler in earshot of the Berghof orderlies, remarking on the army's "cowardice." The final clash with Hitler came on June 30, with disaster threatening General Georg Lindemann's Army Group North in the Baltic states. Zeitzler appealed to Hitler to withdraw the army group to the shorter Dvina River line while there was yet time. Busch's successor—Model—and Lindemann supported Zeitzler from afar, but Hitler would not hear of it; to throw Finland into the arms of Stalin would deprive Germany of her last nickel supplies, with grave effects on arms production. "I bear the responsibility, not you," he acidly reminded Zeitzler. Undaunted, Zeitzler told him that now that the the invasion of France had manifestly succeeded, the war could not be won unless the much-publicized "total war" effort became a reality. He suggested the appointment of the Reichsführer SS Himmler as "dictator" to put teeth into the campaign. Total war alone would release the manpower the eastern front now needed. Hitler felt that Zeitzler's nerve had deserted him and commented spitefully on the defeatism of the General Staff.

Zeitzler left without saluting and suffered a complete nervous and physical collapse later that day. Hitler never saw him again. He managed without a Chief of General Staff for the following three weeks.

Rundstedt, the Commander in Chief West, was also a marked man. For several days—following June 26, 1944—Hitler had invited Field Marshal von Kluge as the heir-apparent to sit in on the Berghof war conferences and thus steep himself in Hitler's forced optimism.

He introduced Kluge to the murderous V-1 flying bomb and explained its strategic purpose. The enemy was already forced to keep 250 fighter aircraft on patrol against the V-1s; to add an element of confusion, Hitler had ordered them painted with the same black-and-white stripes as the Allied invasion aircraft. On June 26 he stepped up the V-1 saturation of London, still hoping to force the Allies to stage a disastrous second invasion in the Pas de Calais; and when the OKL suggested filling 250 V-1s a month with an extradestructive aluminized explosive, Trialen, Hitler responded by ordering ten times that number. He was ecstatic that England was suffering again, and by all accounts even worse than in 1940. "The all-out bombing attacks on our catapult sites are sufficient proof of the effectiveness of our weapons!" two officers of the V-1 regiment assured Hitler at the Berghof on June 29. Hitler proudly explained to Kluge that all the shells fired at Paris by Krupp's Big Bertha in World War I contained less explosive than one V-1. "We spare our men and our aircraft.—The V-1 is aircraft and bomb alike, and it needs no fuel for a return flight!" That night the two-thousandth flying bomb was launched against England.

The latest disheartening Intelligence forwarded by Rundstedt from Rommel's headquarters was that about thirty enemy divisions had already landed in Normandy and that at least *sixty-seven more* were standing by in England.[2] This phantom invasion army overshadowed Hitler's conferences at the Berghof that June 29, 1944. It meant that Salmuth's well-appointed Fifteenth Army, covering the Pas de Calais, still could not be weakened. Thus Hitler had to bow to the "painful verdict," as he called it, of Rundstedt and Rommel that no attack could be sprung on the American army in the Cherbourg peninsula, where isolated pockets of German troops were still fighting a fanatical last stand. On this day he finally accepted that Germany was on the defensive in France too. Rommel's primary concern had to be to prevent the enemy from breaking through into France's open countryside toward Paris, and the main counterattack on the beachhead—first proposed by Hitler at Soissons and subsequently enlarged at Guderian's suggestion to include the 2nd Panzer Division and the crack Panzer-Lehr Division as well as the four SS panzer divisions—was doomed to failure unless certain elementary requirements were first met.

These he spelled out on June 29, first to Rundstedt and Rommel and then that

---

[2] Only fifteen divisions were still in England, awaiting shipment to Normandy. It is not clear whether Hitler was being deliberately misled by German anti-Nazis or by the faulty intelligence of General Staff officers.

evening to Dönitz, Göring, and Sperrle, the Third Air Force commander in France. First, the enemy's offshore battle fleet had to be driven off or sunk, and his transport ships had to be prevented from reaching the invasion coast; Hitler proposed saturating the coastal waters with the new secret mines, sowing them with the same "bulldog tenacity" the enemy had shown in bombing the German ground-transport system. "It's far more effective to sink an entire ship's cargo than to have to deal with the troops and equipment piecemeal after they have been unloaded," he pointed out. He recommended the ruthless employment of every weapon available—circling torpedoes, submarines with snorkel breathing-tubes, radio-controlled launches packed with high explosives, and V-1 flying bombs manned by suicide-pilots.[3] The second requirement was for motor transport to match the enemy's immense mobility; if necessary, trucks and buses would have to be ruthlessly requisitioned from the French. Third, no proposed counterattack could survive long without logistics support; Hitler asked the Luftwaffe to establish certain "convoy highways" to the bridgehead, heavily protected by antiaircraft and fighter cover. The fourth requirement was for at least localized air superiority—an armada of fighters and fighter-bombers to keep the enemy bombers at bay.

While Göring called his generals together to examine Hitler's demand for the Luftwaffe to regain air supremacy in the west, Hitler himself asked Keitel to hint to Field Marshal von Rundstedt that he should take an extended leave. How often in later months—right to the end—Hitler bemoaned the fact that he had to occupy himself with even the most trivial matters; the fact that his Commander in Chief West had on his own initiative reached none of these relatively simple decisions was a persuasive argument against appointing a Commander in Chief East as well. Privately, Hitler blamed the women of France and the good food and liquor for softening his armies in the west. Rundstedt had done nothing to prevent this corruption of the Wehrmacht and erosion of its fighting spirit.

Rundstedt's fatalism was powerfully expressed on July 1, when he submitted to the OKW his own view that no counterattack would ever be possible and advised them to give up the bridgehead at Caen—the main enemy Schwerpunkt of attack—and withdraw the remaining front line beyond the range of the enemy ships' artillery. He enclosed a similar appreciation by General Leo Geyr von Schweppenburg, commander of Panzer Group West; Geyr suggested that there was a choice between tactical mending, which left the initiative with the enemy, and elastic warfare, which would give the defenders the initiative for at least some

---

[3]About a thousand V-1s with cockpits built in were found after the war at a depot south of Hamburg.

of the time. Precisely *how* he hoped to fight an elastic war with the panzer divisions immobilized by lack of fuel and motor transport he did not stipulate. Jodl soberly pointed out that the Rundstedt–Geyr proposals would be the first step toward a catastrophic evacuation of France. There were only two choices: either evacuation, or fighting this decisive battle where they stood at the first possible opportunity. Late that day Hitler signaled to Rommel that "the present lines are to be held. Any further enemy breakthrough is to be prevented by tenacious defense or by local counterattacks." Rundstedt was dismissed—Hitler sent one of his army adjutants, Colonel Heinrich Borgmann, to decorate him with the Oak Leaves and hand him the ominous blue envelope in person—and Kluge took his place. Geyr von Schweppenburg was also sacked, and Hitler nearly dismissed Blumentritt, Rundstedt's Chief of Staff, as well. For a time the energetic commander, fresh from the Berghof, brought new inspiration to the defense of France.

Hitler thus learned the hard way that the key to victory lay in the air defenses —just as the British had in 1940. In four months he hoped to recover air supremacy. The measures proposed by Reichsmarschall Göring to his astounded colleagues on the evening after the Führer's Berghof conference on June 29 were revolutionary. In the future only fighter aircraft would be manufactured—this was the "will of the Führer." Anybody disobeying would be stood before a firing squad.

Hitler's final discontent with the bomber arm had begun smoldering on the twentieth, while discussing with Milch and Saur ways of reaching the Me-262 production target of one thousand a month in the shortest time. But his real anger blazed up against the huge twin-engined Heinkel 177 heavy bomber a few days later: it was backward, plagued by faults, and suffered heavy casualties.[4] Its fuel consumption was so high that there was no future for it in a Germany clearly entering upon a crippling fuel crisis as one refinery after another was destroyed by enemy air raids. On June 25, at his midday conference, anguished by General von Schlieben's harrowing last appeals for the promised air support for Cherbourg, Hitler first remarked that mass production of fighters was more important than bomber production now. As for the four-engined version of the Heinkel 177, only now did he learn that the squadrons would not see it before 1946! But by then four-engined propellor-driven bombers would be in museums—rendered

---

[4]On June 27, 1944, General Karl Koller, the OKL chief of operations, was provided with statistics on the Heinkel 177: 179 conventional bombing sorties had been flown in the first four months of 1944, resulting in 26 planes lost. From November 1943 to June 1944, 192 sorties carrying remote-controlled bombs had resulted in 43 planes lost and only 3 destroyers and 5 merchant ships definitely sunk.

obsolete by mass-produced jet fighters like the Me-262. He telephoned Saur and asked him, "How many fighters can I build for one Heinkel 177?" Saur replied that "five thousand workers making two hundred Heinkel 177s a month could produce a thousand fighters more." That settled it. At the next day's war conference, Hitler reiterated: "What matters in our situation is to build fighters and still more fighters—and high-speed bombers too. We've got to get that air umbrella over our home base and our infantrymen! And if that means going without a strategic bomber force for years on end, then so be it!" At a midnight conference with Guderian two days later, Hitler happened to ask the general's Chief of Staff, Colonel Wolfgang Thomale, if he had seen the Luftwaffe in evidence in France that day. "No," the colonel replied. "That is, apart from two fighters between Paris and Chartres."

Such was the background to Hitler's final decision to scrap most bomber production, announced on July 1. General Koller forcefully argued that if only fighters were produced, there would be no minelaying, no guided bombs, no air launching of the V-1, and no Fourth Air Corps operations in the east—their only strategic bombing experiment; moreover, if the enemy began to use poison gas, the Luftwaffe would be powerless to reply. Thus Hitler's ax fell only on the Heinkel 177—but that decision was final. The next day he asked Saur on the phone how fighter production would now rise. "In June we turned out twenty-six hundred single- and twin-engined fighters," came the reply. "In July I hope to top the three thousand mark. In August thirty-three hundred, and then rising three hundred a month to forty-five hundred fighters in December. This will make our total aircraft output eventually sixty-five hundred, of which five thousand will be single- and twin-engined fighter types." As he replaced the receiver, Hitler recognized that the strategic issue was now this: could the bulging, straining battlefronts be kept from the Reich long enough for these figures to be attained? Much would depend on the courage and convictions of his field marshals.

The Führer lectured Kesselring on this when the field marshal came to the Berghof on July 3. After weeks of unremitting, hard-fought retreats, Kesselring had brought the enemy's advance in Italy to a standstill, still some way south of the as yet unfortified Apennine line. Kesselring depicted his plight in Italy—with insufficient troops, air cover, and civilian manpower—vividly. General Koller wrote that day:

> The Führer replied in great detail to all this, and explains just why we have to fight for every square meter of ground—because for us gaining time is everything now. The longer we can hold the enemy off at the periphery the better. Perhaps the individual soldier or NCO may not grasp why he is asked

to fight in the Abruzzi mountains instead of the Apennines, but his Supreme Commander must understand why and comply, because the interests of Germany's fight transcend those of the individual soldier.

Kesselring fears that he will be breached in his present position if he holds it too long, and he wants to fall back on the Apennine line early on. But the Führer wants that postponed as long as possible, as there is nothing else behind the Apennines, and if the enemy gets through there, the entire lowlands of Upper Italy will be lost; nor is that all, because the troops will find their escape cut off by the leapfrogging Allied tank formations. Another reason is that any withdrawal to the north increases the threat to the coasts of Greece, Albania, and Dalmatia.

Turning to the war in the air, the Führer again emphasizes how enormously different the situation would be if we still had the air superiority we used to. We are going to win it back—at least partially—but for that we need time, and we must not give up ground before then.

In the east, the catastrophic eclipse of Army Group Center was all but complete. At the midday conference on July 6, 1944, the Führer again rejected Model's view that four divisions could be extracted from Army Group North by ordering its withdrawal. It was an illusion, he said, to expect any savings; all that would happen was that the group would lose its fortified positions and its heavy guns and equipment. Turning to General Heusinger, Hitler quietly asked what the disaster had cost them so far in the Center and was told: "Twelve to fifteen divisions are encircled, but the overall losses will run to twenty-eight divisions."

Twenty-eight! Since June 22—in just two weeks—Hitler had lost 350,000 trained German soldiers to the Russians. Another might have lost his nerve, but Hitler's restless mind thought only of winning time for a few more months until the new Luftwaffe and the secret weapons reversed this trend. "I don't mind saying," he reminisced later, "it would be hard to imagine a graver crisis than the one in the east. When Field Marshal Model took over, Army Group Center was all gap. There was more gap than front—but then at last there was more front than gap." He had given Model a more realistic directive than had been given to his predecessor: the "fortified places" were only to be held long enough for a cohesive new front to be established farther back; but even this was a labor of Sisyphus, for by July 3, when Minsk itself had been overrun, the enemy had poured 126 infantry and 6 cavalry divisions with 45 tank brigades through a breach now over two hundred miles wide. Model had only 8 divisions worthy of the name!

At first the cause of this defeat was a mystery. Zeitzler's faulty strategic appreciation alone was not to blame; more serious was the Luftwaffe's virtual impotence—thrown into confusion by the sudden loss of its forward airfields and paralyzed by the first serious fuel shortage to affect the eastern front. Hitler's demands for an airlift to the encircled Fourth Army southeast of Minsk could not be fulfilled; the Messerschmitt 323 giant transport planes were grounded, and the entire Sixth Air Force was hamstrung by the lack of refined aviation fuel. Most ominous of the causes was the sudden unwillingness of leading army officers to continue the fight. As General Jodl put it soon after: "Practically the entire Army Group Center surrendered to the enemy this summer." There was evidence that Soviet-trained "Seydlitz officers" had infiltrated the battle zone, in German uniforms, and issued false orders to sabotage the army group's defense. Others seemed to have been active in Moscow's cause even longer. After the Fourth Army surrendered on July 8, Hitler was shown an order signed by General Vinzenz Müller of the Twelfth Army Corps[5] in which that army's soldiers were instructed to put an "end to the pointless bloodshed":

> The Russian command have promised (a) to care for the injured and (b) to let officers retain daggers and medals, and other ranks their decorations. All weapons and equipment are to be collected and handed over in good condition.

Two weeks later Müller and fifteen fellow generals of Army Group Center signed a long pamphlet attacking Hitler and denigrating their colleagues' continued defense of the Reich. Millions of facsimiles were scattered over the German lines. The text was personally broadcast by the generals on Moscow radio. Shortly afterward, the same generals, abetted by Paulus and Seydlitz, appealed to Army Group North officers to desert or disobey Hitler's "murderous orders" to stand fast. "Now," said Hitler, "I am beginning to understand how such frightful things could have happened in the Center."

The collapse had brought the Red Army to the very frontiers of East Prussia. Hordes of weary refugees had fled before them, swamping the province from White Russia. There were fears that if the enemy penetrated farther into Poland a general uprising would break out there. "When will the first task force of fifteen Me-262s begin operations?" the Führer impatiently asked on July 2.

He had still not abandoned hope. Somehow, however, the Soviet tide had to be stemmed before it engulfed East Prussia. Late on July 5 he decided to create new army divisions at an unprecedented speed to act as an emergency breakwater. He announced this to Himmler, Speer, Buhle, and half a dozen others at the Berghof the next day. Fifteen "blocking divisions" for the army would be raised

---

[5]Müller, fifty, was one of the little circle of dissidents around Hans Oster as early as 1939. After the war, he lived in the Soviet zone of Germany, where his memoirs, *Ich fand das wahre Vaterland (I Found the True Fatherland),* were published.

immediately from the navy and Luftwaffe; Speer's arms factories must contribute fifty thousand of their young workers. The Reichsführer SS would temporarily supervise the training of six such divisions. In addition, ten or twelve panzer brigades were to be created, each with perhaps fifty tanks. Hitler instructed Saur to institute a crash program to manufacture the necessary extra infantry equipment over the next weeks.

At this urgent conference, and an additional one called toward midnight, Hitler noticed the same one-armed colonel who had been at the Berghof a month before —a black patch on one eye, and two fingers missing from his one good arm; Schmundt had selected this officer, who seemed particularly fanatical, to be Chief of Staff to General Fromm, a man patently weary of his job as commander of the Replacement Army. This time the colonel was armed with a bulging yellow leather briefcase.

Very early on July 9, Hitler flew back to Rastenburg for a day of urgent talks there. With him he took Himmler, Keitel, Dönitz, Jodl, and Korten, while from the eastern front came Model, General Friessner (of Army Group North), and Greim. The Wolf's Lair was in a turmoil of noise and activity, for the strengthening of the bunkers was far from complete. Hitler again ruled against any weakening of Army Group North. He was seconded in this by Admiral Dönitz, who rehearsed the familiar strategic arguments against allowing Stalin free access to the Baltic Sea. The first new divisions were promised to Model by July 17, and Hitler explained how he intended to replace the Center's lost twenty-eight divisions: some of the new divisions would arrive in the second half of July, but the rest not before the end of August; three refurbished Crimea divisions would follow, joined by two from Norway and the 6th and 19th panzer divisions. Gauleiter Koch and the Party were to be put in charge of fortifying the East Prussian frontier. On balance, both Model and Friessner were optimistic about the Center and North; but within one or two days, Model warned, he expected the Russians to attack his other army group, North-Ukraine, at Kovel.

Hitler flew back to the Berghof that evening, his mind at peace. General Korten had informed him that during the night the first V-1s would be air-launched from Heinkel bombers against England and that the first four Messerschmitt 262 jet bombers would attack the invasion area within ten days. "The Allies only like advancing when air power is on their side," said Hitler. "That is why everything now depends on our fighter production. We must keep it top-secret and start stockpiling in a big way. Then just watch the enemy gape when we turn the tables on them four months from now—as far as air supremacy is concerned!"

Yet suddenly a mood of despair gripped the Führer and he decided abruptly to return to Rastenburg, even though the Wolf's Lair was still unready. The battle for Vilna, the last bastion before East Prussia, had just begun. He had already ordered the General Staff and OKL to stand by to evacuate their East Prussian headquarters to Potsdam "if need arose." But the cancer of defeatism he had discovered in the General Staff had deeply shocked him, and he felt that only his physical presence in East Prussia could prevent a rout. At the Berghof on the eleventh, the news was that both Model and Friessner admitted their assessments of two days earlier might have been overoptimistic. The colonel with the yellow briefcase had again come, to discuss the new blocking-divisions—now referred to as "grenadier divisions"; but as Himmler did not appear, the colonel left—his business uncompleted.

Hitler had asked Himmler to supervise all 15 embryo new divisions. He would trust the General Staff no longer.[6] On July 13 he personally addressed the generals and staff officers selected for these and the 10 panzer brigades, perhaps 160 men. Never again would he possess the physical strength to deliver such a speech, but of this, his last to his generals, there is no surviving record.

That morning Marshal Konev's attack on Army Group North-Ukraine had begun. East of East Prussia, Vilna had fallen, and Hitler was airlifting reliable SS troops to defend Kauen, the next town. The next morning he would himself fly back to Rastenburg. Desolately, he wandered through the Berghof rooms with the young wives of Dr. Brandt, his surgeon, and Colonel von Below, Luftwaffe adjutant, pausing affectionately in front of each familiar painting or tapestry as though taking leave of an old friend for the last time. One painting was of a rather plump young lady, whom Speer had always threatened to deflate with a knife. At last, the Führer bid the ladies courtly good night and kissed their hands. But shortly afterward he returned to the Great Hall and bid them farewell. At this Frau Brandt began to weep. Frau von Below said reassuringly, "But, mein Führer —you will be coming back in a week or two, won't you?"e Great Hall and bid them

Hitler did not reply.

---

[6] In Berchtesgaden on July 9, 1944, Speer had chanced upon the army's Quartermaster General Wagner—who had just reported to Hitler on the equipment lost in the Center—and Generals Erich Fellgiebel, Helmuth Stieff, and Fritz Lindemann, who were conniving in a luxury hotel. Zeitzler was also in the hotel, "convalescing." "The hotel ambience of coffee and cigarettes formed a distasteful contrast to the topic under discussion," recorded Speer's office chronicler; "—namely the divisions lost on the Russian front . . . [Wagner] makes the problems in the east all seem so trivial and it is hard to understand why his comments as Quartermaster General do not show greater concern, as he is responsible for the all-important military supplies. Inroads like these into the armaments sphere would have had the Minister [Speer] speaking in a very serious tone of voice. But this afternoon the generals were nonchalantly referring to the various eastern situations as mere trifles." (All were plotting, and suffered the consequences.)

"Do You Recognize My Voice?"

"We got back to the Wolf's Lair yesterday," wrote Martin Bormann on July 15, 1944. "With its twenty-two-foot-thick bunkers it is now really a fortress of the most modern kind." As Hitler's Condor touched down at Rastenburg airfield, fifteen minutes' drive away, thousands of Todt Organization laborers were still working on the strengthening of the Führer's headquarters. The old site used for "Barbarossa" was now barely recognizable: the mammoth concrete bunkers rearing up out of the trees had been expertly camouflaged against enemy reconnaissance; there was grass on the flat roofs, and both natural and artificial trees. It was an idyllic setting. "How beautiful it is out here," one of Hitler's stenographers noted in his diary. "The whole site is resplendent with luscious greenery. The woods breathe a magnificent tranquillity. The wooden hutments, including ours, have meantime been heavily bricked-in to afford protection against bomb-splinters. We all feel well at ease here. It's become a second home to us."

As Hitler's bunker proper was still incomplete, he moved into the former guest bunker in the heart of a top security zone compound which had been wired-off in the southwest corner of Zone I since September 1943. The noon war conferences were accordingly transferred to one of the gray-painted wood and brick hutments some forty yards west of this temporary home; at one end of the hut a forty-foot-long conference room had been created by simply knocking down two partition walls. The room thus had windows on three sides—it was light and airy and filled with the fragrances of the surrounding woods.

This peaceful setting belied the grimness of the dark crisis into which Germany was descending. For the first time Keitel and Fromm—commander of the Replacement Army—had plunged into discussions with Bormann and the Party chiefs on command relationships in the likely event that the Reich itself became a battleground. The trickle of refugees from the east had become a flood. At long last Hitler had bowed to pressure to *implement* the doctrine of total war. Some of this pressure came from Speer, but most came from Goebbels and Bormann.

On about July 15 Hitler instructed Bormann's three-man "cabinet"[1] to summon the principal ministers to find ways of stepping up the Reich's defense effort still further. On July 18, Goebbels sent Hitler a long letter protesting the continued underexploitation of the Reich's vast manpower resources. "At this moment, with East Prussia preparing to defend her soil as best she can, every mail delivery here in Berlin brings fresh invitations from every corner of the Reich to official receptions, to parties, to games, or to displays that today do more harm than good." Red tape was choking the Wehrmacht and civil service. Goebbels scorned the ability of any three-man committee to undo the damage that the failure to implement total war had done to public feeling, and he reminded Hitler that in October 1926 he had not suggested using a "committee" to capture "Red Berlin" for the Nazi party. "My suggestion is this: give absolute power to one man you can trust for every problem requiring a rapid solution. . . . Every time I see you, I look into your eyes and face to see what your health is like. When you came to Berlin by plane for the state funeral of General Hube—risking death from American fighter or bomber aircraft—I was shaking with fear, I confess. I dare not think what might have happened. You alone, mein Führer, are our guarantee of victory."

This was unquestionably true. No man possessed the affection of and authority over the German people that Hitler did, even at this gloomy pass in their fortunes. If he succumbed now, nothing would halt the Soviet avalanche—least of all his querulous generals. The Red Army would stand astride the Rhine within a month. Yet the Germans waited for Hitler's ultimate appeal, an appeal he seemed ashamed to issue. Goebbels besought him: "By calling all England to arms after Dunkirk did Churchill thereby condemn her to die? And Stalin—when he proclaimed during our advance on Moscow 'Better to die on your feet than live on your knees!'—did he imperil the whole USSR? On the contrary!" Joseph Goebbels, propaganda minister and veteran of the Party struggle since its earliest days, reminded Hitler he had always stood at his side in his hour of need.

"Our return was very timely," wrote Martin Bormann on July 15. "Surprisingly, this war has shown with increasing clarity that it is the Führer and his Party faithfuls who are inspired by a savage determination to keep fighting and resisting, rather than the military—among whom passion and intensity ought to have increased with their rank. The Führer has had to come here in person to stiffen the often shamefully weak-kneed attitude of the officers and hence their troops."

The optimism of the "Party faithfuls" was certainly limitless. Himmler, who

[1]See page 471.

visited Hitler that day, was soon writing to Kaltenbrunner: "How are we going
to rule and pacify Russia when we reconquer large parts of her, as we certainly
shall in the next years?" Jodl shared Bormann's criticisms of the army generals'
defeatism. The German civilian public was showing far greater courage, though
it had far worse to suffer. In East Prussia everybody from university professors
to fifteen-year-olds had rallied to Gauleiter Koch's call to build defenses and
fortifications. A dispiriting torrent of disorganized army units and refugee columns was making for the Reich frontiers, and Hitler had to issue stern orders
before the rot became an outright rout. He ordered a new defensive line rapidly
built along the entire eastern front, following the rivers San and Vistula to the
Warsaw bridgehead, and then the Narev and a line forward of the Reich frontier
to the Baltic; but it was touch-and-go whether there would be either the manpower to build it or the troops to man it before the Russian avalanche swept
westward into Germany.

Fifteen new "grenadier divisions" ordered by Hitler were being raised in
the Reich. The army had issued the first order over General Stieff's signature
on July 8, but Hitler wanted more urgency, and a week later, on July 15, he
summoned to the Wolf's Lair both General Fromm and his Chief of Staff—
the colonel with the now familiar yellow briefcase. Most midday war conferences here were interminably long and the humid air was heavy with recriminations, as Hitler saw no way of checking the present trend until the autumn
at least, when Germany might well regain fighter and U-boat supremacy. But
this conference lasted only half an hour, from 1:10 to 1:40 P.M., as a special
session on the reconstitution of the shattered eastern front followed until 2:20
P.M. Hitler cold-heartedly laid down that the refugee families were to be
stopped east of the new line and the able-bodied members diverted to the fortification works. Nothing else could stop the Bolshevik hordes. "Things are
pretty grim here," wrote Martin Bormann three days later. "The Russians
are at Augustov near the East Prussian frontier, and if their armored units
press on any farther, we've got nothing to stop them with for the time being.
. . . The new divisions which are being formed still lack the necessary antitank weapons! . . . We have plenty of worries, and it's a good thing that the
Führer is here." On July 19, Hitler ordered two East Prussian divisions raised
from the province's elderly home guard. In this connection Fromm's Chief of
Staff was detailed to report to Hitler the next day.

In France the Allies were mercilessly bombing and strafing the Germans containing the beachhead. For the first time napalm bombs were being used, and flame-
throwing tanks of immense range were incinerating the inmates of the stubborn
pillbox bunkers. Late on July 17, Field Marshal Kluge telephoned with the

shattering news that Rommel's car had been strafed by an Allied plane; the driver had crashed into a ditch and Rommel's skull had been split; he would be in the hospital for many months.[2] The next day two thousand bombers hit the stronghold built by Rommel at Caen. Over two thousand French civilians were found dead in the ruins by British troops when they advanced on the nineteenth.

Hitler's world was thus beginning to crash. In Italy the German Fourteenth Army pulled out of Leghorn (Livorno). In Denmark Communist resistance cells were waging overt partisan warfare, and they aggravated the crisis by calling a general strike. Reich Commissioner Werner Best had ignored Hitler's instructions to deal with the terrorists *sub rosa,* as formal trial and execution just created martyrs; to Best and Ribbentrop the Führer grumbled, "You gentlemen always want to be smarter than I am!" When Best interjected, "May I say something?" Hitler replied, "I don't want to hear it. Get out!"

In Hungary too there were still ominous rumblings of distant thunder: a pro-German prime minister, General Döme Sztójay, had replaced Kállay in March, but Horthy and his advisers had maintained their clamor for Hitler to withdraw the German troops from Hungary. Horthy had still not kept his part of the Klessheim bargain—the total expulsion of the Jews from Hungary; moreover, after July 8 he refused to deport any more Jews, and a few days later he announced his intention of replacing Sztójay by a military regime. Ribbentrop telegraphed Hitler's furious reply to Budapest on July 17, after Hitler had consulted with Himmler again on the Hungarian Jews: "The Führer expects the Hungarian government to take action against the Budapest Jews forthwith and without further delay." Otherwise he would withdraw his approval of certain exceptions from the expulsion order—artists, musicians, and notably forty-six members of the Manfréd-Weiss industrial family, who had leased their important factory in Hungary to the Hermann Göring works in May in return for exit visas. But now Himmler's ghastly secret was coming out, for two Slovak Jews had escaped from Auschwitz extermination camp, and their horrifying revelations were published in two reputable Swiss newspapers early in July. Horthy refused to deport the Jews from Budapest; instead, he announced that a general would bring Hitler a letter on July 21.

The reasons for Hitler's discontent were therefore manifold. His irritation was such that on July 18 he dismissed one of his adjutants, SS Colonel Fritz Darges, transferring him to the eastern front because of a minor incident in the conference

---

[2]Rommel had been earmarked for a British assassination operation a few days later anyway. There are papers in secret British files on this.

hut.[3] He lunched in his bunker that day virtually alone, as always now, sharing the vegetarian repast with his secretary Fräulein Christa Schroeder. He was ill at ease, and he exclaimed, "Nothing must happen to me now, because there is nobody else who could take over!" He had premonitions of trouble; two days later he admitted to Mussolini that he had first experienced them during the flight to the Wolf's Lair on the fourteenth. At lunch with Fräulein Schroeder he commented uneasily, "There is something in the air."

There were several abscesses of opposition, but they were hard to identify and lance. Perhaps Hitler had learned through Himmler's agents of the current wave of rumors about an imminent attempt on his life. (On July 29 he was to say, "I admit I long expected an assassination attempt.") But from which quarter? He was cool toward the Prussian Junkers and the nobility, but they had served Germany well in the past. The field marshals or generals? Some, like General Fellgiebel, Chief of Signals, were conspicuous by their hostile remarks, but as Jodl was to note on the twenty-fourth: "The Führer always good-naturedly overlooked them and held a protecting hand over them." More likely assassins were the civilians—like ex-Mayor Carl Goerdeler of Leipzig, for whom the Gestapo had just asked Himmler to authorize an arrest warrant. Alternatively, the enemy might launch a paratroop attack right here, on the Wolf's Lair itself; Himmler discussed this very possibility with Hitler on the fifteenth. An entire battalion was concealed in the woods with tanks and both assault and antiaircraft guns; the very enticing green lawns of the Security Zones were in fact deadly minefields—but the possibility of enemy paratroop attack always remained.

Rommel's Army Group B now considered that the enemy had landed forty divisions in France and that about as many more were still available in Britain. By late on July 18 the enemy breakthrough east of Caen called for urgent remedial action. Three thousand Allied fighters and fighter-bombers were roaming the battlefield and supply roads as far as the Seine. Saturation bombing had taken a heavy toll of German tanks and men. Kluge telephoned early on July 19 to demand that the 116th Panzer Division be withdrawn from the Fifteenth Army and thrown into the breach. Hitler authorized this immediately, thus accepting for the first time that the Fifteenth Army was waiting for an invasion of the Pas de Calais that might never come. After a long talk that night with Schmundt and Keitel, he instructed Field Marshal Kluge to take permanent command of Rommel's army group as well, "as no other suitable person can be found." Kluge telephoned Keitel at noon: "Without doubt we've got a crisis here on our hands."

[3]The deeper reason was that Fritz Darges had broken off his relationship with Eva Braun's sister Gretl; she had then married Himmler's liaison officer, Hermann Fegelein, on June 3.

He said he was planning to address his senior commanders immediately behind the battlefront the next morning, July 20. "Good luck," said Keitel. "Take care of yourself!" Hitler trusted Kluge implicitly.

These were Hitler's principal worries that day, therefore: the threat to East Prussia and Silesia; the possible loss of France; the proclamation of total war designed to mobilize Germany's untapped resources; the seemingly unavoidable defection of Hungary. Nor were Germany's relations with Italy satisfactory: they were burdened by the continued internment of a million Italian troops and the annexation of the northern provinces. For political reasons Hitler had conceded to Mussolini the right to raise four new divisions of troops loyal to fascism. The first two, equipped with the best German weaponry, were at this very moment being inspected by Mussolini and Marshal Graziani in Germany, but on July 19, Hitler tentatively decided to disband all four divisions. On consideration, he felt that no good could come of them and that their German training personnel and equipment were badly needed for the new German divisions. He sent Boden-schatz to air this suggestion with Graziani: perhaps the Italian troops could be used for the antiaircraft defenses of key German factories instead. Mussolini himself was due to arrive at the Wolf's Lair after lunch on July 20. Bodenschatz reported to Hitler that morning that Graziani had not taken to the idea at all. Hitler replied, "Come and join the war conference with me."

The conference had been brought forward thirty minutes, to 12:30 P.M., because of the Duce's visit. Schaub arrived about 12:25 P.M. to tell him that the officers were assembled. As Hitler walked the forty yards to the gray conference hut, he saw Warlimont and various other officers waiting outside; the others were already in the oppressively hot conference room. General Heusinger, standing to his right, began briefing him on the eastern front. Shortly afterward, Keitel arrived, accompanied by General Buhle—who was an armaments expert—an adjutant, and Fromm's Chief of Staff, the colonel with the black eyepatch and yellow briefcase. "Mein Führer," Keitel announced, "this is Colonel Count Schenk von Stauffen-berg, who is to brief you on the new divisions." He stepped back a pace to the left of Hitler, his customary position. Hitler shook the colonel's mutilated hand, then resumed his seat on a wicker stool, his back to the door, facing the open windows. Once he asked Buhle for a detail and the general suggested that Stauffenberg might reply; but to his evident chagrin the colonel had stepped outside. There were now twenty-four men in the room. From the other side of the heavy trestle table, the Luftwaffe Chief of Staff, General Korten, was just referring to an air reconnaissance report, and Hitler leaned across the maps, propping himself on his right elbow; there was a bunch of pencils in his right hand and in his left a magnifying glass with which to read the fine print.

For Hitler, this was the dividing instant of time between an old world and a new one. At that instant a blinding sheet of dazzling yellow flame engulfed him as two pounds of explosives detonated less than six feet away. His back was half turned to the blast, but his impression was that it came from just to the right of Colonel Heinz Brandt, Heusinger's chief assistant, who was waiting to lay out fresh situation maps. "The swine are bombing us!" thought Hitler as the blast wave caught him. He heard a distinct double-crack—probably the initial blast, and then the noise of his own eardrums bursting. Dense, opaque smoke filled the room. He found himself lying near the left doorjamb; he was covered with lathes and timbers from the ceiling, he could feel his hair and clothes on fire, and his right elbow was hurting savagely. As the choking fumes parted, his smarting eyes made out disheveled figures groping in the wreckage, and faces contorted by screams of pain which he could not hear. Perhaps an enemy paratroop attack had begun! If he tried to get out of the windows, he might blunder straight into their guns. He painfully extricated himself and stumbled into the corridor, beating out the flames on his ragged black trousers. He felt blood trickling down his legs and out of his ears. With his plaster-caked hair standing on end, he felt he must look like "a baboon"; but he was alive.

Supported by Keitel, who like a doused poodle had just shaken his towering frame free of debris, he limped out of the hut's middle exit as charred documents spiraled down from the sky and guards converged on him. Horribly maimed men were being carried out of the wrecked conference room and laid on the grass as Otto Günsche, his bodyguard, led the Führer back to his bunker. "Somebody must have thrown a hand grenade into the room," exclaimed Hitler; but the sentries had seen nobody. While a manservant ran for Dr. Morell, Hitler sat down unsteadily and took his own pulse—pleased at his self-composure. Then he thrust his injured arm inside his tunic, Napoleon-style, to ease the pain. His secretaries came in, and he grinned at them. "Well, ladies, things turned out well again!" Then he withdrew to his bedroom, walking taller and more cheerfully than he had for some time. Morell and the surgeon Hasselbach removed the shredded trousers, revealing that the skin on the lower third of both thighs had been badly torn by the explosions; altogether they removed over a hundred splinters of the fragmented oaken trestle from his legs. His face had been cut in a score of places by flying splinters, and his forehead was scarred by a falling roof timber. He began to mutter that this incident would give him the long-wanted opportunity of dealing with his critics, and the prospect evidently pleased him.

"It was the work of a coward!" he exclaimed, his mind still grappling with the identity of the perpetrator. "Probably one of the Todt Organization workmen installed a bomb." He sent guards out to search for the hidden fuse cable and for possible additional bombs. He instructed his press chief to telephone Dr. Goebbels, and he sent his Luftwaffe adjutant, Colonel von Below, bloodstained and deafened, to the telephone exchange a hundred yards away to summon Göring —who had stayed away that day as he could not abide Mussolini—and Himmler.

He ordered absolute secrecy about the incident. Below returned after having removed all the jacks from the telephone switchboard and forbidden the telephonists to go near them. But presently Hitler learned that the blast wave had evidently originated *above* floor level. Moreover, only a handful of officers had known that the war conference would be brought forward because of Mussolini's visit. And that yellow flame could only be from an English explosive. Whatever the truth, Himmler and the Gestapo investigators summoned with Kaltenbrunner from Berlin would find it out.

At about 1:15 P.M. he reemerged into the warm sunshine, wearing a fresh uniform over bandages covering all injuries but those to his head. To General Fellgiebel, the signals chief, whom he espied strolling deliberately up and down outside the security zone's perimeter fence, Hitler must have appeared unscathed. He sent for Colonel Ludolf Sander, his own headquarters signals chief, and asked for arrangements to be made for him to broadcast to the German people as soon as possible; but it would take several hours for the sound truck to arrive from Königsberg. Now Hitler learned of the carnage the explosion had caused. Those who had been on his right hand had suffered the worst: Colonel Heinz Brandt had lost a foot, the stenographer Heinrich Berger had lost both legs, Korten had been impaled by a jagged table fragment, Schmundt had ghastly leg injuries and an eye gouged out; nobody had escaped the burns and blast entirely. Stenographer Berger's colleague had been able to talk with him—Berger hoped he would survive but committed his wife and children to his friend's care if he should not. Hitler appointed Berger to a high civil-service grade forthwith, so that the widow could draw a pension—a provident gesture, for Berger died in agony that afternoon.

Hitler drew fresh energy from his narrow escape from death. Had he believed in God, he would have credited the Almighty with this miracle. His private secretary, Christa Schroeder, vividly recalled those hours, under later interrogation:

> I did not expect that July 20, 1944, to be called in for lunch with him after the assassination attempt. But nonetheless I was sent for to join him. I was astounded to see how fresh he looked, and how spritely he stepped toward me. He described to me how his servants had reacted to the news: [Heinz] Linge was indignant, Arndt had begun to cry. Then he said, verbatim, "Believe me, this is the turning point for Germany. From now on things will look up again. I'm glad the *Schweinehunde* have unmasked themselves!"
>
> I told him he couldn't possibly meet the Duce now. "On the contrary!" he retorted, "I must—what would the world press say if I did not!"

"Duce, I have just had the most enormous stroke of good fortune," Hitler said in greeting to the Italian dictator as he emerged from his train at 2:30 P.M. He had brought his entire staff to the local railroad station—Himmler, Keitel, Göring, Ribbentrop, and Bormann were all there. Security Zone I was packed with SS officers and armored vehicles which had crawled out of the woods. The Führer and the Duce drove to the shattered conference hut and inspected the gaping hole in the floor and the buckled floors of the adjacent rooms, where the blast wave had come up through the floor cavity. It was now that Martin Bormann brought to Hitler the corporal who had tended the telephone outside the conference room. This man had seen an officer leave in a hurry just before the explosion, a colonel with one arm; in fact he had left his briefcase, cap, and belt in the hut. The army officers had angrily rejected the corporal's implied libel on the worthy Colonel von Stauffenberg, but Bormann had taken him seriously. Stauffenberg certainly was nowhere to be found. Perhaps he had flown to Russia?

Suspicion against him hardened during the afternoon. The Gestapo investigators found shreds of the yellow leather briefcase embedded in the wreckage. Stauffenberg had bluffed his way past the cordons and left Rastenburg airfield at 1:13 P.M., ostensibly for Berlin's Rangsdorf airfield; but he had not arrived there. Moreover, shortly before four o'clock his chief, General Fromm, telephoned Keitel from Berlin and said that rumors were flying around the capital and ought he declare a state of emergency? "The Führer is alive. There is no cause whatever for that. Is Stauffenberg in Berlin?" Keitel rasped. Fromm, taken aback, replied, "No, I thought he was at Führer Headquarters." Keitel promised to keep him up-to-date. Almost at once the Wolf's Lair began monitoring the most extraordinary orders emanating from Fromm's Bendlerstrasse office to the territorial army commands *(Wehrkreise)*, proclaiming a state of emergency by the code word "Valkyrie." By telephone too the commands were being instructed that Field Marshal Erwin von Witzleben, Rundstedt's predecessor, was now Supreme Commander of the Wehrmacht and that he had appointed General Erich Hoepner commander of home forces.[4] These were names from the past indeed.

The emergence from obscurity of these forgotten, forcibly retired, or cashiered army officers could only mean that an army putsch was being attempted in Berlin. Hitler forthwith accepted Himmler's proposal that the Gestapo be given powers to arrest army officers. Since Fromm was *prima facie* one of the conspirators, Hitler neatly legalized the move by appointing Himmler his successor, thus giving the SS leader control over all army units in the Reich; a secretary typed the decree, Hitler signed it, and with this and Hitler's specific directive to restore order, Himmler and Kaltenbrunner took off by plane for Berlin at once. Himmler's mission was a delicate one. He felt he had been chosen not as the army's arch rival, that is, as Reichsführer SS, but "as the Führer's loyal thane, as a soldier,

---

[4]The conspirators had not realized that a special network fed all orders issued to the Wehrkreise to the Führer's headquarters automatically as well. This slip was crucial to the crushing of the putsch.

as a National Socialist, and as a *Germanic* German," as he put it; but would the army see it that way? Hitler had ordered him on no account to allow his Waffen SS to come into direct confrontation with the army; that would be the first step toward the ultimate tragedy of civil war.

Keitel's energetic countermeasures crushed the putsch in the provinces before it even began. At 4:15 P.M. his dramatic message went out to the Wehrkreise: "Most Immediate! . . . The Führer is alive! Safe and sound! Reichsführer SS new commander of Replacement Army, only his orders valid. Do not obey orders issued by General Fromm, Field Marshal von Witzleben, or General (ret.) Hoepner! Maintain contact with local Gauleiter and police commander!" Shortly afterward, General Helmuth Stieff telephoned Keitel on the orders of the army Quartermaster General, Eduard Wagner, at Zossen. Fromm's office was proclaiming that the army had taken power; at 4 P.M., said Stieff, Stauffenberg, and General Ludwig Beck—the army Chief of Staff Hitler had dismissed in 1938— had phoned Wagner from Berlin.[5] Beck was claiming to have "taken over"; Witzleben, the "new Supreme Commander," was said to be on his way to Zossen at that moment.

Toward five o'clock this was confirmed beyond doubt. A long telegram signed by Witzleben (and countersigned by Stauffenberg) was monitored, being transmitted to the Wehrkreis commands. It exploited the overwhelming loyalty of these officers to Hitler by suggesting that not they but Party malcontents were behind the putsch. The telegram was timed 4:45 P.M.:

I. Internal unrest. An unscrupulous clique of combat-shy Party leaders has exploited the situation to stab the hard-pressed armies in the back and seize power for their own selfish purposes.
II. In this hour of supreme danger the Reich government has declared martial law to preserve law and order, and appointed me Supreme Commander of the Wehrmacht with absolute executive authority.

Long, detailed instructions for the incorporation of the Waffen SS, the "elimination" of the Gestapo, and the ruthless breaking of any opposition followed. Accordingly, a warning was radioed by Hitler's HQ to Himmler's aircraft to divert to a Berlin airfield heavily guarded by reliable SS troops. Field Marshal Model, commanding Army Group Center, telephoned: he had received from Bendlerstrasse an order commencing "The Führer Adolf Hitler is dead"—but he had refused to obey it. Hitler sent for his press chief and ordered a succinct communiqué broadcast to the people. It would announce: "A bomb attack was

---

[5]Stauffenberg did not reach the war ministry in Bendlerstrasse until about 4:30 P.M., as he had cautiously landed elsewhere than at Rangsdorf airfield, only to find neither car, driver, nor gasoline waiting there for the drive into the city; this evidently cost him ninety minutes' delay.

made on the Führer today. . . . Apart from minor burns and bruises the Führer was uninjured. He resumed work immediately afterward and—as planned—received the Duce for a lengthy discussion."

The Italian visitors had been treated almost like embarrassments by their hosts. Hitler had subjected Mussolini to the usual impressive statistics of Speer's forthcoming production of tanks, guns, and ammunition, and had secretly confided that fighter-aircraft output would soon reach 5,000 per month compared with the 3,400 turned out by the Allies. The V-1 was a triumph, and soon there would be a V-2. He was resolved to "raze London to the ground"—and "after August, September, or October" the new secret U-boats would also enter service.

At five o'clock tea was served in the headquarters mess. Hitler began to brood; Ribbentrop began to blame the generals for Germany's plight; the generals blamed Ribbentrop and Dönitz, and somebody tactlessly referred to the Röhm purge of June 1934.

After a while Julius Schaub was called to the telephone. Hitler's personal adjutant, Alwin-Broder Albrecht, was calling from the Reich Chancellery: strange events were afoot in Berlin. A detachment of the Guards Battalion had just tried to occupy the Chancellery. Streetcars were rattling through the government quarter without halting. The whole area was being cordoned off by troops. Simultaneously, Joseph Goebbels telephoned on his private line from Berlin. The Party "commissar" attached to the Guards Battalion had just revealed to him that its commander, Major Otto Ernst Remer, had been instructed to occupy the government quarter. "Has the army gone mad?" the propaganda minister asked Hitler. At six o'clock the dissidents began issuing a new telegram to the Wehrkreise, this time signed by "General Fromm."[6] The commanders were being instructed to "secure" all radio and communications stations and arrest all ministers and leading Party and police officials. The concentration camps were to be occupied (but no prisoners were to be released as yet).

Hitler began to fear he was losing control of events in Berlin. He telephoned Goebbels to find out when the radio communiqué announcing his survival would be broadcast. Goebbels replied that he was sitting on it until he had composed a fitting commentary to go with it. Hitler exploded in anger. "I didn't ask you for a commentary. I just want the news broadcast as fast as possible!" At 6:28 P.M. the radio service was interrupted with the startling news flash. This dealt the first body-blow to the putsch, for a *live* Hitler's word was still law.

The awkward tea party with Mussolini continued until about seven o'clock.

---

[6]Fromm had not in fact signed the order.

Then the doors were opened and he was ushered out into the light drizzle. "The Duce's cloak!" ordered Hitler. Then they parted, never to meet again. Almost immediately, Goebbels was on the telephone again, this time with a highly suspicious Major Remer at his side—unable to discern whether his own army superiors or the wily propaganda minister was attempting to overthrow Hitler. Hitler was heard shouting into the telephone, demanding to know why Himmler had not yet arrived in Berlin. But with his ears deafened, the Führer could hardly hear the answers, so he asked to speak to Remer himself. "Major Remer, can you hear—do you recognize my voice?" Remer had spent forty-five minutes with him some months before, collecting the Oak Leaf cluster for bravery; once heard, Hitler's voice was unforgettable. "Major Remer," continued Hitler, "they tried to kill me, but I'm alive. Major Remer, I'm speaking to you as your Supreme Commander. Only my orders are to be obeyed. You are to restore order in Berlin for me. Use whatever force you consider necessary. Shoot anybody who tries to disobey my orders." This was the second, deadliest blow to the plot—for it enabled Hitler to use the army itself to put down the conspiracy.

Hours of suspense passed at the Wolf's Lair, while Keitel and Bormann telephoned and cabled orders to every command, canceling the plotters' moves. The injuries began to tell on Hitler's physique. He slumped into a chair, morosely consuming quantities of colored pastilles from a dish in front of him. "I am beginning to doubt that the German people is worthy of my genius," he exclaimed —a sullen outburst that provoked a clamor of loyal protestations. Dönitz reminded him of the navy's achievements. Göring could not match this, so he picked a quarrel with Ribbentrop, who retorted, "*I* am still the foreign minister, and my name is *von* Ribbentrop!" Göring brandished his marshal's baton at him. Hitler named General Guderian to succeed the ostensibly "sick" Zeitzler as Chief of the General Staff, and he assigned the youthful General Walther Wenck—a tough Chief of Staff from an eastern front army group—to take the injured General Heusinger's place. Martin Bormann meanwhile purveyed what scanty information he could to the Gauleiters, using his modern teleprinter linkup.[7] "The reactionary criminal vermin evidently staged the attack on the Führer and his loyal officers in conjunction with the National Committee 'Free Germany' in Moscow (General von Seydlitz and Count [Haubold von] Einsiedel). Should the attack succeed, the generals' clique comprising Fromm, [Friedrich] Olbricht, and Hoepner would take over power and make peace with Moscow; that this so-called

[7]This was another circuit the plotters had failed to immobilize. They had duly "secured" the Berlin radio building, but nobody had instructed this army detail as to what to do then—let alone interrupt the programs broadcast. These were the officers who criticized Hitler's generalship. "They should have gone to school with us Nazis," Hitler scoffed to Schaub. "Then they would have learned how to do it!"

peace would cost the German people their lives is obvious. That the attempt has misfired means the salvation of Germany, because now the hopes reposed in these traitorous generals have been smashed for good." And at 9:40 P.M. Bormann warned the Gauleiters: "A General Beck wants to take over the government. The one-time Field Marshal von Witzleben is posing as the Führer's successor. Of course no National Socialist Gauleiter will allow himself to be taken in by, or accept orders from, these criminals, who are just miniature worms in format."

Dining with his secretaries in his bunker that evening, Hitler voiced his anger at the assassins. "What cowards! If they had drawn a gun on me, I might still respect them. But they didn't dare risk their own lives." He snorted: "The idiots cannot even imagine the chaos there would be if the reins slipped out of my grasp. I'm going to make an example of them that will make anybody else think twice about betraying the German people. . . . These criminals! They don't realize that our enemies are planning to destroy Germany so thoroughly that she can never rise again." At the 10 P.M. war conference, Hitler began by expressing his regrets to the two duty stenographers over the death of their colleague. As a reaction to the murder attempt, he ordered a particularly violent V-1 attack on London during the night—to show that he was less inclined to compromise than ever.

The radio sound-truck from Königsberg had now arrived. Hitler's entire staff assembled in the teahouse at 11:30 P.M.—General Jodl with a white bandage around his head, Keitel with bandaged hands, others with sticking plasters; many men were missing. In a voice trembling with anger and emotion, Hitler recorded a fiery speech to the nation "So that you can hear my voice . . .":

A minuscule clique of ambitious, unscrupulous officers of criminal stupidity has been plotting to get rid of me and to liquidate virtually the entire German Wehrmacht command staff at the same time. The bomb was placed by Colonel Count von Stauffenberg and exploded six feet away to my right. Several of my dear colleagues were gravely injured, one has died. I myself am completely uninjured apart from a few minor scratches, bruises, and burns. I regard this as a fresh confirmation of the mission given me by Providence to continue toward my goal. . . .

The speech was broadcast ninety minutes later. By that time Hitler had heard from a general who had escaped from the Bendlerstrasse building that Stauffenberg and Olbricht had locked Fromm in an office after he had refused to believe that Hitler was dead; Stauffenberg had sworn to the assembled staff officers that he "had seen the Führer's corpse being carried past on a stretcher."[8] Many

---

[8]"Keitel is lying," Stauffenberg assured Olbricht and Hoepner. He had seen an explosion like the impact of a 150-millimeter shell and doctors running over. "Hardly anybody can have survived!"— This emerged from the trials and interrogations.

idealists were eventually propelled to the hangman's noose by this easy lie, but Stauffenberg had nothing more to lose. Already the arrest-list was swelling: General Fellgiebel's very presence, uninvited, at the Wolf's Lair had compromised him; Keitel sent for him at midnight and arrested him. Hitler was mystified that the army's Chief of Signals had failed to gun him down when their eyes had met that very afternoon, as Hitler strolled with Schaub outside his bunker. "There he was, ambling up and down like a lamb, as though he'd had nothing to do with this conspiracy!" In Vienna and Prague the dissidents' orders had been largely carried out. In Paris the military governor had actually put the Gestapo and SS chiefs under lock and key, until Hitler's broadcast revealed the hollowness of Stauffenberg's claim. The position of Field Marshal von Kluge was ambiguous, for in an instant of black comedy the loyal General Hermann Reinecke, attempting to telephone General Fromm that evening, had found the doomed General Beck on the line, and Beck had imagined he had reached Kluge in France ("Kluge, is that you?"). Witzleben telephoned Keitel from his hideout during the night; the OKW chief kept him talking long enough to find out where he was, and then ordered his arrest too. A telegram from Fromm in the small hours spelled out the end of the putsch:

> Attempted putsch by irresponsible generals has been bloodily put down. All the ringleaders shot. . . . I have resumed control, after having been temporarily held under armed arrest.

Undeceived, Hitler ordered General Fromm's arrest as well. At 3:40 A.M. Martin Bormann circulated the triumphant teleprinter message to the Gauleiters: "The traitors' action can be regarded as at an end." Dizzy with euphoria, Hitler retired to bed.

Hitler saw the day's events as a temporary aberration, the product of a wayward clique of disgruntled army officers—a kind of blood poisoning which the army would get out of its own system. The perpetrators had been "shot by the army's own battalions," the press announced in special editions the next day—an infelicitous choice of words which caused many ordinary Germans to ask just how large the "minuscule clique" of traitors was? The Führer pushed the occurrence itself out of his mind, after emotionally sending the torn gray uniform jacket and black trousers to Eva Braun as a memento (they still exist). Himmler would no doubt see that the guilty did not escape unpunished.

Remarkably, the Allies had failed to exploit the hiatus in High Command operations; but the situation in France was already grave enough, and the bulging Normandy beachhead might burst into the rest of France at any moment. From Field Marshal Kluge's forward headquarters at La Roche-Guyon—Rommel's old HQ—a special courier arrived in the Wolf's Lair with two top-secret letters. The first was a letter from Kluge dated July 21; it endorsed the second—a strong recommendation by Rommel, written on July 15, that Hitler end the war. Rommel complained vigorously that although he had lost 97,000 men since June 6, he had been sent only 6,000 replacements; 225 tanks had been lost, but only 17 replaced. His infantry divisions lacked artillery, armor-piercing weapons, and above all bazookas. Given the enemy's harrowing air supremacy, their breakthrough into France was inevitable. "Our troops are fighting heroically all along the line, but the unequal battle is nearing its end. In my view you should draw the necessary conclusions. I feel bound as the army group's Commander in Chief to say this quite bluntly." Kluge's letter made its point in the words, "Unfortunately the field marshal's view is right." Nonetheless he had concluded a speech to his generals south of Caen the day before thus: "We must stand fast, and if there should be no way to turn the tide in our favor, then we must die honorably on the field of battle!"

Hitherto Hitler had worshiped Günther Hans von Kluge: physically and mentally alert, with an erudite high forehead, he was known through the army as *"kluge* Hans"—clever Hans. But evidently he and Rommel still did not appreciate, said Hitler a few days later, that this was Germany's fight for her destiny— "a struggle which cannot be discharged or disposed of by negotiation, by 'clever' politics, or by tactical sleight-of-hand." Obviously it was a temptation for Kluge to withdraw his hard-pressed armies from Normandy to some more distant line of defense, though such a line would certainly be far longer; but Hitler told Jodl on July 31: "If we lose France, we lose the basis of our U-boat campaign." Moreover, France was Germany's last source of tungsten—indispensable for high-grade steel manufacture and electronic equipment. It was pointless for his generals to calculate how they might better employ the Normandy divisions elsewhere in the west. Most were immobilized by lack of transportation; of the rest only a few would ever reach whatever new line the generals might propose to defend. Thus Kluge and his generals—Rommel, of course, was still hospitalized—must stand fast where they were until Göring had recovered at least partial air supremacy for the Luftwaffe in the west.

Nonetheless, Hitler also prepared for the worst. On July 23, spurred perhaps by these two letters, he ordered the West Wall fortifications which had been built in 1938 and 1939 to be readied for the defense of Germany. Two days later the Allied offensive began in Normandy. The British thrust toward Falaise was halted by a countermove of the First SS Panzer Corps, but late on the thirtieth the Americans managed to punch a dangerous hole through the line at the coastal town of Avranches. Hitler and Jodl now began secret deliberations envisaging the total loss of France, while resolved to insist that Kluge must defend the Normandy line to the utmost. The upshot was that Hitler instructed the OKW to prepare the Somme-Marne-Saône-Jura line for immediate occupation in the event of a collapse. (Hitler had ordered Rundstedt to reconnoiter this line ten months before.)[9] Hitler displayed the ability to reach hard decisions: if need be he would sacrifice the entire Balkans to recover enough military strength to defend Germany's last conquests elsewhere. Meanwhile he must inflict months of delay on the Allies; strong garrisons commanded by officers of proven courage and resourcefulness must be sacrificed to defend the main French ports and deprive the enemy of their use; the French railways must be destroyed down to the last freight car and track tie. On no account was any hint of these "horrific" strategic decisions to reach the army group headquarters in France, for who knew how many traitors still lurked there, waiting to pass the word to the enemy? After all, the military commander of France, General Carl-Heinrich von Stülpnagel, had made common cause with the putschists of July 20. "Let's be quite clear on one score," Hitler expounded to Jodl. "The tide in France cannot turn until we manage—even just for a short time—to regain air superiority." Meanwhile the French population watched and waited in the wings: now they began to rejoice at each enemy battle victory.

Hitler's ambition to regain the strategic initiative in the autumn was not pure fantasy. He had asked Göring to amass a great secret reserve of fighter aircraft, and he hoped some day to throw two thousand fighters into the struggle for France. Six new Mark XXI submarines had been delivered in July, and 144 were to have been built by the end of 1944. This was why the coming battles in the west must not go against Germany. Hitler himself would fly west to take command as he had in 1940—but his damaged eardrums made it impossible for him to fly anywhere for many days to come: the constant roaring and the pressure differences might provoke an inner-ear infection. "Obviously, if all the dams burst, I would do anything and wouldn't care—I'd go as gunner in a single-engined plane to get there as fast as possible. . . . Normally, I should have gone to bed for ten or fourteen days, but every day I've had to work at least eight hours not even counting the hours of reading of dispatches. . . . Apart from that the miracle is that the shock got rid of my nerve complaint almost entirely. My left leg still trembles somewhat if conferences go on too long, but previously this leg used to shake in bed. With this shock, that's vanished almost completely—not that I would recommend this kind of remedy."

The assassin's bomb had affected Hitler more than he liked to admit. On July 21 he suffered violent ear pains, and his right ear began to bleed. His eyes constantly

[9]A rare foresight by Hitler: see page 580.

flicked to the right (nystagmus); alone in his bunker, he kept thinking he was falling over to the right. That evening he went for a short walk in the twilight and twice found himself wandering off the path. There was a constant taste of blood in his mouth. An army ear-nose-and-throat expert, Dr. Erwin Giesing, was fetched; Hitler confessed that he could not sleep despite Morell's Phanodorm tablets, and Giesing noticed that his voice was unnaturally loud and that he was lip-reading replies. The next day Giesing cauterized a large rupture to Hitler's right eardrum, and on July 23, Professor Carl von Eicken—a specialist who had operated on Hitler's vocal cords in 1935—came to find out why the ear was still bleeding despite the hemostatic pills and injections being administered by Morell. Hitler joked: "Perhaps I'm just a natural bleeder!" The next day he asked Giesing to cauterize the ear again regardless of the pain. "I stopped feeling pain long ago," he observed. "Besides, pain exists to make a man of you."

He visited the army hospital at Rastenburg and talked with Schmundt and the other adjutants injured in the blast. "There are you," he remarked to Admiral Heinz Assmann, "seriously injured—yet you were not the one that was marked down for assassination. These gentlemen were after me and only me: yet I escaped entirely. Four times in this war my enemies have tried to take my life, and now the Almighty has stayed their hands once again. This can have only one historical interpretation, that Providence has elected me to lead the German people." Thus he had redoubled his resolve to lead them on, "not to final defeat but to victory." Two of the hospital beds were empty: Günther Korten, Chief of Air Staff, had died of his injuries on July 22; and Colonel Brandt—promoted to General to benefit his widow—had succumbed the same day. Korten would get a state funeral, but not Brandt: Scherff, Hitler's court historian, had shared his ward and reported that in his delirium the colonel had complained at Stauffenberg's callousness in placing the bomb at his feet when he, Brandt, was one of the conspirators himself; Brandt had even incriminated Heusinger, but the latter swore on oath that the colonel was lying and thus survived.

Each day revealed fresh names of conspirators. Himmler, who had decided to arrest even those who had only the most marginal association with the conspiracy, was appalled to find the eventual list totaling over six thousand. Zeitzler's adjutant was arrested and contritely confessed. Virtually every section head of the army General Staff except Reinhard Gehlen (Foreign Armies East) and Rudolf Gercke (transport) was involved. The implication of Colonels Hansen and Roenne, the Intelligence chiefs in the west, seemed to throw light on many otherwise inexplicable failures; so did the sudden suicide of General Eduard Wagner, the army's quartermaster general, and the disappearance of General Lindemann, the director of artillery. Hitler became convinced that General Fellgiebel's signals organization had instantly flashed his secrets to the enemy and was still doing so, as the accuracy of the British-controlled Soldatensender Calais transmitter showed. "Fellgiebel must confess," he raged, "if he has to be skinned alive!" Even Arthur Nebe, the Gestapo department chief—who had been a guard of honor on Heydrich's bier in 1942—had vanished without trace, as had Carl Goerdeler, twice appointed mayor of Leipzig and then provided with an abundant pension by the Führer. Goerdeler's papers were located in a hotel safe; they revealed that Goerdeler had been chosen to succeed Hitler, and they listed additional conspirators; these were arrested, and fresh chain reactions were established by their interrogation. On July 23, Admiral Canaris was picked up by the Gestapo, but since both Keitel and Himmler intervened on his behalf, his early imprisonment was more comfortable than that of his fellow conspirators. Franz Halder and Hjalmar Schacht, prewar governor of the Reichsbank, were also pulled in, as their opposition to Hitler was well documented.

Meanwhile Bormann began showing Hitler the lengthy interrogation reports compiled by Kaltenbrunner's staff. Kaltenbrunner clearly did not intend to spare the Führer's feelings. "I could not bear to watch this man running amok," one conspirator (General Stieff) had blurted out; "smashing his own great works by his obstinacy: we are defending Kirkenes and Crete, but we shall be losing Königsberg and Cracow in the process!" A physical revulsion took hold of Hitler as he realized the true scope of the plot; over half the traitors were army officers, but there were also trade-union officials, lawyers, civil servants, academics, and clergy. Even Count Wolf Heinrich von Helldorf, the pre-1933 brownshirt rowdy and Jew-baiter whom Hitler had made police president of Berlin, now confessed to being one of Stauffenberg's minions—not because he opposed National Socialism, but because he despised its plebeian aura and its creation of a nonaristocratic elite. None of the prisoners had much clue as to what system they were proposing in Hitler's place. The army generals, he reasoned, had failed to appreciate his *political* imperatives, and the politicians had criticized his generalship. They questioned his orders for the rigid defense of the Demyansk pocket, the Donets bend, the Dnieper line, the Nikopol bridgehead, the Crimea, the Narva line, the Vitebsk salient, and the Cherkassy pocket; one after another these positions had been lost until by July 1944 the core of the German army was destroyed. They blamed him for these military reverses; but there was a class element too, for he was the son of an Austrian customs official to whom the officer corps felt bound by neither blood nor brotherhood.

Gradually, the Gestapo investigators reconstructed the assassination attempt. The yellow briefcase was pieced together from its fragments. An English time-fuse had been used to detonate the explosive, evidently from Abwehr stocks. A second package of explosive was found where Stauffenberg's adjutant had jettisoned it from their car as they sped back to the airfield; had it also been used, their plot might have succeeded. Stauffenberg had also carried the assassination implements to the Berghof on July 11 and to Rastenburg four days later, but he had used neither those weapons then nor the second explosive charge on the twentieth. The riddles would remain unanswered, for General Fromm had invited Beck to put a bullet in his brains, and he had rushed Stauffenberg and his adjutant in front of a firing squad before the Gestapo could get at them. "He wanted to silence Beck before he unmasked him as his accomplice," Hitler aggressively declared.

Count von Helldorf's full confession was handed to Hitler as he was once again being treated by Dr. Giesing. Helldorf had blamed General Olbricht, who had advised him that Hitler's vaunted secret weapons were a myth and that even the A-4 rocket would not enter service before 1945. "Who would have thought Helldorf was such a rat?" asked Hitler. "That he was irresponsible was obvious enough from his gambling debts. How often I had to settle them for him—four or five times, and never less than one hundred thousand marks! A gambler like that was bound to fall into the hands of enemy agents, and the British secret service no doubt settled even bigger debts on his behalf. I'm sorry for his wife and pleasant children," he added, laying the report aside. "But I must clean out this Augean stable with an iron broom, and there can be no mercy. If I don't wipe out these traitors now, there may be more *Schweinereien* later, and the poor German soldier in the trenches has to pay for their stupidity with his life. How thankful I am to Remer [the Berlin garrison commander]. . . . A few more fine, clear-thinking officers like him and I wouldn't have to worry about the future. But this yellow gang sends me an even yellower Stauffenberg from Berlin—if he'd at least had the courage to stay there with his briefcase! But no! It was a pity to waste even one bullet on him. I keep asking myself what they were all after. To stop the war and start peace talks with the enemy—with *these* Tom Thumbs as the government? Because this gang had neither the guts nor the gumption to fight on. As though Stalin or Churchill or Roosevelt would have been bothered one instant by our sudden desire for peace! In eight days the Russians would have been in Berlin and it would have been all over for Germany—for good."

Hitler's escape had once more brought the entire German population together; for many weeks their fury against the plotters was said to be intense. It was reported that army generals in Berlin had to conceal their uniforms beneath raincoats to escape the people's indignation. Goebbels opened a fund to enable people and troops alike to express their feelings. "I just heard the frightful news," a Viennese widow wrote to Hitler on the evening of July 20. "Hatred—a deep, indelible hatred—fills me against these wretched creatures! Did nothing happen to you, really? Mein Führer—you are all that is left to me in this world. I had a child, but he died in action in Russia at Mayevka. He had passed his examinations and had a place waiting at technical college. I had been saving up for this, but now he'll never return, my darling child! Take my money, out of joy that nothing befell the Führer." A lock of hair and a picture of the boy accompanied the letter.

Goebbels himself arrived at the Wolf's Lair on July 22 and asked that semidictatorial powers be given him.[10] Goebbels was deeply moved by Hitler's appearance. "He was just coming out of his little headquarters bunker, not weary, but relaxed, not bowed, but with his head slightly sunk—a picture to melt the sternest heart. At that moment I wished the entire German people could have seen him; nobody in Germany would ever have doubted again." Two days earlier, he and Speer had vigorously informed an audience of government officials that despite total war and the efforts of Gauleiter Sauckel, manpower was still being criminally wasted: 500,000 women were working as domestics. While Speer had 6,-000,000 armaments workers, another 3,200,000 men were being soaked up by office work in government and industry. A preliminary conference with Bormann, Speer, and Goebbels preceded the full session on July 23 with Hitler, Göring, and Himmler. Goebbels promised to procure half a million more men immediately for the war effort. Hitler ordered Göring to appoint the propaganda minister "Reich Commissar for Total War Mobilization" and announced—despite the misgivings of his doctors—that he would speak to the Gauleiters in one week's time.

The plot's side effects on government opinion in wavering countries like Turkey, Finland, Romania, and Bulgaria must have been grave, but the psychological damage to Hitler was also vast. Though he claimed the contrary, he now trusted nobody. Robert Ley's broadcast blaming "blue-blooded swine" for plotting Hitler's death brought Field Marshal von Richthofen in full-dress regalia to the Wolf's Lair formally protesting this slur on his fellow aristocrats who had unquestioningly obeyed their oaths of allegiance; Hitler pointed to his adjutants *von* Below, *von* Puttkamer, and Erik *von* Amsberg, as proof that he valued men only for their accomplishments. However, he himself would soon be heard mimicking an aristocratic general (General von Schlieben of Cherbourg) justifying a decision to choose dishonorable captivity to the hero's death he had demanded of his troops: "After all, what harm can possibly come to us? We'll be taken prisoner and get decent treatment—particularly we who are of noble families. We won't get put together with those frightful plebs." And although Hitler himself signed an order forbidding any intemperate criticism of the officer corps, the generals, and the nobility at large, in private he regretfully speculated that Stalin had been right to purge his regular officer corps in 1937, and that in 1934 he would have done better to opt for the SA against the Reichswehr. Every officer who now came

[10]As he had in his letter of July 18. See page 658.

to his headquarters was frisked for hidden weapons before being allowed into his presence. His food was tasted and tested for poison, and his medicines were purchased only from approved SS clinics in Berlin. Hitler trusted nobody; he even ordered the still-uniformed and bemedaled corpses of Stauffenberg and the others allegedly shot in Berlin to be exhumed, lest the army had deceived him about their execution.

Treachery and treason became the only explanation he could find for his defeats. While the Sixth Army, fighting in the Carpathians, had more than enough bazookas, the Seventh and Fifteenth armies in France had barely any. "Who issues these weapons?" asked Hitler angrily. Keitel shrugged his shoulders. "That was the quartermaster general, Wagner." "Aha!" Hitler said triumphantly. "The swine! He did well to shoot himself, otherwise I would have hanged him. In the open countryside of the Ukraine we have bazookas in abundance. And in the hedgerows of Normandy where our troops can only ward off the enemy's superabundance of tanks with such bazookas, we have none! He did it on purpose —it was treason!" He exclaimed, "These criminals won't go before a court-martial, because their accomplices will preside and spin the trials out. They will be thrown out of the Wehrmacht and tried by the People's Court. Nor will they die honorably before the firing squad, but like common criminals in the hangman's noose. . . . And above all, they'll get no time to make long speeches. Freisler will see to that—he's our Vishinsky!"[11]

Göring did what he could to restore Hitler's trust in the Wehrmacht. On July 22 a staff stenographer noted in his diary: "Before today's noon war conference, the Reichsmarschall delivered a short speech to the Führer proposing that as an outward token of gratitude for his miraculous escape the entire Wehrmacht should adopt the Hitler salute forthwith. The Führer signed the decree, whereupon there was a spontaneous ovation from everybody present." But all the raised hands in Germany could not erase the cancer of suspicion from Hitler's mind, and each fresh report from Kaltenbrunner started fresh tumors malignantly festering. By the end of July 1944 two names had cropped up that Hitler had never expected to see among his enemies: Field Marshals Kluge and Rommel. The allegation was so awesome that two weeks passed before Hitler could decide how to act on it.

[11]Roland Freisler was president of the Nazi People's Court; Andrei Vishinsky presided over the notorious Moscow Purge Trials.

He Who Rides a Tiger

August 1944 saw many of the intricate problems facing Hitler solved of their own accord, though not as he had wished. When September arrived, he no longer had to concern himself with Pétain's puppet government in France, for France was lost; nor with keeping Finland and Romania in the alliance, for both had defected; nor with impressing Turkey, for she had bowed to the enemy's pressure and broken off diplomatic relations with Germany. In Europe, Hungary alone remained an ally of any substance; but Admiral Horthy too regarded Germany as doomed, and had begun tactical maneuvering to regain his country's lost sovereignty—once again evoking from Hitler the warning that Germany and her allies were in one boat and there could be no disembarking in mid-tempest. Or as he put it in another context—reading Kaltenbrunner's reports on the renegades of July 20—"He who rides a tiger will find he can't dismount."

In France, the American breakthrough succeeded at Avranches. In the east the Red Army reached the Baltic on August 1, cutting off General Schörner's entire Army Group North from East Prussia. Russian troops were only an hour's drive from Hitler's headquarters. In Italy, the British occupied Florence. In Warsaw, a fresh uprising broke out.

Hitler fought a gigantic delaying action, but his health was now uncertain. General Heinz Guderian—the new Chief of General Staff—thus had a free hand. Hitler was disposed to accept this modern general's advice, for Guderian was born at Culm and it was his own homeland he was now defending; his forefathers had farmed West Prussian soil since the seventeenth century, and even now his wife was living in Hohensalza, close enough to hear the rumble of distant gunfire from the Warsaw front. "May the Führer's faith in you persist," she wrote him on July 30, "so that you really get the opportunity to go to work." "And so that you can save Germany's East," she added a few days later, "and our newfound ancestral homeland stays in our hands."

Guderian thrived on tough decisions. He was appalled at the neglect of the frontier defenses and issued dramatic orders for their renovation on July 27. "All eastern Germany must become a fortress in depth." Local Gauleiters and military commanders were to work together on the rapid construction of defensive positions—the Pilica line, the Narev-Bobr line, and the Vistula line from Warsaw northward to Danzig, with well-armed bridgeheads east of the most important cities along the river. Guderian signed these orders with Hitler's name; the Führer grumbled but allowed them to pass. A Russian invasion of East Prussia or the Upper Silesian industrial region would bring psychological disaster in its train. Indeed, now Hitler claimed to find positive advantages in the shrinking of his eastern empire—for it was the sheer distance of the eastern front of 1942 that had proved its undoing. Hundreds of thousands of men and women, young and old, began digging antitank trenches running southward from Stolp, across ripening harvest fields and farms. In Pomerania, seventy thousand women volunteered. Nothing had been done in the ancient fortresses of Königsberg and Lötzen; Guderian soon had them bristling with minefields and captured guns. Moreover, word of Hitler's presence in East Prussia was spread from mouth to mouth. Thus the miracle was achieved: the Red Army was halted at Augustov and Grodno, and Field Marshal Model's emaciated Army Group Center, with its fewer than forty divisions, undertrained and exhausted, withstood for a while the weight of one-third of the entire Soviet forces—143 rifle divisions, 19 rifle brigades, 12 cavalry divisions, and a host of armored brigades and regiments mustering over 2,000 tanks along its four-hundred-mile front line.

In Warsaw, astride the main access routes to Army Group Center, the Polish underground army rose in arms against the Germans as soon as the Russians showed across the river. Himmler came at once to Hitler. "Mein Führer," he orated with determined optimism, "the moment is an awkward one, but viewed historically what the Poles are doing is a blessing. We'll survive the next five or six weeks. But by then Warsaw, the capital, the brains, the nerve center of this former sixteen- or seventeen-million-strong nation of Poles, will have been wiped out—this nation that has barred our passage to the east for seven centuries and lain foul of us ever since the first Battle of Tannenberg." The Reichsführer ordered the total destruction of the city; it was to be burned down and blown up block by block. SS General von dem Bach-Zelewski fought a cruel battle against the partisans; but the Poles' commander, General Bor-Komorowski, was every inch his equal and rejected every demand to surrender, despite the around-the-clock bombardment of the city by 600-millimeter artillery and despite the dawning realization that the Russian relief attack across the river would not come in time. "I wish we had a multitude of men like General Bor," exclaimed Himmler on September 21, and when the last Polish insurgents finally surrendered ten days later, he ordered that Bor be treated well.

In Finland voices could again be heard in Parliament demanding an armistice.

The Red Army had reached Tukkum on the Gulf of Riga, thus cutting off Schörner's Army Group North. The importance the Russians attached to destroying Hitler's position in the north was clear from the appeals by Moscow radio urging his generals to defect while there was still time. It was to General Kinzel, the army group's Chief of Staff, that Stauffenberg and Beck had issued late on July 20 the "order" to retreat immediately. A catastrophe would have befallen the army group; bereft of artillery and ammunition it would have been devoured. But evidently the Berlin dissidents had failed to win any frontline commanders to their cause.

Hitler's major worry on this account was the German generals in Moscow. The OKW warned every headquarters of repeated cases in which unfamiliar officers in German uniforms and with valid identity cards had issued damaging orders to the troops. This became a standard explanation for each fresh reverse. "The Bolsheviks grow more useless every day," complained Schörner in a private letter to Hitler. "Recent days' prisoners range from fourteen-year-olds to old men. But what is astounding is the sheer hordes of human beings. . . ." Hitler had prepared calmly for the army group's temporary isolation: on July 12 he had already instructed the admiralty to coordinate the seaborne supplies to any such enclave. Schörner shared his confidence. He had ruthlessly stripped the entire command area of soldiers and packed them into the combat zone. "I am convinced the enemy is staking everything on one card," he wrote. "I am convinced that . . . what matters now is to survive this phase of the battle, then we shall have won." Guderian had planned a counterattack in August, confident that it would restore land contact to Schörner (and it did).

By early August, Army Group North-Ukraine had also weathered its crisis. The Soviet attack in mid-July had extended on the twenty-third to the sector of the First Hungarian Army, putting the headquarters unit to an unseemly flight which was only just halted forward of the Hungarian frontier. The Germans conceded that "German troops also gave way in places, which is attributed to the failings of individual commanders and the infiltration of panic-mongers and saboteurs from Russia." A few days later the army personnel branch recommended that in the future the families of German traitors should be punished, as a deterrent; Hitler approved the recommendation.

Farther south, Army Group South-Ukraine had been becalmed since the rout of April 1944, when it had fallen back on Romanian territory. At that time General Schörner had bitterly rebuked the OKW's General Erich Hansen—the military liaison to Marshal Antonescu—for the inadequate provision made to receive the struggling army group. The military chaos, the refugees, the abandoned equipment, and above all the added financial burden on the Romanian economy put a strain on German-Romanian relations. Hansen was nearly sixty and what Guderian described as "a man of General Beck"; but he had Antonescu's confidence, and thus Hitler refused Schörner's repeated recommendations for a replacement. As he later in August told General Alfred Gerstenberg, the Luftwaffe commander of the Romanian oil regions: "We are staking all we've got. If we lose the oil regions, we cannot win the war."

General Guderian had transferred six panzer and four infantry divisions away from Army Group South-Ukraine, and he had sent Schörner to Army Group North, where his particular skills were urgently needed. This brought Marshal Antonescu protesting to Rastenburg on August 5. Guderian—speaking French, for the marshal spoke no German—explained the military situation. Hitler spoke through his interpreter to Antonescu for hours on end, assuring him that the Stauffenberg putsch was of no importance, that impressive new German tanks and guns were under construction, that a new explosive "at the experimental stage" was capable of killing everybody within two miles of its point of impact, that he had failed to keep his promise about the Crimea and Ukraine because of "traitors" in the General Staff who had encouraged the decay of the lines of communication, and that pro-Soviet traitors had also procured the collapse of Army Group Center. But Antonescu was disturbed at the growing financial burden of enemy air raids on Romania—particularly now that the enemy might begin using Turkish airfields—and the discussion was sometimes heated. He assured Hitler that his army was completely loyal to him, that "he would remain at Germany's side and be the last country to abandon the Reich"; but Hitler mistrusted King Michael as he mistrusted every monarch.

It was a warm summer's day as Hitler took leave of Antonescu. He did not drive to the airfield with him, but as the column of cars moved off he suddenly stepped forward and called out in German, "Antonescu! Antonescu! On no account set foot inside the king's castle!" Antonescu had not understood him and stopped the car. Hitler repeated, "Don't go into the king's castle!" A sudden instinct had warned him that he might otherwise not see Antonescu again.

Before July was over, Himmler's drastic measures had provided the army with forty new reserve battalions, of which thirty were earmarked for Army Group North alone. The new divisions were divisions with a difference; they were now called *Volksgrenadier* divisions, for Himmler had obtained Hitler's approval to raise a People's Army which would eventually supplant and replace the army of Hans von Seeckt, Werner von Fritsch, and Walther von Brauchitsch—which he identified only with obstructionism, defeatism, and retreat. The Himmler divisions were designed to attract German youth untainted by the spirit of the older generation. Whereas General Fromm had grudgingly furnished Hitler with

60,000 new soldiers a month, by mid-August Himmler had already raised 450,000 new troops, and 250,000 more recruits were already in the barracks.

When Bormann assembled the Gauleiters at Posen on August 3, Himmler boasted of his prowess as the new de facto Commander in Chief of the army. He boasted too of having prepared since Stalingrad for such a putsch as the one on July 20, insisting for example on a separate training ground for the SS in Lausitz, near Berlin. But he could not explain how the rambling, ill-concealed Stauffenberg network had escaped his scrutiny. Speer then spoke of how future arms production would restore Germany's freedom of action and air supremacy by December. Production of the excellent MPi 44 submachine gun would increase fivefold to 100,000 a month; of tanks from 1,680 to 3,200; of V-1 flying bombs from 3,000 to 9,000; and of fighter aircraft from 2,927 to 4,800.[1]

Thus encouraged, the Gauleiters came to hear Hitler speak on August 4. He was still unwell—at times he felt dizzy and there was a ringing in his ears *(tinnitus aurium)*. One diarist wrote: "The Führer walked in very slowly and stiffly, and proffered only his left hand; but later, when he began his speech, he loosened up and became more lively." No transcript has survived, but he evidently disclosed that he had set up an Army Court of Honor under Rundstedt to discharge the conspirators from the Wehrmacht so that they could be tried by the People's Court; those found guilty would be hanged. "What annoyed him most was that a clown like Goerdeler had been chosen to succeed him." Another diarist, Helmút Sündermann, the deputy press chief, wrote:

> The speech's beginning was delayed a bit as the Führer ordered the prepared desk to be removed; he had a small table and chair brought, sat down, and began to speak so softly at first that I had difficulty hearing from the back row. Then his voice rapidly rose. "I always knew that shots would be fired at me one day from this quarter; but I never dreamed the blow would be struck so far below the belt!" He said he was now "old and shaky," not because of his fight against Germany's enemies but because of the perpetual conflict with "this clique which always eluded me." This numerically small but highly influential group would have been totally incapable of any real political achievements, as they were wholly out of touch with the broad public. . . . Now we were in the position of somebody who had been poisoned—if we could surmount this crisis then we would not be dead, but in superb health. Although he had spoken virtually nothing of substance, his speech had an obvious impact on the Gauleiters. As the senior man present, [Konstantin] Hierl [leader of the Reich Labor Service] spoke a few words of thanks to the Führer: "There is only one kind of loyalty. There is no 'loyal, more loyal, loyalest.' There is only 'loyal,' and that says everything."

---

[1]Martin Bormann later warned Hitler that several Gauleiters had proof that Speer's figures were dishonest. Speer now admits that they were deliberately exaggerated, though justifiably so.

The Führer's insomnia had returned, and with it his nervous twitch. He scoffed at Stauffenberg's "bungling," but the injuries to his legs and arms were very painful, and Morell's treatment of his right elbow—a bandage soaked in acid aluminum acetate—had resulted in dermatitis and pruritis which left it so swollen that he could not sign state documents; when unsuspecting frontline generals heartily grasped his right hand he winced at the pain. Morell was also treating him with massive doses of Ultraseptyl, a sulfonamide-type drug (as Germany had no penicillin); the other doctors noted with concern that the Führer's health had begun to deteriorate. An oxygen bottle now stood permanently hissing in one corner of his bedroom, but still he could not sleep. One night, just after he had drifted off, the emergency lighting suddenly came on. "I had to clamber about like a monkey," he grumbled to his manservant. "I dragged a table over, but the fixture was right up in the ceiling, and then of course the bulb was so tightly screwed in that it was all I could do to unscrew it."

An unsettling predicament had confronted him since August 1. One of the confessed putschists, Lieutenant-Colonel Caesar von Hofacker, had convincingly implicated both Field Marshal von Kluge and the invalid Field Marshal Rommel in the July 20 plot. The degree of their involvement was uncertain, but neither had reported the conspiracy to Hitler. Both these officers enjoyed an immense popularity in the army—it would be unthinkable to stand them before the People's Court. Hitler decided to wait and see. He told Guderian: "Kluge is an accessory, but we cannot dispense with him." He sent for Jodl privately on August 1, showed him the Hofacker interrogation report, and indicated that as soon as Rommel had recovered, he would personally question him and then retire him from the army without fuss. As he said a few weeks later, "He has done the worst possible thing a soldier can do under such circumstances—sought for some way out other than the purely military."

The Allies had now landed a million and a half troops on the Normandy beachhead. The attempted British breakthrough from Caumont had been checked; but through the breach at Avranches on the coast, at the extreme southwestern end of the German containing line, American armor and troops were pouring into Brittany—General George S. Patton's Third Army. To Hitler it seemed that the Americans had suddenly mastered the German knack of exploiting God-given opportunities, but there was an obvious countermove: if German tanks struck through to the coast again, it would sever the one artery on which Patton's bold thrust relied. "We must strike like lightning," he announced. "When we reach the sea the American spearheads will be cut off. Obviously they are trying all-out for a major decision here, because otherwise they wouldn't have sent in their best general, Patton. That's the most dangerous man they have. But the more troops they squeeze through the gap, and the better they are, the better for us when we reach the sea and cut them off! We might even be able to eliminate their whole beachhead. We mustn't get bogged down with mopping up the Americans that have broken through; their turn will come later. We must wheel north like lightning and turn the entire enemy front from the rear." If Hitler's stroke of genius came off, the Allies would scarcely have time to beat a disorderly retreat to their artificial harbors off the Normandy beaches—and then he, Hitler, could turn his attention to Russia once again.

It was an intoxicating prospect, though with obvious fallacies. Hitler issued the order for the attack late on August 2. It was to be spearheaded by General von Funck's Forty-seventh Panzer Corps. Hitler planned to employ eight of his nine panzer divisions in Normandy, and a thousand fighter planes. He sent Jodl's deputy, General Warlimont, to "sit in" on Kluge's headquarters personally, and the generals there assured Warlimont that the attack might well succeed. During the sixth, Hitler drafted a powerfully worded message to Funck's troops:

> The outcome of the Battle for France depends on the success of the attack on the southern wing of the Seventh Army. Commander in Chief West [Kluge] will have a unique and unrepeatable opportunity of thrusting into a region largely devoid of the enemy, and to change the whole situation thereby.

While the spearheads were thrust boldly through to the sea, fresh panzer divisions were to follow in their wake and wheel north, where they would turn the enemy front in Normandy. "The utmost boldness, determination, and imagination must inspire every commander down to the lowest levels," Hitler's order continued. "Each man must believe in victory. The restoration of order in the rear areas and in Brittany can be left until later." But in a series of telephone conversations that afternoon General Jodl learned that Kluge was planning to start the attack before midnight, without waiting for the fighter squadrons to arrive. In addition, only four of the planned eight panzer divisions could be extricated from the battlefield in the north in time, and those that had arrived were still short of tanks and artillery. So far Funck would command only 75 Mark IV tanks, 70 Mark Vs, and 32 self-propelled assault guns. Kluge explained that the enemy had already detected their preparations, and he was prepared to take the responsibility for jumping off now even though understrength.

Hitler mistrusted Kluge's judgment. Above all, he wanted Kluge to wait for the right weather. He sent his best infantry general, Walter Buhle—whom he had earmarked as Zeitzler's eventual successor—by plane to France to influence Kluge, but it was too late: the half-cocked thrust toward Avranches had already begun by the time Buhle arrived. The first big town, Mortain, was recaptured by an SS panzer division, but then the fog lifted and a murderous enemy air assault began. Over a thousand Allied fighter-bombers roamed the battlefield virtually unchecked; the Luftwaffe could provide only 300 fighter planes, and by the next day, August 8, only 110 were still in action. Kluge's grenadiers unflinchingly faced slaughter by the enemy's strategic bomber squadrons, but the tanks themselves could proceed no farther. At eleven that evening Kluge informed Jodl that he had failed. When General Warlimont reported back from France that day, Hitler terminated his battle narrative with one rasping sentence—as ominous as the judgment the People's Court passed that same day on Witzleben, Hoepner, and their fellow conspirators: "The attack failed because Kluge *wanted* it to fail."[2]

Kluge's headquarters warned that the enemy's objective was becoming plainer every day: "Target Paris!"

At Hitler's headquarters the fiasco of Kluge's first counterattack was openly blamed on the Luftwaffe. But Reichsmarschall Göring had not been seen here since July 23, and he still had to introduce to Hitler a successor to the fatally injured Chief of Staff. Korten's deputy—an able Bavarian general, Karl Koller —officiated in their absence. Göring recognized that his own star was waning. After the July 20 putsch attempt, Admiral Dönitz had preceded him in a broadcast to the nation, and he was no match for the new Himmler-Bormann-Goebbels triumvirate; he had therefore retired to bed, surrounded by medicines. He eventually named Werner Kreipe as Korten's successor over the far more capable Koller, although Kreipe was many years the latter's junior. Until Göring had "recovered," Koller had to bear the brunt of Hitler's intemperate attacks. "At every conference the Führer goes on for hours on end about the Luftwaffe," lamented Koller in his fragmentary shorthand diary on August 8. "He strongly reproaches the Luftwaffe. The reasons are our lack of aircraft, technological shortcomings, and noncompletion of the replacement squadrons in the Reich, the Me-262, etc. . . . How am I to know what claims the Reichsmarschall and General Korten made, or undo the wrongs committed from 1939 to 1942 through the total absence of any planning? It's a hard lot to have to answer for these errors."

Six squadrons, each of sixty-eight fighters, had been transferred to the Reich for rehabilitation in July; now that Hitler ordered Kluge to prepare a second attack on Avranches, a tug-of-war began over these squadrons. He instructed Jodl late on the eighth to transfer four squadrons to the west by August 12. Kreipe was horrified and telephoned Göring and General Galland. "Both agree with me: the squadrons aren't ready, they will sink without trace in the chaos of the west

---

[2] The principal cause for the failure of Hitler's plan, here as elsewhere, was that OKW code signals were being deciphered by the British.

and then they are lost to the home defense." (This was sheer shortsightedness, because if the enemy overran France, his intensified bombing operations from French airfields would take more than four extra squadrons of fighters to prevent.) The next day Hitler increased his demand to six squadrons and ordered Kluge to be ready to attack Avranches again on the eleventh. "The Forty-seventh Panzer Corps attack failed because it was launched prematurely and was thus too weak, and under weather conditions favoring the enemy. It is to be repeated elsewhere with powerful forces." Kluge was to employ six panzer divisions in a more southwesterly direction than on the seventh; and General Hans Eberbach was to be in command instead of Funck (who had been on Fritsch's staff before the war and therefore could not be trusted).

General Kreipe was finally introduced to Hitler on August 11, and wrote in his diary: "The Führer has become very bent, with cotton wool in his ears, and frequently trembles uncontrollably; one must not shake his hand too violently. ... First the Führer asked me about my career, then spoke at length on the origins of what he called the collapse and failure of the Luftwaffe—primarily the errors of the Reichsmarschall's technical advisers, who had made overhasty promises about the quality and quantity of new aircraft types. The air staff had probably also been deceived, and—through negligence or ignorance—made false statements to him on which he [Hitler] had unhappily based his decision. He mentioned Milch, Udet, and Jeschonnek in this context." Kreipe swore to speak only the unadulterated truth to him.

In France, meanwhile, the Goddess of Fortune had eluded Hitler's grasp and would not return. Suffice to say that events now overtook General Eberbach. The force he had assembled invited envelopment by the enemy, and the invitation was accepted. On the twelfth, the Allies captured Alençon in Eberbach's rear, and by late on the thirteenth the jaws closing on him—the British and Canadians from Falaise in the north, and the Americans from Argentan—were barely twenty miles apart. Desperate fighting ensued in the Falaise pocket to prevent the encirclement of the bulk of the German Seventh Army and Eberbach's Fifth Panzer Army. Small personal tragedies occurred, hurting Hitler deeply. Hans Pfeiffer, his one-time adjutant, died in a blazing tank in Normandy. Hans Junge, the young SS captain who had been his orderly, was struck down by a strafing Spitfire far behind the lines. Frau Traudl Junge was Hitler's youngest secretary—he kept the gloomy secret to himself until it was confirmed some days later, then broke it to her in person. "Ach, child, I am so sorry; your husband had a fine character." Bormann's private letters testify to Hitler's dejection over this one episode.

Field Marshal Kluge's tactics in Normandy, meanwhile, defied explanation. Despite Hitler's clear orders, he was still holding Eberbach's tank forces too far to the north, thus positively aiding Patton's encirclement operation. On August 14 Hitler again ordered Eberbach to attack the American Fifteenth Corps at Alençon; Kluge was to use the Nineteenth Army to defend the Mediterranean coast of France against the invasion now known to be imminent there as well.[3] Patton's tanks were already roaming across Brittany. The fortress commandant of Saint-Malo—a port Hitler had ordered strongly defended—radioed: "The enemy is putting German prisoners on his tanks so as to get close to our strong-points." A Luftwaffe general attending Hitler's midday conference recorded: "Tense atmosphere. Fegelein [Himmler's liaison officer to Hitler] dropped hints that even more generals and field marshals are involved in July 20." That after-noon Heinrich Himmler, conferring alone with Hitler in the now restored confer-ence barracks where Stauffenberg's bomb had exploded, arrived with still firmer proof that both Kluge and Rommel had been in the anti-Hitler conspiracy up to their necks. Late that evening, news reached Hitler's conference that the invasion of the French Riviera was underway.

Thus August 15, 1944, arrived. "The worst day of my life," Hitler subsequently admitted. It brought one of the war's great unsolved riddles. At the morning conference the news was that the Americans had started their big attack on the Falaise pocket, and the fate of Eberbach's panzer divisions was in the balance; but Field Marshal von Kluge had disappeared. He had ostensibly set out to confer with Eberbach on whether to abandon the panzer attack on Alençon. But he had not arrived, and an *enemy* radio signal was monitored asking where Kluge was! Was it coincidence that Major General Henning von Tresckow and so many other leading conspirators of July 20 had served under Kluge in Russia until 1943? The clouds of suspicion suddenly loomed up. As evening came, Hitler learned that Kluge's radio truck had been silent since last signaling at 9:30 A.M., and neither Eberbach, nor SS General Hausser, nor SS General Sepp Dietrich had seen him. Either he was dead, gunned down like Hans Junge by a strafing aircraft—or he was at that very moment secretly negotiating the surrender of the entire western front to the enemy. "To change our destiny by surrendering to the British and joining forces against Russia—what an idiotic notion!" Hitler scoffed a few days later. From his own sources he had long decided that Churchill had sold out the Balkans and all Europe east of the river Elbe—if not indeed the Weser—to Stalin.

---

[3]Largely by close surveillance of enemy ships passing Gibraltar, the German naval staff deduced that an invasion of southern France was imminent, although most of the evidence gained by German secret agents (*i.e.,* those leftovers of the Canaris era) pointed the other way. General Charles de Gaulle provided the necessary confirmation in a radio broadcast to France on August 7, boasting that "a mighty French army" (*i.e.,* that in North Africa) would shortly set foot in France.

He had recently described Britain's standpoint as *"Après moi le déluge—*if only we can get rid of the hated National Socialist Germany."

At 7:30 P.M. on August 15 Hitler ordered SS General Hausser to take over Army Group B and stop the enemy onrush threatening to envelope the Fifth Panzer Army. Kluge was still missing. Hitler spent a sleepless night, swallowed fresh sedatives to no avail at 6 A.M., and asked for a doctor again at eleven. He learned that Eberbach's HQ had reported Kluge's arrival late that night in the heart of the Falaise pocket; there was no explanation of where he had been all day.

Hitler could trust him no longer, and he radioed the order "Field Marshal von Kluge is to leave the danger area immediately for Fifth Panzer Army HQ, from which he is to direct the withdrawal movement." (From outside the pocket, Kluge could no longer secretly contact the Allies.) Field Marshal Model, to whom Hitler had only the day before pinned the Diamonds award for his magnificent reconstruction of Army Group Center, and who was already back at the eastern front, was now recalled to the Wolf's Lair and secretly appointed Kluge's successor. His instructions were to build up a new front in France as far forward of the Seine-Yonne line as possible, using to that end divisions evacuated from southern France step by step (any other line would mean the loss of the French coast and the V-1 launching sites).

Model was sent by plane to Kluge with a sealed letter ordering him back to Germany. He arrived unannounced at Kluge's headquarters late on the seventeenth and immediately issued orders which resulted three days later in the almost unhoped-for escape of the main German forces from the Falaise encirclement. Kluge returned to his native village—but in a coffin, having been killed on the nineteenth by a cerebral hemorrhage, according to the army doctors. Hitler, thwarted of his prey, ordered a second autopsy; but even Model's doctors again reported natural causes. According to his Chief of Staff, General Blumentritt, Kluge had been shocked by the failure of his counterattack on Avranches on August 7 and upset by Hitler's reproaches; he had sent his son into the Falaise pocket with the words "Let nobody accuse me of sparing my son and heir"; on the road to Nécy, the prearranged rendezvous with Eberbach and Hausser on the fifteenth, Kluge had seen four of his staff killed when their radio truck was strafed —hence, apparently, the day-long silence on his movements. Blumentritt had last seen him on the eighteenth, tapping a battle chart and moaning, "Avranches, Avranches! This town has cost me my reputation as a soldier. I'll go down in history as the Benedeck of the western front.[4] D'you know Count Moltke's book

---

[4] Ludwig von Benedeck commanded the Austrian army crushingly defeated at the Battle of König-gratz by General Helmuth von Moltke during the Austro-Prussian War (1866).

on Benedeck? I did my best, but that's fate for you." It seemed that an aged field marshal had faded away, his heart worn out by the burden of being both Commander in Chief West and Commander of Army Group B. Hitler allowed preparations for a state funeral to proceed; but mistrustfully he ordered SS doctors to stage yet a third autopsy, and meanwhile the death was to remain a state secret.

American forces had reached the Seine on August 18 and were only thirty-six miles from Paris. The German army was in full flight across the river, by barge, pontoon bridge, and raft, abandoning its heavy gear to the enemy in a panic-stricken scramble for the German frontier. Some German soldiers blamed the lack of fuel and motor transportation for the German defeat in France; others, the age and indolence of their commanders. The Luftwaffe's General Koller returned from Paris with grim reports on the moral decay of the army after four years of occupation and a carefree life as demigods.

Hitler had foreseen that all this would happen if the Normandy front collapsed; his generals had their "war of movement" with a vengeance. On the nineteenth he called in Keitel, Speer, and Jodl and soberly ordered them to lay the material foundations for a new western army, as he was planning a great counteroffensive in November when the enemy air forces would be grounded by bad weather. Twenty-five divisions must be raised and equipped for this. (Thus was born the Ardennes offensive of December.)

Martin Bormann steered most of the odium for the defeat onto the Luftwaffe. Göring was still malingering, and Hitler asked caustically how long the Reichsmarschall's illness might be expected to last; not until August 26 did Göring reappear at the Wolf's Lair, after an absence of five weeks. Meanwhile Bormann, aided by Goebbels, had initiated a "Luftwaffe Scandals" file to which the Gauleiters contributed profusely. Bombs had been shunted out of bombproof stores to make room for contraband from Italy and Greece. At Rechlin, the main experimental airfield, a technician tipped off Bormann that a villa was being built for the commandant at Lake Ammersee at Luftwaffe expense and that Luftwaffe workmen were flying down to Bavaria each weekend to finish the job. Göring's sacked deputy, Milch, was accused of having fostered bad aircraft and aeroengine projects for the sake of old Lufthansa business cronies. Gauleiter Hartmann Lauterbacher reported that four hundred flying instructors and pupils who had volunteered for an immediate special Reich-defense mission had been idle ever since. In Italy, General Maximilian Ritter von Pohl's staff had swollen while his squadrons had diminished; his officers were said to be idling in luxury hotels, with ample cigarettes, cognac, and coffee, or lazing on beaches with their female personnel.

Small wonder that Hitler unfavorably compared the Luftwaffe's squandering of manpower with the way that Himmler had conjured up new battalions for the army. Air Chief of Staff General Kreipe could not even find out how many men were in the Luftwaffe. Hitler began to think of dissolving the entire Luftwaffe and building up the antiaircraft defenses instead. On August 17 he had angrily telephoned Kreipe and instructed him to replace Field Marshal Sperrle, the fat Luftwaffe commander in France, by General Dessloch; it was typical of Hitler to have delayed this decision until now, when it was too late. The future of the Messerschmitt 262 jet was again debated. The first jet bomber squadron was still to enter service; Göring, Kreipe, Speer, and Galland all wanted the Me-262 used as a fighter after all. But now the enemy's bombing of the oil plants had reduced aviation fuel supplies to a trickle. The bombproof refineries would not begin operating until March 1945, but by December the OKW fuel reserve would have been consumed. Small wonder that Hitler began complaining of splitting headaches to his doctors; the ringing in his ears just would not stop.

On August 20, 1944, the Red Army launched its main offensive of the late summer on General Friessner's army group on the Romanian frontier—twenty-seven German and twenty Romanian divisions on a three-hundred-mile front from the Carpathians to the Black Sea. Within three days the Sixth Army would be all but encircled here, but Hitler's eyes were still on France. In Paris, armed partisan bands had risen against the German garrison. General Dietrich von Choltitz, the arrogant, feckless military commander Hitler had only recently appointed in place of General Hans von Boineburg—who had allowed the capital to decay into a rotten *Etappenstadt* of draft dodgers, malingerers, and army scroungers—asked the insurgents for a three-day armistice to prevent harm from coming to life, limb, or the capital. The insurgents agreed, Choltitz withdrew his pitifully few troops to the east bank of the Seine, and then, to his injured surprise, the uprising began again the next day. Paris, however, was vital both militarily and politically, and Hitler had emphatically demanded its defense in an order of the twentieth; and not just the city, but a cordon well outside the city. Every Seine bridge between Paris and the sea had been destroyed; Hitler ordered those intact in Paris heavily defended by antiaircraft guns. If, however, the bridges fell undemolished into enemy hands—and Choltitz had not even mined them yet—then the enemy could prise open Hitler's coastal defenses from the rear and rob him of his V-1 launching sites as well. "In all history the loss of Paris has meant the loss of France," Hitler reminded Model in an order on August 22. "Inside the city the first signs of revolt are to be harshly put down, *e.g.,* by blowing up entire street blocks, by public execution of the ringleaders, or by evacuation of any districts involved, as only this will stop things getting out of hand. The Seine bridges are to be prepared for demolition. Paris must not fall into enemy hands—or if it does, then only as a field of ruins."

Where previously he had relied on his army generals, now Hitler leaned increasingly on his trusted Party comrades—particularly on Martin Bormann and Heinrich Himmler, both of whom took to attending the regular war conferences. It was Bormann who mobilized the Gauleiters and Reich officials to construct deep frontier defenses in the west. When Hitler's two southeastern commanders, Weichs and Löhr, came for a conference on August 22, Himmler was also inexplicably hovering in the background. Weichs had brought news of a remarkable rapprochement between General Nedić, the puppet prime minister of Serbia, and Draža Mihajlović, leader of the Četnik guerrillas, who proposed to unite in the face of the threat to the Serbs posed by Tito's Communist partisans; together they had offered to help Hitler in the Balkans if he would provide the necessary ammunition—three million rounds—and allow them to raise an army of fifty thousand men from the Četniks. Weichs admitted that these two men would have 90 percent of the Serbs behind them and proposed a modified acceptance of their terms—perhaps a quarter of a million rounds and six thousand troops at first. All Hitler's latent Austrian resentment against the Serbs welled up within him. "The Serbs are the only eternally consistent people in the Balkans," Jodl's diary quoted him as warning. "They alone have the strength and the ability to keep pursuing their pan-Serbian aims." Hitler's experiences in arming helpful friends and neighbors had chastened him; too often the ammunition had ended up in the bodies of German troops. He would therefore permit the new experiment proposed by Weichs on only the smallest scale.

Joseph Goebbels came the next day to confer with Hitler and Bormann. All Germany's erstwhile allies were scampering off the sinking ship. On August 17, Keitel had decorated Marshal Mannerheim with a high German award; but Mannerheim had pointedly responded that the Finnish people had made him president in place of Ryti because they objected to the latter's pro-German policies. This gave the marshal "a free hand."

On the southern Russian front, Marshal Rodion Malinovski's armies were pouring into Romania. Far into the night Hitler—his inflamed sinuses preventing sleep—conferred from his bed with Generals Guderian and Jodl. He trusted Marshal Antonescu, but not the Romanian army; indeed, only recently he had secretly authorized General Friessner to withdraw Army Group South-Ukraine to the obvious best line—from Galatz on the Danube to the Carpathians—the instant the Russians attacked. But to say that the Romanian divisions were failing would be a euphemism. Friessner's Chief of Staff wrote: "It was obvious they were deliberately not fighting, so as to shorten the war." As Friessner fell back, Hitler obviously felt he could defend the new line and the vital oil fields, for on August

22 he ordered experts to find out if a seventy-foot-wide canal could be excavated immediately—using hordes of slave laborers—from the Danube to the Black Sea at Constanta; because if the Russians could blockade the Danube at its delta, the strategic implications would be vast. Rumors multiplied—for instance from the air attaché in Hungary—that a coup d'etat was imminent in Romania, but the German envoys in Bucharest itself reassured Hitler that all was well. Hitler rebuked Kreipe on August 21: "Your air attachés shouldn't poke their noses into what doesn't concern them. The SS report the opposite." Nonetheless Hitler at last decided to replace General Hansen as his military representative in Bucharest.

Again he was overtaken by the rudeness of events. He was having tea with his staff in his bunker late that day, August 23, when his Wehrmacht adjutant, Amsberg, called him to the telephone. A voice announced that Marshal Antonescu had just been arrested after seeking an audience with his king. Hitler replaced the receiver and commented to Amsberg: "Why on earth didn't he listen to me! I knew this would happen!" Shortly afterward, Romanian radio broadcast a proclamation by King Michael: "The Romanian government has accepted the armistice offered by Russia and the United Nations." The Allies had promised to restore Transylvania to Romania, to guarantee her independence, and to fight side by side with her against the Hungarian dictatorship. The king ordered his forces not to open hostilities with the German Wehrmacht, however. This was cold comfort for Hitler, for much of his current oil requirements were met from the Romanian wells. But his men in Bucharest were not men of action—indeed, as in Warsaw and Paris, the German agencies were scattered throughout the capital of Romania and the surrounding country with a blithe disregard for a potential emergency such as this; the embassy's radio station was in a distant suburb, which left Hitler reliant on the ancient Romanian telephone service. Kreipe wrote that evening: "Telephone conversation with Ambassador [Manfred] von Killinger, and Gerstenberg [the Luftwaffe attaché] in Bucharest. Both trapped in the legation, Killinger a complete wreck, sends greetings to the Führer. Gerstenberg suggests dive-bomber attack and using the [German] antiaircraft division at Ploesti to seize the city! I phone Hitler several times, he approves Gerstenberg's proposals, demands the arrest of the king. Contact established with Bucharest once more, then interrupted."

From 9:45 P.M. until far into the night Hitler's headquarters issued orders to Friessner's army group and General Hansen—still the German military representative in the Bucharest legation. Friessner was to prepare for a German takeover of the oil fields and plan means for getting the oil to the Reich. Every German serviceman in Romania was placed at his disposal. Hansen was to put down the putsch, the Fifth Antiaircraft Division at Ploesti was to occupy the capital as Gersternberg had suggested, and Admiral Brinkmann was to seize the

Black Sea harbor of Constanta. A pro-Nazi Romanian general was to be appointed head of the government. Friessner promptly dismissed Hansen and commanded Gerstenberg to execute Hitler's orders.

Hitler began his delayed evening war conference at 2 A.M. and afterward again discussed the wholly altered Balkan situation with Field Marshal von Weichs. He had decided to abandon Greece to the enemy the moment they attacked, particularly the Peloponnesus.[5] He would shift his Schwerpunkt to northern Greece. This made it vital to prevent the Bulgarians—whose defection was clearly only hours away—from seizing the railway line from Nis to Skoplje for the Allies, as this was the only link with Greece.

At 3:30 A.M. Gerstenberg radioed from Ploesti to Hitler's headquarters: "Fought my way out and took command in Ploesti together with SS General Hoffmeyer." But both Hansen and Killinger had already given up hope. Their telephone message reached East Prussia an hour later: "This is no putsch by some court camarilla, but a well-laid coup d'etat from above with the complete backing of the army and people." Not one Romanian general sympathetic to Nazi Germany could now be found. The Romanians controlled the means of communication. "Given the balance of forces, there is at present no prospect of a military or political success." However, Hitler repeated his orders and detailed Ribbentrop to broadcast a proclamation to the Romanians; Horia Sima, the leader of the Iron Guard which had with Heydrich's clandestine backing unsuccessfully attempted to overthrow Antonescu in January 1941—after helping him to power in 1940—would be brought out of German exile, where he had languished then on Antonescu's insistence, and appointed his successor.

Hitler had ordered Gerstenberg to advance on Bucharest at 6:30 A.M., and five hours later the two thousand antiaircraft troops were at the city's northern outskirts. Gerstenberg emphatically disowned Hansen's gloomy assessment and called down three bombing attacks on the city center. But he was outnumbered 4 to 1; the Romanians had mined the approach roads and they were bringing up tanks and artillery. Gerstenburg captured the radio station, but without proper combat troops he could proceed no farther. Hitler ordered more troops in. "War conference with the Führer," a Luftwaffe general wrote at midday. "Everyone busy with Romania. Hitler very optimistic, curses SS Intelligence service and foreign ministry, mimicks Ribbentrop.—Goebbels and Bormann also present." But the new troops were slow in arriving, and the Romanians were master of their capital still.

The midday conference next day was long and acrimonious. "Ribbentrop

---

[5]This and his recent secret order to General Friessner (page 691) again refute the postwar legend that Hitler never voluntarily abandoned territory when it was strategically desirable that he do so.

pleads extenuating circumstances, is sure Killinger and Gerstenberg will restore the situation. Hitler accepts this view." Using the bombing attacks as an excuse, the Romanians declared war on Germany on the twenty-fifth. Hitler transferred General Stahel, the Luftwaffe troubleshooter-general who had had served him well in Sicily and more recently in Vilna and Warsaw, to take command in Bucharest. But within four days of his arriving in Romania he and Gerstenberg were captives of the Red Army now debouching into the country. Baron Manfred von Killinger committed suicide as his legation was stormed.

With the now hostile Romanians in the rear, Friessner's army group collapsed; sixteen German divisions were wiped out in the debacle. Finland and Bulgaria trembled, and from Hungary too came sounds of an imminent earthquake that needed no seismograph for Hitler to detect.

To his war staff Hitler still radiated confidence and dynamism. A young SS captain, fresh from the street-fighting in Warsaw, who now joined the conferences as Fegelein's adjutant, jotted down his first impressions on August 27, 1944:

> After supper at 10 P.M. work goes on until 3 A.M. or even later. Every day I see the Führer for several hours and stand only a pace or two away; each day it is the same great experience anew, one I will never forget. I am filled with the most ineffable admiration of him; he is unique as a man, as a politician, as a military commander. He radiates such a comforting calmness. But more than once I have heard him speak harshly—and each occasion was when on purpose or sometimes out of ignorance less than the full and brutal truth had been spoken, or even an outright lie. He seems to sense it at once; it is enormously impressive for me. . . . The Führer is never angry if, as I have myself found several times, you tell him you have to make an immediate inquiry before you can answer a question or questions. What astounds me again and again is the radiance emanating from the Führer: I have seen the highest ranking officers come to report laden with problems and worries. They always leave his presence full of new confidence and hope.

Yet the secret image of Hitler was not always what the public then believed or history has come to accept of him. The sequel to July 20 provides many examples. He was revolted by the newsreel film of the People's Court hearing against Field Marshal Witzleben and the other putschists, and he sent a sharp rebuke to Roland Freisler over his melodramatic and insulting behavior as the judge. "He is behaving like a ham actor, instead of getting the trial of these common criminals over as quickly as possible," Hitler told Schaub. The hangings were also filmed, but Hitler refused to see the films; when Fegelein produced photographs of the naked corpses, Hitler irritably tossed the pictures aside. Helldorf—on his instructions—was required to witness his fellow-conspirators' execution before his turn came. Hitler ordered their property sold to benefit the "frontline troops" they had betrayed. Most remarkable was his instruction to Himmler at the end of August to provide proper monthly subsistence payments to the next-of-kin of the hanged men "to spare them the worst hardships as in the case of the next-of-kin left by those shot after [the Röhm purge of] June 30, 1934."

About 140 people were executed after July 20, and perhaps 700 more arrested. Investigations still continued.

Choltitz's feeble surrender of Paris on August 25 now made it impossible to build a Somme-Marne position in time. Warsaw, Paris, and now Bucharest had seen disgraceful scenes of German officialdom—and above all Wehrmacht officers —in full flight. Hitler issued an angry order to his viceroys to prevent any recurrence by evacuating their main staffs immediately from the biggest non-German cities:

> Our military and civilian authorities are often living irresponsibly and opulently without the slightest warlike preparations, sometimes even surrounded by their families and female employees. Defeats at the front coupled with uprisings in the cities result in their being paralyzed the moment a crisis breaks out. The upshot is that our troops are witness to a panic-stricken headlong flight, encumbered by a disgraceful load of German and alien womenfolk and their own or other people's ill-gotten goods, streaming across the countryside.
>
> Nothing is more likely to tarnish the image of these German authorities and thus of the Reich in the eyes of our troops and foreign populations. When their escape is cut off and the German authorities are trapped by the enemy or insurgents, moreover, it is the combat troops who have to go in and risk their own lives to protect them or rescue them from their luxurious quarters.

Shameful word reached Hitler of the scenes of rout and degradation in France. In one area, five chaotic columns—two of them out in the fields—belonging to five different divisions streamed eastward down the same road toward Belgium or the West Wall. In another, officers forced their cars past bridge bottlenecks at pistol point, or Luftwaffe trucks laden with furniture and loot pulled out of bases in which irreplaceable radar gear or artillery or ammunition would fall intact into enemy hands. All the while enemy aircraft leisurely strafed the columns from a hundred feet up with cannon and machine-gun fire.

Scapegoats were sought in Rommel's old headquarters most of all. General Speidel, the Chief of Staff, was indicted by several of the putschists as an accomplice, but Model demurred at his release, and two weeks passed before Speidel was turned over to the Gestapo. Hitler assumed that all Rommel's associates had become infected by the spirit of July 20.

Kluge's mortal remains were still at his village church, awaiting burial while rumor and speculation spread. On August 28, General Burgdorf, chief of army personnel, showed Hitler the long-awaited report on the third autopsy, by SS doctors—and with it a long, penciled letter Kluge had addressed to his Führer. Martin Bormann noted triumphantly in his diary:

> On the evening of August 28, SS General Fegelein disclosed to me that analysis by the RSHA [Reich Main Security Office] has established that Field Marshal Kluge poisoned himself with cyanide! And that Kluge wrote the Führer a farewell letter, which General Burgdorf handed to him.
> Kluge wrote that as a soldier he has drawn the consequences of his defeat, which he had predicted and dreaded all along. In Kluge's view Germany's defeat is inevitable; hence the Führer should realize this and act accordingly.

The letter was a strange amalgam of Nazi fanaticism, personal asseverations of loyalty, and defeatism. The next day cross-examination of Kluge's nephew in the People's Court elicited clear proof that the field marshal was linked with the plotters—evidence so damning that a stunned Judge Freisler adjourned the trial to send for Kluge, not realizing that he was long dead. To Speidel's successor, General Hans Krebs, Hitler vented his bitter disgust thus: "Twice I personally promoted him, I gave him the highest medals, a big cash gift to buy an estate, and a supplement to his field marshal's pay. . . . Maybe he just slid in, I don't know; maybe he saw no other way out: he saw one officer after another being arrested, and feared what they might testify."

Hitler ordered a quiet funeral, with military pallbearers but no other honors. Now he could interpret the army's reports on that "blackest day"—August 15—more certainly: obviously Kluge *had* tried to contact the enemy, only to have a chance fighter-bomber destroy his only radio truck. Why else had he stopped halfway and sent off his staff officer, Major Behr, to go on alone to the alleged rendezvous planned with Eberbach and the other generals? "It was the purest chance that his plan was not carried out," Hitler marveled on August 31. "The army group's entire actions are explicable only in this light." But all of this was only of academic interest now.[6]

Kluge, at sixty-two, had given up the fight; Hitler, at fifty-five, would fight on. "We shall fight on, if need be on the Rhine. Where, matters not the least to me.

---

[6]I know of only one clue to the mystery on the Allied side. In American files is a reported statement of Lieutenant Colonel George R. Pfann, secretary of General Patton's Third Army General Staff, in 1945. Pfann explained that Patton had vanished from Third Army HQ for an entire day in mid-August, 1944; when he returned, he stated he had been out to try to make contact with a German emissary, who had not, however, shown up at the appointed place. On the German side is the CIC interrogation of Kluge's son-in-law, Dr. Udo Esch (of the German army medical corps), on July 27, 1945. It was he who had supplied Kluge with the cyanide. Kluge, said Esch, discussed with him the possibility of surrendering the entire western front. "He went to the front lines but was unable to get in touch with the Allied commanders."

Come what may we will keep fighting this fight until—as Frederick the Great once said—one of our accursed enemies tires of the struggle, and we can get a peace assuring the German nation's livelihood for the next fifty or a hundred years—and above all a peace that does not drag our honor in the mire as happened in 1918."

Rommel Gets a Choice

"I have always said," remarked Hitler as autumn 1944 approached, "the time is not ripe for a *political* decision. I think I may say I have shown often enough in my life that I know how to score political triumphs; I need hardly add that I won't let a suitable opportunity pass. But obviously it is infantile and naïve to look for a favorable political initiative at a moment of grave military defeats. There may be such initiatives once one has the upper hand again. . . ." The outburst was directed as much against Foreign Minister Ribbentrop as against Field Marshal Kluge. The day before, August 30, Ribbentrop had submitted a memorandum asking for authority to put out peace feelers; it began with a quotation from *Mein Kampf:* "The job of diplomatists is to ensure that a people does not founder heroically, but survives. Any means to this end is justified; to spurn such means can only be termed a contemptible crime."

But Hitler was waiting, yearning for a wholly different event—the moment when the differences between East and West finally brought the Russians into open conflict with their allies. He hinted to a French diplomat on September 1 that this was one hidden blessing of the German retreats: when the Bolsheviks filled the vacuum, their true brutal nature was not concealed for long. Was this perhaps the secret reason for Hitler's new readiness to evacuate his troops from the Balkans—to provide bait for his enemies to squabble over? One remarkable episode suggests that it was.

On September 2, Field Marshal von Weichs cabled Hitler's headquarters that British officers had asked for a meeting in which to coordinate Germany's step-by-step withdrawal from Greece with the British advance, so as to leave no such momentary vacuum for Communists to fill. Weichs reminded Jodl that the Führer had disclosed his intention of abandoning southern Greece.[1] But captured

---

[1]See page 693.

documents clearly betrayed the Communists' intentions of seizing the key posts there before the British could take over. Dr. Hermann Neubacher, the foreign minister's special envoy to the Balkans, supported Weichs's appeal for permission to meet the British. But Hitler—his eye now on more distant aims—refused. Already the Russians were south of Bucharest, thrusting toward the Danube— probably, in Hitler's view, racing for the Aegean Sea and the Dardanelles before the British could get there. As the great German withdrawal from southern Greece began, the British took no action to disrupt it—another sign, in his view, that Stalin had laid claim to the entire Balkans. "It is politically desirable to foment trouble between Communists and nationalists in every region we abandon," quoted Jodl in his diary.

Besides, Hitler had another card up his sleeve. By way of Japan, loud and unmistakable hints reached Hitler late in August that Stalin was reluctant to destroy Germany, as Russia would need all Germany's industrial expertise in the coming conflict with the West. "Stalin is evidently willing to conclude a peace treaty even with a National Socialist Germany under Adolf Hitler," the telegram from Tokyo read. This was why the Soviet offensive had stopped short of Russia's 1940 frontiers, and this was why Stalin had not emulated his western allies' terror-bombing of German cities. General Guderian agreed with Hitler that Germany still held some trump cards. If only Germany could survive the next months—"and that means holding the eastern and western fronts at all costs"— her military and political position could only get better.

Not sharing Hitler's strategic motivation, Finland and Bulgaria shortly followed Romania's distressing example. On August 21 a German counteroffensive by the Third Panzer Army had restored contact with Schörner's isolated Army Group North, and he came to see Hitler six days later to plead for permission to abandon Estonia. On this occasion Hitler's silence alone persuaded Schörner to withdraw his request. But a few days later the political situation altered, for Hitler learned that Finland had begun armistice talks in Moscow. On September 2, General Kreipe wrote in his diary: "The Finns jump overboard. At war conference [Führer] swears about Mannerheim, takes immediate decisions." Himmler warned Hitler the same day of secret reports that Hungary was also planning to defect. Bulgaria too was unmistakably steering a course out of the war, and Hitler had to rule against any armed German intervention in Sofia; on the eighth the Bulgarian government formally declared war on the Reich. Finally, in Slovakia, smoldering partisan troubles blazed into open rebellion late in August, obliging Hitler to send in security forces and disarm the Slovak divisions.

All these diminutions of Hitler's empire produced one certainty: that within months his arms factories would no longer have the oil or raw materials to manufacture the weapons the Wehrmacht would need. It was a trend which did not take Hitler by surprise, for in August he had instructed Albert Speer to analyze just how long the war could be protracted, given a "minimum economic region." These instructions anticipated the German evacuation of Finland, Norway, and all southern Europe as far as the Alps in Italy, the Sava River in Yugoslavia and the Tisza River in Hungary. With France overrun by the enemy, all the machine tools and materials sent to the French factories by Speer were lost.[2]

The Reich had lost Ukrainian manganese, Turkish chrome, Portuguese and Spanish tungsten, Romanian petroleum, Balkan ores, southern France's bauxite, and probably the Finnish nickel of Petsamo. How long Sweden would supply iron ore was uncertain. On September 3, Speer had assured Dönitz he already had enough iron ore for the whole of 1945. But later, his experts' final verdict on Hitler's "minimum economic region" came to a very different conclusion: "If the present production of special steels is continued, chrome supplies will be exhausted by January 1, 1945. Then armament production will come to a complete standstill." Assuming this bottleneck could somehow be surmounted, steel output would end by August 31, 1945. This prognosis reached Hitler on September 5, 1944. "Hitler suddenly began talking of the war," a doctor treating him at this time recalled. "He said the British and American gentlemen had made a huge miscalculation. They had not been able to meet their invasion deadline. And he still had all the raw materials he needed to last one year; we even had enough gasoline stockpiled for eleven months." And his experts had talked of a new electrosteel process for hardening armor plate which would make them independent of foreign chrome and tungsten.

Even so, "one year" put a very clear deadline on any breach between East and West—if such a breach was to avail Hitler's Germany.

Under Albert Speer and Karl-Otto Saur, arms production was still soaring. A new peak had been reached in August 1944. With trembling and barely legible handwriting Hitler put the finishing touches and signature to a document commending his arms manufacturers.

His arm was still far from healed. He jokingly said to his secretaries, "Before the bomb I had this shake in my left leg; now it's in my right hand. I'm glad it

[2]Martin Bormann observed in an uncharitable memorandum of August 17, 1944: "This shows again how wrong Minister Speer's agreements with the French economics minister [Jean] Bichelonne [in October 1943] were. It would have been far better to follow Sauckel's demands to fetch as many [French] workers as possible into the Reich. . . . Now we have lost both the machine tools and the materials Herr Speer sent over to them."

hasn't reached my head yet. It'll be a bad day when I can't keep my head from nodding!" Worse, he had caught a head cold from his barber—for he still couldn't shave himself—and now sinus headaches kept him awake all night. His head felt as though it was bursting, and Morell's treatment did not improve it. Another doctor elicited the fact that Morell was using a sulfonamide drug, Ultraseptyl—preferring this to the more usual I. G. Farben sulfa drug Tibatin because it was made by a Budapest firm in which Morell had a controlling interest. At the end of this Ultraseptyl treatment, Hitler was almost paralyzed by stomach pains and lay awake with dreadful nightmares. On August 18, Professor von Eicken had examined him and recommended a different drug; but Morell sharply rebuked him: "Out of the question—the Führer is allergic to anything else." The army doctor, Erwin Giesing, tested the drug on himself and experienced the same side effects after five days. To ease the sinus pains, he began cocaine treatment of Hitler, using a 10 percent solution supplied—like everything else—by the SS pharmacy in Berlin. Hitler sensed an immediate relief, though the cocaine reaction often brought out a sweat; on one occasion Giesing suspected it had brought on a mild heart attack, because Hitler felt giddy, things went black in front of his eyes, and for a full ninety seconds he had to lean heavily on the table in order not to fall over.

Over the next weeks the Führer began begging—indeed, importunately imploring—the army doctor to prolong the cocaine treatments; and in return he obediently found time to sit hunched over inhaling apparatus or in front of shortwave radiation equipment. He began to take a morbid interest in his own body, borrowed medical lexicons from Giesing, and experimented on his orderlies with Giesing's mirrors and instruments after the doctor had gone. He came to look forward to the cocaine and once said admonishingly to the doctor, "I hope you are not making an addict out of me." No longer did he have to salute with his left arm; no longer was his pillow bloodstained when he awoke each morning. But his memory was fading, he noted with concern; he forgot names and faces too easily. "But what does my health matter, when the entire nation's existence is at stake?" he would hoarsely ask the doctor.

At war conferences with his generals, Hitler awkwardly fumbled with vitamin and other unlabeled tablets and consumed them in seemingly random quantities.

He trusted only Martin Bormann, and he spent many hours alone with him. But July 20 had left him increasingly irritable and snarling. Emerging from his bunker to walk to the conference hut, he found his six-foot SS adjutant, Schulze, waiting to escort him. "Herrgott!" Hitler burst out. "Must somebody always follow me? Can't I ever go alone!" Everybody was suspect, new or old: the new Luftwaffe Chief of Staff, Kreipe, was under telephone surveillance, but SS bloodhounds were also following every movement of Rommel now that he had risen from his sickbed.

To be out of Hitler's favor was to be persona non grata with his staff as well. General Blumentritt related how he reported to the Wolf's Lair on September 13 with a cloud over his head after being replaced by General Siegfried Westphal in Hitler's housecleaning of Kluge's and Rommel's staffs. Guderian cut him dead outside the hut with a loud rebuke: "You dare come *here*—after what happened in the west?" But then Hitler approached through the woods, with slow and weary steps, escorted by five or six men, and greeted Blumentritt most courteously. At this the other generals were also nice to him, and Keitel invited him to tea.

In the west, at Keitel's suggestion, Hitler had reappointed Field Marshal von Rundstedt as Supreme Commander; his loyalty was beyond reproach. Model had tactical command, as commander of Army Group B; Rommel was formally relegated to the "Führer-reserve." On September 3, Brussels fell, and the next day the Allies captured the port of Antwerp with hardly any resistance; almost no effort had been made to destroy the port installations. Thus a huge breach was torn in the German line from Liège to the North Sea, through which a determined enemy might well sweep forward into northern Germany or encircle the Ruhr. Model reported that the Allies had two thousand five hundred tanks; the entire German tank strength in the west was less than one hundred. Without air cover he was helpless. The first Me-262 jets had still not arrived.

The V-1 flying-bomb organization in northern France had been overrun but on September 3, Hitler ordered air launchings of the deadly weapon from Heinkel launching-aircraft to continue. Production had just reached 3,419 a month. The damage inflicted on London had been enormous—in one suburb during August over 20,000 houses a day had been severely damaged by flying-bomb explosions. The British government now conceded that 450 aircraft with 2,900 flying personnel had been lost in the fight against this weapon. And now Hitler opened fire with what he called V-2—the army's fourteen-ton A-4 rocket designed at Peenemünde. Launching sites for the V-2 were in Holland, and to ensure that all went well the Führer appointed one of Himmler's best SS generals, Hans Kammler, to direct the V-weapon attack. The rocket had overcome its chronic "air burst" problem, and 374 had been manufactured by slave labor during August in an underground factory in the Harz Mountains. The initial attack on Paris was called off after two launchings miscarried on September 6, but two evenings later the first missiles slammed into Central London without warning. Hitler triumphantly ordered Himmler to decorate Wernher von Braun and his chief engineers, and he instructed Speer to step up V-2 output to 900 a month. (In

September and October, 629 and 628 were produced, and in November 662.)

Hitler angrily forbade any discussion of the Me-262 as a jet fighter but grudgingly conceded that every twentieth Me-262 manufactured could be supplied to the fighter squadrons. His discontent with the Luftwaffe was almost pathological. After General Kreipe set out the fuel situation on September 3—it was now so grave that all bomber and some fighter and dive-bomber operations would have to be curtailed—he stunned the Chief of Staff by remarking: "I am considering disbanding the air force altogether and tripling the antiaircraft artillery instead." He repeated his attack on the Luftwaffe when Göring again deigned to appear at the Wolf's Lair on the fifth. Kreipe's diary recorded:

Führer spoke first: a tirade against the Luftwaffe. No good, gets worse year after year, he was lied to permanently about production figures and also about aircraft performances. Absolute collapse in France, ground staff and signals troops had left their airfields in headlong flight to save their own skins instead of helping the army to fight.

Again the question of Me-262 operations was ventilated. The same arguments as to why only "high-speed bomber" can be considered. In milder form he again developed his idea of manufacturing only Me-262s in the future, while tripling the antiaircraft instead. . . . Our fighter designs were all wrong. What we need to fight the four-engined bombers are heavy twin-engined fighters with large-caliber armament. At the Reichsmarschall's request, Colonel [Hans] Boehm-Tettelbach, who had commanded a fighter squadron, was called in. From his own experience he explained why even heavy fighter aircraft with fighter escorts were not the best way of combatting heavy bombers. Boehm-Tettlbach was rudely sent away.

For about ten minutes Hitler and Göring then talked privately. Then I was called in again. The Führer promoted me very cordially to full general and said I had been an excellent representative of the Luftwaffe these last weeks. . . . Afterward I sat a long time with Göring, who was extremely pleased with himself and said the idea of disbanding the air force was a dead duck. He promised to get Himmler to stop tapping my telephone.

Göring had provided Hitler with the means to plug the yawning breech between the Seventh Army on the German frontier and the North Sea: his paratroop regiments, training or reequipping under General Kurt Student in Germany. On September 4, Hitler ordered Student to establish a new army, the First Parachute Army, along the Albert Canal in Belgium—a meager force with twenty-five tanks and thirty-five batteries of 88-millimeter antiaircraft guns to defend a sixty-mile line from Maastricht to Antwerp; the line from Antwerp to the sea would be taken over by the remnants of the Fifteenth Army struggling over the Scheldt Estuary.

Farther south the rout was also halted, after Hitler, Keitel, and Bormann issued draconian orders to the commanding generals and the Gauleiters. Squads of military police separated even the highest-ranking officers from their truck-loads of chaises-longues and French women, and caught deserters fleeing from their units. When the Gauleiters warned Bormann that the military headquarters were moving into luxury hotels and chateaux inside the German frontier, Hitler stepped in with an order to his generals to house their staffs in the most humble quarters practicable; in one case a general had even tried to take over a military hospital. All along the western frontier women and children, young and old, were digging hastily improvised fortifications, an operation for which Gauleiter Koch's achievements in East Prussia served as an example. To halt the Allied invasion, the factories were turning out bazookas by the hundred thousand, in addition to the extra tanks, artillery, and ammunition Hitler had ordered for his great winter counterattack—the "great opportunity" that "fog, night, and snow" would afford him, as he prophesied on September 1.

Hitler's first plan had been to counterattack from Lorraine into the inviting flank of the American thrust toward Belgium. The Allies were short of fuel, as the best and closest French ports were still denied them by determined German garrisons. But Jodl argued against launching any attack until November 1, which would allow for time to replenish the divisions concerned; besides, Himmler's Volksgrenadier training program and Speer's special arms production effort were geared to the November 1 date Hitler had set in mid-August.

Hitler accepted Jodl's advice. The hours of inactivity forced on him by his doctors gave him time to think. As he gazed for hours on end at the ceiling of his shabbily furnished bunker bedroom, hearing only the hiss of the oxygen bottle in the corner, a far more adventurous campaign took shape in his mind. On about September 12 he sent for Jodl, who fetched a map which they spread out on the white bedspread. Together they sketched the direction of the attack and its necessary breadth and depth. Hitler had decided to strike again through the Ardennes—scene of his 1940 triumph—and seize Antwerp as soon as winter closed in. That day he established a new SS panzer army in Germany and transferred the robust SS General Sepp Dietrich from the Fifth Panzer Army to command it, camouflaging the move's importance by telling General Hasso von Manteuffel, his successor, that he felt better use could be made of Dietrich at home than in the field.

The Sixth SS Panzer Army was to be the spearhead of Rundstedt's Ardennes campaign. But Dietrich's skills were at best questionable. So, why the SS? The answer lay in the regular army's unencouraging record in the west. Besides, the Gestapo reports on the army's renegades—remorselessly fed to Hitler by Bormann and Fegelein—laid bare the moral decay into which most army generals had apparently relapsed: Beck, an amiable procrastinator, an Olympian academic, and embittered ponderer; Witzleben, the pessimist whose only reading was schoolgirl books from his wife's library; Eduard Wagner, a bureaucratic empire builder of pathological vanity; Tresckow, whose rebellion had been initiated when Schmundt had rebuffed his ambitions to succeed Heusinger as chief of operations in the General Staff. In a Germany bomb-blasted and rationed, these army plotters had lived the easy lives of grand gourmets. In Olbricht's cellars investigators found a thousand bottles of wine. A champagne orgy lasting far into the night had been their reaction to news of Hitler's "death." Fromm had flown regularly by plane on private hunting parties, sending his empty Mercedes on ahead by road. While the armies cried out for troops, the conspirators had squandered able-bodied soldiers on petty household jobs or on guarding their damaged homes. Because of the fuel crisis, teams of oxen were now having to haul the Me-262 jet aircraft onto the runways of German airfields. But according to Gestapo reports Stauffenberg had had his army chauffeur drive him a hundred miles a day or more on private excursions—in addition, his home was said to have been full of black-market alcohol and other scarce goods.

These reports must have made some impression on the prudish and ascetic Hitler in September—although it was he himself who had initiated the army's decline by leaving it leaderless when he dismissed Brauchitsch in December 1941.

After the regular war conference on September 16, Hitler asked certain men to remain behind—among them Jodl, Guderian, Buhle, Fegelein, and Hewel. Kreipe's diary records that Jodl began by stating that some fifty-five German divisions at present confronted ninety-six enemy divisions in the west, and that ten more Allied divisions were en route from England; the enemy's main strategic reserve—an airborne army—was still in Britain. The German divisions were short of heavy guns, ammunition, and tanks. "The Führer interrupts Jodl: he has resolved to mount a counterattack from the Ardennes, with Antwerp as the target." He considered that the German defensive position was strong enough to outweigh the enemy's numerical advantage. "The present front can easily be held! Our own attacking force will consist of thirty new Volksgrenadier divisions and new panzer divisions, plus panzer divisions from the eastern front. Split the British and American armies at their seam, then a new Dunkirk!" But with Antwerp in German hands, this time the encircled enemy armies would have no port from which to escape. "Guderian objects because of situation on eastern front," Kreipe's diary adds. "Jodl refers to enemy air supremacy and fears of parachute landings in Holland, Denmark, and northern Germany. Hitler demands one thousand five hundred fighters by November 1!" Kreipe's reasoned objections were overruled. "Acid comments. That's why our offensive will begin in a bad-weather period, when the enemy air force is grounded too. Von Rundstedt will take command. All preparations by November 1. The Führer sums up his decision in a lengthy speech." On pain of death, he ordered them to keep this secret to themselves and their most trustworthy staff officers.

———

American troops were now standing on German soil, and a bloody fight for Aachen, the first big German city, had begun. The Party ordered the city evacuated, but the German divisional commander, General Gerd von Schwerin, rescinded the order and provided a city official with a letter in English commending the citizens to the American troops' mercy. Schwerin was relieved of his command at once. Hitler issued the following secret message to his commanders, instructing them to pass it on to their troops by word of mouth.

> The fighting in the west has now spilled over onto German soil. German towns and villages will become battlefields. This fact must instill fanaticism into our fight and spur on every able-bodied man in the combat zone to make a supreme effort, so that every pillbox, every city block, every village becomes a fortress against which the enemy bleeds to death or which entombs its defenders in the man-to-man fight.
>
> No longer will this be a war of movement, but a choice between holding the line or annihilation. . . .

On the Russian front, the Red Army had begun a new stubborn attack on Schörner's Army Group North: twenty Soviet armies (equivalent to German corps) were pitted against Schörner's Sixteenth and Eighteenth armies. The Narva line was breached, and on September 16, Guderian and Schörner both came to Hitler to appeal for permission to abandon Estonia and withdraw Army Group North to a bridgehead at Riga. With Finland now out of the Nazi coalition, the political arguments no longer weighed; but Hitler was still reluctant, as Schörner's thirty-three divisions were tying down over a hundred of the enemy —the familiar "Crimea" argument. Besides, he disclosed to the generals, he had to keep some pawns in hands, as the Russians were currently extending feelers to him. One of Ribbentrop's staff had passed this news to him; this time Hitler authorized his minister to put out counterfeelers—but the Russian intermediary never showed up at the rendezvous. Perhaps an overeager agent had misinterpreted a sign. When some weeks later Frau von Ribbentrop wrote to Hitler suggesting that she should unofficially contact the Soviet ambassadress in Stockholm, Madame Kollontay, Hitler forbade her to. "Probing the Soviet attitude," he reflected, "is like touching a glowing stove to find out if it's hot."

On September 17, 1944, German speculation about the Allies' next move in the west was dramatically terminated. Instead of attempting a direct frontal assault on the West Wall, the Allies launched a sudden airborne attack on key river bridges in Holland; the attack was designed to capture a succession of important crossings from Eindhoven as far as the Rhine bridge at Arnhem, fifty miles to the north. British and American armored spearheads plunged northward along the corridor thus created toward the Zuider Zee; their mission was to cut off all Hitler's troops in Holland and destroy the V-2 rocket-launching sites near The Hague. If the Arnhem bridge was captured, the Allies could circumvent the billion-Reichsmark West Wall altogether. Small wonder that Hitler's heart sank at the news. His Luftwaffe chief recorded in his diary: "Nonstop telephoning and issuing of orders for the defense. Führer telephones. Afternoon, to see him and Jodl again. Quite a flap on."

The bold assault took the Germans completely by surprise, even though their Intelligence had been watching the enemy's airborne army for some weeks. Over fifteen hundred Allied troop transports and five hundred gliders had taken part. The Luftwaffe flew six hundred and fifty sorties against the airborne landings that day.

Arnhem was not even in the German combat zone—for the first hour only the proverbial cookhouse parties could defend the town. The town commandant had been killed in an air raid that morning, leaving only his elderly operations officer, one Major Ernst Schleifenbaum, in charge—an unlikely Horatio to hold the bridge. But for some reason the British paratroops had been set down five miles west of the bridge, at Oosterbeek (by chance the very place where Model had his army group headquarters); and this gave Schleifenbaum time to raise an emergency force for Arnhem's initial defense. In one unit were men of twenty-eight different commands, World War I veterans every one; each was given a captured gun and twenty rounds, and sent out to defend Arnhem against ten thousand enemy paratroops until help arrived. Schleifenbaum was to write some weeks later: "When Field Marshal Model came on the telephone and said, 'You are responsible to me for holding Arnhem!' I felt quite faint, until the old Siegerland nerves came to my aid. . . . We old fellows still have something in us yet." Undetected by the enemy, the Second SS Panzer Corps was only fifteen miles away and licking its wounds after defeat in France. Of these two divisions, Model threw Colonel Walter Harzer's 9th SS, the "Hohenstaufen" Panzer Division, into the fight. Moreover, the entire Allied battle plan was captured from a wrecked glider that same day. Although the Allies threw in fresh airborne forces the next morning, September 18, Arnhem and the bridge remained in German hands— after Aachen, the second defensive triumph for Hitler following a long run of defeats in the west. When the exhausted British fell back toward Nijmegen, they left over 1,000 dead and 6,450 prisoners at Arnhem.

Hitler did not at first recognize it as a tactical success. He thundered at the "idiocy of allowing the enemy to capture bridges [at Nijmegen] undestroyed"; and although the Luftwaffe's General Student deserved much credit, it could not offset the Party's campaign against Reichsmarschall Göring. Gauleiter Lauterbacher had just detected nine hundred Luftwaffe troops idling at Güstrow airfield; another one thousand five hundred at a camp near Flensburg wondered why they still had neither uniforms nor work. In addition, the British night raids had begun again. Ancient Königsberg was now in ruins, and one recent saturation attack on Darmstadt's center had left twelve thousand civilian dead in half an hour. The Me-262 jet had been unable to intervene at Arnhem, as its home airfield at Rheine had been plowed over by night raids. In consequence of all this, Hitler began to consider replacing Göring—at least *de facto*—by a real Luftwaffe commander like General von Greim; Richthofen, alas, had undergone a brain operation and might not live much longer.

The gathering storm is clearly described in Kreipe's diary on September 18— a day already made grim for Hitler by a painful headache which had allowed him no sleep. "During the Führer's conference," wrote Kreipe, "there are fresh reports of airborne landings in Holland. The Führer loses his temper and rages at the Luftwaffe's failure; he demands to know immediately what fighter sorties were flown in Holland to engage the enemy. I telephone Luftflotte 'Reich' and find out that because of the weather hardly any sorties were flown today. The Führer takes my report to this effect as an excuse for the most biting criticism. 'The entire air force is incompetent, yellow, and leaving me in the lurch. I've had fresh reports that numerous Luftwaffe units are retreating across the Rhine.' I inform him that under General Putzier we have set up an organization along the roads and at the Rhine crossings to catch them. I asked for concrete examples for me to follow up. Hitler retorted, 'I have no desire to speak with you again. Tomorrow I want to talk to the Reichsmarschall—no doubt you can arrange *that!*'" Göring still refused to see the danger signals. "When I warn him the whole witch-hunt is aimed at him, he just scoffs," wrote Kreipe the next day. "The Führer's war conference follows: icy atmosphere. I am ignored completely. At its end Göring sees Hitler. He tries to take me too, but Hitler indicates that he wants to speak with him alone. About 8 P.M. the Reichsmarschall comes back from the Führer, absolutely broken and washed up. After a long silence he tells me the Führer doesn't like me, as I have no faith in him, I am a typical staff-officer type and calculating machine, defeatist and unreliable; I am just full of objections and contradictions. . . . I responded that he must realize that the whole campaign is really directed against himself. Göring shot up and angrily rejected this. 'The Führer has expressly assured me of his confidence in me!'"

Shortly after midnight Fegelein informed General Kreipe that Hitler had forbidden him to set foot within the Wolf's Lair again. For the next two months the Luftwaffe had no Chief of Staff, and Göring kept a safe distance between himself and Hitler.

———

Deep-rooted factors contributed to this arbitrary and irrational behavior. One was that on the eighteenth he had just authorized Schörner's army group to abandon Estonia on the Baltic after all. Many thousands of Estonians who had fought to keep out the Red Army would be suffering now. Another factor was his own failing health, and the unspoken fear that with each cumulating illness since July 20 his own life was slipping inconclusively away as surely as was that of his beloved General Schmundt, who was dying of his wounds at Rastenburg hospital two miles away.

With his splitting headache undiminished, he drove to the hospital for head X-rays to be made on September 19. The X-ray department was searched for bombs, and guards were posted on every exit. After three X-ray photographs had been taken—all of which were found by the Allies in 1945[3]—he shook hands with the Catholic nursing sisters, then asked his doctor, Hasselbach, to guide him around the wards where the victims of July 20 lay. Schmundt was now in high fever (his wife wrote in her diary: "Afternoon: Führer here again, works like medicine"); at his bedside Hitler began to weep, because the doctors had advised him his adjutant had not long to live: gangrene had set in. "I was called in too late," Morell had gravely assured him that morning. "Otherwise I could have saved him with my penicillin." (In fact his "penicillin"—analyzed by Giesing— proved quite valueless.)

Word of Hitler's presence had spread, and when he rejoined his car he found several hundred people thronging outside, who burst out cheering as they recognized him. Half were civilians from Rastenburg town, the rest were invalid troops —including many cripples, many on stretchers, and many without an arm or leg, whose emotion at this, their first encounter with their Führer at such close quarters, could be seen glistening in their eyes. Even now his very proximity still infused many Germans with the certainty of eventual victory. A few days before, one of his SS staff had written privately: "Never have I been so confident as to our war position. Up here one gets a far broader view, you see things with a different eye. . . . With our Führer, nothing can possibly go wrong for Germany or any of us; he is quite simply *wunderbar.*"

---

[3]I obtained these X-rays in 1967; they do indeed show a cloudiness of the left maxillary sinus, needing irrigation. In 1968 the Soviet author Lev Bezymenski published good photographs of the jaw taken from a corpse found in the Chancellery garden in Berlin in 1945. As I first demonstrated in *Die Zeit* (Hamburg) on January 14, 1972, this jaw was identical to that in the X-rays *and* to that sketched from memory by Hitler's dentist, Professor Blaschke, under American interrogation in 1945. More recently the Norwegian-born dental expert Dr. Reidar F. Sognnaes, of the section of oral biology at the University of California, confirmed this at a symposium on forensic medicine in Edinburgh.

Over the next week Hitler's dimly lit bunker rooms seemed crowded with doctors. Professor von Eicken came from Berlin to perform the sinus irrigation. Giesing and Hasselbach were treating his other injuries. A fresh electrocardiogram was made to test the progress of his coronary sclerosis. His stomach spasms had returned, and even Dr. Koester's antigas pills were failing to exorcise them—Hitler's valet, Heinz Linge, showed the little black pills to Giesing at his request. In the daylight more than one of Hitler's staff thought his skin and eyes were turning an unhealthy yellow. General Nikolaus von Vormann, the retiring commander of the Ninth Army, visited him on September 26; he has described how he was frisked for hidden weapons, then led into a small room some ten feet square, with a small round table and some chairs.

Through a curtain, Hitler came in alone from the next room; it was a tired, broken man who greeted me, then shuffled over to a chair, his shoulders drooping, and asked me to sit down. Without waiting to find out my business, he began to speak of our coming final victory and the new secret weapons. When I tried to tell him of the impossible situation on the Vistula and in Warsaw, from whence I came, he interrupted me, "Your successor [General Smilo Freiherr von] Lüttwitz will get help." He spoke so softly and hesitantly it was hard to understand him. His hands trembled so much he had to grip them between his knees. This was not the same Hitler I had last seen at war conferences on July 15 and 18—before the murder attempt of the twentieth.

Later that day, September 26, Heinrich Himmler arrived with a bulging briefcase of things to discuss. The real blockbuster was noted on his agenda simply as "Treason since 1939." In a locked safe at Abwehr headquarters outside Berlin Gestapo investigators had found documents proving that Mayor Goerdeler, General Oster, General Beck, and above all Admiral Canaris—the slippery former chief of Intelligence—had been plotting Hitler's overthrow since 1939 at least. More revolting still for Hitler was the proof that it was Canaris and his men who had deliberately betrayed the plans and dates of his 1940 western campaign ("Yellow") to the enemy. These documents extended only to mid-1940. They had been assembled by two of the admiral's staff—General Oster and Hans von Dohnanyi—with a view toward someday prosecuting Brauchitsch, then the army's Commander in Chief, for refusing to aid the anti-Hitler plotters. Hitler could only speculate on the harm Canaris had done to Germany since then. From General Muñoz Grandes, who had commanded Spain's contingent in Russia, he had learned some time ago that Canaris had personally warned Franco against bringing Spain in to the war on Hitler's side; but this clue had not been followed up.

It was all of only academic interest now, with the Russians poised to invade East Prussia and the Allies massing on the West Wall. Since his arrest in July, Canaris had told ingenious tales to save his neck, but those who had rejected the

Third Reich—Oster and Dohnanyi—betrayed their friend Canaris as their accomplice under Gestapo questioning and in a face-to-face encounter. General Alexander von Pfuhlstein, former commander of the "Brandenburg" (Commando) Division, was arrested on September 4, and he had strongly implicated Canaris in the murder plot as well: the admiral had once discussed using the division to storm the Wolf's Lair. (Canaris hotly denied it: "I only discussed with you using the division to protect Abwehr buildings if such a revolution should break out!") Pfuhlstein told his interrogators that Canaris had confidently predicted Germany's defeat for December 1943. Colonel Georg Hansen advised his questioners to search for Canaris's diaries, and these other damning documents had been found in the locked safe of another Abwehr colonel who had succumbed to the suicide epidemic after July 20.

The documents showed that the plotters had sent the then Colonel Georg Thomas—another of Keitel's department heads—to win Halder and Brauchitsch over in November 1939. Halder had refused: Brauchitsch would never join in, the German army would not rebel, and besides Britain's fight was against Germany, not Hitler. A 1939 "study" by Oster dealt explicitly with a coup d'etat. There were voluminous memoranda by General Beck, and scattered pages of the fabled Canaris diary throwing a revealing new light on the 1943 Black Chapel case and Abwehr dealings with the Vatican.[4] In April 1940, the documents indicated, Thomas had shown Halder a message from one Dr. Josef Müller—a Bavarian lawyer friendly with the Pope: the Vatican was willing to intercede with the British and French provided Hitler and Ribbentrop were first eliminated. On being informed of this approach, Brauchitsch had proposed to Halder that Thomas be arrested. The same Josef Müller had betrayed the date of "Yellow" to the Vatican—evidently on Abwehr instructions, since when Abwehr investigations of the leak led to Müller, Canaris ordered the affair hushed up. This explained how the Belgian envoy to the Vatican had been able to telegraph a coded warning to Brüssels, as Hitler had learned from the Forschungsamt in May 1940.[5] Oster had also warned the Dutch directly. This must explain why the "Brandenburg" agents detailed to capture the Meuse bridges in Holland had been massacred and why the bridges were blown before the Germans could make use of them. Hitler grimly informed Jodl of the news Himmler had brought. The facts about Admiral Canaris were so terrible that he could not make them public until the war was over; then there would be a state trial at which the German people could take their revenge.[6]

---

[4]See page 503.

[5]See page 106.

[6]After months of investigation, in November 1945 a British Intelligence report concluded that the Abwehr under Canaris had opposed Hitler only because of its jealousy over the inroads made into their domain by Himmler's agencies. "The role of Admiral Canaris has never been entirely clear, but

A personal catastrophe was about to fall upon Hitler, immobilizing him for two weeks.

First, Martin Bormann secured from him one last signature on September 26, 1944, ordering the Party to raise a people's army, a *Volkssturm,* by public levy on every able-bodied man between sixteen and sixty for the defense of German soil. The original idea was Guderian's. Alarmed to see his siege-defense troops in the east drained off to the West Wall, he had proposed a local territorial reserve *(Landsturm)* for temporarily plugging any breaches in his eastern defenses. Guderian had suggested Wilhelm Schepmann, chief of the SA, as their leader, because since 1934 the army had always got on well with the paramilitary Brownshirt organization. Bormann, however, could point to the results the Party had achieved in the west; Rundstedt had highly praised him. On the twenty-third the field marshal had sent four thousand sets of the necessary army blueprints to the seven western Gauleiters, and already the Party had half a million men erecting tank obstacles, bunkers, and fortifications. Hitler trusted Bormann, and the Party got the job of raising the Volkssturm—to mobilize "the people" just as Stalin had mobilized the factory workers of Moscow and Leningrad in 1941.

During the night Hitler was attacked by stomach cramps of such intensity that he had to bite back his need to scream. The next morning he refused to get up; wearing a gray flannel dressing gown over his shapeless army nightshirt, he lay with empty and expressionless eyes on his bed. A loaded revolver was on the night table. He refused to eat that day or the next. Morell was summoned, diagnosed only the old intestinal troubles, and gave him liver-extract injections; but the pains got worse. The fat doctor was seen leaving the bunker pale and sweating, for his medical experience had its limitations. Professor von Eicken arrived on the twenty-seventh from Berlin, but Morell sent him back without allowing him near his patient. Martin Bormann, sick with worry, remained constantly in the bunker for three days. Doctor Giesing recognized a case of jaundice, but Morell angrily denied it and attributed Hitler's yellow color and spasms to a gall bladder blockage caused by nervous worry; he began dosing his agonized patient with castor oil at one end and warm camomile-tea enemas at the other in the hope of

it is now demonstrable that he drew into the Abwehr men whom he knew to be engaged in anti-Hitler activities and on several occasions took steps to defend them. The fact that his attitude concerning the war seems from the first to have been strongly defeatist provides the only clue to the behavior of one of the most obscure figures in the history of the Nazi period."

unblocking the intestinal tracts. The pain got worse, and between September 28 and 30, Hitler lost six pounds. Blood tests and urinalyses were taken, but Morell refused to show them to his fellow doctors.[7] The Wolf's Lair was paralyzed. The war conferences were canceled for days on end. Admiral Puttkamer, recovering from his bomb injuries, hobbled in on crutches to read to Hitler the daily notes on the war situation. But for days Hitler just lay there with no comment or reaction at all.

By October 2 he had begun to dress again but still stayed in his little bedroom, where Blondi and her new puppies lay in a big wooden box in the corner. On the night before, General Schmundt—his chief adjutant since 1938 and one of the organizing architects of the Wehrmacht—had died of his injuries from Stauffenberg's bomb. Richard Schulze, his SS adjutant, found Hitler sitting on the edge of his bed in black trousers, collarless shirt, and suspenders. It was Schulze's thirtieth birthday. Hitler summoned up a smile and handed him the obligatory Glashütte gold watch. "I don't suppose I'll be presenting any more of these!" he exclaimed. Three days later, Puttkamer ushered in Schmundt's widow. Hitler was still frail and ill, and began to weep as she came in. "It is you who must console me," he sighed, "for mine was the greater loss."

Frau Schmundt then explained that the Gestapo were harrying her for access to Schmundt's secret diaries. She begged Hitler to take them into his personal custody. "Jawohl," agreed Hitler after some reflection. "Will it suffice if they are locked up in the Chancellery safe, and you have one key and Puttkamer the other?"

During Hitler's illness, Giesing sampled the little black antigas pills himself and suffered the same testiness, aversion to light, thirst, loss of appetite, enhanced sense of taste, and stomach cramps that had afflicted Hitler; it might even explain his jaundice too. From the Latin label it seemed that the quantities Hitler had consumed since Stalingrad must have *cumulatively poisoned* him with strychnine and atropine. Hitler somberly thanked Giesing; he had thought them just charcoal tablets for absorbing stomach gases.

All Morell's rivals—and they were many—closed in for the kill. Professor Brandt, Hitler's surgeon since 1934 and a staunch adviser of Speer's ministry, hurried from Berlin and accused Morell of criminal negligence. But Bormann was now out for Speer's blood, and he knew of Hitler's irrational affection for Morell as the only doctor who had helped him earlier. "Every other German has the right to choose his own doctor," Hitler confirmed. "I have chosen Morell." Morell,

---

[7]The reports are in Morell's papers. The urine tests revealed the presence of bile pigments and increased amounts of urobilinogen and urobilin—both consistent with an attack of jaundice.

pale and frightened, apologized profusely for his oversight. Bormann dismissed both Brandt and Hasselbach—using the latter's indiscreet revelations on the pills affair to Hitler's adjutants during the journey back from Schmundt's funeral at Tannenberg as a formal pretext. On October 9, Giesing too was paid off. Even Himmler was cold and unsympathetic to the doctors. He was next seen heading toward Hitler's bunker with his own personal doctor in tow—the thirty-six-year-old orthopedic surgeon, Dr. Ludwig Stumpfegger, a tall slim SS major with a brilliant reputation for bone and muscle surgery. Morell remained Hitler's doctor, but the consumption of the antigas pills was stopped. And Stumpfegger, Himmler's nominee, replaced Brandt, Hasselbach, and Giesing on Hitler's staff.

Hitler's irrational and often infuriating loyalty to his old faithfuls saved Göring as it had saved Morell.

Enraged by the Luftwaffe record, he had sacked Kreipe and determined to get rid of Göring too. On September 21 he interviewed General von Greim, commander of the Sixth Air Force, from the eastern front and asked him to become Göring's "Deputy Commander in Chief"; it would be a new position, and Greim discussed it thoroughly with Himmler, Fegelein, and Bormann over the next two weeks before Göring rebelled and sent him back to the east. The Reichsmarschall then sent for General Kurt Pflugbeil, commander of the First Air Force, and offered him Kreipe's job; Pflugbeil took one look at the situation at Luftwaffe headquarters and fled back to his own command. Göring gave up. In mid-October he went hunting on Rominten Heide, and here, he remarked, he proposed to stay —"keeping a strict eye on Himmler and Bormann" nonetheless, for the Reichsführer had now demanded air force squadrons of its own for the SS. At the Wolf's Lair, General Eckhard Christian alone represented the Luftwaffe when Hitler's war conferences resumed.

Fortunately, Hitler's adjutants remarked, the war stagnated during his two-week illness. Ominous rumblings still came from Hungary; the auguries of an East-West split became louder; planning for the Ardennes offensive continued; in Warsaw the Polish uprising collapsed; in northern Norway, Hitler authorized the Twentieth Army to fall back on the Lyngen Fjord–Narvik line; in the Balkans he ordered all Greece, southern Macedonia, and southern Albania abandoned to the enemy.

A melancholy report reached him on the last days of German rule in Estonia, too. Schörner had allowed ten days for the evacuation starting on September 18. In seventy ships the German navy had snatched the last Germans from the Baltic ports and evacuated a hundred thousand Estonian refugees as well. The oil-shale works were demolished, and the last Germans embarked in Revel (Tallin) on September 21. The local population could hardly believe that the Germans were letting the Russians return, and many announced that they would vanish into the forests and wait for the Germans to come back, as come they surely must. "On the twenty-first, knots of civilians gathered in the streets of Revel, armed with rifles. The last Germans to sail out could see a huge Estonian flag unfurled from the tower of the ancient Teutonic castle, 'Lanky Hermann,' and the German war ensign flew alongside—a sign that there were still Estonians minded to put up a fight, however hopeless, against the Bolsheviks. As far as we know," the report concluded on the twenty-eighth, "the Bolsheviks have liquidated all Estonians suspected of collaboration with the German administration and transported the able-bodied as slaves."

On October 7 a big Russian attack began, and the news that East Prussia itself was threatened brought Hitler out of his sickroom and back into the conference hut again. The generals urged him to leave the Wolf's Lair, but his answer was always the same: "The East Prussians would say I was leaving them to the Russians, and they'd be right. However secret we kept it, they'd still find out. The wretched people here have already had one taste of the Russian reign of terror in 1914 and 1915. I want to spare them a second dose."

In mid-October one problem could no longer be shelved: the future of Erwin Rommel. The field marshal, Hitler's favorite until recently, the first commandant of his HQ (in 1939), had recovered from his crash injuries at the family home near Ulm. The agents shadowing his movements reported that he went for walks "leaning on his son"; but local Nazi officials reported that Rommel was still uttering mutinous remarks. If any one popular hero could persuade the Germans to call a halt to the war, it was Rommel. The evidence against him seemed also complete: Lieutenant Colonel Hofacker had before his execution testified in writing that Rommel had assured the putschists that they could count on him if the plot succeeded.

Hitler showed Keitel the Hofacker document. Keitel sent for Rommel, but the field marshal declined to come. This left only a direct appeal to Rommel's sense of dignity.

At Hitler's dictation, Keitel wrote Rommel a letter advising him to come to see the Führer if he considered himself innocent or to behave as an officer should if he did not; otherwise he would be arrested and put on trial by the People's Court. General Wilhelm Burgdorf—Schmundt's burly successor as Hitler's adjutant and chief of army personnel—and his deputy, General Ernst Maisel, took the letter and the Hofacker statement in person to Rommel's home at Ulm, using a small unmarked Mercedes from Schaub's motor pool; the autobahns were closed to prevent Rommel's escape. At the evening war conference on October 14, Hitler was informed briefly that Rommel had just "died of his injuries." His only comment was an expressionless "There goes another of the Old Guard." He ordered no press announcement for the moment. Burgdorf returned to the Wolf's Lair with the field marshal's cap and baton and reported to Hitler and Keitel. Rommel had asked him if the Führer was aware of the Hofacker statement and then asked for time to think. Burgdorf had asked him to choose poison rather than the conventional pistol, to avoid causing public speculation. The Führer had, he said, promised a state funeral with full honors to preserve Rommel's popular reputation. The alternative would be trial and—if found guilty—dishonor, and execution.

Secret and promise were well kept. Even Hitler's adjutants did not find out. On October 15 or 16, Colonel von Amsberg drafted the usual obituary announcement for the *Army Gazette*. For a field marshal only the Führer himself could sign; Amsberg left it on Hitler's tray. Days passed, until Amsberg inquired whether the wording ought perhaps to be altered in some way. Hitler bit his lip and virtuously exclaimed, "I will not sign this obituary. I will not lie!"

On the Brink of a Volcano

On October 15, 1944, the day after Rommel's sudden death, Hitler's agents deposed the Hungarian regent, Admiral Nikolaus Horthy, and brought "a thousand years of Hungarian history" to an end.

The Nazi coup in Budapest had its origins in July, when Horthy had stopped the deportation of Hungarian Jews to Germany and sent his then adjutant General Béla Miklós to Hitler with a letter announcing his intention of appointing a military government; Hitler had received the general on July 21, claimed to be entitled to interfere in Hungarian affairs given the country's key position in the Balkans, and evidently also made some promise about the Jews, because four days later Himmler ordered the deportations to cease until further notice. He had already started talks with Allied intermediaries on an alternative means of disposing of the Jews—by barter, in exchange for goods or foreign currency from the Allies; on July 20, Ribbentrop had advised Edmund Veesenmayer, his representative in Budapest, that according to the BBC the Allies had rejected the barter proposal as an impudent attempt at weakening them. As his own penciled notes for the discussion reveal, at about this time Himmler debated with Hitler the "transfer of the Jews abroad." "Setting them free against foreign currency, [while retaining] the most important as hostages" was the proposal—to which the Reichsführer added his own comment: "Am against it"; as he subsequently checked the proposal, with the proviso that the currency must come "from abroad," Hitler evidently overruled him. By the end of July, Adolf Eichmann had left Hungary, and his task force was disbanded soon after. The first 318 Hungarian Jews were released from Bergen-Belsen camp and transferred to Switzerland to prove Germany's intention of keeping the bargain; but Himmler's intermediaries were asking for trucks in exchange ("to be used only on the eastern front"), and although further consignments of Jews were allowed to leave—1,355 in December and 1,100 in February 1945—the deal collapsed.

In October 1944, Himmler ordered the extermination of the Jews to stop. What led to this order is uncertain. SS General Ernst Kaltenbrunner, chief of the Reich Main Security Office, stated in his closing speech to the Allied tribunal at Nuremberg two years later that he had received a stunning report from an investigating judge he had appointed in 1943 to prosecute corruption at top level in the concentration camp system: this lawyer, Dr. Konrad Morgen, had been drafted into the SS for the purpose, and his early inquiries at Buchenwald convinced him that illegal murders of witnesses of the commandant's corrupt practices had occurred. Morgen had secured the execution of the commandant, Karl Koch, and eventually procured indictments in two hundred other cases. Late in 1943 he had realized that a systematic mass murder was proceeding at two camps—Auschwitz and Lublin. The commandant at Lublin, a former Stuttgart lawyer named Wirth, told him "they were destroying the Jews on the Führer's orders," and he was running altogether four extermination camps in the eastern Generalgouvernement of Poland, including Majdanek near Treblinka, in which five thousand Jews were themselves operating the machinery (before being systematically liquidated themselves). Shortly after telling him this, Morgen later reported, Wirth vanished from Lublin, having been instructed to raze his extermination camps to the ground. Late in 1943, he continued, while following up a major gold-smuggling racket, he stumbled on the truth about Auschwitz, where one Rudolf Hoess was commandant. Believing at that time that Hitler himself had ordered all this, Morgen felt powerless to intervene. He began a merciless prosecution of the camp officials over the "lesser" murders, however—outside the general massacre program, hoping in this way to ventilate the whole issue. But an investigating judge sent to scrutinize the files of the Reich Main Security Office itself—under whose Departments IV and IVb the massacre had begun—found that no general order for the massacre had ever been received or issued. Morgen himself was the target of harassment; his staff's barracks were burned down one night, with all their files, but he fought on and eventually laid the dossier before Kaltenbrunner.

Kaltenbrunner stated (in August 1946) that he was "stunned by the report." He himself had been interested only in the Intelligence side of his office. He sent the document by special courier that October 1944 day to Hitler. Hitler sent for him in person next day, and after a long discussion agreed to call Himmler and Oswald Pohl, chief of the concentration camps, to account for their actions. In Kaltenbrunner's presence—as he described at Nuremberg—the Führer ordered SS General Fegelein to ensure that Himmler reported to him immediately. (According to the manservant's register, Himmler came on October 17, and then again on November 7.) Hitler gave Kaltenbrunner his word, as they shook hands and parted, that he would put an immediate end to the massacre. (We have only Kaltenbrunner's account of all this; he himself was hanged at Nuremberg, and his widow possesses none of his personal papers which might have thrown light on the truth. Morgen, now a respected lawyer in Frankfurt, supports only part of the SS general's account, while motivated by an obvious and understandable antipathy toward him.)

The following scene is, however, independently testified to. On October 27, 1944, news reports reached Hitler that the Russians claimed to have found a former concentration camp, Majdanek, near Lublin, at which 1,500,000 people had been liquidated; according to Heinz Lorenz, his press officer, Hitler angrily dismissed the reports as propaganda—just as German troops had been accused of "hacking off children's hands in Belgium" in 1914. When Ribbentrop pressed him for an answer, the Führer replied more revealingly, "That is Himmler's affair and his alone." He betrayed no flicker of emotion.

There was no act of violence Hitler was not prepared to commit to keep Hungary —his only remaining petroleum supplier and a large foodstuffs exporter—within his domain, his "minimum economic region." From the end of August 1944, when Horthy openly courted Hitler's disapproval and announced that he had appointed General Geisa Lákatos to head a military government in place of the ailing and pro-German Döme Sztójay, one alarm signal after another was reported to Hitler indicating that the regent was plotting to follow Romania's—or even better— Finland's path out of the war while there was still time.

Initially, Hitler fought to win time, hoping for a spectacular military victory in the defense of Hungary by General Friessner to restore the Hungarian Cabinet's flagging spirit. When on September 7 Horthy issued a semi-ultimatum demanding five fresh German panzer divisions within "twenty-four hours" or he would ask the enemy governments for an armistice, Hitler ordered Guderian to accept the demand insofar as possible; and the first divisions began moving into Hungary the next day. But the next morning, the eighth, the German air attaché telephoned urgent warnings from Budapest about "goings-on similar to Romania." Hitler took him seriously, since this general, Cuno Heribert Fuetterer, had also provided the earliest alert of the coup in Bucharest. This warning gave him five weeks' clear notice to stage in Hungary a countercoup of the kind he had tried and failed to achieve in Romania in August.

After Antonescu's overthrow in August, the Hungarian and German general staffs had agreed to launch an offensive from Klausenburg to capture the Romanian half of Transylvania and then to hold and fortify the general line of the Carpathian Mountains. But the German troops movements, two hundred trainloads, would take ten days, and the Romanians and Russians reached and blocked the passes first. When the offensive began on the fifth, it rapidly fell apart—leaving Guderian no option but to abandon the easternmost tip of Hungary and fall back on the Maros River. What unsettled Hitler was that the Hungarian

Lakatos regime suddenly stopped the invasion of Romanian Transylvania at the eleventh hour without consulting him—evidently for political reasons. This excited his distrust. When General Janos Vörös, Guderian's Hungarian counterpart, pleaded for more military assistance on the twelfth, the Führer told him to his face: "I have no faith in your Lakatos government." This evoked from Vörös an assurance, given with Hungarian flamboyance and feeling, that Horthy would remain loyal and would fight at Germany's side until the end of the war. Hitler again promised to send the rest of the five panzer divisions, and at that night's war conference he outlined to Vörös his plans for a great new offensive to reconquer all of Romania.

He suspected Admiral Horthy of plotting a Badoglio-type betrayal. The admiral wanted high-grade German troops moved to eastern Hungary; then he would sign a sudden pact with Stalin—the British and Americans having evidently given him the cold shoulder—and deliver these now isolated German divisions to the enemy sword. East of the Tisza River Hitler had evidently already written off Hungary; but if he was not to lose western Hungary as well, he had no option but to take just that risk of treachery and pack every good division he had into the front line.

Together with SS Major Otto Skorzeny, Hitler began plotting ways of eliminating Horthy's now baneful influence on his generals. Horthy and his entourage lived ensconced in the Citadel at Budapest. Immediately after Antonescu's overthrow, the SS commander in Budapest, SS General Otto Winkelmann, had investigated the layout and security organization of the Citadel. Now Hitler spent hours each day poring over the original building-plans of the Citadel and its labyrinthine underground tunnels, plotting Horthy's capture and overthrow with all the Machiavellian attention to detail that had accompanied his planning for the Dirschau bridge and Eben-Emael fortress operations in 1939 and 1940.

Hitler's strategy in Hungary in September 1944 had derived from the comforting conviction that having digested Romania, the Red Army would wheel south to realize Russia's historic ambitions in the Dardanelles—and to reach the Balkans before Britain and the United States. The planned German offensive from Klausenburg had been a product of this belief: the Red Army was assumed to be leaving only covering forces along its Carpathian flank. The Russian offensive from this very region, spilling out *northward* into the Hungarian lowlands and capturing Arad, proved the falseness of Hitler's assumption—and this was the very eve of his debilitating two-week illness.

Immediately, on September 23, fresh alarms began sounding at the Wolf's Lair. German Intelligence networks evidently learned that Horthy was putting out increasingly urgent feelers to the western Allies in Italy and Switzerland, because

Hitler ordered the Luftwaffe to keep a close watch on all Hungarian airfields to prevent Horthy from sending his family out to safety in Switzerland. The Führer also discussed with Jodl the possibility of using three or four paratroop battalions to arrest the regent if he tried to move into the Hungarian army headquarters; some days later the plan was amended to include Skorzeny and five hundred Waffen SS troops in gliders. The scale of these operations was inevitable, because Winkelmann had learned that the Hungarian commandant of Budapest, General Bakay, was already plotting a large-scale military operation to round up every major German sympathizer. It was an undeclared war, in which Hitler was determined to keep the initiative. On September 25 he designated all Hungary a German "operations zone," thus bringing it under unified German General Staff control to avoid the clashes of interest that had hamstrung the German counter-coup in Bucharest.[1] Ferenc Szálasi, the extreme right-wing Hungarian General Staff major and Fascist leader, declared his willingness to take over the government. Millions of Hungarian pamphlets were printed in Vienna and transported to Budapest in sealed police trucks ready for the coup.

But Hitler was now ill, and the coup was postponed day after day—whether because of this or because he wanted Horthy to make the first move, we cannot tell. He must have found out that early in October Horthy had at last sent a team of negotiators to Moscow, because on October 3 he ordered the fight for Hungary's defense to continue even though "we are standing on the brink of a volcano." Some facts spoke for themselves. Although the Red Army had long been ready at Arad, it was still postponing its offensive, so evidently somebody was negotiating somewhere.[2] On the sixth—without any authority from Hitler or Himmler—Winkelmann decided to force Horthy's hand, because (as he later explained to the Reichsführer) "you can't just keep on postponing a putsch that's all ready and waiting." He ordered four top Horthy men kidnapped, including General Bakay and Horthy's own son and heir, who was believed to be dealing with the enemy himself. Bakay was netted at dawn on October 10. Later that day Himmler, Winkelmann, and probably SS General von dem Bach-Zelewski as well reported to Hitler for further orders; Bach-Zelewski—who had just cruelly put down the Polish uprising in Warsaw and was now ordered to raze the entire city to the ground—was directed to take his giant 650-millimeter mortar to Budapest

[1] Romania had been partly an OKW and partly a General Staff theater; operational control was shared by General Gerstenberg, General Friessner, General Hansen, and Admiral Brinkmann.

[2] They were indeed. The severe armistice terms dictated by Molotov to the Hungarian delegation on October 8, 1944, required the Hungarian armies not only to declare war on Germany "immediately," but to commence hostilities against them at the same time—just as Hitler had feared. Horthy cabled his acceptance of these terms on the tenth, as the secret Hungarian telegrams show. After the war, however, Horthy frequently denied he had ever accepted.

and help Skorzeny's operation. He arrived on the thirteenth. The same day Hitler directed Rudolf Rahn, one of Ribbentrop's best troubleshooting ambassadors, to follow him to Budapest and supervise the political aspects of the anti-Horthy coup, which was code-named *Panzerfaust*—"Bazooka."

To put teeth into their political pressure on Horthy, the Russians launched a big offensive on October 6 from the area between Arad and Klausenburg, across the plains toward Debrecen and Szolnok, which is on the Tisza. If this push had succeeded, it would have trapped Friessner's army group in the Carpathians, but at Debrecen Hitler had assembled three panzer divisions and on the tenth began a four-day tank battle which resulted in the destruction of several Soviet armored corps. This triumph should have stiffened Horthy's resolve to fight on; but he had already crossed the political Rubicon and secret orders had been issued to the First and Second Hungarian armies to retreat—the first phase of the betrayal of his erstwhile ally. Friessner was bewildered. His operations officer later wrote: "A major crisis occurred when on October 13 a section of the Hungarians—in fact the very ones who had been most effusive in their friendship toward us gullible soldiers—changed to the enemy side in mid-battle, no doubt in the misguided hope of a better future."[3]

During the following night, the first instructions were telegraphed to Veesenmayer in Budapest. The next morning, October 14, the crisis reports from Budapest multiplied. But Rudolf Rahn had now arrived there, and so had forty-two Tiger tanks which were being conspicuously unloaded at one of the main stations. It was the day of Rommel's sudden death; Goebbels, Speer, and Keitel were visiting the Wolf's Lair. Hitler himself attended his war conference ninety minutes after midnight; at a quarter to four in the morning he sent for his two secretaries and gossiped with them until five, when he went to bed. The news from Budapest was that Horthy had demanded to see Veesenmayer at noon the next day, and that the regent's Cabinet was meeting at ten; this probably meant that the hour for Hungary's defection had arrived. During the night the Hungarian General Staff telegraphed a threat to Guderian to withdraw the Hungarian troops from the front because Germany had not kept her promises. Guderian sent his deputy, General Wenck, flying to Budapest with his reply—an ultimatum to the Hungarians to stop meddling with the Hungarian divisions in Friessner's army group, as all Hungary was a German theater of operations now; and to rescind within twelve hours the orders to the First and Second Hungarian armies to

---

[3]His manuscript continued: "At the end of September we had transferred our army group headquarters to a picturesque but modern sanatorium for railwaymen in the Matra Mountains north of Gyöngyös. The accommodation and surroundings could not have been more beautiful. I refused to be robbed of my daily midday ride on Yutta through the brightly colored autumn beech forest. In the evening the deer were calling!!"—The general was a passionate huntsman.

retreat, failing which the Reich would take such measures as seemed necessary to attain her objectives. As this ultimatum was being delivered at 10 A.M., Skorzeny's team in Budapest was kidnapping Horthy's son—luring him to an ambush by telling him that an emissary from Marshal Tito was waiting for him.

Thus by the time Hitler was awakened by his staff on October 15 at half-past noon, the die had been cast; Horthy's son, the pawn in Hitler's hand, had been rolled—bloodstained and senseless—into a carpet and bundled into a plane bound for Vienna. At that very moment, unaware that at noon "Panzerfaust" had begun to roll, the regent was receiving the German envoy, Veesenmayer. Let us hear Winkelmann's coarsely worded narrative of that day, in his proud report to Himmler:

> Veesenmayer showed up at Horthy's punctually at 12 noon; Horthy immediately launched into a violent tirade, complaining we had kidnapped his son— we'd ambushed him. The old fellow said he had always warned him, but his son had refused to listen. He demanded that we release his son from custody, etc.
>
> Veesenmayer stood up to him like a man and didn't have to wheel out the biggest gun we had agreed on, namely to tell the old chap that if there was the least whiff of treachery we would stand his son up against a wall. Horthy threatened to quit the war, but did not commit himself positively as to when. Shortly afterward, his radio broadcast the foul proclamation.
>
> Meantime Ambassador Rahn had driven over to Horthy to appeal to his conscience. Horthy was crying like a little boy, kept clutching Rahn's hand and promising to call everything off, running to the telephone and then not speaking into it, and in general acting like somebody demented.

Horthy's armistice announcement had been broadcast at 2 P.M. Almost immediately the radio building was seized by a German police lieutenant and a handful of men—even before Bach-Zelewski's Tigers had arrived. A proclamation was broadcast, apparently signed by General Vörös, declaring Horthy's announcement of an armistice null and void and ordering the fight against the Red Army continued. Hungarian and German march music was broadcast, and then came Ferenc Szálasi's pronouncement that he had assumed power. Horthy's own troops in the capital deserted him. He and his dwindling supporters retreated into the Citadel; other Hungarian ministers, "pale and evil-smelling" in SS General Winkelmann's words, sought German protection. The Citadel was well guarded, and its approaches were mined; but Hitler had twenty-five thousand men in the city and more than forty Tigers—and he had the seventy-two-year-old statesman's son as hostage. The deal was put to the regent during the evening hours: at 6 A.M. the Citadel would be stormed; alternatively, if the regent would resign, legally transfer power to Szálasi, and leave the country, his son would be restored to him. Horthy's prime minister, General Lakatos, acted as the go-between. Horthy must have heard the Tigers raising a horrendous clatter as they pawed their way around the inclines to his Citadel.

Hitler canceled the midnight war conference and retired to his bunker at 1:15 A.M. to gossip with his secretaries Frau Christian and Fräulein Schroeder. Shortly before 4 A.M. Budapest telephoned: General Lakatos had told Veesenmayer that his government would resign, and that Horthy would abdicate the next day. Horthy was asking in return for asylum in Germany for himself, his family, and some friends, and for promises that the Reich would not blacken his name over the events of the previous day and would prevent any civil war in Hungary. Hitler agreed, and went to bed at four.

Thus Hungary remained in his *Festung Europa,* such as it now was, with Ferenc Szálasi as the constitutionally appointed head of state; Stalin's hopes of trapping Friessner's Army Group South were crushed. Horthy's orders to his First and Second armies—of which Hitler seemingly never learned—had been squashed before they even left the Budapest ministry.⁴ General Miklós, commanding the First Army, deserted with a handful of his staff to the Russians. General Lajos von Veress, commanding the Second Army, was arrested by Friessner for ordering his army to retreat. A second great tank battle was fought by Friessner at Debrecen, and a new defeat inflicted on the Red Army. A brief respite was thus granted the Nazis in Hungary.

In anticipation of the battle for East Prussia, Hitler had moved over into Bunker Eleven, a monstrous rebuilt complex of dormitories, operations rooms, and offices for himself and his principal minions; there was even space for his own diet kitchen in it. It would be proof against the heaviest known bombs, and against poison-gas attack, since it had its own compressed air and oxygen supplies and a U-boat air-conditioning plant in case all else broke down.⁵ On the day of Arnhem, Hitler had ordered a realistic reassessment of the Wolf's Lair's defenses against mass paratroop attack. "We can't afford to take rash risks any longer. . . . If a *Schweinerei* happens here—then myself, my entire High Command, the Reichsmarschall, the OKH, the Reichsführer SS, and the foreign minister, we are all sitting ducks! What a catch we would be! If I could get my hands on the entire

---

⁴Upon receiving a certain code message ("Carry out order of March 1, 1920"), Generals Veress and Miklós were to contact the Russians and turn their guns immediately on the Germans instead; the Third Army's General Heszlény was not trusted enough to be taken into Horthy's confidence. Horthy issued the code message on October 15, but the Hungarian defense ministry officers were suspicious and refused to transmit it.

⁵The air-conditioning plant installed by the Dräger firm had poison-gas filters; should these filters perish, canaries in the bunker rooms would provide an early warning. But Hitler declined to have canaries in his own rooms.

Russian High Command at one fell swoop, I would risk two paratroop divisions for it immediately!" On the day the Russian attack on Memel had begun, he had demanded twelve heavy antiaircraft batteries for his headquarters' defense immediately.

Here on the eastern front, Hitler, now tired and ailing, had long lost the initiative in the face of the baffling Russian superiority; his only strategic prerogative was to decide which towns to defend and which to abandon. An avalanche of enemy tanks had again swamped across Army Group North and reached the Baltic coast in the second week of October. Memel was surrounded, but Hitler ordered this ancient port fortified and held. Along the Memel River, the northern border of East Prussia itself, he managed to establish a new front line on the twelfth, while the long-range guns of the German battle fleet held the enemy at bay. But Schörner's attempts to drive a fresh corridor through to East Prussia failed, and the twenty-six divisions of his Army Group North were again cut off —this time in Kurland, a fifty-mile-square promontory into the Baltic. Hitler accepted Dönitz's arguments that the port of Libau, at its closest end, was more important than Riga, and the latter port was abandoned on the fifteenth. In this pocket the army group remained, attracting a disproportionate number of Russian divisions away from the main front—a controversial appendix of Hitler's "Barbarossa" campaign until the war was over, surviving six bloody battles undefeated.

On October 16, 1944, the day of Horthy's abdication, as Göring, Ribbentrop, and Goebbels joined in Hitler's noon war conference, the Red Army suddenly stormed into East Prussia itself, with two big armored spearheads thrusting into the eastern flank of the province toward Gumbinnen and Goldap, evidently making for Königsberg itself. Refugee columns began streaming past Hitler's headquarters. The German divisions were outnumbered 4 to 1. Gumbinnen fell, burning from end to end. By the twenty-second many of Hitler's staff considered East Prussia already lost. At Hitler's noon conference that day Keitel pleaded with him to leave for Berlin. Martin Bormann privately instructed the stenographers to begin packing for the move to the Chancellery and ordered the transcription section to make the transfer in three days.

Why did Hitler not tour the nearby battlefield now? He was far from well. Half the evening war conferences were canceled so that he could retire to bed, swooning with nameless pains against which neither Drs. Morell nor Stumpfegger, nor Eicken, summoned again from Berlin, could effectively prescribe. Morell thought it was an inflammation of the nasopharyngeal area. His dentist, Professor Hugo Blaschke, X-rayed the jaw, found an agonizing defect to the second bicuspid about which Hitler had kept silent, and after days of pleading was allowed to extract it.

An atmosphere of imminent defeat lay heavily in his private rooms—an air which no conditioning plant could dispel. One secretary wrote: "It made us despair to see the one man who could end all the misery with a stroke of his pen lying apathetically in bed, gazing at us with weary eyes, while all around us all Hell was loose. It was as though the Flesh had suddenly realized the futility of the efforts of his Will and had just gone on strike; and Hitler, who had never run into such disobedience before, was caught unawares by it."

Dr. Theo Morell gloomily wrote on October 23, "It's real autumn here, with dense fogbanks everywhere." Hitler's secretaries sat each evening gossiping at his bedside. At midnight an adjutant—Puttkamer, Below, or Major Willi Johann-meyer—would bring the brief war report. Sometimes Colonel von Amsberg, his Wehrmacht adjutant, spent the day touring the battlefields, where the Russians had now broken into Rominten Heide. Other times he would stand dutifully at the foot of Hitler's bed listening to the Führer ruminating on the errors he had committed in the past. In the darkness, after the secretaries left at four or five, Hitler made up his mind to stay at the Wolf's Lair and to die fighting for the Reich's frontier, rather than return to Berlin.

Then the miracle happened—Hitler believed it was just because his riflemen knew that he was still there. General Hossbach's Fourth Army halted the Russian onslaught and launched a courageous counterattack; first he deliberately accepted the risk to Goldap and concentrated on the enemy spearhead west of Gumbinnen. Here the Russians were put to flight and Gumbinnen recaptured. As Hossbach then swung south to deal with the Goldap spearhead, the devastation and carnage left by the Russian General Galizki's Eleventh Guards Army were witnessed for the first time. General Kreipe, touring the combat zone, wrote in his diary: "Visited 'Hermann Göring' Panzer Corps, in combat at Gumbinnen. Gumbinnen ablaze. Refugee columns. In and around Nemmendorf women and children crucified on barn doors and shot. I order photographs taken as evidence." The Gumbinnen atrocities made a deep impression on Hitler. The same secretary wrote: "Gone was his good temper. When we arrived at night for tea, he looked grim and careworn and he had to make an effort to put these pictures and reports from the eastern front out of his mind: women raped, children massacred, men mutilated . . . He swore revenge for them. 'They aren't human,' he said. 'They're the beasts of the Asiatic steppes. The war I am waging against them is a fight for the dignity of European man. No price is too high for victory. We must be harsh and fight with every means at our disposal.' "

On October 25, Hitler told Bormann he would definitely not consider leaving the Wolf's Lair until the crisis in East Prussia was over. "We would prefer rather more safety for the Führer," Bormann wrote nervously that day. "After all, forty or fifty miles are nothing for modern tanks to cover. Besides, we would prefer a more congenial place for the Führer to convalesce. But the Führer commands, and we obey." His secretaries asked if they ought to learn to handle pistols. Hitler loftily excused them from this need. "No, thank you, ladies: I have no desire to die at the hands of one of my secretaries!"

Amsberg, leaving to take up a frontline command, reported for one last time to the Führer in his bunker living room and asked what he ought to tell the officers of his new unit. "I know what I must not say, but not what I should." With a sigh of resignation Hitler told him: "You know for yourself how black things look. Tell them I am thinking and fighting all day and night for the German people and that my thoughts are always out there with my troops. I did try— and I will keep trying—to bring this war to a happy conclusion yet. But you know the way our Luftwaffe is, and there's no point in concealing it."

Sepp Dietrich, raising the new SS Sixth Panzer Army for the Ardennes offensive, visited Hitler and lectured him: if there was no Luftwaffe available even for reconnaissance, then the most heroic fight the infantry or U-boats could put up would be in vain. Göring called the criticisms libel and bitterly resented Bormann's daily rapid teleprinter reports submitted by the Gauleiters direct through him and Schaub to Hitler; these Party chiefs had no praise for the Reichsmarschall. By day and night the most devastating rain of fire in history was eating out the heart of Hitler's war industry. A five-thousand-ton deluge of bombs dropped on one city center within twenty minutes was a commonplace; nine thousand tons of bombs cascaded on Duisburg in one October day. With France lost, the Luftwaffe had no early-warning systems; conversely the enemy had stationed radar guidance systems in France enabling them to pinpoint towns as small as Bonn despite the most adverse weather. These saturation raids began to cause severe shortages throughout the German economy. By October all medical supplies—drugs, serums, bandages, anesthetics, and analgesics—were scarce or even unobtainable, as the factories had been destroyed. But the American daylight raids were a rapier thrust to the heart; synthetic rubber production was hit, and this alone limited the number of the new secret Mark XXI submarines Hitler could build. The loss of synthetic gasoline was so severe that a vicious cycle set in: by October over three thousand day fighters were available, but their fuel supplies were low; the refineries were inadequately defended; and those pilots that did engage the enemy had been undertrained because of the lack of gasoline.

Four times in the last two weeks of October Hitler taxed Göring in person about the Luftwaffe. Göring told him he had agreed with Adolf Galland and Albert Speer on a policy of conservation; he had now saved up three thousand one hundred fighter aircraft to throw en masse against the enemy bombers on a day when the weather was good enough. To Hitler it seemed a strategy designed to conserve only the pilots. He again began considering supplanting Göring with Greim. On November 1 he had another ninety-minute talk with the general. Greim had suggested appointing a chief of air warfare—namely himself—with operational command over the entire Luftwaffe. Göring came to the Wolf's Lair on November 3 and again on the fifth, and talked Hitler out of it. Evidently the price Hitler demanded in return was that Göring must appoint General Karl Koller, the Bavarian who had worked his way up from the ranks, as Luftwaffe Chief of Staff. Göring told Koller that day about the fight being waged against him by the SS, the army, and the Party. "He talked about the situation and declared that he is just fed up," wrote Koller that day. "He wished he were dead. He would like to join the paratroop army and fight with it at the front, but the Führer won't let him go and has told him that only he can rebuild the Luftwaffe."

Be that as it may, Hitler's consultations with Göring about major Luftwaffe policy were now only pro forma. He had just ordered Speer to triple antiaircraft artillery production at the expense of aircraft production, and he had decided that antiaircraft batteries should be concentrated on the defense of the steel industry, major factories, and railway centers; Allied airmen described the German batteries as their deadliest enemies. And it was thanks to Hitler that the Me-262 was in service as a jet bomber—though five months later than he had planned. As he had predicted, the Me-262 was proving an unwieldy disappointment as a fighter—it was vulnerable to enemy fighters during its takeoff and landing. But the bomber version was performing well against the large enemy troop assemblies around Nijmegen. Hitler accepted Speer's advice and ordered the rapid design and mass production (without trial) of a single-jet fighter, the Volksjäger; Heinkel's design was accepted, and the new plane was incorporated in the special production decree Speer asked Hitler to sign on October 12, concentrating aircraft production capacity on the new high-performance planes.

Meanwhile the devastation continued. General Galland kept delaying his fighters' *Grosser Schlag*—the Grand Slam. Finally Hitler lost patience, calculated for himself that Galland's arithmetic was full of fallacies, and announced at a war conference on November 6: "It's pure madness to go on turning out new aircraft all the time just so that the Luftwaffe can juggle with figures." On the twelfth, Galland claimed he had three thousand seven hundred fighter aircraft ready, but that same day an episode in Norway dealt the death blow to his plan. A small force of British heavy bombers attacked the crippled battleship *Tirpitz* at anchor in Tromsö Fjord. The local Luftwaffe fighter squadron was given more than adequate warning of the attack, and the Lancaster bombers, each carrying a ten-ton earthquake bomb, would have made easy targets; but—as Admiral Dönitz furiously telegraphed to Hitler—the fighters arrived too late. After eight minutes it was all over, and the huge battleship suddenly capsized, entombing one thousand sailors in the hull. Hitler angrily ordered Galland to surrender his hoard of fighters for his own Grosser Schlag—the coming top-secret Ardennes offensive —instead.

After the *Tirpitz* incident, he did not spare Göring's feelings even in public. Some days later, Göring showed him a memorandum. Hitler tossed it contemptuously aside. "There's no point in my reading that, it's all a pack of lies!"—and he turned his back on him. Galland was also on the way out.

To balance his grudges, Hitler showed special favor to some. Only recently he had ordered Bormann to find a suitable estate to present to Field Marshal von Manstein, and he did not take it amiss when Rundstedt asked for the services of Manstein, Leeb, or Kleist on the western front; he hinted to his staff that if ever Germany began great military offensives in the east he would again send for Manstein to command. Even Field Marshal von Brauchitsch—whom one officer claimed to have seen riding through Berlin in full field marshal's uniform on July 20 and whose conduct in 1939 and 1940 was not above reproach, as the Oster/Dohnanyi documents revealed—was restored to Hitler's favor. On August 3 he had written Hitler a letter offering his services and dissociating himself from Stauffenberg and the putschists; and now that Hitler's secret order creating the Volkssturm under Himmler had been made public, the elderly field marshal wrote again offering his life for Germany. Brauchitsch was given high marks in Hitler's book for having fostered Peenemünde and the V-2 rocket project: the V-1 flying bomb was still in action against the port of Antwerp, to which the enemy had now forced access by clearing the Scheldt Estuary, but only the V-2 rocket could still reach London. Every day he asked Jodl for the latest V-2 launching figures. Twenty or thirty times a day the missiles hit the British capital, each time with a one-ton warhead and the dynamic force of an express train. "No population can hold out under such an uninterrupted bombardment," Hitler gloated to his secretaries. "Their nerves won't stand it, because there is no warning from the sirens. The bomb can impact at any instant. Sheer panic will grip the masses and drive them out into the open countryside. But just imagine what that means—for the millions of people of a city almost twice as big as Berlin to swarm out to where there is neither roof nor rafter to accommodate them. . . . It will be an avalanche of misery and suffering, because even when the people get there, the local villagers will regard them as a plague. What parliamentary government can survive that! There will be such a storm of protest and war-weariness that the government will be overthrown. And that will mean peace at last."

By early November the British government had still not admitted that London was under enemy missile attack. But the repeated appeals to the evacuees not to return to the capital, and the lengthening obituary notices in London newspapers, gave all the confirmation Hitler needed.

From his two-week illness onward, Hitler, who had avoided as much contact with the civil affairs of the Reich as possible since 1939, concerned himself exclusively with military command decisions.

Dr. Hans Lammers, chief of the Reich Chancellery, had secured his last conference with him on September 24, 1944. That day the Führer signed his last law into the statute book (a minor item permitting Wehrmacht members to belong to the Nazi party).

In the east and west, in the Balkans, in Italy and in Norway, he was having to yield ground to the enemy which he might have been able to defend with his new strategic reserves but for his unshakable decision to concentrate those reserves in a great new counteroffensive in the Ardennes. Every day saw him in secret consultation with the handful of associates he had taken into his confidence —Fegelein, Himmler's liaison officer; Jodl, his chief strategic adviser; Buhle, who was scouring the Reich for every available piece of artillery. But even the military burden was now proving too much for him. He could seldom muster enough strength to hold his evening war conference. Several times he lay awake all night, sick with worry about the future—and about an aching throat which stirred in him the same cancer fears that had led to an operation in 1935. After supper on October 29, for example, he received Fegelein, Puttkamer, and Dr. Franz von Sonnleitner—Hewel's stand-in—for their reports on SS, Wehrmacht, and foreign affairs, then he sat sipping tea until 3:30 A.M. But he could not sleep: Dr. Morell was fetched at 6:10 A.M.—no doubt with sedatives—and again after breakfast eight hours later. Even the most vital evening conferences were transferred to this shabby, semidarkened bedroom. There was room for only one stenographer. "10:50 to 11:21 P.M.: took down conference of General Buhle and SS General Fegelein in Führer's bedroom," noted the stenographer Karl Thöt, on the thirty-first. "The Führer was lying in bed, but no less vigorous than usual. I sat behind his two visitors at a round table with a lamp."

His Ardennes gamble depended on the eastern front remaining stable until then. Here the war gods aided Hitler. Although fierce fighting would rage all winter in Hungary, elsewhere the Red Army was evidently exhausted. General Guderian predicted that Stalin would delay his main offensive until the frost— probably later than usual this year. Thwarted in East Prussia by Hossbach's counterattack, the Red Army had stormed Schörner's army group in Kurland on October 27, again hoping for a quick victory. But again they lost heavily. On the eleventh day of this fierce battle General Wenck said triumphantly to Hitler, "We have already knocked out five hundred twenty-two tanks." When Hitler soberly pointed out that the Russians had "huge numbers of tanks," Wenck continued, "—against which our own material losses are only three 75-millimeter guns, seven light field-howitzers, nine 122-millimeter Russian guns, and one 150-millimeter." "Slight losses indeed!" conceded Hitler. "When we stand fast! All our losses have come from our 'glorious' retreats—the kind of retreat one makes to 'regain one's tactical freedom.' "

By November 5 the Red Army had also been thrown out of the East Prussian town of Goldap, leaving a battlefield strewn with so much equipment in comparison to the meager haul of Russian captives that Hitler concluded—probably rightly—that the Red Army's "divisions" were of only regimental troop strength. "They are staking everything on their artillery," he pronounced. "Their 'divisions' are all understrength, just conglomerations of a few thousand men." Wenck agreed; it was remarkable, he pointed out, that they had scraped reinforcements together from quite far afield to try to save their foothold in Goldap. Hitler tried to read Stalin's mind. Where would it be best to launch the great winter offensive? In East Prussia or in Poland? "He must have had his doubts," commented Hitler, reflecting on the barely-hoped-for German victory in East Prussia. "He has always been wary of sending his troops into a highly developed area, as they would be bound to realize the absurdity of bolshevism after seeing it. So it is possible he'll move them into here"—indicating the Vistula bridgeheads in Poland—"and that up here [on the Baltic] he'll say he's got what he wanted by snapping off this thing," meaning Army Group North. Some minutes later, after hearing of an aircraft reconnaissance report on the menacing Soviet bridgehead across the Vistula at Baranov, Hitler again postulated: "That's where we must be on the lookout. Everything he's doing up here is just a diversion. . . . Besides, he must sense that up here on German soil [*i.e.,* East Prussia] he'll have to shed a lot of blood—a lot."

The Führer felt he had good reason to expect an early clash between Russia and her Allies. Throughout the autumn the unnatural three-year-old alliance between the capitalist democracies and the Bolshevik dictatorship had been closely examined in Berlin for signs of "metal fatigue."

Hairline cracks were already appearing. Stalin had given British and American military delegations twenty-four hours to get out of Bulgaria. His invasion of Romania and Bulgaria, and the spread of Communist subversion in the Balkans, flagrantly violated the Teheran agreements of 1943—as the Cicero documents showed. Stalin's annexation of eastern Poland was causing uproar in London and Washington if the foreign press dispatches and code intercepts were to be trusted: Hitler and Ribbentrop soon believed they could name their own price—once the "East-West war" began. On October 10, Himmler had shown Hitler a strong clue that Stalin was again putting out oblique feelers to him.

Foreign Minister Anthony Eden admitted in Parliament that relations with Stalin were strained, but he advised Goebbels not to fasten any hopes on it. However, actions spoke louder than words. Neither Stalin nor Hitler could fail to see that the British were still purposefully allowing the Wehrmacht to escape unhindered from the southern Balkans to the battlefields in Hungary. "It's obvious the British could have done something here, given the position we're in," Jodl commented to Hitler. "They only had to invade somewhere along here"—indicating the Adriatic coast of the Balkans—"and they would have cut us off completely down there." In the United States meanwhile, the Hearst press quoted Washington officials' predictions of an early outright conflict. In Iran, British and American oil interests had already provoked a government crisis over their dispute with the Russian oil interests. In Greece the government appointed by the British military commander had disbanded the Communist guerrilla units—on paper, if not in fact. Most encouraging of all for Hitler was the Luftwaffe's discovery that an entire British tactical air force wing had vanished from the Italian front despite Field Marshal Sir Harold Alexander's warning that the Germans were not weakening. At the same time German Intelligence had reported *Russian* troops and tanks appearing on Bulgaria's frontier with Turkey, only a hundred miles from the coveted Dardanelles. A tactical air force needed prepared bases—like those airfields the British had demanded of Turkey last winter. Hitler speculated:

> Perhaps they have disengaged a tactical wing to be on the safe side. Because for all the polite phrases they are swapping, the tension seems to be building up. Perhaps they are disengaging it to transfer it to Greece or to *here*—

and at this point Hitler's finger must have tapped eastern Thrace, that is, northern Turkey.

> It's quite definite that the Russians will attack there. I estimate it'll take them two to three weeks to deal with that. And when you're on one shore of the Dardanelles you don't just stop there, because you've got to occupy the other shore as well. You can only use the waterway if you control both shores. So he'll have to take the second bit as well [southern Turkey].

"And that," concluded Hitler logically, "will start the whole structure toppling. . . . My view is the British are standing by, because vital interests are at stake." A few weeks later Ribbentrop summarized Hitler's current strategy as follows: "If we are asked whether we would consider a political settlement, we reply that we are intent only on fighting on, and are not thinking of any political settlement—because this stance in itself might bring such a political settlement that much nearer."

Meanwhile the OKW instructed German military attachés not to discuss the coming East-West conflict at all.

———

With Hitler's last European ally gone, and the German nation nevertheless unbowed by bombing or military reverses, the Allies could only hope for a speedy victory if the Führer was ill or a power struggle broke out. Rumors abounded in the foreign press that he was ill, exhausted, in an asylum, or even Himmler's captive. "According to this one," Hitler guffawed, reading one news report aloud to his staff, "I'm a prisoner in my own house, my own 'residence' on the Obersalzberg!"

No doubt his increasing dependence on doctors and specialists caused some of the rumors. Morell had temporarily abandoned him—pleading a heart complaint —and was now far from the autumn fogs and military alarms of East Prussia. His assistant, Dr. Richard Weber, proved equally acceptable; on some days he was called to Hitler's bunker three or four times, and on November 13, Hitler was examined by the dentist, Blaschke, and by Major Stumpfegger as well. His throat was very sore, and he was finding it difficult to eat. He postponed the necessary X-rays, fearing they might reveal a malignancy.

The preparations for his top-secret counterattack in the Ardennes were nearing completion. Rundstedt had capably fulfilled Hitler's main requirement—that the western front be stabilized until the attack was launched. At Arnhem, Aachen, and now Antwerp, a series of costly battles had been forced on the Allies: Antwerp had fallen into enemy hands in early September, but for three months Hitler had prevented any convoys reaching the port. Aachen, the westernmost town of the Reich, had barred Lieutenant General Omar Bradley's advance across the West Wall. For purely prestige reasons he had begun a heavy attack here on October 2, but Hitler had ordered the town defended house by house, as Stalingrad had been, and when the Americans poured artillery shells into it he repeated his Paris order—that on entering, the enemy was to find only a field of ruins. When Aachen was finally encircled and overrun on October 21, the Allies found to their chagrin that Hitler had used the vital respite to rebuild the West Wall line to the east. Every ton of equipment and supplies that the enemy moved to the Aachen area for the later drive to the Ruhr pleased Hitler more—for then the booty from the Ardennes attack would be bigger. He told his staff he would not be tempted to divert reinforcements from his own Ardennes buildup "even if the enemy pushes through to Cologne."

This *was* General Eisenhower's main objective for early November: the British and American armies would exploit the Aachen gap to reach the Rhine on a one-hundred-mile front; they would then envelope the Ruhr industrial region from north and south. But Rundstedt launched a strong spoiling attack on

October 27, and Eisenhower's plans were delayed by two weeks. Meanwhile General Patton, south of the Ardennes, had assured his superiors that he could reach the Saar in three days—with a quarter of a million troops, his Third U.S. Army outnumbered the Germans 3 to 1 in that sector—and then "easily breach the West Wall." Patton's attack began on November 8, but confronted with pouring rain, mud, and minefields he advanced only fifteen miles toward the West Wall in eight days before the elastic tactics of General Hermann Balck and the stubborn defense of the city of Metz finally halted him.

Hitler had not lost his nerve. In his secret order for the Ardennes attack signed on November 10 he expressly accepted all the risks inherent in his Ardennes buildup "even if the enemy offensive on either side of Metz, and the imminent attack on the Ruhr region, should create major inroads into our territory or fortifications." It was a calculated risk, but one largely justified by events.

Hitler had provisionally ordered the Ardennes attack to begin on December 1. The eastern front was still quiet, with the exception of Hungary. But on November 14 the Allies began a renewed assault on the Alsace region; two days later the delayed American attack through the Aachen gap also began, while bombers devastated the minor towns between there and the Rhine: 2,703 tons were dropped on Düren in one attack—leaving it 95 percent wiped out—1,917 tons on Jülich, and 1,020 tons on Heinsberg. A steady drain on the German fuel and ammunition resources buildup for the Ardennes attack began. Thus Keitel and Jodl had a powerful case for Hitler to transfer his headquarters to the west. Moreover, his throat had now been X-rayed, and on the eighteenth it was again examined at Karlshof hospital (near Rastenburg) by Eicken, Morell, Stumpfegger —who had transferred his loyalties completely from Himmler to the Führer— and Dr. Brandt; a laryngeal polyp, not a malignant tumor, had been found on the anterior third of his left vocal cord, but Eicken would have to operate on Hitler's throat in Berlin at once.

The Führer's departure from East Prussia was kept secret. The special train would have to arrive in Berlin in the dark small hours for that reason. At 3:15 P.M. on November 20, while the noise and clatter of the construction gangs working on the last bunkers still continued, Hitler left the Wolf's Lair for Görlitz station and boarded his train. After tea he slept for a while, and then he invited his private staff to dine with him at 8:30 P.M. An SS orderly listed those at dinner as Martin Bormann, Dr. Morell, the dietician Fräulein Manzialy, Julius Schaub, the impresario Benno von Arent, and two secretaries. One of the latter wrote evocatively of the journey:

I had come to love the forest life and East Prussia's landscape. Now we were leaving them forever. Hitler probably knew that too. And although he ordered the construction work continued as though he intended to return one day, he too was in a farewell mood. Had he not always maintained that so long as he personally commanded any sector it had never been abandoned? His carriage windows were blacked out. He sat in his compartment with the light switched on . . . a twilight like a mausoleum.

I had never seen Hitler as dejected and distant as on this day. His voice barely rose above a whisper. His eyes were rooted to a spot on the white tablecloth. An oppressive atmosphere crowded in on the narrow, swaying cage around us.

Hitler suddenly began to talk about an operation and about his confidence in Professor von Eicken's skill. "It's a great responsibility for him, but he's the only one who can do it. An operation on the vocal cords isn't dangerous, but it may leave me with no voice . . ."

At 5:30 A.M., the train arrived at Berlin's Grunewald station. The usual station, the Silesian station, had been damaged in an air raid. With the car's headlights picking out only ruins to the right and left, Hitler was driven back to his Chancellery.

His sojourn here lasted three weeks, as circumstances obliged him to keep postponing the Ardennes attack. Fräulein Eva Braun joined him, and lunched and dined with him almost every day. Eicken operated on him on November 22; the pathologist confirmed that the polyp—a piece of flesh the size of a millet seed—was quite benign, more commonly referred to as a "singer's knot." The morphine injection Eicken used to anesthetize the Führer proved an alarming overdose, however, for he was knocked out by it for nearly eight hours; the professor had failed to take into account Hitler's total abstinence from alcohol and nicotine in calculating the dose. Gradually Hitler's voice returned, although by early December he could still only whisper; soon the entire Chancellery was talking in whispers too. He remained out of sight, kept company only by Eva and the three older secretaries; an adjutant brought him the war reports. When Albert Speer came for a conference on the twenty-eighth, it was obvious Hitler had recovered.

During Hitler's fresh physical incapacity, the enemy inflicted an unexpected defeat on General Balck's Army Group G. It was of little strategic significance, but a further blow to German morale. On November 23, American tanks pushed into Strasbourg and reached the Upper Rhine, after the German First and Nineteenth armies had been put to flight. On the twenty-sixth Hitler put Himmler himself in command of this Upper Rhine sector, with control over all army, Waffen SS, and even Luftwaffe units in his area.

On December 10, Hitler left Berlin at 5 P.M.; ten hours later, in pitch darkness, he switched from his train to a car and drove on to the Eagle's Nest, the bunker headquarters built in 1940 at Bad Nauheim near the western front. That afternoon and the next he forcefully addressed two audiences of twenty senior generals whose divisions would begin the Ardennes attack on the sixteenth (his voice was not strong enough to command a larger audience). He suggested that evil forces had blocked Germany's unification ever since the Treaty of Westphalia in 1648. Peoples suffered the hardships of war bravely, but only so long as victory was still possible. If that hope was now suddenly removed from the enemy, their people must turn against the war. "Whatever they do, they cannot expect me to surrender. Never, never!" He reminded his audiences of how Frederick the Great had fought on in the Seven Years' War although all his generals and even his own brother had lost hope. "His state presidents, his ministers, turned up from Berlin in droves to beg him to stop the war because it could no longer be won. But the tenacity of that one man made it possible to fight on until finally the tide miraculously turned. To suggest that if the throne hadn't changed hands in Russia the tide would not have changed, is quite beside the point; because if they had stopped the war in the *fifth* year a throne change in the seventh year would have been neither here nor there. It is that moment we have to wait for!"

Never in history had heterogeneous coalitions such as existed between East and West in 1944 survived long. The enemy powers were already almost at each other's throats. "If you sit at the center of the web, like a spider, and follow this trend, you can see how from hour to hour the contrasts between them grow. So if we throw in a few really powerful punches, we may at any moment see this entire artificially erected common front suddenly collapse with a mighty clap of thunder."

The Ardennes offensive began at 5:30 A.M. on December 16. The weather was perfect for the attack.

PART 6

ENDKAMPF

The Gamble

It was a calculated risk that Hitler was taking, but he and his military advisers recognized that they had no choice.

Hitler himself reflected early in December 1944 that his own life was virtually spent in any case: before World War I he had been too impoverished to enjoy it; during that war itself he had been consigned to the Flanders battlefields; afterward, he had committed himself body and soul to his fight for power. Now a new war, more terrible than the first, had robbed the former infantryman turned Führer of the fruits of success. This is how Hitler viewed his career in retrospect. He insisted that now his one aim was to fight the war through to a victorious conclusion that would make fresh passages of arms impossible in Europe for at least a century. "Frederick II earned his title 'the Great' not because he was victorious, but because he did not despair in adversity; equally, posterity will come to recognize me because I too will never have surrendered after grievous misfortunes."

Hitler had commenced an order to his commanders on November 25 as follows: "This war will determine the survival or extinction of the German people. It demands the unqualified commitment of every individual. Even seemingly hopeless situations have been mastered by the blind courage and bravery of the troops, the stubborn steadfastness of all ranks, and by calm, unyielding leadership."

This was not just a war to decide frontiers or systems of government; it was a war against the destruction of the German race. In his view, the enemy had made their purposes quite plain. Whether Germany was defeated or surrendered "unconditionally," the Americans planned to convert Germany into "a country primarily agricultural and pastoral in its character"; the plan drafted by Henry Morgenthau, U.S. Secretary of the Treasury, to that end had been secretly initialed by Churchill and Roosevelt in mid-September. The American press had obtained and published it—a gift to Goebbels's anti-Semitic propaganda.[1] He and Hitler proclaimed that the enemy leaders were agreed on the extermination of forty million Germans, for such would be the necessary outcome of the plan. The resumption of the saturation bombing and firestorm raids seemingly added authority to the claim. Over 2,200 tons of fire bombs were dropped by night on ancient Heilbronn, massacring 7,147 civilians within ten minutes. On December 15—the very eve of the Ardennes gamble—Churchill announced in Parliament his approval of Stalin's demands on eastern Poland; the Poles could in return have all East Prussia and much of eastern Germany, from which the Germans would be expelled—"Because expulsion is the most satisfactory and lasting means, so far as we are in a position to judge." "Earlier," Hitler reminded his generals, "that kind of thing would have been dismissed as a propaganda slogan, as a propaganda lie. Here we have it from the horse's mouth, but even so it falls a long way short of reality, because if Germany collapses, Britain has no hope whatever of making a stand against bolshevism anywhere." From Guderian's eastern Intelligence branch Hitler knew that Russian deserters had reported that Stalin had recently ordered that while the Red Army was to behave properly in Poland, in German territory the troops might loot and rob and "do as they pleased." The whirlwind Hitler had sown in 1941 was approaching.

To surrender on terms like these would be a betrayal of the three million Germans who had now been lost in battle or enemy air raids. He had not invested billions of Reichsmarks in this war[2] just to see ten million Germans cast onto the winter roads of East Prussia and Silesia as refugees, while the unindustrious Poles confiscated their neat farms and homesteads.

But Hitler saw sound political and strategic reasons for launching his big winter counterattack, and in the west rather than the east. The British and Americans were obviously experiencing supply problems; their armies were thinly spread along the five-hundred-mile western front; they were low in fuel and ammunition, and experiencing manpower shortages. Keitel on the other hand planned to raise half a million new German troops by February 1945. "Our position is no different from that of the Russians in 1941–42," Hitler comforted his generals. "They too were in the most straitened circumstances, but then they began to launch isolated offensives along our long battlefront—on which we ourselves were on the defen-

---

[1] The full Morgenthau Plan approved by "F.D.R." and "W.S.C." provided for any people trying to flee Germany's frontiers to be gunned down by armed guards; a long list of categories of officials was to be summarily executed. A photocopy of the thirty-page document is in my possession.

[2] The German finance minister's papers reveal that Wehrmacht costs from September 1, 1939, to November 30, 1944, had totaled 398,760 million Reichsmarks; a further 199,700 million had been spent on the civil sector. Against this, the Reich had raised only 288,550 million Reichsmarks by direct and indirect taxation and by occupation charges.

sive—and slowly maneuvered us back again." Once the German public saw this process start there would be a great sigh of relief, and the young would volunteer enthusiastically for battle. "And this I must say—our nation is as decent as one could ask for. It would be impossible to find a better people than the Germans." He did not mention the difference between Russia in 1942 and Germany now: that the ticking time-bomb left by the raw-materials crisis gave him only a limited number of months in which to succeed.

Recognizing that General Eisenhower's command abilities were questioned by the British, Hitler hoped for most *political* gain by puncturing the enemy front where it was held by the U.S. First Army—which had already suffered heavy losses in the battle for Aachen. In any case, the Americans had left only four or five divisions to hold a one-hundred-mile Ardennes front. In his view, the United States was such a potpourri of inferior races, a country with so little tradition of heroic national sacrifice, that a great bloodletting here would invite fundamental political controversies across the Atlantic. In short, the demeaning label applied by Goebbels and Rommel to the American troops in North Africa—"the Italians" of the western alliance—had stuck in his mind. And what Stalin had done to the Italians at Stalingrad, Hitler would repeat with the Americans here in the Ardennes. "If we succeed," he explained on December 2 to Generals Hasso von Manteuffel and Sepp Dietrich, the two panzer army commanders involved, "we will have knocked out half the enemy front. Then let's see what happens!" Most probably, he would then transport his spare divisions back to the eastern front in time to buttress it against the coming big Soviet offensive.

This meant a further gamble within the main one. The chief of Guderian's operations branch, Colonel Bogislaw von Bonin, was confident about the strength of certain sectors of the eastern front—notably East Prussia, Warsaw, and Cracow—but Hitler knew that Stalin would not forever postpone the big offensive he was clearly preparing in the Vistula bridgeheads from Warsaw to Cracow.[3] The gamble was, how long did Hitler have? On December 2, Army Group A predicted the Soviet attack within one week and asked that the moment the offensive began

---

[3]Hitler emphasized this to the new Hungarian leader, Ferenc Szálasi, when they first met on December 4.

The General Staff's insouciance of early December about the eastern front is understandably muted in postwar memoirs. But in captivity in August 1945 Major General Burkhart Mueller-Hillebrand was overheard telling a fellow general how Guderian had summoned the chiefs of staff of the eastern armies to an OKH conference at Zossen on December 5: "First there was a tremendous grubfest with enough food to burst, and then a binge. Guderian stayed until 2 A.M., by which time they were standing on the tables. I was revolted." Every evening the OKH, including the operations branch, were drunk as lords, he said.

the navy, army, and air force destroy the numerous wooden bridges erected by the Russians over the Vistula. Guderian believed the attack would be in mid-December, when the first frosts hardened the ground. Russian prisoners gave "December 20" as the date. Had the Ardennes offensive begun in mid-November as originally planned, the risk would have been less; but it had already been delayed nearly a month by logistics problems. It was due to begin on December 16. Guderian was sure Stalin would march westward the moment Hitler had committed his strategic reserve in the Ardennes. But Hitler was equally convinced of the opposite—that while Stalin was not bluffing, he would wait until Germany and the Allies had exhausted their reserves in the west, just as he had waited in vain in 1940.

Hitler's conviction proved correct. Not until mid-January 1945 did Stalin show his hand. Hitler also won his second extraordinary gamble, on concealing his Ardennes intentions for three months from the enemy. He had ordered absolute radio silence before the attack; no preparatory orders were to be conveyed by plane or transmitted even in code by radio; special war diaries were to be kept for the preparatory phase; potentially unreliable troops, like those born in the Alsace, were to be withdrawn from the front line; reprisals were threatened against the next-of-kin of any deserters; and any hint that the enemy had wind of the attack was to be reported immediately.

No hints came. In the first twelve days of December 1944 there were only five known or probable desertions from the western front. Hitler's security measures proved almost perfect; besides, the renegades who had betrayed his moves in the past were now in Himmler's custody awaiting trial. Not until the second day of the actual offensive did an enemy aircraft suddenly sight "thousands of vehicles" massing in the mountainous Eifel plateau. Hitler concluded that Eisenhower, Bradley, and General Bernard Law Montgomery had been living only in their own dreamworld of future campaigns. "Perhaps," he was to say, "there was also the belief that I might already be dead, or at least suffering from cancer somewhere—unable to drink or live on much longer, which would rule me out as a danger."

The only order known to have fallen into enemy hands was one for the formation of a special reconnaissance unit in the west—about two battalions of volunteers with one common qualification: an ability to speak American; captured American uniforms and equipment were also to be sent in. Hitler—with his predilection for the adventuresome—had sent for SS Colonel Otto Skorzeny on October 21, told him that three captured German tanks flying German colors had been put to devastating use by the Americans in the fight for Aachen, and directed him to build up a phony "American" task force to seize key bridges across the Meuse River between Liège and Namur when the Ardennes attack began. Other American-uniformed units were to spread alarm and confusion behind the American lines.

The rapid seizure of bridgeheads across the Meuse would be vital. At a tightly restricted late October conference, Hitler had revealed his Ardennes plan to the chiefs of staff of Rundstedt and Model (Generals Westphal and Krebs) and informed them that the strategic object of the offensive would be to destroy enemy forces, not capture territory as such. Model and his generals were urging that the knife be plunged in only as far as the Meuse, to excise merely the American forces massing for the attack on the Ruhr. However, if the knife was forced right through to the coast at Antwerp, it would also trap the British armies in the Netherlands. Göring had promised two thousand planes for the attack. Model and Rundstedt accepted this, but warned that they were not strong enough to reach Antwerp. They favored the more limited solution—turning at the Meuse instead. Throughout November the tactical controversy raged until Hitler, on the twenty-fifth, insisted that his own decision to go for the "big solution" was final. The small solution might prolong the war; the big one might end it—at least in the west. To use the General Staff's own jarring phrase, it was time for a *Ganzer Entschluss,* a "total decision." Therefore the Meuse must be forded by the second day and Antwerp itself captured by the seventh, for no bad-weather period could be relied on to last longer and keep Allied planes grounded.

Hitler jealously watched over the planning, from the infantrymen's winter boots and blankets to the deployment of the formidable Jagd-Tiger tanks with their 128-millimeter guns. He had remorselessly herded artillery units into the western front. During November, 1,349 tanks and assault guns were sent to Rundstedt, and 1,000 more would follow before Christmas. Snow-clearing troops were put on standby. Special tanks had to be built to spread sand on the icy mountain roads. Victory was certain: he began drafting orders to ensure that this time no German soldiers set foot inside Paris the germ center of the recent Wehrmacht defeat. A special SS squad was detailed to round up and execute civic and Party officials in towns and villages that had surrendered too readily to the enemy. Hitler dictated orders for the initial artillery bombardment to concentrate on the enemy-occupied villages and headquarters. It was to be followed by a further one-minute barrage and by a saturation bombardment of the enemy artillery positions. "There must not be one gun barrel that does not join in this artillery preparation!" During lulls in the bombardment, the troops were to simulate infantry assaults ("Shouts of 'Hurrah,' and machine-gun bursts") to get on the American defenders' nerves. Hitler had learned a vital lesson from the Russian June 1944 offensive against Army Group Center: to conserve his tank strength, the initial breach in the enemy line would be made by the *infantry* with assault-gun support. The panzer divisions would not follow until the following night; these were the "thousands of vehicles" the Allied spotter aircraft had sighted massing in the Eifel district. On November 26, Hitler set December 10 as the first possible date; and at a conference with Model, Dietrich, Manteuffel, and Westphal on December 2 zero hour was fixed at 5:30 A.M.

———

Twice more the attack was postponed briefly, while the last supplies arrived. The requested stockpile of 3.8 million gallons of gasoline had been built up, and more than the 50 trainloads of ammunition. The morale of the troops was high. Some 170 bombers, 90 ground-attack planes, and nearly 1,500 fighter aircraft were standing by. Twenty-eight German divisions were about to fall upon only 5 American divisions. At 3 P.M. on December 15, Hitler held a final war conference with Himmler and Rundstedt's Chief of Staff, General Westphal. Model wanted another postponement, but Rundstedt's advice was to go ahead before their intentions were unmasked. Hitler agreed, and at 3:30, Westphal telephoned the Führer's decision to Rundstedt's command post nearby. The Luftwaffe meteorologist forecast poor weather for several days. The enemy air force would be virtually grounded. Hitler telegraphed once more to Model forbidding him to turn the knife before crossing the Meuse. He assured him that "if you comply with all these basic operational guidelines, a great victory is certain." The Führer dined with his secretaries, sat talking with Bormann or Hewel, went briefly with Bormann to hear the latest war report from Colonel von Below and Major Johannmeyer at 1:10 A.M., and retired to bed at five—half an hour before the artillery barrage began—satisfied that no ugly surprises were in store.

By the time he was awakened, at 11:30 A.M. on December 16, the American front had been engulfed at many places along a seventy-mile sector between Monschau and Echternach, and the German infantry was already eight and ten miles inside enemy territory. Jodl confirmed that they had taken the Americans completely by surprise. A glow of confidence warmed the bleak bunker headquarters. After Hitler had been tended by Drs. Morell and Blaschke for an hour, he went for a casual stroll with Bormann's younger brother and lunched with the secretaries. The thunder of gunfire could clearly be heard. One of his staff stenographers wrote in his diary: "When [Stenographer Ewald] Reynitz and I went over at 3 P.M. for the war conference, an imposing number of German fighter planes swept low overhead, and Major Büchs [a Luftwaffe adjutant] . . . turned to all of us as we excitedly watched our fighters roaring past after so many months of German air inferiority, and said challengingly, 'Who dares say anything against the Luftwaffe now!' . . . When we reached the conference room the Führer was already there, contrary to his custom. It was only too evident how delighted he was at the first magnificent news of our offensive. Even before the conference the Reich press chief, Dr. [Otto] Dietrich, told us: 'Well—now at last you're going to get something cheerful to take down!' And so it was." To Hitler the battle was already as good as won. That day he ordered the German navy to do everything possible to prevent British ships escaping from Antwerp before—and after—Sepp Dietrich's SS Sixth Panzer Army got there.

It will serve no purpose to follow here the next month's events on the Ardennes battlefields. It is more interesting to see how opinion at the Eagle's Nest, inspired by Hitler's hardy optimism, persistently failed to grasp the harsh realities of the campaign. Hitler's tanks never recaptured Antwerp—perhaps he had deliberately set his armies' sights too high. Worse, they never even saw the Meuse, let alone crossed it.

What caused this tactical defeat? Some factors came as a shock to Hitler: the Americans had established an unexpected main line of defense two or three miles behind their battle front; and they fought with inexplicable bravery. But other factors should have caused less surprise. The Luftwaffe radio operators newly transferred to man Sepp Dietrich's tanks were unfamiliar with battle procedures. The battalion of superheavy Jagd-Tiger tanks—each weighing seventy-two tons and equipped with 128-millimeter guns—sent by Hitler to block the roads on the northern flank against American forces concentrated around Aachen was not even deployed; Hitler learned twelve days later it had never crossed the Rhine. "They must be insane!" he announced. "If the enemy attacks our defenses with ten or twelve heavy tanks, there's enough screaming to bring the house down; but when we've got twenty-four of the heaviest tanks in the world, they aren't even used!" Those tanks that did attack ran out of gasoline too soon, as they churned in low gear through the narrow, twisting valleys and defiles. The fuel shortage was aggravated by the overmotorization of attacking divisions. Convoys of empty trucks were following so they could be stuffed with booty. The roads were blocked by blown bridges and by obstacles the Germans themselves had created in their retreat some weeks earlier. Gasoline tankers could not get through, as immense traffic jams built up in the narrow roads leading to the battlefields. Finally, although General von Manteuffel's Fifth Panzer Army broke through first, Hitler continued to attach the Schwerpunkt to the SS Sixth Panzer Army—perhaps for political reasons.

Despite all this Hitler kept his eye on the strategic blessings of his counterstroke. He betrayed no signs of disappointment at the offensive's slow progress. Within five days 25,000 American prisoners were taken and 350 enemy tanks claimed destroyed; the Allied air force was still grounded by the weather. The Luftwaffe and paratroop support operations were rolling like clockwork. Skorzeny's "American" units were spreading consternation behind the lines. There were signs among the Americans in Belgium of the same sort of panic that had gripped the Germans after the enemy breakthrough at Avranches that summer. By December 22, Eisenhower had had to call off his attacks along the rest of the western front, and he even relinquished hard-won bridgeheads along the Saar. Sixteen to twenty enemy divisions were estimated to be bearing down on the

Ardennes battlefield, but Hitler's slow advance on the Meuse had not yet been checked, and the weather was still against the Allies. At a war conference Hitler chuckled: "Mr. Churchill, now *you* must make a *Ganzer Entschluss!*"—and he mimicked the British prime minister's speech impediment as he did so.

With an offensive against East Prussia and Silesia now, Stalin could immediately have disembarrassed his western Allies. But apart from the continuing struggle in Hungary he made no move.

In Italy, France, Belgium, and Britain Communist underground movements were stirring at Moscow's command. Reports reached Hitler of open warfare between the pro-Stalin elements in Greece and the British troops. After a luckless attempt to bring the warring factions to heel, Churchill flew out of Athens "with his tail between his legs," mocked Hitler. "And now he wants people to believe him capable of stopping the tide of bolshevism into Europe as a whole!" Meanwhile Churchill's frank Poland speech in Parliament had evoked a response which promised a storm to come. At his Washington press conference Roosevelt was asked whether the Atlantic Charter—which Stalin's annexation of eastern Poland so flagrantly violated—had ever existed in writing, and if so where; he replied that it had not. This lie did nothing to still the Polish exiles' discontent. The Soviet attack on Schörner's army group in Kurland, resumed on December 22, did not cause one German division to be withdrawn from the west. (Nor was it any more profitable than the Red Army's previous two attempts to capture this rump of northern Latvia.) The Intelligence now reaching Hitler was that Stalin had attached outrageous political demands to the unleashing of his big offensive. December 20, the date given by interrogated Russian prisoners as the one set for launching a Soviet offensive, had now passed. Hitler slapped the map table at the Eagle's Nest and crowed to his staff: "You see, perhaps we've made it after all!"

On the seventh day of Hitler's offensive, December 23, the skies cleared. By day and by night the Allied air force regained control of the Ardennes battlefield. The knife had now plunged forty miles into the enemy front; but the railroad stations in the German rear, at Koblenz, Gerolstein, and Bingen, were devastated, and Allied fighter-bombers created havoc on the roads. General Patton's Third Army had begun a counteroffensive on Rundstedt's southern flank. The 2nd Panzer Division was only five miles from the Meuse. Hitler stood outside his blockhouse impassively watching as two thousand enemy bombers swarmed eastward over his head, glittering solemnly in the weak winter sun, spelling the end of his hopes of an easy triumph in the west. Over lunch, his sharp-tongued secretary Christa Schroeder challenged him. "Mein Führer, we *have* lost the war —haven't we?" He stonily replied that they had not.

He had begun rereading the *Collected Letters* of Frederick the Great, and found one letter written in the fifth year of what was to be a seven-year war:

I first went to war with the finest army Europe ever saw. I now have a rabble; I have no commanders left, my generals are incompetent, the officers can't lead, the troops are hopeless.

Yet Frederick had finally won through. And it was this obdurate tenacity that alone assured victory: "When all goes well people are on top of the world," Hitler explained to a panzer general at 2 A.M. one morning. "But when everything starts going wrong they just fold up and give in." So if Hitler's troops now asked him, Why all this sacrifice? he would answer, "The war cannot last as long again as it has already lasted. Nobody could stand it, neither we nor the others. The question is, Which side will crack first? And I say that the side that lasts longer will do so only if it stands to lose everything. *We* stand to lose everything. If the other side announces one day, 'We've had enough!' no harm will come to them. If America says, 'Cut! Stop! No more American boys for Europe!' it won't hurt them. New York remains New York, Chicago remains Chicago, Detroit remains Detroit, San Francisco remains San Francisco. Nothing changes. But if we say today, 'We've had enough, we're packing up'—then Germany will cease to exist."

This was the "cornered tiger" logic into which Allied insistence on unconditional surrender had forced him. But it was not illogical, for cracks kept appearing in the monolithic enemy front. Hitler learned secretly that Stalin was willing to negotiate with him now, before beginning his main eastern front attack. But Hitler was no more inclined to throw in the towel than Stalin had been in 1941. When Ribbentrop gamely offered to fly with his family to Moscow now, as a surety for Germany's honest intent, Hitler begged him not to. "Ribbentrop, don't pull a Rudolf Hess on me!" Stalin's offer seemed to confirm that the Red Army was exhausted; and had not the General Staff proclaimed its confidence in the strength of the main eastern front?[4]

Surviving documents indicate that both Guderian and Hitler were preoccupied with Hungary in December 1944, rather than with the rest of the Russian front. Without Hungary there would be neither aluminum to build aircraft nor aviation fuel to fly them. "This is why Hungary is so vital," agreed Guderian. Late in November Stalin committed two army groups to the fight for Budapest and western Hungary—the cornerstone of Hitler's "minimum economic region"; Hitler's strategy was to force Stalin to throw even more weight into Hungary. Now that Hungary was at stake, it did not occur to either Hitler or the Hungarians to declare Budapest an "open city": on December 4, Ferenc Szálasi sanctioned the house-by-house defense of the beautiful city in return for an undertak-

[4]See the statement of Colonel von Bonin, chief of the General Staff operations branch, as quoted by the navy on December 1, 1944 (page 741).

ing by Hitler not to make a deal with Stalin at Hungary's expense. Throughout December the Soviet pincer attack continued. General Friessner moved seventy thousand German and Hungarian troops into the city's defenses. On the twentieth the final Russian offensive began. When Guderian arrived that day for two days of talks and a privileged invitation to tea at Hitler's headquarters, Hungary was the first point on his agenda, followed by the need to reshuffle divisions southward along the eastern front; the other sectors in Poland, East Prussia, and Kurland were relegated to points 7, 10, and 11 of Guderian's agenda. But Hitler's Hungarian strategy began to fail. The Soviet thrust bypassing the city to the west met so little German resistance that Hitler dismissed Friessner and the Sixth Army's General Fretter Pico on December 23; by the twenty-fourth, Budapest was totally invested by the enemy.

It was Christmas Eve 1944, but at the Eagle's Nest near Frankfurt—where Hitler was still directing the Ardennes battle—there was little respite.[5] Not until December 26 did Guderian again arrive from Berlin. Jodl's diary and General Staff records show that Hitler agreed to move what meager forces he could to the Second Panzer Army holding the "Margaret line," in Hungary, between the Drava River and Lake Balaton, in defense of the vital petroleum fields at Nagykanisza; an infantry division would be moved from the west to Budapest. Two more would follow to the main eastern front. In particular, Guderian had sent out an order late on December 24 for the Fourth SS Panzer Corps, commanded by the redoubtable Herbert Gille, to entrain from Warsaw (Army Group A) to Hungary—where its two panzer divisions, "Death's Head," followed by "Viking," would begin a counterattack on New Year's Day to relieve the besieged city of Budapest. As Guderian wrote on December 31 to his Hungarian counterpart: "By deliberately taking a very grave risk on the rest of the eastern front we have done everything possible to restore firm contact with Budapest."[6]

[5]The manservant's duty-register shows that on December 24, 1944, Hitler lunched with his two middle-aged secretaries, invited Keitel, Jodl, Burgdorf, Buhle, Scherff, Bormann, and Fegelein to tea, slept three hours, then dined with the same secretaries and his dietician until the midnight war conference. An SS major wrote the next day: "After a short break, we worked on during the night. Supper last night was quite good. Field Marshal Keitel made a speech, short and sweet, then we all sat around a candlelit Christmas tree for a while before going back to work. This morning I ran into the Chief [Hitler]. He shook my hand, asked about the family, and even remembered that we have two children and that the daughter was born the day I joined him. I could do and sacrifice anything for this man."

[6]I have seen no documentary evidence that Guderian expressed concern for the main eastern front comparable to his concern about Hungary until early 1945. The General Staff's subsequent failure to prevent the Soviet invasion in mid-January resulted in many durable postwar legends; aided by Jodl's little-known diary, by the fragmentary stenograms and Admiral Voss's digests of Hitler's daily conferences, and by the manservant's visitors' record, I have done my best to untangle these legends. There is no contemporary evidence to support Guderian's 1951 version, which has him at the Eagle's Nest on December 24 for the sole purpose of pleading with Hitler to transfer the defensive Schwer-

In the west, Model now estimated that 38 of Eisenhower's 70 divisions were battling to contain the Ardennes bulge. Hitler was cock-a-hoop. "We have knocked out at least six or seven hundred enemy tanks; about six or seven divisions have presumably been completely destroyed." In the tank battle between Vaux and Grandmenil on December 27, Manteuffel destroyed 62 enemy tanks and captured 8. But General Patton's counterattack into the flank south of the bulge was causing concern; with the failure to reach the Meuse, Hitler lifted his prohibition on dealing with the tough American pocket of forces contained at Bastogne; and to ease the logjam in the Ardennes, he began plotting with Rundstedt a series of rapid blows along the denuded American front further south.

The first would be "North Wind"—an attack by eight divisions from the Saarbrücken region, designed to take from the rear the Americans advancing through northern Alsace. The second would be toward Metz, to restore Germany's iron-ore position. "The purpose of all these attacks," Hitler theatrically announced to his generals, "will mainly be to eliminate the Americans south of our [Ardennes] entry point—to destroy them bit by bit, to eliminate [*ausrotten*] them division by division." This would damage Eisenhower's plans and reputation, and it would cost him heavily in fuel for regrouping and ammunition—all of which Eisenhower had to bring up over greater distances than Hitler.

If these body blows succeeded, then Manteuffel and Dietrich could resume their attack in the Ardennes. "If not," Rundstedt's war diary recognized, "it will mean the end of our offensive operations and a transition to a defensive war of attrition. But no matter what, the important result remains that for the time being we have rid the Rhine and Palatinate of the threat of an enemy offensive."

One other strategic success of these weeks should not be overlooked: as Field Marshal von Weichs, Commander in Chief Southeast, wrote in his diary on December 30 1944: "The auspicious return of our troops from Greece . . . is akin to a great battle won." The soldiers of General Löhr's Army Group E had force-marched up to a thousand miles from the torrid heat of the Mediterranean to the midwinter snowstorms of the Croatian mountains and had still managed to fight off the Russians, Bulgarians, and Communist partisans harrying their flanks. Had Hitler delayed his secret oral order to Weichs to evacuate Greece in

---

punkt from west to east and Hitler snubbing him—"The eastern front must manage with what it's got." Not until January 14—two days *after* the Soviet invasion began—did Admiral Voss report from Hitler's conference that "[Guderian] has now asked the Führer to transfer the war's Schwerpunkt to the eastern front."

August, or had Löhr shown less resolution in adversity, the entire army group would have been lost.

Crossing this last high plateau of his fortunes, Hitler still radiated determination, the nameless energy of a Messiah, to his visitors: Szálasi noticed it; Bormann cultivated it; Guderian succumbed to it. But he had aged: his back was bent, his spine had lost its symmetry (Scoliosis); his face was haggard and his voice quavered; his hair was gray, and the famous moustache—which he clung to as he did to his "postman's cap" in spite of all Eva Braun's remonstrances—was snow-white. Admiral Heinz Assmann wrote: "His handclasp was weak and soft, all his movements were those of a senile man; only his eyes retained their flickering gleam and penetrating look." His "midday" conference rarely began before 5 P.M.; after that his doctors ordered him to sleep three hours each day. He went for frequent strolls in the snow around his bunker. Wieland Wagner, the composer's grandson, found the convalescent Führer's manner "even tamer and kindlier than before"; Blaskowitz, conferring with him about "North Wind" on December 28, observed that his left shoulder drooped and his hand was shaking; Baron von Steengracht felt he "still put a brave face on, but he was frail and his hand trembled." Indeed, Hitler could now hardly write; since December a trusted civil servant had had to forge his signature on official citations and awards. All this worried Martin Bormann badly. Professors Eicken and Morell, and the SS doctor, Stumpfegger, examined Hitler on the thirtieth and found him medically recovered from his operation; and his throat was well enough for him to prerecord that day his radio speech for New Year's Eve. But the speech itself lacked the wit and bite of his earlier annual addresses. Goebbels may have told him later that the public missed any references to the new weapons or campaigns which might yet bring them the promised victory.

This was as well, for at the end of the plateau there was an abyss. Göring's Luftwaffe delivered its grand slam attack on January 1, 1945, with 1,035 fighters and fighter-bombers attacking the enemy airfields in the Low Countries. Five hundred planes were claimed destroyed, but Göring also lost 277 planes, nearly two-thirds of them to his own antiaircraft guns, which had not been warned. Hitler was unimpressed. In 1944 Allied heavy bombers had dropped a hundred times more bombs on Germany than Göring had on Britain in 1940. This proved what he had all along said about the value of the four-engined bomber. The Luftwaffe's aircraft were powerless against them. The 217 rocket-propelled Me-163 interceptor aircraft built and launched had claimed only 5 bombers; Hitler ordered Me-163 production canceled. Antiaircraft artillery alone could defend Germany now. Meanwhile the devastation of the railway and canal system was resulting in crippling coal, steel, and munitions shortages. At a meeting with Hitler on January 3, Speer blamed Göring and the Luftwaffe; but others blamed Speer himself. Martin Bormann brought to Hitler's attention convincing reports that Speer had misled both the Gauleiters and Hitler on the real output figures of the arms and aircraft factories.

The transport, munitions, and fuel crises were directly affecting Hitler's strategy. Coal was piling up in the Ruhr pitheads, but the railroads could not carry it to the factories. The loss of France, Lorraine, and Belgium had cut German steel output by the autumn from 3,100,000 to 2,000,000 tons a month; but the colossal air attack on German transportation since mid-October had cut Ruhr production alone from 700,000 to only 400,000 tons in November. There were frustrating side effects on the new secret weapons Hitler had relied on to turn the tide in the eleventh hour: prefabricated sections of the secret Mark XXI submarine could not be brought to the assembly points because of wrecked canals. In November only 9 instead of 17 had been assembled, and in December only 18 instead of 28, because now air raids had stopped submarine-battery production too. How right Hitler had been to press his "lunatic" demand late in 1939 for keeping Germany's air frontiers as far apart as possible! "Herr Beck and his memoranda!" he scorned. "Those gentlemen wanted to fight in the pre-airpower age!" He could not even strike back equally at Eisenhower's transportation. "We can't rely on the V-1 or V-2 bombardment alone."[7] On January 8 he again insisted on equipping the Me-262 jet aircraft with 500-kilo bombs to disrupt the enemy's railroads and dockyards behind the western front.

Hitler's counterattacks were also failing. "North Wind" caused Eisenhower momentary alarm—he abandoned hard-won ground and even contemplated evacuating Strasbourg after Himmler, commanding Army Group Upper Rhine, succeeded in throwing a bridgehead across the fast-flowing Rhine north of the city; but the enemy sidestepped fast enough to escape encirclement in Alsace. In Hungary, Gille's relief attack slowed to a halt six days later, still short of Budapest. On January 3—even as Hitler was debating the transportation crisis with Speer, Goebbels and Dr. Albert Ganzenmüller, the transport minister—Britain's Field Marshal Montgomery began his carefully planned offensive on the northern flank of the Ardennes bulge; Patton was still relentlessly attacking it from the south. Hitler—whose generals had now claimed to have destroyed 1,230 Allied tanks in the battle and captured 400 guns and 24,000 American prisoners—decided to cut his losses. At a conference with Hitler and Göring on the seventh, Rundstedt asked the Führer to authorize Model's request to pull back the westernmost attack spearhead, the Forty-seventh Panzer Corps; Hitler agreed, and decided that if he was not to lose the initiative entirely, he must also pull out Sepp

[7]Allied-held Antwerp had been under continual rocket attack and flying-bomb bombardment since October 1944. Damage was severe. On December 17 one V-2 rocket killed seven hundred people in the packed Rex cinema, half of them soldiers.

Dietrich's SS Sixth Panzer Army to establish a tactical reserve while he could, for there was no knowing what the enemy might do with the divisions he could now release from the Ardennes battlefield. This order—Hitler's tacit admission that he had lost the Ardennes gamble—was issued from the Eagle's Nest at 2 A.M. on January 8, 1945.

Deep snow drifts blanketed Hitler's headquarters. It was 20°F. In Poland, the ground had frozen, but Stalin had still not begun his big push from the Vistula bridgeheads toward Berlin. On January 3 the General Staff's eastern expert, General Gehlen, announced: "Various signs indicate that the attack has again been postponed to mid-January."

When General Guderian came to Hitler's headquarters on January 9, the Führer speculated: "If the Russians aren't attacking, then it's for political reasons." Guderian seconded that: "It's because of the British." But he now expressed extreme alarm about the eight-hundred-mile front between the Carpathian Mountains and the Baltic, where the Russians—ignoring Hitler's attempt to lure their reserves south into Hungary—had built up an immense superiority in tanks, artillery, and troops. Guderian had just visited General Josef Harpe— commanding the army group astride Warsaw—and now fearlessly put to Hitler Harpe's proposals for the army group to fall back on a "given word" from the winding Vistula River line to a more economical one; this would create two strong groups of reserves for a counterattack after Stalin's big offensive began. Guderian's adjutant later wrote a dispassionate account of the heated argument that followed:

Guderian was very spirited and waded in with gusto. His program was in effect that we should give up and move the forces farther west. Guderian showed on the map how critical Harpe's situation at Cracow was. . . . The Baranov bridgehead salient was being continually reinforced by the Russians; reconnaissance planes had sighted innumerable tanks and aircraft. For twenty miles the front line was stretched to breaking point. . . . From the mountains up to as far as Warsaw the army group had only six divisions. That was far too few, they could never halt a serious attack. . . .

A "given word" had therefore been prearranged, upon which the troops in the German salient were to be pulled back to a shorter chord line. . . . Hitler was curt and skeptical, and belittled everything. He kept repeating that the Russians didn't have much—their formations were exhausted, they hadn't any tanks, and to talk of superiority was nonsense. He minimized the Russian enemy and exaggerated our own strength in a most irresponsible manner. He began to tear the general's arguments to shreds. When he raised his voice, the others fell silent. Guderian explained the situation and again mentioned the "given word" plan. After a few words Hitler interrupted: "Out of the question. Where a German soldier is, there he stays!" Guderian tried to talk him around, but in vain.

Guderian's object had been to win the entire Sixth SS Panzer Army from the west for the eastern front, but Hitler would grant him only two divisions. "The others present listened in silence," concluded the adjutant's account. "Only Göring butted in once or twice."

Hitler's reasons for rejecting Guderian's appeal on January 9 are plain from the fragments of stenographic record. Firstly, if Stalin's attack was due in mid-January, it was too late to begin rethinking their strategy; secondly, he believed that with nine panzer and three panzer-grenadier divisions (sited north and south of Cracow, southwest of Warsaw, and in East Prussia) Guderian already held sufficient in reserve to stave off the threat; thirdly, he was inspired by the fortifications dug by the Gauleiters and east Germans over the last months; and fourthly, as he admitted in private to his own adjutants the next day, "I always shudder when I hear talk of 'withdrawing here' in order to be able to 'operate there'; I've been hearing that tune for two years now, and every time it's been a disaster."

Guderian's statistics failed to impress Hitler either. The German army already had 3,000 tanks and assault guns in the east; by Hitler's reckoning, Stalin would need a 3 to 1 superiority to begin an offensive (although his own superiority in the Ardennes had fallen far short of that in December). "At any rate, they don't have nine thousand tanks." As for artillery, if Stalin really had "150 guns per kilometer" he must have 20,000 in his bridgeheads altogether, which was absurd. The hordes of Soviet divisions listed by the General Staff reminded Hitler of "Chinese divisions": each probably had only a few thousand men. Here Guderian could retort that his own panzer divisions each had only 70 or 80 tanks compared with 250 in June 1941. When the general bewailed the crippling ammunition shortage—"If only we could get the ammunition now, we could put up a tremendous showing!"—Hitler lectured him: "Now you see what nobody wanted to see at the time: the potential harm of our retreats in the east. From our factories down there"—pointing to the Donets Basin—"we would probably already be supplying the eastern front with two or three million shells a month. But people told me, 'What's the point, just for a few iron-ore mines!' And the front line was shorter then than it is now."

That evening, January 9, an army adjutant gave Hitler the first *documented* hint that Stalin's attack was imminent. "Over the last few days there have been continued heavy movements into the Baranov bridgehead [across the Vistula]. The impression there is that they are going to start soon after all."

Over the next two days the warning signs multiplied: "ice-bridges" were being laid; minefields were being cleared; and radio monitoring posts heard of reinforcements being moved up. Prisoners confirmed that the offensive would begin between the eleventh and sixteenth. The Russian artillery was in place, and the infantry had taken up its assault positions. So Hitler learned on the eleventh; before he fell asleep at 4:20 A.M. the next morning, he probably had word that an all-out hour-long Russian artillery bombardment had just taken place in the Baranov bridgehead; and when he rose at noon Jodl's adjutant, Colonel Heinz Waizenegger, came almost at once to announce that after a further hour-long barrage between 7 and 8 A.M. Stalin's great offensive had begun. At the Eagle's Nest they now wondered, Was this the Russians' last desperate exertion? Or would still further attacks follow?

Hitler was still on the western front. Two of his secretaries—the young but widowed Frau Junge and the elderly Frau Wolf—had just returned from leave and lunched with him at two. Frau Junge had hitched a truck ride through Munich the morning after British bombers had blasted the city with two thousand tons of bombs, and her emotional description made his blood boil. "In a very few weeks this nightmare will suddenly stop," he pronounced. "Our new jet aircraft are now in mass production. Soon the Allies will think twice about flying over Reich territory."

One anecdote remained in Frau Junge's memory of that day, and it illustrates Hitler's bantering manner with his immediate entourage. His dog Blondi urgently needed to go out, and sprang delightedly through the bunker door with the manservant summoned for the purpose. "Amazing what little things can please a dog," Frau Junge remarked, at which Hitler laughed, adding: "Not to mention us human beings too! I was once on the road for hours on end with my men, and I had to go on to Magdeburg to open the first stretch of autobahn there. But when my convoy of cars was spotted, more and more cars would fall in behind. It was often quite impossible to make an urgently necessary stop in some wood or other and be alone. And when we reached this autobahn there was almost a calamity. Hour after hour we drove on, dying for a break, but everywhere they were lining the autobahn—Hitler Youth, League of German Girls, Brownshirts, SS, the lot —I had no idea the Party had so many formations. I felt at that moment it was too many. Brückner and Schaub sat petrified with masklike faces next to me. I had to keep standing, too, with a fixed grin. Then Brückner suddenly reminded us: 'Mein Führer, I had your special train sent to Magdeburg station!' How glad we were to see that train."

Julius Schaub cupped his hand over one ear and grunted in appreciation of the story. "Mein Führer, do you remember The Elephant at Weimar!" "Ja," Hitler laughed. "That was an old-fashioned hotel prewar, but well managed. My regular rooms had running water but no bathroom or W.C., so I had to walk down this long corridor and vanish into the little room at the end. It was sheer purgatory every time, because when I left my room word spread around the hotel like wildfire, and when I emerged from the awkward closet they were all waiting to cheer me and I had to give the Hitler salute and a rather embarrassed smile all the way back to my room. Later on I had that hotel rebuilt." As Frau Junge afterward wrote, it was as though there was no war and Hitler had no cares. "But those who, like us, knew him well, recognized that he had recourse to such small talk as a kind of anesthetic to distract him from the losses of territory, equipment, and human life of which every hour brought fresh report."

At Hitler's main war conference that day, January 12, the news was that Marshal Konev's powerful infantry and tank forces had swept through the three German divisions containing the Baranov bridgehead and had already advanced ten miles westward. By the next day they had advanced twenty miles; nothing was halting the onrushing enemy. The German panzer divisions had been split up and mauled, and now after a two-hour artillery barrage by 350 batteries a new deluge of tanks and infantry hit the eastern flank of East Prussia. On the fourteenth the two other Vistula bridgeheads also debouched into southern Poland south of Warsaw, and a second offensive began against East Prussia, this time on the southern flank. The deadline for the offensive here was known, and the Germans drenched the massing Russian forces and artillery with shells, briefly throwing Marshal Rokossovski's forces off balance. But although 245 enemy tanks had already been destroyed, by the fifteenth the whole eastern front was ablaze, and it was clear that the enemy had achieved his strategic breakthrough. Kielce in southern Poland fell. Warsaw, still in German hands, was bypassed to the north and south. Hitler, aghast at the sudden collapse after his armies in Kurland and East Prussia had held off the enemy so well before, admitted to Colonel von Below, one of his most trusted adjutants: "We have no hope." Only a miracle could save Germany now.

Stalin had committed 180 divisions to his front in Poland. Hitler had 133 in the east, but 30 were in the Kurland and Memel pockets and 28 were in Hungary. Stalin's "divisions" had barely more than 4,000 men, but his superiority in aircraft, tanks, and guns was overwhelming. On the fourteenth, Guderian at last cabled an appeal to Hitler to transfer the war's Schwerpunkt to the eastern front. Hitler held a last conference with Rundstedt and Model on January 15, instructing them to hold off the Allies for as long as possible. At 6 P.M. he drove with his staff to the station and boarded his special train. At 7:15 P.M. he held another war conference. Five minutes later Guderian again telephoned, appealing for "everything to be thrown into the eastern front." (In fact, Hitler was to order over forty divisions moved to the east over the next six weeks.) As the train gathered speed toward Berlin, one of his staff—the SS colonel who was later to fulfill Hitler's last and hardest order—remarked within his hearing: "Berlin will be most practical as our headquarters: we'll soon be able to take the streetcar from the eastern to the western front!"[8] Hitler laughed wanly at this witticism, and the rest of his staff joined in.

[8]This was SS Colonel Otto Günsche. See page 822 below.

Waiting for a Telegram

When he awoke at 9 A.M. on January 16, 1945, his train was approaching the capital. Snowdrifts concealed Berlin's cruelest injuries. Forty minutes later he was being driven from Grunewald station to the Reich Chancellery.

The old wing, scene of his prewar political triumphs, had suffered unmistakably, and he could make out snow-filled craters in the gardens. A rectangular concrete slab elevated some feet above ground level marked the site of the deep shelter which Albert Speer had built for him. It looked an inhospitable place. Hitler decided to sleep in his usual first-floor bedroom for the time being—a hurricane seemed to have blasted through it, but it had been repaired—and to continue holding his war conferences in the ornate study overlooking the ravaged Chancellery gardens.

No stenograms of the next conferences survive, but they were clearly charged with high drama. General Harpe's Army Group A had collapsed; since Schörner's army group had fought brilliant defensive actions in Kurland, Hitler send for him that afternoon, awarded him the Diamonds, and appointed him Harpe's successor. He also instructed the navy to embark two panzer and two infantry divisions at the Kurland port of Libau immediately and to bring them by sea to reinforce the main eastern front. In Poland and East Prussia he designated several cities as "fortresses," to be held as breakwaters and buttresses, slowing down the swirling enemy advance.

Postmortems on the catastrophe in Poland began. Hitler learned that the Twenty-fourth Panzer Corps (General Nehring), stationed southwest of Kielce —much too close to the Russian Schwerpunkt—had received telephone orders from Harpe to hold Kielce as a "hinge," without counterattacking, although that was what panzer divisions were for. Now that the front line had been overrun so "unexpectedly rapidly," the corps was engulfed. Seething with anger, Hitler ordered Harpe to report to him in person. The general calmly produced a Führer Order explicitly reserving these divisions—the 16th and 17th panzer divisions—

to Hitler's whim. Hitler had never seen the order before, and concluded that Guderian's staff was responsible.

The loss of Warsaw produced another example of the General Staff's wayward-ness. Hitler had ordered the Polish capital defended as a fortress, but when Guderian next appeared at the Chancellery he told the startled Führer that the city had already fallen to the Russians, and he had redrawn the situation map accordingly. But even as they were conferring, a radio message arrived from the German battle commandant in Warsaw: he was still holding out, though en-veloped on all sides. Hitler ordered the city held at all costs—like Budapest, which was still surviving the Soviet onslaught. However, it was now too late, as Guderian's earlier order to the contrary had been obeyed.

Asked for an explanation, Guderian blamed his chief of operations, Colonel Bogislaw von Bonin, for the inaccurate report (the same officer had expressed the General Staff's confidence in the eastern front's defenses in December). Hitler ordered Bonin arrested, and when Guderian guiltily objected, Hitler retorted, "I'm out for the General Staff's blood. This General Staff clique has got to be stamped out!"[1] On the eighteenth he instructed Jodl to draft a firmly worded order that in the future no commander was to commence any attack or retreat without first having informed the Führer in sufficient time for the order to be countermanded; any future inaccurate reports submitted to him—"whether by design or through negligence"—would be severely punished. The order was issued three days later.

Faced with this Soviet invasion, Hitler skeptically authorized Ribbentrop's first cautious feelers to the western powers. His mind was clear on the general terms. (Once he had said he would fight on until "a peace that is honorable, acceptable to Germany, and will safeguard the life of her coming generations becomes possible; because I need hardly add how distasteful I find this war.") Failing that, Ribbentrop's feelers might still drive a wedge into the enemy alliance. Sources strongly suggested that it was falling apart. Both Roosevelt and Churchill refused to accept Stalin's "Lublin Committee" puppet government and his proposed frontiers for Poland. Hitler confidently expected the alliance to founder on this rock—a misjudgment as monumental as his Dunkirk error five years before.

Whereas then, in 1940, Hitler had assumed that Churchill could not honorably

---

[1]Bonin stayed in prison until the end of the war. Subsequently he was involved in strange dealings with the Soviet occupation authorities in East Germany in the 1950s. As for Hitler's remarks about the General Staff, several officers present testified later that General Jodl (one of the General Staff's most illustrious products) coldly informed him that it was small wonder that "the spirit of July 20" was prevalent if Hitler cast its officers into prison on such flimsy pretexts.

abandon the French in battle, now in 1945 he could not believe that Churchill would bring himself to abandon Poland to bolshevism; after all, Britain had gone to war over Poland's integrity in 1939. Surely the British would now see that Germany was central Europe's last bulwark against the hordes of Asia? "There must be people in Britain who can see what it is they are demolishing!" he exclaimed in exasperation to his adjutants.

On January 2, German Intelligence sources reported that Moscow's Comintern had ordered anti-British agitation to begin. With his Ardennes offensive still causing acute embarrassment to the Allies, Hitler authorized Ribbentrop—probably that same day—to draw up proposals for the western governments; the form of these proposals was to be such that they could not be attributed to Hitler himself. By the nineteenth, when Ribbentrop brought the document to him, the political climate seemed even more propitious; London and Washington could surely find little comfort in the Red Army's immense offensive. The document proposed that Germany retain her national frontiers and renounce both her economic autarky and her ambitions to a hegemony over Europe; that she cooperate in her foreign policy and in economic affairs; that freedom of religion would be restored and the Jews resettled somewhere in an international community. The proposals were stated to be the views of "authoritative sources in Berlin including the foreign minister." Hitler approved it. Ribbentrop signed it and sent one of his most experienced diplomats, Dr. Werner von Schmieden, who had a distinguished League of Nations record, to Switzerland to make contact with a Mr. Allen Dulles—Roosevelt's Intelligence chief there—and an equivalent British official. Now Berlin could only wait for the reply.

Hitler confidently prepared fresh military undertakings in the east meanwhile. His health must have improved, for his doctors only rarely visited him. But his milieu changed. Martin Bormann—who returned from a two-week leave on January 19, bringing Eva Braun to Berlin with him—held regular morning conferences with Hitler. Goebbels and Ley were frequent guests. Admiral Dönitz attended the war conferences almost daily—for his warships were to evacuate hundreds of thousands of civilians from the threatened eastern provinces. On January 20, the admiral offered Hitler twenty thousand naval troops for the land battles. That same day Hitler conferred with Speer and Saur on ways of restoring the Luftwaffe's supremacy; Göring, Messerschmitt, and other experts crowded the Chancellery study. Hitler ordered—once again—the heaviest cannon, and air-to-air missiles like the R4M rocket, to be mass-produced for the fighter squadrons. Jet-fighter development was to continue at top priority, and the Führer called for a long-range heavy bomber to be designed using the jet-engine principle. Göring was ignored. General Galland was not present—having been replaced that day in disgrace by Colonel Gollob as commander of the fighter force.

This long-term industrial planning showed that Hitler still expected a Seven Years' War. Jodl's staff had formulated a new master plan to stave off an earlier defeat: by weakening the western front to the utmost degree compatible with safety, an assault army would be built up in the east before the end of February 1945; this would head off the Russian invasion. Meanwhile the western enemy would be harried by more aggressive warfare from Hitler's Atlantic "fortresses" —Lorient, Saint-Nazaire, La Rochelle, and North Gironde—and their long lines of communication would be disrupted by U-boat, minelaying, midget-submarine operations, and Luftwaffe attacks. On January 19, Dönitz endorsed Hitler's delaying strategy. One hundred and seven of the secret Mark XXI electro-U-boats were already fitting out, and the first were to begin operations in March.

Before the eastern front had caved in, Hitler had ordered the powerful Sixth SS Panzer Army disengaged from the Ardennes battlefield as a tactical reserve for Rundstedt. Late on January 19, Hitler began to consider transferring the army to the east instead, and the next day he ordered its First Panzer Corps to Berlin before heading for the eastern front as rapidly as possible. But events were rapidly overtaking him, and he knew that weeks had to pass before the panzer army could complete its transfer. Martin Bormann, who saw him at 1:45 P.M., wrote in his diary: "Midday: situation in the east growing increasingly menacing. Evacuation of the Warthe Gau. Tank spearheads approaching Kattowitz, etcetera." Hitler blotted from his mind the almost audible sounds of the battle approaching Berlin, and he tried to envisage the Wehrmacht's plight several weeks hence. He concluded that the *strategic* danger to the Reich lay in Hungary and Austria, where Stalin was preparing with an army of inferior troops and Balkan allies to capture the last remaining petroleum fields south of Lake Balaton and in the Viennese region. On January 20, Hitler confided to press chief Otto Dietrich: "I'm going to attack the Russians where they least expect it. The Sixth SS Panzer Army's off to Budapest! If we start an offensive in Hungary, the Russians will have to go too."

His plan was for a rapid pincer attack, launched from both ends of the fifty-mile-long Lake Balaton to unhinge the southern end of the Russian front. On January 21 he cabled Weichs, the Commander in Chief Southeast, to investigate the feasibility of a simultaneous thrust by three or four divisions from Croatia across the Drava into southern Hungary; Weichs replied the next day in terms of conditional approval. Hitler forthwith ordered the Sixth Panzer Army sent to Hungary. When Guderian, exhausted by poor health, protested that he needed the army to defend Berlin, Hitler caustically replied, "You intend operating without gasoline. Fine! How far do you think your tanks will get!" The counter-offensive in Hungary must come first. But it took longer to prepare than Hitler had calculated.

In Poland, Cracow and Lodz were overrun. To release a corps for East Prussia, Hitler ordered Memel abandoned and its dockyard destroyed; on January 21 he authorized General Hossbach's badly mauled Fourth Army to fall back on the line of lakes on either side of the well-provided fortress town of Lötzen. The Russians had torn a huge breach between the German armies fighting in East Prussia—Army Group Center—and Schörner's Army Group A; now virtually nothing stood between them and the Baltic. At a conference with Guderian and Jodl on January 21, Hitler announced that the Reichsführer SS, Himmler, would take over command of a new Army Group Vistula to plug this gap and thereby prevent the enemy from breaking right through to Danzig and Posen and even isolating East Prussia; Himmler was also to "organize the national defense on German soil behind the entire eastern front." When Guderian proposed that this would be an ideal assignment for Field Marshal von Weichs instead—he had an army group staff available and Himmler had not—Hitler rejected the suggestion. Himmler's unorthodox talents had impressed him during the Reichsführer's brief command on the Upper Rhine front; he hoped for a ruthlessness and tenacity from the Reichsführer that was lacking in the elderly, worn-out army generals.

Two days later the Russians reached the coast at Elbing (Elblag), cutting off East Prussia. On the twenty-fourth Hossbach withdrew the Fourth Army to the west and abandoned the Lötzen fortifications without a fight. Hitler's permission was not asked—in flagrant violation of an explicit order; he was not even told. Confronted with this fresh *fait accompli* Hitler exploded: "Hossbach and the Russians are hand in glove!" The general and his entire staff were dismissed immediately; and the same rough justice was meted out to the army group commander, the badly injured General Hans Reinhardt, who was replaced by General Rendulic. To Jodl, Hitler privately compared the Lötzen "treachery" with the August 1944 "Avranches affair" which had presaged the fall of France.

Russian tanks were now rolling into Upper Silesia—the industrial province to which Hitler had evacuated his most precious war factories. The Oder was reached and bridged by the enemy at Steinau. Auschwitz was overrun. The fortress of Posen was encircled, and on January 27 the long, hard fight for possession of the city began; comparable in ferocity with the battles for Stalingrad and the Alcázar of Toledo, it would end only one month later with the death of its commandant and surrender to the Russians after they had threatened to massacre the injured Germans in their hands. Millions of Germans began fleeing westward before the advancing Russians. In East Prussia there were 2,000,000: the navy would evacuate 450,000 from the port of Pillau over the next weeks; 900,000 more set out on foot despite sub-zero temperatures, along the forty-mile causeway to Danzig or across the frozen lagoon known as the Frisches Haff. Behind them the invading Russians—incited by Stalin and by an order signed by Marshal Zhukov himself[2]—raped, pillaged, burned, and plundered. Gehlen's Intelligence branch confirmed that the Russians were shooting civilians quite indiscriminately. "Refugee columns overtaken by Soviet tanks are often machine-gunned and then crushed beneath them."

Every road to Berlin, Dresden, and the west was choked with fleeing refugees. All Germany listened on January 30 to Hitler's radio broadcast, the last he would ever make. His private adjutant, Alwin-Broder Albrecht, wrote the next day: "From all sides the response to the Führer's speech has been indescribably positive, however gloomy the omens may be. . . . What moved me most deeply was one telegram that arrived today from a refugee column trekking from the east. It just read: 'Führer, we trust in you!'—signed, 'A column passing through so-and-so.'" And a few days later Albrecht wrote from Hitler's Chancellery to a querulous mother uncomfortably billeted in Schleswig-Holstein: "It should be sheer ecstasy to hear children noisily playing and shouting. Imagine what a mother feels when her children freeze to death and must be left at the roadside, as happens in countless cases now." Hitler ordered Berlin's buses to rush bread to the refugee columns.

The war he had started had bred inhumanity. To exploit the refugee chaos in Berlin, the Americans sent over nine hundred heavy bombers at noon on February 3. Hitler was awakened in time and took shelter as two thousand tons of bombs rained down, but it was a near thing: his dining room collapsed onto his staff's prepared luncheon table, and the city's casualties were immense. But on the eastern front the slaying of prisoners—an atrocity rare in the west—was commonplace, as neither belligerent had the protection of the Geneva Convention. On February 16, Himmler's Chief of Staff signaled his army commanders: "Führer Order: When villages are captured, and particularly during assault-troop raids, the prisoners are not to be slain near the front line as the civil population has to pay for it afterward." The world's newspapers shortly reported what the Russians had found at Majdanek and other concentration camp sites.

Ever westward and northward the Russians swept, across frozen rivers and frosted fields, exploiting the Polish and east German railroads and autobahns

---

[2]Zhukov's long Order of the Day fell into German hands. It was headed, "Death to the Germans!" and announced in uncompromising terms that the hour had come for the Red Army to wreak revenge on "Hitler's cannibals." "We'll take revenge for all those burned to death in the Devil's furnaces, poisoned in the gas chambers, shot and martyred. We'll take cruel revenge for them all. . . . Woe betide the land of murderers! . . . *This time we will destroy the German breed once and for all.*"

which the withdrawing armies had not had time to destroy. On January 27, Schörner had to order the Upper Silesian industrial region abandoned. Two days later Königsberg, capital of East Prussia, was isolated by the enemy, and on the thirtieth the Russians reached and bridged the Oder on both sides of Küstrin (Kostrzyn)—only fifty miles from the center of Berlin. The German command structure in the east had collapsed. Hitler had lost contact with entire armies; he did not know which cities had fallen and which were still in his troops' hands. He instructed Guderian: "Over the next few days I must be told everything that is known about the enemy's movements and the most likely directions of attack and assembly areas, because our own countermeasures will depend on them." "Jawohl," answered Guderian.

One thought consoled Hitler: the Soviet avalanche must be causing concern in London and Washington. A decoded directive of the Allied "combined chiefs of staff" showed this concern quite clearly. The Allies' strategic air forces were shortly to begin a series of annihilating attacks on east and central German railway centers, ostensibly in aid of the Russians but in fact designed to hinder their westward progress.[3] The Berlin raid was clearly the first. Hitler instructed Ribbentrop to feed to the British Intelligence networks a phony report that Stalin was raising an army of two hundred thousand German Communists; under General Paulus and other captured German officers, this "army" was to march westward and set up a puppet government, for example in Königsberg. "That'll shake them—like being jabbed with a cobbler's awl!"

A dialogue between Hitler, Jodl, and Göring on January 27 illustrates how firmly rooted their daydreams had become. Hitler mused, "I don't know—do you think the British can still be watching this entire Russian development with a thrill of excitement?" "No, definitely not," replied Jodl. "Their plans were quite different. . . ." "They certainly never bargained for us standing firm in the west and letting the Russians conquer all Germany meanwhile," seconded Göring. "If it goes on like this we'll be getting a telegram in a few days' time. . . . They went to war to stop us moving east, not to have the east coming right up to the Atlantic!" "Absolutely right!" said Hitler. "It doesn't make sense. The British newspapers are already bitterly asking, What's the point of this war?"

It was in this mood of *Schadenfreude* that Hitler conducted two lengthy conferences with Ribbentrop early in February 1945, and then on the seventh with SS General Karl Wolff—his chief police representative in occupied Italy—as well. No note survives, but Wolff later described having drawn Hitler's attention to the

---

[3]The directive, dated January 24, 1945, was intercepted—together with two others issued by General Carl F. Spaatz, the American bomber force commander—and decoded by the Luftwaffe Intelligence branch. A copy of the intercept is in classified files in London.

military stalemate in Italy and to the western Allies' "increasingly concrete peace feelers extended via Switzerland," coupled with similar offers of mediation by the Vatican. Hitler took note of his remarks and pointedly refrained from forbidding him to pursue these channels to the West. Ribbentrop notified Wolff that Hitler's reaction was thus one of guarded approval. Wolff then began secret talks in Switzerland with the same Mr. Dulles whom Herr von Schmieden had been sent to contact.

At the Reich Chancellery the broadcast of Hitler's January 30 speech was followed by the premiere of Goebbels's most ambitious color film ever, *Kolberg:* the story of one of the most stirring battles in the Seven Years' War. Hitler never saw it, but throughout his rapidly shrinking domain the film revived failing spirits; it was even dispatched by fighter aircraft to inspire the German garrisons of the remaining Atlantic fortresses. "These times require lionhearts," wrote one of his adjutants after seeing *Kolberg,* "so it is salutary to be reminded of what previous generations suffered in the fight for our nation's survival. . . . The film matches present history so well that its originators—and work began on the film in 1942 —must have had clairvoyant powers." History in the besieged Baltic port of Kolberg would indeed soon be repeated.

Two weeks had passed since the Soviet invasion. Schörner's army group had now claimed 1,356 enemy tanks and the army group in East Prussia an equal number; but the enemy losses were being replaced with equal rapidity. The fortress city of Posen—where German-speaking officers in German uniforms had infiltrated the lines—was still holding out; but other strongholds were being engulfed one after the other. Chelmno, Thorn, and Marienwerder (Kwidzyn) had to be relinquished by Himmler's makeshift army group; Hitler and Guderian authorized these painful retreats. Hitler's day ended later and later: on January 30–31 it was five-thirty before he retired, only to be awakened at noon by Martin Bormann with the alarming news that Russian tanks were approaching Krossen and had just crossed the frozen Oder River between Küstrin and Wriezen.

The Oder was the last major river before Berlin. Its western banks were defended only by the Volkssturm battalions rushed into position from the capital itself, from central Germany, and even from Austria. These elderly soldiers—the ill-armed home guard which the Party had been organizing since autumn— slowed down the Russian onslaught and without support manned the Oder line, fighting off the Red Army for the whole first week of February until regular army reinforcements arrived. Meanwhile Hitler directed that over three hundred heavy antiaircraft batteries be transferred from the Reich's air defense to the Oder line to provide a formidable if immobile antitank defense. All fighter planes were committed to the Silesian and East Prussian battlefields, because most could now carry bombs—as Hitler had always demanded. Thus the crisis was overcome, though it took stamina: even Himmler had called his army group staff together one evening and announced that there was no hope of withstanding the Russian pressure any longer. ("But then it began to drip outside," he recalled later. "The thaw had come—we had been saved as though by a miracle. Now we would have time to build up the Oder defenses after all. Since then I have never doubted we'll win the war.") Ten weeks would pass before the Russians could recover the impetus they had lost so close to their final objective—Berlin.

In weakening the Reich's air defenses to keep the Russians at bay, Hitler perhaps hoped the Allied bombers might be called off—just as those still German-occupied islands in the Aegean were very obviously being left unmolested by the British. ("So that the British do not need to defend them against the Russians or any other usurpers," the German naval staff observed.) This fear was borne out by evidence that the British were fortifying the isles of Lemnos and Chios which the Germans had evacuated; in addition, the German commandant of the eastern Aegean had received a secret British offer to carry supplies to the German-held islands on British steamships. From February 5 onward the Americans in the Saar began appealing by loudspeaker to the opposing German troops to concern themselves with the Russians, their common enemy, and make common cause with the Allies; this was a particularly worrying form of propaganda for the German High Command. But against all these auguries Hitler had to set one new hard fact: since early February, somewhere in the world, Churchill, Roosevelt, and Stalin were meeting to settle their differences.

Almost all Silesia had been overrun. In Breslau, the capital, 38 Volkssturm battalions had been raised from the city's quarter-million population and from the surrounding countryside. With these 15,000 men and 30,000 regular troops, Breslau defied air and artillery bombardment and ground attack in a long siege that was not ended until a week after Hitler himself had perished. Here Bormann had a more than usually fanatical Gauleiter—Karl Hanke, Goebbels's former state secretary and an intimate friend of Albert Speer. "Hanke's a devil of a fellow," said Hitler approvingly. "He's a Silesian himself." Hitler knew, however, what the loss of the Silesian coal would mean, now that the Ruhr was virtually isolated by the rail and canal destruction. Germany's economic collapse seemed inevitable. Japan was in a similar plight. The enemy blockade of her seaways to the south—now that the Philippines had been retaken by the United States—would deprive her of rice, oil, bauxite, and iron ore; Hitler's attaché in Tokyo warned that Japan could not fight on longer than another year.

This was the economic background to his "nod" to Karl Wolff and Ribbentrop early in February—the go-ahead to contact the western Allies. The oil crisis had already forced on Hitler a strategic choice between East and West anyway. In January the bomb-battered refineries had produced only 50,000 tons of gasoline and 12,000 tons of aviation fuel; the latter figure represented only 6 percent of the May 1944 output. It was unlikely that the new U-boats and jet aircraft—145 Me-262 jets had been produced in January alone—would get the diesel and J-2 kerosene they needed. Because of the fuel shortage, the air war against Antwerp was now restricted to single-engined fighter-bombers. At the end of January Hitler ruled that in the future the western front must go short of fuel and ammunition to aid the eastern front: Rundstedt had to forfeit fuel to replenish the Sixth SS Panzer Army before its departure for Hungary, although at any moment Eisenhower might begin his new offensive toward the Ruhr and Rundstedt lacked the fuel to move up his own reserves accordingly.

Along the Oder the ice was still thawing. Hitler ordered ice-breakers and explosives used to speed up the process. By February 8, the immediate danger to Berlin had passed. During the previous week the OKW had taken forceful action to prevent a panic-stricken flight from the capital; but important Wehrmacht command posts were ordered to leave, and provision was made for the ministries to follow if a new crisis should develop. For Hitler himself Bormann began preparing an emergency headquarters at Stolpe, in his own earlier stamping-ground, Mecklenburg.

The ruinous American daylight raid had left Berlin's government quarter a shambles. The railroads and stations were obliterated. Bormann wrote: "The Reich Chancellery garden is an amazing sight—deep craters, fallen trees, and the paths blotted out by rubble and debris. The Führer's residence was badly hit several times. Only fragments remain of the Winter Garden and the Banquet Hall walls. . . . Vossstrasse is pitted with enormous craters, and the houses opposite in Hermann-Göringstrasse have been completely burned out." Hitler's residence and Bormann's Party Chancellery lost all telephone contact with the outside world. An adjutant wrote on the fifth: "Some twenty-five bombs fell on our district. There's no water, no heat, no electricity. . . . By roundabout route water reached the main points again after twenty hours, but we'll have to wait another two weeks for heat—unless the visitors return in the meantime—for which possibility we are steeling ourselves."

Every night the sirens wailed in Berlin. The Russians had captured 130 airfields since mid-January, nearly all intact, and Soviet bombers joined the British and American campaign. Many cities like Dresden had lost all their antiaircraft guns to the eastern front. With the fighter squadrons still committed to the Oder battlefront, the big cities were defenseless. Not one aircraft had climbed to the defense of Berlin on February 3 for this reason. Every sea or land disaster was now laid at the Luftwaffe's door. When a Soviet submarine sank the liner *Wilhelm Gustloff,* drowning five thousand refugees from East Prussia, and when the hospital ship *Steuben* was torpedoed some days later, drowning nearly all the twenty-five hundred casualties and one thousand refugees aboard her, Dönitz blamed the Luftwaffe for failing to provide antisubmarine patrols. Hitler—confined to his air raid shelter yet again by a small raiding force of Mosquitoes—received from the Ninth SS Panzer Corps in the heart of beleaguered Budapest the radio message familiar ever since Stalingrad: the Luftwaffe airlift was letting them down. The Luftwaffe war diary shows that Hitler strongly attacked Göring for the failure, without even checking on the justice of the allegation.

In vain the anxious Reichsmarschall signed strings of belated death sentences on Luftwaffe officers—including a full general, Waber, his commander in the northern Balkans—for offenses ranging from desertion, cowardice, slackness, espionage, corruption, and loose living to precipitate flight from airfields and depots, and allowing new aircraft, fuel, and bomb dumps to fall into enemy hands. For every sin that Göring punished, Bormann could always prove the commission of ten more.

When Lammers ventilated the delicate matter of Hitler's heir, Bormann contemptuously advised him that Göring was out of the running. Hitler openly ridiculed the Reichsmarschall's visit to the Oder front, and no word of it reached the press. Göring's very presence in the cramped air raid shelter revolted the Führer, since both the Reichsmarschall and his adjutant Dr. Ramon Ondarza made liberal use of conflicting perfumes, with which the shelter's air purification system could not cope. Eventually Hitler loudly commanded Göring: "Tell your man Ondarza that he stinks like a cesspit, and he's not to perfume himself when he comes visiting again!" Göring fully understood Hitler's characteristically oblique hint.

No word had yet come from the western powers—no "telegram." Nor was there word of Stalin's meeting with the western leaders, except that it was somewhere on the Black Sea. In Bulgaria, King Boris's successors had just been shot by the new Communist regime. In Poland, Stalin's new satellite government proclaimed the forthcoming annexation of Silesia and East Prussia.

The very simultaneity of action in east and west suggested there was a disconcertingly high degree of collaboration between the enemy powers after all. On February 8, Marshal Konev attacked from the Steinau bridgehead across the Oder with the obvious aim of encircling Breslau. On the same day a big Allied offensive developed between the Rhine and the Meuse.[4] Far into the night Hitler sat talking with Bormann, Speer, the latter's fellow architect, Professor Hermann

---

[4]Rundstedt had asked permission to make local tactical withdrawals where necessary. Hitler granted this but forbade the surrender of any fortifications or city. "The enemy may well be able to storm the ruins of a bunker line or city, but they are never to be evacuated—except on the Führer's orders."

Giesler—who had replaced Speer as Hitler's principal confidant on city planning —and Eva Braun, who was returning to Munich the next day now that the immediate danger to Berlin had passed. Toward morning Hitler was informed that the British had destroyed the Pölitz synthetic refinery, the Luftwaffe's last gasoline source. It had been defended by 429 guns, but Hitler shortly learned that a nameless Luftwaffe officer had ordered its entire searchlight defenses removed. With the Luftwaffe's dwindling fuel stocks now down to only 6,000 tons, it would receive only 400 more tons in February.

Professor Giesler had come to Berlin for a specific reason. Late on February 9 he unveiled to Hitler his model for the reconstruction of the bomb-desecrated city of Linz—where Hitler had first heard Wagner's *Rienzi* and decided to become a statesman. Hitler had decreed that Linz must replace Budapest as the Danube's fairest city; it was to have fine Party buildings, a concert hall seating thirty-five thousand, and a bell tower five hundred feet high—with Hitler's parents entombed in a crypt at its base—on the north bank, and a major replanning of the old city on the south. A wide ceremonial mall was to extend from the railroad station to the city center, flanked by opera houses, theaters, a museum, library, and immense art gallery. Now in Giesler's model it all took shape before Hitler's eyes. At 4 A.M. that morning he again stole into the shelter where the model was laid out, and he returned at 3 A.M. the morning after.

When SS General Kaltenbrunner came with alarming reports of declining public morale, Hitler took the Gestapo chief, himself a native of Linz, into the model room. For many minutes Hitler described how Linz would arise anew when victory was theirs—how he would be the art gallery's principal benefactor, and he would found a medical academy there as well. When the ponderous general himself warmed to the theme, Hitler challenged him with his haunting eyes. "My dear Kaltenbrunner, do you imagine I could talk like this about my plans for the future if I did not believe deep down that we really are going to win this war in the end!"

In their advance toward Berlin, the Russians had been held off about seventy miles from the Pomeranian coast by Himmler's army group, leaving an inviting three-hundred-mile flank for the Germans to attack. Since early February Guderian had been planning to exploit this, to relieve the pressure on Berlin. But the rate of buildup for this counterattack was slow, partly because only one bridge was available across the Oder at Stettin. Hitler's enthusiasm waned; the odds were heavily against them, and Himmler expressed a marked reluctance to risk his forces. At one meeting Hitler was stung into rebuking Himmler: "Now you too have turned defeatist!"—and showed him the door. On February 10 he called both Guderian and Himmler to the Chancellery. Guderian pleaded for the attack to be brought forward—"We can't wait until every last can of gasoline has arrived!" —and demanded a capable army general for Himmler's command staff. He suggested his own deputy, General Wenck. According to Guderian the argument lasted two and a half hours. Eventually he got his way, because Hitler smiled wearily and instructed Himmler: "Wenck will be attached to your staff." The attack would be brought forward to the fifteenth.

In the event, the operation, from south of Stargard, was a failure. On the third day Wenck was injured in a motor accident. Perhaps because of this the attack lost all further impetus, and Hitler called it off.

Guderian's star began to wane as rapidly as Zeitzler's had after the failure of "Citadel" in 1943. When Hitler learned that the general had recently advised Ribbentrop that the war was lost, he made a terrible scene at the next war conference. "In a situation like this any sign of defeatism is open treachery. That is just what General Guderian's recent discussion with Ribbentrop amounts to. I expect every one of my colleagues to stand by me—the greater the peril, the more your tenacity. It must be clear to everybody, if I throw an ordinary work-man who mutters defeatist remarks in an air raid shelter into a concentration camp or hang him, or if the same thing happens to a soldier who loses his nerve and runs away, that I must expect at least as much from you. This kind of sedition has got to stop."

The outcome of Stalin's meeting with Churchill and Roosevelt at Yalta, in the Crimea, had produced this shift in Hitler's stance. The mere fact that the Allied and Soviet military staffs were also conferring there had persuaded him that the western leaders were blind to Stalin's ambitions. He cannot have been surprised when Werner von Schmieden now returned from Switzerland having failed "for technical reasons" to contact Allen Dulles. From Yalta the enemy leaders announced on February 13 that Hitler's Reich was to be destroyed and carved up between the victors as "occupation zones." The Yalta communiqué—sent in to Hitler page by page as it came over the teleprinters—produced a hoot of triumph from him. "So much for the drivel talked by our coffeehouse diplomats and foreign ministry politicos! Here they have it in black and white: if we lose the war, Germany will cease to exist. What matters now is to keep our nerve and not give in." He dictated to his press officer his own brutal response, deliberately burning any bridges that might still exist. He would never surrender; nor would he allow his people to.

That evening, February 13, 1945, to distract himself with dividers and magnifying glass from the ugly world of war outside, Hitler again walked down to view the models for the rebuilding of Linz. He dined at eight with two secretaries, then slept until it was time for the midnight war conference.

Here the news was that since midday Breslau had been totally encircled by the Soviet armies and that three hundred heavy bombers had just set the ancient heart of Dresden—alive with a million homeless refugees—on fire. A firestorm like that in Hamburg had broken out there. Before the conference was over, word arrived that a new attack, heavier than the first, had begun on Dresden. The city had had no antiaircraft guns; and only that day the Luftwaffe had decided that jet-fighter and ground-attack operations in the east and west must take precedence over Reich defense, so no fighters had operated. Fire brigades were converging on Dresden from all over Germany. From the city itself there was a merciful silence, as all the telephone lines were down. It was 6:15 A.M. before Hitler retired to his cramped bunker bedroom. At 1 P.M. he was awakened with the news that the American bomber forces were continuing the carnage in Dresden which the British had left incomplete the night before; huge fires were still raging in the city.

After the all clear sounded in Berlin, Hitler was surprised to meet in the Chancellery hall the army doctor who had treated his ear injuries after July 20; Dr. Giesing had been visiting an adjutant in the Chancellery when the alert sounded. He wrote some weeks later: "Hitler and I sat down on a corner bench in the big hall upstairs. Now that I could see his face better by daylight, I was astounded at the change. He looked older and more bowed than ever. His complexion was as pale as before, and there were pronounced bags under his eyes. His speech was clear but very soft. . . ." Twice the Führer asked the doctor where his family was; twice he replied, "They are in Krefeld, mein Führer." Hitler seemed distant; he looked exhausted. His hands were white and his fingernails devoid of blood. Twice he asked Giesing which hospital he worked at, and twice the doctor told him.

Then Hitler suddenly turned to the war. "Germany is in a tough spot, but I'll get her out of it. The British and Americans have miscalculated badly. . . . In no time at all I'm going to start using my Victory weapon (Siegwaffe) and then the war will come to a glorious end. Some time ago we solved the problem of nuclear fission, and we have developed it so far that we can exploit the energy for armaments purposes (Rüstungszwecke). They won't even know what hit them! It's the weapon of the future. With it Germany's future is assured. It was Providence that allowed me to perceive this final path to victory."[5] His gaze remained

[5]Hitler had already hinted at atomic bombs in his last talk with Antonescu in August 1944. Giesing in fact wrote his account of this conversation with Hitler from memory on June 21, 1945—six weeks before Hiroshima! The origin of Hitler's optimism is puzzling. Scientists under Professors Werner Heisenberg and Carl-Friedrich von Weizsäcker had been studying nuclear fission and atomic bomb physics since 1939, and they had started building an experimental atomic pile at Haigerloch in 1944; in December the Reich chief of nuclear research, Professor Walther Gerlach, appealed to Bormann for exemption for them from Volkssturm service and speciously mentioned their "atomic bomb" research as justification. I suspect that Bormann was Hitler's source.

rooted to the floor. All at once he again asked the doctor where his family was. "In Krefeld, mein Führer." "Nothing can happen to them there, that's for sure," Hitler replied. "The West Wall will stand fast and then our *Siegwaffe* will decide the war in a very short time. . . . And if the war should go against us, then we must all die bravely. I shall remain at the head of my forces and die in action. But Providence has brought me this far unscathed, and I shall continue along this prescribed path undeterred by whatever may befall me."

The night's death toll in Dresden was estimated at a quarter-million. Hitler was intrigued that the British bombers had not instead been employed against Himmler's armies, which were winding up for a counterattack in Pomerania. "They flatten the Dresden opera house and wipe out refugees—but Stettin harbor, which is jam-packed with troop transports, they leave alone!" At 7:15 P.M. on February 14, Hitler discussed Dresden for forty-five minutes with Goebbels. The propaganda minister suggested retaliating with the Luftwaffe's huge stocks of top-secret nerve gases, but without a bomber force this was impossible.

Goebbels's alternative proposal was to execute one Allied prisoner for every German civilian killed in air raids. It would invite reprisals against German prisoners in Allied hands, but to Hitler this was not without its attractions. Since the renewed British offensive in the west, German desertions had assumed epidemic proportions; not without reason the German infantryman was attracted to the carefree prison-camp existence and the Allies' humane treatment of prisoners. "This constant sniveling about humanity will cost us the war," Hitler complained. "Neither the Russians in the east nor these hypocrites in the west stick to the Geneva Convention—just look at their attacks on the civilian population!" According to the staff stenographer present, Heinz Buchholz, Hitler emphasized that the Russians had demonstrated what could be achieved by ruthlessly punishing enemy airmen. "Our airmen couldn't be persuaded to fly over Moscow or Leningrad for their lives, after the Russians began executing Luftwaffe airmen. They just published that 'enemy paratroopers had been found and exterminated.'"

The idea of dropping the Geneva Convention appealed to Hitler, but not to the Party or the Wehrmacht. Keitel, Jodl, and Dönitz opposed it (the latter recommended that at least they should not announce publicly that they were going to disregard the convention). Ribbentrop—summoned by his horrified liaison officer Walther Hewel—ultimately talked Hitler out of the idea during a forty-minute stroll with him in the blitzed Chancellery gardens on February 21. But their conversation also revolved around Ribbentrop's latest clandestine peace approach to the Allies—four days previously Ribbentrop had sent a sixteen-page telegram to certain German ambassadors outlining arguments to use in favor of an armistice. Germany proposed to fight on until her enemies realized she could not be defeated; Stalin's aim was to rule Europe; he would abide by none of his solemn undertakings—already he was raising a Soviet German army. Ribbentrop argued that this was Europe's last chance to unite against Stalin. But on February 21, after his talk with Hitler, he had to recall the telegram and tell his ambassadors to ignore it.

Hitler had seen the photographs of Dresden. In heaps of five hundred at a time, the city's air raid victims were now being publicly cremated on makeshift grids of steel girders in the ruined town center. The pictures showed the thousands of men and women and children, still in their Mardi Gras fancy dress costumes, being stacked like rotting cabbages onto the bonfires. Where was the justice in history if an enemy could vanquish Germany by means such as these? This was the mood that impelled Hitler now.

Two vivid descriptions of Hitler in late February 1945 exist. One was by a General Staff officer who had last seen him in 1941 and was now brought by Schörner to the Chancellery on February 19. "—Older, stooping, an unhealthy pink tinge in his bloated face. But his eyes were as clear and calm as ever, though harsher than I recalled them. His voice was still gruff and self-possessed. He asked his questions calmly and listened patiently until I finished." A clammy, oppressive heat gripped the bunker under the Chancellery—the central heating had been restored two weeks after the Berlin raid. "What repelled me was the atmosphere and the attitude of what we called 'the scum' in the anterooms. Well-dressed and handsome young adjutants, many with the highest medals—which they unquestionably had once deserved—some of them SS officers, lolling around with bored expressions and criticizing everything. . . ."

The second description was by a Gauleiter, summoned along with other Party dignitaries at short notice to the Chancellery at 2 P.M. on February 24. On the previous day the Americans had unexpectedly begun their big offensive across the Roer River east of Aachen—even though the flood waters Rundstedt had released by breaching the Roer dams on the eighth had not subsided. North of this, the Canadian First Army had already penetrated deeply into Germany west of the Rhine. On this February 24, the Red Army had just begun an equally unexpected attack on Himmler's thin line defending Pomerania. Only in Hungary had a modest success been achieved, with the destruction that day of a Russian bridgehead across the Gran River after days of arduous fighting.

When Hitler entered one of the few still undamaged Chancellery halls, followed by Bormann, he found sixty or seventy of the Gauleiters and officials lined up around three sides. He shook hands with each of them, then invited them to a simple luncheon—stew, followed by real coffee. Afterward he made a speech, sitting at a small table on which he had spread out his notes—an old man, his back bent, his left hand shaking so violently that his entire frame trembled. His voice gained in strength as the customary climax was reached, but the sensational news his Party faithfuls had all anticipated was not forthcoming; no mention here of "nuclear fission." He talked of a forthcoming counterattack in the east, an operation which had been delayed by the losses of heavy weapons. He referred wistfully to the deceased General Hube and wished he had more generals "carved of the same oak." He asked for a supreme final effort from the Party so that the war might still be won—they must bring out a *furor teutonicus* in the people. If the people now gave up, this would prove they had no moral worth: they would deserve annihilation.

He lavished praise on the West Wall, the new U-boats, and the jet aircraft. Politically, he now expected Britain to hold out to the end, unshakable in her alliance with Russia; but he predicted the day when serious conflict would arise between Russia and the United States.

In conclusion Hitler mentioned to the Gauleiters his own declining health. Frederick the Great, he said, had also returned from his wars an ill and broken man, and now he too felt this burden. At one stage he tried to convey a glass of water to his mouth, but his hand trembled so much that he abandoned the attempt. Perhaps it was an act of showmanship, for he concluded with a smile: "I used to have this tremor in my leg. Now it's in my arm. I can only hope it won't proceed to my head. But even if it does I can only say this: my heart will never quaver." Over the next few weeks, he warned them, he might be forced to adopt some harsh measures which they might not understand; he asked the Gauleiters not to misjudge him.

Six to eight thousand Russian tanks had been claimed destroyed since mid-January. Still the General Staff's belief was that the Red Army's next move would be the assault on Berlin—regardless of the danger from Himmler's army group. General Ritter Bruno von Hauenschildt was designated commander of the Berlin district. He attended Hitler's daily war conferences. The city's antiaircraft batteries were regrouped into tight clusters situated where they could also command the main approach roads.

The very day of Hitler's speech to the Gauleiters proved Guderian's experts wrong. Instead of continuing westward toward Berlin, Marshal Zhukov turned north against Himmler's army group in Pomerania. Gehlen conceded the new situation in a belated appreciation the next day. On the twenty-seventh, Zhukov achieved a massive breakthrough in Himmler's lines; two enemy tank armies which Gehlen had believed on the Oder front preparing to exploit the Küstrin bridgehead now emerged far to the northeast, racing toward Köslin and the Baltic coast. At a conference that day Hitler promised immediate reinforcements to Himmler for a counterattack, and he ordered the historic rail and road corridor

—cause of the 1939 dispute with Poland—held at all costs. Meanwhile all manner of deception was to be used to persuade the Russians that between the Oder front and Berlin a deep and impregnable defense had been established. Phonograph records of moving tanks, marching troops, and construction work were to be played over loudspeakers toward the enemy lines. Unless Himmler's counter-attack succeeded, the loss of East and West Prussia seemed inevitable.

Germany's military reserves were long since exhausted. On February 27, Jodl showed Hitler a telegram from Rundstedt, forcefully complaining that of the 52,215 soldiers promised him in February, only 11,902 had come. Martin Bormann believed that over 500,000 deserters were concealing themselves in the Reich, and he had campaigned since mid-February for action against this "epidemic of cowardice." His staff proposed public hangings of such men under the slogan Gauleiter Karl Hanke had recently found effective in his fanatical defense of Breslau: "Death and dishonor to those who fear an honorable death!" Hitler proposed to Himmler two radical solutions designed to shame the deserters back into their units: to attain "a suitable effect on the men's attitude" the Reich women's leader, Frau Scholtze-Klink, should be consulted on the creation of a women's battalion. Secondly, 6,000 youths of fifteen were to be recruited to reinforce Himmler's rear lines of defense. Bormann acidly observed to his staff in a memorandum: "This means that we are now calling up women and fifteen-year-olds to strengthen the front."

Turkey, Egypt, Finland, and a host of South American countries now declared war on Germany. Turkey gave one week's notice; Finland backdated her declaration to September 15, 1944, there being nothing in the rules against such an action.

In the west, the Americans broke out of their Roer bridgehead on February 28 and began advancing with tanks on the Rhine between Düsseldorf and Venlo. Hitler ordered every available jet- and propellor-driven aircraft to engage them. American tanks flying German colors tried to rush the Rhine bridges at Düsseldorf and Uerdingen, but these—and every other bridge from Duisburg down to Koblenz—were destroyed in the nick of time. The apathy of the German people west of the Rhine shocked Hitler. Weeks of terror-bombing, which had lately extended to even the smallest villages, had reduced the people's former defiance to a simpering servility. White flags waited for the enemy. Local farmers attacked German troops with pitchforks when they tried to blow up minor bridges to hamper the enemy invasion; other gangs of farmers removed tank obstacles. At Bingen the citizens refused to complete tank obstacles. The deputy mayor of Ingelheim was publicly hanged for advising his citizens to let the enemy in. At Trier the Volkssturm melted away; other Volkssturm units were reported throwing their bazookas, machine guns, and ammunition into lakes and rivers. At

Remagen, American troops entering the town were astonished (and delighted) to find the railway bridge across the Rhine still intact and flung an immediate armored bridgehead onto the eastern shore. Most of Cologne was overrun. The crisis developed so suddenly that Hitler voiced to the OKW a lingering suspicion that Rundstedt might be secretly dealing with the western powers; why else had his headquarters at Ziegenberg still not been bombed?[6]

By March 8 the situation in the east was also worse. Pomerania seemed lost, and with it Hitler's faith in Himmler was finally destroyed. Pleading angina, the Reichsführer SS had abandoned his command staff for a health clinic at Hohen-lychen; his staff described as "utopian" Hitler's orders to seal the breach torn by Zhukov in Pomerania's defenses. On March 4, General Hans Krebs—deputizing for the injured Wenck—quoted to Hitler the blunt objections telephoned by General Kinzel, Himmler's operations officer: "This war is being fought on paper, it's quite divorced from reality!"

A year before Hitler would not have tolerated such criticism; but now he had to swallow it, because each military defeat eroded his authority. He decided on a more limited eastward counterattack from Stettin instead. General Erich Raus's Fourth Panzer Army would receive the necessary reinforcements by March 6. Shortly afterward his Third SS Panzer Corps (under General Martin Unrein's command) announced that it was ready, or at least had enough ammunition for the first two days' attack. Hitler, cautious ever since Avranches, sent an SS adjutant to Stettin to check. SS Major Johannes Göhler reported back that the divisions had no ammunition at all. "On the drive up to Stettin," wrote Göhler privately, "we passed endless columns of refugees who had set out weeks ago. A shocking sight. It was freezing cold and the roads were like glass. The roads were jammed again and again, so I had time to speak with many of them. I can scarcely comprehend their faith in victory. As for the troops I spoke with, everybody from corps commander downward wanted to know about the Führer's health, about how things are on other sectors of the front, and more than anything about whether we can hope for further V-weapons. What could I say? I radiated what optimism I could. How young are the faces one sees among the soldiers, and what devotion! Among the divisional commanders I found frequent skepticism but also a fierce determination to stand fast and do their duty. Don't ask me my own thoughts—I'd often like to believe in miracles."

On the afternoon of March 8, General Raus came in person to the bunker to explain his army's defeat in Pomerania. He pointed out that his army's 8 divisions —with only 70 tanks among them—had held a line 150 miles long against 8 Soviet

---

[6]Hitler replaced Rundstedt by Kesselring as Commander in Chief West two days after the Remagen incident; however, he stressed that Rundstedt still enjoyed his "fullest confidence."

armies and 1,600 tanks. Hitler interrupted nigglingly: *"Fourteen* hundred!" Raus
had built dense thickets of tank obstacles with the help of the Party and local
authorities. The Volkssturm had manned positions at every village entrance. The
battle for Pomerania was illuminated by countless acts of bravery by puny defenders against Stalin's armored invaders. Naval personnel armed with antitank weapons had wrought particular havoc. Out of 34 tanks attacking the naval-held
bridgehead at Divenow on March 7 only one had escaped destruction; and this
very morning the same naval troops had fearlessly charged across open country
and wiped out all 36 attacking Russian tanks—though not without heavy loss to
themselves. In the battle for Pomerania, 580 enemy tanks had been knocked out
—360 by bazooka at close range. But Hitler was unimpressed by Raus and sent
him from the room. "Where does he come from—Berlin? East Prussia?" he
inquired. Guderian replied, "He's one of your fellow countrymen: an Austrian!"
Hitler decided to dismiss Raus. "He's too nondescript, bogged down in petty
details." Manteuffel would replace him. That day, March 8, 1945, Guderian
predicted that since the Pomeranian threat to the Red Army's northern flank had
now collapsed, Stalin's main attack on Berlin would begin "in about one week."[7]

How high Hitler set his chances we do not know. On March 13 he lightly
assured Hindenburg's wizened old state secretary, Otto Meissner, that he was to
stay on to enjoy Germany's peacetime reconstruction. "I can't let you retire until
you're seventy"—in 1950. Two nights later Hitler was inspiring Kesselring, Rundstedt's successor, with promise of a great "defensive victory" coming in the east,
after which Germany's main tank output would revert to the western front.

His new master plan must not fail: a sudden northward thrust from the Ninth
Army's narrow bridgehead at Frankfurt-on-Oder would destroy Zhukov's forces
massing at Küstrin and thus disrupt the big offensive for weeks to come. In
conference with Himmler, Göring, and Guderian on March 15, Hitler instructed
them to deceive the Russians into expecting the thrust to turn south, not north.
That day he drove to the corps headquarters in the Frankfurt bridgehead to
inspect for himself the unit strengths and their stocks of ammunition. Refugees
swirled past his car windows in anonymous multitudes; ten million were now
fleeing the Russian tanks and guns.

On the road back from the Oder River to his capital, Hitler remained sunk deep
in thought.

---

[7]The General Staff misjudged again. Not until mid-April 1945 did the Soviet attack on Berlin begin.

Hitler Goes to Ground

What intangible forces sustained Hitler during these last dark weeks and in turn allowed him to sustain others? Schopenhauer identifies a certain rare character whom Fate has raised from total obscurity to eminence and who ever afterward believes that the same forces will never wholly desert him in his hour of misfortune—that no abyss is really bottomless, but that when he has plumbed its depths he will once again be lifted to the heights. Such a man was Hitler. He had been tutored, years before the war, by Lloyd George, too. The elderly British statesman had revealed to him in conversation that only the Armistice of 1918 had saved the Allies and dashed the cup of victory from Germany's lips—a perhaps ill-considered remark which the Führer never tired of quoting.

While in Italy the stalemate continued, the "race for Berlin" between East and West convinced Hitler that the two world hemispheres must within months be at war with each other, a war from which Germany would emerge as the *lachender Dritte*. His analysis was correct in all but one essential detail: the time scale. Had his war lasted the full seven years, he might have reaped the Cold War rewards that fell to his successors. Yet Hitler had good reason to expect them to come sooner. Until the very last days of his life his Intelligence experts nourished his beliefs with evidence of the coming conflict—evidence of the most concrete kind. For example, a group of Soviet agents parachuted into Templin on the night of April 7–8, 1945, admitted under interrogation that their mission had been to find out what plans the Allies had made for attacking the Russians; if the Allies reached Berlin first, the agents were to destroy their papers and lie low, "on no account revealing themselves as agents."

If Stalin himself expected such a clash, then Hitler intended to keep his Reich in existence—however battered and however diminished—until then.

———

Since late February 1945, and a further ruinous American air raid on Berlin, Hitler and his staff had spent their nights in the Reich Chancellery's shelters. Albert Speer had begun building the main deep shelter for Hitler in mid-1944, and now it lay becalmed and impregnable—compared by Julius Schaub to "a U-boat prowling the depths below Berlin's sea of houses and ministry buildings." Such was the scene of this final chapter of Hitler's life, with its narrow concrete passageway and cell-like rooms, the constant hum of air-conditioning machinery, the glare of artificial light, the throng of military and Party officials—some curious, some concerned, but most clinging to Hitler and his infectious belief that this crisis would be overcome.[1] The Führer's shelter was entered down a short flight of steps and through gas-tight doors from the older, weaker shelter built in 1938 beneath the Chancellery's ceremonial hall. Right of the passageway after the machine room was Martin Bormann's office with the main telephone switchboard and his teleprinter units; the office was wallpapered with maps of Germany and Berlin, each covered with a celluloid sheet on which a five-man unit marked in blue chinagraph pencil the progress of each enemy bomber-stream hour by hour. Here Hitler spent the hours of the big alerts, watching with tired eyes the arrows approaching Berlin; each week the tracks grew more complex, for now the British bombers attacked from behind "screens" of radio-jamming and electronic countermeasures, feinting first toward one city, then another, while "fast raiding forces" mounted diversionary attacks far from the main targets of the night. Since the holocaust of Dresden, British bomber forces had cascaded incendiaries and explosives into Chemnitz (Karl-Marx Stadt), Duisburg, Worms, Kassel, ancient Würzburg—the list was endless.

The Americans too had begun attacking area targets. Nuremberg and Munich were laid waste. But by day the tide was beginning to turn, as the Me-262 jets with the heavier armament and air-to-air rockets joined the squadrons. The grim pages of the Luftwaffe High Command's war diary reported: "Four Me-262s shot down four bombers. . . ." But as the Luftwaffe's fuel stocks ran out, this last hope expired. General Peltz (Ninth Air Corps) and Colonel Hajo Herrmann (Ninth Fighter Division) had secured in February Göring's permission in principle for a mass attack by suicide pilots on American bomber formations. Originally 600 Messerschmitt 109s were set aside for this, but the Chief of Air Staff, General Karl Koller, objected that since the Me-109 was ceasing manufacture and only 1,800 still survived, the suicide attack ("Werewolf") would accelerate the end of piston-engined fighter operations and tactical reconnaissance missions until the improved Ta-152 fighter arrived.

---

[1] Thus Admiral Dönitz advised his commanders on March 3, 1945: "Let us place our trust unconditionally in Adolf Hitler's leadership. Believe me, in my two years as Navy Commander in Chief I have found that his strategic views always turned out right."

The suicide operation—almost overlooked by history—was vivid proof of the anger and bitterness fomented by the bombing war. After weeks of hesitation Koller made available 180 Me-109s with high-performance engines on April 3; 150 pilots were released, but far more, 184, volunteered and flew in "Werewolf" four days later—emptying their cannon into the bombers at point-blank range and then ramming them. The battle took place west of Hanover on April 7, 1945. Of the "suicide" Me-109s, 133 were lost after destroying 23 American bombers; 77 pilots were killed; the escorting jet fighters claimed 28 more American bombers that day.

Left of the red-carpeted main passageway in Hitler's shelter—with its incongruously lavish decor of priceless paintings and furniture rescued from the Chancellery upstairs—were his private rooms: a bedroom with army bed, wardrobe, chest of drawers, and a safe; and a tiny, low-ceilinged living room with desk, table, and hard upholstered sofa; a portrait of Frederick the Great hung over the desk. Between the bedroom and passageway was the small conference room, filled with a map table surrounded by a wooden bench. Through the doors at the passageway's far end a spiral staircase led up into the Chancellery gardens.

A filtration system protected the shelter against poison-gas attack. Recently it had been improved after fumes were detected during a war conference; inquiry revealed that Göring's chauffeur had parked his car near the air-intake duct and had left its engine running to keep warm! In February 1945 Hitler was also fitted with a gas mask in case of emergencies.

This bunker was connected to the Voss Bunker under the Chancellery, which could house two thousand people. In 1939 Hitler had opened it to Berlin's hospital and welfare services, and many an "Adolf" had first seen the light of day here, the birth being marked by flowers for the mother and a bankbook with a hundred marks for the child. During April 1945 an SS Life Guard battalion moved in, as did Bormann's staff and a field hospital, and the maternity clinic was moved to a shelter underneath the Reichstag. Every evening a line formed in the street for access to the Voss Bunker. Hitler ordered a concrete shelter built for those waiting, but weeks later his order had still not been carried out. "I have to attend to every minor detail myself," he exclaimed angrily at lunch to his secretaries. "And yet there's nobody suitable as a successor. Hess went off his rocker. Göring's lost the public's sympathy. Himmler is unacceptable to the Party." Fräulein Schroeder, the sharpest of his secretaries, pointed out: "But Himmler's name is often mentioned by the people." "The man's got no artistic sense at all!" retorted Hitler, to which Fräulein Schroeder tartly replied, "In our present straits artistic sense hardly matters!" Hitler stopped eating and angrily stalked out. "Carry on—rack your brains to think of a successor!" Some days later he repeated this injured challenge. "Why not Admiral Dönitz?" Julius Schaub suggested. Hitler did not reply.

The Luftwaffe's impotence against the air raids began to corrode his mind. A million people in Germany's domains had been slain by the enemy's bombers or machine-gunned to death in fields, streets, and trains. He was obsessed by the idea that those responsible were escaping unpunished.

One day early in April Bormann read to Hitler an Allied newspaper report that German troops had saved an American bomber crew about to be lynched by angry townsfolk after a raid. Hitler was furious and looked around at General Koller, standing to the left of his chair. "These are the men who are murdering German women and children! It's incredible!" Since Kaltenbrunner was hovering in the background, Hitler turned to him too. "I order that all bomber crews shot down these last few months or in the future are to be turned over by the Luftwaffe to the SD at once and liquidated." This sweeping order was greeted with hostile silence by the officers present in the cramped conference room. Koller pointed out that the enemy might then simply take reprisals against their Luftwaffe prisoners; Hitler retorted that they could arrest one hundred thousand French civilians in Germany and hold them hostage to prevent such reprisals.

In the passageway outside, Keitel, Kaltenbrunner, and Koller agreed that the order should be ignored. But Hitler buttonholed Koller a few minutes later and appealed to him. "You must help me—we can't go on like this. Our air defenses have failed. What am I to do against this nightmare terror-bombing and the murder of our women and children?" Koller urged patience. "When our jet squadrons get stronger the war in the air over Germany will turn in our favor again." Hitler replied, "I cannot wait until then. If these airmen realize that in the future they will be liquidated as terrorists, they'll think twice about whether to fly over." Koller replied that neither the Luftwaffe—into whose officers the laws and articles of war had been painfully drummed—nor the SD would lend themselves to such an order; he also pointed out that Luftwaffe pilots would themselves suffer in enemy hands. Hitler replied without emotion, "In other words the Luftwaffe is afraid. Fair enough, but I am in charge of the German people's safety, and I know no other way."

The failure to execute this latest order showed again that as the end approached Hitler's authority was crumbling. Yet another instance was his ministers' unauthorized peace feelers to the enemy. Since Yalta, Hitler had emphatically opposed all such feelers, but Ribbentrop persisted nonetheless. He sent his English affairs expert, Fritz Hesse, to Stockholm, and when the Swedish press exposed Hesse's mission on March 15—earning for Ribbentrop a thunderous rebuke from Hitler —a few days later the foreign minister again sent Werner von Schmieden to

Switzerland and Consul Eitel Friedrich Moellhausen to Madrid, to contact Allen Dulles and the American ambassador, Robert Murphy, respectively, about terms for a halt to the "frightful bombing and carnage"; but Schmieden was still waiting for an entry visa to Switzerland when the war ended, and Murphy had evidently just left Madrid for Washington before Moellhausen could get to see him. Reichsmarschall Göring referred to Hitler's stubbornness in a private conversation late in March; General Koller noted that when he complained to Göring about the lack of clear directives from Hitler "the Reichsmarschall agreed—he is just as much in the dark. F[ührer] told him nothing. Nor is it permissible to make the slightest political move, for example, the attempt of a British diplomat in Sweden to contact us was strictly rebuffed by F. The Führer flatly forbids Reichsmarschall to make any use of his own comprehensive contacts abroad . . ."[2] Again and again the foreign minister [Ribbentrop] submits fresh possibilities to F., but he just turns them down." Thus nobody knew how long a war still to plan for: another year or longer? or just a few last desperate months?

By the date of Göring's remarks, March 28, 1945, Germany's position was militarily hopeless. Asked by Hitler ten days earlier to comment on the loss of Saar coal and its effect on their arms production, Albert Speer had answered in one sentence, "It will speed up the general collapse." When Gauleiter Forster had arrived from Danzig late on the nineteenth with word that "four thousand" Russian tanks were converging on that city, Hitler had still confidently sworn that Danzig would be saved. But in the west a catastrophe had already occurred. All attempts at destroying the Remagen bridge across the Rhine failed until too late; by the time the German naval frogmen and jet bombers had between them brought it down, the Americans had another bridge in service and the enemy bridgehead had swollen to unmanageable proportions.

Kolberg had fallen in mid-March after holding out against the Polish and Russian enemy—some in German uniforms—long enough for sixty thousand of the port's civilians to escape by sea. The civilian evacuation of Königsberg and Danzig was in full swing. In Hungary and Pomerania the counterattacks in which Hitler had vested his hopes had failed dismally. In the west one disaster overtook another. On the night of March 22, American amphibious tanks had sprung a surprise bridgehead across the Rhine at Oppenheim at a cost of only eight

---

[2]Some words are missing from Koller's note, as his papers decayed during the postwar years of burial and concealment. Count Lutz Schwerin von Krosigk also noted in his unpublished diary a talk with Goebbels on April 9, 1945, in which Goebbels described how Germany had put out cautious peace feelers. The Russians and Americans had reacted positively, but the British had rejected them out of hand.

casualties. At 3 A.M. on the twenty-fourth, Montgomery's main Rhine crossing began at Wesel. By March 28 it was clear that the Ruhr was about to be encircled. Whole companies of German troops were throwing away their weapons and deserting. There were reports that German civilians had actually helped the Americans cross the Main near Frankfurt and were dancing with them in the streets at night. General Koller confided to Göring: "My own faith in our army commanders and in our striking power is exhausted." He regarded the southern American operation as strategically the most dangerous: it was the old French interwar strategy of thrusting eastward astride the Main toward Czechoslovakia so as to slice Germany in two.

The speed of events in the west stunned Hitler, who had been confident that in the east a great German defensive triumph lay in store. On March 25 he told Gauleiter Fritz Sauckel that for the first time he feared the war was lost. But as General Jodl explained to Allied interrogators: "For our leaders there was no alternative but to fight on to their last breath; your propaganda itself fostered this attitude." American troop indoctrination manuals had reached the Chancellery; as one Führer adjutant wrote: "The implacable hatred preached in them against the entire German nation seems little short of the Old Testament language to me." Early in April, Hitler was shown a captured British manual ominously code-named "Eclipse": evidently the end product of the Morgenthau Plan, it named numerous categories of Germans for "automatic arrest" and contained maps of the ultimate dissection of Germany and Berlin into occupation zones. At the same time army Intelligence secured a copy of Stalin's infamous "Order Number Five": "The German people is to be destroyed. All German factories and property are to be laid waste. The German animal must be battered to death in its hovels." Brief German reconquests of ground in East Prussia brought fresh reports on the fate of the Germans who had not escaped in time. "It shall not be! These illiterate brutes shall not inundate all Europe!" Hitler raged. "I am the last bulwark against this peril. If there is any justice, then we shall emerge victorious. One day the world will see the moral of this struggle!"

Defeat seemed certain to all but the most blindly loyal. The hours Hitler spent with them increased, for they alone still displayed the kind of caged fanaticism that might even now see Germany through her misfortunes. He rewarded their loyalty well. When Goebbels late in March abused the Reich press chief, Dr. Otto Dietrich, for his overconservative press policies toward the Allies, Hitler sent for Dietrich and told him: "I'm sending you on six weeks' leave. By then it will all be over one way or the other." Dr. Robert Ley, leader of the Labor Front and previously the butt of many cruel witticisms in Hitler's milieu, was now like Goebbels favored with many hours of Hitler's private conversation. He left Berlin inflated with new courage and conviction, to organize an "Adolf Hitler" Free Corps in Austria—tank-killer teams trained and equipped to operate behind the

Russian lines. "The Führer was head and shoulders above us all," wrote Ley after the war. "And we were too puny for this Titan." Hitler's earlier sycophants discreetly bowed out or were impatiently dismissed. As the end approached, old scores were settled all around—by Goebbels against Ribbentrop, by Bormann against Speer, by Speer against Göring, and by Ley against "that petty and pitiable" Heinrich Himmler. On March 20, Hitler relieved the Reichsführer of command of Army Group Vistula. "The Führer saw through Himmler," wrote Ley. "I had a long talk with the Führer at the time, in which he bitterly complained of Himmler's disobedience, dishonesty, and incompetence."

Fundamental to Hitler's predicament was that many of his generals and ministers were already secretly preparing window-dressing for the war crimes trials they regarded as inevitable: Gotthard Heinrici, the mild-mannered, church-going general Hitler was forced to appoint as Himmler's successor—for want of any better commanders—lacked the wholehearted commitment of a Schörner or Model: Model held out with Army Group B in the encircled Ruhr pocket until his guns had fired their last ammunition; he then took his own life to cheat the enemy. This was the bold spirit which had saved Stalin's Russia in 1941 and 1942. But Hitler's lieutenants lacked even the will to cheat the enemy of the spoils of war: the arms factories of Upper Silesia had fallen intact into Russian hands and were now adding to the arms and ammunition stockpiles being built up on the eastern bank of the Oder. Speer had not hesitated to order the destruction of Hungarian oil refineries in January—a premature destruction that the OKW was just able to stop in time. But by March he was planning less for Germany's defense than for his own.[3]

Speer's character was ambivalent and complex, and Hitler evidently changed his mind about him; after a half-hearted attempt at dismissing him late in March he cut him out of his political testament entirely one month later. He was disappointed by the failure of Me-262 jet aircraft production to reach Speer's predictions, and he appointed SS General Hans Kammler—already special commissioner for V-weapons—to take charge. Another of Speer's projects—codenamed "Iron Hammer"—had also fallen short of expectations: 82 special aircraft, arranged in tandem, had been built for a daredevil attack on the main Soviet power stations, producing between them 1,904,000,000 kilowatts for Stalin's tank and arms factories. Since February, Göring had strongly backed the project, and enough fuel had been set aside while the bomber and Pathfinder crews were trained. But on March 18, Speer had advised Hitler to divert nearly half the special

---

[3]Perhaps Speer was exaggerating when he claimed under Allied interrogation a few weeks later that he "had counted up all the acts of high treason which he had committed from the end of January onward and had arrived at a total of over sixty."

aircraft to destroy the Soviet bridges across the Oder or Vistula rivers the moment the big enemy offensive began. Hitler was torn between the two alternatives but reverted in Speer's absence on March 26 to his order for an attack on the Soviet power stations. "Imagine what it would have meant for us if the enemy had attacked all *our* power stations simultaneously! It is just the same for the enemy. I'd rather forgo the attack on the Vistula bridges—we can do them sometime later." But when the full moon came, the weather conditions were wrong and "Iron Hammer" had to be postponed indefinitely.

Hitler did not even resent Speer's uncomfortably frank March 15 memorandum on the economic situation. He told Guderian he had stuffed it, "unread," into the man-high safe at the foot of his bed. It bravely exposed Speer's conviction that the war was hopelessly lost: the enemy air raids, and the loss of the coal-bearing regions, made Germany's "final economic collapse" inevitable within four to eight weeks. *"After this collapse the war cannot even be militarily continued."* Speer's memorandum urged Hitler to remember the government's obligation in the coming hours of trial to aid its people; and he demanded strict orders prohibiting the destruction of factories and bridges, as this could now only harm Germany. Hitler turned a deaf ear on Speer when he again argued these points, in person this time, late on the eighteenth. Speer was an intellectual foreign to the dictates of strategy; and it was the minister's fortieth birthday next day. But his indulgence toward Speer cooled when he learned a week later through Party channels that Speer had secretly driven to the west to sabotage Hitler's orders for a scorched-earth policy to slow down the enemy advance. Hitler had issued these orders on March 19, after Keitel's orders issued in January had failed to prevent the scandalous events of Upper Silesia and the Saar, where entire industries had fallen intact into enemy hands. Hitler's emphatic directive called for the destruction of all military installations and transport-, communications- and public-utility equipment "insofar as they may be of use to the enemy in the furtherance of his fight."[4]

Both Speer and his energetic deputy, Karl-Otto Saur, shuttled between Berlin and the Ruhr, but Hitler soon learned that their purposes were very different. Saur admitted that further production in the Ruhr was hopeless, but he bitterly criticized the response of the General Staff officers there to his own expressions of optimism. Speer on the other hand had spread despondency and gloom, infecting everybody he had met and urging them to turn their factories over to the enemy intact. Meanwhile the American spearheads were plunging deeper and deeper into Germany. At Hanau and Aschaffenburg two more key bridges fell undemolished into their hands. Probably only Speer's friendship with Hitler and

---

[4]In his memoirs Speer omits the words I quote.

Eva Braun now spared him from an unkinder fate. Late on March 28 the Führer coldly received him and instructed him to stand down as armaments minister, giving the customary ill-health plea as an excuse. Speer clearly lacked the necessary faith that the tide could still turn in their favor, the Führer pointed out. Speer flushed and protested, but Hitler challenged him outright. "Do you still hope for a successful continuation of the war, or is your faith shattered?" When after twenty-four hours Speer had still not given him a straight answer, Hitler virtually sacked him, although he continued to value his presence at the Chancellery as a friend. Meanwhile, Jodl and his military staff attempted to put Hitler's defense doctrines into practice—instilling into the western army group commanders the need to bring home to the enemy that they were plunging into a Germany "fanatical with fighting spirit." Only this would enable the western front to be stabilized. "This is not the time or place for considering the civilian population," the OKW order concluded.

Bormann added his own characteristic warning to his Gauleiters: "Devil take the one who deserts his Gau under enemy attack except with express orders from the Führer, or who does not fight to the last breath in his body—he will be cast out as a deserter and dealt with accordingly."

Hitler spent the last week in March 1945 purging his followers of the faint of heart. Hans Lammers, his chief of Chancellery, came for the last time on the twenty-seventh and mentioned his high blood pressure; Hitler sent him to Berchtesgaden on sick leave. On March 29 he dismissed General Guderian too, fearing that when the crisis came his poor health would produce a breakdown similar to his collapse in the Moscow winter of 1941. General Hans Krebs, a young and tough idealist strongly reminiscent of Zeitzler in his heyday, took over as Chief of the General Staff. Heinrich Himmler had also fallen from grace, for the SS Sixth Panzer Army in Hungary under SS General Sepp Dietrich had not only failed in its big counterattack north of Lake Balaton, but had been routed and thrown back onto the Austrian frontier. Nothing could stop the Russians from pouring into Vienna; the Hungarian oil fields were lost. "If we lose the war, it will be his fault!" Hitler raged, and ordered that as a punishment Sepp Dietrich's principal divisions were to be stripped of their brassards and insignia for three days. Himmler was packed off to Vienna to issue a stern reprimand to his Waffen SS generals.

Guderian's dismissal resulted from a similar defeat just east of Berlin. Hitler had clung to the ancient city of Küstrin to deny its important Oder bridges and road junctions to the Russians; since mid-March he had been preparing a limited counterattack toward Küstrin from his own Frankfurt bridgehead, hoping to destroy the enemy assault forces massing for the attack on Berlin. But before General Theodor Busse's Ninth Army could begin the counterattack, the Russians struck and encircled Küstrin completely; Busse's own attack on March 22 failed, but Hitler insisted that it must be repeated immediately. General Heinrici, Himmler's successor as army group commander, came to the bunker in person on March 25 to argue for Küstrin to be abandoned to the enemy so that he could conserve what ammunition and gasoline he had for the big defensive battle looming ahead. But again Hitler insisted on a policy of attack. A purely defensive stance would allow the Russians to pounce at will—the German reserves would be tied down in hasty repair jobs, and then Heinrici would begin clamoring for new reserves all over again. "Since the enemy will always be stronger than us," Hitler wearily reminded him, "they will then ultimately break through and that will be your downfall." Their only hope was to throw rapid punches at the enemy before they were ready to attack, delaying them week after week while Hitler stockpiled ammunition for the major battle. Most Russian strength was massing south of Küstrin—particularly artillery. Hitler admitted that a renewed counterattack here would be a gamble, but with the necessary faith, he insisted, it would succeed.[5]

The new attack began on March 28. The German tanks reached Küstrin's outskirts, but once again the infantry failed to follow through and the tanks were brought back. Against Hitler's explicit orders the Küstrin garrison then broke out to the west, knifing through Russian lines which Heinrici and Busse had described as impenetrable. Hitler summoned General Busse to the bunker and informed him of his displeasure. Guderian loudly and intemperately defended him, purpling with rage. Hitler cleared the bunker conference room and advised Guderian: "You need sick leave. I don't think your heart can stand the strain. Come back in six weeks."

Along the Oder, Marshal Zhukov had assembled over 750,000 troops for the offensive; farther south along the Neisse Marshal Konev had 500,000 more under his command. Additional Soviet forces were approaching from the battlefields of East and West Prussia, but Hitler believed that the attack might begin without them, because the Russians were determined to reach Berlin before the Americans.

On the day after Guderian's dismissal Hitler issued a clear-sighted appraisal of the situation "now that we have failed to shatter the enemy preparations by counterattack." He demanded a fanatical defense effort by Army Group Vistula, from General Heinrici himself right down to the youngest recruit. In particular Hitler ordered Heinrici to construct a "main battle line" two to four miles behind

---

[5]Cornelius Ryan omitted mention of this conference of March 25, 1945, in *The Last Battle* (New York, 1966) and—relying on an alleged "diary" of General Heinrici—refers to a conference on April 6 as the first with Hitler. The war diaries of Army Group Vistula and the OKH operations staff establish the correct date as the fourth.

the present front line—a bitter lesson he had learned from the Americans on the dawn of his own Ardennes offensive. The moment the Russian offensive was seriously anticipated, Heinrici was to fall back on this second line; the huge enemy artillery bombardment would then fall on the empty trenches of the original front line. Heinrici was also ordered to resite his artillery farther back, where it could saturate the countryside between the present front and the "main battle line" when the Russian attack began.[6]

Thus his malevolently brilliant brain was still functioning logically and flexibly, even though his physical frame was a palsied shadow of the Hitler that had sprung this war on central Europe in 1939. His doctors were unanimous in agreeing that his sanity remained intact until the end, even though he could not walk more than thirty paces without gripping something firm for support, and his bloodshot eyes became so poor that he had to put on his spectacles even to read documents typed on the special big-face typewriters. His hair had turned an ashen gray, and Morell observed in Hitler for the first time now *fetor ex ore*—the clinical description of bad breath. But when frontline commanders were brought down to the shelter, his willpower and perseverance appeared undiminished—the central powerhouse, coordinating and commanding, that alone seemed to enable Germany to withstand the onslaught of the whole world in indignant coalition against her. A year before he had dominated all Europe from the North Cape to the Crimea and the Spanish frontier; now millions of enemy troops were only an hour's drive away, east and west of his capital, and his headquarters was this shelter. Yet the admiration of his strategic advisers was unimpaired. "Looking at the whole picture," General Jodl unashamedly told his interrogators, "I am convinced that he was a great military leader. Certainly no historian can say that Hannibal was a poor general just because ultimately Carthage was destroyed." Admiral Dönitz, himself no simpleton, unreservedly echoed this judgment on Hitler.

For Hitler the spring had brought encouraging signs for the future, which blinded him to the remorseless approach of the enemy armies. Hundreds of the new jets were now reaching the squadrons. Jet reconnaissance planes had re-opened the skies over England and Scotland. On March 17 the first Mark XXI submarine—capable of voyaging submerged to Japan—had set forth, bound eventually for the east coast of the United States. Underground oil plants were being built by the SS. He and the General Staff believed that Stalin could be held off, for Soviet tank losses were outrunning production: in February, Stalin had lost 4,600, against a monthly output of only 2,300; in the first twenty-two days of March no fewer than 5,452 Soviet tanks were claimed destroyed. "The enemy's

[6]Unaware of this Hitler Order of March 30, 1945, Cornelius Ryan in *The Last Battle,* pages 299, 342, and 351, gives Heinrici the credit for this stratagem.

reserves will shortly be exhausted," the General Staff assured the Führer. Stalin had been provoked into launching a sixth attack on Hitler's besieged army in Kurland; again he had suffered a bloody defeat, and he made no further attempts. In the beleaguered fortresses of Breslau and Königsberg German garrisons were still holding out. "And as long as I have Königsberg I can still claim to the German people that East Prussia is not lost," Hitler explained in private. On the Czech frontier, the tough General Ferdinand Schörner fought a grim twenty-day defensive battle for the industrial city of Moravian Ostrau (Ostrava) which ended on April 3 in a convincing victory for his Army Group Center. Hitler appointed him field marshal.

During the first week of April 1945 this optimism was severely shaken. On April 2 the Reich surgeon general, Dr. Karl Brandt, privately warned him that one-fifth of all essential medical items was already unobtainable, and that stocks of two-fifths more would run out completely in two months. This put the shortest time-fuse yet on Hitler's strategy: without medicines disease and epidemic would cut his people down. Now that the Ruhr and Saar arsenals had been overrun, crippling production shortages in weapons, small arms, ammunition, and explosives made a mockery of his efforts to raise fresh divisions from the Hitler Youth or Reich Labor Service battalions. Virtually all aircraft production had ceased; the ground-attack and air-transport squadrons were already running out of replacement aircraft. An airlift to Field Marshal Model's Army Group B, encircled in the Ruhr pocket, was out of the question. The Breslau garrison was barely surviving, but in Königsberg—despite Hitler's repeated instructions that the fortress was to be held to the last man—the commandant, General Otto Lasch, surrendered to the Russians on April 9; during the following night Hitler ordered a message sent to all surviving command posts and radio units at Königsberg: "General Lasch is to be shot as a traitor immediately."

But which generals heeded Hitler's orders now? His authority was waning, and they were beginning to act arbitrarily, in disregard and ignorance of the central strategy laid down in Berlin. "Blomberg always told me that obedience stops short at generals," Hitler was to recall a few days before the end. At his midday war conference on April 1, Hitler had expressly laid down: "Anybody retreating in Austria is to be shot!" But now every day Martin Bormann submitted sheafs of telegrams from the angry and bewildered Gauleiters reporting the Wehrmacht's headlong retreat from across the Hungarian frontier. During the afternoon of April 5, General Otto Wöhler's Army Group South retreated *fifty miles;* Bormann jotted in his diary: *"The Bolsheviks are outside Vienna!"* But Hitler merely sacked the general and replaced him with Lothar Rendulić, the gritty general who had just thwarted Stalin's last assault on the Kurland army group. One of Bormann's Party officials had telephoned that night: "None of the army group gentlemen"—meaning Wöhler's staff—"has the slightest faith in their ability to hold off the enemy penetration into the [Zisterdorf] petroleum fields;

nor in fact, and this I must state plainly, do they believe we can still win. The Luftwaffe blew up all Vienna's searchlight sites on the night of April 3 without a word to the army group. In the Lower Danube Gau the Wehrmacht rout goes on."

Zisterdorf, outside Vienna, was Hitler's only remaining source of petroleum. On April 6 he ordered its defense until the last possible moment. Vienna itself seemed bent on suicide. From there SS Colonel Skorzeny reported on the tenth that while the tank brigades were running out of gasoline, retreating Luftwaffe units were passing through with truckloads of "girls and furniture"; a handful of tough SS commanders could stop the rout—he himself had just ordered three traitors hanged from a bridge. Three days later Vienna was overrun.

Warily—because he knew Hitler's loathing of astrologers—Dr. Goebbels had sent for the Führer's horoscope, which the Gestapo kept filed away. Two separate horoscopes came to a remarkably unanimous conclusion—and both could be interpreted as having already predicted the outbreak of war in 1939, the victories until 1941, and the hammer blows of defeat since then; the hardest blows, they prophesised, would fall in this first half of April, while the second half would temporarily give Germany the upper hand again. A period of stalemate would follow until August 1945, in which month peace would return. After three cruel years, the horoscopes concluded, Germany's ascent to greatness would be resumed in 1948.

Stalin's big Oder offensive might begin any day now. General Theodor Busse was confident that his Ninth Army could stop it from reaching Berlin. In the west, Hitler planned to launch in mid-April a counterattack against the long exposed American flank as they thrust eastward. Goebbels strove to persuade Hitler not to lose hope, for he was sure the clash between Russia and the West must come within the next three to four months—by August 1945, in short. Early in April he came to the shelter and, in his melodious and theatrical voice, read aloud to Hitler from Carlyle's fine description of the darkest hours of the Seven Years' War. It was a moment in which Frederick the Great saw no way out, his generals and ministers were convinced of imminent defeat, and Prussia's enemies already gloated over its fall. With an uncertain future stretching darkly before him the great king wrote one last letter to Count Finckenstein proclaiming that if the tide had not turned by a certain date he would accept defeat and swallow poison.

Here Carlyle apostrophized:
Brave King! Tarry awhile, because your days of travail will soon pass. Already the sun has risen behind the clouds of your misfortune, and soon it will shine forth.

Three days before the king's deadline, the Czarina Elizabeth died, the accession of Peter III took Russia out of the war, and thus the House of Brandenburg was saved. Goebbels saw tears starting in Hitler's eyes as he laid the book aside.

Putting himself in Stalin's now enviable shoes, Hitler himself believed the buildup before Berlin was only a feint and that the real Russian offensive would first be toward Prague. Stalin must surely intend to embrace the important Czech industrial region before his American rivals could reach it—just as Hitler had striven for the Donets Basin and the Caucasus in 1941. Hitler had chided General Guderian: "The Russians won't be as stupid as us. We were dazzled by our nearness to Moscow and just had to capture the capital. Remember, Guderian —*you* were the one who wanted to be first into Moscow at the head of your army! And just look at the consequences!" Whether this was intuition or on General Staff advice the records do not disclose, but at this crucial juncture, he impulsively ordered General Busse to relinquish four SS panzer divisions to Schörner's army group defending Czechoslovakia.

In early March, Schörner had commanded 413,000 troops, and 527,000 more were under Heinrici's command; since then Hitler had moved strong reinforcements to the Oder and Neisse fronts. The Soviet forces were not so overwhelming in terms of troop strength as they were in purely *material* strength: tens of thousands of Russian guns and rocket launchers waited mutely on the Oder's higher eastern bank overlooking the German positions; the Luftwaffe was powerless to interfere. Against the enemy's frightening tank superiority, Hitler could set only his own antitank and antiaircraft batteries, and the bravery of individual tank-killer squads equipped with hand-held bazookas. Yet he was confident of a swift victory. He summoned General Heinrici to the shelter again on April 4 and subjected the Oder defenses to a mile-by-mile scrutiny. He reminded Heinrici of the need to lay down deadly minefields at the obvious Schwerpunkt positions; he ordered the Ninth Army to drive tunnels into the strategically crucial Seelow Heights—which commanded the marshy valley west of Küstrin through which the Russian attack must advance—to protect the army's reserves from enemy artillery. He gave Heinrici control of all army and Luftwaffe antiaircraft batteries and warned him against "Seydlitz officers" infiltrating in German uniforms. Behind the main front line, thousands of trees were being felled and antitank trenches dug. Evidence of Russian occupation methods, seen by General Busse's officers and troops in villages they had recaptured, determined them to keep Soviet forces from advancing one more yard into Europe.

By April 11 American forces had reached the Elbe at Magdeburg—only sixty miles from Berlin. Hitler was told that a Russian deserter had revealed that the Oder offensive would begin in four days' time, but he suspected it might come even earlier, as the Russians would want to reach Berlin before the Americans. Again he asked for a complete report on Heinrici's army group. He was assured that no other sector in Germany was so powerfully manned with troops and artillery. He congratulated Heinrici's officers. "The Russians are going to suffer their bloodiest defeat ever!" But late on April 12 he admitted to his staff that he was uneasy about the sector east of Cottbus—where Schörner's and Heinrici's army groups met at the junction of Oder and Neisse.

One thing was certain: he could not fight a long battle of attrition because his stocks of aviation fuel would keep the Luftwaffe airborne over the Oder battlefield for only a few days, and—as the quartermaster general warned explicitly on April 15—all German munitions supplies would shortly cease. Their munitions factories and dumps were almost all in enemy hands. "There may shortly occur the most momentous consequences for our entire war effort," the general had warned.

As American troops advanced across Thuringia, Hitler was confronted with the problem of the concentration camps. Göring advised him to turn them over intact and under guard to the Western Allies, who would sort out the criminals from the foreign laborers and Russian prisoners, thus preventing hordes of embittered ex-convicts from roaming the countryside and inflicting additional horrors on the law-abiding. Hitler did not share Göring's trust in the enemy. Sitting casually on the edge of the map table after one war conference, he instructed Himmler's representative to ensure that all inmates were liquidated or evacuated before the camps were overrun.

Nor had he forgotten his special collection of prominent prisoners—among them his star defendants for planned postwar trials. On April 8 prison officials loaded them aboard prison vans for transfer to the south. There was a kaleidoscope of famous names: the Schuschnigg family, General Thomas, Dr. Schacht, General Halder, Molotov's nephew, Captain S. Payne Best (a British Intelligence officer kidnapped in Venlo, Holland, in November 1939), and Colonel Bogislaw von Bonin. Behind them at Flossenbürg camp they left Admiral Canaris and General Oster. A few days before, General Buhle had stumbled by chance on the long-sought secret diaries of Canaris, and they sealed the Abwehr chief's fate. He and General Oster were hanged after a summary court-martial on the ninth. The surviving VIPs were moved to Dachau, near Munich. A vague notion of continuing the war from the easily defended mountain region of Bohemia, Bavaria, and northern Italy had begun to crystalize in Hitler's brain. When Gauleiter Franz Hofer came from the Tirol on April 9 and urged Hitler to abandon most of northern Italy—arguing that the only arms production of any significance came from the South Tirol—the Führer pointed out that virtually the entire arms effort now relied on electrosteel supplied by northern Italy. Late on April 10 he ordered Karl-Otto Saur—Speer's *de facto* successor as armaments minister—to investigate the possibility of creating an independent arms industry in the Alps.

If the remaining Reich was cut in two by the American and Russian spearheads, military governments under Admiral Dönitz and Field Marshal Kesselring would rule the northern and southern Reich respectively—a curious but significant rebuff by Hitler to the Party's ambitions. He briefed Kesselring at length late on April 12. Kesselring ever after recalled the Führer's radiant optimism. "I'd even say, in retrospect, he was a man possessed by the idea that he might yet be saved—he clutched at it like a drowning man at straws." Hitler talked of the coming great victory on the Oder, of his new secret weapons, of the Twelfth Army he was raising under General Wenck to defeat the Allies on the Elbe, and of the coming rupture between the Russians and the West. General Busse, commanding the Ninth Army on the Oder, shared Hitler's confidence. "If need be, we'll stand fast here until the Americans are kicking us in the arse," he said, earthily expressing his strategic convictions to Goebbels that evening; and the propaganda minister assured Busse's more skeptical staff that if there was any justice, some miracle would surely save the Reich, just as the House of Brandenburg had been saved in 1762. With gentle irony an officer inquired, "Which Czarina is going to die, then?" All along the Oder, a troublesome Russian artillery activity had just begun.

The news of President Franklin Delano Roosevelt's sudden death on April 12 in Warm Springs, Georgia, reached Hitler only a few minutes after an American news agency announced it that night. Goebbels telephoned, his voice shrill with excitement. "Mein Führer, I congratulate you! Now Roosevelt is dead! It is written in the stars that the second half of April will be the turning point for us. This *is* the turning point!" All Hitler's ministers agreed that God had wrought a swift and terrible Judgment on their hated enemy. Speer and other doubting Thomases were fetched. Hitler brandished the news agency report at them. "Do you *still* say we have lost the war!"

The next morning he began dictating his famous proclamation to his soldiers on the eastern front—to be released the moment Stalin's offensive began:

For one last time our mortal enemies, the Jewish Bolsheviks, are throwing their weight into the attack. They are attempting to shatter Germany and annihilate our people. You soldiers in the east already know full well the fate awaiting German women and children. The older men and children will be murdered, women and girls will be debased to barrack-room whores. The rest will go on foot to Siberia.

We have been expecting this attack, and since this January everything has been done to build up a strong front. A mighty artillery is waiting to greet the enemy. Our infantry losses have been made good by innumerable new units. . . . This time the Bolsheviks will meet the old fate of Asia—they must and shall bleed to death at the gates of the German Reich's capital.

Whoever fails in his duty now is a traitor to our people. The regiment or division that abandons its position will be a disgrace to the women and children who have withstood the bombing terror in our cities.

Again Hitler warned them to be on guard against German traitors in the pay of Stalin and perhaps even wearing German uniforms. "Berlin stays German! Vienna"—which the Russians had overrun that very April 13—"will be German again. Europe will never be Russian."

He issued the proclamation to the army groups that night. It closed with a reference to Roosevelt. "At this moment when fate has carried off the greatest War Criminal of all times from the face of this earth, the war's turning point has come."

Hitler seemed to have shut his eyes to the possibility that Berlin itself might become a battlefield; but late on April 13, 1945, when Ribbentrop spoke with him, he gave permission for the nervous diplomatic corps to leave the capital for southern Germany. The next day the shelling of Busse's positions increased, and two hundred Russian tanks launched attacks of up to regimental strength; ninety-eight tanks were destroyed. April 15 brought a lull. According to a Russian prisoner, the attacks had been for reconnaissance purposes.

It was on this day that Eva Braun unexpectedly arrived back in Berlin. Some of those who knew Hitler intimately found the decision to remain at his side comparatively easy. The last letter from one of his adjutants to his wife admitted, however: "It is certainly hard for us men to stand in our last battle far from our families, knowing that our wives and children will later have to face the trials of life alone. But hundreds of thousands of others have found the strength, and I am trying to set an example, however humble, to all my compatriots."

During the night General Wenck's new army succeeded in destroying one American bridgehead on the Elbe south of Magdeburg and in reducing another. But a Russian prisoner taken south of Küstrin revealed that the big Oder offensive would begin the next morning, April 16—he spoke of a colossal artillery barrage and of mighty new tanks and howitzers standing by, and he reported that the Red Army troops had been ordered to tidy up their uniforms and wash and shave every day "to make a cultivated impression" from now on. This had the ring of authenticity; Hitler ordered Busse's Ninth Army pulled back during the remaining hours of darkness into the secret second line of defense (a line which, he now learned, Heinrici had built without much enthusiasm). At his midnight conference Hitler learned with stabbing misgivings of a puzzling request by General Heinrici—for permission to transfer his army group HQ to a new site which Hitler found, after much searching on the map, to be to the *rear* of Berlin and thus *behind* the Führer's own headquarters.[7] He flatly forbade such a transfer and again ordered General Krebs to telephone instructions to the army group to build up its rear positions as fast as possible.

Too late, these afterthoughts. At 5 A.M. the next morning, April 16, a mighty Russian artillery barrage began all along the Oder and Neisse rivers. Nearly half a million shells thundered down on the—now virtually abandoned—German forward positions. At 6:30 A.M. Zhukov's tanks and infantry began pouring across both sides of the Frankfurt-on-Oder strongpoint still held by Busse's Ninth Army; an hour later the main assault on the Fourth Panzer Army defending the Neisse front began. Savage battles developed between tank and gun, while overhead two thousand Russian planes bombed and harrassed the defenders; the German air force threw all it had into the battle. Sixty planes manned by suicide pilots crash-bombed the Oder bridges across which the enemy was flooding westward. By nightfall, although a five-mile-deep breach had been torn into the front near Wriezen, held only by the ill-experienced 9th Paratroop Division, there was no doubt in the Chancellery that a resounding defeat had been inflicted on the enemy.

Christa Schroeder asked quietly whether they would now be leaving Berlin. Hitler answered almost resentfully, "No. Calm down—Berlin will always be German!" The secretary replied that she was not afraid and regarded her life as spent already. "But I can't quite see how it's all going to end, with the Americans coming closer every day on one side and the Russians on the other."

"Time!" explained Hitler. "We've just got to gain time!"

---

[7]In defiance of the orders he had accepted from Hitler, Heinrici had secretly decided that if his Oder front collapsed, he would abandon Berlin to the enemy without even the pretense of a fight. He did not inform Hitler of this—although the decision affected not only his own two armies, but also the defenders of Berlin and the capital's three million civilian inhabitants. Albert Speer claimed to have brought about Heinrici's remarkable decision in a secret conference with him on April 15, 1945.

"Eclipse"

Hitler recognized that the end of what he envisioned as his lone fight against bolshevism was approaching, and there are clues in the documents as to how long he believed he could postpone it: for example, he had ordered the General Staff to provide the Berlin area with logistics sufficient for three divisions to hold out for twenty days, should the city be surrounded. If open conflict had not broken out between Stalin and the Americans by then, Hitler realized, his gamble had failed; it would be his "Eclipse," to use the code name assigned by his victorious enemies to the postwar carve-up of the Reich. By April 15, 1945, the document outlining this plan—captured from the British in the west—had been fully translated and was in the hands of Hitler, Himmler, and the military authorities; its appended maps revealed that Berlin was to be an enclave far inside the Russian occupation zone, divided like Germany itself into British, American, and Russian zones.

What encouraged Hitler was the fact that the American spearheads, in reaching the Elbe, had already encroached on Stalin's zone, while the Russians had duly halted at the demarcation line on reaching Saint-Pölten in Austria late on April 15. A clash seemed inevitable, and Hitler's General Staff toadied to this desperate belief. Colonel Gerhard Wessel, the new chief of Foreign Armies East, reported with emphasis on the fifteenth[1] that Russian officers were apprehensive that the Americans were preparing an attack ("We must drench the Americans *'accidentally'* with our artillery fire to let them taste the lash of the Red Army"); Wessel also disclosed that the British too were adopting a dangerous new propaganda line to subvert German security forces in Slovenia. "Britain is shortly going to start fighting the Soviet Union herself, and with better prospects than the Reich; Britain has already begun raising Russian units for this purpose." Over

---

[1] He succeeded General Gehlen in 1968 as chief of the West German Intelligence service.

and over during the next two weeks Hitler restated the belief that sustained him: "Perhaps the others"—meaning Britain and the United States—"can be convinced, after all, that there is only one man capable of halting the Bolshevik colossus, and that is me." This was the real point of fighting an otherwise hopeless battle for Berlin.

Since Roosevelt's death, Foreign Minister Ribbentrop had secretly circulated to German diplomatic channels abroad a fourteen-page memorandum designed for Allied consumption—a forbidding and not wholly inaccurate prophecy of Stalin's postwar position as the cruel and authoritarian ruler of both a Soviet Union of proven "biological strength" and of three hundred million non-Soviet eastern Europeans too. German technicians and factories captured by Stalin were already working to expand Stalin's power; could England, asked the memorandum, afford to abet this menace to her traditional routes to the Middle East and India, particularly once the United States had withdrawn her forces from western Europe as one day she must?

So far the British had been blinded by their hatred, but the Americans suddenly proved more amenable. On the night of April 17, SS General Fegelein —Himmler's representative—adroitly informed Hitler that the secret talks between SS General Wolff and Allen Dulles in Switzerland had resulted in principle on terms for an armistice on the Italian front. The Americans were still talking of unconditional surrender, but that was a minor problem if thereby the enemy alliance could be torn asunder. At 3 A.M. the Führer sent for Wolff and congratulated him. "I hear that you and your skill have managed to establish the first official contacts to top Americans." He asked Wolff not to leave Berlin until the next evening, to give him time to think it over. "I am grateful that you've succeeded in opening the first doorway to the West and America. Of course, the terms are very bad—there can be no talk of unconditional surrender, obviously." But by 5 P.M. his mood had hardened again. Strolling with Wolff, Kaltenbrunner, and Fegelein in the Chancellery garden, Hitler enlarged on his own hopeful theories. "I want the front to hold for eight more weeks. I am waiting for East and West to fall out. We are going to hold the Italian fortress at all costs, and Berlin too." This was the message Hitler gave Wolff to pass on to General Heinrich von Vietinghoff, Kesselring's colorless successor as Commander in Chief in Italy.

Hitler took harsh action against every vestige of defeatism. After consultation with Bormann, he ordered the arrest of his handsome former staff surgeon, Dr. Brandt, for sending his wife and family to Bad Liebenstein, where they would fall into American hands; on April 18, Brandt was summarily condemned to death for the offense.[2] Similar sentences would follow.

But entire armies could not be court-martialed for losing heart. Zisterdorf fell to the Russians. On the seventeenth Gauleiter August Eigruber cabled from Linz that "the petroleum fields are in jeopardy"; by the next day General Hans Kreysing's Eighth Army had already abandoned them precipitately, after prematurely destroying the installations. Himmler reported to Hitler that in Austria the army's tendency was to retreat everywhere even though "Ivan is obviously both wary and weary of fighting."

This was Hitler's second motive for making a last stand in Berlin: to set an example to his generals and thereby restore his personal authority over them.

Great slaughter had been inflicted on the Russians, but by early April 18 alarming fissures were appearing in the defenses. On the sixteenth Busse's Ninth Army had destroyed 211 tanks—and 106 more the next day—on the Oder front; while General Fritz Gräser's adjacent Fourth Panzer Army had knocked out 93 and 140 tanks on the Neisse front. Busse's front was still intact, though mauled and buckled by the sheer weight of Zhukov's onslaught; at Wriezen in particular a deep wedge had been hammered into the main German line. But southeast of Berlin Marshal Konev's army group had thrown two bridgeheads across the Neisse on the very first day—in fact just where Hitler had foreseen the Russian Schwerpunkt, though angled differently. Russian tanks were already approaching Cottbus and the Spree River at Spremberg: Konev's objective, like Zhukov's, was obviously Berlin and not Prague. This gave Hitler less time than he had thought.

Counterattacks by Heinrici and Schörner failed to restore the old battle line. On April 17, Hitler ordered the autobahn bridges blown up and every available aircraft, including the Messerschmitt jets, thrown in to stop the enemy from reaching Cottbus. At his midday conference he proclaimed: "The Russians are in for the bloodiest defeat imaginable before they reach Berlin!" But the failure of the counterattacks unsettled him. He sat brooding far into the night with Eva Braun and his secretaries, trying to convince them and himself that the wedge at Wriezen was just the natural luck of the attacker, but that such luck would not hold for long. Now he had to agree to pull troops out of the German bridgehead east of Frankfurt-on-Oder to strengthen the fortress's flanks. He began to blame General Heinrici for the sudden plight of the Oder front—calling him "a plodding, irresolute pedant lacking the necessary enthusiasm for the job."

---

[2] Himmler and Speer together prevented Brandt's execution by a series of maneuvers. He survived the war, only to be hanged by the Americans at Landsberg.

During the eighteenth a furious battle was fought for Seelow, the high plateau commanding the Russian assault area. By evening it was firmly in Zhukov's hands, and Hitler learned that only the SS "Nederland" Division—a volunteer unit of Dutch mercenaries—had been thrown into a counterattack. Perhaps this was the cause of his petulant outburst to General Karl Hilpert, the new commander of the Kurland army group, that day: "If the German nation loses this war, that will prove it was unworthy of me." A further eruption came when he learned that Goebbels had sent five battalions of wholly unsuitable Volkssturm troops to the Oder front—although Hitler had insisted that such troops were only to be used as a last resort in defense of their own towns and villages. There were enough able-bodied airmen and sailors who could have been sent—if only they had had the guns and ammunition.

From now until the end, Hitler slept only fitfully and irregularly. The long days were punctuated by an unending series of ill tidings, each one bringing the end much closer than its predecessor. Restless and pallid, Hitler rambled around the shelter, took brief strolls upstairs, then sat in the telephone exchange or machine room—where he had never set foot before—or visited his dogs in their makeshift kennels behind the lavatories; he took to sitting in the passageway with one of the puppies on his lap, silently staring at the officers passing in and out of the shelter.

He had news that separatist movements were stirring in Württemberg, Bavaria, and Austria. Late on April 19, Saur reported back to Hitler from the south, where he had conferred two days earlier with Gauleiter Hofer and SS General Kammler on the possibility of establishing an "Alpine Redoubt." In one of the Chancellery's few remaining rooms, Saur laid the unpalatable news squarely on the line: there was not enough time left to start large-scale arms production in the Alps; the most they could count on would be small factories for re-machining captured ammunition to fit German weapons. It was an uninspiring end to the armaments empire Speer had created. As Hitler accompanied Saur to the exit, he talked nostalgically of Speer's deceased predecessor. "Who knows—if Todt hadn't been killed, the war might have gone very differently!" He gave the stocky arms expert his hand, and he prophesied: "Within the next twenty-four hours we shall have won or lost the war."

This echoed the latest dispatch of Heinrici's army group: at Müncheberg, due east of Berlin, and at Wriezen, farther north, the Russians had finally broken through into open country between 5 and 6 P.M. Immense tank forces were pouring through the two breaches; at Müncheberg alone tank-killer squads and aircraft destroyed 60 tanks during the next few hours, while the Ninth Army's total that day was 226 Russian tanks knocked out. "The battle," Heinrici's army group reported that evening, "is about to be decided." A stabbing headache assailed Hitler as this news reached his bunker. He weakly called for a servant to fetch Dr. Morell, and at his behest the physician crudely drained a quantity of blood from Hitler's right arm until it blocked the hypodermic needle and Morell had to force a somewhat larger needle into the veins. The servant blanched as the blood ran into a beaker, but wisecracked: "Mein Führer, all we need do now is mix the blood with some fat and we could put it on sale as Führer blood sausage!" Hitler repeated the unpleasant witticism to Eva Braun and the secretaries over tea that evening.

Midnight would bring his fifty-sixth birthday. Bormann wanly observed in his diary that it was "not exactly a birthday situation." Hitler had asked his staff to refrain from ceremony, but Eva Braun cajoled him into stepping into the anteroom and shaking hands with the adjutants who had gathered there. Saur had brought a perfect scale-model of a 350-millimeter mortar for Hitler's collection. Hitler spoke for a while with Goebbels and Ley about his determination to defend the Alpine Redoubt and Bohemia-Moravia in the south, and Norway in the north; then he retired to drink tea with Eva in his low-ceilinged drawing room-cum-study.

All night after that he lay awake, until the knocking of Heinz Linge, his valet, told him it was morning. General Burgdorf, the chief Wehrmacht adjutant, was outside the door. He shouted that during the night the Russians had broken through Schörner's army group on both sides of Spremberg; the Fourth Panzer Army was trying to repair the breaches by a counterattack. Hitler merely said, "Linge, I haven't slept yet. Wake me an hour later than usual, at 2 P.M."

When he awoke Berlin was under heavy air attack—a birthday bombardment that continued all day. His eyes were stinging, but the pain subsided after Linge administered cocaine eyedrops.[3] Morell gave him a glucose injection, then Hitler fondled a puppy for a while before lunching with Eva and the two duty-secretaries, Johanna Wolf and Christa Schroeder. There was no conversation. After lunch they picked their way along the duckboards into the Voss Bunker, to steal another look at the model of Linz; he identified to them the house where he had spent his youth.

---

[3] A desk calendar later found in the shelter shows that Linge had to administer eyedrops at an ever-increasing rate—rising from one a day on April 16 to thirteen on April 28, the last page with entries.

Wrapped in a gray coat with its collar turned up, he climbed the spiral staircase to the Chancellery garden followed by Goebbels. The Berlin air was thick with the dust and smoke from a hundred fires. A short line of fresh-faced Hitler Youths awaited decoration for bravery against enemy tanks on the Oder front. The once well-tended lawns and paths were now pocked with holes and craters and strewn with branches and empty canisters. The perimeter wall was punctuated by dug-outs and piles of bazookas at the ready. Near the music room a small parade of troops from the Kurland battlefield awaited inspection. Himmler saluted, and Hitler—stooping and shuffling—passed along the line. They crowded around in a semicircle. He apologized for not being able to speak very loudly, but he did promise that victory would be theirs and that they could tell their children that they had been there when it was finally won.

At about 4 P.M. that afternoon, April 20, 1945, he retraced his steps into the shelter, having seen the sky for the last time.

Before the main war conference began, he allowed his principal ministers in singly to proffer formal birthday greetings. Ribbentrop stayed about ten minutes, the others—Göring, Dönitz, Keitel, and Jodl—rather less. Keitel dropped a broad hint that it was time for Hitler to leave Berlin, but Hitler interrupted: "Keitel, I know what I want—I am going to fight in front of Berlin, fight in Berlin, and fight behind Berlin!" With this Clemenceau-like utterance he extended his trembling hand to the field marshal and sent for the next well-wisher.

The main conference began immediately. Both north and south of Berlin the Russians had indeed decided the battle, and armored spearheads were dashing westward. Unless Schörner's counterattack succeeded, the last main road out of Berlin to the south would be cut off in a matter of hours. Göring echoed Keitel's feeling that it was time for a far-reaching military decision on the future of Berlin. General Koller pointed out that the truckloads of OKW equipment and documents would have to leave Berlin for the south immediately—certainly there was neither the fuel nor the fighter escort for the OKW to evacuate Berlin by air. Hitler authorized an immediate splitting of the command: Dönitz and part of the OKW staff were to leave for northern Germany; another part were to leave at once for the south. He gave the impression that he would in due course follow. Bormann left the room at once to organize sufficient armored transport and omnibuses for the transfer. Göring—whose own truckloads of property were already at Karinhall waiting for the word to go—inquired, "Mein Führer, do you have any objection to my leaving for Berchtesgaden now?" Hitler was dumbfounded that Göring could so casually desert him but did not betray his disappointment; he frigidly granted Göring's plea.

At 6 P.M. Spremberg fell to the Russians; they were now only a few miles from the vital autobahn from Berlin to the south. At 9:30 P.M., as a new air raid started, Hitler sent for the two older secretaries with whom he had lunched. Christa Schroeder wrote a few days after:

> Pale, tired, and listless, he met us in his tiny shelter study where we had eaten our meals or had tea with him of late. He said that the situation had changed for the worse over the last four days. "I find myself compelled to split up my staff, and as you are the more senior you go first. A car is leaving for the south in one hour. You can each take two suitcases, Martin Bormann will tell you the rest." I asked to stay in Berlin, so that my younger colleague could go as her mother lived in Munich. He replied, "No, I'm going to start a resistance movement and I'll need you two for that. You mean the most to me. If worse comes to worst, the younger ones will always get through—Frau Christian at any rate—and if one of the young ones doesn't make it, that's just Fate." He put out his hand to stop any further argument. He noticed how downcast we were, and tried to console us. "We'll see you soon, I'm coming down myself in a few days' time!" Absolutely numbed, my colleague and I left his room, to pack the two suitcases permitted us in the Voss Bunker where we four secretaries had shared a bedroom for some time. The hall outside was packed with pedestrians who had taken refuge from the air raid outside. In the midst of our packing the phone rang. I answered it—it was the Chief. In a toneless voice he said, "Girls, we're cut off"—we were going to drive down through Bohemia —"your car won't get through there now. You'll have to fly at dawn." But soon after he phoned again. "Girls, you'll have to hurry. The plane's leaving as soon as the all clear sounds." His voice sounded melancholy and dull and he stopped in mid-sentence. I said something, but although he still had not hung up, he made no reply.

The Russians had now reached Baruth—just ten miles south of OKW and OKH headquarters at Zossen, south of Berlin, and still more tanks were pouring through the big gap between the Fourth Panzer and Ninth armies. Schörner's counterattack had begun, but when Hitler called on Heinrici to attack, in order to close this gap, the army group commander demurred, demanding permission to pull back the Ninth Army's right flank instead, as it seemed in danger of encirclement. But Heinrici could give Hitler no assurances that this would not cost the flank corps its entire artillery, so Hitler—after hours of deliberation—ordered the line held where it was. Heinrici dramatically telephoned the General Staff half an hour after midnight to protest that Hitler's order was "unrealizable and hopeless." "I ought to declare: 'Mein Führer, as the order is against your interests I request you to relieve me of my command . . . then I can go into battle as an ordinary Volkssturm man with a gun in my hand!' " General Krebs drily pointed out: "The Führer expects you to make a supreme effort to plug the gaps as far east as possible, using everything you can scrape together, regardless of Berlin's later defense." Again Hitler ordered every available jet to attack the Russians south of Berlin.

In fact General Heinrici had already decided to "override" Hitler's order to stand fast. The Ninth Army, he felt, should withdraw westward while it still could. Thus the breach which must eventually seal Berlin's fate—and Hitler's too if he stayed for the capital's defense—was further widened. But at the time Hitler believed that his orders were being obeyed.

That night he resolved not to leave Berlin.

Cramped with his two remaining secretaries in his study he had explained, "I'd feel like some Tibetan lama, turning a useless, empty prayer wheel. I must force the decision here in Berlin or go down fighting." Hardly anybody arrived for the night conference—most of his staff, like his secretaries, were packing feverishly. Kreb's operations officer brought the grim news that the breach in the Fourth Panzer Army had widened still farther. Hitler calmly blamed this on that army's "betrayal." The general challenged him. "Mein Führer, you often talk of your betrayal by your commanders and troops. Do you really believe so much has been betrayed?" Hitler cast him a pitying look. "All our defeats in the east are solely the result of treachery"—and he spoke with deep conviction. At 1 A.M., Hitler dismissed the two stenographers, Kurt Peschel and Hans Jonuschat, so that they too could catch that night's plane south. As the general also departed, Ambassador Walther Hewel stuck his head around the door. "Mein Führer, do you have any orders for me yet?" Hitler shook his head. Ribbentrop's representative exclaimed, "Mein Führer, the zero hour is about to strike! If you still plan to achieve anything by political means, it's high time now!" Hitler replied with an exhausted air, "Politics? I'm through with politics. It sickens me. When I'm dead you'll have more than enough politics to contend with."

Outside, the all clear was just sounding. Puttkamer—his naval adjutant since 1935—was leaving, evacuating too General Schmundt's dangerous diaries in a suitcase; Saur joined him on the plane, with orders to organize in the Alps what arms production he could. About eighty other staff members and their families flew south that night. But in the early hours Martin Bormann cabled to the Berghof: "Wolf [i.e., Hitler] is staying here, because if anybody can master the situation here, it is only he."

The next morning, April 21, 1945, there was a hammering on Hitler's bedroom door. Linge shouted that Russian artillery had begun pouring shells into the heart of Berlin. Hitler shaved rapidly—"I can't stand anybody else hovering near my throat with an open razor," he used to say—and stepped into his study. General Burgdorf announced that the Russians had evidently brought up a heavy battery by rail across the Oder. Hitler telephoned orders to the OKL to identify and attack the battery at once; General Koller assured him: "The Russians have *no* railway bridges across the Oder. Perhaps they have captured and turned around one of our heavy batteries." Soon after, Koller came on the phone again; the offending Russian battery had been spotted from the observation post atop the towering antiaircraft bunker at the zoo. It was just eight miles away—at Marzahn.

Throughout the day, as the rain of shells on Berlin continued, a growing sense of isolation gripped Hitler's bunker. Koller was unable to brief Hitler on the Luftwaffe operations south of the city because of communications failures. Nothing had been heard from General Helmuth Weidling's Fifty-sixth Panzer Corps, due east of the city, since 8 P.M. the previous evening. According to one incredible report, Weidling himself had fled with his staff to the Olympic village *west* of Berlin; his arrest was ordered. The jets had been prevented by enemy fighter patrols from operating from Prague airfields against the Russian spearheads south of Berlin. Hitler angrily phoned Koller. "Then the jets are quite useless, the Luftwaffe is quite superfluous!" Infuriated by a Saar industrialist's letter with further disclosures about the Luftwaffe, Hitler again angrily called up Koller. "The entire Luftwaffe command ought to be strung up!" and he slammed the phone down. Heinrici—ordered to report in person to the shelter that day—asked to be excused as he was "completely overburdened." He successfully avoided having to look his Führer in the eye ever again.

During the afternoon Hitler began planning a last attempt at plugging the widening breach torn in Heinrici's front between Eberswalde and Werneuchen, northeast of Berlin. An *ad hoc* battle group under the bullet-headed SS General Felix Steiner must—like a sliding door—push south during the night from Eberswalde to Werneuchen; if Steiner succeeded, Zhukov's advanced forces north of Berlin would be cut off. But north of Eberswalde the Soviet Marshal Rokossovski had now breached the Oder front sector held by General von Manteuffel's Third Panzer Army, and Hitler's detailed order to Steiner, issued about 5 P.M., had an hysterical undertone:

> Any officers failing to accept this order without reservations are to be arrested and shot at once. You will account with your life for the execution of this order. The fate of the German capital depends on the success of your mission.

Krebs repeated this to the over-busy Heinrici by telephone, but Heinrici was also preoccupied with salvaging his right flank—the Ninth Army's flank corps —from Russian encirclement at Fürstenwalde. "All I can manage now is to pull it back *south* of the string of lakes southeast of Berlin," Heinrici warned. This was tantamount to abandoning Berlin. As for the Steiner attack, if the Führer insisted on it, then Heinrici asked to be replaced as Steiner's superior.

Hitler insisted, but did not replace him; perhaps Krebs did not report the conversation to him, for Hitler now pinned all his hopes on Steiner's attack. At 9 P.M. he learned that a battalion of the "Hermann Göring" Division was still defending the Reichsmarschall's abandoned stately home at Karinhall. He ordered the force handed to Steiner, and when Koller plaintively telephoned at 10:30 P.M. to ask where Steiner was, the Führer snatched the phone from Krebs's hand and rasped, "The Luftwaffe is to transfer every man available for ground fighting in the north to Steiner. Any commander holding men back will have breathed his last breath within five hours. . . . You yourself will pay with your life unless every last man is thrown in." Krebs confirmed this. "Everybody into the attack from Eberswalde to the south!"—and then hung up.

What orders Heinrici now issued to Steiner we do not know. But even Steiner was no fool, and to attack Zhukov's flank with a motley collection of demoralized, ill-armed, and undermunitioned troops would be courting disaster. He stalled while ostensibly girding himself for the attack.

The SS general's inactivity—to put the best possible interpretation on it—was the last straw for Hitler after Sepp Dietrich's fiasco in Hungary. In the narrow confines of his bunker, the Führer suffered an apparent nervous breakdown on April 22, as the Russians closed in from the east, north, and south on Berlin's outer ring of defense. Little now stood between Berlin and a seemingly inevitable defeat. Although crippled by 90 percent power failures, Daimler-Benz, Alkett, and the other arms factories were still sending their remaining tanks and assault guns straight to the nearest front line. But fuel and ammunition were running out, and there was already heavy street fighting in the suburbs. The Russians were in Köpenick and approaching Spandau. By evening they might well be fighting in the government quarter itself. This was the military position as Krebs finally secured Hitler's authorization for the garrison at Frankfurt-on-Oder to abandon that city to the enemy as well.

The war conference on April 22 began routinely at about 3 P.M. First Goebbels telephoned, and later Ribbentrop; but then Hitler asked about the operation which had obviously been in the foreground of his mind all night—Steiner's counterattack in the north. An SS authority assured him the attack had begun well, but Hitler mistrustfully asked the Luftwaffe to check; within the hour General Koller came on the phone with word that Steiner had not yet begun his attack and would not begin before nightfall. This betrayal and deceit by the SS, of all people, shook Hitler to the core.[4] He asked if the Luftwaffe troops had duly come under Steiner's command; General Christian replied that they had still not received any orders from Steiner. Hitler straightened up and purpled. He suspected a *fait accompli,* to force him to leave Berlin. His eyes bulged. "That's it,"

[4]Steiner wrote in postwar memoirs that he had decided against the relief attack as it was pointless.

he shouted. "How am I supposed to direct the war in such circumstances! The war's lost! But if you gentlemen imagine I'll leave Berlin now, then you've another think coming. I'd sooner put a bullet in my brains!" Everybody stared. Hitler abruptly stalked out, while the adjutant Otto Günsche started after him, calling out, "But, mein Führer . . ." Walther Hewel telephoned Foreign Minister Ribbentrop in extreme agitation: "The Führer's had a nervous breakdown—he's going to shoot himself!"

Hitler ordered a telephone call put through to Goebbels. When the propaganda minister's voice came on the line, he dictated to him an announcement: "I have decided to stay to the end of the battle in Berlin." He ordered Goebbels to bring his family to the shelter and sent for Julius Schaub, his lifelong factotum. By the time Schaub hobbled in, Hitler had recovered some of his composure. "Schaub—we must destroy all the documents here at once. Get some gasoline." He fumbled with his ring of safe keys, handed them to Schaub, and went into the tiny bedroom. While Schaub opened the small safe at the foot of the bed and stuffed its contents into a brown suitcase on the bed, Hitler took his lightweight 6.35-millimeter Walther pistol from his trouser pocket and exchanged it for the more lethal 7.65-millimeter Walther from the bedside table. The bulging suitcase was carried upstairs; from the upstairs safes more suitcases were filled, and then emptied into a crater in the garden. For a while Hitler stood with Schaub, watching his collection of memoirs, memoranda, and secret letters from world statesmen consumed by the flames. "Richelieu once said, give me five lines one man has penned!" Hitler lamented afterward. "What I have lost! My dearest memories! But what's the point—sooner or later you've got to get rid of all that stuff." He indicated that Schaub must leave for Munich and the Berghof and destroy the papers there too.[5] But first there was something he wanted to dictate—evidently something for posterity.

Hitler's anguished staff realized that he intended to remain in Berlin and brave the coming storm. "I have been betrayed by those I trusted most," he declaimed. "I'm going to stay here in Berlin, the capital of our crusade against bolshevism, and direct its defense myself." Goebbels, Bormann, Keitel, and Jodl begged him to reconsider. Dönitz and Himmler telephoned. Ribbentrop arrived, but was not even given a hearing. Keitel cornered Hitler alone but was interrupted almost at once. "I know what you're going to say: It's time to take a *Ganzer Entschluss!* I've taken it already. I'm going to defend Berlin to the bitter end. Either I restore my command here in the capital—assuming Wenck keeps the Americans off my

[5] I have reason to believe that Schaub did not complete this latter task but sold Hitler's papers to a former magistrate now living on Lake Starnberg in Bavaria. This gentleman has so far proved unapproachable.

back and throws them back over the Elbe—or I go down here in Berlin with my troops fighting for the symbol of the Reich." He felt that if he had stayed in East Prussia in November, the Russians would never have got through there. That was why, he disclosed to the furious field marshal, he had just ordered his decision to stay in Berlin announced to the people; he could not change his mind now.

Jodl joined the argument and pointed out that if at the last moment Hitler committed suicide in Berlin, the German army would be leaderless. (He also candidly explained that given the Führer's trembling hands he was too infirm to handle a rifle or bazooka in the street fighting and that in any case there was the danger that he might be captured.) Hitler called Martin Bormann in, and ordered him, Keitel, and Jodl to fly to Berchtesgaden that night to continue the war with Göring as acting Führer. All three refused. Somebody objected that there was not one German soldier who would be willing to fight for the Reichsmarschall. Hitler retorted, "There's not much fighting left to be done. And when it comes to negotiating, the Reichsmarschall will be better at that than I."

It was nearly 5 P.M., and the Russians had now taken the Silesia station. The Führer's bunker vibrated with the distant echoes of exploding shells. His petrified staff was clustered in the passageway, many of them expecting to hear pistol shots announcing that Hitler had abandoned them. In a private aside to Eva Braun, General Burgdorf put their chances now at only 10 percent. But Jodl argued on —pointing out that Hitler still held powerful trump cards in the form of Schörner's undefeated army group and the armies on the Elbe and in Norway. He reminded Hitler of the demarcation line shown on the captured "Eclipse" maps and suggested that now they should swing Wenck's Twelfth Army around from west to east and use it to relieve Berlin. Hitler shrugged. "Do whatever you want!" Secretly he may have been relieved, like a convict granted a last-minute reprieve. Perhaps, as Jodl argued, *now* the Allies would take his anti-Bolshevik intent seriously. Keitel announced that he would drive in person to give the necessary orders to Wenck that night. Hitler ordered a hearty meal prepared for the field marshal before he set out.

Hitler was not appalled at the prospect of imminent death. At an August 1944 war conference he had told his generals he was almost looking forward to it, just as an artisan savors the coming of the evening, when he can set his gnarled hands to rest; in death Hitler looked for "a release from my sorrows and sleepless nights and from this nervous suffering. It takes only the fraction of a second—then one is cast free from all that and rests in eternal peace." Ever since World War I he had lived on borrowed time. Besides, as he told Schörner, his death might remove the last obstacle preventing the Allies from making common cause with Germany. If Model could find the courage to take his own life, so would he; he, Hitler, was no Paulus. "Did not Varus command his slave: 'Now kill me!' " he noted in a comparison to the Roman general who had led three legions to their destruction.

He gruffly instructed Eva Braun and the two remaining secretaries to get changed and fly south. "It's all over—it's quite hopeless." Eva took both his hands in hers. "But you know I am going to stay here with you!" Hitler's eyes glistened, and he did something nobody had seen him do before—he kissed her lightly on the lips. Frau Junge chimed in, "I'll stay too!" and Frau Christian echoed her. "I wish my generals were as brave as you," Hitler replied.

Despite a telephone call from his liaison officer, Hermann Fegelein, Himmler had failed to show up at the shelter, evidently fearing from what Fegelein told him that he would be arrested for SS General Steiner's passivity; Fegelein was sent to meet him halfway but failed to return. Instead Himmler's doctor, Karl Gebhardt, a potbellied, bespectacled Bavarian, arrived about 11 P.M.; he pleaded with Hitler to leave or at least to let the women and children sheltering in the adjacent Voss Bunker escape under Red Cross cover. Hitler learned that Himmler had a battalion of six hundred SS troops for his own safety outside Berlin; he invited Himmler through Gebhardt to contribute them to the defense of the Chancellery. Some time after, Himmler's chief lieutenant, General Gottlob Berger, arrived. Hitler repeated to him his reproaches about the SS's disloyalty and asked Berger to go to Bavaria to crush the dissident and separatist movements stirring there and in Württemberg and Austria. "Everybody has deceived me! Nobody has been telling me the truth! The Wehrmacht has lied to me! Even the SS has left me in the lurch!" His last instruction to Berger before the latter flew south was to round up as many British and American officer-prisoners as possible and transport them under guard to the Alpine Redoubt—as hostages; though for what purpose even Hitler did not seem clear.

Under cover of darkness, still more of his staff left Berlin. General Koller flew to Bavaria. Morell came to the shelter, clutching his heart and gasping that he needed a change of climate; he offered Hitler a last injection before he left, a morphine pick-me-up, but Hitler suspected that a plot might be afoot to drug him and evacuate him from Berlin by force. He contemptuously dismissed the gaudily bedecked professor. "You can take off that uniform and go back to your practice in the Kurfürstendamm!" Morell chose Munich instead and flew out that night. Hitler sent out the remaining two staff stenographers as well; their orders were to take the last shorthand records to the "outside world."

Hitler's press officer, Heinz Lorenz, was instructed to take down the remaining historic war conferences as best he could. His fragmentary notes—which begin with Keitel's exhausted return with Jodl from the battlefield at 3 P.M. on April 23—reveal the growing desperation at Hitler's shelter. East of Berlin the Fifty-sixth Panzer Corps had vanished without trace, as had General Weidling, its commander. "It is all so abominable! When you come to think it over, what's the point of living on!" exclaimed Hitler. Steiner had made no discernible move with his 25th Panzer-Grenadier and 7th Panzer divisions at Eberswalde, north of the capital. The Russians had swarmed across the Havel River between Oranienburg and Spandau—unless the Havel lakes could be defended, the city would be completely encircled at any moment.

The situation on Germany's other fronts no longer occupied Hitler. With tanks swarming as far as the eye could see toward the heart of Berlin along the Landsberg Chaussee from the east—and the new "Stalin" tanks at that, virtu-ally impregnable to German shells—the bunker conferences devolved only on the defenses of Berlin. Hitler's last stratagem began unfolding. At noon Goeb-bels's ministry released the news. "The Führer is in Berlin. . . . Our leadership has resolved to remain in Berlin and defend the Reich capital to the end." Perhaps if Stalin knew that Hitler was still in Berlin, his armies might over-reach themselves and suffer the same kind of defeat Hitler himself had suffered at Moscow. Lorenz recorded Hitler's belief thus: "The enemy now knows I am here. They will do all they can to concentrate on us. That gives us an excellent opportunity of luring them into an ambush. But this depends on all our people realizing the importance of this hour and genuinely obeying the orders they get from above; they must be honest about it! This business up here"—indicating Steiner on the map—"was downright dishonest! Steiner had too many nagging doubts about the defenses confronting him." General Krebs interjected, "I be-lieve we still have four days' time." "In four days we'll know the outcome," agreed Hitler.

The "ambush" to which Hitler referred was the plan Keitel and Jodl had proposed—for the army on the Elbe and Mulde fronts, facing the Americans, to be turned around, to link up south of Berlin with Busse's Ninth Army and then strike northward toward Potsdam and Berlin, mopping up the elite Russian troops they thereby cut off. Wenck's objective would be the autobahn at Ferch, near Potsdam. At the same time the Forty-first Panzer Corps—commanded by the reliable General Rudolf Holste, an old regimental comrade of Keitel's—would be brought back across the Elbe, to counterattack between Spandau and Oranienburg; Steiner was to turn over his mechanized divisions (the 25th Panzer-Grenadiers and the 7th Panzer) to Holste, northwest of Berlin.

The realist in Hitler whispered that defeat was inevitable, and he made no secret of this to his intimates, even if he felt constrained to put on a braver face to his generals. Eva Braun wrote that April 23: "The Führer himself has lost all hope of a happy ending. But while we still live all of us have hope, including me."

Later she added: "At present things are said to be looking up. General Burgdorf who gave us only a 10 percent chance yesterday has raised the odds to 50–50 today. Perhaps things may turn out well after all!" Hitler drank chocolate with Goebbels's five little girls and son Helmuth, who had now moved into Morell's quarters. Helmuth read aloud his school essay on the Führer's birthday. Helga squawked, "You stole that from Papa!" "You mean Papa stole it from me!" retorted Helmuth, to the delight of the adult listeners. The children seemed oblivious of the fate their parents planned for them.

Before Keitel returned to Wenck's headquarters, he came in to see Hitler and quietly inquired whether any talks at all were proceeding with the enemy. Hitler replied that before he could start talks he must win "one more" victory—the Battle for Berlin. He disclosed that he had opened up one channel to the Allies through Italy and that he had asked Ribbentrop to discuss further steps with him that evening. Ribbentrop's only proposal of substance was to have top Czech industrialists flown that night to France, where they would attempt to persuade the Americans to protect Bohemia and Moravia from the Bolsheviks. "The Führer has agreed to this," Ribbentrop informed Karl-Hermann Frank by letter. For the first time Hitler now admitted to Ribbentrop that the war was lost—but he insisted that he had been right all along, that Britain would have done better to have fought at his side and not against him. He dictated to Ribbentrop four secret negotiation points to put to the British if he got the chance, points vital to the future of Europe. If the Continent was to survive in a world dominated by bolshevism, then somehow London and Berlin must bury the hatchet between them. He instructed Ribbentrop to write secretly to Churchill in this sense. "You will see," Hitler predicted. "My spirit will arise from the grave. One day people will see that I was right."

When Ribbentrop left—eventually attaching his diplomatic staff to General Wenck's Twelfth Army staff—an adjutant announced that Albert Speer had just arrived in the Chancellery, having made a venturesome landing by light plane on the East-West Axis across the Tiergarten after a flight escorted by a whole fighter squadron from Rechlin. Eva Braun, who like Hitler had been troubled by the recurring rumors of Speer's inexplicable behavior, greeted him warmly. "I knew you'd return—you won't desert the Führer!" Speer grinned. "I'm leaving Berlin again tonight!" According to Julius Schaub—who also left that night—when Hitler asked his friend's opinion on his decision to fight the battle for Berlin to its end, Speer's almost brutal advice was that it was better to die there than in his weekend cottage on the Obersalzberg, that is, if the Führer attached any importance to the verdict of history. The remark reveals much about Speer's own motives. Hitler, unaware that Speer had secretly arranged with Heinrici for Berlin to be abandoned to the Russians, agreed.

After the war conference, Bormann brought to Hitler a startling telegram just received from Göring at Berchtesgaden. Göring, it seemed, was seizing power.

> Mein Führer!
> In view of your decision to remain in the fortress of Berlin, are you agreed that I immediately assume overall leadership of the Reich as your Deputy, in accordance with your decree of June 29, 1941, with complete freedom of action at home and abroad?
> Unless an answer is given by 10 P.M. I will assume you have been deprived of your freedom of action. I shall then regard the conditions laid down by your Decree as being met, and shall act in the best interests of the people and Fatherland.
> You know my feelings for you in these the hardest hours of my life. I cannot express them adequately.
> May God protect you and allow you to come here soon despite everything.
> > Your loyal Hermann Göring.

Bormann no doubt read this aloud to Hitler in tones worthy of a public prosecutor. But that Ribbentrop and Speer, Göring's other archenemies, were by chance also in Hitler's bunker was a double misfortune for the Reichsmarschall. Ribbentrop had received from Göring a telegram asking him to fly down immediately unless ordered to the contrary by 10 P.M. Keitel also heard from Göring. Somehow Hitler learned that Göring's plan was to fly to the American supreme commander, General Eisenhower, and ask for peace terms. Hitler immediately cabled Göring that he alone would decide when the Decree of June 29, 1941, took effect; Göring was forbidden to undertake any steps in the direction he had hinted at. The Führer then ordered Göring and his staff on the Obersalzberg placed under house arrest. The shelter was in an uproar over Göring's "treachery." Speer undoubtedly fanned the flames, for that same day he wrote to General Galland, now a jet-fighter squadron commander in Bavaria, enclosing a copy of Göring's telegram to Ribbentrop. "This telegram is clear. The Führer has reacted to it accordingly and ordered Göring's arrest. I request you and your comrades to do everything to prevent an airplane flight by Göring as discussed."[6]

Thus with characteristic hesitancy and with prodding from Bormann, Hitler took the decision with which he had been grappling since September 1944—

---

[6]Speer does not refer to this in his memoirs. The only acceptable explanation is that if Göring tried to fly to Eisenhower, Galland was to have him shot down. Speer evidently feared Göring would get the credit for peace moves, leaving high and dry his own hesitant preparations—which included a radio speech prerecorded at Hamburg ordering the German people to stop fighting.

dismissing Göring. But even then he spared his feelings, telegraphing the Reichs-marschall: "Your actions are punishable by the death sentence, but because of your valuable services in the past I will refrain from instituting proceedings if you will voluntarily relinquish your offices and titles. Otherwise steps will have to be taken." Göring hastened to comply. Hitler meanwhile ordered General Robert von Greim from Munich to Berlin; Koller was also instructed to return, and the Luftwaffe's General Josef Kammhuber was sent for as well. Greim's take-off was, however, prevented by an air raid; Koller pleaded ill-health, and Kammhuber also avoided coming to the capital. The Luftwaffe was in chaos anyway. General Galland's fighter squadron had somehow amassed ninety-five new Me-262 jets on its Munich airfield, but the squadron had only twenty pilots; on the other hand, the crack jet-fighter wing JG.7 had only twenty Me-262s left and could not obtain replacements. Nothing had prevented the British bomber squadrons from execut-ing a precision attack in broad daylight on the Obersalzberg early on April 25, leaving the Berghof a smoking ruin.

The last week of Hitler's leadership was plagued by the crumbling communica-tions system. From April 24, 1945, onward, it is difficult to relate the orders emanating from his bomb- and shell-shattered Chancellery building to either the war information reaching him or the actions of his commanders in the field. On April 24, Hitler himself contributed to the command chaos by an order upending the existing command structure and subordinating the General Staff's eastern front to the OKW operations staff. But three days later Hitler's only radiotele-phone link with Jodl's headquarters was silenced, and Hitler could communicate with the outside world only via a telephone to the admiralty's still-functioning signals room. Jodl's clear instructions to the armies were repeated by Hitler on April 24: Generals Holste, Wenck, Schörner, and Busse were to speed up their relief attacks toward Berlin, from northwest, southwest, and south, respectively, and "restore a broad land contact with Berlin again, thereby bringing the Battle of Berlin to a victorious conclusion." But apart from Wenck and Schörner, Hitler's commanders no longer even paid lip service to his authority—they were driven only by the compulsion to escape the Russian grasp themselves before the final collapse came.

Apart from word that part of the Ninth Army had been encircled southeast of Berlin, there was no news of the army until Weidling, the "missing" comman-der of its Fifty-sixth Panzer Corps, whose arrest for desertion Hitler had ordered, reached Berlin's outskirts and the public telephone; he then stormed into the Chancellery to establish his innocence. On April 24, Hitler willingly appointed this fiery general battle-commandant of Berlin.

Weidling set about reorganizing the capital's defenses, laying down new signals networks and dismissing indifferent sector commanders; but his task was nigh impossible. Hitler and Goebbels had optimistically sacrificed the capital's resources of men, ammunition, and gasoline to the forward defenses on the Oder, and little now remained for Berlin. According to Keitel, a decamping army commandant had blown up Berlin's last major ammunition dump at Krampnitz. Weidling would have little infantry, no artillery, and hardly any tanks. Apart from the shattered remnants of his own corps, the coming street battles would be fought between trained, professional Russian combat troops with the glint of final victory in their eyes, and a few thousand antiaircraft soldiers, Volkssturm men, and police armed with captured rifles, broken-down tanks, or makeshift rocket-launchers. About 2,700 youths—hardly more than children—had been mustered into a "tank-killer brigade"; Hitler assigned this Hitler Youth offering to the defense of the bridges across which the relief armies must march into Berlin. Late on April 24, Hitler appealed to the navy for troops; from Flensburg, Admiral Dönitz promised to airlift 2,000 of his best sailors and fortress troops into Berlin in the next forty-eight hours and to put 3,500 more of his most cherished fleet personnel—including crews trained to operate the new secret U-boats—on standby for the fight; unless Berlin won this last battle—which Hitler described to Dönitz as "a battle for Germany's whole future" outranking all other theaters in importance—those U-boats would never operate.

Dönitz kept this promise—unlike Himmler, who had eventually parted with only half his personal security battalion. (According to stenographer Ewald Reynitz, in these last days of his life Hitler refused to speak to Himmler even over the telephone and flatly forbade Himmler to participate in the war conferences.) Even Ribbentrop courageously requested permission to take up arms in Berlin. But Hitler forbade this: Ribbentrop knew too many secrets to be allowed to fall into enemy hands; and Walther Hewel—whom Hitler urged with the rest of his staff to take poison before the Russians could capture them[7]—telegraphed the foreign minister in Mecklenburg: "The Führer appreciates your intentions but has turned you down. Until the ring encircling Berlin has been broken open or until you receive further instructions, you are to stand by outside the combat area." Hewel added significantly: "I have no political information whatever." Schörner, whose army group had just recaptured Bautzen and Weissenberg, south of Berlin, inflicting heavy losses on the Russians, also began moving northward toward the capital. "The attack by Schörner's army group proves," Dönitz was signaled by Hitler's staff on April 26, "that given the will, we are still capable of beating the enemy even today." These distant victories glowed faintly through the thickening gloom of the communications breakdowns besetting Hitler's shelter.

---

[7]Hewel, Krebs, Burgdorf, the Goebbels family, and many others followed Hitler's request.

"The British and Americans along the Elbe are holding back," Hitler observed. ". . . I think the time has now come when out of a sheer instinct for self-preservation they must act against this bloated proletarian Colossus, this Bolshevik Moloch. . . . If I can win through here and hang on to the capital, perhaps hope will spring in British and American hearts that with our Nazi Germany they may after all have some chance against this entire danger. And the only man capable of this is me. . . . But I am only Führer as long as I can really *lead*. I can't lead if I go south and sit on some mountain, but only if I have authority over armies and those armies obey me. Give me one victory here—however high the price—and then I'll regain the right to eliminate the deadweights who constantly obstruct. After that I will work with the generals who've proved their worth." Later he again digressed on this theme. "First I must set an example to everybody I blamed for retreating, by not retreating myself. It is possible that I will die here, but then at least I shall have died an honorable death." Hitler proclaimed that this Battle of Berlin was as important as the 1683 Battle of Vienna, which had turned the tide of the Turkish conquest of Europe.

The first battalion of Dönitz's naval troops arrived, and Weidling threw them straight into the fight. The makeshift hospital in the Voss Bunker next to Hitler's bunker filled with casualties. The streets were strewn with burning vehicles and tanks. The government quarter was under nonstop bombardment by artillery and bombers. But Weidling reported to Hitler that it was proving difficult to demolish bridges—for example along the Teltow Canal defense line—because Speer's staff had decamped with all the bridge plans. Speer had also fought tooth and nail against the dismantling of the bronze lampposts along the East-West Axis, as Hitler had ordered, to prepare an emergency landing strip. (Speer had protested to Weidling's predecessor: "You seem to forget I am responsible for the reconstruction of Berlin.")

During April 26 spirits soared in Hitler's bunker, as the news of Wenck's approaching army and Schörner's successes trickled in. That evening General Greim limped into the shelter with a female admirer, having been shot in the leg as he piloted his light plane to the East-West Axis and made a crash-landing on the boulevard. His injuries were tended, then he was put to bed in a room opposite Hitler's conference room. For many hours Hitler sat at his bedside, morosely describing Göring's "ultimatum" and the history of the Luftwaffe's failure—only General Koller had dared tell him the truth about the technical inferiority of German planes. At 10 P.M., German radio broadcast Greim's promotion to field marshal and his appointment as Göring's successor. Hitler urged suicide capsules on Greim and his woman friend, and instructed them—if worse came to worst —to arrange their own cremation so that the Russians would find nothing. "I firmly believed that Berlin could be saved on the banks of the Oder. Everything we had here was moved forward to that position. You must believe me—when all our efforts there failed I was the most stunned of all," he mused. But Wenck was now approaching Berlin. "If he can relieve Berlin, we shall fall back to a new line and fight on." He ordered his new Luftwaffe commander to concentrate the Messerschmitt jet squadrons around Prague.

At night Hitler was kept awake by the shell fire and by his own vivid memories. This was Stalingrad all over again, but this time the miracle would happen. "Imagine! Like wildfire the word spreads throughout Berlin: one of our armies has broken through from the west and restored contact with us!" How could Stalin hope to reduce a great city of four million people with only four hundred tanks, especially if fifty were being knocked out each day? "The Russians have already exhausted their strength in crossing the Oder, particularly the northern army group [Zhukov's]."

Against this Hitler had to set his own virtual helplessness and lack of precise information on the battle. Schörner's forces were approaching, and within one day this pressure should begin embarrassing the Russians in the south. According to Keitel, General Holste's battle group in the northwest had gained ground at Nauen and Kremmen and would gather its last reinforcements for its main attack early on the twenty-eighth. Hitler impatiently told Krebs, "It's high time they got a move on!" General Wenck's relief offensive from the southwest—three well-fueled divisions under General Karl-Erik Koehler—had already reached the Schwielow lake, and during the morning the Party announced that it had reached Potsdam, thus attaining the tactical objective laid down four days before. But a tough ring of Soviet troops still barred the way to Berlin.

Hitler realized that time was running out fast. At 5 A.M. on April 27 a big Russian push along the Hohenzollerndamm Boulevard had begun. As Goebbels nervously put it: "I keep getting this nightmare picture: Wenck is at Potsdam, and here the Russians are pouring into Potsdamer Platz!" "—And I'm here at Potsdamer Platz, not Potsdam!" agreed Hitler uneasily. His eyes were transfixed by the colored arrows marking the relief armies on the map. He recognized the problem his dwindling authority was causing. Wenck had the drive, the gasoline, and the loyalty to get to Potsdam, but he lacked the tanks to smash the Russian armor. General Busse's Ninth Army—encircled southeast of Berlin—had the tanks, but its westward movement seemed designed to *bypass* Berlin to the south. Hitler was puzzled by this defiance of his orders.[8] Late on the twenty-sixth he had

---

[8]Busse had decided to drive with his army remnants toward the American lines—unaware at that time of Hitler's plan to denude the Elbe battlefront in favor of Berlin.

radioed to Jodl: "Make it clear to Ninth Army that it is to wheel sharply north with Twelfth Army to take weight off Battle for Berlin." Throughout the twenty-seventh he speculated on this puzzle. "I just don't understand the direction of its attack. Busse's driving into a complete vacuum." "If he had pushed northwest instead, and covered as much distance as he has now, he would have accomplished much more." "Wenck and the Ninth Army would already have linked up." And, late that day, it occurred to him at last why the Ninth Army had pleaded its radio failure. "If there's a long radio silence, it is always the sign that things are going badly." "It's impossible to command if every plan that's drawn up is adapted by every army commander as he sees fit." "What's happened now is just what I predicted: they've been encircled."

North of Berlin, the generals' disobedience to orders was even more blatant. Heinrici's remaining Oder sector, south of Stettin, had collapsed under the weight of Marshal Rokossovski's attack. Since noon on April 26, Heinrici had begged Jodl to allow General Steiner's two armored divisions to repair the damage. But Hitler and Jodl mistrusted Steiner, and these divisions had been ordered to support Holste's more promising relief attack instead. This order was ignored. Heinrici assured Keitel he was holding a line from Angermünde to Ücker-heim, but when the field marshal set out on a surprise visit to the battle-field he found the front line only a few miles away, in the midst of what was a well-prepared retreat; and the 5th Light Infantry Division—although its troops were still eager for combat with the Russians—was being pulled back westward because "its officers have decided not to fight any longer." Keitel telephoned Hitler about Heinrici's deceit. Far from holding the line, Heinrici and Manteuffel —commanding the Third Panzer Army on the breached Oder sector—were deliberately herding their troops across Mecklenburg toward the haven of the Allied lines. At about 5 P.M. Jodl radiotelephoned his grim decision to Hitler: Steiner's two armored divisions would have to be thrown northward—away from Berlin—into the southern flank of the Russian spearheads pursuing Manteuffel's troops.

Up to now Hitler had been sustained by the hope of relief. "If we can just hold on two, three, or four days more here, Wenck's army may arrive and perhaps even Busse's too," he had said. Admiral Voss had assured him: "Wenck's coming, mein Führer! The only question is—can he manage by himself!" And Hitler had responded, "I'll sleep a bit better tonight. I don't want to be awakened unless a Russian tank's outside my sleeping cubicle. Then I must be given time to do what has to be done." But the new hysterical atmosphere created by Jodl's radiotele-phone message can be judged from the words Martin Bormann jotted in his diary:

> The divisions marching to relieve us have been halted by Himmler and Jodl!
> We shall stand by and die with our Führer, loyal unto death. If others think

they must act "out of superior judgment," then they are sacrificing the Führer. And their loyalty—Devil take them!—is no better than their sense of "honor"!

A premature dusk had fallen over Berlin outside the shelter, as smoke clouds and mortar dust blotted out the sun. Gatow and Tempelhof airfields had been cut off. Junkers transport planes were redirected to the Axis landing strip, but the Russians had strung out antiaircraft batteries along the flight path and many planes were lost. A hundred of Dönitz's crack troops had been sent to the Chancellery for Hitler's personal protection. Camouflaged by swastika pennants, four enemy tanks had reached Wilhelms Platz before they were detected and destroyed. "Identification regulations are to be strictly obeyed!" Hitler ordered. The Russians announced that they were bringing up 406-millimeter and 370-millimeter mortars to reduce the last citadel of Hitler's capital. Hitler handed his adjutants more of the brass-encased cyanide capsules, to use if absolutely necessary. When the time came he would order a general breakout toward Wenck's army at Potsdam. He disclosed privately to Colonel von Below, his Luftwaffe adjutant ever since 1937: "Only my wife and I will stay behind." He compared Eva Braun's loyalty with the gross disloyalty displayed by Göring and Himmler —whom he intuitively blamed for Steiner's disobedience.

At the late night conference, General Krebs reassured Hitler that the battle lines in Berlin itself were stable again. Hitler Youth units were holding a big bridgehead south of the Pichelsdorf bridge in anticipation of Wenck's arrival; isolated trucks from Wenck's army had already broken through. But the first Russian snipers were roaming Potsdamer Platz and Hitler pointed out: "The subway and streetcar tunnels are a source of danger." Transport planes with more troops were standing by, but one had just crashed and was blocking the Axis Boulevard. Colonel von Below announced that the first air drops of ammunition had begun.

A ticking clock coming over the radio loudspeakers warned that enemy bombers were still over Germany. Hitler brooded on the evening's bulletin that Benito Mussolini had just been captured alive by Italian Communist guerrillas. He could hear the distant singing of the Goebbels children in sixfold chorus as they prepared for bed. During the evening he had unpinned his own golden Party medallion and bestowed it on their red-eyed mother, Magda. She wrote: "Our children are wonderful! . . . Never a whimper or word of complaint. The thudding of shells is getting even on my nerves, but the little ones soothe their younger sisters, and their presence here is a boon to us because now and again they manage to prise a smile from the Führer." They told "Uncle Hitler" they were longing for the day when the new soldiers he had promised would come and drive the Russians away. For their sake Hitler hoped too, though he himself had long decided to stay.

"In this city I have had the right to command others; now I must heed the commands of Fate. Even if I could save myself here, I will not do so. The captain too goes down with his ship."

At 3 A.M.—it was now April 28—Krebs telephoned Keitel at the OKW's field headquarters. "The Führer is most anxious to know about the relief attack west of Oranienburg. What's the news? Is it making any headway? The Führer doesn't *want* Steiner to be commander there!! Hasn't Holste taken over there yet? If help doesn't reach us in the next thirty-six or forty-eight hours, it'll be too late!!!" Keitel replied that he was going to see Steiner in person. Some hours later Hitler learned that a small separatist uprising had begun in Bavaria; a Munich radio station had been seized, and it was broadcasting seditious proclamations to the local workers and foreigners.

It is unlikely that Hitler slept that night. The Chancellery was under direct and heavy shellfire. The Munich separatists had been bloodily suppressed by local forces, but in Berlin the Russians had now penetrated the last lines of defense. The Führer restlessly paced the bunker passageways, gripping a Berlin street map that was disintegrating in his clammy hands. Over three hundred Russian tanks had been destroyed in the street fighting. Busse's Ninth Army had at last linked up with General Wenck's Twelfth, but both were beyond the limits of exhaustion. Moreover, by 4:30 P.M. General Krebs had learned from Jodl the full extent of Heinrici's disobedience north of Berlin: Keitel had discovered the southern flank of Manteuffel's Third Panzer Army retreating across the Schorf Heide in compliance with secret *orders* which Heinrici had concealed from both the OKW and Hitler. Steiner was covering this illicit retreat and doing nothing to seal off the breach at Prenzlau. Keitel was apoplectic with anger and instructed Heinrici and Manteuffel to meet him at a lonely crossroads to account for their actions. One thing was certain: Berlin's northern defenses were wide open.

Hitler had hardly seen Himmler's liaison officer SS General Fegelein, or the Gestapo chief, Müller, this last week. But on April 28 his staff began receiving erratic and surreptitious telephone calls from Fegelein. Hitler suspected he was absconding, and he debated with Greim the possibility that the Reichsführer SS was condoning this—which might have sinister implications. Late that afternoon Bormann showed him yet another stunning news report: Allied radio had proclaimed that Himmler had contacted the United States and Britain and guaranteed them Germany's unconditional surrender! But the Western Allies were insisting on including Russia in the surrender terms.

This bombshell caused a furor. Bormann sneered, "I always said *loyalty* has to be stamped on your heart and not on your belt buckle!" Fegelein's effects were searched and papers relating to Himmler's treachery were found, along with two money belts of gold sovereigns and other enemy currencies. Eva Braun, whose sister had married Fegelein, mournfully noted: "The Führer is spared nothing. With his life drawing to a close even the SS and his trusted Fegelein are deserting him." Fegelein's adjutant stated he had last seen him changing into civilian clothes at his Kurfürstendamm apartment; Bormann sent men out into the inferno to search for him. He cabled his Party headquarters in Munich at 8 P.M.: "Instead of spurring on the troops to fight us free with orders and appeals, just silence from the top men. Loyalty apparently yielding to disloyalty. We remain here. Reich Chancellery already in ruins."

Two hours later General Weidling, the city commandant, reported that the Russians were hammering Wenck's relief army into the ground. The situation in the city was desperate. Food and medical stores were exhausted. He read out an appeal by Professor Ferdinand Sauerbruch, of the Charité hospital, to consider the plight of the injured. Finally Weidling outlined his plan for a mass breakout by the remaining troops, but Hitler replied that he would not himself leave the Chancellery. His naval liaison admiral radioed to Dönitz: "We are holding on to the very end." At midnight Keitel's telegram arrived. At the crossroads rendezvous Heinrici had suavely promised to obey orders, but at 11:30 P.M. he admitted he had in fact ordered a further retreat; Keitel had dismissed him and his Chief of Staff General Ivo-Thilo von Trotha, who appeared to be equally guilty.[9] At about the same time Eva Braun was phoned by Fegelein. "Eva, you must abandon the Führer if you can't persuade him to leave Berlin. Don't be stupid, it's a matter of life and death now!" Within the hour he had been brought back to the bunker, still in civilian clothes. Hitler told Bormann to hand him over to SS General Wilhelm Mohnke, to help the fight for central Berlin; but Bormann and Günsche —Hitler's personal adjutant—pointed out that Fegelein would just run away again, so the Führer ordered him summarily court-martialed and executed.

"Our Reich Chancellery is reduced to rubble," wrote Bormann in his diary. " 'On dagger's edge the world now stands'! Treason and treachery by Himmler —unconditional surrender—announced abroad. Fegelein disgraced—the coward tried to clear out of Berlin in civilian clothes!" Hitler, reeling with suspicion, saw this as the origin of Steiner's failure too. Perhaps at this very moment Himmler was plotting to kill or kidnap him? Suddenly he mistrusted the cyanide capsules supplied by the SS's Dr. Stumpfegger. He sent for Professor Werner Haase from the Voss Bunker operating theater and ordered him to test a sample capsule on Blondi—the largest animal available in the shelter. The dog's jaws were forced

---

[9]It is hard to fault Dönitz's opinion that Heinrici and Trotha "should have been court-martialed, not just dismissed"; Keitel was surprised to find that Trotha gravitated to Speer's staff on his arrival in Flensburg.

open and an ampoule was broken inside them with pliers; a bitter almond smell wafted toward the expressionless Führer; the dog howled briefly and then stiffened. A short council followed on the best methods of suicide; then Hitler handed ampoules to the rest of his staff, apologizing for being unable to offer them no kinder farewell gift.

More Russian tanks were reported massing south of Potsdamer Platz for the assault on the Chancellery. Hitler was informed that Wenck's guns were already shelling the Russian positions here. While Eva Braun, Goebbels, and Hewel hastily wrote last letters to their relatives, a chalk-faced Hitler slumped on Field Marshal Greim's bed. "Our only hope is Wenck. We must throw in every plane we've got to cover his breakthrough." An Arado training plane had just made a brilliant landing on the shell-cratered Axis; Hitler ordered the injured Greim to betake himself and his female admirer to Rechlin air base to command the Luftwaffe attack—and to arrest Himmler, if his treason were found to be proved. The woman became hysterical, and both begged to stay and share Hitler's end. The Führer dismissed them with "God protect you." Bormann and Krebs signed a joint appeal to Wenck to break through as soon as he could, so as to furnish Hitler with a basis for political maneuver. But Hitler himself was already writing finis: Himmler's treachery and the failure of the relief divisions left him with no desire to live on.

With the shelter's concrete membranes reverberating under the blast of Russian shells, and a table being laid for eight in his small study, he sent for his youngest secretary the widowed Traudl Junge. "Perhaps I can just dictate something to you now." For a while Hitler stood at his usual midtable place, leaning on the now bare map-room table with both hands and staring at her shorthand pad. Suddenly he barked out: "My Political Testament" and began dictating without notes—part *pièce justificative,* part paean of praise for his brave troops' accomplishments against such odds. "From the sacrifice of our soldiers and my own comradeship with them unto death, we have sown a seed which one day in Germany's history will blossom forth into a glorious rebirth of the National Socialist movement and thus bring about a truly united nation." Even dictated under stress, and without notes, the document betrayed, at least in its drafting and construction, no trace of any mental disequilibrium. Hitler formally expelled Göring and Himmler from the Party and appointed Dönitz as his own successor; Speer was also sacked. Field Marshal Schörner—"the only man to shine as a real warlord on the entire eastern front," Hitler had sighed a day before —was appointed Commander in Chief of the German army.

It was about 2 A.M., April 29, 1945. Another notable event lay ahead, and this was at the forefront of Hitler's private testament, that he now dictated. "During my years of struggle I believed I ought not to engage in marriage; but now my mortal span is at its end I have resolved to take as my wife the woman who came to this city when it was already virtually under siege, after long years of true friendship, to link her fate with my own. It is her wish to go with me to her death, as my wife. This will make up for all I could not give her because of my work on behalf of my people." Hitler bequeathed his effects to the Party; or if it no longer existed, to the state. With neat realism he added that should the state also have been destroyed "further dispositions on my part would seem superfluous." He asked Martin Bormann as his executor and most loyal henchman to take care of his next of kin, his private staff and secretaries, his housekeeper, and Eva's mother.

Elsewhere in the shelter the small wedding party had assembled. A city official had been fetched from Goebbels's ministry as registrar, a slight, quiet-spoken man in Party uniform and a Volkssturm armband. Hitler signed with his most legible signature in months; Eva—wearing the black silk afternoon dress that was Hitler's favorite—signed more nervously. From time to time during the funereal wedding supper Hitler left to discuss with Goebbels and Bormann the constitution of the Cabinet with which Dönitz must carry forward the war against "the poisoner of all nations, international Jewry." Goebbels was included as Reich Chancellor, but Goebbels warned Hitler that he would not leave Berlin. Most of the rest were "moderates" like Seyss-Inquart, Schwerin von Krosigk, and Backe. Gauleiter Karl Hanke, still defending his embattled Breslau, was to replace Himmler as Reichsführer SS and chief of police.

Bormann, the new Party minister, was still transmitting strongly worded messages to Dönitz at Flensburg. "Foreign press reports fresh treason. The Führer expects you to strike like lightning and tough as steel against every traitor in north zone. Without fear or favor. Schörner, Wenck, and rest must prove their loyalty to the Führer by fastest relief of Führer. Bormann." In his diary he recorded Himmler's treason, Hitler's wedding, and the dictating of the political and private testaments. "The traitors Jodl, Himmler, and Steiner are abandoning us to the Bolsheviks! Yet another heavy barrage! Enemy reports state Americans penetrated Munich." By 4 A.M. Frau Junge had finished typing the testaments in triplicate (Hitler wanted to make certain that one copy reached the outside world). Hitler himself was still reminiscing softly with Goebbels about the exhilarating struggle for power and empire which was now approaching its end. Death would be a merciful release—and all the easier now that he had been betrayed by so many of the living.

Hitler's conferences over the next thirty-six hours were irregular and brief, for a Stygian information blackout was descending: his armies were silent and for days he had seen no diplomatic cables. The street fighting in Berlin could be followed only by ringing up telephone numbers at random. Often Russian voices answered. During the night, rain had grounded the OKW's aerial-carrying balloon, so VHF radiotelephone contact was interrupted. At noon on April 29, Jodl reported briefly that Wenck was at a standstill, but at 12:50 P.M. the VHF channel again went dead.

From now on the enemy news bulletins provided Hitler's main information on his own armies. Italian radio was monitored describing the scene as the corpses of Mussolini and a dozen other Fascist leaders "shot in the back" were strung up at the Standard Oil station in a Milan square. Admiral Voss signaled from the shelter to Dönitz at 4 P.M.: "All contact with army authorities outside cut off. Urgently request information on fighting outside Berlin via naval signals channel." Hitler's now idle liaison staff began edging toward the exits. Krebs's aide, Captain Gerhardt Boldt, suggested that he and two fellow officers attempt to contact the Twelfth Army. Hitler willingly dispatched them. "My regards to Wenck—and tell him to hurry, or it'll be too late!" The three sets of testaments were entrusted to three other hardy souls who were ordered to smuggle them out to Dönitz, Schörner, and to the Berghof. General Burgdorf wrote to Schörner: "The testament is to be published as soon as the Führer so orders or his death is confirmed."

Heavy fighting was going on at the Anhalt railroad station. With the tattered street map in his hand, Hitler spoke to his chauffeur, Erich Kempka, who had driven him on so many historic journeys since 1933. Kempka told him his motor pool was ferrying supplies to the troops guarding the Chancellery, from the Brandenburg Gate to Potsdamer Platz: "Their courage is exceptional. They're waiting for General Wenck's relief columns to arrive." Hitler calmly responded, "We're all waiting for Wenck." In his study he wrote a last letter to Keitel: the fight would soon end, he would commit suicide, and Dönitz would succeed him as Reich President; Keitel was to support the admiral to the end. "My people and Wehrmacht have given their all in this long hard struggle. The sacrifice has been immense. Many people have abused my trust in them. Disloyalty and betrayal have undermined our resistance throughout this war. This was why it was not granted to me to lead my people to victory." He refused to believe that such great sacrifice could have been in vain. "The aim must still be to win territory in the east for the German people."

The Russians were pushing down Saarlandstrasse and Wilhelmstrasse and were nearly at the air ministry. At 7:52 P.M. Hitler signaled five urgent questions to Jodl. "I am to be informed at once: 1. Where are Wenck's spearheads? 2. When do they attack? 3. Where is the Ninth Army? 4. In which direction is Ninth Army breaking through? 5. Where are Holste's spearheads?" Hours passed without any answer. Bormann issued two signals. The first reflected the ugly atmosphere of the bunker and read: "Our own impression is increasingly clear that for many days the divisions in Berlin battle zone have been marking time instead of hacking-out the Führer. We only receive information supervised, suppressed, or doctored by Teilhaus [Keitel]. We can only transmit via Teilhaus. Führer orders you to take rapid and ruthless action against all traitors." The second signal was briefer: "The Führer's alive and directing defense Berlin."

At the last battle conference on the twenty-ninth, General Weidling announced that there was heavy fighting at the nearby Potsdam Station. There were no bazookas left. Tanks could no longer be repaired. He predicted that the fighting would end within twenty-four hours. A long silence followed this. Hitler wearily asked Mohnke, the Citadel commandant, if he agreed; Mohnke said he did. With great effort, Hitler lifted himself from his chair and turned to go. Weidling asked what his troops should do when their ammunition ran out. Hitler replied, "I cannot permit the *surrender* of Berlin. Your men will have to break out in small groups." He restated this in a letter to Weidling and Mohnke during the night. Soon after, he received Keitel's telegram replying to his questions. It left no hope whatever that Berlin would be relieved. "1. Wenck's spearhead is stalled south of Schwielow lake. 2. Twelfth Army is therefore unable to continue attack to Berlin. 3. Bulk of Ninth Army encircled. 4. Holste's Corps forced onto defensive."

At Eva's suggestion, all the women in the Chancellery shelters—refugees fleeing the Russians, nurses from the Voss Bunker hospital, cooks, and officers' wives —were brought to one of the passages. His eyes bleary and unseeing, Hitler went and shook hands with them and spoke a few words in a low voice to each. One of the nurses began a hysterical speech, insisting that the Führer would bring them victory after all, but Hitler brusquely silenced her. "One must accept one's fate like a man." He knew he had taken a deliberate gamble by staying in Berlin; his gamble had failed. By morning, on April 30, 1945, he had decided to die at 3 P.M.

He shaved and dressed as punctiliously as ever, donning the olive-green shirt, and black shoes, socks, and trousers for the last time. Eva was pale but composed; she wore a blue dress with white trimmings and a favorite gold bracelet set with a green jewel which "meant a lot" to her. The Russians were now fighting in the subway tunnels under Friedrichstrasse and Vossstrasse; they were at Weidendamm bridge and on the edge of Potsdamer Platz, where a counterattack had begun.

Hitler sent for Bormann and then for Otto Günsche, his personal adjutant. He told them he and his wife would commit suicide that afternoon; Günsche was to ensure that both were really dead—by delivering coups de grâce if necessary— and then burn both bodies to ashes. "I would not want my body put on display in some waxworks in the future." His shelter was to remain intact. "I want the Russians to realize that I stayed here to the very last moment." Choking with emotion, Günsche replied, "Jawohl, mein Führer. I will see to it." Frau Goebbels sank to her knees and pleaded with him to stay, but he gently raised her and explained that his death was necessary to remove the last obstacle in Dönitz's path, if Germany was to be saved. His female staff was assembled, and a last lunch was taken together. When he walked through the bunker for the last time to say farewell, accompanied by Eva, he probably noticed a handful of officers of his escort waiting with two stretchers near the exit staircase.

It was about three-thirty when Hitler and Eva withdrew into the little green-and-white tiled study. Hitler closed the double doors, leaving Goebbels, Krebs, Burgdorf, and Bormann in the conference room. The doors sealed out all sounds but the murmur of the ventilation plant and the echoing explosion of shells. Eva sat on the narrow couch, kicked off her shoes, and swung her legs up onto the faded blue and white upholstery beside her. Hitler sat next to her, with his mother's photograph to his right and the portrait of Frederick the Great frowning down in front of him. They unscrewed the brass casings—like lipstick containers—and extracted the thin glass phials with their amber liquid content. Eva bit the glass and sank her head on his shoulder. Her knees drew up sharply in agony. Controlling his trembling hand, Adolf Hitler raised the heavy 7.65-millimeter Walther to his right temple, clenched his teeth on the phial in his mouth, and squeezed the trigger.

A Select Bibliography
of Published Literature on Hitler

ABETZ, OTTO. *Das offene Problem* (Löln, 1951).

ADÁM, MAGDA (ed., with G. Juhász, L. Kerekes). *Allianz Hitler–Horthy–Mussolini. Dokumente zur ungarischen Aussenpolitik* (Budapest, 1966).

ALFIERI, DINO. *Deux dictateurs face à face* (Paris, 1948).

ANFUSO, FILIPPO. *Roma–Berlino–Salò* (Italy, 1950).

ASSMANN, HEINZ. *Deutsche Schicksalsjahre* (Wiesbaden, 1951).

AUSWÄRTIGES AMT, Berlin. *Weissbuch Nr. 3—Polnische Dokumente zur Vorgeschichte des Krieges* (Berlin, 1940).

———. *Weissbuch Nr. 4—Dokumente zur englische-französischen Politik der Kriegsausweitung* (Berlin, 1940).

———. *Weissbuch Nr. 5—Weitere Dokumente zur Kriegsausweiterungspolitik der Westmächte. Die Generalstabsbesprechungen Englands und Frankreichs mit Belgien und den Niederländen* (Berlin, 1940)

———. *Weissbuch Nr. 6—Die Geheimakten des französischen Generalstabes* (Berlin, 1940).

———. *Weissbuch Nr. 7—Dokumente zum Konflikt mit Jugoslawien und Griechenland* (Berlin, 1941).

———. *Weissbuch Nr. 8—Dokumente über die Alleinschuld Englands am Bombenkrieg gegen die Zivilbevölkerung* (Berlin, 1943).

BAUR, HANS. *Ich flog Mächtige der Erde* (Kempten, 1956).

BAYLE, FRANCOIS. *Croix gammée contre caducée. Les experiences humanies en Allemagne pendant la deuxième guerre mondiale* (Berlin & Neustadt/Pfalz, 1950).

BEST, S. PAYNE. *The Venlo Incident* (London, 1950).

BEZYMENSKI, LEV. *Der Tod des Adolf Hitler* (Hamburg, 1968).

———. *Die letzten Notizen von Martin Bormann* (Stuttgart, 1974).

———. *Sonderakte Barbarossa* (Stuttgart, 1968).

BLAU, GEORGE E. *The German Campaign in the Balkans, Spring 1941* (Washington, 1953).

———. *The German Campaign in Russia, Planning and Operations (1940–1942)* (Washington, 1955).

BOELCKE, WILLI A. *Kriegspropaganda 1939–1941* (Stuttgart, 1966).

———. *Deutschlands Rüstung im Zweiten Weltkrieg* (Frankfurt, 1969).

———. *Wollt Ihr den totalen Krieg?* (Stuttgart, 1967).

BOLDT, G. *Die letzten Tage der Reichskanzlei* (Hamburg, 1947).

BONDY, L. W. *Racketeers of Hatred. Julius Streicher and the Jew-Baiters' International* (London, 1946).

BOR, PETER. *Gespräche mit Halder* (Wiesbaden, 1950).

BORMANN, MARTIN. *The Bormann Letters* (London, 1954).

BRITISH AIR MINISTRY. *The Rise and Fall of the German Air Force (1933–1945)* (London, 1948).

BROSZAT, MARTIN. *Nationalsozialistische Polenpolitik 1939–1945* (Stuttgart, 1961).

BUCHHEIM, HANS. *Anatomie des SS-Staates* (Freiburg i.Br., 1965).

BULLITT, ORVILLE H. *For the President* (Boston, 1972).

BURDICK, CHARLES. *Germany's Military Strategy and Spain in World War II* (Syracuse, N.Y., 1968).

BUTLER, J. R. M. *Grand Strategy,* Vol. 2 (London, H.M.S.O.).

CAVALLERO, UGO. *Diario* (Rome, 1948).

CHURCHILL, W. S. *The Second World War,* Vols. 1–6 (London, 1948–54).

COLLIER, BASIL. *The Defence of the United Kingdom* (London, H.M.S.O., 1957).

CSIMA, JANOS. *Adalékok a Horthy hadsereg szervezetének és haborús tevékenységének tanulmányozásához 1938–1945* (Budapest, 1961).

DEAKIN, F. W. *The Brutal Friendship. Mussolini, Hitler, and the Fall of Italian Fascism* (New York, 1962).

DETWILER, D. S. *Hitler, Franco und Gibraltar* (Wiesbaden, 1962).

DIETRICH, OTTO. *Zwölf Jahre mit Hitler* (Köln, 1955).

DILKS, DAVID (ed.). *The Diaries of Sir Alexander Cadogan 1938–1945* (London, 1971).

Documents on British Foreign Policy (London, H.M.S.O.)

Documents Diplomatiques Français 1932–1939, Vols. 3–6 (Paris, 1968–70).

Documenti Diplomatici Italiani (Rome, 1954 *et seq.*).

Documents on German Foreign Policy (London, H.M.S.O.)

DOMARUS, MAX. *Hitler—Reden und Proklamationen 1932–1945,* Vols. 1, 2 (Neustadt and Aisch, 1962–63).

DÖNITZ, KARL. *Zehn Jahre und Zwanzig Tage* (Bonn, 1958).

ERICKSON, JOHN. *The Soviet High Command* (London, 1962).

FABRY, PHILIPP W. *Die Sowjetunion und das Dritte Reich* (Stuttgart, 1971).

FENYO, MARIO D. *Hitler, Horthy and Hungary* (New Haven, 1972).

FOOT, M. R. D. *S.O.E. in France* (London, H.M.S.O., 1966).

Foreign Relations of the United States (Washington, D.C.).

FRANK, K. H. *Confessions of Karl-Hermann Frank* (Prague, 1946).

FRIESSNER, HANS. *Verratene Schlachten, die Tragödie der deutschen Wehrmacht in Rumänien und Ungarn* (Hamburg, 1956).

GOEBBELS, JOSEPH. *Tagebücher aus den Jahren 1942–1943* (Zürich, 1948).

GÖRLITZ, WALTER (ed.). *Generalfeldmarschall Keitel—Verbrecher oder Offizier* (Göttingen, 1961).

GREINER, HELMUTH. *Die Oberste Wehrmachtführung 1939–1943* (Wiesbaden, 1951).

GROSCURTH, HELMUTH. *Tagebücher eines Abwehroffiziers 1938–1940* (Stuttgart, 1970).

GUDERIAN, HEINZ. *Erinnerungen eines Soldaten* (Heidelberg, 1951).

HAGEN, HANS W. *Zwischen Eid und Befehl* (München, 1959).

HALDER, FRANZ. *Kriegstagebuch 1939–1942,* Vols. 1–3 (Stuttgart, 1962–64).

HASSELL, ULRICH VON. *Vom andern Deutschland, Tagebüchern 1938–1944* (Frankfurt, 1964).

HEDIN, SVEN. *Ohne Auftrag in Berlin* (Buenos Aires, 1949).

HEIBER, HELMUT (ed.). *Hitlers Lagebesprechungen, Die Protokollfragmente seiner militärischen Konferenzen 1942–1945* (Stuttgart 1962).

———. *Reichsführer! Briefe an und von Himmler* (Stuttgart, 1968).

HESSE, FRITZ. *Das Spiel um Deutschland* (Munich, 1953).

HILGER, GUSTAV. *Wir und der Kreml* (Frankfurt, 1956).

HILL, LEONIDAS E. (ed.). *Die Weizsäcker Papiere 1933–1950.*

HILLGRUBER, ANDREAS. *Staatsmänner und Diplomaten bei Hitler 1939–1941* (Frankfurt, 1967); Vol. 2: 1942–1944 (Frankfurt, 1970).

———. *Hitler, König Carol und Marschall Antonescu* (Wiesbaden, 1954).

HITLER, ADOLF. *Hitlers Zweites Buch* (Stuttgart, 1961).

———. *Mein Kampf* (Munich, 1936).

HOENSCH, JÖRG K. *Die Slowakei und Hitlers Ostpolitik* (Cologne & Graz, 1965).

HOFFMANN, PETER. *Widerstand, Staatsstreich, Attentat* (Munich, 1969).

HUBATSCH, WALTHER. *Hitlers Weisungen für die Kriegführung 1939–1945* (Frankfurt, 1962).

———. *Weserübung. Die deutsche Besetzung von Dänemark und Norwegen 1940* (Göttingen, 1960).

JÄCKEL, EBERHARD. *Frankreich in Hitlers Europa* (Stuttgart, 1966).

JACOBSEN, HANS-ADOLF. *Fall Gelb* (Wiesbaden, 1957).

KEHRIG, MANFRED. *Stalingrad. Analyse und Dokumentation einer Schlacht* (Stuttgart, 1975).

KEHRL, HANS. *Krisenmanager im Dritten Reich* (Düsseldorf, 1973).

KEMPKA, ERICH. *Ich habe Adolf Hitler verbrannt* (Munich, 1948).

KESSELRING, ALBERT. *Soldat bis zum Letzten Tag* (Bonn, 1953).

KLEE, K. *Das Unternehmen Seelöwe* (Göttingen, 1958).

KLEIST, PETER. *Zwischen Hitler und Stalin 1939–1945* (Bonn, 1950).

KLINK, ERNST. *Das Gesetz des Handelns. Die Operation Zitadelle 1943* (Stuttgart, 1966).

KOLLER, KARL. *Der letzte Monat* (Mannheim, 1949).

KOTZE, HILDEGARD VON (ed.). *Es spricht der Führer* (Gütersloh, 1966).

KRAUSE, KARL-WILHELM. *Zehn Jahre lang Tag und Nacht Kammerdiener bei Adolf Hitler* (Hamburg, 1949).

KRECKER, LOTHAR. *Deutschland und die Türkei im Zweiten Weltkrieg* (Frankfurt, 1964).

Kriegstagebuch des Oberkommandos der Wehrmacht (Wehrmachtführungsstab) 1940–1945, Vols. 1–4 (Frankfurt, 1965, 1963, 1963, 1961).

LASCH, OTTO. *So fiel Königsberg* (München, 1958).

LIDDELL HART, SIR BASIL (ed.). *The Rommel Papers* (London, 195).

———. *The Other Side of the Hill* (London, 1948)

LOSSBERG, BERNHARD VON. *Im Wehrmachtführungsstab* (Hamburg, 1949).

LÜDDE-NEURATH, W. *Regierung Dönitz* (Berlin, 1964).

LUTHER, HANS. *Der französische Widerstand gegen die deutsche Besatzungsmacht und seine Bekämpfung* (Tübingen, 1957).

MACARTNEY, C. A. *October Fifteenth, a History of Modern Hungary 1929–1945*, Vols. 1–2 (Edinburgh, 1956–57).

MANSTEIN, ERICH VON. *Verlorene Siege* (Bonn, 1955).

MARTIN, BERND. *Deutschland und Japan im Zweiten Weltkrieg* (Göttingen, 1969).

———. *Friedensinitiativen und Machtpolitik im Zweiten Weltkrieg 1939–1942* (Düsseldorf, 1974).

MEISSNER, OTTO. *Staatssekretär unter Ebert–Hindenburg–Hitler* (Hamburg, 1950).

Militärgeschichtliches Forschungsamt: Operationsgebiet östliche Ostsee und der Finnisch-Baltische Raum 1944 (Stuttgart, 1961).

MILWARD, ALAN S. *The German Economy at War* (London, 1965).

MOELLHAUSEN, EITEL FRIEDRICH. *Die gebrochene Achse* (Alfeld, 1949).

Monatshefte für Auswärtige Politik, Bd. VII (1940).

MÜLLER, KLAUS-JÜRGEN. *Das Heer und Hitler* (Stuttgart, 1969).

NEUBACHER, HERMANN. *Sonderauftrag Südost 1940–1945* (Göttingen, 1956).

NEVAKIVI, JUKKA. *Apu jota ei pyydetty* (Helsinki, 1972).

ORLOW, DIETRICH. *The Nazis in the Balkans. A Case Study of Totalitarian Politics* (Pittsburgh, 1968).

OVEN, WILFRIED VON. *Mit Goebbels bis zum Ende*, Vols. 1–2 (Buenos Aires, 1949).

OVERSTRAETEN, GENERAL VAN. *Albert I–Leopold III* (Brussels, no year).

PAPEN, FRANZ VON. *Der Wahrheit eine Gasse* (Munich, 1952).

PHILIPPI, ALFRED (FERDINAND HEIM). *Der Feldzug gegen Sowjetrussland 1941–1945* (Stuttgart, 1962).
PICKER, HENRY. *Hitlers Tischgespräche im Führerhauptquartier 1941–1942* (Stuttgart, 1963).
PLATEN-HALLERMUND, ALICE. *Die Tötung Geisteskranker* (Frankfurt, 1948).
Der Prozess gegen die Hauptkriegsverbrecher vor dem Internationalen Militärgerichtshof Nürnberg, 14. November 1945–1. Oktober 1946 (Nürnberg, 1947–49).
POULSSON, E. *Lehrbuch für Pharmakologie* (10.Aufl., ? Berlin, 1934).
PUTTKAMER, KARL-JESKO VON. *Die unheimliche See—Hitler und die Kriegsmarine* (Munich, Vienna, 1952).
RAEDER, ERICH. *Mein Leben,* Vol. 2 (Tübingen, 1957).
RAHN, RUDOLF. *Ruheloses Leben* (Düsseldorf, 1949).
Reichsgesetztblatt, Teil I (published in Berlin).
REINHARDT, K. *Die Wende vor Moskau. Das Scheitern der Strategie Hitlers im Winter 1941–42* (Stuttgart, 1972).
REITLINGER, GERALD. *Die Endlösung, Hitlers Versuch der Ausrottung der Juden Europas 1939–1945* (Berlin, 1956).
RIBBENTROP, JOACHIM VON. *Zwischen London und Moskau* (Leoni, 1961).
RINTELEN, ENNO VON. *Mussolini als Bundesgenosse* (Tübingen, 1951).
ROOSEVELT, F. D. *Nothing to Fear. The Selected Addresses of F. D. Roosevelt 1932–1945* (New York, 1961).
ROSKILL, S. W. *The War at Sea,* Vols. 1–3 (London, H.M.S.O., 1960).
ROTHFELS, HANS. *Die deutsche Opposition gegen Hitler* (Frankfurt, 1958).
SALEWSKI, MICHAEL. *Die deutsche Seekriegsleitung 1935–1945* (Frankfurt, 1970).
SCHENCK, ERNST-GÜNTHER. *Ich sah Berlin sterben* (Herford, 1970).
SCHEURIG, BODO. *Free Germany* (Middletown, Conn., 1970).
SCHMIDT, PAUL. *Statist auf diplomatischer Bühne 1923–1945* (Bonn, 1949).
SCHRAMM, E. (VON THADDEN). *Griechenland und die Grossmächte im Zweiten Weltkrieg* (Weisbaden, 1955).
SCHRAMM, PERCY ERNST. *Das Ende des Krieges* (Cologne, 1965).
SCHRÖDER, JOSEF. *Italiens Kriegsaustritt 1943* (Göttingen, 1969).
SERAPHIM, HANS-GUNTHER (ed.). *Das politische Tagebuch Alfred Rosenbergs* (Göttingen, 1956).
SIEGLER, FRITZ VON. *Die höheren Dienststellen der Deutschen Wehrmacht 1933–1945* (Munich, 1955).
SKORZENY, OTTO. *Geheimkommando Skorzeny* (Hamburg, 1950).
SPEER, ALBERT. *Erinnerungen* (Berlin, 1969).
STEINER, FELIX. *Die Freiwilligen* (Göttingen, 1958).
STOCKHORST, ERICH. *Fünftausend Köpfe—Wer war was im 3. Reich* (Velbert, 1967).
SÜNDERMANN, HELMUT. *Deutsche Notizen, 1945–1965* (Leoni, 1966).
A Szálasi-per [*The Szálasi Trial*] (Budapest, 1946).
TANNER, VÄINÖ. *Olin ulkoministerinä talvisodan aikana* (Helsinki, 1950).
TANSILL, CHARLES C. *Back Door to War* (Chicago, 1952).
THOMAS, GEORG. *Geschichte der deutschen Wehr-und Rüstungswirtschaft* (Boppard am Rhein, 1966).
TREVOR-ROPER, HUGH. *The Last Days of Hitler* (London, 1947).
———. *Hitler's Table Talk* (London, 1953).
TURNEY, ALFRED W. *Disaster at Moscow. Von Bock's Campaigns 1941–42* (London, 1971).
U.S. ARMY. *The German Campaign in Poland 1939* (Washington, 1956).
U.S. Strategic Bombing Survey: The Effects of Strategic Bombing on the German War Economy (Washington, D.C.)
VÖLKER, KARL-HEINZ. *Die deutsche Luftwaffe 1933–1939* (Stuttgart, 1967).

———: *Dokumente und Dokumentarfotos zur Geschichte der deutschen Luftwaffe* (Stuttgart, 1968).

Völkischer Beobachter, Berlin or Munich editions, 1939–1945.

VORMANN, NIKOLAUS VON. *Der Feldzug in Polen 1939* (Weissenburg, 1958).

WAGNER, EDUARD. *Der Generalquartiermeister, Briefe und Tagebuchaufzeichnungen* (Munich, Vienna, 1963).

WAGNER, GERHARD (ed.). *Lagevorträge des Oberbefehlshabers der Kriegsmarine vor Hitler 1939–1945* (Munich, 1972).

WARLIMONT, WALTER. *Im Hauptquartier der deutschen Wehrmacht 1939–1945* (Frankfurt, 1962).

WEBSTER, SIR CHARLES (NOBLE FRANKLAND). *The Strategic Air Offensive against Germany 1939–1945* (London, H.M.S.O., 1961).

WEIZSÄCKER, ERNST VON. *Erinnerungen* (Munich, 1950).

WILMOT, CHESTER. *The Struggle for Europe* (London, 1952).

WOODWARD, SIR LLEWELLYN. *British Foreign Policy in the Second World War* (London, H.M.S.O., 1962).

ZIEMKE, EARL F. *The German Northern Theater of Operations 1940–1945* (Washington, D.C., 1959).

ZOLLER, ALBERT. *Hitler privat. Erlebnisbericht seiner Geheimsekretärin* (Dusseldorf, 1949).

Notes

ABBREVIATION USED IN NOTES

AA Auswärtiges Amt, German foreign ministry. For a listing of Serials against NA microfilm numbers, see George A. Kent, *A Catalog of Files and Microfilms of the German Foreign Ministry Archives 1920–1945,* Vol. III, pages 525 *et seq.*

ADI(K) British Air Ministry's Assistant Directorate of Intelligence, interrogation and captured documents section.

AL/ File number assigned by CO Enemy Documents Section; document now in IWM

BA Bundesarchiv, the German federal archives, based on Koblenz (civil agencies) and Freiburg (military)

BDC Berlin Document Center (of U.S. Mission, Berlin)

—C A Nuremberg Document Series (*e.g.,* 100–C)

CAB Cabinet File (in British Public Records Office)

CCPWE U.S. Army Interrogation series (now in NA)

CIC Counter intelligence Corps of the U.S. Army

CIOS Combined Intelligence Objectives Survey

CIR Consolidated Interrogation Report (U.S. army)

CO Cabinet Office files

CP Cabinet Paper (British)

CSDIC Combined Services Detailed Interrogation Center (these British reports are still top secret)

D— Nuremberg document series

DBFP *Documents on British Foreign Policy*

DDI *Documenti Diplomatici Italiani*

DGFP *Documents on German Foreign Policy*

DIC Detailed Interrogation Center (*see* CSDIC)

DIS Detailed Interrogation Summary (U.S. army)

EC— A Nuremberg Document series

ED— An IfZ document series

ETHINT European Theater Interrogation (U.S. Army series)

F— An IfZ document series

FA   Forschungsamt, literally Research Office: Göring's wiretap agency

FD—   Foreign Documents, a British series of unpublished captured documents, currently held by Imperial War Museum, London

FIR   Final Interrogation Report (U.S. Army interrogation)

FIAT   Field Intelligence Agency, Technical

FO   Foreign Office, London

FRUS   *Foreign Relations of the United States*

GB—   British documentary exhibit at Nuremberg

GRGG   CSDIC document series

II H—   German army document, in BA, Freiburg

IfZ   Institut für Zeitgeschichte, Institute of Contemporary History, Munich

IIR   Interim Interrogation Report (U.S. Army interrogation)

IMT   International Military Tribunal: *Trial of the Major German War Criminals at Nuremberg*

KTB   Kriegstagebuch, war diary of a German operational unit

Kl. Erw.   Kleine Erwerbung, a minor accession by BA, Koblenz

L—   A Nuremberg document series

46—M   Interrogations at Berchtesgaden, 1945, now in library of University of Pennsylvania

MA—   IfZ microfilm series

MD   Milch Documents, original RLM files recently restituted by British government to BA, Freiburg; microfilms of them are available from Imperial War Museum, London, and soon from NA too. (The citation MD 64/3456 refers to Vol. 64, page 3456.)

MGFA   Militärgeschichtliches Forschungsamt, German defense ministry historical research section in Freiburg

MI   Military Intelligence branch (British)

MISC   Military Intelligence Service Center (U.S. Army interrogations)

ML—   NA microfilm series

N   *Nachlass,* the papers of a German military personage, now held by BA, Freiburg

NA   National Archives, Washington, D.C.

ND   Nuremberg Document

NG—   A Nuremberg document series

NCA   *Nazi Conspiracy and Aggression* (U.S. publication of selected Nuremberg documents)

NO—   A Nuremberg document series

NOKW—   A Nuremberg document series

NS—   Collections of Nazi documents in BA, Koblenz

OCMH   Office of the Chief of Military History, Washington, D.C.

ONI   Office of Naval Intelligence

O.QU.   *Oberquartiermeister,* Quartermaster

OUSCC   Office of U.S. Chief of Counsel (IMT)

P—   MS series of U.S. Army: postwar writings of German officers in prison camps (complete collection in NA)

PG/   Files of German admiralty, now held by BA, Freiburg

PID   Political Intelligence Division of the FO

PRO   Public Record Office, London

—PS   A Nuremberg document series

R—   A Nuremberg document series (*e.g.,* R–100)

R   Collections of Reich documents in BA, Koblenz (*e.g.,* R 43II/606)

REP   Document series of Bavarian State Archives, Nuremberg

RGBl.   *Reichsgesetzblatt,* the Reich government gazette

RH   German army document in BA, Freiburg

RIIA   Royal Institute of International Affairs, London

RIR   Reinterrogation Report (U.S. Army)

RLM   Reichsluftfahrt-Ministerium, Reich air ministry

SAIC   U.S. Seventh Army Interrogation Center

SAO   C. Webster and N. Frankland, *The Strategic Air Offensive against Germany,* 4 vols (London, 1961)

SS—   BDC document series

T   NA microfilm series. (The citation T78/300/1364 refers to Micropcopy T78, roll 300, page 1364.)

USNIP   U.S. Naval Institute *Proceedings*

USFET   U.S. Forces, European Theater

USSBS   U.S. Strategic Bombing Survey

VB   Völkischer Beobachter, the Nazis' national newspaper

VfZ   *Vierteljahrshefte für Zeitgeschichte,* quarterly published by IfZ.

WR   *Wehrwissenschaftliche Rundschau,* German military science monthly journal

X—   OCMH document series, now in NA

X—P   DIC interrogation series (prisoners' conversations, recorded by hidden microphones, as at CSDIC's)

ZS—   *Zeugenschrift,* collection by IfZ of written and oral testimonies

ZSg.—   Zeitungs-Sammlung, newspaper cuttings collection in BA, Koblenz

I HITLER'S WAR BEGINS

"White"

p. 4   Colonel Eduard Wagner echoed Vormann's awe in a letter of September 4. "Even so not a shot has been fired in the west yet, a funny war so far. It's official that France hesitated to the last moment and was only pulled in by Britain. Once again you can only say *Gott strafe England!*"

Apart from reference to the published sources, I based my account of the Polish campaign on the diaries of Jodl, Bock, Halder, Helmuth Groscurth, Milch, Vormann, the naval staff, Wagner, Lahousen, Rosenberg, and the commandant of Hitler's HQ; and on interrogations of Hans von Greiffenberg, Blaskowitz, Göring, Dönitz, Scheidt, Warlimont, Keitel, and others.

pp. 8–9   Hitler's policies are well defined in Professor Martin Broszat's *Nationalsozialistische Polenpolitik 1939–1945* (Stuttgart, 1961). On the Bromberg massacre see the war diary of Rear Army Command 580 (General Braemer) in BA files (page 824), and of the Military Commander of West Prussia (RH 53–20/v. 16). A sample of lower Party officials was Kreisleiter Werner Kampe, appointed lord mayor of Bromberg with the job of "extracting compensation for ethnic Germans who suffered Polish atrocities"; Kampe swindled the victims out of millions of marks to benefit befriended Party and civic officials. The Reich ministry of justice indicted him, but Gauleiter Albert Forster secured his release

(BA file R 22/4087). About seven thousand Germans were massacred by the Poles in Bromberg.

p. 10   Three copies of Canaris's memorandum on his conference in Hitler's train on September 12, 1939, exist: one in the "Canaris-Lahousen fragments"—a hitherto neglected file of key documents and extracts from the Canaris diary obtained by the Cabinet Office (AL/1933); one in Groscurth's papers (N 104/3); and an abbreviated copy in Lahousen's IMT file (3047–PS); *cf* Lahousen's pretrial interrogation of September 19, 1945, and Vormann's diary, September 12, 1939: "Göring and Brauchitsch here at Ilnau. Canaris on account of Polish population."

p. 13   Read in sequence, Heydrich's R.S.H.A. (Reich Main Security Office) conferences (on NA film T175/239) during September and October 1939 show a gradual shift in emphasis and urgency. Professor H. Krausnick also published Heydrich's related memorandum of May 1941 in *VfZ*, 1963, page 197; and see Heydrich's frank memorandum of July 1940, in Kurt Daluege's papers (BA, R 19), on the role of his task forces.

p. 14   The purge in Poland: I used W. Huppenkothen's 1945 essays, in BDC files; a CSDIC interrogation of Udo von Woyrsch; Dr. Rudolf Lehmann's testimony; Halder's diary; Heydrich's conferences; and army documents.

p. 48   The earlier assassination attempts are touched on in Hitler's Table Talks on September 6, 1941 (Koeppen's note) and May 3, 1942 (Heim's note); Peter Hoffmann, who investigated them in Swiss archives, informs me that Bavaud was beheaded in May 1942.

p. 50   Dr. Anton Hoch published a study on the Bürgerbräu murder attempt in *VfZ*, 1969, pages 383 *et seq.*, effectively demolishing the many postwar legends by referring to the Gestapo interrogation of Georg Elser, the lone assassin (now in BA file R 22/3100). I also used the diaries of Bormann and Groscurth, the day's detailed program (NS–10/126), and testimonies of Below, Grolmann, Schaub, and Baron Karl von Eberstein; the Gestapo finally listed eight dead and sixty-three injured (T175/473/4876). On Hitler's orders later trials of Elser and his former employer, whose negligence enabled him to steal the quarry explosives, were adjourned sine die (file R22/4087), and Elser was executed in April 1945.

p. 53   Jodl's diary and postwar testimony, coupled with his adjutant Wilhelm Deyhle's notes (1786–PS), show that until November 13 Hitler was convinced he could amicably come to terms with Holland. An entry in the diary of Halder's Intelligence chief, General Kurt von Tippelskirch (BA file III H36/1), on November 12 proves that Hitler himself ordered the kidnapping of the two British agents, and he himself decorated the SS officers who achieved this at a Reich Chancellery ceremony two days later (BDC file on SS Major Helmuth Knochen).

pp. 54–55   Admiral von Puttkamer first told me of the Ardennes relief map; it was also observed by Lieutenant Colonel Lahousen in the Chancellery on November 20, 1939, as he testified under interrogation six years later, and Hitler himself referred to the relief map "we used at that time in Berlin" in a war conference on September 17, 1944 (Heiber, page 660).

p. 55   The two Abwehr officers were Captain Fleck and Lieutenant Hokke, according to the diaries of Groscurth, Lahousen, Jodl, and Halder. Lahousen noted: "The Führer has asked for every demolition charge's touch-hole [*Zündloch*] to be described to him." A full record of the secret conference of November 20, 1939, is in the Canaris-Lahousen fragments (AL/1933).

p. 57   The completest records of Hitler's harangue of November 23, 1939 (Milch's diary called it a "spunk-jab"), are the shorthand note in General von Leeb's diary and the anonymous ND, 789–PS, which agrees well with a text in Groscurth's files (N104/3). I also found a summary in the diary of Colonel Hoffmann von Waldau—Deputy Chief of Air Staff—and the diaries of Bock and Halder. General Hoth used it as the basis for a speech to the Fifteenth Army Corps' generals (BA file W.2005/2), and Admiral Raeder likewise for his section heads (PG/31762a).

Clearing the Decks

p. 60 Goebbels's memorandum—"Thoughts on the Outbreak of War 1939"—is in BA file NS–10/37. It described the public's mood in the first September days as very grave but calm: "There is thus nothing of the bravo-spirit of 1914."

p. 65 I have been unable to resolve the conflict of evidence on Quisling's two meetings with Hitler in December 1939. Jodl's diary dates one the 13th; Raeder's note on Rosenberg's memo dates it the 14th; Rosenberg's diary dates it the 15th; the otherwise very informative survey drawn up by his *Aussenpolitisches Amt* (NS–43/25) states with equal confidence "Quisling was received for a personal audience by the Führer on the 16th and again on the 18th."

p. 68 Raeder's adjutant (Freiwald) recalls that as they left the Chancellery he hinted to Raeder they might at least add to the vague and indecisive signal the words, "I wish you a safe further *voyage.*" Raeder refused however to tie Langsdorff's hands in any way.

p. 69 The then chief of Foreign Armies West, Ulrich Liss, wrote a bitter criticism of Canaris's Intelligence failure in 1940 in *WR*, 1958, pages 208 *et seq.*

p. 70 Professor Broszat covers some of the ground on Hitler's Polish policies (see my note to pages 8–9). I also used the Groscurth, Halder, and Milch diaries; Frank's verbatim remarks at a police conference on May 30, 1940 (2233–PS); an SS investigation of Soldau (NO–1073); testimony of General von Gienanth—Blaskowitz's successor—and Karl Wolff; and documents in Chancellery files R 43 II/1332 and /1411a. Himmler's notes are on NA microfilm T175/94. As early as November 1, 1935, incidentally, they show that he had to explain "deaths in concentration camps."

p. 72 Without explanation, Professor Broszat omits the first sentence I quote from the adjutant Gerhard Engel's note.

p. 73 For the case of the magistrate—Otto Christian von Hirschfeld—see the Reich justice ministry file R 22/4087 and Lammer's memo in file R 43II/1411a.

"We Must Destroy Them, Too!"

p. 76 The 922-page ledger kept by Walther Hewel of the diplomatic papers submitted to Hitler from January 1940 to August 1942 is in AA files; it lists many of the Forschungs-samt's achievements, including for example a decoded Belgian telegram of February 11, 1940, reporting Ciano's comments to the Belgian envoy in Rome. For evidence that Ciano betrayed "Yellow" to the Belgians see Groscurth's diary of January 2, and Halder's diary. On the seventh the general noted: "Other side knows date . . . Führer aware of this"; and next day Major Hasso von Etzdorf, his liaison officer to the foreign ministry, told him of a "telegram (Kerchove)." The latter was Belgian envoy in Rome. On January 18, Weiz-säcker wrote to Ambassador von Mackensen in Rome: "I believe Herr von Ribbentrop has briefed you about certain goings-on between Rome and Brussels . . . but I found it most important that you should be shown or sent the actual texts concerned" (AA, Serial 100, pages 64885 *et seq.*). On Janury 22, Halder's Intelligence chief wrote in his diary: "It [alian] betrayal to Belg[ians] of German intentions and preparations."

p. 77 The report by Halder's Intelligence chief (Tippelskirch) on Belgium is in the files of Foreign Armies West (AL/1329). For an opposing view on Belgium's neutrality, see Professor H. A. Jacobsen's study in *WR*, 1957, pages 275 *et seq.*

p. 78 My account of the Mechelen affair is based on Jacobsen's study in *WR*, 1954, pages 497 *et seq.*, Jean Vanwelkenhuyzen, *ibid.*, 1955, pages 66 *et seq.*, and the diaries of Jodl, Halder, Groscurth, Milch, Hassell, and Deyhle; on the Weizsäcker file on Belgium; and on interrogations of Göring and Below. About a dozen damning fragments of typed pages and directives did in fact survive the flames; the general geography of "Yellow" could be deduced from them. "On day 1 of the attack" the Eigth Air Corps job would be to destroy the Belgian army west of the Meuse "in close cooperation with the Sixth Army Schwerpunkt at and west of Maastricht." The 7th Air Division (paratroops) had targets at Namur and Dinant. Another fragment stated: "Additionally it is intended to occupy

Holland with the exception of the Fortress Holland itself, using part of the forces (Tenth Corps, incorporating 1st Cavalry Division)."

p. 81   Quite apart from the construction of the Ardennes relief map, a postcard written by the Luftwaffe adjutant to an uncle on May 14, 1940, confirms that Hitler struck on the victorious strategy in *1939*. "I hinted at it to you at Christmas," Colonel von Below reminded his uncle. The date of Schmundt's visit to Manstein is fixed beyond doubt by the private diary of Frau Schmundt. Engel noted afterward: "Schmundt was very excited and told me that he had found M[anstein] expressing precisely the same opinions . . . as the Führer is constantly expressing." Hitler had thereupon instructed Schmundt to send secretly for Manstein, without informing either Brauchitsch or Halder in advance. After meeting Hitler, Manstein scribbled in his diary: "What an extraordinary conformity with my own views!" According to Warlimont (MS P–215) Hitler saw the general off with the words: "Manstein is the only person to see what I'm getting at."

p. 82   Several versions exist of Hitler's dinner on February 17, 1940—Manstein's, Rommel's private letter (T84/R273a/0866), and General Geyr von Schweppenburg's (IfZ, ZS–680).

pp. 82–83   Winston Churchill's version of the *Altmark* affair must be faulted on essential details—if not on its wealth of color. I relied on the naval staff's war diary and its special case file (PG/33730)—with its full-length report by the captain—the Jodl diary, and diplomatic papers in Weizsäcker's and Ernst Woermann's AA files. On the legal aspects, see Heinz Knackstedt, in *WR*, 1959, pages 391 and 466 *et seq.,* and the study by the U.S. Naval War College in *International Law Situation and Documents,* 1956, pages 3 *et seq.*

p. 84   I based my account of the developing plan to invade Norway on the war diaries of Milch, Jodl, Halder, Tippelskirch, and the naval staff. Raeder's powerful support is clear in the latter diary entry on March 2, 1940, for example. I also employed the war diary of the army's XXI Gruppe (BA file E. 180/5), and Raeder's two important postwar manuscripts, "My Relations with Adolf Hitler" and "The Occupation of Norway on April 9, 1940" (1546–PS).

p. 85   For the Allies' rather undignified attempts to prolong the Russo-Finnish war, see the naval staff war diary, March 8–14, 1940. Weizsäcker also hinted at the Forschungsamt's remarkable coup in his diary entry of March 13, noting that the western powers had tried to prevent the armistice by offering empty promises to Finland: "We have hard evidence of this." After Ribbentrop disclosed German knowledge of the Finnish envoy's message, in his White Book published on April 27, an official inquiry resulted in Helsinki; eventually Dr. Pakaslahti, chief of the Finnish's FO's political department, cabled the guilty envoy in Paris—Harri Holma—on May 14, identifying the telephone call which the Germans must have intercepted as that at 3:30 P.M. on March 12 (Finnish FO archives, 109/C2e, Tel. R.145). The telephone call is also mentioned in the diary of Finnish Foreign Minister Väinö Tanner (see his memoirs, *Olin ulkoministerinä talvisodan aikana,* Helsinki, 1950, page 387). Holma was an intimate of both Daladier and Reynaud, and pursued his own interventionist foreign policy in Paris—100 percent pro-western. It appears that he feared that his telegram to Helsinki might be delayed in transmission, so he dictated it over the phone as well. Interestingly, Ulrich Kittel—one of the Forschungsamt's section heads —confirmed the whole episode in ZS–1734.

p. 89   According to the Hewel Ledger (see my note to page 76) two Forschungsamt reports on the Italian talks with Sumner Welles were submitted to Hitler. The Italians evidently told Hitler little, for Hewel endorsed the entry as follows: "The Führer has instructed that the Italians are to be handed a protocol on the Sumner Welles talks with the Führer and the foreign minister [on March 2] conforming in length and content to that supplied by the Italians." This mistrust was also plain in Hitler's directive on April 4 on strategic cooperation with Italy (PG/33316): "Neither 'Yellow' nor [the invasion of Scandinavia] are to be discussed in any form before the operations begin."

p. 91 It is worth observing that in his speech to commanders on April 1, 1940, prior to the invasion of Norway, Hitler described their relations with Russia at present as just about as favorable as they could wish; but how long this would *remain* so could in practical foreign policy never be predicted (Appendix to war diary of XXI Gruppe).

Hors d'oeuvre

p. 93 Hitler frequently referred to the incautious utterances of Churchill and Reynaud afterward, *e.g.,* in conversation with the Norwegian envoy Arne Scheel and the Swedish admiral Fabian Tamm on April 13 and 16; in a letter to Mussolini on the 26th; and in his famous Reichstag speech of July 19, 1940; see also his remarks in Table Talk, July 1, 1942, evening.

p. 95 The FA intercept is reported in the naval staff war diary, April 7, 1940. I also read the testimony of Major Sas (ZS–1626).

p. 99 The naval attaché in Oslo lectured the naval staff in Berlin on April 21 that in his view Norway would return to normal only if Hitler directed the troops to adopt the slogan "We come as your friends to *protect* Norway" and did not attempt to repeat "the Poland method" there. For the very complicated situation in Norway created by the king's defection, see Weizsäcker's and Hassell's diaries, and particularly the long report submitted by one of Rosenberg's staff to Colonel Schmundt—Hitler's adjutant—on April 17, 1940 (NS–43/25) and Hitler's talk with Quisling on August 18 (NG–2948).

p. 100 Jodl's deputy—Warlimont—ordered Lossberg to write down an account of Hitler's nervous actions for the OKW war diary kept by Greiner. A copy survived among Greiner's papers. Schmundt was aghast; as Lossberg later wrote (in an unpublished manuscript): "He felt it was sacrilege to write down one of the ostensibly infallible Führer's weak moments in black and white." The page was stricken from the official diary text. To get behind the OKW scenes, I used not only Jodl's diary and Deyhle's notes of April 24 (1781–PS) but also manuscripts by Lossberg and by the navy captains Wolf Junge and Heinz Assmann on Jodl's staff, and interviews of Baron Sigismund von Falkenstein (his Luftwaffe staff officer) and General Ottomar Hansen (Keitel's adjutant).

p. 103 Details of the extraordinary British documents captured in Norway can be reconstructed from Jodl's diary, April 23–27; from the naval staff diary, April 27; from Hitler's letter to Mussolini on the 26th—pontificating about "the perfidious mendacity" of the Englishman—and from Goebbels's confidential remarks at his ministerial conference the same day and on May 3 and 19; from Colonel Wagner's private letter of May 7; and from the AA's White Book publishing the most important of the documents on April 27, 1940.

p. 106 From the text of Reynaud's telephone conversation with Chamberlain at 10:10 P.M. on April 30, published in *Völkischer Beobachter,* May 7, 1940, they appear in fact to have been discussing French plans to bomb the Caucasus oil fields of Baku and Batum (a plan of which the Germans learned in detail only when numbers of Allied planning documents fell into their hands during "Yellow"). Reynaud assured Chamberlain that General Weygand, the French Commander in Chief Middle East, had promised to be ready by May 15, at which Chamberlain retorted that his impression was that people down there were taking their time. Reynaud explained that Turkey was raising "steeper demands each day" for overflight permission; he talked of certain *difficultés mentales.* For the French documents later captured relating to the bombing plan, see Weizsäcker's AA files (Serial 121). My researches establish prima facie the authenticity of the transcript of the conversation: it was obtained by the SS agent Fritz Lorenz, a language expert who had been on Ribbentrop's staff since 1935 and transferred to the RSHA in January 1940. From his personnel records I established that he traveled with forged documents through Switzerland and Italy to Paris on April 23, with the delectable job of seducing the telephone operator Marguerite T_____; at their last rendezvous on May 1 she handed him the transcript, which she herself had made. See his amusing correspondence in Himmler's files,

T175/124/9424 *et seq.*, and in his personnel file in the BDC; his insistent demand for a decoration went up to Hitler himself (see Hewel Ledger, January 15, 1942) but was vetoed because of his uncouth behavior in Italy—he had fired a revolver in a hotel when in an alcoholic stupor.

p. 106   On the FA intercepts, see Jodl's diary, the testimony of Sas, and Hermann Graml's study of the Oster affair in *VfZ*, 1966, pages 26 *et seq.* On May 8, 1940, there is also a cryptic reference in Tippelskirch's diary to alerts proclaimed in the Low Countries: "Luxembourg: Telephone conversation [overheard on] May 6: 'Are they coming or aren't they?' 'It's in the air.' " In the AA files of Ambassador von Mackensen (Rome) is extensive correspondence from May 17, 1940, to July 28, 1941, relating to the SD's attempts to identify the German citizen in Rome who had tipped off the Vatican's Father Robert Leiber, S.J., about "Yellow" deadlines.

2 "War of Liberation"

The Warlord at the Western Front

p. 115   General von Trotha provided me with original documents relating to his mission. I also used the annexes to the war diary of the Führer's HQ, diaries of Jodl and Tippelskirch, Hitler's recollections in Table Talk, October 17–18, 1941 (Heim's note), and Gerhard Schacht's study on Eben Emael in *WR*, 1954, pages 217 *et seq.*

p. 116   The definitive account of the Luftwaffe attack on Rotterdam is still Professor H. A. Jacobsen's, in *WR*, 1958, pages 257 *et seq.;* and I used Kesselring's interrogation by the USSBS.

p. 118   Raeder's verbal account of his meeting with Hitler is in the naval staff diary; it is more explicit than his own written summary.

p. 120   The simple explanation that it never occurred to Hitler that the British army was decamping from Dunkirk and leaving the French in the lurch escaped most historians; it is hinted at by Ulrich Liss—chief of Foreign Armies West at the time—in his article in *WR*, 1958, pages 325 *et seq.*, but neither Jacobsen (in *Allgemeine Schweizerische Militärzeitschrift*, 1953, page 845 and elsewhere) nor H. Meier-Welcker, in *VfZ*, 1954, pages 274 *et seq.*, nor the British official historians L. F. Ellis and J. R. M. Butler grasped this point. Liss's daily situation reports are none too emphatic; and the entry in the diary of his superior, Tippelskirch, on May 31—"What picture emerged over the last few days to suggest that the British and French were embarking by sea?"—suggests that the search for a scapegoat was beginning.

p. 121   That the initial decision to halt the German tanks outside Dunkirk was Rundstedt's—and only subsequently given Hitler's blessing—is proven beyond doubt by the war diary of Rundstedt's Army Group A; Rundstedt indignantly denied paternity of the decision when interrogated after the war. But the facts are plain. Late on May 24 an impatient Halder radioed permission to Army Groups A and B to attack Dunkirk. Rundstedt (Army Group A) refused, as "the mechanized groups must first be allowed to pull themselves together." His operations officer, Günther Blumentritt, marked the file copy of Halder's signal, "Submitted to OC [Rundstedt] and Chief of Staff, but has not been forwarded to Fourth Army as Führer wants OC Army Group A to decide." This did not prevent Bock (diary) and Fourth Army (war diary, May 27) from attributing the order to Hitler; the Führer never blamed Rundstedt in later years, however. I also used the diaries of Jodl, Richthofen, Waldau, and Halder; the interrogations of Halder, Kesselring, Scheidt, Jodl, Warlimont, Rundstedt, and Heusinger; and the memoirs of Keitel, Lossberg, and Junge. Engel also noted (allegedly on May 27): "Contrary to expectations the Führer left the decision largely to Rundstedt."

p. 123   Himmler's written proposals for dealing with the eastern populations are in his files (T175/119/5133 *et seq.*); a genesis of these ideas will be found in his speech notes of March 13, 1940. For Hitler's broadly similar views, note his remark in Table Talk, February

4, 1942 (Heim's note): "Wherever in the world there is some Germanic blood, we'll be taking the best of it for ourselves." Himmler's eight-page plan of June 1940 (pages 123–24) is on IfZ microfilm MA–360.

Himmler's notes written before his meeting give a good impression of his varied interests, *e.g.,* May 22, 1940, Führer, at Felsennest [HQ]. (1) Chief of SS and Police for Holland: Bach or Rauter? ('Warmly approves of Rauter, as Austrian'). (2) Pistol with spotlights. (3) Identity photos (Waffen SS). (4) Book by Divinger, Atrocities in Poland. (5) Memorandum on Poland. ('Not yet read'). (6) Legal proceedings against [British agents] Best and Stevens. ('Führer will fix the date')" (T175/94/5221).

p. 125   My account of Hitler's secret speech of June 2, 1940, is based principally on Leeb's diary, but also on accounts by Rommel, Weichs, Bock, and Salmuth.

p. 126   For Leopold's fury, see Army Group B's telex to the OKH on May 31, 1940 (Weizsäcker's AA files, Serial 141).

p. 128   Hitler's caustic comments about Italy were reported, respectively, by General Thomas (1456–PS), Weizsäcker in a private letter of June 5 and diary July 10, Junge, Puttkamer, and Engel in a note on June 10, 1940.

p. 129 *(footnote)*   In Etzdorf's files is a further dispatch by Karl von Wiegand from Paris, transmitted with Hitler's consent on June 15, 1940, in typical newspaper jargon. Paris was quiet and undamaged, the population was curious, the police were saluting German officers, and German soldiers were voluntarily saluting the tomb of the Unknown Soldier at the Arc de Triomphe. "Tonight hotel dining rooms filled German officers who obviously happy but maintain astonishingly quiet dignified demeanor considering they've taken one greatest cities world."

p. 130   The only record of Hitler's private talk with Mussolini is in Italian, in the Duce's handwriting (Mussolini papers, T586/406/769 *et seq.*); he had talked with Hitler for a long time about the French fleet, but Hitler had persuaded him that modern bombers rendered big warships obsolete. "Since France wanted this war and declared it on us, despite my repeated offers of agreement," continued Hitler, "my terms will be such as to solve once and for all the outstanding problems"—and he pointed to the Colmar-Mühlhausen area on the map, indicating that the present (German) inhabitants of Alto Adige, in the Tyrol, would be resettled there. For Russia Hitler expressed only "enormous contempt." He concluded: "Now Germany can be compared with a lucky and audacious gambler, who has kept winning but kept on doubling his stake. Now he is a little bit nervous and wants to take home his winnings quickly." Mussolini's protocol makes much of Hitler's admiration of Italy; but Waldau's diary, June 20, reports that the Führer returned to HQ "bitterly upset about the complete inactivity of the Italians."

p. 130   It was Admiral Puttkamer who overheard—and told me of—Hitler's refusal to Raeder to assign the French fleet to Germany.

p. 131   In Weizsäcker's files is a detailed list of all the "insulting and degrading conditions of the Versailles Treaty" drawn up for comparative purposes (Serial 1892H).

p. 131   Hitler had learnt the measurements of the world's most famous theaters by heart, having steeped himself years earlier in the British architect Sachs's *Modern Opera Houses and Theatres.*

p. 131   The origins of Hitler's belief that the British would give way are clear enough. On June 17, 1940, Lord Halifax's undersecretary R. A. Butler saw the Swedish envoy in London, Björn Prytz, who promptly telegraphed Stockholm: "Mr. Butler's official attitude will for the present be that the war should continue, but he must be certain that no opportunity should be missed of compromise if reasonable conditions could be agreed, and no diehards would be allowed to stay in the way. He [Butler] was called in to Lord Halifax and came out with a message to me that common sense and not bravado would dictate the British government's policy. Halifax had said that he felt such a message would be welcome to [Prytz] but it must not be taken to mean 'peace at any price.' " Two days later Weizsäcker was told of this telegram in broad outline by Prytz's Berlin counterpart,

Richert, who added on June 22—the day before Hitler's talk with Brauchitsch, on which the OKW note exists in CO files—that Halifax took the peace line in opposition to Churchill, Duff Cooper, Chamberlain, and Simon. (See Weizsäcker's AA file, "Anglo-German Relations," Vol. III.) Swedish government publication of Prytz's remarkable telegram was twice (in 1946 and 1964) successfully blocked by the British FO.

Churchill had not always opposed a compromise with Hitler, nor had the British Cabinet. On May 28, 1940, according to its minutes now available for inspection, Chamberlain "said that it was our duty to look at the situation realistically. He felt bound to say that he was in agreement with the foreign secretary [Halifax] in taking the view that if we thought it was possible that we could now get terms which, although grievous, would not threaten our independence, we should be right to consider such terms." According to Halifax's private diary, on June 6 Churchill also confirmed that "any peace terms now as hereafter offered must not be destructive of our independence."

The Big Decision

p. 133   Telegrams of congratulation are in the files of *Adjutantur des Führers,* NS–10/18 and /19.

p. 134   Canaris reported his talk with Hitler in a report on June 11, 1940 (T77/1450/0899).

pp. 135–36   On July 1, 1940, one of Ribbentrop's officials learned that "the Führer has directed that as little as possible is to be committed to paper about the whole business" —meaning his secret plans for annexing French territory. The official promptly wrote this down (Weizsäcker's files, Serial 1892H). A well-informed study is Professor Eberhard Jäckel, *Frankreich in Hitler's Europa,* (Stuttgart, 1966), especially Chap. IV. I also used Pierre Crenesse, *Le Proces de Wagner* (Paris, 1946), and interrogations of Dr. Wilhelm Stuckart's aides Dr. Hans Globke and Klas. See the naval staff diary, June 2, 1940, and Goebbels unpublished diary, May 30, 1942—Hitler told him that Brabant, Belgium, and Flanders were to become German Gaul and that the Netherlands and France were to be thrown back to "the frontiers of 1500."

p. 136   Greiser and Streckenbach are quoted verbatim in Hans Frank's diary, July 31, 1940. On the Madagascar plan and the developing Jewish problem, see Hitler's conference with Raeder on June 20, 1940. On the 24th Heydrich wrote reminding Ribbentrop that he had been promoting Jewish emigration on Göring's instructions since January 1939; two hundred thousand had already emigrated, and he asked the AA to inform him should there be any conferences on the Final Solution of the Jewish Problem. In fact an AA file with this title had existed since 1938, Serial 1513. Ribbentrop's staff had pressed him since June 3 at least to lay down Germany's policy on this—for example they might all be excluded from Europe; or the eastern Jews might be sorted out from the western Jews; or they might be given a national home in Palestine (which brought the "danger of a second Rome!") On the Madagascar idea see *inter alia* Rademacher's AA memo of July 3; Hitler's talk with Ambassador Abetz on August 3 (NG–1838); Luther's AA memo of August 15, 1940, and again of August 21, 1942 ("The R.S.H.A. enthusiastically adopted the Madagascar plan"); and Hitler's talk with Count Teleki on November 20, 1940.

p. 138   According to General Curt Siewert, Brauchitsch's staff officer, it was Brauchitsch who first egged Hitler on to tackle the problem of Russia (IfZ, ZS–345). We note also that late on June 21, 1940, the AA cabled the German military attaché in Moscow to be on guard for the first signs of Russian aggression against Romania, as Halder was "urgently interested." See in general J. W. Brügel's informative study on the Soviet ultimatum to Romania, in *VfZ,* 1963, pages 404 *et seq.*

p. 139   Many of the captured French documents were published in an AA White Book on air war in 1943. Churchill's postwar account of his meeting with Daladier on May 16, 1940 (memoirs, Vol. II), mentions neither his own bombing proposals nor Daladier's compelling arguments; nor does he publish his harshly worded telegram to Reynaud of

May 23, 1940, now in Weizsäcker's AA files, Serial 121, page 119942. See the files of Unterstaatssekretär Woermann, "War West II," for 104 more of the Allied documents.

p. 142   Invited by British officers to comment on his diary, Halder volunteered, re July 2, 1940 ("The Commander in Chief has flown to Berlin") the remark: "About this time Commander in Chief. Army asked me to begin operational thinking about Russia." Re the entry of July 3 ("Greiffenberg must take over as my deputy [OQu.I]"), Halder commented for the British: "For the planned operation in Russia." The political situation was already acute, as the naval staff diary, July 5, demonstrates. "Early further advances by Russians feared, objective: bolshevization of the Balkans . . ." Halder's frank commentary proves that the General Staff showed a more positive interest in attacking Russia—and earlier—than has hitherto been supposed.

p. 142   Lossberg described the origins of his historic study for a Russian campaign ("Fritz") in a private letter of September 7, 1956. For certain reasons he had omitted reference to this from his memoirs ("which were heavily altered by the publishers anyway"); in particular Helmuth Greiner, the OKW war diarist, had urged Lossberg to make Hitler appear solely responsible for the campaign. Note that in a speech to Gauleiters on November 7, 1943 (ND, 172–L) Jodl apparently admitted: "The Führer himself . . . apprised me as early as during the western campaign of his fundamental decision to tackle this [Soviet] danger as soon as our military situation made it at all possible."

p. 142   Lossberg, Jodl, and Puttkamer all stressed the psychological aspect—the need to tackle Russia while the German people were still in the mood. On February 17, 1941, Halder quoted Hitler as saying, "If Britain were finished, he would never manage to summon up the German nation against Russia again; so Russia must be dealt with first." As Hitler said in his famous speech of December 12, 1944, "You can't extract enthusiasm and self-sacrifice like something tangible, and bottle and preserve them. They are generated just once in course of a revolution, and will gradually die away. The grayness of day and the conveniences of life will then take hold on men again and turn them into solid citizens in gray flannel suits."

p. 143   His refusal to unleash the Luftwaffe against England appears in many documents. Major von Etzdorf noted on July 10, 1940: "Britain, three options: *Air war:* Führer opposed, as desires to draw up fresh requests; foreign minister in favor. *Blockade:* Führer in favor, hopes for effect within two and a half months. [*Peace*] *offer:* Reichstag has been postponed sine die . . ." And Tippelskirch noted similarly that Hitler was weighing several possibilities: "Fresh rubble heaps [*i.e.,* bombing war]; intensification of blockade?—Two months [suffice]. Ri[bbentrop] tougher line. Late autumn Russia?" On July 16, Major Etzdorf noted: "Britain: common sense may have to be bludgeoned into them." On July 23, Weizsäcker commented: "The fact is that Churchill's resistance is not logical but psychological in origin. Churchill has gone out on a limb and can't get back." (Private diary.)

p. 144   Apart from the many unpublished cables in AA files, I used Walter Schellenberg's unpublished manuscript memoirs—the handwriting is daunting but not illegible— and the Tippelskirch diary, July 11, 1940, in following the Duke of Windsor episode.

p. 145   The most important *FA* and other Intelligence intercepts were communicated to the German ambassador in Moscow and are in his embassy's files; remarkably, most have not been published. Echoes of them can be traced in the Etzdorf, Halder, and Tippelskirch diaries. A highly important summary of them will be found in *Pol. V* files in AA archives, Serial 104, pages 113176 *et seq.*

p. 146   OKW files reflect the economic chaos caused by the withdrawal of barges for invasion preparations. By July 22 a thousand German barges had been requisitioned, and nine hundred more in Holland and Belgium (T77/201/7513).

p. 148   On July 15, 1940, Papen also warned that Stalin had 180 divisions available. General Halder's experts were more optimistic: Colonel Eberhard Kinzel (Foreign Armies East) allowed the Russians 20 infantry, 4 cavalry, and 4 mechanized divisions or brigades in Poland; 20 infantry, 4 cavalry divisions, and 6 mechanized brigades in the Baltic states; 15 infantry divisions in Finland; and 15 infantry, 9 cavalry divisions, and 10 mechanized brigades in the annexed part of Romania (AL/1367).

p. 149   Hitler's private meeting with Jodl is often stated to have been on July 29, 1940. It was certainly between July 27 and 30. I relied on Jodl's various postwar accounts and on what he told his staff—Warlimont, Lossberg, Falkenstein, and Junge.

The Dilemma

p. 153   See Professor A. Haushofer's note on his conversation with Rudolf Hess on September 8, 1940 (T253/46/9921) and Walter Stubbe's memorial essay in *VfZ*, 1960, pages 246 *et seq.* Rather sinisterly, Haushofer's letters to the Duke of Hamilton were intercepted by the British secret service and never reached him (PRO, Hess files, FO 371/26566).

p. 153   According to the—unpublished—dispatch of the German minister in Paris on August 3, the French lady's maid of the duchess reported that "the Duke has no intention of embarking to take up his new post but would await further events in Europe in Lisbon." This bore out the reports of the envoys—Eberhard von Stohrer in Madrid and Baron Oswald von Hoyningen Huene in Lisbon.

p. 155   Raeder admitted Hitler had duped him in a note for the admiralty historian K. Assmann, April 10, 1944 (Assmann's files, PG/33945b). Note too the extreme reticence of the OKW war diary. Although Hitler was explicit on July 31, 1940, about his intention to attack Russia, it is buried in the OKW diary of Greiner thus: "For further utterances of the Führer to Army Commander in Chief see [Warlimont's] note of August 1." Eberhard recalled in an interview with me in 1970 that when Greiner visited OKH headquarters at Fontainebleau in the summer of 1940 he hinted to the Luftwaffe liaison team there that there was to be no invasion of England. "You'll see well enough next spring why nobody's putting any weight into it." And on August 6, Tippelskirch—Halder's chief of Intelligence —noted: "Engel [Führer's army adjutant] says, Führer has powerful hangup [over England] . . . If no decision this autumn, lock up shop until May." Finally, we observe that after Hitler's speech on August 14 the chief of naval operations approached Jodl thus: "Should the Führer inwardly have resolved not to execute [the invasion of Britain], we propose it should be called off so as to take the pressure off our economy, while keeping this top secret. In its place a special deception operation should be mounted to maintain the threat on the enemy" (naval staff war diary). On August 22, Tippelskirch then recorded the further ripples of Hitler's new strategy: "[Foreign Armies East] briefing notes on Russia . . . Etzdorf: general policy against Russia? . . . Don't throw Russia and Britain into each other's arms. Führer against Russia. Molotov's speech [on August 1, in Moscow]. A long war . . ."

p. 159   Weizsäcker, Ribbentrop's number-two man, was not pleased by Hitler's move into Romania. He wrote in his diary on September 1, 1940: "Our relations with Russia are beginning to suffer. Molotov announces that the Arbitration Award between Hungary and Romania violates last year's [German-Soviet] pact—the joint consultation requirement. Of course it's our guarantee to Romania that the Russians regard as an obstacle and a slight to them. There'll be more slights yet, as we're beginning to favor Finland and to occupy northern Norway in force. In my own view this is exposing our hand too soon, because we still have eight months ahead of us in which we can't properly get to military grips with Russia."

Schmundt's flight to seek out a new HQ site in East Prussia—the later famous Wolf's Lair—is fixed by his widow's diary as August 27–29, 1940. Halder's diary shows that the army had begun looking by August 14.

p. 160   On August 29, 1940, the naval staff prepared for Admiral Raeder a survey on "Warfare against Britain if 'Sea Lion' [the invasion] is dropped" (PG/31762c). Raeder discussed it with Hitler on September 6. As the British translator evidently did not realize the significance of "the *S*-problem," he simply omitted the whole paragraph and renumbered the rest (*Brassey's Naval Annual,* 1949, page 135).

p. 161   I used mainly Milch's transcript of Hitler's secret conference of September 14, 1940; but also Halder's diary, the OKW and naval staff diaries. In a speech the day before, Hitler had already decided against an invasion of England, according to the OKW diary; and General von Weichs recalled Hitler's closing words as: "The war is all but over. I no longer need to take such a risk."

p. 162   Jodl's order of September 6, 1940, included the ambiguous words, "The impression must not be allowed to arise in Russia from these redeployments that we are preparing an eastern offensive."

p. 162   Lossberg's operations study "East" (Fritz), of September 15, 1940, is in Moscow archives and published by L. Bezymenski in *Sonderakte Barbarossa,* pages 307 *et seq.* Lossberg's family confirmed its authenticity to me.

Molotov

p. 165   Göring—his staff under interrogation testified to this too—argued for a German attack on Gibraltar, the occupation of French North Africa and Dakar, and the sealing-off of the Mediterranean instead of a Russian campaign; he also wanted the navy to invade the Azores as a German Atlantic base.

p. 166   Hitler's phrase "fraud on a grand scale" is quoted by Weizsäcker and appears in the notes of Etzdorf, Halder, and Tippelskirch as well at this time.

p. 167   The Finnish military attaché in Moscow quoted to his German counterparts information that the Russians were beginning to spread anti-German propaganda in the factories (T77/1027/0207).

p. 172   Although Mussolini's letter to Hitler is dated "October 19, 1940," Hewel's receipt for it, signed in Hitler's train at Montoire, shows it did not arrive until the 24th (AA files, Büro RAM). The original teletype from Ribbentrop's train *Heinrich* is in Hewel's private papers.

p. 173   The available documents suggest that—perhaps on October 4, 1940—Hitler had given Mussolini a free hand against Greece, but in the distant future and only if unavoidable. On October 21 Weizsäcker noted (diary): "Toward Italy we are right respectful. We're not restraining the Italian intention of dropping on Greece soon. Axis loyalty." On October 23 the OKW diary noted Jodl's suspicion that the Führer had agreed without telling his closer staff. This was echoed by the naval staff diary on the 25th, while Weizsäcker noted that day that Mussolini "announces he'll intervene in Greece simultaneously with next offensive against Egypt." See the naval staff file PG/33316, Tippelskirch's diary —with its minute-by-minute account of October 28—and Badoglio's memoirs, *Italien im Zweiten Weltkrieg* (Munich) pages 51 *et seq.,* and Karl Ritter's memo of November 7, 1940 (NG–3303)

p. 174   The adjutant was Engel. Tippelskirch wrote on November 1, 1940: "Führer in filthy temper about Greece. [Italians are] just amateurs, getting nowhere. Duce complains about his generals, if only he had some like ours."

p. 174   I have quoted the Führer's lament with some reluctance from M. Bormann's notes on Hitler's last Table Talk conversations—that on February 20, 1945. These notes have survived only in French translation, upon which British and German (!) translations have since been based.

p. 175   Etzdorf analyzed the divergence of German and Italian policy on November 14, 1940, in these words: "Italians want to state their claims [on French territories] right now. Führer against this as France would then drift away, as she wouldn't swallow [loss of] Corsica and Tunisia. Hitler wants to play it cool, there's still time yet, forbids [Ribbentrop] to let Ciano raise the matter if he meets Laval and Ciano. Question: Peace with Britain at France's or Italy's expense?"

p. 180   I suspect that Hitler deliberately allowed some of his ministers to spread the impression that the Molotov talks had gone harmoniously. (Evidence of this is in Raeder's files, PG/31762c; in naval staff diary, November 16, 1940; in Weizsäcker's circular to diplomatic missions, November 15; in the diaries of Halder and Tippelskirch). Goebbels's press directive of November 14 was unctuous and oily in its tone. But Heinrich Himmler was more succinct in his secret speech to Party district leaders on November 28, 1940. "Upshot is: all treaties and economic agreements are to be exploited to the full; then shaken off the moment they become a burden after the war and lose their importance."

The "Barbarossa" Directive

p. 185   German records on the British operational plans in Ireland will be found in Etzdorf's file ("Misc.") and the diaries of the OKW, the naval staff, Tippelskirch, and Halder.

p. 188   Hitler still smarted under Franco's rebuff three years later. He described Franco's excuses as "threadbare" to Hewel, who wrote in a letter of February 1, 1944: "At the time the Führer commented, 'The man has missed the historic chance offered him by fate. This he'll never be able to make up for.' " In January 1944, Hewel supplied Hitler with a comparison of Spain's 1940 "minimum existence" demands, and the actual supplies the Allies had since made to her, "which had enabled her not only to survive but to rebuild her economy." Thus in 1940 Franco had demanded 103,000 tons of petroleum a month; but in the whole of 1942 the Allies had supplied only 15,000 tons.

p. 190   On January 21, 1941, Etzdorf recorded this note on German policy toward the U.S.: "Roosevelt made two speeches, one 'fireside' and one to Congress. [Führer] is not to reply, so as not to help Roosevelt fan the flames. Roosevelt's line is to provide maximum assistance to Britain short of war, with soonest possible provocations so *we'll* declare war."

p. 190   The final "Barbarossa" directive of December 18, 1940, will be recognized as an awkward compromise between the OKW and General Staff proposals, which were in part incompatible.

p. 193   Goebbels's speech draft—amended in Hitler's handwriting—is in BA file NS–10/37.

Let Europe Hold Its Breath

p. 200   I have used Erwin Rommel's memoirs, *Krieg ohne Hass* (Heidenheim, 1950) and his private correspondence (T84/R274 *et seq.*).

p. 206   The oil factor in the "Barbarossa" campaign is emphasized in the war diary of Keitel's OKW economics staff (T77/668).

p. 207   Besides other standard sources on the North Africa fighting, like the war diaries of Rommel's various commands, I have used his writings and correspondence with his wife, Lucie, and with Colonel Schmundt, which reveal his strong dependence on Hitler. Thus on March 3, 1941, he wrote: "Major Grünow brought back from Berlin the Führer's greetings and news that he is delighted at the change in our fortunes since my arrival and intervention here. He supports my actions to the hilt. That pleased me, it gives me strength to do greater deeds." And on April 4: "Führer congratulates me on the unexpected successes, sends guidelines for continuation which wholly conform with my own ideas" (T84/R274).

Behind the Door

p. 209   Fearing an injunction from the Soviet embassy in Bonn, my German publishers have omitted the description of the Soviet embassy in Paris. Heydrich's report to Ribbentrop, dated July 2, 1941, is in Weizsäcker's file, Serial 105. In Ritter's AA file, Serial 1386, page 358996, is Canaris's report: "A side wing of the embassy was equipped as a GPU base complete with instruments for torturing, executions, and the disposal of corpses." Colonel Lahousen's eyewitness description is in CO files, AL/1933. Hewel's Ledger proves the reports went to Hitler on July 25, 1941. Goebbels also refers to them in his (unpublished) diary of August 10, 1941 (T84/267).

p. 216   Paula Hitler was interrogated at Berchtesgaden on May 26, 1945.

p. 217   Ribbentrop, in *Zwischen London und Moskau,* page 224, recalls Hitler describing the Yugoslav ministers' gloom "as though they were at a funeral." Prince Paul himself was more of a realist, however; under German interrogation, Dragizha Tsvetkovich and his secretary related that when he was forced to abdicate a few days later the prince declared he was convinced that an alliance with Britain would result in the ruination of their country (AA, files of task force Künsberg, Serial 2013H, pages 443373 *et seq.*). For the bribery employed by Churchill's government to secure the prince's overthrow, see *The Cadogan Diaries,* page 366.

p. 218   The events of March 27–28, 1941, are described from the diaries of Halder, Hewel, Waldau; the German records of Hitler's talks with Sztójay and Parvan Draganoff; Hungarian records in the national archives of Budapest; and the OKW operations staff note on Hitler's conference of March 27 (1746–PS).

p. 219   The immediate fear of the naval staff (war diary, April 3, 1941) was, "Through the Balkan operation, "Operation B[arbarossa]" is going to be held up by around five weeks, initially." That the heavy rains would in fact have delayed it anyway becomes clear from the postwar testimony of Heusinger, Gyldenfeldt, and others.

p. 220   The German record of Hitler's most important meetings with the Japanese ambassador and foreign minister has not always survived, but the Japanese texts of Oshima's cables are in Tokyo archives, usefully translated into German in *WR,* 1968, pages 312 *et seq.*

pp. 221–22   Summaries of Hitler's secret speech of March 30, 1941, are in the diaries of Bock, Halder, Waldau, and Milch, and in the war diaries of the OKW and naval staff and the latter's volume of appendices C (Part VII). Raeder was particularly pleased by Hitler's undertaking to expand the German battle fleet—particularly with battleships and aircraft carriers—"after the army's big tasks were dealt with." (On April 7, General Friedrich Fromm's Chief of Staff was to note in his diary Brauchitsch's statement: " 'Barbarossa' on June 22 or 23. Create operational reserve . . . What happens after 'Barbarossa's' dealt with? Schwerpunkt switches to navy and Luftwaffe.")

A Bitter Victory

p. 224   Colonel von Lossberg delivered a useful lecture on the Balkan campaign as early as May 5, 1941 (T77/792).

p. 227   The difficulties with the Italians are eloquently recapitulated in a memo by the German military attaché, Rintelen, dated April 23, 1941, in Ritter's AA files, and by Keitel (memoirs, page 264). On April 28, Keitel explained to Canaris: "The Führer has disowned any interest in the Balkan affairs insofar as no regions occupied by German troops are concerned, and is leaving these questions entirely up to the Italians. . . . We want to see the Italians—who are just like children, wanting to gobble up everything—spoil their appetite with things they just can't digest. For the time being we must control our temper to the utmost, and above all do nothing in those territories that might be interpreted in any way as being anti-Italian. Otherwise, the Führer regards himself—as far as the Croats are concerned—as an Austrian" (Lahousen diary).

p. 231   Scherff's appointment aroused strong antagonism from the two OKW war diarists Schramm and Greiner. Before committing suicide in May 1945, Scherff ordered the stenograms of Hitler's war conferences destroyed lest the enemy abuse them for their own ends. Fortunately Scherff's adjutant, Wilhelm Scheidt, took notes on which he based a useful series of articles in *Echo der Woche,* September–November 1949. His widow also turned his papers over to me.

p. 232   Weizsäcker, who was even more hostile to "Barbarossa" than Ribbentrop, recorded in his diary: "Schulenburg was alone with the Führer, instructed—by Ribbentrop—to outline to him the view 'as seen from Moscow'. . . . The Führer saw him barely thirty minutes and described his military preparations as defensive, rather as he did to Matsuoka." Months later Goebbels would mockingly note in his diary that Schulenburg steadfastly refused to believe the enormous military preparations being made by Stalin against Germany. Weizsäcker's famous comment on Schulenburg's memo was this: "If every Russian town burned down was worth as much to us as one British warship sunk, then I would speak up for a German-Russian war this summer." On April 29 he explained in his diary: "Ribbentrop is basically averse to the war because of his so recent speeches in favor of friendship with Russia." The next day, however, Hitler flattered Ribbentrop by appearing at his birthday party in Berlin-Dahlem; and on May 1, 1941, Weizsäcker noted with resignation: "Ribbentrop has now come out in writing in favor of the war against Russia in a letter to the Führer. He reproaches me for being negative about yet one more Great Decision."

p. 233   Hitler's speech of April 29, 1941, is recorded on discs in BA files (discs Le 5 EW 66,319 *et seq.*)

p. 234   Eden visited Athens from March 30. In *The Reckoning,* page 200, he suggests that he had learned "from the Americans" there of what Hitler told Prince Paul. On March 31 this was reported to London, and Eden repeated it on April 6 both to London and to the British ambassador in Athens, who stated that Eden had learned it via King George II of Greece from Prince Paul (see AA's cable to Ritter, April 18, 1941, AA Serial 4467, page E221085). Meanwhile on April 2 the Abwehr had learned from agents in the Soviet embassy in Berlin that Moscow was convinced that war with Germany was a certainty: "The war is inevitable, as sure as two times two is four" (T77/792/1141).

pp. 234–35   Stalin's extraordinary embrace is described in many telegrams from Moscow (PG/33738), the Weizsäcker diary, and Table Talk, July 27, 1942; Hewel also showed Hitler a Forschungsamt report on "Incidents on Matsuoka's departure from Moscow."

p. 235   The charred, undated memo by Canaris on Jodl's cynical disclosure is transcribed in CO file AL/1933.

p. 236   The naval staff war diary, March 27, 1941, punctuates the Soviet warship statistics with double exclamation marks. Heinrich Himmler referred very pertinently to the dramatic Soviet arms production effort in a secret speech to Gauleiters on August 3, 1944. "People say, 'We had no need to make war on Russia, Stalin wouldn't have touched us ever.' But the very fact that this Mr. Stalin had stocked up with twenty thousand tanks speaks for itself. So does everything we then found by way of troop concentrations and preparations. Only a few days ago I told someone, 'You know—it's obvious you're quite right: Stalin laid on this army just to play a bit of soldiers. For that you've got to stockpile twenty thousand tanks and a gigantic air force.' " In fact—as John Erickson's standard work, *The Soviet High Command* (London, 1962), pages 584 *et seq.,* states, in June 1941 Stalin had organized twenty-four thousand tanks in sixty tank-brigades or divisions.

p. 238   Zhukov glosses over Stalin's secret speeches of May 5, 1941, in the Russian edition of his memoirs; in western editions he omits them entirely. But several generals who had been present were captured and interrogated by the Nazis in 1942 and 1943; they believed Stalin was preparing an offensive for August or September 1941. The reports are in AA files, Serials 1083 and 1699; see also Ribbentrop's remarks to the Bulgarians on October 19, 1943; interrogations of Göring and Ribbentrop; and Weichs's memoirs, N19/9.

Hess and Bormann

p. 242   Rudolf Hess was interrogated in Britain in May 1941 (ND, M-117). I also relied on the diaries of Bormann, Hewel, Halder, and Weizsäcker, and Goebbels's ministerial conferences; unpublished memoirs of Below, Schellenberg, Schaub, Ley, and Linge—the latter in Russian archives; and postwar testimonies of Speer, Bohle, Darré, Puttkamer, Dr. Erich Isselhorst, and Hess's secretary Laura Schrödl. General Bodenschatz amplified my account in an interview in 1970.

p. 247   The official Party statement late on May 12, 1941, ran: "Despite a strict order from the Führer forbidding any further flying activity, on account of a progressive illness from which Party-member Hess has suffered for some years, he recently managed to get possession of an aircraft again. Toward 6 P.M. on Sunday, May 10, Hess took off from Augsburg on a flight from which he has not returned. A letter he left behind is so incoherent as to give evidence of a mental derangement, which gives rise to fears that he is the victim of hallucinations. The Führer has ordered the immediate arrest of the adjutants of Hess, who alone knew of his flight and despite the Führer's orders did nothing to hinder or report it. Under the circumstances it is to be feared that Party-member Hess has crashed or met with an accident somewhere."

The BBC repeated this without comment at 10 P.M., and at 11 P.M. added the comment that Hess had "been bumped off by the Gestapo" just as Mussolini had murdered Marshal Italo Balbo (who had in fact been shot down in error by his own antiaircraft guns). Not until 6 A.M. on May 13 did the BBC announce that Hess was on British soil, speciously adding: "Great Britain is the only country in which Hess felt safe from the Gestapo."

p. 249   Dr. Robert Ley wrote privately in August 1945: "I found a number of reasons to suspect that Bormann at least knew of the strange flight to Britain. For example, his complete indifference to the Führer's deep emotion during that remarkable assembly at the Berghof [on May 13, 1941] where the Führer told us—as shattered as he was—of Hess's act and passed judgment on it. Bormann was ice-cold, as though it did not affect him in the least; indeed some seemed to detect signs of pleasure in him" (from Ley's private papers).

p. 250   The timely death of Gauleiter Röver: see Heydrich's letter to Himmler, May 13, 1942 (T175/139/7452 *et seq.*).

p. 251   Professor Andreas Hillgruber has published several studies on the structure of Hitler's coalition war—*e.g.*, in *WR,* 1960, pages 659 *et seq.;* see too Hitler's order of May 1, 1941 (T77/792/1209, and in file PG/31025), and the files of General Staff and OKW conferences with the Finns on T78/458, and Ritter's AA files, Serial 833. As Ernst Klink points out in his study of the German-Finnish coalition, in *WR,* 1958, page 391, Field Marshal Mannerheim's memoirs are unduly reticent on the extent of Finland's collaboration with Hitler in the preparation of "Barbarossa."

p. 254   Puttkamer told me, in interviews in 1967 and 1968, of Hitler's uneasiness upon learning that the *Bismarck* had sailed. Captain Wolf Junge, Jodl's naval aide, also wrote of it in his unpublished memoirs, and it is indirectly confirmed by the naval staff's war diary on June 7–two weeks later. "He [the Führer] requests to be informed *in advance* of future naval staff decisions on the operations of surface warships!" From the same diary, June 13, 1941, we learn that naval security was so poor that the *Bismarck* sailed from Gotenhafen with bands playing.

p. 255   The naval staff war diary of May 13, 1941, bears eloquent testimony to Hitler's determination to avoid war with the United States: the German navy was to use extreme caution both inside and outside the declared blockade area when American ships were concerned, even if this put the German sailors at a great disadvantage, "as the Führer has *no intention whatever* of provoking an American entry into the war by some incident or other at the present moment." This determination was repeated on May 22 *(ibid.)*.

p. 258   That the *Bismarck* scuttled herself—and was not "sunk"—was later confirmed by Captain Junak, her turbine officer, who himself opened the sea cocks.

p. 260   Halder exuded confidence when army chiefs of staff met for an OKH conference on June 4, 1941. The Russian deployment on the frontier was purely defensive. "The whole fight may take several days, or perhaps even a considerable number of days; but then there will follow a vacuum, if the enemy retains his present formation, and he will scarcely have time to change it now" (Appendix to Seventeenth Army war diary, BA file 14,499/5).

Pricking the Bubble

p. 261   There is a wealth of detail on the hitherto neglected Iraq affair in Hewel's diary. On May 30, 1941, Hitler realized the German force might be ejected from Iraq, but told Hewel: "The last to leave must be the Germans, particularly if Italians are still fighting there. The Mossul position is important as an attack base during 'Barbarossa.' " On May 31, Hewel recorded a long conference of Hitler, Keitel, Jodl, and Ribbentrop from 9 A.M. onward, unusually early because the Iraqis were demanding to know whether Germany could aid them or not by 11 A.M. The British had a hundred tanks there; but Turkey was refusing permission to Germany to send in tanks and guns. After a further evening conference with Ribbentrop, Göring, Jeschonnek, Keitel, and Jodl, the Führer decided he could not help although "we must realize that if we go back the whole Arab uprising will die down." Hewel noted: "Meantime a telegram arrives from Mossul announcing the collapse of resistance there; so there is nothing else to discuss."

p. 262   Hitler's "Barbarossa" hint to Mussolini is confirmed in the German embassy's telegram from Rome to Berlin on June 22, 1941: "As the Duce claims to have told the Führer already, during their last conference at the Brenner [on June 2], he completely shares the Führer's view that the Russian problem demands an immediate solution, and that if this cannot be attained by negotiations then it must be by force." By 1943 Mussolini had changed his tune—claiming to have warned the Führer "early in 1941" against a Russian campaign (Weizsäcker diary, February 7, 1943).

p. 262   Hitler's similar hint to Oshima is also recorded in Hewel's diary, June 3, 1941. "Berghof . . . Führer spends afternoon with Reichsmarschall. 7 P.M. Oshima: [Führer] hints at 'Barbarossa'; I write the protocol." Dr. Bernd Martin summarizes in *Deutschland und Japan im Zweiten Weltkrieg* (Stuttgart, 1967), page 97, the Japanese-language sources confirming that Oshima understood the hint.

p. 263   Task Force Künsberg's telegram of June 6, 1941, about "Pendlebury"—which was shown to Hitler—is in Ritter's file, Serial 4667.

p. 263   Key documents on the "Commissar" Order will be found on microfilms T77/792 and T78/458. I also used the Nuremberg documents 1471–PS, 2884–PS, NOKW–209, NOKW–484, NOKW–1076, NOKW–3357, and 886–PS. As Keitel admitted to his son, in a private talk in his Nuremberg death cell on September 25, 1946: "Jawohl, I know it was wrong. But either we won, or it was all over for the German nation anyway" (Keitel family papers).

p. 267   Hitler recalled his warning to Göring, both in conversation with Marshal Antonescu on January 10, 1943, and in a secret speech to his generals on May 26, 1944 (T175/94/4963). Below also quotes the warning in his unpublished memoirs.

p. 270   On Hitler's interim plan to dump western Europe's Jews in Hans Frank's Generalgouvernement, see Lammers's letter to Schirach, December 3, 1940 (1950–PS); General Alfred Streccius's letter to General Fromm, February 24, 1941 (BA, RH 1/v. 58); Bormann's memo of October 2, 1940 (USSR-172), and the corresponding entries in Hans Frank's diary on October 27 and 31, November 6, 1940, January 11, and July 17, 1941. Rosenberg's speech of June 20, 1941 (page 271) is in CO file AL/1933; see also the war diaries of the OKW, June 20, and naval staff, June 21, 1941.

p. 273   A private letter of Hitler's adjutant Alwin-Broder Albrecht on Saturday June 21, 1941, reveals the late hours that were kept. "The tempo since then has been hectic, with me on duty until 2:30 A.M. on Thursday, until 3:30 A.M. yesterday, and today it's going to be late—that is, early—again."

As for Hitler's final decision to attack—Jodl's relevant signal of June 20 is in naval file PG/31025—years later Hitler's staff still recalled how he sweated over it. Hewel wrote privately on February 1, 1944: "The decision which the Führer had to take, to attack Russia, was unimaginably tough, and he had to take it quite alone. He grappled for months with it before making his mind up to go ahead—certainly against his hopes and desires, but because he had seen the danger and realized that those who trifle with a danger only enlarge it all the more."

3 CRUSADE INTO RUSSIA

The Country Poacher

p. 281 The Abwehr's clandestine operations had contributed heavily to the initial success of "Barbarossa." Important bridges, including those at Dvinsk, were seized in advance by units of the "Brandenburg" Regiment, and held at a cost of twenty-three lives until Leeb's main force arrived. Abwehr-trained Lithuanian activists lost some four hundred dead in similar operations to secure twenty-four key bridges along the attack route of the Sixteenth Army. See Lahousen's diary, June 28, and July 10, 1941, and Colonel Erwin Stolze's written testimony of December 25, 1945 (ND, USSR-231).

p. 283 On July 26, 1941, Etzdorf noted that Hitler had decided "Sweden is to be 'left to fall by the wayside,' since she doesn't want to join the Axis." Hitler refused permission for Swedish officers to visit the battlefront.

p. 284 Hitler's order of July 13, 1941, will be found in naval file PG/32020. The order of July 14 is on film T77/545.

p. 285 Weizsäcker, Ribbentrop's number-two man, at least recognized Hitler's long-term aim of war with the New World. On August 13, 1941, he wrote cryptically in his diary: " 'People' think that Germany and Britain are winning such mutual admiration in the present duel that sometime later they will march together against the U.S.A." And on September 15: "England is the country of 'our' [*i.e.,* Hitler's] respect, indeed almost of 'our' love. To advance with her against the U.S.A.—that is the dream of the future." Careful readers will also find traces of Hitler's aim in his talk with Ciano on October 25, 1941.

p. 285 Lieutenant Jacob Jugashvili, Stalin's son from his first marriage, committed suicide in 1943 after British fellow-prisoners made life unbearable for him because of his uncouth behavior. (See U.S. State Dept. files.) His interrogations are in AA files, Serial 1386, pages 358994 *et seq;* and see Hitler's Table Talk, May 18–19, 1942.

p. 285 On the unknown Russian tanks, see the war diary of Army Group North, June 24–25, 1941 (T311/53); the Waldau diary, July 3 and 15; Halder's diary, July 24–25; Hitler's remarks to Oshima on July 14 and to Goebbels (unpublished diary, August 18, 1941). The German official historian Klaus Reinhard, in *Die Wende vor Moskau* (Stuttgart, 1972), pages 18 and 25, comes to the same conclusion as I do: Halder wholly misinformed Hitler on the Russian strengths, realized this only in mid-August 1941, but continued to make the same error.

p. 286 Colonel Erwin Lahousen's memo of July 20, 1941, is in CO file AL/1933. Later, Canaris indignantly propagated the self-defense that he had correctly predicted the Russian tank potential and particularly their supertanks, but that nobody had listened to him (Goebbels diary, April 9, 1943). This was quite untrue.

p. 286 Stalin's speech will be found in BA file NS–26/v. 1194. Hitler ordered Hewel to destroy his copy of it. See his Table Talk on July 11–12, 1941, and particularly the passage in Bormann's note on the meeting of July 16 (1221–PS) quoting Hitler: "The Russians have now issued orders for partisan warfare behind our lines. But this has its advantages—it enables us to exterminate anybody who stands in our way." As early as July 5, Hitler ordered the police brigades equipped with captured tanks for their mopping-up operations (T77/792 1414).

p. 288 In Marshal Antonescu's papers (ND, USSR-237) is the letter Hitler wrote him on July 27, 1941, explaining that he was not trying to capture territory but to destroy enemy material. "It may be easy enough for the Russians to replace men; to replace well-trained combat troops is not so easy for them, while the replacement of arms and material on this scale is quite impossible, particularly once we have occupied their main production centers." Besides, as Hitler explained to Minister Fritz Todt on June 20, Germany had not yet attained self-sufficiency in certain raw materials and had to conquer those regions of Russia for that purpose (2353–PS, and Todt diary).

p. 289 Bormann's note on Hitler's conference of July 16, 1941, survives (1221–PS); I also used Colonel Georg Thomas's papers; he learned on July 17: "The Führer desires that no military power factor should remain west of the Urals" (T77/441). Further versions of the conference are in Consul Otto Bräutigam's hitherto unexploited diary in the Library of Congress manuscripts division; in interrogations of Rosenberg, Lammers, and Göring; and in Etzdorf's notes of July 16 and August 12 1941. The latter quotes Bräutigam thus: "Führer has commanded that Crimea with its hinterland Tauria will belong to Germany. The Russian inhabitants are to be brought out to Russia, 'I don't care where, Russia's big enough.' Reichskommissar Koch is very reluctant to take up the new job; he'll do it only as long as necessary for the Four-Year Plan. He's only interested in East Prussia." Hitler's decrees resulting from the conference are on films T77/545 and T175/145.

p. 290   Werner Koeppen remained at Führer HQ until February 1943, writing a total of 192 lengthy summaries of Hitler's table talk and conferences for Rosenberg's information. Of these, Nos. 27–55 survived, as duplicates were supplied to Gauleiter Alfred Meyer (T84/387); Koeppen kindly authenticated them for me. I believe nobody has exploited them before me.

p. 290   On the Lithuanian pogroms, see the war diary of Army Group North; Hitler's talk with Kvaternik on July 22, 1941; and the report of the AA liaison officer in Riga on April 5, 1943 (Serial 1513, pages 372208 *et seq.*). Hitler frequently used the "Jewish bacillus" imagery, *e.g.,* in his talk with Horthy on April 17, 1943. See in this connection Alexander Bein's interesting analysis, "The Jewish Parasite—Comments on the Semantics of the Jewish Problem" in *VfZ,* 1965, pages 121 *et seq.*

p. 292   Hitler's deduction that Churchill and Roosevelt were conspiring to stage a suitable "incident" is confirmed by a cynical memorandum in Churchill's secret papers on the search for the *Prinz Eugen.* He wrote: "It is most desirable that the United States navy should play a part in this. It would be far better, for instance, that she should be located by a United States ship, as this might tempt her to fire upon that ship, thus providing the incident for which the United States would be so thankful." Churchill never published this; but Ludovic Kennedy did, in *Pursuit* (London, 1974), page 222.

p. 293   Weizsäcker, who saw Ribbentrop for the first time after six weeks on September 5, 1941, wrote in his diary: "[Ribbentrop] asked me to avoid anything that might give the Führer—who's immersed in military affairs—cause for political worry; his health has temporarily suffered from the bunker life, so we must spare him every anxiety we can. He, Ribbentrop, is only feeding good news to him too. He says that consecutive on our victory in Russia the Führer's planning to advance southward, probably into Iran or Egypt." But Ribbentrop admitted that the strength of the Russian resistance had surprised him.

p. 294   I had Hitler's electrocardiograms reinterpreted by a competent British expert, who also noted a progressive abnormality of repolarization, of which in a man of fifty-one the most likely cause would be coronary artery disease. Morell's medication was, according to an appreciation made for me by Professor Ernst-Günther Schenck—who was familiar with the proprietary medicines used by Morell—proper for this disease. According to Schenck, however, most of Morell's other medicines were either placebos or deliberately underdosed, no doubt to document his indispensability as Hitler's physician.

Kiev

p. 297   On Stalin's strength, Goebbels wrote in his unpublished diary on August 8, 1941: "The number of enemy tanks was originally estimated at ten thousand, but is now assumed to be twenty thousand." Moreover there was no doubt that Stalin had built up a major armaments industry beyond the Ural mountains (T84/267).

p. 301   On the Bishop Galen affair: Bormann's memorandum of August 13, 1941 (3702–PS); Goebbels diary, August 14, 1941, March 21, 1942, and May 12, 1943; Table Talk, July 4 1942; Rosenberg memo, May 8, 1942 (1520–PS); Hasselbach manuscript, September 26, 1945 (BA, Kl.Erw. 441–3); M.Bormann, circular of April 26, 1943 (T175/68/1860).

p. 301   Dr. Karl Brandt testified to Hitler's order stopping the euthanasia operation during his Nuremberg war crimes trial (Case I, protocol page 2443); see his interrogation, October 1, 1945. Only a few days earlier, on August 21, 1941, the pro-euthanasia film *Ich Klage an* (I Accuse) had met an enthusiastic reception at the Führer's HQ (Hewel diary). Up to one hundred thousand bedridden incurably insane people were mercy-killed by the war's end. The Germans argued that once the full weight of Allied saturation bombing fell on the cities, lunatic asylums were nowhere safe from air raids; that the existing hospital space was inadequate for the one million Wehrmacht casualties that were hospitalized; and that this space was further reduced by the necessity to leave all the upper floors of hospitals empty as an air raid precaution. The local authorities considered they had little choice but to empty hospital beds by euthanasia of the "useless" insane.

p. 302 Goebbels's brief for his discussion of anti-Jewish measures with the Führer, dated August 17, 1941, is on film T81/676/5739 *et seq.*, and see his diary, August 13–20. I also used his ministerial conferences of July 19, September 6 and 17, 1940, and May 27, 1942, and foreign ministry documents on AA Serial 4851H, pages 247680–8 and 247716. On the introduction of the Yellow Star emblem, see the Reich Law Gazette *(RGBl.)* I, 1941, page 547, and Heydrich's ordinances in BDC file 240, II, pages 167 *et seq.* ("Everything is to be done to prevent arbitrary and illegal excesses against the Jews now marked in this way. Swift action is to be taken against such transgressions.")

p. 308 Anti-German feeling in Italy ran high. According to the Hassell diary, September 20, 1941, Italian officers had declared to Admiral Canaris that there was to be a military putsch against Mussolini that winter. Two days later Major von Etzdorf noted that an Italian staff officer in the Balkans had muttered to a German officer, *"Meglio perdere que vincere con la Germania!"* (Better to lose than to win with Germany.)

pp. 310–11 The only record of Hitler's conversation with Abetz is in Etzdorf's files, AA Serial 1247, pages 337765 *et seq.* A summary by the quartermaster general went to the economic staff in France on September 24 (IfZ microfilm MA–167); and compare Koeppen's report of September 18, 1941. Weizsäcker's diary of September 15 adds ominously: "Switzerland will be meted out her punishment in a quite special manner."

p. 312 Late on September 3, 1941—a few hours after Field Marshal von Leeb had already authorized sporadic artillery fire on Leningrad—Keitel assured him that Hitler had no objection to the city's shelling or air bombardment (war diary, Army Group North).

p. 313 On the cruel conditions in beleaguered Leningrad, see Himmler's report to Hitler of October 23, 1942 (T175/194/3896), and an interrogation report of September 22, 1941 (T77/32/0896 *et seq.*) According to Lossberg, *Im Wehrmachtführungsstab*, page 132, Hitler had learned from an ancient paper by Ludendorff of the difficulties of feeding Leningrad and had then "against his soldiers" ordered the elimination of the population by starvation, freezing, and air raids. But OKW files contain Lossberg's *own* draft recommendations, dated September 21, 1941, for the fencing off of the city "if possible by electrified wire," with machine-gun guards; Lossberg admitted there might be epidemics, and it was "furthermore questionable whether we can trust our soldiers to open fire on women and children breaking out" (T77/792/1456 *et seq.*). After lunch with the Führer on September 18, Koeppen noted that the idea was to destroy all Russia's cities as a prerequisite to the lasting German domination of the country.

p. 314 The secret AA record of Hitler's remarks to Seyss-Inquart on September 26, 1941, was produced as evidence at the later Nuremberg trials (NG–3513).

p. 316 My account of Heydrich's posting to Prague is based on Koeppen's notes; Bormann's diary; the Reich justice ministry files R22/4070 and /4087; interrogations of Neurath, Karl-Hermann Frank, and Kurt Daluege; and Schellenberg's original manuscript, Vol. II, page 243; I also used an AA memo on Hitler's secret discussion with Neurath, Frank, and Gürtner, dated October 5, 1940 (ND, GB–521). The transcript of Heydrich's revealing speech of October 2, 1941, is in Czech state archives.

Cold Harvest

p. 318   On Russian winters, see the German air ministry summary dated September 22, 1941 (T77/32/0786 *et seq.*). After it was all over—on November 10, 1942—Field Marshal Milch told his staff that he and Albert Speer had just gone over the Russian meteorological records. "Last winter [*i.e.,* 1941–1942] was by no means abnormal, but by Russian standards a medium winter, as were the two previous winters. . . . Last winter was somewhat worse than the notorious winter of 1812 in October, November, and December. *But afterward,* when the French army [of Napoleon] had already been wiped out, in January, February, and March [1812], that was just about the coldest there had ever been; but not at the time Napoleon was on his retreat, that was still a medium winter" (MD 17/3128).

p. 319   Weizsäcker (diary, September 30, 1941) had evidently hoped for a more definitive speech by Hitler. "The Russian campaign has cost us only one tenth the casualties of World War I; at its end there is to be a speech by the Führer. Theme: We stand invincible astride this continent. For all we care the war can go on another thirty years." On October 5, Weizsäcker revised this. "The Führer made his speech yesterday, but only as an entr'acte, primarily for home consumption. The British can hardly have failed to notice the Führer's silent affection for them, which he still has today; Japan got short shrift indeed."

p. 321   A tactical controversy surrounds the Vyazma-Bryansk encirclement operations. General Hoepner's own comments, dated October 4, 1941, are in his papers (N51/2).

pp. 324–25   The journey reports written by Canaris and Lahousen in October 1941 are in CO file AL/1933; see also Lahousen's interrogations, and the diaries of Halder, November 12–14, 1941, and especially of Bock, October 20: "A nightmare picture of tens of thousands of Russian prisoners of war, marching with hardly any guards toward Smolensk. Half dead from exhaustion and starvation, these pitiful souls trudge on."

p. 325   The quotation is from Colonel Erwin Lahousen's journey report, October 23, 1941. In a further report on October 28, on his visit to Bock's HQ at Smolensk, Lahousen wrote: "At the conference with his G-2 [intelligence officer], Tarbuk raised the shooting of Jews at Borissov [Bock's former HQ]. Seven thousand Jews had been liquidated there 'in the manner of tinned sardines.' The scenes that had resulted were indescribable—often even the SD could not go on, and had to keep going by heavy consumption of alcohol" (AL/1933). In the report of an armaments inspector in the Ukraine to the OKW's General Thomas, December 2, 1941, the active assistance of the Ukrainian militia in the mass killings of the Jews is also emphasized (3257-PS).

p. 326   Himmler's letter to Greiser, September 18, 1941, is in SS files (T175/54/8695). See also his letter to SS Brigadier Uebelhör, the governor of Lodz, dated October 10 in the same file. The governor had protested that he had no room to accommodate the influx of Jews; Himmler sharply rebuked him: "It is in the Reich's interests that you accommodate the Jews, as it is the Führer's will that the Jews must be driven out from the west to east, step by step."

In addition to Hitler's adjutants (*e.g.,* Below, Puttkamer, Günsche, Engel, Wolff) whom I interviewed or whose testimony is available, all the (non-Party) Reichstag stenographers who recorded all his war and staff conferences, however secret, after September 1942, were closely interrogated about Hitler's involvement in the Jewish atrocities. Among the private papers of the stenographer Ludwig Krieger I found a note dated December 13, 1945. "In the Führer conferences which I reported in shorthand there was never any mention of the atrocities against the Jews. For the present it must remain an unanswered question, whether Hitler himself issued specific orders . . . or whether orders issued in generalized terms were executed by subordinates and sadists in this brutal and vile manner." Karl-Wilhelm Krause, Hitler's manservant from 1934 to 1943, believed the latter reason, explaining: "Hitler lived in a world of his own—he liked to believe good rather than evil of people." While Himmler's last adjutant, Werner Grothmann, whom I interviewed in 1970, felt it unlikely that the Reichsführer SS would have dared act on his own initiative, and Himmler's surviving brother Gebhard—formerly a high civil servant—told me the same in 1968, the written testimony of Karl Wolff is persuasive (IfZ, ZS–317); Wolff, who was also Himmler's Chief of Staff, believes that Himmler desired, in some bizarre way, to perform great deeds for the "Messiah of the next two thousand years"—without having to involve his Führer in them. Writing a confidential study on Hitler in his Nuremberg prison cell, Ribbentrop also exonerated him wholly. "How things came to the destruction of the Jews, I just don't know. As to whether Himmler began it, or Hitler put up with it, I don't know. But that he *ordered* it I refuse to believe, because such an act would be wholly incompatible with the picture I always had of him . . ." (Bavarian State Archives, Rep. 502 AXA 131).

p. 328 Weizsäcker summarized in his diary on October 21, 1941: "The peace compromise with Britain which we are ready to accept consists of this: the British Empire remains intact (woe, if India fell into other hands or chaos); in Europe of course Britain must stand back. . . . Britain—which will shortly be ruled by Beaverbrook—will come to realize that Germany's mission is to organize Europe against the Mongol flood from the east and that Germany and Britain will eventually have to stand side by side against the U.S.A."

p. 330 For Eichmann's conferences right up to October 1941 on the Madagascar project, see the reports—and Dieter Wisliceny's written testimony—in the IfZ collection F–71/8. Himmler's telephone notes are on film T84/95. Greiser's letter of May 1, 1942 (page 330) is answered by Himmler on July 27, 1942, to the effect that he had no objections to liquidating "with the utmost discretion" the tens of thousands of incurable tuberculosis cases that were also burdening Greiser's economy (NO–244). The February 1942 document quoted in my footnote on page 330 is Nuremberg document NG–5770; the original is in AA file "Undersecretary of State, *re* Colonies," Serial 2554.

p. 330 Heydrich's letter to Himmler, October 19, 1941, is in SS files (T175/54/8645).

p. 332 In view of Himmler's note of November 30, 1941, I cannot accept the view of Dr. Kubovy, of the Jewish Document Center, Tel Aviv, expressed in *La Terre Retrouvé* on December 15, 1960, that "there exists no document signed by Hitler, Himmler, or Heydrich speaking of the extermination of the Jews." Of equal evidentiary interest is Himmler's telephone call to Heydrich on April 20, 1942—after a day with Hitler—on which the Reichsführer noted: "No annihilation of gypsies." Yet the gypsies were also deported en masse to the death camps by the SS.

p. 333 The quartermaster general, Eduard Wagner, referred to his meeting with Hitler in private letters; there is more detail in Koeppen's report. On January 10, 1942, Wagner frankly admitted to Etzdorf that he had been misled by the General Staff's assessment that the Russian campaign would end in October, which would have released rail capacity for the transportation of winter clothing. "But the winter came a month earlier than usual . . . On December 15 the troops had their winter clothing, but it could not cope with temperatures of minus 10°F. and worse." On January 25, Keitel gave his OKW staff a similar explanation, and Göring told Mussolini much the same three days later. Popular legend—inspired after the war by the real culprits of the General Staff—ascribes to Hitler a categorical prohibition on preparing for a winter war in Russia. There is not even a hint of this in the contemporary records.

p. 334 There is information on Hitler's inspection of Wagner's winter equipment display on November 1, 1941, in Bormann's diary, Wagner's letters, and the testimony of Heinz von Gyldenfeldt, Baron Ulrich von Canstein, and Puttkamer.

p. 335 Raeder's anxiety about the Mediterranean is mirrored in the naval staff war diary and in the diaries of Waldau and Weizsäcker. The latter believed (diary, October 30, 1941): "We ought to be hitting Britain in the heart [*i.e.,* the Atlantic] and not on her limbs [Mediterranean]. What we've got now is a case of Not Only but Also." See also Göring's conference with Italians on October 2 (MD 65/7111 *et seq.*), Hitler's directives of October 29 and December 2, Jodl's note of October 22 (Annex XIV to naval staff war diary Part C) and Commander Wolf Junge's letter to the naval staff of November 3 (PG/33213), and above all Hitler's letter to Mussolini of October 16 and his conference with Admiral Fricke on October 27, 1941 (PG/31762e).

A Test of Endurance

p. 337   Erich Hoepner's critique of October 16, 1941, is in his papers (N51/2).

p. 338   Hassell's dealings are mentioned in his diary, September 20 and October 4, 1941. The correspondence between Heydrich, Ribbentrop, Himmler, and Hitler's staff (T175/125/0248 *et seq.*) disprove Dr. Hedwig Maier's theory that Himmler conspiratorially kept his knowledge of such dealings to himself *(VfZ,* 1966, pages 302 *et seq.)*

p. 340   In a telephone conversation with General Greiffenberg, Chief of Staff of Army Group Center, Halder expressed the following beliefs: "The Russians will try and hang on to the Moscow area as long as possible. This area—which is excellently linked with the Asiatic power sources—can be regarded as the bridgehead of Asiatic Russia in Europe. . . . In contrast to this, the possession of the Caucasus is not strategically necessary for the Russians and they can replace the oil fields they'll lose there by other adequate sources in the Urals and Asia. Their defense of Caucasus serves more of a negative purpose—to keep Germany out of the energy sources we so desperately need" (war diary of Army Group Center).

p. 341   Todt's private meeting with Hitler on November 29, 1941—immediately before the one mentioned on page 342—was also attended by the tank specialist Dr. Walter Rohland, who made available to me his pocket diary and unpublished manuscript memoirs.

p. 341   Notes on Hitler's tank-design symposia in February, May, and November 1941 are—with related correspondence—in the OKW war diary, Vol. I, and microfilm T77/17; I also used Todt's notebooks and the postwar testimony of Saur, his deputy (FD–3049/49).

p. 342   Milch's documents prove that the Luftwaffe "cold-start" technique—whereby basically a little gasoline was added to the engine oil while still warm to thin it ready for the next morning—was demonstrated to army liaison officers by Udet at Rechlin in Hitler's presence on July 6, 1939 (MD56/2678). Halder's diary shows that on December 6, 1941, Hitler advised the army to investigate the "Udet" cold-start technique, which was probably that described.

p. 343   Ribbentrop's full speech will be found in the BA's Reich Chancellery file R43II/606. Under interrogation (August 29, 1945) he stated that Hitler gave him express permission to make this reply to the—very shrewd—British propaganda motif that Ribbentrop had misinformed the Führer. For a recent—and surprisingly well-researched— examination of the origins of that canard see his widow's book *Die Kriegsschuld des Widerstandes* (Starnberg, 1974). In fact Ribbentrop warned Hitler in writing in his last report as ambassador in London that the British would be Germany's "deadliest enemies" and would stop at nothing to join war with her; this report, A 5522 of December 28, 1937, was allegedly "not found" by the Allied editors of the published German documents. (I found it in the Library of the British FO—where one would have expected to find it.) I have placed copies in the German AA library and the IfZ archives.

p. 343   Hewel later showed Hitler the AA's intercept of Ciano's coded telegram reporting their interview. According to Koeppen's note, Ciano and his entourage ate with Hitler and Ribbentrop alone. "The individual members of the Führer's HQ made virtually no attempt to conceal their dislike of him [Ciano]."

p. 344   On October 21, 1941, Marshal Pétain had written to Hitler reminding him of his offer at Montoire, adding: "The victory of your arms over bolshevism now gives even greater cause than there was one year ago to cooperate on peaceful works for the greatness of a changed Europe" (T77/851/5971).

p. 344   On the employment of Russian prisoners in German industry, see Milch's diary and Göring's conference of November 7, 1941 (1193–PS), and Speer's unpublished office chronicle, November 21 and 29. Despite opposition from the army—who could not handle the task—from the food minister, Darré, and from the Party, who feared Bolshevik contamination of Germany, Hitler insisted on the immediate employment and proper nutrition of the Russian prisoners. In this Fritz Sauckel, whom he appointed manpower commissioner in March 1942, supported him, as did Dr. Herbert Backe, Darré's number-two man. On March 22, Albert Speer recorded the Führer's categorical order: "The Russians are to receive absolutely adequate nutrition and Sauckel is to ensure that the food is provided by Backe." Moreover: "The Führer is surprised that the Russian civilians are still being treated like prisoners of war behind barbed wire. I [Speer] explain that this results from an order he issued. The Führer is aware of *no* such order." Hitler's attitude is confirmed by Frau Backe's private diary: on April 11 she summarized Backe's many conferences with Sauckel on the injection of one million Russians into the German arms industry. Hitler had told Sauckel, "Go to Backe first—it all depends on whether he can agree to feed them." Herbert Backe assured Sauckel the Russians would get "normal rations." "At the next conference Sauckel thanked Herbert for his help. Herbert's opinion tallies exactly with the Führer's, he said. Then he announced that he wants to import five hundred thousand foreign girls as home helps! Herbert was shocked at this and wouldn't quiet down all day because of it—how can such a thing be planned as though the Führer seriously desires it?"

p. 345 Unknown to Hitler, the German military attaché in Washington, General Friedrich von Boetticher, took pains to suppress any evidence that his theory that war with Japan would make it impossible for Roosevelt to intervene in Europe was wrong.

p. 346 My text is translated from Oshima's Japanese telegram to Tokyo—which was, significantly, intercepted by American cryptanalysts (ND, D-656). The German record describes Ribbentrop's remarks to Oshima even more clearly: "He didn't believe that Japan would avoid the conflict with America, and the situation could hardly be more favorable to the Japanese than now. He [Ribbentrop] thought they should exploit it now, while they were so strong" (T120/606/0025 *et seq.*).

p. 346 Baron von Weizsäcker summarized in his diary on December 6, 1941: "For four or five days now the Japanese have been afraid they will scarcely avoid their clash with the U.S.A. The Japanese navy has stepped up the pressure, for seasonal reasons. We have been asked if we'd be willing if need be to bind ourselves not to sign an armistice or peace without Japan's consent with the U.S.A. and Britain, and in the event of war with the U.S.A. breaking out to regard ourselves as at war with the U.S.A. as well. In my view we can't say No, but on the second count we must demand reciprocity. This is the line our negotiations have been taking. Today we'll probably reach agreement."

p. 347 Autopsy reports revealing that Waffen SS troops killed in battle had been partially eaten by the Russians will be found in the unpublished files of SS. division Nord (annexes to war diary, T175/120/5322 *et seq.*). On several occasions Hitler referred in private to Russian cannibalism—*e.g.*, to the new Croat envoy Budak on February 14, 1942 ("hundreds of bones and bits of human body" were found after a long siege of a Russian unit was ended), in Table Talk on the evening of April 5, to Goebbels (diary of April 21 and 26), and to the Belgian Fascist Anton Mussert (remarking on the "big stocks of human flesh" found on Russian prisoners of war) on December 10, 1942 (BA file NS–19/neu 1556).

p. 348 Timoshenko's secret speech was reported by the German military attaché in Berne (First Panzer Army, war diary, annex, N63/53). Timoshenko commanded the Soviet Southwest Front (*i.e.*, army group) from mid-September 1941, and was a member of the Soviet supreme command, the Stavka. Göring mentioned this speech to Mussolini on January 28, and Hitler to Antonescu on February 11, 1942.

p. 349 My version of events at Rundstedt's HQ is based on the diaries of Halder, Richthofen, Waldau, and Bock; the war diaries of Army Group South and the First Panzer Army; and an OKW note of December 3, 1941, as well as on postwar interrogations.

p. 349   The crisis in the Battle of Moscow: I used the diaries of Bock, Waldau, Richthofen, Halder, and Hewel; the war diaries of Army Group Center and the Second Panzer Army; interrogations of Guderian, Heusinger, Brauchitsch; G. Blumentritt's study of the Fourth Army's role in *WR,* 1954, pages 105 *et seq;* and especially Klaus Reinhard, *Die Wende vor Moskau* (Stuttgart, 1972). Guderian's son also supplied me with letters of his father, and diary extracts of General Liebenstein, his father's Chief of Staff, and of Lieutenant Joachim von Lehsten, Guderian's aide-de-camp.

p. 351   The Soviet counteroffensives opening on December 5–6, 1941, clearly accelerated Brauchitsch's decision to resign. On the 4th his chief staff officer, Colonel Gyldenfeldt, wrote in his diary: "With utter candor he has admitted that he just can't go on any longer, particularly since he feels completely incapable of holding his own in discussions with the Führer. Therefore he intends to take the necessary measures to wind up the eastern campaign, which must be regarded as not won, and to take responsibility for this; then he'll ask the Führer to relieve him of his post." See too Halder's testimony in the OKW Trial at Nuremberg, page 1891, and the recollections of Siewert, Engel, and Frau von Brauchitsch.

Hitler Takes Command

pp. 355–56   Commander Wolf Junge and General Ivo-Thilo von Throtha both referred in their unpublished memoirs to frontline rumors of Hitler's presence. The long quotation is from Hitler's remarks to Speer and Milch on May 24, 1942 (in Milch's papers).

p. 357   There is an OKW record of Hitler's midnight conference with Fromm (T77/792/1485); I also used the diary of Fromm's Chief of Staff, General Karl-Erik Koehler, and Halder's diary.

p. 358   On December 16, 1941, Richthofen had already referred to the grapevine reports in his diary. "Führer seems to have made up his mind on major reshuffle: Brauchitsch, Halder, Keitel, and Bock are out—at last." (Warlimont confirmed under interrogation that Halder was also originally earmarked for dismissal.) But on January 18, 1942, Richthofen wrote: "According to Jeschonnek, Keitel and Halder are 'unfortunately' staying on for the time being."

p. 360   Halder's satisfaction with Hitler as the new Commander in Chief was evident for many months. On March 25, 1942, Greiner, the OKW war diarist, quoted Warlimont thus in a private diary: "[Hitler's] 'marriage' to Halder is good, Halder has developed a freer hand since Brauchitsch's departure; Jodl has adopted the roll of 'joint adviser' at the daily war conferences." General Wagner, who accompanied Halder daily to the Führer's HQ, wrote on January 21, 1942: "I don't get away from my desk or telephone before 2:30 A.M. each day, and three hours are taken up each midday by the war conference and journeys to and from the Führer . . . The Führer looks well, and working directly with him is a pleasure." Two years later both Halder and Wagner were among the anti-Hitler conspirators.

p. 362   Hitler's "scorched earth" policy can be traced back to December 8, 1941, when Keitel telephoned to Army Group North the Führer's instruction that every kind of accommodation was to be ruthlessly destroyed before regions were evacuated: "In the interests of the military operations there is to be no respect whatever for the population's situation." Hitler's remarks on December 20 were communicated by telegram to the three army groups the next day (NOKW–539); and see the OKW signal to the OKH (T77/792/1489), Halder's diary, and Manstein's order to the Eleventh Army, December 23, 1941 (NOKW–1726).

p. 364   Hitler's telephone conversations with Kluge are reported in Army Group Center's war diary; I also used the diaries of Hewel and Bormann, and postwar testimony of the adjutants Puttkamer and Below.

p. 366   The Luftwaffe General von Richthofen, whose reports had caused Foerster's downfall, was himself given command of his Sixth Army Corps—a command of which he hurriedly divested himself. (See Richthofen's papers.)

p. 366   For Hoepner's dismissal from the army "with all legal consequences" see Halder's diary, Keitel's memoirs (page 290), and the unpublished memoirs of Weichs. In Hoepner's papers (N51/7) is a 1944 memo by a Major Frankenberg. Schmundt had told him how he had reproached the Führer—"You've sacked one of our most capable army commanders"—to which a remorseful Hitler replied, "I had to make an example of him. Have him told that the family will be taken care of." But on January 13, 1942, Hoepner sent to Schmundt a *pièce justificative* (N51/3), listing his many vain attempts to contact Halder by telephone on the eighth before issuing the order to retreat; Hoepner demanded a court-martial. After the July 20, 1944, bomb plot Hitler lost what little sympathy he had for him (War Conference, August 31, 1944) and allowed his execution. A thoughtful analysis of the legal aspects of the Hoepner, Sponeck, and related cases was published by the German senior assize-court judge Dr. Günter Gribbohm in the judges' journal, *Deutsche Richterzeitung,* May 1972 and February 1973.

p. 367   In narrating the withdrawal of the German battleships from Brest, I used Puttkamer's memoirs and his letters to Raeder on December 26, 1941 (PG/31780), and January 4, 1942 (PG/31762e), Junge's memoirs, the naval staff war diary, the diary of Luftwaffe General Karl Koller, and Captain Wolfgang Kähler's article in *WR,* 1952, pages 171 *et seq.*

p. 368   In a private letter on April 12, 1942, Greiner described the casualties on the Russian front up to March 20 as tolerable: 6.63 percent fatalities, 1.5 percent missing, 23.43 percent injured. "Frost casualties number 133,000, including 17,500 third-degree cases [amputees]." By March 31 the latter figure had risen to 18,337 (Goebbels, diary, April 17, 1942).

pp. 368–69   The original letter of February 10, 1942 is on microfilm, T175/125/9983 *et seq.*

pp. 369–70   On June 5, 1942, Hitler explained: "Fanatical loyalty toward your allies—that's the secret behind keeping them in line" (war diary, OKW historical division).

p. 370   Todt himself stressed that the plan to simplify arms production "resulted from one of the Führer's own ideas" (naval staff war diary, January 22, 1942). My narrative here is based on Saur's files (FD–1434/46 and 3049/49), Milch's files (MD51/435 *et seq.*), and the microfilms T77/194, /313, /441, and /545; on Goebbels's and Bormann's diaries, February 6–7, 1942, and Speer's Chronik.

p. 371   Hitler's order for a "black box" type cockpit-recorder to be designed is referred to in Milch's conferences on February 28 (MD 34/1954), April 14, and October 16, 1942 (MD 13/130 and 34/2300).

p. 372   According to Goebbels's unpublished diary, Hitler still expected the sudden overthrow of Churchill by the British. (Goebbels did not.) On February 8, 1942, Weizsäcker argued in his diary: "Isn't Britain the all-ways loser in this war? Won't the loss of Hongkong, soon of Singapore, and perhaps Burma too rouse spirits against Churchill? Won't there soon be a crack in London, and a peace offer to us?" He himself did not expect to hear such a crack until Russia had been defeated, "for the peace Germany is envisaging would be a calamity for Britain." There is a similar passage in Etzdorf's papers, April 1942.

p. 373   Weizsäcker mirrored Hitler's uneasiness at events in the Far East. "We express great joy at the fall of Singapore. And yet our feelings are mixed. The European yearning for great achievements with the British awakes in us" (diary, February 13, 1942).

Hitler's Word Is Law

p. 374   The Japanese navy actively urged Germany to make peace with Russia. But Ribbentrop cabled his ambassador in Tokyo on March 7: "It is of course out of the question for Germany ever to take the initiative in seeking a rapprochement with the Soviet Union."

p. 376   Hitler spoke of Stalin's shortage of coking coal to the diplomats Alfieri and

Draganoff on August 4 and 14, 1942, respectively; in fact—as Manstein wrote in *Verlorene Siege,* page 429—there were further great coal reserves in the Kusnetsk region, as her continued war production showed.

p. 376   That Hitler had convinced Halder of the importance of the Caucasus campaign is evident from a report by the naval liaison officer to the General Staff, in the naval staff war diary on April 8, 1942. "The region has in his [Halder's] view the same significance as the province of Silesia has to Prussia . . . But it will no longer be possible this year to operate *across* the Caucasus mountains," *i.e.,* to aid Rommel's simultaneous offensive toward the Suez Canal.

p. 379   Greiner's diary shows that the Saint-Nazaire raid occurred at a time when Hitler was disenchanted with the navy. On March 26, 1942, he noted: "Führer anti-navy as technically inadequate. Quickly disposed of. . . . Navy in last place. R[aeder] already tried to resign several times." The next day: "Navy should write fewer memoranda." And on March 28: "2:15 A.M., British raid at Saint-Nazaire, which while completely beaten off has enjoyed an element of success, resulting in intensified hostility of Führer to navy." At a war conference on April 7, Hitler contemptuously referred to the "Sleeping Beauty" slumber of his troops in the west.

p. 379   German interrogation results on the British prisoners of war at Dieppe will be found in interpreter Paul Schmidt's AA files, Serial 1993, and in Etzdorf's file, Serial 364, and Weizsäcker's file Serial 98, page 109234. See also the diaries of the naval staff, April 12, and of Goebbels, April 15, 1942. Hitler drew his own conclusions from the interrogations, as Greiner noted in his diary on April 7. "Führer thinks a different end to war with Britain can't be ruled out. British prisoners' hatred of U.S.A."

p. 382   According to Karl Ritter's AA file on the German-Turkish arms negotiations (Serial 1089) Hitler offered 150 million Reichsmarks' value of U-boats, 50-millimeter anti-tank guns, 20-millimeter and heavy antiaircraft, machine guns, ammunition, and the equipment for a light tank brigade. See also Lothar Krecker, *Deutschland und die Türkei im Zweiten Weltkrieg* (Frankfurt, 1964).

p. 382   Colonel Schmundt took a detailed note of the military part of Mussolini's conference with Hitler on April 30, 1942 (naval staff war diary, annexes, Part C, Vol. XIV). See also the full note in Mussolini's handwriting (T586/405/545 *et seq.*) and Ugo Cavallero, *Diario* (Rome, 1948), and Admiral Eberhard Weichold's published study of the Mediterranean campaign in *WR,* 1959, pages 164 *et seq.*

p. 384   Himmler submitted to Hitler the ministry of post's report on the success of its *Forschungsanstalt* (Research Division) in unscrambling the transatlantic radiotelephone used by the enemy on March 6, 1942 (T175/129/4865 *et seq.*). He enclosed a sample conversation of September 7, 1941. See also *ibid.,* pages 9924 *et seq.,* and the memo of May 1, 1942, which shows that these top-secret intercepts were fed straight to the document shredder after Hitler read them (T175/122/7620).

p. 384   There are traces of the intercepted U.S. signals between Washington and Cairo in Hewel's Ledger (*e.g.,* on February 21, 1942), in the naval staff war diary of April 30, and in Table Talk, June 28, 1942, evening. See also David Kahn, *The Codebreakers: The Story of Secret Writing* (London, 1968), pages 473 *et seq.*

p. 385   Göring's remark will be found in his conference with air force *(Luftflotte)* commanders on April 19, 1942 (MD 62/5193). But Goebbels argued (diary, April 25): "A truncheon across the head is not always a convincing argument—even for Ukrainians and Russians."

p. 388   After the unprecedented German victory at Kharkov, everybody claimed paternity of the crucial decision to go ahead with "Fridericus" as planned. Thus Halder—who had written in his diary only that Bock's proposal (to abandon "Fridericus" in favor of a frontal defense) was "turned down"—expanded this with a postwar footnote that this decision was taken on his own advice to Hitler. Bock's diary however shows beyond a shadow of doubt that Halder had fought tooth and nail against the decision. As Keitel—

writing in a prison cell, from memory—correctly wrote (memoirs, page 302): "Hitler interceded and quite simply ordered the operation ["Fridericus"] to be fought his way."

See also the war diary of the OKW historical division, May 14–19; Goebbels's diary, May 22 and 31 (unpublished); and Table Talk, June 2, 1942, evening. Hans Doerr, at the time Chief of Staff of Fifty-second Corps, analyzed the battle in *WR*, 1954, pages 9 *et seq.*

p. 388   The Luftwaffe Deputy Chief of Staff, General von Waldau, noted skeptically on January 2, 1942 (diary): "Reports from Japanese sources that the Russians have now exhausted their strategic reserves are willingly believed." Halder demonstrated such willingness in his diary on January 4 and February 13. On March 1, Bock submitted a dissenting appreciation to Hitler—warning that the Russians might well have sufficient in reserve not only to foil Germany's spring offensive but to raise complete new armies in the hinterland. Halder telephoned him on March 5 that he had disputed Bock's fears to the Führer: the General Staff calculated that Stalin still had some twenty-five divisions in the Caucasus, but no Intelligence—even from abroad—indicated the raising of new armies. On March 7, after hearing his eastern expert's views, Halder noted: "In short: they are gradually being worn down." But on March 20 the same expert, Colonel Kinzel, revised his views; he now believed the Russians could raise fifty to sixty new divisions! Bock uneasily pointed out the discrepancy in his own diary, March 25. Halder's complacency however continued. On April 2, Hitler suggested that the Russians could scarcely raise worthwhile new armies because of industrial problems alone; on April 19, Halder responded that the Russians had already used up most of their available strength (war diary, OKW historical division). The same source shows that even on June 25, Halder interpreted Intelligence reports that Stalin was moving reinforcements into Sevastopol by submarine as "a fresh proof that the enemy lacks reserves."

p. 388   Hitler's speech is on discs at BA, Le7EW 68,953 to 68,976.

p. 390   Hitler realistically commented on the "thousand-bomber" raid on Cologne: "Given the mendacity of British propaganda it's possible they're exaggerating by a factor of two or three; but the British couldn't exaggerate by a factor of *ten* and look their own troops in the face" (war diary, OKW historical division, June 3, 1942); see also his remarks to Goebbels (diary, March 9, 1943) and war conference, January 28, 1944 (Heiber, pages 544 *et seq.*)

p. 390 (Footnote)   On Himmler's *"Generalplan* East" see Helmut Heiber's documentation in *VfZ*, 1958, pages 281 *et seq.*

p. 391   The AA file on the Final Solution of the Jewish Problem (Serial 1513) contains the original R.S.H.A. memorandum on the so-called Wannsee Conference of January 20, 1942; see also Luther's memo of August 21 (*ibid.,* and NG–2586). On January 21, Himmler noted after telephoning Heydrich, "Jewish problem," and "Berlin conference"; four days later, in the Wolf's Lair, Himmler spoke to Heydrich by telephone about "[putting] Jews in concentration camps"; on January 27 their telephone conversation revolved around "Jew arrests," and the next day about "a roundup of Jews" (T84/25). Further sources on the planning and results of the Wannsee Conference are documents 709–PS and NG–5770, introduced at the Nuremberg trials; the testimony there of Dr. Lammers both in the main trial (IMT, Vol. XI, page 61) and in Case XI (September 23, 1948); and a memo by the East Ministry, January 29, 1942, AA Serial 7117H.

p. 391   For Heydrich's March 6, 1942, conference see Franz Rademacher's note (Serial 1513, pages 372020 *et seq.*) and the record of March 14 (Serial 1512, pages 371961 *et seq.*); the March "detailed memorandum" has survived only in the summary in Goebbels's diary, March 7, 1942. Nowhere in the entire Goebbels diaries—*including* the recently discovered unpublished years being prepared for publication by Hoffmann & Campe—is there any reference to Hitler's alleged initiative in the extermination of the Jews.

p. 391   Globocnik was quoted by SS Brigadier Viktor Brack in a letter to Himmler on June 26, 1942 (NO–206). Brack also proposed that the two to three million able-bodied Jews among Europe's ten million Jews should be sorted out and sterilized.

p. 392 Hitler still referred to the "Madagascar plan" in Table Talk, July 24, 1942. SS General Karl Wolff estimated—in a confidential postwar manuscript—that altogether probably only some seventy men, from Himmler down to Höss, were involved in the liquidation program. The only evidence of a "Führer Order" behind the program came from postwar testimony of SS Major Dieter Wisliceny, Eichmann's thirty-one-year-old adviser on Jewish problems attached to the Slovak government (*e.g.,* in pretrial interrogations at Nuremberg on November 11 and 24, 1945, and a written narrative dated Bratislava, November 18, 1946). He claimed the Slovaks had sent him to Berlin in July or August 1942 to check up on the fate of 33,000 next of kin of the 17,000 able-bodied Jews supplied for the German arms industry. Eichmann admitted to him that the 33,000 had been liquidated, and—said Wisliceny—pulled from his safe a red-bordered Immediate Letter, stamped "Top State Secret," with Himmler's signature and addressed to Heydrich and Pohl. It read (from memory): "The Führer has decided that the Final Solution of the Jewish Question is to begin at once. I herewith designate [Heydrich and Pohl] responsible for the execution of this order." However, there is a marked difference between Wisliceny's 1945 and 1946 recollections of this text; and when years later Eichmann was cross-examined about this in his trial on April 10, 1961, he testified that he had neither received any such written order nor shown one to Wisliceny (who had long since been executed himself). He had only told Wisliceny verbally, "Heydrich sent for me and informed me that the Führer has ordered the physical annihilation of the Jews."

This kind of evidence, of course, would not suffice in an English magistrate's court to convict a vagabond of bicycle stealing, let alone assign the responsibility for the mass murder of six million Jews, given the powerful written evidence that Hitler again and again ordered the "Jewish Problem" set aside until the war was won.

p. 392 On the "resettlement" of the Jews from Poland, see Himmler's letter of July 19, 1942, to SS General Friedrich Krüger, the SS and police chief at Cracow (T175/122/7914); and the report by the Reich transport ministry's state secretary, Theodor Ganzenmüller, nine days later to Himmler's adjutant Karl Wolff that since July 22 one train per day with five thousand Jews was leaving Warsaw for Treblinka, and that twice a week a train was leaving Przemysl with five thousand Jews for Belzek. Wolff replied on August 13 that it gave him "special pleasure" to learn this—that "daily trainloads of five thousand members of the Chosen People are going to Treblinka and that we are thus being enabled to accelerate this migration." He assured Ganzenmüller he would do all he could to smooth their way. Wolff—as ignorant as Ganzenmüller of the true functions of Treblinka extermination camp—was tried in 1964 by a Munich court and sentenced to fifteen years in prison. In the Wolff trial, the notorious SS General von dem Bach-Zelewski testified on July 24, 1964, that in his view "Hitler knew nothing of the mass destruction of the Jews" and that "the entire thing began with Himmler."

The Wolff-Ganzenmüller letters are in Himmler's files (T175/54/8626 et seq.); Sztójay's report from Berlin, dated August 15, 1942, is in Budapest archives.

p. 400 Baron von Weisäcker was less optimistic—in a private letter to his mother on June 28, 1942—than others "here" that there would be peace talks as early as that autumn; but he hoped that by the following spring both Germany and Britain would have realized that they were bashing each other's brains out to the good of other continents. He thought a settlement might then be reached along these lines: restoration of the status quo in the west, and a free hand for Germany in the east. In his diary on June 24 he referred to "test-attempts," e.g. by the British consul-general Cable in Zürich and (far plainer) by the British air attaché George in Ankara, as being symptomatic of the dilemma of the British —some of whom must be asking themselves the classic *cui bono* question, as the bloody duel between Britain and Germany progressed.

p. 400 The evidence on Russian reserves as submitted by Halder to Hitler is plain enough: e.g. he referred on June 25, 1942, to "fresh proof that the enemy lacks reserves" (war diary, OKW historical division); and on July 6 Halder noted in his diary that while the Führer expected Timoshenko to adopt an "elastic" defence, Halder adhered to his view that the Red Army had been overestimated and completely destroyed by operation "Blue." I am aware of Colonel Gehlen's regular Intelligence reports to Halder, which spoke a very different language about the Red Army's potential growth; but there is no indication whatever that Halder forwarded these unpalatable warnings to Hitler. On June 28, 1942, Gehlen assessed Stalin's current strength at 375 rifle divisions, 26 cavalry divisions, and 68 tank divisions and brigades; he did not believe that "Blue" would dispose of all the 160 divisions confronting Army Group South (Bock). Even if one hundred—or upward of 700,000 men—were destroyed, the Russians would still have some 350 rifle divisions, taking those to be raised in the coming winter into account, plus corresponding numbers of cavalry and tank divisions by early 1943. This was hardly the "military collapse" Halder prophesied. In retrospect Field Marshal von Bock wrote on March 1, 1943 (diary); "From all the various accounts it is pretty plain to me that—just as in the winter of 1941—the collapse of the Russians was expected by us at top level, we split up our forces having overestimated our success, and finally ended up too weak everywhere."

p. 400   On the Voronezh controversy, and Hitler's flight to Poltava, I used the diaries of Bock, Halder, and the commandant of the Führer's HQ. Bock's diary, incidentally, establishes that in Halder's view Voronezh should be fully captured first—a view he amended on July 5 when he realized the damage that the delay was inflicting on the main thrust south. By the time Halder published his diaries he characteristically claimed in a footnote (Vol. III, page 471) that he had *recommended* that Hitler leave Voronezh alone! Not so.

p. 401   On the reasons for Bock's dismissal, see his diary entries for October 10, December 4 and 9, 1942, and January 3, March 22 and 26, 1943; also the unpublished memoirs of Weichs, commanding the Second Army (N19/10); the naval staff war diary, July 17, 1942, and Hitler's remarks at the war conference on December 12, 1942 (Heiber, page 84).

p. 402   The invasion force assembling in southern England is reported by the Commander in Chief. West in the OKW historical division's war diary, June 23; in Hanns Rauter's letter to Himmler, June 25 (T175/122/7940); in the naval staff war diary, annexes C, Vol. X (PG/32201), and the war diary of the Admiral Commanding France, June 26, 1942.

p. 403   Hitler's policies for colonizing Russia are outlined in Himmler's letters to Gauleiter Alfred Frauenfeld, July 10, 1942 (NO–2417) and to Schellenberg, July 17 (T175/55/9345); in Canaris's diary, August 10 (AL/1933); in Bormann's letter to Rosenberg, July 23 (T175/194/4061 *et seq.*); and in a memo on a Rovno conference August 26–28, 1942, in Etzdorf's AA file, Serial 1247.

p. 403–404   Himmler quoted Hitler's remarks on education in a secret speech on September 16, 1942 (T175/103/4970 *et seq.*). Two days previously he had a telephone conversation with Bormann about "illegitimate children in Russia."

On the food problem, see Göring's conference with the Gauleiters on August 6 (ND, USSR–170); Etzdorf's memo of August 7; Göring's personal assistant's notes for Führer conferences dated July 24, 27, and 29, and August 11 (Microfilm T84/8); and Hassell's diary, September 4, 1942.

p. 404   Halder's confident advice to Hitler on Russian reserves is indisputable; as late as August 24, 1942, for example, he believed they would not need the Eleventh Army in the south (*vide* Manstein, pages 291 *et seq.*). Halder's postwar protestations that he had warned Hitler cannot therefore refer to this period. ("The proof I submitted each day at the war conference . . . he took as a personal insult." And "My calm, sober arguments on the enemy's reserves position resulted in hysterical outbursts of anger." Thus he is quoted by Peter Bor in *Gespräche mit Halder,* page 226.)

p. 405   In the Luftwaffe General von Richthofen's diary, July 19, 1942, is entered the first impatient criticism of what he regarded as the army's lethargic tempo. "The armies aren't going to attack Nikolevskaya for two more days—by which time the Russians will have bolted! . . . Führer ordered the day before yesterday that everything destined for the attack on Rostov (from north and northeast) is to be united under Kleist's command. . . . But even by today this order still hasn't reached the armies!" Richthofen was particularly unsympathetic to the "aging and doubtless weary" General Hoth.

p. 406   General von Weichs wrote in his manuscript memoirs: "I felt obliged to telephone Hitler myself to demand aid for my army, and fast. But I ran into unexpected difficulties: Hitler obviously couldn't use the telephone correctly. Normally his speech was fast and fluent, but on the phone he stuttered, or paused so long that it was by no means certain he was still there. Moreover his stuttering was very hard to understand on the phone. Even my Intelligence officer, who had been listening in, couldn't tell me afterward what Hitler's actual answers had been. So that was the first and last telephone conversation I ever had with Hitler." (General Engel's "diary" must therefore be mistaken in referring to another conversation on November 19, 1942.)

p. 407   Halder's revealing telephone conversation with List on July 30, 1942, is in the war diary of Army Group A. His signal to Army Groups A and B next day transferring the Fourth Panzer Army (with its two German and one Romanian panzer corps) to the Stalingrad front is in Vol. II of the published OKW war diary, page 1285. In a 1964 footnote to his own diaries (page 494) Halder disowns the signal, and suggests it was sent "on Hitler's instructions"; but the diary clearly reveals—as of course does Halder's conversation with List—that he shared Hitler's appreciation of the situation.

p. 407   Samples of the intercepted Churchill telephone conversations shown to Hitler are on film T175/122/7449 *et seq.*); that of July 22 was recorded on "Reel 599"—which gives a hint as to the volume of the intercepted traffic, as one on July 13 is on "Reel 553" and one on July 14 is on "Reel 562." Penciled marginal notes indicate that SS General Karl Wolff showed them to the Führer.

p. 408   The same Abwehr agent who reported the Dieppe raid also correctly warned of the November 1942 invasion and of a heavy air raid due on Berlin (naval staff war diary, October 31, 1942, and March 15, 1943). Of curiosity value is the British interrogation on March 7, 1943, of a Luftwaffe lieutenant, operations officer of a KG.26 torpedo-bomber squadron; he described how four days before the Dieppe raid a "war game" had been held at Luftflotte 3 HQ, Versailles, to plan the defense of Dieppe. "On August 17 all squadron and flight commanders of units on the western front were summoned to a conference at the HQ of director of air operations, Atlantic, General [Ulrich] Kessler at Angers, where they were told that we [the British] were planning an attack on Dieppe."—ADI(K) Report, 114/1943. From Rundstedt's postaction report of September 3, 1942 (T312/505/9435 *et seq.*) it seems most unlikely that the Luftwaffe passed its prior information on to the army.

p. 408   For Hitler's Atlantic Wall conferences of August 2 and 13, 1942, see General Alfred Jacob's record on film T78/317/1594 *et seq.* and *ibid.*, 1090 *et seq.;* and PG/32201, and the naval staff war diary, August 6, 11, 13, 17, and 21. Halder's diary, August 15, shows the spirit in which the OKH embarked on the new fortifications. "General Jacob: Führer's new demands for permanent improvement of western coastal fortifications (impossible demands!)"

p. 409   In describing the Dieppe debacle I have used the war diaries of the Ninth Air Corps, the naval staff, and its special file, "Enemy Landing at Dieppe" (annexes, Part C, Vol. IIb); the diary of Koller (Third Air Force), and Junge's memoirs. On August 20, 1942, Admiral Theodor Krancke was able to report to Raeder from Werewolf: "The enemy landing at Dieppe has been contemplated with extreme calmness at Führer HQ."

p. 409   Paul Schmidt's remark is quoted from his letter to one "Jasper," September 6, 1942 (AA Serial 1993); his interrogation report is in Serial 67, pages 47914 *et seq.*

p. 410   The quotation is from Hitler's secret speech to commanders on September 29, 1942 (a record taken by the First Army, in its war diary, annexes, T312/23/9706 *et seq.)*

p. 411   The OKW records of the joint German-Japanese staff talks will be found in naval archives (war diary, annexes, Part C, Vol. XV); they are invaluable surveys of German long-term strategy and planning.

The Black Spot for Halder

p. 412 Halder quoted Göring's words: Dittmar diary, August 17, 1945, and CSDIC report GRGG 346, August 14, 1945. On the supply and logistics problems that summer, 1942, see Richthofen's blistering speech at Rostov, August 15, and especially his annex to his diary, August 23, 1942.

p. 413 Small wonder that on February 11, 1943, Hitler blamed the Stalingrad disaster —besides on his weak allies—on the fact that the OKH "had either not carried out a series of his orders at all, or had done so badly" (Richthofen diary).

p. 414 Richthofen's opinion was at growing variance with the General Staff's. On August 12, 1942, he wrote in his diary: "My impression is still this—the Russian southern army is destroyed. Parts of it are in rout along the Georgian Army Road"—beyond the Caucasus mountains!

p. 415 I base my account of "Operation Whirlwind" on Greiner's original draft OKW war diary (of which I have deposited a complete *correct* transcript with the IfZ) and on Halder's diary. In his postwar diary, March 27, 1946, General von Salmuth suggested that "Whirlwind," which he had helped prepare as acting commander of the Fourth Army, was one instance of Hitler's military inability. "It was worked out as a double pincer from north and south. Right in the middle burst the Russian offensive at Rzhev, which meant the loss of the pincer's main arm. Kluge asked the Führer more than once to call off what would now be a one-armed "Whirlwind" . . . Adolf Hitler just retorted—when Kluge reproached him that he would be sacrificing thirty or forty thousand men for nothing— 'Just see, the offensive will cut through them like butter!' "

pp. 415–16 The quotation is from Hitler's war conference on December 12, 1942 (Heiber, page 92). Greiner's original draft proves that on August 12, 1942—*i.e.*, right at the start of "Whirlwind"—Hitler had told Halder, "The forces are to be held tightly together in the main direction of attack, Sukhinichi."

p. 416 Several versions of Hitler's famous row with Halder on August 24, 1942, exist: Heusinger's, Manstein's, and Warlimont's memoirs; but I used especially Halder's private conversation with General Heim on August 13, 1945 (recorded by hidden microphones at CSDIC). Engel's "diary" falsely dates the episode on September 4.

p. 418 I have reconstructed Rommel's supply problems in the desert from his private letters (T84/R274); from the diary of General von Waldau, now director of air operations (Africa), with its many appendices; from Greiner's draft war diary; from the daily reports of Rommel's Panzer Army Africa; from the naval staff war diary and from Ritter's AA file on Egypt, Serial 1442.

p. 420 Hitler's plan to "dispose of" Stalingrad's male population is referred to in both Halder's diary, August 31, and in Greiner's draft of September 2, 1942. Halder was presumably Weizsäcker's source in writing (diary, September 13) "So our plan is to destroy bolshevism *and* the Russian empire. To this end Stalingrad and Leningrad are to be destroyed."

p. 420 For Richthofen's hostility to Hoth see his diary, July 22–23, and August 23–25, and 27, 1942; and Greiner's and Halder's diaries, August 28, 1942.

pp. 420–21 List's visit to Hitler is recounted in the diaries of Richthofen, Greiner, Halder, and Army Group A, August 31; and the naval staff war diary, September 1–2, 1942.

p. 422 I base my account on Jodl's own papers. Milch, who was present, wrote in his diary on September 7, 1942: "Vinnitsa, to see Führer. Noon conference on Central Planning and aviation. Row over List. Göring had already left." And Speer's deputy Saur told me in 1965, "It was the worst depression I have ever experienced at the HQ, because Jodl's report was such a shock—up to then nobody had wanted to believe it, and the Führer wouldn't have found out for a long time either if Jodl, who was an extraordinarily honest man, hadn't told him."

p. 422   Julius Schaub's papers contain a full account of the recruiting of the conference stenographers. I also used Bormann's diary, September 7, 1942; Heiber's introduction to the war conferences, pages 14 *et seq.;* and the correspondence between Lammers and Göring's staff in September and October (T84/8).

p. 422   One of the stenographers who served Hitler from September 11, 1942, to the very end wrote a diary, which is in my possession. Hitler evidently went to great lengths to win their respect, for on December 25, 1942, the diary records how the Führer received the two duty stenographers a few minutes early, invited them to sit down while he stood, and explained, "In earlier times I often used stenographers. In 1931 or 1932 I was called to testify in a trial against Dr. Goebbels in Berlin. The lawyer—a half-Jew—fired one question after another at me from 9 A.M. to 7 P.M. trying to trap me; and I was well aware that the press was just waiting to use my testimony to accuse me of just about anything, to get a stranglehold on me. But the trial report of one day's proceedings was usually only three or at most four pages long, so nothing precise could be proven from them, so for this day I hired two stenographers from the Bavarian Diet, and these gentlemen really saved my bacon"—a remark he had already introduced the speech with—"as everything happened just as I had imagined. The next day the press published completely distorted reports of my testimony hoping to bring about my own prosecution." Hitler's only regret was the expense, as the hiring had cost him eight hundred Reichsmarks. "Anyway, I'm glad to have you here now and only regret I didn't fetch you in earlier as I want to pin down the responsibility for events once and for all by a shorthand record. As you see, I have to busy myself with even the smallest trivia here. Moreover these things must be taken down for later historical research. Anyway I'm glad you're here now."

p. 423   J. Daniel Chamier's biography, *Ein Fabeltier unserer Zeit: Glanz und Tragödie Kaiser Wilhelm II,* was incidentally proscribed reading in the Third Reich, according to the records of the Nazi party censorship commission (NS-II/22).

pp. 425-26   On September 16, 1942, Rommel wrote after a talk with Kesselring: "He came from the Führer's HQ. The battle for Stalingrad seems to be very hard and it's tying down a lot of strength we could use better in the south. Field Marshal L[ist] is to be retired. . . . It didn't work out with H[alder] either in the long run, as I predicted" (T84/R274/0890). Two days later the OKW diarist Greiner wrote in his diary: "Warlimont tells me that Halder's out, Zeitzler takes his place, Blumentritt his, and Manstein List's. Reshuffle not over yet. Jodl and Warlimont dodgy." Zeitzler's name was *not* mentioned as early as September 9—the last four paragraphs of Greiner's published war diary (OKW war diary, Vol. II, pages 704 *et seq.*) are a postwar fabrication. On September 27, Greiner privately summarized: "The last three weeks haven't been pleasant—a major crisis of confidence caused by the unsatisfactory situation on the eastern front. The first victim was Halder, but he really wasn't up to much anymore as he was a nervous wreck. His successor is now the diminutive, stocky, ambitious, bustling, and definitely highly energetic Zeitzler." The rest of my narrative is based on Zeitzler's papers (N63/1 and /18) and the diaries of Frau Schmundt, Bormann, and Halder.

p. 426   The order is in the war diary of the chief of army personnel (*i.e.,* Schmundt), October 5, 1942 (T 78/39). Schmundt replaced Keitel's ailing brother Bodewin. As Goebbels observed in his unpublished diary on September 29, 1942: "Here was the real cancer in our Wehrmacht. In the personnel branch are a host of officers who've already been there fifteen years and done nothing but deal with personnel problems."

p. 426   I extracted information on the "Red Orchestra" spy case from the interrogations of Puttkamer and Kraell, Goebbels's unpublished diary, September 23 and 30, and Milch's remarks on October 20, 1942 (MD 16/2731 *et seq.*); further, from the 1945 OCMH interrogation of Frau Ingeborg Havemann (née Harnack), and SS General Müller's letter to Himmler afterward (T175/129/5161).

p. 428   On the "missing ten percent" effort see Goebbels's unpublished diary, September 25–30, 1942, and Speer's remarks in Central Planning, October 30, 1942 (MD 46/9014 *et seq.*). "I recently talked over this whole question with Goebbels; his view is that the people are only waiting to be called upon to make this last effort."

p. 428   King Christian's lapidary telegram read simply: "To Reich Chancellor Adolf Hitler. Best thanks for your congratulations. Christian *Rex.*" I also referred to the diaries of Goebbels, Hassell, Weizsäcker, and the naval staff, and an interrogation of Baron von Steengracht. For Best's appointment see his manuscripts written in 1949 (IfZ, ZS–207) and his report on his first six months in Himmler's files (T175/119/4942 *et seq.*).

pp. 428–29   A General Staff transcript of the speech is on microfilm, T78/317/1567 *et seq.*

Africa and Stalingrad

p. 432   On October 26, 1942, Admiral Krancke reported to the naval staff the "perceptible relaxation" of tension at the Führer HQ since Zeitzler had replaced Halder. "Though the Führer's personal relationship to the headquarters generals hasn't yet completely regained its old form." Goebbels also commented on the change in his diary, December 20—Zeitzler was doing his utmost to relieve Hitler of unnecessary work, which would, Goebbels hoped, leave the Führer with more time to attend to the neglected affairs of state.

p. 433   For my investigation of the origins of Hitler's Commando Order, I used Hitler's letter to the Wehrmacht commands, October 18, 1942 (503–PS), and interrogations of Keitel and Jodl. I myself have seen the British commando-training manual which fell into German hands (in private possession). On the sinking of the minelayer *Ulm* and Hitler's outburst, see naval staff war diary, September 11 and 14, and Table Talk September 6, evening.

pp. 433–34   The Sark raid which provoked the Commando Order is dealt with by the British official historian Professor M. R. D. Foot, in *S.O.E. in France,* page 186; he no doubt accurately described the raiding force as "highly skilled and intelligent toughs of several nationalities." Foot appears unaware of the reports by Warlimont (T77/1428/1077 *et seq.*) and the First Army (T312/23/9771 *et seq.*) on the Sark raid. For the consequences, see Greiner's record of Warlimont's report on Hitler's conference on October 5; the naval staff war diary, October 8, 9, and 11; Weizsäcker's diary, October 11, 1942; interrogations of Warlimont and Baron Horst treusch von Bottlar-Brandenfels—who testified to Keitel's and Jodl's refusal to draft the actual Commando Order (dated October 18, 1942, in naval file PG/31755, or document 498–PS)—and the memoirs of Engel and Scheidt. I also referred to Jodl's own private papers on this controversial affair.

p. 434   The Gestapo interrogation of Paul Evans, who initially survived the brave attack on the *Tirpitz* was submitted to Hitler on November 10 and 11, 1942 (T175/124). For the glider attack on Norway, see my book *The Virus House* (London, 1967; *The German Atomic Bomb,* New York, 1968) and the May 1943 correspondence between OKW and foreign ministry on microfilm T77/1428/1071 *et seq.*

p. 436   The laconic report by Himmler to Hitler that 363,211 Russian Jews had been executed as "partisan accomplices and suspects" from August to November 1942 will be found on film T175/124.

p. 436   Richthofen added in his diary, quoting Goring: "Führer wants me to take over List's army group"; but nothing came of it. On the same day Helmuth Greiner confided to his private diary: "Witchhunt by Luftwaffe brass against the army goes on. Frightful arse-licking."

p. 437   On the nonexploitation of the Maykop oil, see the Seventeenth Army's report of August 19, 1942, in OKW war diary, Vol. II, page 581; the unpublished war diary of the OKW economics staff, September 12, 1942 (T77/668); and George Blau's first-rate study, *The German Campaign in Russia* (U.S. Army, 1955), which uses the records of the staff's "Technical Brigade (Petroleum, Russia)."

p. 437   As early as February 6, 1943, Hitler admitted to Manstein (diary) that the Luftwaffe field divisions had been a mistake. See in general Lieutenant General Meindl's report on their operations, May 15, 1943, submitted to Hitler (MD 51/551 *et seq.*)

pp. 437–38   Gehlen's reports and appreciations will be found in his branch files (BA files H3/185 and H3/420). See also Greiner's notes on the Führer conferences of October 6, 7, 14, and 30. As Jodl said under Russian interrogation, June 18, 1945 "The biggest [Intelligence] failure was in November 1942 when we totally missed the assembly of strong Russian troops on the Sixth Army's flank on the Don. . . . There was nothing there before, then suddenly powerful forces launched a big push that won decisive significance. After that mistake the Führer mistrusted the General Staff's reconnaissance work." Jodl had leveled much the same criticism at the General Staff in his study of Hitler dated May 22, 1945 (Jodl papers). In the naval staff war diary, November 8, 1942, is a hard-hitting analysis of the Abwehr's total failure to detect the North African invasion planning. Specific references to "Cherbourg" are in Greiner's notes of October 5 and 9; the Keitel quotation is from the diary of General Karl-Erik Koehler, Fromm's Chief of Staff.

p. 438   That Hitler anticipated the Soviet thrust toward Rostov: Greiner's unpublished notes on the Führer's conferences, October 25–26, and Admiral Krancke's report in naval staff war diary, October 26, 1942.

p. 439   The Luftwaffe commander was General Hoffmann von Waldau (Tenth Air Corps), whose private diaries proved singularly illegible here—a faded blue carbon copy written in a minute hand and German script. (I have handed my transcription to the IfZ in Munich.) Among Antonescu's papers the Russians found Keitel's letter of October 31, 1942, appealing urgently for more oil for the Italian navy to support North African supply operations (ND, USSR-244).

p. 440   Rommel had copies of the main signals made six months later for his personal papers (T84/R276/0887 *et seq.*). According to the texts decoded by the British intercept service, he also tried other sly tactics—like asking for Hitler's "hold fast" order to be repeated to him. My account also derives from the files of Panzer Army Africa, the diaries of Greiner and Waldau, and postwar testimony of Warlimont, Below, Junge, Scheidt, Kesselring, and others. On November 3, Rommel wrote to his wife: "The battle rages on in unremitting violence. I can't believe in a happy ending, not any longer. [Alfred] Berndt [Rommel's staff officer, a SS brigadier from Goebbels's staff] is flying to report to the Führer" (T84/R274/0891). Rommel's furtive methods were undoubtedly the reason for Hitler's order on November 5—recorded by Greiner—"Command staffs subordinated to the OKW are to be instructed not to report special happenings in routine daily reports."

p. 444   My description of Hitler's train journey on November 7–8, 1942, relies on the naval staff war diary, and postwar manuscripts by Christian (U.S. army MS D–166), Engel, Below, and Speer; Saur—interviewed in 1965—stressed to me that Hitler took the news absolutely calmly. Ribbentrop's account of his proposals remained consistent through many interrogations by the Allies and in his unpublished manuscripts.

p. 446   Herbert Backe, the food minister, spent November 8, 1942—the day of the Allied invasion of North Africa—with Hitler in Munich, not leaving him until 3 A.M. "The Führer spoke on every possible subject, art, the theater, etc., and even artificial fertilizers (Herbert did not contradict, although his views differed)," wrote Frau Backe in her diary on the eleventh. "Once the Führer said, 'Today it's wonderful, just like when we were fighting for power—every bulletin brings a fresh situation.' Just how tense he was inside only became evident when he jumped up immediately as the foreign ministry men came in, and he went over to meet them."

p. 447   My account of the occupation of the rest of France derives from the diary of General Koller, the war diary of the naval staff, the handwritten record kept by Greiner of the OKW, and documents submitted by Himmler to Hitler (T175/124); for a reliable narrative based additionally on French sources, see Eberhard Jäckel, *Frankreich in Hitlers Europa* (Stuttgart, 1966), Chap. XIV.

p. 449 (footnote)   Italian hoarding of oil was evidently a national trait. According to the war diary of Rommel's Afrika Korps, they unexpectedly stumbled on thirteen thousand tons of Italian oil near Tripoli in December 1941 (T314/16/0035–37). See also the naval staff war diary, November 11, 24, and 28, 1942; Hitler's remarks to Antonescu on February 26, 1944; and especially Göring's outburst at a conference with Speer on October 27, 1943: "They [the Italians] had bigger stocks of copper than we have! But the most astounding thing is the fuel oil: in two tunnels we found enough oil to keep their entire navy operational for a year! The swine tucked it away, barrel after barrel, and then came whining to me for more: 'We would dearly love to fly, but we need the fuel!' I gave them another thousand tons—and now we find they had sixty-five thousand tons tucked away" (MD 31/754).

p. 449   Weizsäcker quoted the public's stoic foresight in his diary, November 16, 1942.

p. 449   For the onset of the Russian attack I used Greiner's handwritten note of November 19, 1942; the published version in OKW war diary, Vol. II, page 988, is an entirely postwar concoction.

4 TOTAL WAR

Trauma and Tragedy

p. 453   My chapters on Stalingrad are largely based on the records of the Sixth Army, of Gehlen's Intelligence branch, and the diary of the chief of army personnel; on the personal diaries of Richthofen, Milch, Manstein, and Generals Fiebig and Pickert (CO's of the Eighth Air Corps and the Stalingrad antiaircraft division, respectively); on the notes, letters, and manuscripts of staff at Hitler's HQ (Captain Junge, Below, Greiner, Engel, Scheidt); on Zeitzler's manuscripts written in about 1951 (N63/79, 80, and 101) and interrogations of Heusinger, Göring, Christian, and others; and on fragmentary documents like Hitler's war conference stenograms and Jodl's staff talks with the Japanese (naval staff war diary, annexes, Part C, Vol. XV). I was also fortunate to find among Milch's private papers the only copy of Major Werner Beumelburg's official manuscript on Stalingrad, dated June 8, 1943, and "based on official files and individual testimony."

p. 454   On the Heim affair, see Kehrig, *op. cit.*, pages 133 *et seq.*, citing the war diary of The Forty-Eighth Panzer Corps. Weichs dealt with it in his manuscript (N19/12). Heim's own version—in *Der Feldzug gegen Sowjetrussland* (Stuttgart, 1962)—is justifiably bitter. See also the war diary of the chief of army personnel, November 26, 1942, July 28, August 16, and September 23, 1944. By September 25, 1944, Heim was talking freely to his British captors about secret events at Hitler's HQ (CSDIC report SRGG 1063C, top secret).

p. 455   For the recriminations between the German and Romanian commanders over the collapse, see Greiner's unpublished notes of December 8 and 11; and Hitler's war conference on December 12, and talk with Antonescu on January 10.

p. 455   Hitler's signal was repeated by Weichs' Army Group B to the Sixth Army at 3:25 P.M., November 21 (BA file 75167/6). Richthofen noted in his diary that day: "Sixth Army thinks it can be kept supplied in its pocket by my Luftflotte. Trying all I can to prove to them it won't work out." See in general Colonel Johannes Fischer's semiofficial study of the Stalingrad airlift decision in *Militärgeschichtliche Mitteilungen*, 1969, pages 7 *et seq.* —which however relies heavily on the since-discredited "Engel diary" for its dates.

p. 456   According to Milch's diary, Colonel Artur Eschenauer—Jeschonnek's supply adviser—described to him how he had warned Jeschonnek that the so-called 1000-kilo supply container could only carry 500–680 kilograms of supplies, and the "250-kilo" container only 170 kilograms; their names derived from their *shapes* only. Göring refused to pass this fact on to Hitler (diary, May 21, 1946). See also Hitler's conference with Speer, January 18, 1943. The first reference to a "transport Schwerpunkt with the Fourth Air Force" is in the air ministry files on November 24, 1942 (MD17/3390).

On February 10, 1943, Göring admitted to Richthofen (diary) that "at the beginning of the Stalingrad episode he had played the optimist and supported the Führer in his decision to stand fast there." But when Richthofen asked Hitler the next day, Hitler replied that "he had promised [Sixth Army] the five hundred tons [daily], apparently without the Reichsmarschall's knowledge." In a speech to Luftwaffe generals on February 15, (Koller diary) Göring defended the Stalingrad decision. "Initially there was no reason to evacuate [Sixth Army], as there was justification for the view that the strong forces could hold out until they were relieved. But then fuel ran out in Stalingrad. 'Well, they could still have evacuated on foot!' But there was still the hope that Stalingrad could be relieved. Then the Italian front caved in, and with the breakthrough at Kolnikovo the front was torn wide open for hundreds of miles and was beyond repair. If we had fought much harder—in Stalingrad itself too—we would still be in Stalingrad today and it would not have surrendered. Paulus was too soft, didn't make a fortress out of this Stalingrad."

p. 456   From his comments to his doctors in 1944, and even as early as the war conference on December 12, 1942, it is clear that the twenty-four hour incommunicado train journey became a standby-alibi to Hitler for his defeat at Stalingrad. Linge's diary shows that an identical train journey, in November 1943, did indeed last from 4:30 P.M. on the ninth to 6:50 P.M. on the tenth; added to which, while Hitler arrived at the Wolf's Lair in the small hours of November 24, 1942, the OKW operations staff train did not arrive until a day later (according to the diaries of Greiner and one of the stenographers).

p. 457   An air force table of airlift sorties to the Sixth Army, November 24, 1942, to February 3, 1943 (microfilm T321/18/8846 *et seq.*), suggests that Greiner's figures are on the low side. Greiner's note on the food situation at Stalingrad echoes an entry in General Martin Fiebig's diary, November 26. "The Sixth Army does not take an unfavorable view of its tactical position, if it can get 300 cubic meters [about 210 tons] of gasoline and 30 tons of tank ammunition a day; food is said to be adequate for one month."

p. 458   Initially Hitler's optimism about Stalingrad was widely shared. The OKW diarist Greiner wrote in a private letter on November 27, 1942: "The Russian offensive still gives us fewest headaches, as we are entitled to the confident expectation that the situation can be cleared up in a short time. . . . Far worse is our situation in North Africa: everything depends on hanging on to Tunis and western Libya and Tripoli at least, and that's not going to be easy against the onrush of superior British and American forces from east and west." Jodl echoed this attitude to the Japanese on December 4. "Russian attackers will soon be deadlocked. Manstein is on the way. Perhaps next Russian attack on Italian army. German forces standing by. Situation in Russia indubitably more difficult. We now assume Soviet Union has some thirteen thousand aircraft and three thousand tanks; quality declining." (The naval staff queried whether *"thirteen thousand"* should not read *"——— hundred"!*) And the unusually well-informed Weizsäcker wrote in his diary, December 9: "From the eastern front too our military HQ is emitting favorable noises. Even Stalingrad, where some two hundred thousand men are cut off, no longer impresses our command: the view is that the eastern front won't suffer any grave strategic collapse this winter." On December 11, Ribbentrop cabled to all his missions instructions to refute enemy propaganda claims that Germany was badgering Japan to attack Russia in the Far East; until January 20, 1943, this was in fact true.

p. 458   Manstein's situation appreciation of November 24, 1942, is in BA file 39694/3b and in the war diary of Manstein's Army Group Don (N507/1). Under OCMH interrogation on September 10, 1945, General Heusinger confirmed that Manstein was initially of this view, that the Sixth Army's withdrawal from Stalingrad was *not* necessary. Major Engel's "diary" entry of November 26 ("Long discussion on Manstein's appreciation of situation, proposal to withdraw Sixth Army . . .") is further reason to treat this source with extreme caution—as Colonel Manfred Kehrig, the official West German historian (*Stalingrad,* Stuttgart, 1974), has also recently warned. Kehrig's history also uses the diaries of Count Johann von Kielmansegg, who headed Group East of the General Staff operations branch, and Major Thilo, who dealt with Army Group B affairs in that branch; but Kehrig did not procure either the *original* Richthofen diary or Greiner's papers, both of which I have used.

p. 459 A typed narrative of Rommel's meeting with Hitler and Göring is in the war diary of Panzer Army Africa (T313/472/1016ff); the shorthand record by his adjutant is in his papers (T84/259).

p. 461 On Abwehr subversive operations in North Africa, I used Greiner's record of Warlimont's conference on December 6, 1942; a memo by Canaris of December 14 (Ritter's AA files, Serial 1105); Lahousen's diary, December 21; and Canaris's memos for Keitel, dated December 9, and talk with him on December 11 (AL/1933). According to newspaper reports, U.S. courts-martial sentenced 174 Arabs to death for sabotaging railroads.

p. 462 Bormann's memo on Hitler's conversation with Anton Mussert on December 10, 1942, is in BA file NS–19/*neu* 1556. Keitel made similar remarks to Canaris on December 20 (AL/1933).

p. 462 Himmler's own handwritten agenda for discussion with Hitler on December 10 survives (T175/94/5330); against Item 3, "Jews in France," Himmler put a tick and the word *abschaffen*—dispose of. In his subsequent memo to the Gestapo chief, Müller, however, he used the milder words *verhaftet und abtransportiert*—arrested and transported away (T175/103/5558).

There are other illuminating references to the "Jewish problem" in Himmler's files at this time. On October 2, 1942, he wrote to Pohl, Krüger, Globocnik, and Wolff about his determination to extract the Jews from their protected status within important arms factories in Poland too. "It will then be our aim to replace these Jewish workers by Poles and to merge most of these Jewish concentration-camp workshops into a very few big Jewish concentration-camp factories, as far as practicable in the east of the General-gouvernement. But there too the Jews must one day, in accordance with the Führer's wish, disappear [*verschwinden*]" (T175/22/7359). On November 30, Himmler sent to Gestapo Chief Müller a "very interesting [press] announcement about a memorandum written by Dr. [Stephen F.] Wise [President of the American Jewish Congress] in September 1942," and commented: "Given the scale of the Jewish migration, I'm not surprised that such rumors crop up somewhere in the world. We both know there's a high death rate among the Jews who are put to work. But you are to guarantee to me that at each location the cadavers of these deceased Jews are either burned or buried, and that nothing else can happen with the cadavers wherever they are. You are to investigate at once in all quarters to find out whether there have been any such abuses as the—no doubt mendacious—rumors disseminated around the world claim. All such abuses are to be reported to me on the SS oath of honor" (T175/68/4325). This letter was the purest humbug, and Himmler's suave reaction to two specific Allied press reports on the extermination of the European Jews proves it. On November 24, 1942, *The Times* (London) published a dispatch from the Jewish Agency in Jerusalem on the holocaust, partly fanciful but with an unmistakable hard core of truth. Himmler's office obtained it from Sweden and forwarded it with a noncommittal letter to the SS Reich Main Security Office in Berlin "for your attention" (T175/68/4406). On February 14, 1943, the same newspaper published a report received by the British Section of the World Jewish Congress from Central Europe, claiming that the extermination of Jews was being accelerated: Bohemia-Moravia was to be "*judenrein*" by March 31, deportations from Germany were continuing, and the mass exterminations in Poland were proceeding, in one place at the rate of six thousand daily. "Before being massacred, the Jews are ordered to strip and their clothes are sent to Germany." Rudolf Brandt, Himmler's adjutant, sent the news report to Kaltenbrunner's office. "On the instructions of the Reichsführer SS I am transmitting herewith to you a press dispatch on the accelerated extermination [*Ausrottung*] of the Jews in Occupied Europe" (T175/68/4398).

p. 464 Hitler's thought processes can be reconstructed from the stenogram of his war conference on December 12, 1942, and from Greiner's unpublished note of the same date. By this time, according to the diary of the Eighth Air Corps commander, Fiebig (December 11), Paulus's casualties were increasing at the rate of 1,000 a day; he still had 270,000 men, of whom 40,000 were infantry combat troops.

p. 466   I used both German and Italian accounts of the conference: the latter are in *comando supremo* files (T821/21/951 *et seq.*, and T821/457/409 *et seq.*). On December 19, 1942, Greiner noted: "Italians had urged some kind of arrangement with Stalin, but this is rejected by Führer out of hand, as even without weakening eastern front there is enough strength for the southern." As Weizsäcker commented (diary, December 25), it was hardly surprising that Ciano got this reply: "Talk like this can only be direct and without witnesses, and between the Duce and the Führer—not by Duce to General von Rintelen, Duce to Göring, Ciano to the Führer."

p. 467   Zeitzler nervously retorted to Richthofen: "But you were one of the first to advise us to hang on to the Volga.!" Richthofen denied this in his diary *("Impertinence.!")*.

For Hitler's order to raise two SS divisions, see his adjutant Pfeiffer's teletype to Himmler, December 19, (T175/145/2277); Greiner's note, January 23; Wolff's memo, January 13 (IfZ, MA–333, page 8079); Himmler's letter to Bormann, March 13 (T175/70/6813), and speech, October 6, 1943.

Retreat

p. 471   From the diaries of Goebbels and Bormann, and Speer's Chronik (FD–3037/49) it is possible to reconstruct the origins of the formidable three-man cabal established by Keitel, Bormann, and Lammers late in 1942, to extract every last ounce of effort out of the nation—and in particular "one million new soldiers" (as Goebbels secretly announced at a ministerial conference on January 5). Goebbels was however given only a consultative role by Hitler's formal decree setting up the Council of Three on January 13, 1943 (IfZ, MA–470, pages 4910 *et seq.*) See also Speer, *Erinnerungen,* pages 265 *et seq.*, and the diary of Colonel Gerhard Kühne of the OKH.

p. 472   Despite the apparent entry in Engel's "diary" for December 29, 1942, there is no proof that Hitler ordered the Taman bridgehead held until one month later (see Greiner's note of January 23). According to the stenographer's diary, the special conference at which Hitler presumably planned the Kharkov offensive lasted from 10 to 11:45 P.M. on New Year's Eve.

p. 472   The number of transport aircraft on hand always vastly outnumbered those that actually flew, as Milch's records show. From January 1 to 14 the daily availability of Junkers 52s and Heinkel 111s was: 481, 473, 482, 485, 480, 467, 464, 437, 466, 470, 472, 466, 498, 539, to which were added 20 four-engined FW 200s and 28 big Heinkel 177s on January 9; but over the same period the sorties actually flown were only 78, 0, 97, 145, 53, 29, 63, 76, 102, 102, 95, 51, 69, 74.

p. 473   The cassette was handed to Göring on his splendid fiftieth birthday, January 12, 1943, by Keitel.

Hitler's private sources of Intelligence—like the letter from Winrich Behr to Colonel von Below quoted—must not be underestimated. Hewel will certainly have shown him the letter he received, dated January 9, from an arms specialist attached to Army Group Center. "The fighting is hard, perhaps harder than ever before, but even so the feeling is that the Russians are also at the end of their tether; it is a war of annihilation in which the one who keeps his nerve in the last quarter-hour will emerge victorious—and that will be us" (Hewel's private correspondence, AA files).

p. 473   On the Arctic fiasco, I used the naval staff war diary (especially January 23 and March 10, 1943) and the report in Raeder's personal file (PG/31762); and material from Puttkamer and Junge. For Speer's campaign against Raeder and the admiral's resignation, I used manuscripts in Raeder's files, Speer's note on his discussion with Hitler on January 3–5 (Point 78: Speer "reported in detail to the Führer the worries of the U-boat people that, owing to Admiral Dönitz's partly bad standing with the naval staff, he could come to harm"), and his frank postwar admission to Milch that he had caused Raeder's downfall (Milch diary, July 13, 1947). In fact, as Raeder wrote reminding Hitler on January 14, 1943, he had "thrice given Admiral Dönitz preferential promotion" during the war. See also Krancke's memo of February 13, 1943 (PG/31747).

p. 474 A month after Hitler's remark to Antonescu, Göring also privately admitted that while he was not worried about the situation "it's not quite clear to me how we are intending to end this war" (Weizsäcker diary, February 17, 1943).

p. 476 Dönitz's visit to Hitler on January 25, 1943, is confirmed by Bormann's diary and Puttkamer's memoirs; there exists no transcript, but his "connivance" at the scrapping of the capital ships emerges from a telephone call recorded in the next day's naval staff war diary.

The appointment of Milch to manage the Stalingrad airlift is described in his diaries, in an OCMH interrogation of Göring, July 20, 1945, in Greiner's note for January 16, 1943, and in Milch's unpublished manuscript memoirs. Speer announced to Central Planning on January 26 that Milch would be "away in the east for probably six to eight weeks" (MD 47/9236). A few days earlier, Hitler had ordered mass production of airdrop containers on the biggest scale.

pp. 476–77 Göring is quoted in Koller's diary, February 15, 1943.

pp. 477–78 On Hitler's new propaganda directive to Goebbels after Stalingrad see Goebbels's ministerial conference on January 24, 1943; Gottlob Berger's letter to Himmler, January 29, (T175/124/9596); naval staff diary January 24, Weizsäcker's diary February 12, and Goebbels's diary March 9, 1943.

p. 479 Allied "plans to invade Portugal" were presumably misinformation fed deliberately to Hitler. They are mentioned in the naval staff diary, February 4, and Hitler's meeting with Dönitz on the ninth, and in Canaris's diary February 9 (AL/1933), and a memo of the tenth in naval file PG/31747. Canaris admittedly saw no reason to believe them, but pointed toward Spanish Morocco (naval staff diary, February 13). Finally, on April 25, 1943, the naval staff diary sarcastically asked what had happened to the invasion so confidently predicted by the OKW in Portugal for the February 22.

p. 480 Traudl Humps, who had joined his staff in November and in April 1943 married SS Lieutenant Hans Junge, his manservant; she kindly made her unpublished memoirs available to me. The army doctor mentioned was Dr. Erwin Giesing.

p. 481 The material on Hitler's foreign policy comes from Ritter's AA file on Japan (Serial 1028), with its notes on Oshima's meetings with Hitler and Ribbentrop; from Weizsäcker's diary, January 27–30, and February 6, 1943; and from Ribbentrop's memoirs, page 263.

p. 481 Rosenberg's querulous conferences with Hitler are dealt with in Himmler's files, in Etzdorf's note of February 23, 1943, and in Goebbels's unpublished diary, February 16.

p. 482 The Russian document—originating from General Krupennikov, 1941–42 deputy chief of Soviet replacements—is in naval files, PG/32602-3; the statistics are quoted by Greiner in an unpublished note of January 8 and January 23; by Hitler to Antonescu on April 12, and by Gehlen's department to the war academy in a lecture on April 16 (BA file H3/319).

The quotation on Hitler's speech, February 7, 1943, is from Frau Ursula Backe's diary, February 8. There are similar words in a letter by an SS captain on Hitler's staff, writing on September 7, 1944, about the present trials of German fortitude. "On this point even the Führer yesterday said, 'Those who don't want to fight don't deserve to survive.' "

p. 483 Hitler's remarks are quoted in Milch's conferences soon after (MD35/4685 and /3226, and MD18/4735).

pp. 483–84 Richthofen was disappointed when Manstein told him the outcome of his talk with Hitler (diary, February 8, 1943). "Führer was calm and composed, Manstein visibly bucked up. Naturally no discussion whatsoever of another kind of command or command-organization, although this was just what Manstein was there for." (Manstein humanly gives the opposite impression in his postwar memoirs.) Richthofen advised the field marshal to keep a tighter grip on the panzer divisions, with short sharp forays, leaving behind their "dead wood" and carving up the enemy front piece by piece—copying Russian tactics; Manstein replied that his commanders would not oblige. Richthofen wrote: "I told him quite cheerfully that in my far-off youth I had once heard a rumor that in military affairs it was possible to issue *orders.*"

On Kluge's similar trip to Hitler, I used Schlabendorff's August 1944 testimony under Gestapo interrogation (NS–6/41), Zeitzler's manuscripts (N63/80 and 101), and Engel's notes.

p. 485   The quotation is from Hitler's secret speech on June 22, 1944 (NS–26/51).

p. 486   The late Fritz Todt—Speer's predecessor—had described the power radiated by Hitler thus, in a private letter to a professor dated September 30, 1933, which I found amongst Todt's personal effects: "The most beautiful thing about my work is that it takes me close to the Führer. I am convinced that any man who can spend ten minutes a week with the Führer achieves many times his normal output of work."

Strychnine

p. 489   The medical details are from interrogations of Morell, Giesing, and Gebhardt; Professor Ernst-Günther Schenck identified Prostakrinum for me from the 1939 *Gehe Codex* as a product of Morell's own firm, Hamma A. G., used to combat a hypertrophied prostate and general sex-hormone insufficiency in the male.

p. 489   The appointment book kept by Hitler's servants Hans Junge and Heinz Linge from March 22 to June 20, 1943, lay in a waterlogged condition in 1945, and ended up in the Hoover Library, California; it was restored at my request in 1965. I have deposited a transcript with the IfZ.

p. 490   The panzer Lieutenant General Karl Eibl (Twenty-fourth Panzer Corps), holder of Germany's second highest medal, lost his leg in the blast and died under the subsequent emergency operation (performed without anesthetic). Hitler did not tell Mussolini of the incident until April 23, 1944.

p. 490   Hitler's anxiety to spare his allies' feelings is plain from his order to Eighth Army, February 14, 1943 (in its war diary appendices, file 36199/9); from Ritter's memo to Ribbentrop, March 20 (Serial 1006); and from Scherff's letter to Jodl, June 25 (T77/1035/7945).

p. 492   Professor Charles Burdick wrote a convincing account of the German planning for an invasion of Spain, 1942–43, in *WR*, 1964, pages 164 *et seq.;* I also used the unpublished diaries of Greiner and Canaris (especially February 9, 1943: AL/1933) and of Richthofen, and Junge's memo on Hitler's conference of February 10 (PG/31747). Burdick does not mention the German-Spanish secret protocol of February 11, 1943; it will be found on AA microfilms of Ribbentrop's office files, Serial F3, page 0355.

p. 494   Hitler made his remark about Rommel at the conference on August 31, 1944 (Heiber, page 614); Goebbels quoted Göring similarly on March 2, 1943. Canaris also reported at length on Tunis after a visit there on February 27, 1943, is in file AL/1933.

p. 494   On the fighting in Tunis: Goebbels's unpublished diary, February 1943; war conference stenogram, March 4; Rommel's private letters (T84/R274); Kesselring's memoirs; the war diaries of the naval staff and OKW, and Greiner's handwritten draft for the latter; correspondence between Hitler and Mussolini (T586/405), and Ritter's AA files, Serial 5757. On March 15 Richthofen entered Jeschonnek's observations in his diary: "Rommel very low, nerves finished too. For the first time Kesselring's fixed grin was wiped off his face. Only the Führer is still optimistic. What's certain is that in the long run Africa can't be held for supply reasons."

p. 498   The undeniable restoration of the generals' faith in Hitler that spring emerges from Greiner's unpublished note of March 14, and from an entry in the anti-Hitler conspirator Hassell's diary two weeks later. "The generals are enough to drive you around the bend," Etzdorf had told him in despair. "Now that everything's going better again, everything's apparently okay: 'The Führer has turned out right again.'—Hopeless!"

My footnote is based on security documents in the BA Schumacher Collection, file 487, and Canaris's journey report (AL/1933). On the fabled assassination attempt at Smolensk, see Fabian von Schlabrendorff, *Offiziere gegen Hitler* (Zürich 1946), and Peter Hoffmann, *Widerstand, Staatsstreich, Attentat* (Munich, 1969), Chap. IX. In the conspirators' earlier accounts—*e.g.,* the British Consolidated Interrogation Report "The Political and Social Background of the 20 July Incident" (Secret, September 10, 1945) and the USFET interrogation of Baron Rudolf von Gersdorff himself (OI-IIR/34, dated February 18, 1946)—there are irritating discrepancies. Was their alleged bomb disguised as brandy (round) or Cointreau (square) bottles? Was the Abwehr explosive that Canaris mentioned used? or British-made Clam explosives with magnetic fastenings? Was the packet handed to Colonel Heinz Brandt to carry—he and Tresckow, the other main conspirator, died in 1944—or did Schlabrendorff himself "place it under Hitler's seat"? We can only speculate—particularly since Brandt in fact *never* flew in Hitler's plane, according to Schaub's manuscripts.

p. 500   The effect of strychnine and atropine is described in E. Poulsson's *Lehrbuch für Pharmakologie* (10th ed., 1934); it is only proper to point out that from the composition of "Dr. Koester's Antigas Pills" as described in the 1937 *Gehe Codex,* Professor Schenck —whom I consulted—doubted whether Hitler could have imbibed enough to have a serious effect. Hitler's doctors, going by the figures printed on the pillbox, thought differently.

p. 503   For the Abwehr Intelligence failures see Eberhard's diary, September 28, 1938; Colonel Ulrich Liss's remarks in Groscurth's diary, October 5 and 10, 1939; Tippelskirch's diary, September 19, 1939, etc.; but also Canaris's spirited self-defense in Goebbels's diary, April 9 and 11, 1943—he claimed that he had predicted everything in good time, but the truth had been withheld from Hitler. Not so.

p. 503   Canaris sardonically quoted Keitel's remark in a memo of October 23, 1941 (AL/1933). Lahousen heard Keitel say much the same that spring, as he recalled under interrogation. There is evidence that the Army's chief judge advocate, Karl Sack—one of the conspirators—gulled Keitel into believing that the SS was out to undermine the OKW's Abwehr, thus persuading him to stifle the Gestapo investigations.

p. 503 (footnote 6)   Himmler's report on population movements dated January 20, 1943, is in BA file R 43 II/1411a. A major statistical study by his analyst, Dr. Richard Korherr, on the Soviet manpower reservoir definitely went to Hitler as well; it was retyped on the "Führer typewriter" and shown him in May 1943 (Himmler files, T175/54/6437 *et seq.*).

p. 503   Himmler had ordered Korherr to make a statistical analysis of the Final Solution, by letter of January 18, 1943 (T175/18/1557) explaining that Kaltenbrunner's office "lacked the necessary expert precision." The draft and shortened final reports, and Himmler's related correspondence, are on microfilm T175/103/5017 *et seq.*). As the ribbon copy of the shorter version is still in Himmler's files, it may not even have gone to Hitler. Nor did several letters which at about this time reached Dr. Hans Lammers alleging that Jews were being methodically exterminated in Poland (ND, NG–1903). At the Nuremberg war crimes trials, Lammers stated that he followed up these reports by asking Himmler. "Himmler denied that there was any authorized killing going on and told me—making reference to the Führer's orders—'I have to evacuate the Jews and in such evacuations there are . . . obviously fatalities. Apart from those, the people are being housed in camps in the East.' And he fetched a mass of pictures and albums and showed me how the Jews were being put to work in the camps on war production, in shoe factories, tailors' shops, and the like. Then he told me: 'This job comes from the Führer. If you think you must put a stop to it, then go and tell the Führer' " (IMT, Vol. XI, page 62).

Clutching at Straws

p. 508   For the contingency planning for an invasion of Sweden, see Wolf Junge's manuscript; the naval staff plans in its war diary annex, Part C, Vol. III; the naval staff war diary, October 23, 1943; and the OKW war diary.

p. 509   According to the manservant's register, Hitler saw Horthy three times: at 5:30
P.M. on April 16, and at 12:10 and 5 P.M. on the 17th; three corresponding records exist,
by interpreter Paul Schmidt, but as both Horthy and Schmidt claim in their memoirs that
the interpreter was absent during at least the first meeting, it is probable that as in 1944
(see Jodl diary, March 17, 1944) the conference room at Klessheim was bugged with hidden
microphones.

p. 509   On the deportation of Hungary's Jews, see the AA's letter to Bormann, March
9, 1943 (Serial 5231 pages E310707 *et seq.*), and the Abwehr's security objections—in a letter
to the AA—against allowing large units of Hungarian Jews to come near German military
movements (*ibid.,* K206893). According to Schmidt's notes, Ribbentrop went even further
than Hitler in one outburst to Horthy, exclaiming "that the Jews must either be destroyed
or put in concentration camps—there is no other way" (a wording which caused Ribbentrop some discomfiture in the witness box at Nuremberg). Horthy copied the wording into
his 1953 memoirs (page 254) but put them in Hitler's mouth! Secret Hungarian records do
not echo the wording in such bluntness. In a draft letter to Hitler on May 7, Horthy
included a sentence—later deleted—"Your Excellency further reproached me that my
government does not proceed with stamping out Jewry with the same radicalism as is
practiced in Germany." And in his discussion with the Hungarian envoy Sztójay a few
days later Ribbentrop went no further than to remind him that Hitler had (in the summer
of 1942) decreed that "by the summer of 1943 all Jews of Germany and the German
occupied countries are to be moved to the eastern, *i.e.,* Russian, territories." Ribbentrop
added that for security reasons Germany required her allies to conform—Mussolini had,
for instance, just undertaken to intern the Jews in Italy (documents in National Archives,
Budapest).

p. 510   Many sources exist highlighting the Rosenberg-Koch squabble over policies in
Russia: the Goebbels diaries and Himmler files (T175/124 and /171); BDC file SS 981;
Richthofen's diary, May 24, 1943; the stenogram of Hitler's conference with Keitel and
Zeitzler on June 8; Etzdorf's note of April 13; Ribbentrop's memo on the Vlasov operation,
April 6 (Etzdorf's file, Serial 1247); Bormann's memo of May 19 (BA file R 58/1005);
Gehlen's files, containing Hewel's memo of May 24 (T81/219/9474 *et seq.*); the diary of
Colonel Heinz-Danko Herre, of Gehlen's staff; Kluge's conference with General Reinhardt
of the Third Panzer Army, June 17 (in the Army's war diary, annexes, H 12–33/5);
Etzdorf's teletype to the AA, June 17 (Serial 364), and Lahousen's diary, June 21, 1943.

p. 512   The best history of "Citadel" so far is unquestionably the German official
historian Dr. Ernst Klink's *Das Gesetz des Handelns* (Stuttgart, 1966); it supersedes earlier
studies by Generals F.W. Hauck and Gotthard Heinrici in *WR,* 1965, and by Eike Middel-
dorf, *ibid.,* 1953. Klink kindly read and commented on my own "Citadel" narrative, which
benefits from a number of sources not available to him—notably the Richthofen diary and
the manservant's diary, which helps, for example, to pinpoint the date of Zeitzler's visit
as April 21, 1943.

p. 513   On Model's visit: Ninth Army war diary, April 27–28, (BA, 34739/2) and
annexes, Vol. VIII (35212/2); Model's appreciation, April 25 (35939/12); Junge diary,
April 27, 1943; war conference, May 18, 1944 (stenogram); and Guderian's manuscript,
March 1949 (IfZ, ZS–57).

Hitler's order of April 29 is mentioned in the OKW war diary, July 5; the resulting OKH
order of April 30 is in the Fourth Panzer Army's war diary, annexes (34888/23) and the
Ninth Army's war diary, annexes (34890/1); for the Luftwaffe view, Richthofen's diary
contains an appreciation dated May 1, 1943.

p. 513   Guderian's notes on his tank conferences with Hitler are on microfilm T78/622.
I also used Saur's testimony (FD–3049/49).

p. 514   Richthofen glued a lengthy memo on Jeschonnek's account of the May 4, 1943,
Munich conference into his diary, May 25. On the fifth Richthofen himself wrote: "Rumor
has it that some kind of conferences between Guderian and the Führer and Zeitzler have

brought an element of uncertainty into opinions. Perhaps—and the interpolation of Guderian indicates this—it is hoped that minor technical improvements will result in major military changes. Of course this is pure rubbish—they haven't resulted in decisive victories in any war yet, but again and again they are tried for by us." On May 24, Richthofen flatly told Jeschonnek that the Russians would build far more by way of defensive positions in six weeks than the Germans could hope to increase their striking power.

There is no evidence that either Guderian or Manstein opposed the delay. In 1958 correspondence with Zeitzler, General Theodor Busse loyally quoted Manstein as telling Hitler, "The attack will be tough, but I think it'll succeed." But Kempf clearly recalled in 1958 telephoning Zeitzler three days later, furious at the delay; Zeitzler had replied that the general's call was "grist to his mill. He [Zeitzler] had desperately opposed any further postponement of 'Citadel,' but only Field Marshal von Kluge had supported him" (N63/12). This is supported by Kempf's memo on the telephone conversation in the Eighth Army war diary (36188/20).

p. 515 Hitler's words to Warlimont are quoted in a naval staff memo on Hitler's Berghof conference, May 1, 1943 (PG/31747).

p. 515 On Hitler's speech of May 7, 1943, I used the diaries of Junge, Bormann, Himmler, and Goebbels.

p. 516 From May 1943 onward, a diary, kept by Rommel, exists in British hands— as far as I know I am the first to have exploited it (AL/1708). For Rommel's fierce anti-Italian feelings, see also the Goebbels diary, May 10–13, and Rommel's letters of May 10–13 (T84/R274).

p. 517 Connoisseurs of British Intelligence operations will find the complete file on the corpse and its documents in German naval archives, PG/33216; they should also read the naval staff diary, May 1943, and microfilm T78/343. On May 25, Goebbels wrote in his diary that Canaris "energetically refuted" his hypothesis that the documents were deliberately planted. The duty stenographer who noted that Hitler shared Goebbels's skepticism —initially—was the late Ludwig Krieger, who described the scene in his private papers in 1945 and to me in a 1972 interview.

p. 518 Dönitz's famous admission to Hitler on May 14, 1943, that his U-boat offensive had collapsed, caused a sensation at the Wolf's Lair; see Goebbels's diary, and Rommel's diary and private letters (T84/R275/0324).

For Hitler's plan to strengthen the Balkans, see his war conference on May 20 (Heiber, pages 238 *et seq.*); the date of this is now firmly established by the manservant's diary.

p. 519 Captain Wolf Junge's handwritten account of Hitler's conference of May 15 is in naval archives (PG/31747). Rommel's diary also refers to it. "Following the situation report the Führer speaks on probable developments in Italy and Greece. There are prospects for my early employment."

p. 520 An early meeting with Mussolini was probably the topic raised by Hitler with Prince Philip of Hesse at 4:45 P.M. on May 20, 1943; the prince—who had married Princess Mafalda, daughter of the king of Italy, in 1923—was frequently used by Hitler as a special courier to Rome.

p. 520 Hewel's memo for Ribbentrop, June 25, 1943, is in Ritter's AA file (Serial 1462). See also Scherff's letter to Jodl, June 25 (T77/1035/7945), and the naval staff's indignant protests at aspersions cast by Hitler on German shortcomings in supplying North Africa (war diary, June 29 and August 5). Hitler even summarily deleted three pages of Goebbels's proposed speech of June 5 because they referred to North Africa (NS-6/129).

p. 521 The quotations are from Hitler's conference with Konstantin von Neurath— son of the famous pre-1938 foreign minister—on May 20, 1943 (Heiber, pages 220 *et seq.*); see also Rommel's diary. Winston Churchill alleged with his characteristic attention to accuracy (*The Second World War,* Vol. V, page 29) that "Neurath, the foreign secretary," was present.

p. 522 The Berghof menu is pasted into Eva Braun's album (NA, 242–EB–22–33a). In his unpublished diary Goebbels wrote on June 25 after a day with Hitler: "Little is left of the physical fitness we always used to marvel at in him."

pp. 522–23 Canaris's record of his talks with Warlimont and Rommel's chief of staff General Alfred Gause is in the Canaris diary file AL/1933, which unfortunately ends at this point; see also the Lahousen diary, June 4.

Correcting the Front Line

p. 526 Guderian's note on his June 16 conference with Hitler is in BA file H16/236. According to the naval staff war diary, June 25, the General Staff expected tank production to increase from four hundred to one thousand three hundred a month by autumn. Zeitzler's naval liaison officer emphasized the uncertainty being injected into the eastern front by the Mediterranean situation. But "the troops' morale is high, offset only by the bad news reaching them on the effects of enemy air raids at home" *(ibid.)*. According to Goebbels's unpublished diary, June 25, Zeitzler had visited Hitler on the twenty-fourth —no doubt to agree to the final postponement of "Citadel."

p. 528 On the dispute between Frank and the SS, I relied on Nuremburg trial documents NG–3556, 2233–PS, NO–2202, and 437–PS; see also Hassell's diary, May 15, 1943, with its authentic detail by Frank's administration chief on the SS mass extermination of Jews in Poland. On Frank's meeting with Hitler on May 9, I used the diaries of Goebbels, Frank, and Bormann, and the latter's memo of May 11 (BA, Schumacher Collection, file 371). On May 31, Frank called a big security-conference in Cracow; Himmler agreed to send representatives, apologizing in a letter to Frank on May 26: "The evacuation of the last two hundred fifty thousand Jews, which will doubtless cause unrest for some weeks, must be completed as rapidly as possible despite all the difficulties" (T175/128/4157 *et seq.*).

p. 529 Himmler's talk with Hitler, June 19, 1943: see his files, T175/94/5096 *et seq.*, T175/40 and T175/76; and T175/94/5098.

p. 529 On the Schirachs' last visit to the Berghof (June 1943) I collected testimony from both Schirachs, Otto Günsche, secretary Christa Schroeder, Marion Schönmann—whose wording I have followed—Traudl Humps (who learned about it from her husband, Hans Junge), and the cameraman Walter Frentz; also from the Goebbels diary, June 25, 1943, and Table Talk, June 24 (evening).

Traces of Hitler's "scalepan" argument recur in Table Talks on September 14 and November 5, 1941, and in Goebbels's diary, May 23 and 30, 1942.

pp. 530–31 Professor Ernst Heinkel describes the aircraft designers' conference with Hitler on June 27, 1943, in his memoirs, pages 459 *et seq.* I also used Bormann's diary, Speer's notes, Messerschmitt's interrogations and personal papers (FD–4355/45, Vol. 6), and Wolf Junge's manuscript.

p. 531 The "Hektor" and "Josephine" reports (see pages 572–73) will be found in Baron Gustav Adolf Steengracht von Moyland's AA file, Serial 98. Controller of these alleged "agents" was Counsellor of Legation Karl-Heinz Kraemer, at the Stockholm legation; he has declined to identify them.

p. 532 Envoy Hans Thomsen's telegram of June 21, 1943, is in Steengracht's file, Serial 191. The "gentleman" was Peter Kleist (see his book *European Tragedy*, pages 144 *et seq.*) Subsequently the Russians claimed that Alexandrov—a former counsellor of their Berlin embassy, by June 1943 head of the German division of the Soviet foreign ministry—was in Australia in June 1943 (see *Izvestia*, July 29, 1947). Not so. The June 22, 1943, announcement was made in *Pravda*. The July 1 article was by N. Malinin in *Voina i rabochnii klass* (War and the Working Class).

p. 532 General Hans Friessner (Twenty-Third Corps) wrote the manuscript record of Hitler's speech which I quote. I found it in his personal papers, BA file H 14–23/1, pages 121–9. In his diary, Rommel wrote: "Evening, big conference in outbuilding [of General Staff HQ]. Every field marshal and field commander present, and some corps commanders.

Führer gives picture of the situation and the planned operations. Afterward a gettogether until 2:50 A.M." A short verbatim extract of the speech (pages 55 to 61 only) is on microfilm T77/778/0773 *et seq.* See also Manstein, pages 495 *et seq.*

The panzer general von Knobelsdorff was overheard on May 14, 1945, describing the evening to a fellow prisoner thus: "Hitler promised us the world there. . . . Naturally we never got it. Hermann [Göring] sat next to him, wilting more and more from one quarter-hour to the next until his face looked downright sheepish—a complete dullard. He kept eating pills and then perked up for a while. . . . We sat together with the Führer for a while, but Hermann went off with his Luftwaffe men" (X–P4).

p. 534   In fact about three *thousand* Allied ships were involved. Rommel's diary states, July 10, 1943: "Noon war conference with Führer. British and Americans landed on Sicily with paratroops and landing craft. Three hundred ships.—9:30 P.M. to 1:40 A.M. discussion with Führer."

p. 535   The view at Hitler's HQ was that Stalin's July 12, 1943, counteroffensive was a last desperate fling. Milch—who saw Hitler the next day—reassured his staff on the nineteenth: "The Russians have *got* to attack. They have no option. They have such ghastly domestic problems, and so little hope that things will get better, that they say, 'If we don't finish the war this summer and winter at the latest, then for me it'll be all over.' The Russians will not survive this winter as a fighting force—and that's definite" (MD22/6076). And see the food minister Herbert Backe's remarks, quoted by his wife in a letter to Heydrich's widow on July 25: "He says it's very important for us not to have a bad harvest in this critical year. America's harvest has failed; Russia is starving. Besides this, my husband thinks it good that the Russians are attacking—it's a sign of their weakness: they *have* to." Richthofen's words, written after Hitler's noon conference on July 28, are very similar (diary), as are Goebbels's that same day.

pp. 535–36   The captured letters are analyzed in a report of July 7, 1943, shown to Hitler (H3/644).

p. 538   Rommel's diary, July 13, 1943, encapsulates Germany's growing military plight. "Noon, Führer's war conference; ditto evening.—"Hermann Göring" Division has not met desired success in attack [in Sicily]. Syracuse occupied by British. Two battalions of enemy paratroops landed west of Catania destroyed by our own paratroops. Field Marshals von Kluge and von Manstein report to Führer, evening General Guderian too. Russians staging counterattacks. Model's [Ninth] Army can't keep up."

p. 540   There is a record of the talk with the Italian ambassador in Milch's files (MD53/1116 *et seq.*)

p. 540   Rommel's diary on July 16, 1943, reads: "At noon conference. Göring wants General Stahel as Commander in Chief [Sicily] and not Hube. I get Hube accepted and suggest General Bayerlein as his Chief of Staff. The Führer acquiesces.—Heavy tank losses on eastern front. The breach at Bryansk [Second Panzer Army] has been sealed off.— Phoned General Bayerlein, didn't reach him. Went over to Führer's evening conference. Hube is called on to operate offensively." And the next day Rommel continued: "At noon conference with Führer. Ambassador [Hans George] von Mackensen [Rome] with Führer. General Bayerlein expected in afternoon.—Situation in east for a time at crisis point, eases again. Russian attacks beaten back. Italy: British air raids. . . . 4 P.M.: summoned to Führer. Initially Admiral Dönitz, Field Marshal Keitel, General Jodl, and myself present; later General Bayerlein. Bayerlein not taking on new job as still ill. Colonel Kriebel is then proposed. I suggest von Bonin instead and he gets the job.—To Führer's evening conference."

On Hitler's mid-July strategy prior to Mussolini's overthrow, see his remarks to the Bulgarian leaders on October 18, 1943.

pp. 541–42   This fragment of Mussolini's diary, dated August 19, 1943, is in secret AA files, Serial 715, pages 263729 *et seq.;* for the official Italian record, see Mussolini's papers (T586/405/394 *et seq.*) and the records of the *comando supremo* (T821/251/955 *et seq.*).

p. 543   Himmler's Intelligence report to Bormann, July 19, 1943, is in the Reichsführer's files (T175/53/7178ff).

p. 543   For the Abwehr's mistaken belief that the Allies would soon invade the Balkans —which culminated in Hitler's directive of July 26, 1943—see the naval staff and OKW war diaries, July 28.

pp. 543–45   My narrative of events at Hitler's HQ is based on Milch's diary, on Admiral Krancke's reports (in naval staff diary), on Goebbels's diary, and on the stenograms of Hitler's dramatic war conferences on July 25.

"Axis"

p. 546   I drew on signals in the naval staff war diary's annexes, Part C, Vol. XIV (PG/32216), the diaries of Rommel, Richthofen, the OKW, and other sources complementing Josef Schröder's authoritative history *Italiens Kriegsaustritt 1943* (Göttingen, 1969).

p. 547   Himmler's telephone log shows that he telephoned R.S.H.A. chief General Kaltenbrunner at noon on July 28: "Reports from Italy.—Grab all dissidents.—Morale [after raids on] Hamburg."

p. 548   Rommel's diary expands on Richthofen's dramatic record of July 26, 1943. "12 noon land at Rastenburg [on return from Greece]. Drive to Wolf's Lair immediately. . . . Situation in Italy still confused. No news yet on how Mussolini's overthrow happened. On king's orders Marshal Badoglio has taken office as head of government. It's to be expected that despite pronouncements by king and Badoglio Italy will drop out of the war, or at least that the British will undertake fresh major landings in Upper Italy. . . . I'm hoping to be sent into Italy soon." See also the record of Hitler's conferences with Admiral Dönitz over these days.

Skorzeny himself described (in a 1970 interview) how he was picked by Hitler. Richthofen did not think much of General Student. "He's personally an absolute fool and hasn't the faintest idea of how to get on with his ('somewhat fantastic') mission, or what it's consequences may be" (diary, July 27). Captain Wolf Junge—Jodl's naval staff officer— also wrote fully about this episode in his unpublished manuscript memoirs.

p. 550   Junge described the huge relief created at Hitler's HQ by Churchill's gloating speech. The naval staff war diary commented, on July 27, that it was ideal for German purposes, and added the next day: "In comments on Churchill's speech the Italians point out that it has unmasked as pure hypocrisy the British claim to be fighting only fascism."

p. 550   On the German-monitored Churchill telephone conversation, see OKW war diary July 29 and August 3, 1943; and Himmler's telephone call to SS General Gottlob Berger at 11 P.M. on July 29 ("Churchill-Roosevelt conversation"). According to Sir Alexander Cadogan's diary, there had been a meeting of the Defence Committee at 10:30 P.M. that July 28: "Discussed armistice terms and Ike's mad idea of broadcasting a bowdlerized version. PM got Pres[ident] on the telephone and squashed latter idea. But Ike authorized to put out a proclamation. PM mainly preoccupied about our prisoners." Knowledge of this intercept was undoubtedly behind Admiral Hans-Erich Voss's warning from the Wolf's Lair to the naval staff on July 30 that the situation toward Italy was more acute "as there is further evidence that the Italian government is playing a double game." See also Rommel's diary, August 4, 1943.

The Americans were alarmed at Churchill's foolish noncompliance with telephone security rules. General Marshal advised Harry Hopkins that U.S. Army censors had listened in to one such recent conversation; while Hopkins had tactfully kept urging Churchill to guard his tongue, "the prime minister cited names and places in such a way as to create possible danger for himself and others." The U.S. Army warned that the Germans were known to be able to unscramble the radiotelephone (NA, letter from J. McCarthy to Hopkins, October 12, 1943, in Hopkins Papers, Box 136, Winston Churchill file.) Unfortunately no British or U.S. recordings of the actual conversations seem to exist, so we can only speculate on precisely what secrets were compromised.

p. 551   Rommel wrote with relish on July 30, 1943: "I'm going to enjoy this new job far more than the Southeast command. . . . We can guess what the Italians have up their sleeve now that Mussolini's resigned: they'll change sides, lock, stock, and barrel. Question is—will they find the actual courage to take the plunge."

For the faulty Intelligence on Italy, see the war diaries of the OKW, July 30–31, and August 3 and 5, 1943, and of the naval staff, July 29. On Canaris's role: Lahousen diary, July 29–August 3, 1943, and Walther Huppenkothen's 1945 manuscript "Canaris und Abwehr" in BDC files.

p. 551   Ribbentrop described his telephone call to Hitler in a later (December 30, 1944) talk with Ambassador Filippo Anfuso (in AA files). The Italian records of the talks with Keitel and Ribbentrop on August 6 are in *comando supremo* files (T821/251/777 *et seq.*).

pp. 552–53   Professor Hermann Giesler's record of the Führer's conference with Ley and himself on August 20, 1943, is in the present files of the Munich city planning bureau.

p. 554   Rommel commented on the Stalin rumors in his diary, August 9, 1943. "If they are founded on truth, they open up undreamed of new possibilities to us." Hitler's reflection is quoted from his conference with Dönitz a few days later.

p. 555   Rommel's letter commenting on Mussolini's departure from the European stage was written on August 6 to his wife (T84/R27/0352).

p. 556   Rommel's diary contains a complete account of the August 15, 1943, meeting at Bologna. (The Italian map was later published in *Das Reich,* October 10; and see the *Völkischer Beobachter,* October 23–24.) On August 16, Rommel noted: "General Jodl reports by phone from Sicily that by tomorrow provisionally 90 to 95 percent of the German troops will have been withdrawn." The evacuation was completed by 6:30 A.M. the next day, including all trucks and guns, despite the huge Allied superiority (see naval staff diary, August 20).

p. 556   Helmut Heiber wrote a fine study of King Boris's mysterious decease in *VfZ,* 1961, pages 384 *et seq.* The three German doctors are all dead—Eppinger and de Crinis as 1945 suicides and Seitz (as my researches in Madrid established) of natural causes there some years ago. The HQ stenographer Krieger recalled—in a postwar letter—that Hitler issued strict instructions to Raeder, Keitel, and the other prominent guests at the funeral in Sophia "on no account to accept food or drink offered to them there, but to feign stomach upsets and only eat the food they had brought with them from the Führer's HQ."

p. 557   Nonetheless Prince Philipp of Hesse retained his admiration for Hitler, despite his subsequent incarceration. He described under American interrogation (July 21, 1945) how Hitler had treated him almost like a son, spending hours every night talking with him of his plans for the reconstruction of Germany. Philip—who was Oberpräsident of Hesse-Nassau province—"had realized that he was probably in some sense a prisoner [at Hitler's HQ], and his urgent requests to return to his post when Kassel came in for heavy air attacks [on July 28 and 30, 1943] had been refused."

p. 558   The quotation is from Himmler's speech to Reich propaganda officials, January 28, 1944 (T175/94/4784 *et seq.*).

p. 559   The code name "Baroque" figures in Himmler's agenda for discussion with Hitler about March 17, 1943 ("Overall 'Operation Baroque' ") and in several telephone conversations, *e.g.,* with Kaltenbrunner on November 2, 1943 (T84/25). Himmler laughingly revealed the whole story in his speech to the Gauleiters on August 3, 1944 (see *VfZ,* 1953, pages 375 *et seq.*). Under CIC interrogation the Gestapo officials Walther Huppenkothen and Willi Litzenberg testified to Hitler's knowledge of the Himmler-Popitz rendezvous (which is also noted in Himmler's pocket diary, August 23, 1943). As Dr. Franz Reuter related in his monograph, "Der 20. Juli und seine Vorgeschichte" (in British secret files), Popitz spoke less than Himmler, who "seemed not satisfied at all with the outcome of the conversation." See also Goebbels's diary, September 23, 1943, and the Hassell diaries.

p. 560 The agent's message was cabled by Himmler's staff to Fritz Darges, Bormann's adjutant at Hitler's HQ, late on August 25, 1943 (T175/117/2393).

p. 561 In addition to the AA record of Hitler's talk with Antonescu, a Romanian version exists in Antonescu's files, "Conversatia dintre Domnul Maresal Antonescu si Fuhrerul Adolf Hitler" (ND, USSR–235).

p. 563 For the events of September 8, 1943, I used the diaries of Linge, Goebbels, the naval staff (and the latter's annexes, Part C, Vol. XIV), and the OKW. Hitler and Ribbentrop described the events—with Badoglio's and Roatta's manifold protestations of loyalty—frequently afterward, *e.g.,* to the Bulgarian envoy Sagoroff on October 6 (AA Serial 68, pages 49298 *et seq.*); to Saffet Arikan, the Turkish ambassador, on October 7 (AA Serial 5452, pages E366598 *et seq.*); and in Hitler's secret speech on January 27, 1944 (BA Schumacher collection, file 365). The actual timing of the Italian announcement clearly took Hitler by surprise. Himmler—as his diary shows—had flown away on leave to Bavaria that morning, only to be recalled by a telephone call from Hitler's HQ at 8:20 P.M., the very moment that Jodl's order was being cabled to the various HQ's: "Marshal Badoglio has confirmed accuracy of Allied radio broadcasts about Italian capitulation. Code word 'Axis' takes effect immediately" (T77/792/1641). For Field Marshal Kesselring the first sign that the betrayal was imminent was that morning's air raid on his HQ at Frascati, outside Rome: in a crashed Allied bomber were found target maps showing his and Richthofen's HQ's in such detail that official Italian collaboration was obvious. Besides, Rome's fire brigade was waiting outside Frascati just before the attack began— which did not prevent the villagers from losing many dead (the Germans alone lost ninety killed). See also Jodl's version of events, in his notes for a speech to Gauleiters on November 7 and in staff talks with the Japanese on September 29, 1943.

p. 564 The prince's arrest is described by Goebbels; and by Baron von Steengracht in an overheard conversation with Papen on June 27, 1945 (X–P 18); and by the prince himself under interrogation by the U.S. State Department.

Feelers to Stalin

pp. 565–66 On the East Wall controversy I relied on Speer's records of conferences with Hitler, and his Chronik; on Führer decrees in file FD–3049/49; on the naval staff war diary, July 19, 1943; on OKW staff papers on the wall's positioning, on microfilm T77/778; and on Field Marshal von Küchler's memo on his conference with Hitler on September 11, 1943 (Army Group North, war diary).

p. 567 Vice Admiral Wilhelm Meisel first recorded Hitler's hopes for an East-West split at the Führer's evening war conference on August 28, 1943.

p. 568 A report by Likus on Soviet feelers, addressed to Ribbentrop on August 9, 1943, is in AA files (Serial 146, pages 130779 *et seq.*). Kleist describes his contact with Edgar Klauss in *Zwischen Hitler und Stalin,* (Bonn, 1950). From Klauss's original documents now in possession of my friend and colleague Dr. Bernd Martin of Freiburg there can be no doubt that Klauss's Soviet contacts were genuine. Significantly, it was not until late September that these indirect German approaches were reported by the Soviet legation in Stockholm to their U.S. colleagues (see Mr. Herschel Johnson's telegram from there to Washington, September 29, 1943, in *FRUS,* 1943, Vol. III, pages 698 *et seq.*).

p. 569 Hitler's decrees carving up northern Italy will be found in file FD–3049/49.

p. 571 A number of entries in Himmler's telephone notes relate to problems with the Ciano family. After Himmler and Kaltenbrunner visited Hitler on September 15, 1943, the two SS potentates talked about "Situation in Rome. Commun[ists]. Italian guests; villa for Musso family. Jewish Question [in Italy]." And at 6 P.M. Himmler telephoned Hewel at Hitler's HQ: "Edda Ciano telephone [conversation] with Mussolini." On September 20, after talking with Kaltenbrunner about "Ciano family's behavior," Himmler jotted on his agenda for discussion with Hitler that evening, "Journeys of Countess [Edda] Ciano: smashing up furniture."

p. 573 (footnote)   The air staff report exposing these phony "star agents" is dated December 14, 1944 (BA file RL2/547).

pp. 573–74   The narrative of the air offensive is based on unpublished documents in Milch's files, volumes 31, 39, 51, 53, 62, and 63; on Milch's secret speech to the Gauleiters on October 6 (T175/119/5054 *et seq.*); on Speer's notes on Führer conferences; on Hitler's war conference of October 4 and his remarks to the Bulgarian regents on October 18, 1943.

p. 575   The telegram from Consul Eitel Friedrich Moellhausen, October 6, 1943, is ND, NG–5027; Hitler's negation of the SS order is in Franz von Sonnleitner's teletype dated October 9, 1943. For the SS report on the roundup of Rome's Jews, October 17, see T175/53/7133.

pp. 575–76   At one stage in his speech of October 6, 1943—according to the wire-recording archived in Washington (NA, 242–299)—Himmler directly addressed himself to "You, Herr Reichsminister," which indicates that Speer was a listener. Few generals later admitted that they had known; perhaps they did not realize the enormity of what they were being told in such dry sentences. Field Marshal Weichs frankly told interrogators of the U.S. Seventh Army on May 30, 1945, that Himmler had once visited him in the Balkans and confirmed that the rumors were true—that the (unspecified) victims were loaded into railroad trucks without knowing that a sudden, painless death awaited them. "They are just criminals of whom we must rid ourselves," was Himmler's explanation.

p. 577   The fragmentary record of Hitler's remarks—in the war conference of October 27, 1943—was found by my Soviet colleague Lev Bezymenski in Moscow archives. Hitler had just had a long talk with Himmler, who had seen Schellenberg during the afternoon. Schellenberg's report on "MacEvan" is in AA file Serial 1755, pages 404620 *et seq.*

p. 578   Rommel himself wrote to his wife on October 26, 1943: "Anyway, he hasn't signed the order for the new job. . . . Perhaps I didn't inspire much hope that the position could be held. Perhaps my hesitation whether to take over the command was cause enough. Perhaps there are quite different groundss. So K[esselring] stays for the time being" (T84/R275/0379). And Richthofen added his own comment (diary, October 21): "Apparently Rommel's not getting overall command in Italy after all. Evidently made a bad impression during his report to Führer, from which he came back yesterday—an impression which doesn't surprise me."

p. 579   The case history of the Melitopol-Zaporozh'ye Line needs examining in detail, as it shows how justified Hitler's suspicions of his field commanders were. Kleist's Sixth Army had withdrawn to this line, which Manstein described as a "well-built position," but in *Verlorene Siege*, pages 537 *et seq.*, Manstein himself admits that Kleist was thrown out of the line "surprisingly rapidly" by the Red Army in October 1943. At the end of the year Hitler fulminated, "That was the spirit then—*Retreat!* . . . Everybody lost their nerve, even Kleist. *Everybody, retreat!*" In the same war conference (December 28) he scoffed "Nobody's going to maintain that this line here [forward of Melitopol] would have been tougher than that [the new line] or the entire front we have now [December]. But now from here down we have to hold this whole line now; while there we only had this little bit to defend. Then we wouldn't be having our Crimea difficulties either." Over the months that followed, Hitler learned the truth. Luftwaffe General Karl Kitzinger, an expert on lines of fortification, had offered to take over the job in 1943. The army had indignantly refused, saying that only Manstein's army group could do it. "The upshot was," snarled Hitler on July 31, 1944, to Jodl, "that nothing—nothing whatsoever—was done. Not one shovelful. The positions they claimed to have built from Melitipol to Zaporozh'ye were a lie from start to finish. They told me downright lies. They cheated me. There was nothing." (See Heiber, page 605.)

Hitler's letter to Antonescu, October 25, 2943, is in the marshal's papers (ND, USSR–240).

p. 581   Hitler's order to Rundstedt to reconnoiter a *rear* line in France was cabled by Jodl to the Commander in Chief West on October 31 (T78/317/1448); see too the OKW war diary. The teletype is entered under November 2 in the war diary of Commander in Chief West, but was not forwarded by Blumentritt to the army and corps commanders concerned until the eleventh. See too Hitler's conference with Jodl, July 31, 1944 (Heiber, page 594).

"And So It Will Be, Mein Führer!"

p. 583   On the Balkan situation: Weichs's appreciation of November 1, 1943, is in naval staff war diary, annexes, Part C, Vol. XIV (PG/32217); I also used the OKW war diary, Weichs's private diary (N 19/3), and the files of the German envoy at Zagreb, Kasche (AA Serial 1770), and interrogations of Dr. Hermann Neubacher, who later published an erudite history, *Sonderauftrag Südost 1940–45* (Göttingen, 1958).

p. 584   Much has been written about "Cicero." I have relied only on the contemporary records, in Cabinet Office file AL 2656, secret AA files (Serial 1553), and Steengracht's AA file on Turkey (Serial 61). There are cautious references to his work in the naval staff diary (*e.g.,* November 12) and Ribbentrop's discussions with Dobri Bozhiloff, the Bulgarian Prime Minister, and Oshima, and in Goebbels's diary, November 13 and 20, 1943. As the summary in Jodl's diary, February 1944, shows, the authenticity of Cicero's documents was accepted at every level right up to Hitler.

p. 585   On Hoth's dismissal: war diary of chief of army personnel, November 3, 1943. On January 7, 1944, Hitler remarked to Keitel, on the army's poor political record. "I hear hideous reports on this score. Worst of all, I don't mind saying, was how it was in Hoth's army: in his generals' presence Hoth constantly criticized all the *Weltanschauung*-measures. This is why the Fourth Panzer Army has made the worst showing" (NS–6/162).

p. 586   In Central Planning on March 1, 1944, Milch recalled: "On March 5 [last year] I stated to the Führer that there was already enough manpower in the army, air force, and navy for them to mobilize the necessary combat troops from within. In November the Führer ordered a census and found out that there are only 265,000 combat troops permanently at the eastern front. . . . Remember, I had that job at Stalingrad [directing the airlift to the Sixth Army in January 1943]: at Taganrog [far to the rear] there were 65,000 army troops, while every kilometer at the front was being held by one lieutenant and six men, who would have been delighted to get twenty or thirty men to help them" (MD 48/9983 *et seq.*).

p. 587   I used an investigation by U.S. authorities of the underground Central Works factory in May 1945 (FD–3268/45), its production records (held in London), and the excellent reports made by the special mission of Colonel T. R. B. Sanders on the V-weapon sites in France, February 21, 1945, top secret; also a manuscript by Colonel Eugen Walter (MS B–689) of the "Sixty-Fifth Army Corps" set up to control the V-weapons, and Milch's documents and Jodl's diary.

p. 589   On the planning of the Luftwaffe's winter attack on London see Goebbels's diary, December 7, 1943; Koller's files (T321/90/0413 *et seq.*), and the annexes to the OKL war diary on T321/10. Hitler is quoted from his war conference on January 28, 1944.

p. 590   The original FO telegrams to Ankara are in PRO files, *e.g.,* FO 371/37478–9.

p. 592   Küchler's account of his meeting with Hitler is an annex to the war diary of Army Group North (T311/79/2814 *et seq.*). See also Admiral Heinz Assmann's letter to the naval staff, December 29, 1943 (PG/31747), which I quote at length on pages 592–93.

p. 593   There is a file on the *Scharnhorst*'s end in naval staff war diary annexes, Part C, Vol. II. I also used the entries for December 2 and 23–28, 1943, and January 8, 1944, and Dönitz's conference with Commander in Chief Naval Group North (PG/31747).

p. 594   A Colonel Lersner's record of Hitler's speech on October 16, 1943, is on microfilm T77/1039/2937 *et seq.* On Nazi indoctrination proposals, see the papers by Waldemar Besson, Gerhard L. Weinberg, and Volker Berghahn published in *VfZ*, in 1961 (page 76), 1964 (page 443), and 1969 (page 17), respectively. General Schörner's correspondence is in British files (AL/2831).

p. 594   See the stenogram of Reinecke's discussion with Hitler on January 7, 1944, in Party files (NS–6/162). I also used interrogations of Reinecke and Göring by OCMH.

p. 596   Many sources on the January 4, 1944, conference exist: by Lammers, (ND, 1292–PS) and a circular (T84/175/4886 *et seq.*); by Sauckel, (1292–PS) and memo (T175/71/8037 *et seq.*); by Speer, in his Chronik; references in Central Planning meetings on February 16 and March 1, 1944 (MD48/10066 *et seq.*, and 9953 *et seq.*), and in the diaries of Milch and Himmler.

p. 596   Edda Mussolini's letters are in AA files Serial 738, pages 267674 *et seq.*

p. 597   Encouraged by Cicero's reports, Hitler began withdrawing forces from the Balkans in December: see Jodl's diary for December 23, 28, and 29, 1943, and February 10 (?), 1944.

pp. 597–98   The shorthand record of Hitler's January 27, 1944, secret address is in the BA Schumacher collection, file 365. It is referred to also in the diaries of the naval staff, Jodl, Weichs (March 3, 1944), and Salmuth (March 27, 1946), and of the chief of army personnel (Schmundt), January 27, 1944: Hitler had "delivered a speech in very grave tones," during which "Field Marshal von Manstein made an interruption. In connection with this interruption and the various tensions of late the question of retiring Field Marshal Manstein is again debated."

p. 599   Bormann's record of Hitler's remarks on January 27–28, 1944, is on IfZ microfilm MA–340.

Trouble from Providence

p. 600   Walter Schellenberg, who saw Hitler that spring, wrote in his manuscript memoirs: "His eyes—once the dominating feature of his face—were now tired and lusterless; his left arm shook so strongly that he almost constantly had to clutch it with his right hand; he made a conscious effort to conceal his clumsy movements, which began not with the limbs but with the body itself."

p. 602   Dr. Werner Best quoted Hitler's remark of December 30, 1943, in his manuscript (ZS–207/1)

p. 603   A file of Rommel's daily diarylike reports is held by the OCMH in Washington (X–501). Salmuth was to write (on March 18, 1946): "Whether Rommel was really a great commander in the European theater—as opposed to the African—I will not comment." Salmuth was irritated by Rommel's "unpleasant manner" of shouting at officers and men alike on these inspection tours, and by his "highly superficial and abrupt tone." Nonetheless Salmuth was the first to recommend to Rundstedt that Rommel's Army Group B should assume tactical command of both the Seventh and the Fifteenth armies (Salmuth, private papers).

p. 604   Rommel reported in detail on his anti-invasion measures on April 22, 1944 (AL/510/1/4).

p. 605   Telegrams from Istanbul, Ankara, and Sofia relating to the damaging defection of Erich Vermehren are in Steengracht's AA files, Serial 61, pages 41960 *et seq.* The rest of the story, resulting in Canaris's dismissal, is built up from the naval staff war diary, February 19 and 22, and March 2, 4, and 7; Himmler's diary, February 9 and 11; a memo by Wagner, July 1, 1944 (Bobrick's papers, Serial 738, pages 267624 *et seq.*); Hitler's order of February 12 (file H3/1539); and Walther Huppenkothen's 1945 manuscript (BDC files). Canaris was appointed "Chief of the Special Staff for Economic Warfare and Measures" as of July 1, according to the naval staff war diary, July 10; twelve days later he was arrested for high treason.

p. 606   On the operations of the turncoat German officers in the Cherkassy pocket: CSDIC interrogation of Lieutenant General Kruse; and the diaries of the chief of army personnel and of Weichs, March 3, 1944, and of Ulrich von Hassell, February 23.

p. 608   Professor W. Löhlein's record of his examination of Hitler's eyes on March 2, 1944, is in American files (OI-CIR/4); I also used Dr. Erwin Giesing's manuscript.

p. 610   Count Gerd von Schwerin wrote a note on his personal impressions of Hitler at Nuremberg on November 12, 1945.

p. 610   Schellenberg recorded his conversation with Ribbentrop in his handwritten manuscript (IfZ files).

p. 611   The preparations for the occupation of Hungary are described from the diaries of Jodl, Weichs, and the OKW; and OKW files (T77/791) and Steengracht's file on Hungary, Serial 99.

p. 612   Of descending value on Hitler's confrontation with Horthy are these sources: Captain Assmann's report to the naval staff (war diary, March 19, 1944); Jodl's diary, March 18; Horthy's account to his Crown Council in Budapest, March 19 (in the Horthy papers). The version in the OKW war diary, Vol. IV, pages 200 *et seq.* and 230, is marred by inaccuracies. See particularly the OKH attaché section's lengthy "Report on the Journey with [Hungarian] General Homlok to Salzburg from March 17 to 20, 1944" (T78/451/6889 *et seq.*): Hitler reproached Horthy for the attitude of the Hungarian press. He would be forced "to clear things up" and asked Horthy to agree in writing that the German troops which would invade on March 19 were doing so "at his request"; Horthy refused, as this would be unconstitutional. I also used postwar interrogations of Horthy, Ribbentrop, Carl Rekowski, Edmund Veesenmayer, and General Greiffenberg; and Zeitzler's manuscript (N63/117).

p. 613   Jodl also took a lengthy note of Hitler's March 28, 1944, conference.

p. 614   General Alexander von Falkenhausen, military governor of Belgium, also observed Rommel's extreme optimism when the field marshal visited him early in March 1944 in Brussels. "Our views on the political and military situation could not have been more divergent. But when I repaid the visit on June 1, 1944, at La Roche-Guyon [Rommel's HQ] he had changed and wholeheartedly adopted my view" (U.S. Army, MS B–289).

p. 614   On the proposed execution of Allied airmen, see the OKW file on film T77/778; Hewel's memo of March 24, 1944 (NG–4059); Milch's diary, February 23–24, 1946; Bormann's circular of May 15, 1944 (BDC file 182); and a memo by Ribbentrop's bureau, July 17, 1944 (Ritter's files, Serial 6530).

p. 616   Below and Günsche both told me of Hitler's affection for Manstein. I also referred to Backe's letter to Manstein of October 17, 1944, and Hitler's remarks in the noon war conference on March 2, 1945: "Manstein has in my eyes the greatest talent for operational strategy. No doubt about it. I'm the last person to deny that."

The Most Reviled

p. 617   Gauleiter Frauenfeld's study on the administration of the occupied east, dated February 10, 1944, is in Himmler's files (T175/125/0419 *et seq.*).

p. 618   For Hitler's military policies in southern Russia, see his conversation with the Romanian General Garbea on March 29, 1944 (T78/366/8829 et seq.).

p. 618   Saur reported Hitler's remarks to the Fighter Staff on April 8 (MD5/2388 *et seq.*); I also use Göring's version of the Führer's conference with Dönitz on April 13 (MD64/6480 *et seq.*).

p. 620   In addition to the better known materials on the evacuation of the Crimea— like the OKW war diaries, and papers by Baron von Weitershausen and by H. D. von Conrady in *WR* in 1954 (pages 209 *et seq.*, and 327 *et seq.*) and in 1961 (pages 312 *et seq.*, respectively)—I used the naval staff war diary and the hitherto unknown diaries of the army liaison officer to Dönitz (T608/1/529 *et seq.*) and the army's special evacuation staff under General Lindemann (T78/269/7187 *et seq.*); further documents from the naval side will be found in OKW files (T77/778) and in Schörner's papers (AL/2831/2).

pp. 622–23   General von Trotha, Schörner's operations officer, flew into Sevastopol at this time. In his 1946 manuscript he described: "As our plane approached we could see the waves tinged red at one place. There were high cliffs there, on top of which our troops had shot hundreds of horses and thrown them over into the sea, so they wouldn't fall into enemy hands."

p. 623   That Jaenecke's tongue had failed him is eloquently shown in the opening words of his letter to Hitler the next day, April 30, 1944: "At yesterday's conference there were one or two points I unfortunately omitted to make . . ." (AL/2831/3).

p. 625   German Intelligence had obtained a proof copy of Eisenhower's still-secret Proclamation to the French people, announcing the disembarcation of French and Allied troops in France; see the naval staff war diary, April 13, 1944, and file PG/33399 for a full translation.

p. 625   According to Army Group B's war diary, on May 1 and 6 Hitler again stressed his belief that the invasion would strike Normandy and Cherbourg and demanded close scrutiny of the readiness of General Erich Marcks's Eighty-Fourth Corps, defending that sector; Rundstedt's war diary records that Jodl telephoned on May 9 that the Führer expected the invasion in mid-May—perhaps on the eighteenth—and that the main effort would be against Normandy, followed by a subsidiary push into Brittany. On May 27, Hitler repeated this to the Japanese ambassador, Oshima; anything other than the invasions of Brittany and Normandy would be "just diversions."

p. 627   The final report of Admiral, Black Sea, is in naval staff war diary annexes, Part C, Vol. XIV.

p. 628   Koller's studies on the shrinking Luftwaffe bomber force are in his private papers (in my possession) and in OKL war diary annexes (T321/1) and Milch's papers (MD53/706 *et seq.*). What follows is also based on Göring's conferences (MD64) and on a memo in Bormann's files on the Me-262 jet (NS-6/152).

p. 630   Horthy's assent is implicit in Ribbentrop's telegram to Veesenmayer some weeks later, on July 16—after Horthy had just stopped the transports of Jews—protesting that this was a departure from "the measures agreed on at Klessheim" (AA Serial K789). Himmler's views are evident from his handwritten speech notes, *e.g.*, for his speech to field commanders at Posen on January 26, 1944." Jewish question. In the General gouvernement [Poland] huge calmdown since Jewish problem solved. —Racial struggle.—Total solution. —Don't let avengers arise to take revenge on our children" (T175/94/4835 *et seq.*). His May 5 speech is on microfilm T175/92/3475 *et seq.*, and that of May 24, T175/94/4609 *et seq.* That Himmler only talked of "expulsion" of Jews *(Aussiedlung)* to Hitler is clear from his handwritten agenda of July (or August) 1944 *(ibid.,* page 5065).

pp. 631–32   Hitler's speech is recorded in Himmler's files *(ibid.,* 4972 *et seq.).* He used similar language to Sztójay on June 7, 1944.

p. 632   Korten's optimism (MD64/6998) and Speer's in Central Planning the next day (MD55/2170) are echoed in a letter written by the food minister, Herbert Backe, on May 17, 1944. "Apparently the invasion's got to be taken seriously after all. There's talk of May 18—that means tomorrow. I won't believe it until they are actually ashore. . . . Our generals are very optimistic, without exception. . . . Immense preparations have been made on our side. I am not particularly worried about it. Here everybody is longing for it to start" (Backe's private papers).

p. 633   Not only had Dönitz gone on leave—see the naval staff diary of June 6, 1944, and his interrogation on August 6, 1945—but Salmuth (Fifteenth Army) went on a two-day hunting party, and Rommel returned briefly to Germany.

5. THE WORMS TURN

Man with a Yellow Leather Briefcase

p. 637   Little is known of the actual events at the Berghof during the night of the invasion. I have pieced them together from statements of Hitler's adjutants, of Keitel, Jodl, and Zeitzler, and from the times recorded in the war diaries of the naval staff, Commander in Chief West, and the OKW. What is certain is that Chester Wilmot's version in *Struggle for Europe* (pages 248 and 287), which has Hitler "forbidding" Jodl at 4 A.M. to release the OKW reserves, is pure fantasy. The situation crystalized far too slowly for even the OKW to be blamed for delaying this decision.

Hitler probably stayed awake until 3 A.M. (Milch diary, May 7, 1947, quoting Speer). Twenty minutes earlier (according to the naval staff diary) the "Admiral, Channel Coast" had telephoned the OKW tersely: "Advance report: from 2 A.M. on, large number of paratroops and gliders, east coast Cotentin peninsula and east of Trouville." Not until 3:45 A.M. was this enlarged upon. By 5:45 A.M. Naval Group West believed the invasion had begun—but neither Rundstedt's staff nor the OKW shared this conviction. At 7:30 A.M. Naval Group West convincingly reported: "Invasion area extends from Saint-Vaast to Deauville, main efforts evidently Quistreham and Saint-Vaast. North of Barfleur major invasion force heading south. Cargo ships with the invasion forces . . ." At 8:15 A.M. this was forwarded to Jodl's staff at Berchtesgaden by telephone, and they now agreed that their earlier skepticism seemed misplaced. At 9:30 A.M. Reuter officially confirmed the invasion, and a string of intercepted Allied wireless messages reached the Berghof: "No details so far, but we are ashore." "Front line overrun." "Situation on Red Beach isn't too good."

p. 638   The SD report that the BBC invasion-alerts had been monitored was forwarded by Kaltenbrunner to the OKW on June 1; thence to Foreign Armies West on June 2, 6:50 P.M. (T78/451/6880 *et seq.*). Under Nuremberg interrogation, Walter Schellenberg blamed the military for failing to appreciate the significance of this scoop. This seems justified, for on the very eve of the invasion—June 5, 1944—Rommel's much-praised Chief of Staff, General Hans Speidel, sanguinely dismissed the invasion-alert signals which the BBC had broadcast with increasing frequency since June 1 as "not providing any evidence of an imminent invasion" (Army Group B, weekly report, T311/3/2156 *et seq.*). See also the war diaries of the Fifteenth Army, which independently monitored the BBC messages and warned Speidel. Note that the war diary of Commander in Chief West was *retrospectively* written up—one forms a different impression altogether of the army's readiness and alertness from sources like the naval staff diary of June 11, 1944. The admiralty was certainly warned on June 2 (see file PG/33399), and on June 3 the naval staff noted: "Foreign Armies West regards June 5 to 13 as favorable invasion date."

In later months the naval staff painstakingly analyzed all the Abwehr agents' reports on the coming invasion. Of the 173 received prior to June 6, 1944, only 8 percent had been right; 14 percent had been partially correct; the rest had been wrong or worthless (diary, March 23, 1945). What is a staggering indictment of German army Intelligence methods is the treatment of the Operational Plan of the U.S. Fifth Corps—*i.e.,* of the entire American sector in Normandy—which fell into the hands of the German 351st Infantry Division on June 7, 1944, and can thereafter be traced (through postwar statements) up to the Eighty-Fourth German Corps (General Marcks) and thence to Seventh Army, which forwarded it to Rommel's HQ on June 11. Blumentritt—Rundstedt's Chief of Staff —believes in manuscript B637 that he saw it and sent it up by courier on June 12 to the OKW. Had this document ever reached the OKW or Hitler it would have left no doubt that Normandy was *the* main invasion area. Having been seized from the corpse of an American officer killed in a gunfight, an enemy trick was ruled out. But there is no mention of the document in the files of either the OKW or Commander-in-Chief West.

p. 639   Salmuth's March 1946 manuscript on the invasion is in his private papers. Not until 9:12 A.M. did the German naval commandant in Normandy forward from the big gun battery at Marcouf to the naval staff the pregnant signal: "Very many landing craft are approaching under cover of battleships and cruisers."

p. 639   The hardy optimism of the Germans in the face of the colossal invasion is evident wherever we look in their records. Hitler's personal adjutant, Alwin-Broder Albrecht, wrote on June 9: "Anyway, everybody here's breathing a sigh of relief." Hitler told Sztójay that they had been looking forward to it, because it would end with the defeat of the British. And the naval staff recorded on June 7: "As for the invasion operations in the west, the Führer and Field Marshal Rommel view the situation positively and confidently, in anticipation of the success of our countermeasures." These included the laying of the new top-secret German "pressure mines" off the invasion coast, which Hitler authorized at his noon conference that day.

p. 639 There are sparse references to the "suicide pilot" project in General Koller's papers, among which I found a sequence of daily air staff reports. Speer heard of the project, because on July 28, 1944, he wrote to Hitler: "The endeavors to throw these men into action against the enemy invasion fleet are to be condemned, as long as using them against Russian power stations would be capable of procuring quite different results in the long run."

p. 640 The war diary of Colonel Max Wachtel's "Antiaircraft Regiment 155(W)"— the V-1 flying-bomb launchers—has survived intact.

p. 642 Schramm's account of Hitler's visit to Soissons on June 17, 1944 (OKW war diary, Vol. IV, pages 316 *et seq.*), is unreliable. Koller's papers make it plain that Hitler went on his own initiative. My account depends on Heinz Assmann's description (naval staff diary), on Jodl's diary, on signals in the war diaries of Rundstedt and Army Group B (T84/281), and on the typed narrative of the conference in the volume of appendices to Army Group B's war diary (T311/278).

pp. 642–43 Rommel's exuberance is clear from a diary entry of Admiral Friedrich Ruge and from Rommel's own weekly report of June 19: "Despite the enemy's vast superiority in air power and ships' artillery and ruthless expenditure of troops and equipment in repeated heavy attacks, they have gained no successes, but actually lost ground at Caumont. . . . Our Intelligence and captured documents show that the enemy has not reached one of his far-flung objectives, but has had to throw in considerably more forces than originally intended. . . . In the fighting so far the enemy has lost over five hundred tanks and over one thousand planes. . . . The population in the combat area is friendly toward us; there has been a perceptible decrease in the sabotage and other resistance activity that sprang up in the first postinvasion days" (Army Group B, war diary, annexes).

p. 643 In August 1944 Hermann Gackenholz wrote a full report on the disastrous collapse of Army Group Center for its war diary; the war diary is in OCMH files. Gackenholz kept the report and published it in *VfZ,* 1955, pages 317 *et seq.* The faulty appreciations of Stalin's intentions by Gehlen's branch of the General Staff can be followed in this, in the naval staff war diary, and above all in Koller's daily reports.

p. 644 General Student described on September 22, 1945, to fellow generals how in his presence, two days before the Russian offensive began, "Zeitzler explained his reasons for expecting the main enemy effort to come in the south. He considered a big attack in the center quite improbable. Hitler thought otherwise and at the last moment ordered reserves sent to Army Group Center" (General Kurt Dittmar, diary).

p. 645 Himmler's speech of June 21, 1944, is on microfilm T175/93/3950 *et seq.;* Hitler's of the next day is on microfilm T580/871.

p. 647 Hitler later learned from Allied press reports that General von Schlieben's surrender had been somewhat inglorious. "A braggart," Hitler complained to Jodl on July 31. "He issues a defiant proclamation . . . and then waits for the others [the Americans] to arrive, whereupon he immediately runs up a white flag. When they ask him, 'How can you square issuing such a proclamation with your own honor?' he just shrugs."

p. 647 Dollmann's Chief of Staff, Max Pemsel—who hitherto has always denied this —admitted to me for the first time that it was indeed suicide; Dollmann had retired for the first time to Pemsel's vacant bed and was found in it the next morning.

p. 648 Even if Hitler had authorized the withdrawal of Army Group North, its divisions could not have reached the crisis area of Army Group Center in less than four weeks (see Hitler's conference with Dönitz, July 9, 1944).

p. 648 Zeitzler described his last row with Hitler in various postwar manuscripts (N63/1, /80, and /96); his adjutant Günther Smend described it to the Gestapo on August 1, 1944 (T84/22/4535 *et seq.*) By July 1 he was—according to Gackenholz's report—already "off sick."

p. 649   The quotations are from the war diary of Antiaircraft Regiment 155(W). See too Rommel's appreciation, dated June 26, 1944, on the internal situation in France." The population affected continues to be embittered by the Allies' ruthless mode of warfare, especially by their use of air power, while otherwise the population is reserved. Coastal population in Belgium is tending to migrate away. Combat operations by the new weapon [V-1] against England evoked interest and in some parts satisfaction." For Rommel's conference with Hitler on June 28, see the note taken by his adjutant (Appendix to Army Group B war diary, T311/278).

p. 651   Koller's formal record of Hitler's remarks on June 29, 1944, is in his papers; he also jotted down a shorthand record of both these and Göring's subsequent outbursts about "the cowardly fighter pilots."

pp. 652–53   Again I quote Koller's lengthy record, but equally explicit accounts of Hitler's speech are to be found in both Jodl's diary and the naval staff war diary of July 3, 1944.

p. 653   Koller noted Hitler's question to Heusinger; his later reminiscence is quoted from his conference with Generals Siegfried Westphal and Hans Krebs on August 31, 1944 (Heiber, page 615). He had said the same to Antonescu on August 5.

p. 654   General Vinzenz Müller's order of July 8, 1944, will be found on microfilm T77/1038/0780 *et seq.*, together with other similar documents emanating from the renegades. See also the war diary of the chief of army personnel, July 27.

pp. 654–655   This war diary (see note for page 654, above), together with Koller's, Speer's, Thomale's, and Himmler's papers, was used to trace the origins of the fifteen "blocking divisions" *(Sperrverbände)*—out of which the *Volksgrenadier* divisions were born.

p. 655   With the exception of Peter Hoffmann, no historian noticed that Hitler undertook this lightning one-day visit back to the Wolf's Lair on July 9, 1944. From the records of Jodl, Dönitz, and Koller there can, however, be no doubt. It is also referred to by Major General Peter von Groeben in his study "The Collapse of Army Group Center" (U.S. army manuscripts, T31). It was here too—as Himmler wrote to Rosenberg on July 14—that Hitler ordered every available man in Estonia to be recruited into the SS (T175/125/0532).

p. 656   According to the stenographer's diary, Hitler's July 13, 1944, secret speech lasted from 10:22 to 11:40 P.M. Eighteen days later, his health shattered by the bomb attempt, Hitler admitted to Jodl: "Obviously I can stand up and even speak for a certain length of time, but then I suddenly have to sit down again. I would not trust myself to speak to ten thousand people today. Nor would I trust myself to make a speech like that one I recently did on the Obersalzberg, because I might suddenly faint and collapse" (Heiber, page 608). Its content was evidently the familiar litany. On April 11, 1945, General Fellgiebel's adjutant told British interrogation officers that General Stieff—chief of the OKH organization branch—had privately muttered, 'If I hear that phonograph record played once more I'll go crazy!'—to which Fellgiebel, a fellow-conspirator, replied with heavy irony, "Well, Stieff, that was the last time."

"Do You Recognize My Voice?"

p. 657   On the implementation of total war, see Lammers's letter to Keitel, July 17, 1944, and subsequent correspondence (T175/71/7972 *et seq.*). Only the French text of Goebbels's letter survives in British files, AL/1904/4; the original may be in France.

p. 659   The infantry general Edgar Röhricht mentions Stieff's order of July 8, 1944, in his March 1946 study "Himmler's Struggle for Military Power" (in IfZ files). Significantly, when Stauffenberg returned from Hitler's HQ on July 11 or 15, 1944, and exclaimed that the whole HQ ought to be blown sky high, Colonel Georg Hansen—Canaris's successor and a fellow-conspirator—"attributed this exclamation to Stauffenberg's very powerful irritation that the fifteen new divisions being raised were to be subordinated to the Reichsführer SS [Himmler]" (Gestapo interrogation of Hansen, July 29, 1944, T84/19/0257).

p. 661   See the verbatim interrogation of Fräulein Schroeder at Berchtesgaden, May 22, 1945.

p. 661   See the brief record of Hitler's speech to Nazi indoctrination officers on July 29, 1944 (T78/80/0603 *et seq.*); Jodl's speech of July 24 (T77/1432), and Himmler's speech of August 3, 1944, about Fellgiebel's defeatist utterances.

p. 661   These first withdrawals from the idle Fifteenth Army are referred to in the diaries of the OKW, Kluge's staff, and the naval staff, July 20, 1944, and their strategic importance is underlined in Jodl's diary.

pp. 662–63   Percy Schramm wrote several annexes to the OKW war diary on the July 20, 1944, bomb incident, based on Warlimont's verbal information; they were not published, but are on T77/1432/0620 *et seq.* I also used the diary of one staff stenographer, the version in Schmundt's official diary, and above all Peter Hoffmann's excellent study in *VfZ*, 1964, pages 254 *et seq.*, and his full-length book, *Widerstand, Staatsstreich, Attentat* (Munich, 1969), Chap. XI. In addition I assembled a voluminous collection of statements and interrogations of the officers in the hut, largely from secret British files.

p. 663   Hitler related his personal impressions on several occasions: on August 15, 1944, to the envoy Siegfried Kasche (whose record is in his papers, AA Serial 1770, pages 405808 *et seq.*); to the staff stenographer Ludwig Krieger; to his ENT-specialist Erwin Giesing; and to the Gauleiters on August 4. The wife of Food Minister Herbert Backe wrote in a diary on August 7, 1944: "Herbert came straight from the Führer conference. At lunch he was only three places away from the Führer. Gauleiter Giesler [of Munich] asked the Führer. 'What did you feel at the moment of the blast?' The Führer said, 'I thought I had heard three detonations and suspected hand grenades had been tossed in from outside. The generals jumped out of the windows. But I thought I would then be running right into the killers' arms. I went out through the door, putting out the flames in my hair. . . .' "

p. 663   On Hitler's injuries I used manuscripts or testimony of Morell, his wife, Hasselbach, Brandt, and Giesing.

p. 665   Keitel's alacrity is evident from the documents. The Berlin conspirators had begun issuing their "Valkyrie" signals a few minutes before 4 P.M.—misusing Fromm's signature and making reference in them to Witzleben and Hoepner. Just *fifteen* minutes later Keitel was already issuing the first teletypes from Hitler's HQ overriding these spurious signals. By 4:05 P.M. the OKH General Staff already had evidence that Stauffenberg had failed, for staff at Zossen monitored a telephone conversation between Hermann Fegelein (Himmler's liaison officer at Hitler's HQ) and SS General Hans Jüttner on the explosion's failure—it had been "similar to Munich [in November 1939], but Führer safe and well."

pp. 665–66   Himmler emphasized the delicacy of his role in speeches on July 21 and 26, 1944 (T175/93/3904 and 4146). See also Keitel's memoirs, page 222.

p. 666   Eduard Wagner's role is an enigma. He wrote on July 21 to Zeitzler: "I swear to you on my word of honor that I had nothing to do with the events of July 20," and enclosed a full account of the events at Zossen as he remembered them (IfZ file, ED–95).

p. 666   A complete sequence of the key July 20, 1944, telegrams was captured by British Intelligence in the files of the Nazi party office in Schleswig-Holstein. This particular one omitted the first sentence: "The Führer Adolf Hitler is dead." But it is included in the later versions—e.g., in naval staff war diary, 8:05 P.M.; and Kluge's Paris staff received by teletype at 8:10 P.M. an assurance that the 6:28 P.M. radio broadcast (page 666) was a lie and that the Führer *was* dead and that all steps were to be taken as swiftly as possible.

p. 667   I used Schaub's unpublished manuscript, and a private letter by the adjutant Albrecht dated July 22, 1944.

p. 668   See the report by Dr. Hans Hagen on his visit to Goebbels (T84/19/0022 et seq.). The propaganda minister had a direct telephone line to Hitler, unknown to the plotters (OCMH interrogation of General Wilhelm Arnold, OKH signals chief, August 25, 1945).

p. 668 The interpreter present, Eugen Dollmann, gives a spirited account of Hitler's conversation with Mussolini, Göring, and Ribbentrop in a prison-cell conversation monitored by the British on July 22, 1945 (CSDIC/CMF/X194).

p. 669 The engineer General Werner Kennes—Fromm's armaments expert—had slipped out of the Bendlerstrasse building at midnight. Generals Hoepner and von Thüngen were also witnesses to Stauffenberg's bland assurance that he had seen Hitler's corpse; so was another—anonymous—officer, of whose testimony before the People's Court only the sound recording survives.

p. 671 Rommel's "Observations on the Situation," dated July 15, 1944, are in Army Group B's war diary annexes (T311/3/2241 *et seq.*); Kluge forwarded the document with a letter to Hitler dated July 21 *(ibid.)*. They are mentioned in his war diary, but the annexes referred to are missing. Professor H. A. Jacobsen and other historians have uncritically quoted from the erroneous text given (from memory) by General Hans Speidel in *Invasion 1944.* Note that Rommel's letter was *not* addressed to Hitler.

p. 672 The quote is from Hitler's talk with Jodl on July 31, 1944 (Heiber).

p. 673 Eicken's treatment notes on Hitler survive (NA special microfilm, ML–125 and 131). He was also interrogated by the British.

p. 673 At Christmas 1944 Himmler told Admiral von Puttkamer: "If only we'd known the scale right from the start, we'd have proceeded quite differently; then we'd have differentiated more—we wouldn't have hanged people just because they had heard talk of something."

p. 674 Helmuth Maurer—Canaris's pianist neighbor, who wrote a long unpublished manuscript on the Abwehr chief—had been with him on the afternoon of July 20, 1944. About 3 P.M. Stauffenberg telephoned that the Führer was dead. Canaris knew his phone was tapped and responded, "Was it the Russians?" Maurer says that the admiral's nerves went to pieces over the next three days until his arrest. According to the SS investigator Horst Kopkow (under British CSDIC interrogation), Canaris pressed Schellenberg to know whether that "petty staff officer" Hansen hadn't been jotting down pettifogging notes again. Only Canaris's most recent diary was immediately found, and that was not incriminating.

p. 675 Reinicke described the Berliners' indignation under OCMH interrogation in July 1945. The diary of the Catholic Field Marshal von Weichs mirrors the fury of the unimplicated officers. "*21 July.* Putsch. Frightful situation—this internal unrest too. Success would have produced chaos. Madness to think a rapid peace can be achieved by such means. A stab in the back like 1918, but worse as it comes from a quarter from which one might have expected the opposite. Horrifying, the names that participated in this revolt. How will the army sit this terrible upheaval out, now that its officers and generals will forfeit every shred of confidence in them? How will our allies take this blow?" And on *22 July:* ". . . because even if the assassination had worked, the putsch would still have collapsed, as not one soldier would have accepted orders from these leaders."

p. 675 A bulky collection of letters to Hitler after the plot is in Goebbels's files (BA, R55DC/145).

p. 677 Rommel had warned Hitler of the bazooka shortage at his mid-March 1944 conference; the Seventh Army needed 5,190 but had only 644; the Fifteenth Army needed 6,228 but had only 781 (war diary, Army Group B, quartermaster, annexes). Wagner in fact shared responsibility for distribution with Kluge's quartermaster, Colonel Eberhard Finkh—who was one of the conspirators and was sentenced to death on August 30, 1944. According to the naval staff diary, August 9, the OKW noted: "Despite adequate supplies of ammunition, weapons, and equipment at home Commander in Chief West keeps reporting shortages of specific types, particularly armor-piercing ammunition and bazookas."

Historians dissatisfied with Schramm's summary treatment of the war's theaters in the OKW war diary will find excellent daily reports on Hitler's war conferences as submitted to the naval staff by the attending admiral (usually Voss) from August 1944 to January 1945 (PG/32122b); and from December 1944 to April 7, 1945 (PG/31742).

He Who Rides the Tiger

p. 680   A minute on Stauffenberg's telephone call to Army Group North at 7:55 P.M., July 20, is in German army files (T78/352/2592); Beck himself took the phone, declaring, "To let yourselves be shut in—just as in Stalingrad—that is no way to lead an army!"

p. 681   In addition to the German record of Hitler's meeting with Antonescu there exists the marshal's own account, published on January 15, 1953, in *La Nation Roumaine* in Paris. I also used Guderian's manuscript (ZS–57), the army conferences with General Garbea (T78/366/8704 *et seq.*), and—with caution—Professor Andreas Hillgruber's study of the last months of the German-Romanian alliance in *WR,* 1957, pages 377 *et seq.:* Hillgruber relies perhaps too heavily on Erik Hansen as a source. Hitler's warning was witnessed by his adjutant Colonel Erik von Amsberg, whom I interviewed in 1971; and Hitler himself later referred to it, according to Wolf Junge's manuscript.

p. 682   The diarist was Herbert Backe's wife. I also used the account written by Hitler's deputy press chief Dr. Helmut Sündermann—at the time, according to his son.

p. 683   See Jodl's diary, August 1, 1944. "5 P.M.: Führer has me read Kaltenbrunner's report [dated July 30] on the testimony of Lieutenant Colonel Hofacker about discussions with K[luge] and R[ommel]. Führer is looking for a new Commander in Chief West. Plans to question R[ommel] after he's better again and then to retire him without further ado."

Kluge appears to have remained on the sidelines as an interested observer of the conspiracy and little more. At an emergency conference late on July 20 with Stülpnagel, Hofacker, and Blumentritt he had dissociated himself from the deed, but he had noticeably failed to report these meetings to the Gestapo investigators. Salmuth later wrote: "It became clear to me that Kluge had known what was planned on July 20 when I paid a visit to him the next day, because when I asked him for his view he only answered, 'Well, it didn't work out!' and these few words told me enough."

p. 684   On Hitler's and Jodl's attempts to prevent Kluge launching the Avranches counterattack prematurely, see the war diary of Commander in Chief West, annexes. That the panzer divisions were unready is clear from the telephone log of the Seventh Army (AL/528/1).

p. 685   General Werner Kreipe's diary (transcribed by the Americans as MS P–069) and Koller's papers provide extensive information on Hitler and the Luftwaffe at this stage.

p. 687   Of 192 agents' reports, only 15 accurately predicted the Allied invasion of southern France. See the naval staff war diary, August 8, 10, 13, and 15, 1944; and its annex, "Investigation of the Value of R.S.H.A. Intelligence on Enemy Invasion Plans," October 16, 1944 (PG/32218).

p. 687   Blumentritt stated under British interrogation that Keitel had told him of the intercepted enemy signal to Kluge. Guderian told much the same to Milch (diary, October 28, 1945). "Kluge tried in France to contact the enemy to surrender, but this misfired. . . . Moreover Kluge is to blame for the false use of the tanks—he seems to have deliberately tried to lead the tank units into the pocket at Falaise!!" Salmuth also heard of this story from Gauleiter Greiser in January 1945—but dismissed it as "a rumor probably spread by the Party on orders from above." I also used a conversation between General Eberbach and Blumentritt on August 19, 1945, recorded by CSDIC, the diary of chief of army personnel, and Blumentritt's letters to Jodl (AL/1720) and Burgdorf (X–967).

p. 689   Jodl recorded Hitler's meeting of August 19, 1944, in his diary; Buhle—also present—told the OKH artillery branch of Hitler's intention to raise fourteen new artillery brigades on August 24: "By these means a concentration of one thousand guns is to be achieved for a decisive job in the west." And, "The armament of the twenty-five divisions demanded is to be German" (T78/269/7521 *et seq.*)

p. 689   Martin Bormann's file on "Luftwaffe Scandals" is in the BA Schumacher collection file 315.

p. 690   According to the unpublished manuscript of the Abwehr colonel Friedrich-Wilhelm Heinz on "Canaris and Nicolai" (NA special film ML–690), a trusted crony of

Canaris's placed on Choltitz's staff persuaded the general to turn over Paris intact to the enemy. Hitler's order to the contrary (page 690) is in the annexes both of Army Group B's war diary and of Commander in Chief West's war diary.

pp. 691–92 Hitler's startling—but short-lived—project for a canal is reported by Admiral Voss in the naval staff war diary.

pp. 692–93 My narrative of Antonescu's overthrow—and Hitler's attempted counter-measures—relies on the naval staff diary (which is far preferable to the OKW war diary here); General Hans Friessner's memoirs, *Verratene Schlachten* (Hamburg, 1956); and a report by the Fourth Air Force on events in Romania in 1944, dated February 11, 1945.

p. 693 Hitler's immediate decision to abandon Greece is recorded in Weichs's private diary, August 23–24, 1944. The formal OKW directive followed on August 26; see also OKW war diary, Vol. IV, page 681.

p. 694 Hitler's rebuke to Freisler is confirmed by Schaub's unpublished manuscript, by interviews of Heinz Lorenz and Otto Günsche in 1967, and by a U.S. Seventh Army interrogation of Dr. Immanuel Schäffer of the propaganda ministry in June 1945. British files contain an account by one of the guards at Plötzensee, describing the hangings; Helldorf's grim treatment is described by the Gestapo official Dr. Georg Kiessel in his account of "The Plot of July 20, 1944, and its Origins," August 6, 1946 (British files), and by SS Captain Otto Prochnow under CSDIC interrogation, March 1946. The rest is based on Himmler's letters to Thierack, November 7, 1944 (BDC, SS–4465), and to Lammers and SS General Franz Breithaupt, August 27, 1944 (BDC file 242). British files list 81 such executions at Plötzensee prison after July 20, 1944; a separate list of 130 names altogether also exists. Kiessel puts the final figure at 140. There is no support for the figure of "4,890" put about by the Allies in 1945, nor for the *New Statesman*'s "official estimate" of "over twenty thousand executed."

p. 696 The original page in Bormann's handwriting is in OCMH files, Washington (X–967). Kluge's penciled letter to Hitler is in London files (MI.14/7). The version published in the OKW war diary, Vol. IV, pages 1574 *et seq.,* is only a translation of an English translation.

p. 696 On the Kluge mystery, see the memo by Colonel Hugh M. Cole, historical officer attached to the U.S. Third Army, in OCMH file X–967 (and *Time* magazine, June 25, 1945). According to the CSDIC interrogation of Blumentritt, Kluge's first reaction to the spurious word of Hitler's death on July 20, 1944, had been: "If the Führer's dead, we ought to get in touch with the people on the other side right away." So the idea was not anathema to him. And note his curious words on the telephone to Blumentritt at 11:55 A.M. on August 16, after his miraculous return from his "vanishing act" the day before: "Pass word up to the top that I'm now 'back from abroad' again and that I didn't let the reins of government out of my hands for one instant" (war diary, Commander in Chief West, annex 1450).

Rommel Gets a Choice

p. 698 Ribbentrop's description of his peace proposal is partially confirmed by an entry in Kreipe's diary on September 13, 1944. After telling Göring bluntly how hopeless the Luftwaffe situation was, he inquired whether it was not time for the Reichsmarschall to make a political intervention. This question "was answered with bitter criticism of Ribbentrop—he [Göring] was the last person who should now make the Führer feel uncertain."

p. 698 Weichs's telegram to Hitler's HQ, and the reply, are in Ritter's AA files, Serial 1487, pages 368686 *et seq.;* the fieldmarshal also referred to this after the war (N 19/12), as did Hermann Neubacher—under U.S. State Department interrogation—who stated that the British local commander, General Sir R. M. Scobie, had contacted both himself and the German Commander in Chief, Northern Greece, the mountain corps general Hubert Lanz. Ribbentrop confirmed the "bait" strategy in a conversation with the Belgian Fascist leader Léon Degrelle on December 8, 1944 (AA Serial B 16): see also naval staff diary, September 6 and 14, and Jodl's diary, September 14, and directive to Weichs (AA Serial 1487); and OKW war diary, Vol. IV page 719.

p. 699 Two Japanese admiralty officers informed the German naval attaché of Stalin's alleged views on August 25; Ambassador Heinrich Georg Stahmer's telegram from Tokyo reporting this reached Ribbentrop's train on August 26 (AA, Ritter's files, Serial 1436, page 363344). Most probably this was connected with the recent return of the Soviet ambassador Jakob Malik to Tokyo from Moscow. A few days later the Japanese foreign minister, Mamoru Shigemitsu, visited Stahmer in the same connection. Finally, on September 4, Ambassador Oshima came from Berlin to the Wolf's Lair to put the same proposals directly to Hitler. (Ribbentrop's report on this talk to Stahmer two days later is in Ritter's file, Serial 1436.) Hitler however painted an optimistic picture of Germany's sound strategic position—a coming counteroffensive with fresh divisions, new fighter aircraft, new submarine types, and adequate raw materials for two years—and emphasized that there was so far not the slightest sign that Stalin wanted peace. Only a military impasse would convince Stalin; for the time being Hitler asked the Japanese to refrain from such steps. Thus the Japanese attempt to mediate between Hitler and Stalin failed. On this whole episode see also naval staff war diary, September 5, 1944, and Speer's testimony at Nuremberg, Vol. XVI, page 533. That Guderian shared Hitler's view was reported by his liaison officer to the naval staff (diary, September 17).

p. 700 Speer's prognosis on the nickel supply was also inconsistent. On September 13, 1944, the naval staff noted Speer's clear announcement that the Petsamo nickel supply was no longer of great importance to Germany's arms industry—a view the naval staff diary strongly disputed five days later.

pp. 703–704 See Keitel's draconian order to the infantry General Hans-Karl von Scheele on September 10, 1944, ordering immediate court martialing and public execution of deserters (T77/869/5928 *et seq.*)

p. 704 The plan for a western counteroffensive began to crystalize in Hitler's order of August 29, 1944: "There is only one possibility, and that is to wade into the American right flank and thus endanger the enemy's advance into Belgium itself from the rear" (Army Group B, war diary annexes); the plan took clearer shape in his order of September 3 to Rundstedt (*ibid.,* and war diary, Commander in Chief West). Kreipe's diary of September 11 shows that Hitler was still half-looking at the Vosges offensive idea, but then he switched attention to the Ardennes. See the ETHINT interrogations of Jodl and his staff officer Major Herbert Büchs.

p. 704 Kaltenbrunner's damning reports are in BA file N6/41.

p. 706 Schörner's visit is recorded in Jodl's diary, September 16, 1944. When Dönitz heard of the plan to abandon Estonia, he hurried to Hitler but could not change his mind; on the eighteenth the evacuation began (naval staff diary, September 15; and see Schörner's teletype to Keitel, September 9, in film T77/778).

p. 706 Frau von Ribbentrop confirmed the episode of Madame Kollonti to me. Both Ribbentrop and Colonel Bogislav von Bonin—of the General Staff—reported Hitler's "pawn in hand" argument under interrogation in 1945. Interestingly, on September 12, 1944, Himmler jotted down as Item 9 on his agenda for discussion with Hitler the words "Britain or Russia"; and as Item 10, "Russia—Japan." Both items are endorsed "dealt with" (T175/94/5062).

pp. 706–707 On the Arnhem operation I used General Kurt Student's account in the journal *Der Frontsoldat Erzählt,* 1952; Schleifenbaum's letter to a Herman Giesler, January 11, 1945 (T81/122/4665 *et seq.*); an unpublished letter by Colonel W. Harzer to *Quick* magazine, December 1955; and entries in the naval staff war diary.

p. 710 Himmler's visit to Hitler on September 26, 1944, is reconstructed from his handwritten agenda (T175/94/5056); from Bormann's letter to his wife that day; from Kaltenbrunner's interrogation of Canaris and Pfuhlstein, September 21, (NS–6/41); the war diary of the chief of army personnel, September 4; manuscripts of Jodl, 1944 (T77/775) and Huppenkothen, 1945 (BDC), and Kiessel and Georg Thomas; and interrogations of Jodl, Lahousen—who privately confirmed in Nuremberg on November 12, 1945, that Canaris and Oster had betrayed the date of "Yellow," but declined to say more as both were now dead—and of Huppenkothen, Kopkow, and Thomas.

p. 712   Hitler's confinement to bed with jaundice is testified to by Giesing, Hasselbach, and Brandt; it is referred to in Bormann's letters of September 30 and October 1 and 4, in the manuscripts of the secretary Traudl Junge and Assmann, and in my 1965 interview with Saur and Puttkamer. After visiting him on October 5, 1944, Schmundt's widow wrote in her diary: "With Puttkamer this afternoon in the Wolf's Lair. Führer bedridden. Said he had lost his finest man."

p. 713   As Professor Morell wrote on October 23, 1944: "The last few weeks have not been too pleasant for me. There was a lot of trouble. But the Führer was so charming to me that this more than makes up for it."

pp. 714–15   Alfred Rosenberg's report to Hitler on the evacuation of Estonia, dated September 28, 1944 (NG–1094).

pp. 715–16   A primary source on Rommel's suicide is the testimony of Julius Schaub's chauffeur, Heinz Doose, who drove the car in which Rommel swallowed the poison. When Doose handed the field marshal's cap and baton in to Schaub, the latter went pale. "I didn't know about this . . . I want nothing to do with it!" The rest of my narrative relies on interrogations of Keitel and Jodl; my interviews of the adjutants Günsche, Amsberg, and Göhler; written statements of the staff stenographers Buchholz and Krieger; and a hand-written note on Keitel's talk with his son in the Nuremberg cells on September 21, 1946.

On the Brink of a Volcano

p. 717   In Himmler's files is a teletype report from SS Colonel Kurt Becher dated August 25, 1944. The fact that "three hundred items [Jews] had unconditionally crossed the frontier" would amend the other side's opinion that "we only want their agreement to exploit it for propaganda purposes" (T175/59/4473 *et seq.*). See too in this connection Schellenberg's interesting explanation noted by Count Schwerin von Krosigk in his diary on April 15, 1945: the treatment of the Jews had been worse than a crime—it was a folly, he said, as two thirds of all Jews lived outside the German domain. Quite wrongly the Reichsführer was being blamed for what "admittedly occurred in his name, but not at his behest." Therefore they had now allowed one thousand two hundred Jews to go to Switzerland, with the object of improving the Reichsführer's image abroad.

On April 19, 1945, Himmler himself claimed to Krosigk "that for two years nothing else has happened to the Jews still left in Germany—we need them as a pawn for all the coming negotiations."

p. 718   Kaltenbrunner's closing speech is in IMT, Vol. XXII, pages 431 *et seq.* His widow, now living in Linz, Austria, was unable to provide me with any further documentary support for his—on the face of it, implausible—account. I traced Dr. Konrad Morgen, now a respected Frankfurt attorney; he displayed understandable animus toward Kaltenbrunner, but his replies to my questions largely supported the SS general's claim. Morgen himself had reported voluntarily to the U.S. Seventh Army on September 22, 1945, and was regarded by them as a reliable witness on SS atrocities (SAIC report PIR/313); but when Kaltenbrunner's defense counsel applied for Morgen's appearance at Nuremberg, the Americans denied knowledge of his whereabouts until July 1, 1946, when they admitted that he was being held at Dachau. Thus Morgen's testimony came too late for Kaltenbrunner to be cross-examined on it (IMT, Vol. XX, pages 532 *et seq.*). Kaltenbrunner made his claim about showing the Morgen report to Hitler in his Closing Speech at Nuremberg, August 1946 (IMT, Vol. XXII, pages 431 *et seq.*). I also used his testimony earlier (Vol. XI, pages 306 and 338). Dr. Konrad Morgen's testimony is in IMT, Vol. XX, pages 532 *et seq.*: and I corresponded with him in 1974. Heinz Lorenz several times described how Hitler reacted to the Majdanek reports (*e.g.*, in CSDIC interrogation); and see Helmut Sündermann's diary, October 27, 1944.

In Himmler's files are only faint echoes of Morgen's long investigations; thus on January 29, 1944, Martin Bormann asked him "please to read for *yourself*" a horrifying report on conditions at Lublin concentration camp. Himmler replied suavely that the commandant concerned, SS Major Hermann Florstedt, was already under arrest: "The abuses are being ruthlessly remedied [*ausgerottet*] and redressed by a sweeping judicial process" (T175/53/7290).

p. 719   On Hungary's preparations for defection: OCMH and U.S. State Department interrogations of Greiffenberg and Veesenmayer; Kasche's note on Hitler's talk with the Croat "Poglavnik," September 18, 1944 (AA Serial 1770); and naval staff diary, September 26–28.

p. 720   For Hitler's remarks to Vörös, see Greiffenberg's telegram to Berlin on his talk with Geisa Lakatos, the Hungarian Prime Minister, September 15, (T77/869/5914).

p. 720   SS General Winkelmann's sometimes hilarious account of events in Budapest, dated October 25, 1944, is in Himmler's files (T175/59/4489 et seq.). Even Otto Skorzeny deprecates Winkelmann's choice of words.

p. 721   I adopt the word "shameful" used by Professor C. A. Macartney in his publication of the secret Hungarian telegrams in *VfZ*, 1966, pages 79 *et seq.* From Lakatos's testimony in the trial of Szálasi we know that in the decisive Budapest government meeting of October 10, 1944, he had spoken in favor of accepting the Soviet terms—and even proposed they invite the Red Army to halt briefly outside Budapest to give Béla Miklos's First Army time to withdraw "so that we can really attack the Germans properly."

p. 722   The appointment book kept by manservant Heinz Linge for the Führer from October 14, 1944, to February 28, 1945, was found by British Intelligence officers on September 10, 1945, in the ruins of the Chancellery (T84/22); with it was Hitler's desk appointment pad of April 1945 (AL/1488/4).

p. 724   Hitler kept his promise not to blacken Horthy's name. See the D.N.B. (German News Agency) dispatch of October 17, and Helmut Sündermann's diary of the same date. Editors had been instructed, "No attacks are to be made on the former regent."

p. 724   A folder of documents on the bunker's air-conditioning plant is in the BA, file R 58/1057.

p. 726   Hitler told Keitel and Jodl, in conversation on April 22, 1945, that he had resolved to die at the Wolf's Lair.

p. 726   Jodl's note on the Führer's war conference of October 25, 1944, survives. "Russian atrocities during occupation of East Prussian territory must be publicized by Wehrmacht propaganda branch. Photographs, eyewitness accounts, documentary reports, etc., for this" (1787–PS).

p. 728   On the decline in Göring's role: interrogations of Göring and Galland; Speer's chronicle, October 7, 1944; the Kreipe diary; and Koller's note on a talk with Göring, November 5.

p. 728   The disappointing performance of the Me-262 jet as a fighter is highlighted in Messerschmitt director Fritz Seiler's papers (FD–4924/45)—a report by Ludwig Bölkow dated October 25—and a memo in Bormann's files, dated October 21 (NS–6/152). The first Heinkel 162 "Volks" fighter flew on December 6, 1944; it was an aerodynamic disaster.

p. 733   The quotation is from Hitler's war conference on November 6, 1944 (Heiber, page 711). See the *Neue Zürcher Zeitung* November 14, and Himmler's files (T175/524) for such rumors. Hitler also mentioned them during lunch with Szálasi on December 4. Baron Gabriel von Kemény, the Hungarian foreign minister, later reported: "The Führer said with a laugh that the enemy camp has repeatedly proclaimed him dead—crediting him with a complete nervous breakdown or rumoring a cancer of the throat" (T175/130/6884).

PART SIX: END KAMPF

The Gamble

p. 739   Hitler's reflection that his life was already spent: see his conversation with the Hungarian Fascist leader Szálasi, December 4, 1944.

p. 740 (footnote)   The figures are from a financial survey of the previous five and one quarter war years prepared by the finance ministry on November 30, 1944 (T178/16/2913 *et seq.*).

pp. 740–41   The quotation is from Hitler's secret speech of December 28.

p. 741   According to the invaluable naval staff diary, December 1, 1944, Colonel von Bonin expressed great confidence in the German defensive strength along the eastern front, "especially in the areas of East Prussia, Warsaw, and Cracow."

p. 743   On the planning of the Ardennes offensive, I used interrogations of Westphal, Jodl, Keitel, Koller, Manteuffel, and Büchs; the diaries of Jodl, Commander in Chief West, the OKW, and the naval staff; Jodl's notes on Führer conferences (1787–PS); Wilhelm Scheidt's manuscript and various published monographs.

p. 744   On the gasoline allocation for the offensive, see Jodl's diary, November 10 and December 18. From the OKW diary, January 4, 1945, it is clear that in fact *more* that the amount requested was supplied; but the actual consumption was higher than foreseen. It was precisely with this fear in mind that Keitel—who was responsible for fuel allocation —had ordered Rundstedt and others on December 7 to take stern action against unauthorized motorization of the troops (T77/778). The effect of the emphasis on the western front was grave in the east. From the draft General Staff war diary (T78/339) we learn that General von Greim's Sixth Air Force had only enough fuel reserve for about three major combat days by January 5, 1945.

p. 745   The excessive gasoline consumption is mentioned in the naval staff diary as early as December 17, 1944—Day Two of the offensive. See Hitler's postmortem account of their errors on December 28, 1944 (Heiber, page 746); SS General Bach-Zelewski, who attended the speech, stated that Rundstedt thanked Hitler for the "harsh but just" criticism (U.S. Army manuscript B-252: "Fourteenth SS Corps in Nov.–Dec. 1944").

p. 746   The navy's Captain Wolf Junge heard Hitler's mocking words to Churchill and mentions them in his manuscript.

p. 747   The quotation is from Hitler's talk with General Wolfgang Thomale, December 30, 1944 (Heiber, pages 779 *et seq.*).

p. 747   Under CSDIC interrogation on May 23, 1945, Milch said, "Hewel, the representative of the foreign office with the Führer, told me of Stalin's offer of negotiations fourteen days before the Russians staged their offensive on the Vistula front" (SRGG 1255C).

pp. 747–48   In addition to the German version of Hitler's talk with Szálasi and Baron Kemény's version in Himmler's files, two Hungarian versions exist (T973/1 and /14).

p. 752   Gehlen's Intelligence report of January 3, 1945, is in file H3/179.

pp. 752–53   For Guderian's visit to Hitler on January 9, 1945, I used—with caution— his own memoirs and the IfZ file ZS–57, and with greater confidence the fragmentary remarks by Hitler in his war conferences later that day and on January 10 and 27, and a manuscript by Colonel Freytag von Loringhofen (Guderian's adjutant) found among the general's papers for me by his son.

p. 753   For Germany's overconfidence in the eastern fortifications, see *e.g.*, Jodl's speech to allied military attachés in Berlin on January 13, 1945, 4 P.M. (T77/775/0754 *et seq.*) and the OCMH interrogation of Bonin.

p. 754   The conversation is recorded in Traudl Junge's manuscript.

p. 755   Gehlen assessed Stalin's attack strength at: 225 rifle divisions, 22 tank corps, 29 other tank formations, and 3 cavalry corps. But at Yalta Stalin—who surely had no reason to play down his contribution—stated he had only 180 divisions in Poland. Were

Guderian and Gehlen hoodwinked by the Russians? And as far as the Soviet divisions' strengths are concerned, General S. M. Shtemenko wrote in the Russian history, *The General Staff in the War Years* (Moscow, 1968): "At the time our divisions averaged only about four thousand men each."

p. 755   Guderian's cable to Hitler, dated January 14, 1945, is in the war diary of the General Staff operations branch (annexes, T78/305/6032 *et seq.*). He reported that Army Groups A and Center were fighting desperate defensive battles and that the enemy had now succeeded in making a strategic breakthrough from the western part of the Baranov bridgehead. "I therefore request the immediate transfer of several panzer and further infantry divisions from the west to the eastern front." And see naval staff war diary, January 14 for Admiral Voss's account.

pp. 755–56   Jodl records Guderian's phone call in his diary. It was followed by a telegram at 7:30 P.M., dictated by telephone to Hitler's train at 2:25 A.M., repeating the demand for reinforcements for Army Group A. Traudl Junge recorded Otto Günsche's witticism.

Waiting for a Telegram

pp. 757–58   Dönitz's adjutant, W. Lüdde-Neurath, described the scene with Harpe on January 19, 1945, in his book *Regierung Dönitz* (Berlin, 1964).

p. 759   Dr. Werner von Schmieden described his mission under OCMH interrogation; I also used the testimony of Fritz Hesse, interpreter Paul Schmidt, and Ribbentrop's colleague Fräulein Blank.

p. 759   The new OKW master plan is summarized in the naval staff diary, January 19, 1945, but is not mentioned at all in Schramm's OKW war diary.

p. 760   On the withdrawal of the Sixth SS Panzer Army to Hungary—instead of the eastern front—I used the annexes to the General Staff operations branch war diary (T78/305), the OKW war diary, and Jodl's notes after Führer conferences (1787–PS); see also Helmut Sündermann's diary, January 20, 1945, and Hitler's conference with Dönitz three days later, which clearly puts the Hungarian and Viennese oil fields foremost among their defense priorities.

p. 761   The conference leading to Himmler's appointment is in Jodl's diary, January 21, 1945. Hitler's resulting order was sent by Bormann to the Gauleiters (IfZ file ED–36) and to Himmler himself; see the war diary of Army Group Vistula, T311/167/8516 *et seq.*, and the General Staff war diary, T78/305/5979.

p. 762   Zhukov's order is appended to Gehlen's report of February 22, 1945, "Red Army's Behavior on German Soil" (T311/168/0014); a copy in big typescript for Hitler is in General Staff files (T78/304/5627).

p. 763   The astounding decoded directive of the Allied Combined Chiefs of Staff is retranslated into English as an Appendix to a British Intelligence report on the achievements of the German Intelligence branches (Appendix III to ADI(K) Report 395/1945). It begins: "The Soviet Union has achieved successes in the east to an extent not expected by the Anglo-American command. In the event of any further rapid advance towards the West, a situation may thus develop which would be extremely unwelcome to the Anglo-American Governments and Commands. Experience has shown that the Soviet Union does not release—except under strongest military pressure—any territory it has occupied. . . . *Our military measures must therefore be such as to permit the Germans to reinforce their Eastern Front, a reinforcement they can mainly achieve by weakening their Western Front.* . . ." The directive lists ways of deceiving the Russians as to this shift in Allied aims —by cunning propaganda techniques, for example. Its authenticity seems vouched for by the subsequent realization of much of the directive: "Maximum 'terror' effort to shake the war morale of the German people . . . The bombing of the communications system should receive the first priority. . . . The preparation of a strong 'terror' mission against Berlin of some 1,200 four-engined bombers in several streams. . . ."

pp. 763–64   I used Karl Wolff's testimony at Nuremberg, December 1, 1947, and in IfZ file ZS–317. He evidently saw Hitler on January 6 or 7, 1945 (Linge and Bormann diaries).

p. 764   See Hans Kissel's study of the Volkssturm 1944–45 in *WR*, 1960, pages 219 *et seq.*

p. 764   On the transfer of antiaircraft batteries from the Reich to the Oder front see Jodl's note on Hitler's conference of February 1, 1945, and the war diary of the OKL operations staff (T321/10/6799 *et seq.*).

pp. 764–65   Himmler recalled the crisis in conversation with Schwerin von Krosigk on April 19 (diary); and see the Reichsführer's order of February 1, 1945: "The thaw which has begun at this precise stage in the conflict is a gift of Fate . . . The Lord God has not forgotten his worthy German people" (T78/304/5774).

p. 767   For Göring's punitive measures, see his order of January 16, 1945 (T177/3/5007 *et seq.*). Lammers quotes Bormann's advice in a letter of April 24 (T580/265).

p. 768   I corresponded with Professor Hermann Giesler on his model for Linz; Hitler's plans are described by the local Gauleiter, August Eigruber, in a speech there on November 25, 1942 (T175/124/9670 *et seq.*); I also used Linge's diary, February 9–10, and Sündermann's, February 14, 1945, and Wilhelm Scheidt's manuscript.

p. 769   On Ribbentrop's last peace attempt, I used Guderian's testimony, and an overheard conversation of Ribbentrop's state secretary, Steengracht, on July 14, 1945: "So Guderian came to Ribbentrop and told him, 'It's all over. The game's up. Their tank superiority is one to eight, their aircraft one to sixteen.' Then Ribbentrop went to Hitler and told him that. Hitler retorted that he would not allow the foreign office to concern itself with such criticism. 'Secondly the figures are all wrong, and thirdly the soldiers don't know what they're talking about anyway' " (X–P–18).

p. 771   On the proposal to kill Allied prisoners in reprisal, I relied on the testimony of Ribbentrop, Scheidt, Steengracht, Sündermann, Jodl, and the stenographer Krieger—who particularly recalled Keitel's opposition. Also, Hitler's talks with Dönitz, February 19–21, and a memo by Jodl (ND, 606–D). Linge's diary of February 21 actually records: "3:15–3:55 P.M. [Hitler] strolls with foreign minister." The other main topic was clearly Ribbentrop's unauthorized peace feelers, for that same day according to the Weizsäcker diary, Ribbentrop urgently canceled his previous instructions to ventilate armistice proposals through neutral channels.

p. 772   The first description is by General von Trotha; the second is by Gauleiter Karl Wahl, under U.S. Army interrogation, June 1, 1945.

p. 773   Gauleiter Friedrich Rainer also described the "glass of water" scene. And see the account in Helmut Sündermann's diary, February 25, 1945. "He [Hitler] spoke with a firm voice, and particularly moved the Gauleiters with one sentence: 'You may see my hand tremble sometimes today, and perhaps even my head now and then; but my heart —never!' " Herbert Backe, who had scribbled notes on his shirtcuff during the speech, quoted the identical words to his wife for her diary on March 10, 1945.

p. 774   Bormann's memorandum is in the BA Schumacher collection, file 368. The women's battalion is also mentioned by Göring under interrogation on May 24.

p. 775   There is an invaluable file of telephone conversations between the General Staff and Army Group Vistula in the latter's war diary annexes (T311/167–169); I also used General Erhard Raus's postwar manuscript, "The Pomeranian Battle and the Command in the East" (D-189).

p. 776   Meissner related this under U.S. State Department interrogation, August 31, 1945.

p. 776   The conference is in Jodl's diary. General Eberhard Kinzel telephoned Army Group Vistula afterward that Hitler had ordered the Third Panzer Army to revert to the defensive at once, as "the imminent attack on Berlin" would necessitate the disengagement of various panzer and panzer-grenadier divisions for that front sector (T311/169/0913).

Hitler Goes to Ground

p. 777   See *e.g.*, the teletype from Foreign Armies East to the General Staff on April 16, 1945 (T78/304/5405).

p. 778   Copies of Admiral Dönitz's notes to his commanders are in Bormann's files (T81/5/2954 *et seq.*)

pp. 778–79   On "Operation *Werewolf*"—the Luftwaffe kamikaze attack—see the OKL war diary, March 18 and April 3, 6, and 7, 1945. It is not even mentioned in Schramm's OKW war diary.

p. 779   In generally describing life in Hitler's Berlin bunker I used the manuscripts or testimony of Schaub, Christa Schroeder, Speer, Puttkamer, Göhler, Below, Scheidt, Guderian, Saur, Jodl, Keitel, Günsche, General Erich Dethleffsen, and others.

p. 780   The outburst is described by General Koller in a letter to the Nuremberg lawyer Professor Franz Exner dated March 25, 1946, and independently by the attending staff stenographer Gerhard Herrgesell, July 19, 1945. A few days beforehand, Professor Giesler's mother had been killed on the road from Stuttgart to Ulm by an Allied fighter plane, which may have influenced Hitler.

pp. 780–81   Schmieden's failure is related in his interrogations. Fritz Hesse went to Sweden on February 17 with Ribbentrop's peace proposals; but on March 15 the Swedish journalist Arvid Fredborg compromised them in a *Svenska Dagbladet* article, "Nazistis fredstrevare gjordes via Stockholm?"—which, according to Karl Wolff, Kaltenbrunner at once reported to Hitler. See Sündermann's diary, March 18, on this.

Ribbentrop described the Moellhausen mission in some detail, but the diplomat touches on it only barely in *Die gebrochene Achse* (Alfeld/Leine, 1949), page 280. An interrogation of Dr. Ernst Jahr, chief of the ecclesiastical affairs branch of the Gestapo, stated on May 3, 1946, that Ribbentrop had also sent Bishop Heckel—director of the foreign affairs section of the German Evangelical church—to Stockholm during March 1945 to open up ecclesiastical channels to London.

p. 781   The quotation is from General Koller's diary, March 28, 1945. See too Göring's OCMH interrogation, July 20, 1945.

p. 781   At Hitler's conference on March 8, 1945, after the Remagen bridge scandal, Sündermann noted in his diary: "The Führer also plans to send in flying courts-martial to stamp out these signs of dissolution. I have noted down two of his angry outbursts: 'Only Russian methods can help us now,' and 'If we lose the war the Germans will be exterminated anyway—so it's a good thing to exterminate some of these creatures now.'" The Remagen culprits were executed.

pp. 782–83   Among Robert Ley's papers I found a long manuscript he wrote about Hitler in August 1945. It is among the files of the American prosecutor Justice Robert H. Jackson, who recommended that Ley's papers should be destroyed after his Nuremberg suicide.

pp. 783–84   For my account of "Iron Hammer" I used Koller's papers, the OKL war diary, Gehlen's files (H3/653), and a teletype from Himmler to Fegelein, March 13, 1945 (T311/169/0831).

p. 785   Speer gives his version of his talk with Hitler in a letter to him dated March 29, 1945—but he never delivered it. His Allied interrogators recorded that although Speer had hoped to withhold the letter from them because of its "purely personal" language, they "found it nonetheless." But there can be no doubt that Speer did put up a tough fight against the destruction orders. On April 3, 1945, Milch noted in his diary a session of the transport staff Hitler had set up under Speer in mid-February: "Speer relates his battle with F[ührer] over demolitions."

p. 785   Bormann circulated the OKW order (signed by Jodl) to all Gauleiters on March 30, 1945 (T81/5/3034 *et seq.*).

p. 786   In addition to Heinrici's notes—appended to the war diary of his army group

(T311/169)—a valuable source is General Theodor Busse's article on the Ninth Army's operations in *WR*, 1955, pages 159 *et seq.* I also used the daily notes written by Guderian's and Krebs's adjutants after Hitler's conferences (T78/305).

p. 787 In an OCMH interrogation of July 21, 1945, Admiral Dönitz echoed Jodl's words to the USSBS on June 29: "Despite the defeat at Carthage the people admired Hannibal, didn't they? And despite our German defeat the people still admire Hitler." The admiral added, "Hitler was a man with an abundance of good nature. His mistake was that he was *too* noble. He persisted too much in his loyalty toward people who didn't deserve it." This trait in Hitler was also referred to by Göring—of all people (OCMH interrogation, July 23).

p. 787 The first Mark XXI submarine (U-2511, Captain Adalbert Schnee) put out on March 17, 1945, but was delayed in home waters by air raids and did not finally commence operations from Bergen until April 30—only to be recalled almost immediately by Dönitz upon Hitler's death.

pp. 788–89 There is a folder of the Gauleiters' teletype reports to Bormann during April 1945 on microfilm T580/43; I also used his diary, which was found on a corpse—presumably his—in Berlin early in May.

p. 789 Goebbels related all this to Schwerin von Krosigk; see the latter's diary, April 15, 1945.

p. 790 Hitler's erroneous supposition that Stalin would first drive into Bohemia is clear from the adjutants' notes on his war conferences from March 28 to April 6 (T78/305).

p. 791 Quartermaster general Alfred Toppe's letter to Keitel, April 15, 1945, is on microfilm T77/778.

p. 791 One of the participants in the conferences where Hitler ordered the liquidation of the convicts gave me the information; himself an SS major, he asked for his identity not to be divulged.

p. 792 Busse's words are quoted by Goebbels in the Schwerin von Krosigk diary.

p. 793 On the evacuation of the diplomatic corps, see the memo of May 1, 1945, in the Ribbentrop papers (T580/266). The adjutant quoted is Albrecht. After his letter of April 9, his wife heard no more of him—he was presumed killed in the defense of the Chancellery.

p. 793 The prisoner interrogations were reported by Colonel Gerhard Wessel on April 15, 1945 (T78/305).

p. 794 After the war Speer made little secret of his part in persuading Heinrici to abandon Berlin to the Russians without much fight. See his CIOS interrogation, June 1, 1945, and his conversation with Milch shortly before his departure to Spandau prison (diary, July 1947). "Hitler stayed in Berlin to organize the resistance. This Speer thwarted with General Heinrici and his Chief of Staff Kinzel, who sacrificed Berlin at his request. Only thus could be prevented the large-scale demolition of Berlin bridges and factories which Hitler had ordained should the battle come." In his recent *Memoirs,* Speer rather identifies Heinrici himself as the mastermind. The general had disclosed: "There won't be any fight over Berlin." Speer: "So Berlin will be swiftly captured?" Heinrici: "Well, there won't be any real resistance." There is a record of Speer's visit to Heinrici's HQ on April 15, 1945, in the army group war diary (T311/169/1719), but it is vague on this point: Speer was against any battle for Berlin because of the civilian casualties—a sound argument—and because of the destruction of vital industrial and traffic bridges Hitler had ordered. The record then states that should Army Group Vistula's front be breached, it proposed to "pull back Ninth Army on both sides past Berlin." (Hitler, of course, was never told this.) However, Hitler himself had on April 4, 1945, personally instructed Heinrici that "a commission must immediately be set up to prepare and supervise the demolition of bridges in Greater Berlin," but that *on no account* were the principal traffic bridges to be so prepared (General Staff diary, annexes, T78/305/6931 and 6945). In the circumstances it is difficult to understand Albert Speer's meddling in purely military affairs.

p. 794   The words are from Fräulein Christa Schroeder's shorthand notes written in May 1945 and transcribed at my request.

"Eclipse"

p. 795   My narrative of the last battle for Berlin is largely based on the war diaries of the General Staff (T78/304) and its annexes (*ibid.,* and T78/305), and of Army Group Vistula (T311/169 and /170); on the private diaries of Martin Bormann, of the Luftwaffe General Karl Koller (ADI[K] Report 348/1945), and of Jodl; on numerous interrogations and interviews of those concerned; and on the fragmentary shorthand notes of Hitler's last staff conferences salvaged by Heinz Lorenz in 1945 and published in *Der Spiegel,* No. 3, 1966 (their authenticity is established beyond doubt by official British papers I have seen).

p. 795   A German translation of the British 21st Army Group's *"Eclipse"* folder, typed on Hitler's large-face typewriter, is in General Staff records (T78/434/5864 *et seq.*). Keitel initialed it on April 15; I find no evidence to support Cornelius Ryan's contention in *The Last Battle* that the document was captured as early as January.

p. 795   Wessel's report of April 15, 1945, is on microfilm T78/304/4862.

p. 796   Ribbentrop's renewed feelers: the memorandum is on film T77/775/1439 *et seq;* from its contents, it was written between the capture of Vienna (April 13) and the Soviet attack across the Oder (April 16)—and not in mid-February 1945 as Reimer Hansen surmises in *Geschichte in Wissenschaft und Unterricht,* 1967, pages 716 *et seq.*

p. 796   On dealings with the British and Americans: Schwerin von Krosigk diary, April 15, 1945, and interrogations of Karl Wolff in December 1947. Wolff's appointment with Hitler "before staff conference" on April 18 is in fact noted on Hitler's desk pad, in British Cabinet Office files.

p. 797   Hitler's remarks in private were recalled under Soviet interrogation by his staff —Heinz Linge and Otto Günsche; their manuscript is in my possession—and by his secretary Traudl Junge in her manuscript memoirs.

p. 800   Axmann described Hitler's short speech under interrogation on January 14, 1946.

p. 800   Bormann certainly gained the impression that Hitler would leave for the south soon; see the manuscript by Bormann's secretary, Ilse Krüger, in British files. So did Jodl: his wife wrote in her diary that April 20: "A[lfred] told me this evening that we may fall back briefly to the north, but that F[ührer's] intention is to go to the south." (Cornelius Ryan's version of this entry—in the opposite sense—must be a misunderstanding.) Milch, who met Speer the next day, noted in his own diary Speer's "good impression of Führer, bad impression of 'that dodger Göring.'"

p. 801   Quoted from her May 1945 shorthand note.

p. 803   Weidling died in Soviet captivity, but fortunately wrote a long account of the battle for Berlin first which was published in *Voennoistoricheskii Zhurnal,* Moscow, October–November 1961.

p. 804   The tumultuous events of April 22, 1945, are described by the diaries of Koller and Jodl April 22–23; by memos of Koller, and Lieutenant Volck, April 25; in interrogations of Keitel, Jodl, Christian, Freytag von Loringhoven, Below, Colonel von Brauchitsch, Lorenz, and the stenographers Haagen and Herrgesell; and in written manuscripts of Günsche, Linge, Ilse Krüger, Traudl Junge, and Keitel.

p. 804   Felix Steiner, *Die Freiwilligen* (Göttingen, 1958), pages 324 *et seq.*

p. 806   An important private letter by Eva Braun to her sister, dated April 23, 1945, describes the contemporary mood.

The decision to turn round the Twelfth Army to fight the Russians—no less than an invitation to the Allies to take Berlin—was made by 5 P.M., for at that time Krebs telephoned it to Heinrici (T311/170/2182 *et seq.*).

p. 808   German Radio broadcast Hitler's decision to stay in Berlin at 12:40 P.M., April 23, 1945 (BBC Monitoring Report). Among the papers of Ribbentrop's Nuremberg defense counsel I found an eleven-page account by the foreign minister of the last days of Hitler (Rep. 502 AXA 132). He describes arriving at Hitler's shelter after the regular war conference on April 23: "While I was there I learned that it was by no means certain whether the Führer would be leaving for southern Germany, even temporarily. I thereupon spoke to Fräulein Eva Braun and asked her to influence the Führer to go to southern Germany, because if he was cut off in Berlin he could no longer lead and then the front lines might easily just cave in. Fräulein Braun told me she couldn't understand either—the previous day the Führer had been talking of probably flying down south; apparently somebody had talked him around to the opposite view."

p. 809   Ribbentrop's secret letter to Churchill was circulated as a memorandum, CP (45) 48 to the British Cabinet. It is in PRO file CAB 66/66. Ribbentrop swore in it that both he and Hitler had always striven for rapprochement with Britain; Ribbentrop "had always regarded England as my second home." Churchill sent the letter to Stalin on July 12, 1945—"I assume its content may be of some interest to you, although it is exceptionally long and tedious."

Ribbentrop described his last meeting with Hitler in several interrogations, in Rep. 502 AXA 132, and his memoirs. In his other manuscript, Rep. 502 AXA 122, he proposed repeating the four main points of the offer to the British prosecuting counsel Sir David Maxwell-Fyfe, since he had had no reply from Churchill or Eden. According to an overheard conversation of his state secretary, Steengracht, on July 14, Ribbentrop told him after that April 23, 1945, meeting: "You know, the Führer has proved right after all. The last thing he told me was, 'I actually came to power ten years too soon. Another ten years and I would really have kneaded the Party into shape.' . . . I wrote that letter to Churchill because I had to. In our last discussion the Führer—he was quite calm—told me he had never wanted any harm to come to Britain. The big handshake with 'Germanic' England —that had always been his goal" (X–P 18).

p. 810   The telegram draft was found in Göring's possession as a prisoner (DE 426/DIS 202). I also used an interrogation of Below, and the manuscripts of Ilse Krüger and Hans Rattenhuber (in Russian archives); and Koller's secondhand version (diary, April 23). Göring's telegram to Ribbentrop and Speer's letter to Galland are on microfilm T77/775. In Donitz's last diary (T608/1) we find a telephone call from Bormann on April 23, after which—at 10:45 P.M.—the admiral phoned General Stumpff, the Luftwaffe commander in Germany. "I have the following Führer order for you: 'The Reichsmarschall who's down in the south has off his own bat ordered that the Reich government elements that fell back to the north are to fly down to the south. The Führer does not want that at all. It is to be prevented at all costs. You [Stumpff] are to see to that. Have you understood that?' "

p. 810   Göring certainly found little support at the Chancellery. On April 25, 1945, Koller explained to the new Luftwaffe Commander in Chief Greim: "He hadn't one friend there. He was just surrounded by enemies who fought him and the Luftwaffe in the most malicious manner these last two years and more, instead of helping" (diary). And Göring's personal assistant Dr. Fritz Goernnert told American interrogators on May 12: "He [Göring] realized more and more that [the Luftwaffe's decline] was no accident. The Luftwaffe depended entirely on raw material allocations. You just couldn't get them for the Luftwaffe. Reichsminister Speer played the biggest part against Göring, because that's just the way he was—highly ambitious. He thought that in this way he could satisfy his ambitions still further" (46M–8).

This is my own view too, after having intensively studied the interplay of Luftwaffe and German army arms production (which was Speer's domain, along with raw material allocations). On the basic question as to whether Speer deliberately obstructed Luftwaffe production as a means of humiliating Göring and obtaining control over it himself, see Göring's USSBS interrogation of June 29, 1945; Milch's resignation speech of June 30, 1944, (MD56/2701 *et seq.*); and the air ministry study of the reasons for the huge increase in aircraft production from March to June 1944–i.e., from the moment Speer's ministry took over (FD–4439/45).

p. 811 Hitler's order of April 24, 1945 (evening), is in OKW files (T77/775/1198 *et seq.*). Koller inadequately summarized it in his diary two days later, which text is unfortunately adopted by the OKW diary, Vol. IV, page 1590.

p. 813 A long U.S. DIC interrogation report on Hanna Reitsch—Greim's female admirer—is in my possession.

pp. 816–17 Transcripts of the last letters written by Joseph and Magda Goebbels to their surviving son—by her first marriage—Harald Quandt, on April 28, 1945, are also in my possession.

p. 817 The texts—not always accurate—of the last days' signals from the Chancellery are in the war diaries of the OKW command staffs north and/or south.

p. 817 The BBC Monitoring Report of April 28, 1945, noted that a "Freedom Action Bavaria" began broadcasting at 5:50 A.M. to workers to protect their installations against "Nazi sabotage"; Gauleiter Paul Giesler quickly broadcast his counterattack at 9:56 A.M., and at 4:48 P.M. he announced that the "traitors" had been "summarily dealt with."

p. 817 The BBC Monitoring Report noted the first Allied report of Himmler's surrender offer at 1:55 P.M. About 5 P.M. Dönitz asked if the OKW was aware of this report. Himmler denied it, and Schwerin von Krosigk—Ribbentrop's successor—repeated this dementi in a telegram to Ambassador Stahmer in Tokyo on May 6, 1945. Precisely how far Himmler did in fact go is uncertain. Reporting an earlier meeting between him and Count Folke Bernadotte, the British envoy in Stockholm cabled London on April 13 that Himmler had refused to consider a surrender as he was bound by his oath to the Führer, to whom he owed everything and whom he could not desert; Hitler was now interested only in the future architecture of Germany's cities, according to Himmler. (The telegram is in British files.)

p. 818 Bormann's cable to Munich is quoted in Dönitz's files, T608/1; so is Admiral Voss's radio message.

p. 818 In an order to Heinrici and Manteuffel that April 28, 1945, Keitel refused to cancel the dismissal decision and put General von Tippelskirch (Twenty-First Army) in command of the army group (T77/779/5697; and T77/1432/0025).

Dönitz's opinion is cited by W. Baum in his study of the German military collapse, *WR*, 1960, page 251. Keitel's view is in his *Memoirs*.

p. 819 To his stepson Harald Quandt, Joseph Goebbels wrote: "Germany will survive this frightful war but only if our people have vivid examples before their eyes upon which to righten themselves. We want to set such an example. . . . One day the lies will collapse and truth will again triumph over them. The hour will come when we shall stand above them all, pure and immaculate, just as our faith and endeavor have always been. Farewell, my dear Harald! Whether we shall ever meet again is in the hands of God. If not, then be proud to have belonged to a family that was loyal to the Führer and his pure and holy mission even in misfortune." Frau Goebbels wrote in the same vein. Hanna Reitsch read the letters and decided not to forward them; the farewell letter of Eva Braun ("With the Führer I have had everything. To die now beside him completes my happiness") she tore up—no doubt out of jealous pique.

p. 819 The letter to Wenck read as follows: "Esteemed General Wenck! As can be seen from the attached dispatches, the SS Reichsführer Himmler made the Anglo-Americans an offer which would have surrendered our nation unconditionally to the plutocrats. Only the Führer—and he alone—can bring about a turning point. The prerequisite to that is the immediate establishment of contact between the Wenck Army and ourselves, so that the Führer regains freedom of action for domestic and diplomatic moves. Yours, Krebs, Chief of the General Staff. Heil Hitler, yours, M. Bormann."

p. 819 For Hitler's coming suicide the generals blamed the Party, and vice versa. General Wilhelm Burgdorf wrote on April 29 to Schörner that Hitler had signed his will "today under the shattering news of the Reichsführer's treachery." Bormann emphasized the failure of the generals in his letter to Dönitz: "As our position seems hopeless because of the nonarrival of every division, the Führer last night dictated the enclosed Political Testament."

p. 821   Hitler's last letter to Keitel was destroyed by the courier, Colonel von Below, on May 2, 1945; but he reconstructed it under CSDIC interrogation in March 1946.

pp. 822–23   My principal witness is Otto Günsche himself, who tape-recorded many hours of his recollections in 1967 and again in 1971 for me. Furthermore, I used interrogations of Kempka—who helped in burning the bodies—the secretaries Gerda Christian, Traudl Junge, and Ilse Krüger, and Goebbels's adjutant Günther Schwägermann. Contrary to the otherwise reliable account of Lev Bezymenski, *Der Tod des Adolf Hitler* (Hamburg, 1968)—based on Soviet documents—there is not the least doubt that Hitler shot himself as well as took poison, as in fact Artur Axmann privately told Milch in prison on March 1, 1948 (diary). Fragments of the cyanide phial were found in Hitler's jaw. And *Life* magazine published in July 1945 William Vandivert's excellent photographs of the bunker room and couch, on which the blood stains are clearly visible. Both Kempka and SS Brigadier Hans Rattenhuber (manuscript dated May 20, 1945, Moscow) noticed the bloodstains on the carpet too. The Walther pistol with which Hitler killed himself is now in private German hands.

According to Goebbels's telegram to Admiral Dönitz, May 1, 1945, Hitler died at 3:30 P.M., April 30, 1945.

Index

NORWEGIAN SEA

Narvik
Namsos
Trondheim
Andalsnes

NORWAY

SWEDEN

Oslo
Stavanger
Stockholm
Kristiansand

UNITED KINGDOM

SCOTLAND

Glasgow
Edinburgh

NORTH SEA

DENMARK

Copenhagen

KUR
Libau

BALTIC SEA

EIRE

Belfast
Dublin

Liverpool
Manchester

Flensburg

Königsberg
Gumbi

Gdynia
Danzig
Elblag
Rastenbu

ATLANTIC OCEAN

Birmingham

ENGLAND

HOLLAND

Wilhelmshaven
Hamburg
Lübeck

Prenzlau
Eberswalde
Oranienburg
Potsdam
Berlin

Szczecin (Stettin)
Stargard
Thorn

Poznań
Kutno

Vistula

Bristol
London
Portsmouth

Amsterdam
Rotterdam

Nijmegen
Arnhem

Bremen

Essen
Dortmund
Duisburg
Kassel

GERMANY

POLAND

Lodz
Wroclaw

ENGLISH CHANNEL

Le Havre
Dieppe
Cherbourg
Caumont
Caen

Arras
Amiens
Soissons

Antwerp
Brussels
BELG.
Liege
Aachen
LUX.
Echternach
Luxembourg
Saarbrücken

Leipzig
Cottbus
Dresden
Spremberg

Kattowitz
Ostrau
(Ostrava)

Prague

Plzen

CZECHOSLOVAKIA

Crac
Pr

Brest

Avranches
Lorient
Mortain
Argentan
Alençon
Paris

Metz
Nancy
Strasbourg

Frankfurt
Mannheim
Nuremberg
Stuttgart

Kosic
Debre

Saint-Nazaire
Nantes
Montoire

FRANCE

Munich

Zisterdorf
Salzburg
Vienna
Bratislava

La Rochelle

Vichy
Lyons
St.-Étienne

Zurich
Bern
Geneva
SWITZ.

AUSTRIA

Tarvisium

Nagykanizsa

Budapest
HUNGAR
LAKE BALATON
Szeged

Bordeaux

Turin
Milan
Venice
Trieste

Zagreb

Tisza
Drava River

Bilbao
Hendaye
Toulouse

Monaco
Genoa
La Spezia

Po River

Belgrade

YUGOSLAVIA

Oporto

PORTUGAL

SPAIN

Marseilles
Nice

Leghorn
(Livorno)
Florence

Sarajevo

Dubrovnik

ADRIATIC SEA

Lisbon

Madrid
Toledo

CORSICA

Rome

ITALY

Tirane
ALBANIA

Valencia

SARDINIA

Gaeta
Cassino
Foggia

Naples
Salerno
Taranto

Seville
Cordoba

Cádiz
Málaga
Granada
Gibraltar

M E D I T E R

Palermo

SICILY

R A N E A N

SP. MOROCCO

Algiers

Bizerte
Tunis

PANTELLERIA

MALTA

Rabat
Casablanca

MOROCCO

ALGERIA

TUNISIA

Tripoli

Benghazi

LIBYA

- - - - - - Eastern Front, late 1942
————— Eastern Front, 1945